THE OXFORD HANDBOOK OF

COMPARATIVE
SYNTAX

THE OXFORD HANDBOOK OF

COMPARATIVE SYNTAX

Edited by

GUGLIELMO CINQUE
RICHARD S. KAYNE

OXFORD

UNIVERSITY PRESS

2005

OXFORD
UNIVERSITY PRESS

Oxford   New York
Auckland   Bangkok   Buenos Aires   Cape Town   Chennai
Dar es Salaam   Delhi   Hong Kong   Istanbul   Karachi   Kolkata
Kuala Lumpur   Madrid   Melbourne   Mexico City   Mumbai   Nairobi
São Paulo   Shanghai   Taipei   Tokyo   Toronto

Published by Oxford University Press, Inc.
198 Madison Avenue, New York, New York 10016

www.oup.com

Oxford is a registered trademark of Oxford University Press

Library of Congress Cataloging-in-Publication Data
The Oxford handbook of comparative syntax / edited by
Guglielmo Cinque, Richard S. Kayne.
p. cm.
Includes bibliographical references and index.
ISBN-13 978-0-19-513650-0
ISBN 0-19-513650-0
1. Grammar, Comparative and general—Syntax.   I. Cinque, Guglielmo.
II. Kayne, Richard S.
P291.O95 2004
415—dc22   2003064925

2 4 6 8 9 7 5 3 1

Printed in the United States of America
on acid-free paper

PREFACE

....

THIS volume contains a set of essays representing work done in what is called comparative syntax. Comparative syntax, which has grown into an indispensable part of the field of syntax, studies the precise ways in which languages differ from one another (in their syntax). In so doing, it attempts to deepen our understanding of the "parameters" side of the human language faculty, to discover the form and extent and limits of the syntactic parameters of variation that underlie the extraordinary range and richness of the syntax of human languages.

At the same time, comparative syntax provides us with a new and highly promising tool with which to deepen our understanding of the "principles" side, the invariant core, of the human language faculty. The principles and parameters of universal grammar (UG) can hardly be dissociated from one another. What is common to all human languages can hardly be understood in abstraction from an acute understanding of how those languages can and do differ. The "minimalist" question why UG is as it is has little chance of finding an answer without the kind of work being done that we have tried to illustrate in this volume.

The essays included here are heterogeneous in style, in content, and in length. Yet taken together, they provide a sense of the range and power of the methods and results of comparative syntax. They do not cover all languages. That would simply be impossible, no matter how many extra pages were added. Nevertheless, we have tried to include work covering a fair range of currently existing families, with the choices in practice of course limited by considerations involving how much work had already been done (at the time we made the choices) on one family or another. (At the same time, practical constraints made it impossible to cover as many families as we might have liked to.)

To a large extent, these chapters are organized around particular families of languages (as opposed to "all languages" or to extremely heterogeneous groups of languages). This structure reflects in part simply who was available and willing to contribute but also in part our belief that comparative work is (all other things being equal) more readily doable when the languages considered are relatively more similar to one another. As the field of comparative syntax expands, as more and more work is done on more and more languages, the set of feasible groupings should grow correspondingly.

Contents

Contributors

ENOCH OLADÉ ABOH   University of Amsterdam, Netherlands

R. AMRITAVALLI   Central Institute of English and Foreign Languages, Hyderabad, India

PAOLA BENINCÀ   University of Padua, Italy

LISA L.-S. CHENG   Leiden University, Netherlands

MICHEL DEGRAFF   Massachusetts Institute of Technology, United States

STEVEN FRANKS   Indiana University, United States

ANDERS HOLMBERG   University of Durham, United Kingdom

K. A. JAYASEELAN   Central Institute of English and Foreign Languages, Hyderabad, India

RICHARD S. KAYNE   New York University, United States

ALAIN KIHM   Centre National de la Recherche Scientifique, Paris, France

JAKLIN KORNFILT   Syracuse University, United States

NICOLA MUNARO   University of Venice, Italy

JAMAL OUHALLA   University College Dublin, Ireland

CHRISTER PLATZACK   Lund University, Sweden

CECILIA POLETTO   Consiglio Nazionale delle Ricerche, Padua, Italy

JEAN-YVES POLLOCK   Université de Picardie à Amiens, France

EDUARDO P. RAPOSO   University of California at Santa Barbara, United States

KEREN RICE   University of Toronto, Canada

GEMMA RIGAU   Autonomous University of Barcelona, Spain

LUIGI RIZZI   University of Siena, Italy

LESLIE SAXON   University of Victoria, Canada

ANDREW SIMPSON   School of Oriental and African Studies, London, United Kingdom

RINT SYBESMA   Leiden University, Netherlands

MAGGIE TALLERMAN   University of Durham, United Kingdom

ARHONTO TERZI   Technological Educational Institute of Patras, Greece

JUAN URIAGEREKA   University of Maryland, United States

JOHN WHITMAN   Cornell University, United States

JAN-WOUTER ZWART   University of Groningen, Netherlands

COMPARATIVE SYNTAX

CHAPTER 1

SOME NOTES ON COMPARATIVE SYNTAX, WITH SPECIAL REFERENCE TO ENGLISH AND FRENCH

RICHARD S. KAYNE

1 GENERALITIES

1.1 Parameters

COMPARATIVE syntax necessarily involves work on more than one language, but it is not simply that. On the one hand, it attempts to characterize and delineate the parameters that ultimately underlie cross-linguistic differences in syntax. On the other, it attempts to exploit those differences as a new and often exciting source of evidence bearing on the characterization and delineation of the principles of Universal Grammar (UG), of the properties that, by virtue of holding of the (syntactic component of the) human language faculty, will be found to hold of every human language.

The term "parameter" has itself been used in more than one way—in turn related to the ways in which the terms "lexical" and "lexicon" are used. In one sense, lexical is opposed to "functional," as when one distinguishes lexical categories like N and V from functional categories like C, D, and Asp. One correspondingly speaks of nouns (like *cat* and *table*) and verbs (like *die* and *break*) as lexical morphemes, as opposed to the functional morphemes *for, the* and *-ing*. At the same time, it is often said that *for, the*, and *-ing* belong to the lexicon of English, where one takes the lexicon to include both lexical and functional elements.

As long as one has these distinctions clearly in mind, I see no objection to this usage of lexical and lexicon, and I will consequently speak of the lexicon (of a given language) as containing both lexical and functional elements. Now a widespread idea about syntactic parameters is that they are limited to being features/properties of functional elements,[1] as opposed to ever being features of lexical elements. But since functional elements are part of the lexicon, then this limitation means that syntactic parameters are nonetheless necessarily features, or properties, of elements of the lexicon. This seems like a perfectly reasonable way of speaking, given the above-mentioned way of using the word "lexicon."

Limiting syntactic parameters to features of functional heads is also intended to exclude the possibility that there could be a syntactic parameter that is a feature of no element of the lexicon at all—for example, there could presumably not be a parameter of the sort "language L_i has or does not have bottom-to-top derivations." This is similar to (though more obvious than) Chomsky's (1995: 160) proposal that there cannot be a parameter attributing Case chains to some languages but not to others (as had been suggested by Koopman 1992).[2]

The restriction that parameters are invariably features of functional elements needs to be sharpened, however. One would presumably not want to allow English *the* and Dutch *de* 'the' to differ in that *the* "can be part of a Case chain" while *de* cannot be? A parameter of that sort ("can or cannot be part of a Case chain") could be formulated as a feature of a functional element (instead of being formulated as a property of a language), but clearly that would go strongly against the spirit of Chomsky's proposed restriction.

What this brings out is something that I think has always been implicit in the proposal that parameters are restricted to features of functional elements— namely, that the features in question must be simple and limited in type, in some sense to be made precise. Being (or not) part of a Case chain would not count as an appropriate feature. Reaching an adequate characterization of what it means to be an appropriate feature in this sense is one of the primary challenges faced by (comparative) syntax.

What form syntactic parameters take is itself a question that is, I think, quite separate from another that has occasionally led to some confusion in the literature. This other question has to do with the effects of different parameter settings, and, more specifically, with the "size" of those effects. For example, the pro-drop parameter, as discussed in the late 1970s and early 1980s, had multiple effects. In addition to differing with respect to the expression or non-expression of un-stressed pronominal subjects, non-pro-drop and pro-drop languages also differed with respect to the possibility of having postverbal subjects and in whether or not they allowed "that"-trace violations. The range of effects traceable back to that one parameter was notable.[3]

It has occasionally been thought that the term "parameter" itself should only be used when there is such a notable, or dramatic, range of effects. I do not pursue that way of thinking here however, in part because what seems "dramatic" depends on expectations that may themselves be somewhat arbitrary.[4]

For example, French and English differ in that in restrictive relatives English *who* is possible as a direct object, whereas in French the corresponding word *qui* is not (though it is possible as the object of a preposition). Let us set aside the (important) question of what exactly the parameter is that underlies this French/ English difference and ask whether that difference carries over to nonrestrictive relatives. The answer is that it does—that is, restrictives and nonrestrictives act alike in the relevant respect.[5] Assuming the same parametric difference to be at work in restrictives and nonrestrictives, is this then an example of a parameter with a notable/dramatic/impressive range of effects or not? I'm not sure that the answer to this last question is clear (it depends on expectations about—and on one's theory of—how similar the two types of relatives should be); and I'm not sure how important the answer is.

For syntactic theory (and linguistic theory more generally) to merit being thought of as a theoretical field in the most ambitious sense of the term, syntactic theory must provide some results of nontrivial deductive depth (the more the better, of course, all other things being equal). In the subarea of syntax that we call comparative syntax, these results can in some cases indeed take the form of a single parametric difference having a multiplicity of effects. (A different type of nontrivial result would be a successful restrictive—and deep[6]—characterization, in terms of possible parameters, of the range of human languages, in the area of syntax.)

From that, it does not follow that every parameter, understood as a (simple) feature of some functional element, need have an equally wide range of effects.[7] Take, for example, the well-known French/English difference concerning the po-sition of *assez/enough* relative to an associated adjective. In English, *enough* differs from related words like *too, so,* and *how* in following, rather than preceding, the adjective (*rich enough* vs. *too rich,* etc.). In French, *assez* does not differ from the corresponding set of related degree elements: they all precede the adjective (*assez riche, trop riche,* etc.). English *enough* plausibly has some feature that induces movement of the adjective to its left; French *assez* plausibly lacks that feature.

This seems like a reasonable enough parameter, which might (or might not) turn out to have other, unexpected effects (in other areas of syntax). If it turned out to have no other effects, it would be an example of a relatively less dramatic parameter than, say, the pro-drop parameter, although even then it might still be of substantial interest for the construction of a general theory of parameters.

A partially similar point was made several years ago by Holmberg and Sandström (1996), in their discussion of prenominal and postnominal possessors in northern Swedish dialects. There is significant parametric variation in those dialects, in that area of syntax. Holmberg and Sandström speak of "minor" versus "major" parameters. For example, a parametric property of the functional element that hosts possessors in its specifier might not have effects that go beyond sentences containing an overt possessor, and in that sense might be minor (compared to a parametric property of the "agreement" morpheme found with finite verbs, which is likely to have a much more pervasive set of visible effects). Again, minor in this sense is perfectly compatible with "theoretically important," if, for example, the parameter(s) in question should turn out to tell us something important about the general status of parameters in UG, and/or (as in the case of *enough*) about the general question of how exactly movement is triggered.

Consequently, I freely use the term "parameter" to characterize all cross-linguistic syntactic differences, independently of the degree of "drama" or range of effects associated with any particular parameter.

1.2 Microcomparative Syntax and Microparameters

Another dimension of interest in the universe of parameters has to do with a potential distinction between microparameters and macroparameters. Let me approach this via the partially related distinction between microcomparative syntax[8] and macrocomparative syntax. Microcomparative syntax can be thought of as comparative syntax work done on a set of very closely related languages or dialects. However, since "very closely related" is an informal characterization, let me recast this in more relative terms: some comparative syntax work is more microcomparative (less macrocomparative) than other comparative syntax work. Work on a more closely related set of languages or dialects is more microcomparative than work on a less closely related set. In some cases, the distinction is quite clear (in others, two sets of languages or dialects might not be readily comparable). Thus, work on a set of Northern Italian dialects would be more microcomparative than work on a set of Indo-European languages including Italian, Greek, and English. (As a first approximation, we can take degree of historical relatedness as an informal guideline for degree of syntactic "closeness."[9]) Work on a set of Indo-European languages in turn would be more microcomparative/less macrocomparative than work on a set including some Indo-European and some Afro-Asiatic.

It might be that one can distinguish in a similar vein microparameters and macroparameters. Different settings of microparameters would characterize differences between very closely related languages or dialects such as American English and British English. One example would involve *do*-support and in particular the fact that British English, but not American English, has what looks like nonfinite *do*-support, in sentences like *He may do, He may have done.*

Still, it is not clear a priori that the parameter(s) underlying this difference (however best formulated) have effects only within English.[10] More generally put, although there will certainly be syntactic parameters distinguishing pairs of very closely related languages, the same parameter(s) might be active in unrelated families, with effects that might look superficially rather different (due to interactions with other properties of that other family).

We can thus use the term "microparameter" for those parameters that at least in some cases differentiate two very closely related languages. Whether microparameters in this sense (or minor parameters as above) differ in any systematically interesting way from other parameters should be considered an open question at this (early) stage of comparative syntax work.

A similar degree of caution would be appropriate for the notion of macroparameter as in Baker (1996: 8). Baker might be correct in thinking that there are some (macro)parameters that compactly characterize a significant group of (historically not necessarily related) languages such as the so-called polysynthetic ones.[11] However, one of the key properties of polysynthetic languages—namely the obligatory appearance of a pronominal agreement element in addition to the (nonincorporated) lexical argument (if there is one)—is also found within languages of an apparently rather different sort. For example, the Italian CLLD construction (clitic left-dislocation; Cinque 1990) requires the presence of a pronominal clitic in addition to the dislocated direct object argument. In Italian this does not carry over to indirect prepositional (dative) arguments, but in Spanish it does. In Spanish, dative arguments (preceded by a preposition) must to a large extent be accompanied by a pronominal clitic even when not "dislocated." In many Northern Italian dialects, this is an absolute requirement. Some Northern Italian dialects impose the presence of a pronominal subject clitic in addition to a lexical subject.

Although these varying requirements found in language families like Romance that are not polysynthetic in any general way might turn out to be unrelated to Baker's polysynthesis parameter, it could alternatively be the case that the systematic obligatoriness of pronominal agreement morphemes in Mohawk is just an extreme example of what is found to a lesser extent in (some) Romance.[12] (A theoretical reason for remaining cautious about the polysynthesis parameter is that, as Baker (1996: 505) notes, it leads to an expansion of the universe of possible parameters (which would have to be allowed to contain some parameters of a certain "visibility condition" sort).

Uncertainty concerning the importance of a micro- versus macroparametric distinction does not affect the special status of microcomparative syntax, which I think has a certain special importance. (Macrocomparative syntax work is essential, too, of course). This special status of microcomparative syntax resides in the fact that it is the closest we can come, at the present time, to a controlled experiment in comparative syntax.[13]

In a universe (very substantially) unlike the one we live in, we could imagine experimenting on individual languages. We could take a particular language—say Italian (in which pronominal clitics follow infinitives)—and alter it minimally, for example, by giving it a "twist" in such a way as to change the position of its clitics relative to infinitives. We would then look carefully at this new language (variant of Italian) to see if any other syntactic properties have changed as an automatic result of our experimental twist. If some have, then we can conclude that there must be some parameter(s) that link these other properties to the position of clitics relative to infinitives.

By performing many such experiments (on many languages), we would develop a substantial body of evidence concerning which syntactic properties are parametrically linked to which others. These experiments would dramatically increase our knowledge of what clusters of syntactic properties are linguistically significant and would dramatically facilitate our discovering the correct theory of syntax. Not only would our increased knowledge facilitate delineating the primitive parameters of the syntactic component of the language faculty, but also a deeper understanding of the working of syntactic parameters could only facilitate our making progress toward understanding the universal principles that these syntactic parameters are so tightly connected to.

We cannot do such experiments. But by examining sets of very closely related languages, languages that differ from one another in only a relatively small number of syntactic ways, we can hope to achieve something of the same effect. We can take one language or dialect, then look for another very similar one that differs with respect to a property we are interested in. The closeness of the languages or dialects in question will make it relatively more likely that any other syntactic property that we discover to vary between the two will be parametrically related to the first.

It is not that microcomparative syntax is easy to do, nor that one is guaranteed of success nor that there is a black-and-white distinction between micro- and macrocomparative syntax. It is rather, I think, that the probability of correctly figuring out what syntactic property is parametrically linked to what other one (and consequently the probability of discovering what the relevant parameter(s) may be) is higher when the "experiment" approaches to a greater extent the ideal of a controlled one, with fewer variables to be taken into account. Intra-Romance comparisons can at least sometimes be pursued without one being forced (in a crucial way) to look further afield than Romance, whereas comparative work taking, for example, English and Japanese as a starting point might lead almost anywhere, at the risk of making the comparative work not impossibly difficult but certainly more difficult.[14]

Putting things another way, we might say that microcomparative syntax work provides us with a new kind of microscope with which to look into the workings of syntax.[15] That it is syntax in general that is at issue, and not just comparative syntax proper, is a point worth emphasizing: study of the principles of syntax is not and cannot be a separate enterprise from study of the parameters.

Let me illustrate this with one example. English allows embedded infinitival interrogatives such as:

(1)   We don't know where to go.

(2)   We don't know whether to leave.

But it does not allow:

(3)   *We don't know if to leave.

Romance languages very often allow infinitival interrogatives in the way that English does. They typically have no word corresponding directly to *whether*, but they do have a general counterpart to *if*. Some Romance languages are just like English in disallowing a controlled infinitive with (their counterpart of) *if*—for example, French:

(4)   *Jean ne sait pas si partir. (J neg know not if leave$_{infin}$)

What is surprising is that some Romance languages do allow it—for example, Italian:

(5)   Gianni non sa se partire. (G neg knows if leave$_{infin}$)

A standard comparative syntax question would be to ask what this intra-Romance (French, Italian) difference might correlate or cluster with (and then to bring in English and other languages). Although it is of course logically possible that the answer to this sort of question might in a given case be "nothing" (i.e., that we are looking at an isolated differential property),[16] the best working strategy at the present stage of development of the field is to assume, I think, that there exists some positive answer (i.e., some clustering of properties), and then to look hard for it.

In the particular case at hand, there is a very good candidate, since those Romance languages which, like French, disallow *if* + infinitive appear to differ systematically in another way from those which, like Italian, allow it. This other way has to do with the relative placement of pronominal clitic and infinitive. The Romance languages that are French-like (with respect to (4)) have the order clitic–infinitive, while the Italian-like ones have the order infinitive–clitic.

This correlation within Romance between control with *if* and the order infinitive–clitic is of obvious importance to any attempt to delineate the parameter(s) underlying the syntactic differences at issue. At least as important, however, is the fact that this correlation within Romance promises to provide an invaluable clue to a general understanding of the theory of control. Put another way, it is entirely reasonable to impose on any proposed theory of control the requirement that it lend itself to a natural account of this correlation. (This kind of cross-Romance correlation could by definition come to the fore only as the result of comparative syntax work.)

Since, in the spirit of Emonds (1978) and Pollock (1989), the difference between clitic–infinitive order and infinitive–clitic order almost certainly involves a difference (or differences) in verb movement, it is plausible that, in part, verb movement is what underlies the French/Italian difference with respect to control with *if* seen in (4) versus (5). If so, then the correct theory of control must be sensitive to verb movement.

Kayne (1991) suggested that a theory of control embedded in the version of the government-based binding theory put forth in Chomsky (1986, 170ff.) meets this criterion in the desired way (although Chomsky's more recent minimalist work has attempted to move away from the use of government). If that evolution is on the right track, then the correct theory of control cannot depend on government yet must continue to meet the unyielding requirement that it be able to express the Romance correlation at issue.[17]

The study of (what underlies) (1)–(5) is also relevant to the earlier discussion of micro- versus macroparameters, in particular to the idea that apparently macroparametric differences might all turn out to dissolve into arrays of microparametric ones (i.e., into differences produced by the additive effects of some number of microparameters). This idea could be elevated to a general conjecture:

(6)   Every parameter is a microparameter.

What this would mean is that every syntactic parameter is such that each of its (two) values yield (when all other factors are held constant) a pair of UG-admissible grammars that characterize two languages that we would all (informally) agree are very closely related.

The importance of (1)–(5) lies in showing that microparameters (e.g., the relatively microparametric one(s) responsible for clitic–infinitive vs. infinitive–clitic order) are perfectly capable of participating in an explanation of a "cluster of properties," in this case of the correlation with control in interrogative *if*-

clauses. It may be that (some of) the clusters of syntactic properties that were under prominent discussion twenty-five years ago were too coarsely characterized. It may be that as research progresses a much finer-grained picture of syntax will substantially displace the one current twenty-five years ago (not to mention even earlier ones). Yet it may, and very likely will, also turn out that the type of parametric explanation put forth twenty-five years ago in the early stages of comparative syntax will have long-term validity and long-term importance.

2 How Many Parameters? How Many Languages?

2.1 How Many Functional Elements?

The hypothesis that syntactic parameters are invariably features of functional elements does not imply that every functional element is associated with some parameter, but that additional hypothesis is a plausible one that I would like to entertain:

(7)   Every functional element made available by UG is associated with some syntactic parameter.

If (7) is correct, then we have a minimum number of parameters. There must be at least as many syntactic parameters as there are functional elements in the syntax.

How many functional elements are there, then? Before hazarding a guess, let me separate this question from the question of the proper analysis of such elements. Consider, for example, the English suffix -*ish* (meaning approximately 'more or less'), as in:

(8)   We're ready-ish.

(9)   John looks thirty-five-ish.

(10)   It must be a quarter after five-ish.

The last example (in which -*ish* has scope over *a quarter after five*) surely suggests a strongly syntactic approach,[18] in which case the absence of a direct counterpart of -*ish* in French is of immediate interest to (comparative) syntax.

But even suffixes that cannot follow phrases can readily have syntactic import—for example, the agentive -er or the nominalizing -ion which interact with the expression of arguments—not to mention (inflectional) tense suffixes, going back to Chomsky (1957). Let us therefore take such "derivational" suffixes as -er and -ion (as well as standard inflectional suffixes) to be part of the syntax, broadly construed. More specifically, let us assume that such suffixes are subject to parameterization that affects the syntax, whether or not they are to be analyzed as functional heads or as elements that trigger movement to a higher functional head. (An informal conjecture would be that, as more and more comparative work is done on derivational suffixes, they will come to be seen more and more clearly as part of syntax.)

Thinking of Cinque (1999), we of course want to take into account, in building up our inventory of functional elements, as many languages as possible and to count as relevant functional elements even those elements that occur overtly only in some languages. A list of functional elements relevant to syntax would now plausibly include (in no particular order):

(11)   Complementizers like *that* or *for*

(12)   Elements expressing mood; also subjunctive and indicative morphemes, imperative morphemes

(13)   Modals of different sorts

(14)   Tense elements

(15)   Aspectual elements

(16)   Negation morphemes; emphatic and affirmative morphemes

(17)   Person morphemes—in particular, first and second person

(18)   *Se*-type reflexive morphemes (related to person) and morphemes like French *on*

(19)   Number agreement morphemes; gender morphemes and word markers; noun class markers

(20)   Third-person pronouns; locative clitics like French *en, y*; nonclitic locatives

(21)   Pro- "predicate" morphemes like French *le*

(22)   Demonstratives

(23)   Definite articles; specific articles

(24)   Indefinite articles

(25)   Elements like *some, any*

(26) Numerals and the arguably related *several*

(27) Universal quantifiers

(28) Quantity words like *many* and *few*

(29) Classifiers

(30) Degree words, including comparatives and superlatives; *very*

(31) *Have/be*; copula versus existential

(32) Possessive morphemes such as *of*, *'s*; suffixes as in French *mon* (=*m-* + *-on*), and as in Russian

(33) Nouns like *body, thing, place, one* that have special (functional) behavior, as in *somebody else*

(34) Filler nouns like *one* in *a blue one*

(35) *Body, self, -même* in complex reflexives

(36) Wh-words in interrogatives, in relatives, in free relatives, and in exclamatives

(37) *-ever*, as in *whoever*

(38) Functional adpositions; perhaps all adpositions

(39) Case morphemes; direct-object-marking morpheme sensitive to animacy or definiteness

(40) Particles like *up* and *down* and directionals like German *hin* and *her*

(41) Prefixes of all sorts—e.g., *re-, out-, over-*; negative *un-*; reversative *un-*

(42) Adverbial *-ly*

(43) Suffixes like *-less, -ful, -ish, -y*; also *-th* as in *two hundred and fiftieth*; also *-ity, -ness*

(44) Nominalizing morphology like *-ion*, gerundive *-ing*, infinitive suffixes like Romance *-r*

(45) Functional verbs like causatives and *get*; also restructuring verbs a la Cinque (2001; 2002)

(46) Functional adjectives like *other, same, good*

(47) Focusing elements like *only, just, even, also, too*

(48) *As, than*

(49) Conjunctions like *and, or, but*

(50) *(Al)though, while, after, before, if, because, since*

I have certainly forgotten some, if not many, functional elements. Others I am not aware of because they are found overtly only in languages that I have never come into contact with (in most cases because the languages in question have not come into existence yet or else have disappeared without leaving a trace). In other words, the above list is no doubt too short. That is so despite the fact that it mentions over fifty English morphemes and indirectly alludes to many more (from English and other languages—see in particular Cinque 1999).

In some cases (e.g., *any*) I may have included elements that are actually bimorphemic (*an* + *-y*, thinking of *every* as possibly being *ever* + *y*). The conclusion is that the number of functional elements in syntax is not easy to estimate, but at the same time that 100 would be a low estimate.

Let us take that low estimate and let us associate each functional element with one (binary-valued) parameter, making the additional simplifying assumption that the resulting 100 parameters are all independent of one another—that is, each can be set independently of all the others. The number of syntactically distinct grammars characterizable even by this (in all probability artificially small) set of 100 independent parameters is large, on the order of 10^{30}, or 1 followed by 30 zeros.[19]

There is no problem here (except, perhaps, for those who think that linguists must study every possible language), since neither the language learner nor the linguist is obliged to work directly with the set of possible grammars. The learner needs only to be able to manage the task of setting the 100 parameters (or whatever the number is), and the linguist needs only to figure out what they are (and what the accompanying principles are, and why they are as they are).

2.2 How Many Parameters per Functional Element?

The number of syntactic parameters would increase (while still remaining manageable) if a given functional element could be associated with a (small) number of distinct parameters. The exent to which this is likely to hold is not entirely clear. The answer is in part dependent on a proper understanding of the extent to which syntax is "decompositional."

Consider the contrast within English:

(51) They've written few (*number) articles.

(52) (?)They've written the fewest number of articles of anybody I know.

Although *few* cannot be immediately followed by *number*, the superlative counterpart is much more acceptable. For this and other reasons it is plausible that *few articles* is to be analyzed as *few NUMBER articles* (where the capital letters indicate nonpronunciation), with *few* taken to be an adjective similar to *little/small*, but restricted to modifying the noun *number*/NUMBER. In the same vein, *a red car* is arguably to be analyzed as *a red COLOR car*, where *red* necessarily modifies COLOR, rather than *car* (which is itself modified by *red COLOR*).[20]

If these analyses are correct, we need to ask why the learner of English would have ended up with them. The simplest answer is that there was no choice, in the sense that these analyses are the only ones that UG makes available for such phrases. (I am setting aside the question whether *few NUMBER* and *red COLOR* are reduced relatives.) As to why these would be the only analyses made available by UG, a plausible proposal is that UG respects a "principle of decompositionality" that can be formulated as follows:[21]

(53) UG imposes a maximum of one interpretable syntactic feature per lexical or functional element.

The idea is, for example, that *a red car* simultaneously expresses, in addition to what is attributable to *car* and to *a*, the notion of color plus a distinct notion having to do with the particular position or interval on the color scale. What (53) says is that UG requires that those two notions correspond to two separate elements (two separate nodes).[22] (The range of implications of (53) will depend on the correct characterization of "interpretable syntactic feature.")

3 SOME PARAMETERS HAVING TO DO WITH NONPRONUNCIATION

3.1 Pronunciation versus Nonpronunciation: The Case of French *-aine* and English -AINE

Returning to parameters, it seems clear that the more decompositional syntax is, the more likely it is to be true that each functional element can be associated with just one syntactic parameter. However, there is one type of parameter (that can be thought of as straddling syntax and phonology) that might be readily able to coexist with another (more purely syntactic) parameter. What I have in mind here is cross-linguistic variation with respect to the pronunciation versus non-pronunciation of a given functional element.

While it is logically possible that the absence of an overt functional element in language A corresponding to a functional element visible in language B could indicate that language A entirely lacks that functional element, there is a substantial tradition that has profitably taken the opposite position—namely, that if language B visibly has some functional element, then all languages must have it, even if in some or many it fails to be pronounced at all.

The postulation of unpronounced functional elements is familiar from the area of inflectional morphology—for example, in Vergnaud's work on Case, in much work on agreement (and pro-drop), and more widely in Cinque (1999).[23] Let me mention here one potentially interesting example from what would be called derivational morphology. French has a (nominal) suffix -aine (feminine in gender) that can readily follow certain numerals (10, 12, 15, 20, 30, 40, 50, 60, 100), with an interpretation akin to *about*.[24] An example is:

(54)   Elle a déjà publié une vingtaine d'articles cette année (she has already published a$_{fem.}$ twenty -*aine* of articles this year = ... about twenty articles ...).

English has no visible suffix that matches -*aine*.

Yet there is some evidence that English does have an unpronounced counterpart of this -*aine*.[25] This is suggested by the contrast:

(55)   a hundred (*of) articles

(56)   hundreds *(of) articles

As an ordinary numeral, *hundred* cannot be followed by *of* (apart from partitives containing definites like *a hundred of these articles*), but plural *hundreds* must be followed by *of* (unless the following NP is itself left unpronounced). Moreover, (56) has an "approximate" rather than a precise numerical interpretation and would be translated in French by *centaine*:

(57)   des centaines d'articles (of-the hundred-*aine*-s of articles)

rather than with the simple numeral *cent* (hundred).

Now the presence of *of* in (56) versus its absence in (55) is plausibly to be thought of as reflecting the nominal behavior of *hundreds* versus the adjectival behavior of *hundred*, with the strong unacceptability of:

(58)   *three hundreds articles

as opposed to:

(59)   three hundred articles

then parallel to that of:

(60)   *three excellents articles

versus:[26]

(61)   three excellent articles

Why, though, should *hundreds* be nominal if *hundred* is adjectival? The answer must be that *hundreds* necessarily contains a nominal suffix (that I will
represent as -AINE) akin to overt French -*aine*:

(62)   hundred + -AINE + -s of articles

with the nominal character of that suffix responsible for the appearance of *of*,
much as in *a box of apples*, et cetera. The fact that this nominal *hundreds* is not
compatible with a further numeral, as in:

(63)   *seven hundreds of articles

means that its nominal suffix has something in common with *oodles* and *numbers*
in:

(64)   They have (*seven) oodles of money.
(65)   We've invited (*seven) large numbers of linguists to the party.

If English has an unpronounced suffix -AINE comparable to French -*aine*,[27]
we can ask whether the two of them differ in some other parametric way, beyond
the phonological difference. A good candidate has to do with singular versus
plural. French has both singular:

(66)   une centaine d'articles (a hundred -*aine* of articles = about a hundred
       articles)

and plural:

(67)   des centaines d'articles (of-the . . . = 'hundreds of articles')

whereas alongside (56) English does not allow:

(68)   *a hundred of articles

(In addition, (55) does not have the approximative interpretation.[28])

What looks like a similar restriction to plural holds for me in the contrast between (64) and (69):[29]

(69)   *They have an oodle of money.

On the reasonable assumption that this is an intrinsic property of *oodle* and of English -AINE (and that (68) and (69) are one phenomenon), we seem to have, in the case of *-aine*/-AINE, an example of two parametric differences—pronunciation (French) versus nonpronunciation (English)—and compatibility with singular (French) versus incompatibility with singular (English)—associated with a single derivational suffix.

Still, it might be that incompatibility with singular follows from nonpronunciation, in particular if English -AINE needs to be licensed by overt plural *-s*, and if that licensing requirement is imposed by the nonpronunciation of -AINE.[30] In this case, the two parametric differences in question would reduce to one (pronunciation versus nonpronunciation).

In the universe of inflectional suffixes, postulation of two parametric properties for one functional element is not unfamiliar. For example, Spanish and Italian differ from Paduan in robustly allowing null subjects in the third-person singular (and plural). Taking Harris (1969) to be correct in arguing that the third singular suffix in Spanish is zero (and generalizing to Italian), we seem to reach the conclusion that this zero suffix, in addition to its phonological property (which distinguishes it from the third singular, present-tense,[31] suffix of German), has, in Spanish (and Italian), some further property that licenses a null subject (as opposed to the apparently similar zero third-singular suffix of Paduan). Alternatively, one might try to reinterpret this second property by reducing it to the fact that Paduan (but not Spanish or Italian) has subject clitics.[32]

3.2 Nonpronunciation and Licensing: The Case of *Something Heavy*

Pronunciation versus nonpronunciation of a given functional element has in some cross-linguistic cases effects that seem likely to follow at least in part from UG principles. Such cases (as perhaps the case of French *-aine* vs. English -AINE just mentioned) seem to indicate that pronunciation versus nonpronunciation is unlike a simple difference between one non-zero phonological realization and an-other.[33] Another example of interest is the following.

English has:[34]

(70)   somebody famous, something heavy

whereas French has:

(71)   quelqu'un de célèbre (some-one of famous)

(72)   quelque chose de lourd (some thing of heavy)

with an obligatory preposition *de*:

(73)   *quelqu'un célèbre

(74)   *quelque chose lourd

that English cannot have:

(75)   *somebody of famous, *something of heavy

That (70) and (71)/(72) are essentially the same phenomenon (as suggested to me by Hans Bennis), modulo the preposition, is reinforced by the fact that both languages fail to allow this with fully lexical nouns:

(76)   *Some linguist famous just walked in.

(77)   *Some book heavy just fell off the table.

and similarly in French (if we abstract away from focalization effects). In addition, there is a determiner restriction that holds for (70):

(78)   *thebody famous, *thatthing heavy

that also holds for French (again abstracting away from focalization effects).[35] That French (71)/(72) is strongly parallel to English (70) is further suggested by their common limitation to singular:[36]

(79)   *somethings heavy/abnormal

(80)   *quelques choses de lourds/anormaux (some things of heavy/abnormal)

3.3 Determiners and Unpronounced EVER

A way in which English and French contrast here has to do with the range of allowable determiners. English allows fairly well:

(81)   Everybody famous is happy.

(82)   Everything expensive is worth buying.

As in (76)/(77), a fully lexical noun is not possible:

(83)   *Every writer famous is happy.

(84)   *Every book expensive is worth buying.

French normally expresses *everything* as *tout*, a single morpheme, and *everybody* as *tout le monde*, literally 'all the world'. Combining these with *de* plus adjective is not possible, however, in contrast to (71)/(72):

(85)   *tout le monde de célèbre (all the world of famous)

(86)   *tout de cher (all of expensive)

   A possible account might be the following. First, note that *tout* is identical in form to the masculine singular French counterpart of *all* in *toutes les filles* (all$_{\text{fem.,pl.}}$ the girls).[37] Second, we might claim that *all* and *every* differ in definiteness, with *all* definite and *every* indefinite.[38] Third, it might be that indefiniteness is a necessary condition for (70)–(72) and (81)–(82).
   Parametrically speaking, this would point up the importance of the fact that English *each, every,* and *all* have only two counterparts in French: *chaque* and *tout*. If *chaque* is a close counterpart of *each*, as seems very likely, and if *tout* corresponds to *all*,[39] then it looks as if it is *every* that is missing in French. This, in turn, might (if we are willing to think of *every* as *ever + y*, perhaps parallel to *any* as *an + y*) be linked to the absence in French of any overt morpheme corresponding to nontemporal *ever*,[40] as found in English in:

(87)   Wherever he goes, they'll be unhappy.

What French would have is:

(88)   Où qu'il aille, . . . (where that he goes, . . .)

with no *ever*, but with an overt complementizer (and the verb in the subjunctive). It may be that the overt complementizer *que* (normally impossible in standard French in combination with a wh-word) is necessary in (88) to license an unpronounced counterpart of *ever*[41]—that is, French may have:

(89)   Où EVER qu'il aille, . . .

But this unpronounced French EVER would be unable to occur as a (part of a) determiner (perhaps because French has no *-y*).

What this seems to indicate, in a way that is partly familiar from earlier work on the Empty Category Principle (ECP),[42] is that languages may differ in that one language may associate no pronunciation with a functional element that is pronounced in the other, yet the unpronounced version will be subject to licensing requirements that may in some cases force the presence of an element (here, *que* in (88)) not otherwise needed, and at the same time in other cases result in the unpronounced version being unusable (as with the absence of a French counterpart to *every*).

3.4 "Extraposition" Differences

This brings us to a second way in which French and English differ in the area of syntax under discussion. On the one hand, the French counterpart of *someone else, something heavy* contains the preposition *de* (of), which we saw in (71)–(74) to be obligatory; in English the corresponding overt preposition is impossible, as seen in (75). On the other hand, there are major similarities between French and English (restriction to nouns like *one* and *thing*; restriction to indefinite determiners; restriction to singular), as seen in (76)–(80). A natural proposal, therefore, is to take English *something heavy*, et cetera, to contain an unpronounced counterpart to French *de*, call it OF:

(90)   something OF heavy

Now the difference between pronounced *de* and unpronounced OF seems to correlate with the fact that French allows combining this construction with "extraposition" to a greater extent than English does. For example, French has:

(91)   Rien n'est arrivé de très intéressant. (nothing neg is happened of very interesting)

while:

(92)   ??Nothing happened very interesting yesterday.

is not very good, as opposed to all of these:

(93)   Nothing very interesting happened yesterday.

(94)   Nothing happened that was very interesting yesterday.

(95)   Nothing happened of much interest yesterday.

with the last of these showing an overt *of* that is arguably responsible for the contrast with (92), parallel to (92) versus (91). Similarly, in wh-cases, French allows:

(96)   Qui as-tu invité de célèbre? (who have you invited of famous)

while English is not very happy with:

(97)   ??Who did you invite famous?

as opposed to (cf. (94) and (95)):

(98)   Who did you invite that/who was famous?

(99)   Who did you invite of interest?

    That extraposition of OF + adj. is less successful than extraposition of *de* + adj. has a familiar ring to it: it recalls the well-known fact that, within English, relative clause extraposition is degraded if the complementizer is unpronounced:

(100)   Something just happened *?(that) John isn't aware of.

Thus the French/English contrast concerning extraposition with adjectives will plausibly follow from general principles of licensing (again, in the spirit of the ECP[43]), interacting with the parametric difference between a pronounced and an unpronounced preposition.

3.5 Quantity Word Differences and Nonpronunciation

This parametric difference concerning *de* versus OF is in one sense more complex than the apparently similar one discussed earlier concerning the French derivational suffix *-aine* and its unpronounced English counterpart, in that English *of/*

OF is often pronounced, so its nonpronunciation with adjectives cannot simply be a general feature.[44]

A perhaps related case in which French has *de* and English has no visible preposition is the case of quantity words. The closest French counterparts of:

(101)   too few tables

(102)   so few tables

are:

(103)   trop peu de tables (too *peu* of tables)

(104)   si peu de tables (so . . .)

and similarly for *little* in:

(105)   too little sugar

(106)   so little sugar

which in French are:

(107)   trop peu de sucre (too *peu* of sugar)

(108)   si peu de sucre (so . . .)

with *peu* translating both *few* and *little*. (I return later to the question of what exactly *peu* corresponds to.)

Note in passing that the very fact that English distinguishes *few* and *little* on the basis of plural versus mass, while French uses *peu* in all of (103)–(108), itself reflects a parametric difference of interest similar to the fact that English has both *someone* and *somebody*, whereas French has a close counterpart only of the former—*quelqu'un*.

These parametric differences are of course "in the lexicon," in the specific sense that they are based on features of particular functional elements, but they are equally "of the syntax" and raise all sorts of interesting questions—for example, how best to characterize the relative distribution of -*one* versus -*body*, or of *few* versus *little*, and how best to understand the principles that underlie the distributional differences. In the case of *few/little*, we have a distinction that is clearly related to the distinction between *number* and *amount* (and *quantity*), leading to interesting questions concerning the contrast:

(109)   (?)That library has a large amount of books in it.

(110)   *John has a large amount of sisters and brothers.

The parallelism between *someone* and *quelqu'un*, while certainly real, leads to the question whether *some* and *quelque* are quite the same, given:

(111)   Some are interesting.

versus:[45]

(112)   Quelques*(-uns) sont intéressants.

and the ensuing thought that *quelque* is actually *quel* (which) + complementizer *que*.[46] The idea that *quelque* is not a perfect match for *some*, in turn, may be supported by the arguable absence in French of any simple counterpart to *any*. Whether French has a (closer) covert counterpart of *some* (and *any*) (and if not, why not?) is a (valid and important) question that I will not try to pursue here.

More generally, all work in (comparative) syntax depends in part on (often implicit) hypotheses concerning correspondences between morphemes across languages. In many cases, discerning what French morpheme corresponds to what English morpheme, for example, is straightforward, in other cases less so, as in the example just mentioned of *some* and *quelque*. (It seems highly likely that the proportion of straightforward cases is greater the more microcomparative the work.) As we shall see later in this chapter, the similarity between *peu* and *few/little* in (101)–(108) in fact is misleading.

Before taking on the correspondence question, let us focus again on the *de* that appears in (103)/(104) and (107)/(108), as well as in the corresponding examples without a degree element:

(113)   peu de tables

(114)   peu de sucre

These contrast with *few* and *little* in (101)/(102) and (105)/(106) and in:

(115)   few tables

(116)   little sugar

which do not have *of* (and cannot).

In this respect one can see a parallel to (70)–(75) that, in turn, may be related to an English/French contrast concerning (relative clause) complementizers, exemplified by the contrast:

(117)   the books (that) you have read

(118)   les livres *(que) vous avez lus

The fact that English has no overt preposition in *something interesting* might perhaps (and perhaps similarly for (115)/(116)) depend on English allowing an unpronounced counterpart of *that* in (some) finite relative clauses. (Whether this is an intrinsic feature of *that* or follows from something else about English remains to be understood.)

In contrast to French, the Italian counterparts of (113)–(116)—namely:

(119)   poche (*di) tavole

(120)   poco (*di) zucchero

do not show the preposition *di* (of) that one might expect, given that the Italian relative clause complementizer *che* is more like French *que* than like English *that*. But this contrast between French and Italian is probably related to the fact that Italian *poco/poca/pochi/poche* agrees with the noun in number and gender, while the corresponding French *peu* does not agree at all. Put another way, Italian may allow a covert preposition here (like English does, but for a different reason) if that covert preposition in Italian is licensed by the overt agreement morphology.[47]

The English/French contrast concerning *of* and *de* with *few/little* versus *peu* carries over to:

(121)   too many (*of) tables

(122)   too much (*of) sugar

versus:

(123)   trop *(de) tables (too of tables)

(124)   trop *(de) sucre (too of sugar)

despite the fact that (123)/(124) contain no overt element corresponding to *many/much*. The obvious proposal is that these French examples contain an unpronounced counterpart of *many/much* (which I'll represent as MUCH):

(125)   trop MUCH de tables/sucre

Licensing is once again required; in the absence of any appropriate element like *trop*, unpronounced MUCH would be impossible—for example, alongside *Have they eaten much sugar?*, there is no French:

(126)   *Ont-ils mangé de sucre? (have they eaten of sugar)

Not every degree word is a possible licenser, however. *Assez* (enough) does act like *trop*; for example, like (124)/(125) is:

(127)   assez de sucre

with the analysis:

(128)   assez MUCH de sucre

and like (107) is:

(129)   assez peu de sucre (enough *peu* of sugar = little enough sugar)

On the other hand:

(130)   si peu de sucre (so *peu* of sugar)

has no counterpart:

(131)   *si de sucre

It might be that the licenser of unpronounced MUCH in French must be + N, and that while *trop* and *assez* are or can be +N, *si* cannot be, just like *très*:

(132)   très peu de sucre (very *peu* of sugar = very little sugar)

(133)   *très de sucre

Given that alongside the possible (124)/(127), we have the impossible (126), (131), and (133), the question arises as to how French does express what they were intended to express. Let me focus on *much sugar*, which would normally be translated as:

(134)   beaucoup de sucre

Yet *beaucoup* does not seem to be a true counterpart of *many/much*. For example, it cannot be modified by *trop* (too), *si* (so), or *très* (very):

(135)   *Jean a mangé trop beaucoup de sucre. (J. has eaten too *beaucoup* of sugar)

(136)   *Jean a mangé si beaucoup de sucre.

(137)   *Jean a mangé très beaucoup de sucre.

In addition, *beaucoup* is not a polarity item in the way that *much* is:[48]

(138)   Jean a mangé beaucoup de sucre.

(139)   *?John has eaten much sugar.

Rather, *beaucoup* looks more like a French counterpart of *a good deal*, as in:

(140)   He's spent a good deal of time in London.

It is not that the two morphemes that make up *beaucoup* correspond exactly to *good* and *deal* (although *beau* and *good* have something in common),[49] but, rather, that there are two; that the first is adjectival and the second nominal; that the restrictions against modification in French seen in (135)–(137) carry over to a *good deal*:

(141)   *He's spent too/so good a deal of time in London.

(142)   *?He's spent a very good deal of time in London.[50]

and that neither *beaucoup* nor *a good deal* can be preadjectival modifiers (comparatives aside):

(143)   *Jean est beaucoup riche. (J. is *beaucoup* rich)

(144)   *John is a good deal rich.

The conclusion that *beaucoup* is more like *a good deal* than like *many/much* (despite the fact that *a good deal* (unlike *beaucoup*) is less natural with plurals than with mass nouns) seems solid and might be taken to indicate that French simply has no overt morpheme corresponding to *many/much*. Yet, in fact, one candidate does come to the fore: (107), (129), (130), and (132) have parallels with adjectives, in the sense that *trop, assez, si,* and *très* occur in:

(145)   trop petit, assez petit, si petit, très petit (too/enough/so/very small)

Against the background of (145), consider now:

(146)   Jean a mangé tant de sucre. (J. has eaten *tant* of sugar)

which would normally be translated as *J. has eaten so much sugar*. Given the proposal made earlier in (125) that *trop de sucre* is really *trop MUCH de sucre*, one could well think the same of *tant de sucre*. But *tant* is crucially unlike the degree words *trop*, *assez*, and *si* (and also *très*) in that it cannot directly modify adjectives:

(147)   *Jean est tant petit. (J. is *tant* petit)

This suggests the possibility that (146) is better analyzed as:

(148)   SO tant de sucre

with SO unpronounced and with *tant* then a truly close counterpart of *many/ much* (except that overt *tant* is (parametrically) restricted to cooccurring with SO).[51]

Taking *tant* to be essentially like *many/much* allows us to relate (147) to:

(149)   *John isn't much intelligent.

that is, to the fact that English *much* is normally impossible with adjectives. The fact that one can say:

(150)   That book isn't much good.

is almost certainly due to *good* being able to act as a noun, as suggested by:

(151)   It isn't of much good to anybody.

since overt *of* can normally not go with adjectives in English (cf. (90)), and by:

(152)   What good is that?

since *what* otherwise requires a noun.

An additional similarity between *tant* and *much* lies in the observation that *so*, in the case where it takes an adjective as antecedent, is sometimes compatible with a preceding *much* (in a way that the adjective itself would not be):[52]

(153)   John is intelligent, too much so, in fact.

combined with the observation that the closest French counterpart of this *so*, namely clitic *le*, is also compatible with *tant*, even when *le* takes an adjective as antecedent:

(154)   Jean ne l'est pas tant que ça. (J. neg so is not much *que* that)

Like (146) versus (147) is:

(155)   Jean a mangé autant de sucre que Paul. (J. has eaten as much of sugar *que* P.)

(156)   *Jean est autant petit que Paul. (J. is as much small *que* P.)

If *tant* is strongly parallel to *much*, then *autant* can readily be decomposed into *au* + *tant*, with *au*- parallel to the English comparative *as* that precedes adjectives or (adjectival) quantity words. The way French expresses the adjectival counterpart of (155) is:

(157)   Jean est aussi petit que Paul.

where *aussi* is clearly composed of the *au*- of (155) plus the *si* of (130) and (145).[53] Transposing back to English, we reach:

(158)   *John is as so small as Paul.

which is not possible, but which suggests that the following:

(159)   John is as small as Paul.

is really:[54]

(160)   ... as SO small ...

with an unpronounced SO, and similarly for:

(161)   John has eaten as much sugar as Paul.

(162)   ... as SO much ...

in which case (155) must be:

(163)   ... au SO tant ...

unifying it with (148).

This analysis of (159) and (161) amounts to saying that the degree element in these examples is the unpronounced SO rather than *as*, which thereby makes it possible that the second *as* in (159) and (161) is the same functional element as the first (rather than an accidental homonym, though its exact status needs to be elucidated).

This in turn makes it interesting (and imperative) to ask why French does not use *au-* twice:

(164)   *Jean est aussi petit au Paul.

(165)   *Jean a mangé autant de sucre au Paul.

and, conversely, why English does not use a correspondent of the *que* seen in (155) and (157):

(166)   *John is as small that/what Paul.

(167)   *John has eaten as much sugar that/what Paul.

Since saying that *au-* cannot appear in (164)/(165) because it cannot be an independent "word" is not much of an answer (why could it not be?),[55] I will leave that question open. (The question posed by (166)/(167) is not easy, either.)

Given that French overt *tant* is akin to *much/many*, except that it is restricted to occurring with the unpronounced degree element SO, we have a parametric difference of a noteworthy sort, about which we can begin to ask further questions. For example, we can wonder why SO is the only degree element that can occur unpronounced with *tant* ((146) cannot be interpreted as if it had an unpronounced TROP or ASSEZ). Relevant may be sentences like:

(168)   He can stand only so much noise.

in which *so* has a demonstrative-like interpretation, suggesting that *so* itself may have less interpretive content than *too* or *enough*,[56] and thereby be more recoverable (in a sense to be made precise, thinking of the fact that pronouns are cross-linguistically often unpronounced) than *too* or *enough*.

If so, we can then ask why English does not follow the same path as French (in which case English would allow 'SO *much*') and vice versa (in which case French would allow *si tant* (so much)). That French does not allow *si tant* would appear to be part of a clear generalization to the effect that *tant* (unlike *many/much*) cannot occur with any overt degree modifier (recall that from the present perspective the *au-* of (155) is not a degree element):

(169)   *Jean a mangé trop/si/assez/très tant de sucre. (J. has eaten too/so/enough/
         very much of sugar)

In turn, this looks like the other side of the coin represented by (125) and (128)—that is, in place of the impossible *trop tant* and *assez tant*, French has '*trop* MUCH' and '*assez* MUCH'. The question now is how best to state this. Tentatively assume the following:

(170)   If in a given language a given functional (or lexical) element can be pronounced, then it must be.

(171)   Principle (170) can be overridden.

From this perspective, English *too *(much)* sugar* is expected, while French must have recourse to (171)

3.6 A Licensing Parameter Possibly Reinterpreted as a Movement Parameter

From the preceding perspective, French and English differ in that in French MANY/MUCH can be unpronounced in the context of certain +N licensers like *trop* (too)—for example, *trop de sucre*.[57] As is so often the case, this is less a difference between the two languages taken as wholes than it might appear. The reason is that English itself allows unpronounced MANY/MUCH in the specific instance of *enough sugar*. This contrast within English between *enough sugar* and *too sugar* appears to be related to *smart enough* versus *smart too*—that is, the only degree word that allows *many/much* to be unpronounced in English is precisely the one that requires its adjectival complement to move to its left.

This leads to an alternative approach: instead of just attributing to *trop* a licensing ability with respect to MUCH denied to its counterpart *too*, it might be that in French (but not in English) MUCH moves leftward past *trop* in a way parallel to what happens overtly in English with *enough* and adjectives (despite the fact that it does not happen in French with overt adjectives).

This would make the licensing configuration (for unpronounced MUCH) the same in *enough sugar* and *trop de sucre*:[58]

(172)   MUCH enough sugar

(173)   MUCH trop de sucre

and might alter our view of the French/English difference here from simply being a parameter concerning licensing to being a parametric difference that (also) concerns movement. Put another way, it might be that the licensing of MUCH (a case of (171)) would be automatic whenever MUCH moved leftward past its degree modifier. If so, then *too much sugar* versus *trop de sucre* would reduce to the same general kind of movement parameter that one sees within English in *smart enough* versus **smart too* (apparently, a feature of the degree word itself).

In English, the adjective must cross *enough*:

(174)   *John is enough smart.

On the natural assumption that the obligatoriness of this movement carries over to the relevant French cases,[59] we have an immediate account, parallel to (174), of:

(175)   *Jean a mangé trop tant de sucre. (J. has eaten too much of sugar)

Instead, the question is now why French excludes (given (173)):

(176)   *Jean a mangé tant trop de sucre.

The answer must be the same as for English:

(177)   *John has eaten much enough sugar.

and could be attributed to:

(178)   If (171) comes into play, it does so obligatorily.

In other words (in a way parallel to the obligatoriness of movement; see note 59):

(179)   If the nonpronunciation of an otherwise pronounceable element is licensed
        in some environment, then pronunciation of that element in that envi-
        ronment is impossible.

We can think of (178)/(179) as imposing a kind of blocking effect, but if we do, we must keep it distinct from the weaker notion of morphological blocking that favors *sincerity* over *sincereness* and *invisible* over *unvisible*. I say "weaker" because both *sincereness* and *unvisible* seem to me essentially acceptable, and in any event appreciably more acceptable than (177).[60]

As is well known, (177) contrasts with:

(180)   John has eaten little enough sugar.

which, in turn, correlates with the fact that the following:

(181)   John has eaten enough sugar.

cannot have the interpretation of (180). Put another way, *little* must be pronounced, unlike *much*, even when preposed to *enough*. As in the discussion of
(168), some notion of recoverability must be at issue. (For example, it might be
that (180) contains an unpronounced negation that must be licensed by overt
little.)

The word order in (180) does not match French:

(182)   Jean a mangé assez peu / *peu assez de sucre.

Similarly, alongside the proposed (173), we have:

(183)   Jean a mangé trop peu / *peu trop de sucre.

French *peu* does not move past degree words in the way that French MUCH has
been postulated to. This may correlate in part with the fact that *peu* does not
correspond as closely to *little* as it might seem to. (Again, I return to this later.)

Recall from (131) that *si* (so) acts differently from *assez* and *trop* in that *si* is
incompatible with unpronounced MUCH:

(184)   Jean a mangé si peu de sucre. (J. has eaten so *peu* of sugar)

(185)   *Jean a mangé si de sucre.

In place of (185), French has:

(186)   Jean a mangé tant de sucre.

which I have argued to be 'SO *tant*', with *tant* corresponding to English *much*.
The question now is how exactly to exclude (185). One possibility was mentioned
at (131), using the feature +N. Another might be that if *si* is just the pronounced
counterpart of SO, then (179) provides an answer, in particular if the nonpronunciation of SO in (186) is licensed prior to the point in the derivation at which
MUCH could move. (The fact that overt *tant* in French, unlike overt *much* in
English, licenses SO needs further elucidation.)

Apparently like (184)/(185) is:

(187)   Jean a mangé très peu de sucre. (J. has eaten very *peu* of sugar)

(188)   *Jean a mangé très de sucre.

But there is an important difference—namely, there is no obvious candidate to express (188) in the way that (186) expresses what (185) might have. Put another way, English has, in particular in polarity contexts, pairs like:

(189)   John didn't eat very much sugar.

(190)   John didn't eat much sugar.

but French, it would seem, has nothing comparable. (We may be able to exclude (188) on the basis of *très* not being +N,[61] as just mentioned for *si*.)

The absence of a word-for-word counterpart in French of *too much sugar* (see (175)) has a partial parallel in the absence in French of a word-for-word counterpart of interrogative *how much sugar*. The parallel is partial in the sense that while French does have *trop petit* as a good match for *too small*, it has no two-word equivalent at all for interrogative *how small*, and more generally for interrogative *how* + adjective.[62] The translation of *how much sugar* would normally be:

(191)   combien de sucre

but there is no interrogative:

(192)   *combien petit

3.7 Missing wh-Words

Now the word *combien* is itself arguably bimorphemic, with the second morpheme equal to *bien* (well) and the first essentially the same as the *comme* that occurs in exclamative:

(193)   Comme il est petit! (how he is small)

in:

(194)   Vous considérez Jean comme un homme intelligent. (you consider J. as/like a man intelligent)

and in:

(195)   Comme j'ai dit . . . (as/like I have said)

The range of English glosses here might be taken to suggest that French *comme/com-* corresponds homonymously to (at least) two distinct elements of English. Yet while homonyms surely exist (cf. the usual (*river*) *bank* and (*savings*) *bank*), the set here (*how, as, like*) does not seem to be sufficiently arbitrary, so we should feel obliged, I think, to consider the stronger hypothesis that takes *comme/com-* to be a single element. (In a general way, we should be as skeptical as possible about allowing homonyms within the universe of (non-zero) functional elements.)

Comparing *comme* to *as* and *like*, we can note the contrast within English:

(196)   As is obvious, . . .

(197)   *Like is obvious, . . .

and the fact that in this respect *comme* acts like *like*:

(198)   *Comme est évident, . . .

If we add to this the fact that neither instance of *as* in comparatives like *Mary is as smart as Ann* translates as *comme* in French (see the discussion of (155) and (166)), we can conclude that *comme* is closer to *like* than to *as*. Thinking further of the nonstandard:

(199)   We were saying like as how we'd been there long enough.

it might be that *comme* in (195) is to be analyzed as:[63]

(200)   comme HOW j'ai dit (like HOW I have said)

and similarly for *combien de sucre*, which would be:

(201)   com-HOW bien MUCH de sucre (like HOW well MUCH of sugar = how much sugar)

If interrogative *comme/com-* were to require *bien* to appear (for reasons that would remain to be elucidated), and if *bien* were to require MUCH and if MUCH requires the presence of a noun (rather than an adjective), we would have a way of accounting for the absence in French of interrogative *how small*, in part by denying that French has any overt counterpart to *how* at all.

In which case, we could try to relate the absence of *how* in French to the absence in French of any true counterpart of *why*.[64] French *pourquoi* appears to be used in the same way, but is bimorphemic, and in that sense it corresponds closely to English *what . . . for?*, apart from the preposition stranding.[65]

French may seem to have *how* in interrogatives like:

(202)   Comment ont-ils résolu le problème? (*comment* have they resolved the problem)

but following the preceding discussion, *comment* may itself be bimorphemic—*comme* + *-ent* (like + HOW + *-ent*, with the status of *-ent* needing to be understood)—with that perhaps related to its incompatibility with the EVER of free relatives mentioned earlier (see the discussion of (88)). While French has counterparts of *whoever*..., *whatever*..., and *wherever*...with *qui* (who), *quoi* (what), and *où* (where)—for example:

(203)   Qui que tu invites, ... (who EVER that you invite)

there is none using *comment*:

(204)   However you solve this problem, ...

(205)   *Comment que tu résolves ce problème, ... (*comment* that you solve this problem)

and similarly for *combien*:

(206)   However much money you have, ...

(207)   *Combien d'argent que vous ayez, ... (*combien* of money that you have)

It may be that unpronounced EVER in French must directly follow the wh-word, but cannot with *comment* or *combien*, because of the presence of *-ent* and *bien*.[66]

Taking French to lack direct counterparts of overt *how* and *why* leads us to *when*, whose apparent French counterpart *quand* acts like *comment* in being impossible in free relatives:

(208)   Whenever we see them, ...

(209)   *Quand que nous les voyions, ... (when that we them see)

and also in simple relatives (see note 66):

(210)   the year when we met them

(211)   *l'année quand ...

Thus *quand*, along with *comment* and *pourquoi*, may be (bi- or) multimorphemic (presumably at least *qu- + -and*[67]) in French in a way that it is not in English (whereas *qui, quoi,* and *où* would correspond more directly to (the possibly bimorphemic) *who, what,* and *where*).

Assuming, then, that French lacks "simple" overt counterparts to *when, how,* and *why,* we can ask why it does (though I have no specific proposal for this case). More generally put, whenever one language lacks an overt element corresponding to one found in another language, one can (and must) ask whether the absence of such in the first language is an irreducible parametric property of the particular element in question, since it might alternatively be that that absence can be derived from independent factors.

A relevant example is:

(212)   At the age of seven (years), John . . .

(213)   A l'âge de sept *(ans), Jean . . .

English readily omits *years,* whereas French cannot omit *ans.* Although this might appear to be an irreducible property of *year(s)* versus *an(s),* there is reason to think that this English/French contrast is related to and follows from another difference between them concerning number morphology[68]—namely, that English prenominal adjectives (as opposed to French prenominal adjectives) are not accompanied by a plural morpheme. If so, then the availability of unpronounced *year(s)* in English versus French is not irreducible.

4 RELATED PARAMETERS

4.1 The Indefinite Article

I suggested earlier at (140) that French *beaucoup* is more akin to *a good deal* than it is to *many/much,* while neglecting the fact that English *a good deal* contains an *a* that *beaucoup* lacks entirely. While important, this contrast between *a good deal* and *beaucoup* is, I think, orthogonal to the idea put forth that *beaucoup* is bimorphemic and that it does not correspond directly to *many/much.* The basic reason for this orthogonality is that the presence of *a* in *a good deal* versus *beaucoup* seems to be part of a wider difference between the two languages.

It is not that French lacks an indefinite article. (In fact, except for various special cases, French prohibits arguments from being bare singulars.[69]) French *un* behaves in many ways like a typical indefinite article (in addition to being used as the stressed numeral corresponding to *one*), fitting in naturally with Perlmutter's (1970) hypothesis that indefinite articles are unstressed forms of the numeral *one*.

Rather, it is that English imposes an indefinite article in a class of cases where French either does not impose it or does not allow it at all. One concerns predicate nominals. English has:

(214)   Mary is *(a) doctor.

whereas French allows the indefinite article to be absent:[70]

(215)   Marie est médecin.

A second is:

(216)   What *(an) imbecile!

(217)   Quel (*un) imbécile!

a third:

(218)   Mary has published *(a) hundred/*(a) thousand articles.

(219)   Marie a publié (*un) cent / (*un) mille articles.

This last pair is moderately close to *a good deal* versus *beaucoup*. Even closer is:

(220)   Unfortunately, *(a) good number of linguists disagree with you.

(221)   Bon nombre de linguistes ... (good number of linguists)

where this French example lacks an overt indefinite article.

This last pair indirectly establishes a link between *a good deal* and *a good number* (and between *beaucoup* and *bon nombre*). Another point in common (this time internal to English) between *a good number* and *a good deal* lies in their nonpluralizability:[71]

(222)   *?Unfortunately, good numbers of linguists disagree with you.

(223)   *Mary has eaten good deals of sugar.

Also:

(224)   *three good numbers of linguists

(225)   *three good deals of sugar

In turn, this nonpluralizability recalls the fact that *that long a book* has no plural counterpart:

(226)   *that long books

The indefinite article of *that long a book* cannot be replaced by any other determiner:

(227)   *that long some book

I think this carries back over to:

(228)   *?Unfortunately, some good number of linguists disagree with you.

(229)   *Mary has eaten some good deal of sugar.

It may be that for *that long* to precede the determiner in *that long a book*, the determiner must not only be unstressed, as Perlmutter had the indefinite article, but also be cliticized, in the strong sense of occupying some special clitic position, one available to *a/an*, but not to any other determiner. In which case, we could say that the same holds (as the result of some UG requirement) of the *a/an* of *a good number, a good deal*—that is, it must occupy a special clitic position—and then add that French *un* (generally) lacks that option (for reasons to be discovered). The (general) lack of that option in French would, following this reasoning, preclude the appearance of *un* in (217) and (219), and arguably also with *beaucoup*.[72] (French also lacks any word-for-word counterpart of *that long a book*.)

If the preceding is on the right track, the article difference between *a good deal* and *beaucoup* is orthogonal to the real parallelism between them. Both involve adjective plus noun; *beaucoup* is closer to *a good deal* than it is to *many/ much* (which is (usually) not expressed in French). (A separate question is whether French has an unpronounced counterpart of the indefinite article in (some of) the cases mentioned above.)

4.2 The Categorial Status of *few/little* versus *peu*

Unlike *a good deal* and *beaucoup*, which agree in taking a following preposition:

(230)   a good deal of sugar

(231)   beaucoup de sucre

few/little and *peu* diverge in that *de* must intervene between *peu* and the noun:

(232)   peu *(de) livres (*peu* of books)

(233)   peu *(de) sucre

as opposed to English:

(234)   few (*of) books

(235)   little (*of) sugar

A natural proposal, in part motivated by the appearance of *de/of* with *beaucoup* and *a good deal* (where *deal* is obviously nominal), is that *de* appears with *peu* because *peu* is nominal, and that *of* fails to appear with *few* and *little* because they are adjectival.

Taking *little* in *little sugar* to be adjectival has the immediate advantage of relating it strongly to the *little* of *a little boy*.[73] In addition, it straightforwardly accounts for *very little sugar, so little sugar*, and so on, where *little* takes modifiers/ degree words typical of adjectives, as opposed to nouns. The adjectival character of *little* is brought out, too, by the contrast between *a little* and *a lot*, with *lot* acting clearly like a noun. This is seen in the contrast:

(236)   a little (*of) sugar

(237)   a lot *(of) sugar

and similarly for:

(238)   *a whole little sugar

(239)   a whole lot of sugar

as well as:

(240)   (?)They want only a very little sugar.

(241)   *They want (only) a very lot of sugar.

In pretty much the same way, *few* is clearly adjectival[74]—*very few books, so few books, fewer books, the fewest books*; also **a whole few books* and (?) *They need only a very few books*.

More intriguing is the question of the categorial status of French *peu*, whose *de* suggests nominal status, as noted. One might object, though, that nominal status for *peu* is difficult to maintain, given:

(242)   si peu *(de) livres

(243)   très peu *(de) sucre

where *de* appears even in the presence of *si* (so) and *très* (very), which otherwise modify adjectives: For example, *si grand* (so big), *très grand* (very big).[75]

But that would be to miss the importance of sentences like:

(244)   Jean a faim. (J. has hunger)

This kind of sentence, the normal way of expressing *John is hungry* is French, has an interesting property. Although *faim* is a noun by familiar criteria (it has intrinsic gender (fem.), it does not agree with anything else in the manner of an adjective, it can take determiners and relative clauses the way nouns do), *faim* has the property that in these sentences with *avoir* (have) it needs no determiner and can be modified by adjectival modifiers:

(245)   Jean a si faim. (J. has so hunger = J. is so hungry)

(246)   Jean a très faim. (J. has very hunger = J. is very hungry).

Somewhat similarly, French allows, with nouns like *professeur*:

(247)   Jean fait très professeur. (J. makes very professor = J. looks very much like a professor)

with no determiner and a modifier that otherwise normally goes with adjectives.

Yet when *professeur* (and the same holds for *faim*) does have a determiner, this kind of modifier becomes impossible:

(248)   Jean ressemble à un (*très) professeur. (J. resembles to a very professor)

(249)   Jean a une (*très) faim extraordinaire. (J. has a very hunger extraordinary)

Let me take (245)–(247) to involve NPs that are not part of any larger DP at all—that is, are not associated with any determiner at all, not even an unpronounced one.[76]

The idea now is that the way to understand the combined presence of *si/très* and *de* in (242)/(243) is to take *peu* there to be a noun that is behaving like *faim* and *professeur* in (245)–(247) (i.e., *peu*, though a noun, is not associated with any determiner).[77] It is the nominal status of *peu* that determines the presence of *de*; yet in French, nominal status is not necessarily incompatible with modification by *si* (so) and *très* (very), as we have seen.

That *peu* is a noun is supported by its ability to occur with an overt determiner in examples like:

(250)   un peu de sucre (a *peu* of sugar)

Of interest is the fact that when *peu* is preceded by *un*, it can no longer be modified by *très* (just as we saw in (248)/(249) for *faim* and *professeur*):

(251)   *un si/très peu de sucre

Rather, it acts like a normal noun embedded within DP and can take an adjective:

(252)   un petit peu de sucre (a little *peu* of sugar)

When there is no determiner, *petit* is not possible:

(253)   *Jean a mangé petit peu de sucre. (J. has eaten little *peu* of sugar)

There is obviously now a problem of sorts with the glosses. In (252), *peu* can hardly be glossed as *little*, given the presence of *petit* = little. Rather, what comes to mind is:

(254)   a little bit of sugar

In fact, if we take *peu* to be the French counterpart of English *bit*, we have an immediate understanding of the fact that *peu* requires a following *de* in, for example, (242)/(243), since *bit* in English is clearly a noun (that requires *of* before the associated NP):

(255)   a bit *(of) sugar

Further indication of the nominal (as opposed to adjectival) character of *bit* comes from (254) versus:

(256)   *a very bit of sugar

(Moreover, *a bit of* N shares with *un peu de* N a strong preference for mass over count.) The possibility of (242)/(243) in French is compatible with the nominal character of *peu*, as we saw from the discussion of (245)–(247).

Against the background of the conclusion that *peu* corresponds to *bit*,[78] let us turn to some explicit questions of parameters. The fact that French allows (245)–(247), and English does not, may well reduce to the fact that in (apparently) simpler cases French allows (215) and:

(257)   Jean est professeur. (J. is professor)

while English does not allow:[79]

(258)   *John is professor/teacher/doctor.

(If so, then *faim* in (245)–(246) and *professeur* in (247) will probably turn out not to be arguments.)

Taking:

(259)   un peu de sucre

to match (almost) perfectly:

(260)   a bit of sugar

we can ask why there is a sharp contrast when the indefinite article is omitted:

(261)   Marie a mangé peu de sucre.

(262)   *Mary has eaten bit of sugar.

To express (261) English has:

(263)   Mary has eaten little sugar.

whose word-for-word equivalent in French is ill-formed:

(264)   *Marie a mangé petit sucre.

Let me suggest that the answer might lie in aligning (252) and (254) and in claiming that *a bit* and *un peu* always require adjectival modification, which need not be overt—that is, that (259)/(260) are:[80]

(265)   un LITTLE peu de sucre

(266)   a LITTLE bit of sugar

From this perspective, we could say, first, that (262) reflects the greater English need for a determiner discussed in (214) ff.,[81] second, that that need is waived if *bit* is unpronounced (and licensed by *little*), as it arguably is in (263):

(267)   . . . little BIT sugar

third, that French does not allow *peu* to be unpronounced at all, so that (264) is not available:

(268)   . . . *petit PEU sucre

and fourth, that (267) generalizes to:

(269)   a little BIT sugar

with the indefinite article.

4.3 In What Sense Can a Difference in Category Be a Parameter?

Although (263) and (261) are natural translations of each other in French and English, the proposal here is that *little* is an adjective while *peu* is a noun. At the same time, taking into account (265)–(269), we can see that the claim is definitely not that *little* is the English equivalent of the noun *peu* in an adjectival guise. Rather, *little* corresponds strongly to the French adjective *petit*, and *peu* corresponds strongly to the English noun *bit*. The differences between English and French in this area of syntax depend on what can or cannot be pronounced and under what conditions.

Put another way, this is NOT an example of a parameter of the sort:

(270)   Some element X in UG is realized as category A in one language but as a distinct category B in some other language.

The question is, is (270) ever an admissible type of parameter? In the spirit of Baker's (1988, 46) UTAH principle, the answer should arguably be negative. Yet there do seem to be cases that one might be tempted to look at as instances of (270). In fact, there is (at least) one revealing case internal to English itself that bears, I think, on the correctness or incorrectness of (270). Consider:

(271)   John has enough/sufficient money to buy a new house.

Although it is very hard to see any difference in interpretation between *enough* and *sufficient*, there are some very sharp syntactic differences:

(272)   John is sufficiently/*enoughly rich.

(273)   John has a sufficient/*enough amount of money.

(274)   insufficient(ly); *unenough/*inenough

In these various ways, *sufficient* looks like an adjective (in allowing -*ly* and *in*- and in occurring between determiner and noun), but *enough* does not. *Enough* is usually called a degree word (as distinct from adjective) that in English has a specific word order property mentioned earlier at (174):

(275)   John has rich enough friends.

which is not possible with:

(276)   *John has rich sufficiently friends.

In light of all this, one might be tempted to conclude that *enough* and *sufficient* correspond to one and the same UG element, except that *enough* is that element realized as a degree word, whereas *sufficient* is its realization as an adjective.

This is not so much wrong, I think, as incomplete, as one can see by extending the discussion to:

(277)   That argument does not suffice to make the point.

(278)   That argument is not enough to make the point.

In light of the verb *suffice*, it is natural to take *sufficient* to be a derived form—to be an adjective (or participial adjective) composed of *suffice* plus an adjectival suffix. If this is correct, then it is primarily the relation between *enough* and *suffice* that we need to ask about. A clue comes from German, whose counterpart of *enough* is *genug*, and in which *suffice* can be translated as the verb *genügen*, transparently based on *genug*. Taking this to be an instance of "incorporation" (perhaps in the sense of Hale and Keyser 1993 and related work) and transposing back to English, we arrive at the proposal that *suffice* has (in suppletive fashion) incorporated *enough*, and that it is only in that sense that *suffice* and *enough* correspond to the same UG element.

Saying that *suffice* incorporates *enough* can be interpreted to mean simply that sentences with *suffice* contain a nonverbal node corresponding to the degree element ordinarily realized in English as *enough*. A possible, more precise, proposal would have (277) derived from a structure resembling (278)—to have *enough* incorporated into *be* (or perhaps just moved to *be*), whether by head movement or (see note 12) by phrasal movement. Generalizing, we reach the principle (cf. Grimshaw 1979; Pesetsky (1995: 3):

(279)   A given UG element is invariably associated with only one syntactic category.

By itself (279) underdetermines the answer to the question which of such a pair is to be analyzed as incorporated into which, and how exactly that is to be done. In addition (cf. Pesetsky's 1995: chap. 3 discussion of the range of theta roles associated with psych verbs), it does not provide an algorithm for determining when two morphemes or words reflect a common UG element. *Suffice* and *enough* seem to constitute a very plausible pair; other cases may be more complex.

An interesting cross-linguistic case is mentioned by Cinque (2001: 111):

(280)   John almost fell.

(281)   Jean a failli tomber. (J. has *failli* fall$_{infin}$)

The French example (281) appears to be an extremely faithful rendition of (280), although it contains an auxiliary verb *faillir* in past participle form (in addition to a finite form of auxiliary *have*). Example (281) is quite different in shape from (280), despite the apparent (absolute) synonymy. It might be that, along the lines of (270), this is an instance of a single UG element being realized variously as an adverb in English and a verb in French (which would be incompatible with (279)).

Note that this question cuts across the cross-linguistic/one-language dimension, since within English we have:

(282)   John just missed falling.

which seems very close in interpretation to (280) and quite close in shape to (281). English also allows:

(283)   John came close to falling.

If (280)–(283) (or some subset of them) do reflect a common UG element, then (279) becomes relevant and imposes (some version of) an "incorporation" analysis (as opposed to having *almost, miss/faillir,* and/or *close* as varying categorial realizations of one UG element).[82]

Ultimately, the correct theory of UG will provide a restrictive characterization of the set of available incorporation analyses that will, in turn, impose limits on what pairs/sets of sentences can be related in that fashion. Examples (277)/(278) seem very likely to constitute a pair that can (and must) be so related. Whether that is also true of (280)–(282) is a little less clear, though for those to be syntactically related seems plausible. Whether that relation should extend to (283) seems a bit more uncertain, but still possible. (How wide the range of sentences will turn out to be that fall under this kind of relation will depend in part on the limits imposed by the theory of incorporation/movement and in part on how impoverished the (functional part of the) UG lexicon is.[83])

5 COMPARATIVE SYNTAX AND GREENBERGIAN TYPOLOGY

5.1 Syntactic Data

Comparative syntax must subsume the kinds of universals discovered within the Greenbergian typological tradition.[84] That tradition is obviously highly macro-comparative in the sense of macrocomparative mentioned earlier in section 1.2. But before going on to say something about the relation between Greenbergian universals and generative comparative syntax, let me make a digression to the question of syntactic data.

Generative syntax taught us early on that in working on a given language, a native speaker has an advantage over a nonnative speaker. Being able to provide acceptability judgments oneself is an advantage. It saves time and energy, which are finite. I can work on English faster than I can work on French. I can see no disadvantage to that whatsoever. (When necessary, I can also do informant work with speakers of English, as I always must with speakers of French.)

It is almost certainly the case (although not literally provable, as usual) that I can go deeper into the syntax of English, and learn more about the human language faculty from it, than I ever could by devoting myself in isolation to the study of a language that no linguist had ever worked on, no matter how many years I devoted to it. The reason is not simply one of how fast I can work on one or the other. In working on English I can see, if not actually feel, connections between phenomena. In working on one problem, on one kind of sentence, I can readily jump to others that are relevant. Other data always come to mind because I am a native speaker of English. That can happen to some extent when I work on French, but appreciably less. If I were to try to work on Chinese, it would happen not at all, and my chances of achieving descriptive adequacy in Chomsky's (1965: 24) sense would be greatly reduced. (Every syntactician is a full-fledged native speaker of at least one language, and occasionally of some very small number of languages. Which language that is is an accident of history that is of practical importance in that it determines which language, or languages, we have an advantage working on.)

The disadvantages that we all face when working on a language not our own can fortunately be reduced. We can enlist the help of syntacticians who are native speakers of that language (as I have done for the past thirty-five or so years for French). They can make the connections that we cannot (or not as readily). Our chances of achieving descriptive adequacy can increase substantially.

All syntacticians face a problem when it comes to languages for which there are at a given time no native-speaking syntacticians available. Sometimes there are non-linguist informants available who are gifted at syntax, who can make connections, who can suggest other sentences that we haven't thought of, who can point out interpretations that would have escaped us. Sometimes there are not (or not to a sufficient degree), and in that case we have to accept that that language (at that time) may not be fertile ground for syntactic study (or at least not to the degree desired) and that it cannot participate to the same degree as others in the construction of syntactic theory.

To a certain extent, these considerations cut across macro- and microcomparative syntax. There may be a Northern Italian dialect that I am particularly interested in, but for which I can find no native-speaking syntactician. Or even worse, if it is a dialect once spoken in France, I may be able to find no native speaker at all. In that case, even if there is a very good grammar available, my chances of gleaning something of theoretical importance are reduced even further (though not necessarily to zero). However, in the case of Northern Italian (or French) dialects, I would be dealing with a language whose broad outlines are familiar and many (but not all) of whose properties are well understood, by transposition from related dialects for which there are native speakers or native-speaking syntacticians. In that sense, the challenges of this sort posed by microcomparative syntax (in well-studied families) are on the whole more manageable than the corresponding problems that arise with work in macrocomparative syntax, where a potentially interesting language may be inaccessible to a more substantial degree.

Cutting across all of this is the question of accuracy of the data, as well as accuracy of the descriptive generalizations. For languages like English, Japanese, et cetera, for which there are many native-speaking syntacticians, replicability of data is readily at hand. Inaccurate or unclear data or generalizations can be picked up and criticized widely and quickly. The fewer the number of native-speaking syntacticians for a given language, the greater the danger that a mistake will fail to be pointed out. In which case, those of us who try to keep track of and use work from many languages (whether in a micro- or macrocomparative vein) risk incorporating misinformation into our own work. There is no perfect solution, only the need to remain consistently skeptical, taking into account the range and variety of sources for the data and generalizations from a given language. (The judging of analyses and theoretical proposals involves additional factors of a more language-independent sort.)

There is no implication here that every individual syntactician needs to take into account many languages. But the field as a whole does, and has. The number of languages taken into account has increased dramatically over the past forty years, in part simply as the result of the increase in the number of languages spoken natively by syntacticians from around the world. (The number of languages or dialects for which there exist native-speaking syntacticians is, of course, still modest, compared to the number of currently spoken languages and dialects, not to mention the number of possible human languages—see section 2.)

Greenbergian typological (highly macrocomparative) work has emphasized large numbers of languages (where "large" must be kept in the perspective just mentioned),[85] some or perhaps many of which have not been worked on by native-speaking linguists. To some extent the ensuing potential problems of observational and especially descriptive adequacy have been mitigated by a restriction to relatively more accessible syntactic properties (word order and agreement, for example, as compared with parasitic gaps, quantifier scope, weak crossover, and so on). The resulting universals (more precisely, hypotheses concerning UG) have sometimes failed to hold up over time (as happens in all varieties of syntax and science).[86] At other times, the proposed universals seem to have substantial solidity.

5.2 Missing Languages

Comparative syntax can and must take these Greenbergian universals (the ones that seem to be solid) as facts to be explained, as facts that are likely to tell us something important about the human language faculty. It seems, for example, that verb-initial and complementizer-final are mutually exclusive—that is, that one never finds a language whose normal order is:[87]

(284)   *V IP C

At first glance, this is surprising, in particular against the background of the widespread mixed-headedness found across languages. (The idea that languages are predominantly either head-initial or head-final looks thoroughly wrong, especially when one takes into account a wide variety of heads, including those that are not pronounced.) The question, then, is why the order within CP should "affect" the relative order of CP and V. I have proposed elsewhere that (284) can be made sense of (only) if one gives up the idea that there is a constituent CP composed of C and IP. Rather, C is merged outside VP and IP moves to it. In languages like English of the "V C IP" sort, the visible word order is in part the result of VP-movement to the Spec of C. That is possible only if C is "initial." No reasonable combination of movements will yield (284).[88]

Generative syntax has taught us the importance of paying close attention to what is not there. Sentences that are unacceptable in a given language have a central role in telling us about the grammar of that language (and about UG). In a parallel fashion, comparative syntax teaches us the importance of observing what a priori plausible types of languages are not there, the Greenbergian case of (284) being one example.

In a rather different area of (less macrocomparative) syntax, there is the case of ECM constructions. The existence in English of sentences like:

(285)   Everybody believes John to have made a mistake.

is well known, and various analyses have been proposed. But the proper analysis of (285) must allow us to understand why (285) is not possible (or much less widely possible) in many other languages, as French, for example. Some analyses are too powerful (that is, they reflect theories that are too powerful) in that they make it "too easy" to generate one or other kind of sentence. In that sense, an approach to (285) based on S-bar (CP) deletion is unsatisfactory—it gives us no immediate way to understand why (285) is not available in all languages.[89] Another example, closer to (284), lies in the area of "heavy-NP-shift," as exemplified in English by:

(286)   They put back on the table the book that had just fallen.

Again, various analyses have been proposed over the years that I think again (despite their increasingly positive contributions) have made it "too easy" to generate such sentences, and that have not made it easy to understand why some VO languages such as Haitian lack (286) entirely.[90] That they do, must, I think, be accounted for by any proposal about (286) in English.

5.3 English and Haitian

In other words, crucial data bearing on (286) in English come from Haitian. There is no paradox. As soon as we grant that all human languages have a common

UG "infrastructure," it follows (since evidence bearing on that common infra-structure can come from any language, and since any analysis of a particular type of sentence in any language will rest in part on hypotheses about that infrastruc-ture) that evidence bearing on one language can readily and unsurprisingly come from another.

As for why heavy-NP-shift is absent in Haitian, I think the key is the obser-vation that Haitian has D following NP, rather than NP following D as in English. What this means is that for Haitian to have (286), it would have to allow:

(287)   *V . . . NP D

which is arguably impossible in a way parallel to the similar (284), with D in (287) playing the role of C in (284).[91]

Similarly, Haitian lacks right-dislocation, and also right-node raising;[92] that is, it lacks counterparts of:

(288)   We like him a lot, the guy over there.

(289)   We like, but they dislike, the young man who was just elected mayor.

Again, any analysis of English right-dislocation or English RNR, must (together with the theory in which it is embedded) allow an account of their absence in Haitian.[93] (An initial proposal would be that both right-dislocation and RNR involve D in a way parallel to heavy-NP-shift, despite various ways in which the three constructions diverge.[94])

5.4 Adpositions

Closer still to (284) than (287) is is the following (with P an adposition, not a particle):

(290)   *V DP P

which is a way of stating the Greenbergian near-universal that postpositional languages are generally not verb-initial.[95] To this generalization there are some apparent counterexamples, but it is at least possible that they are in fact instances of V P DP P with a phonetically unrealized preposition (and a final P that is better analyzed as nominal). Assuming that to be so, we need an account of (290).

As in the discussion of (284), I think that the traditional approach to P, which has it merged with DP as complement, provides no way of understanding the apparent "effect" of the relative order of P and DP on their relative order with respect to V. Instead, we need to give up the idea that P is merged with DP, in favor of having P introduced outside VP, as in the derivation (292), for (291):

(291)   They're looking at us.

(292)   . . . looking us → merger of K
        . . . K looking us → movement of DP to Spec,K[96]
        . . . us$_i$ K looking t$_i$ → merger of P
        . . . at [us$_i$ K looking t$_i$] → movement of VP to Spec,P
        . . . [looking t$_i$]$_j$ at [us$_i$ K t$_j$]

K in (292) is a Case element of the sort that is paired with P in a visible fashion in some languages such as German and Russian (but unpronounced in English). VP-movement in the last step is remnant movement of a familiar sort.

The key idea with respect to word order here is that V can come to precede P only via such VP-preposing, and that that preposing depends on P having an available Spec position. If P (and categories in general) can have only one Spec position, then VP-preposing in (292) is incompatible with DP being in Spec, P. In which case, given the antisymmetric claim (which I take to be valid) that DP in (290) could not be in complement position of P, (290) is excluded.

We can readily recast (290) in terms of clustering of properties. According to (290), the property of a language "being postpositional" clusters with the property "being V-final." The proposal sketched in (292) is part of the explanation. Another piece of the whole picture must of course be the distinction between prepositions and postpositions. If a language is prepositional, it has VP-preposing of the sort illustrated in (292). But from the perspective of a theory that attributes to sentences with prepositions a derivation like (292), what kind of derivation should be attributed to sentences with postpositions? And what kind of parameter underlies the difference between prepositions and postpositions?

In Kayne (1994) I had taken prepositions to in effect be merged with their associated DP as complement, and postpositions to be the same except that postpositions further had that DP complement move to their Spec. Postpositions from that perspective could have been thought of as having a feature inducing movement to Spec (and lacking in prepositions). However if (292) is correct in denying the existence of PP and in using K in an essential way, the preposition/postposition difference needs to be rethought.

5.5 Movement as a Side Effect of Doubling

The proposal made in Kayne (2003a) has the following components. First, just as Spec,P in (292) does not contain DP, so it does not with postpositions, either.

Second, K is uniformly introduced outside VP (as P is, but earlier), in both prepositional and postpositional languages. Third, postpositional languages with overt K seem to have DP K P order rather than *DP P K order. Putting these together leads to the idea that postpositions are necessarily accompanied by an unpronounced double (called P') that is merged later than K but earlier than P itself. A derivation would be (using English morphemes):

(293)   ... looking us → merger of K
        ... K looking us → movement of DP to Spec, K
        ... us$_i$ K looking t$_i$

At this point, the unpronounced double of P (P') is introduced, with VP moving to its Spec (just as VP moves to Spec,P in (292), with prepositions):

(294)   ... us$_i$ K looking t$_i$ → merger of P'
        ... P' us$_i$ K looking t$_i$ → movement of VP to Spec,P'
        ... [looking t$_i$]$_j$ P' us$_i$ K t$_j$

Then P itself is merged, with KP moving to its Spec:

(295)   ... [looking t$_i$]$_j$ P' us$_i$ K t$_j$ → merger of P
        ... at [looking t$_i$]$_j$ P' us$_i$ K t$_j$ → movement of KP to Spec, P
        ... [us$_i$ K t$_j$]$_k$ at [looking t$_i$]$_j$ P' t$_k$

The analysis reflected in the derivation (293)–(295) has the property that it locates the difference between prepositions and postpositions in the unpronounced double P', which is present with postpositions but absent with prepositions.[97] It thereby establishes a link (though how close a link remains to be ascertained) with other parametric differences involving doubling, such as the difference between Spanish and French with respect to overt dative clitic doubling (widespread in Spanish, absent in French with nondislocated lexical DPs).

The derivation in (292) differs from that in (293)–(295) in that the latter has P' and the former does not. We can ask how that kind of parameter (and similarly for clitic doubling) fits in with the idea that parameters are invariably (simple) features of functional heads. An immediate question is whether French has unpronounced clitic doubles in those cases in which Spanish has overt clitic doubles. If the answer is positive,[98] then Spanish versus French clitic doubling simply becomes another instance of pronunciation versus nonpronunciation, with the question remaining as to how exactly to assure the correct distribution of pronounced and unpronounced clitic doubles. The same holds for unpronounced P' versus pronounced P'—that is pronounced adpositional doubles, as mentioned in note

97—with the additional (open) question whether pronounced adpositional doubles are ever found with postpositions.

A potentially interesting property of (292) versus (293)–(295) is that there is
no irreducible movement difference involved (between prepositions and postpositions). DP moves to Spec,K in both. VP moves to Spec,P with prepositions and
to Spec,P' with postpositions, but that is less a movement difference than just the
difference between pronounced P and unpronounced P'. The only salient difference in movement appears to be that what moves to Spec,P in (292) is VP, whereas
what moves to Spec,P in (293)–(295) is KP.

5.6 Feature-driven Movement or "Closeness-driven" Movement?

However, focusing on the category difference VP versus KP obscures an important
similarity between the two derivations. In both, what moves to Spec,P is the
complement of the head just below P (K in (292), P' in (295)).

We can express this similarity by saying in part that P must have some phrase
move to its Spec (P has an EPP feature).[99] The question is, which phrase. Assume:[100]

(296)   The complement of a given head H can never move to the Spec of H.

(In feature-checking terms, this could be achieved if upon Merge the maximal set
of matching features had to be checked.[101]) Then VP-movement to Spec,P in (292)
and KP-movement to Spec,P in (295) would both follow from:

(297)   Move to Spec,P the category closest to P (that is not excluded by (296)).

Statement (297) recalls Chomsky's (1995, 296) MLC and Rizzi's (1990) relativized
minimality, except that (297) is blind to specific categorial (and other) features.

In essence what (296)/(297) says is that what gets moved to Spec,P is determined by what was merged below P and in what order. For example, KP is moved
to Spec,P in (295) as the result of P' being merged just between K and P—that
is, just above K and just below P.

Generalizing (297) to all (phrasal) movement would yield:

(298)   Move to Spec,H the category closest to H (that is not excluded by (296)).

If (298) is true, it means that what is moved where is entirely determined by what
is merged (in a given derivation) and in what order.

Setting aside the question of the validity of (298) as being beyond the scope of this article, we can still see that (297) has the effect that prepositions and postpositions will not differ with respect to movement in any way that is not a consequence of the merger or nonmerger of P'. Put another way, the parameter underlying prepositional and postpositional languages has to do at bottom with the presence or absence of P'—that is, of a certain kind of doubling.

This approach to adpositions is compatible with the antisymmetry claim that every word-order difference rests on a difference in movement, though the discussion underscored the point that that claim does not by itself determine exactly what these cross-linguistic movement differences themselves rest on.

Orthogonal to the question whether movement is feature-driven in Chomsky's sense or subject to (298) or both is the question whether a movement approach to cross-linguistic word-order differences should also extend to cross-linguistic morpheme-order differences involving affixes (i.e., morphemes not considered to be words) and to those involving clitics. Let me assume without discussion that ordering differences involving clitics—as, for example, those alluded to in the discussion of (4)/(5) and more generally those discussed in Kayne (1991)—definitely do rest on movement differences, whether on differences in clitic movement or on differences in verb or verb phrase movement (or both).

Turning to affixes, one example of a morpheme-order difference would hold between, say, Bambara, which has a causative prefix (see Koopman 1992), and Bantu languages that have a causative suffix. I think the key observation here was already made by Greenberg (1966: 93), whose Universal 27 pointed out a certain correlation between prefixation/suffixation and the position of adpositions relative to object. What Greenberg's correlation suggests is not merely that movement is involved in establishing whether some affix ends up looking like a prefix or like a suffix (which could hold via movement within the "word"), but something much stronger—namely, that movement not only underlies all cross-linguistic morpheme-order differences, but those movements that affect affix order are not segregated from phrasal movement of the familiar sort.[102]

6 CONCLUSION

In these "notes," I have touched on some (and only some) of the ways in which comparative syntax can shed light on a wide variety of questions concerning the human language faculty. In many or most or perhaps even all of the cases treated, the same results could not have been reached otherwise. Comparative syntax has become an indispensable, if not privileged, part of our attempt to understand the (syntactic component of the) human language faculty.

NOTES

For helpful comments on an earlier draft, I am indebted to Guglielmo Cinque and to Jean-Yves Pollock.

1. Cf. Chomsky (1995: 6) and references cited there; also Webelhuth (1992).

2. Whether Chomsky's (2001: 35) proposed parameter for OS would fit into a restrictive theory of parameters is not clear.

3. It may be that "pro-drop" in the third person is quite different from pro-drop in the first or second person, even in Romance. See Poletto (2000) and Kayne (2001).

4. Cf. Baker's (1996, 35n) point about the difficulty of deciding how to (numerically) count the effects of a given parameter.

5. Though not in all respects. For further details, see Kayne (1976) and Cinque (1982).

6. In the sense of "beautiful" or "inevitable," as discussed by Weinberg (1992: chap. 6).

7. Cf. Chomsky's (1981: 6) use of "may" in his "change in a single parameter may have complex effects."

8. The term may have been used first by Hellan and Christensen (1986: 1).

9. It may be possible to go further than this; see Guardiano and Longobardi (2003) and Longobardi (2003).

10. Compare the fact that some Romance has *do*-support of a sort close to that of English; Benincà and Poletto (1998).

11. For arguments against the head-initial/head-final parameter, see Kayne (1994, 2003a). For recent argument against "nonconfigurationality," see Legate (2002).

12. Baker (1996: 20, 282) states that full-fledged referential Noun Incorporation implies that the language in question also has obligatory subject and object agreement (with the exception of inanimate objects, recalling the fact that animacy is a large factor in the appearance of *a* preceding direct objects in Spanish). This is reminiscent of Cinque's (1990) discussion of Italian CLLD and may suggest that Noun Incorporation involves (phrasal) movement to a specifier position in the sentential projection.

13. Compare Kayne (1996) and Benincà (1994: 7). Controlled experiments of a different sort can be done in (the syntactic part of) comparative acquisition work; comparative neurolinguistics (of syntax) may be expected to become relevant in the future.

14. Kuroda's (1988) interesting proposal about English versus Japanese runs into difficulty when one takes into account, for example, Dravidian languages that have subject-verb agreement. The probability that intra-Romance work will have to pay central attention to Dravidian is lower; even more so for comparative work based on a set of Italian dialects.

15. Baker (1996: 7) notes that microcomparative work can lead to the "fragmentation" of parameters. This seems rather similar in a general way to what happens in the natural sciences, as microscopes of different types come into being. We can expect that clusterings of properties and correlations will continue to be found, though the properties themselves will be much finer-grained than in the past.

16. As in the case of *enough* mentioned earlier, perhaps.

17. It might be possible to alternatively relate the control difference within Romance to another well-known difference within Romance concerning postverbal subjects (in turn arguably related to verb movement). (On the limited way in which French reaches sentences with postverbal subjects, see Kayne and Pollock 2001. On other Romance languages, see Kayne 1991: 657.) In turn, this might depend on having control involve movement, not so much in the manner of O'Neil (1995; 1997) or of Hornstein (1999, 2001) (recently criticized by Landau 2003) as in the manner of Kayne (2002a), where movement is paired with a doubling structure (the controller would be the double of PRO). (The proposals concerning control in Chomsky and Lasnik 1993 do not by themselves account for the Romance correlation in question.)

18. Cf. Julien (2002), Koopman and Szabolcsi (2000) and note 102.

19. For additional discussion, see Kayne (1996).

20. Note that *a red color car*, with overt *color*, is fairly acceptable, and that *What color car did they buy?* is fully so. Compare Lanham's (1971: 310) proposal that the *mu* of *Ngimude* (I *mu* tall) appears because one really has the intermediate 'Mina muntu ngili mude' (1sg. absolute pronoun + person + *ngi* + ultimately unpronounced copula *li* + *mu* + *de*), and *mu* is agreeing with *muntu*. He also notes that postulating *mina-muntu* as an abstract subject is supported by the fact that it is a possible NP in Zulu; compare Postal (1966) with Delorme and Dougherty (1972).

21. See Kayne (2005). An early suggestion for a decompositional approach (to causatives) can be found in Chomsky (1965: 189). Note that the kind of counterargument given by Fodor (1970) and Ruwet (1972: chap. 4) was weakened by the subsequent development of the notion of "small clause," which allows one to say that *cause to die* and *kill* differ in that the latter lacks, for example, an embedded tense of the sort that the former has.

22. It seems very plausible that both *few* and *number* in the text examples fall on the functional element side of the distinction between functional element and lexical element. *Color* may well, too, be more likely than *red* to fall on the functional element side.

23. See also Chomsky's (2001: 2) uniformity principle. On Case, see Rouveret and Vergnaud (1980) and Vergnaud (1985).

24. Jean-Yves Pollock reminds me that *douzaine* can also sometimes be exactly twelve.

25. See Carstens's (1993) proposal for an unpronounced zero-affix in the case of diminutives and augmentatives in Bantu; for much relevant discussion, see Pesetsky (1995).

26. Similarly for *thousands versus thousand, millions versus million*, and so on. Note in particular *zillions of articles versus a zillion articles*, implying that *zillion* in the latter is adjectival (i.e., without any nominal -AINE suffix), in which case the imprecision of *zillion* should be attributed to its *z*-prefix (cf. the *ump-* of *umpteen*).

In French, *cent* (hundred) and *mille* (thousand) are adjectival in that they do not take *de* (of), but *million* is nominal, perhaps because it is *mill-* + *-ion*, with *-ion* nominal (whereas English *million* is *m-* + *-illion*, with *-illion* adjectival). The presence of *a* in *a hundred articles* is licensed by the unpronounced singular noun NUMBER: 'a hundred NUMBER articles' (see Kayne 2005).

Italian *cento* (hundred) is adjectival in that it does not take *di* (of), yet it shows no number agreement (unlike the general case for Italian adjectives), probably like *meno* (less) and *abbastanza* (enough).

27. It seems unlikely that *dozen* is to be analyzed as *doz-* + *en*, with *-en* comparable to French *-aine*. Like French *douzaine* (see note 24), *dozen* can be either exact, as in (i), or inexact, as in (ii):

(i)   He's spent a dozen years on that paper.

(ii)   There are dozens of typos in your paper.

Yet while plural *dozens* is quite parallel to plural *douzaines*, singular *dozen* differs from singular *douzaine* in not by itself being able to express approximation and in not taking *of*, suggesting that *dozen* does not contain an *-en* parallel to *-aine* but is rather a variant of *twelve* that has the syntax of *hundred* (including the ability to take -AINE) except for:

(iii)   three hundred/*dozen and two days

(iv)   two thousand three hundred/*dozen days

28. Note that *a good hundred articles* does not have that interpretation, either, and that the possible presence of *good* does not imply that *hundred* is a noun (vs. Jackendoff 1977: 128), any more than it does for *many* in *a good many articles*. Rather, both *hundred* and *many* are adjectival, modifying unpronounced NUMBER; see Kayne (2005) on *many* and *few*; see also note 26. Alternatively, there are differences between adjectival numerals and ordinary adjectives that remain to be understood—for example, with respect to agreement.

Moderately acceptable is *She's written twenty-ish (*of) articles this year*. The impossibility of *of* suggests that *-ish* cannot be nominal (as opposed to adjectival).

29. The restriction against numerals seen in (64) and that against the indefinite article may have something in common, but they diverge in:

(i)   They have tons / a ton/*seven tons of money.

The idiomatic 'very large quantity' reading is lost with the numeral; similarly for *lots / a lot / *seven lots* and for *large amounts / a large amount / *seven large amounts*.

30. Jean-Yves Pollock (pers. comm.) suggests that the licensing of -AINE by plural might be linked to the licensing by plural of the indefinite determiner; for relevant discussion, see Delfitto and Schroten (1991), Longobardi (1994), and Déprez (n.d.).

Guglielmo Cinque (pers. comm.) points out that *-aine* and -AINE may well correspond to a functional head in the (sentential) syntax (cf. note 102), given in particular the "approximative inversion" (NP-movement) that seems to be induced by their (unpronounced) counterpart in Russian and Ukrainian, as discussed by Franks (1995: 165ff.).

Note the contrast:

(i)   John has hundreds/*fifties of friends.

(ii)   John has tens/hundreds/*fifties of thousands of dollars.

as opposed to:

(iii)   John is in his fifties.

(iv)   John was born in the fifties.

Why *fifty* (and other non-powers of ten) is incompatible with -AINE in (i)/(ii), yet compatible with YEAR(S) in (iii)/(iv) (see Kayne (2003b)) remains to be understood, as does the analysis of:

(v)   ?Your articles must number in the fifties.

perhaps with an unpronounced pronominal:

(vi)   ... in the fifty N -s

which would recall French (cf. Gross 1977):

(vii)   Vous avez publié dans les cinquante articles. (you have published in the 50 articles = ... about 50 ...)

31. The fact that German -*t* for third singular occurs in the present but not the past recalls English -*s*, but cannot be attributed to German disallowing two inflectional suffixes, contrary to (the spirit of) Bobaljik and Thráinsson (1998: 59).

32. Though that might not extend to Hebrew or Finnish, which resemble Paduan; for some relevant discussion, see Kayne (2001).

33. Compare the possibility that irregular morphology is associated only with phonological features, as in Kayne (2003b, (116)).

34. For one recent approach, see Kishimoto (2000). The text discussion will need to be extended to cover *something else, everything else.*

35. On these effects, see Azoulay-Vicente (1985).

36. If the suggestion in notes 26 and 28—to the effect that *three hundred(*s) books* is impossible with -*s* because *hundred* is adjectival—is correct, then either *thing* in *something(*s) heavy* is adjectival (which seems odd), or these two cases of plural -*s* being impossible are to be kept apart. The latter solution may receive support from **three / a thing heavy / heavys.*

French does allow:

(i)   quelques-uns de célèbres (some-ones of famous)

but (i) is not the plural of (71) (and is not limited to animate the way (71) is). Rather it corresponds to English *some famous ones*, with an understood antecedent.

37. The paradigm is *tout* (m. sg.), *toute* (f. sg.), *tous* (m. pl.), *toutes* (f. pl.).

38. On *every* as indefinite, see Beghelli and Stowell (1997).

39. In which case, the limited *all else* needs to be looked into. An alternative approach, at least for (86), might involve a link with:

(i)   tout *(ce) que tu vois (all that that you see)

although there would be a problem with:

(ii)   *tout ce de cher

40. French does have *jamais* corresponding to English temporal *ever/never*; all three of these arguably cooccur with an unpronounced TIME.

41. French also lacks any visible counterpart of the *ever* of:

(i)   We'll go wherever you go.

though here there would be no *que*, for reasons that need looking into.

42. See Chomsky (1981) on the Empty Category Principle.

43. Example (100) is better for me with *he* in place of *John* (see Kayne 1994: 156). Interestingly, French and English also differ in the nonextraposed wh-cases. Although *Who else did you invite?* and *Qui d'autre as-tu invité?* are both fine, *??Who famous did you invite?* is less good than *Qui de célèbre as-tu invité?* The deviance of the former might be relatable to that of (97) if *who famous* can never be a derivation-final constituent. See Kayne (2000: chap. 15, (18); 2004: appendix).

For an analysis of "extraposition" that involves no rightward movement, but rather leftward movement keyed to the complementizer, see Kayne (2000: chap. 15, sect. 3) and Cinque (2003).

44. In addition, there are cases of English *of* that cannot be transposed to French— for example, *all of the books, all three of the books, the three of us.* Here, there may be a link to the fact that English is unusual, too, in having a complementizer *for* that is responsible for objective Case on a following subject (see Kayne 1981a).

45. The appearance of *-uns* (ones) here is atypical of French; for relevant discussion, see Pollock (1998).

46. Here I am thinking of the (interpretive) similarity within English between *We'll buy any book you recommend* and *We'll buy whichever book you recommend,* and the earlier postulation of unpronounced EVER (for French). (Note also that Italian *qualche* takes a singular noun.) Whether French has any exact counterpart of *some* is an open and important question; for relevant discussion, see Jayaseelan (2000).

47. Cf. Kester (1996) on English versus other languages with respect to *John bought a big *(one).* Overt versus covert is too simple (as it is in the area of pro-drop), since Italian *abbastanza* (enough) does not agree, yet occurs without *di,* as opposed to English *enough* and French *assez.* (Of importance, too, is the fact that Catalan sometimes has agreement coocurring with a preposition; see Martí Girbau 2001.) On the relevance of paradigmatic considerations, see Pollock (1994).

48. In my (colloquial) English, *many* is a polarity item, too, though to a lesser degree:

(i)   ?They have many students this year.

49. In some respects, *beaucoup* is more like *a great deal*—for example:

(i)   You haven't spent a great/good deal of time in London.

In the sense of *not very much,* (i) seems appreciably more possible with *great* than with *good.* (With *good,* (i) seems possible only as a denial.) *Beaucoup* is natural in the scope of ordinary negation. For my purposes here, the important point is that *beau* in *beaucoup* is an adjective. How exactly it matches up with *good, great,* and *beautiful* (to which *beau* often corresponds) is an important question that I will not pursue.

50. Here *a great deal* diverges from *beaucoup,* in that *a very great deal of time* is fairly acceptable.

51. Alternatively, the required unpronounced modifier of *tant* might be THAT, thinking of English *that much sugar,* which has no overt counterpart in French. Extended to Italian *tanto zucchero,* the hypothesis that *tant/tanto* corresponds to *many/ much* raises the question of the status of Italian *molto zucchero,* readily translated as *much sugar.* Alternatively, *molto* is an Italian counterpart of *very*:

(i)   molto MUCH zucchero

This might help with an understanding of *moltissimo intelligente* versus ?*pochissimo intelligente*.

52. I take this to mean that this *so* (like French *le*—on which, see Sportiche 1995a)— is not an adjective (see Corver 1997: 160, versus his p. 128), as also suggested by:

(i)   ... enough so to ...

(ii)   ... *so enough to ...

and by:

(iii)   a big enough room

(iv)   *a so enough / enough so room

53. The doubling of the *s* is orthographic; no third morpheme is involved.

54. See note 51.

55. See Julien (2002) for systematic doubts about the syntactic importance of the notion 'word'.

56. In which case the exclamative sense of:

(i)   He's eaten so much sugar!

must be attributed to a distinct (unpronounced) element or elements.

57. Also *énormément de sucre* versus *enormously (of) sugar*. For additional details, see Kayne (2002b).

58. The link between the licensing of an unpronounced element and movement recalls Rizzi's (2000, 316) discussion of null topics in German, which suggests that the movement of MUCH may be forced by UG.

59. Ideally, because universally, movement is never optional; compare Chomsky's (1995: 256) "Last Resort."

60. Some cases of sharp judgments in "morphology," such as:

(i)   John saw/*seed Paul.

might actually fall under (179), at least in part.

61. There may be a parametric difference here between French and Italian; see note 51.

62. In some cases, French can use something like *to what extent*. I leave aside the more complex question of exclamative *combien*, as well as the related question of what happens when *combien* or *tant* is separated from the adjective.

63. Compare den Besten (1978) and Larson (1987).

64. See Benincà and Poletto, chapter 6 in this volume.

65. For a parametric proposal about preposition stranding, see Kayne (1981a).

66. They may be a link here to the absence in French of a direct counterpart to the nonstandard relative *how* of:

(i)   the way how they solved the problem

(ii)   *la façon comment ...

67. This -and does not participate in a pairing with any non-wh element in the manner of when/then. (French does not have a good counterpart to the then of We saw her just then.) According to Houngues (1997: 130), Mina (Gengbè) lacks simple wh-words entirely (apart from a counterpart of which).

68. See Kayne (2003b). There is a partial similarity here to Carstens's (1997) proposal concerning unpronounced locative nouns in Bantu. Unpronounced pronominals have long been thought of as licensed by the presence of other "morphology"—see, for example, Rizzi (1982) on null subjects; see also Kester (1996), Lobeck (1995), and Delfitto and Schroten (1991).

69. For relevant discussion, see Déprez (n.d.).

70. For a comparative analysis, see Pollock (1983).

71. Some adjectives are fully compatible with numbers:

(i)   Large numbers of linguists have been coming to the talks.

(ii)   *Large deals of sugar have been eaten.

72. Un is possible, however, in (221).

73. A more thorough analysis of little sugar would have little directly modifying an unpronounced AMOUNT. See Kayne (2005).

74. As noted by Jespersen (1970: 106).

75. Why English and French contrast with respect to:

(i)   Mary is so very intelligent!

(ii)   *Marie est si très intelligente!

remains to be understood.

76. Whether très is part of that NP is not entirely clear. Relevant is Jean a trop (*de) faim (J. has too of hunger).

77. The parallel between très peu de sucre and . . . très professeur suggests taking très peu, when followed by de, to originate within a relative clause-like structure with a copula, thinking of the relation between (very) few books and books that are (very) few (in number).
The impossibility of de in:

(i)   Jean a très peu (*de) faim. ('J. has very peu of hunger)

would then be linked to:

(ii)   Jean a faim (*qui est étonnante). (J. has hunger that is astonishing)

(iii)   Jean est professeur (*qui est célèbre). (J. is professor who is famous)

with the generalization being that relative clauses (and APs that originate as reduced relatives; and possessives like de Marie) require a DP (cf. Kayne 1994: 87) and cannot combine with a bare NP. On (i) without de, see note 76.

78. This correspondence holds strongly in the singular, but English plural bits, as in:

(i)   ?John has bits of money in various bank accounts.

has no French counterpart with peu.

Note also that *peu*, when not embedded within DP, is compatible with a plural N/NP:

(ii)   Jean a peu d'amis. (J. has *peu* of friends)

though here there is no direct comparison available with English, given (262).

79. Compare Pollock (1983). With titles, English does allow *John is professor of history at . . .*

80. If (179) is correct, then either the unpronounced adjective here is not exactly the equivalent of *little* or else the structure of (265)/(266) is not identical to that of (256) (which in any event shows that LITTLE could not be modified by *very*).

The special relation between *little* and *bit* is also suggested by:

(i)   a little/?small/*large bit of sugar

(ii)   a small/large/?little amount of sugar

This contrast is sharper in:

(iii)   John is a little/*small/*large bit tired.

Note also:

(iv)   *John is a small/large amount tired.

Why there is a contrast:

(v)   John has quite a (little) bit of money.

(vi)   *John is quite a (little) bit tired.

needs to be looked into. Compare:

(vii)   John is (*quite) a little unhappy.

suggesting that (viii) is really (ix):

(viii) John is a little unhappy.

(ix)   . . . a little BIT unhappy

81. When French leaves out the determiner, an ordinary adjective becomes impossible, as in (253). Note that Italian would render (252) as:

(i)   un pochino di zucchero (a bit *-ino* of sugar)

where *-ino* is a suffix arguably equivalent to *little*, and presumably requiring movement across it.

82. Alternatively, as Guglielmo Cinque (pers. comm.) suggests, it might be that (281) contains an unpronounced ALMOST and (280) an unpronounced verb MISS comparable to *faillir*; see Cinque (2001: 111). In the same spirit, (277) might contain an unpronounced ENOUGH, thinking of the near-possible:

(i)   ?That won't suffice enough.

83. Relevant here is Ronat's (1972) criticism of Postal (1970). See also note 21.

84. Compare Greenberg (1966) and later work, for example, Dryer (1992).

85. Work on large numbers of languages is, of course, not specific to the typological tradition; see, for example, Cinque (1999) and Julien (2002).

86. See Dryer (1988) on adjectives.

87. See Dryer (1992). Specifying "normal order" is necessary since, as Bayer (2001, 32) points out, postverbal C-final clauses are possible in Marathi, Telugu, and Malayalam. See also the following discussion of (290).

88. For details, see Kayne (2000: chap. 15, 2003a) and Cinque (2003).

89. The government-based approach of Kayne (1981a) needs to be rejuvenated but is probably closer to the truth. On the causative subtype of ECM, leading to the question why some languages, but not others, need to dativize the embedded subject, see Rouveret and Vergnaud (1980), Kayne (1981b, 2004). The *want*-subtype of ECM found in English is almost certainly dependent on English having a *for*-complementizer that can fail to be pronounced; see Kayne (1981b) and note 44 above.

90. On Haitian, see Dejean (1993).

91. More exactly, what is parallel to C is a D merged high, not a low one; for details, see Kayne (2003c).

92. I am indebted for these data to Michel DeGraff.

93. And the same for English Q-floating/stranding and its absence (Michel DeGraff, pers. comm.) in Haitian.

94. For example, RNR allows preposition-stranding more readily than heavy-NP-shift. Michel DeGraff tells me that (non-Gallicized) Haitian also disallows sentences like:

(i)   John knows and appreciates classical music.

(see also Dejean (1993 (102b))), supporting the proposal in Kayne (1994: 61) that such apparent verb-coordination is really RNR.

95. See Dryer (1992: 83).

96. Compare in part McCloskey (1984).

97. Absent in (292), that is. Whether prepositions can have unpronounced doubles in more complex constructions such as quantifier stranding and right- and left-dislocation is a related but separate question. I also leave aside here the question of visible doubles of prepositions, as found to some extent in Italian (Rizzi 1988: 514) and more marginally in French (Kayne 1975: 154n).

98. As seems plausible; see Sportiche (1995b).

99. Possibly, every functional head has an EPP feature, or better, there is no such feature, but rather a general need for functional heads to have filled Specs. See Kayne (2000: 322).

100. Contrary to Kayne (1994). Having P (and similarly for K, C, and—as in Sportiche (2002)—D) introduced outside VP makes it unnecessary (and impossible) for DP-P order to be produced by complement-to-specifier movement.

101. Alternatively, thinking in part of Nunes (2001), it might be that H-XP and XP-H are contradictory orders.

102. On the lack of segregation between morpheme order within "words" and order at the phrasal level, see Kayne (1994: 40) (and (10)). A still stronger position (which I think is likely to be correct) is taken by Julien (2002) and by Koopman and Szabolcsi (2000).

REFERENCES

Azoulay-Vicente, A. (1985) *Les tours comportant l'expression de + adjectif.* Droz, Geneva.

Baker, M. C. (1988) *Incorporation: A theory of Grammatical Function Changing.* University of Chicago Press, Chicago, Ill.

Baker, M. C. (1996) *The Polysynthesis Parameter.* Oxford University Press, New York.

Bayer, J. (2001) "Two Grammars in One: Sentential Complements and Complementizers in Bengali and Other South Asian Languages," in P. Bhaskararao and K. V. Subbarao (eds.) *The Yearbook of South Asian Languages: Tokyo Symposium on South Asian Languages—Contact, Convergence and Typology.* Sage, New Dehli, 11–36.

Beghelli, F., and Stowell, T. (1997) "Distributivity and Negation: The Syntax of *Each* and *Every*," in A. Szabolcsi (ed.) *Ways of Scope Taking.* Kluwer, Dordrecht, 71–107.

Benincà, P. (1994) *La variazione sintattica: Studi di dialettologia romanza.* Il Mulino, Bologna.

Benincà, P., and C. Poletto (1998) "A Case of *Do*-Support in Romance." *University of Venice Working Papers in Linguistics* 8: 27–64.

Bobaljik, J. D., and H. Thráinsson (1998) "Two Heads Aren't Always Better Than One." *Syntax* 1: 37–71.

Carstens, V. (1993) "On Nominal Morphology and DP Structure," in S. A. Mchombo (ed.) *Theoretical Aspects of Bantu Grammar 1.* CSLI Publications, Stanford, Calif., 151–180.

Carstens, V. (1997) "Empty Nouns in Bantu Locatives." *Linguistic Review* 14: 361–410.

Chomsky, N. (1957) *Syntactic Structures.* Mouton, The Hague.

Chomsky, N. (1965) *Aspects of the Theory of Syntax.* MIT Press, Cambridge, Mass.

Chomsky, N. (1981) *Lectures on Government and Binding.* Foris, Dordrecht.

Chomsky, N. (1986) *Knowledge of Language.* Praeger, New York.

Chomsky, N. (1995) *The Minimalist Program.* MIT Press, Cambridge, Mass.

Chomsky, N. (2001) "Derivation by Phase," in M. Kenstowicz (ed.) *Ken Hale: A Life in Language.* MIT Press, Cambridge, Mass., 1–52.

Chomsky, N., and H. Lasnik (1993) "Principles and Parameters Theory," in J. Jacobs, A. von Stechow, W. Sternefeld, and T. Vennemann (eds.) *Syntax: An International Handbook of Contemporary Research.* Walter de Gruyter, Berlin.

Cinque, G. (1982) "On the Theory of Relative Clauses and Markedness." *Linguistic Review* 1:247–294.

Cinque, G. (1990) *Types of A'-Dependencies.* MIT Press, Cambridge, Mass.

Cinque, G. (1999) *Adverbs and Functional Heads: A Cross-Linguistic Perspective.* Oxford University Press. New York.

Cinque, G. (2001) " 'Restructuring' and Functional Structure." *University of Venice Working Papers in Linguistics* 11: 45–127.

Cinque, G. (2002) "A Note on Restructuring and Quantifier Climbing in French." *University of Venice Working Papers in Linguistics* 12: 7–30.

Cinque, G. (2003) "A Note on Verb/Object Order and Head/Relative Clause Order." Unpublished ms., University of Venice.

Corver, N. (1997) "*Much*-Support as a Last Resort." *Linguistic Inquiry* 28: 119–164.

Dejean, Y. (1993) "Manifestations en créole haïtien du principe d'adjacence stricte." Unpublished ms.

Delfitto, D., and J. Schroten (1991) "Bare Plurals and the Number Affix in DP." *Probus* 3: 155–185.

Delorme, E., and R. C. Dougherty (1972) "Appositive NP Constructions: *we, the men; we men; I, a man; etc.*" *Foundations of Language* 8: 2–29.

den Besten, H. (1978) "On the Presence and Absence of *Wh*-Elements in Dutch Comparatives." *Linguistic Inquiry* 9: 641–671.

Déprez, V. (n.d.) "Morphological Number, Semantic Number and Bare Nouns." Unpublished ms.

Dryer, M. S. (1988) "Object–Verb Order and Adjective–Noun Order: Dispelling a Myth." *Lingua* 74: 185–217.

Dryer, M. S. (1992) "The Greenbergian Word Order Correlations." *Language* 68: 81–138.

Emonds, J. (1978) "The Verbal Complex V'-V in French." *Linguistic Inquiry* 9: 151–175.

Fodor, J. A. (1970) "Three Reasons for Not Deriving *kill* from *cause to die.*" *Linguistic Inquiry* 1: 429–438.

Franks, S. (1995) *Parameters of Slavic Morphosyntax.* Oxford University Press, New York.

Greenberg, J. H. (1966) "Some Universals of Grammar with Particular Reference to the Order of Meaningful Elements," in J. H. Greenberg (ed.) *Universals of Language,* 2nd ed. MIT Press, Cambridge, Mass., 73–113.

Grimshaw, J. (1979) "Complement Selection and the Lexicon." *Linguistic Inquiry* 10: 279–326.

Gross, M. (1977) *Grammaire transformationnelle du français: Syntaxe du nom.* Paris, Larousse.

Guardiano, C., and G. Longobardi (2003) "Parametric Syntax as a Source of Historical-Comparative Generalisations." Unpublished ms., University of Pisa/University of Trieste.

Hale, K., and S. J. Keyser (1993) "On Argument Structure and the Lexical Expression of Syntactic Relations," in K. Hale and S. J. Keyser (eds.) *The View from Building 20: Essays in Linguistics in Honor of Sylvain Bromberger.* MIT Press, Cambridge, Mass., 53–109.

Harris, J. W. (1969) *Spanish Phonology.* MIT Press, Cambridge, Mass.

Hellan, L., and K. K. Christensen (1986) "Introduction," in L. Hellan and K. K. Christensen (eds.) *Topics in Scandinavian Syntax.* Reidel, Dordrecht, 1–29.

Holmberg, A., and G. Sandström (1996) "Scandinavian Possessive Constructions from a Northern Swedish Viewpoint," in J. R. Black and V. Motapanyane (eds.) *Microparametric Syntax and Dialect Variation.* John Benjamins, Amsterdam, 95–120.

Hornstein, N. (1999) "Movement and Control." *Linguistic Inquiry* 30: 69–96.

Hornstein, N. (2001) *Move! A Minimalist Theory of Construal.* Blackwell, Malden, Mass, and Oxford.

Houngues, D. M. K. (1997) "Topics in the Syntax of Mina." Ph.D. diss., Boston University.

Jackendoff, R. (1977) *X' Syntax: A Study of Phrase Structure.* MIT Press, Cambridge, Mass.

Jayaseelan, K.A. (2000) "Questions and Question-Word-Incorporating Quantifiers in Malayalam." Unpublish ms., CIEFL, Hyderabad.

Jespersen, O. (1970 [1914]) *A Modern English Grammar on Historical Principles. Part II: Syntax (First Volume).* George Allen & Unwin, London, and Ejnar Munksgaard, Copenhagen.

Julien, M. (2002) *Syntactic Heads and Word Formation*. Oxford University Press, New York.

Kayne, R. S. (1975) *French Syntax: The Transformational Cycle*. MIT Press, Cambridge, Mass.

Kayne, R. S. (1976) "French Relative 'que'," in F. Hensey and M. Luján (eds.) *Current Studies in Romance Linguistics*. Georgetown University Press, Washington, D.C., 255–299.

Kayne, R. S. (1981a) "On Certain Differences between French and English." *Linguistic Inquiry* 12: 349–371.

Kayne, R. S. (1981b) "Two Notes on the NIC," in A. Belletti, L. Brandi, and L. Rizzi (eds.) *Theory of Markedness in Generative Grammar: Proceedings of the 1979 GLOW Conference*. Scuola Normale Superiore, Pisa, 317–346.

Kayne, R. S. (1991) "Romance Clitics, Verb Movement and PRO." *Linguistic Inquiry* 22: 647–686. (Reprinted in Kayne 2000.)

Kayne, R. S. (1994) *The Antisymmetry of Syntax*. MIT Press, Cambridge, Mass.

Kayne, R. S. (1996) "Microparametric Syntax: Some Introductory Remarks," in J. R. Black and V. Motapanyane (eds.) *Microparametric Syntax and Dialect Variation*. John Benjamins, Amsterdam, ix–xviii.

Kayne, R. S. (2000) *Parameters and Universals*. Oxford University Press, New York.

Kayne, R. S. (2001) "A Note on Clitic Doubling in French," in Guglielmo Cinque and Giampaolo Salvi (eds.) *Current Studies in Italian Syntax: Essays Offered to Lorenzo Renzi*. North-Holland, Amsterdam, 189–212 (Reprinted in Kayne 2000.)

Kayne, R. S. (2002a) "Pronouns and Their Antecedents," in S. Epstein and D. Seely (eds.) *Derivation and Explanation in the Minimalist Program*. Blackwell, Malden, Mass., 133–166.

Kayne, R. S. (2002b) "On Some Prepositions That Look DP-internal: English *of* and French *de*." *Catalan Journal of Linguistics* 1: 71–115.

Kayne, R. S. (2003a) "Antisymmetry and Japanese" *English Linguistics* 20: 1–40.

Kayne, R. S. (2003b) "Silent Years, Silent Hours," in L.-O. Delsing et al. (eds.) *Grammar in Focus. Festschrift for Christer Platzack, Volume 2*. Wallin and Dalholm, Lund, 209–226.

Kayne, R. S. (2003c) "Some Remarks on Agreement and on Heavy-NP-Shift," in M. Ukaji, M. Ike-Uchi, and Y. Nishimara (eds.) *Current Issues in English Linguistics* (Special Publications of the English Linguistic Society of Japan, volume 2). Kaitaku-sha, Tokyo, 67–86.

Kayne, R. S. (2004) "Prepositions as Probes," in A. Belletti (ed.), *Structures and Beyond*, Oxford University Press, New York.

Kayne, R. S. (2005) "On the Syntax of Quantity in English," in R. S. Kayne *Movement and Silence*. Oxford University Press, New York.

Kayne, R. S., and J.-Y. Pollock (2001) "New Thoughts on Stylistic Inversion," in A. Hulk and J.-Y. Pollock (eds.) *Inversion in Romance*. Oxford University Press, New York, 107–162.

Kester, E.-P. (1996) "The Nature of Adjectival Inflection." Ph.D. diss., University of Utrecht.

Kishimoto, H. (2000) "Indefinite Pronouns and Overt N-Raising." *Linguistic Inquiry* 31: 557–566.

Koopman, H. (1992) "On the Absence of Case Chains in Bambara." *Natural Language and Linguistic Theory* 10: 555–594.

Koopman, H., and A. Szabolcsi (2000) *Verbal Complexes.* MIT Press, Cambridge, Mass.

Kuroda, S.-Y. (1988) "Whether We Agree or Not: A Comparative Syntax of English and Japanese." *Lingvisticae Investigationes* 12: 1–47.

Landau, I. (2003) "Movement out of Control." *Linguistic Inquiry* 34: 471–498.

Lanham, L. W. (1971) "The Noun as the Deep-Structure Source for Nguni Adjectives and Relatives." *African Studies* 30: 299–311.

Larson, R. K. (1987) " 'Missing Prepositions' and the Analysis of English Free Relative Clauses." *Linguistic Inquiry* 18: 239–266.

Legate, J. A. (2002) "Warlpiri: Theoretical Implications." Ph.D. diss., Massachusetts Institute of Technology, Cambridge, Mass.

Lobeck, A. (1995) *Ellipsis: Functional heads, Licensing, and Identification.* Oxford University Press, New York.

Longobardi, G. (1994) "Reference and Proper Names." *Linguistic Inquiry* 25: 609–665.

Longobardi, G. (2003) "Methods in Parametric Linguistics and Cognitive History." Unpublished ms., University of Trieste.

Martí Girbau, N. (2001) "*De* in Quantitative Constructions: A Marker of Unspecificity." Presented at *Going Romance 2001, Main Session: Workshop on Determiners, Abstracts.* University of Amsterdam, 58–59.

McCloskey, J. (1984) "Raising, Subcategorization and Selection in Modern Irish." *Natural Language and Linguistic Theory* 1: 441–485.

Nunes, J. (2001) "Sideward Movement." *Linguistic Inquiry* 32: 303–344.

O'Neil, J. (1995) "Out of Control," in J. N. Beckman (ed.) *Proceedings of NELS 25.* GLSA, University of Massachusetts, Amherst, 361–371.

O'Neil, J. (1997) "Means of Control: Deriving the Properties of PRO in the Minimalist Program." Ph.D. diss., Harvard University.

Perlmutter, D. M. (1970) "On the Article in English," in M. Bierwisch and K. E. Heidolph (eds.) *Progress in Linguistics.* Mouton, The Hague, 233–248.

Pesetsky, D. (1995) *Zero Syntax: Experiencers and Cascades.* MIT Press, Cambridge, Mass.

Poletto, C. (2000) *The Higher Functional Field in the Northern Italian Dialects.* Oxford University Press, New York.

Pollock, J.-Y. (1983) "Sur quelques propriétés des phrases copulatives en français." *Langue Française* 58: 89–125.

Pollock, J.-Y. (1989) "Verb Movement, Universal Grammar, and the Structure of IP." *Linguistic Inquiry* 20: 365–424.

Pollock, J.-Y. (1994) "Checking Theory and Bare Verbs," in G. Cinque, J. Koster, J.-Y. Pollock, L. Rizzi, and R. Zanuttini (eds.) *Paths toward Universal Grammar: Studies in Honor of Richard S. Kayne.* Georgetown University Press, Washington, D.C., 293–310.

Pollock, J.-Y. (1998) "On the Syntax of Subnominal Clitics: Cliticization and Ellipsis." *Syntax* 1: 300–330.

Postal, P. M. (1966) "On So-Called 'Pronouns' in English," in F. P. Dineen (ed.) *Report of the Seventeenth Annual Roundtable Meeting on Linguistics and Language Studies.* Georgetown University Press, Washington, D.C., 177–206.

Postal, P. M. (1970) "On the Surface Verb 'Remind'." *Linguistic Inquiry* 1: 37–120.

Rizzi, L. (1982) *Issues in Italian Syntax.* Foris, Dordrecht.

Rizzi, L. (1988) "Il sintagma preposizionale," in L. Renzi (ed.) *Grande grammatica itali-*

ana di consultazione. Vol. I: *La frase. I sintagmi nominale e preposizionale*. II Mulino, Bologna, 507–531.

Rizzi, L. (1990) *Relativized Minimality*. MIT Press, Cambridge, Mass.

Rizzi, L. (2000) *Comparative Syntax and Language Acquisition*. Routledge, London.

Ronat, M. (1972) "A propos du verbe 'Remind' selon P. M. Postal: La sémantique générative—une réminiscence du structuralisme?" *Studi Italiani di Linguistica Teorica ed Applicata* 1: 233–267.

Rouveret, A., and J. R. Vergnaud (1980) "Specifying Reference to the Subject: French Causatives and Conditions on Representations." *Linguistic Inquiry* 11: 97–202.

Ruwet, N. (1972) *Théorie syntaxique et syntaxe du français*. Editions du Seuil, Paris.

Sportiche, D. (1995a) "French Predicate Clitics and Clause Structure," in A. Cardinaletti and M. T. Guasti (eds.) *Small Clauses*. Academic Press, San Diego, Calif.

Sportiche, D. (1995b) "Clitic Constructions," in L. Zaring and J. Rooryck (eds.) *Phrase Structure and the Lexicon*. Kluwer, Dordrecht.

Sportiche, D. (2002) "Movement Types and Triggers." *GLOW Newsletter* 48: 116–117.

Vergnaud, J.-R. (1985) *Dépendances et niveaux de représentation en syntaxe*. John Benjamins, Amsterdam.

Webelhuth, G. (1992) *Principles and Parameters of Syntactic Saturation*. Oxford University Press, New York.

Weinberg, S. (1992) *Dreams of a Final Theory*. Vintage Books, New York.

CHAPTER 2

ON THE GRAMMATICAL BASIS OF LANGUAGE DEVELOPMENT

A Case Study

LUIGI RIZZI

1 INTRODUCTION

MODERN linguistics has often stressed the rapidity of the language-acquisition process: when children start the systematic acquisition of structured domains of knowledge at school, they already have acquired the fundamental structures of their native language. Language acquisition is remarkably rapid, given the complexity of the acquired system and the fact that acquisition takes place naturally, without an explicit teaching. This remarkable cognitive achievement sets strong empirical conditions for the study of language as a cognitive capacity: linguistic models must be able to capture the fact that every normal child succeeds in acquiring language within the observed limits of time and exposure to data.

Acquisition is rapid, but not instantaneous. This is immediately obvious if we consider production: newborn babies don't talk, and when children start producing the first recognizable linguistic sounds, the first words, and then the first word combinations, they do not talk like adults. There is observable development: for a few years, the child's system undergoes systematic changes and recognizable phases, to eventually stabilize and converge to the target system.

This chapter reports on a trend of developmental research which is characterized by the use of sophisticated linguistic models of the "Principles and Parameters / Minimalism" type, and by the adoption of the comparative perspective, with full use of the theoretical apparatus of modern comparative syntax.

The theory-conscious study of language development is defined by three fundamental questions:

1. What is the nature of early grammatical systems?
2. What makes early grammatical systems change over time?
3. What is the time course of grammatical development?

The first question bears on the basic ingredients that early grammars are made of. The crucial issue is the validity and range of the hypothesis that there is a fundamental continuity in language development (Pinker 1984); this issue can be addressed through the detailed comparative study of early and adult grammatical systems: Is the internalized grammar of the child cast in the same mold as adult grammars, or is it different in fundamental respects? Is continuity the prevailing factor in development, or are there critical points of discontinuity?

The second question bears on the identification and study of the causal factors of development: What is the respective role of learning (of lexical inventories, of morphological paradigms, etc.) and of inner maturational schedules in language development?

The third question aims at designing a temporal chart of the sequence of events which take place in normal language development, also in view of defining a baseline for the study of developmental pathologies.

Over the last twenty years or so, a lot of progress has been made on the first question, and the hypothesis of a fundamental continuity between early and adult systems has received strong empirical support. This progress took place under the impulse of the parametric approach to comparative syntax, which offered a conceptual framework and formal tools well suited for comparing grammatical systems. Much work was also devoted to the second question, but the progress has been more limited, and the level of controversy is greater. This is not surprising, as conceptual and formal advances in the theory of syntax are less immediately of help for addressing this question: the motor of development must somehow lie outside grammatical theory. As for the third question, the drawing of the temporal chart has proceeded steadily for production, with the constitution and study of natural production corpora and with much experimental work on elicited production and other aspects. As for comprehension, there has been progress in certain areas, but much of the experimental work remains to be done. Here we restrict our attention to the study of early production, with only occasional reference to the (potential) relevance of the developmental study of comprehension.

This chapter is organized as follows. After a short historical excursus on the influence and relevance of the theory of parameters for the study of development, I consider a central case study to illustrate this recent research trend: the analysis of subject drop in early linguistic production.

I try to show that early subject drop is a genuine grammatical option available in early systems, not the mere effect of performance limitations. After studying in some detail the structural conditions in which subject drop is possible in early grammars, I discuss some cases of argument drop in adult systems that are structurally akin or identical: Topic Drop and Root Subject Drop. I then address the question of why the Root Subject Drop parameter (and other parameters connected to the dropping of material) seem to permit a delayed resetting on the negative value, thus giving rise to observable developmental effects, while other parameters appear to have already been correctly fixed when syntactically relevant production begins, in compliance with Wexler's (1998) Very Early Parameter Setting. I try to address this split in the time course of parameter fixation within an approach in which language development is grammatically based, but keyed to the growth of the performance systems.

2 HISTORY

The study of language acquisition is a fundamental component of the program of generative grammar ever since its origins. So much so that Chomsky's "Conditions on Transformations," the first full-fledged attempt to structure the theory of Universal Grammar, starts with the following statement: "From the point of view that I adopt here, the fundamental empirical problem of linguistics is to explain how a person can acquire knowledge of language" (Chomsky 1973: 232). In the same vein, about a decade earlier, Chomsky had defined "explanatory adequacy"—the most ambitious level of empirical adequacy that a linguistic analysis can achieve—as the level reached when the acquisition process is captured (see, e.g., Chomsky 1964, and, for a recent discussion of this notion within the Minimalist Program, Chomsky 2001 and 2002). Nevertheless, apart from few noticeable early attempts (e.g., Edward Klima's collaborative work with Ursula

Bellugi in the 1960s—see Klima and Bellugi 1966), till relatively recently, little attention was paid by theoretical linguists to the actual process of language development. Rather, the acquisition problem was addressed as an abstract logical problem, characterized by Chomsky (1986) (and in much related work) as the variant of Plato's problem pertaining to linguistic knowledge: What kind of inner structure should we presuppose in the learning mechanism to account for the acquisition of a system as rich and structured as the adult knowledge of language on the basis of the linguistic evidence available to the child? This question can be asked at an abstract level, abstracting away from the actual time course of acquisition, and can be modeled as an achronic, or instantaneous, process; these issues are often discussed informally but can be phrased precisely through the formal techniques of Learnability Theory (Pinker 1979, Wexler and Culicover 1980).

Models of generative grammar till the mid-1970s were based on the idea that the adult speaker's knowledge of his native language is expressed by a Particular Grammar, a system of rules that are construction specific and language specific. Universal Grammar (UG) is a grammatical metatheory, expressing the general format of grammatical rules, and some very general conditions on rule application (such as the "A over A" condition, etc.). In this model, language acquisition is a process of grammatical induction: children must figure out, on the basis of individual linguistic experience, the grammatical rules of the language they are exposed to, within the grammatical space defined by UG. A major problem confronting this approach was that no clear and effective ideas about how grammatical induction could work were available.

A major change took place in the late 1970s with the introduction of the Principles and Parameters model of UG. The first step was the observation that principles on rule application gave rise to slightly different results across languages, and the variation could be expressed by assuming that they contained certain parameters (like the class of bounding nodes for subjacency, which was responsible for the selective violability of Wh-islands in some languages—see Rizzi 1978 and Chomsky 1981). Then it was quickly realized that this approach could be deemed responsible for the whole cross-linguistic variation (at least in syntax), thus making it possible to dispense with the concept of "language-specific rules" altogether. In this conception, UG is a system of principles with certain choice points, the parameters, that allow a restricted variability. A particular grammar is simply UG with the parameters set in a particular way: UG plus a specific set of parametric values.

Within this model, language acquisition is an operation of parameter setting: language learners, equipped with the innate UG structure, set the parameters of the system on the basis of their linguistic experience. There is no process of rule induction, because there is no language-specific rule system to figure out: acquiring the computational properties of a natural language amounts to selecting some internally generated options and discarding, or "forgetting," other options, on the basis of experience (on "learning by forgetting" in phonology, see Mehler and Dupoux 1992).

This approach had an extraordinary effect on comparative syntax: parametric models offered a theoretical language that permitted natural capture of the cross-linguistic invariants while concisely expressing the domains of variation, thus quickly enhancing the empirical and theoretical dimension of syntactic comparison.

As for language acquisition, not only did the theory of parameters lead to a radical reformulation of the logical problem of language acquisition, it also profoundly affected the study of language development. Language development raises descriptive problems that are analogous to those raised by comparative syntax: the domain involves the comparison of systems that are similar (say, the comparison between early English, early French, and early Chinese, as well as the comparison between these systems and their adult counterparts), but with local points of divergence; the theoretical language of parameters thus offered an attractive opportunity to address the issues of development, at the same time potentially extending the explanatory coverage of the theory and adding a new dimension, the comparison of early and adult systems, to the comparative endeavor (see also the introductory chapters of Rizzi 2000a and Friedemann and Rizzi 2000). I will now illustrate this direction of research through a representative case study.

3 SUBJECT OMISSION IN THE EARLY PHASES OF THE ACQUISITION OF A NON-NSL

Some adult languages, such as Italian and most of the Romance languages, allow null pronominal subjects in tensed clauses (*(Io) parlo italiano* (I speak Italian)); other languages, such as English and other Germanic languages, do not have this option and require the overt expression of pronominal subjects (*(I) speak English*). This distinction led researchers to the postulation of a parameter of Universal Grammar, the Null Subject Parameter (NSL), the first extensively studied case of parameter, ever since the early 1980s (Rizzi 1982: ch. 4 and Jaeggli and Safir 1989, among much other work).

Child languages would appear to be more uniform in this respect. In early linguistic productions, children tend to omit subjects even when the target language is not an NSL. Examples like the following are typically found in natural production corpora (speakers' names and ages—years; months; days—in parentheses):

(1)   English (Brown 1973)
     a. _____ was a green one (Eve, 1;10)

     b. _____ falled in the briefcase (Eve 1;10)

(2)   French (Hamann et al. 1996)
     a. _____ a tout tout tout mangé (Augustin 2;0)
     '_____ has all all all eaten'

     b. _____ ôter tout ta (Augustin 2;0)
     '_____ empty all that'

(3)   Danish (Hamann & Plunkett 1997, 1998)
     a. _____ er ikke synd (Jens 2,1)
     '_____ is not a pity'

     b. _____ ikke køre traktor (Jens 2,0)
     '_____ not drive tractor'

Subject omission in early production cannot be reduced to a subcase of a general tendency to speak "telegraphically," omitting pronouns and other functional material (on the hypothesis that there may be a "prefunctional stage" in development, see Radford 1990). Subject omission is selective with regard to object omission for instance: Bloom (1990) counted subject and obligatory object omissions in the natural productions of children acquiring English (Adam (2;3–2;7), Eve (1;6–1;10), Sarah (2;3–2;7), corpus available through CHILDES, see MacWhinney and Snow 1985) and found a huge discrepancy: 55% of subjects were omitted, while only 9% of obligatory objects were (see Hyams and Wexler 1993 for similar results and discussion). Moreover, subject omission is strongly sensitive to the structural position of the subject, a property that would be totally unexpected under a generalized strategy of deletion of pronouns and other functional elements.

In addition, subject omission is a very stable phenomenon in development. Consider the following table, concerning omissions in nonimperative clauses in the natural production of a child acquiring French:

(4)   **Hamann, et al. (1996)**
      Early Null subjects in French (Augustin)
      Proportion of Null Subjects

Age[a]	Verbal utterances (no.)	Null subjects (no.)	%
2;0;2	49	23	46.9
2;0;23	23	14	60.8
2;1;15	15	7	46.6
2;2;13	44	16	36.3
2;3;10	33	10	30.3
2;4;1	53	29	54.7
2;4;22	46	22	47.8
2;6;16	100	37	37.0
2;9;2	141	35	24.8
2;9;30	133	19	14.2

[a] The first column expresses the age of the child (years; months; days); the second gives the number of nonimperative verbal utterances; the third the number of null subjects; and the fourth the proportion of null subjects.

Subject omission oscillates between 60% and 30% throughout the first part of the third year of life; around age 2;9 it still involves about a quarter of the relevant verbal utterances, and only in the last recording, around age 2;10, it falls under the bar of 20%. The persistency of the phenomenon throughout the third year of life is not at all a peculiarity of this particular child: it appears to be the general case in the acquisition of Non-Null Subject Languages. Early subject drop thus appears to be a kind of developmental universal.

Why is it so? Hyams (1986) put forth the influential hypothesis that early subject drop results from a missetting of the Null Subject Parameter. Suppose that the Null Subject Parameter (whatever its appropriate formulation) is initially set on the positive value, the one licensing null pronominal subjects in tensed clauses. Then nothing happens in the acquisition of Italian, Spanish, and other languages; the evidence available to the child is consistent with the initial value, and no development is observed. In contrast, the child learning English, French, and other languages must eventually realize that the target system is not a NSL; but this takes time, whence the developmental effect and the observed null subject phase.

This hypothesis gave rise to a major interdisciplinary debate on the relevance of theoretical linguistic tools for the study of language development and was at the source of the current theory-conscious trend of developmental studies. One direction of research that was pursued was to verify if other parameters of UG would give rise to similar developmental effects. Another direction was to pursue a more fine-grained analysis of the structural properties of early subject drop, to verify if they matched what is observed in adult NSL's.

4 The Time Course in the Fixation of Some Major Parameters

It is a rather traditional observation in developmental studies that word-order properties of the target system are by and large respected when syntactically significant production starts, in the so-called two-words stage, around the end of the second year of life or shortly thereafter. Children learning English, French, or Italian, typically produce VO structures, while children learning Japanese or Korean typically produce OV structures, not the other way around. In parametric terminology, the headedness parameter (or its equivalent in a system like Kayne 1994) appears to be already fixed when (syntactically relevant) production begins.

The same conclusion seems to be true for more subtle parameters, such as the amount of verb movement in the inflectional structure. So, Pierce (1989, 1992) showed that, already in the two-word stage, children acquiring French raise finite verbs to an inflectional position higher than negation (*Il (ne) mange pas* 'he eats not') and leave nonfinite verbs in VP internal position (*(ne) pas manger* 'not to eat'); Stromswald (1990) observed that children acquiring English never attempt to produce nontarget consistent "French-like" structures with the lexical verbs raised past negation (**He eats not*); again, the V-movement parameter(s) studied in Emonds (1978), Pollock (1989), and much subsequent work appears to be correctly fixed as soon as syntactically significant production starts. The same conclusion was reached by Poeppel and Wexler (1993) on the fixation of the Verb Second parameter in Early German; and by Hamann, et al. (1996) on the fixation of the clitic parameter(s) (primarily, the parametric choice of the structural host of the clitic), at least in the sense that, as soon as children acquiring French start producing object clitics, they place them in the correct clitic position.

These observations led Wexler (1998) to postulate that parameter setting is done perceptually, before the onset of production (Very Early Parameter Setting): when syntactically significant production begins, major parameters have already been set on the target-consistent values, which are faithfully reflected by early production.

But then what about the early null subject stage? If VEPS may well be valid for major word-order parameters, it may not hold for other kinds of parametric choices. In fact, other cases involving the dropping of material seem to give rise to a delayed fixation.

A potential case is the dropping of the copula. Becker (2000) showed that children acquiring English tend to drop the copula honoring structural or interpretive distinctions along lines similar to those governing the syntax of copulas in some adult languages. Becker observed that four children learning English (Nina 2;0–2;2, Peter 2;0–2;3, Naomi 2;0–2;7, Adam 2;7–3;4) dropped copulas selectively, much more frequently when the predicate was a locative PP, as in (5)b, then when it was a DP, as in (5)a:

(5)   a. It (is) a dog (overt copula: 72.4%)

       b. It (is) in the garden (overt copula: 20.9%)

She interpreted this difference not as a primitive structural difference, but as a reflex of the interpretive properties of the two types of predicates, with locative PP's typically expressing a temporary property (or stage level) and DP predicates normally expressing a permanent property (individual level) of the subject. She also connected the children's pattern to the fact that some adult languages formally sanction the same interpretive divide with distinct forms of the copula (Spanish *ser* vs. *estar* for individual- and stage-level predicates, respectively) and even with selective copula drop, a phenomenon restricted, in Modern Hebrew, to stage-level predicates (with many complications discussed by Becker and in references quoted there):

(6)   a. Ha-kli   ha-ze   hu   patis.
          the tool   the this   COP   hammer

       'This tool is a hammer.'

       b. Dani   _____   me'od   'ayef   ha-yom.
          Dani   COP   very   tired   the day

       'Dani is very tired today'

Other cases may be amenable to a similar analysis. The omission of the copula is often treated as akin to another characteristic feature of child language: the use of Root (or Optional) Infinitives. Around the age of two, children typically use infinitival verbs in main clauses in nontarget-consistent ways—for instance, to describe an event that they just observed. The following examples are taken from Child French:

(7)   a. Voiture partir (Grégoire 1;11)

          'Car leave'

       b. Misette lancer la balle dans la cour (Philippe 2;1)

          'Misette throw the ball in the court'

    c. Maman faire boum sur le camion (Philippe 2;1)

      'Mommy make boum on the truck'

    d. Michel dormir là (Philippe 2;2)

      'Michel sleep there'

    e. Pas marcher toboggan (Philippe 2;2)

      'Not work toboggan

According to some analyses, this major case of nontarget consistency is related to a maturational process, somehow permitting the extra option of omitting the tense specification in child systems (this is a primitive option in Wexler 1994; the consequence of the option of omitting external structural layers in Rizzi's 1993–94 truncation approach; and the consequence of a more abstract computational principle, the Unique Checking Constraint, in Wexler 1998[1]); other analyses, such as that by Avrutin (1998), point out that some adult languages can make a rather extensive use of nonfinite main clauses, even in descriptive environments. One case is the Russian construction "[which] indicates the beginning of an action that follows immediately some event assumed to be known" (Avrutin 1998: 66):

(8)   a. Carevna xoxotat.
       princess to-laugh

       'The princess started to laugh, right after something funny happened.'

    b. Zriteli applodirovat.
       'spectators to-applaud

       'The spectators started to applaud right after something exciting was done.'

So even though the point is controversial, it is not inconceivable that this case too may be amenable to an initial parameter missetting (see also Lasser 1997 on main infinitival constrictions in adult and child German).

Along partly analogous lines, Chierchia, et al. (2000) analyzed determiner drop in child language as akin to the parametric choice of determiner-less adult languages, again a case of initial parametric missetting.

If these analyses are on the right track, the question arises of why certain parameters, roughly characterizable as involving the grammatically driven dropping of material should differ from major word-order parameters in not respecting VEPS and in giving rise to observable developmental effects. I go back to this important question in section 11.

5 EARLY SUBJECT DROP REVISITED: ROOT SUBJECT DROP

Going back to early subject drop, one line of inquiry to test the hypothesis of the early missetting of the Null Subject Parameter is to study the fine structural properties of the phenomenon, to verify if they match the structural context in which null pronominals are licensed in Null Subject Languages.

A preliminary hint that this was not the case came from an observation in Valian (1991): in her rather extensive corpus (21 learners of English, ages 1;10–2;8) she found only 9 null subjects out of 552 non-subject Wh questions (1.6%). That is, while the subject omission in environment (9a) is robustly attested, it is virtually absent in environment (9b):

(9)   a. (dis) goes there

      b. Where *(dis) goes?

Valian's observation prompted the conjecture (Rizzi 1992) that early subject drop in the acquisition of a non-Null Subject language is limited to the highest position of the clause—the specifier of the root. If the sentence starts with a Wh-element in the C system, as in (9b), the subject is not the specifier of the root, and cannot be dropped:

(10)   Early Subject Drop in the acquisition of a non-NSL is only possible in the Specifier of the root.

The root subject drop conjecture was quickly confirmed in other languages. Crisma (1992) observed plenty of subject drop in Philippe's corpus (ages 2;1–2;3; see Suppes et al. 1973)) in declaratives like (11a) (406 out of 1,002, or 40.5%), and virtually no subject drop in post-Wh-environments like (11b) (1 out of 114, or 0.9%):

(11)   a. _____ est perdu xxx celui-la (Philippe 2;2)

            '_____is lost that one'

       b. Où il est le fil? (Philippe 2;1)
           'Where it is the wire?'

Crisma's finding was confirmed by Levow (1995) based on a larger French corpus (Grégoire 1;9–2;3 [CHILDES], Nathalie 1;9–2;3, Daniel 1;8–1;11—see Lightbown 1977): she found 55% of null subjects in declaratives versus only 5% of null subjects in the post-Wh-environment.

Hamann (2000) brought an interesting addendum: null subjects in French in situ (i.e., unmoved) Wh-questions are about as frequent as in declaratives. In Augustin's corpus, in the period 2–2;4 we find that 49% of the in situ Wh-questions have null subjects, and in the period 2;6–2;10 the proportion lowers to 26%, about as in declaratives. This observation is important because it shows that there is no inherent incompatibility between null subjects and Wh-questions: what counts is the initial or noninitial position of the subject (in the following examples the final subject is presumably right dislocated):

(12)   a. _____ marche sur quoi Cedric? (Augustin 2;6,16)
          ‘_____ walks on what Cedric?’

       b. _____ est où maman? (Augustin 2;6;16)
          ‘_____ is where mummy?’

Haegeman (1995, 1996a) validated the root null subject conjecture for Child Dutch. Her corpus (Thomas 2;3–2;11, Hein 2;4–3;1, Niek 2;8–3;10) shows stability of subject omissions in initial position at 24.4% to 23%. But in noninitial position in post-Wh-environments (in fact, with order Wh V S . . . , as the language is V-2), null subjects are near absent (at 2.8% to 1.3%).

Along similar lines, Clahsen, et al. (1995) looked at an extensive corpus of Child German: 134 recordings from 9 children ages 1;7–3;8. Only 4% of post-Wh-subjects were null. It is not possible to determine from this study the number and proportion of initial null subjects in the same corpus, but initial null subjects are a robust phenomenon in Child German (e.g., Duffield 1993 reports over 2,000 null subjects in Simone's files 3–22—i.e., over a quarter of the subject environments), so that it's very likely that early German will reproduce the sharp asymmetry that Haegeman found in Early Dutch.

An independent indication of the validity of the Root Null Subject conjecture comes from the study of the acquisition of subordination. Subordinate clauses become robustly attested in child corpora about at the time when subject drop is disappearing. Nevertheless, there is some overlap; in this period, we typically find examples with main subjects dropped and embedded subjects expressed, such as the following:

(13)   a. _____ went in the basement . . . that what we do . . . after supper (Eve 19)

       b. _____ know what I maked (Adam 31)

Valian (1991) found no null subjects out of 123 finite embedded clauses in her corpus of Early English. The same observation was made in Roeper and Weissenborn (1990) for Early German. The limitation to the specifier of the root strongly separates early subject drop from the null subjects resulting from the positive fixation of the Null Subject Parameter. Null Subject languages allow null subjects in initial and noninitial (post-Wh, or embedded) position. In these systems, the highest subject position does not seem to have any privileged status, and the null pronominal subject is licensed under a local (Agreement) relation with the verbal inflection, regardless of the position of the *pro*-Agr complex with respect to other elements in the structure:

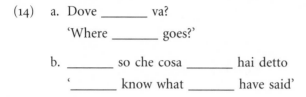

(14) a. Dove _____ va?

         'Where _____ goes?'

      b. _____ so che cosa _____ hai detto

         '_____ know what _____ have said'

Thus the Early Subject drop is a very different phenomenon from the licensing of *pro* in NSL's: the structural environments in which the two phenomena are legitimate are sharply different. We thus have clear evidence against the analysis of Early Subject Drop as a missetting of the Null Subject Parameter.

At this point we should ask the question: What happens in the acquisition of a NSL? Do young learners of Italian drop subjects like adult Italians? Or rather like their peer learners of English and French?

In fact, in natural production corpora we find plenty of examples of subject drop in the post-Wh-environment (the following data are from Cipriani et al. 1993):

(15) a. Ov'è? (1;8)   c. Pecché piangi? (2;3)

         'Where is?'   'Why (you) cry?'

      b. Cos'è ? (1;10)   d. Quetto cosa fa? (2;5)

         'What is?'   'This what does?'

Guasti (1995) calculated the proportion of subject drop in post-Wh-environments. In the corpus of Child Italian she took into account (Martina 1;8–2;7, Diana 1;10–2;6, Guglielmo 2;2–2;11), she found that, out of 171 nonsubject Wh-questions, 104 had null subjects (or 60.8%).

In conclusion: the Null Subject Parameter appears to be correctly fixed early on, as is shown by the sharp difference between Early Italian and Early English,

French, Dutch, German in the noninitial (post-Wh)-environments. Learners of Null Subject Languages freely drop subjects in this environment, in which learners of non-NSL's virtually allow no subject drop. So, it appears that the Null Subject parameter is quickly fixed on the correct value, in accordance with VEPS. On top of the negative fixation of the Null Subject Parameter, learners of non-NSL have the independent option of dropping subjects in the Spec of the root. Once the distinct structural properties of this option are recognized, the question arises of its exact nature, and of its independent existence in adult systems. Is root subject drop an independent parameter of UG, an option adopted by some adult languages? Before addressing this question, I need to introduce an important refinement in the analysis: child language seems to allow two structurally distinct kinds of null subjects.

6 Two Kinds of Early Null Subjects: Licensing Conditions and Development

We have already seen that children can use nonfinite structures more freely than adults; in particular, as main clauses. Roeper and Rohrbacher (1994) studied the distribution of null subjects in finite and nonfinite clauses; they confirmed the observation that early null subjects are restricted to the initial position, but they added the important proviso that this constraint only holds in finite clauses, not in (root) infinitives: while examples like (16a), with a clause-initial Wh-element and a null subject, are virtually absent, cases like (16b) are numerous in the corpus they considered (Adam 2;3–2;11):

(16)   a. (*)Where _____ goes / went is his going?

       b. Where _____ go(ing)?

    This is not too surprising: nonfinite clauses typically allow (or require) null subjects in the adult grammar. Children allow nonfinite structures as main clauses: under continuity assumptions, we thus expect null subjects to be possible in such cases. And, also not surprisingly, we find that the kind of null subject occurring in (main) nonfinite clauses is insensitive to first position; its occurrence is legitimate because it is the subject of a nonfinite clause, irrespective of any other positional constraint. Integrating Roeper and Rohrbacher's observation, we are thus led to conclude that two distinct kinds of early null subjects must be postulated: null subjects that are legitimate in the Spec of the root, typically occurring in finite clauses, and null subjects occurring in nonfinite clauses, which are legitimate in both initial and noninitial position (see also O'Grady et al. 1989, Hyams and Sano 1994, Bromberg and Wexler 1995 on English, and Rasetti 2000 on French).

What about the nature of the two types of null subjects? As for the kind occurring in nonfinite structures, an immediate answer seems to be that it is PRO, the null subject typically occurring in untensed structures in adult grammars. We may then assume that PRO will be licensed in the Spec of an untensed I, as in the adult grammar (via the PRO theorem, or the Null Case approach of Chomsky and Lasnik 1995), the only relevant difference being that children in the Root Infinitive phase permit untensed structures more liberally than in the target systems.

As for the empty category allowed to occur in the Spec of the Root, things are less straightforward. When the distributional generalization was discovered, syntactic theory didn't offer an obvious theoretical principle, based on adult models, to deduce a descriptive statement like the following:

(17)   *ec* is licensed in Spec of the root.

One possibility was to capitalize on the fact that the Spec of the Root is the highest position in the structure, the one that c-commands everything else, and isn't c-commanded by any other category. In the general case, a null element must satisfy a requirement of identification clause-internally. For instance, one cannot leave an unidentified gap in an object position, as in (18a); (18b) is fine because the gap is connected, through a syntactic chain, to the head of the relative, which recovers the content of the null object:

(18)   a. * John put _____ on the table.

       b. The book which John put _____ on the table.

The null elements, which are locally licensed in a Spec-head configuration, are identified by the licensing head (*pro* is identified by the Strong Agr of Null Subject Language in the analysis of Rizzi 1986, and PRO is arguably identified by the local Agr under the Anaphoric Agreement approach of Borer 1989); other types of null elements need a c-commanding identifier, as in (18b). This requirement has sometimes been expressed as the identification component of the Empty Category Principle:

(19) ECP (Identification): *ec* must be identified through chain-connection to a c-commanding antecedent.

This suggests a possibility to capture the special property of the Spec of the root. Suppose that principle (19) must be met up to virtual satisfiability: it must be satisfied if it can be satisfied—if the structure offers the ingredients for a possible satisfaction (this interpretation is inspired by the approach to the theory of Binding in Chomsky 1986: the local domain of an element is the smallest category with a subject in which the element's binding requirement is virtually satisfiable). The Spec of the root is not c-commanded by any category, so that there is no potential identifier for it, under (19); then, under the "virtual satisfiability" interpretation, it is the only position exempted from the clause internal identification requirement: it can host a null element not identified clause internally and available for identification in the discourse.

We now have to deal with the fact that both types of null subjects disappear in the development of a non-NS Language. What is the causal factor of development? As for null subjects in main clause infinitives, things are rather straightforward: they disappear when Root Infinitives (RI) disappear. The disappearance of RI in development is no trivial issue in and of itself, but it is pretty obvious that this developmental event will determine the loss of the structural environment for this kind of early null subject.

As for the loss of root null subjects in finite main clauses, some additional assumption is needed. Why are they impossible, for example, in adult French? Suppose that the following principle holds in adult grammars:

(20) Root = CP

If not only questions but also declaratives are CPs, the subject position (Spec IP) is never the specifier of the root; hence, it cannot host a root null subject. In this approach, one is led to identify the factor that triggers development in principle (20): perhaps this principle is not operative in early grammars, but as soon as it becomes effective, in accordance with an inner maturational schedule, the subject position ceases to be a possible host for an unidentified null element, in terms of the approach presented in this section, and the early null subject option is lost. This is the proposal in Rizzi (1992), which I come back to and revise in section 10 (see also, for relevant discussion on this approach, Prévost and White and other chapters in Friedemann and Rizzi, 2000).

7 AGAINST EXTRAGRAMMATICAL EXPLANATIONS

In the previous discussion I have followed Hyams's (1986) original hypothesis that early null subjects are a grammatically based phenomenon: there is a property in the early grammars that makes subject drop grammatically licit in certain positions.

An alternative view has often been proposed, based on the competence-performance divide. Perhaps early grammars are even closer to the target systems than early production suggests. Linguistic production is a complex task, involving the fine coordination of different systems, the system computing abstract linguistic representations and the articulatory system, with its complex motor programs. Fine-tuning, automatization, and short-term memory growth (to integrate the different kinds of relevant information) take time, so that production may start with a production system that is not fully up to its tasks. So it could be that early production does not fully mirror the underlying grammar because of performance limitations. It could be, for instance, that subject drop and other nontarget-consistent omissions of material are dictated by performance limitations, rather than grammar based.

This line of argument raises immediate questions, though. As we have seen, the dropping of material is not generalized and unstructured: it appears to obey certain structural patterns. So, extragrammatical approaches must rely on grammar-independent factors to address such regularities. One particular extra-grammatical approach relies on pragmatics (Greenfield and Smith 1976). Perhaps, in order to facilitate the task of the immature production system, the child tends to produce only new, focal information, freely omitting old information even when it is grammatically required. Subjects tend to express old information more than objects do, and this may account for the fact that subjects are more frequently omitted, quite independently from grammar-driven options—so the "pragmatic" account of subject drop goes.

But as soon as a more detailed analysis of the structural properties of the phenomena is available, this approach appears untenable. Consider the root null subject generalization, in particular the fact that subject drop is virtually absent in post-Wh environments. In such structures as *Where DP goes*, and *Où DP est*, the Wh-element takes up the focus of the structure (as is directly shown by the fact that Wh-consituents are often overtly marked as focal in languages using overt focus particles, such as Gungbe; see Aboh 1998), so that the rest of the structure, and the subject position in particular, is presupposed, old information. So, the post-Wh-environment should be a particularly favorable environment for subject drop, contrary to fact. Clearly, the relevant generalization is not naturally expressible in informational terms.

Or consider Roeper and Rohrbacher's observation that in post-Wh-environments only nonfinite, uninflected clauses allow null subjects: again, an information-based approach does not seem to have anything to say on this distributional constraint. So this variant of the extragrammatical approach seems unable to capture the basic structural patterns of early subject drop.

A different kind of extragrammatical approach appeals directly to the fact that different positions in the clause may involve different levels of processing difficulty, thus determining selective droppings of material in the positions in which the production system is more heavily solicited. Along such lines, Bloom assumes a processing theory according to which "the processing load at every point is proportional to the number of yet-to-be-expanded nodes that must be kept in working memory" (1990: 501), so that the processing load will be maximal at the beginning of the sentence and then decrease from left to right. Then, Bloom argues, subjects are more likely to be dropped than objects because they occur earlier in the sentence, in the structural environment in which the processing load is maximal. This approach would seem to predict a slow decrease of the frequency of pronoun drop from left to right, in parallel with the decrease of yet-to-be-expanded nodes. But this is not what the detailed structural study has observed: rather, what has been observed is a sharp distinction between the first position, freely allowing pronoun drop, and every other position, basically banning it (in inflected clauses). In particular, the processing account seems to be unable to account for the obligatory overtness of subjects in post-Wh-position like (16a): here the yet-to-be-expanded nodes after the subject involve the whole IP structure, exactly as in the corresponding declarative, so that there seems to be no basis to expect the impossibility of subject drop in this environment. Or, consider again Roeper and Rohrbacher's observation: inflected and uninflected clauses have the same configurational structure, under standard assumptions, so that there is no basis to predict the sharp observed difference between the two cases.[2]

These indications seem to me to strongly argue against an extragrammatical account: early subject drop takes place in initial position and in the subject position of uninflected clauses, a state of affairs that can be naturally traced back to grammatical principles and parameters.

Nevertheless, Bloom (1990) provides interesting evidence for the relevance of processing considerations in early subject drop. He shows that sentences with null subjects tend to have longer VPs in Child English: perhaps, the child planning a more complex VP is more likely to drop the subject, thus reducing the processing load. Other indications that early subject drop may correlate with other factors of syntactic complexity come from previous work. For instance, Bloom (1970) had observed that early subject drop is more frequent when certain factors of complexity are added—for instance, in negated versus nonnegated sentences. Mazuka et al. (1986) and Valian (1991) also argued for the relevance of processing limitations in the dropping of structural material.

All these observations give plausibility to the idea that early subject drop is somehow connected to the facilitation of the task of an immature production system, but they must be reconciled with the clear evidence for the grammatical nature of the phenomenon. In fact, in my opinion, there is no contradiction between the two findings: it could very well be that early subject drop is a genuine grammatical option of the early system *and* that the child may use it to alleviate a processing problem. This functional role is responsible for the effects found by Bloom and others but does not affect the status of subject drop as a grammatical option, a formally legitimate computational operation allowed by the early grammatical system.

That a genuine grammatical option may be used to alleviate a performance problem is obvious and uncontroversial. Consider, for instance, a classical performance problem: the difficulty of parsing center-embedded structures (Miller and Chomsky 1963): (21a) is as unparsable in Italian as the English gloss is. But Italian has the option of leaving subjects in VP final position. If we use this option and place the subject of the first relative clause *L'editore che il governo ha finanziato* (the publisher that the government funded) after its predicate *ha pubblicato* (published), we obtain the much more parsable sentence (21b):

(21)   a. Il libro che l'editore che il governo ha finanziato ha pubblicato ha vinto un premio. (Unparsable)

'The book that the publisher that the government funded published won a prize.'

b. Il libro che *pro* ha pubblicato l'editore che il governo ha finanziato ha vinto un premio. (Parsable)

'The book that *pro* published the publisher that the government funded won a prize.'

What happens in inverted structures? Consider the two representations:

(22)   a. Il libro$_i$ [che [l'editore$_k$ [che [il governo ha finanziato _____$_k$] ha pubblicato_____$_i$]]] ha vinto un premio.

'The book that the publisher that the government funded published won a prize.'

b. Il libro$_i$ [che [*pro* ha pubblicato _____$_i$ [l'editore$_k$ [che il governo ha finanziato _____$_k$]]] ha vinto un premio.

'The book that *pro* published the publisher that the government funded won a prize.'

What seems to be problematic in (21a) is that we have an antecedent-gap dependency embedded within a dependency of the same kind: in Miller and Chomsky's terms, the procedure for relative clause interpretation cannot be called upon a second time while it is being used. Subject inversion in (21b) has the effect of putting the two antecedent-gap dependencies in linear succession, a configuration which is not problematic for the human parser:

(23)   NP$_i$ NP$_k$ _____$_k$ _____$_i$

(24)   NP$_i$ _____$_i$ NP$_k$ _____$_k$

Clearly, subject inversion is a grammatical option, a property that some languages have and others (English, for instance) don't have. It is a grammatical option which may be used to alleviate a performance problem, such as the difficulty with center embedding, an interpretation that seems to be fully legitimate and uncontroversial for the case of subject inversion. I would like to claim that the case of early subject drop is entirely analogous.

8 SOME ADULT MANIFESTATIONS OF THE "PRIVILEGE OF THE SPEC/ROOT"

Under continuity assumptions, we expect adult languages to manifest in some form the special status that the Spec of the root appears to have in child language. So continuity assumptions led researcher to look for adult analogs of the privileged status that the specifier of the root appears to have in licensing null elements in child grammars.

The first case that was discussed in direct connection with early subject drop concerned certain special written registers of adult languages. In previous work Liliane Haegeman had observed that initial subject drop is possible in special abbreviated registers, such as the "diary register," of adult English, French, and other languages; the limitation to the main subject position suggested an immediate parallel with the child phenomenon (see Haegeman 2000 and references quoted therein; see also Haegeman and Ihsane 1997 for the identification of a more "liberal" diary register, permitting subject drop also in internal positions).

(25)   a.   A very sensible day yesterday. _____ saw no one. _____ took the bus to Southwark Bridge.

b. _____ walked along ... (Virginia Woolf, *Diary*, from Haegeman 1990)

c. _____ m'accompagne au Mercure, puis à la gare ...

'(he) takes me to Mercure, then to the station ... '

d. _____ me demande si ... je lui eus montré les notes

'(I) ask myself if ... I would have shown him the notes' (Paul Léautaud, *Le Fléau, Journal Particulier, 1917–1930*, pp. 60–70, from Haegeman 1990)

At least partial analogs were quickly observed also in spoken registers. A relevant case is Topic Drop, as it manifests itself in colloquial German, Dutch, and other Germanic languages, as per Ross's (1982) original discussion. The option of a null pronominal topic is found when the pronoun is in the left periphery, as in (26a), and excluded when the pronoun is in IP internal position, with the left peripheral position in a V-2 configuration filled by another constituent, as in (26b–c); in embedded clauses (whether V-2 or not) a null topic is disallowed (as in (26d–e)). So, only the Spec of the root appears to be a possible position for a null topic in these languages.

(26) Topic Drop in Colloquial German (Dutch, Swedish, but not Flemish)

a. (Ich) habe es gestern gekauft.

'(I) have it yesterday bought.'

b. Gestern habe *(ich) es gekauft.

'Yesterday have (I) it bought.'

c. Wann hat *(er) angerufen?

'When has he telephoned?'

d. Hans glaubt *(ich) habe es gestern gekauft

'Hans believes I have it yesterday bought.'

e. Hans glaubt dass *(ich) es gestern gekauft habe.

'Hans believes that I it yesterday bought have.'

Topic Drop differs from the child phenomenon in that it can involve not just subjects, but other topicalized constituent—for instance, object topics, as in (27); moreover, it is restricted to topics, and as such it does not extend to nontopic elements such as expletives (see (28)), which are typically dropped by children. (This is true in the varieties exhibiting a restrictive version of Topic Drop, such as the one described by Cardinaletti 1990; other less-restrictive varieties of German and other Germanic languages also admit expletive drop: consider, e.g., the paradigm in colloquial Swedish discussed in Rizzi 1992 and the detailed discussion in Haegeman 1996b):

(27) _____ habe ich t gestern gekauft

‘_____ have I yesterday bought’

(28) a. *_____ wurde viel getanzt

‘_____ was a lot danced’

b. *_____ hat viel geregnet

‘_____ has a lot rained’

The option of dropping material in the Spec of the Root is not found in all V-2 languages: it does not seem to exist in West Flemish (Haegeman 1996b: 141). It is also not limited to adult V-2 languages. For instance, Brazilian Portuguese lost the status of Null Subject Language in the twentieth century (see Kato and Negrão 2000, and section 11 later); nevertheless, Figueiredo (1996) observes that the language retained the possibility of dropping a referential subject in initial position:

(29) a. _____ comprei um carro ontem

‘(I) bought a car yesterday.’

b. * O que que _____ comprei ontem?

‘What that (I) bought yesterday?’

c. * A Maria disse que _____ vendi o carro muito caro.

‘Maria said that (I) sold the car too expensive.’

Along similar lines, Kenstowicz (1989) observed that Arabic dialects, such as Levantine Arabic, while disallowing Infl-licensed null subjects, permitted null subjects in main declaratives:

(30) a. _____ istarat l-fustaan.

‘_____ bought the dress.’

b. *Fariid kaal innu _____ istarat l-fustaan.

‘Fariid said that _____ bought the dress.’

c. Fariid kaal inn-ha istarat l-fustaan.

‘Fariid said that she bought the dress.’

And De Crousaz and Shlonsky (2000) pointed out that in Gruyère Franco-Provençal the subject clitic, obligatory in post-Wh-environment (31b), is optional both in main declaratives and in situ Wh-questions (31a–c), much as in Child French:

(31)　a. (I) travayè pra.

　　　　'(She/He) works a lot.'

　　b. Portyè *(i) travayè?

　　　　'Why she/he works?'

　　c. (I) travayè kan?

　　　　'She/He works when?'

In fact, the option of dropping initial subjects (and, more generally, clause-initial material) is found also in oral colloquial registers of English. Thrasher (1977) describes such a register with the following properties:

(32)　a. (I) thought I heard something.

　　b. I thought *(I) heard something.

　　c. _____ can't do it, can I/you/he/she/they/we?

　　d. More problems, *(I) don't need.

　　e. What do *(you) want?

In this colloquial register, subject drop is possible in main but not in embedded environments; it may concern any subject personal pronoun, as the tag in (32c) shows; and it is not possible when the subject is preceded by a topic or by a Wh-element.

9 BACK TO PARAMETER SETTING: TOPIC DROP LANGUAGES AND ROOT SUBJECT DROP LANGUAGES

The existence of adult systems like those analyzed in the previous section, which take advantage of the "privilege of the Spec of the Root" to allow a null element not identified clause-internally, has a number of consequences for the analysis of the developmental phenomenon. On the one hand, it lends further support to the grammatical nature of the process: children seem to use a grammatical option, one that some adult systems also exploit. On the other hand, the existence of such adult systems makes a maturational account of the child phenomenon implausible and suggests that genuine parameters of UG are involved. So, starting from the latter point, the first step of the analysis should be to explore possible parametric accounts to express the fact that different adult languages make different uses of the "privilege of the root."

Let us start from Topic Drop languages. How can one formally express the Topic Drop Parameter? Say, how can one formally distinguish Dutch and West Flemish, two very close grammars sharing core formal properties (e.g., both languages are V-2) but distinct, among other things in that only the first allows Topic Drop? One could argue that this is a simple lexical difference: perhaps, only Topic Drop languages have, in their functional lexicon, a null pronoun licensed in topic position, in the left periphery of the clause. But this account would not express the fundamental structural property of the phenomenon—the fact that it appears to be restricted to the left periphery in main clauses. Why should the licensing of the null topic be restricted to the unselected C system and be excluded from embedded clauses (which, in general, can host overt topics)? The traditional one-layer theory of CP does not offer a natural way to express the parametrization.

More recent approaches to the C system, assuming a richer structure for the left periphery of the clause, appear to be more promising in this respect.

Rizzi (1997, 2004a) argues that the C system is a structural zone delimited by two heads and their projections: Force expresses the clausal type (declarative, question, imperative, exclamative) and delimits the system upward; Fin agrees in finiteness with the adjacent IP and delimits the C system downward. In between, the Topic-Focus field is generated, which hosts topic, focus, and various types of left-peripheral operators. For instance, the finite complementizer in Romance is typically expressed under Force, while the prepositional infinitival complementizers are in Fin, so that topics typically precede the latter and follow the former in languages like Italian:

(33)　a. Credo che dovrei parlare a Gianni domani.
　　　　　'I believe that I should talk to Gianni tomorrow.'

　　　b. Credo di dover parlare a Gianni domani.
　　　　　'I believe of to have to talk to Gianni tomorrow.'

(34)　a. Credo che, a Gianni, gli dovrei parlare domani.
　　　　　'I believe that, to Gianni, I should talk to him tomorrow.'

b. Credo, a Gianni, di dovergli parlare domani.

'I believe, to Gianni, of to have to talk to him tomorrow.'

Languages may differ on which head(s) of the C system they choose to lexicalize. Irish appears to lexicalize Fin also in finite clauses, so that the element translated as *that* appears after the Topic-Focus field; Welsh appears to lexicalize both Force and Fin, so that the Topic-Focus field appears sandwiched in between the two particles:

(35)   Is doíche   [faoi cheann   cúpla   lá   [*go*   bhféadfaí   imeacht]]

'Is probable   at-the-end-of   couple   day   that   could   leave'
(Irish: McCloskey 1996)

(36)   Dywedais   i   [*mai*   'r   dynion   fel   arfer   a   [werthith   y

'Said   I   C   the   men   as   usual   C   will-sell   the
ci]]

dog.' (Welsh: Roberts 2004)

So, according to this approach, the theory of the left periphery includes at least the following structure:

(37)   Force . . . Top . . . Foc . . . Fin IP (Rizzi 1997, 2004a)

Some parametrization on the arrangement of left-peripheral projections is necessary. For instance, Italian appears to allow for a Top position lower than Foc, while other languages—for example, Hungarian and Gungbe—require a strict ordering Top Foc (see also various papers in Rizzi 2004 for different views on the nature of this lower position).

This approach to the left periphery offers an immediate possibility for expressing the Topic Drop parameter while capitalizing on the theoretical analysis of the "privilege of the root" sketched out here in section 6. It is conceivable that languages may vary in the set of categories that may be taken as the root of the syntactic tree. Suppose that some languages may allow the TopP to be the root: in this case, the topic would be the highest position of the clause, a possible site for a null element not identified clause internally, whence the Topic Drop property. A language requiring root clauses to be ForceP's would not allow topics to appear high enough to be null, in the terms of the proposed approach to the "privilege of the root."

Consider now a system allowing null subjects in root environments, not as a subcase of the null topic option (i.e., if no object topic drop is allowed, and subject drop extends to expletives, which cannot occur in TopP): colloquial English as described in paradigm (32) may be a good approximation to this case. Following the logic of the proposal for Topic Drop languages, we could assume that this case involves the option of taking the bare IP as the root, so that the canonical subject position (the Spec of the highest head of the IP system) will enjoy the "privilege of the root."

This approach has been called elsewhere the "truncation" approach. Updating and integrating it with recent theoretical work, we can phrase it as follows: UG defines the clausal structure as a hierarchy of positions, starting from the left periphery, along the lines investigated by the "cartographic" approach (Cinque 2002, Rizzi 2004b, Belletti 2004 and references quoted therein). In its maximal expression, the system starts from the Force position, continues with the positions of the left periphery investigated in Rizzi (1997) and related work, and then with the positions of the IP system investigated in Cinque (1999) and related work, with some obligatory positions which form the structural backbone of the clause (Force, Tense, etc.) and other positions that are there only if called for by the content to be expressed (Top, Neg, etc.).

The truncation parametrization is now expressible as follows. Suppose that languages can vary in the inventory of categories that can be taken as the root, Force being the unmarked case always available to function as the root, but other categories (TopP, IP, . . .) being admissible options which some languages may choose. Then, external slices of the universal structure (including the obligatory backbone) may be omitted, while the hierarchy is respected from the first expressed element downward. So, what I am now suggesting is that languages may vary in the amount of "truncation" permitted in root clauses, as a matter of parametric choice. Topic Drop languages allow the root category to be TopP, and Root Subject Drop languages allow the root to be IP (or, more accurately, the higher projection of the inflectional system, hosting the subject in its Spec). Notice that no actual deletion of structure is involved in this approach: different languages simply have the option of starting the generation of a structure at different levels of the universal hierarchy, thus "truncating" the portion of the hierarchy higher than the category selected as the root.[3]

10 DEVELOPMENT REVISITED

This generalized truncation approach raises the possibility of the following scenario for the observed development of early subject drop. When syntactically relevant production starts, children uniformly entertain the parametric value allowing root subject drop (in the proposed terms, the possibility of selecting a bare IP as the root). This gives rise to a phase of systematic omissions of root subjects throughout the third year of life, presumably a developmental universal. If the target language is RSD (the variety of colloquial English described by Thrasher 1977), nothing changes; if the target language is not RSD (French, for example), the learner must reset the parameter on the negative value, but this takes time, whence the developmental effect.

So, we are back to the logic of Hyams (1986), except that the Null Subject Parameter is replaced by the empirically more accurate parametrization involved in the choice of the root, and the different truncation options.[4]

A number of questions are immediately raised by this scenario. The first question has to do with the initial parametric value: Why is it that all early systems start out with the RSD option? What is the principled basis for selecting the positive value as the initial value? Learnability considerations, such as the Subset Principle, would lead to the opposite expectation.[5]

The second question has to do with the time course of parameter fixation: Why does it take so long for the child learning French, for example, to abandon the RSD option, while other parameters (involving basic word order, V movement to I and C, cliticisation, etc.) appear to be fixed correctly from the start of syntactically relevant production, in accordance with Wexler's (1998) Very Early Parameter Setting (VEPS)? In particular, both the Null Subject Parameter and the Root Subject Drop parameter have to do with subject drop, and their empirical consequences overlap to a certain extent, along the lines discussed in the previous sections. So, why is it that the former is set quickly in accordance with VEPS, while the latter is not? The same question arises for copular drop, and possibly for the Root Infinitive construction, determiner drop, and possibly other parameters involving the dropping of functional material, if these early options also correspond to genuine parametric values. So we seem to need a principled way to split parameters into two classes—those set in accordance to VEPS and those that show a delayed fixation on the negative value.[6]

The third question has to do with delearning in a countersubset situation. On what basis does the child learning French, for example, delearn the positive fixation of the RSD parameter (and the other delayed parameters involving the dropping of functional material)?

While answering these questions, we would like to express the fact that subject drop seems to have the effect of facilitating performance, as Bloom's observation on the inverse correlation between overtness of the subject and VP length, and other similar observations from the developmental literature, would seem to indicate.

11 A CONJECTURE

When language production begins, the system is immature in a number of respects. Certain fine coordinations between the abstract computational system and the articulatory system require time and practice to be fully in place, fine tuned, and fully automatized. And there are working memory limitations that affect the rapidity of the integration of different kinds of information, as efficient linguistic production requires. I would like to put forth the conjecture that, in order to cope with such limitations, the child adopts the following strategy:

(38)   When production begins, the child initially assumes all the parametric values which facilitate the task of the immature production system by reducing the computational load, and which are consistent with her current grammatical knowledge.

Thus the system of linguistic knowledge that the child possesses is set up so that all the possible parametric values are recruited to facilitate the task of the immature production system. In particular, the grammatical options involving the dropping of material considerably facilitate the task of the production system by saving the activation of motor programs and various complex instructions to the articulatory system. So, under (38), parametric values allowing pronoun drop, the dropping of functional verbs and, possibly, of finite inflections—perhaps even the dropping of determiners—are recruited and shape the properties of early linguistic production.[7]

The dropping options are grammatically based, but their initial choice is dictated by the immaturity of the performance system. We thus intend to capture Bloom's observations and integrate them into a grammatically based account. There are two kinds of grammatical constraints, according to (38). The first is provided by Universal Grammar: the facilitating options are parametric options offered by UG, so there is no wild dropping of material, but there are grammatically based omissions. The second constraint is provided by the knowledge that the child has already acquired on the particular grammar of the target language, under (38). This is crucial, among other things, for understanding why RSD and NSP are fixed with such different time courses.

It is a traditional observation that the NSP can be set positively (at least for referential null subjects: we omit here, for the sake of brevity, the distinction between formal licensing and identification of *pro*; see Rizzi 1986) only if the verbal morphology manifests "rich agreement," with distinct morphological forms for different persons and numbers, at least a good approximation to a full differentiation (with some degree of morphological overlap tolerated by the system); this is Taraldsen's (1978) generalization. This view was questioned by the observation that a subject drop option exists in languages lacking morphological agreement altogether, such as Chinese and Japanese (Huang 1984), but in these languages subject drop appears to be a particular case of more general argument drop options, of the topic drop type, which casts doubts on the relevance of such cases for Taraldsen's generalization. Nevertheless, the evidence for the validity of the generalization is strong and varied. Of special relevance is the study of language change, illustrating the concomitance between the loss of rich agreement and the loss of an Infl-licensed referential null subject.

One case that has recently been discussed in great detail is the progressive loss of the Null Subject option in Brazilian Portuguese in the course of the twentieth century. (Kato and Negrão 2000, Duarte 2000). The agreement paradigm was simplified not because of a phonological change (as in the history of French), but because of a simplification in the paradigm of personal pronouns, with second-person pronouns *tu* and *vós* replaced by the indirect form *você(s)* (from *Vossa Mercê*, 'Your Grace') triggering third-person agreement (singular or plural), and, later in the twentieth century, with first-person plural *nós* replaced by the pronominal expression *a gente* (akin to French *on*, Italian *si*, etc.), also triggering third-person singular agreement. This triggered an impoverishment from a six-forms paradigm (*amo, amas, ama, amamos, amais, aman* in the present indicative) to a four-forms paradigm (*amo, ama, ama, amamos, aman, aman*), and then to a three-forms paradigm (*amo, ama, ama, ama, aman, aman*). Concomitantly, the option of null pronominal subjects progressively shrank. Duarte (2000) calculated the proportion of overt subjects in popular plays, supposed to somehow capture the way people speak, over the century; she found that overt subjects shifted from 20% to 25% at the beginning of the century, to 46% to 50% around the middle of the century, to 67% to 74% in the second half of the century.[8]

Synchronic evidence supporting the same conclusion is offered by certain contrasts found in different verbal paradigms with varying morphological richness within the same Null Subject Language: for instance, in Italian, the infinitival construction permitting (at a literary stylistic level) lexical nominative subjects with Aux to C does not allow referential null subjects, which are possible in the corresponding finite construction carrying agreement:

(39)   Ritengo che (lei) sia disposta ad aiutarci.
       'I believe that (she) is ready to help us.'

(40)   Ritengo esser *(lei) disposta ad aiutarci.
       'I believe to be (she) ready to help us.'

Even more minimal is the contrast between present and past subjunctive: the first involves identical forms for first-, second-, and third-person singular (*parta,*

parta, parta); the second involves a distinct form for the third-person singular (*partissi, partissi, partisse*). The double ambiguity of the past subjunctive is perfectly tolerable—(41) is acceptable on both interpretations, while the triple ambiguity of (42) is not—and an overt second-person pronoun becomes obligatory here:

(41)   Credevano che _____ partissi.
           'They believed that I/you would leave.'

(42)   Credono che _____ parta.
           'They believe that I/*you/he leave(s).'

(43)   Credono che tu parta.
           'They believe that you leave.'

The minimal contrast between present and past subjunctive thus offers a cue as to what "rich agreement" means: one syncretism is tolerable, but two are not. An isolated case like the paradigm of Italian present subjunctive can be solved by locally reducing the ambiguity: that is, by making the overt subject obligatory for some morphological specifications without affecting the global positive fixation of the Null Subject Parameter. If verbal paradigms are more massively impoverished the effect will be global, a negative fixation of the parameter.[9]

The properties of partial Null Subject languages (Irish, Modern Hebrew) also provide indications along similar lines; see McCloskey and Hale (1984), Borer (1989), and Rizzi (1993) for discussion.

In conclusion, there seems to be clear evidence that the positive setting of the Null Subject Parameter (at least as far as the option of referential null subjects is concerned) is causally linked to the richness of the agreement paradigm. It has been observed that children figure out the basic properties of the Agr system very early on. Guasti (1993–94) observed that the use of agreement in Italian is virtually error-free. Weak agreement of the English kind (the use of -s for third-person singular of present indicative) is frequently omitted, but when it is used it is almost always correct (Wexler 1994), so children appear to have knowledge of the agreement paradigm very early on, basically from the onset of syntactically significant production (the vast majority of agreement errors being cases of omission, not of inappropriate use).

Then we have an answer for why, under (38), children do not misset the NSP; their early knowledge of the impoverished agreement system of languages of the English type makes it impossible for them to entertain the positive value of the NSP, because, under (38), that hypothesis would violate already acquired language-specific knowledge. So, the fixation of the NSP takes place in accordance with VEPS.

The situation of RSD is different. Here assuming a positive value is not in contradiction with any element of knowledge of the target language that the learner may have (the evidence available to the child, sentences always with overt subjects, does not support the RSD option, but does not overtly contradict it either): therefore the positive value is assumed, under (38).

12 Delearning

What about development? We may assume that when the production system is fully in place, strategy (38) ceases to be operative; what happens at this point is that the positive fixation is kept if it is supported by experience (sentences manifesting RSD, as, say, in Gruyère Franco-Provençal), and abandoned otherwise (say, French).

This latter step, the "delearning" of the positive fixation, would seem to be problematic, given certain restrictive assumptions on the acquisition process. We are in a countersubset situation: the positive evidence that the learner has access to (sentences always with overt subjects) is compatible with both parametric values of the RSD parameter (also the positive fixation is consistent with the expression of the subject). So on what empirical basis can language learners decide that the target language is not RSD, if they start with the assumption of a positive fixation of the parameter?[10]

I will sketch out a possibility, partly along the lines of Rizzi (2000). The following is a plausible principle concerning the syntax-semantics interface:

(44)   Categorial Uniformity: Assume a unique canonical structural realization for a given semantic type.

This is a rather natural economy principle ruling the mapping from meaning to categories. The mapping should be as transparent as possible, ideally a one-to-one correspondence: individuals correspond to the category DP, propositions to the category CP (ForceP), and so on—what has been called the Canonical Structural Realization of semantic types (Grimshaw 1979). We also know that (44) defines the unmarked case: marked categorial realizations are possible. For instance, we have bare IP complements (in Exceptional Case Marking environments), and Small clauses as possible categorial realizations of propositions (alongside the unmarked realization as ForceP), depending on the lexical selectional requirements of the main verbs:

(45)   I say that Mary is happy.

(46)   I believe Mary to be happy.

(47)   I consider Mary happy.

(See Granfeld and Schlyter 2001 for an application of this principle to the study of the acquisition of clitics in second language acquisition (L2)).

So, Categorial Uniformity (CU) defines the unmarked case, but it is violable, for example, if lexical selection dictates otherwise. I am assuming that CU is a principle governing the form-meaning interface through the definition of the unmarked cases, this is very different from the principles operative in the computational system proper, which I assume to be inviolable. CU is operative in the absence of a countering force, in which case it enforces the choice of the unmarked case; but, as soon as it encounters an opposing pressure (by a lexical requirement, by a competing principle pushing in the opposite direction, or by overt evidence that the unmarked case must be abandoned), CU gives in, and a marked case arises.

Consider now the issue of the categorial status of main clauses from the vantage point offered by Categorial Uniformity. Embedded clauses, with their overt complementizer system, provide direct evidence that propositions are CPs (ForcePs) in the unmarked case. Thus, CU creates some pressure for analyzing also main clauses as ForcePs, and in the absence of overt indications opposing this pressure, this will be the assumption made by the speaker of French, Standard English, and so on; whence, the lack of root subject drop and other phenomena taking advantage of the privilege of the root in such systems.

Colloquial German, Dutch, and other languages manifest Topic Drop, which provides evidence for truncation at the TopP level; Gruyère Franco-Provençal and colloquial English manifest Root Subject Drop, providing overt evidence for truncation at the IP level (here I am simplifying: see note 4). Hence in these systems CU is countered by overt evidence that enforces a departure from the unmarked case; therefore CU can be violated to allow root categories permitting these phenomena (truncation at the TopP level and IP level, respectively, according to the proposal of section 10).

What about Child French, Child Standard English, and other child languages? We have assumed that Categorial Uniformity is a weak principle, not an inviolable computational principle, but an interface principle optimizing the form-meaning mapping in the unmarked case; it is operative only when no other force counters it and violable otherwise. As long as strategy (38) is operative, Categorial Uniformity is silent, because the need to adopt grammatical options facilitating the production system counters its effects. When the production system is fully in place and (38) ceases to be operative, nothing counters CU in French or Standard English, hence, under CU, main clauses must now project up to ForceP, and the conditions for RSD cease to exist. Then the dropping option gets out of the system. Because Topic Drop and Root Subject Drop languages provide positive evidence for assuming the appropriate levels of truncation (at TopP and IP, respectively), after (38) has ceased to be operative, the learner of a Topic Drop or of a Root Subject Drop language has evidence for assuming or keeping the relevant parametric values, thus departing from the unmarked case defined by CU.[11]

13 CONCLUSION

Early grammatical systems are UG-constrained systems. They are accessible to comparison with other early systems and with the target systems through the basic tools of adult comparative syntax: the theory of principles and parameters. I have illustrated this research trend through the analysis of subject drop in child language. Early subject drop in the acquisition of non-Null Subject Languages is not a mere performance effect. It is possible in selective structural environments: the specifier of the root and the specifier position of uninflected clauses. None of these cases is amenable to the Null Subject Parameter, licensing referential null subjects in local construal with rich verbal inflections. Nevertheless, continuity guidelines raise the expectation that some adult systems may license null subjects in the same structural environments as in child grammars. This is obviously true for PRO null subjects in uninflected clauses, but there are also adult systems taking advantage of the "privilege of the root" for the licensing of null arguments in the highest Spec position of the clause. The case of root subject drop raises the issue of parameters which apparently can be reset: it seems to be the case that some parameters are already correctly set when syntactically relevant production starts, while others are not, and then give rise to observable developmental effects. A principled way to distinguish between the two kinds of parameters seems to be in order. I have speculated that the persistency of certain non-target-consistent parametric values is amenable to a grammatically driven strategy to alleviate the task of the immature production system. If this is correct, language development is grammatically based but performance driven: non-target-consistent properties observed in language development correspond to genuine UG options, but the factors determining their temporary adoption by children lie in the growth of performance systems, outside the grammatical system proper.

NOTES

1. The Unique Checking Constraint (UCC) states the following: "The D-Feature of DP can only check against one functional category" (Wexler 1998: 9); it is assumed to hold in the grammar at age 2, and to cease to be operative at later stages according to a maturational schedule. If the clausal structure involves both Agr and T projections, both endowed with EPP features, the subject normally has to pass through both Spec's, thus violating UCC. According to this approach, one option that the child has is to omit either Agr or T projection (the Agr/T Omission Model of Schuetze and Wexler 1996), thus giving rise to a structure which is then "read" by the morphology as uninflected. On truncation, see section 9.

2. In fact, as Schuetze (1997) points out, uninflected clauses are simpler than inflected clauses, at least in terms of overt morphemes; so a processing account would expect more subject drop with the more complex inflected structure, in sharp contrast with what Roeper and Rohrbacher found.

3. In fact, in terms of the structure-building algorithm based on "merge at the root," as in Chomsky (1995) and subsequent work, the root category is the one at which the last application of "merge" applies: so the relevant parameter can be seen as involving the inventory of categories at which the syntactic computation can stop. A V-2 language allowing for expletive subject drop would then differ from a "pure" topic drop language in allowing truncation at the level occupied by local subjects in V-2 contexts, a level lower than Top. This may be the regular subject position, if an asymmetric theory of V-2 is adopted, à la Zwart (1997). Under a symmetric theory of V-2, with the finite verb always moving (at least) to Fin, the position of initial subjects in V-2 structures could be Spec Fin, or an argument position in the C-system immediately above Fin, and truncation could take place at this level.

4. For some of the systems discussed in section 8, we do not have enough evidence to decide if they are Topic Drop or Root Subject Drop languages, or have both properties, but this doesn't affect the logic of the approach, as the diagnostic properties are clear: a "pure" RSD language allows dropping of both referential and expletive root subjects, but no dropping of object topics; a "pure" Topic Drop language cannot drop expletive subjects, which can never reach the Top position, but can drop both subject and object topics; a mixed language combines the latter property with the possibility of dropping expletive subjects. In terms of the proposed truncation parametrization, a Topic Drop language allows TopP as the root, an RSD language allows IP as the root (with the possible extra option of truncation at the CP projection hosting local subjects in V-2 languages, see note 3), and a mixed language has both options.

5. The Subset Principle claims that when two options generate languages that are in a subset-superset relation, the option generating the smaller language is the unmarked option, assumed by the learner by default, while the option generating the

larger language is adopted only in presence of overt evidence supporting it. See Berwick (1985) and Manzini and Wexler (1986).

6. If some adult languages allow genuine cases of root infinitives (see the discussion in section 4), we could extend the proposed parametrization to permit a deeper truncation within the IP system, allowing the choice of a root category lower than Tense in the universal hierarchy. This is, in essence, an extension of the analysis of root infinitives in Rizzi (1993–94) to potential adult analogs.

7. Does this strategy affect grammatical knowledge tout court or grammatical knowledge "as implemented in the production system"? This question could only be addressed by studying language production and perception in parallel. Do children producing early null subjects have this option in their receptive grammar—does their receptive system naturally integrate subjectless sentences? This can only be determined by a detailed experimental study of the receptive system. Notice that if it turns out that the receptive system is more "advanced" than the production system, as is quite plausible, this would not affect at all the conclusions we have reached on the grammatical basis of the phenomena. Rather, it would show that grammatical knowledge is implemented in partially distinct forms in production and perception, and following partially distinct developmental courses, this would hardly be a surprising conclusion.

I will not try, in this chapter, to compare and connect the present attempt to other proposals to relate grammatical development to the growth of performance systems, most notably Phillips (1995).

8. The process of change was also visible in generational differences at the same time. Duarte calculated that around 1995, speakers over age 45 expressed subjects between 50% and 80% of the time (depending on the person), while speakers between ages 25 and 35 expressed subjects between 71% and 92% of the time.

9. Certain details remain to be understood: Why is second person selected to regularize the Italian subjunctive paradigm? Poverty of stimulus consideration suggests that this choice is dictated by principled reasons. A possible link may exist with the fact that the Northern Italian dialects, exhibiting a large range of variation in the systems of subject clitics, converge in requiring second-person singular clitics, while the obligatoriness or optionality of other subject clitics varies considerably from dialect to dialect (see Renzi and Vanelli 1983).

10. Notice that the problem exists if the evidence that children have access to is strictly limited to positive evidence (as in Wexler and Culicover's 1980 approach to the logical problem of language acquisition) and they have no way of inferring a negative fixation from the nonoccurrence of a given structure: this kind of inference is what is sometimes called "indirect negative evidence," which could be available through statistical considerations (if a structural option is selected by the target system, there will be a certain non-null probability that it will be manifested in the primary data; if I don't hear any such manifestation in a sizable body of data, I can conclude that the option is not selected). If children have access to some form of indirect negative evidence, the delayed refixation of RSD parameter, once strategy (38) ceases to be operative, is not problematic.

I believe the access to some kinds of indirect negative evidence in the acquisition process is not implausible; if such access is assumed in the case at issue, it would provide a solution to the delearning problem. Nevertheless, the point is controversial, so it is worthwhile to explore other possible reasons that may lead a child to reset the parameter, once the production system is fully mature.

11. In terms of the proposed analysis, the gradual character of the abandonment of the RSD in the acquisition of French and other languages may be understandable. The maturation of the production system, triggering strategy (38) clearly is a gradual process—for example, the working memory capacity grows gradually, the fine tuning and coordination of the complex motor programs get progressively automatized, and so on—so it is conceivable that the recruitment of grammatical options to alleviate the burden of the production system decreases in a symmetrically gradual fashion. This may be formally expressed, in terms of grammar competition: for instance, it could be that the child simultaneously entertains two grammars, one with a positive fixation of RSD, in compliance with strategy (38), and one with the negative fixation, in compliance with CU. As the production system matures, the grammar built in accordance with (38) weakens, and the grammar complying with CU progressively takes over.

Does the child entertain the Topic Drop option under (38), on top of the RSD option? The low rate of null objects in Child English (see section 3) suggests that the answer is no. Perhaps Topic Drop does not fall within the parametric values recruited under (38) because the facilitating effect linked to the possibility of not pronouncing the object may be counterbalanced by the added computational load of necessarily displacing the object to the left periphery (hence this option does not globally "reduce the computational load").

I do not address here the developmental curve of root infinitives and other developmental effects that are possibly related to parameter setting under strategy (38). Let us just notice that if root null subjects in finite clauses and root infinitives are developmentally related, as was shown in a particularly clear way by Hamann and Plunkett (1998) for Child Danish, the link should be found in the weakening and disappearance of (38) in concomitance with the growth of the production system.

REFERENCES

Aboh, E. (1998) "From the Syntax of Gungbe to the Grammar of Gbe." Ph.D. diss., University of Geneva.

Avrutin, S. (1998) "EVENTS as Units of Discourse Representation in Root Infinitives," in J. Schaeffer (ed.) *The Interpretation of Root Infinitives and Bare Nouns in Child Language*. Occasional Papers 12. MIT Press, Cambridge, Mass., 65–91.

Becker, M. (2000) "The Development of the Copula in Child English." Ph.D. diss., UCLA.

Belletti, A. (ed). (2004) *Structures and Beyond: The Cartography of Syntactic Structures*, Vol. 3. Oxford University Press, New York.

Berwick (1985) *The Acquisition of Syntactic Knowledge*. MIT Press, Cambridge, Mass.

Bloom, L. (1970) *Language Development: Form and Function in Emerging Grammars*. MIT Press, Cambridge, Mass.

Bloom, P. (1990) "Subjectless Sentences in Child Language." *Linguistic Inquiry* 21: 491–504.

Borer, H. (1989) "Anaphoric Agreement," in O. Jaeggli and K. Safir (eds.) *The Null Subject Parameter*. Kluwer, Dordrecht, 69–110.

Bromberg, H., and K. Wexler (1995) "Null Subjects in Wh Questions." *MIT Working Papers* 26.

Brown, R. (1973) *A First Language: The Early Stages*. Harvard University Press, Cambridge, Mass.

Cardinaletti, A. (1990) "Pronomi nulli e pleonastici nelle lingue germaniche e romanze." Ph.D. diss., University of Venice.

Chierchia, G., T. Guasti, and A. Gualmini (2001) "Nouns and Articles in Child Grammar: A Syntax/Semantics Map." Unpublished ms., University of Milano-Bicocca.

Chomsky, N. (1964) "Current Issues in Linguistic Theory," in J. Fodor and J. Katz (eds.) *The Structure of Language*. Prentice Hall, New York, 50–118.

Chomsky, N. (1973) "Conditions on Transformations," in S. Anderson and P. Kiparsky (eds.) *A Festschrift for Morris Halle*. Holt, Rinehart and Winston, New York, 232–286

Chomsky, N. (1981) *Lectures on Government and Binding*. Foris, Dordrecht.

Chomsky, N. (1986) *Knowledge of Language*. Praeger, New York.

Chomsky, N. (1995) *The Minimalist Program*. MIT Press, Cambridge, Mass.

Chomsky, N. (2001) "An Interview on Minimalism," with A. Belletti and L. Rizzi. *Su Natura e Linguaggio*. University of Siena, 151–198.

Chomsky, N. (2002) "Beyond Explanatory Adequacy," in A. Belletti (ed.) *Structures and Beyond*. Oxford University Press, New York.

Chomsky, N., and H. Lasnik (1995) "Principles and Parameters Theory," in N. Chomsky, *The Minimalist Program*. MIT Press, Cambridge, Mass.

Cipriani, P., A. M. Chilosi, P. Bottari, and L. Pfanner (1993) *L'acquisizione della morfosintassi in italiano: fasi e processi*. Unipress, Padua.

Cinque, G. (1999) *Adverbs and Functional Heads*. Oxford University Press, New York.

Cinque, G., (ed.) (2002) *The Structure of DP and IP: The Cartography of Syntactic Structures, Vol. 1*. Oxford University Press, New York.

Clahsen, H. C. Kursawe, and M. Penke (1995) "Introducing CP." *GALA Proceedings* 1995: 5–22.

Crisma, P. (1992) "On the Acquisition of Wh Questions in French." *GenGenP* 115–122.

De Crousaz, I., and U. Shlonsky (2000) "The Distribution of a Subject Clitic Pronoun in a Franco-Provençal Dialect." Unpublished ms., University of Geneva.

Duarte, E. (2000) "The Loss of the Avoid Pronoun Principle in Brazilian Portuguese," in M. Kato and E. Negrão (eds.) *Brazilian Portuguese and the Null Subject Parameter*. Vervuert-Iberoamericana, Frankfurt and Madrid, 17–36.

Duffield, N. (1993) "Roots and Rogues: Null Subjects in German Child Language." Unpublished ms., University of Düsseldorf.

Emonds, J. (1978) "The Verbal Complex [V'-V] in French." *Linguistic Inquiry* 9: 151–175.

Figueiredo, M. C. (1996) *La position sujet en Portugais Brésilien*. Unicamp, Campinas, Brazil.

Friedemann, M.A., and L. Rizzi (eds.) (2000) *The Acquisition of Syntax*. Longman, New York.

Granfeld, J., and S. Schlyter (2001) "Cliticisation in the Acquisition of French as L1 and L2." Unpublished ms., University of Lund.

Greenfield, P., and J. Smith (1976) *The Structure of Communication in Early Language Development*. Academic Press, New York.

Grimshaw, J. (1979) "Complement Selection and the Lexicon." *Linguistic Inquiry* 10: 279–326.

Guasti, T. (1993–94) "Verb Syntax in Italian Grammar: Finite and Non-finite Verbs." *Language Acquisition* 3: 1–40.

Guasti, T. (1995) "The Acquisition of Italian Interrogatives." Unpublished manuscript, Fondazione S. Raffaele, Milan.

Haegeman, L. (1990) "Non overt subjects in diary contexts." in J. Mascaro and M. Nespor (eds.) *Grammar in Progress*. Foris, Dordrecht.

Haegeman, L. (1995) "Root Infinitives, Tense and Truncated Structures in Dutch." *Language Acquisition* 4: 205–255.

Haegeman (1996a) "Root Infinitives and Initial Null Subjects in Early Dutch." *GALA Proceedings* 1996: 239–250.

Haegeman, L. (1996b) "Verb Second, the Split CP and Null Subjects in Early Dutch Finite Clauses." *GenGenP* 4: 133–175.

Haegeman, L. (2000) "Adult Null Subjects in non-Pro Drop Languages," in M. A. Friedemann and L. Rizzi (eds.) *The Acquisition of Syntax*. Longman, New York, 129–169.

Haegeman, L., and T. Ihsane (1997) "Subject Ellipsis in Embedded Clauses in English." *GenGenP* 5: 1–20.

Hamann, C. (2000) "The Acquisition of Constituent Questions and the Requirements of Interpretation," in M. A. Friedemann and L. Rizzi (eds.) *The Acquisition of Syntax*. Longman, New York.

Hamann, C., and K. Plunkett (1997) "Subject Omission in Child Danish." *BUCLD* 21: 220–231.

Hamann, C., and K. Plunkett (1998) "Subjectless Sentences in Child Danish." *Cognition* 69: 35–72.

Hamann, C., L. Rizzi, and U. Frauenfelder (1996) "On the Acquisition of Subject and Object Clitics in French," in H. Clahsen (ed.) *Generative Perspectives on Language Acquisition*. Benjamins, Amsterdam/Philadelphia, 309–334.

Huang, J. (1984) "On the Distribution and Reference of Empty Pronouns." *Linguistic Inquiry* 15: 531–574.

Hyams, N. (1986) *Language Acquisition and the Theory of Parameters*. Reidel, Dordrecht.

Hyams, N., and T. Sano (1994) "Agreement, Finiteness and the Development of Null Arguments." *NELS* 24.

Hyams, N., and K. Wexler (1993) "On the Grammatical Basis of Null Subjects in Child Language." *Linguistic Inquiry* 24: 421–459.

Jaeggli, O., and K. Safir (eds.) (1989) *The Null Subject Parameter*. Kluwer, Dordrecht.

Kato, M., and E. Negrão, eds. (2000) *Brazilian Portuguese and the Null Subject Parameter*. Vervuert-Iberoamericana, Frankfurt and Madrid.

Kayne (1994) *The Antisymmetry of Syntax*. MIT Press, Cambridge, Mass.

Kenstowicz, M. (1989) "The Null Subject Parameter in Modern Arabic Dialects," in O. Jaeggli and K. Safir (eds.) *The Null Subject Parameter*. Kluwer, Dordrect, 263–276.

Klima, E., and U. Bellugi (1966) "Syntactic Regularities in the Speech of Children," in J. Lyons and R. Wales (eds.) *Psycholinguistic Papers*. Edinburgh University Press, Edinburgh.

Lasser, I. (1997) *Finiteness in Adult and Child German*. MPI Series in Psycholinguistics. Wageningen.

Levow, G. (1995) "Tense and Subject Position in Interrogatives and Negatives in Child French." *MIT Working Papers* 26: 281–304.

Lightbown, P. (1977) "Constituency and Variation in the Acquisition of French." Ph.D. diss., Columbia University, New York.

MacWhinney, B., and C. Snow (1985) "The Child Language Data Exchange System." *Journal of Child Language* 17: 457–472.

Manzini, R., and K. Wexler (1986) "Parameters, Binding Theory and Learnability." *Linguistic Inquiry* 18: 413–444.

Mazuka, R., B. Lust, T. Wakayama, and W. Snyder (1986) "Distinguishing Effects of Parameters in Early Syntax Acquisition: A Cross-Linguistic Study of Japanese and English." *Papers and Reports on Child Language Development* 25.

McCloskey, J. (1996) "On the Scope of Verb Movement in Irish." *Natural Language and Linguistic Theory* 14: 47–104.

McCloskey, J., and K. Hale (1984) "On the Syntax of Person-Number Inflection in Modern Irish." *Natural Language and Linguistic Theory* 1: 487–533.

Mehler, J., and E. Dupoux (1992) *Naître humain*. Editions Odile Jacob, Paris.

Miller, G., and N. Chomsky (1963) "Finitary Models of Language Users," in R. Luce, R. Bush, and E. Galanter (eds.) *Handbook of Mathematical Psychology*, Vol. 2. Wiley, New York, 419–492.

O'Grady, W., A. M. Peters, and D. Masterson (1989) "The Transition from Optional to Required Subjects." *Journal of Child Language* 16: 513–529.

Phillips, C. (1995) "Syntax at Age Two: Cross-linguistic Differences." *MIT Working Papers* 26: 325–382.

Pierce, A. (1989) "On the Emergence of Syntax: A Crosslinguistic Study." Ph.D. diss., MIT, Cambridge, Mass.

Pierce, A. (1992) *Language Acquisition and Syntactic Theory*. Kluwer, Dordrecht.

Pinker, S. (1979) "Formal Models of Language Learning." *Cognition* 1: 217–283.

Pinker, S. (1984) *Language Learnability and Language Development*. Cambridge University Press, Cambridge.

Prévost, P., and L. White (2000) "Truncation and Missing Inflection in Second Language Acquisition," in M. A. Friedemann and L. Rizzi (eds.) *The Acquisition of Syntax*. Longman, New York, 202–235.

Radford, A. (1990) *The Acquisition of Syntactic Structures*. Basil Blackwell, London.

Rasetti, L. (2000) "Null Subjects and Root Infinitives in the Child Grammar of French," in M. A. Friedemann and L. Rizzi (eds.) *The Acquisition of Syntax*. Longman, New York, 236–268.

Renzi, L., and L. Vanelli (1983) "I pronomi soggetto in alcune varietà romanze," in *Scritti linguistici in onore di G. B. Pellegrini*. Pisa, Pacimi, 121–145.

Rizzi, L. (1978) "Violations of the Wh Island Constraint in Italian and the Subjacency Condition." *Montreal Working Papers in Linguistics* 11: 155–190.

Rizzi, L. (1982) *Issues in Italian Syntax*. Foris, Dordrecht.

Rizzi, L. (1986) "Null Objects in Italian and the Theory of pro." *Linguistic Inquiry* 17: 501–557.

Rizzi, L. (1992) "Early Null Subjects and Root Null Subjects," in T. Hoekstra and B.

Schwartz (eds.) *Language Acquisition Studies in Generative Grammar*. John Benjamins, Amsterdam/Philadelphia, 151–176.

Rizzi, L. (1993) "A Parametric Approach to Comparative Syntax: Properties of the Pronominal System." *English Linguistics* (Tokyo) 10: 1–27.

Rizzi, L. (1993–94) "Some Notes on Linguistic Theory and Language Development: The Case of Root Infinitives." *Language Acquisition* 3: 341–393.

Rizzi (1997) "The Fine Structure of the Left Periphery," in L. Haegeman, (ed.) *Elements of Grammar*. Kluwer, Dordrecht, 281–338.

Rizzi, L. (2000a) *Comparative Syntax and Language Acquisition*. Routledge, London.

Rizzi, L. (2000b) "Remarks on Early Null Subjects," in M. A. Friedeman and L. Rizzi (eds.) *The Acquisition of Syntax*. Longman, New York, 269–292.

Rizzi, L. (2004a) "Locality and Left Periphery," in Belletti (ed.) *Structures and Beyond*. Oxford University Press, New York.

Rizzi, L. (2004b) *The Structure of CP and IP: The Cartography of Syntactic Structures, Vol. 2*, Oxford University Press, New York.

Roberts, I. (2004) "The C-System in Brythonic Celtic Languages, V2 and the EPP," in L. Rizzi (ed.) *The Structure of CP and IP*. Oxford University Press, New York, 297–328.

Roeper, T., and B. Rohrbacher (1994) "True pro-drop in Child English and the Principle of Economy of Projection." Unpublished ms., University of Massachusetts, Amherst

Roeper, T., and J. Weissenborn (1990) "How to Make Parameters Work," in L. Frazier and J. De Villiers (eds.) Reidel, Dordrecht.

Ross, J. R. (1982) "Pronoun Deletion Processes in German." Paper presented at the Annual Meeting of the Linguistics Society of America, San Diego, California.

Schuetze, C. (1997) "Infl in Child and Adult Language: Agreement, Case and Licensing." Ph.D. diss., MIT, Cambridge, Mass.

Schuetze, C., and K. Wexler (1996) "Subject Case Licensing and English Root Infinitives." *BUCLD* 20: 670–681.

Stromswald, K. (1990) "Learnability and the Acquisition of Auxiliaries." Ph.D. diss., MIT, Cambridge, Mass.

Suppes, P., R. Smith, and M. Leveillé (1973) The French Syntax of a Child's Noun Phrases." *Archives de psychologie* 42: 207–269.

Taraldsen, T. (1978) "On the NIC, Vacuous Application, and the That-t Filter." Unpublished ms., MIT, Cambridge Mass.

Thrasher, R. (1977) *One Way to Say More by Saying Less: A Study of So-Called Subjectless Sentences*. Eihosha, Tokyo.

Valian, V. (1991) "Syntactic Subjects in the Early Speech of American and Italian Children." *Cognition* 40: 21–81.

Wexler, K. (1994) "Optional Infinitives, Head Movement and the Economy of Derivations in Child Grammar," in D. Lightfoot and N. Horstein (eds.) *Verb Movement*. Cambridge University Press, Cambridge, 305–350.

Wexler, K. (1998) "Very Early Parameter Setting and the Unique Checking Constraint: A New Explanation of the Optional Infinitive Stage." *Lingua* 106: 23–79.

Wexler, K., and P. Culicover (1980) *Formal Principles of Language Acquisition*. MIT Press, Cambridge, Mass.

Zwart, J. W. (1997) *Morphosyntax of Verb Movement: A Minimalist Approach to the Syntax of Dutch*. Kluwer, Dordrecht.

CHAPTER 3

COMPARATIVE SYNTAX AND LANGUAGE DISORDERS

ARHONTO TERZI

1 INTRODUCTION

IT seems to me that for the framework of generative linguistics, within which this volume is situated, the importance of the study of language disorders—although not usually made explicit—is inescapably implicated. The fact that the study of generative grammar shifted attention from the study of language regarded as an externalized system to the study of the system attained and represented in the mind, and ultimately in the brain,[1] where the cause of several language disorders is also found, is a fundamental reason for this implication. Taking this a step further, and considering the theoretical constructs that have been proposed by linguists to stand for the principles and procedures guiding the system of language to also be represented in some physical configurations in the brain, we are in a position to see the relevance of (some) language disorders for syntactic theory in particular. The fact that these configurations, or physical mechanisms, may not be currently known does not imply that the corresponding principles and procedures are less credible or the quest for them less worth pursuing. Such a conviction is apparently expressed in the following passage from Chomsky (1989: 6), in which the parallelism between linguistic theory and "hard sciences" is drawn:

This is a familiar story in the physical sciences. Thus, nineteenth century chemistry was concerned with the properties of the chemical elements and provided models of compounds (for example, the benzene ring). It developed such notions as valence, molecule, and the periodic table of elements. All of this proceeded at a level that was highly abstract. How all of this might relate to more fundamental physical mechanisms was unknown, and there was in fact much debate over whether these notions had any "physical reality" or were just convenient myths devised to help organize experience. This abstract inquiry set problems for the physicist: to discover physical mechanisms that exhibit these properties. The remarkable success of twentieth-century physics have provided increasingly more sophisticated and compelling solutions for these problems in a quest that some feel may be approaching a kind of "ultimate and complete answer."

It is not clear whether neuroscience has reached the stage of twentieth- (or twenty-first!)-century physics in terms of discovering the physical mechanisms that underlie the properties of the theoretical constructs proposed by linguists since this passage was written—or whether linguists have been particularly concerned with providing neuroscience the relevant input for such discoveries. It seems perfectly clear to me, however, that for a language research program along these lines the study of the structural properties of impaired language, regardless of whether it has received the deserved attention until now, is certainly welcome on conceptual grounds.[2]

Two reasons (at least) render research on language disorders of interest for contemporary linguistics: the first derives from the need to identify detailed physical mechanisms of the brain that correspond to the various domains of grammar and its structure, and this is especially pertinent to the disorders known as aphasias. The core idea is that if a certain (and known) part of the brain is damaged by some lesion that has resulted in aphasia and it is observed that a number of language forms or structures begin to function unlike what is expected by linguistic theory, and unlike how they were functioning before the lesion occurred, it must be the case that these structures are stored in this particular part of the brain.[3]

The second reason is more pertinent to linguistic theory per se, confined to syntactic theory in this essay:[4] the behavior of impaired language (with respect to various syntactic concepts and proposals) may be able to provide independent evidence of the concepts and their interaction and thereby contribute to current developments of syntactic theory. Just as it has become obvious and established in studies of language acquisition, research on language disorders can serve as a terrain within which syntactic proposals may be tested and evaluated.[5]

As suggested by its title, this chapter falls more within the second type of inquiry into the properties of human language; hence, it aims at demonstrating ways in which research on impaired language interacts with syntactic theory. And it does so, at least in the beginning, in an even more modest and indirect manner than the studies mentioned in passing in note 5 do. That is, I am committed here to demonstrating how the study of impaired language interacts with comparative syntax in particular, a research program which aims at understanding human language by comparing and contrasting the behavior (or properties) of several languages with respect to certain syntactic structures or (types of) phenomena.

I approach the aforementioned interaction from two directions, which will also determine the structure of this chapter: in section 2, I examine ways in which the study of language disorders contributes to and influences research in comparative syntax. Subsequently, in section 3, I turn to the contribution that comparative syntax has to make to the study and understanding of language disorders. It will become evident that, although I try to detect and pinpoint direct contributions from one research area to the other and vice versa, the whole enterprise should rather be thought of as a continuous interaction between research areas whose borders are becoming less rigidly defined and whose discoveries feed each other's research program. In section 4, I outline the relevance of language therapy for the issues discussed. Although a number of syntactic structures are used to illustrate the points at stake, the empirical bulk is drawn from the domain of clitic placement, and the language most often discussed is Greek.

2 THE CONTRIBUTION OF IMPAIRED LANGUAGE(S) TO COMPARATIVE SYNTAX

The various types of language disorders, or conditions that affect language, are standardly grouped into two major categories, depending on the time in the individual's life that the impairment occurred—that is, before or after birth. Accordingly, they are distinguished as developmental and acquired. Here, I focus primarily on Specific Language Impairment (SLI) a disorder falling into the first category. I also often refer to Broca's aphasia, however—an acquired condition that results from lesions in Broca's area, giving rise to the linguistic behavior known as "agrammatism." These two disorders are chosen because their occurrence is manifested in the morphosyntactic domain of language and, presumably as a result of this, they have attracted and continue to attract the attention of syntacticians.

In both SLI and Broca's aphasia minimal (although a precise definition of what is "minimal" is rather difficult, and, most probably, uninteresting) deviations from the corresponding normal language are observed, examples of which will follow throughout the article. They make one wonder at first glance, therefore, whether these differences are important for microparametric syntax, since this is a line of research within which the behavior of closely related linguistic varieties (or languages that differ in all but a few factors) is studied. If impaired language were comparable to a "variety" (or dialect) of normal language, its study would be of potential value for microparametric syntax in the same manner that comparisons and contrasts between closely related varieties have been instrumental in understanding a number of syntactic phenomena.[6]

One notices immediately, however, that a crucial difference between "impaired varieties" and the dialects of a normal language employed in comparative syntax is that the former may not constitute real language, in the sense that their behavior and properties do not necessarily reflect properties of UG, but deviations from it. Therefore, comparisons of the impaired variant with the normal or standard pattern may not able to say much about UG and the language faculty per se (although they may be telling of several other things, a number of which I will soon discuss). It seems to me at first inspection that the various manifestations of impaired language(s) cannot be employed in the manner dialects are employed by comparative syntax, despite the fact that they may also differ in few and crucial factors from a (normal) language and the languages and dialects that are related to it.

Conclusions along these lines follow even from those views that consider (some) impaired varieties as close to the normal language as possible, in the sense of attributing them an intact syntactic domain. An example of the sort is Avrutin's (2000) work on the comprehension of wh-questions by Broca's aphasics. Avrutin found that the behavior of Broca's aphasics in comprehension tasks of wh-questions contradicts expectations deriving from claims of contemporary syntactic theory (the latter based on normal language, obviously). More precisely, he found that while the Broca's aphasics of his study did well at non-D-linked wh-questions such as in (1), they did not perform equally well on D-linked wh-questions, (2), and this is a surprising behavior in light of the fact that extraction of D-linked questions is more easily acceptable in normal language—(4) versus (3)—for principled reasons. Contrasts such as in (3) and (4) have been the focus of extensive research in the syntactic literature (see Cinque 1990), hence, the behavior manifested by Broca's aphasics with respect to sentences such as (1) and (2) raise questions as to what is responsible for the picture they present but also as to what may be the relevance of such examples for syntactic theory:

(1)   Who did the tiger chase?

(2)   Which lion did the tiger chase?

(3)   *Mary wants to know what who read.

(4)   Mary wants to know which of the books which man read.

Rather than concluding that Broca's aphasics do badly at sentences such as (2) because their syntax is somehow impaired, Avrutin proposes that they have problems incorporating world knowledge in their syntactic structures, a process involved in D-linked questions only. Assuming that incorporation of world knowledge in the grammar requires more "energy" than that involved in non-D-linked wh-questions (which rely on the syntax of the sentence solely), D-linked wh-questions are rendered more "costly" and therefore problematic for aphasics. Hence, the claims of syntactic theory concerning wh-questions are not challenged by the behavior of the aphasics just described. At the same time, however, interesting contrasts as in (1) and (2) do not contribute much as they stand to claims of syntactic theory revolving around these issues.

Put in other words: while studies such as the one reported are important for the understanding of impaired language, they do not necessarily contribute to the understanding of the nature of normal grammar. Had a normal population exhibited the behavior of the paradigm in (1)–(2), the theoretical claims around A'-movement and binding would probably have to be reexamined. Unlike normal microparametric variations, however, impaired "microparametric deviations" cannot initiate such an inquiry for the syntactic structure of normal language.

Similar considerations follow from those studies on Specific Language Impairment which consider SLI to be as close to normal language as possible, in the sense of considering it to be delayed language (Wexler 1996).[7] That is, just as in the case of agrammatic language, the study of language manifesting SLI may not necessarily reveal a great deal about the properties of normal language per se or add to its understanding, in the way a related dialect would within the research paradigm of comparative syntax. This is not a statement meant to downplay the importance of such studies but to set the record straight from the outset.

Studying the syntax of SLI in particular is important for several other reasons. First, in order to establish that SLI is indeed delayed language in the descriptive sense of patterning the corresponding early language in all domains of grammar (since there are still unexplored areas within which the two language "varieties"—namely, early and SLI—language—may be found to differ).[8] The second reason depends on the first in the sense that it is fed by its data but is more of a conceptual type: it has to do with the need to express in syntactic terms (a legitimate means since the impairment affects the morphosyntactic domain) the factor(s) that underlie or are responsible for SLI. According to Wexler (2000), the impairment is best characterized in terms of an extended period during which the individual's grammar is restricted by the Unique Checking Constraint (UCC). According to the UCC, which was originally proposed for early language (Wexler 1998), a DP can check only one D feature on functional categories as a result of which Tense or Agr are forced to be omitted—hence, there is a period in the individual's grammar during which Tense is used optionally. The direct manifestation of the constraint is an extended period during which nonfinite and finite forms are produced interchangeably in root contexts, and this is known as the Extended Optional Infinitive stage.[9] Needless to say that this, or any other, theoretical claim is much more credible if it has explanatory power over all domains in which SLI differs from normal language, as well as across several languages— hence, the importance of collecting evidence from various aspects of syntax, as well as from various languages manifesting SLI.

These we see in this context as the basic issues to be pursued and the questions to be posed at the present stage of research in language disorders—that is, to cover empirically the various domains of impaired language and to express in syntactic terms the nature of the impairment. In the time required for addressing these issues, a number of discoveries will emerge and answers to further questions concerning the properties of both impaired and normal language will be offered. Precise formulation of these questions will be taking place along the way.

In addition to these issues we can see two more as pertinent to this discussion. The first concerns one particular aspect of (non)resemblance between SLI and early language. The second addresses the new "reality" and possibilities that emerge as a consequence of the ongoing research on impaired language(s), regardless of its precise objectives. With respect to the resemblance between SLI and early language, the question to be asked is of methodological nature and may sound somehow provocative. If SLI is indeed delayed language, is it justified to pose a distinct research area for its study, especially if one considers the extent to which research on early language has progressed? Provocative as this question may sound, I think it is still worth taking a bit of time to answer it. A distinct field for the study of SLI is justified first because the issue of whether SLI is different from early language is not entirely settled (see Tsimpli 2001; Stavrakaki 2001a, 2001b). Furthermore, at least one factor behaves differently in SLI than in early language in ways that can benefit the study of both; this is the "factor" of time. The very simple fact that a language stage lasts much longer in SLI than in early normal language results in easier exposure of the phenomenon to more careful observation.

By bringing the second issue into the discussion, I intend to moderate and qualify the statement that impaired varieties may not able to contribute much to the study of normal language in the narrow sense of comparative syntax. While this may be so, for the reasons explained—that is, by virtue of the fact that impaired varieties are qualitatively different from dialects and therefore cannot be compared with them—the various studies on language disorders, even if conducted for the sake of understanding the disorder per se, are in fact able to contribute to proposals concerning normal language in an alternative manner. This is how I see this contribution to take place in the immediate future: if a certain phenomenon has been offered a similar account cross-linguistically for normal language, one expects that its impaired, let's say SLI, variant, should manifest similar behavior as well across the same languages. If not, the account offered on the basis of normal adult language may have to be reexamined. The cross-linguistic evidence from (the various types of) impaired language(s) that continues to accumulate offers this opportunity and will inevitably provide further input and stir research into the syntax of normal language in this entirely novel way, it seems to me. In the remainder of this section, the above two points are confirmed empirically through the relatively detailed presentation of work we recently conducted on the position of clitics in early and SLI Cypriot Greek (Petinou and Terzi 2002).

2.1 SLI and Early Normal Language

In adult (normal) Cypriot Greek, pronominal clitics are often found to follow the verb in finite contexts (5a). This ordering does not hold when some functional head precedes the verb, in which case clitics must precede (and be immediately adjacent to) the finite verb, as in (6a) and (7a). The relevant functional heads in these examples are the subjunctive and negative particles, respectively (and see Terzi 1999b for more environments):

(5) a. (I Maria) edhkiavasen to.
         (Maria)   read-3s   it-cl

     b. *(I Maria) to edhkiavasen.
        (Maria) it-cl read-3s

        'Mary read it.'

(6) a. Thelo na tin dho.
        want-1s M her-cl see-1s

     b. *Thelo na dho tin.
        want-1s M see-1s her

        'I want to see her.'

(7) a. En ton iksero.
        neg him-cl know-1s

     b. *En iksero ton.
        neg know-1s him-cl

        'I don't know him.'

The clitic positioning pattern of Cypriot Greek is not unfamiliar. Similar ordering facts hold for Western Romance languages (with Portuguese and Galician as the best-known representatives) in which pronominal clitics are also often found to follow the finite verb (Uriagereka 1995, Martins 1994).[10] In Terzi (1999a) finite enclisis was attributed to movement of the verb to a position past Agr/T and past the clitics. This position is taken to be M (the head of Mood Phrase) and is considered to host various Infl elements, including negation. The movement of the finite verb to M is attributed to properties of M (clearly not present in the M of Standard Greek, from which comparable verb movement and finite enclisis are absent). Very briefly, the distinct properties of the Cypriot clausal structure which are crucially attributed to the M(P) projection (and to which I return at a later point in this chapter) is the absence of a number of auxiliaries, such as of the future particle *tha* and the perfective *have/had,* hence the lack of compound tenses. The view according to which finite enclisis is the result of verb movement to a position higher than Agr/T and past the clitics is comparable to proposals for Portuguese and Galician (Martins 1994, Uriagereka 1995, among others), and is illustrated in (8) for the Cypriot Greek clausal structure.

(8)

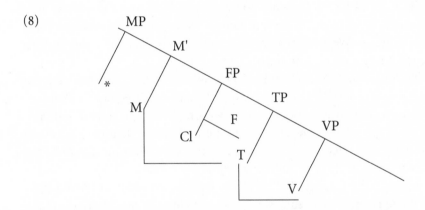

With the structure of Cypriot in mind, let us now shift our attention to the early and SLI language. It has been known about Cypriot Greek that children do not comply to the pattern of clitic placement just outlined and produce finite enclisis even in contexts in which it is not allowed by adult grammar—namely, they produce sentences such as (6b) and (7b). Similar considerations hold for children diagnosed with SLI, from which the following examples have been taken:

(9)   A kolisume *ta* tetadio mu. (Normal adult: Na *ta* kolisume sto tetradio mou.)
       M stick-1p them-cl (on the) notebook mine

       'To stick them on my notebook.'

(10) E telo *tin*. (Normal adult: En *tin* thelo.)
      neg want-1s her-cl

      'I don't want her.'

(11) Oi fori *ta* touta. (Normal adult: Oi, en *ta* fori touta. / En *ta* fori touta.)
      no wear-3s them-cl these

      'He doesn't wear these.'

The picture presented by these (and other similar examples) is striking, especially in light of the fact that clitics have not been encountered in nonadult position cross-linguistically, although they may often be omitted from contexts in which their presence is obligatory in adult grammar (Jakubowicz et al. 1998, Marinis 2000). Therefore, this phenomenon, which I earlier called Clitic Misplacement (a rather misleading term, as it will turn out), raises several questions concerning its rareness and the factors responsible for it.

To obtain an understanding of the phenomenon, we collected data from both early and SLI Cypriot Greek-speaking populations, which we subsequently analyzed and compared in terms of the position of clitics with respect to the finite verb in the sentence. We collected spontaneous speech data from five normal children, aged 2;8 to 3;0 (years;months), with whom we met every two months and recorded for 45 minutes each time. These were matched with five children of the same language level (in terms of Mean Length of Utterance in Words— MLU/W), gender and socioeconomic status who had been diagnosed with SLI. The diagnosis of the impairment was based on criteria other than the position of clitics. I do not present here the actual numbers that resulted from the study, but the reader may refer to Petinou and Terzi (2002) for details.

We found that the pattern of clitic placement was invariant in the SLI population, in the sense that children always produced clitics in nonadult position in the relevant contexts—that is, in contexts involving either the subjunctive particle or a negative particle, or both. For early language, the percentage of misplaced clitics varied in all three stages tested; most relevant is that clitics were not encountered in nonadult position across the board in any of the three stages. Moreover, Clitic Misplacement disappeared when children reached age 3, in contrast with the SLI children of the study who continued to produce misplaced clitics as the only pattern until at least age 5. Thus, while the normal children of the study were already placing all their clitics in adult position by age 3, the SLI children were placing all their clitics in nonadult position even at age 5.

In Petinou and Terzi (2002) the persistence of finite enclisis was attributed to the fact that children continue to perform verb movement to M, even in contexts in which this is not allowed by adults. This finding attributes the existence of misplaced clitics to a prolonged stage of verb movement to M, whose result was that clitics surfaced in postverbal position even when this was not allowed in adult grammar.[11]

Once this proposal was made, the next step was to look for independent evidence to support it, with two candidate domains emerging: properties of the finite verb that moves to M or properties of M to which the finite verb moves. We were not able to identify some exceptional property of the finite verb, conceivably responsible for its persistent (and illicit) movement to M. I believe, however, that we found evidence showing that something about the M position itself rendered it problematic in early language: a consequence of the nonadult nature of M was that children performed movement of the finite verb to M even when this position was apparently occupied by some Infl particle that bans finite verb movement and the enclisis in the adult language that is associated with it.

In particular, we discovered that the SLI language sample of our study manifested both misuse of the negative particle and significant omission of the subjunctive particle. Examples of the first type are sentences such as (11), repeated below, and of the second sentences such as (12):

(11)   Oi fori *ta* touta. (Normal adult: Oi, en *ta* fori touta. / En *ta* fori touta.)
       no wear-3s them-cl these

       'He doesn't wear these.'

(12)   (Th)elo (zogr)afiso *to*. (Normal adult: Thelo na *to* zografiso.)
       want-1s (M) paint-1s it-cl

       'I want to paint it.'

The most telling error was the type of substitution SLI children performed when they erroneously employed the negative particle: crucially, they consistently employed the XP-type of negative marker instead of the X° type, but not vice versa. This error, matched with the omission of the subjunctive marker (M), led to a more precise formulation of the problem with the M domain associated with children's illicit verb movement to M, and, consequently, with their illicit (for adult grammar) enclisis.[12]

When we looked at the data we collected from early language, we did not find similar types of errors; that is, no omission of the subjunctive particle or misuse of the negative particle was detected in my early language data. This "discrepancy" was alarming at first as it made us think that perhaps something else was going on in early normal language that could conceivably argue for a qualitatively different pattern. The first move was to look for younger children with normal language development to see whether similar errors in the M domain were associated with stages at which children misplaced clitics across the board. No stage of across-the-board illicit enclisis was identified for normal children speakers of Cypriot Greek, however.

Subsequently, we turned to the CHILDES data base. We found that errors such as the omission of M and the nonadult choice of negative particle (in the direction of the collected data) are typical of early Greek. This amounts to saying that there is in normal language as well a stage during which the behavior of Infl particles is similar to that of the SLI children's we studied. Hence, the normal data of our study did not differ from the SLI data qualitatively, and it was probably an accident of our small sample that we did not encounter in the early language data the types of errors that were found in the SLI language data.

The point I hope I have made via the relatively detailed presentation of this study is that even if it is true that SLI language is qualitatively similar to early language, precisely because of its extremely slow rates of development, it is able to assist in making observations at given points of language growth that are not always easy to make via the study of early language because of the pace at which its development proceeds. In other words, SLI performs the role of a magnifying glass in time, in the sense of making observations and correlations easier to see than in early language. In the particular study on clitic placement I described, it is doubtful that we would have arrived at the conclusions we did regarding the status of the Infl particles in early and SLI language (and the associated proposal concerning illicit enclisis) on the basis of the data from early language alone, since none of the Infl related errors were present in the data collected. The crucial errors came from the SLI data, which I then confirmed via search in larger samples of data based early language. Research in other domains of early language may be benefited by research on SLI language in a comparable manner.[13]

2.2 Cross-Linguistic Studies on Impaired Language

It is well known, and I mentioned it already in passing, that Cypriot Greek is not the only language in which clitics are banned from certain positions, the sentence-initial position being one, and the most relevant for the issues to be brought up immediately afterward. Similar positioning restrictions are present in Portuguese and Galician and make their clitic placement pattern look quite unlike that of the nearby Romance languages, in a contrast similar to that manifested by Cypriot versus Standard Greek. The following examples from Galician are from Uriagereka (1995) and demonstrate that unless some functional head precedes the finite verb, (14), clitics cannot be preverbal, hence sentence-initial, either (13).

(13)   Ouvimo-lo.
        hear-2s it-cl
        'We hear it.'

(14)   Non o ten ouvido.
  not it-cl has heard
  'She/He hasn't heard it.'

Recent work on Berber discusses comparable positioning properties of clitics (Ouhalla, chapter 14 in this volume, and references therein). Ouhalla states explicitly that "CL cannot be the 'first word' in the clause that includes it"; hence, the following examples:

(15)   T-sqad as tfruxt tabratt.
  3fs-send$_{PERF}$ him-cl girl letter
  'The girl (has) sent him the letter.'

(16)   Ur tn 'lix.
  neg them-cl see-1s
  'I have not seen them.'

In addition to Portuguese and Berber, the entire group of Slavic languages, with Serbo-Croatian as its much-discussed representative, are also known for a ban on first position of clitics (Bošković 2001, and many references therein). The situation in Serbo-Croatian is (even at first glance) different, however, since there seems to be a designated position—the "second position"—for clitics to be placed (which, moreover, in contrast to the previous languages, is not limited to pronominal clitics). The following examples are from Stjepanović (1998):

(17)   Tu su mi knjigu dali.
  that are me-DAT book-ACC given
  'They gave that book to me.'

(18)   *Mi Marijinoj prijateljici smo ga dali.
  we Marija's friend-DAT are it-ACC given
  'We gave it to Mary's friend.'

Insufficient research has been conducted on the SLI (and early) "varieties" of these languages with respect to the positioning of clitics so far. Nevertheless, one would tend to think that if it turns out that the counterpart impaired varieties of each of these languages manifest similar behavior, the behavior of clitic placement in the normal languages would have to be the manifestation of the same phenomenon—hence, follow from the same account.

That such data may constitute valuable empirical support to the proper characterization of the phenomenon of clitic placement (and, by extension, of any other phenomenon) becomes clear when faced with facts from normal language which somehow blur the picture. For instance, while only Serbo-Croatian is considered a typical clitic second language, in all (but one) of the examples I have lined up until now—from Cypriot Greek, Portuguese, and Berber and from many other examples in the literature—the position of clitics in the sentence appears to also be the second. A context in which clitics appear in other than the second position is in the presence of an overt preverbal subject, an instance in which clitics surface third in matrix sentences. In Cypriot, such a case appeared in (5) and is repeated here, while the examples from Portuguese, (19), and Galician, (20), also demonstrate enclisis in the presence of an overt subject, thus, the clitic occupies the third position in the clause.

(5)   a. (I Maria)   edhkiavasen   to.
          (Maria)   read-3s   it-cl

       b. *(I Maria) to edhkiavasen.
          (Maria) it-cl read-3s

          'Mary read it.'

(19)   Ele viu-a.
       He saw her. (Duarte and Matos 2000)

(20)   Xan Rodriguez veuno / *o veu
       Xan Rodriguez saw-it / it saw (Uriagereka 1995: 83)

With Berber subjects being postverbal, such a context disappears; hence, it is difficult to encounter clitics in other than the second position, a fact which can create the impression that Berber is a second-position cliticization language, in the fashion of Serbo-Croatian.[14]

With the previous discussion in mind, it is interesting to note that it has been reported for early Portuguese that clitics appear after the finite verb in contexts in which this is not allowed by adults; hence, a sentence such as (21) was produced by a child age 2;9 (Duarte and Matos 2000):

(21)   Não chama-se nada.
       not calls-refl nothing

       'That's not his name at all.'

The situation is very similar to that of Cypriot Greek, not only in terms of the type of early clitic (mis)placement (that is, enclisis where it should be proclisis) but also in terms of clitics attaining adult position at the same age (namely, before age 3, in both Cypriot and Portuguese). This resemblance indicates in a novel way, it seems to me, that the same phenomenon takes place in both languages. Consequently, it also offers empirical support, of an entirely different type, to accounts that attribute finite enclisis to similar factors in both languages. Certainly, the behavior of SLI Portuguese on the same phenomenon would contribute toward a complete account of it.

With respect to Serbo-Croatian, D. Kudra-Stojanović (pers. comm.) informs me that she has not noticed phenomena of nonadult positioning of clitics in the Serbo-Croatian early language on which her research has focused.[15] Therefore, although the overall empirical contribution of the above early and SLI languages is admittedly limited, and several details concerning the precise syntactic analyses of the related structures may need to be further elaborated, some good first evidence is provided to support the different stands usually taken with respect to the treatment of clitic positioning in Serbo-Croatian versus Portuguese and Cypriot. No comparable evidence is available yet for early or SLI Berber (J. Ouhalla, pers. comm.).

In face of the limited SLI (and early) data from the reported languages, it is premature to predict whether when more of this evidence becomes available it will also be able to contribute toward the formulation and evaluation of an even more precise account of clitic placement in normal language, and how exactly. One could certainly envision contributions along these lines, however. Moreover, "misplaced clitics" are found in languages such as Cypriot and Portuguese, while the phenomenon is not attested in other instances (and languages) in which enclisis and proclisis alternate within the same language. The case in mind is the proclisis versus enclisis alternation associated with finiteness in the majority of Romance languages. It is known, at least for Italian, that this alternation does not create confusion to children (Guasti 1993–94) and the same holds for SLI Italian as well (Bottari et al. 2000). The question of why clitics do not appear misplaced across the finite versus nonfinite distinction of most Romance languages is addressed briefly in Petinou and Terzi (2002). The relevant point here is that claims which attribute enclisis of Italian infinitives, gerunds, and imperatives and of Portuguese finite contexts to similar factors (Rizzi 2000) have to be reevaluated in view of the different behavior of early and SLI clitic placement in the above two syntactic contexts. These questions have come up as a result of recent research in early and SLI language, but there is no doubt that answers to them will constitute important contributions to the study of normal language as well.[16]

To conclude, by focusing in this section on a particular domain of grammar, the position of clitics in the sentential structure, I demonstrated how the study of impaired varieties is able to offer insights into the syntactic structure of normal language. The presentation was somehow tentative and sketchy, primarily a result of the insufficient cross-linguistic research in early and SLI language surrounding this phenomenon. I believe I have demonstrated, however, that with the rate at which research on impaired "varieties" proceeds, its contribution to the study of the properties of normal language will be difficult to ignore in the near future, and it may prove crucial for the understanding of a number of phenomena, in a manner that was inconceivable until recently. I hope I have indicated how such empirical evidence will be employed and directions toward which the related outcomes will evolve.

3 COMPARATIVE SYNTAX CONTRIBUTING TO LANGUAGE DISORDERS

Certainly, more research has been conducted on the syntax of normal language than on its various disordered variants cross-linguistically. One is tempted to conclude, therefore, that the overall results of research in comparative syntax, or on the syntax of normal language in general, are in a better position to contribute to the study of (the syntax of) impaired language than vice versa. One is also able to speculate as to why this is so and conceive of ways in which this contribution takes place. Syntactic theory provides the theoretical apparatus to characterize deviations and the ability associated with more advanced fields to offer insights as to how to look for patterns and characteristics in less explored or unusually behaving domains.

When it comes to impaired language, however, understanding its syntactic structure is often not the only issue at stake. Equally important (or more important, perhaps) is to be able to intervene on it in an efficient manner. The very first step in the process of intervention is diagnosis: the ability to detect accurately whether and how a language that gives the impression of being impaired can be (best) characterized for a certain impairment. With respect to SLI in particular, the related issue at stake is that of *clinical markers.* The concept is rather new in the manner used here, since it refers to a particular linguistic form (rather than to various, usually unrelated, characteristics of impaired language), which varies to a certain extent cross-linguistically and which has many chances of identifying the grammar of the individual as being SLI. Identifying such a form has undoubtedly practical value since it amounts to quickly detecting preschool children with the impairment, for instance, so that the child may be referred for further evaluation and language rehabilitation if necessary. However, identifying a clinical marker is also of importance for theoretical considerations, since pinning down a persisting (nonadult) property of impaired language is essentially a step closer to understanding the nature of the impairment.

In what follows I approach the general issue of how research in comparative syntax is able to contribute to the study of language disorders by focusing on just this particular aspect of the latter—namely, the identification of clinical markers. Since the term has been employed with reference to SLI so far, I will limit the discussion to this disorder. I demonstrate the relevant points by speculating on how claims that have been made on the basis of English (and other, similarly behaving languages) can extend to Greek, for which the issue of identifying a clinical marker has not been raised; hence, potential clinical markers have not been evaluated, either, until now. As a result, and given the novelty of the concept, apart from reviewing the relatively limited literature on clinical markers, the section that follows also serves as an exercise in suggesting as to how future research on the topic may proceed.

3.1 Clinical Markers in SLI

It had long been held about SLI, that there is no unique linguistic characteristic for it (Leonard 1987). Accordingly, and in the absence of hearing or cognitive deficits, the diagnosis of the condition by the speech-language pathologist usually takes place via examining a set of characteristics of the language through the utilization of standard tests or tests and methods created by the speech-language pathologist, when assessing languages for which standard tests are not available. Petinou and Terzi (2002) refer to several characteristics that lead the speech-language pathologist to the diagnosis of the children of the study as SLI.[17] For theoretical linguists, and for syntacticians in particular, the criteria used often seem vague and informal, an impression which is not accidental or unjustified. When it comes to English, for example, the set of morphemes that have constituted the basis of normal language development—hence, deviation(s) from them have been considered to signal impairment—are those of Brown (1973). Brown identified 15 such morphemes for investigation, whose use has been instrumental in diagnosis since then but whose choice was clearly atheoretic.[18] This is not the case with clinical markers—hence the important role they are able to play in understanding the nature of the impairment, in addition to just detecting it.

In their pioneering work, Rice et al. (1995) and Rice and Wexler (1996) establish the existence of such a clinical marker for English, proposing that this is the Optional Infinitive in its delayed use—namely, the Extended Optional Infinitive (EOI). The idea is that if the optional omission of Tense persists until after a certain age (approximately the age of 5), as a result of which children produce sentences such as (22) and (23), there is some serious indication that their language is SLI:

(22)   She like me.

(23)   She not go.

The identification of such a linguistic form[19] finds a syntactic explanation in what Wexler (1998) calls Unique Checking Constraint (UCC), a constraint that also operates in early normal language. As mentioned, the UCC amounts to the inability of DPs to check more than one D feature on the sentential functional heads, as a consequence of which Tense is often dropped in matrix contexts. An overt manifestation of it is that sentences such as (22) and (23) are produced by children with normal language development until around age 3;04, and by SLI children until much older ages.

It follows from the proposed constraint that we should not be able to find the counterpart of (E)OI in null subject languages, since the D feature of Tense is checked by the verb (Taraldsen 1978, Alexiadou and Anagnostopoulou 1998); consequently, the DP checks one D feature only, in accordance with the UCC.[20] In short, this view of SLI attributes the impairment to the persistence of the UCC, while it proposes that the Extended Optional Infinitive can be considered a clinical marker. Manifestations of the latter are sentences such as (22) and (23), omission of Tense morphemes at a higher rate than other morphemes in the language of the same child, or omission of the same (Tense) morphemes at higher rates when compared with the language of normal children at the same age (see Rice and Wexler 1996). With this information in mind, but also with what is known about the syntactic structure of the Greek sentence from research in comparative syntax, we can explore the predictions made for potential clinical markers in the language and how these are supported empirically by the evidence available so far.[21]

The discovery of a clinical marker such as the EOI in English and structurally related languages, and its concurrent theoretical basis, the UCC, do not seem to predict much about a language such as Greek directly, for a number of reasons. First, Greek does not have infinitives (for details, see Terzi 1997, and references therein); hence, one not only does not expect to find the counterpart structures of English early and SLI language but it is not even obvious what to expect as the corresponding forms. Second, Greek is a null subject language; hence, a stage during which infinitival forms of the verb are used optionally in finite contexts is not expected on the basis of this property of adult language either. At this point a further option emerges, however, one mentioned in passing in Wexler (1998: 73): Wexler predicts the counterpart of the OI stage in null subject languages, which seems to be supported by preliminary data from early Italian. On the basis of the clausal structure of Italian, according to which auxiliaries head a distinct projection (see Belletti 1990), and under the crucial assumption that auxiliaries also have a D feature, the UCC predicts a substantial proportion of auxiliary omission in early language. This prediction seems to be borne out via first in-spection of data from Italian (Lyons 1997, as reported in Wexler 1998).

It is interesting that available (albeit, indirect) evidence from Greek indicates that things may operate in a similar manner in Greek as well, offering support to these views concerning the manifestation of (E)OI in null subject languages, but also insights as to what may be an adequate clinical marker for SLI in the language. I refer to the available evidence as "indirect" because it comes from early language (which is also the case for Italian, as just mentioned). It is es-sential, therefore, to adopt—for the time being at least—the assumption that SLI is structurally parallel to early language, in order to pursue the reasoning that follows.

In a study by Varlokosta, et al. (1998) it is reported that at early stages, child native speakers of Standard Greek erroneously use a form of the verb that is identical to the third-person singular, but also to the participle of adult lan-guage.

(24)   Tuto sel-i. (Normal adult: tuto thel-o.)
        this want-3s
        'I want this.'

(25)   Fa-i. (Normal adult: Tha fa-o.)
        eat-3s
        'I will eat.'

Varlokosta et al. (1998) claim that rather than being third-person singular, the early form they discover corresponds to the past participle. Hence, they conclude, forms such as (24) and (25) constitute an interesting counterpart of the English Optional Infinitive stage and of structures such as in (22) and (23) in the sense that the form of the verb employed by Greek children is also the form minimally inflected for Tense/Agr in the adult language.[22]

The interest of these findings lies in the fact that sentences such as (25) may be interpreted in an alternative manner (not incompatible with the claims in Varlokosta et al.). One can conceivably propose that what is actually happening in examples such as (25) is auxiliary omission rather than use of the participle. Providing that Greek SLI is indeed delayed language—hence is structurally similar to early language—and that the idea of auxiliary omission is on the right track, I may have been able to identify a clinical marker for SLI in Standard Greek.

Of course, numerous details must be elaborated on both conceptual and em-pirical grounds for such a proposal to be credible. It is not clear, for instance, that auxiliary omission and not the extensive use of third-person singular per se is an accurate clinical marker for Greek, and this issue is pending empirical confirmation. If the latter is indeed the case, how does it compare to the findings from Italian, which is also a null subject language, but in which infinitives are available? Moreover, whether the auxiliary omission of Italian (reported in Wexler 1998) is in some way related with the agreement that the past participle following *essere* exhibits with the subject (entirely absent from Greek) is another issue to be examined. All these are possibilities to be considered and issues that have to be addressed and settled. It seems to me, however, that the domains I have pinpointed are precisely those that will offer the answers to the questions posed and that the knowledge obtained via research in comparative syntax will guide the formulation of the optimal hypothesis for evaluating the existing empirical evidence, as well as the search for additional empirical support in case this is necessary.

Regardless of whether I have been successful in identifying and proposing a satisfactory clinical marker for Standard Greek, however, I can proceed with an attempt to identify a clinical marker for Cypriot Greek. The latter is also a null subject language without infinitives, therefore, no Extended Optional Infinitive stage comparable to that of English is to be expected. But, in contrast to Standard Greek, Cypriot Greek also lacks auxiliaries.[23] This is an important difference between the two dialects for our purposes, since, if auxiliary omission turns out to be the appropriate clinical marker for SLI in (at least some) null subject languages, it cannot be of use in Cypriot. It is precisely in this context that the study of nonadult Cypriot clitic placement in Petinou and Terzi (2002) may prove useful. It was hinted there that the across-the-board misplacement of pronominal clitics in the SLI children's language—namely, the fact that clitics were placed after the verb in all contexts where they should be preverbal—has serious chances of serving as a clinical marker. In light of the discussion in this section, and in the absence of auxiliaries from Cypriot, this hint deserves further consideration.[24]

To conclude: this section discussed ways in which research in comparative syntax is able to contribute to current studies on impaired language, and I approached the topic by focusing on one specific domain associated with the latter—the identification of clinical markers.[25] By extending proposals that have been made on the basis of languages other than Greek, I demonstrated how well-established knowledge concerning the syntactic structure of it, along with the structure of other languages, is able to guide research in this domain. In a similar fashion, work on other aspects of impaired language can be benefited and inspired by research in comparative syntax and the knowledge concerning properties of language that has emerged from it.

4 Language Therapy

In this final section I address an area of language disorders that interacts with linguistic theory and research in (comparative) syntax in a particularly bilateral manner and, moreover, in a manner considerably different from what syntacticians have been used to but also from what researchers (and even most practitioners) in language disorders are familiar with. This is the area of (syntactic) theory-motivated therapy, a relatively recent way of practicing language therapy. With the term *theory-motivated therapy* I refer to language therapy that relies crucially on theoretical concepts and proposals of generative syntax. It has been employed primarily with Broca's aphasics so far, and it has demonstrated clearly, it seems to me, that various well-established claims of syntactic theory are able to render therapy more efficient, at least in terms of making it less time- and effort-consuming, as far as I can see.[26] Subsequently, the outcomes of this type of therapy are able to contribute to syntactic theory in an entirely new mode. In the remainder of the chapter, I present existing work in this domain, leaving to the reader most of the task of judging the importance and ramifications of it.

In Thompson (1997) (and a series of earlier references therein) the enterprise of applying therapy to syntactic structures involving movement in English Broca's aphasics is presented, and the various results of it are discussed and evaluated. Assuming the statistics to be on the right track, these results are gratifying for the eyes of a syntactician, not only because of their efficiency in therapy but also because they seem to offer full support to fundamental claims of syntactic theory. In the aforementioned study, for instance, language therapy focused on two types of movement structures, A and A'—the first consisting of passive and raising sentences, and the second of wh-questions and object clefts. One structure from each type was targeted for therapy each time, and the result was that the targeted structure, along with the other structure of the same type, improved simultaneously. This amounts to saying that when only the raising constructions of agrammatics were treated, the performance of the treated individuals on passive sentences also improved while their performance on wh-questions and object clefts was not affected. Comparable results were obtained when object clefts were trained: wh-questions then improved, while performance on passive and raising sentences remained unaffected. In other words, it emerged that a fundamental distinction of syntactic theory was supported empirically by means of an entirely new source. Notice that the empirical support for these two types of movement structures comes from sources different even from those discussed by Grodzinsky and Finkel (1998), and by Avrutin (2000), offering an idea of the wide spectrum of empirical evidence that can be contributed by studies on impaired language.

Since I am also concerned with the other direction of the relationship, however,—that is, with the contribution of syntactic theory to language disorders—

we should keep in mind that, if by targeting one structure from a related group, the rest of the structures of the group are also affected simultaneously, there are some serious time- and effort-saving benefits to be obtained. It is probably the case that such benefits are not easy to trace in other types of language therapy.

More recently, Friedmann et al. (2000) report that they applied therapy of wh-questions to Hebrew Broca's aphasics in a similar manner.[27] The results revealed that once higher nodes or parts of the syntactic tree were trained (wh-questions; hence, the C domain), lower parts of the sentential structure (Agr/Tense inflection; hence, the I domain) also improved simultaneously, while no evidence for the opposite direction was offered. The results from that study are rather preliminary, as they come out of only one patient; nevertheless, they can at least serve as a starting point for a number of issues to be further investigated.[28] The psychological reality of the syntactic tree (Friedmann 2001), the direction to which impairment occurs (higher toward lower nodes, but not vice versa), and also ways in which language therapy can contribute toward evaluating alternative syntactic theories (while benefiting the patient at the same time) are some of these issues.

Thus, despite the novelty of the above-mentioned studies—hence, the need for finer-grained research in order to establish the validity of their results and the associated claims—there is no doubt, it seems to me, that these studies contribute not only to both the understanding of the representation of language in the brain and the nature of the various impairments but also toward a more restrictive syntactic theory (which will have to take the relevant findings into consideration). Of course, the manner and efficiency with which all this can be achieved will depend on the depth and the precision of the studies.

5 CONCLUSION

This chapter has discussed various ways in which research in comparative syntax interacts with research in language disorders that affect the morphosyntactic domain of grammar. By focusing on SLI and Broca's aphasia I held that, although their manifestation in language seems to offer an additional array of "dialects" to be studied by syntacticians, their usefulness is limited if they involve deviations from UG. Their contribution is important in alternative ways, however: for SLI in particular I showed that by being essentially a slowly developing language it offers the opportunity to approach certain syntactic phenomena and correlations between them in ways that are not always feasible when studying early normal language because of the quick rate at which it develops. Furthermore, I pointed out that the available data from both SLI and agrammatism accumulate so fast that we will soon be able to improve our understanding of certain syntactic phenomena by being able to compare how they are manifested in their impaired variants cross-linguistically. It is in this sense, I believe, that the study of language disorders can contribute the most, and in the most ingenious manner, to current syntactic theory and its claims regarding the nature of normal adult language.

In addressing the other direction of the relationship—namely, what and how comparative syntax is able to contribute to research in language disorders—I discussed the identification of clinical markers and the insights that syntactic theory can offer toward an efficient (theory-motivated) therapy. The results of the latter, in turn, can provide new feedback and an entirely novel terrain within which claims of syntactic theory can be reevaluated and further develop.

Finally, the goal of this chapter is to demonstrate that research in these two areas, if communicated properly, is of enormous potential for providing complete answers to fundamental questions regarding the nature and properties of the human language faculty.

NOTES

Several of the ideas expressed in this chapter grew out of discussions and interaction during the semester of my sabbatical (spring 2000) at the department of brain and cognitive sciences of MIT. Many thanks to Ken Wexler for facilitating my stay at the department and for the time he often took in discussing various related issues with me. I would also like to thank him, along with Danny Fox, Phoevos Panagiotidis, and Melita Stavrou, for reading an earlier version of the chapter and commenting on it. This is also the place to express my appreciation to the Greek Ministry of Education for its wise policy of (partially) funding sabbaticals abroad and to the Technological Educational Institute of Patras for having implemented this policy.

1. As Chomsky (1989: 3) puts it: "The shift of focus was from behavior or the products of behavior to states of the mind/brain that enter into behavior. . . . The three basic questions that arise, then, are these:

(i)   What constitutes knowledge of language?

(ii)   How is knowledge of language acquired?

(iii)   How is knowledge of language put to use?"

2. More recently, this is stated as, "to show how a particular choice of parameter values, and lexicon enters into fixing a language L—and to proceed beyond, to the study of use, acquisition, pathology, cellular mechanisms, and a wide range of other questions having to do with the place of language in the biological and social worlds" (Chomsky 2000: 92).

3. The proposals in Grodzinsky (2000) with respect to the localization of a subpart of syntactic abilities, those associated with movement operations, are representative of this type of research.

4. See Levy and Kavé (1999) for the relevance of research on language disorders for other areas of linguistic theory and for cognition.

5. Representative of this type of contribution is the work reported in Grodzinsky and Finkel (1998), according to whom agrammatics demonstrate different behavior in XP than in X° movement structures, arguing (in ways that follow from Grodzinsky's earlier work) that the latter type of movement does not create chains, a finding in accordance with Chomsky (2001). As for Specific Language Impairment, Tsimpli (2001) identifies problems that SLI children have with uninterpretable features of lexical items, supporting the distinction between interpretable and uninterpretable features introduced in Chomsky (1995); see also Clahsen (1989) and Clahsen et al. (1997), for claims along similar lines. Finally, Petinou and Terzi (2002) observe that, despite a number of problems that the SLI children of their study have with respect to Inflectional elements, they seem to obey the requirement on right adjunction that follows from Kayne's (1994) antisymmetry proposals.

6. As Kayne (1991, note 69) states it: "It is advantageous to work with a set of closely related languages, much as in any experiment one tries to keep the number of variables as low as possible." See Poletto (2000) for a typical case of detailed microparametric study of subject clitics in Northern Italian dialects. See also Terzi (1999a) for a study of the ordering of object clitics in minimally different varieties of Greek and subsequent extension of the claims to the standard Romance languages. The work of Ordóñez and Terzi (1999) on clitic ordering in dialects of Spanish falls within the same research paradigm.

7. I should note here that ascribing the status of "delayed" language to a linguistic condition does not necessarily exempt it from being impaired. For the case of Specific Language Impairment in particular, even if we accept that there are no wild cards among the deviant structures manifested by SLI—namely, that we are not to encounter structures which cannot be encountered in the (respective) early language—the mere fact that the deviation persists until a much older age and (unlike with early language) it may not go away entirely, is sufficient to characterize the language as impaired, it seems to me.

8. See Stavrakaki (2001a), for instance, in which the behavior of Greek SLI children with respect to a number of syntactic structures is tested from a psycholinguistic perspective, and it is claimed that the behavior of SLI is different from that of early language for several of them. See also Stavrakaki (2001b).

9. The UCC can capture (at least) one more phenomenon with interesting cross-linguistic variation: the fact that object clitics are omitted in some early and SLI languages (Italian) but not clearly so in others (Spanish) (Wexler 2000).

10. Another language which behaves in a similar manner, and to which we will return in more detail shortly, is Berber (Ouhalla, chapter 14 in this volume).

11. Hence, the term "Clitic Misplacement" used to describe the phenomenon was misleading, since it is not clitics per se that are misplaced but the illicit (for adults) verb movement that makes them look so.

12. In Petinou and Terzi (2002) we put forward a full proposal concerning what it is that children misperceive during the nonadult enclisis stage: we claim that functional

heads (which in adult normal language occupy the M° position and check the verb features of M) are perceived as phrasal by children. More precisely, the Infl particles either occupy the Spec(MP) position, or they are adjuncts; hence, they are unable to check verb-related features. Finite verb-movement to M takes place in order to check verb features of M, resulting in surface structures with finite enclisis that are illicit for adult grammar but presumably not for children since their Infl particles are not in M, but where the asterisk in (8) indicates.

13. One can conceivably raise a number of objections regarding the validity of the points just mentioned. They may want to argue, for instance, that we could have reached the same conclusions after looking at much larger samples of normal language from the very beginning. Or that a powerful syntactic theory, such as the one I employed for the phenomenon under investigation, would have urged me to look directly at the behavior of the Infl particles in the data base from early language. I do believe, however, that it is doubtful whether we would have arrived at the inferences we did, especially within the short time span this was achieved, had I not obtained the nontrivial and transparent "errors" regarding the behavior of the Infl particles from the SLI data I collected.

Some of the results of the Dutch-speaking children discussed in Wexler et al. (2004) constitute a case similar in nature: while predictions of Schütze and Wexler's (1996) Tense/Agr Omission Model do not seem to be borne out clearly by the linguistic behavior of the Dutch-speaking children discussed in Wexler et al. (in terms of the children's usage of present instead of past tense that the model predicts), the predictions are definitely borne out by SLI children.

14. One context in which clitics are found in third position, in Tarifit Berber, is in the presence of the past Tense marker.

(i)   Lla ttarin-n t

PAST write$_{\text{IMPERF}}$-3pl CL$_{\text{3s:ACC}}$

'They were writing it.' (Ouhalla, chapter 14 in this volume).

15. Furthermore, Wexler (2000) reports that, according to Moucka (1999), 92% of second-position clitics appear in second position in young Czech speech. One may want to be slightly cautious with respect to Czech, however, especially if Bošković (2001) is right in that Czech is losing its second-position clitichood properties. Comparable data from Serbo-Croatian would definitely assist in strengthening the point.

16. Within the same line of reasoning, if agrammatics have problems with verb movement in some languages (see also note 28), while it is generally accepted that they have only problems with XP movement, it may be the case, or is at least worth investigating it, that in these languages verb movement is an instance of remnant movement (see Kayne 1994 and subsequent work).

17. "Language samples were analyzed for mean length of utterances in words (MLU/W) and structural errors involving omission or incorrect use of morphological inflection, omission or incorrect use of function words (definite and indefinite articles, prepositions, pronouns) errors in word order, errors in subject-verb agreement for number and person, case and number."

18. These morphemes, in order of acquisition, are progressive -ing; the prepositions in and on; plural -s; past irregular, possessive -s, uncontractible copula, articles a and the, past regular -ed, third-person regular -s, third-person irregular, uncontractible auxiliary, contractible copula, and contractible auxiliary.

19. The term "linguistic form" in this particular case actually refers to a set of morphemes, those marking Tense in English—namely, -s, -ed, BE, and DO. Apart from the theoretical importance of setting apart these four morphemes, the practical value of having to measure the performance on four morphemes rather than the fourteen of the previous note, should not go unnoticed.

20. The prediction is borne out since the Optional Infinitive stage, in the sense of the adult infinitival forms of the verb employed optionally in root sentences, has been found in all Germanic languages and in French, Irish, Russian, and Czech, but not in Italian, Spanish, Catalan, Tamil, or Polish.

21. I refer to both Standard and Cypriot Greek, which essentially differ only in terms of clitic placement. An additional difference is the lack of auxiliaries from the latter, which, however, is a property most probably related to the placement of clitics (see note 23 and section 2).

22. A concrete example of the verbal paradigm is given in order to facilitate the discussion: *exo fai* (have-1s eaten) 'I have eaten', *exis fai* (have-2s eaten) 'You have eaten', *exi fai* (have-3s eaten) 'S/he has eaten', and so on.

23. I mentioned in passing in section 2, that in Terzi (1999a, 1999b) the finite verb movement to M, which results in enclisis in Cypriot, is triggered by properties of M. A fundamental property of the language associated with the M domain is the fact that Cypriot Greek has no compound tenses and therefore no auxiliaries to express them. Thus, the counterparts of Standard Greek forms such as *exis fai* (have-2s eaten) and *ixes fai* (had-2s eaten) are *efa(g)es* (ate-2s). Furthermore, the future particle *tha*, which is typical of the future of the Balkan future, is also absent. Thus, the counterpart of *tha fas* (FUT eat-2s) is *en-na fas*, which is most probably to be glossed as (is SUB eat-2s).

24. I am not implying here that the across-the-board enclisis of Cypriot follows from UCC, or that such an option can be excluded, however. All I intend to say at this stage is that, in the absence of those characteristics of the language (auxiliaries, in particular) that would follow from UCC as potential clinical markers, other possibilities must be investigated. The pattern of clitic positioning is a characteristic that emerges very clearly at this point and is worth investigating whether it can play this role. Whether it follows from UCC or not is a separate issue.

25. I have excluded from the discussion at least two other accounts of SLI that may be reminiscent of the notion of clinical marker, since, despite that fact that they do not employ the term explicitly, they are based on well-defined syntactic structures which are claimed to be characteristic of SLI language. I refer to van der Lely (1996, 1998) in particular, for whom SLI is identified as a disorder with problems in movement structures, and work of Clahsen (1989) and Clahsen et al. (1997), which are concerned with Agreement relationships primarily. Apart from reasons of space, another consideration was the fact that both accounts center around the understanding of the nature of the phenomenon primarily, rather than its manifestation in a way that can assist diagnosis.

26. Language therapy based on syntactic theory is also being employed currently on children with severely persistent SLI by Ebbels and van der Lely (2001).

27. As for the precise manner in which therapy was implemented, it is safer for the reader to refer to the original sources. Very briefly, emphasis was first given on clarifying the argument structure of the active sentences to the patients. Subsequently, the patients were given direct guidance regarding the movement operations.

28. In the context of this study, and taking into account problems Dutch Broca's

aphasics have with verbs and V-second, according to Bastiaanse (1995), it is tempting to want to find out, for instance, what the effect of training wh-questions is, with the hope to shed further light into the issue of whether V-second involves V-to-I or V-to-C movement, in Dutch at least. At the same time, one should not disregard the fact that contradicting experimental results should also be resolved in order for a number of such studies to constitute significant contributions. As we have seen already, it is not entirely clear that agrammatics have problems with X° movement (Grodzinsky and Finkel 1998) while V-second is standardly considered to be such a type of movement (see note 16).

REFERENCES

Alexiadou, A., and E. Anagnostopoulou (1998) "Parametrizing AGR: Word Order, V-Movement and EPP-Checking." *Natural Language and Linguistic Theory* 16: 491–539.

Avrutin, S. (2000) "Comprehension of D-linked and non-D-linked questions by children and Broca's aphasics," in Y. Grodzinsky, L. Shapiro, and D. Swinnie (eds.) *Language and Brain*. Academic Press, San Diego, 295–313.

Bastiaanse, R. (1995) "Broca's aphasia: a syntactic and/or morphological disorder? A case study." *Brain and Language* 48: 1–32.

Belletti, A. (1990) *Generalized Verb Movement*. Rosenberg and Sellier, Turin.

Boskovic, Z. (2001) *On the Nature of the Syntax-Phonology Interface: Cliticization and Related Phenomena*. Elsevier, Amsterdam.

Bottari, P., Cipriani P., and Chilosi, A. M. (2000) "Dissociations in the Acquisition of Clitic Pronouns by Dysphasic Children: A Case Study from Italian," in C. Hamman and S. Powers (eds.) *The Acquisition of Scrambling and Cliticization*. Kluwer, Dordrecht.

Brown, R. (1973) *A First Language: The Early Stages*. Harvard University Press, Cambridge.

Chomsky, N. (1989) *Language and Problems of Knowledge*. MIT Press, Cambridge, Mass.

Chomsky, N. (1995) *The Minimalist Program*. MIT Press, Cambridge, Mass., 1–52.

Chomsky, N. (2000) "Minimalist Inquiries: The Framework," in R. Martin and J. Uriagereka (eds.) *Step by Step*. MIT Press, Cambridge, Mass., 89–155

Chomsky, N. (2001) "Derivation by Phase," in M. Kenstowicz (ed.) *Ken Hale: A Life in Language*. MIT Press, Cambridge, Mass.

Cinque, G. (1990) *Types of A'-Dependencies*. MIT Press, Cambridge, Mass.

Clahsen, H. (1989) "The Grammatical Characterization of Developmental Dysphasia." *Linguistics* 27: 897–920.

Clahsen, H., S. Bartke, and S. Goellner (1997) "Formal Features in Impaired Grammars: A Comparison of English and German SLI Children." *Journal of Neurolinguistics* 10: 151–171.

Duarte, I., and G. Matos (2000) "Romance Clitics and the Minimalist Program," in J. Costa (ed.) *Portuguese Syntax: New Comparative Studies*. Oxford University Press, New York, 116–142.

Ebbels, S., and H. van der Lely (2001) "Meta-syntactic Therapy Using Visual Coding for

Children with Severe Persistent SLI." Unpublished Birkbeck College, University of London.

Friedmann, N. (2001) "Agrammatism and the Psychological Reality of the Syntactic Tree." *Journal of Psycholinguistic Research* 30: 71–90.

Friedmann, N., D. Olenik, and M. Gil (2000) "From Theory to Practice: Treatment of Agrammatic Production in Hebrew Based on the Tree Pruning Hypothesis." *Journal of Neurolinguistics* 13: 250–254.

Grodzinsky, Y. (2000) "The Neurology of Syntax: Language Use without Broca's Area." *Behavioral and Brain Sciences* 23: 1–71.

Grodzinsky, Y., and L. Finkel (1998) "The Neurology of Empty Categories: Aphasics' Failure to Detect Ungrammaticality." *Journal of Cognitive Neuroscience* 10: 281–292.

Guasti, M. T. (1993–94) "Verb Syntax in Italian Child Grammar: Finite and Nonfinite Verbs." *Language Acquisition* 3: 1–40.

Jakubowicz, C., L. Nash, C. Rigaut, and C.-L. Gérard (1998) "Determiners and Clitic Pronouns in French-Speaking Children with SLI." *Language Acquisition* 7: 113–160.

Kayne, R. (1991) "Romance Clitics, Verb Movement, and PRO." *Linguistic Inquiry* 22: 647–686.

Kayne, R. (1994) *The Antisymmetry of Syntax.* MIT Press, Cambridge, Mass.

Leonard, L. (1987) "Is Specific Language Impairment a Useful Construct?" in S. Rosenberg (ed.) *Advances in Applied Psycholinguistics.* Vol. 1: *Disorders of First Language Development.* Cambridge University Press, Cambridge, 1–39.

Levy, Y., and G. Kavé (1999) "Language Breakdown and Linguistic Theory: A Tutorial Overview." *Lingua* 107: 95–143.

Marinis, Th. (2000) "The Acquisition of the DP in Modern Greek." Ph.D. diss., University of Potsdam.

Martins, A. M. (1994) "Enclisis, VP-Deletion and the Nature of Sigma." *Probus* 6: 173–206.

Ordóñez, F., and A. Terzi (2000) "Variation in Clitic Ordering from a Synchronic and Diachronic Perspective." Paper presented at the Conference on Antisymmetry, Cortona.

Petinou, K., and A. Terzi (2002) "Clitic Misplacement among Normally Developing and SLI Children and the Status of Infl Heads." *Language Acquisition* 10: 1–28.

Poletto, C. (2000) *The Higher Functional Field. Evidence from Northern Italian Dialects.* Oxford University Press, New York.

Rice, M. L., and K. Wexler (1996) "Toward Tense as a Clinical Marker of Specific Language Impairment in English-Speaking Children." *Journal of Speech and Hearing Research* 39: 1239–1257.

Rice, M. L., K. Wexler, and P. Cleave (1995) "Specific Language Impairment as a Period of Extended Optional Infinitive." *Journal of Speech, Language and Hearing Research* 38: 850–863.

Rizzi, L. (2000) "Some Notes on Romance cliticization." *Comparative Syntax and Language Acquisition.* Routledge, London, 96–121.

Schütze, C., and K. Wexler (1996) "Subject Case Licensing and English Root Infinitives," in A. Stringfellow, D. Cahan-Amitay, E. Hughes, and A. Zukowski (eds.) *Proceedings of the 20th Annual Conference on Language Development.* Cascadilla Press, Somerville, Mass., 670–681.

Stavrakaki, S. (2001a) "Specific Language Impairment in Greek: Aspects of Syntactic Production and Comprehension." Ph.D. diss., University of Thessaloniki.

Stavrakaki, S. (2001b) "Comprehension of Reversible Relative Clauses in Specifically Language Impaired and Normally Developing Greek Children." *Brain and Language* 77: 419–431.

Stjepanović, S. (1998) "On the Placement of Serbo-Croatian Clitics: Evidence from VP-Ellipsis." *Linguistic Inquiry* 29: 527–537.

Taraldsen, K. (1978) "On the NIC, Vacuous Application and the That-Trace Filter." Unpublished ms., University of Tromsoe.

Terzi, A. (1997) "PRO and Null *Case* in Finite Clauses." *Linguistic Review* 14: 335–360.

Terzi, A. (1999a) "Clitic Combinations, Their Hosts and Their Ordering." *Natural Language and Linguistic Theory* 17: 85–121.

Terzi, A. (1999b) "Cypriot Greek Clitics and Their Positioning Restrictions," in A. Alexiadou, G. Horrocks, and M. Stavrou (eds.) *Studies in Greek Syntax*, Kluwer, Dordrecht, 227–240.

Thompson, C. (1997) "Training and Generalized Production of wh- and NP-Movement Structures in Agrammatic Aphasia." *Journal of Speech, Language and Hearing Research* 40: 228–244.

Tsimpli, I.-M. (2001) "LF-interpretability and Language Development: A Study of Verbal and Nominal Features in Greek Normally Developing and SLI Children." *Brain and Language* 77: 432–448.

Uriagereka, J. (1995) "Aspects of the Syntax of Clitic Placement in Western Romance." *Linguistic Inquiry* 26: 79–123.

van der Lely, H. K. J. (1996) "Specifically Language Impaired and Normally Developing Children: Verbal Passive vs. Adjectival Passive Sentence Interpretation." *Lingua* 98: 243–272.

van der Lely, H. K. J. (1998) "SLI in Children: Movement, Economy and Deficits in the Computational-Syntactic System." *Language Acquisition* 7: 161–192.

Varlokosta, S., A. Vainikka, and B. Rohrbacher (1998) "Functional Projections, Markedness and 'Root Infinitives' in Early Child Greek." *Linguistic Review* 15: 187–207.

Wexler, K. (1996) "The Development of Inflection in a Biologically Based Theory of Language Acquisition," in M. L. Rice (ed.) *Toward a Genetics of Language*. Lawrence Erlbaum. Mahwah, NJ, 113–144.

Wexler, K. (1998) "Very Early Parameter Setting and the Unique Checking Constraint: A New Explanation of the Optional Infinitive Stage." *Lingua* 106: 23–79.

Wexler, K. (2000) "The Unique Checking Constraint and Cross-Linguistic Differences in the Development of Object Clitics, Both Normal and Impaired." Paper presented at the Conference on Determiner and Pronoun Development, Paris.

Wexler, K., J. Schaeffer, and G. Bol (2004) "Verbal Syntax and Morphology in Dutch Normal and SLI Children: How Developmental Data Can Play an Important Role in Morphological Theory." *Syntax* 7.

CHAPTER 4

OBJECT SHIFT, VERB MOVEMENT, AND VERB REDUPLICATION

ENOCH OLADÉ ABOH

1 INTRODUCTION

THE Gbe[1] languages manifest complement-head versus head-complement asymmetries. In the Gungbe determiner phrases (DPs), the noun precedes the determiner head *lɔ́* as in (1a). Similarly, the complement sequence [noun-Det] precedes the postnominal morpheme *jí* that heads the postnominal phrase (*p*P) in (1b).[2] In contrast, the prepositional phrases (PPs) in (1c–d) display head-complement structures: the preposition precedes the DP/*p*P-complements:

(1) a. Kɔ̀jó zán   [$_{DP}$ àmì lɔ́].
       Kojo use-Perf   oil   Det

     'Kojo used the oil.'

   b. Kɔ̀jó xɛ́   [$_{p}$P [$_{DP}$ távò lɔ́] jí].
       Kojo climb-Perf   table Det $P_{[ON]}$

     'Kojo climbed on the table.' [i.e. on the surface of the table]

   c. Kòjó   zé   [$_{DP}$ àmì   lɔ́]   [$_{PP}$ xlán   [Kwésí]].
      Kojo   take-Perf   oil   Det   P$_{[TO]}$ Kwesi

      'Kojo sent the oil to Kwesi.'

   d. Kòjó   zé   [$_{DP}$ àmì   lɔ́]   [$_{PP}$ ɖó   [$_{PP}$ [$_{DP}$ távò   lɔ́]   jí]].
      Kojo   take-Perf   oil   Det   P$_{[AT]}$ table   Det   P$_{[ON]}$

      'Kojo put the oil on the table.'

In addition to the asymmetries found in (1), the Gungbe DP/*p*Ps and PPs show different distributive properties. On the one hand, DP and *p*Ps are subject to movement operations, while PPs are immobile. For instance, the focus sentences (2a–b) involve DP-and *p*P-fronting, respectively. On the other hand, prepositions must be stranded, as in (2c). As the ungrammatical (2d) shows, PPs cannot be pied-piped:

(2)   a. [$_{DP}$ Àmì   lɔ́]   wɛ̀   Kòjó   zán.
             oil   Det   Foc   Kojo   use-Perf

         'Kojo used THE OIL.'

      b. [$_{pP}$ [$_{DP}$ Távò   lɔ́]   jí]   wɛ̀   Kòjó   xé.
                table   Det   P$_{[ON]}$ Foc   Kojo   climb-Perf

         'Kojo climbed ON THE TABLE.'

      c. [Kwésí]   wɛ̀   Kòjó   zé   [$_{DP}$ àmì   lɔ́]   [$_{PP}$ xlán [$_{kwési}$]].
         Kwesi   Foc   Kojo   take-Perf   oil   Det   P$_{[TO]}$

         'Kojo sent the oil to KWESI.'

      d. *[$_{PP}$ Xlán   [Kwésí]]   wɛ̀   Kòjó   zé   [$_{DP}$ àmì   lɔ́].
             P$_{[TO]}$ Kwesi   Foc   Kojo   take-Perf   oil   Det

Under Aboh (1996, 2004a), I assume that the postnominal morphemes (*p*s) are deficient for case. This would mean that DPs and *p*Ps display similar distribution because they must be licensed for case. Witness in (3) that DPs and *p*Ps can surface in subject or object positions:

(3)   a. Távò   lɔ́   flɛ́.
         table   Det   fall-Perf

         'The table fell.'

      b. Távò   lɔ́   jí   zɛ̀.
         table   Det   P$_{[ON]}$ cleave-Perf

         'The surface of the table cracked.'

c. Yé   nyì   távò   ló.
   3pl   throw-Perf   table   Det

'They threw the table (away).'

d. Yé   súnsún   távò   ló   jí.
   3pl   clean-Perf table Det P[ON]

'They cleaned the surface of the table.'

Complement-head sequences also arise within the clause. The imperfective sentence (4) manifests OV order. But the perfective (or nonimperfective) sentence (5) displays VO order:[3]

(4)   Kòjó   tò   [DP àmì   ló]   zân.
      Kojo   Imperf   oil   Det   use-NR

'Kojo is using the oil.'

(5)   Kòjó   zán   [DP àmì   ló].
      Kojo   use-Perf   oil   Det

'Kojo used the oil.'

Under Kayne's (1994) specifier-head-complement hypothesis, the Gbe head-complement versus complement-head asymmetries result from:

1. Movement of the complement to the specifier of the head (6a)
2. Movement of the complement to a position higher than that targeted by the head (6b)
3. Movement of the head to a position higher than that targeted by the complement (6c)[4]

(6)   a.   b.

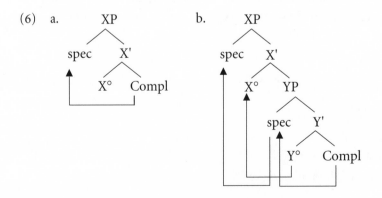

c.

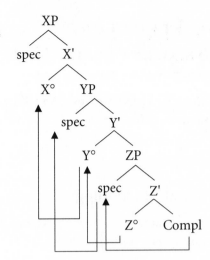

Structure (6a) accounts for the Gungbe DPs and *p*Ps: the complement is moved to the specifier position of its head (Kinyalolo 1995; Aboh 2004a).

This chapter focuses on structures (6b–c). It argues that object shift and verb movement are never optional in Gbe. DP-arguments necessarily move to the relevant licensing position to check their case features or else some strong EPP[5] feature, while the verb moves to check its aspect features. In this regard, I argue in section 2 that VO sequences derive from subsequent V-to-Asp movement to the left of the object, due to aspectual licensing. In section 3 I show that in OV sequences, however, verb movement past the object is blocked because the verb is stuck in an embedded nominalized small clause. This small clause manifests its own left periphery expressed by a nominalizer morpheme and an inflectional system manifested by an aspect marker. Under the EPP, the embedded subject position must be filled in overt syntax. This requirement is met by subsequent movement of the object (via [spec AgroP]) to a position higher than the landing site of the verb (i.e., the embedded aspect position).

I further argue that OV sequences are favorite contexts for verb reduplication. The conclusion reached there is that verb reduplication is a licensing device that legitimates a null subject expletive when no object (or relevant maximal projection) is available that could be moved to the embedded subject position to satisfy the EPP. In section 4 I extend this analysis to OVV sequences (i.e., contexts in which the object precedes a reduplicated verb) and suggests that those constructions necessarily involve reduplication because the object is moved to some specifier position within the left periphery of the small clause. Alternatively, the embedded subject position is filled by a null expletive licensed by the inflected (or reduplicated) verb.

2 CLAUSE STRUCTURE AND THE VO SEQUENCES IN GBE

This section describes the Gbe clause structure and shows that VO sequences involve monoclausal structures unlike OV sequences, which are biclausal.

2.1 A Poor Inflectional Morphology

Gungbe manifests no inflectional morphology. The sentences under (7) show that the verb always surfaces in its bare form and shows no sensitivity to finiteness or subject-verb agreement:

(7) a. Ùn jró   ná   [wlé] xὲ   lɔ́.
          1sg want-Perf Prep catch bird Det

          'I wanted to catch the bird.'

  b. Ùn/yé [wlé]   xὲ   lɔ́.
          1sg/3pl catch-Perf bird Det

          'I/they caught the bird.'

Similarly, example (8) shows that nouns are never inflected for case and number in Gungbe.

(8) a. Àsé lɔ́   wlé   àvú lɔ́.
          cat Det catch-Perf dog Det

          'The cat caught the dog.'

  b. Àvú lɔ́   wlé   àsé lɔ́.
          dog Det catch-Perf cat Det

          'The dog caught the cat.'

  c. Àsé lέ   wlé   àvú lέ.
          cat Numb catch-Perf dog Numb

          'The cats caught the dogs.'

Yet certain pronouns (i.e., 1sg and 2sg) show case morphology—see Agbedor (1996) and Aboh (1996, 2004a):

(9) a. Ùn/à/é/   mí/mì/yé   wlé   àvú   lέ.
          1/2/3sg-NOM   1/2/3pl-NOM   catch-Perf   dog   Numb

          'I, you, s/he, we, you they caught the dogs.'

     b. Àvú   lέ   wlé   mì/wè/è/   mí/mì/yé.
         dog   Numb   catch-Perf   1/2/3sg-ACC   1/2/3pl-ACC

         'The dogs caught me.'

In this chapter, I regard the distinct forms in (9) (i.e., 1/2sg-NOM and 1/2sg-ACC) as empirical evidence that the Gbe clause structure involves case-related functional projections, say AgrP, where nominative and accusative cases are assigned under spec-head relationship (Belletti 1990, Chomsky 1993).

2.2 The Gbe IP-Markers

The Gbe languages involve distinct markers that express the I-features: negation (10a), future (10b), habitual (10c), imperfective (or progressive) (10d), and prospective (10e). The IP-markers surface in a space that is delimited on the left by negation and on the right by the verb (Clements 1972, 1975; Avolonto 1992; Aboh 1996, 2004a; Houngues 1997; Manfredi 1997; Cinque 1999; Essegbey 1999).[6]

(10) a. Àsíbá **má**   xɔ   kèkέ. (Negation)
          Asiba Neg   buy-Perf   bicycle

          'Asiba didn't buy a bicycle.'

     b. Dáwè   lɔ́   **ná**   xɔ   kèkέ. (Future)
         man   Det   Fut   buy   bicycle

         'The man will buy a bicycle.'

     c. Dáwè   lɔ́   **nɔ̀**   xɔ   kèkέ. (Habitual)
         man   Det   Hab   buy   bicycle

         'The man habitually buys a bicycle [e.g. every year]'

     d. Dáwè   lɔ́   **tò**   kèké   xɔ̀. (Imperfective)
         man   Det   Imperf bicycle buy-NR

         'The man is buying a bicycle.'

     e. Dáwè   lɔ́   *(**tò**)   kèké   *(**nà**)   xɔ̀. (Prospective)
         man   Det   Imperf   bicycle Prosp   buy-NR

         'The man is about to buy a bicycle.'

Sentences (10d–e) suggest that the prospective marker *nà* depends on the imperfective marker *tò*. The latter can be realized individually, but not the former. Also, the imperfective and prospective constructions involve a sentence-final low tone, which is marked as an additional stroke [`] on the sentence-final word and glossed as NR.[7] Finally, in example (11), the Gungbe IP-markers can occur simultaneously in the order negation-future-habitual-imperfective-prospective:[8]

(11) Kòfí   mà   ná   nɔ̀   tò   nà   hɔ̀n.
      Kofi   Neg   Fut   Hab   Imperf   Prosp   flee-NR

'Kofi will not be about to flee [e.g., when we get there]'.

In the following sections, I assume that the I-system consists of a series of discrete functional projections whose heads are associated with distinct (bundle of) abstract features, some of which are morphologically realized in Gbe by the markers (Tenny 1987; Pollock 1989; Avolonto 1992; Aboh 1996, 2004a; Cinque 1999). The negation marker *má* realizes feature [+negative]; the tense marker *ná* expresses feature [+future]; and the aspect markers *nɔ̀*, *tò*, and *nà* encode the features [+habitual], [+imperfective], and [+prospective], respectively. I further assume that the I-features that are negatively set have no proper morphological content in Gbe. They represent the default value.

In this regard, sentence (12a) suggests that Gungbe involves only one tense marker *ná* that expresses the feature [+future] on T°. Sentences (12b–d), in contrast, show that past and present tenses are not morphologically realized in Gungbe. In this respect, dynamic verbs that are not associated with any overt tense or aspect marker are assigned the perfective aspect by default, while state verbs receive a present state reading. Sentence (12b) involves a dynamic verb but includes no IP-marker. The verb is interpreted as perfective: the event has an end point in time. Sentence (12c) shows that adding the time adjunct *dìn* 'now' to (12b) sets the event in present time, even though the verb is assigned perfective aspect. Sentence (12d) instead involves a state verb *nyín* 'equative be' and the time adjunct *dìn*: the sentence is assigned a present state reading:

(12) a. Kòfí   ná   ɖù   lésì.
         Kofi   Fut   eat   rice

      'Kofi will eat rice.'

      b. Kòfí   ɖù   lésì.
         Kofi   eat-Perf   rice

      'Kofi ate (or has eaten) rice.'

      c. Kòfí   ɖù   lésì   **dìn.**
         Kofi   eat-Perf   rice   now

      'Kofi has just eaten rice.'

d. Àsíbá   wè   nyín   gán   mítɔ̀n   **dìn.**
Asiba   Foc   is   chief   1pl-Poss   now

'At this moment ASIBA is our chief.'

In accounting for these data, Aboh (1996, 2004a) proposes that past and present tense specifications are expressions of a [−future] T°, the interpretation of which derives from periphrastic time and aspect adverbs or from the default aspect that is assigned to sentences involving no overt tense/aspect marker (Avolonto 1992, Houngues 1997). Put differently, a null T° must be controlled by some time or aspect specification that is available in the sentence or in the discourse. The overt versus null T° asymmetry is further illustrated by the fact that the Gungbe time adjunct sɔ̀, which literally means '[±1 day] from the speech time', is interpreted as [yesterday]—[−1 day]—or [tomorrow] or [+1 day], depending on whether T° is null or overtly realized as ná. Sentence (13a) includes no overt tense or aspect maker. The verb is assigned the default perfective aspect, and the time adjunct sɔ̀ is interpreted as *yesterday*. In sentence (13b), however, T° is realized as ná, and the time adjunct sɔ̀ is necessarily interpreted as *tomorrow*:

(13)   a. Àsíbá   gɔ̀   sɔ̀   (ɖě   wá   yì).
Asiba   return-Perf   day   that   arrive   go

'Asiba returned yesterday.'

b. Àsíbá   ná   gɔ̀   sɔ̀   (ɖě   jà).
Asiba   Fut   return   day   that   come

'Asiba will return tomorrow.'

c. *Àsíbá   gɔ̀   sɔ̀   ɖě   jà.
Asiba   return-Perf   [+1 day]   that   come

'Asiba will return tomorrow.'

d. Àsíbá   ná   gɔ̀   sɔ̀   ɖě   wá   yì.
Asiba   Fut   return   [−1 day]   that   arrive   go

*'Asiba will return yesterday.'
'Asiba should/would have returned yesterday.'

The future reading cannot be forced on the time adjunct sɔ̀ by the relative clause ɖě jà 'that is coming' in (13c). The same holds of the ungrammatical sentence (13d), where the relative clause ɖě wá yì 'that has passed' cannot force past reading on sɔ̀ due to the intervening future marker. The sentences in (12) and (13) clearly show that the presence of ná triggers future interpretation, while its absence generally corresponds either to past or perfective reading for dynamic verbs and present reading for state verbs. This is an indication that T° is always active and encodes the features [±future]. Therefore, the contrast in (12) reduces to the semantic properties of the Gbe lexical verbs (Aboh 2004a).

As shown by sentence (11), repeated below as (14a), the Gungbe IP-markers can cooccur in the fixed order: negation$_{[má]}$ > future$_{[ná]}$ > habitual$_{[nɔ̀]}$ > imperfective$_{[tò]}$ > prospective$_{[nà]}$. In addition, sentence (14b) indicates that there is between the tense marker and the cluster of aspect markers, a position to host certain middle-field adverbs like sɔ́ 'again'. No such position exists though between negation and tense (14c):

(14) a. Kòfí   má   [ná   nɔ̀   tò   nà]   hɔ̃n.
         Kofi Neg   Fut Hab Imperf Prosp flee-NR

      'Kofi will not be habitually about to run away.' [e.g., anytime we see him].

      b. Kòfí   má   ná   sɔ́   nɔ̀   tò   gbádó mìmὲ   sὰ.
         Kofi Neg   Fut again Hab Imperf maize roasted sell-NR

      'Kofi will not be habitually selling roasted maize again.'

      c. *Àsíbá   má   sɔ́   ná   xɔ̀   kèké.
         Asiba   Neg   again Fut buy bicycle

If it is true that precedence relations reproduce asymmetric c-command relations (see Kayne 1994), then the sequence in (14a) suggests that TP manifests a position higher than the aspect markers (i.e., habitual nɔ̀, imperfective tò, and prospective nà) that head their own aspect projections—AspP1, AspP2, and AspP3, respectively. The tense and aspect articulation occurs between the negative marker má that heads NegP and the VP (15) (see Belletti 1990; Ouhalla 1990; Zanuttini 1991, 1997; Chomsky 1995; Haegeman 1995; Cinque 1999):

(15) ... NegP > TP > AspP1 > AspP2 > AspP3 > VP

Assuming this is the right characterization, a possible explanation for the ungrammatical (14c) could be that there is a structural relation between tense and negation so that TP licenses NegP. Put differently, NegP and TP are in local relationship, and nothing can intervene between them (Zanuttini 1991, 1997; Haegeman 1995). Assuming the subject is first merged VP-internally, this analysis is compatible with the idea that the subject moves to [spec AgrsP] via [spec TP] to be licensed for nominative case (Sportiche 1988). This would mean that AgrsP dominates NegP, which, in turn, dominates TP. This analysis extends to accusative case assignment. The object must move to [spec AgroP] where it gets case under spec-head agreement. I further assume, following the relevant literature, that

AgroP immediately dominates VP, as shown in (16) (Larson 1988; Johnson 1991; Chomsky 1993, 1995):

(16)   AgrsP > NegP > TP > AspP1 > AspP2 > AspP3 > AgroP > VP

2.3 Object Shift and Verb Movement in the [−Imperfective] VO Clauses

As briefly mentioned, VO and OV sequences manifest different structures. The former is monoclausal, while the latter is biclausal. To see this, let us first consider the following adjacency facts:

(17)   a. Àsíbá   ná   gbέ   nɔ̀   ɖù   lésì.
           Asiba   Fut   at least   Hab   eat   rice

       'Asiba will at least eat rice habitually.'

       b. ??Àsíbá   nɔ̀   gbέ   ɖù   lésì.
             Asiba   Hab   at least   eat   rice

       'Asiba habitually eats rice at least.'

       c. ??Àsíbá   nɔ̀   gbέ   tò   lésì   ɖ̀ù.
             Asiba   Hab   at least   Imperf   rice   eat-NR

       'Asiba is at least eating rice habitually.'

       d. *Àsíbá   tò   gbέ   lésì   ɖ̀ù.
            Asiba   Imperf   at least   rice   eat-NR

       e. *Àsíbá   tò   lésì   gbέ   ná   ɖ̀ù.
            Asiba   Imperf   rice   at least   Prosp   eat-NR

       f. *Àsíbá   tò   lésì   ná   gbέ   ɖ̀ù.
           Asiba   Imperf   rice   Prosp   at least   eat-NR

Sentence (17a)—also (14b)—shows that there is an intermediate position between the tense marker and the habitual aspect marker that can host a middle-field adverb. Under V-to-I movement, this is strong evidence that T° is not accessible for verb movement in Gungbe (Pollock 1989, Cinque 1999). Yet the marginal sentences (17b–c) indicate that the adverb cannot intervene between the habitual marker and the verb, nor can it surface between the habitual marker and the imperfective marker. A possible conclusion here is that example (17c) is quite degraded because the projections that host the habitual and imperfective markers are in local relationship, in terms of Rizzi (1990). AspP1, headed by the habitual marker *nɔ̀*, immediately dominates AspP2 headed by the imperfective marker *tò*.

In this regard, the sequence to the right of the imperfective marker *tò* (i.e., the object, the prospective marker, and the verb) seems to involve a more local relationship. Observe from the ungrammatical sentence (17d) that nothing can intervene between the imperfective marker and the preverbal object. In a similar vein, the ungrammatical sentence (17e) shows that no element can occur between the object and the prospective marker. The same holds of the ungrammatical (17f), which indicates that nothing can surface between the prospective marker and the verb. In terms of Aboh (1996, 2004a), the sentences (17d–f) are more degraded than those in (17b–c) because the sequence to the right of the imperfective marker *tò* is a constituent on its own. *Tò* selects for a nominalized small clause, whose left periphery encodes the nominal feature specific to the imperfective constructions and whose I-system hosts the prospective aspect marker. This selectional requirement also explains the interactions between imperfective and prospective aspects. Witness from example (10e)—repeated here—that prospective aspect depends on the feature [+imperfective]. Put differently, prospective aspect is available (or projects) if and only if the aspect head that encodes the feature [±imperfective] is positively set (i.e., realized by *tò* or else by some aspectual control verb). I return to this discussion in section 3. (for the discussion on other Gbe and Kwa languages, see also Fabb 1992; Kinyalolo 1992, 1997; Awóyalé 1997; Houngues 1997; Manfredi 1997).

(10)　e. Dáwè　lɔ́　*(tò)　kɛ̀ké　*(nà)　xɔ̀.
　　　　　man　Det　Imperf　bicycle　Prosp　buy-NR

　　　　'The man is about to buy a bicycle.'

Building on this, I conclude that the Gungbe VO sentences involve a less articulated structure than the OV clauses. For example, in (18) the VO (or nonimperfective) sentences never involve the prospective marker *nà* and the sentence-final low tone:

(18)　a. *Dáwè　lɔ́　nà　xɔ̀　kɛ̀kɛ̂.
　　　　　 man　Det　Prosp　buy　bicycle-NR

　　　 b. *Dáwè　lɔ́　xɔ̀　kɛ̀kɛ̂.
　　　　　 man　Det　buy-Perf　bicycle-NR

The data in (18) further support the hypothesis that, in nonimperfective clauses, Asp°2 is set as [−imperfective], an illegitimate licensor for the prospective marker and the sentence-final low tone. There are open questions as to whether the functional projections which encode the nominalizer feature and the prospective aspect are transparent or totally absent from the abstract makeup of those constructions. As a first attempt, I suggest that when AspP2 is marked as [−imperfective], it requires a reduced structure that lacks those projections—that is, NomP and AspP3 (see section 3). This means that a [−imperfective] Asp°2 manifests the structure in (19):

(19)   AgrsP > NegP > TP > AspP1 > AspP2 > AgroP > VP

Granting that verb movement holds in Gbe, I propose that the Gungbe non-imperfective sentences manifest the VO order because the aspect markers are not affixes. The verb cannot attach to them, and subsequent verb movement to their left is prohibited due to the Head Movement Constraint (HMC) (or some of its variant; see Chomsky 1995; Collins 1996). Unlike T°, which is not within the scope of verb movement in Gungbe, the aspect positions (Asp°1, 2) are accessible for verb movement only when they are negatively set. This leads us to conclude that the null counterparts of the aspect markers are affixes. A sequence of the type S-*ná*-VO in (20a) derives from object movement to [spec AgroP] for case reasons. The verb then moves to Asp°1 (via Agr° and Asp°2) to check the features [−imperfective] and [−habitual]. However, the future marker *ná* is first merged in T° to express the feature [+future], as partially represented in (20b):

(20)   a. Kòfí   ná   dín   gólù.
          Kofi   Fut   look   gold

      'Kofi will look for gold.'

      b.

Similarly, a sequence of the type S-nɔ́-VO (21a) involves object movement to [spec AgroP]. But verb movement stops in Asp°2 because the habitual aspect marker nɔ́ is first merged in Asp°1, where it encodes the feature [+habitual]. Accordingly, the verb only checks the uninterpretable feature [−imperfective]. T°, in contrast, is specified as [−future], the latter being interpreted as past or present. The derivation is represented in (21b):

(21) a. Kòfí   nɔ̀   dín   gólù.
         Kofi   Hab   look   gold

      'Kofi habitually looks for gold.'
      'Kofi habitually looked for gold.'

b.

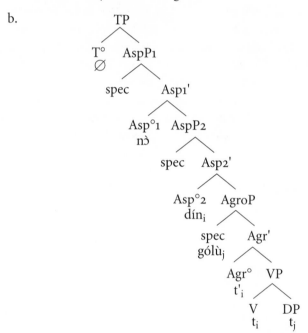

This analysis suggests that T° is not within the scope of verb movement in Gungbe. Recall from the preceding discussion that the verb always surfaces to the right of the tense marker. In addition, sentences (22a–b) indicate that the middle-field adverb must occur to the left of the verb, in a space between the tense and habitual markers:

(22) a. Kòfí   ná   gbέ   nɔ̀   cɔ́   xwé   lɔ́   ná   yé.
         Kofi Fut at least Hab   watch   house   Det Prep 3pl

      'Kofi will at least habitually watch the house for them.'

      b. *Kòfí cɔ́   gbέ   xwé   lɔ́   ná   yé.
          Kofi watch at least house Det Prep 3pl

Granting that Gungbe does not involve V-to-T° movement, I conclude that sentence (22b) is ungrammatical because the verb cannot move past the adverb. In terms of Pollock (1989), Laenzlinger (1998), and Cinque (1999), among others, adverbs are maximal projections that target the specifier of a functional projection within I. This would mean that there is a specifier position between T° and Asp° that hosts the middle-field adverbs (*gbé* 'at least', *só* 'again', *té* 'even'). Building on representation (21b), such a position could be [spec AspP1]. Under this approach, the verb cannot surface to the left of the adverb because verb movement only targets the lower portion of the I-system. Verb movement in Gungbe is short because it is limited to the aspect articulation. In this regard, the Gungbe [−imperfective] VO constructions manifest the feature combinations in (23) that derive from the interactions of verb movement and object shift as illustrated in (24):

(23)   a. [+future; +habitual; − imperfective] → ná nɔ̀ (Future-habitual)

   b. [+future; −habitual; − imperfective] → ná — (Future)

   c. [−future; +habitual; − imperfective] → — nɔ̀ (Habitual)

   d. [−future; −habitual; − imperfective] → — — (Perfective)

(24)

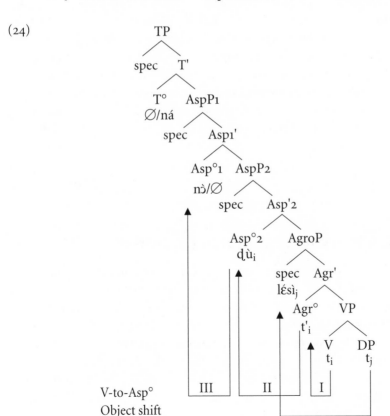

V-to-Asp°
Object shift

On the one hand, the object must move to [spec AgroP] to check its case feature. On the other hand, the verb must move to the aspect heads to check its aspect features. Because they are nonaffixes, however, the Gungbe aspect markers block verb movement. In other words, V-to-Asp movement arises only when an aspect head is not morphologically realized. Since Asp°2 is negatively set (i.e., not morphologically realized) in nonimperfective constructions, I propose that verb movement to Asp°2, via Agr° (i.e., steps 1 and 2) always holds in the Gungbe VO sentences. On the other hand step 3 applies when Asp°1 is negatively set as [−habitual] that is, is not morphologically realized.

When T° and Asp°1 are positively set, as in (23a), the verb only checks the uninterpretable feature [−imperfective], and the sentence is read as future and habitual. On the contrary, when only T° is positively set, the verb checks the features [−imperfective, −habitual], and the sentence is set into the future, as in (23b). Similarly, when T° is negatively set, but Asp°1 is positively set, the verb only checks the feature [−imperfective] and the sentence is read as habitual, as in (23c). Consequently, T° is controlled by some D-linked time specification that is available in the sentence or in the discourse. Finally, when no position is positively set within the tense or aspect articulation, the verb checks off the uninterpretable features [−imperfective; −habitual] by raising cyclically to Asp°1. Since T° is specified as [−future] as expression of the null morpheme $\emptyset$, I conclude that the combination of the features [−imperfective; −habitual]; [−future] is interpreted as perfective by default (23d). This suggests that the Gbe languages do not involve any perfective aspect marker. Instead, perfective aspect is derived by default as a consequence of cyclical verb movement to the relevant Asp°. I further argue that the fact that dynamic verbs are interpreted as perfective in such contexts, while state verbs are assigned some present state reading, does not indicate a difference in structure. Instead, such different interpretations derive from the semantic properties of the Gungbe lexical verbs (Aboh 1996, 2004a).

2.4 On the Theory of Verb Movement in Gbe

The theory of verb movement developed in this chapter suggests that the syntax of V-to-I movement (i.e., V-to-Asp movement in our terms) does not result from a strong inflection system that necessarily correlates with a rich inflectional ending on the verb (Pollock 1989; Rohrbacher 1994; Vikner 1995, 1997). On the contrary, verb movement in the Gbe languages indicates that the term "strong inflection" can also be taken to mean an articulated inflectional system offering room for distinct tense, aspect, and mood markers, each of which heads a functional projection within the clause structure. Assuming that the licensing conditions on the verb are universal, I further conclude that V-to-I movement arises in Gbe because the "bare" V-stem must be licensed for tense and aspect. This amounts to saying that the functional heads T° and Asp° dominate bundles of abstract strong features that must be checked before spell out. This requirement is met either by merge (i.e., a nonaffixal marker is inserted under the relevant head) or by verb movement (i.e., when no marker is available) (Chomsky 1995, 1999; Aboh 1996, 2004a).

Since the Gungbe bare V-stem necessarily surfaces to the right of the tense and aspect markers and certain middle-field adverbs (cf. (21–22)), one may object that there is no empirical evidence for the manifestation of V-to-Asp movement in the Gbe languages. This evidence comes from the Ewegbe-type languages where the aspectual markers are affixes and, therefore, the verb left-adjoins to the aspect marker. Compare the Gungbe sentence (25a) to the Gengbe and Ewegbe examples (25b) and (25c), respectively:

(25) a. Kòfí   nɔ̀   sà   àgásá. (Gungbe)
         Kofi   Hab   sell   crab

         'Kofi habitually sells crabs.'

      b. Kwésí   sà-nà   àglán. (Gengbe)
         Kwesi   sell-Hab   crab

         'Kwesi habitually sells crabs.'

      c. Kwésí   jrà-nà   àkɔɖú. (Ewegbe)
         Kwesi   sell-Hab   banana

         'Kwesi habitually sells bananas.'

Thus, while taking it that the Gbe languages have the same underlying structure, meaning that their aspect markers are generated in the same positions, I assume that the Gungbe-type languages have nonaffixal aspect markers while the Ewegbe-type languages manifest affixal aspect markers. The nonaffixal markers of the Gungbe type can survive on their own and therefore block verb movement, due to the HMC. This is illustrated by the order S-Hab-V-O in (25a). The affixal ones of the Ewegbe-type, in contrast, encliticize on to the verb due to subsequent verb movement, as suggested by the order S-V-Hab-O in sentences (25b–c). That nothing can intervene between the moved verb and the aspect marker to its right further supports this analysis (cf. (26a–b)):

(26) a. *Kwésí   sà   té   nà   àglán. (Gengbe)
          Kofi   sell   even   Hab   crab

      b. *Kwésí   jrà   tete   (n)à   àkɔɖú. (Ewegbe)
          Kofi   sell   at least   Hab   banana

In addition, the contrast in (27) suggests that the Gungbe-type and the Ewegbe-type languages also differ with respect to the target of verb movement. The tense and aspect markers freely combine in the Gungbe-type languages (27a), but not in the Ewegbe-type ones (27b–c):

(27) a. Kòfí ná nò sà àkwékwé. (Gungbe)
         Kofi Fut Hab sell banana

         'Kofi will habitually sell bananas.'

      b. *Kwésí jrà-(n)à-à àkòdú. (Ewegbe)
         Kofi sell-Hab-Fut banana

         'Kofi will habitually sell bananas.'

      c. *Kwésí á jrà-(n)à àkòdú. (Ewegbe)
         Kofi Fut sell-Hab banana

         'Kofi will habitually sell bananas.'

The ungrammatical sentence (27b) shows that, in Ewegbe, the verb cannot move cyclically to Asp°1 and to a morphologically realized T°. This indicates that the Ewegbe tense marker *á* does not qualify for an affix.[9] The ungrammatical sentence (27c) further suggests that there is no intermediate position to the right of an overtly realized T° where the Ewegbe verb could be licensed. I therefore conclude that in the Ewegbe-type languages verb movement targets a higher portion of the I-system, say T°, whereas in the Gungbe-type languages verb movement is limited to the lower portion—that is, the aspect articulation.

Interestingly enough, the Ewegbe tense and aspect markers cooccur in contexts where V-to-T° movement is prohibited. For example, the interpretation of features [+future] and [+habitual] that fails in (27), due to the absence of verb movement, can be conveyed when put to the progressive (28). Like its Gungbe counterpart in (10d), sentence (28) displays OV order and requires the sentence-final nominalizer:

(28) Mì á nò nú hia wó kátaa wò m̀.
      2pl Fut Past-Prog things Dem Num all do NR

      'You would be habitually doing all these things.'

Sentence (28) is compatible with the analysis I propose for the OV sequences in section 3. The conclusion reached there is that verb movement cannot target T° because the verb is stuck in a (nominalized) sequence that includes the VP. In the Gungbe-type languages, however, the verb targets Asp°, and the interpretation in (28) results from a free combination of the tense and aspect markers.

3 THE OV SEQUENCES IN GBE

OV sequences are found in various contexts in Gbe. For example, the following Gungbe sentences show that the object necessarily precedes the verb in imperfective constructions (29a), in prospective constructions (29b), in purpose constructions (29c), and in constructions involving some aspectual control verbs like *start* (29d) and *begin* (29e) (see Koopman 1984; Fabb 1992; Kinyalolo 1992, 1997; Manfredi 1997; Aboh 1996, 2003, 2004a).[10]

(29) a. Kòjó tò   [DP àmì lɔ] zân. (Imperfective)
          Kojo Imperf oil   Det use-NR

       'Kojo is using the oil.'

      b. Kòjó tò   [DP àmì lɔ] nà   zân. (Prospective)
          Kojo Imperf oil   Det Prosp use-NR

       'Kojo is about to use the oil.'

      c. Kòjó yì   [DP àmì lɔ] sà   gbé. (Purpose)
          Kojo go-Perf oil   Det sell Purpose

       'Kofi left in order to sell the oil.'

      d. Séná jè   [DP wémà lɔ] xíá   ná   Kòfí jí.
          Sena begin-Perf book   Det read for Kofi Part
                                                    ("Control V1")

       'Sena began to read the book to Kofi.'

      e. Séná gbé   [DP wémà lɔ] xíá   ná   Kòfí. ("Control V2")
          Sena refuse-Perf book   Det read for Kofi

       'Sena refused to read the book for Kofi.'

Though the sentences in (29) have distinct pragmatic and semantic implications, I propose that they all involve the same underlying structure. For instance, they only differ superficially with respect to (1) the type of aspect marker or control verb that they involve, and/or (2) the type of sentence-final element that they require. Yet, the fact that those sentences manifest verb reduplication further indicates their common underlying structure. Verb reduplication arises when there is no overt material to insert between the aspect marker (or the control verb)[11] and the lexical verb. The sentences in (30) show that object extraction triggers reduplication:

(30) a. Àmì ló wè Kòjó tò   zízân.
         oil   Det Foc Kojo Imperf   RED-use-NR

      'Kojo is using THE OIL.'

      b. Àmì ló wè Kòjó yì   sìsà   gbé.
         oil   Det Foc Kojo go-Perf RED-sell Purpose

      'Kofi left in order to sell THE OIL.'

      c. Wémà ló wè Sèná jè   xìxíá   ná   Kòfí jí.
         book   Det Foc Sena begin-Perf RED-read   for Kofi Part

      'Sena began to read THE BOOK to Kofi.'

      d. Wémà ló wè Séná gbé   xìxíá   ná   Kòfí.
         book   Det Foc Sena refuse-Perf RED-read   for Kofi

      'Sena refused to read THE BOOK for Kofi.'

Similarly, an intransitive verb must reduplicate (31) (I return to verb reduplication in section 3.1):

(31) a. Kòjó tò   sìsàn.
         Kojo Imperf   RED-show off-NR

      'Kojo is showing off.'

      b. Kòjó yì   sìsàn   gbé.
         Kojo go-Perf RED-show off Purpose

      'Kojo left out to show off.'

      c. Séná jè   sìsàn   jí.
         Sena begin-Perf RED-show off Part

      'Sena began to show off.'

      d. Séná gbé   sìsàn.
         Sena refuse-Perf RED-show off

      'Sena refused to show off.'

In the following sections, I show that the OV sequences involve a biclausal structure. The imperfective marker or the aspectual control verb selects for a small clause that has its own I- and C-systems. In the Gungbe prospective clauses, for instance, the sentence-final low tone manifests the left periphery of the small clause, while the prospective marker expresses the I-system. For expository purposes, this chapter focuses on the Gungbe imperfective and prospective clauses (29a–b) only. When relevant, I make specific reference to the OV sequences described in (29c–e) to show that the proposed analysis extends to those constructions as well. For detailed discussions, see Fabb (1992), Kinyalolo (1992), Awóyalé (1997), Manfredi (1997), and Aboh (1996, 2003, 2004a).

3.1 The I-System of the Embedded Small Clause

The discussion in previous sections shows that imperfective and prospective constructions involve object preposing and a sentence-final low tone represented by the additional stroke on the sentence-final syllable. Also, the prospective marker depends on the imperfective marker (32a–b).

(32) a. Kòfí   tò   lésì   ɖà   ná   Súrù.
          Kofi Imperf rice cook for Suru-NR

      'Kofi is cooking rice for Suru.'

      b. Kòfí *(tò)   lésì   nà   ɖà   ná   Súrù.
          Kofi Imperf rice Prosp cook for Suru-NR

      'Kofi is about to cook rice for Suru.'

The preverbal object position may host distinct elements such as headed relatives (cf. 33a), *P*Ps (cf. 33b), and certain reduplicated adverbs (cf. 33c). When the sentence includes an object and a reduplicated adverb, object shift is preferred to adverb preposing (33d–e). This indicates that the object and the reduplicated adverb target the same position in OV sequences:

(33) a. Àsíbá   tò   [[dáwè ɖĕ   mí   mɔ̀n]   lɔ́]   dîn.
          Asiba Imperf   man   that 1pl see-Perf Det   search-NR

      'Asiba is looking for the man that we saw'

      b. Àsíbá   tò   àxì   mè   yì̀.
          Asiba Imperf market *P*[IN] go-NR

      'Asiba is going to market.'

      c. Àsíbá   tò   dédé   zɔ̀n.
          Asiba Imperf slowly walk-NR

      'Asiba is walking slowly.'

      d. Kòfí   tò   lésì   ɖù   dédê
          Kofi Imperf rice eat slowly-NR

      'Kofi is eating rice slowly.'

      e. *Kòfí   tò   dédé   ɖù   lésì̀
          Kofi Imperf slowly eat rice-NR

However, clitic objects are right adjacent to the verb. In prospective constructions the verb-Cl cluster occurs to the right of the prospective marker (34a), but
in imperfective constructions, the clitic is attached to the reduplicated verb (34b):[12]

(34) a. Kòfí ná   nɔ̀   tò   ná   dù-ì̃.
         Kofi Fut Hab Imperf Prosp eat-3sg-NR

         'Kofi will be habitually about to eat it.'

      b. Kòfí ná   nɔ̀   tò   dùdù-ì̃.
         Kofi Fut Hab Imperf RED-eat-3sg-NR

         'Kofi will be habitually eating it.'

The sentences in (32–34) clearly indicate that movement to the preverbal object
position is not case-driven. For example, in (33c), the preverbal object position
may host certain reduplicated adverbs. In addition, sentences (34a–b) show that
object clitics are right adjacent to the verb (see also note 12). Granting that the
clitic checks its case features in Agr° (Friedemann and Siloni 1997), I conclude
that accusative case is assigned in some position to the right of the prospective
marker. In terms of structures (35a–b), the verb-Cl cluster derives from verb
movement to Agr° where it left-adjoins to the clitic. In a similar vein, case-
assigned DPs move to the left of the prospective marker via [spec AgroP] to check
their case features:

(35) a. . . . $[_{AspP3}$ $[_{Asp°3}$ nà $[_{AgroP}$ $[_{Agr°}$ V + Cl $[_{VP}$ t$_v$ t$_{cl}$]]]

      b. . . . $[_{AspP3}$ DP $[_{Asp°3}$ nà $[_{AgroP}$ t'$_{DP}$ $[_{Agr°}$ V $[_{VP}$ t$_v$ t$_{DP}$]]]

This analysis implies that object shift or adverb preposing to the left of the
prospective marker is determined by other principles of the grammar. In this
regard, it is interesting to notice that when there is no overt material to insert
between the imperfective marker and the verb, the latter reduplicates.[13] As briefly
discussed in previous paragraphs, this situation occurs when:

1. The verb is intransitive. Sentence (36b) is derived from (36a). Sentence
   (36c) shows that that reduplication is blocked by the intervening aspect
   marker *nà*:

   (36) a. Sìn   lɔ́   sà.
            water Det pour-Perf

            'The water poured.'

         b. Sìn   lɔ́   tò   sìsà̃.
            water Det Imperf RED-pour-NR

            'The water is pouring'

   c. Sìn   ló   tò   nà   (*sì)sà
      water Det Imperf Prosp (RED)-pour-NR
      'The water is about to pour'

2. Reduplication also arises in Gungbe when the object is a clitic or is being wh-extracted (37a–b):

(37) a. Àsíbá tò   díndín wὲ.
        Asiba Imperf RED-search 2sg-NR
        'Asiba is looking for you.'

      b. Ménù$_i$ wὲ Àsíbá tò   díndîn t$_i$?
        who Foc Asiba Imperf RED-search-NR
        'Who is Asiba looking for?'

      c. Kòjó$_i$ wὲ Àsíbá tò   díndîn t$_i$.
        Kojo Foc Asiba Imperf RED-search-NR
        'Asiba is looking for KOJO.'

The intervening prospective marker blocks reduplication:

(38) a. Àsíbá tò   ná   dín wὲ.
        Asiba Imperf Prosp search 2sg-NR
        'Asiba is about to look for you.'

      b. Ménù wὲ Àsíbá tò   ná   dîn?
        who Foc Asiba Imperf Prosp search-NR
        'Who is Asiba about to look for?'

The data in (36–38) suggest that reduplication is not related to the verb argument structure. It is a syntactic process that depends on the surface constituent string. Verb reduplication occurs when the verb is right adjacent to the imperfective marker *tò* (or to the control verb; see Fabb 1992; Aboh 2003, 2004a). Since verb reduplication is in complementary distribution with object shift and prospective aspect marking, I conclude that those three syntactic properties satisfy the same requirement. They license a subject position within the sequence to the right of the imperfective marker (or the control verb).

In other words, I now account for the OV sequences by assuming that the imperfective marker—a [+imperfective] Asp°2 (or else the control verb that realizes Asp°2)—selects a small clause whose INFL-system is headed by Asp°3, which encodes the features [±prospective]. When Asp°3 is marked as [+prospective], it hosts the prospective marker. But when it is specified [−prospective], it is available for verb movement. Furthermore, [spec AspP3] represents the subject position of the small clause. Under the EPP, this position must be filled in overt syntax. This requirement is met by object movement to [spec AspP3] via [spec AgroP]. This analysis correctly predicts that not just case-assigned elements surface in the preverbal position: the sentences in (32–33) show that [spec AspP3], in addition to hosting ordinary DPs, also hosts headed relatives, pPs, and reduplicated adverbs. In terms of Chomsky (1995, 1999) this would mean that the preposed category checks the strong EPP features of Asp°3.

When no relevant category is available (e.g., due to the verb argument structure, wh-extraction, or cliticization), the verb reduplicates as a reflex of null expletive licensing in [spec AspP3], which is an instance of spec-head relation (Aboh 1996, 2004a; Holmberg 2000). In prospective constructions, however, the prospective marker is first merged in Asp°3 to encode the feature [+prospective]. As a consequence, verb movement to Asp°3 is blocked, and no verb reduplication arises. In this framework, the reduplicated verb and the prospective aspect marker are mutually exclusive because they involve the same position Asp°3. This suggests that the prospective aspect marker and the reduplicated verb share some inflectional strength. The former is specified as [+prospective], while the latter is [+inflected].[14] Accordingly, they can license the null expletive in [spec AspP3] when needed—that is, when no relevant category can raise to [spec AspP3]. This clearly suggests that null expletive licensing is a last resort phenomenon. Similarly, verb reduplication is a last resort strategy contingent on a [−prospective] Asp°3: the verb reduplicates only when XP-raising to [spec AspP3] cannot apply and the prospective marker does not realize Asp°3. The case of intransitive verbs is very telling in this respect; they must reduplicate when put to the imperfective aspect because the verb moves to Asp°3 where it gets inflected through reduplication in order to license the null expletive in [spec AspP3]. But reduplication is blocked in prospective aspect constructions because the verb stays in Agr° and the null expletive is properly licensed by the prospective marker (36).[15]

3.2 The C-System of the Embedded Small Clause

From the preceding discussion, I propose that the Gungbe sentence-final low tone, typical of imperfective and prospective constructions, is a nominalizing morpheme that has been partially deleted (see note 7 and example (29)).

Following Aboh (1996, 2002, 2004a, b), I suggest that the sentence-final morphemes or tonemes better qualify as left peripheral markers (i.e., C-type elements). I further argue that they occur to the right edge because they trigger leftward movement of their complements to their specifier positions.[16] That certain left peripheral markers may occur to the right edge is not limited to OV sequences.

A case in point is the Fongbe sentence-final yes-no question marker (QM). Grant-ing that the QM is a manifestation of the left periphery, I propose that sentence (39b) is derived from the declarative (39a) by movement of the bracketed sequence to [spec InterP] headed by the QM:

(39) a. Kòfí   xɔ   wèmá   ɔ́. (Fongbe)
          Kofi   buy-Perf book   Det

          'Kofi bought the book.'

      b. [$_{InterP}$ [$_{IP}$ Kòfí xɔ   wèmá   ɔ́]$_i$ [$_{Inter°}$ à [$_{IP}$ t$_i$]]]?
          Kofi   buy-Perf book   Det   QM

          'Did Kofi buy the book?'

Similarly, sentence (40a) shows that the Gungbe topic and focus markers occur to the left periphery in a position between the complementizer ɖɔ̀ and the subject. In certain yes-no questions, however, those markers occur to the right edge. Sentence (40b) involves the Gungbe sentence-final yes-no QM represented by the additional low tone on the topic marker. Assuming that each marker heads its own projection within the C-system, I propose that the topic and focus markers occur sentence-finally, due to leftward movement of the clause to the specifier position of FocP. Subsequently, FocP is pied-piped to [spec TopP]; finally, TopP is pied-piped to InterP. In (40b) snowballing movement triggers the order Foc$_{[wɛ̀]}$–Top$_{[yà]}$, contrary to the sequence Top$_{[yà]}$–Foc$_{[wɛ̀]}$ in (40a) (cf. Aboh 2004a, b; Rizzi 1997):

(40) a. Ùn   ɖɔ̀   ɖɔ̀   Kòfí$_j$ yà   òzàn   lɔ́$_i$ **wɛ̀**   é$_j$ xɔ   t$_i$.
          1sg say-Perf that Kofi   Top bed   Det   Foc 3sg buy-Perf

          'I said that as for Kofi he bought THE BED.'

      b. Ùn   kànbíɔ́   ɖɔ̀   [Kòfí xɔ   òzàn   lɔ́] **wɛ̀**   **yà̀**.
          1sg ask-Perf that Kofi buy-Perf bed   Det Foc Top-QM

          'I asked whether KOFI BOUGHT THE BED [as expected].'

Building on this, I argue that the sentence-final morphemes typical of the Gbe OV sequences are expressions of a head, FORCE, that projects as the left periphery of the embedded small clause. FORCE may encode the features [+nom-inal], expressed by a low tone in the imperfective or prospective sentences (29a–b); [+purpose], realized by the morpheme gbé in the purpose constructions, as in (29c); and [+continuous], manifested by jí in sentences involving certain control verbs, as in (29d). The refuse clause (29e) shows that FORCE is not overtly realized in all the relevant cases, and this is a property of left peripheral elements in general. In this framework, FORCE occurs sentence-finally because it requires left-ward movement of the complement to its specifier position [spec FORCEP] in order to meet a spec-head configuration—that is, the expression of nominalization in (29a), of purpose in (29c), and so on.

Sentence (41a) results from object movement to [spec AspP3] via [spec AgroP]. The verb cyclically moves to Agr° and Asp°3, assuming the latter is not already filled by the prospective marker. The whole AspP3 then moves to [spec FORCEP], where it enters into a spec-head relationship with FORCE° which hosts the nominalizer morpheme—the low tone (41b):

(41) a. Àsíbá   tò   [lésì   ɖù̀].
          Asiba   Imperf   rice   eat-NR
          'Asiba is eating rice.'

b.

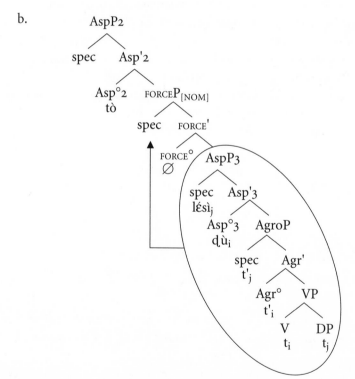

Examples (41c–d) are illustrations of a prospective construction:

(41) c. Àsíbá   tò   [lésì   nà   ɖù̀].
          Asiba   Imperf   rice   Prosp   eat-NR
          'Asiba is about to eat rice.'

d.

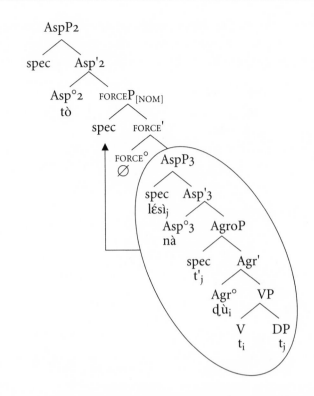

Representations (42b–c) illustrate imperfective and prospective constructions involving an intransitive verb. This analysis also extends to cases that involve cliticization or wh-extraction in Gungbe; see Aboh (2004a):

(42) a. Kòfí tò   hìhɔ̀n.
      Kofi Imperf RED-flee-NR

      'Kofi is fleeing.'

b.

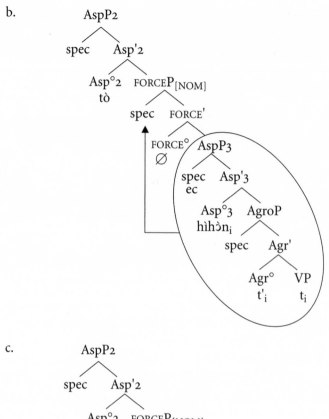

c.

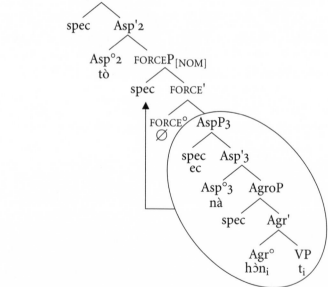

The analysis I propose here assumes that the OV sequences involve biclausal structures as opposed to nonimperfective VO constructions, which involve monoclausal structures. This is compatible with the fact that the sequence to the right of the imperfective marker (or the aspectual control verb) is a constituent. The sentences in (43) show that verb focusing in the imperfective and related clauses requires leftward movement of the sequence [object–prospective–*nà*–verb–indirect object] that occurs to the right of the aspect marker (43a). Under no circumstance can the verb be extracted from that sequence, as is normally the case in VO constructions where the focused verb is moved sentence-initially, leaving a copy in the IP-internal position (43b–c):

(43) a. [lésì ló nà zé xlán Rèmî] Àsíbá tè.
         rice Det Prosp take toward Remi-NR Asiba Imperf

       'Asiba is ABOUT TO SEND THE RICE TO REMI.'

    b. *Zé Àsíbá tò lésì ló zé xlán Rèmî.
       take Asiba Imperf rice Det take toward Remi-NR

    c. Zé$_i$ Àsíbá zé$_i$ lésì ló xlán Rèmí.
       take Asiba take-Perf rice Det toward Remi

       'Asiba SENT the rice to Remi'

If OV sequences are biclausal, we expect that in languages where this structure is being lost, there should be a concomitant loss of the left periphery of the small clause—the loss of the null expletive, together with the loss of verb reduplication. Interestingly enough, this is exactly the situation we find in Gengbe (Jondoh 1980; Houngues 1997; Manfredi 1997).

    Sentence (44) is the Gengbe counterpart of the Gungbe imperfective examples discussed above. The object surfaces between the imperfective marker *lè* (with low tone) and the verb. The sentence-final position is overtly realized by the nominalizer morpheme *ɔ̀*:

(44) Kwésí lè mɔ́lú ɖù ɔ̀.
     Kwesi Imperf rice eat NR

    'Kwesi is eating rice.'

However, Gengbe also manifests imperfective constructions that display VO order. In those cases, the imperfective marker is realized as *lě* (i.e., with a low-high tone) and no nominalizer morpheme occurs sentence-finally (45a–b):

(45) a. Kwésí lě ɖù mɔ́lú.
      Kwesi Imperf eat rice

     'Kwesi is eating rice.'

    b. *Kwésí lě mɔ́lú ɖù ɔ̀.
      Kwesi Imperf rice eat NR

I refer to sentences (44) and (45a) as imperfective I and II, respectively. The two variants are semantically equivalent, and the only difference is purely stylistic. With regard to syntax, imperfective I and II differ sharply. In addition to the loss of OV sequences and the sentence-final nominalizer, imperfective II (i.e., with the marker *lĕ*) never involves verb reduplication. Consider the contrast in (46a–b):

(46) a. Kwésí   lè   vǎvá   ɔ.
         Kwesi   Imperf   RED-come   NR

         'Kwesi is coming.'

      b. Kwésí   lĕ   vá.
         Kwesi   Imperf   come

         'Kwesi is coming.'

In the analysis presented here, the loss of OV sequences, together with the sentence-final nominalizer in the Gengbe imperfective II, indicates that the imperfective II aspect marker *lĕ* requires a less-articulated structure that does not qualify as a constituent (i.e., a small clause).

In the sentences in (47), verb focusing in imperfective I requires that the OV sequence or the reduplicated verb and the sentence-final nominalizer be moved to sentence-initial position (47a–b). This strategy is prohibited in imperfective II, where only the verb is extracted (47c). Recall from the Gungbe example (43c), repeated here as (48), that this strategy is normally restricted to nonimperfective VO constructions:

(47) a. [Vǎvá$_i$ ɔ   yé   mí   lè   t$_i$ lò!
         RED-come   NR   Foc   1pl   Imperf   Exclamation

         'We are just ARRIVING!'

      b. [Mɔ́lú   ɖù   ɔ]$_i$ yè   Kwésí   lè   t$_i$.
         rice   eat   NR   Foc   Kwesi   Imperf

         'Kwesi is EATING RICE.'

      c. Vá$_i$ yé   mí   lĕ   vá$_i$ lò!
         come   Foc   1pl   Imperf   come   Exclamation

         'We are just ARRIVING!'

(48) Zé$_i$ Àsíbá   zé$_i$ lésì   lɔ́   xlán   Rèmí.
      take   Asiba   take-Perf   rice   Det   toward   Remi

      'Asiba SENT the rice to Remi.'

The similarities between (47c) and (48) are strong indications that the Gengbe imperfective II are not biclausal structures. Like the nonimperfective constructions discussed above, they do not involve an embedded small clause endowed with its own left periphery FORCEP. In addition, that imperfective II never involves verb reduplication suggests that they cannot be analyzed on a par with ECM constructions (e.g., I believe [$_{IP}$ John to be a liar]), where the embedded IP (i.e., AspP3 in our terms) has its own subject position. This explains why imperfective II involves neither object movement to [spec AspP3] (i.e., OV sequences) nor the null expletive that is licensed by the reduplicated (or inflected) verb (i.e., VV sequences). In this regard, the loss of the null expletive is contingent on the loss of verb reduplication.

I further conclude that the VO sequences typical of imperfective II constructions result from subsequent verb movement to Asp°3 in a structure like that in (16). In this regard, Gengbe does not have a prospective marker of the Gungbe-type. Instead, Gengbe resorts to adverbial-like elements, as shown in sentences (49a–b), partially represented in (49c):

(49) a. Kwésí lě   ɖù mɔ́lú.
         Kwesi Imperf eat rice

         'Kwesi is eating rice.'

     b. Kwésí lě   já   ɖù   mɔ́lú.
         Kwesi Imperf about eat rice

         'Kwesi is about to eat rice.'

   c.

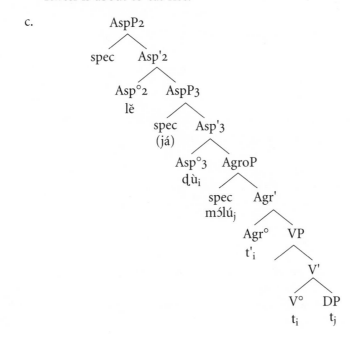

The previous paragraphs showed that a theory that assumes a biclausal structure accounts for the Gbe OV sequences in a straightforward manner. The question may then arise whether the embedded small clause occurs in contexts other
than that of OV sequences. In the following section, I argue that the structure I
propose for OV sequences naturally extends to OVV sequences where the object
precedes a reduplicated verb.

4 OVV Sequences as Small Clauses

The conclusion reached in section 3 is that object movement to [spec AspP3] and
verb reduplication are two expressions of the same principle. The object raises to
[spec AspP3] to check the strong EPP features of Asp°3. When no object is available (e.g., due to wh-extraction, cliticization, or the presence of an intransitive
verb), a null expletive that is licensed by the reduplicated verb is merged. Accordingly, object shift and verb reduplication are mutually exclusive. I further
argue that the embedded small clause involves a C-system—say, FORCEP—whose
specifier hosts the whole AspP3. In the imperfective and prospective constructions,
AspP3 movement to [spec FORCEP] is triggered by the nominalization process,
which necessitates that the nominalized complement be in a spec-head configuration with the nominalizer head. A consequence of this movement is that the
nominalizer head occurs sentence-finally. In terms of this analysis I don't expect
to find situations where the preposed object would precede the reduplicated verb.
Yet, sentence (50a) illustrates such OVV sequences. In sentences (50b–c), the OVV
sequences function as object and subject, respectively:

(50)　a. àzɔ́n　wìwà
　　　　work　RED-do

　　　'The act of doing a work'

　　　b. Kɔ̀jó　kplɔ́n　　[àzɔ́n　wìwà].
　　　　Kojo　learn-Perf　work　RED-do

　　　'Kojo learned the act of working.' [i.e., He learned working.]

　　　c. [àzɔ́n　wìwà]　má　jró　mì　　dîn.
　　　　work　RED-do　Neg　please　1sg-ACC　now

　　　'Working does not please me now.' [i.e., I don't want to work now.]

A priori, the OVV sequences in (50) are counterexamples for our analysis.
However, let's suppose that the preposed object is not in [spec AspP3], as one

could believe, but in the left periphery where it is in a spec-head relationship with the head FORCE°. In other words, the preposed object moves to [spec FORCEP], via [spec AgroP], leaving a trace in its base position. On the other hand, the verb moves to Asp°3, where it reduplicates to license the null expletive in [spec AspP3]. This situation is similar to that of OV sequences discussed above, where the object is focused or wh-extracted. In (51), in such contexts, the verb must reduplicate, too:

(51) a. Yé   kánbíɔ́   ɖɔ̀   ménù$_i$ wè   Àsíbá   tò   díndîn t$_i$.
          3pl ask-Perf that who   Foc Asiba   Imperf RED-search-NR

          'They asked who Asiba is looking for.'

      b. Yé   ɖɔ̀   ɖɔ̀   Kɔjó$_i$ wè   Àsíbá   tò   díndîn t$_i$.
          Kojo say-Perf that Kojo   Foc Asiba   Imperf RED-search-NR

          'They said that Asiba is looking for KOJO.'

We now reach the conclusion that the small clause may involve A-movement to [spec AspP3] or A-bar movement to [spec FORCEP]. In both cases, movement is last resort because "it is triggered by the satisfaction of the quasi-morphological requirements of heads" (Rizzi 1997: 282). The following Yoruba examples lend further support to this analysis. According to Awólayé (1997) Yoruba manifests both OVV and VVO sequences as in (52):

(52) a. kí-kọ-ìwé
          RED-write-letter

          'writing letter (or writing book)'

      b. ìwé$_i$-kí-kọ   t$_i$
          letter-RED-write

          'Letter-writing (or book-writing)'

      c. *ìwé$_i$-kọ   t$_i$
          letter write

In (52a) the object raises to [spec AgroP] to check its case features. In (52b), however, the object subsequently moves to [spec FORCEP] in order to encode the theme-activity articulation—hence, the different interpretations in (52a–b). In both cases, [spec AspP3] is occupied by a null expletive that is licensed by the reduplicated (or inflected) verb, as suggested by the ungrammatical example (52c). The Yoruba situation does not undermine our analysis of reduplication as last resort because each sequence in (52a–b) triggers a distinct interpretation.

Granting that reduplication is contingent on the presence of a null expletive in [spec AspP3], we also expect to find VV sequences only—for instance, when the verb is intransitive. In the analysis presented here, the reduplicated intransitive verb in (53) occurs in a small clause. The verb raises to Asp°3 where it licenses the null expletive in [spec AspP3]. The bracketed interpretation suggests that [spec FORCEP] might host a null operator, in terms of Rizzi (1996):

(53)   Kɔjó   kplɔ́n   [sísá].
       Kojo   learn-Perf   RED-crawl

'Kojo learned crawling.' [i.e., He learned how to crawl.].

Going back to the discussion of transitive verbs, I conclude that sentences (50a–c) are derived as in (54a–c):

(54)   a.

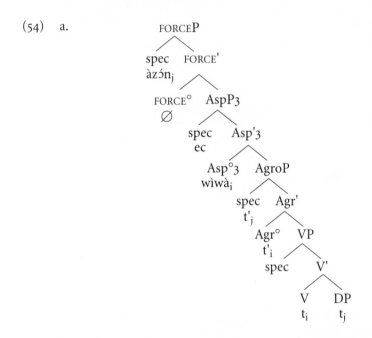

   b. [ᵢₚKɔjó [ᵥₚ kplɔ́n [_FORCEP àzɔ́n [_FORCE°[_AspP3 wìwà]]]]]

   c. [ᵢₚ[_FORCEP àzɔ́ṇ [_FORCE°[_AspP3 wìwà]]] [ᵢ° má jró mì dîn]]

In the representations of (54), unlike OV sequences, OVV constructions cannot involve subsequent AspP3 movement, since [spec FORCEP] is already occupied either by the preposed object or by a null operator. As a consequence, OVV sequences never involve the sentence-final morpheme typical of OV constructions, as shown by the following ungrammatical Fongbe and Gengbe examples:

(55)   a. nù   ɖúɖú (Fongbe)
          thing   RED-eat

b. *nù   ɖúɖú   wὲ
   thing   RED-eat   NR

   'the act of eating something'

(56) a. nú   ɖúɖǔ (Gengbe)
   thing   RED-eat

b. *nú   ɖúɖǔ   ɔ̀
   thing   RED-eat   NR

   'the act of eating something'

The incompatibility between OVV constructions and the sentence-final morpheme is actually expected since movement of the object to [spec FORCEP] is not meant to express nominalization, purpose, continuity, or any other feature typical of the OV sentences but to encode the theme-activity articulation of the embedded small clause. There are open questions why FORCE° is not realized by an overt marker in OVV constructions. For one: Why couldn't we have the sequence O-FORCE-VV? As a first attempt, I propose that this could result from subsequent movement of the reduplicated verb to FORCE° as an expression of I-to-C movement. To my knowledge, the Gbe languages discussed here provide no empirical evidence that favors or disfavors this hypothesis.

It is interesting to observe, however, that the analysis of OVV sequences in terms of small clause makes a number of predictions with respect to their distribution that are borne out across Kwa.

First, like other constituents (e.g., DPs, headed relatives), the OVV sequence can be focused:

(57) a. [Hàn   lɔ́]ᵢ   wὲ   yé   kplɔ́n   tᵢ.
   song   Det   Foc   3pl   learn-Perf

   'They learned THE SONG.'

b. [Hàn   ɖě   mí   jì]   lɔ́]ᵢ   wὲ   yé   kplɔ́n   tᵢ.
   song   that   1pl   sing-Perf   Det   Foc   3pl   learn-Perf

   'They learned THE SONG THAT WE SANG.'

c. [hàn [jìjì]]ᵢ   wὲ   yé   yì   kplɔ́n   tᵢ.
   song   RED-sing   Foc   3pl   go-Perf   learn

   'They left to learn SINGING.'

Second, it can surface in the preverbal position typical of OV constructions—for example, in imperfective or prospective constructions, in purpose constructions, and so on:

(58) a. Yé   wá   [hàn   lɔ́]   kplɔ́n   gbé.
        3pl   come-Perf   song   Det   learn   Purpose
      'They came on the purpose to learn the song.'

      b. Yé   wá   [hàn   ɖě   mí   jì]   lɔ́]   kplɔ́n   gbé.
        3pl   come   song   that   1pl   sing-Perf   Det   learn   Purpose
      'They came on the purpose to learn the song that we sang.'

      c. Yé   wá   [hàn   [jìjì]]   kplɔ́n   gbé.
        3pl   come   song   RED-sing   learn   Purpose
      'They came on the purpose to learn the act of singing.' (i.e., They
      came to learn singing.)

Third, the OVV sequence can occur as the complement of certain locational
postnominal morphemes (Ps):

(59) a. Yé   té   ɖó   [[xó   lɔ́]   gò].
        3pl   stick-Perf   Loc   word   Det   P[AT]
      'They kept on talking about the story.'

      b. Yé   té   ɖó   [[[xó   ɖě   mí   ɖɔ̀]   lɔ́]   gò].
        3pl   stick-Perf   Loc   word   that   1pl   say-Perf   Det   P[AT]
      'They stuck to the words that we said.'

      c. Yé   té   ɖó   [[xó   ɖìɖɔ̀]]   gò].
        3pl   stick-Perf   Loc   word   RED-say   P[AT]
      'They stuck to the act of talking.' (i.e., They kept on talking.)

In terms of the analysis I propose here, that OVV sequences surface in various
contexts is not surprising: they are constituents, and they must target the relevant
licensing positions in the clause. That they involve certain syntactic processes (e.g.,
object preposing and verb reduplication) results from their internal structure as
small clauses.

5 CONCLUSION

This chapter shows that the Gbe languages of the Kwa family manifest an artic-
ulate I-system in which each feature that is traditionally associated with INFL is
the property of a functional head that projects within I. In this respect, I show

that the VO versus OV asymmetries in those languages are better accounted for in terms of the interactions between object shift and verb movement on the one hand and clause structure differences on the other. For instance, VO sequences are monoclausal. In those contexts, the object moves to [spec AgroP] to be licensed for case. But the verb moves to Agr° and subsequently to some aspect head position, due to aspectual licensing. Conversely, OV sequences are biclausal. They involve an embedded small clause that has its own C- and I-systems. Here the object moves to [spec AgroP] to be licensed for case and subsequently to the subject position of the small clause to satisfy the EPP. The verb moves to Agr° and possibly to Asp°3 when the latter is not already filled by the prospective marker. But movement out of the small clause is prohibited. Accordingly, the verb surfaces to the right of the object occupying [spec AspP3]. This analysis extends to OVV contexts, in which the preposed object occurs in the left periphery of the small clause—that is, [spec FORCEP]. A major conclusion reached here is that verb reduplication in OV/OVV sequences does not result from nominalization process, as it is often mentioned in the relevant literature. Instead, it is a last resort phenomenon contingent on the presence of a null expletive in [spec AspP3]. The verb reduplicates (or gets inflected) in order to license the null expletive.

NOTES

Thanks to James Essegbey, Felix Ameka, and Cinque Guglielmo for commenting on various aspects of this chapter.

1. Gbe is a subgroup of Kwa (see Capo 1988). This chapter discusses data from Gungbe, spoken in Porto-Novo in Benin, but reference is made to Fongbe, Gengbe, Ewegbe, and other Kwa languages when necessary.

2. Such postnominal morphemes generally express location but have the semantics of a genitive.

3. The terms "imperfective" and "nonimperfective" are used to distinguish sentences that involve the imperfective marker or some aspect verb occupying the same position and sentences whereby this position is not overtly realized.

4. See Koopman (1984), Lefebvre (1992), Avolonto (1992), Kinyalolo (1992, 1993), Tossa (1994), and others for alternative analyses in terms of SOV or mixed structures.

5. In the Government and Binding framework, the Extended Projection Principle (EPP) is understood as the requirement that sentences must have subjects. Under minimalist assumptions, however, Chomsky (1995, 1999) defines the EPP as the necessity of a head to have a specifier. Whether the EPP is interpreted in its traditional sense or along the lines of Chomsky makes no difference for the proposed analysis.

6. See Aboh (2004a), where is it shown that the Gbe languages also involve other markers of the C-type that typically occur to the left of negation.

7. In certain Gbe languages, the nominalizer is a morpheme. Consider the following Fongbe example:

(i) Àsíbá ɖò   mɔ̃lìnkú ɖù wὲ.
     Asiba Imperf rice   eat NR

'Asiba is eating rice.'

8. This does not hold for all Gbe languages. In Gengbe and Ewegbe, for instance, tense and aspect markers are in complementary distribution. See section 2.4 and Aboh (2004a) for the discussion.

9. But see Essegbey (1999) where it is proposed that the Ewegbe morpheme á encodes mood specifications and not tense.

10. I call the reader's attention to the fact that the OV sequences I discuss in this essay are to be distinguished from serial verb constructions (SVC) where the object surfaces between two lexical verbs, as illustrated. But see Aboh (2003) for extending this analysis to series. See also Baker (1989), da Cruz (1993), Collins (1997), and Stewart (1998) and references cited therein for different analyses on SVCs.

(i) Àsíbá zé   lέsì ɖù.
     Asiba take-Perf rice eat

'Asiba took the rice and ate it.'

11. Aboh (2004a) also shows that the control verb and the imperfective marker compete for the same position.

12. Certain Gungbe speakers allow for the DP-object to follow the reduplicated verb (see Aboh 2004a):

(i) Kòfí tò   ɖùɖù   lέsì.
     Kofi Imperf RED-eat rice-NR

'Kofi is eating rice.'

Ewegbe, on the contrary, uses a weak or strong pronoun and maintains the SOV order in such contexts.

13. See Aboh (2004a) and Pulleyblank (1988) and references cited therein for the discussion on the morphophonological properties of verb reduplication in Gungbe.

14. This is also supported by the fact that the reduplicated verb can be used as type of past participle (and interpreted as adjective) in the following examples:

(i) àvɔ̀   xúxú
     cloth RED-dry

'a dried cloth'

(ii) sìn   fífá
     water RED-cool

'fresh water'

15. See Ndayiragije (2000) for extending this analysis to the Fongbe OV structures.

16. This is compatible with the idea that the Gbe determiners and postnominal morphemes are left peripheral markers of the nominal sequence, as suggested by struc-

ture (6a). See Aboh (2002, 2004a) and references cited therein for the discussion of the Gbe C-system.

REFERENCES

Aboh, O. E. (1996) "A propos de la syntaxe du gungbe." *Rivista di Grammatica Generativa* 21: 3–56.

Aboh, O. E. (2002) "La morphosyntaxe de la périphérie gauche nominale." *Recherches Linguistiques de Vincennes* 31: 9–26.

Aboh, O. E. (2003) "Les constructions à objet préposé et les série verbales dans les langues Kwa," in P. Sauzet and A. Zribi-Hertz (eds.) *Typologie des langues d'Afrique et Universaux de la grammaire*, vol. 2. L'Harmattan, Paris, 15–40.

Aboh, O. E. (2004a) *The Morphosyntax of Complement-Head Sequences: Clause Structure and Word Order Patterns in Kwa*. Oxford University Press, New York.

Aboh, O. E. (2004b) "Left or Right? A View from the Kwa Periphery," in D. Adger, C. de Cat, and G. Tsoulas (eds.) *Peripheries*. Kluwer, Dordrecht, 165–189.

Agbedor, P. (1996) "The Syntax of Ewe Personal Pronouns." *Linguistique Africaine* 16: 19–53.

Avolonto, A. (1992) "Les particules modales en fongbe et la nature de INFL dans les phrases injonctives." *MIT Working Papers in Linguistics* 17: 1–25

Awóyalé, Y. (1997) "Object Positions in Yoruba," in R.-M. Déchaine and V. Manfredi (eds.) *Object Position in Benue-Kwa*. Holland Institute of Generative Linguistics, Holland Academic Graphics, The Hague, 7–30.

Baker, C. M. (1989) "Object Sharing and Projection in Serial Verb Constructions." *Linguistic Inquiry* 20: 513–553.

Belletti, A. (1990) *Generalized Verb Movement*. Rosenberg and Sellier, Turin.

Capo, H. B. C. (1988) *Renaissance du Gbe: Réflexions critiques et constructives sur l'Eve, le Fon, le Gen, l'Aja, le Gun, etc.* Helmut Buske, Hamburg.

Chomsky, N. (1993) "A Minimalist Program for Linguistic Theory," in K. Hale and S. J. Keyser (eds.) *The View from Building 20: Essays in Linguistics in Honor of Sylvain.* MIT Press, Cambridge, Mass, 1–52.

Chomsky, N. (1995) *The Minimalist Program*. MIT Press, Cambridge, Mass.

Chomsky, N. (1999) "Derivation by Phase." MIT *Occasional Papers in Linguistics* 18.

Cinque, G. (1999) *Adverbs and Functional Heads: A Cross-Linguistic Perspective*. Oxford University Press, New York.

Clements, G. N. (1972) "The Verbal Syntax of Ewe." Ph.D. diss., University of London.

Clements, G. N. (1975) "Analogical Reanalysis in Syntax: The Case of Ewe Tree-Grafting." *Linguistic Inquiry* 6: 3–51.

Collins, C. (1996) *Local Economy*. MIT Press, Cambridge, Mass.

Collins, C. (1997) "Argument Sharing in Serial Verb Constructions." *Linguistic Inquiry* 28: 461–497.

da Cruz, M. (1993) "Les constructions sérielles du fongbe: approches sémantique et syntaxique." Ph.D. diss., Université du Québec à Montréal.

Essegbey, J. (1999) *Inherent Complement Verbs Revisited: Towards an Understanding of*

Argument Structure in Ewe. M.P.I. Series in Psycholinguistics 10. Ponsen and Looijen bv, Wageningen.

Fabb, N. (1992) "Reduplication and Object Movement in Ewe and Fon." *Journal of African Languages and Linguistics* 13: 1–39.

Friedemann, M-A., and T. Siloni (1997) 'Agr$_{object}$ Is Not Agr$_{participle}$'. *Linguistic Review* 14: 69–96.

Haegeman, L. (1995) *The Syntax of Negation*. Studies in Linguistics. Cambridge University Press, Cambridge.

Holmberg, A. (2000) "Scandinavian Stylistic Fronting: How Any Category Can Become an Expletive." *Linguistic Inquiry* 31: 445–483.

Houngues, M. K. D. (1997) "Topics in the Syntax of Mina." Ph.D. diss., Boston University Graduate School of Arts and Sciences.

Johnson, K. (1991) "Object Positions." *Natural Language and Linguistic Theory* 9: 577–635.

Jondoh, E. E. (1980) "Some Aspects of the Predicate Phrase in Gengbe." UMI Dissertation Series.

Kayne, R. S. (1994) *The Antisymmetry of Syntax*. MIT Press, Cambridge, Mass.

Kinyalolo, K. K. W. (1992) "A Note on Word Order in the Progressive and Prospective in Fon." *Journal of West African Languages* 22: 35–51.

Kinyalolo, K. K. W. (1993) "On Some Syntactic Properties of ɖɔ̀ in Fon." *Lingua* 91: 201–233.

Kinyalolo, K. K. W. (1995) "Licensing in DP in Fɔ̀n." *Linguistique Africaine* 14: 61–92.

Kinyalolo, K. K. W. (1997) "The Verbal Gerund in Fon," in R.-M. Déchaine and V. Manfredi (eds.) *Object Position in Benue-Kwa*. Holland Institute of Generative Linguistics, Holland Academic Graphics, The Hague, 67–86.

Koopman, H. (1984) *The Syntax of Verbs: From Verb Movement Rules in the Kru Languages to Universal Grammar*. Foris, Dordrecht.

Laenzlinger C. (1998) *Comparative Studies in Word Order Variation: Adverbs, Pronouns, and Clause Structure in Romance and Germanic*. John Benjamins, Amsterdam.

Larson, K. R. (1988) "On the Double Object Construction." *Linguistic Inquiry* 19: 335–391.

Lefebvre, C. (1992) "Agr in Languages without Person and Number Agreement: The Case of the Clausal Determiner in Haitian and Fon." *Canadian Journal of Linguistics* 37: 137–156.

Manfredi, V. (1997) "Aspectual Licensing and Object Shift," in R.-M. Déchaine and V. Manfredi (eds.,) *Object Position in Benue-Kwa*. Holland Institute of Generative Linguistics, Holland Academic Graphics, The Hague, 87–122.

Ndayiragije, J. (2000) "Strengthening PF." *Linguistic Inquiry* 31: 485–512.

Ouhalla, J. (1990) "Sentential Negation, Relativized Minimality and the Aspectual Status of Auxiliaries" *Linguistic Review* 7: 183–231.

Pollock, J.-Y. (1989) "Verb Movement, Universal Grammar, and the Structure of IP." *Linguistic Inquiry* 20: 356–424.

Pulleyblank, D. (1988) "Vocalic Underspecification in Yoruba." *Linguistic Inquiry* 19: 233–270.

Rizzi, L. (1990) *Relativized Minimality*. MIT Press, Cambridge, Mass.

Rizzi, L. (1996) "Residual Verb Second and the wh-criterion," in A. Belletti and L. Rizzi (eds.) *Parameters and Functional Heads: Essays in Comparative Syntax*. Oxford University Press, New York, 63–90.

Rizzi, L. (1997) "The Fine Structure of the Left Periphery," in L. Haegeman (ed.) *Elements of Grammar*. Kluwer, Dordrecht, 281–337.

Rohrbacher, W. B. (1994) "The Germanic Languages and the Full Paradigm: A Theory of V to I Raising." Ph.D. diss., University of Massachusetts, Amherst.

Sportiche, D. (1988) "A Theory of Floating Quantifiers and Its Corollaries for Constituent Structure." *Linguistic Inquiry* 19: 425–449.

Stewart, O. T. (1998) "The Serial Verb Construction Parameter." Ph.D. diss., McGill University, Montreal.

Tenny, C. L. (1987) "Grammaticalizing Aspect and Affectedness." Ph.D. diss., MIT, Cambridge, Mass.

Tossa Comlan, Z. (1994) "Adjonctions et séries verbales dans les langues Gbe." Ph.D. diss., University of Ottawa.

Vikner, S. (1995) *Verb Movement and Expletive Subjects in the Germanic Languages*. Oxford University Press, New York.

Vikner, S. (1997) "V-to-I Movement and Inflection for Person in All Tenses," in L. Haegeman (ed.) *The New Comparative Syntax*. Longman Linguistics Library. Longman, London, 189–213.

Zanuttini, R. (1991) "Syntactic Properties of Sentential Negation: A Comparative Study of Romance Languages." Ph.D. diss., University of Pennsylvania.

Zanuttini, R. (1997) *Negation and Clausal Structure: A Comparative Study of Romance Languages*. Oxford University Press, New York.

CHAPTER 5

FINITENESS AND NEGATION IN DRAVIDIAN

R. AMRITAVALLI AND

K. A. JAYASEELAN

1 INTRODUCTION

THE identification of finiteness with Tense is a very widely accepted tenet of generative theory. Thus we have definitive statements like the following, from Ur Shlonsky analyzing Semitic languages (which have problematic "verbless" finite copular clauses, just like Dravidian):

> My starting point is that every clause, by definition contains a TP. I will argue ... that the essential difference between a full clause and a small clause is that only the former contains a TP. (Shlonsky 1997: 3)
>
> Independent or full clauses must by definition contain a TP projection.... Clauses lacking a TP are, to adapt a familiar terminology, "small clauses" and cannot occur, for example, as root clauses. (55)

This is also the position of most European traditional grammars. When we come to the Dravidian linguistic tradition, however, we find that the question of what constitutes finiteness in a Dravidian clause has been a matter of long-standing debate. This tradition has noticed both that there are finite verb forms with no tense morpheme and that there are nonfinite verb forms that apparently incorporate a tense morpheme. There are also "verbless" finite copular clauses, where the nominal predicate exhibits agreement. Agreement appears to be a more dependable diagnostic of finiteness than tense in Dravidian. The suggestion in this tradition has been that, insofar as a "morphological" definition of finiteness is possible at all, it is agreement, or a combination of tense and agreement, that constitutes finiteness. Thus Sridhar (1990: xxiii) writes: "Finiteness is a function of agreement, not tense." (See also note 13.) Again, Steever (1988: 121, n.3) notes that the "personal verb forms" (i.e., verbs inflected for agreement) in the Dravidian languages are finite, whether or not they encode tense as a morpheme.[1]

In this chapter, we attempt to show that Dravidian clause structure does not project a Tense Phrase. Hence, 'Finiteness-is-Tense' cannot be universal. We suggest that finiteness in Dravidian is constituted by the presence of a Mood Phrase. If agreement morphology lodges in the Mood Phrase (say, as a reflex of Indicative Mood), this would explain the observed correlation of agreement with finiteness.[2]

Our analysis is a partial vindication of the Dravidian linguistic tradition, which has stopped short of a definitive identification of finiteness with agreement, for perhaps the following reasons, among others. First, alone among the four major contemporary Dravidian languages, Malayalam lacks agreement morphology. A simple identification of finiteness with agreement morphology would thus create a typological divide between Malayalam on the one hand and Tamil, Telugu, and Kannada on the other. But if agreement morphology is a reflex of Indicative Mood, we can posit a null morphological reflex of Indicative Mood in Malayalam and thus accommodate this language in our picture.

Second, agreement morphology appears on predicate nominals; and in Kannada, Tamil, and Telugu, but not Malayalam, the predicate of the copular clause consists merely of this nominal marked for agreement, with no overt verb. This is a problem for the position that "morphological finiteness" is a property of the verb (cf. Steever 1988: 2 and 121, n.3). Under the agreement-as-mood analysis, however, we can straightforwardly integrate agreement in verbless copular clauses, traditionally called "nominal" clauses, into the general proposal for clause structure in these languages.

Our proposals are thus an exercise in comparative syntax at two levels: one considering the Dravidian languages with respect to other languages—for example, European languages; the other considering these languages, in particular Kannada and Malayalam, with respect to each other. (At a finer level, the analysis of the Kannada infinitive presented here draws crucially on evidence that has been obliterated from the written language, but is preserved in two standard spoken dialects.)

We begin our argument from an examination of how negative sentences are formed in Kannada and Malayalam. In section 2, we develop an analysis of negation in Kannada that assigns finiteness to the Neg element *illa*. The tense interpretation of negative clauses is shown to arise from the aspectual properties of particular nonfinite clause types (section 2.4). The structure of negative clauses, in which *illa* is licensed by a finiteness head in MoodP, is then generalized to other (affirmative or modal) clauses in the language (section 2.6).

In section 3, the superficially dissimilar facts of Malayalam negation are assimilated into the proposed analysis; the reanalysis is shown to yield a more complete account of the Malayalam facts, and (in the case of serial verbs and gerunds, discussed in section 3.2) to correct a misanalysis of aspect as tense. Section 4 establishes that there are two elements *illa* (a verb of negative existence, and a Neg) in Kannada as well as Malayalam; the striking superficial differences in the negative clauses of these two languages are suggested to follow from the absence of overt agreement in Malayalam.

2 NEGATION IN KANNADA

2.1 Kannada and Malayalam: Some Differences

Superficially, the Kannada clause exemplifies a familiar pattern in the languages of the world: the finite verb is inflected for tense and agreement (in that order):

(1)   (Kannada)
    a. Avanu   bar-utt-aane.
       he   come-present-3msg
       'He comes.'

    b. Avanu   ban-d-anu.
       he   come-past-3msg
       'He came.'

The Kannada pattern is found in the other major Dravidian languages, with the exception of Malayalam. In Malayalam, the verb is inflected only for tense:

(2)   (Malayalam)
    a. Avan   var-unnu.
       he   come-present
       'He comes.'

    b. Avan   van-nu.
       he   come-past

    'He came.'

The Malayalam verb had agreement in an earlier historical period but has lost it completely in the modern language.[3]

The differences between Kannada and Malayalam become more prominent when we look at negative sentences. Consider how the sentences of (1) are negated:

(3) (Kannada)
     a. Avanu   bar-uvud(u)   illa.
        he   come-gerund   neg

        'He does not come.'

     b. Avanu   bar-al(u)   illa.
        he   come-inf.   neg

        'He did not come.'

We have glossed *illa* as "neg." Tense and agreement are not present; we are faced with a matrix gerund in (3a), and with a matrix infinitive in (3b), raising the question of what marks the clauses in (3) as finite.

At first glance, negation in Malayalam—unlike in Kannada—seems to be a straightforward affair. The sentences of (2) are negated as shown in (4):

(4) (Malayalam)
     a. Avan   var-unn(u)   illa.
        he   come-present neg

        'He does not come.'

     b. Avan   van-n(u)   illa.
        he   come-past   neg

        'He did not come.'

It would seem that we negate an affirmative sentence in Malayalam by adding a negative marker *illa* to it, very much like in English; the clauses in (4) appear to contain Tense and Neg, in that order.

We shall, however, argue that the finite element in both the Kannada examples (3) and the Malayalam examples (4), is the Neg element *illa*. We will show, therefore, that what we have glossed as "present" or "past" in (4) cannot be tense (or else the clause would be doubly marked for finiteness). This element in (4), we shall say, is aspect; and aspect is also the element present in the Kannada matrix gerund and matrix infinitive in (3), which gives these examples the "tense interpretations" indicated in translation. Thus the Malayalam verb phrases in (4) and the Kannada verb phrases in (3), superficial differences notwithstanding, are structurally parallel.

We shall first make the argument about *illa*, finiteness, and tense-marking for Kannada, and then show how extending the analysis to Malayalam solves a number of problems in Malayalam syntax.

2.2 The Gerundive and Infinitive Complement of Negation in Kannada

Consider again the Kannada negative sentences (3) (repeated here):

(3)   a. Avanu   bar-uvud(u)   illa.
         he   come-gerund   neg

   'He does not come.'

      b. Avanu   bar-al(u)   illa.
         he   come-inf.   neg

   'He did not come.'

In (3), we glossed *illa* as "neg"; but since the main verbs are in the gerundive and infinitive forms, the question arises what finiteness element the clauses carry. In view of this difficulty, it has been customary in traditional analyses to treat *illa* as a "finite negative verb." We shall retain the insight that *illa* is finite; we shall however show, in section 4, that a more complex analysis is necessary to treat only some instances of *illa* as a negative existential verb. Hence, the traditional insight needs a different execution.

In support of the analysis of *illa* as finite, it should be pointed out that negation by *illa* is not licensed in genuinely nonfinite clauses—that is in nonroot gerundive and infinitive complement clauses. This is shown by (5)–(6): the gerundive or infinitive of the (a) sentence cannot be negated by adding *illa*; see the (b) sentence:

(5)   a. [Avanu   ivattu   bar-uvudu]   aas'carya.
         he   today   come-gerund   surprise

   'His coming today is a surprise.'

      b. *[Avanu   ivattu   bar-uvud(u)   illa]   aas'carya.
         he   today   come-gerund   neg   surprise

   'His not coming today is a surprise.'

(6)   a. Avanu [PRO   iij-alu]   nooDidanu.
          he   swim-inf.   saw (i.e., tried)

      'He tried to swim.'

      b. *Avanu [PRO   iij-al(u)   illa]   nooDidanu.
          he   swim-inf.   neg   saw (i.e., tried)

      'He tried not to swim.'

If, as this shows, *illa* can occur only in finite clauses, it seems reasonable to say
that it incorporates the notion of finiteness.

Before we proceed, let us make sure that *bar-uvudu* is indeed a gerund and
that *bar-alu* is indeed an infinitive. First, *bar-uvudu* can be case-marked and the
case-marker in each case is that of the grammatical relation of the gerundive
phrase to the rest of the sentence:

(7)   a. [[Avanu   ivattu   bar-uvud-]   annu]   yaarig-uu   tiLisa   beeDa.
          he   today   come-gerund   acc.   anyone   inform   do not

      'Do not inform anyone (about) his coming today.'

      b. [[Avanu   ivattu   bar-uvud-]   akke]   yella   yeerpaaDugaLuu
          he   today   come-gerund   dat.   all   preparations
          aagive.
          have happened

      'All preparations have taken place for his coming today.'

However, while the phrase behaves like an NP with respect to the sentence,
it has internally a VP. This is shown by two facts: first, the subject of gerunds in
Kannada, but not of derived nominals or underived nouns, takes the nominative
case.[4] Consider thus the verb *bare-* 'write,' which has related forms in the gerund
bare(y)-uvudu 'writing,' and the derived nominals *bara-ha, bara-ha-gaLu* 'writing,
writings.' The latter forms (observe the possibility of a plural variant) take a
genitive subject, exactly as other, underived nouns such as 'letter, picture' do (8a);
whereas the *-uvudu* gerund form of *bare-* takes a nominative subject (8b) (and
this form cannot be pluralized):

(8)   a. avan-a   bara-ha / bara-ha-gaLu / patra (gaLu) / chitra (gaLu)
          he   gen.   writing   writings   letter (pl.)   picture (pl.)

      'his writing/writings/letter(s)/picture(s)'

      b. avan-u   bare-y-uvudu (*gaLu)
          he   nom.   write-gerund

      'his writing (*writings)'

Second, the *-uvudu* form takes the entire range of complements of the corresponding verb. Thus, *bar-uvudu* 'come-gerund' may be modified by time and place adverbials, and *bare-y-uvudu* 'write-gerund' can take direct and indirect objects; but underived nouns like *pravees'a* 'entry' cannot be adverbially modified, and derived nominals like *baraha* '(the) writing' cannot take an object:

(9) a. i. avan-u   ivattu   beLagge   mane-ge   bar-uvudu
             he   nom.   today   in the morning   home-dat.   come-gerund

             'his coming home today in the morning'

        ii. avan-a   (*ivattu   beLagge   mane-ge)   pravees'a
             he   gen.   today   in the morning   home-dat.   entry

             'his entry (*home today in the morning)'

     b. i. avan-u   nanage   patra   bare-y-uvudu
             he   nom.   I dat.   letter   write-gerund

             'his writing letters to me'

        ii. avan-a   (*nanage   patra)   bara-ha
             he   gen.   I dat.   letter   write-gerund

             'his writing (*letters to me)'

As regards the form *bar-alu*, the *-alu* form of the verb occurs typically in purpose adjuncts, and in control complements to verbs like 'try' (cf. (6a)). We illustrate this briefly, returning to an extended discussion of the *-alu* form in subsection 4, on case-marked and bare infinitives:

(10) a. Avaru [PRO   neNTar-anna   kare-y-alu]   horaTiddaare.
             they   relatives-acc.   call-inf.   have set out.

             'They have set out to invite relatives.'

      b. Ninage [PRO   makkaL-anna   hoDe-y-alu]   yaaru   heeLidaru?
             you dat.   children-acc.   beat-inf.   who   said

             'Who told you to beat the children?'

Returning to negation in Kannada, if it is granted that we have rightly analyzed *bar-uvudu* and *bar-alu* as nonfinite forms, we have immediately two problems with the negative sentences in (3). The first problem is that the negative sentences look radically different from the corresponding affirmative sentences (1). In an English-type language, negation is simply a matter of generating an optional Neg Phrase in the functional architecture of the clause. But in Kannada, Tense and Agreement seem to have been "knocked off," syntactically speaking, by the introduction of negation.

But Tense nevertheless surfaces in the meaning. The second problem (then) is how Tense is "read off" from two nonfinite forms.

By way of an answer to the first question, let us say (continuing to assume a Tense projection in Kannada) that tense is "absorbed" by the negative element *illa*. We can execute this proposal as follows: assuming very "surfacy" structures like (11a, b) for affirmative and negative sentences,

(11)   a. V]$_{VP}$ ±past]$_{TP}$ PNG]$_{AgrP}$

      b. V]$_{VP}$ illa]$_{NegP}$ ±past]$_{TP}$ PNG]$_{AgrP}$

we can say that *illa* adjoins to Tense (and possibly also to Agreement). Tense (or agreement) does not appear on the surface in the output of (11b) because *illa* is morphologically defective. (In fact, *illa* is historically a "defective verb" of negative existence.) In effect, we are claiming that the two *illa*'s of (3a) and (3b) are covertly marked, respectively, as [−past] and [+past].

Turning now to the second problem: How does the tense of the negated sentence get "read off" the nonfinite morphology on the main verb? Assuming a covert tense feature located in the negative, this must be the result of a "match" between that tense feature and the nonfinite morphology. There exists a mechanism in the theory to achieve such a match—namely, selection of an appropriate complement type by the tense feature. For the learner, the indication of whether the tense feature of *illa* is [−past] or [+past] is in fact only this selection.

But such an account (we should not fail to realize) gives only half an answer. For there remains the central question: What makes the match (of nonpast tense with gerundive morphology, and past tense with infinitival morphology) nonarbitrary, and therefore learnable?

We shall argue that what makes the putative match nonarbitrary is the aspectual specification of the complement of *illa*: the infinitive is specified for perfect aspect, the gerund for imperfect aspect. That is, a careful analysis of Kannada shows that the aspectual specifications of nonfinite clauses are more complex than is currently recognized, and the parallels we note with English suggest that at least some such aspectual specifications are independent of particular languages. Having thus explained the complement selection facts of Kannada negation, we shall raise the question whether the category of Tense is necessary for our analysis.

2.3 Aspect in the Gerund

In an important analysis of the interpretation of infinitives, Stowell (1982) proposed that infinitives have a tense interpretation—namely, "unrealized" (or "possible future")—and that the tense operator is located in COMP. Stowell further contrasted gerunds with infinitives: gerunds, lacking both a COMP and a tense operator, are simply transparent or "completely malleable" to the semantics of the matrix verb.

Thus Stowell contrasts (12a) and (12b):

(12)   a. Jim tried [PRO to lock the door].

         b. Jim tried [PRO locking the door].

There is an inference in (a), but not in (b), that at the point of time of the "trying," Jim did not lock the door. The familiar purposive interpretation of infinitival adjuncts—cf. 'He turned the key to open the door'—would thus be explained, as also the inference in (13a), where the bringing of the wine is un-realized with respect to the point of time of the remembering:

(13)   a. Jim remembered [PRO to bring the wine].

Gerunds, in contrast, have no tense operator to fix the tense interpretation, so they have differing interpretations, depending on the matrix verb. Thus, since remembering refers to the past, the wine-bringing is in the past in (13b), whereas the locking of the door in (12b) is simultaneous with the trying, or even unrealized with respect to it:

(13)   b. Jim remembered [PRO bringing the wine].

Now both these analyses appear to present serious difficulties for our Kannada data. If gerunds have no tense operator and are "completely malleable to the semantics of the governing verb," we expect the Kannada negative sentence con-taining the gerund to be interpretable as having (indifferently) either tense, past or nonpast. (There is, of course, no matrix verb in this case to determine the gerund's tense interpretation, but perhaps we can take the "governing verb" here to be Neg + Tense, specified as [±past].) The prediction is wrong, however; the gerund occurs only in the nonpast tense.

The Kannada infinitive is even more recalcitrant. The Kannada negative sen-tence containing the infinitival is interpreted as signifying past tense, but Stowell's suggested tense specification of infinitives is "unrealized," or possible future!

How can we make sense of this situation? As a first step, we can look at the paradigm of gerunds in Kannada. We note that, in fact, there are three gerund forms in the language. The *V-uvudu* form that occurs in the negative sentence (3a) is the "imperfect gerund"; besides it, there are the "perfect gerund" and the "negative gerund." The three forms are illustrated in (14):

(14) bar-uv-udu   ban-d-addu   ba-a-r-addu
      come-imperf-nom   come-perf-nom   come-neg-nom
      'coming'   'having come'   'not coming'

(15) a. [Avanu   ivattu   bar-uv-udu]   aas'carya.
         he   today   come-imperf. gerund   surprise

         'His coming today is a surprise.'

      b. [Avanu   ivattu   ban-d-addu]   aas'carya.
         he   today   come-perf. gerund   surprise

         'His having come today is a surprise.'

      c. [Avanu   ba-a-r-addu]   yaarige   gott-ittu?
         he   come-neg.gerund   to whom   was known

         'Who knew about his not coming?'

The negative gerund *ba-a-r-addu* exhibits a negative infix -*a*- in the verb *bar*-.
The negative infix is a survivor from an erstwhile "negative conjugation" of Dravidian, and the negative infixed verb currently occurs only in nonfinite contexts,
like (15c). Apparently fulfilling Stowell's prediction, this form indeed has no inherent tense interpretation but can be interpreted as "present" or "past" depending on the matrix clause.[5]

   For us, it is the perfect and nonperfect gerunds that are of immediate interest.
And the significant thing about them is that they contain Aspect. We now see
that in (3a), it is the nonperfect gerund that must match with a putative tense
feature [nonpast], absorbed by *illa*. This now seems to provide a good reason for
the selection.

   As regards (3b), can we similarly "match" the hidden tense feature [past] in
illa with perfect aspect in the infinitive? There is indeed some relevant evidence.
The Kannada passive auxiliary is *aag*- 'happen', which takes as its complement a
verb in the infinitive:

(16) Alli   ondu   mane   kaTT-al-aagide.
      there   one   house build-inf. aux

      'There is a house being built over there.'

Consider the comparable fact from English: the verb form selected by the passive
auxiliary is the perfect, or -*en*, form.

   Passives, it is well known, have a stative interpretation; and stativity is also a
feature associated with perfectivity. Given this reasoning, it would appear plausible
that the selection of a perfect complement is a principled fact about passives in
general. If this is so, it is possible to draw the inference that the Kannada infinitive

is parallel to the perfect form of the English verb, insofar as its aspectual interpretation is concerned.

Before we can proceed further, however, we need to sort out two different
types of infinitives. Kannada (too), exactly like English, has both purposive infinitives and infinitival complements to verbs like 'try', and these infinitives have
Stowell's "unrealized" interpretation. Compare our (6a), repeated here, and the
purposive (17) (compare also (10a,b)):

(6) a. Avanu [PRO   iij-alu]   nooDidanu.
        he   swim-inf.   saw (i.e., tried)

      'He tried to swim.'

(17)   Naanu [PRO   tarkaari   taralu]   horaTe.
       I   vegetables   to bring   set off

      'I set off to get vegetables.'

If we wish to claim that there is an infinitive which has a perfective interpretation,
we need to maintain a distinction between this and the Stowell-type infinitive by
some diagnostic means.

In the following discussion, we first look at Kannada and show that case-
marking can distinguish between these infinitives. We then show that case-marking distinguishes two types of infinitives in English as well.

2.4 Case-Marked Infinitives and Bare Infinitives

Infinitival complements to verbs like 'try' and purposive adjuncts both have the
"unrealized" interpretation. The form of the verb cited in (6a) and in (17) exhibits
no case-marking; and this is indeed the standard, literary citation form for the
verb in such sentences. However, the same, standard dialect of Kannada allows
the "unrealized" infinitive to carry an overt dative case, especially in the spoken
language. Thus (6a), repeated as (18a), has the variant (18b):

(18)   a. Avanu [PRO   iij-alu]   nooDidanu.
          he   swim-inf.   saw
        b. Avanu [PRO   iij-al-ikke]   nooDidanu.
          he   swim-inf.-dat.   saw

        'He tried to swim.'

Indeed, the spoken variety of the same standard dialect (the Bangalore-Mysore
dialect) exhibits an even more intriguing variation. The dative case can appear on
the (imperfect) gerund, instead of on the infinitive; that is, the case-marked in-

finitive can be realized as a case-marked imperfect gerund in the spoken language (as also noted in Sridhar 1990: 43):

(18)   c. Avanu [PRO   iij-uvud-ikke]   nooDidanu.
          he   swim-gerund-dat.   saw

       'He tried to swim.'

The bare infinitive, in contrast, has only the expected form *V-alu* in both the literary and the spoken language.

There are, then, revealing differences between the bare infinitive and the dative case-marked infinitive in the spoken language, which are neutralized in the literary variety. Significantly, the bare infinitive, which we argue occurs in the past tense negative sentence (3b), and as a complement to the passive auxiliary (16), can neither be optionally case-marked nor substituted by a gerund (case-marked or otherwise), in any variety of the standard language.[6] Thus (3b) and (16) do not have variants (19–20):

(19)   a. *Avanu bar-al-ikke illa. (* on the relevant reading)

          'He did not come.'

       b. *Avanu bar-uvud-ikke illa. (* on the relevant reading)

          'He did not come.'

(20)   *Alli ondu mane kaTT-al-ikke / kaTT-uvud-ikke aagide. (* on the relevant reading)

       'There is a house being built over there.'

Turning now to English, let us point out that what Stowell investigates is actually only the 'for-to' infinitive in English. (This is obscured by the fact that in "standard" English, the 'for' is usually dropped.) English also has another type of infinitive, with a different "tense" specification.[7]

This latter infinitive, indistinguishable from a "bare" or simply tenseless verb, occurs as a complement to perception verbs. Most of these verbs also take *-ing* or gerundive complements. Akmajian (1977) noted—crediting the observation to Emonds (1972)—that these two types of complements have different semantics: the gerundive signifies an "incompleted" action, but the infinitive signifies a completed one:

(21)   (= Akmajian's (52))
       a. We watched the prisoners dying. (Incompleted)

       b. We watched the prisoners die. (Completed)

Akmajian further showed that the same distinction holds for certain nonperception verbs, which take both kinds of complements:

(22)   (= Akmajian's (53))

    a. We had them marching into the mess hall.

    b. We had them march into the mess hall.

(23)   (= Akmajian's (54))

    a. We kept them marching into the mess hall.

    b. We made them march into the mess hall.

He concluded that the semantic distinction therefore has nothing to do with perception verbs per se but "seems rather to be a function of a more general structural distinction between 'gerundive' and 'infinitive' verb phrase complements."[8]

We suggest that this "more general structural distinction" is a distinction of Aspect. Specifically, we suggest that there is a bare infinitive of English which inherently has the perfective aspect. The parallel with the Kannada -*al* infinitive should now be obvious.

Further, we suggest that what Stowell analyzed as Tense in infinitives is actually Aspect. Saying this obviates many problems; it is very difficult to claim that bare infinitives have a tense operator: they occur in "small clauses," which lack the functional baggage of full clauses. In the selection of the bare infinitive by the passive auxiliary in Kannada, too, it seems to be Aspect that is the operative factor.

Again, we avoid a problem with respect to the Kannada gerund. Stowell rightly argued against Tense in gerunds: gerunds lack a COMP, and if Tense is in COMP, gerunds cannot have Tense. But Aspect is a "content" category, a property often intrinsic to verbs as part of their semantic specification. It does not require a COMP for its realization.

2.5 A Finiteness Head in MoodP

We now have an account of why the selection of complement types by *illa* is nonarbitrary; that is, why *illa* which is [−past] selects a *V-uvudu* complement, and *illa* which is [+past] selects a *V-al* complement.[9]

But we are now in a position to ask whether our initial postulation of a covert tense feature [+past]/[−past], which is "absorbed" by Neg *illa*, and which selects the nonfinite complement, is really necessary. The aspectual specifications of the nonfinite complements are inherent to them and obtain independently of the matrix tense. (Thus, in the English sentence *We shall watch*[*the prisoners die*], although the matrix tense is nonpast or future, the bare infinitive is interpeted as a completed action: the "watching" will go on until the prisoners are dead.) In other words, the inherent aspect we have discovered is different from "anaphoric" tense, such as what obtains in tensed pseudorelative complements to perception verbs in Romance (where the tense of the pseudorelative must be the same as the tense of the matrix verb; cf. Guasti 1993: 148).

If the tense interpretation of (3a, b) can be obtained from the aspectual spec-ifications of the verb forms, the tense feature [±past], or a Tense projection, becomes redundant. It would seem that all that we need in a Kannada negative sentence is a finiteness element that sanctions the nonfinite clause in a matrix context, allowing its aspect to be interpreted as Tense. This finiteness head, we suggest, is incorporated in the Neg *illa*. Not having to postulate *illa* as an element that can have *opposite* tense specifications is a happy result, since such an element involves learnability problems.

Sentences with modals pattern with sentences with negatives, and so they seem to ask for a structure without a Tense projection. Like negatives, modals surface with neither tense nor agreement, taking an infinitive complement. Cf. (24a):

(24) a. Avanu bar-beeku;   avanu   bar-bahudu.
         he   come-must   he   come-may

      'He must come; he may come.'

The verb form in (24a) looks like a stem, but it is an infinitival, as becomes apparent when the emphatic morphemes *-ee* and *-uu* attach to the verb. The *-al* of the infinitive now surfaces:

      b. Avanu bar-al-ee   beeku; avanu bar-al-uu   bahudu.
         he   come-inf.-emph   must   he   come-inf.-emph   may

      'He certainly must come; he might even come.'

Thus modals induce a "matrix infinitive."

In English, the current assumption is that modals select a bare or stem form of the main verb. However at least the modal 'ought' (standardly cited as 'ought to') clearly selects an infinitive. Further cross-linguistic investigations may perhaps show that modals universally select an infinitive as complement.

The complement of a modal has the "tense" interpretation of "unrealized." But the Kannada modal's complement does not (in any dialect, to the best of our knowledge) allow a dative case-marker:

(25) *Avanu bar-al-ikk-ee   beeku; avanu bar-al-ikk-uu
      he   come-inf.-dat.-emph must   he   come-inf.-dat.-emph
      bahudu.
      may

      *'He certainly must come; he might even come.'

In English, too, while one modal allows (in fact, requires) 'to' in its complement, no modal allows 'for'. There may be independent reasons that disallow a case-marker in the modal's infinitival complement, both in English and in Kannada, which are still unclear to us.

   Let us now propose that Kannada has a Mood Phrase. And (importantly for the focus of this essay), that finiteness *is* Mood (in Kannada). That is, the presence of the Mood Phrase makes a Kannada clause finite.[10] MoodP takes as its complement an Aspect Phrase, which takes a VP complement:

(26)

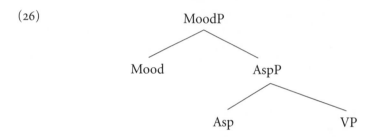

The head of MoodP can be a modal. It can also be Agr; for although Agr itself is not a Mood, it can be taken to be a reflex of the Indicative Mood. When negation is introduced into the clause, a NegP is generated immediately below MoodP.[11] The element *illa* is licensed by a null finiteness head in MoodP, to which it raises. (We shall take up a more detailed analysis of *illa* in section 4.) This picture now enables us to understand why Modal and Agr are in complementary distribution and why *illa* is in complementary distribution with both Modal and Agr.

2.6 "Tense" in Affirmative Sentences

An apparent problem for the elimination of a Tense projection in the negative and modal sentences of Kannada is presented by the structure of the affirmative sentences. For these were shown as containing Tense, in (1). If the structure of a negative sentence is $]_{VP}]_{AspP}]_{NegP}]_{MoodP}$, and that of a modal sentence is $]_{VP}]_{AspP}]_{MoodP}$ (as we have just argued), the structure of an affirmative sentence in Kannada seems to be $]_{VP}]_{TP}]_{AgrP}$.

Comparing the structures, if we assume that agreement morphology is a reflex of Indicative Mood (often taken to be the "default" or null mood), AgrP can be taken to be an instantiation of MoodP. The essential difference of the affirmative structure from the negative and modal structures then seems to be that it has a Tense Phrase in place of the Aspect Phrase of the other structures. But this is an important difference, which returns us to an initial question: Why would a language have such a radical difference between its affirmative and other (negative and modal) sentences? Such a result is surely unintuitive.

In this section we provide arguments against a category Tense in the affirmative sentences of Kannada—sentences like (1) (repeated here), which have a verb marked for (what is standardly analyzed as) tense and agreement:

(1)   a. Avanu   bar-utt-aane.
         he   come-present-3msg

      'He comes.'

      b. Avanu   ban-d-anu.
         he   come-past-3msg

      'He came.'

Clearly, the putative tense morphemes in Kannada are identical with the corresponding aspect morphemes. Thus -*utt*-, glossed as nonpast tense in (1a), marks progressive aspect in (27a); and -*d*-, glossed as past tense in (1b), marks perfect aspect in (27b). In (27a–b), we instantiate the "compound tenses"—the progressive and the perfect; both of these are formed with the auxiliary *iru* 'be,' which carries "tense"—in (27), "past tense"—while the main verb is marked for aspect: progressive aspect in (27a), perfect aspect in (27b):[12]

(27)   a. Avanu   bar-utt-id-d-anu.
          he   come-progressive-be-past-3msg

       'He was coming.'

       b. Avanu   ban-d-id-d-anu.
          he   come-perfect-be-past-3msg

       'He had come.'

For further evidence, let us look more closely at these tense-aspect morphemes -*utt*- and -*d*-. The *tt* in -*utt*- is actually an "augment"; it occurs also in other Dravidian languages (e.g., Malayalam). Its function may be purely phonological (possibly breaking up a sequence of vowels). The nonpast 'tense-aspect' morpheme then is just -*u*-. Compare now the imperfective gerund form *bar-uv-udu* 'come-imperf.-nom.' of (14). In *bar-uv-udu*, as indicated, -*udu*- is a nominalizing suffix. Thus the imperfective suffix in the gerund is, again, -*u*-, taking the /v/ of -*uv*- to be epenthetic. There is an even more obvious homophony between the -*d*- which is the past tense suffix, and the perfective suffix -*d*- of the perfective gerund form *ban-d-addu* 'come-perf.-nom.' of (14).

This homophony has sometimes led to claims in the literature that in Dravidian, Tense is present in the gerundive and participial forms of the verb.[13] But this is rather implausible, for there is clear evidence that (returning to the paradigm in (14)) the negative gerund, at least, is a nonfinite form. Thus, it is the only negative form that is licit in nonfinite complement clauses that exclude Neg *illa* because the latter is finite. Cf. (5b, 6b) (repeated here), and the corresponding permitted negative forms:

(28)   a. (=(5b))

          *[Avanu   ivattu   bar-uvud(u)   illa]   aas'carya.
          he   today   come-gerund   neg   surprise

          'His not coming today is a surprise.'

    b. [Avanu   ivattu   ba-a-r-addu]   aas'carya.
          he   today   come-neg-gerund   surprise

          'His not coming today is a surprise.'

    c. (=(6b))

          *Avanu [PRO   iij-al(u)   illa]   nooDidanu.
          he   swim-inf.   neg   saw (i.e., tried)

          'He tried not to swim.'

    d. Avanu [PRO   iij-a-d-e   ir-alu]   nooDidanu[14]
          he   swim-neg.-nom.-part.   be-inf.   saw (i.e., tried)

          'He tried not to swim.'

If we take the negative gerund as typical of its paradigm, gerund forms in Kannada are nonfinite. They cannot carry a tense morpheme; the apparent tense morpheme is an aspect morpheme.

We have shown that the aspect and putative tense morphemes in Kannada are homophonous, and that this has led to a misdiagnosis of the category Tense in verb forms that are demonstrably nonfinite. We can rest the argument at this point, treating the morphological facts as accidental. Alternatively, we could take the morphological facts to accurately reflect the functional structure: tense and aspect morphemes in Kannada are "homophonous" because they in fact belong to a single functional category. (This is indeed the assumption that has led to the misanalysis of the gerund as tensed.) This single functional category, however, we shall maintain, is not Tense but Aspect.

The advantage of taking the position that the "tense" morphemes are actually aspect morphemes is that affirmative sentences in Kannada now have an Aspect Phrase complement to a MoodP, just as negatives and modal sentences do. Again, affirmative sentences in Kannada now have the main verb instantiated in a non-finite form, just as negatives and modal sentences do. In all these clause types, finiteness is marked, not by "tense" in the verb but by an element in the MoodP: agreement in the case of affirmative sentences, Neg *illa* in the case of negatives, and the modal in sentences with modals.

We thus unify the structures of the affirmative, negative, and modal sentences of Kannada. Kannada clauses now have the general structure (29):

(29) a. bar]$_{VP}$ utt   ]$_{AspP}$ [aane   ]$_{Agr}$]$_{Mood P}$ '(he) comes'

    b. bar]$_{VP}$ uvud   ]$_{AspP}$ [illa   ]$_{Neg}$]$_{Mood P}$ 'does not come'

    c. bar]$_{VP}$ al   ]$_{AspP}$ [bahudu]$_{Modal}$]$_{Mood P}$ 'may come'

3 NEGATION IN MALAYALAM

3.1 Negation and Finiteness in Malayalam

As we said earlier, negation in Malayalam appears to be a straightforward affair of adding a negative marker to an affirmative sentence. The affirmative and negative sentences (2) and (4) are repeated:

(2) a. Avan   var-unnu.
       he   come-present
       'He comes.'

    b. Avan   van-nu.
       he   come-past
       'He came.'

(4) a. Avan   var-unn(u)   illa.
       he   come-present   neg
       'He does not come.'

    b. Avan   van-n(u)   illa.
       he   come-past   neg
       'He did not come.'

In (2) as well as in (4), what looks like a tense morpheme occurs on the main verb. The negative sentences in (4) differ from the corresponding affirmative sentences only by the presence of *illa*.

Illa in Malayalam, then, would seem to be quite different from *illa* in Kannada. In Kannada, it is the occurrence of the matrix gerund or infinitive with *illa* that prompts the analysis of *illa* as a finite element. In the corresponding Malayalam sentences of (4), there appears to be no similar need to say that *illa* is finite, since finiteness seems obviously to reside in the tensed verbs.

The first problem for this apparently commonsensical account is that in nonfinite complement clauses, Malayalam *illa* is not licensed, just as its Kannada counterpart is not licensed in nonfinite complement clauses. The Malayalam examples (30–31) are the counterparts of the Kannada examples (5–6); the (b) examples of (30–31) show that *illa* cannot occur in gerundive and infinitival complements. In (32), we see that the negative element permitted in these clauses is the infix *-a-*; the corresponding Kannada examples are (28b) and (28d):

(30) a. [Avan   var-unn-atə]   nannaayi.
          he   come-present-nom.   is good

      'His coming is good.' (i.e., 'It is good that he is coming.')

      b. * [Avan   var-unn-atə   illa]   nannaayi.
            he   come-present-nom.   not   is good

      *'His not coming is good.'

(31) a. Avan [PRO   niint-uvaan]   nookki.
          he   swim-inf.   looked (i.e., tried)

      'He tried to swim.'

      b. * Avan [PRO   niint-uvaan   illa]   nookki.
            he   swim-inf.   not   looked (i.e., tried)

      *'He tried not to swim.'

(32) a. [Avan   var-aa-tt-atə]   nannaayi.
          he   come-neg-(aug)-nom.   is good

      'His not coming is good.'

      b. Avan [PRO   niint-aa-t-e[15]   irikk-uvaan]   nookki.
          he   swim-neg-nom.-part.   be-inf.   looked (i.e., tried)

      'He tried not to swim.'

Now if Malayalam *illa* were indeed a simple Neg element like English *not*, there would be no accounting for this restriction against its occurrence in nonfinite clauses. But if Malayalam *illa*, like Kannada *illa*, were to occur in a Mood Phrase, the data just presented would be explained.

It thus seems reasonable to claim that the *illa* in the sentences of (4) is finite. But if this is correct, we have the problem of two finite elements in a simple sentence, since, apparently, the verbs *war-unnu* and *wan-nu* in the negative sentences of (4) are inflected for Tense, just as they are in the affirmative sentences (2). We say "apparently" because for Kannada, we reanalyzed the putative tense morphemes as aspect morphemes. The question arises whether a similar resolution of the problem is possible, or desirable, for Malayalam. Let us therefore look more closely at the verb forms in (4).

3.2 Aspect in Gerunds and Serial Verbs in Malayalam

We straightaway note that Malayalam in fact exhibits the apparent homophony of "tense" and aspect morphemes familiar from the Kannada data presented earlier.

(33) a. Avan   var-unn(u)   uNDə.
           he   come-imperf.   be (exis.) (present)

       'He is coming.'

      b. Avan   van-n(u)   irun-nu.
           he   come-perf.   be-past

       'He had come.'

The standard analysis of verb forms such as *var-unnu* and *van-nu* as "tensed" forms ignores this homophony. We show in the following discussion that at least two other instantiations of these verb forms—namely, in the gerund and in the serial verb construction—should be analyzed as aspectual forms and not as tensed forms. Pursuing this logic of correcting a tendency to misdiagnose the category Tense in verb forms that are at best ambiguous between tensed and aspectual forms, we raise the question whether Tense is projected at all in the Malayalam clause.

3.2.1 *Gerunds*

In (34) we illustrate the occurrence of verb forms such as *var-unnu* and *van-nu* inside nominalized clauses (i.e., gerunds). (As demonstrated earlier for Kannada, the gerund is marked with the case appropriate to its position in the sentence.)

(34) a. [Avan   var-unn-at]-ine   patti   ñangaL   samsaari-ccu.
          he   come-nonpast-nomin.-acc.   about   we   talk-past

      'We talked about his coming.'

      b. [Avan   van-n-at]-ine   patti   ñangaL
          he   come-past-nomin.-acc.   about   we
          samsaari-ccu.
          talk-past

      'We talked about his having come.'

Notice the problem already encountered in Kannada: if we analyze *-unn(u)* and
-n(u) as tense inflections, we have the embarrassment of tense inside gerunds. If
these are aspect morphemes, however, their occurrence in the gerund is not unexpected.

Further confirmation that *-unn(u)* and *-n(u)* in the gerunds in (34) are aspect
morphemes comes from the other member of the gerund paradigm, the negative
gerund. (The gerunds illustrated in (34a,b) are the imperfect and the perfect members, respectively, of this paradigm.) The negative gerund is illustrated in (35); it
may be recalled that this is a nonfinite form. (It is its lack of finiteness that allows
it to occur in the negation of nonfinite complement clauses which disallow *illa*:
cf. our examples in (32).)

(35) [Avan   var-aa-tt-at]-ine   patti   ñangaL   samsaari-ccu.
         he   come-neg-(aug)-nomin.-acc.   about   we   talk-past

      'We talked about his not coming.'

The fact that at least one member of the gerund paradigm is demonstrably nonfinite is, of course, supportive of the analysis of its other members (e.g., *var-unnu*
and *van-nu*) as containing nonfinite aspect morphemes rather than finite tense
morphemes. But we can make a stronger argument: namely, that the negative
gerund in Malayalam can also be marked for temporal aspect, without affecting
its nonfinite status. (The facts here diverge from Kannada, which requires a
dummy verb *iru* to carry markers of temporal aspect in the negative gerund
construction; see note 5.) This is illustrated in (36):

(36) [Avan   var-aa-ññ-at][16]-ine   patti   ñangaL   samsaari-ccu.
         he   come-neg-perf.-nomin.-acc.   about   we   talk-past

      'We talked about his not having come.'

Thus temporal marking in the gerund paradigm in general, we claim, is diagnostic
of the category of Aspect, rather than Tense.

3.2.2 *Serial Verbs*

The argument that certain apparently "tensed" forms of the Malayalam verb are actually aspectual forms is especially attractive when we consider the so-called conjunctive participles of the Dravidian languages.[17] This is a ubiquitous type of phrase in Dravidian; its superficial manifestation is as a string of content verbs, which have a conjunction-like semantics. Consider (37) (the serial verb examples are adapted from Jayaseelan 1984: 623):

(37) a. Ñaan   oru   maanga   poTTicc-u   tin-nu.
         I   a   mango   pluck-past   eat-past

      'I plucked and ate a mango.'

      b. Ñaan   oru   maanga   poTTicc-u   kazhuk-i   tin-nu.
         I   a   mango   pluck-past   wash-past   eat-past

      'I plucked, washed, and ate a mango.'

      c. Ñaan   oru   maanga   poTTicc-u   kazhuk-i   muRicc-u   tin-nu.
         I   a   mango   pluck-past   wash-past   cut-past   eat-past

      'I plucked, washed, cut, and ate a mango.'

In the construction illustrated in (37), only the last verb shows evidence of finiteness. (Thus in the Dravidian languages which have agreement morphology, such morphology appears on the final verb.) In Malayalam (which has no agreement), only the last verb shows tense (or mood) alternation. Compare (37a) with (38a) and (38b), and (37c) with (39a) and (39b): only the final verb *tinn-* varies in form, and the interpretation of the entire sentence follows from the tense (or mood) of this final verb:

(38) a. Ñaan   oru   maanga   poTTicc-u   tinn-unnu.
         I   a   mango   pluck-past   eat-present

      'I pluck and eat (or am plucking and eating) a mango.'

      b. Ñaan   oru   maanga   poTTicc-u   tinn-aam.
         I   a   mango   pluck-past   eat-Modal

      'I may pluck and eat a mango.'

(39) a. Ñaan   oru   maanga   poTTicc-u   kazhuk-i   muRicc-u
         I   a   mango   pluck-past   wash-past   cut-past
      tinn-unnu.
      eat-present

      'I pluck, wash, cut, and eat (or am plucking, washing, cutting, and eating) a mango.'

b. Ñaan   oru   maanga   poTTicc-u   kazhuk-i   muRicc-u   tinn-aam.
   I   a   mango   pluck-past   wash-past   cut-past   eat-Modal

'I may pluck, wash, cut and eat a mango.'

The point to note is that the nonfinal verbs are all in an invariant form, apparently a "past tense" form, irrespective of the tense or modality of the sentence as a whole. In Jayaseelan (2003), these verbs were said to be in a "frozen" past tense form, which therefore did not contribute any past tense meaning to the sentence. These verbs were then claimed to be in fact nonfinite.[18]

This analysis left unexplained the "doubling" of a past tense form as a nonfinite form. But if these verbs are not past tense forms, but perfective forms, their nonfiniteness, as well as the conjunctive or sequential interpretation of the actions denoted by these strings of verbs, is straightforwardly explained. The nonfinite, participial status of all but the last in the string of verbs that make up the serial verb is confirmed by examples such as (40), which attest the negative participle in this construction:

(40)   Ñaan   oru   maanga   kazhuk-aa-t-e   tin-nu.
       I   a   mango   wash-neg-nom.-part.   eat-past

'I ate a mango, without washing it.'

3.3 A Reanalysis of Tense in Malayalam

We have shown that the homophony of the aspect and (putative) tense morphemes in Malayalam has led to a misdiagnosis of the category Tense in verb forms that are at best ambiguous between tensed and aspectual forms. A reanalysis of "tense" morphemes as aspect morphemes is necessary for at least the gerund, and the nonfinal verbs in the serial verb construction, in Malayalam. A natural question that now arises is whether the Malayalam facts are indicative merely of a homophony of tense and aspect, or whether the morphology reflects a generalization at the level of functional structure, such as we have argued for in Kannada. On the first view, Malayalam would differ from Kannada (this language would project Tense).

Main clause negation in Malayalam does not provide as salient an argument against Tense as Kannada does: there are no matrix gerunds or infinitives. However, negation in nontensed complement clauses in Malayalam exhibits the same asymmetry as in Kannada: the Neg element licensed here is not *illa* but the *-a-* infix that occurs in nonfinite forms. (The comparative syntax perspective thus highlights and centralizes a fact that has so far remained marginal in accounts of

Malayalam negation: Malayalam, like Kannada, exhibits separate negative elements in finite and nonfinite clauses.) It is this crucial fact that a reanalysis of the Malayalam "tense" morphemes as aspect morphemes explains. It allows us to analyze *illa* as finite in matrix negative clauses such as (4) (repeated here):[19]

(4) a. Avan var-unn(u)   illa.
       he   come-present neg

      'He does not come.'

    b. Avan van-n(u)   illa.
       he   come-past   neg

      'He did not come.'

Treating *illa* as the finite element in (4) allows us to explain why this form of Neg is not licensed in gerunds and infinitives; see examples (30–31). But if, in (4), finiteness is "absorbed" by *illa*, then the so-called tense morphemes in (4) cannot be finite. Nothing now distinguishes them from the homophonous aspect morphemes.

Modal clauses in Malayalam pattern like their Kannada counterparts: they surface without tense, taking an infinitive complement. Compare (41) (which also illustrates the fact that modals and *illa* are in complementary distribution and that the negation of modals is done by "negative modal" forms).

(41) avan var-uka-(y)ee   veeNDa[20]
      he   come-inf.-emph. need not

     'He need not come at all.'

Malayalam modal clauses thus present a matrix infinitive.

There thus seem to be convincing reasons for extending our analysis of Kannada to Malayalam: the suffixes standardly analyzed as present tense and past tense markers (*-unnu* and *-nu*, respectively, in (2)) are actually markers of imperfect and perfect aspect. Having assimilated Malayalam to the pattern we discovered in Kannada, we can now generalize and say the following: Dravidian languages do not project Tense. The "tense" morphology that in some clauses appears on verbs is nonfinite and therefore is more appropriately labeled "aspect." In the presence of Mood, the tense interpretation of the sentence is "read off" the aspectual specification of the verb. The Indicative Mood has its morphological reflex in Agreement in all the Dravidian languages except Malayalam. In Malayalam, the Indicative Mood has a null morphological reflex.[21]

4 *ILLA* IN MALAYALAM AND KANNADA

4.1 *Illa* as Neg and *illa* as a Verb of Negative Existence in Malayalam

Historically, *illa* contains a verbal root *ir-*, which may be variously translated as 'sit', 'remain', or 'be'.[22] (It would appear to be the combination of *ir-* with *aa*, the Dravidian negative morpheme currently instantiated in nonfinite verb forms such as the negative gerund.) The meaning of *ir-* 'be' in *illa* is still unmistakably present where *illa* is a negative existential verb. We illustrate this first for Malayalam and then for Kannada.

Malayalam has a verb *uNTǝ*, generally described as the "existential copula." It is a defective verb: it does not inflect for tense (i.e., aspect, under our analysis). (Its cognate in the other Dravidian languages does not inflect for either tense *or* agreement.) In (42a), *uNTǝ* is interpreted as having present tense and is obviously finite. The point is that in (42b), *illa* is the negative counterpart of *uNTǝ* ; it is a negative existential copula which is finite.

(42)   a. Avan   iviDe   uNTǝ.
          he   here   be (exist.)(present)

          'He is here.'

       b. Avan   iviDe   illa.
          he   here   neg

          'He is not here.'

Hany-Babu (1996, 1997) argues that there are two *illa*s in Malayalam. Besides the *illa* illustrated in (42b), there is a "purely neg" *illa*, which has no meaning of negative existence. Thus (43a) (= (4b)) has no counterpart with *uNTǝ* (43b):

(43)   a. Avan   van-n(u)   illa.
          he   come-perf.   neg

          'He did not come.'

       b. *Avan van-n(u) uNTǝ.
          'He came.'

Let us call *illa* in (42) the verb of negative existence, *illa₁*, and let us call the *illa* of "pure negation," *illa₂*. Both *illa*s are finite—they incorporate Mood—and thus neither of them can take a modal suffix ((44a) instantiates the verb of negative existence, and (44b) the *illa* of "pure negation"):

(44) a. *Avan   iviDe   ill(a)-aam.
            he   here   neg-may

      'He may not be here.'

      b. *Avan   van-n(u)   ill(a)-aam.
            he   come-perf.   neg-may

      'He may not have come.'

Let us say that the *illa* of negation, *illa₂*, differs from the first *illa* (the verb of negative existence) in not containing the verb 'be'. In effect, we are saying that *illa₂*, which historically has *ir-* 'be' as its root, has been reanalyzed in some cases in Malayalam as merely a negativity and finiteness marker.

The verb of negative existence, *illa₁*, has a participial form that occurs in nonfinite clauses. Thus it occurs in relative clauses, which in Dravidian must be nonfinite (as traditionally noted, but for yet unexplained reasons).[23] Note the occurrence of *illa* in (45b):

(45) a. Suuci-kkə   kaNNə   illa.
            needle-dat.   eye   be-neg

      'There is no eye in the needle.'

      b. kaNN-   ill-aa-tt-a   suuci
            eye   be-neg-(aug)-rel.   needle

      'the needle without an eye'

Let us call the nonfinite *illa*, *illa₃*, characterizing it as an element that incorporates just the existential copula and Neg, and does not incorporate Mood.[24]

4.2 An Account of the Three *illa*s in Malayalam and in Kannada

We can generate the three *illa*s noted in the preceding discussion with their relevant properties, assuming a clause structure like the following:

(46)

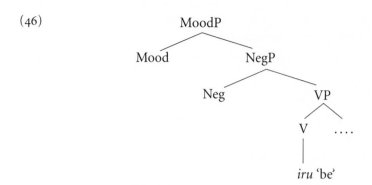

We can get the "three *illas*" by incorporation of these elements in three ways:

illa₁   be + Neg + Mood
illa₂   Neg + Mood
illa₃   be + Neg

That is, the negative existential *illa* originates under V and raises to incorporate Neg and Mood; whereas the *illa* of negation originates under Neg and raises to incorporate Mood. The participle *illa*, which occurs in nonfinite clauses, originates under V and raises to Neg, but does not incorporate Mood.

Interestingly, what we do not get in Malayalam is a simple Neg, which does not incorporate either the verb 'be' or Mood. Thus the *illa* of negation cannot occur in nonfinite contexts, whereas the *illa* of existence can (see note 24).

Our account of *illa* in Malayalam straightforwardly generalizes to Kannada. Thus Kannada has a verb of negative existence, *illa₁*, which has a nonfinite participial form (*illa₃*). Examples (47a–b) and (48a–b) correspond to the Malayalam examples (42) and (45):

(47) a. Avanu   illi   idd-aane.
         he   here   is-3pmsg.

         'He is here.'

      b. Avanu   illi   illa.
         he   here   is not

         'He is not here.'

(48) a. Suuji-ge   kaNNu   illa.
         needle-dat.   eye   be-neg

         'There is no eye in the needle.'

      b. kaNN-ill-a-d-a   suuji
         eye be-neg-part.-rel.   needle

         'the needle without an eye'

That *illa*₁ (the verb of negative existence) is distinct from *illa*₂ (the Neg element) in Kannada can be seen from (49). In (49), the affirmative sentences again have the verb *iru* 'be.' But the negative counterparts of these sentences are formed in the now-familiar way, by adding *illa* to a gerundive or an infinitive form of the verb *iru*:

(49)   a. (i) Avanu   illi   ir-utt-aane.
                 he   here   be-imperf.-3pmsg.
             'He will be here.'

       (ii) Avanu   illi   iruvud-   illa.
               he   here   be.gerund   -neg
            'He will not be here'

   b. (i) Avanu   illi   id-d-anu.
             he   here   be-perf.-3pmsg.
           'He was here'

      (ii) Avanu   illi   iral-   illa.
              he   here   be.infinitive   -neg
           'He was not here'

That is, the Neg *illa* of (49) cooccurs with the *iru* to negate it; it does not replace *iru* as in (47).

As we saw at the outset (in examples (5–6)), the negative element *illa*₂ is finite and cannot occur in nonfinite complement clauses (gerunds and infinitives). Nor can it occur as negation in relative clauses:

(50)   a. MakkaLu   bar-al-   illa.
            children   come-inf.   neg
          'The children did not come.'

       b. *baral-ill-a-d-a   makkaLu
           come.inf.-neg-rel   children
          'the children who did not come'

The evidence (thus) is that our teasing apart of the Malayalam *illa* into three *illas* extends to Kannada, and there is nothing to suggest that an analysis similar to (46) is not appropriate to Kannada.

4.3 The Two Verbs *iru* in Kannada and Their Counterparts in Malayalam

A peculiarity of the Kannada verb *iru* 'be' emerges from the data in (47) and (49): *iru* occurs in three forms. Two of these are the familiar forms of all Kannada verbs: the imperfect, *V-utt-*, and the perfect, *V-d-*. The third form of *iru* is peculiar to this verb, cf. (51c):

(51)   a. ir-utt-aane
           be-imperf.-3pmsg.

           '(he) will be'
           cf. bar-utt-aane
           come-imperf.-3pmsg.

       b. id-d-anu
           be-perf.-3pmsg.

           '(he) was'
           cf. ban-d-anu
           come-perf.-3pmsg.

       c. idd-aane
           be-3pmsg.

           '(he) is'
           cf. *band-aane

The form of *iru* in (51c) is morphologically unique. The agreement suffixes of the verbs in its paradigm are homophonous with those of the imperfect paradigm; compare (51a, 51c), and (52a, 52c). But in (51c) and (52c), these suffixes do not attach to the *-utt-* of imperfect aspect.

The stem *idd-* in (51c) in fact looks like the stem *id-d-* of the perfect *iru*. However, a consideration of the full paradigm shows that the stems in (c) are not identical with the perfect stem, either. Compare the third-person neuter forms in (52):

(52)   a. ir-utt-e
           be-imperf.-3pnsg.

           '(it) will be'

       b. it-t-u
           be-perf.-3pnsg.

           '(it) was'

c. id-e
    be-3pnsg.
    '(it) is'

A nongeminate *-d-* such as occurs in *ide* in (52c) is unattested in the perfect paradigm for *iru*; the perfect *-d-*, when it attaches to *ir-*, always results in a geminate *-dd-* on the surface.

How do we account for the "extra" *iru* in Kannada? We suggest that just as there are two *illa*s (in Malayalam and Kannada), there are two *iru*s (in Kannada). There is a "regular" verb *iru*, which we now term *iru₂*. This verb occurs with regular perfect and imperfect morphology (in affirmative sentences) and as an infinitive or gerund plus *illa₂* (in negative sentences—see (49)). There is in addition a verb *iru* that is unspecified for aspect. (This appears to be in consonance with its permitting a "timeless" reading: *suuryanu iddaane* 'the sun exists'.) This *iru*, which we now term *iru₁*, is the counterpart of the negative existential verb *illa*, or *illa₁*. We have analyzed *illa₁* as 'be' + Neg + Mood, or *ir* + *aa* (negation)+Mood; we now analyze *idd-aane* (etc.) as 'be' + Mood, or *ir* + agreement.

The clause structure necessary for this analysis of Kannada *iru* has already been motivated for Malayalam *illa*. Thus in the schema (46) (reproduced here),

(46)

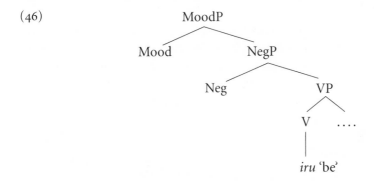

generating a verb *iru₁* 'be' without an intervening NegP will give us, when this verb raises to MoodP, the forms *idd-aane* and so on (recall that agreement suffixes are reflexes of Indicative Mood). When a NegP is generated and *iru₁* raises to it, what surfaces is *illa₁*, the verb of negative existence. We thus explain how *iddaane* in (47a) appears to be "replaced" by *illa* in (47b).

The regular verb *iru₂* is generated (like all verbs) in a VP that is the complement of an AspectP; that is, in the more articulated clause structure (53) (which is a combination of (46) with the already suggested (26)), we conjecture that the AspectP is projected by all verbs except *iru₁* and *illa₁*:

(53)

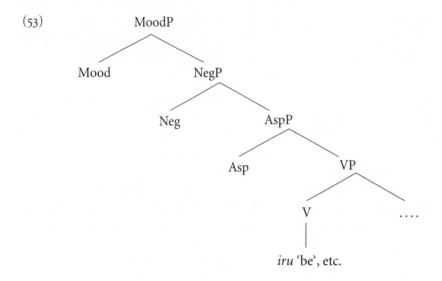

iru 'be', etc.

The regular *iru* (like all verbs) raises to Aspect and Mood in affirmative sentences. In Aspect it picks up aspectual morphology, and in Mood it picks up agreement morphology; so we get forms like (51a), *ir-utt-aane* 'be-imperf.-3msg.' and (51b), *id-d-anu* 'be-perf.-3msg.' In negative sentences it (again) raises to Aspect but raises no further; a Neg *illa* that originates in NegP (i.e., *illa₂*) raises to Mood. So we get forms like *ir-uvud-illa* 'be-gerund-neg' (cf. (49aii)) and *ir-al-illa* 'be-infinitive-neg' (cf. (49bii)).[25]

Either *iru* may occur in the "compound tenses" as the second verb—that is, as the auxiliary. The patterns of negation in these verb forms fall out straightforwardly from the negations illustrated for *iru*: *iru₁* is negated by *illa₁*, the verb of negative existence; *iru₂* is negated by Neg *illa*, or *illa₂*. We illustrate these facts in the following. (Example (54) is the paradigm of the imperfect tenses, with the imperfect suffix *-utt-* on the main verb. The paradigm of the perfect tenses is similar.)[26]

(54) a. Verb + *iru₁*

Bar-utt   idd-aane.
come-imperf.   be-agr

'(He) is coming'

b. Verb + *iru₂*

(i) Bar-utt   ir-utt -aane.
    come-imperf.   be-imperf. -agr

'(He) often comes, he keeps
   coming.'
(lit. (He) will be coming.)

Verb + *illa₁*

Bar-utt   illa.
come-imperf.   not be

'(He) is not coming.'

Verb + *illa₂*

Bar-utt   ir-uvud(u)   illa
come-imperf.   be-gerund   neg

lit. '(He) will not be coming.'

(ii) Bar-utt   id-d-anu.
    come-imperf. be-perf. agr

    '(He) used to come.'
    (lit. (He) was coming.)

    Bar-utt   iral(u)   illa.
    come-imperf. be-infinitive neg

    '(He) did not use to come.'
    (lit. (he) was not coming)

In Malayalam, the verb corresponding to iru_1 of Kannada is *uNDə*, which we have already seen in (33a) and (42a). In a negative sentence, it is replaced by *illa₁*, exactly like in Kannada, and as already illustrated in (42). Since Malayalam has no agreement, and since iru_1/ *uNDə* takes no aspectual morphology, Malayalam *uNDə* has only the one invariant form.[27] In a "compound tense" it can occur as the second verb:

(55) Avan   var-unn(u)-uNDə.
    he   come-imperf.- be (present)

    'He is coming.'

The Malayalam verb corresponding to iru_2 of Kannada is *ir-*. It can occur as the second verb of a "compound tense" and take aspectual morphology:

(56) a. Avan   van-n(u)-irikk-unnu.
       he   come-perf.-be-imperf.

      'He has come.'

    b. Avan   van-n(u)-irun-nu.
       he   come-perf.-be-perf.

      'He had come.'

4.4 Two Remaining Questions

We shall now attempt to answer two questions. First, can a Tense projection still be postulated in Dravidian languages, which can be shown to be consistent with the range of data we have examined? Second, given our demonstration that Kannada and Malayalam share not only the fundamentals of clause structure but even the detail of having two negative elements *illa* with identical properties (viz., a verb of negative existence with a corresponding relative participle, and a "pure" Neg), why are the simplest negative sentences in Kannada and Malayalam so different from each other?

Taking up the first question, the central claim of this chapter has been that in Dravidian languages, finiteness and "tense" information are realized in different projections—the first in a Mood Phrase, and the second in Aspect Phrases—

without ever taking recourse to a Tense projection. The head Tense in the current theory can be argued to "syncretize" two different types of elements—namely, the finiteness feature (which is deictic and "absolute") and features that provide temporal information (which are always "relative"). While this type of head may serve well for English-type languages, we are suggesting that there may be languages in which the two classes of features are realized on different heads. Even in English (it need hardly be pointed out), temporal information is often expressed by Aspect (as in adjunct participles: "Once bitten, . . ."); our claim is that in Dravidian, all temporal information is expressed by this means. (See Comrie 1977: 82ff. for typological evidence of "tenseless" languages.)

But (it could be argued) perhaps a "parametric" solution is not really called for here: Dravidian still can have "covert" tense. In a sentence like (1a) (repeated here), we could maintain that there is a present tense; being unmarked, it has no morphology to express it. But its covert presence makes the imperfective -utt yield a present (non-past) tense meaning:

(1)   a. Avanu   bar-utt-aane.
         he   come-imperf.-3msg
         'He comes.'

Whereas, when a past tense morpheme -d- follows -utt in the "compound tense" illustrated by (27a), it yields a past progressive meaning:

(27)   a. Avanu   bar-utt-id-d-anu.
            he   come-imperf.-be-past-3msg
            'He was coming.'

The homophony of the "past tense" morpheme, expressing absolute past, and the perfective aspect morpheme, expressing relative past, is a type of homophony noticed in many languages; so that (27b) should not be surprising:[28]

(27)   b. Avanu   ban-d-id-d-anu.
            he   come-perf.-be-past-3msg
            'He had come.'

Suppose we grant this analysis. Considering this possibility, let us note in its support that our analysis of iru_1 in Kannada as a finite verb of existence with no overt tense or aspect morpheme could be taken as evidence for just such a "covert present tense" (which, as expected, now restricts the imperfect form $ir-utt-$ to a future time interpretation: cf. note 26). But then, this "covert present tense" is not substantively different from what we have called a "finiteness feature in MoodP." Its reflex in affirmative clauses would have to be agreement (cf. *idd-aane*). It does not really carry any temporal information: the label "present tense" in the case of *iru*₁ seems to be a term for an "eternal now," "in the real world." Crucially, its function is to license the overt, so-called tense morphemes -*utt*- and -*d*-. The latter are not in themselves finite.

It is this latter claim that we are interested in preserving, for Kannada as well as for Malayalam: that the verb forms standardly analyzed as tensed are in fact nonfinite forms specified with temporal information. Our point of departure was the puzzle of negation in Kannada, which exhibits clearly nonfinite verb forms which are (we saw) specified with temporal information; in these clauses finiteness lodges in Neg *illa*. In the case of sentences with *illa* again, it is possible to argue that there is an abstract Tense head which is the locus of finiteness, to which *illa* adjoins. But now we are back to the analysis with a Tense head which can be either [+past] or [−past] (see note 28). The alternative (which is close to the traditional analysis) is to say that only in the Kannada negative clause, temporal features are clearly differentiated from the finiteness feature, and this is a peculiarity of these clauses. Affirmative clauses instantiate "tense" in the usual way, as a head with finiteness, as well as temporal features. But surely a more plausible account is that languages that allow finiteness and temporal information to reside in different heads in one type of clause do so because they consistently allow this in other clause types as well. This is the position that we have tried to defend: that what obtains in the Kannada negative clause is a principled fact, not merely of Kannada but, more generally, of the language family that Kannada belongs to.[29]

Let us now turn to the question why negative clauses in Kannada and Malayalam are superficially so different. Recall that the complement of Neg *illa* in Malayalam is the same verb form as in the affirmative, whereas the complement of Neg *illa* in Kannada is an infinitive or gerund. So robust is this fact in each of these languages that the superficially identical morpheme sequences in (57) receive very different analyses and interpretations in Malayalam and Kannada. What is understood as the negation of a "simple past tense" in Malayalam is understood as the negation of a "present perfect tense" in Kannada:

(57)   van-n(u) illa 'did not come' (Malayalam)
       come-perf. neg

       ban-d(u) illa 'has not come' (Kannada)
       come-perf. neg

In the Kannada example, there is an additional VP layer: the regular perfect verb is the complement of a verb *iru*₁ occurring as an "auxiliary." Thus *illa* in the

Kannada example is *illa*$_1$, the negative of this verb of existence, whereas in the Malayalam example it is the "pure" Neg *illa*, or *illa*$_2$:

(58) [[[[van] n(u)]$_{AspectP}$ t$_i$]$_{NegP}$ illa $_i$]$_{MoodP}$ (Malayalam)
      come perf.   neg

      [[[[[ban] d(u)]$_{AspectP}$ t$_i$]$_{VP}$ t$_i$,t$_j$]$_{NegP}$ il$_i$ -la$_j$]$_{MoodP}$ (Kannada)
      come perf.   be neg

There is an obvious difference between these two languages, and this is that Malayalam lacks agreement morphology. Now if in languages with overt agreement (e.g., Kannada), the "regular" perfect and imperfect suffixes (that occur in affirmative clauses) are generated along with agreement features, and these features need to raise to the Mood head for checking, an intervening NegP with *illa* as its head would block this movement. (The shapes of the agreement morphemes in Kannada do indeed vary with perfect and imperfect aspect, arguing for a single complex of features.) Then the "regular"-suffixed verbs could not occur with NegP. We thus predict a correlation: Dravidian languages with overt agreement will not instantiate the same verb forms in negative clauses as in affirmative clauses; negative clauses will look very different from affirmative clauses in these languages.[30]

This correlation holds for Tamil and Telugu, the other two "major" Dravidian languages, both of which have overt agreement morphology. Negative clauses in both these languages have matrix infinitives:

(59) (Tamil)
      a. Avan   viZə- r- aan.   Avan   viZən- d- aan.
         he   fall nonpast 3pmsg   he   fall past 3pmsg

         'He falls.'   'He fell.'

      b. Avan   viZ-əlle.   Avan   viZ-əlle[31]
         he   fall inf. neg   he   fall inf. neg

         'He does not / did not fall.' 'He does not / did not fall.'

(60) (Telugu)
      a. Neenu   baazaar-ku   weLL-æ-nu.
         I   bazaar-dat. go-nonfuture-agr

         'I went to the bazaar.'

      b. Neenu   baazaar-ku   weLL-a   leedu.[32]
         I   bazaar-dat. go-inf. neg

NOTES

1. Actually, the debate on finiteness in Dravidian has centered less on the determinants of finiteness in the clause than on a typological claim that the Dravidian sentence permits only a single finite predicate. (That is, only the root clause is finite; all embeddings must be nonfinite.)

This claim (first put forward by the father of Dravidian linguistics, Bishop Robert Caldwell, in his monumental work *A Comparative Grammar of the Dravidian or South-Indian Family of Languages* [1856]) is still a tenet of "Dravidianist" studies; for example, it is extensively discussed by Steever (1988), who attempts to reconcile recalcitrant data. In this chapter we shall have nothing to say about this claim; but see Jayaseelan (1991) for a critique of Steever (1988). (We note, incidentally, that the position taken here as regards the finiteness of particular Dravidian constructions—for instance, the relative clause—is different from that of Jayaseelan (1991), the difference being due to the different analysis of finiteness proposed here.)

2. Here we consider two of the four "major" Dravidian languages: Malayalam and Kannada. Much of our analysis extends to Tamil and Telugu (the other two major languages) as well. The analysis of Kannada negation outlined here was originally proposed in Amritavalli (2000).

3. The Dravidian verb has two stems: Compare *bar/ban* in the Kannada examples (1) and *var/van* in the Malayalam examples (2). The first member of each pair exemplifies what is referred to (in the literature) as the non-past stem or present tense stem, and the other exemplifies the past tense stem. See Madhavan (1983) for a discussion of this stem alternation in Malayalam. (Madhavan refers to the two stems (neutrally) as Stem 1 and Stem 2.)

Although it is convenient in a synchronic treatment of the language to speak about stem alternation, what we have treated as the "past tense stem" was historically derived through morphophonemic changes from a form that incorporated an older "past tense" suffix. Thus Kannada *ban-d-* is derived from *bar* + *-nd*, where *-nd* was the "past tense" suffix; similarly, Malayalam *van-n(u)* is derived from *var* + *-nt* (the final /u/ being just an "enunciative" vowel); see Subrahmanyam (1971: 113, 131, 133). For our purposes, what matters is only the claimed presence of a tense suffix in the forms cited, not its exact shape or "boundary."

4. The English gerund takes only genitive or accusative case (cf. 'I don't like [his/him/*he smoking cigars]', except in nominative absolute adverbial constructions such as 'he being a confirmed bachelor, . . . ' (Reuland 1983).

5. Temporal aspect can be specified for the negative gerund if desired by using a dummy verb *iru* 'to be': *bar-a-d-ee ir-uvu-du* 'be without coming' (= 'to not come'), *bar-a-d-ee id-da-ddu* 'having not come'.

Regarding the now-absent "negative conjugation" of Dravidian, we may add that the matrix verbs that were negated with the infix were apparently free with respect to the interpretation of tense. Hence the emphasis in Kittel (1908: 332) on how "the modern dialect expresses clearly" or "in a clear way" the negations of particular tenses: "Forms like *iruvadilla, baruvadilla, kaaNuvadilla, aaguvadilla*, in the modern dialect, *take the place of the simple negative to express the present tense* of the negative in a clear way;

kaLeyalilla, paDeyalilla, keeLalilla, sigalilla are used in the modern dialect *to express clearly the past tense* of the simple negative" (emphases in the original).

See Steever (1988) for an account of the evolution of negation in early Dravidian. (See Jayaseelan (1991) for a summary of Steever's account.)

6. The significance of this fact—namely, that "the truly 'bare' infinitive" cannot be substituted by a gerund—is that insofar as the dialectal facts argue for a neutralization of gerunds and infinitives into a single nonfinite category in Kannada, this neutralization is restricted to the dative case-marked context. (The first author thanks Hans Kamp for drawing her attention to the possibility of such a neutral nonfinite category.)

The point that in non-dative-marked contexts, gerunds and infinitives have different privileges of occurrence irrespective of dialect, can be illustrated both ways. While only infinitives are permitted in past negative and in passive sentences, only gerunds are permitted in noun phrase positions such as (5a, 7a–b) in the text (cf. (i)), and in *-aagi* 'as' complements to raising verbs such as 'be' (ii):

(i) Avanu   baruvudu/* baralu   aas'carya.
     he   come-ger.   come-inf.   surprise

   'His coming is a surprise.'

(ii) Avanu   baruvud-aagi/*baral-aagi   iddare   barali.
     he   come-ger.- *aagi* come-inf.- *aagi* be (cond.)   let come

   'If he is coming / is to come, let him come.'

We shall come back to the question of the commonalities between gerunds and infinitives.

7. English certainly has still other types of infinitives (besides the 'for-to' infinitive and the "bare" infinitive that we are interested in). Thus Jayaseelan (1987) argued that the complements of exceptional case marking verbs and raising verbs show "tense inheritance," which can now be understood (in the context of our analyses of gerunds and infinitives) as a claim that these complements have no inherent aspectual specification. We can leave the question of the types of infinitives in English and Kannada open.

8. Guasti (1993: 150) reiterates the facts about English bare infinitives. She notes, however, that the accusative-infinitive complement to perception verbs in Romance may have an imperfective aspect; it is in this respect like the English "acc-*ing*" construction.

9. Our account does not say why other verb forms with similar aspectual specifications are excluded from the negative clause, however. For example, since Kannada has a perfect gerund (see (15b)), why cannot *illa* [+past] select this form, instead of the infinitive? This may be related to case-marking: the perfect gerund patterns with the case-marked imperfect gerund. Both occur, for example, in clausal complements to the negative existential verb *illa*. Thus in (19b), *avanu bar-uvud-ikke illa* (starred on the present tense negative reading) has a reading 'He is not (allowed) to come.' Correspondingly, *avanu ban-d-add illa* has the reading 'it is not the case that he has (ever) come.' This last form differs (again) from the present perfect negation *ban-d-illa*: *avanu inna ban-d-illa* 'he hasn't yet come,' **avanu inna ban-d-add-illa* (no coherent reading).

We leave these details for future research, noting that the problem extends to contexts other than negation. For example, why does the Kannada passive auxiliary select a perfect infinitive instead of the "regular" perfect?

10. Pollock (1994) proposes that "the seldom recognized functional category of mood ... should be the head of a MoodP, which ... is the highest functional projection in French and Romance as well as Old, Middle and Modern English clauses."

11. Modals and Neg *illa* are in complementary distribution in Kannada. Instead of analytic "modal + *illa*" phrases, we have "negative modals," such as *baaradu, beeDa*. (In (i–ii), the modal scopes over negation; this seems to be true of all the negative modals.)

> (i) Avanu bar-al-ee   baaradu.
>   he   come-inf.-emph   must not
>
>   'He must not (under any circumstances) come.'

> (ii) Niinu bara   beeDa.
>   you come-inf. do not
>
>   'Don't come/You must not come.'

Modals can (however) cooccur with the negative infix *-a-* (in a verb that presumably stays within VP: note the dummy *iru* carrying infinitival morphology in (iii–iv). Compare note 5 and example (28d), with note 14); (in this case, too, modals scope over negation):

> (iii) Avanu bar -a-d-e   ira- bahudu.
>   he   come-neg-ger.-part.   be-inf. may
>
>   'He may not come.' (i.e., it may be the case that he does not come)

> (iv) Niinu maataaD-a-d-e   ira-baaradu.
>   you speak-neg-ger.-part.   be-inf. must not
>
>   'You mustn't not speak.'

12. We discuss the patterns of negation of these verb forms in section 4.3.

13. Thus Sridhar (1990: 41), in a discussion of noun clauses in Kannada, makes the following statement: "Tense is *not* a determinant of finiteness, since gerund clauses also show tense, though not agreement."

14. The infinitive suffix here appears on a dummy verb *iru* 'to be'. Example (28b) also has variants with the dummy verb *iru*; see note 5. What is glossed here as "particle", *-e*, has a counterpart in Malayalam also, see (32b). The nature of this particle is unclear.

15. See note 14.

16. The perfective morpheme *-ññ-* is actually derived from the proto-Dravidian perfective morpheme (traditionally analyzed as the past tense morpheme) *-nt-*; see note 3. Historically, therefore, it is the same morpheme as the "past tense" morpheme *-nu* of *van-nu*. What may superficially appear to be a "corresponding" morpheme *-tt-* in (35), is only an augment and not an aspect marker; the form *var-aa-tt-at* is in fact neutral with respect to aspectual interpretation (like the Kannada negative gerund). Example (36) also has a variant in which the aspect is carried by the "dummy" verb *iru* 'be', on the pattern of (32b).

17. See Jayaseelan (1984, 2003) for earlier analyses of this construction. In the later article, it is analyzed as a serial verb construction.

18. In Jayaseelan (1984), the conjunctive participle was called a "schwa adjunct."

This was a misanalysis, induced by the fact that the final /u/ of the past tense forms of verbs—strictly, of most verbs; there are some verbs whose past tense forms end in /i/—are reduced to a schwa in the spoken language. (The schwa was wrongly taken to be a new suffix that attached to the so-called past tense stem, to yield a participial adjunct.) But the fact that the conjunctive participle is the same as the past tense form of the verb can be easily seen in the case of verbs whose past tense forms end in /i/:

(i) a. Avan   paaTTə   paaD-i.
         he   song   sing-past

         'He sang a song.'

(i) b. Avan   paaTTə   paaD-i   naDan-nu
         he   song   sing-past walk-past

         'He went about, singing a song.'

Here, *paaD-i* is the same when it is the main verb and when it is the participle.

19. This account also irons out a wrinkle in the standard analysis that assumes a Tense projection: in (4), Neg seems to be higher than Tense (looking at the surface order). (This would be so, regardless of whether we say that *illa* takes the rest of the clause as its complement to its left, assuming a Spec-Complement-Head order for SOV languages; or that *illa* takes its complement to the right—assuming a universal Spec–Head–Complement order—with a "roll-up" type of operation.) This is a potential problem for the claim that in the universal hierarchy of functional categories, Neg must be c-commanded by Tense (Laka 1990). Under the proposed analysis, Neg will not be higher than Tense; it will only be higher than Aspect, which is in consonance with the universal hierarchy of functional categories. (In some languages Neg is actually higher than future and past tense, however; see Cinque 1999.)

20. We have used an emphasis marker -*ee* to "help" the infinitive marker to surface, since the latter tends to be elided otherwise, in both written and spoken language. Thus (41) without the emphasis marker would be realized as:

(i) Avan   var-aNDa.
     he   come-need not

     'He need not come.'

The -*uka* suffix in (41) is the bare infinitive. The -*uvaan* suffix of infinitives illustrated in (31a) and (32b) corresponds to the dative-case-marked infinitive form of Kannada and the 'for-to' infinitive of English (see Jayaseelan 1985). (As in Kannada and English, the complement of the modal in Malayalam does not allow dative case marking.)

21. Wexler (1994: 331–334) moots the possibility of an "empty dummy modal" (EDM) stage in child language acquisition. Evidence from seven languages (English, French, German, Dutch, Swedish, Danish, and Norwegian) argues for an "optional infinitive" (OI) stage, in which children allow nonfinite verbs in matrix clauses, although they distinguish the clause positions (with respect to verb movement) that finite and nonfinite verbs may appear in. One explanation, Wexler suggests, could be a pleonastic null modal auxiliary, "an empty version of the dummy modal *do* in English." (The modal has to be pleonastic because the nonfinite verbs are "used to describe real activity.")

Wexler does not pursue this proposal. However, his facts all fall into place if children start out with a MoodP instead of a TenseP: the finiteness feature in MoodP would be the "pleonastic modal" that licenses matrix infinitives. Interestingly, the OI stage in English lacks dummy *do* in negatives: that is, there is no stranded Tense. Agreement, however, *is* present in the OI grammar; this would follow if agreement is a reflex of Indicative Mood, as we have suggested.

Wexler speculates that the OI stage is preceded by a stage where "only infinitival forms are produced" (p. 329). Significantly, he briefly entertains the possibility that "the underlying cause of children's optional infinitives is optionality of T" (p. 335).

Zanuttini (1991) discusses a matrix infinitive that occurs in the negation of the "true imperative" in Italian. She reports Kayne (2000) as postulating an empty modal in this construction. (Zanuttini herself takes the infinitival morphology to be a vestigial inflection, akin to tense.)

22. *Ir-* is still used in Malayalam as a main verb to mean 'sit', as in (i). (In Kannada, *ir-* is an existential and copular verb.)

(i) Avan   irun-nu.
     he   sit-perf.

     'He sat.'

Ir- is also currently an auxiliary verb in both Malayalam and Kannada in the "compound" (progressive and perfect) tenses; compare the Kannada examples in (27) and the Malayalam example (33b). The occurrence of *ir-* as a "dummy" verb to carry stranded inflection is seen in negative gerunds marked for temporal aspect in Kannada; see note 5.

23. This can be shown by both the tests of finiteness we employ—namely, the verb's ability to take an agreement suffix (in Dravidian languages other than Malayalam), and the verb's ability to take a modal suffix (in all Dravidian languages, including Malayalam):

(i) (Kannada)
     *nenne   ban-d-   anu-(v)a   magu/*nenne   band-ira-bahud-a
     yesterday   come-perf. -3msg-rel. child/yesterday come-inf.-may-rel.
     magu
     child

     'the child who came / may have come yesterday'

(ii) (Malayalam)
     *innale   van-n(u)-aam-a   kuTTi
     yesterday   come-Asp.-may-relat.   child

     'the child who may have come yesterday'

In other words, the relative clause does not allow the Mood Phrase.

24. As expected (under the assumption that only fully lexical verbs have corresponding nonfinite participial forms), *illa₂* or the *illa* of negation has no nonfinite counterpart that can occur in a relative clause:

(i) *innale   van-n-illaa-tt-a   kuTTi-kaL
     yesterday   come-Asp-Neg-Aug-relat.   child-pl.

     'the children who did not come yesterday'

25. There is a question about the nominal morphology -ud- in *bar-uv-ud-*. Possibly there is a nominal projection (like the projection headed by -*ing* in English gerunds (Reuland 1983)) in this case.

26. The verb forms here labeled "compound tenses" have essentially the structure of "serial verbs" in Kannada and Malayalam; the label "compound tense" may be a misnomer. See the discussion in Jayaseelan (1996). We note that for the verb *iru*, the interpretation of the "nonpast" morpheme -*utt*- (and the corresponding gerundive morphology -*uvudu* in negative sentences) is restricted to future time, regardless of whether this verb occurs as the "main verb" or the "auxiliary."

27. But in a relative clause, *uNDə* 'be' + -*a* (relativizer) is realized as *uLLa*.

28. Having a morphologically expressed past tense (with the present tense an abstract element) also seems to avoid the "learning problem" noted earlier, of an abstract Tense head which can be either +past or −past.

29. The separation of finiteness from temporal information (typically marked on the category V) allows us to take at face value the Kannada "nominal" copular clause, as a verbless but finite clause instantiating agreement on the predicate nominal. Two kinds of copular sentences are extant in Kannada, with and without the verb 'be'. It is tempting to view (i) as the verbless counterpart of (ii) but there are differences in the two sentence types that argue against such a reduction (see Amritavalli 1997):

(i) Avanu   oLLey-   avanu.
     he   good   pro3p.msg

    'He is a good man.'

(ii) Avanu   oLLey-avan   -aagi   idd-aane.
     he   good pro3p.msg   *aagi* be 3pmsg

    'He is a good man.'

First, sentence (i) is negated by *alla*, a negative element that appears in noun phrases and (so-called) postpositional phrases, but not in verb phrases or in the clause; sentence (ii) is negated by *illa*.

Second, the verbless clause (i) is a finite clause. (It is introduced in embedded contexts by the regular complementizer *anta*.) The other is a small clause complement to *iru* 'be'. Notice the element *aagi*, a postpositional complementizer like English *for*. *Aagi*-clauses typically occur in "object complement" constructions and with "raising verbs" such as *kaaN*- 'seem,' *tiLi*- 'know, think' (Amritavalli 1977: 48).

30. We are indebted to Guglielmo Cinque for suggesting this analysis to us.

31. The Tamil negative clause appears not to preserve temporal information.

32. The Telugu data are from Hariprasad (1989: 58). Hariprasad describes the tense system of Telugu as [+future] or [−future]. The nonfuture tense is negated by a matrix infinitive followed by a neg element (in an invariant third person neuter form) The future tense is negated by the infix -*a*- in the place of the tense morpheme, followed by agreement suffixes, reminiscent of the erstwhile "negative conjugation" of Dravidian (see note 5)

REFERENCES

Akmajian, Adrian (1977) "The Complement Structure of Perception Verbs in an Auton-omous Syntax Framework," in Peter Culicover, Thomas Wasow, and Adrian Akma-jian (eds.) *Formal Syntax*. Academic Press, New York, 427–460.

Amritavalli, R. (1977) "Negation in Kannada." M.A. thesis. Simon Fraser University, Burnaby.

Amritavalli, R. (1997) "Copular Sentences in Kannada." Paper presented at the seminar on Null elements, Delhi University.

Amritavalli, R. (2000) "Kannada Clause Structure," in Rajendra Singh (ed.) *Yearbook of South Asian Languages and Linguistics*. Sage India, New Delhi, 11–30.

Cinque, Guglielmo (1999) *Adverbs and Functional Heads: A Cross-Linguistic Perspective*. Oxford University Press, New York.

Comrie, Bernard (1977) *Aspect*. Cambridge University Press, Cambridge.

Emonds, Joseph (1972) "A Reformulation of Certain Syntactic Transformations," in Stanley Peters (ed.) *Goals of Linguistic Theory*. Prentice-Hall, Englewood Cliffs, NJ.

Guasti, Maria Teresa (1993) *Causative and Perception Verbs: A Comparative Study*. Rosen-berg and Sellier, Turin.

Hany-Babu, M. T. (1996) "The Structure of Malayalam Sentential Negation." *Interna-tional Journal of Dravidian Linguistics* 25: 1–15.

Hany-Babu, M. T. (1997) "The Syntax of Functional Categories." Ph.D. diss., Central In-stitute of English and Foreign Languages, Hyderabad, India.

Hariprasad, M. (1989) "Negation in Telugu and English." M.Litt. diss., Central Institute of English and Foreign Languages, Hyderabad, India.

Jayaseelan, K. A. (1984) "Control in Some Sentential Adjuncts of Malayalam." *Proceed-ings of the Berkeley Linguistic Society* 10: 623–633.

Jayaseelan, K. A. (1985) "Infinitivals in Malayalam: Some Preliminary Observations." *CIEFL Working Papers in Linguistics* 2:247–258.

Jayaseelan, K. A. (1987) "Remarks on *for-to* Complements." *CIEFL Working Papers in Linguistics* 4:19–35.

Jayaseelan, K. A. (1991) "Review of Sanford B. Steever, *The Serial Verb Formation in the Dravidian Languages*." *Linguistics* 29: 543–549.

Jayaseelan, K. A. (2003) "The Serial Verb Construction in Malayalam," in Veneeta Dayal and Anoop Mahajan (eds.) *Clause Structure in South Asian Languages*. Dordrecht, Kluwer Academic Publishers, 2003, 67–91.

Kayne, Richard S. (2000) "Italian Negative Infinitival Imperatives and Clitic Climbing," in Richard S. Kayne *Parameters and Universals*. Oxford University Press, New York, 2000, 98–106.

Kittel, F. (1908 [1982]) *A Grammar of the Kannada Language*. Asian Educational Services, New Delhi.

Laka, Imtiaz M. (1990) "Negation in Syntax: On the Nature of Functional Categories and Projections." Ph.D. diss., MIT, Cambridge, Mass.

Madhavan, P. (1983) "Word Formation and the Lexicon in English and Malayalam." M.Litt. diss., Central Institute of English and Foreign Languages, Hyderabad, India.

Pollock, Jean-Yves (1994) "Notes on Clause structure." Unpublished ms., Universite de Picardie, Amiens.

Reuland, Eric (1983) "Governing -*ing*." *Linguistic Inquiry* 4: 101–136.

Shlonsky, Ur (1997) *Clause Structure and Word Order in Hebrew and Arabic: An Essay in Comparative Semitic Syntax.* Oxford University Press, New York.

Sridhar, S. N. (1990) *Kannada.* Routledge, London.

Steever, Sanford B. (1988) *The Serial Verb Formation in the Dravidian Languages.* Motilal Banarsidass, Delhi.

Stowell, Tim. (1982) "The Tense of Infinitives." *Linguistic Inquiry* 13:561–570.

Subrahmanyam, P. S. (1971) *Dravidian Verb Morphology: A Comparative Study.* Annamalai University, Annamalainagar.

Wexler, Ken (1994) "Finiteness and Head Movement in Early Child Grammars," in David Lightfoot and Norbert Hornstein (eds.) *Verb Movement.* Cambridge University Press, Cambridge, 305–350.

Zanuttini, Raffaella (1991) "Syntactic Properties of Sentential Negation: A Comparative Study of Romance Languages." Ph.D. diss., University of Pennsylvania.

CHAPTER 6

ON SOME DESCRIPTIVE GENERALIZATIONS IN ROMANCE

PAOLA BENINCÀ AND
CECILIA POLETTO

1 INTRODUCTION

In this work we present a number of cross-linguistic descriptive generalizations concerning Romance languages and point out their theoretical relevance for syntactic theory. We make extensive use of dialectal variation, viewing it as a way to shed light on diachronic processes on the one side and on the complexity of syntactic structure on the other.

We restrict the empirical domain, considering in general only some areas of Romance languages and Italian dialects. The linguistic domain that we take into consideration includes three distinct areas of syntactic processes: *wh*-items and questions in general, personal pronouns, and negation. The choice of the grammatical topics is due to both practical and theoretical reasons, as these three domains have been—and still are—central to the development of syntactic theory and have been systematically explored during fieldwork in the last ten years. The geographical area we have chosen is the one whose microvariation has been more extensively investigated, both with respect to modern and preceding stages (going back to the thirteenth century).

The aim of this chapter is not to provide new analyses for a single phenomenon but to show how cross-linguistic variation can direct our research toward a precise path and thereby narrow down the number of possible analyses of a given phenomenon. In what follows, descriptive generalizations are formulated in their strongest form, but this does not mean that we are particularly sure that they cannot be falsified if the domain of languages studied is widened. We think that a generalization has an empirical side, which has the function of a challenge: it provokes further, more detailed, observations and possibly more accurate description. Even if a generalization ends up being falsified, we will have increased our empirical basis and, more generally, our knowledge of how languages work.

In section 2 we examine the pattern of clitic *wh*-elements and illustrate some empirical generalizations that are valid both diachronically and cross-linguistically; in section 3 we do the same with respect to the emergence of pronominal clitics.[1] A comparison between the two evolutionary patterns is presented in section 4, where we isolate some properties common to both *wh*-items and pronouns. In section 5, we present and discuss some empirical generalizations that lead us to analyze *wh*-in situ and *wh*-doubling in Romance as closely related phenomena. Section 6 illustrates the factors that influence the cliticization process of a preverbal negation marker—namely, modality and verb movement. Section 7 deals with the common properties of cliticization phenomena. Although the factors favoring cliticization are different for the various classes of elements (*wh*-items, pronouns, and negative markers) that undergo the process, it appears that the pattern of cliticization is essentially the same wherever it is manifested. The clitic elements appear in positions where the strong counterpart used to move to; this can either be hypothesized or attested for past stages of a language or directly observed in the present, in closely related dialects or inside the same one as an option with slightly different interpretations.

2 THE CP LAYER AND *WH*-CLITICS

We first consider a number of cross-linguistic descriptive generalizations concerning the CP layer and precisely the different forms and behavior of *wh*-items. It has been argued that some *wh*-items display clitic-like properties in Romance (cf., among others, Bouchard and Hirschbühler 1986, Obenauer 1994, Friedemann 1997, Munaro 1997, and Poletto 2000). A closer examination of cross-linguistic patterns of the elements that can or cannot be clitics reveals an interesting picture of the relations between the morphological makeup of *wh*-elements and their syntactic properties.

We adopt here a pretheoretical, though precise, notion of clitic as an element that has a strong counterpart; contrary to its strong opponent, it has severe limitations on its distribution and, in general, can only occur in a fixed position inside the clausal structure. This definition excludes from our investigation all functional heads that indeed have a fixed position in the clause but do not have a strong counterpart.

Using the tests first formulated by Kayne (1975) for pronouns, we notice that some *wh*-items more easily than others develop cross-linguistically and diachronically a clitic/tonic pair; moreover, some other *wh*-elements never undergo a process of this kind. The facts can be illustrated by means of cross-linguistic descriptive generalizations expressed in the form of implications. Among the *wh*-items that can display clitic properties in Romance languages, we observe the following:

(1)   a. If only one *wh-* behaves like a clitic, it is either *what* or *where*.[2]

      b. Elements like *who* and *how* can also display clitic-like properties, but this is less frequently the case; moreover, the presence of clitic/tonic pairs for *who* and *how* in a language implies that both *where* and *what* also behave as such.

      c. The *wh*-element corresponding to *why* never behaves as a clitic and is always expressed by a compound.

In what follows, we illustrate each generalization with examples of various languages.

2.1 The *wh*-Item *What*

Consider (1a): it expresses the fact that there are languages that display a single clitic/strong opposition only for the *wh*-item 'what' or 'where' but not for other *wh*-items (1a), and there are languages that have a clitic/strong opposition for both of them; to our knowledge there is no language that displays a clitic form for either 'how' or 'who' without also displaying a clitic form for both 'what' and 'where' (cf. (1b)). The same seems to be true from the diachronic point of view: the first elements displaying the clitic/strong opposition can be either 'what' or 'where', while the *wh*-items corresponding to 'who' and 'how' can only become clitics if 'what' and 'where' already are such.

Languages like French only have a morphologically distinct clitic form for 'what'—namely, *que*. The analysis of *que* as a clitic element to explain its distributional properties has a long tradition in the studies on French syntax (we only mention here, among others, Bouchard and Hirschbühler 1986).

It is well known that *que* cannot be coordinated, modified, used in isolation, or stressed and can only occur adjacent to the inflected verb; its strong opponent, *quoi*, is restricted to the in situ position, and in embedded inflected interrogatives the form substituting *que* is *ce que*:

(2)   a. *Que ou qui a-t-il vu?
          what or who has he seen
          'What or who did he see?'

      b. *Que d'interessant a-t-il dit?[3]
          what interesting has he said
          'Did he say anything interesting?'

      c. *Que?
          What?

      d. Que fais-tu?
          what do-you
          'What are you doing?'

      e. Qu'a fait Jean?
          what has done Jean
          'What has John done?'

      f. *Que il fait?
          what he does
          'What is he doing?'

      g. *Il a fait que?
          he has done what
          'What has he done?'

      h. Je ne sais pas *(ce) qu'il a fait.[4]
          I not know not (what) that he has done
          'I do not know what he did.'

A clitic/strong opposition concerning *what* seems to be present also in the standard Italian spoken in Central Italy, using both *che* and *cosa*: *che* is restricted the way *que* is in French, while *cosa* is a full form that can occur in main and embedded interrogatives and can be used in isolation, coordinated, modified, and stressed (see Poletto and Pollock 2004 for a detailed presentation of the various classes of Italian speakers). The same type of partition between a clitic and a strong form has been proposed by Ambar et al. (1998) for Portuguese *que* and *o que, que* being the clitic form.[5]

2.2 The Clitic Element *Where*

Further comparison with other languages and dialects strengthens the earlier generalizations: in the dialect spoken in S. Michele al Tagliamento (in the Italian region Friuli), two distinct forms can be used for the *wh*-item 'where' (*do* and *dulà*). One of them (*do*) displays clitic properties:

(3) a. *Do e quant (a) van-u? (S. Michele al T.)
          where and when (*cl*) go.they
          'Where and when do they go?'

     b. Dulà?/ *Do?
          where
          'Where?'

     c. Di dulà / *di do al ven-ja?
          from where he comes he
          'Where does he come from?'

     d. I so-tu zut dulà? / *I so-tu zut do?
          cl are.you gone where
          'Where have you gone?'

(4) a. *Do a van-u?
          where *cl* go.they
          'Where are they going?'

     b. Dulà a van-u?
          where *cl* go.they
          'Where are they going?'

(5) a. A mi an domandat dulà ch al era zut.
          cl to-me have asked where that he was gone
          'They asked me where he had gone.'

b. *A mi an domandat do ch al era zut.

    cl to-me have asked where that he was gone

    'They asked me where he had gone.'

Examples (3) to (5) exemplify the characteristics that we consider in order to attribute the locative *wh*-item *do* the status of clitic element. The clitic *wh*-item *do* 'where' cannot be coordinated, used in isolation, modified, or stressed (cf. (3)). Moreover, it has to occur close to the verb (just like French *que*; cf. (4)) and does not occur in embedded clauses, where *wh*-items have to be followed by a complementizer (cf. (5)). None of these restrictions is found with the full form *dulà* or with the element *sé* corresponding to 'what'. In this dialect the *wh*-item *sé* 'what' has just one form, the strong one: this *wh*- behaves like the strong *dulà* and has none of the restrictions met by the clitic form *do*.

Other languages have a wider set of clitic *wh*-items. In the dialect of Pera di Fassa the *wh*-item *co* 'how' patterns with *che* 'what' and contrasts with *can* 'when' in requiring strict adjacency to the inflected verb:

(6)   a. Can vas-to pa? (Pera di Fassa)

       when go.you *particle*?

       'When are you leaving?'

    b. Can pa tu vas?

       when *particle* you go

(7)   a. Co l fas-to pa?

       how it do.you *particle*

       'How do you do it?'

    b. *Co pa tu l fas?

       how *particle* you it do

(8)   a. Che compres-to pa?

       what buy.you *particle*

       'What are you buying?'

    b. *Che pa tu compre?[6]

       what *particle* you buy?

The last generalization concerns the *wh*-item corresponding to 'why': to our knowledge, there are no languages that have a clitic form for 'why', even if in several dialects the morphological makeup of the form is different from the typical Romance pattern formed by the preposition corresponding to 'for' and the item corresponding to 'what', as French *pourquoi*, Italian *perché*, Spanish *porqué*, and

Paduan *parcossa*. Some Rhaeto-Romance dialects have the form *ciuldì*, which can be decomposed in *what-wants-say*—namely, 'What does it mean?' Although this form is nowadays perceived as a single item, it has developed no clitic counterpart; moreover, a survey of the AIS (1928–1940) data (showing that there are no Italian dialects that have developed a noncompound form for the *wh*-item corresponding to 'why') further strengthens our claim.

The descriptive generalizations in (1) point toward an implicational scale that has interesting similarities with the one of object clitics, as we show in the next paragraph.

3 IMPLICATIONS IN THE EMERGENCE OF PRONOMINAL CLITICS

In this section we present and illustrate with examples some descriptive generalizations concerning the presence of clitic forms in the pronominal paradigm across languages. The implications that will emerge suggest hypotheses concerning the diachronic stages of cliticization processes in Romance. The descriptive generalizations we formulate in (9) are obviously to be limited to nominal elements in the Romance languages; first, it is well known that in other languages the set of clitic elements is much wider than in Romance. Slavic languages, for instance, also have clitic auxiliaries: Rivero (1994) and Alexiadou (1995) analyze some adverbial forms as clitics in Greek. At present we cannot make statements concerning the relation between these different areas in which cliticization processes are found. Moreover, even in Romance some adverbials are weak elements in the sense of Cardinaletti and Starke (1999), and negative markers can also undergo the process of cliticization (as we illustrate later). Thus, what the generalizations in (9) describe is not a general prohibition against having clitic adverbials, which is immediately falsified by other language groups and by Romance languages, but a diachronic and cross-linguistic implicational scale concerning nominals, which goes from the direct object to nonselected items.[7] This suggests that clitic pronouns represent the functional part of DP and, as such, have to do with its case or argumental status.[8] With these provisos, we expect that the weaker implication (that nonselected elements can be clitics only if arguments are[9]) to be correct even outside the domain of Romance languages:[10]

(9) a. If a Romance language has clitics, it has direct object clitics.

   a'. If a Romance language has dative clitics, it has direct object clitics.

b. If a Romance language has partitive or locative clitics, it has dative clitics.

c. If a Romance language has subject clitics, it also has direct and indirect object clitics.

d. There is no implication between locative/partitive and subject clitics.

e. Adverbial clitic forms for elements that are never selected by a verb are much rarer and imply the presence of argument clitics.

It is common opinion that all Romance languages have clitics, but there exist a few that do not have any. Although this fact of Romance languages that do not have a clitic system at all can be surprising at first, the data are quite clear in this respect: see in Gartner (1910: 88ff) samples of compared translations of the parable of the Prodigal Son, and see a description in Haiman and Benincà (1992: 126). The AIS data show that the Rhaeto-Romance dialects of Brigels and Camischollas (in the Grisons region) have only tonic pronouns. The data reported here (from AIS VI 1110; VIII 1597, 1650, 1651, 1667) are the counterpart of standard Italian sentences with clitics (and not with tonic pronouns), as the Italian translations (10a'–d') show:

(10) a. Ša ti vol *al*.
          if you want it

     a'. Se *lo* vuoi.
          if it.you-want

      b. Vus amflayas bec *el*.
          you find not it

     b'. Non *lo* trovate.
          not it.you-find
          'You do not find it.'

      c. Yu amfla netur *el*.
          I find nowhere it

     c'. Non *lo* trovo in nessun posto.
          not it.I-find in no place
          'I cannot find it anywhere.'

      d. I an caciau giodor *el*.
          they have chased away him

d'. *Lo* hanno cacciato.
   him.they-have chased-away
   'They chased him away.'

As example (10a) shows, the object pronoun occurs at the right of the verb. Examples (10b–d) show that the pronoun is not in enclitic position, as it can perfectly well be separated from the verb by the postverbal negative morpheme or by other elements. These dialects do not have any other dative, locative or partitive clitic, either proclitic or enclitic (the examples are from AIS VI 1110, 1113; VII 1345; VIII 1638, 1659):[11]

(11)   a.   Gi *kuai ad el.*
            tell that to him

       a'. Di*glielo.*
            tell.to-him it

       b.   Dai *e a nus.*
            give of-it to us

       b'. Da*ccene.*
            give.to-us.of-it

       c.   k eu mondi
            that I go (there)

       c'. che *ci* vada
            that there.I-go

       d.   Koy figesas *kun el*?
            what would-you-do with it
            'What do you do with it?'

       d.' Cosa *ne* fareste?
            what with-it.you-would-do[12]

This peculiar area of Romance can provide further, more detailed, evidence in favor of our generalization, because other dialects only have direct object clitics (cf. (12a)) but no dative, locative, or partitive clitics (12b,c), a system of this type is not attested elsewhere in the Romance family. The dialects exemplified here are those of Ardez and Remüs (AIS VI 1110; VIII 1638, 1659):

(12)   a.   Se tu *il* vos.
            if you it.want

a'. Se *lo* vuoi.

b. Di *ad el*.
   tell to him

b.' Di*gli*.
   tell.him

c. k e ia
   that I go (there)

c'. che io *ci* vada
   that I there go

d. T∫e fessat cun el?
   what do-you-do with it

d'. Cosa *ne* farete?
   what with-it.you-will-do

As for the other arguments, there are no Romance languages that have partitive clitics but do not have dative clitics, while there exist languages that have dative clitics but no partitive or locative (for instance, Spanish or Friulian; cf. Chomsky 1981)—hence, the implication in (9b):

(13)   a. Gli parlo.
         to-him.I-talk
         'I talk to him'

       b. Ne voglio una.
         of-it.I-want one
         'I want one.'

       c. Ci.vado.
         there I-go
         'I go there.'

We have not found other implicational relations concerning the presence of locative and partitive clitics and subject clitics, as there are languages that have subject clitics but no locative or partitive, like some Friulian dialects, and there are languages like standard Italian (see 14 b', c') that have locative and partitive clitics but no subject clitics:

(14)　a. Toni al ven. (Friulian)
　　　　　Toni he comes

　　　　　'Toni is coming.'

　　　　b. Toni al è.
　　　　　Toni he is

　　　　　'Toni is there.'

　　　　b' Toni c'è.
　　　　　'Toni there.is

　　　　c. Toni al compre doi.
　　　　　Toni he buys two

　　　　c'. Toni *ne* compra due.
　　　　　Toni of-those.buys two

　　　　　'Toni buys two of those.'

Looking for an implication between locative and partitive clitics we have noticed that, for example, some Friulian dialects have a partitive, which appears in limited contexts, and no locative, while Spanish has no partitive clitic but preserves traces of the locative *y* "there" (15d):

(15)　a. Nd ai vjodut nome doi. (Friulian, Clauzetto)
　　　　　of-them I-have seen only two

　　　　b. O viodi nome doi
　　　　　I see only two

　　　　c. Juan ha ido (allì). (Spanish)
　　　　　Juan has gone (there)

　　　　d. Hay un muchacho.
　　　　　has.there a boy

　　　　　'There is a boy'

However, the evidence provided by the latter case is not very strong, as it can be just a lexicalized relic. Scrutinizing the ASIS data from over 140 NIDs, Penello (1993) has found no dialect with a locative and no partitive clitic; there are, on the contrary, various dialects from different places that have a partitive and no locative clitic. The marginality of the implication might be tied to the fact that originally the partitive clitic *ne* is also a locative indicating movement out of a place, so that we can suppose that both locative arguments tend to develop together into clitic elements[13]. Another argument in favor of the idea that the emergence of clitics is tied to case and that direct objects and indirect objects are the first elements developing a clitic series comes from clitic clusters, which interestingly behave in some languages as compounds belonging to a complex but unique syntactic object. Benincà (1988) noted that, although standard Italian is not in general a language that permits doubling of a dative DP, when the dative clitic is combined with a direct object, clitic doubling of the dative becomes possible, as if the dative clitic (differently from the object clitic) were not "visible" anymore, in some respects:[14]

(16)   a. *Gli regalo a Mario il mio violino.
           to-him.I-give to Mario the my violin
           'I give Mario my violin.'

        b. Glielo regalo a Mario.
           to-him.it.I-give to Mario
           'I give this to Mario.'

        c. *Glielo regalo a Mario il violino.
           to-him.it.I-give to Mario the violin
           'I give Mario my violin.'

Locative and partitive clitics also cluster, giving rise to a compound. The following data exemplify the few cases of its functions in Italian and some Veneto dialects:

(17)   a. Ce ne sono due. (Italian)
           *loc.part.*are two
           'There are two of them.'

        b. Ci sono due ragazzi.
           *loc.*are two boys

        c. (Di ragazzi) ce n'è due.[15]
           (of boys) *loc part* is two
           'There are two (boys).'

        d. *C'è due ragazzi.[16]
           *loc.*is two boys

        e. Ghe ne zé do.(Venetian)
           *loc.part.*are two

        f. Ghe ne compro do.
           *loc.part.*I-buy two
           'I will buy two of them.'

   g. Te (*ghe) ne compro do.
      to-you.(*loc*).*part*.I-buy two

      'I will buy two of those for you.'

   h. Ghi *(n')è un tozo. (Coneglianese)
      loc.(part).is a boy

      'There is a boy.'

   i. Ngègghi na fiola. (Borgomanerese)
      loc.part.is.*loc* a girl

      'There is a girl.'

In Italian a locative + partitive cluster *ce ne* is properly connected with a locative and a partitive argument, but the cluster has more features than the sum of its components, as the agreement facts in (17b–d) show. The cluster appears to optionally perform as a subject clitic, triggering agreement. In Veneto dialects the cluster obligatorily appears when the partitive is selected, but the locative disappears if a dative clitic is required (17e–g). In other dialects, such as Coneglianese (17h), the existential construction with the locative element *ghi* requires also the realization of a partitive clitic *n*. In the dialect of Borgomanero studied in Tortora (1997), this type of locative + partitive cluster surfaces only with unaccusative verbs that have a locative argument. All these cases may suggest that within the positions of clitic elements located in the high portion of the IP layer we have to identify some clitic clusters that are activated together in the sense that the occurrence of one element of the cluster implies the presence of the other element. This seems to be true for third-person dative and accusative object clitics, and for locative and partitive. We have not found any cluster formed by three elements.

4 A Comparison Between Pronominal and *WH*-Clitics

The comparison between the descriptive generalizations concerning *wh*-items and pronouns leads us to observe the following parallels.[17]

(18)   a. In both cases, the first elements that give rise to a clitic/strong opposition are those that can be internal[18] arguments.[19]

b. In both cases, the clitic corresponding to the external argument is less frequent and implies the presence of direct and indirect object clitics.

c. Nonargumental clitic forms are rare and imply the presence of argumental clitics.

Concerning (18a), the factors ruling the emergence of a *wh*-clitic element are two. The first factor is connected to the number of semantic features expressed by the *wh*-. Elements like *what* become clitics before elements like *who*, although both can be objects. This leads us to think that inanimacy also plays a role. An example of object *wh*-clitic is the case of French *que*, studied (among others) by Obenauer (1976, 1994). He proposes to connect the special status of *que* to the poverty of semantic features that characterize it. He starts from the assumption that the unmarked value of the feature [± animate] is [−animate], which corresponds to the morphological realization of the item *que*. Therefore, in his account the inanimate object is the "least marked" element in the *wh*- series; this poverty is syntactically encoded as nonexpansion of the internal structure of the *wh*-item itself, which is a head and behaves as a clitic. The second factor is the grammatical function of the element: it appears evident that the fact that *que* is a direct object also plays a role in its evolution as a clitic. In modern French, *que* cannot be a subject, as the following contrast illustrates:

(19)   a. *Que s'est passé?
            what itself.is happened
            'What happened?'

       b. Que s'est-il passé?
           what itself.is.it happened?

Sentence (19a), in which *que* is the subject of the unaccusative verb, is ungrammatical. On the contrary, (19b), where a subject clitic appears in enclisis to the inflected verb, is possible. The presence of a subject clitic was not necessary at earlier stages of French, when the language was pro drop; a sentence like (19a) was then possible. However, *que* did not have the typical clitic behavior it displays in modern French, as it was not restricted to main clauses and could be stressed, modified, and found in isolation (cf. Pollock 2001).

These data show that another factor playing a role in the change has to do with the object nature of *que*. In other words, it seems that when *que* becomes a clitic it is always interpreted as a direct object (cf. (19)): the "prototypical selected element" is the direct object, which is in fact the one which displays clitic properties with the highest frequency.

As for why there is such an implicational scale inside the arguments of the verb and why adverbial clitics are much rarer, we cannot put forth at this point a detailed proposal but can only sketch a possible line of research. The correlations in (18) can be seen as indicating that the development of a given element as a clitic is sensitive to a well-defined hierarchy, which is ultimately connected to the way thematic roles are encoded in the syntax. It seems that those elements connected to case (in the sense of Kayne 2001, where prepositions are an instance of case) more often develop clitic forms than those that are not. We will not develop this intuition any further, as it lies beyond the scope of this chapter, which is simply to show how a wide empirical basis can drastically reduce the number of potential explanations for a given phenomenon. We limit ourselves to point out that semantic factors, through the filter of their syntactic realization possibly as case, are at work in the development of clitic forms.

As for why clitic forms emerge, many authors have put forth their analyses, which can be summed up into roughly three major lines of thought: the first and more traditional view is that the origin of clitics is due to a progressive phonological reduction of the pronouns, which at a second stage induces the well-known syntactic phenomena typical of clitics. This approach does not provide any explanation of the process. Another view sees a syntactic process pruning some functional projections internal to the DP—ultimately due to a minimal effort strategy—as the triggering factor for clitic-formation (cf. Halpern 1995, Barbosa 1996, etc.). A third view (Jelinek 1996) conceives cliticization as the answer to a semantic problem concerning the interpretation of nonexistential variables.

In section 7 we claim that a conspiracy of phonological, syntactic, and semantic factors leads to the emergence of clitics in a language. This is in agreement with the new view on the phenomenon put forth by Cardinaletti and Starke (1999), who consider also semantic factors to be essential to the process of weakening, which only at a second stage of evolution becomes syntactically and phonologically relevant.

5 *WH*-DOUBLING AND *WH*-IN SITU

Another interesting phenomenon connected to the clitic status of *wh*-items is the one of *wh*-in situ[20] and *wh*-doubling found in the NIDs: the following generalizations illustrate the connection between the appearance of clitics in the *wh*-paradigm and the possibility of *wh*-in situ on one side and the connection between *wh*-in situ and *wh*-doubling (already noted by Munaro 1997) on the other:

(20) a. If *wh*-in situ is found with a single *wh*-item, this *wh*-item corresponds to 'what.'

   a'. If *wh*-doubling is found with a single *wh*-item, this *wh*-item corresponds to 'what'.

   b. If a language allows *wh*-in situ cooccurring with subject clitic inversion (SCLI), the only *wh*-items that can be left in situ are those that can become clitics.[21]

   b'. If a language allows *wh*-doubling cooccurring with SCLI, the only *wh*-items that can be left in situ are those that can become clitics.

   c. If a language allows a *wh*-in situ strategy, this is applied to *wh*-phrases only if it applies to *wh*-words.

   c'. If a language allows a *wh*-doubling strategy, this is applied to *wh*-phrases only if it applies to *wh*-words.

   d. *Wh*-doubling in embedded interrogatives is possible only when the complementizer is not lexicalized.

The first generalization can be illustrated by data reported in Tortora (1997: 7). In Borgomanerese—which has two forms (*kus* and *kwe*) for 'what'—only *kwe* can be left in situ; all other *wh*-items cannot:

(21) a. Kus tal ʃerki? (Borgomanerese)
       what you look-for
       'What are you looking for?'

   a'. *Tal ʃerki kus?
       you look-for what

   b. Tal ʃerki kwe?
       you look-for what

   b'. *Kwe tal ʃerki?
       what you look-for

The same is true of doubling cases for older stages of the Veneto dialects spoken in Belluno and Illasi (Verona). Munaro (1999) notes that the first element displaying the doubling structure is precisely 'what', as in the following example (from Munaro 1999: 2.28):

(22) Ché olè-u che epia metù ché? (Bellunese)
       what want.you that I-have put what

In the dialect of Illasi the older generation (older than 60) only admits doubling with the *wh*-item *sa* 'what', while younger speakers admit doubling with 'what', 'where', and 'who':[22]

(23)   S a-lo fato ché? (Illasi)
        what has.he done what
        'What did he do?'

(24)   a. %Ndo va-lo andóe?
           where goes.he where
           'Where is he going?'

        b. %Ci e-to visto ci?
           who have.you seen who
           'Whom did you see?'

The generalization in (20b) can be illustrated on the basis of Bellunese data, reported from Munaro (1997, 1999). In modern Bellunese the class of *wh*-items that occur obligatorily *in situ* are precisely those that display clitic properties cross-linguistically:

(25)   a. *Ché a-tu fat? (Tignes d'Alpago; Munaro 1997: 3.62)
           what have.you done
           'What have you done?'

        b. A-tu fat ché?
           have.you done what

(26)   a. *Chi laore-lo?
           who works.he
           'Who is working?'

        b. E-lo chi che laora?
           is.he who that works?

(27)   a. Va-lo andè?
           goes.he where
           'Where is he going?'

        b. ??Andè va-lo?
           where goes.he

(28)   a. Se ciame-lo comè?
           himself.calls.he how
           'What is his name?'

       b. ??Come se ciame-lo?
           how himself calls.he

(29)   a. In che botega a-tu comprà sta borsa?
           in which shop have.you bought this bag
           'In which shop did you buy this bag?'

       b. *A-tu comprà sta borsa in che botega?
           have.you bought this bag in which shop

All *wh*-phrases are excluded from the in situ position, but the crucial datum showing that the distinction is not the one between *wh*-phrases and *wh*-words is the following:

(30)   a. Parché sié-o vegnesti incói?
           why are.you come today
           'Why did you come today?'

       b. *Sié-o vegnesti incói parché?
           are.you come today why

Hence, the property cutting across elements that can be left in situ and elements that cannot is the same that underlies the process of clitic-formation. Moreover, it seems to underlie also the process of clitic doubling, as the second generalization suggests. *Wh*-doubling is limited to the *wh*-items that have clitic forms: in the dialect of Monno (cf. Munaro 1999), only the *wh*-items corresponding to 'what', 'where', and 'who' can be doubled:

(31)   a. Ché fè-t majà què?
           what do.you eat what
           'What are you eating?'

       b. Ch'è-l chi che vè al to post?
           what is.it who that goes to the your place
           'Who is going in your place?'

       c. Ngo è-l ndat ngont?
           where is.he gone where
           'Where has he gone?'

This is parallel to the behavior of pronominal clitics, which only display doubling when one of the two elements is a clitic. We analyze this property in section 7.

The generalizations in (20c) and (20c′) express the empirical observation that, to our knowledge, there is no variety of Romance that admits *wh*-in situ or *wh*-doubling with *wh*-phrases without admitting it with the subset of *wh*-words that can display clitic properties. The generalization in (20d) can be illustrated with data of the dialects of Illasi, Monno, and Bellunese, where *wh*-doubling in embedded clauses is marginally possible only when the complementizer is not present; the following Bellunese data provide an insight of what the relation between doubling and cliticization of *wh*-items could be:

(32) a. I m à domandà cossa ho fato stamatina. (Bellunese)
          they to-me asked what I-have done this morning
          'They asked me what I did this morning'

      b. I m à domandà cossa che ho fato stamatina.
          they to-me asked what that I-have done this morning

      c. I m à domandà sa ho fato stamatina.
          they to-me asked what I-have done this morning

      d. *I m à domandà sa che ho fato stamatina.
          they to-me asked what that I-have this morning

      e. ?I m à domandà sa ho fato ché stamatina.
          they to-me asked what I-have done what this morning

      f. À-lo fato ché stamatina?
          has.he done what this morning
          'What did he do this morning?'

      g. *Cossa à-lo fato ché stamatina?
          what has.he done what this morning

In this dialect there are two possible elements for 'what', and they occur to the left of the clause: *sa* and *cossa*. *Cossa* can occur either with or without a lexical complementizer, as shown in (32a) and (32b). On the contrary, *sa* can occur only when no complementizer is present (cf. the ungrammaticality of (32d)). Doubling is only possible with *sa* and not with *cossa* (cf. the contrast between (23) and (32g)), both in main and in embedded clauses. In other words, the form that tolerates doubling is the same that does not tolerate a complementizer; hence, the form occurring in the highest position in the CP when doubling occurs is precisely a clitic. In turn, this shows that the generalization in (20d) concerning the un-grammaticality of clitic doubling in embedded contexts when a complementizer is present has to be derived from the fact that clitic *wh*-items cannot cooccur with a lexical complementizer, contrary to non-clitic *wh*-items. Whatever the explanation for this turns out to be, (20d) depends on (33):

(33)   Clitic *wh*-items are not compatible with a complementizer.[23]

We do not try to propose an analysis for (33) but notice that there is a striking parallel between the pattern of emergence of *wh*-in situ and the pattern of emer-gence of *wh*-doubling: the generalizations (20a–a') to (20c–c') suggest that both diachronically and cross-linguistically the development of *wh*-in situ and *wh*-doubling follow the same path that is typical of the emergence of a clitic pattern: the first element is the inanimate direct object, followed by other arguments; only at the last stage (represented by languages like spoken French and some Western Lombard dialects) *wh*-in situ is generalized to all elements, including complex phrases.

The fact that *wh*-in situ is tied to *wh*-doubling on one side and to the emer-gence of *wh*-clitics on the other has to be taken into account in any theory aiming to explain the *wh*-in situ phenomenon in general and its variational and dia-chronic pattern.

The preceding descriptive generalizations clearly point to a direction that excludes analyses of *wh*-in situ which do not encode any relation between the phenomenon and the emergence of a clitic series for at least some *wh*s. This immediately excludes analyses as the one usually found in the literature for lan-guages like French which views *wh*-in situ structures as "pure IPs" where the *wh*-item is left in its argumental position and moves to SpecC only at LF or is not moved at all and the sequence is interpreted as an interrogative by pragmatic strategies.

It also excludes more refined analyses as the one proposed by Cheng and Rooryck (2000), where the *wh*-in situ strategy is attributed to the presence of an intonational morpheme in C° realized on the lowest element of the clause, namely the *wh*-item itself.

The only set of solutions compatible with the descriptive generalizations here is the one that takes into account the link between *wh*-clitics and *wh*-in situ structures, which might lead us to postulate that in the languages that only have *wh*-in situ but not *wh*-doubling there is a "null doublet" occupying the same position the overt clitic fills in doubling structures.

6 NEGATION AND THE CLITIC PATTERN

An apparent counterexample to the idea that clitics correspond to elements that can be arguments is negation, which is an adverbial element and nevertheless has apparently developed a clitic status in many Romance languages (cf. Pollock's 1989 proposal for French *ne* and Belletti's 1990 proposal for Italian *non*). Before taking into account the pattern of cliticization of the negative marker in Romance and discussing the properties it shares with the development of *wh*-clitics, we provide a brief sketch of the distribution of sentential negation across Romance languages, which we need for the comparison between negation and *wh*- items.

Romance languages have by and large three systems for negating a clause:

(34) a. preverbal negation (Neg1)

  b. pre- and postverbal negation (Neg 1/2)

  c. postverbal negation (Neg2)

The languages that have only a preverbal negative marker are the most conservative ones; those that have a pre- and a postverbal negative marker have innovated creating a clitic/strong pattern in which the preverbal element is clitic and the postverbal element is not; those languages that only have postverbal negation have lost their preverbal morpheme entirely and have maintained the strong postverbal negative marker. Anticipating the conclusion we reach in section 7, we point out that, on a par with *wh*-doubling and pronominal clitic doubling, negation displays doubling when one of the two elements (the higher one) is a clitic form.

This type of evolution is quite common across languages and was first described by Otto Jespersen (1917), so that the progressive loss of a preverbal negative marker in favor of a postverbal element is known as "Jespersen's cycle." The term "cycle" can be misleading, since the change has a beginning and an end, and, as far as we know, there are no languages that have undergone the opposite process, developing a preverbal negative morpheme starting from a postverbal one. This is a curious fact in itself, which we try to explain in section 7. As for now, we focus on those languages that have both a pre- and a postverbal morpheme, showing that the emergence of the complex pattern in (34b) is sensitive to a series of factors, including modality and sentence type. We adopt the theory proposed by Zanuttini (1997) for Romance, who distinguishes between two positions for preverbal negation (a clitic and an independent negative head; see also Cinque 1999: 21) and three positions for postverbal negation (whose specifiers are occupied by negative elements). We use these five positions to account for dialectal data, showing which might be the factors that influence Jespersen's cycle, the various steps of evolution of postverbal negation, and finally what negation has in common with *wh*-clitic and pronominal clitics.

Among the languages that have both pre- and postverbal negative markers, there are syntactic contexts in which only one out of two elements is possible. We are now going to illustrate some of these cases.

6.1 Negation and Verb Movement

The first factor that plays a role in the emergence of a postverbal negative marker seems to be sentence type: in some Veneto dialects, interrogative structures show a different negative pattern with respect to declarative clauses.

Most Veneto dialects normally only have a preverbal negative marker and insert a postverbal negative morpheme only when a presuppositional meaning is possible:[24]

(35)   a. No l vien. (Paduan)
          not he comes

          "He is not coming."

       b. No l vien miga.
          not he comes not

The presuppositions activated by the postverbal negative particle in these languages is similar to those related to *mica* in Italian (see Cinque 1976). In these languages, preverbal negation is impossible in main interrogative clauses if subject clitic inversion applies: for example, a sentence like (35a) cannot have a corresponding interrogative with SCLI:

(36)   *No vien-lo?
        not comes.he

        'Isn't he coming?'

A sentence like (36) becomes grammatical if a postverbal negation is added:

(37)   No vien-lo miga?
        not comes.he not

        'Isn't he coming?'

In this case, the preverbal negative marker becomes optional, giving rise to a structure which only has a postverbal negative marker, a possibility which is excluded in declaratives:

(38)   a. Vien-lo miga?
           comes.he not

           'Isn't he coming?'

       b. *El vien miga.
           he comes not

Before analyzing these data, let us consider another Veneto dialect, where a preverbal nonclitic negative head blocks V to C. The case is represented by the dialect of S. Anna, a Veneto dialect spoken south of Venice.[25] In this dialect, negation is usually expressed by a pre- and a postverbal morpheme, and both elements are obligatory, contrary to Paduan:

(39)   Ne l vien *(mina). (S. Anna)
       not he comes not

       'He is not coming.'

In a negative interrogative clause—which displays SCLI, on a par with nonnegative interrogative—the preverbal negative morpheme is obligatorily deleted:

(40)   Vien-lo mina?
       comes.he not

       'Isn't he coming?'

(41)   *Ne vien-lo mina?
       not comes.he not

What in Paduan is simply a possibility, in the S. Anna dialect becomes a necessity. This pattern is widely attested: postverbal negation becomes the only negative marker when the verb has moved to the Comp domain, as it does in main interrogative clauses (as SCLI indicates).

Hence, in a dialect like the one of S. Anna, preverbal negation is incompatible with V to C movement (cf. Poletto 2000 for arguments showing that SCLI corresponds to syntactic movement). This contrasts with French-type languages, where the preverbal negative morpheme has no effect on the interrogative structure with SCLI. Therefore, the preverbal negative morpheme, which cooccurs with the postverbal negative marker *mina* in the S. Anna dialect, must be different from French *ne*. This difference can be explained within Zanuttini's (1997) framework. She proposes that preverbal negative markers are of two types: independent heads and clitic elements. Independent heads block verb movement; clitics do not. As main interrogative clauses have obligatory V to C movement, the independent head *ne* blocking verb movement cannot be present in main interrogatives. According to what we said so far, Paduan has both the "French option" of using a preverbal clitic, which does not interfere with verb movement, and the "S. Anna option" of using an independent negative head, which cannot surface when V to C applies.[26]

Our analysis assumes, then, that independent heads can also cooccur with a postverbal negative marker, and this might lead us to a better understanding of the way postverbal negation arises: in the first stage, negation is only preverbal and is probably to be analyzed as an independent head (cf. Zanuttini 1997 for arguments in favor of this hypothesis); in the second, a postverbal negative element is inserted in contexts of presupposition, as Cinque shows for Italian *mica*, but, if we are on the right track in our analysis of the S. Anna data, even in languages that normally have both pre- and postverbal negative markers, the preverbal negative marker can maintain its properties of independent head. In other words, the number of stages a language undergoes within the Jespersen's cycle must be more than the ones we have roughly sketched in (34). Moreover, even within the same language stage, there are contexts in which postverbal negation is favored for independent reasons (in our case, verb movement combined with the X° status of preverbal negation).[27]

There also exist contexts where the presence of a preverbal negative marker is favored even in languages that normally have only postverbal negation, and this seems to be tied to the second factor influencing the complex pattern of pre- and postverbal negation—namely, modality: in some Northern Lombard dialects, which display only postverbal negation with indicative verbs, preverbal negation occurs at least in modal contexts as subjunctive and conditional (Vai 1996 and pers. comm.).

The preverbal negative marker surfaces only when the verb is a subjunctive or a conditional, while when the verb is in its indicative form, preverbal negation is not attested, and the only morpheme is a postverbal one. In the languages examined above, there is a ban against the occurrence of a preverbal negative marker, which is the usual form for sentential negation, but here there is a requirement that forces the presence of a preverbal negative marker, that does not occur in other contexts. Hence, the loss of a preverbal negative marker is also influenced by modality, a fact that should not be surprising because it matches what we find in other languages (such as Greek, for instance) in which negation also displays sensitivity to mood. What is more interesting is that subjunctive, which probably raises higher than indicative (cf. Poletto 2000), requires a preverbal negative morpheme, while indicative does not, and not vice versa.

6.2 Mood and Negation

Another typical context in which negation changes its form according to modality
are imperative clauses. Negative imperatives often display a peculiar pattern different from all other contexts: the imperative form is substituted by a suppletive
form when combined with preverbal negation. Benincà (1992) and Zanuttini
(1997) note that this is true only for those languages that have only a preverbal
negative marker, while postverbal negation is perfectly compatible with a true
imperative form:

(42) a. Mangia! (Standard Italian)
          eat-imperative
          'Eat!'

      b. *Non mangia!
          not eat-imperative

(43)   Non mangiare!
          not eat-infinitive
          'Don't eat!'

(44) a. Bùgia! (Piedmontese)
          move
          'Move!'

      b. Bùgia nen!
          move not
          'Don't move!'

While the standard Italian sentence in (42b) combining preverbal negation with
a true imperative form is excluded, in Piedmontese there is no restriction to the
combination of a true imperative form with postverbal negation, as the grammaticality of (44b) shows.

   However, some cases of postverbal negation are not compatible with a true
imperative form (Emilian *mia*, Rhaeto-Romance *buca*: cf. AIS VIII, 1647):

(45) Movrat mia! (Albinea [Emilian])
      move-infinit.yourself not
      'Don't move!'

Here the infinitive substitutes for the true imperative even if the negative marker
is postverbal.[28]

Zanuttini's analysis of this asymmetry between pre- and postverbal negation does not explain why cases like (45) should exist. She proposes that preverbal negation requires the presence of a modal projection, whose features cannot be checked by the defective true imperative form. Therefore, a suppletive form able to check the modal feature is used. On the contrary, postverbal negation, being located lower in the structural tree, is not sensitive to mood at all, and it is compatible with a true imperative form. How can cases like the ones in (45) be analyzed within such a framework? The generalization can be maintained in a weaker form: preverbal negation is incompatible with imperatives. Therefore, we would like to preserve Zanuttini's intuition that in general preverbal negation is sensitive to mood while postverbal negation is not, given that the majority of languages and dialects confirm her generalization. But how can we integrate somewhat exceptional cases like (45) into her account? We propose that some languages, although they only display a lexical postverbal negative marker, have a phonetically null preverbal negation imposing the same requirement that its phonetically realized counterpart imposes in languages with preverbal negation. If this is correct, we are facing once again a case in which negation is not what it seems to be by simply looking at the position of the visible negative marker. In other words, in some languages that already seem to have undergone the whole process which transforms preverbal negation into postverbal negation still retain some of the typical features of preverbal negation, leading to the idea that it is still somehow present even where we do not see it. This view agrees in general terms with what we proposed for the S. Anna dialect, where a preverbal negative marker, which looks at first sight like French clitic *ne*, is not clitic at all, although it obligatorily cooccurs with a postverbal negative element.

In a diachronic perspective, we can better understand this state of affairs: some dialects that used to have a preverbal negation maintained that preverbal NegP active, even when they stopped inserting a morpheme there. This can be thought of as a stage in the diachronic process, which is recognized and becomes visible in those contexts in which preverbal negation clearly differs from postverbal negation, as imperative clauses.

Postverbal negation is also sensitive to the presence of Neg-words inside the clause. In general, as originally noted by Rizzi (1982), in languages with preverbal negation, the preverbal negative marker is obligatory if the sentence contains a postverbal Neg-word; in languages with postverbal negation, the negative marker is not obligatory in this case. However, the concept of postverbal negation is in itself misleading; as has been shown by Zanuttini (1997), the data of NIDs provide evidence for at least three postverbal positions for negation: one position corresponds to the presuppositional negation (cf. Italian *mica*), and is located higher than the adverb 'already' in Cinque's (1999) hierarchy of lower adverbials; a second position is located lower than 'already' but higher than 'no longer'; a third position is located lower than 'no longer' and 'always' and is usually focalized. We report here Zanuttini's (1997) scheme for possible positions of postverbal negation:

(46) [NegP1 non [TP2 [NegP2 pa [TP2 [NegP3 nen [Asp perf [Asp gen/progr
      [NegP4 no]]]]]]]]

The three distinct postverbal negative markers in (46) correspond to three different etymological types; the highest element usually derives from a word meaning 'small quantity' (Italian *mica*, Emilian *brisa*, French *pas*, Milanese *minga*, Rhaeto-Romance *minne*, Polesano *mina*, Lombard *mia*), the second from the N-word corresponding to 'nothing' (Piedmontese *nen*, Rhaeto-Romance *nia*), and the third is the same morpheme used as pro-negative sentence (Lombard *no*).

These three types of postverbal negation obey different constraints with respect to the cooccurrence with an N-word. In some dialects both the *mica*-type and the *niente*-type can cooccur with N-words, while the lowest postverbal negation *no* does not tolerate any type of N-word:[29]

(47) A ne l'è mina vignù nisun. (Loreo [Rovigo])
      cl not *cl* is not come nobody

      'Nobody came.'

(48) A l'à nen vist gnun. (Piedmontese [Zanuttini])
      cl cl has not seen nobody

      'He saw nobody.'

(49) *A l'à vist no nisun.(Milanese)
      cl cl has seen not nobody

      'He saw nobody.'

Although it is probably not possible to identify each position with a distinct etymological type, clearly each type corresponds to different negative markers located in structurally contiguous positions. In this view, belonging to a given etymological type does not constitute sufficient evidence to place the negative marker in a single position, but at least it provides evidence for isolating a small set of possible contiguous positions among which the negative marker selects its own. If we are on the right track, the three distinct etymological types might also correspond to three distinct possible ways of negating a clause: taking Cinque's (1999) hierarchy of functional projections, Zanuttini (1997) proposes that a presuppositional negation is located immediately above the Anterior Tense projection and that a nonpresuppositional negation is located immediately above a Perfective Aspect projection. However, French *pas* occurs in a position that should always give rise to a presupposition, although this is not the case. Hence, the NegP higher than Anterior Tense is not necessarily bound to be presuppositional.

Whatever the original functions of these elements, when they become a negative marker, they lose their peculiar features, but apparently they preserve the position they had in connection with their function.

The etymological origin of these negative markers will possibly result in matching their position in the clause only in part; the connection is, first of all, a diachronic one: when they took over the function of the preverbal negative marker, their original function weakened, and it is surprising to find their position to still correspond to the one they used to occupy before losing their original meaning. It could also be found that in some cases they have moved upward. About their position we point out only the following: the type of negative marker deriving from the negative direct object 'nothing', like Piedmontese *nen*, occurs immediately above Terminative Aspect in Cinque's hierarchy (or Perfective Aspect in Zanuttini's approach); negative markers originally indicating "small quantity," which add a presuppositional content to negation, are located above perfective Aspect. For the moment we leave this argument to future research.

The etymological origin of negative markers is also connected to their possibility to become an expletive negation. As Portner and Zanuttini (1996) show, the "expletive negation" in exclamative contexts is not expletive at all but has a specific function: it widens the scale of implicature of the exclamative clause. A potentially interesting generalization connected to this concerns the type of negative marker that can act as expletive negation: it has been proposed that only preverbal negative markers can perform this function. This is clearly not true, as German *nicht*, which is located quite low in the structure of the clause, can be found in exclamative clauses with expletive value. However, the generalization is not entirely incorrect but needs to be refined as follows: the negative markers that can function as expletive negation in exclamative contexts are those that contain a negative morpheme. Since, in general, preverbal negative markers are composed precisely by a negative morpheme, they all have the relevant property that enables them to behave as expletive negation. Nevertheless, reformulating the generalization has consequences on postverbal negative markers: it predicts that among the postverbal negative markers, only those containing a negative morpheme— like German *nicht*, but not those which do not contain any (for instance French *pas*)—can be used as expletive negation. Again, this descriptive generalization makes reference to the internal form of the negative marker and not to a specific position, which is probably only indirectly connected to the morphological makeup.

After having recognized some interesting properties that characterize the various types of negative elements, and the way they are localized in the structure in relation to their form and original value, we can observe how the general developmental path of negation, starting from a very high position in the clause and ending up in a low position, shows interesting similarities to *wh*-in situ cases.[30] In particular, the intermediate stage with pre- and postverbal negative markers is similar to *wh*-doubling cases. Moreover, the higher *wh*-in doubling structures and the preverbal negative marker in pre- and postverbal cases are similar in their feature composition: in both cases, the higher element encodes only part of the information encoded in the lower element; in both cases, there are good reasons to believe that this is due to the clitic nature of the higher element. The same is obviously true for pronominal clitics, where the clitic is only a partial copy of the information contained in the full DP.

Postulating preverbal empty negative elements as we have done leads us to another interesting comparison with clitics, which across the Romance languages also alternate with an empty category, namely *pro*. The case of subject clitics is probably the best known case of this type: some languages have different types of subject clitics, others have pro. The same would be true for preverbal negation, which probably also has a null counterpart in some languages. But pronominal clitics do not seem to follow the same diachronic path that negation and *wh*-items display—namely, a pattern that starts from a high position that is progressively abandoned through a mechanism of doubling of a clitic and a full form. However, what has been noticed in the evolutionary path of negation and *wh*-items might be helpful for reinterpreting an old idea proposed originally by Antinucci and Marcantonio (1980), who viewed the position of clitics as marking the position where direct and indirect objects used to appear in Latin. Assuming Kayne's (1994) hypothesis that in SOV languages the object moves to a position higher than the verb, we might interpret the change from SOV to SVO that has occurred in the early development of Romance from Latin as related to the loss of object movement to a very high position in the clausal structure. Hence, the emergence of object clitics would also be, on a par with negation and *wh*-items, related to a change in the movement pattern, in this case of objects, objects which used to raise to a very high position and have lost this property by creating a clitic counterpart that still moves high in the structural tree. In what follows, we try to develop this intuition on the rising of clitic series as related to the progressive loss of syntactic movement.

7 SOME THEORETICAL OBSERVATIONS

In the preceding sections, we have shown that the development of clitic forms for *wh*-items, pronouns, and negative markers is influenced by a number of factors. These factors vary according with the type of element that is undergoing the process. Pronominal elements become clitics following a well-defined hierarchy: indirect object clitics imply the presence of direct object clitics, and both direct and indirect object clitics are present in languages that have subject clitics. *Wh*-items are also sensitive to the same hierarchy (as the ban against subject *que* in modern French shows), but their development as clitic forms is also influenced by the number of semantic features that the *wh*-elements encode: the poorer the semantics of an element is, the easier it becomes a clitic. Moreover, clitic *wh*-forms are banned from embedded contexts, while strong forms are not. Hence, clitic *wh*-forms are sensitive to some form of verb movement to the C domain. Verb movement also influences negation: preverbal negative markers that are independent heads are not allowed in V to C contexts, as shown by the distribution of preverbal and postverbal negative markers in main interrogatives. In turn, negation is also sensitive to mood, as preverbal forms are preferred in some usages of subjunctive, while being banned in indicative clauses. Clitic formation is thus sensitive to both semantic (as the intrinsic semantic poverty of some *wh*-items which are more frequently clitics testifies) and syntactic factors (as verb movement).

More generally, it is possible to characterize all cases of cliticization along the following lines: the first common property characterizing the process is well known. Clitic forms generally display only part of the semantic features that strong forms encode. In a parallel way, it seems that the morphological and phonological reduction that the elements undergo leads to an X° containing only part of the functional information and no lexical information of the full form (see note 3). Again, it is well known that third-person pronominal clitics are very similar to determiners, while the preverbal negative marker that becomes a clitic contains only the -n- morpheme, indicating that an element is negative and does not derive from a form indicating "small quantity" or from a negative quantifier like "nothing" as postverbal negation does (see section 6). In other words, preverbal negation does not encode any quantificational feature, while postverbal negation apparently does. The same seems true also for *wh*-items: in Friulian the clitic form *do* loses precisely the "locative" indicator *là* (where) that the strong form *dulà* still retains; *que* has been noticed (cf. Obenauer 1976) to be identical to the complementizer, a purely functional element. Therefore, the morphological makeup of clitic elements preserves the functional information, lacking the lexical part, which is probably located lower in the internal structure of the element itself.

We formalize the observation that clitic forms encode only the functional portion of their strong counterpart by proposing that clitics forms are the overt counterpart of the mechanism of feature movement at Logical Form proposed by Chomsky (1995): pied-piping of the whole category is not necessary, only the feature(s) that has to be checked moves to the target projection. The clitic form checks the semantic features of an element in a high functional projection without pied-piping the whole complex category: pronominal clitics check agreement feature in a high Agr projection without pied-piping the whole DP.[31] The same is true for *wh*-doubling structures,[32] where the clitic checks the interrogative features of the sentence-initial projection in the interrogative CP without moving the whole *wh*-, located in a lower position. Our account also derives the observation that diachronically clitics seem to develop when movement of the independent category gets lost: if the connection originally noted by Antinucci and Marcantonio (1980) between the development of pronominal clitics and the change from SOV to SVO from Latin to Romance has to be interpreted as we propose in section 6.2, clitic forms develop when movement of an independent element to a high functional projection is lost. This appears quite evident in the case of *wh*-doubling and *wh*-in situ, which substitute for *wh*-movement to the clause-initial position and is also transparent in Jespersen's cycle, where an independent preverbal negative head is substituted by a preverbal clitic form cooccurring with a postverbal negative marker.

If the relation between the rising of SVO and the development of clitics is to be analyzed as a loss of object movement to a very high Agreement projection, the interpretation of clitics as a case of more economical, non-pied-piped version of movement due to feature checking also applies to pronouns. Negation also checks a negative feature in a high NegP projection, without pied-piping the whole XP, which remains in a postverbal position. Evidently, the rising of clitic forms constitutes the first step toward the loss of movement to the high functional projection: negation in spoken French, Piedmontese, Lombard, and some Rhaeto-Romance dialects has undergone the whole of Jespersen's cycle, as postverbal negation is the only element occurring in these languages. The same seems to be true for *wh*- in situ of the French and Northern Lombard type: *wh*-in situ is possible with all *wh*-elements, showing that this is not more related to any clitic phonetically realized or null form and that in these structures *wh*-movement to the initial CP projection has been completely lost. As for why Romance languages have maintained pronominal clitics retaining just postverbal objects, although the evolution of a clitic pattern is quite ancient, there must be some independent acquisitional evidence that agreement projections are strong in Romance, hence must be checked in overt syntax by the "smallest possible element," namely, a clitic.

The idea that clitics are connected to the loss of movement provides some interesting insight into some of the facts noted in the previous sections. In section 3 we noticed that adverbial clitic forms other than negation (i.e. corresponding to lower adverbs like *più* 'anymore', *già* 'already', *mai* 'never', and *sempre* 'always', or to higher adverbs like *forse* 'perhaps', *fortunatamente* 'luckily', *francamente* 'honestly', etc.) are virtually absent from Romance languages: if clitics are developed as a sort of more economical strategy to check a high projection, it is straightforward that elements that do not move do not develop clitic forms. According to Cinque's (1999) analysis of adverbs in Romance, these elements do not move to check any functional features located in higher projections. The only movement that adverbs can undergo in Romance is focalization, which is clearly a different kind of movement with respect to the checking of some functional features. Hence, if adverbials do not move in Romance, they are not expected to develop clitic forms.

NOTES

Our heartfelt thanks go to the editors of the volume, Guglielmo Cinque and Richie Kayne, for their comments and suggestions on the first draft of this chapter. We are also deeply grateful to M. M. Parry and G. Salvi, who carefully read the chapter and provided precious comments. We are finally indebted to the participants in the ASIS weekly seminars in Padua for insightful discussions and data. When not otherwise indicated, the source of the examples is the ASIS corpus. For the concerns of the Italian academy, Cecilia Poletto takes responsibility over sections 1–4 and Paola Benincà over sections 5–7.

1. In this work we only examine head clitics, leaving weak pronouns as defined by Cardinaletti and Starke (1999) aside.

2. This is true in general for Northern Italian dialects, but is also the case in standard French, standard Portuguese, and Southern Italian dialects, although our empirical basis with respect to Southern Italian dialects is far more limited than for the dialects of Northern Italy.

3. Apparently clitic *que* is different from object clitics in languages such as some Northern Italian dialects (NIDs), where it is possible to cliticize the pronoun to a preposition (see (i)); hence, the contrast between (i) and (ii):

(i)   El vien drio-ghe.
      he comes behind.him

(ii) *Avec que s'est-il blessé?
      With what has he hurt himself?

4. Cliticization is not a simple matter of adjacency, as *que* is ungrammatical in embedded stylistic inversion interrogatives, where it is adjacent to the verb:

(i)   *Je ne sais pas qu'a fait Jean.
      I not know not what has done Jean

For an analysis of this effect, see Poletto and Pollock (2004).

5. As Richard Kayne pointed out to us, most of the restrictions on *que* also apply to *que diable*, thus suggesting that they are not due to the clitic status of *que* but to the "semantic poverty" of this item. However, the fact that *que diable* can violate the constraint on adjacency leads us to think that *que* is indeed a clitic element and that its semantic poverty has probably contributed to its development as a clitic element. In Old

and Middle French *que* was not a clitic, as cases of nonadjacency are attested; some speakers probably still have that type of grammar. As for the constraints on its in situ counterpart *quoi*, we cannot even begin to do justice to its complex syntax here; we limit ourselves to refer to Poletto and Pollock (2004) for the idea that the opposition between *que* and *quoi* cannot simply be described in terms of strong versus clitic.

6. Some speakers find these sentences acceptable with a pitch intonation on the *wh*-item. This changes the interpretation of the question, which becomes of the type: "tell me exactly how you do it, or what you buy."

7. This recalls a concept developed in various works on grammaticalization, namely 'persistence' (see Hopper 1991; Vincent 1998, among others): in our case, a lexical item behaves as a phrase since it originates from one.

8. See also, in a different perspective, Salvi (2001), who develops the idea that clitics express first of all 'central functions'.

9. In this respect, clitic formation is parallel to article formation; an interesting theoretical problem appears to be how to differentiate the two classes properly. See Giusti (1998), Renzi (1992), and Vincent (1997, 1998) for analogous intuitions and interesting analyses.

10. On some interesting topics, such as possessives, adnominal genitives, and object pronouns in Brazilian Portuguese, we do not have detailed enough data or descriptions.

11. G. Salvi (pers. comm.) points out that a very common situation in this area presents only one clitic form, which can be used for both dative and accusative (obviously, only for one of the two arguments at a time); moreover, the clitic can be freely replaced by a tonic form without any emphasis. This situation is described by Gartner (1893) as characteristic of the Engadinese area. Anyway, this system does not conflict with our generalization, since the only existing clitic has the form of a direct object.

12. There could still be the doubt that this dialect does not lack clitics but is, in fact, like Borgomanerese (see Tortora (1997, 2002)), which has clitic pronouns appearing in enclisis after the inflected verb or a special class of adverbs and prepositions. The evidence in favor of our interpretation is probably not compelling; however, we point out that in Borgomanerese the pronoun is phonologically reduced and fused with its host (a process typical of enclisis), while this is not the case in the dialects we analyze here. Moreover, the order in clitic clusters is Dative–Accusative, and not the opposite.

13. While direct and indirect object clitics and subject clitics still preserve in their morphological makeup at least person (frequently also gender or number information), locative arguments—apart from the very special clitic for 'out of a place', which only survives in formal Italian and French—reduce to just one clitic, completely void of any feature with respect to their strong counterpart: they encode neither any directional information nor any information concerning the reference to the speaker or to the hearer. We will come back to this in section 7.

14. As Giampaolo Salvi pointed out to us, in support of this vague intuition on the opacity of this kind of compound some phenomena can be taken into account: in Old French the plural ending -*s* was added at the end of the compound *le+me*, *te* 'it *obj.*+me, you *dat.**; in modern Italian *glielo* obliterates the distinction between masculine *gli* and feminine *le* clitic pronouns. Other phenomena from Catalan are reported by Mascaró (1985).

15. The presence of the left-dislocated element *di ragazzi*, of which *ne* becomes a copy, has no consequence.

16. The sentence is only acceptable in the colloquial registers of some regional varieties of Italian.

17. The two sets of descriptive generalizations also display one major difference concerning datives: datives can be clitics in the personal pronominal series, but they never are clitics in the interrogative series.

18. As for *wh*-items, the fulfilling of this requirement is not enough; the internal argument has to be inanimate, while this is not the case for pronouns. This difference is clearly tied to the fact that inanimacy is not morphologically encoded in pronouns, while it is in *wh*-items.

19. We are aware of the fact that we are simplifying the relation between argumentality and case, if we think, for example, of cases like inalienable, benefactive, and ethic dative clitics, which are not arguments but still have the form of a dative clitic. These generalizations should be seen in a diachronic perspective: the clitic form arises in correspondence with the argumental usages and is then extended to the nonargumental cases. A topic related to this concerns the number and type of features that two elements must share in order to be affected by the extension of the pronominal clitic form. For some tests distinguishing argumental and nonargumental *ci* in Italian, see Benincà (1988).

20. Here we use *wh*-in situ as a pretheoretical term and do not imply any analysis of the phenomenon, which could be handled as a case of covert movement to the CP domain; if much recent work on *wh*-in situ (cf. Pollock 2001, Munaro and Poletto 1998, Extepare and Uribe-Extebarria 2000) is on the right track, the low position of the *wh*-in situ is not a true in situ one but a low position in the CP domain.

21. Munaro and Poletto (1998) show that *wh*-in situ is not a unitary phenomenon and that it is important to distinguish between *wh*-in situ with SCLI and *wh*-in situ without SCLI.

22. The *in situ* form of *sa* is *che*, which cannot appear fronted:

(i)   *Ché a-lo fato (ché)?

       what has.he done what?

The symbol % marks the difference among different classes of speakers.

23. This is probably due to the fact that *wh*-clitics have to cliticize onto a verbal form (see Poletto and Pollock 2004) and are then "dragged along" by the verbal complex moving to the Comp domain. As R. Kayne pointed out to us, the incompatibility of *wh*-clitics and the complementizer contrasts a bit mysteriously with the close combination of subject clitics and complementizers. Still, there is an interesting similarity between *wh*-clitics and one specific type of subject clitic, namely *a*: they can never be in enclisis to a verb.

24. The presuppositional value is similar but not completely parallel to that of standard Italian *mica*, analyzed in Cinque (1976).

25. The data have been collected through fieldwork; they are not available in the ASIS corpus.

26. Italian can be interpreted in the same way, given that the data are the same.

27. At the first stage of evolution the presence of a Neg-word like *niente* 'nothing' as the internal argument favors the loss of preverbal negation: see Vai (1996) for Old Milanese, but see also the following standard Italian examples:

(i)   Sarà niente.
       it-will-be nothing
       'It is nothing serious.'

(ii)   Sembra niente.
       it-seems nothing
       'It does not seem serious.'

(iii) L'ha ridotta a niente.
       her.he-has reduced to nothing
       'He destroyed her.'

In the same contexts, French *ne* can be omitted.

28. There are also interesting instances of negative imperative in Emilian dialects in which the negation *briza*, normally postverbal, appears preposed and the imperative is replaced with the infinitive; cf. AIS VIII, 1647: *briza móvrat* "don't move *infin.* yourself!"; Parry (1996: 251) from Fusignano (Emilia): *briza kórar* "don't run!"; here an interesting parallel is also pointed out with the position of negation in gerundive clauses: in Fusignano dialect we have *briza avéndla lezýa* "not having.it read" as opposed for example to Milanese *avendola minga lezýa* "having.it not read."

29. See also Berruto (1990: 14–15) and Parry (1996: 246–249; 1997) for more detailed data. Here interesting phenomena concerning the interaction between the clitic preverbal negative morpheme and other clitics are also described.

30. This parallel development between negation and *wh-* was first pointed out to us by Massimo Vai (pers. comm.).

31. Compare Sportiche (1996) for a similar idea that clitics check Agr features that are checked by scrambled DPs in languages like German. However, this technical execution of Sportiche is quite different from ours.

32. On the view that *wh-*in situ is the null counterpart of *wh-*doubling, as Poletto and Pollock (2004) propose, *wh-*in situ—at least when it is restricted to *wh-*items that can become clitics—is totally equivalent to *wh-*doubling with a null clitic.

REFERENCES

AIS. (1928–1940) *Sprach- und Sachatlas Italiens und der Südschweiz.* Rengien, Zofingen.

Alexiadou, A. (1995) "Word Order Alternation in Modern Greek." Paper presented at the Fifth Colloquium on Generative Grammar, La Coruña, Spain.

Ambar M., H. Obenauer, I. Pereira, and R. Veloso (1998) "The Internal Structure of *wh-*Phrases in Portuguese and French." Paper presented at the round table on *Structures formelles du langage* (UPRESA 7023), Paris.

Antinucci, F., & A. Marcantonio (1980) "I meccanismi del mutamento diacronico: il cambiamento d'ordine dei pronomi clitici in italiano." *Rivista di Grammatica Generativa* 5: 3–50.

ASIS. Atlante sintattico dell'Italia Settentrionale. Unpublished material. Consiglio Nazionale delle Ricerche and Department of Linguistics, University of Padua.

Barbosa, P. (1996) "A New Look at the Null Subject Parameter," in J. Costa et al. (eds.) *Proceedings of ConSOLE 3.* Leiden University, Leiden.

Belletti, A. (1990) *Generalized Verb Movement.* Rosenberg and Sellier, Turin.

Belletti, A., and L. Rizzi (1988) "Psych-verbs and Theta Theory." *Natural Language and Linguistic Theory* 6: 291–352.

Benincà, P. (1988) "L'ordine degli elementi della frase e le costruzioni marcate," in L. Renzi (ed.) *Grande Grammatica Italiana di Consultazione.* Il Mulino, Bologna, 1: 129–194.

Benincà, P. (1992) "Geolinguistica e sintassi," in G. Ruffino (ed.) *Atlanti linguistici italiani e romanzi.* Centro di Studi Filologici e Linguistici Siciliani, Palermo, 29–40.

Berruto, G. (1990) *Studi di Sociolinguistica e Dialettologia Italiana.* Congedo, Galatina.

Bouchard D., and P. Hirschbühler (1986) "French *QUOI* and Its Clitic Allomorph *QUE*," in C. Neidle and R. A. Nuñez (eds.) *Studies in Romance Languages.* Foris, Dordrecht, 39–60.

Cardinaletti, A., and M. Starke (1999) "The Typology of Structural Deficiency: On the Three Grammatical Classes," in H. van Riemsdijk (ed.) *Clitics in the Languages of Europe.* Vol. 8 of *Empirical Approaches to Language Typology.* Mouton de Gruyter, Berlin, 145–234.

Cheng, L.S., and J. Rooryck (2000) "Licensing *Wh*-in-Situ." *Syntax* 3: 1–19.

Chomsky, N. (1981) *Lectures on Government and Binding.* Foris, Dordrecht.

Chomsky, N. (1995) *The Minimalist Program.* MIT Press, Cambridge, Mass.

Cinque, G. (1976) "Mica." *Annali della Facoltà di Lettere e Filosofia dell'Università di Padova* 1: 101–112.

Cinque G. (1999) *Adverbs and Functional Heads.* Oxford University Press, New York.

Dobrovie Sorin, C. (1994) *The Syntax of Romanian: Comparative Studies in Romance.* Mouton de Gruyter, Berlin.

Etxepare R., and M. Uribe-Extebarria (2000) "On the Properties of in Situ *Wh*-Questions in Spanish." Talk delivered at the Workshop on *Minimal Elements of Linguistic Variation*, Paris.

Friedemann, M.-A. (1997) *Sujets syntaxiques: positions, inversions et* pro. Peter Lang, Bern.

Gartner, T. (1893) *Raetoromanische Grammatik*, Henninger, Heilbronn.

Gartner, T. (1910) *Handbuch der raetoromanischen Sprache und Literatur.* Niemeyer, Halle.

Giusti, G. (1998) "The Categorial Status of Determiners," in L. Haegeman (ed.) *The New Comparative Syntax.* Longman, London, 95–123.

Haiman, J., and P. Benincà (1992) *The Rhaeto-Romance Languages.* Routledge, London.

Halpern, A. (1995) *On the Placement and Morphology of Clitics.* CSLI Publications, Stanford, Calif.

Hopper, P. (1991) "On Some Principles of Grammaticization," in E. Traugott & B. Heine (eds.) *Approaches to Grammaticalization.* John Benjamins, Amsterdam, 17–35.

Jelinek, E. (1996) "Definiteness and Second Position Clitics in Straits Salish," in A. Halpern and A. M. Zwicky (eds.) *Approaching Second: Second Position Clitics and Related Phenomena.* CSLI Publications, Stanford, Calif., 271–298.

Jespersen, O. (1917) *Negation in English and Other Languages.* Host, Copenhagen.

Kayne, R.S. (1975) *French Syntax*. MIT Press, Cambridge, Mass.

Kayne, R.S. (1994) *The Antisymmetry of Syntax*. MIT Press, Cambridge, Mass.

Kayne, R.S. (2001) "Prepositions as Probes." Unpublished ms., New York University.

Mascaró, J. (1985) *Morfologia*. Enciclopédia Catalana, Barcelona.

Munaro N. (1997) "Proprietà strutturali e distribuzionali dei sintagmi interrogativi in alcuni dialetti italiani settentrionali." Ph.D. thesis, University of Padua.

Munaro, N. (1999) *Sintagmi interrogativi nei dialetti italiani settentrionali*. Unipress, Padua.

Munaro, N., and C. Poletto (1998) On Two Types of *wh*-in situ. Unpublished ms., University of Venice and Consiglio Nazionale delle Ricerche.

Obenauer, H.-G. (1976) *Etudes de syntaxe interrogative du français. 'Quoi', 'combien' et le complémenteur*. Niemeyer, Tübingen.

Obenauer, H.-G. (1994) "Aspects de la syntaxe A-barre: Effets d'intervention et mouvements des quantifieurs." Ph.D. thesis, University of Paris VIII.

Parry, M. M. (1996) "La negazione italo-romanza: variazioine tipologica e variazione strutturale," in P. Benincà, G. Cinque, and T. De Mauro (eds.) *Italiano e Dialetti nel tempo: Saggi di grammatica per Giulio Lepschy*. Rome, Bulzoni, 225–257.

Parry, M. M. (1997) "Preverbal Negation and Clitic Ordering, with Particular Reference to a Group of North-West Italian Dialects." *Zeitschrift für Romanische Philologie* 113.2: 243–270.

Penello, N. (1993) "Capitoli di sintassi veneta: Uno studio di microvariazione." Ph.D thesis, University of Padua.

Poletto, C. (2000) *The Higher Functional Field in the Northern Italian Dialects*. Oxford University Press, New York.

Poletto, C., and J.-Y. Pollock (2004) "On the Left Periphery of Some Romance Wh-Questions," in L. Rizzi (ed.) *The Structure of CP and LP: The Cartography of Syntactic Structures, Volume 2*. Oxford University Press, New York, 251–296.

Pollock, J.-Y. (1989) "Verb Movement, Universal Grammar, and the Structure of IP." *Linguistic Inquiry* 20: 365–424.

Pollock, J.-Y. (2001) "Subject Clitics, Subject Clitic Inversion and Complex Inversion: Generalizing Remnant Movement to the Comp Area." Unpublished ms., University of Amiens.

Portner, P., and R. Zanuttini (1996) "The Syntax and Semantics of Scalar Negation: Evidence from Paduan," in K. Kusumoto (ed.) *Proceedings of NELS XXVI*. University of Massachusetts, Amherst, 257–271.

Renzi, L. (1992) "Le développement de l'article en Roman." *Revue Roumaine de Linguistique* 37: 161–176.

Rivero, M. L. (1994) "Clause Structure and V-movement in the Languages of the Balkans." *Natural Language and Linguistic Theory* 12: 63–120.

Rizzi, L. (1982) *Issues in Italian Syntax*. Foris, Dordrecht.

Salvi, G. (2001) "La nascita dei clitici romanzi." *Romanische Forschungen* 113.3: 423–475.

Sportiche, D. (1996) "Clitic Constructions," in L. Zaring and J. Rooryck (eds.) *Phrase Structure and the Lexicon*. Kluwer, Dordrecht.

Tortora, C. (1997) "The Syntax and Semantics of the Locative Expletive." Ph.D. diss., University of Delaware.

Tortora, C. (2002) "On Prepositions and Spatial Inalienable Possession." Talk delivered at the Linguistic Symposium on Romance Languages XXXII.

Vai, M. (1996) "Per una storia della negazione in milanese in comparazione con altre varietà altoitaliane." *Acme* 49: 57–98.

Vincent, N. (1997) "The Emergence of the D-System in Romance," in A. van Kemenade & N. Vincent (eds.) *Parameters of Morphosyntactic Change.* Cambridge University Press, Cambridge, 149–169.

Vincent, N. (1998) "Tra grammatica e grammaticalizzazione: articoli e clitici nelle lingue (italo)-romanze," in L. Roma & P. Ramat (eds.) *Sintassi storica*, Atti del XXX Congresso. Società di Linguistica Italiana. Bulzoni, Rome, 411–440.

Zanuttini R. (1997) *Negation and Clausal Structure: A Comparative Study of Romance Languages.* Oxford University Press, New York.

CHAPTER 7

CLASSIFIERS IN FOUR VARIETIES OF CHINESE

LISA L.-S. CHENG AND RINT SYBESMA

1 INTRODUCTION

This chapter deals with the use of classifiers in four varieties of Chinese: Mandarin, Wu, Min, and Cantonese (or "Yue"). The main aim is to account for the distribution and interpretation of the different forms of nominal expressions in these languages, as well as for the variation that they display in this regard. To this end, we investigate the question of what parameters play a role and attempt to find deeper reasons for some of the systematic contrasts.

It is generally assumed that there are seven major Chinese language groups (or "dialects"), four of which are looked at in this essay. The term "Mandarin" is ambiguous: it either is an alternative name for the natural variety of Chinese otherwise referred to as "the Northern-Chinese dialect," or it is the name for the standard language, adopted as the official language on the mainland, as well as on Taiwan. Roughly speaking, as a natural (as opposed to standard) language, Mandarin is spoken north of the Yangtze River and in the southern provinces of Yunnan and Guizhou. Wu is spoken in Zhejiang and the southern tip of Jiangsu. Min is the language of Fujian and neighboring parts of Guangdong, and of Hainan and Taiwan. Cantonese is spoken in most of Guangdong and Guangxi, as well as in Hong Kong. For an excellent introduction to several aspects of Chinese and its varieties, see Norman 1988.[1]

Despite the fact that the area where Mandarin is spoken is vast, the internal variation is not very great: in essence, the Mandarin subvarieties are mutually intelligible. This does not apply to the other dialect groups (see Ramsey 1987 for a suggestion why this would be so): the respective areas in which each of these is spoken is much smaller, but the variation is enormous, typically to the point of mutual unintelligibility. This is especially true of Wu and Min, which are standardly divided into Northern and Southern Wu and Northern and Southern Min.

Unless explicitly mentioned otherwise, our Mandarin data belong to the variety spoken in the north-northeastern regions of China. For Wu, we concentrate on the Southern Wu variety of Wenzhou, but now and then we mention Shanghainese, as a representative of the northern branch. The Min data belong to the Southern Min variety spoken on Taiwan. The variety of Cantonese we use is spoken in Hong Kong.

2 THE FACTS

In this section we lay out the facts that will concern us in this chapter, concentrating on the correlations between form, interpretation, and distribution of three different types of nominal expressions in Mandarin, Min, Wu, and Cantonese: bare nouns (to be referred to as "Bare NPs"), phrases consisting of a classifier and a nominal ("Cl-NPs") and expressions made up of a numeral, a classifier, and a nominal ("Num-Cl-NPs"). We present the facts language by language, going from north to south.

2.1 Mandarin

2.1.1 *Bare NPs*

As the following examples show, Bare NPs may receive an indefinite, a definite, or a generic interpretation. What interpretation it gets is essentially determined by the nature of the predicate; in this chapter we do not go into this matter. In sentences with an unbounded activity verb as in (1a), the Bare NP is interpreted as indefinite. In bounded events, like the one expressed in (1b), the Bare NP gets a definite reading. With unbounded states, the Bare NP is generic, as is shown in (1c). (For discussion of (1b), see Sybesma 1992, 176–178.)

(1) a. Hufei   maishu   qu   le.
        Hufei   buy   book   go SFP[2]

     'Hufei went to buy a book/books.'

     b. Hufei   he-wan-le   tang.
        Hufei   drink-finished-PRF   soup

     'Hufei finished the soup.'

     c. Wo   xihuan   gou.
        I   like   dog

     'I like dogs.'

In preverbal position, however, Mandarin Bare NPs cannot be interpreted as indefinite. They get either a definite or a generic interpretation:

(2) a. Gou   yao   guo   malu.
        dog   want   cross   road

     'The dog/the dogs want/s to cross the road.'
     not: 'A dog/dogs want/s to cross the road.'

     b. Gou   jintian   tebie   tinghua.
        dog   today   very   obedient

     'The dog/dogs was/were very obedient today' (not: indefinite)

     c. Gou   ai   chi   rou.
        dog   love   eat   meat

     'Dogs love to eat meat'

2.1.2 Cl-NPs

Interpretationally, the Cl-NP in Mandarin is limited to a nonspecific indefinite reading. As a result, it is limited distributionally, to the object position in un-bounded activity predicates, as is exemplified in (3): (3a) is fine, but in the bounded predicate of (3b), which forces a strong (i.e., specific) interpretation onto indefinites (Sybesma 1992, 176–178), a Cl-NP is not possible. Cl-NPs cannot get a generic interpretation either. In preverbal position, Cl-NPs are also out:

(3) a. Wo   xiang   mai   ben   shu.
        I   want   buy   CL^{volume} book

     'I would like to buy a book.'

     b. *Ta   he-wan-le   wan   tang.
         he   drink-finished-PRF   CL^{bowl} soup

     Intended: 'He finished a (specific) bowl of soup.'

    c. *Wo xihuan wan   tang.
       I   like   CL^{bowl}   soup

    Intended generic reading: 'I love a bowl of soup.'

(4) a. *Zhi gou   yao   guo   malu.
      CL   dog   want   cross road

    Intended: 'A dog wants to cross the road.'

    b. *Zhi gou   xihuan chi   rou.
      CL   dog   like   eat   meat

    Intended generic reading: 'A dog likes to eat meat.'

It is not generally acknowledged that Mandarin has Cl-NPs (but see Paris 1981); Cl-NPs like the one in (3a) are often considered to be the result of phonological reduction of the numeral *yi* 'one'; according to this reasoning, (3a) is the reduced form of the unreduced (5):

(5) Wo   xiang mai   yi-ben   shu.
    I   want   buy   one-CL   book

'I would like to buy a book.'

However, the fact that, as we just saw, Cl-NP is limited to contexts which are definable in semantic, rather than phonological, terms suggests that the reduction view is wrong. There is no phonological reason, for instance, why *yi* could not be reduced in (3b), if (6) were the "unreduced" form of (3b).

(6) Ta   he-wan-le   yi-wan   tang.
    he   drink-finished-PRF   one-CL^{bowl}   soup

'He finished a/one (specific) bowl of soup.'

More arguments for the claim that Cl-NP is a real construct in Mandarin are given in Cheng and Sybesma 1999.

2.1.3 *Num-Cl-NPs*

Mandarin Num-Cl-NP shows basically the same distribution as Cl-NP, the only difference being that it can occur in the object position of bounded predicates (as we just saw in (6)), by virtue of the fact that it can be interpreted as specific. The complete paradigm is given in (7)–(8). Num-Cl-NPs in which the numeral is *yi* (i.e., *yi*-Cl-NP) may be interpreted as specific and nonspecific, comparable to indefinite articles in Germanic languages; it can, of course, also be stressed and mean *one*:

(7) a. Wo   xiang mai   yi-ben   shu.
         I   want   buy   one-CL   book

     'I would like to buy a book.'

     b. Ta   he-wan-le   yi-wan   tang.
         he   drink-finished-PRF   one-CL^{bowl}   soup

     'He finished a/one (specific) bowl of soup.'

     c. *Wo   xihuan   yi-wan   tang.
         I   like   one-CL^{bowl}   soup

     Intended generic reading: 'I love a/one bowl of soup.'

(8) a. *Yi-zhi gou   yao   guo   malu.
         one-CL dog   want   cross   road

     Intended: 'A dog wants to cross the road.'

     b. *Yi-zhi gou   xihuan   chi   rou.
         one-CL dog   like   eat   meat

     Intended generic reading: 'A dog likes to eat meat.'

2.1.4 Summary

In Mandarin, Bare NPs can be interpreted as definite, indefinite, or generic. Num-Cl-NPs and Cl-NPs are invariably indefinite. A difference between the two is that Num-Cl-NPs can be both specific and nonspecific and Cl-NPs are limited to a nonspecific interpretation. All indefinites occur in postverbal position only.

2.2 Wu

2.2.1 Bare NPs

The distribution and interpretation of Bare NPs in Wu is the same as in Mandarin. As objects, they can be interpreted as indefinite, definite, and generic, depending on the nature of the predicate. The following sentences are Wenzhou examples:[3]

(9) a. Vu² Fei¹ tsau³-khe⁵   ma⁴   si¹   fiuɔ²   ba⁴.
         Vu   Fei   go   buy   book SFP   SFP

     'Vu Fei went to buy a book/books.'

     b. ŋ⁴   dei⁶   thuɔ¹   ha⁷   jy²   ba⁴.
         I   take   soup   drink up   SFP

     'I finished the soup'

    c. ŋ⁴   si³-çy¹   kau³.
      I   like   dog

    'I like dogs.'

As to (9b), in bounded predicates Wu disallows objects in postverbal position. Instead, the object appears in preverbal position, following the element *dei⁶* meaning 'take'.[4]

    In preverbal position, Wu displays the same interpretational pattern for Bare NPs as Mandarin, as is exemplified by the following Wenzhou data. They either get a definite or a generic interpretation; an indefinite reading is excluded:

(10) a. Kau³   i⁵   tshi⁷   niou⁸.
       dog   want   eat   meat

      'The dog/the dogs want/s to eat meat.' (Not: indefinite)

    b. kau³   ke⁷-ne⁸   de⁸-bi⁸   teŋ¹-kuɔ³.
      dog   today   very   obedient

      'The dog/the dogs was/were very obedient today.' (Not: indefinite)

    c. kau³   si³-çy¹   tshi⁷   niou⁸.
      dog   like   eat   meat

      'Dogs like to eat meat.'

2.2.2 *Cl-NPs*

With respect to Cl-NPs, the situation is not the same in all Wu dialects. While in some varieties the facts are quite similar to those of Mandarin, Wenzhou is very different. As we saw, in Mandarin Cl-NPs can only be interpreted as indefinite, and their distribution is limited to postverbal position. In contrast, Wenzhou Cl-NPs may occur in both preverbal and postverbal position, and it may be interpreted as definite as well as indefinite (nonspecific). Let us look at Cl-NPs in postverbal position first:

(11) a. ŋ⁴   çi³   ma⁴   paŋ³   si¹   le²   tshi⁵.
       I   want   buy   CL^volume   book come   read

      'I would like to buy a book to read.'

    b. ŋ⁴   dei⁶   y⁷/liɛ⁷   thuɔ¹   ha⁷   jy²   ba⁴.
      I   take   CL^bowl/CL^PL   soup   drink   up   SFP

      'I finished the (bowl of) soup.'

    c. *ŋ⁴   si³-çy¹   ha⁷   y⁷/liɛ⁷   thuɔ¹.
      I   like   drink   CL^bowl/CL^PL   soup

    Intended generic reading: 'I like (a bowl of) soup.'

The use of the Cl-NP in (11a) is similar to (3a): *paŋ³ sɨ¹* 'CL-book' is interpreted as indefinite. However, the Cl-NP in (11b) is interpreted as definite: whether *y⁷* 'bowl' or *liɛ⁷* 'some' is used makes no difference; in both cases the Cl-NP combination translates as 'the soup' (we return to this later).

Let us look at the use of Cl-NPs in preverbal position. Like Mandarin, Wenzhou excludes both an indefinite and a generic interpretation, but unlike Mandarin, preverbal Cl-NPs in Wenzhou can be interpreted as definite:

(12) a. Dɣu⁸ kau⁸ i⁵   tsau³-ku⁵ ka¹-løy⁶.
           CL   dog   want   walk-cross street

      'The dog wants to cross the street.'

     b. *Dɣu⁸ kau³ sɨ³-çy¹ tshɨ⁷ niou⁸.
           CL   dog   like   eat   meat

      Intended generic reading: 'Dogs like to eat meat.'
      (Only possible reading: 'The dog likes to eat meat.')

Interestingly, when Cl-NPs in Wenzhou are interpreted as definite, the tone of the classifier is affected. Wenzhou has eight tones (Norman 1988, Pan 1991), which are divided in four different classes, which for practical reasons we will call A, B, C, and D. Each of these classes, in turn is divided in two subclasses according to register, hi and lo. Thus, we have a hi-A, a lo-A, a hi-B, a lo-B, and so on, and they are numbered accordingly (see table 7.1 and the examples): 1 for hi-A, 2 for lo-A, and so on. Given a five-point scale (1 = low, 5 = high), the tonal contour values are in table 7.1. Chen's (2000: 476) values are partly different, the biggest difference being that, according to him, the D-tones have a dipping contour. The values Chen provides are 313 and 212 for hi-D and lo-D, respectively.

What happens to the tone of the classifier when Cl-NPs are interpreted as definite is that, along register-lines, it invariably is pronounced as a D-tone, whatever its original tone may have been: hi-A (tone number 1), hi-B (number 3), and hi-C (number 5), as well as hi-D (number 7), surface as hi-D (number 7), while lo-A (tone number 2), lo-B (number 4), and lo-C (number 6), as well as lo-D

Table 7.1 Tonal contour values of the eight tones of Wenzhou

Tone	1	2	3	4	5	6	7	8
	hi-A	lo-A	hi-B	lo-B	hi-C	lo-C	hi-D	lo-D
Value	44	31	45 (abrupt)	24 (abrupt)	42	11	23	12

Values are from Norman 1988: 202

(number 8), surface as lo-D (number 8) (You 2000; see also Pan 1991). For now, we call this process "tonal neutralization"; we discuss it more in section 4.1.2.

Let's look at some examples. The original tone of the classifier for dogs *dɣu* is the lo-A (tone number 2): *dɣu²*. In (12a), where the Cl-NP is interpreted as definite, the tone changes to lo-D (tone number 8). If we change the tone in (12a) to its original lo-A (as we do in (13)), the sentence is ungrammatical: because of the tone, we can no longer have a definite reading and, just like in Mandarin, an indefinite reading is excluded in preverbal position:

(13)   *dɣu²   kau⁸   i⁵   tsau³-ku⁵   ka¹-løy⁶
       CL   dog   want   walk-cross   street

In postverbal position, *dɣu² kau⁸* 'CL dog' would of course be grammatical— although it has an indefinite interpretation:

(14)   ŋ⁴   çi³   ma⁴   dɣu²   kau⁸.
       I   want   buy   CL   DOG
       'I would like to buy a dog.'

To illustrate the mechanism one more time, we present a minimal pair in (15) (cf. (11a)):

(15)   a. ŋ̀⁴   çi³   ma⁴   paŋ³   si¹.
          I   want   buy   CL^volume   book
          'I want to buy a book.'

       b. ŋ̀⁴   çi³   ma⁴   paŋ⁷   si¹.
          I   want   buy   CL^volume   book
          'I want to buy the book.'

The only difference between (15a) and (15b) is the tone on the classifier *paŋ* 'volume'. Its orginal tone is hi-B, (number 3). Keeping the original tone, the Cl-NP in (15a) is interpreted as indefinite. In (15b), *paŋ* appears in the hi-D-tone (number 7), and the Cl-NP receives a definite interpretation.

Some classifiers inherently have a D-tone. In the appropriate context, Cl-NPs with these classifiers are ambiguous:

(16)   ŋ⁴   çi³   ha⁷   ɣ⁷/liɛ⁷   thuɔ¹.
       I   want   drink   CL^bowl/CL^PL   soup
       'I would like to drink a bowl of soup/some soup.'
       or: 'I would like to drink the soup.'

In short, Wenzhou Cl-NPs can be interpreted as definite, as long as the classifier is pronounced with a D-tone. For all classifiers that do not inherently have a D-tone, this means a tone change, to be referred to as tonal neutralization (for discussion, see section 4.1.2).[5]

2.2.3 *Num-Cl-NPs*

With respect to Num-Cl-NPs, Wu is the same as Mandarin. They are interpreted as indefinite, either specific or nonspecific. Distributionally, they are limited to postverbal position. Here are some Wenzhou examples. The counterparts of (7c) and (8a,b) are also ungrammatical in Wu/Wenzhou. It should be noted, that the classifier preceded by *i⁷* 'one' keeps its inherent tone:

(17) a. ŋ̀⁴ çi³ ma⁴ i¹ paŋ³ si¹ le² tshɨ⁵.
          I   want buy one CL^{volume} book come read
          'I would like to buy a book to read.' (nonspecific)

    b. ŋ̀⁴ dei⁶ i⁷ y⁷ thuɔ¹ ha⁷ jy² ba⁴.
          I   take one CL^{bowl} soup drink up SFP
          'I finished a bowl of soup.' (specific)

2.2.4 *Summary*

In Wu, Bare NPs can be interpreted as definite, indefinite, or generic. Cl-NPs are interpreted as indefinite in all varieties of Wu (nonspecific only); in some, like Wenzhou, they can also be interpreted as definite, in which case the tone of the classifier is affected in the sense that some neutralization takes place. Num-Cl-NPs are invariably indefinite (specific or nonspecific). All indefinites occur in postverbal position only.

2.3 Min

The situation in Southern Min is the same as Mandarin, with one exception: it has no Cl-NPs, not even in an indefinite reading (Chen 1958, Zhou 1991).

2.3.1 *Bare NPs*

Thus, just like in Mandarin (as was the case in Wu), Bare NPs can be interpreted as definite, indefinite, and generic, depending, partly, on the predicative context and the position vis-à-vis the verb (preverbal position excluding an indefinite interpretation). The sentences in (18) and (19) are parallel to the Mandarin examples in (1) and (2); as to (18b), like Wu, Min disallows postverbal objects in bounded predicates, and, like Wu (see (9b)), it marks the object in preverbal position, using an element meaning 'take':

(18) a. I   be   bue   zhu.
          he   want buy   book
          'He would like to buy a book/books.'

      b. I   ga   teN   lim   liao   a.
          he   take soup drink PRF   SFP
          'He finished the soup.'

      c. I   ai   hue.
          he   like flower
          'He likes flowers.'

(19) a. Gau be   lim   zhui.
          dog want drink water
          'The dog/dogs want/s to drink water.' (definite only)

      b. Gau ai   lim   zhui.
          dog like drink water
          'Dogs like to drink water.' (definite possible; indefinite excluded)

2.3.2 Cl-NPs

It is explicitly mentioned in the literature (e.g., Chen 1958, Zhou 1991) and confirmed by the informants that Southern Min has no Cl-NPs: the classifier can never occur without being preceded by either a numeral or a demonstrative.[6] Thus, the counterparts of Mandarin (3a) and Wenzhou (12a) are ungrammatical in Southern Min:

(20) a. *Ua siuN bue   bun   zhu.
           I   want buy   CL^{volume} book
           Intended: 'I would like to buy a book.'

      b. *Jia gau be   lim   zhui.
          CL   dog want drink water
          Intended: 'The dog wants to drink water.'

2.3.3 Num-Cl-NPs

Just like in Mandarin and Wu, Southern Min Num-Cl-NPs receive a specific or nonspecific indefinite interpretation:

(21) a. Ua   siuN   bue   jit-bun   zhu.
         I   want   buy   one-CL^volume   book

      'I would like to buy a book.' (nonspecific)

      b. I   ga   jit-waN   teN   lim   liao   a.
         he   take one-CL^bowl soup   drink   PRF   SFP

      'He finished a bowl of soup.' (specific)

2.3.4 Summary

In Southern Min, Bare NPs can be interpreted as definite, indefinite, or generic. Num-Cl-NPs are invariably indefinite, either specific or nonspecific. Cl-NPs do not occur in this language in either an indefinite or in a definite interpretation. As before, all indefinites occur in postverbal position only.

2.4 Cantonese

2.4.1 Bare NPs

Cantonese is different from all three varieties of Chinese previously described in that Bare NPs cannot be interpreted as definite: they can receive only a generic and an indefinite reading:

(22) a. Wufei   heoi   maai   syu.
         Wufei   go   buy   book

      'Wufei went to buy a book/books.'

      b. *Wufei   jam-jyun   tong   la.
         Wufei   drink-finish   soup   SFP

      Intended: 'Wufei finished drinking the soup.'

      c. Ngo   zung-ji   gau.
         I   like   dog

      'I like dogs.'

(23) a. *Gau   soeng   gwo   maalou.
         dog   want   cross   road

      Intended: 'The dog wants to cross the road.'

      b. Gau   zung-ji   sek   juk.
         dog   like   eat   meat

      'Dogs love to eat meat.' (only interpretation possible)

2.4.2 *Cl-NPs*

With respect to Cl-NPs, Cantonese is similar to Wenzhou: aside from an indefinite interpretation, Cl-NPs can also be interpreted as definite. In Cantonese, however, there are no tonal effects. The indefinite use is illustrated in (24a); the definite interpretation is exemplified in (24b,c) (cf. (22b) and (23a); also, see the Wenzhou sentences in (11b) and (12a)):

(24) a. Ngo soeng maai bun   syu   lei   taai.
         I   want   buy   CL^{volume} book come read

       'I want to buy a book to read.'

      b. Wufei jam-jyun   wun/di   tong la.
         Wufei drink-finish CL^{bowl}/CL^{PL} soup SFP

       'Wufei finished the soup.'

      c. Zek gau   soeng gwo   maalou.
         CL   dog   want   cross road

       'The dog wants to cross the road.'

2.4.3 *Num-Cl-NPs*

Num-Cl-NPs have the same distribution and interpretation in Cantonese as they do in the other varieties of Chinese, discussed previously.

2.4.4 *Summary*

In Cantonese, Bare NPs can be interpreted as indefinite or generic, but not as definite. Cl-NPs can be either definite or indefinite (nonspecific), with no tonal repercussions. Num-Cl-NPs are invariably indefinite (specific or nonspecific). As in all the other varieties, all indefinites occur in postverbal position only.

2.5 Summary of Form-Interpretation Correlations

The form–interpretation correlations are summarized in table 7.2. Depending on the perspective chosen, these facts can be described in different ways. From the perspective of the formal properties, we can summarize them as follows:

Formal Properties

1. Num-Cl-NPs are the same in all languages: they allow for only an indefinite reading. Later we present a proposal to explain why that is the case.
2. Cl-NPs show more variation. In Min, they are not possible at all. In Mandarin, Cantonese, and Wu, they occur, but while in Mandarin they

Table 7.2 Correlations between form, interpretation, and distribution of nominal expression in four Chinese languages

Interpretation	Form		
	Num-Cl-NP	Cl-NP	Bare NP
Indefinite	Mandarin	Mandarin	Mandarin
	Wu	Wu	Wu
	Min	*Min	Min
	Cantonese	Cantonese	Cantonese
Definite	*Mandarin	*Mandarin	Mandarin
	*Wu	Wu—w. tone neutr.	Wu
	*Min	*Min	Min
	*Cantonese	Cantonese	*Cantonese
Generic	*Mandarin	*Mandarin	Mandarin
	*Wu	*Wu	Wu
	*Min	*Min	Min
	*Cantonese	*Cantonese	Cantonese

*Not found.

can receive only an indefinite reading, in Cantonese and Wenzhou they can be interpreted as definite as well. Wenzhou has the extra feature of tonal neutralization affecting the classifier in definite Cl-NPs, while the indefinite counterpart does not involve such tonal neutralization. In Cantonese, the tones are unaffected. Later, we propose an explanation as to why Cl-NPs can be interpreted as indefinite and definite, why Cl-NPs cannot be definite in Mandarin while they can in Cantonese and Wenzhou, and what the significance of the tonal neutralization in Wenzhou definite Cl-NPs is.

3. Bare NPs can be interpreted as indefinite and generic in all four languages. As far as the definite interpretation is concerned, Bare NPs can be so interpreted in Mandarin, Wenzhou and Min—that is, in the two languages in which Cl-NPs cannot be interpreted as definite (Mandarin and Min) and in the language in which the definite Cl-NP involves tonal neutralization for the classifier. In Cantonese Bare NPs cannot be interpreted as definite. Later, we investigate the question as to how it is possible that Bare NPs can be interpreted as indefinite, definite, and generic, as well as the question why Cantonese is different.

From the perspective of the interpretative properties, the facts in table 7.1 may be summarized as follows:

Interpretive Properties

1. To express an indefinite reading, the four languages are basically the same: Num-Cl-NPs, Cl-NPs, and Bare NPs can be interpreted indefinitely in all cases, the only exception being Min, in which Cl-NP-phrases do not occur at all. Indefinites are only found in postverbal position.

2. The generic interpretation is even more simple: all four languages use only Bare NPs to express genericity.

3. The way to express the definite reading is more complicated. In Mandarin and Min, definiteness is expressed with Bare NPs only. Cantonese employs Cl-NPs to express definiteness. Wenzhou does both, but in the definite Cl-NPs the tone of the classifier is affected.

Later we discuss the form, interpretation, and distribution of the different nominal expressions in the four languages discussed here. We will focus on definite and indefinite phrases, because they show interesting variation.[7] Before investigating the variation, however, we want to take a closer look at the nature and use of classifiers.

3 CLASSIFIERS

3.1 Classifiers and the Functional Domain of N

3.1.1 *The Function of Classifiers*

So far we have been using the term "classifier" loosely, as a cover term for two types of elements, traditionally referred to as "classifiers" and "measure words" and dubbed "count-classifiers" and "mass-classifiers" in Cheng and Sybesma (1998) ("count-classifiers" and "mass-classifiers" were subsequently abbreviated to "classifiers" and "massifiers," respectively). The difference between the two elements is the following (for some discussion, see Croft 1994 and Tai and Wang 1990). Measure words are used to make masses countable; this is the case in Chinese as well as in other languages:

(25) a. a glass of water

b. een   glas   water (Dutch)
   a   glass water

c. yat   bui   seoi (Cantonese)
   one   cup   water

As these examples show, if you want to count a mass like water, you need a counter, a unit to count it with. Measure words make masses countable by creating a unit by which they can be counted. These units have to be created because masses, by their very nature, do not come naturally in units by which they can be counted. WATER does not naturally come in countable units, so we force it into glasses or bottles (or liters or barrels).

Aside from measure words, languages like Chinese have classifiers. In such languages, count nouns look like mass nouns in that they, too, need a counter when you want to count; the examples in (26) show that counting without a counter, in this case the classifier for books, leads to ungrammaticality:

(26)　a.　yi　　*(ben)　shu (Mandarin)

　　　b.　i⁷　　*(paŋ³)　sɨ¹ (Wenzhou)

　　　c.　jit　　*(bun)　zhu (Southern Min)

　　　d.　yat　　*(bun)　syu (Cantonese)
　　　　　one　CLᵛᵒˡᵘᵐᵉ　book

The difference with measure words is that classifiers do not *create* any unit to count by. Unlike mass nouns, count nouns have a built-in semantic partitioning; they come in naturally countable units. Classifiers, then, simply *name* the unit that the semantic representation of the noun naturally provides.

In other words, just like other languages, Chinese languages have count nouns and mass nouns in the sense that they have nouns whose semantic representation does not have a built-in partitioning in natural units and nouns whose semantic representation does have such partitioning. Languages like Chinese, however, need a counter for both noun categories; it simply is a property of these languages that they cannot count anything without the intervention of a counter. In the case of mass nouns, these counters (the measure words, or mass-classifiers) create their unit of counting, in the case of count nouns the counters (the classifiers, or count-classifiers) simply name the unit that the semantic representation of the noun provides.

They are called "classifier" because different nouns have different count-classifiers, depending on the shape or any other property of the individual units that come with the natural partitioning. In Mandarin, for instance, long, tall things like humans are counted with a classifier, *ge*, that goes back to a word meaning 'bamboo'. In this sense they can be seen to classify.

In the following discussion, we will use the term "classifier" either as a cover term for measure words and classifiers or as a shorthand for count-classifier. Only when it really matters do we strictly distinguish between count-classifiers and mass-classifiers.

3.1.2 *Why Count-Classifiers?*

The question that comes up immediately is why we need count-classifiers. If the semantics of the nouns in question already involves a partitioning in natural units, why do we need elements to name them when we start counting?

Doetjes (1996) argues that, in general, for count nouns to be countable, the partitioning that is part of their semantic denotation must be (made) syntactically visible; numerals require the presence of a syntactic marker of countability. She further argues that this countability marker can be realized in different ways: in some languages, number morphology performs this function, while other languages use count-classifiers. In other words, count-classifiers and number morphology have the same function of serving as a syntactic countability marker.[8]

The idea that number and count-classifiers are associated is not new, as Doetjes points out. Greenberg (1963) notes that there is a tendency for languages without grammatical number to make use of count-classifiers. Interesting evidence also comes from language development. Ikoro (1994) describes the development of Kana, a Nigerian Cross River language, which lost its noun class-related number morphology and replaced it with a count-classifier system, while other languages of the same family kept the original system and did not develop count-classifiers. Peyraube (1997) suggests that the development of count-classifiers in Chinese is related to the loss of an element that may have been a plurality marker.

3.1.3 *Association with Number*

Aside from the considerations given previously, there are other indications that classifiers have something to do with number (for discussion, see Paris 1981, 1989). First of all, in the Wenzhou and Cantonese definite Cl-NP phrases, it is the classifier that determines whether we are dealing with plural or singular.

(27) a. bun   syu (Cantonese)
          CL^{volume} book

      'the book(*s)'

      b. di   syu
          CL^{PL} book

      'the book*(s)'

(28) a. paŋ^7 sɨ^1 (Wenzhou)
          CL^{volume} book

      'the book'

      b. liɛ^7 sɨ^1
          CL^{PL} book

      'the book*(s)'

All Chinese languages have a general classifier for the unspecified plural; the same form is used for all nouns—count-nouns, and mass-nouns alike. In Cantonese it is *di*, in Wenzhou *liɛ*⁷, in Mandarin *xie*. A "canonical" classifier like Cantonese *bun* 'volume' in (27a) signals singular, whereas the plural classifier *di* in (27b) marks the whole phrase as plural. The Wenzhou examples in (28) illustrate the same thing. Mandarin can be shown to work in exactly the same way, with indefinite Cl-NP phrases:

(29) a. Wo   xiang   mai   ben   shu. (Mandarin)
         I   want   buy   CL^volume   book

         'I would like to buy a book.'

      b. Wo   xiang   mai   xie   shu.
         I   want   buy   CL^volume   book

         'I would like to buy some books.'

The only difference between these sentences lies in the choice of the classifier. These facts strongly suggest that the classifier is the locus of Number in Chinese.

Second, Iljic (1994) turns the argument around by showing that, in any case, the noun itself is unmarked for number. The following example (somewhat adapted) shows that the phrase *zhe xin* 'DEM letter/s' can be referred back to with a singular, as well as a plural, noun phrase:

(30) a. Ni   zhe   xin   dei   cheng   yi-xia ...
         your   this/ese   letter/s   must   weigh   a-bit

         'This/These letter(s) of yours must be weighed ...

      b. ... ta   chao-zhong-le / liang-feng   dou   chao-zhong-le.
            it   overweight   / two-CL   all   overweight-PRF

         ... it is/they are both overweight.'

If one considers universal quantification as a kind of pluralization, reduplication of the classifier may be seen as constituting a third indication of the connection between number and the classifier, since reduplication of the classifier yields a universal quantification reading (Paris 1981: 69). The flexibility in this respect is not the same in all Chinese languages, but they all allow for classifier reduplication at least to a very basic degree. Here are examples, one from Mandarin and one from Cantonese:

(31) a. ge-ge   xuesheng (Mandarin)
         CL-CL   student

         'every student'

b. zek-zek   gau (Cantonese)
   CL-CL   dog
   'every dog'

In short, the classifier is the locus for grammatical number in Chinese.[9]

3.1.4 *Individuation*

Closely related to the countability function is the "individualizing function" (Croft 1994: 162) of classifiers, a function that is also noticed by Iljic (1994) and Paris (1981), among others. As we just saw in (27) and (28), the canonical classifiers are always singular.

We may rephrase this and state that the classifier singles out one entity from the plurality of entities provided by the semantic representation of the noun in the lexicon; it picks out one instance of what is denoted by N. This is also represented in the Chinese way of saying 'three books': it uses the individuating classifier as shown in (32), not the plural one, as the ungrammaticality of the phrases in (33) asserts:

(32)   san   ben   shu (Mandarin)
       saN   bun   zhu (Southern Min)
       saam   bun   syu (Cantonese)
       three CL^volume book

(33)   *san   xie   shu (Mandarin)
       *saN   se   zhu (Southern Min)
       *saam   di   syu (Cantonese)
       three   CL^PL book

Thus, the literal translation of 'three books' in Chinese is 'three singular units / instances of book'.

The relevance of this discussion will become clear shortly, when we discuss more generally the functional superstructure of the noun in the following section.

3.2 The Functional Superstructure of N

3.2.1 *What It Does*

The discussion in the previous sections is limited to classifiers in Chinese. In this section, we relate this discussion to the issue of the functional superstructure of the noun more generally, especially because we assume that classifiers and D serve similar functions.

Several notions come up in general discussions on the functional domain of the noun phrase. Two of these notions, which seem to be expressed in the nominal domain in all languages of the world, are definiteness and number. All languages have ways of discriminating between definite and indefinite reference. Likewise, they all have ways of distinguishing singular from plural.

Before going into definiteness and number, we prefer to change the perspective and concretely look at what basic functions D, the head of the functional category DP, has been associated with. We single out two. First, it has been associated with what one could call a "subordinating" function (Szabolcsi 1987, 1994; Abney 1987; Stowell 1989). In semantic terms, NPs are predicates, which can be turned into arguments by D (type-shifting; Partee 1987). It is only thanks to being embedded in DP that an NP can be used as an argument at all. Second, Longobardi (1994) argues that the individuating function we associated with the classifier in Chinese is also a typical D-function. He states (1994: 634) that D has the ability to pick out a single instance of whatever is described by N (see also Higginbotham 1985).

We think that these two functions which D is supposed to perform (individuation, syntactic subordination) are closely related to, or even different manifestations of, a more fundamental property of the DP domain: its deictic property—the property to be able to refer at all.

Generally speaking, in language, there is a division of labor between the lexical domain and the functional domain. The division of labor can be summarized as "lexical units describe, functional units refer." It can also be described as "lexical units refer to a concept, functional units refer to actual instantiations of that concept in the real world." The lexical entity *dog*, for instance, "describes" in the sense that it refers to a concept—"dogness." It is only thanks to functional elements like *a* and *the* that we can use lexical items like *dog* to refer to actual instantiations of "dogness" in the real world.

The same division of labor is found in the verbal domain. *Bake cookies* describes a certain type of event. Embedding it in a deictic category like Tense Phrase (TP) enables one to use it to refer to an actual event in the real world that can be described as "bake cookies": *(John) baked cookies*; T explicitly links the lexical phrase *bake cookies* with a specific event associated to the time axis of the real world.

This division of labor between functional and lexical categories is such a fundamental property of language that it must be part of Universal Grammar: all languages have it.

From the literature it may be deduced that this deictic function is a function mainly associated with D. D individuates and, possibly, by doing so, subordinates. The question that arises is this: If this division of labor is such a fundamental property of language, and the deictic function is performed by D, what is going on in languages that lack D?

Before answering this question, we take a look at the nominal phrase in English and French.

3.2.2 *The D in English and French*

Consider the following phrases from English and French. In all these phrases, the determiners (*the*, *a*, and Ø in English; *le*, *les*, *un*, and *des* in French) presumably perform the deictic function. What else do they do?

(34) a. the boy, the boys

     b. a boy, boys

(35) a. le   garçon, les   garçons
          theM:SG boy   thePL boys

     b. un   garçon, des garçons
          aM:SG   boy   aPL   boys

In English, the determiner *the* signals definiteness. It does so in both plural and singular phrases. In other words, *the* does not give us any information with respect to Number. In English definites, Number is marked on the N. *A* signals indefiniteness, but also singularity. The plural indefinite does not have an overt determiner in English.

In French, the determiner is responsible for expressing both number (Delfitto and Schroten 1991) and definiteness. *Garçon* and *garçons* sound exactly the same: whether we are dealing with plural or singular, definiteness or indefiniteness is marked by the determiner. The singularizing function apparent from *a* in English seems to be part of *le*'s function in French as well.[10]

When we look at (36), we see that *le* does even more:

(36) a. le   garçon
          theM:SG boy

     b. la   fille
          theF:SG girl

As Croft (1994) notes, grammatical gender must be seen as a kind of noun classification, and in languages such as French, gender is expressed through the determiner.

In short, D in French expresses definiteness, number, and noun classification. Besides, it has the deictic function we mentioned earlier; it individuates in the sense developed previously and makes it possible for an NP to be used as an argument.

In English, D performs the deictic function, but it only expresses (in)definiteness; it does not express Number, and noun classification does not play a role in English. Number in English is expressed on the noun.

3.2.3 *Cl in Cantonese*

Earlier we posed the question: If Universal Grammar incorporates a describing-referring dichotomy and D takes care of the referring deictic function in the nominal domain, what happens in languages that don't have determiners?

The answer is, of course, that some other functional head will perform that function. When we turn our attention to Cantonese against the backdrop of our discussion of English and French in the previous section, we find that in Chinese the classifier does many things that determiners do in other languages. Consider the basic Cantonese data in (37):

(37) a. bun   syu;   di   syu
         CL^{volume} book;   CL^{PL} book

       'the/a book; the/ø books'

      b. yat-bun   syu;   syu
         one-CL^{volume} book;   book

       'a book; books'

      c. go   jan;   zek   gau
         CL   person;   CL   dog

       'a/the person; a/the dog'

What do these examples tell us? First, the fact that these phrases "refer" means that some element performs the deictic function. Second, the fact that, as was shown in the example sentences in the first section, these phrases can be arguments of predicates indicates that some element functions as the subordinator. Third, these clusters of facts show very clearly that the classifier is the locus of number (see the a-examples) as well as classification (compare the classifiers used in the a-examples with the ones used in the c-examples); the individuation function was elaborated on previously. The definiteness–indefiniteness contrast is less straightforward, at least in the singular (we discuss this fact later); the plural shows a clear presence–absence contrast, as was the case in English.

In short, all the functions the determiner takes care of in French are performed by the classifier in Cantonese: definiteness, number, individuation, noun classification, subordination, and deictism.

This leads to the conclusion that the classifier is the head of a functional projection, ClP, which is in all relevant ways comparable to DP in languages like French and English. (For earlier proposals of ClP, see, for instance, Tang 1990.)

3.3 Conclusion of Classifiers

In this section we have investigated the function of the classifier, in its own right as well as to the background of the more general discussion on the function of the superstructure in the nominal domain. We found that there is one fundamental function to be performed by a functional head in the nominal domain: the deictic function. The lexical NP describes; the functional head deictically refers. We also found that this function is intricately related to the expression of number, definiteness, and even noun classification. It is also linked to the more purely syntactic function of making it possible for the lexical NP to be embedded in a predicate as an argument.

In languages with determiners, the deictic function is performed by D. In Chinese, at least in Cantonese, we concluded, it is taken care of by the classifier. The classifier heads its own functional projection, ClP. This leads to the postulation of the following structure (to be qualified later):

(38)

$$
\begin{array}{c}
\text{ClP} \\
\diagup\diagdown \\
\text{Cl} \\
\diagup\diagdown \\
\text{Cl}^0 \quad \text{NP}
\end{array}
$$

We will see that this is the structure we find in all Chinese languages discussed here. The question is, of course, how we account for the variation we found in section 2.

4 INTERPRETATION AND DISTRIBUTION

In section 2 we saw that both Bare NPs and Cl-NP phrases can be interpreted as either definite or indefinite. (As noted, the position in the sentence plays a role in determining the interpretation.) Among the languages we discuss in this chapter, Wenzhou is unique in allowing both interpretations for both. In Mandarin, Bare NPs can have both interpretations, while Cl-NPs are exclusively indefinite. In contrast, in Cantonese, Cl-NPs can have both interpretations, while Bare NPs are restricted to indefiniteness. In Min, which disallows Cl-NPs altogether, Bare NPs can get both readings.

In section 3 we preliminarily postulated the structure in (38) as the structure for nominal phrases in Chinese. Now in section 4 we investigate the question what determines the variation we found: Why can some phrases be definite in one position but not in the other? Why can some types of NP be definite in the one language but not in the other?

4.1 Definites

4.1.1 *Cantonese, Mandarin, and Min*

Two different types of phrases can be interpreted as definite: Cl-NPs and Bare NPs. Before we turn to Chinese, let us first determine how, in general, definiteness is supposed to arise.

Essentially following the literature, we assume that definiteness arises as the result of the insertion of a certain operator, called the ι operator, into D (Partee 1987). We further assume that the ι operator may be realized as a definite article, as is the case in languages such as English, or may be nonovert, for languages without a definite article. Insertion of the ι operator in D most likely subsequently triggers N-to-D-movement, overtly or nonovertly (see, e.g., Ritter 1989, Longobardi 1994); for enlightening discussion on these matters, see Chierchia (1998).

Let us now turn to Cantonese. In section 3 we reached the conclusion that Cl has many properties in common with D—the singularizing, deictic function being one of them—and we subsequently likened ClP in Chinese-type languages to DP in English and French-type languages. We propose that definite Cl-NPs in Cantonese have the structure in (38): the lexical NP is embedded in a functional structure, ClP, the head of which is filled by an ι operator realized as an overt classifier. The overt classifier has exactly the same function as determiners like English *the*: thanks to the ι operator, insertion in Cl⁰ makes the phrase definite.

As to Mandarin, we suggest that it takes the other option we mentioned: definite Bare NPs also have the structure in (38), but now the ι operator in the head of ClP is nonovert (presumably triggering covert N-to-Cl movement).

This means that all definite nominals in Cantonese and Mandarin have the underlying structure in (38). Cantonese fills the Cl⁰-position with an overt classifier, yielding definite Cl-NPs. Mandarin derives definite Bare NPs by inserting the nonovert ι operator in Cl⁰ (followed by covert N-to-Cl).

Southern Min, of course, is the same as Mandarin. Its definite Bare NPs are derived in exactly the same way: insertion of the empty ι operator in Cl⁰, followed by covert N-to-Cl.

4.1.2 *Definites in Wenzhou*

Among the languages we discuss here, Wenzhou is exceptional because it allows a definite interpretation for both Bare NPs and Cl-NPs. The definite Bare NPs should be unproblematic: their derivation will be the same as in Mandarin and Min: Cl^0 in their underlying structure (38) hosts an empty ι operator, yielding the definiteness.[11]

The definite Cl-NP, in contrast, may be more problematic because of its extra feature, which we have been referring to as tonal neutralization. In definite Cl-NPs, all classifiers with tones belonging to the hi-register subcategory end up being pronounced as a hi-D-tone; all lo-register tones end up being pronounced as lo-D.

In actual fact, what we observe is a general lowering. If we describe the tones of Wenzhou in terms of a three-point scale (H,M,L) instead of a five-point scale, as was done in table 7.1, hi-A, hi-B, and hi-C can be characterized as H, and hi-D as M or L. At the same time, lo-A, lo-B, and lo-C can be characterized as M or L, while lo-D is L.[12] In other words, H goes to M or L; both M and L end up as L.

We propose that in Wenzhou, the ι operator, in addition to being nonovert, can also be realized as a low tone, a nonsegmental unit. When the low tone ι operator is inserted in Cl^0, it must be supported by an element with a richer phonological (i.e., segmental) matrix, like a classifier. As a result of the fusion between the low tone ι operator and the classifier, the classifiers with a tone that is characterizable as H are lowered to M (or L), and the ones with an M or L tone are lowered to L.[13] This proposal is in line with the principle that all tones must be borne by a full syllable (see the work by John Goldsmith—e.g., Goldsmith 1976), as well as the principle that morphemes must always be realized; otherwise we wouldn't know it is there (Lin 1993). In the case at hand, the ι operator in Cl^0 has the form of a low tone, and nothing else; as a consequence, in order for the definiteness to be expressed, the tone has to be realized—on the classifier. Interestingly, the original tone of the classifier is reflected in the register: hi-register tones come out as hi-D, lo-register tones as lo-D (except, of course, if the two D-tones are not distinguished; see note 12).

If this proposal is correct, it means that the ι operator can have a phonological reflex that is anywhere between zero and a lexical, fully segmental element like a determiner or a classifier: it can be realized as something nonsegmental as a tone.

Also, the proposal entails that the formation of definites in Wenzhou involves a certain degree of optionality: it can pick either of two manifestations of the ι operator (discussed further in section 5.2).

4.1.3 Summary

To conclude this section on definites, we have seen that all definite nominals in Chinese we discussed have (38) as their underlying structure. The derivation of definites involves the insertion of an ι operator into the head of ClP. The ι operator has different manifestations. It may be nonovert, as is the case in Mandarin and Min and is an option in Wenzhou; or it may be overt, in which case it is either realized as a full lexical element, a classifier, as is the case in Cantonese, or it may be realized as a low tone, as we saw is an option in Wenzhou. In the latter case, the tone has to be provided with a segmental matrix, like a classifier, which has lowering effects on the tone of the classifier involved.

At least two questions arise: (a) What determines the difference between the different languages? For instance, is there any reason that, say, Mandarin cannot be like Cantonese? And where does the optionality in Wenzhou come from? (b) If Cl-NPs and Bare NPs have the underlying structure in (38), how can they also be interpreted as indefinite? We answer the first question in section 5, after having answered the second question in the next section.

4.2 Indefinites

The only type of phrase that is invariably indefinite in all languages dealt with in this study is the Num-Cl-NP phrase, the one with an overt numeral. In view of the discussion on definites in the previous section, we assume that the indefinite reading is due to the presence of the Numeral; we return to this later. Let us postulate the following structure for indefinite nominal phrases in Chinese, where NumeP stands for NumeralP (instead of NumP, to avoid confusion with NumberP).

(39)

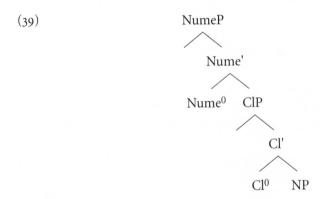

Is there any evidence that (39) is the underlying structure for all different types of indefinite noun phrases, including Cl-NPs and Bare NPs? We think there is.

Longobardi (1994) develops a proposal with respect to the distribution and interpretation of bare nouns in Germanic and Romance. Distributionally, bare nouns in Germanic and Romance are limited to lexically governed positions (in effect, object positions) and interpretationally, they are restricted to an indefinite reading. Longobardi's proposal comes down to the following. Bare nouns are not really bare: they are, of course, embedded in a full-fledged DP projection, the head of which is empty. The assumption of the empty D helps Longobardi explain both the restricted distribution and the limitations on the interpretation in the following way. First, as the empty D is just like any other empty category in having to be lexically governed, the distribution of bare nouns is limited to lexically governed positions. Second, Longobardi argues that an empty D is associated with an existential reading (see also Chierchia 1998).

Turning our attention to indefinite Cl-NP phrases, if they have the same structure as Num-Cl-NPs—that is, the structure in (39), in which the Numeral is empty—we predict that they are limited to lexically governed positions. As the facts in section 2 show, this is the case: Cl-NPs can have an indefinite interpretation only in object position.[14]

For indefinite Bare NPs, the reasoning and the conclusion are the same. The fact that the Bare NPs with an indefinite reading occur only in lexically governed positions suggests that they involve an empty category that has to be governed. If it is the case that in Chinese indefiniteness arises as a result of the presence of a numeral, the Bare NP must have a numeral. In short, we assume that indefinite Bare NPs also have the structure in (39); the difference with indefinite Cl-NPs is that in the case of Bare NPs, not only the Numeral head Nume^0 is empty but also the Cl^0 is empty.[15]

In short, assuming the structure in (39) for indefinite Cl-NPs and Bare NPs explains their limited distribution.

Comparing (39) with (38) we see that (39) actually consists of (38) embedded in a NumeP. Because the structure in (38) is the structure, that underlies all definite nominals in Chinese suggests that the indefinite interpretation arises as a result of the presence of the Numeral. The NumeP, being a quantificational expression, is interpreted as indefinite. "A book" in Chinese languages is literally "[one [the book]]." To get an indefinite reading, a NumeP is required.

In this respect, there seems to be a difference between languages with articles and those without. As was suggested by Teun Hoekstra (class lectures, fall 1996), nominals in Germanic and Romance languages are quantificational expressions—that is, indefinite—unless they are embedded in a DP. Thus, "the book" in English is in fact "[the [(a) book]]." Articled languages have indefinite articles (or, in their absence, the numeral ONE) to pick out singularities, while article-less languages have only classifiers for that purpose. Classifiers, however, are very similar to definite determiners, as we saw earlier.

Before closing off this section, we would like to mention two things. First, definite Cl-NPs and definite Bare NPs do not involve an empty category: in case of the definite Cl-NP, there is no numeral ((38) does not involve a NumeP); in the case of the Bare NP, aside from there being no NumeP, Cl^0 is occupied by the ι operator and N^0 as the result of N-to-Cl. Since they do not involve an empty category, they should not be restricted distributionally, and they aren't.

Second, in section 2 we noted that indefinite nouns with an overt numeral can be interpreted as both specific and nonspecific, while indefinite Bare NPs and Cl-NPs can only be nonspecific. In Cheng and Sybesma (1999: 530–532), we supply ample evidence that indefinite Cl-NPs involve an empty numeral and that they, and indefinite Bare NPs, are excluded from contexts in which a specific interpretation is the only possible option for an indefinite; we have seen some such contexts before, such as (3b). The fact that indefinite Cl-NPs and indefinite Bare NPs may only be nonspecific, while full-fledged Num-Cl-NPs may be both specific and nonspecific, is likely to be related to the empty Numeral in the former: an empty Numeral leads to a nonspecific interpretation. A possible explanation for the difference between an empty Numeral and an overt Numeral is that the latter is a full-fledged quantifier and as such can undergo quantifier raising (QR), yielding a specific reading. In contrast, an empty Numeral lacks the QR option. Instead, it relies on the presence of existential closure to supply the existential quantification, yielding a narrow scope nonspecific reading (cf. Diesing 1992).

4.3 Summary

These are the structures postulated for definite and indefinite nominal phrases in Chinese: all indefinites (Num-Cl-NPs, Cl-NPs, Bare NPs) have the structure in (40a) (=(39)); all definite structures (Cl-NPs, Bare NPs) have the structure in (40b) (=(38)). In the indefinite case of (40a), Nume⁰ and Cl⁰ may be left empty; in the definite (40b), Cl⁰ is filled by the ι operator (possibly realized as an overt classifier) and the covertly moved N⁰:

(40) a. NumeP   b.   ClP

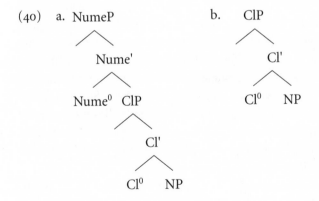

5 How to Account for the Variation

The four varieties of Chinese dealt with here differ from one another in the following ways:

1. Mandarin and Min do not have definite Cl-NPs, they have definite Bare NPs; for Cantonese, exactly the opposite is true.
2. Mandarin has indefinite Cl-NPs, like Cantonese and Wenzhou; Min does not: it is the only variety with no Cl-NPs at all.
3. Cantonese and Wenzhou are the only varieties with definite Cl-NPs, but they differ in that in Wenzhou the tone of the classifier is affected.
4. Wenzhou differs from all others in that it allows a definite reading for both Cl-NPs and Bare NPs; all other languages allow a definite reading for just one of the two.

5.1 Mandarin and Min versus Cantonese

We saw that the derivation of definite nominals involves the ι operator, the difference between the languages discussed in this chapter resulting from the different manifestations the ι operator may take on. Disregarding Wenzhou for the moment, we see that definite nominals are either Cl-NPs (as in Cantonese) or Bare NPs (as in Mandarin and Min): Cantonese involves the insertion of an overt classifier, just as English inserts its overt determiner, while Mandarin and Min have no overt reflex of the ι operator.

From a general point of view, it seems that the option favored by Cantonese is the preferred one (the default). That is to say, in his discussion on noun phrases in English and other languages, Chierchia (1998) suggests that, as far as definiteness is concerned, expressing it overtly is favored over doing it covertly. In other words, if, in principle, there is a choice, languages opt for expressing definiteness overtly, using a definite article (or, we may add now, a classifier). Since the Cantonese option involves insertion of a classifier in Cl⁰, this embodies the preferred procedure. This explains why in Cantonese this is the only option. At the same time, it raises the question what is wrong with Mandarin and Min: What bars them from opting for the preferred choice?

In this context we would like to point at two facts. First, in Min, it is impossible to have an overt classifier without a numeral: as we have mentioned several times, Min has no Cl-NPs at all. Second, in Mandarin, Cl-NPs are always indefinite. If our assumption that indefinites have the underlying structure in (40a) is correct, this means that Mandarin overt classifiers also cannot occur without a numeral, the difference between Mandarin and Min being that Min cannot have empty numerals.

Let us phrase this in the form of a restriction on the appearance of overt classifiers in these varieties of Chinese:

(41)   In Mandarin and Min, overt classifiers are always accompanied by a numeral. (In Min, the numeral must be overt; in Mandarin it may be overt or nonovert.)

Cantonese does not have this property. Although we have no deeper explanation for this difference between Cantonese on the one hand and Mandarin and Min on the other, the restriction explains why it is impossible for Mandarin and Min to get definite nominals in the preferred way. After all, the preferred way involves the insertion of an overt classifier in the head of ClP. For Mandarin and Min, overt classifiers always come with a numeral, and numerals lead to indefiniteness.

5.2 Optionality in Wenzhou

It is not clear how Wenzhou, having both definite Bare NPs (like Mandarin and Min) and definite Cl-NPs (like Cantonese), fits into this picture. Since it does not have the restriction in (41) (as is clear from the data in section 2.2), there is no reason why it should not be like Cantonese.

To be sure, Wenzhou does have definite Cl-NPs, but the tone of the classifier is lowered. Before, we claimed that this is the result of a fusion between a nonsegmental, strictly tonal ι operator and the classifier. In other words: we analyzed definite Cl-NPs in Cantonese and Wenzhou as entirely different. In definite Cl-NPs in Cantonese, the Cl is the classifier in its full form—a segmental ι operator. In the Wenzhou definite Cl-NPs, in contrast, the classifier is there only to provide the nonsegmental ι operator with segmental material.

In section 4.1.2, we suggested that the ι operator can have a phonological manifestation that is anywhere between zero and a fully segmental lexical element like a determiner or a classifier; after all, it can also manifest itself as something nonsegmental, (a low tone, for instance). Let us be less liberal and state that there are three options: segmental, nonsegmental, and empty.

In view of the facts of Cantonese and Wenzhou, we may conclude that only the segmental manifestation counts as fully overt for the purposes of expressing definiteness as discussed previously in the context of Chierchia's hypothesis that definiteness is preferably expressed overtly. Syntactically, the nonsegmental tone does not count as "overt."

This means that the optionality in expressing definiteness displayed by Wen-zhou does not involve the preferred, overt option; it is between two nonovert options. That is why it can have optionality at all. As Chierchia states, *if* there is a choice, and the overt option is one of the alternatives, then that is, really, the only option, the default. Then there can be no optionality.[16]

The answer why Wenzhou is not like Cantonese, then, comes down to the fact that the choice it has for expressing definiteness does not involve the overt option. We don't know why this is the case.

5.3 Parameters Discussed in This Chapter

The first parameter to be mentioned is the one that distinguishes "languages with articles" from "languages with classifiers." Several differences between these two types of languages seem to fall out from one main difference—the fact discussed in section 4.2 that whereas in article languages definites are indefinites-turned-definites, languages with classifiers derive indefinites on the basis of definites. This difference is the consequence of the latter type of language having no indefinite article.

Within the domain of Chinese, the variation may be reducible to the following parameters. The first is whether or not definiteness is expressed by a segmental ι operator in Cl⁰—that is, in the form of a full-fledged classifier—which would set Cantonese apart from the other varieties. A second is whether or not it is possible to have an overt classifier without a numeral (setting apart Mandarin and Min from Wenzhou and Cantonese). Third, Mandarin, Wenzhou, and Cantonese can have empty numerals, whereas Min cannot. The parameters can be charted out as in table 7.3. The claim that the nonovert ι operators involve a (phonologically speaking) truly empty one and one in the manifestation of a low tone is not considered in the table.

It is conceivable that some of these parameters are related to the status of the classifier at a deeper level. As such, they may possibly be connected to phenomena other than the ones discussed in this chapter. There may be a deeper difference, distinguishing "weak classifiers" from "strong classifiers." Aside from the question as to whether they can occur with or without a numeral, we should consider the freedom of reduplication of the classifier (which seems, at a first impression, freer in Cantonese and Wenzhou than in Mandarin and Min), as well as the question whether they are used as the element that links the modifier to its noun (which is the case in Cantonese and some varieties of Wu, but not in Mandarin and Min). More research in this area is necessary to see whether there is such a "deep" parameter.

Table 7.3 Parameters for variation within Chinese

	Classifier or article	ι operator realized segmentally	Overt classifier obligatory with numeral	Can numeral be empty?
		Parameter		
Mandarin	Classifier	No	Yes	Yes
Wenzhou	Classifier	No	No	Yes
Southern Min	Classifier	No	Yes	No
Cantonese	Classifier	Yes	No	Yes

NOTES

This chapter incorporates most of the arguments and conclusions in Cheng and Sybesma (1999). In gathering and sorting the data, we received help and advice from many people, which we gladly and gratefully acknowledge. In particular we acknowledge the input from the following colleagues:

Wu: We thank You Rujie for sharing with us his Wu expertise in general and for providing and discussing the Wenzhou data. Thanks a lot! For Shanghainese we are especially indebted to Hua Dongfan. We also discussed Shanghainese with You Rujie, Eric Zee, Lu Bingfu, and Duanmu San.
Min: The data were provided (and checked with other informants) by C.-C. Jane Tang. Thanks are also due to Tang Ting-chi.
Cantonese: Thomas Lee and Sze-Wing Tang helpfully provided judgments.

We furthermore thank the following colleagues for more general comments and discussion: Thomas Lee, Jane Tang, Dylan Tsai, and especially Richard Kayne, Guglielmo Cinque, and Moira Yip.

Sybesma's research was partly supported by P. Muysken's Spinoza Research Program "Lexicon and syntax" and partly by his own "Vernieuwingsimpuls"-project on syntactic variation in southern China, cofunded by the Dutch Organization for Scientific Research NWO, Universiteit Leiden (main sponsors), and the International Institute for Asian Studies (IIAS).

1. The three varieties of Chinese not mentioned are Hakka, spoken in the area where the provinces of Jiangxi, Guangdong, and Fujian border; Gan, spoken in Jiangxi; and Xiang, the language of Hunan.

2. We use the following abbreviations in the glosses: CL = classifier; PRF = perfectivity/boundedness marker; SFP = sentence-final particle. In case it seems useful to provide the meaning of the classifier, it is added in superscript. Mandarin is transcribed using the pinyin system. For Cantonese we used the Romanization system developed by

the Linguistic Society of Hong Kong. Transcribing Wenzhou, we use the IPA. The Min transcription was provided by Jane Tang (for Min, there does not seem to be a standard); the capital N stands for nasalization. Tones have been left unmarked except in the Wenzhou data, where they are marked using superscript numbers.

3. Without the help of You Rujie we would not have been able to present a complete set of Wenzhou data; especially the presentation of the tone facts would have been much more sketchy.

4. For discussion of the Mandarin counterpart, *ba*, see Sybesma (1999).

5. The situation in Shanghainese is not as clearcut as in Wenzhou. You Rujie (pers. comm.) confirms that the Shanghainese language situation is unstable, or at least that a lot of variation exists among speakers. Qian (1997: 98–99) claims that Shanghai is like Wenzhou the way we described it in the text, in that Cl-NPs can be interpreted as definite, in which case the classifier undergoes a tone change (the precise mechanics of the tonal changes being different from what happens in Wenzhou). Qian says that the younger generation uses it rarely. One of our Shanghainese informants agrees that Cl-NP can be used with a definite reading but is not aware of any tonal change. This is basically the picture sketched by Pan (1991). Three of our informants do not accept Cl-NPs in a definite reading; in an indefinite reading, they are judged fine. The Shanghainese of these speakers is exactly like Mandarin.

6. It seems that the younger generation of Taiwan's Min speakers who are fluent in Mandarin as well do not reject Cl-NPs in Min entirely, in which case they get a nonspecific indefinite interpretation; this may be due to influence from Mandarin.

7. We have included the generic interpretation of noun phrases in this description for the sake of completeness only. Mainly because the languages discussed do not show any variation here (as well as because of space limitations), we do not discuss the generic interpretation of Bare NPs in this chapter. For the same reasons, we leave the derivation of the proper name interpretation of common nouns undiscussed here. For some discussion of generics in Chinese, see Cheng and Sybesma (1999: 532–534) and references cited therein); for proper names, see Cheng and Sybesma (1999: 523–524).

8. We are aware of the fact that languages such as Finnish and Hungarian do not have plural markings when combined with a numeral. However, these languages would still count as "Number" languages. The absence of the plural marking may be a matter of agreement.

9. As a consequence, *men* cannot be a plurality marker—contra Li (1999). We disagree with Li for many reasons, one being that her approach does not explain the lack of productivity of *men*; another reason is that it does no justice to the meaning of *men*, which is much more a collective marker than a plural marker. See Iljic (1994) and Cheng and Sybesma (1999) for discussion.

10. In some cases French nouns do make a plural-singular distinction (*cheval, chevaux*), and in combination with the preposition *à* the determiner loses its number function: *au* and *aux*. Similarly, nouns may express gender, and the gender function of the determiner may be neutralized; both are illustrated by *l'étudiant* and *l'étudiante*. These exceptions do not undermine the system of French as described in the text.

11. We thank Moira Yip for discussion of the phonological side of the discussion in this section.

12. Chen (2000: 476–477) reports that in his informant's speech, the two D-tones are not distinguished. In Chen's tone system of Wenzhou, the D tone is characterized as

L. (Recall that Chen works with partly different values; see the comment under table 7.1 in the text.)

13. The lowering rule apparently does not apply to the D-tones themselves.

14. Indefinites with a numeral can also not occur in subject position; this is due to reasons related to existential closure: see Diesing (1992), Cheng (1991), and Tsai (1994), and, for some discussion, Cheng and Sybesma (1999).

15. We assume that movement of N to Cl (or Nume, for that matter) would only take place if it is triggered.

16. The restriction in (41) bars Mandarin and Min opting for both the segmental and the nonsegmental-only ι operators. At the same time, the reasoning in the text leaves open the possibility that they pick the empty one for reasons not related to (41). After all, we do not have a clear idea as to what factors have a role in determining the choice for any of the three ι operators.

REFERENCES

Abney, Stephen (1987) "The English Noun Phrase in Its Sentential Aspect." Ph.D. diss., MIT, Cambridge, Mass.

Chen, Chuimin (1958) "Minnanhua he Putonghua changyong liangci de bijiao [A comparison of frequently used classifiers in Southern-Min and Standard Mandarin]." *Zhongguo Yuwen* 1958/12: 591–593.

Chen, Matthew Y. (2000) *Tone Sandhi: Patterns across Chinese Dialects*. Cambridge University Press, Cambridge.

Cheng, Lisa L.-S. 1991. On the Typology of wh-Questions. Ph.D. diss., MIT, Cambridge, Mass.

Cheng, Lisa L.-S., and Rint Sybesma (1998) "Yi-wan tang, yi-ge Tang: Classifiers and massifiers." *Tsing-Hua Journal of Chinese Studies*. New Series 28/3: 385–412.

Cheng, Lisa L.-S., and Rint Sybesma (1999) "Bare and Not-So-Bare Nouns and the Structure of NP." *Linguistic Inquiry* 30/4: 509–542.

Chierchia, Gennaro (1998) "Reference to Kinds across Languages." *Natural Language Semantics* 6: 339–405.

Croft, William (1994) "Semantic Universals in Classifier Systems." *Word* 45/2: 145–171.

Delfitto, Denis, and Jan Schroten (1991) Bare Plurals and the Number Affix in DP." *Probus* 3: 155–185.

Diesing, Molly (1992) *Indefinites*. MIT Press, Cambridge, Mass.

Doetjes, Jenny (1996) Mass and count: syntax or semantics? *Meaning on the HIL*. [Occasional Papers in Linguistics.] HIL/Leiden University.

Goldsmith, John (1976) "Autosegmental Phonology." Ph.D. diss., MIT.

Greenberg, Joseph (1963) *Universals of Language*. MIT Press, Cambridge, Mass.

Higginbotham, James (1985) "On Semantics." *Linguistic Inquiry* 16: 547–593.

Ikoro, Suanu (1994) "Numeral Classifiers in Kana." *Journal of African Languages and Linguistics* 15: 7–28.

Iljic, Robert (1994) "Quantification in Mandarin Chinese: Two Markers of Plurality." *Linguistics* 32: 91–116.

Li, Y.-H. Audrey (1999) "Plurality in a Classifier Language." *Journal of East-Asian Linguistics* 8: 75–99.

Lin, Yen-hwei (1993) "Degenerate Affixes and Templatic Constraints: Rhyme Change in Chinese." *Language* 69/4: 649–682.

Longobardi, Giuseppe (1994) "Reference and Proper Names." *Linguistic Inquiry* 25: 609–666.

Norman, Jerry (1988) *Chinese*. Cambridge University Press, Cambridge.

Pan, Wuyun (1991) "An Introduction to the Wu Dialects." William S.-Y. Wang (ed.) *Languages and dialects of China*. Journal of Chinese Linguistics Monograph Series 3: 237–293.

Paris, Marie-Claude (1981) *Problèmes de syntaxe et de sémantique en linguistique chinoise*. Collège de France, Paris.

Paris, Marie-Claude (1989) *Linguistique générale et linguistique chinoise: Quelques exemples d'argumentation*. UFRL, Université Paris 7, Paris.

Partee, Barbara (1987) "Noun Phrase Interpretation and Type-Shifting Principles," in J. Groenendijk and M. Stokhof (eds.) *Studies in Discourse Representation Theory and the Theory of Generalized Quantifiers*. Foris, Dordrecht, 115–143.

Peyraube, Alain (1997) "On the History of Classifiers in Archaic and Medieval Chinese," B. T'sou, A. Peyraube, and L. Xu, (eds.) *Studia Linguistica Sinica*. Hong Kong City University, Hong Kong.

Qian, Nairong (1997) *Shanghaihua yufa* [Shanghainese grammar]. Renmin, Shanghai.

Ramsey, S. Robert (1987) *The Languages of China*. Princeton University Press, Princeton.

Ritter, Elizabeth (1989) "A Head-Movement Approach to Construct-State Noun Phrases." *Linguistics* 26: 909–929.

Stowell, Tim (1989) "Subjects, Specifiers, and X-bar Theory." in M. Baltin and A. Kroch (eds.) *Alternative Conceptions of Phrase Structure*. University of Chicago Press, Chicago.

Sybesma, Rint (1992) "Causatives and accomplishments. The Case of Chinese *ba*." Ph.D. diss., HIL/Leiden University.

Sybesma, Rint (1999) *The Mandarin VP*. Kluwer, Dordrecht.

Szabolsci, Anna (1987) "Functional Categories in the Noun Phrase," I. Kenesei (ed.) *Approaches to Hungarian 2*, JATE, Szeged, 167–190.

Szabolsci, Anna (1994) "The Noun Phrase," in the Ferenc Kiefer and Katalin Kiss (eds.) *Syntactic Structure of Hungarian*, Syntax and semantics, 27. Academic Press, New York, 179–274.

Tai, J. and L. Q. Wang. (1990) A Semantic Study of the Classifier *tiao*. *Journal of the Chinese Language Teachers Association* 25/1: 35–56.

Tang, C.-C. Jane (1990) "Chinese Phrase Structure and the Extended X-theory." Ph.D. diss., Cornell University.

Tsai, Dylan W.-T. (1994) "On Economizing the Theory of A-bar Dependencies." Ph.D. diss., MIT, Cambridge, Mass.

You, Rujie (2000) Wenzhou fangyan yufa gaiyao [Outline of Wenzhou dialect grammar]. *You Rujie zixuanji* [Selected writings of You Rujie]. Anhui Jiaoyu, Hefei.

Zhou, Changji (1991) *Minnanhua yu Putonghua* [Southern Min and Standard Mandarin]. Yuwen, Peking.

CHAPTER 8

MORPHOLOGY AND WORD ORDER IN "CREOLIZATION" AND BEYOND

MICHEL DEGRAFF

1 PROLOGUE

AN introduction to "Creole" morphosyntax would be incomplete without a so-
ciohistorically based discussion of the term Creole and its implications for
comparative-historical linguistics. This essay thus starts with a brief and preliminary critique, in section 2, of certain foundational assumptions in Creole studies.[1]

Then I provide a theoretically grounded overview of a selected subset of VP-
related properties in Haitian Creole (HC)—a bona fide Creole, on the sociohistorical grounds outlined in section 2. Section 3 introduces the basic comparative
data related to verb and object placement in HC and some of its major source
languages. Section 4 contemplates the theoretical implications of verb-placement
contrasts between HC and its European ancestor, French—the principal etymological source of the HC lexicon. Section 5 extends this discussion to the morphosyntax of object pronouns. (The basic data and observations in section 3–5

are taken mostly from DeGraff 1994a, 1994b, 1997, 2000. In fact, this chapter is the payoff of long overdue promissory notes; see DeGraff 1997: 90 n42, 91 n51.)

Section 6 enlarges the discussion to include relevant patterns in Germanic and French diachrony and to inquire about the ("abnormal"?) theoretical status of CREOLE EXCEPTIONALISM—the long-posited opposition between "abnormal" "nongenetic" transmission in Creole genesis, supposedly with "significant discrepancies," and "normal"/"genetic" transmission in "regular" language change, whereby a language is "passed down from one speaker generation to the next with changes spread more or less evenly across all parts of the language" (see, e.g., Thomason and Kaufman 1988: 8–12, 206, 211, etc.).

Section 7 ends the chapter by considering the consequences of the theoretical discussion in sections 3–6 vis-à-vis Creole Exceptionalism. In this section I also compare the Haitian Creole data with germane data from a couple of other Romance-lexifier Creoles: namely, Cape Verdean Creole (lexifier: Portuguese) and Palenquero Creole (lexifier: Spanish). This preliminary comparison suggests that, even within a small sample of Romance-lexified Creoles, there is no structural "Creole" uniformity in the VP and its extended projections. More generally, there is no distinct and uniform "Creole" typology.

My overall conclusion is that, from a Cartesian and Uniformitarian (e.g., a Universal Grammar [UG] based and mentalist) perspective, Creole genesis ultimately, and unsurprisingly, reduces to the same of sort of mental processes that underlie the diachrony of non-Creole languages.

2 Some Histori(ographi)cal Background on Creoles and Creole Studies

2.1 Sociohistorical and Epistemological Assumptions

Creole Exceptionalism—the dogma that Creole languages constitute an exceptional class on either genealogical or typological grounds or both—is a corollary of the twin (neo-)colonial history of Creole speakers and Creole studies (see DeGraff 2001a: 90–105; 2002a).

The languages we call "Creoles" (e.g., Caribbean Creoles) do share well-documented commonalities across sociohistorical profiles (e.g., history of large-scale language contact) and across structural tendencies (e.g., reduction of inflectional paradigms). These commonalities seem uncontroversial, even if these sociohistorical and structural tendencies are also found among other products of language evolution that are not usually labeled "Creole."

What is more controversial is the claim that, across time and across space, Creole languages can be defined as a *typologically* distinct language grouping whose *exceptional diachrony* makes them cluster around an *exceptional structural* "prototype" (see the critiques in, e.g., Givón 1979; Mufwene 1986, 2001; Muysken 1988, and the references in note 1). Such exceptionalist stereotypes have a long history in linguistics—see, for example, the Creole morphological profiles postulated by Jespersen (1922: 233), Hjelmslev (1938), Bickerton (1988: 276), Seuren and Wekker (1986), McWhorter (1998), and Seuren (1998: 292–293). Notwithstanding their long-standing popularity, these stereotypes for Creole morphology have now been shown to be empirically, theoretically, and sociologically problematic.

For my purposes in this chapter, I assume that a valid "Creole" grouping can be reasonably defined on sociohistorical grounds (cf. Mufwene 1986, 2001), not necessarily on genetic, typological, or topological grounds. I thus use "Creole" as an atheoretical ostensive label to point to certain linguistic varieties that are typically perceived as having "abruptly" emerged out of massive language contact as restructured versions of some (erstwhile) "target" language. (I have more to say later in this essay about the terms in quotes.) The most celebrated examples are in the Caribbean, where Creole languages emerged in the seventeenth to nineteenth centuries, as one linguistic side effect of colonization and slave trade by the British, the French, the Portuguese, the Dutch, and the Spaniards. It is thus that the Caribbean has long been known for its history of population contact, and therefore language contact. Prototypical examples of Creole languages usually include the popular vernaculars spoken in the (greater) Caribbean area: Haitian Creole, Jamaican Creole, Papiamentu, Saramaccan, Sranan, and so on.

From the sixteenth and seventeenth centuries onward, the basic ingredients of Europe's imperialist projects in the Caribbean came to typically include the following sociolinguistically relevant factors:

1. Initial contact between Europeans and Africans in and around the slave ports of Africa
2. The enslavement of increasing numbers of Africans and their subsequent dislocation to the "New World"
3. More and more Africans would become exposed to European languages or to approximations thereof by second-language learners with various (European and African) native languages[2]
4. Small homestead settler communities with relatively few slaves, in the early Caribbean colonial stages
5. The gradual and partial replacement, in economically successful colonies

such as Saint-Domingue (i.e., preindependence Haiti), of the original settler communities by large-scale and brutally inegalitarian slave-based plantation economies with a vast majority of Africans and their locally born descendants.

The increased reliance on regimented slave labor for economic expansion would, over time, reduce the ratio of Europeans to non-Europeans, with the two groups becoming more and more segregated, especially at the opposite poles of the power hierarchy and especially so on labor-intensive plantations (e.g., large sugar plantations) like those in Saint-Domingue. This social transformation would, in turn, lead to a complex array of language-contact and language-acquisition settings, with a complex array of linguistic varieties as outputs: a continuum of more or less restructured approximations of European languages with varying amounts of substratum effects and structural innovations. Throughout the colonial period, there existed "middle populations"—"middle" in terms of class, civil status, or race—with relatively close contact with both ends of the continuum. These intermediary populations included the mixed-race (the MU-LATTOES) and the free people of color (the AFFRANCHIS). The Mulattoes were locally born (i.e., "Creole"),[3] and so were many of the Affranchis. These middle populations, specially the Creoles, would play a key stabilizing role in Creole language formation. This is an oversimplified sketch of the extraordinarily complex sociohistorical matrix of Creole genesis (for details, see, e.g., Alleyne 1971; Chaudenson 1992; Chaudenson and Mufwene 2001; Singler 1996; Mufwene 1996, 2001; DeGraff 2002b, 2002c; and the many references therein).

No matter the complexity of, and the horrors inherent in, the sociohistory of Caribbean Creole genesis, it can still be assumed, in Cartesian-Uniformitarian fashion, that native Creole speakers, like native speakers of every other language, have always conformed to UG. Notwithstanding the inhumanity of slavery, the slaves and their descendants were still human. I thus assume, against Creole Exceptionalism, that the cognitive resources and strategies enlisted by language acquirers during Creole genesis are *not* fundamentally different from their analogues in friendlier and better documented cases of language change and creation. Like with any other language acquirers, the cognitive task facing native speakers of (the incipient) Creole languages represents yet another instance of the "poverty of stimulus" paradox, also known as "Plato's Problem" (Chomsky 1986): How does the mind/brain of the language acquirer come to possess complex and abstract linguistic properties for which the Primary Linguistic Data (the PLD) provide relatively little evidence? Linguistic theory's central paradox, namely "Plato's Problem," can be paraphrased as follows: For each speaker, the abstract properties that eventually characterize his or her idiolectal grammar—his or her stable I(NTERNAL)-LANGUAGE, a recursive combinatorial system—are not, and could not be, directly observable from the PLD (a finite set of data) available in the social context of language acquisition. In Creole genesis, too, language learners develop complex I-languages via exposure to relatively impoverished and superficial data sets.

With these basic assumptions in mind, let us proceed to briefly revisit some of the sociology underlying Creole Exceptionalism and its traditional import in comparative-historical linguistics.

2.2 Creole Exceptionalism in Early Creolistics

Creole studies in the colonial period are characterized by the widespread belief that Creole speech originally emerged as radically "corrupted" versions of the colonizers' European languages as spoken by the colonized *non-Europeans*—that is, by people of an "inferior" race. The term "negrified French," which E. F. Gautier coined to refer to French-lexicon Creoles, gained universal appeal in France (Brunot 1966 8:1136).

Racially based classifications of Creole varieties became part of early creolists' orthodoxy as canonized in (e.g.) Larousse (1869), Vinson (1889), and Adam (1883). In Larousse's (1869) dictionary, Creole speech is defined as "corrupted French" and is assumed to be "unintelligible when spoken by an old African [while] extremely sweet when spoken by white Creole women." In Vinson's (1889) encyclopedia, "Creole languages result from the adaptation of a language, especially some Indo-European language, to the (so to speak) phonetic and grammatical genius of a race that is linguistically inferior." In Adam's (1883) treatise on *Hybridologie Linguistique,* Creole languages such as Cayenne Creole (French Guyana) are the structural equivalents of European languages "back in infancy" (p. 157), "*sui generis* new languages . . . to be genetically classified with [West-African] languages, notwithstanding the Aryan nature of [the Creole] lexicon" (p. 5). Adam (1883: 4–7) postulates that African speakers—in his view, speakers of primitive, thus simple, languages—had not evolved the cognitive capacity required to master the structural complexities of European morphosyntax. For Adam, the postulation of race-based cognitive-biological constraints would explain why Cayenne Creole was necessarily African even if its words are etymologically European. Adam's *Hybridologie Linguistique* was thoroughly and explicitly in keeping with the Darwinian evolutionary tropes of the (neo-)Schleicherian linguistics of his era.

More generally, linguists from the seventeenth century onward (see, e.g., Pelleprat (1965 [1655])) have attempted to ascribe generally negative *structural* properties to Creole languages individually or as a group, and this as a matter of (natural) course. Instantiations of this dogma still flourish in twentieth-century linguistics. For example, Seuren, in his 1998 *Western Linguistics: An Historical Introduction,* claims that "Creole grammars . . . lack the more sophisticated features of languages backed by a rich and extended cultural past and a large, well-organized literate society" (p. 292).

It is thus that Creole languages have traditionally been defined by what linguistic features they (allegedly) do not, and cannot, have because of the limited intelligence or the evolutionarily or culturally primitive status of their speakers. (Also see, e.g., Saint-Quentin 1989: 40f. [1872] and Baissac 1880: 23, 32, 92, 103f., for illustrations of Creole Exceptionalism in early Creole studies; the references in note 1 offer extended reviews and critiques of Creole Exceptionalism.)

2.3 Creole Exceptionalism in Contemporary Creolistics

Most contemporary linguists seem to have abandoned the explicitly racist claims of the colonial era. Yet, one widely held dogma in historical linguistics still considers Creole languages to have emerged through "broken," thus "abnormal," transmission. The postulation of such extraordinary "break in transmission" has traditionally forced Creole languages in an exceptional class—namely, the class of "non-genetic [i.e., parentless] languages."[4] In contradistinction, non-Creole languages are taken to gradually evolve "genetically" via the sort of "normal transmission" represented by Stammbaum branches (as, e.g., in Latin-to-Romance or Proto-Germanic-to-English diachrony).

Thomason and Kaufman's (non)genetic-(ab)normal litmus test is primarily structural: broken, or abnormal or nongenetic, transmission implicates "a *significant discrepancy* between the degree of lexical correspondence and the degree of grammatical correspondence—in some or all grammatical subsystems" (1988: 206, emphasis added; see also p. 8–12). But, as I show later in this chapter, "significant discrepancy" as a criterion for "abnormal" creolization as opposed to "normal" language change is, at best, elusive and, at worst, circular: the kind of discrepancies that are manifested in bona fide cases of Creole genesis seems to be on a par with corresponding discrepancies in the diachrony of "genetic" languages (see sections 6–7; see also Mufwene 2001 and some of the references therein).

In a vein somewhat similar to Thomason and Kaufman's classification, both classic and contemporary creolistics postulates sui generis ("abnormal") developmental processes that apply exclusively to Creole genesis. One such process is pidginization that, in the limit, eschews all morphology (Jespersen 1922; Hjelmslev 1938; Bickerton 1984; Seuren and Wekker 1986; McWhorter 1998; Seuren 1998; and others). This hypothetical morphological bottleneck is allegedly one symptom of some "radical break in transmission." More spectacularly, pidginization creates a "born again" proto-Language—a living fossil of prehistoric Language at its evolutionary incipience (see note 4). Such neo-Darwinian hypotheses are empirically disconfirmed by robust data sets and various theoretical observations about Creole diachrony and synchrony (see note 1).

Creole Exceptionalism, implicitly if not explicitly, also underlies the Relexification Hypothesis (Lefebvre 1998). With respect to the genealogy and ontology of Creole languages, Lefebvre (1998: 3) evokes the claims of Adam's (1883) *Hybridologie Linguistique*. Following Adam, Lefebvre argues that Haitian Creole grammar essentially reflects substratum grammar with the French contribution having been strictly limited to phonetic strings "deprived of [syntactic and semantic] features" (pp. 16.f) and to word-order patterns in lexical (e.g., N, V, Adj, P) projections only (pp. 39.f). Given the massive and systematic etymological and word- and affix-order correspondences between French and HC, Lefebvre must assume that the Creole creator was somehow able to segment and (re)analyze French strings and adopt and adapt a great deal of French phonetics and surface order—down to the phonetic shapes and surface distribution of many affixes and grammatical morphemes—while ignoring virtually *all* abstract structural properties of French. Such a feat would make the Creole creator unlike any other language learner documented in the psycholinguistics and language-acquisition literature. After all, word segmentation and word- and affix-order are reflexes of *abstract* morphosyntactic properties. The language acquirer cannot identify, for example, morphemes and their order in the target language without some amount of *abstract* knowledge about morpheme boundaries, morphosyntactic features, lexical categories, and other nonphonetic properties of the target language. Later (in, e.g., section 3.3) I illustrate additional aspects of Haitian Creole morphosyntax that cannot be accounted for by the sort of strict relexification posited by Adam and Lefebvre (see also section 6.2, 6.4; Fattier 1998; DeGraff 2001a, 2002b, 2002c).

In effect, the discussion in this chapter revisits all of the above-mentioned traditional assumptions about Creole languages. I question current dogmas on Creole diachrony and synchrony, using Haitian Creole—a bona fide plantation Creole—as a case study, with a focus on core aspects of Haitian morphosyntax in the domain of the verb phrase and associated functional layers. A preliminary comparison of a small sample of HC versus French morphosyntactic similarities and dissimilarities with counterparts thereof in Germanic and French diachrony suggests that there may be no independent *structural* basis for the now-orthodox dichotomy between Creole languages and non-Creole languages. Furthermore, the sort of language-contact and language-shift effects and structural innovations visible in the formation of HC can also be documented in non-Creole diachrony and in language acquisition (see section 6).[5] Such parallels are neither accidental nor surprising in a mentalist (i.e., Cartesian) framework that assumes UG. The latter offers no conceptual room for a fundamental opposition between Creoles and non-Creoles.

3 THE BASIC COMPARATIVE DATA: VP-RELATED MORPHOSYNTAX

3.1 Some Creole Data

Haitian Creole (HC), like its major source languages, is canonically SVO. The examples that follow illustrate the fact that the majority of HC morphemes—whether lexical or functional, whether free or bound—are etymologically related to French (Fr). HC morphemes with Fr etymology include productive affixes such as the "diminutive" suffix *-èt* (cf. French *-ette*). Also, the HC verb in (1), *konnen* 'to know', has lexico-semantic properties similar to those of its Fr analog in (8), *connaître*. Compare, say, their argument structures and their thematic properties. In fact, such similarities hold for the majority of HC lexical items, from concrete terms (e.g., HC *tab* 'table; cf. Fr *table*) to abstract terms (e.g., the psychological predicate *konnen*). Fattier (1998) provides a wealth of additional evidence for the deep etymological relationship between HC and its lexifier; see also DeGraff (2001a, 2001b, 2002c).

Notwithstanding pervasive etymological connections and structural continuities between HC and Fr, there exist striking and robust morphosyntactic differences between the two languages. One such difference concerns the distribution and inflection of verbs and object pronouns. Here I summarize observations from Dejean (1992), DeGraff (1994a, 1994b, 1997, 2000), and Roberts (1999).

Let's start with the distributional facts. First, consider the HC data. HC pronominal objects, like their nonpronominal counterparts, systematically occur to the *right* of their θ-marking verb:[6]

(1) a. Bouki konnen <u>Boukinèt</u>. (HC)
        Bouki know   Boukinèt

      'Bouki knows Boukinèt.'

     b. Bouki konnen <u>li</u>
        Bouki know   3sg

      'Bouki knows him/her/it.'

(2) a. *Bouki <u>Boukinèt</u> konnen. (HC)

     b. *Bouki <u>li</u> konnen

Not only do HC objects uniformly occur to the right of their θ-marking verb but also, whether pronominal or nonpronominal, they must be *adjacent* to that verb, as in (3). Except for the indirect object in the double-object constructions, clause-internal elements (e.g., adverbs or negation markers) cannot intervene between verb and their objects:

(3) a. Bouki <u>deja</u>   konnen Boukinèt. (HC)
     Bouki already know   Boukinèt

   'Bouki already knows Boukinèt.'

   b. Bouki <u>pa</u>   konnen Boukinèt. (HC)
     Bouki NEG   know   Boukinèt

   'Bouki doesn't know Boukinèt.'

(4) a. *Bouki konnen <u>deja</u> Boukinèt. (HC)

   b. *Bouki konnen <u>pa</u> Boukinèt.

In addition to the distributional uniformity of objects in postverbal position, HC displays another sort of uniformity. Abstracting away from dialectal variation (see, e.g., Fattier 1995) from morphosyntactically conditioned phonological reduction (see, e.g., Cadely 1997) and from a subset of pro-forms that are restricted to certain subject or predicate positions (see, e.g., DeGraff 1992a, 1992b, 1992c, 1992d, 1995a, 1995b, 1998), we find the same pronominal forms occurring in distinct structural positions: as subjects, as objects (of verbs, prepositions, and adjectives) and in the "possessor" position of noun phrases. Outside the eighteenth and nineteenth-century varieties mentioned by Fattier (1995: 138f.) and documented in Ducœurjoly 1802, there is no overt marking of morphological case on HC pronouns. Here's a partial sample of HC personal pronouns (these pronouns are generally atonic; see DeGraff 1992b, 1992c; we return to the etymology of these atonic pronouns, from Fr tonic pronouns, in section 6.4):

(5)   **A sample of HC personal**
              pronouns with no morphological
              Case distinction

Person	Singular	Plural
1	mwen	nou
2	ou	nou
3	li	yo

The inflectional profile of HC pronouns is, in some sense, on a par with the inflectional profile of the HC verb, which is not morphologically inflected for grammatical distinctions such as Tense, Mood, Aspect (TMA), or agreement. A form like *konnen* 'know' in (6) does not morphologically covary with the person, number, or gender features (ϕ-features) of its subject:[7]

(6) {Mwen | Ou | Li | Nou | Yo} konnen Boukinèt. (HC)
    1sg | 2sg | 3sg | 1pl/2pl | 3pl know Boukinèt

    '{I | You | He/She | We | They} know(s) Boukinèt.'

As of TMA features, these are expressed by preverbal free morphemes, as in (7) (also see section 4; in section 6.2 I discuss the etymology of HC TMA markers):

(7) a. Boukinèt te renmen Bouki. (HC)
       Boukinèt ANT renmen Bouki

       'Boukinèt loved Bouki.'

    b. Boukinèt ap renmen Bouki.
       Boukinèt FUT love Bouki

       'Boukinèt will love Bouki.'

    c. Boukinèt a renmen Bouki si . . .
       Boukinèt IRR love Bouki if

       'Boukinèt Would Love Bouki if . . .'

3.2 Some Superstratum Data

The Fr patterns here, which are well known in the comparative-syntax literature (see, e.g., Pollock 1989 and Sportiche 1995), are somewhat the mirror image of the HC patterns in (1)–(7), at least with respect to the following:

1. Object-pronoun placement vis-à-vis the θ-marking verb in nonimperative clauses[8]
2. Placement of the finite verb vis-à-vis clause-internal adverbs and sentential negation
3. Morphological case on pronouns
4. TMA-and agreement-related verbal morphology.

In (8)–(9), Fr object clitics, unlike Fr nonclitic objects, precede the finite verb (when the latter is not in the positive imperative).

(8) a. Bouqui connaît Bouquinette. (Fr)
     Bouqui know   Bouquinette

     'Bouqui knows Bouquinette'.

     b. Bouqui la   connaît.
        Bouqui 3sg-fem   know

     'Bouqui knows her.'

(9) a. *Bouqui Bouquinette connaît. (Fr)

     b. *Bouqui connaît la

Fr IP-internal adverbs and sentence negation follow the finite verb:

(10) a. Bouqui connaît déjà   Bouquinette. (Fr)
        Bouqui know   already   Bouquinette

     'Bouqui already knows Bouquinette.'

     b. Bouqui (ne)   connaît pas   Bouquinette.
        Bouqui NEG   know   NEG   Bouquinette

     'Bouqui doesn't know Bouquinette.'

(11) a. *Bouqui déjà connaît Bouquinette. (Fr)

     b. *Bouqui (ne) pas connaît Bouquinette

Fr *atonic* pronouns are morphologically inflected for case. Here's a sample of Fr atonic personal pronouns and case distinctions therein:

(12) **A sample of Fr (atonic) personal pronouns showing morphological Case distinctions**

Person	NOM	Non-NOM
1sg	je	me
2sg	tu	te
3sg	il (masc.), elle (fem.)	le (masc, ACC), la (fem, ACC), lui (dative)
1pl	nous	nous
2pl	vous	vous
3pl	ils (masc), elles (fem)	les (ACC), leur (DAT)

In Standard French, finite verbs host a relatively robust set of agreement and TMA suffixes:[9]

(13)   J'aime 'ısg-love+ısg'   Nous aim<u>ons</u> 'ıPL love+ıpl'
        Tu aimes '2sg love+2sg'   Vous aim<u>ez</u> '2pl love+2pl'
        Il/Elle aime '3sg+m/f love+3sg'   Ils/Elles aim<u>ent</u> '3pl+m/f love+3pl'

(14)   a. Bouquinette   aim-<u>ait</u>   Bouqui.
           Bouquinette   loved   Bouqui

        b. Bouquinette   aim-<u>era</u>   Bouqui
           Bouquinette   will love   Bouqui

        c. Bouquinette   aim-<u>erait</u>   Bouqui si . . .
           Bouquinette   would love   Bouqui if

The table in (15) sums up the contrasts between HC and Fr with respect to the distribution and morphology of verbs and objects, as sketched so far:

(15)   **Summary of HC-versus-fr VP-related contracts**

	HC	Fr
V Pronoun$_{Obj}$	OK	*
Pronoun$_{Obj}$ V	*	OK
NEG/Adv V$_{+fin}$ Obj	OK	*
V$_{+fin}$ NEG/Adv Obj	*	OK
TMA verbal suffixes	*	OK
Morphological case on pronouns	*	OK

3.3 Some Substratum Data

What could the substratum contribute, *in principle*, to the emergence of the contrasts in (15)? Consider Fongbè, for example, which is often taken as the most influential substrate language for the formation of HC grammar (see Lefebvre 1998 and references therein). First, verbs in Fongbè, as in HC, are not morphologically inflected for TMA or agreement. Second, TMA markers in Fongbè, as in HC, are generally, though not always (see da Cruz 1995), nonaffixal morphemes in preverbal position (Avolonto 1992). Third, verbs in Fongbè and many other West African languages have interpretative properties reminiscent of HC (e.g., all these languages manifest the "factative" effect; Déchaine 1991, Avolonto 1992, Aboh 1999 and chapter 4 in this volume, Ndayiragije 2000, and others).

This said, HC is not structurally isomorphic to its substratum—and neither is it isomorphic to its superstratum. Da Cruz 1995 documents postverbal completive markers in Fongbè, and Aboh (1999: 59f. and this volume) documents suffixal Aspect markers in Gengbe and Ewegbe. As we see in (20), Fongbè verbs do manifest inflectional and syntactic processes that are *not* attested in HC; see also Aboh (1999 and this volume).

For now, let's note that the distributional uniformity of HC objects and the morphological uniformity of HC pronouns—sans morphological case—distinguish HC from its major source languages, including Fr and Fongbè. Take the following four verb-syntax characteristics that have been argued to hold of Fongbè and of the Gbe grouping in general[10] (see Fabb 1992; Kinyalolo 1992; Déchaine and Manfredi 1997; Aboh 1999 and chapter 4 in this volume; Ndayiragije 2000):[11]

(16) a. An IP-internal leftward movement moves objects to the left of the θ-marking verb in certain contexts, as in (18)–(19).

b. The object-movement rule in (16a) distinguishes full NPs, including tonic pronouns, from atonic pronouns: the full NPs may undergo IP-internal object-movement to the left of the verb (as in (18)–(19), whereas the atonic pronouns are generally enclitics hosted by the θ-marking verb, as in (20).

c. Pronouns are overtly marked for morphological case distinctions—compare the first-person singular nominative pronoun in (18) and its nonnominative counterpart in (20).

d. The pattern in (20) illustrates verb reduplication (see Fabb 1992, Déchaine and Manfredi 1997, Ndayiragije 2000, and Aboh 1999 and this volume, for various treatments of reduplication and Object Shift in Gbe; see also note 58).

(17) Ùn ɖú mɔ̌lìnkún. (Fongbè)
     I   eat rice

'I eat rice.' (Adapted from Fabb 1992: 21)

(18) a. Ùn ɖò mɔ̌lìnkún ɖú wè. (Fongbè)
        I   be rice   eat CFP

b. * Ùn ɖò ɖú mɔ̌lìnkún wè.
     I   be eat rice   CFP

'I am eating rice.' (Kinyalolo 1992: 39)

(19) a. Yé ɖídó   nyè   xò gbé. (Fongbè)
        they take-to-the-road me (tonic) beat CFP

b. * Yé dídó xò nyè gbé.

'They took to the road to beat me.' (Adapted from Kinyalolo 1992: 37)

(20) Yé   ɖídó   xixò mì   gbé. (Fongbè)
      they take-to-the-road beat me (atonic)   CFP

(Adapted from Kinyalolo 1992: 37)

None of the four properties in (16) hold of HC. This is unexpected in the strict-relexification proposals of, for example, Adam (1883) and Lefebvre (1998), even though a more moderate sort of substratum influence via L1-transfer in second-language acquisition is quite likely (see the surveys in Mufwene 1990, 2001; DeGraff 1999c, 2001a, 2001b, 2002b, 2002c; Siegel 2003).

To recapitulate, both Fr and Gbe dialects, major source languages of HC, extensively instantiate word-order and case-morphology patterns that are totally absent in HC.[12] Can this be taken as evidence of nongenetic "abnormal transmission" (or "pidginization" or "radical break in transmission") of the kind that would set creolization apart from the diachronic processes that give rise to non-Creole languages?

The main goal of this chapter is to use the observations in this section to revisit the theoretical status of Creole Exceptionalism. In doing so, I'll show that the foundations and desiderata of modern comparative syntax erase the traditional distinction between "nongenetic" creolization and "genetic" language change. Using the Principles-and-Parameters approach to syntax, I will try in sections 4 and 5 to relate the positions of verb and objects in HC to each other and to the morphological profile of the language, enlisting what may be universal grammatical constraints. This is in keeping with the hunch in current generative work that the ultimate locus of language variation is in the lexicon, especially in the inventory and morphosyntactic properties of functional heads (see, e.g., Chomsky 1995). In turn, these theoretical considerations may shed light on the mechanics that underlie, and *unite*, creole genesis and language change (see section 6). In section 7, I examine verb- and pronoun-placement data in two other Romance-lexicon Creoles.

4 THE MORPHOSYNTAX OF HAITIAN CREOLE VERBS

4.1 Basic Facts

Recall the basic verb-placement contrasts that obtain across HC and its lexifier Fr in (3)–(4) versus (10)–(11). These are simplex clauses: the main, and only, verb therein (i.e., the θ-marking verb) occurs without any auxiliary. Let's call such clauses MONOVERBAL CLAUSES. In (Standard) French, these are clauses where the main verb inflects for, at least, person-number agreement and in some cases also evinces TMA suffixes (see (13)–(14)). In contrast, HC verbs evince no inflectional morphology for TMA or agreement, whether or not the main verb is the sole verbal element (see (6)–(7)).

In both languages, there is a class of adverbs that can appear, among other positions, clause-internally—strictly within the space delimited to the left by the subject and to the right by the nonpronominal, unmoved object. It is this clause-internal position that is most relevant for the contrasts at hand, so I abstract away from the other positions (e.g., clause-final) where some of these adverbs can surface, in both languages. (Recall that both HC and Fr are canonically SVO and that only Fr has preverbal object clitics.)

In HC and Fr monoverbal clauses, the clause-internal adverbs and the sentential negation marker appear, respectively, to the left and to the right of the verb. Witness (3a) / (4a) versus (10a) / (11a) and (3b) /(4b) versus (10b) / (11b).[13] The Fr verb-placement facts have been in the limelight of theoretical comparative syntax since Pollock (1989). Dejean (1992) and DeGraff (1994a, 1994b, 1997, 2000) provide additional HC and Fr data with other adverbs. These examples can be schematized approximately as in (21)–(22), abstracting away from the intricate stacking of negation and adverbs à la Cinque:

(21) a. Neg/Adv V   NP$_{Obj}$ (HC)

      b. *   V Neg/Adv NP$_{Obj}$

(22) a. *Neg/Adv V   NP$_{Obj}$ (Fr)

      b.   V Neg/Adv NP$_{Obj}$

4.2 Theoretical Proposals

The analysis proposed in DeGraff (1994a, 1994b, 1997, 2000) is relatively straightforward. In fact, the HC-versus-Fr contrasts shown previously are obviously reminiscent of the English versus Fr contrasts extensively studied in the prolific Pollockian tradition on comparative verb morphosyntax. The central assumption that I'll adopt from this tradition is that there is something like a "verb-placement parameter." The setting of this parameter determines for each given language the absence or presence or, more accurately, the *height* of verb movement to some INFL (inflectional) head within an increasingly intricate Cinquean layer of INFL projections between the CP and VP projections (cf. notes 14, 15, 16, and 18). It is assumed that in all languages the verb is generated within the verb phrase (VP), adjacent to its object (if any). In certain languages, the verb is pronounced inside the VP shell(s)—or their most immediate extended projection(s) such as vP, but I'll gloss over that distinction. When the verb is pronounced in VP, it is pronounced adjacent to its object (if any), in a position that is c-commanded by any material that c-commands the VP. Let's call such languages V-IN-SITU languages. In other languages, the finite verb overtly moves out of the VP into some attracting head within the INFL system below CP. That INFL head—call it x—c-commands the VP. The verb is thus pronounced outside of the VP, to the left of any material that is c-commanded by x, assuming Kayne's (1994) Antisymmetry. Let's call these languages the V-TO-I languages.[14]

In this terminology, HC is V-in-situ while Fr is V-to-I, and the HC-versus-Fr differences in verb placement obtain in a manner similar to analogous word-order contrasts between English and Fr (DeGraff 1994a, 1994b, 1997, 2000). Assume that the relevant clause-internal adverbs and sentential negation markers are generated in some intermediate y_iP projection between VP and some higher xP whose head is the landing site for verb movement, if any. The integer i in y_iP ranges between 1 and some small n, smaller than, say, 29, which is the cardinality of the universal inventory of INFL heads postulated by Cinque (see note 14).[15] The HC-versus-Fr verb-placement contrast follows directly from these assumptions.[16]

The next questions to ask toward explanatory adequacy are: What ultimately forces verb movement in V-to-I languages? What sorts of evidence ("triggers") in the Primary Linguistic Data (PLD) help the language learner decide on the value of the V-to-I/V-in-situ parameter? Is the setting of this parameter an arbitrary property that is free to independently vary across languages, or is this setting reducible to, or deducible from, some more basic, more fine-grained, properties— some Kaynian "microparametric" values?

Here is one tentative generalization to start with.[17] Verb movement seems related to properties of verbal inflectional morphology: (i) languages with relatively larger paradigms of verbal inflections, or with the required distinctions therein, are V-to-I; (ii) languages with relatively smaller inflectional paradigms or without the required distinctions therein, tend to be V-in-situ. In one (here over-simplified) implementation (à la, e.g., Rohrbacher 1994: 114–124; cf. Lasnik 1995), verbal affixes in languages whose paradigms make enough distinctions are listed separately in the lexicon and enter the derivation as syntactically active affixal heads that c-command the VP. Since these affixes need a syntactic host, they force the verb to undergo head-movement in order for the verb to serve as their host under the nodes where the affixes are generated as syntactic heads. This is the Fr case. Otherwise, inflectional morphemes either are nonaffixal (the HC case) or combine with their verbal host postsyntactically, in the morphophonological component (the English case).

In Bobaljik's (2001) recent proposal, it is the *structure* of inflection, not the inventory of the INFL paradigms, that determines verb movement. Multiple inflectional suffixes on the verbal stem diagnose multiple INFL heads in the syntax, leading to the need for V-to-I for the verb to enter into a local checking relation with nonadjacent INFL heads. In absence of multiple INFL heads, as in English, the verb can locally check its inflectional features without movement, thus the possibility of V-in-situ.[18]

In all these proposals, the basic intuition to be captured is that, if the verb is "richly" inflected (with "richness" measured in one way or the other), then the verb must undergo head-movement. No matter what technology is adopted to handle morphology–syntax interactions in verb placement, the HC-Fr comparison already suggests the possibility of a correlation between the respective degrees of verbal inflection and degrees of verb movement (this was first noticed, I believe, in Dejean 1992). For now, let's take HC and Fr to fall on opposite sides of both the V-in-situ/V-to-I and the poor/rich inflectional clines, even though there exist intermediate cases whose positions in the verb-movement and verbal-inflection continua are more ambiguous and problematic. This is perhaps due to still mysterious markedness or change-in-progress factors (see note 20).[19]

Going back to explanatory adequacy, one can ask: How important is verbal inflectional morphology *to the learner* for the setting or resetting of the verb-placement parameter in Creole formation and elsewhere (e.g., in Germanic diachrony)? Let's temporarily assume for the sake of the argument that acquisition of verb placement is completely orthogonal to the presence or absence of verbal affixes. Given the postulation of V-to-I in both Fr (Pollock 1989) and Gbe (Aboh 1999 and chapter 4 in this volume), one could reasonably imagine, pending further data and further insights about learnability, a scenario in which V-to-I would have survived into HC, even in absence of verbal inflectional affixes. This scenario may seem quite reasonable if one assumes that all the language acquirer needs in order to acquire V-to-I is exposure to patterns that instantiate V-to-I (e.g., utterances with the sequence V Neg/Adv NP_{Obj}). French readily provides the relevant V-to-I patterns, so it may seem mysterious why V-to-I did not persist in HC (but see section 6.2 for some relevant speculations regarding the evolution of HC's TMA system from Fr verbal periphrases).

Regardless of the developmental fate of V-to-I, the paradigms of bound inflectional morphology are a well-known casualty in the *initial* stages of language acquisition, *independently of the inflectional profiles represented in the PLD* (see note 9). The reduction of bound inflectional paradigms seems even more spectacular in second-language acquisition under duress in the context of learner-unfriendly language contact with relatively reduced access to native target data (cf. Meillet 1919, Weinreich 1953: sec. 2.3; see DeGraff 1999b: 491–499, 517–518 for an overview). This point was already adumbrated by Schleicher (1852) [1850]) who compared English with its "poor" inflectional morphology and Icelandic with its "rich" inflectional morphology. Schleicher concluded that this spectacular inflectional contrast between these two sister languages is due to the much higher degree of language contact in the history of English (Schleicher 1852: 23–30, [1850]; see DeGraff 2001b: 219 n.5 for some historiographical discussion; also see note 31).

In this vein, that the Fr inflectional paradigms would eventually not survive into HC is not surprising given the nature of language contact on Haiti's colonial plantations and given similar developments in other language-contact situations. Compare Creole genesis to the evolution of Old to Middle to Early Modern English and of Old Norse to Mainland Scandinavian (Danish, Norwegian, Swedish). There, too, the catalyst for inflectional erosion may have been so-called imperfect learning by adult learners in contact situation, *notwithstanding the rich inflectional systems of the languages in contact* (for case studies, data, and analyses, see, e.g., Bunsen 1854; Haugen 1976: 285f, 1982: 14; Kroch and Taylor 1997; Roberts 1999; and Kroch et al. 2000).

In what follows, I'll speculate further on a learnability account in which the "right" configuration of verbal affixes in the PLD is one, *and only one*, of the triggers that force the learner to adopt the V-to-I setting; in this account, the V-in-situ setting (and absence of movement, in general) is an innate preference of the learner (perhaps for economy considerations as in Roberts 1999).

As Bobaljik (2001: 5) points out, such learnability-theoretic considerations are related to, but do not necessarily determine, the synchronic grammatical factors that force V-to-I or V-in-situ in the relevant I-languages. That certain verbal affixes *can* be used as *part* of the triggering evidence vis-à-vis (often quite abstract) verb-placement options does not necessarily entail that it is verbal affixes, and only verbal affixes, that determine verb placement in the adult grammar.[20]

These caveats will lead me to look, in sections 6.2 and 7.1, at the possible contribution of various *syntactic* patterns, alongside inflectional patterns, as acquisition-cum-reanalysis triggers in the diachronic emergence of HC V-in-situ. My learnability considerations will tentatively connect the emergence of V-in-situ in HC to similar diachronic scenarios beyond "creolization" (see, e.g., Roberts 1999; Lightfoot 1999; DeGraff 1999b, 1999d, and references therein; see also V-to-I possibilities in other Creoles such as Capeverdean Creole and Palenquero, as discussed in section 7.3).

Section 5 looks at a wider set of comparative data, including object-placement facts in (the diachrony of) HC, Fr, and Germanic. Section 6 returns to diachronic-cum-learnability issues and entertains a Creole-genesis account whereby certain superstrate and substrate patterns, in tandem with the inflectional-erosion facts, would have tilted the linguistic ecology toward the eventual decline of V-to-I and preverbal object-cliticization in the emergence of HC. The comparative data suggest that such a decline is not an "exceptional" Creole development but a run-of-the-mill diachronic tendency, modulated by UG principles and species-wide language-acquisition mechanisms.

5 THE MORPHOSYNTAX OF HAITIAN CREOLE OBJECT PRONOUNS

5.1 Basic Facts

Can the diachrony of the morphosyntax of HC verb placement, as examined in section 4, be related to the diachrony of the morphosyntax of object pronouns in any theoretically constructive way? Recall these two basic facts from section 3: (i) object (pro)nouns in HC, unlike in Fr in and in Fongbè, are uniformly post-verbal (as in (1)–(2)); (ii) pronouns in HC (see, e.g., (5)), unlike in Fr and Fongbè, do not manifest morphological case distinctions.

5.2 Theoretical Proposals

Is there any theoretical basis for a possible correlation between inflectional mor-phology, verb placement, and object-pronoun placement? Let's keep the working assumption that what induces V-to-I are the morphological properties of certain functional heads above the VP. Does IP-internal object movement rely on some analogous property of functional heads above VP? Are the two types of movement in any sort of dependency? These questions are all the more intriguing in that English diachrony manifests the same sort of "discrepancies" and "losses" that characterize HC's diachrony: (i) loss of V-to-I; (ii) loss of preverbal objects; (iii) loss of inflectional morphology on verbs; and (iv) loss of inflectional (case) mor-phology on (pro)nouns (see section 6.3).[21]

A number of proposals in the generative literature on Germanic and Romance offer an attractive analytical link among inflectional morphology, the placement of verbs, and that of (pronominal) objects. In these proposals, certain sorts of object placement depend on verb movement or on inflectional morphology on the verb and its arguments. Such proposals include Holmberg (1985); Platzack and Holmberg (1989), Holmberg and Platzack (1990), Kayne (1989a, 1989b, 1991), Déprez (1989), Chomsky (1993), Sportiche (1995), Bobaljik and Jonas (1996), and Bobaljik (1995,2002).[22] For Déprez, Kayne, Chomsky, Roberts, Sportiche, and oth-ers, it is inflectional heads dominating VP that are implicated in object cliticization and in other types of clause-internal leftward object movements.[23]

To better understand these proposals, let us first examine cases where *full* NPs behave *somewhat* like object clitics in being pronounced outside of the VP in which they are generated. The prototypical, and much discussed, case is that of OBJECT SHIFT (OS) in Icelandic (IC) and a subset of Germanic; see, for example,

Holmberg (1985), Déprez (1989), Bobaljik and Jonas (1996), Bobaljik (1995, 2002), and, especially, the recent review in Thráinsson (2001). OS is illustrated by the following Icelandic data from Holmberg (1985):

(23) a. Skúli   segir   Sveini   <u>oft</u>   sögur. (IC)
         Skuli   tells   Sveini   often   stories

      'Skuli often tells Sveini stories.' (Holmberg 1985: 161)

      b. Stúdentarnir   stungu   smjörinu   <u>allir</u>   í   vasann.
         the students   put   the butter all   in the pocket

      'The students all put the butter in their pockets.' (Holmberg 1985: 161)

      c. Hann   keypti   bókina   <u>ekki</u>.
         he   bought   the book not

      'He did not buy the book.' (Holmberg 1985: 178)

That *Sveini, smjörinu* 'the butter' and *bókina* 'the book' have "shifted" in (23) is indicated by the position of the objects relative to the underlined items, which are taken to indicate the left boundary of (some extended projection of) VP. Icelandic, unlike English, allows both the verb and the object to overtly move leftward, outside of VP, while the verb moves up higher than the object, giving the surface orders in (23). (Incidentally, nouns and verbs in IC are more richly inflected than in English, for Case and for person and number agreement, respectively; see Holmberg and Platzack 1990; cf. notes 21 and 53.)

Let's (provisionally) assume that OS is related to Case and that its landing site is within the projection of a functional head whose function vis-à-vis the object is somewhat similar to that of the head(s) responsible for V-to-I in section 4 (see Déprez 1989, Chomsky 1993, Sportiche 1995, Bobaljik and Jonas 1996, and others). In this perspective, OS, like V-to-I, is related to some morphological requirements of either the moved element or its landing site (or both). Thus, vis-à-vis morphology and word order, OS versus object-in-situ offer intriguing parallels to the contrast between V-to-I versus V-in-situ discussed in section 4. Compare the Icelandic and English data in (23): Icelandic has OS, while objects in English remain in situ.[24]

Is there a theoretical link between V-to-I and object cliticization (qua OS?) in a way that will give a principled explanation to the emergence of the morphosyntax of verbs and object pronouns in HC? Consider the now familiar, if controversial, claims that (i) elimination (reduction?) of V-to-I typically depends on a prior reduction in verbal inflectional suffixes and (ii) elimination (reduction?) of object cliticization is associated with reduction in morphological case marking (but see note 21.) Is the theory able to relate aspects of (i) and (ii) via independently needed principles?

I now turn to a theoretical proposal whereby overt V-to-I is a necessary condition for object cliticization, here viewed (controversially) as an instance of OS.[25] In such a theory, that HC lacks both V-to-I and preverbal object clitics is not an arbitrary combination of facts. Neither would such combination support Creole Exceptionalism. In the Cartesian-Uniformitarian perspective on Creole genesis that is adopted in this chapter, the constellation of facts in (i)–(ii) would directly fall out from constraints imposed by UG, without any ad hoc assumptions about developmental mechanisms that would apply exclusively in Creole genesis.

The fundamental insight making V-to-I a pre-requisite for OS goes back, I think, to Holmberg (1985).[26]

(24) "Object Shift: Move an object NP leftwards within the X-bar projection of its governing verb, when this verb is phonetically empty." (Holmberg 1985: 184).

For Holmberg, the principle in (24) would explain why OS in IC is not possible in the presence of an auxiliary: in such contexts it is only the auxiliary that moves, not the main verb; the absence of main-verb movement (which entails that the governing verb is *not* phonetically empty) is what bans OS. Compare (23b) with (25):[27]

(25) Stúdentarnir hafa <u>allir</u> stungið smjörinu í vasann
the students have all put the butter in the pocket

"The students have all put the butter in their pockets." (Holmberg 1985: 187)

Holmberg (1985: 189f.) also notices that Swedish (SW), which allows OS only with unstressed personal pronouns ("cliticization" in our terms), allows such cliticization in main clauses only. Interestingly, as observed by, for example, Holmberg and Platzack (1990), the paradigms of verbal and nominal inflections are more restricted in SW than in IC: "Disregarding the genitive, . . . [there is] no Case morphology [in SW], except on pronouns, and no subject-verb agreement" (p. 93). Holmberg and Platzack also observe that SW, unlike IC, has no independent V-to-I: V-to-I in SW only occurs in connection with verb-second (V2)—generally, in main clauses. Given Holmberg's Generalization in (24), it seems no accident that SW has OS in main clauses only: SW object cliticization occurs only when V overtly moves out of VP—on its way to C, since SW lacks independent V-to-I (see Josefsson 1992 for one study of SW object cliticization).[28]

Holmberg's constraint tightly unites V-to-I to OS: the latter happens *only if* the former also happens.[29] If we adopt one of the various implementations of Holmberg's constraints (see note 26) and assume that object cliticization is an instance of OS, then absence of V-to-I in HC would force all objects to surface postverbally in HC: cliticization sans verb movement would entail a violation of an independently motivated principle of grammar. Object cliticization in Fr versus absence thereof in HC is thus related to another morphosyntactic difference between the two languages: namely, Fr V-to-I versus HC V-in-situ (in section 6.4, I explore the possible contributions of both Fr and Gbe source-language patterns to the emergence of the HC patterns). In this perspective, HC and Fr stand in the same typological relation as Swedish and Icelandic: (i) HC and Swedish do not have independent V-to-I movement, modulo the possibility of short verb-movement and of verb-movement outside IP (see notes 14, 15, 16, and 34); (ii) HC and Swedish manifest less verbal inflectional morphology than Fr and Icelandic, respectively; (iii) comparative data from both HC-versus-Fr and Swedish-versus-Icelandic suggest that cliticization is not allowed without verb movement; and (iv) HC and Swedish have a higher degree of case syncretism than Fr and Icelandic, respectively (but see note 21).

6 On the Theoretical Status of Creole Exceptionalism

Is "creolization" *fundamentally* distinct from "language change"? How do the "discrepancies" in HC diachrony, as discussed in sections 3–5, compare with "discrepancies" in the diachrony of non-Creole languages?

This section shows that a deep congruence of morphosyntactic patterns obtains across various sorts of ontogenetic and phylogenetic developments, including "creolization." My claim is that certain VP-related "discrepancies" in the so-called genetic diachrony of Germanic and Romance seem as "significant" as in the so-called nongenetic diachrony of HC. HC morphosyntax does not, *and could not*, isolate HC and its diachrony in some exclusively "Creole" empirical domain of linguistic inquiry.[30]

6.1 Verbal Morphosyntax beyond "Creolization"

In the domain of verb placement and verbal morphology (see sections 3–4), it seems rather clear that there is nothing particularly and exclusively "Creole" about the emergence of the HC V-in-situ patterns with verbs that do not inflect for TMA and agreement. The genesis of HC's VP-related morphosyntax, from the contact of (relatively more) richly inflecting V-to-I languages, falls naturally within a larger domain of developmental "discrepancies" that go beyond creolization proper.

Take first-language acquisition by children (L1A). It is now a celebrated fact that, in the very early stages of acquiring richly inflecting V-to-I languages such as Fr, children may use in situ infinitivals in contexts where the adult language requires finite verbs that undergo V-to-I; when finite forms are used in child French, they tend to undergo V-to-I as in adult French (Pierce 1992, Wexler 1994; see Lardiere 2000 for a recent survey). This is the OPTIONAL (ROOT) INFINITIVE stage which has now been documented in a wide variety of languages (see Wexler 2002 for one recent overview). Here's a sample of "optional root infinitives" in child French:

(26)   a. pas   attraper   une   fleur
          NEG   catch   a   flower

       b. pas   tomber   bébé
          NEG   fall   baby

Each of the words in (26) straightforwardly corresponds to an adult French word, even though these utterances show morphosyntactic "discrepancies" when compared with adult French. In the latter, negated declarative root clauses usually contain a finite verb. One may thus be tempted to conclude *erroneously* that the sample in (26) illustrates "a significant discrepancy between the degree of lexical correspondence and the degree of grammatical correspondence" between child and adult French, thus diagnosing, on a baby scale (so to speak), "abnormal transmission" of the sort envisaged by Thomason and Kaufman (1988: 206). Such a hypothetical claim about "abnormal transmission" seems a theoretical abnormality: pervasive "discrepancies" are quite normal in language learners' developmental paths.

The sort of "discrepancies" exemplified in (26) and in related child-versus-adult developmental mismatches are fully expected in any model of L1A in which language-specific, and often quite abstract, parameter settings must be set (and thus, possibly, 'mis-set') from necessarily spare and often structurally ambiguous cues in the Primary Linguistic data (PLD) (see, e.g., Rizzi 1999 and Roberts 1999). This is what Rizzi (1999: 463f.) calls "grammatical invention"—that is, "the 'trying out' of various UG options [a.k.a. parameter settings] not adopted by the target system." As Chomsky (1995: 6) puts it, "language acquisition is interpreted as the process of fixing the parameters of the initial state [UG] in one of the permissible ways." Discrepancies in L1A are also expected if certain grammatical and processing constraints are in the scope of a maturational schedule, some biological clock (see, e.g., Wexler 2002). In fact, the morphological and syntactic "discrepancies" illustrated in (26) have been replicated in a wide range of acquisition scenarios, both within and across groups of children acquiring typologically different languages (with and without V-to-I, with and without verb-second, etc.). (See Schütze 1997, Roberts 1999: 294–301, and Rizzi 1999: 456–462 for some theoretical alternatives, and see the literature surveys in Lardiere 2000 and Wexler 2002.)

Second-language acquisition (L2A) by adults and even by children seems to allow an even larger scale of morphosyntactic "discrepancies" than in L1A. Furthermore, these "discrepancies" seem to extend over a longer period than in L1A—in some cases, until L2A's endstate. And that, too, is considered a "normal" property of L2A (see the papers in Archibald 2000 for recent discussion—in particular, Lardiere's comparison of L1A and L2A morphosyntactic development in verb placement; see also Prévost and White 2000, Wexler 2002, and Ionin and Wexler 2002): "Adult [second-language] learners have much more difficulty than young child [first-language] learners in learning the exact properties of inflections" (Wexler 2002; for further discussion and references in the context of Creole genesis and its similarities to language change, see DeGraff 1999b: 491–499, 517–518).

What seems particularly affected in L2A is the learning of inflectional paradigms and their relations to morphosyntactic features in the narrow syntax. For example, Prévost and White (2000: 125–130) report that second-language (L2) learners, unlike first-language (L1) learners, often overgeneralize the use of "default" infinitivals to structural positions that are reserved for finite verbs (e.g., VP-external heads in V-to-I languages). More generally, it is argued that "aquisition of L1 morphology is always successful (except in pathological cases)," while "L2 learners have difficulty with the overt realization of morphology" (Prévost and White 2000: 104, 128). These and similar results can be taken as evidence for "morphological non-convergence (or 'fossilization') with respect to the target language [in L2A] as opposed to virtually inevitable convergence in [L1A]" (Lardiere 2000: 113); see also Klein and Perdue's (1992: 302f., 312f.) similar results in the context of a cross-linguistic survey of migrant adult learners with various source and target languages.

This L1A-versus-L2A contrast is crucial: the output of L2A by adults—under "duress," in many cases—has a crucial role in language change, particularly in the context of language contact. In such contexts, L2A's output, including widespread morphological fossilization, substantially contributes to the PLD used by subsequent generations of nonnative and native learners; this is the "cascade" relationship discussed in DeGraff (1999b: 497f., 504, 511, etc.) in the context of creolization and language change. The important—if familiar, but often neglected—point here is that the nature of the PLD, obviously a key factor in language change and creation, is greatly influenced by the absence or presence of adult learners and by their cognitive and psychosocial limitations—for example, take the aforementioned morphological fossilization, which is a hallmark of adult learners' early interlanguages.

In the context of VP-related morphology–syntax interaction in the formation of HC, the L2A–L1A "cascade" relationship suggests the following hypothetical, and overly idealized, sequence. The adult learner, who in effect is the ultimate locus of language contact, is chiefly, but not singly, responsible for various degrees of inflectional "fossilization," depending on the specific and gradient conditions of the contact situation.[31] If rich verbal inflection is an unambiguous morphological trigger for V-to-I, the initial contact interlanguages, or most likely some subset thereof, may well be V-to-I, structurally on a par with the Fr target varieties, but with infinitival-like forms often substituted as default for targetlike finite forms in V-to-I environments (see note 19). Among substrate speakers of proto-HC, the substitution of invariant forms for inflecting forms, although presumably common across early interlanguages (independently of source languages; see Klein and Perdue 1992: 302f., 312f.), may have been more natural for the Kwa speakers than, say, the Bantu speakers: Kwa, unlike Bantu, generally do not manifest Tense and Agreement affixes.

Another class of input that competes with, and reduces, the proportion of finite verbs in the linguistic ecology are targetlike verbal periphrases that are built around in situ infinitival and participle forms (see section 6.2). These verbal periphrases, which are quite frequent in regional and colloquial Fr varieties (Gougenheim 1929), would "conspire" with early learners' inflectionally fossilized interlanguages to weaken the robustness of V-to-I triggers in the evolving linguistic ecology of incoming learners. The latter will have fewer and fewer instances of finite verbs and V Neg/Adv NP_{Obj} patterns in their PLD then will the PLD of the initial "cohorts" of learners. That is, the linguistic ecology will witness a gradual decrease of morphological and syntactic triggers for V-to-I, along with an increase in the frequency of infinitival- and participial-like forms, thus the increased possibility for the development of stable V-in-situ grammars with verb forms that, overall, show less inflection than their counterparts in the original target language. In turn, these changes may be favored by other (arguably) converging factors such as the unmarkedness and economy of V-in-situ; the relative frequency, transparency, and saliency of verbal periphrases as opposed to their synthetic counterparts; the use of tonic pronouns alongside, or instead of, atonic clitics in colloquial regional varieties, and so on. (These grammatical, learnability-theoretic, stochastic, and processing factors are further speculated on in following paragraphs and in sections 6.2 and 6.4.)[32]

For now, note that "discrepancies" of various sort are indeed expected in ontogenetic and phylogenetic developments—in the history of *both* Creole and non-Creole languages. V-in-situ patterns that do not replicate the morphosyntax of the erstwhile "target" languages have emerged in the history of English, for example. It is well established that Middle English (ME) until the sixteenth century was a robustly V-to-I language. Consider the following examples—a staple in the literature on Germanic syntactic change:

(27) a. Wepyng and teres <u>counforteth</u> not dissolute laghers.
         weeping and tears comfort   not dissolute laughers
         (1400–1450: N. Love, The Myrour of the Blessyd Lyf of J.C.; quoted in
         Roberts 1993: 250)

     b. Quene Ester <u>looked</u> never with switch an eye.
         "Queen Esther never looked with such an eye." (Chaucer, *Merchant's
         Tale, line 1744*; (quoted in Kroch 1989b)

     c. . . . if man <u>grounde</u> not his doinges altogether upon nature. (Ellegård
         1953: 40; cited in Kroch 1989a: 143)

     d. How <u>like</u> you this sonnet? (Ellegård 1953: 84; cited in Kroch 1989a:
         143)

Yet, notwithstanding the V-to-I nature of its ancestor, Modern English (NE) is a V-in-situ language:

(28) a. *Peter understands <u>never</u> his lesson.

      b. *Jane comforts <u>not</u> Mary.

      c. *How <u>like</u> you this sonnet?

In the diachrony of English, an erosion in verbal inflectional morphology seems to have been a precondition, although not a sufficient condition, for the subsequent transition from V-to-I to V-in-situ (this is a gross oversimplification that abstracts away from intricate facts of dialectal and register variation). At least as long as English verbal inflection was approximately on a paradigmatic and structural par with that of Fr, English exhibited V-to-I, on a syntactic par with Fr. Witness, from selected ME dialects, the paradigmatic distinctions in (29) and the morphosyntactic structure of the doubly inflected verb in (30) with the stacking of Tense and Agreement suffixes:

(29) sing<u>e</u> '1sg'; sing<u>est</u> '2sg'; sing<u>en</u>, '3sg'; sing<u>en</u> '1pl, 2pl, 3pl' (Midland ME,
      Mossé 1968; cited in Roberts 1993: 256)

(30) [[show + ed] + st] '[[show + PAST] + 2sg]' (Kroch 1989b: 238)

The morphology–syntax correlations in (27)–(30) and their (arguable) parallels elsewhere (e.g., in the diachrony of Mainland Scandinavian; see, e.g., Holmberg and Platzack 1995: 76f.; Vikner 1995: 161–163, 1997: 205–207) suggest a parameter-setting approach in which verbal inflectional morphology serves as one class of triggers, *perhaps alongside word-order triggers*, for the acquisition of verb place-ment.[33]

From such a perspective, there is nothing particularly "Creole" (as opposed to non-"Creole") with the fact that HC is V-in-situ while its lexifier is V-to-I. Modern English and Mainland Scandinavian—neither of which fits the sociohis-torical profile of Caribbean Creoles—are, like HC, languages without V-to-I[34] and with ancestors that are robustly V-to-I and robustly inflecting (see Falk 1993; Rohrbacher 1994; Vikner 1995, 1997; Roberts 1999, and references therein). Again, this is not surprising: as already discussed, L2A often entails a reduction in in-flectional paradigms, and the reduction is greater in the learner-unfriendly situ-ations of abrupt language contact (see note 31). It may thus be expected that parameter-setting in such contexts—in the history of HC as in the history of English and Mainland Scandinavian—would witness a decline in V-to-I.

For this argument to go through, we must assume (i) that V-in-situ is the innately preferred option (i.e., the one initially entertained by the language ac-quirer, in absence of contrary evidence) and (ii) that V-to-I is partly triggered by the right set of inflectional affixes on the verb (see sections 6.2, 6.4, and 7.1 for other syntactic factors in the decline of V-to-I in HC diachrony; see also Roberts 1999 and Lightfoot 1999 on the general issue of morphological and syntactic trig-gers). Once the V-in-situ/V-to-I parameter is set, UG will constrain which other morphosyntactic options can or cannot be adopted in the steady-state grammar. For example, V-in-situ will rule out Object Shift, if the discussion in section 5.2 is on the right track (also see sections 6.3–6.4).

At this point, even the nonalert reader should have noticed the empirical and theoretical fragility of our speculations about the learner's acquisition, and the linguist's analysis, of morphology–syntax interactions in verb placement in on-togeny and phylogeny. Yet the central observation here, independently of one's favorite theory of verb placement, is that the diachrony and synchrony of V-in-situ in HC—a natural language, no matter one's definition of "Creole"—do not, *and could not*, constitute a litmus test that would set "creolization" and its prod-ucts apart from the "normal" and "genetic" processes and products of language change (qua parameter-setting and resetting), as in the diachrony of English and Mainland Scandinavian. On the contrary, the HC data support the hypothesis that—perhaps since Meillet—has posited a deep cross-linguistic connection be-tween (degrees of) syntactic movement and (degrees of) inflectional morphology, at least in certain domains (e.g., in verb and noun-phrase placement).

6.2 Reanalysis in the Emergence of HC Verb Syntax

Corroborating the nonexceptionalism of creolization are the Tense-Mood-Aspect (TMA) morphemes that project the IP layers in HC and other French-lexicon Creoles. Bickerton (1981 and subsequently) has popularized the claims that the morphosyntax and semantics of TMA markers are virtually identical across Creole languages, independently of their respective superstrate and substrate languages. Such pan-Creole similarity is often considered a telltale of massive diachronic "discrepancies" in the history of Creole languages. Yet it can be reasonably argued that Creole TMA markers are not Bickertonian entirely new creations and, thus, do not diagnose any "radical break in transmission." Instead, these morphemes can be analyzed as the product of, inter alia, run-of-the-mill reanalysis or grammaticalization (cf. Mufwene 2001: 28f., 54f., 77f., 2002). Here, too, I argue that, once we look at the appropriate data sets with the appropriate theoretical lenses, creolization reduces to UG-guided restructuring of patterns in the PLD.[35]

In DeGraff (2000: 102–108, 2002c), I point out a number of VP-related structural similarities and dissimilarities among HC and its source languages (e.g., Fongbè and regional varieties of vernacular French). Here it will suffice to point out that *all* the preverbal TMA morphemes in HC, including those illustrated in (7) can be straightforwardly traced back to seventeenth- and eighteenth-century Fr etyma, some of which still exist in certain contemporary French dialects, including sometimes the "standard" dialect. Such similarities between a French-lexicon Creole and its lexifier were already noted, explicitly or implicitly, by, for example, J. J. Thomas (1869), Van Name (1870), Baissac (1880), Gougenheim (1929), Denis (1935), and Sylvain (1936) (see notes 37 and 44). The Fr etyma of HC's TMA morphemes are used preverbally as verbal auxiliaries and as prepositional markers for mood and aspect. These auxiliaries and prepositions are used in the kind of verbal periphrases that were—and, in some cases, are still—popular in vernacular and regional varieties of French (Gougenheim 1929). The sketchy comparison in (31)–(39) highlights the relevant correspondences. In most of these examples, I underline the Fr etymon in its verbal periphrase and its reanalyzed TMA-marker counterpart in HC:

(31)   a. Il   était   (déjà)   allé. (Fr)
           3sg+masc was   (already) go

           'He had gone.'

       b. Li   te   (deja)   ale. (HC)
          3sg ANT   already   go

          'He had (already) gone.'

(32) a. Il <u>était</u> au cinéma. (Fr)
      He was at-the movie-theater
      'He was at the movies.'

      b. Il a <u>été</u> au cinéma. (Fr.)
      He has been to-the movie-theater
      'He has been to the movies.'

      c. Il <u>était</u> malade. (Fr)
      'He was sick.'

      d. Il a <u>été</u> malade. (Fr)
      'He has been sick.'

      e. Li <u>te</u> nan sinema. (HC)
      3sg ANT in movie-theater
      'He/She was at the movies.'

      f. Li <u>te</u> malad.
      3sg ANT sick
      'He/She was sick' or 'He/She has been sick.'

(33) a. Je suis maintenant <u>après</u> à demesler le
      1sg be now after PREP untangle the
      cahos. (17th-c. Fr)
      chaos
      'I am now untangling the chaos.'

      b. M <u>ap(e)</u> demele pwoblèm. (HC)
      1sg PROG untangle problem
      'I am untangling problems'.

(34) a. Je suis <u>pour</u> me marier la semaine
      1sg am for 1sg+ACC marry the week
      prochaine. (Canadian Fr)
      next
      'I am to get married next week.' (Gougenheim 1929: 120)

      b. Mwen <u>pou</u> marye semèn pwochèn. (HC)
      1sg for marry week next

(35) a. Tu <u>vas</u> aller demain. (Fr)
      'You will go tomorrow.'

b. W <u>ava</u> ale demen. (HC)

c. To <u>va</u> allé demain. (18th-c. HC; Ducœurjoly 1802: 377)

(36) a. Nous avons <u>fini</u> de sarcler. (Fr)
          we   have   finished to weed
          'We have finished weeding.'

b. Nou <u>fin(i)</u> sakle. (HC)

c. Nou <u>fini</u> sarclé. (18th-c. HC; Ducœurjoly 1802: 376)

The data in (31)–(36) only begin to illustrate semantic, distributional, and phonological correspondences between Fr verbal periphrases and their grammaticalized counterparts in HC (for a much more detailed comparison, see Fattier 1998: 864–888). As is typical of grammaticalization (see, e.g., Meillet 1912), these HC preverbal markers generally have more reduced phonology than their Fr counterparts, and they have their own specialized distribution and semantics, some of which is unsurprisingly influenced by the substrate languages (cf. Sylvain 1936). Let's flesh this out a bit.

The parallels in (31)–(32) suggest that etyma of HC *te* 'ANTERIOR' include two sorts of inflected forms for Fr *être* 'be': (i) the singular-imparfait *étais/était* and (ii) the past participle *été*. In (33), HC *ap(e)* 'PROGRESSIVE/FUTURE' is from the Fr preposition *après* 'after'. The Fr preposition *après* enters the periphrastic template *être après (à/de)* V_{-fin} with V_{-fin} an infinitival verb. This ... *après* ... periphrase expresses the same sort of progressive that is now expressed by Modern French *être en train de* V_{-fin}. In his Early Creole manual, Ducœurjoly's (1802: 307) reports *ly té après couyé café* 'he was picking coffee' (lit.: '3sg ANT PROG pick coffee') alongside the eighteenth-century Standard French translation *il ceuilloit du café*; contrast with modern HC *li te ap keyi kafe*. In Modern HC, unlike in its eighteenth- or nineteenth-century ancestor that is reported in the available texts, the preposition *apre* 'after' is not homophonous with the TMA marker for PROGRESSIVE/FUTURE *ap(e)*. Judging from the eighteenth- and nineteenth-century written samples,[36] it can be concluded that, over the years, grammaticalization has reduced the phonetic and lexical heft of the erstwhile preposition; thus, *après* > *ap(e)*; this reduction eventually led to a syntactic-category change from prepositional to TMA-marker (i.e., from lexical, or quasi functional, to fully functional). In turn, this categorical reanalysis would lead to a pruning of structure and to higher attachment in the tree, as in the cases of grammaticalization considered in, for example, Roberts (1999).

Similar paths of reanalysis cum grammaticalization can be sketched for HC *pou, ava, fini*, and others. HC *pou* 'DEONTIC' (as in (34b)) is from the Fr preposition *pour* 'for', which enters the periphrastic template *être pour* V*-fin* expressing futurity, likelihood, and obligation (Fattier 1998: 872). HC *ava* 'IRREALIS' (as in (35b)), along with its variants *a / av / va*, is from Fr *va(s)*, present singular forms of the verb *aller* 'to go' (cf. HC *al(e)* 'to go'). The Fr periphrastic template *aller* V*-fin* expresses certain kinds of future (cf. English *to be going to*.) Reanalysis cum grammaticalization has also produced the HC future marker *(a)pral(e)* 'to be going to' via the "pruning" of the seventeenth-century French verbal periphrase *après (de/à) aller*.

Thus far, this is a simplistic distillation of a complex set of correspondences. Similar patterns are found, by and large, in the eighteenth-to nineteenth-century Early Creole samples that I consulted for this essay (see note 36). More extensive etymologies for these and other HC preverbal markers are discussed in Fattier 1998: 864–888.[37] A relatively straightforward case can be made that the syntax of the HC extended VP emerged via parameter resetting (from V-to-I to V-in-situ) in tandem with the reanalysis cum grammaticalization of French verbal periphrases.

One other reanalysis case vividly supports such a scenario: the evolution of the HC sentential negation marker *pa* from Fr *n'a(s) pas* (*NEG HAVE-Auxiliary NEG*) via Early HC / *napa* / (DeGraff 1993: 90). The negative marker in the nineteenth-century Creoles of Réunion and Mauritius in the Indian Ocean is also /*napa*/ (Chaudenson 1992: 166 n52, Chaudenson and Mufwene 2001: 193 n20). The following reanalysis path can be hypothesized, skipping some intermediate stages: Fr *n'a(s) pas* / *n'es (t) pas* > Early Creole (*na*) *pa* > Modern Creole *pa*, with HC *pa* now the head Neg⁰ of NegP, while Fr *pas* is in Spec(NegP) (see DeGraff (1993):

(37) a. Il   n'a pas   parlé. (Fr)
          3sg+masc   NEG+has NEG   spoken

      'He has not spoken.'

      b. Li   napa   pale. (Hypothetical Early 'HC')
          3sg   NEG   spoken

      'He/She has not spoken.'

      c. Li   pa   pale. (Modern HC)
          3sg   NEG   spoken

      'He/She has not spoken.'

(38) a. Tout   être   qui   peut   parler   n'est pas   un   cheval. (Fr)
          all   being   that   can   speak   is not   a   horse

      'Any being that can speak is not a horse.'

b. Monde   qui   konn   parler   n'a pas
person   who   knows   speak   NEG
chouval . . . (Early HC c. 1796)
horse (from an official proclamation; Denis 1935: 347)

c. Moun ki konn pale pa chwal. (Modern HC)

In the mentalist approach adopted here vis-à-vis the mechanisms responsible for both creolization and language change, the ultimate locus of reanalysis (of, e.g., *n'a(s)* and *n'est pas* into *napa* / *nepa* then *pa*) is the language learner. As it turns out, adult learners of French from diverse LIs (e.g., Arabic and Spanish) also reanalyze *n'a(s) pas* and *n'est pas* as monomorphemic sentential negation markers / *napa* / and / *nepa* / in their early interlanguages. Abdelmalek, a Moroccan learner of French, produced / *Mwa napa kone* /.[38] Compare with HC *Mwen pa konnen* and the French *moi, je (ne) connais pas*. Abdelmalek also produces *Les français nepa kone l'espagnol* instead of the targetlike *Les français (ne) connaissent pas l'espagnol* 'The French don't now Spanish' (also notice the invariant verb form /kone/) (Véronique 2000: 307). Other sentential negation markers in Abdelmalek's interlanguage include *ne . . . pas, non, pas*, etc. (idem). We also find / *nepa* / as one of the sentential negation markers in the early interlanguages of Hispanophone learners, as in / *nepa puve* / instead of *(ne) pouvait pas* 'could not'.[39]

Keeping acquisition-based reanalysis in mind, there is another hypothetical, and possibly convergent, scenario for the evolution of HC *pa*. Ducœurjoly's (1802) Creole manual, whose Creole utterances are etymologically transcribed, explicitly notes the Early Creole use of / *napa* / in negative imperatives (e.g., on pp. 292, 325, 332, and 393) alongside the use of *pa* in negative declaratives with verbal predicates (e.g., on pp. 287, 290, 305, and 392). Fattier (1998: 882f.) proposes a reanalysis path whereby *napa* derives historically from the reanalysis of yet another type of verbal periphrase—namely, the singular negative imperative with *aller*: *ne va pas* V*-fin* 'Don't go V*-fin*' as in *Ne va pas croire que . . .* 'Don't go believe that. . . .' In Fattier's words: "The French colonists would use, it seems, this 'future associated with the imperative' to express prohibition" (p. 883; my translation). Fattier considers that this usage may have been widespread in the colonial French varieties spoken in the Caribbean and the Indian Ocean, as she notes parallel constraints on the use of *pa* across (the diachrony of) the Creoles of Haiti and Réunion.[40] We can thus posit the etymon *ne va pas* for the Early HC negative marker *napa* in imperatives, which, in turn, seeded *pa* in modern HC: that is, Fr *ne va pas* > Early HC *napa* (in negative imperatives) > Modern HC *pa*. Fattier (1998: 883) also mentions, as one other possible etymon for *napa*, the negative subjunctive of *aller* 'to go'—namely, *n'ailles pas*—which she rejects in favor of the Fr *ne va pas* V*-fin* periphrase.

With respect to verb placement, contrast the colloquial *Ne va pas tarder dav-*

antage 'Don't go delay any further', where the main verb is in the infinite and stays to the right of *pas*, with Standard French *Ne tarde pas davantage*, where the main verb is finite and undergoes V-to-I to the left of *pas*. Now compare both kinds of imperatives with their Early Creole equivalent (e.g., in (39a)) where the verb is invariant and in situ. The reanalysis of Fr *ne va pas*, in the *ne va pas* V_{-fin} periphrase, into Early Creole *napa*, then into Modern HC *pa*, instantiates yet another developmental path both toward V-in-situ in Modern HC (e.g., *pa tade* 'don't delay' vs. **tade pa*) and toward the phonological shape of the HC verb, with the /e/ ending (in, e.g., *tade*) identical to that of French first-conjugation infinitivals (in, e.g., *tarder*).

It is worth noting that, in Ducœurjoly (1802), both imperative /napa/, as in (39a), and declarative /pa/ with verbal predicates, as in (39c), can coexist in a single text—namely, in the "classic" eighteenth-century Creole chanson *Lisette quitté la plaine* on p. 392f.[41] There we also find /napa/ with nonverbal predicates, as in (39b), a construction where French would use *n'est pas*: contrast *na pas* in (39b) with *n'est pas* in Fr *Le manger n'est pas doux*. Denis (1935: 347 n21) explicitly notes the *n'est pas* > *n'a pas* connection, noting that this substitution, as illustrated in (38b) and (39b), is already "populaire" in Normandie and elsewhere:

(39)   a. <u>N'a pas</u>   tardé   davantage.
          NEG   delay   anymore

          'Do not delay any further.' (18th-c. HC; Ducœurjoly 1802: 392f)

       b. Mangé   <u>na pas</u>   dou.
          Food   NEG   sweet

          'Food is not sweet.'

       c. Mo   <u>pa</u>   mire   toué.
          1sg   NEG   look   2sg

          'I don't see you.'

As for the *Lisette* song, its lyric is presumably all from the same Creole idiolect. Moreau de Saint-Méry (1958: 81 [1797]) attributes it to a certain Duvivier de la Mahautière and dates it to circa 1760.[42] The coexistence in this eighteenth-century Creole idiolect of / pa / and / napa /, as illustrated in (39), seems a signpost in the reanalysis-cum-grammaticalization path of Fr *ne va pas*, *n'a pas*, and *n'est pas* into Early HC (*na)pa*, then into modern HC *pa*. It is thus possible that the negative markers in eighteenth-century Creole are related to at least three distinct reanalysis paths: (i) negative imperative /napa /, as in (39a), is from Fr *ne va pas*, as suggested in Fattier (1998: 882f.); (ii) negative declarative / napa / with nonverbal predicates, as in (38b) and (39b), is from French *n'est pas*, perhaps via an earlier Creole form / nepa / or directly from the dialectal (Norman?) French variant *n'a pas* (for *n'est pas*), which is noted in Denis (1935: 247 n21); (iii) declarative / *pa* /, as in (39c) is from Fr *n'a(s) pas*, perhaps via an earlier Creole form *napa*. In modern HC, the negative markers in (i)–(iii) have all "converged" to a uniform realization of clausal negation as the shorter form *pa*. The longer form *napa*, in imperatives and in nonverbal predication, has undergone the sort of phonetic reduction that is typical of grammaticalization, perhaps concomitantly with changes in categorial status (i.e., reanalysis). (DeGraff 1993 speculates on the transition of clausal negation from Spec(NegP) to Neg^0 in the course of HC genesis; cf. Jespersen's famous "cycle".)[43]

The correspondences in (37)–(39) lend further credence to a scenario in which Fr verbal periphrases like those in (31)–(36) triggered the formation of the HC-extended VP system, via language learners' reanalysis of target strings that are delimited to the right by the thematically main predicate and to the left by the subject in Spec(IP), which is either covert in imperatives or overt in declaratives. (See Fattier 1998: 864–888 and Howe 2000 for larger empirical samples and for more extensive discussions of the combinatorial and interpretive properties of TMA markers in HC.)

This hypothesis is buttressed by a comparison of the inflectional morphology of first-conjugation verbs in Fr periphrases and the default verb marker in HC. As attested in various examples in (31)–(39), main verbs in Fr verbal periphrases are either in the infinitive or in the past participle. It is important to note that most Fr verbs, and generally all new verbs (e.g., borrowings from English), enter the language through the first conjugation, whose infinitives and past participles are marked with the verbal suffixes *-er* and *-é(e)*, respectively, both of which are pronounced /e/.

I have already noted the key role of imperative constructions in the structuring and restructuring of HC's VP-related syntax; see (39) and surrounding comments (later we return to other cases that involve the restructuring of imperative patterns; see note 56). I have also noted that L2 learners of French often substitute infinitival-like invariant forms, most of which end in /e/, for finite forms (Prévost and White 2000: 125–130). It is thus no surprise that the HC verbal marker par excellence is the etymologically related suffix *-e*, which in Fr is found not only in the infinitive (e.g., *chanter* 'to sing') but also in the participle (e.g., *chanté(e)* 'sung(+FEM)') and the second-plural present indicative and imperative (e.g., *chantez*). Although not all HC verbs end with the verbal marker *-e*, the latter is the sole overt productive verbal marker in HC, as in the English-based neologisms *klipse* 'to clip', *ploge* 'to plug,' and *tepe* 'to tape' (see note 7). This, too, alongside the parallels and reanalysis paths previously discussed, indicates that the prototypical etyma for HC verbs include Fr infinitives, past participles and the second-plural of the indicative present and of the imperative, all from the first conjugation (cf. Denis 1935: 435 n4). That this is so seems a straightforward consequence of, inter alia, the sort of L2A tendencies studied in, for instance, Prévost and White (2000).

These recurrent parallels suggest that the distributions and environments of the nonfinite verbal forms both in Fr and in interlanguages with Fr targets provided the creator of early HC with an important class of triggers for the creation of HC's verbal morphosyntax—in particular, the formation of its verbal morphology and its verb-placement syntax. As documented, phonetic and structural pruning characterizes the diachrony of each TMA marker in HC. In some cases, this pruning is associated with an elimination of head-to-head movement and with base-generation higher in the clause: whereas some of the French etyma of HC's TMA markers are lexical heads that in some cases undergo V-to-I, their HC descendants are invariably generated as functional heads high up in the INFL domain, thus obviating head-to-head dependencies (cf. Roberts 1999). Fr verbal periphrases and the reanalysis and grammaticalization thereof—perhaps in tandem with the fossilization of inflection that is independently known to occur in L2A—would have thus conspired to induce the loss of V-to-I in HC grammar. The erosion of inflection would have weakened the morphological triggers for the V-to-I setting, whereas the (presumed) preponderance of verbal periphrasis over synthetic forms would have weakened the word-order triggers for that setting— thus the "conspiracy" toward the emergence of a uniform V-in-situ setting alongside the grammaticalization of key items in certain Fr verbal periphrases (e.g., *étais / était, été, après, pour, va,* and *ne va pas, n'a(s) pas, n'es(t) pas*). (See section 7.1 for additional learnability-related comments.)

At any rate, the systematic correspondences sketched here are quite unlike what one might expect from a "radical break in transmission." And they also disconfirm Lefebvre's (1998: 16f, 39f, etc.) relexification-based claims that the French contribution to HC genesis was limited strictly to phonetic strings "deprived of [abstract, e.g., syntactic and semantic] features" and to major-category word order (see also Adam 1883; cf. sections 2.2, 2.3, 3.3 earlier). These correspondences suggest that, in creating their NEG + TMA system and much else in their lexicon and grammar, the creators of HC not only had to segment and reinterpret French phonetic shapes but also reanalyzed and grammaticalized certain French configurations.

The reanalysis of Fr verbal periphrases into the HC-extended VP system may have also been favored by substratal features, via L2A by Kwa-speaking adults. Recall from section 3 that Fongbè verbs (like HC verbs) are not morphologically inflected for TMA or agreement and that Fongbè TMA markers are, like in HC, nonaffixal morphemes in preverbal position (Avolonto 1992), except for the postverbal completive markers (see, e.g., da Cruz 1995).

This said, it must be noted that Aboh (1999 and chapter 4 in this volume), with respect to a variety of Gbe dialects, argues for (i) V-to-I; (ii) verbal inflection (e.g., aspectual suffixation and morphosyntactically conditioned reduplication); (iii) Object Shift (with Object-Verb order); and (iv) pronominal case morphology. These four morphosyntactic properties, like many others (e.g., postverbal completive markers; da Cruz 1995), have no counterpart in HC (see section 3.3), which suggests that HC and Fongbè differ vis-à-vis the formal specifications of their respective functional heads in the relevant domains, pace the relexificationist claims in Lefebvre (1998). Moreover, some of the Object Shift patterns, in Gbe and in Kwa more generally, are related to specific TMA configurations, and this is well documented in the Africanist literature (see, e.g., Déchaine and Manfredi 1997; Aboh 1999 and chapter 4 in this volume, and references therein; see also note 10). It thus seems unlikely that it is *specifically* the Gbe substratum that was crucial to the emergence in HC of preverbal TMA morphemes alongside verb and object both in-situ. Robust morphosyntactic discrepancies between HC and its substratum remain unaccounted for in Creole-genesis theories based on strict relexification (à la Adam 1883 and Lefebvre 1998); see DeGraff (2002b, 2002c).

Furthermore, HC-like extended TMA systems—with preverbal markers originating from the reanalysis of Fr verbal periphrases—exist in non-Creole French varieties and in non-Caribbean Creoles, including Indian Ocean Creoles (see references in note 37). The linguistic ecology in the formative period of these varieties was quite different from that of HC. In particular, the Indian Ocean Creoles had a much lesser, if any, Kwa input than HC, and it appears unreasonable to claim Kwa influence whenever "Creole-like" preverbal TMA markers are used in regional Fr varieties such as Québec French in (34a) (also see examples from Cajun French and Missouri French in (43)).

Regarding Mauritian Creole (MC), Baissac (1880: 24) calls the MC utterance *Mo va allé* 'I will go' a "pure calque" from Fr (cf. (35)). Also compare MC *Li va vini* 'He will come' with Fr *Il va venir*; cf. Baissac (1880: 80).[44] Brunot (1966 8: 1137 n3) also notes that "[i]n [MC], it's obvious that the periphrastic system of popular and vernacular French . . . has essentially been analyzed, assimilated and utilized."

Regarding non-Creole French varieties, it has been shown that some of the HC preverbal markers find contemporary counterparts in regional dialects of vernacular French—dialects that obviously did not emerge through the sort of pidginization or relexification invoked in, respectively, Bickerton's and Lefebvre's Creole-genesis scenarios (for relevant data and observations, see, e.g., Sylvain 1936: 79–105, 136–139; Chaudenson 1974: 684, 840, 1992: 162–167; Chaudenson and Mufwene 2001: 154–163, 178–182; Chaudenson, et al. (1993: 81–97), Fattier (1998: 863–888); see also note 37, the examples in (43), and the surrounding comments).

One last comparative note on the evolution of "Creole-like" TMA systems in non-Creole languages: Roberts (1999: 317) contemplates "creolization-like" reanalysis in the history of the English auxiliary system. As a closed class of functional heads with restricted distribution and specialized semantics, Modern English modals have emerged from the reanalysis of a subset of erstwhile main (i.e., lexical/thematic) verbs with full θ-marking capacities. More generally, reanalysis and grammaticalization have been extensively documented in the formation of TMA systems across genetic families (see, e.g., Bybee, et al., 1994). Pending solid evidence that the creators of Creole languages constitute a cognitively exceptional subspecies of *Homo sapiens*, our ongoing observations suggest a Uniformitarian scenario for Creole genesis, one that seriously considers parameter-(re)setting in language acquisition, alongside substrate-influenced reanalysis and grammaticalization of superstrate patterns, as crucial factors in the emergence of HC's extended VP (see DeGraff 1999b, 1999d; Roberts 1999; Lightfoot 1999; Mufwene 2002 for related arguments).

6.3 Object-Pronoun Morphosyntax beyond "Creolization"

The object-placement "discrepancies" that differentiate HC from Fr in sections 3 and 5 find analogs outside of "creolization" proper. Let's look, say, at the morphology and placement of object nouns and pronouns through English diachrony.[45]

I take as empirical starting point van Kemenade's (1987) data and observations on English diachrony. She shows that, throughout Old English (OE) and, to a lesser degree, during the early stages of Middle English (ME) until the mid-1300s, object and subject pronouns cliticized leftward in various positions throughout the clause, as far up as COMP.[46] Consider the following data from van Kemenade (1987) and focus on the underlined object pronouns:

(40) a. Fela   spella   <u>him</u>   sœdon   þa   Beormans, . . . (OE)
         many   stories   <u>him</u>   told   the   Permians

         'The Permians told him many stories.' (van Kemenade 1987: 130)

     b. þa   sticode   <u>him</u>   mon   þa   eagan   ut. (OE)
         then   stuck   <u>him</u>   someone   the   eyes   out

         'Then his eyes were gouged out.' (van Kemenade 1987: 130)

     c. . . .þet   he   <u>him</u>   ȝeaue   uyftene   ponds   of
             that   he   <u>him</u>   gave   fifteen   pounds   in
         gold. (ME, c. 1340)
         gold

         ' . . . that he would give him fifteen pounds in gold.' (van Kemenade 1987: 195)

A few preliminaries are in order before discussing the position of object pronouns in (40). OE is controversially considered to be a verb-second (V2) language, *somewhat* on a par with contemporary Germanic languages, with the exception of Modern English (NE). One current controversy concerns the exact nature of

V2 in OE. The following question summarizes, and oversimplifies, the debate: Is OE "asymmetrically" V2 like German and Dutch—with V2 in COMP and with the sentence-initial constituent in Spec(CP) whenever COMP is not lexicalized (e.g., in main clauses)—or is OE "symmetrically" V2 like Icelandic and Yiddish, with V2 in INFL and with the sentence-initial constituent in Spec(IP), which makes V2 applicable, with certain exceptions, in both root and embedded contexts?

Van Kemenade (1987, 1997) takes OE to have the underlying order Subject–Object–Verb (SOV) with V2 in COMP, not in INFL. However, German and Dutch do not allow the "verb-third" (V3) patterns in (40a). This can perhaps be accounted by the absence in German and Dutch of OE-type pronominal clitics adjoining to the left of V in COMP (but see van Kemenade 1987: 52, 126–141 for a rapprochement between OE, German, and Dutch clitics). Alternately, V3 orders in OE, as in (40a), have been taken to result from movement of some XP into Spec(CP) in sentence-initial position, followed by the clitic left-adjoined to IP and the verb in medial INFL (i.e., in "third" position); see Kroch and Taylor 1997: 305f.[47]

One last, but surely not least, bit of background: According to van Kemenade, two major changes occurred in the transition to late ME: English went from SOV to SVO by 1200 (and presumably from head-final IP to head-medial IP), and V2 was "lost" by 1400 (but see note 52). Van Kemenade connects these two changes—SOV-to-SVO and loss of V2—to radical reductions in nominal and verbal inflections, respectively.

Going back to the OE object clitics in (40), two of them (in (40a) and (40c)) surface to the left of their θ-marking verbs. The pattern in (40a) might not surprise us given OE's widespread SOV order, whether it be base-generated (à la van Kemenade) or derived from an underling Kaynian SVO order (à la Roberts 1997). But note that (40b) has the object clitic to the left of the subject *mon* and that (40c) is from circa 1340; at that time, ME—or, perhaps more accurately, most ME idiolects—had already switched from OV to VO.[48] Thus, as van Kemenade argues, the data in (40) suggest that OE and Early ME had a rule that, under certain conditions, forces the verb's complement to be pronounced outside of VP, to the left of the verb. A somewhat similar rule exists in Fr (see, e.g., (41)), but not in NE or HC. A direct comparison of (40a) and (40c) with (41) accentuates the parallels between English and HC diachrony and advances our agenda against Creole Exceptionalism: OE, Early ME, and Fr manifest preverbal object clitics, whereas both NE and HC lack such clitics:[49]

(41)   a. Quelles   histoires   <u>lui</u>   raconteront   ils? (Fr)
            what   stories   3sg-DAT   tell   3pl
        'What stories will they tell him/her?'

b. Il lui   donna quinze livres   d'or.
   he 3sg-DAT   gave   fifteen pounds   of gold

'He gave him/her fifteen pounds of gold.'

As amply documented by van Kemenade (1987), cliticization started disappearing in English around the time when morphological case marking on OE nouns was also disappearing. Van Kemenade (1987: 101) gives the following example of nominal case markings, on *stan* 'stone' (similar markings are found on pronouns):

(42)   **Nominal declension of *stan*
            'stone' in OE**

	Sg	Pl
NOM	stan	stanas
ACC	stan	stanas
GEN	stanes	stana
DAT	stane	stanum

From van Kemenade 1987: 101.

It is estimated that by 1200 a substantial reduction in morphological case paradigms had taken place. In van Kemenade's analysis, this reduction in morphological case directly led to the demise of cliticization: "Clitics are in a sense case affixes and thus are dependent on the presence of inflectional morphology. Accordingly, when inflectional morphology was lost, case affixing was lost" (p. 204).

Van Kemenade (1987: 188–205) further notices that among the various sites where cliticization was lost, C^0 was the last stronghold. The presence of (object) clitics hosted by V in C^0, as in (40a), outlasted IP-internal cliticization, as in (40c) where V remains in IP.[50] She surmises that, unlike IP-internal cliticization which is directly connected with *nominal* case morphology, the (late) C^0-cliticization patterns are connected to V2 effects and to *verbal* morphology; both V2 and a (somewhat) 'rich' system of verbal inflections survived until 1400, along with C^0 clitics (pp. 188–205), whereas (most) IP-internal cliticization and 'rich' nominal case inflections disappeared by 1200. Thus, in addition to morphological case on NPs, cliticization in English diachrony would also be associated to properties of verbal inflections and to V-movement (in this case, V-to-C movement and V2).[51]

Roberts (1997) tentatively couches some of van Kemenade's observations (on the correlation between cliticization and overt case morphology) within "classic" Minimalist assumptions (as in Chomsky 1993). He takes OE object cliticization to be driven by some "strong" features in the INFL layers dominating VP. These strong features are morphologically diagnosed by OE's case declensions (see (42)).

These strong inflectional features are "affixal" in some abstract way, somewhat on a par with the overt affixal heads that trigger V-to-I in Fr and in OE/ME. Thus, "strong" or "affixal" inflectional features of verbs and of nouns, as manifested by "rich" verbal inflections and "rich" nominal case morphology, correlate with the possibility of overt leftward movement out of VP of both V and its object (if any). The loss of preverbal object clitics, in Roberts's (as in van Kemenade's) account is connected to the massive weakening of nominal case morphology in ME: the INFL head that formerly attracted objects from within VP became "weak" or non-"affixal" and stopped driving object movement[52] (see Roberts 1997 for details and Thráinsson 2001 for a critique).

Roberts's and van Kemenade's accounts of the morphology–syntax interface in English diachrony are not without theoretical and empirical problems.[53] But what matters most here is the attractive, if controversial, speculation that the collapse of OE's morphological case system was a necessary, although not sufficient, condition for the subsequent loss of cliticization. This is similar in spirit to the hypothesis that the loss of rich verbal inflection is a precondition for the loss of verb movement.[54]

In Roberts's (1997) scenario, in situ settings have a learnability edge over settings that force movement (see, e.g., p. 421). When a parameter has both a movement option and an in situ option, the latter is taken as the default setting for reasons of economy: "The simplest representation compatible with the input is chosen, where representations lacking overt movement are defined as simpler than those featuring movement dependencies" (this is in keeping with Minimalist conceptual desiderata). *Ceteris paribus*, any reduction in morphological triggers for the movement setting makes it more likely that the language acquirers will adopt the nonmovement alternative. (See Roberts 1999 for learnability considerations and for their relevance to Creole patterns, including V-in-situ and unmoved object pronouns; see also section 7.1.)

The diachronic similarities vis-à-vis morphology and word-order in VP's extended projections in creolization and in language change weaken any empirical basis for Creole Exceptionalism, with its alleged nongenetic "discrepancies." In the history of both HC and Germanic, we have somewhat congruent word-order and morphological changes in VP's extended projections.

6.4 Reanalysis in the Emergence of HC's Object Placement

On a par with the Haitian TMA markers surveyed in section 6.2, the morphosyntax of HC objects was not created ab-ovo from some hypothetical radically impoverished pidgin.[55]

To begin, HC has not incorporated any restructured forms from the Fr *clitic* and *atonic* system: HC pronouns (e.g., those in (5)) are all derived from Fr *non-clitic* and *tonic* pronouns; for example, HC *mwen* '1sg' from Fr *moi*, HC *li* '3sg' from Fr *lui*, HC *yo* '3pl' from Fr *eux* (cf. the Gascony and Auvergne variant *yo* discussed in Sylvain 1936: 36), and HC *nou* '1pl, 2pl' and *ou* '2sg' can be argued to etymologically derive from the nonclitic uses of Fr *nous* and *vous*. As recently argued by Fattier (1995), the relevant regional French vernaculars may have readily provided the Creole creator with at least the basic patterns to be reanalyzed toward the pronominal system of Early HC. Let's elaborate.

It has long been argued (see, e.g., Meillet 1958 [1920]; Brunot and Bruneau 1949) that the Fr clitic pronouns are better analyzed as subject- and object-agreement markers—or as inflectional heads in modern parlance (see, e.g., Sportiche 1995). For Meillet (1958: 177–178 [1920]), Fr subject clitics such as *je, tu,* and *il* should be analyzed as "grammatical markers of person inflection." Meillet adduces the use of (presumably nontopicalized) nonclitic subjects followed by subject clitics—as in *Moi, je dis* 'Me, I say' and *La vache, elle mange* 'The cow, she eats'—as evidence that the subject clitics are really marks of "verbal inflection" that are part of the verbal forms. In the same vein, Brunot and Bruneau (1969: 225 [1949]) write:

> Very early on ... *moi, toi, lui, eux* (which had "more body") replaced ... *je, tu, il, ils* (which were pronounced *j, t, i, i*). As early as the end of the thirteenth century ... *moi* can serve as subject of the verb. ... As a logical conclusion of this evolution, the former pronouns *je, tu, il,* etc., have become "person markers" and become an integral part of the verbal forms. (my translation)

Thus, Brunot and Bruneau distinguish the pronouns *moi, toi, lui,* and so on from the "prefixes" *je, tu, il,* and so on. In contemporary terms, the former would be subjects in Spec(IP), whereas the latter would function as affixal agreement markers, associated with some functional heads above VP, and thus their cooccurrence ("double-marking") in preverbal position, as in *Moi j(e)* ..., *Toi t(u)* ..., *Lui, i(l)* ..., et cetera.

More recently, Chaudenson (1992: 157–162); Chaudenson et al. (1993: 103–107), and Chaudenson and Mufwene (2001: 172–176) have noted related facts in regional varieties of French, such as Cajun French, Louisiana French, and Missouri French. Chaudenson et al. note that, in these regional varieties, object clitics in Standard French (*me, te, le, la, les,* etc.), along with (other) verbal inflections, are "instable," "phonetically fragile," and "disappearing" as a result of "self-regulating processes" (104–106, 120). Chaudenson et al. (1993: 105) give the following examples in (43), to be contrasted with their Standard French counterparts in (44) (focus on the underlined object pronouns):

(43) a. I   v'nont   voir   <u>moi</u>. (Cajun French)
        3pl   FUT+3pl   see   1sg

      'They will see me.'

b. J'   vas   mettre   <u>toué</u>   tout   en
   1sg+NOM   FUT   put   2sg   all   in
   blanc. (Missouri French)
   white

   "I will dress you all in white."

c. M'   as   enterrer   <u>elle</u>   dans   les
   1sg   FUT   bury   3sg+fem   in   the+PL
   feuilles. (Missouri French)
   leaves

   "I will bury her in the leaves."

(44) a. Ils   <u>me</u>   verront. (Standard French)
          3pl   1sg+ACC   see+FUT+3pl

      b. Je   <u>te</u>   mettrai   tout   en   blanc.
         1sg+NOM   2sg+ACC   put+FUT+1sg   all   in   white

      c. Je   <u>l'</u>   enterrerai   dans   les   feuilles.
         1sg+NOM   3sg+ACC   bury+FUT+1sg   in   the+PL leaves

In (43), Cajun French and Missouri French, like HC, exhibit postverbal object pronouns such as *moi, toué,* and *elle* (cf. HC *mwen, ou,* and *li*) in contexts where Standard French requires preverbal object clitics (cf. *me, te,* and *l'* in (44)). Also note the periphrastic future marking in (43c), which is phonetically, structurally, and semantically similar to its HC analog: *M a antere li* 'I will bury him/her/it'. Baissac (1880), Brunot (1966), Chaudenson (1992), Chaudenson et al. (1993), Chaudenson and Mufwene (2001), and Fattier (1998) observe similar periphrastic-future patterns across an array of French-lexicon Creoles and regional varieties of vernacular French, including Québecois (see section 6.1–6.2 and the references in notes 37 and 44). Here, we have "creole-like" restructuring of French morpho-syntax, sans "creolization" (*and* sans relexification; cf. note 57).

The diachrony of pronouns in these regional varieties of French and in French-lexicon Creoles—in some, though not all, respects—is similar to what has occurred in English diachrony, where preverbal object clitics have given way to postverbal counterparts. It is also quite possible that the French varieties that were fed into the genesis of HC were more like Cajun French and Missouri French than Standard French vis-à-vis cliticization possibilities; this would be in line with the previous comments by Meillet (1958 [1920]) and Brunot and Bruneau (1969 [1949]) about popular vernacular varieties (see also note 32, in particular Frei's and Gadet's comments to the effect that popular French uses more postverbal tonic object pronouns than Standard French).

It can also be argued that the preference for tonic pronouns may make sense from a processing or acquisition perspective: Fr tonic object pronouns, unlike their Fr atonic counterparts, are uniformly postverbal and obey the canonical placement rule of full-NP objects—this is very much like the system of HC (atonic) object pronouns. By overgeneralizing the use of Fr tonic pronouns, early learners sidestep the extra complications of preverbal object cliticization, which in any case applies to inflectionallike phonologically and semantically weak elements—namely, the atonic clitics (cf. Fattier 1995: 140–142). The latter belongs to what, in the early stages of L2A, seems to constitute a "brittle" morphological component of the target language (see note 32). Moreover, Fr tonic pronouns are often phonologically and semantically stressed; they are thus made more salient. To wit: MOI, *j'l'ai vu*, LUI, *pas* ELLE 'I myself, I have seen HIM, not HER'.

At any rate, van Kemenade's (1987: 204) generalization—about the loss of OE clitics—can be adapted to fit the emergence of object-placement patterns in HC, Cajun French, and Missouri French: "[Syntactic] clitics are in a sense case affixes and thus are dependent on the presence of inflectional morphology. Accordingly, when inflectional morphology [is] lost, case affixing [is also] lost." Let's suppose that the ancestors of NE, HC, Cajun French, and Missouri French all had robust preverbal clitics. In turn, it can be speculated that their descendants all witnessed a reduction in inflectional paradigms alongside a reduction in cliticization possibilities: object clitics, or some subset thereof, got lost along with other "inflectional" markings on the verb. This is the sort of inflectional erosion that seems typical of language change (via L2A in contact situations), as pointed out by Meillet (1958 [1919]) and Weinreich (1968 [1953]) among many others, and as experimentally confirmed in recent theoretical L2A studies such as Klein and Perdue (1992), Perdue (1995), Lardiere (2000), Prévost and White (2000), and Ionin and Wexler (2002).

More generally, the link noted by van Kemenade between inflectional erosion and loss of cliticization can also be captured in Sportiche's (1995) more recent approach, which "treats [Romance pronominal] clitics as complex agreement morphemes" that head "clitic voices" in the extended projection of the VP (pp. 237, 265, but see 270 n18): in such an approach, the loss of cliticization in HC and its congeners naturally becomes part of the larger loss of agreement morphology—a recurrent phenomenon in the early interlanguages created by L2 learners.[56]

Yet another potential influence toward uniform V-Obj order in HC can be found in the Gbe substratum as the native languages of some of the L2 learners that were exposed to regional French varieties in colonial Haiti. Given the demographics and sociolinguistics of the colony, some of these French varieties would have been nonnative or, in Chaudenson's (1992) term, "approximations of approximations" (i.e., recursive approximations). As for the Gbe languages, they are canonically SVO, with both pronominal and nonnominal objects, once we abstract away from the complex verbal constructions with OV order (see section

3.3). Furthermore, Gbe *atonic* pronominal objects are postverbal, even in the contexts where full NP objects and tonic pronouns shift to a preverbal position (see Aboh, chapter 4 in this volume); such postverbal atonic pronouns are, in their surface distribution, on a par with HC pronominal objects and in contradistinction with their Fr analogs, independently of how pronominal enclisis should be analyzed in these languages. In any case, current results in acquisition research make it quite likely that VO patterns in the substratum would have favored the adoption by L2A learners of congruent VO patterns into the incipient Creole. Similar "substratum" effects (e.g., influence from English in North America) may have contributed to the postverbal pronoun patterns in (43).[57]

7 "Creole Genesis" versus "Language Change": A Mythical Dualism?

7.1 Recapitulation: Creolization, Language Change, and Language Acquisition

Robust VP-related differences between HC and its source languages have been argued to depend on prior erosion of inflectional morphology in the emergence of HC. This scenario makes the emergence of V-in-situ in HC syntax quite similar to its analog in English diachrony (see section 6.1; see also Roberts 1999 and Lightfoot 1999). In turn, HC's lack of preverbal objects can be taken as a corollary of its V-in-situ setting, assuming some implementation of Holmberg's Generalization (see Bobaljik 2002 for one recent proposal). Object-in-situ patterns in HC have analogs in Modern English (NE) and in a subset of Scandinavian languages: these patterns conform to a constraint that is presumably rooted in UG (see section 5). In this account, the reason why the syntax of HC objects differs so robustly from that of its major source languages is rather straightforward: Holmberg's Generalization, to the extent that it applies to the placement of object pronouns, predicts that object cliticization, as an instance of Object Shift to the left of the verb, could not (stably) exist in HC in the absence of V-to-I.[58]

The VP-related divergences between HC and its source languages have recurrent analogs in language acquisition and in language change (section 6). Such congruences suggest that key aspects of Creole genesis can be apprehended by an investigation of the same UG principles that are known to constrain paths of parameter setting (or resetting) in developmental patterns arising outside of "creolization."

Let's also recapitulate our learnability-theoretic speculations vis-à-vis this scenario. It is second-language acquisition (L2A) under duress that, in the development of HC, led to the eventual reduction of inflectional paradigms and thus to the loss through L2A of one class of potential triggers for V-to-I in Creole genesis. The relative salience-cum-transparency of the Fr verbal periphrases, as compared with their synthetic counterparts, may have further biased the language learner toward the V-in-situ setting. If verbal periphrases are, for one reason or another (e.g., salience and transparency), preferred over their synthetic counterparts in popular and second-language varieties of French, then the net effect is a proportional reduction of unambiguous V-to-I syntactic triggers (e.g., instances of verb negation—V_{+fin} *pas*—order with thematic verbs) in the Primary Linguistic Data (PLD) of incoming learners, including the locally born (i.e., Creole) children that created the first native varieties of proto-HC—the first proto-HC I-languages (see the sociohistorical sketch in section 2.1). The main verb in Fr verbal periphrases is in the infinitive or the past participle and always to the right of sentential negation. Thus, every use of a negated clause with a verbal periphrasis instead of its synthetic counterpart entails that the learner is exposed to one less utterance that robustly "expresses" the V-to-I setting with a lexical thematic verb. (See Roberts 1999: 293f. and Lightfoot 1999: 438–441 on the structural and frequency factors that affect the reliability of the PLD with respect to the "expression" of the V-to-I setting.)

In the context of HC's development, the conspiracy between fossilization of inflection in L2A and the processing benefits of verbal periphrases in either language use or language acquisition may thus attract more and more learners toward the V-in-situ option. Besides, V-in-situ may be the unmarked setting since it entails more economical representations (à la Robert's 1999; see section 6.3). In turn, the adoption of the V-in-situ would bias the learner toward PLD patterns that are superficially compatible with, and thus reinforce, the adopted V-in-situ option. Such patterns would include utterances where objects are postverbal, as in Fr positive imperatives (see note 56), independently of the actual representations of these utterances in the grammars that provide some of the PLD. In other words, specific PLD patterns (e.g., Fr imperatives and their postverbal objects) are assigned underlying structures that are distinct from their targetlike representations. Because the latter, in any case, are not directly accessible to the learner, we have the possibility and pervasiveness of reanalysis.

The phenomena described in this chapter vis-à-vis the development of VP-related morphosyntax in HC (namely, paradigmatic reduction in inflectional morphology, the switch to V-in-situ and object-in-situ, reanalysis-cum-grammaticalization, and substrate influence) all make "creolization" look quite similar to contact-induced language change in the diachrony of so-called genetic languages. Independently of which account of the relevant facts ultimately prevails, what matters here is the relevance of the non-Creole diachronic patterns vis-à-vis Creole Exceptionalism as the allegation of a fundamental (developmental and structural) divide between creolization and language change. The admittedly partial evidence available thus far offers recurrent parallels between the patterns of verb and object morphosyntax in HC, English, and French diachrony. The "discrepancies" that obtain in the genesis of HC (see sections 3–5) also obtain outside of "creolization." For example, if we take HC and NE as end points of diachronic developments, we find in both scenarios that a reduction in inflectional morphology is associated with a reduction in IP-internal leftward movement outside of VP.

Once "creolization" and "language change" are viewed from the Cartesian-Uniformitarian perspective, what we're dealing with throughout are individual speakers engaged in UG-guided language creation and re-creation (see DeGraff 1999b, 1999d, 2001a, 2001b). The task of *any* such learner is to use whatever cues are available in the PLD to create or re-create an I-language that is compatible with UG, thereby leading to the intrinsic possibility of "grammatical inventions" (à la Rizzi 1999) alongside the systematic congruence previously observed vis-à-vis morphosyntactic development across various types of linguistic ecologies. As with the PLD in other situations of language contact, the PLD in the creation by Creole children of Creole I-languages would have been influenced by adult learners' early interlanguages and the latter's substrate-influenced innovations. In this perspective, "Creole" and "creolization" do not, and cannot, refer to typological profiles and processes of "grammatical invention" that are qualitatively and fundamentally distinct from their counterparts in non-Creole synchrony and diachrony, as in the Romance and English cases, which I now summarize.

7.2 "Abnormal" Discrepancies in "Normal" (i.e., "Genetic") Diachrony?

The evolution of Latin into Romance (e.g., Fr) constitutes one case of "genetic," "normal," and "continuous" development par excellence. Yet this is what Meillet, who very much believed in "genetic" families, had to say about the evolution of Romance:

(45)   "From a linguistic standpoint, Romance languages, while maintaining many Latin features . . . have structures that are *fundamentally different* from their Latin counterparts: total ruin of case inflection which entails and is conditioned by the relatively fixed word order; the creation of articles; the total restructuring of verb conjugation where, notably, person features are expressed more often by preverbal pronouns than by verbal inflection. *All*

> *this makes neo-Latin languages fall into a typological class that is quite remote from the structural type represented by Latin."*
>
> (Meillet 1951: 80 [1929]; my translation; emphases added)

Now, recall Thomason and Kaufman's litmus test for so-called nongenetic diachrony: "a *significant discrepancy* between the degree of lexical correspondence and the degree of grammatical correspondence—in some or all grammatical subsystems" (1998: 206; my emphasis; see also pp. 8–12). So, are the discrepancies alluded to by Meillet in (45) of a "significant" degree? Meillet, as a pro-Stammbaumtheorie historical linguist, had this to say about discrepancies in the evolution of classic Stammbaumtheorie phyla:

(46)   The use of word order in French and English to express relations between phrases is a *creation* of these languages: such innovation did not have any model in Latin or Old Germanic. (Meillet 1958:148 [1912], my translation)

So, for Meillet, the "discrepant" word-order innovations in French and English diachrony are a matter of language "creation." A generative-grammar spin on Meillet's words in (45)–(46) would then suggest that the creation of French and English morphosyntax in diachrony is quite commensurable with the mechanics of Creole genesis: both are UG-guided language "creation" in the face of necessarily sparse and heterogeneous PLD made available in contingent linguistic ecologies. This Cartesian-Uniformitarian view leaves no room for the orthodox dualism between "genetic" versus "nongenetic" phylogeny.

Indeed, it could also be argued that along *certain* parameters, such as lexical case morphology and movement-related properties like so-called free word-order scrambling, French and HC are more similar to each other than French and Latin are (see DeGraff 2001b: secs. 3.2–3.3). It can also be argued that, again along certain parameters, English and Jamaican Creole are closer to each other than English and Old Germanic are. Such dissimilarities are, it must be stressed, an artifact of what parameters we choose to compare, how, and why. But the comparison so far teaches us that there is no precise and operational structural litmus test, and no coherent theoretical framework, that consistently and reliably discriminates where "language change" ends and where "creolization" begins (for a sustained argument along similar lines, see Mufwene 1986, 1997, 2001). More generally, there is much debate on the feasibility of syntactic reconstruction in the establishment of phylogenetic correspondences (for one recent argument against such reconstruction, see, e.g., Lightfoot 2002).

7.3 VP-related Morphology and Word Order in a Creole Sample

Given the comparative data in this chapter, should we expect *all* Creoles to be like HC in having both verbs and objects uninflected for TMA, agreement, and case and being pronounced where they are generated—that is, in situ within the VP? To the extent that language acquisition under duress, as in abrupt language contact, entails a certain degree of inflectional erosion, à la Weinreich, Meillet, and others, and to the extent that inflectional "erosion" contributes to a diachronic decrease in clause-internal movement out of VP, à la van Kemenade, Roberts, and others, then one may be tempted to answer "yes." Yet, language contact happens in the diachrony of virtually *all* languages, be they Creoles or not (cf. Mufwene 2001)—to wit, the history of Romance and of English. Of course, the degree of contact and the degree of inflectional erosion are not uniform across all instances (cf. note 31). Compare, say, inflectional morphology in HC with Cape Verdean Creole (see later) or within and across Germanic, Romance, and others. Within Germanic, the most celebrated cases include the inflectional contrasts between English and Icelandic and between English and German. Besides, alongside morphological erosion, there is grammaticalization where free morphemes are reanalyzed as bound elements, for one example. In Givón's phrase, "yesterday's syntax is today's morphology," à la Bopp, Humboldt, Meillet, and the like (see DeGraff 2001b: sec. 6).

Be that as it may, language contact, like many other sociolinguistic phenomena, does happen along a continuum, both across time and across space. Given that each contact situation will vary with respect to, among many other things, the degrees of contact and the inventories of the languages, dialects, and idiolects in contact, there is no a priori reason that the outcome of "creolization" should uniformly fall within a predetermined and exclusive typological subspace of variations. Furthermore, as we saw in the comparison of HC and English diachrony, there exist robust development parallels (e.g., vis-à-vis morphology and word order) that cut across phenomena that go by the traditional labels of "creolization" and "language change." At the same time, there exist substantial differences even among Creoles, and even among Creoles with Romance-based lexicons. For example, both Cape Verdean Creole (CVC), with a Portuguese-based lexicon, and Palenquero (PL), with a Spanish-based lexicon, differ from HC along the verb-placement parameter. Both CVC and PL, unlike HC, are V-to-I, as indicated by the verb-adverb-object order in (47) and (48):[59]

(47) a. *João   xina   ben   se   lison.* (CVC)
        João   learned   well   his   lesson

      'João learned his lesson well.' (Baptista 1997: 90; see also p. 225)

b. *João   ta   ama   mutu Eliza.*
João   TMA   love   Eliza

'João loves Eliza too much.' (Baptista 1997: 207)

(48)   *I   asé   ammirá   mucho   ese   monasito.* (PL)
I   HAB   admire   much   this   boy

'I admire this boy (very) much.' (Armin Schwegler, pers. comm. October 9, 2000)[60]

And it is perhaps not accidental that both CVC and PL, unlike HC, express some of their TMA values via affixes. CVC has an affix *-ba* for "past," "past perfect," and "present perfect" (Baptista 1997: 69).[61] PL has a similar affix *-ba* for "past imperfective," in addition to an affixal progressive marker *-ndo*; and the two affixes can cooccur in the same word, as in *toká-ndo-ba* in *Ata la sei músika toká-ndo-ba* 'Until six (in the morning) the band was playing' (see Schwegler and Green, in press, for further details). The link between TMA affixes and verb movement in CVC and PL, modulo the caveats in notes 59 and 61, can be made by postulating that CVC and PL, like Fr and unlike HC, carry abstract affixal features in their inflectional heads. Like their Fr counterparts, CVC and PL affixal features are associated with the verb moving to the corresponding inflectional heads in order to provide a host to these affixal heads (see sections 4 and 6).[62]

Do CVC and PL have movement of objects outside of VP? This is a more difficult question to answer in the space remaining. Both Creoles have their object pronouns in postverbal positions, but there may be some evidence that object pronouns cliticize onto the verb and then ride along with the latter when it moves outside of VP.

Let's start with the CVC data. Baptista (1997: 90) notes that, at PF, adverbs like *ben* 'well' sit most comfortably in the clause-internal position, between the verb and its object, as in (49a). She observes the following contrast, noting some dialect variation in (un)grammaticality with respect to the clause-final position of *ben* in (49d):

(49)   a.   João   xina   ben   se   lison. (CVC)
João   learned   well   his   lesson

'João learned his lesson well.'

b.   *Ben João xina se lison.

c.   *João ben xina se lison.

d.   ?João xina se lison ben.

When the object of *xina* is a clitic (e.g., *l* '3sg'), *ben* becomes perfectly acceptable in clause-final position. Compare (49d) and (50):

(50)   João   xina+*l*   ben. (CVC)
        João   learnt+it   well

Here is Baptista's analysis of (50) (her example (71b)):

(51)   'The [object] clitic [*l* '3sg'] originates in the VP complement and incorpo-
       rates to V [*xina*]. When the verb raises across a VP-internal adverbial [e.g.,
       ben] . . . the object clitic raises with it. (Baptista 1997: 262)

Alternatively, one could take (50) to arise in three successive steps (cf. the analysis of Portuguese enclisis in Raposo 2000: 285f.): (i) V-to-I; (ii) object cliticization to a functional head (say, F) higher than INFL, the landing site in (i); (iii) movement of the V+I complex created in (i) to a landing site still higher of F. In (i)–(iii), "higher than" implies "to the left of," adopting Kayne's (1994) Antisymmetry. In Duarte and Matos's (2000: 130) account of Portuguese enclisis, the clitic and then the verb left-adjoin to an inflectional head that c-commands VP.

    Somewhat similar verb- and clitic-placement facts hold in PL, to which similar analyses can be given. Compare (48), with a nonpronominal object, with (52), with a pronominal object:

(52)   *I*   *asé*   *ammiré+lo*   *mucho.* (PL)
       I   HAB   admire+him   much

      'I admire him (very) much.'

Further evidence suggesting movement of objects outside of VP in PL is given in (53) (courtesy of Armin Schwegler, pers. comm. October 11, 2000):

(53)   a. *I miná+lo+ba.*

       'I looked at him.'

     b. **I miná+ba+lo*

Schwegler and Green (in press) note that object pronouns (e.g., *lo* 'him' in (53a)) are allowed to cliticize onto a verbal host, to the right of the verbal stem and to the left of the suffixal TMA marker *-ba*, thus mesoclisis of *lo* in *miná+lo+ba* of (53a). This is reminiscent of certain forms in Caribbean Spanish (Rivera-Castillo 1992); and in European Portuguese, Galician, and Old Iberian (Durate and Matos 2000; Raposo 2000: 283–287). Assuming that the verb undergoes head movement (out of VP, as in (48)) and moves to adjoin to the left of, and host, the TMA head -*ba*, then the object pronoun must also be able to shift out of VP for it to occur to the left of -*ba*, perhaps along the lines proposed in Baptista's (1997: 262) analysis in (51) (see also the accounts of similar cases of mesoclisis in Rivera-Castillo 1992 and Raposo 2000: 285f.: there, too, mesoclisis depends on instances of verb movement to a variety of VP-external landing sites). The word-order and morphological patterns exemplified in (53a) may thus count as triggers for PL's V-to-I setting (see note 62).

These are all tentative arguments, but the lesson here is that VP syntax in both CVC and PL is *not* isomorphic to that of HC, despite the fact that CVC, PL, and HC are all Romance-lexicon Creoles. VP-related facts seem to draw HC closer to Modern English (both have verbs and objects in situ) than to HC's fellow Romance-lexicon Creoles like CVC and PL (both have verbs and objects outside VP). Conversely, the V-to-I properties of CVC and PL draw them closer to, say, Fr and OE, both of which are non-Creole V-to-I languages, than to HC, a V-in-situ Creole language. Of course, going outside the realm of Romance-lexicon Creoles should, I suspect, afford us even greater variation in the VP domain and elsewhere (see DeGraff 2001b). The implication is that there is no uniform VP syntax across Creole languages—there is no sui generis "Creole" typology (see, e.g., Givón 1979; Mufwene 1986, 2001; Muysken 1988: 300; DeGraff 1999a, 1999b, 2001a, 2001b).

This chapter can thus be read as one more plea for constructively combining research on creolization, language change, and language acquisition toward a triangulation of the mental bases of language creation. At any rate, UG itself offers no conceptual room for any fundamental (diachronic or synchronic) opposition between Creoles and non-Creoles. If "language acquisition is interpreted as the process of fixing the parameters of the initial state [UG] in one of the permissible ways" (Chomsky 1995: 6), then acquisition is not "transmission" *sensu stricto*, but UG-guided "creation" or "re-creation," with contingent, limited, and heterogeneous PLD. "Language creation" happens everywhere and always, and each and every I-language develops in accordance with necessarily invariant UG and necessarily contingent and heterogeneous ecologies.

NOTES

This project has been supported by, inter alia, a much-appreciated fellowship from the National Endowment for the Humanities (Grant no. FA-37500-02).

This chapter's insights, if any, are due entirely to constructive discussions with colleagues and friends, too numerous to all be named. This chapter's shortcomings, and there are many (witness the notes!), are due to my not being yet able to incorporate a long series of questions, suggestions, and disagreements from said colleagues and friends. My future work will be vastly improved once I can take into account all the comments that have so kindly been offered while I was writing this chapter and its fore-runners in the past few years.

In the meantime, heartiest thanks are due specially to Marlyse Baptista, Jonathan Bobaljik, Robert Chaudenson, Yves Dejean, Dominique Fattier, Morris Halle, Richard Kayne, Alec Marantz, Salikoko Mufwene, Juvénal Ndayiragije, Marilene Phipps, Fer-nanda Pratas, Carson Schütze, Armin Schwegler, Almeida Jacqueline Toribio, Daniel Vé-ronique, Cecília Vieira, and Ken Wexler. I am eternally indebted to Richie Kayne and Salikoko Mufwene for many pointed comments at various stages of this chapter's long gestation. The main proposal in this chapter and much else I am thankful for, I owe to the ground-breaking work, constant inspiration, and joyful camaraderie of Yves Dejean (*Papa Iv*).

1. See DeGraff (1999a, 1999b, 2001a, 2001b, 2002a, 2002b, 2000c, 2003) for more thorough reviews; also see Mufwene (2001) for a related critique in a different theoreti-cal framework.

2. In Caribbean Creole-genesis scenarios, the SUPERSTRATE language is the Euro-pean language (e.g., French, English, Portuguese, Spanish, and Dutch), as spoken by those in the socioeconomically dominant positions in the language-contact situation. The superstrate language, in all its varieties and approximations, is the most popular language-acquisition target for those who are newly born or newly arrived into the language-contact situation. Among the newly arrived, we find adult second-language learners from Africa, speakers of the so-called substrate languages; these speakers are typically in subordinate positions vis-à-vis the superstrate speakers. On a structural-phylogenetic note, the superstrate is, inter alia, the LEXIFIER of the Creole—that is, the etymological source of the Creole lexicon. One example: In the context of Haitian Cre-ole's genesis, seventeenth- and eighteenth-century regional varieties of French—and whatever koiné they produced upon contact (see Mufwene 2001: 34–38)—constitute the superstratum/lexifier, while Niger-Congo languages constitute the substratum. (See Goodman 1993 for useful terminological caveats regarding creolists' uses of the terms *substrate* and *superstrate*.)

3. In the Caribbean colonial context, the use of "Creole" vis-à-vis human beings and other biological species seems to have preceded its use vis-à-vis speech varieties. In both the biological and the linguistic cases, certain locally grown varieties were identified as "Creole" in opposition to their imported counterparts. In the Caribbean, the label "Creole" was thus initially used to contrast certain nonlinguistic entities indigenous to the New World of the islands with the analogous varieties that developed in the Old World of Europe and Africa. In colonial Haiti, for example, the locally born descendants of expatriates from the Old World came to be known as Creoles. Subsequently, the de-notation of the label was extended from Creole individuals to the latter's locally grown speech varieties, which were often contrasted with the corresponding metropolitan vari-eties. (For more complex terminological-cum-historical details, see, e.g., Moreau de Saint-Méry 1958: 28–111; Mufwene 1997, 2001: 3–11; Chaudenson and Mufwene 2001: ch. 1 and references therein.)

4. If Proto-Human exists—a big "if"—then Creole languages cannot really be "nongenetic" in a strict interpretation: since Creole speakers are human beings, there

must exist some "genetic" branch relating each Creole language to Proto-Human. This conclusion can be avoided by claiming either that Creole languages are effectively artificial languages that altogether lie outside the scope of (normal) human languages or that Creole languages are "born again" instantiations of Proto-Human grammar, modulo the etymologies of Creole lexicons—these etymologies unmistakably link Creole languages to their lexifiers (i.e., to *non*-Proto-Human languages). As it turns out, Creole studies are rife with claims that Creoles are (direct descendants of) born-again Proto-languages or that they are artificial languages (see DeGraff 2001a, 2001b, for details and critiques).

5. See, for example, DeGraff 1994a, 1994b, 1997, 1999a, 1999b, 2000, 2001a, 2002c; also see DeGraff 1998, 2001b, and the references therein.

6. The following abbreviations are used throughout: ACC, accusative; ANT, anterior; ASP, aspectual marker; CFP, clause-final particle (with discourse-presupposition functions); COMPL, completive marker; DAT, dative, FUT, future; HAB, habitual; IN-DEF, indefinite; IRR, irrealis; NEG, negation; PL, plural; PROG, progressive; SG, sing; 1sg, first singular; . . . , 3pl, third plural; masc, masculine; fem, feminine.

Abbreviations for languages: CVC, Cape Verdean Creole; Fr, French; HC, Haitian Creole; IC, Icelandic; LC, Louisiana Creole; MC, Mauritian Creole; ME, Middle English; NE, New English (i.e., Modern English); OE, Old English; PL, Palenquero; SW, Swedish.

7. This does not mean that HC verbs are morphologically simplex. In fact, an argument can be made that *konnen* itself is made up of a root *konn* and a verbal marker *-en* (the nasalized variant of *-e*, which is etymologically related to the Fr infinitival *-er* and participial *-é(e)*). HC *-e/-en* is subject to apocope (e.g., *konn* from *konnen*) under conditions that I still don't understand (but see DeGraff 2001a: 74f.). The HC verbal marker *-e/-en* is also used productively, for example, to derive verbs from nouns as, say, in *klipse* 'to clip', *ploge* 'to plug', and *tepe* 'to tape' from the nouns *klips* 'clip', *plòg* 'plug', and *tep* 'tape', all of which are English borrowings. As noted by Clark (1993), the Fr suffix *-er* is also the one that language learners use as a default verbal marker in their spontaneous, nonconventionalized, verb coinages. See also related remarks in Van Name (1870: 139–149) and Baissac 1880: 52–55; I return to the origins of the HC verbal marker in section 6.2.

8. I come back to Fr imperatives in Section 6.2 and note 56.

9. When it comes to elucidate Creole genesis, we must consider cross-dialectal and diachronic variations in colloquial speech to better delineate the kind of patterns the Creole creators were exposed to (Chaudenson 1992; Chaudenson et al. 1993; Fattier 1995, 1998; Chaudenson and Mufwene 2001; Mufwene 2001). In the case of HC's genesis, it can be safely assumed that Standard French as we know it today played little, if any, role in Creole formation (see section 2.1). Chaudenson et al. (1993) discuss the paradigmatically sparser inflectional suffixes on verbs in various regional varieties of popular spoken French.

In spoken varieties, *nous aimons* in (13) is giving way to *on aime* with the second-person plural *vous aimez* becoming the only form that is distinguishable from /ɛm/. Notwithstanding this "erosion" of agreement, agreement marking still exists in popular varieties. In addition to second-person plural forms, we also find a distinct third-person plural present for certain verbs (Chaudenson et al. 1993: 57), and certain irregular and frequently used verbs such as *être* 'to be', *avoir* 'to have', and *aller* 'to go' manifest a larger set of inflected forms. It can also be argued that popular colloquial French is gradually replacing the agreement suffixes underlined in (13) with prefixes derived from subject clitics (see section 6.4).

Regarding TMA marking, regional varieties of vernacular French seem to favor, when available, verbal periphrases over their synthetic counterparts illustrated in (14). In section 6.2, I consider the role of such Fr periphrastic verbal constructions in the genesis of the TMA system in HC.

10. All examples are from Kinyalolo's (1992) study of Fongbè word order. See Fabb 1992, Aboh, 1999 and chapter 4 this volume, and Ndayiragije 2000 for more NP_{Obj}-V examples in the Gbe languages. Various chapters in Déchaine and Manfredi (1997) and Mchombo (1993) suggest that the Obj-V order is actually quite widespread in Kwa and in Bantu, which means that Obj-V is quite widespread in HC's substratum. This makes absence of Obj-V in HC a thorny counterexample to the Relexification Hypothesis (see DeGraff 2002b, 2002c, for further discussion).

11. The Fongbè NP_{Obj}-V sequences mentioned in (16a) and illustrated in (18)–(19) are also found after verbs meaning 'start', 'end', 'stop', 'can'/'know', 'refuse', 'make'/'order', etc. (Fabb 1992: 6–7).

12. See DeGraff 2000: 106–108 for further differences between HC and Fongbè (e.g., with respect to the syntax of sentential negation and the placement of certain adverbs).

13. Fr clauses with auxiliaries preceding the main verb (as in compound tenses of the *passé composé*, the *plus-que-parfait*, etc.) introduce more complicated patterns. I return to these in section 6.2.

14. As for the target of "V-to-I" movement, it is worth stressing that we need not assume a unique target position x (some INFL-related head) for all languages. Things are most likely much more complex. Verbs may move to different heights across languages; within a language, verb movement may occur in one fell swoop or cyclically via a number of potential landing sites. By and large I abstract away from these subtleties. In other words, I am letting "I(NFL)" in "V-to-I" stands for a range of INFL-related head positions—possible targets of IP-internal verb-movement to a position that c-commands the VP and that is c-commanded by the (highest) IP-internal subject's surface position. Cinque's (1997: 106) elaborate proposal offers an innate—species-uniform—hierarchy of some 29 "INFL" heads; but see Bobaljik (1999) for a critique and for some possible refinements.

I am purposefully abstracting away, for now, from verb-movement to COMP (aka, V-to-C) and from any intermediate V-to-I steps on V's way to COMP (but see section 6.3). A language can have V-(to-I)-to-C without having *independent* V-to-I (i.e., without verb-movement to INFL as the *final* landing site). According to Vikner (1994: 119; 1995: 142–147), Danish is such a language, along with other Mainland Scandinavian languages. The latter somewhat resemble HC to the extent that they (arguably) lack independent verb-movement to INFL (e.g., in embedded clauses where verb-second is excluded); although see Déprez (1989: 242f.), Thráinsson (1994: 151), and Kroch and Taylor (1997: 319, 325, nn25, 26) for more complex possibilities regarding Scandinavian IP-internal verb placement, including short verb-movement to a *low* inflectional head (cf. Lightfoot 1999: 449 n3). HC does not have V-to-C movement of the sort found in verb-second (V2) languages and does not manifest any type of (dependent or independent) V-to-I, modulo the caveat in note 16. (Also see note 34 for CP-level occurrences of V in HC and Kroch and Taylor 1997 and Kroch et al. 2000 for hypothetical V2-related diachronic implications of V-to-C with or without independent V-movement to INFL heads.)

15. The exact values for y_i, like that for x, may vary across languages and, within a given language, across adverb classes. Furthermore, Pollock shows that Fr *pas* 'NEG' is generated higher than clause-internal adverbs like *souvent* 'often' and that there is an intermediate landing site for verb movement "halfway" between *pas* and such clause-internal adverbs. Infinitives only reach that intermediate landing site, as in *Ne pas lire souvent le journal* versus **Ne lire pas souvent le journal*. (See Cinque 1999 for further elaboration and for additional relevant data.)

16. The Fr negation-placement facts are more complex: in certain dialects, they involve cliticization of *ne* to the finite verb, and movement of the $[ne \ V_{+fin}]$ complex to the left of *pas*; see Pollock (1989) for details. In other (vernacular) dialects, *pas* is often used without *ne*.

Another way to account for the HC-versus-Fr verb-movement contrast would be to posit that both HC and Fr are V-to-I languages but that the landing site of verb-movement in HC, x_{HC}, is lower than the positions of the clause-internal adverbs and negation marker y_iP, and that the y_iP projections are, in turn, lower than the Fr verb-movement landing site x_{Fr}; that is, $x_{HC} < y < x_{Fr}$ ('<' stands for 'lower than'). In other words, HC verb movement (if any) is shorter than Fr verb movement. (In the main text, I abstract away from any possibility of (short) verb-movement in HC.)

17. What follows is a summary and update of DeGraff (1994a, 1994b, 1997, 2000), where I adopted as a working hypothesis a controversial proposal that combines insights from, among many others, Platzack and Holmberg (1989), Pollock (1989), Dejean (1992), Chomsky (1993), Roberts (1995), Rohrbacher (1994), and Vikner (1995, 1997). See also notes 18 and 19.

18. Although attractive, Bobaljik's (2001) treatment of morphology–syntax interactions in Germanic—or perhaps my (mis)interpretation of it—faces its own theoretical and empirical challenges.

Bobaljik assumes DISTRIBUTED MORPHOLOGY (DM) (Halle and Marantz 1993; Noyer 1997; Halle 1997; Harley and Noyer 1997; and others). DM instantiates "a realizational or 'Late Insertion' view [of grammar] in which the syntax concatenates abstract morphemes which are subsequently provided with phonological exponents (also called VOCABULARY ITEMS) via post-syntactic vocabulary insertion or morpheme realization rules" (Bobaljik 2001: 4).

Bobaljik's proposal relies on a one-way entailment from the complexity of verbal inflection to the complexity of the INFL layer: "I will argue here that the correct conception of morphological richness should be stated in terms of structural complexity and not paradigms . . ." (Bobaljik 2001: 5). In this proposal, the "structural complexity" of IP is a *necessary* condition for the "morphological richness" of verbal inflection, and "morphological richness" is diagnosed by stacking of the *phonological exponents* of inflectional affixes: (i) "If a language has rich [verbal] inflection then it has verb movement to Infl" (Bobaljik 2001: 4); (ii) "Verbal inflection is RICH iff finite verbs may bear multiple distinct inflectional morphemes."

A theory-internal tension immediately arises. In DM, the narrow syntax handles "*abstract* morphemes" that are *devoid of phonological exponence*. The phonological pieces of morphemes are inserted "late," postsyntax, in the morphophonology. Now, consider that, in Bobaljik's account, the stacking on the verb stem of *overt* inflectional affixes (i.e., phonological exponents aka "Vocabulary Items") counts as *unambiguous* evidence for the determination of "rich" inflection, which, in turn, entails V-to-I. Yet the morphology-to-syntax entailment in (i) holds only in a model where inflectional affix stacking *necessarily* reflects structural complexity in the narrow syntax; the necessity of such isomorphism is alluded to in Bobaljik (2001: 21 n33). Is DM such a model?

In DM, not only "syntax may be sensitive to distinctions that are not systematically reflected in the overt morphology" (Bobaljik 2001: 13), but, vice versa, the morphology itself may manipulate (inflectional) forms that are introduced *postsyntax*, without being associated with distinct (INFL) head in the narrow syntax. Such forms have no direct structural reflexes in the narrow syntax. Indeed, DM entertains a number of *autonomous* morphophonological operations that routinely break down any one-to-one mapping between abstract morphemes in the syntax (e.g., INFL heads) and their postsyntactic late-inserted phonological exponents (e.g., inflectional affixes). Such postsyntactic operations (e.g., "Impoverishment" of morphosyntactic features, and the "Splitting" or "Fission" and "Fusion" of morphosyntactic units) create "mismatches between syntax and morphology" (Halle and Marantz 1993: 115–121; Noyer 1997: xx, lxvi; Halle 1997: 426, 431f.; and others).

These mismatches seem to defuse the morphology-to-syntax entailment posited by Bobaljik. Because of DM's autonomous, strictly morphophonological licensing of inflectional affixes, multiple inflectional affixes on the verb are not an unambiguous telltale of multiple INFL heads in the syntax. Conversely, Impoverishment and zero-affixation can create affixation patterns that do not unambiguously reflect the structural complexity that is licensed in the narrow syntax.

Can we ban Fission altogether or ensure that it is "constrained so as not to be able to apply in the cases under investigation" (Bobaljik 2001: 21 n33)? Noyer (1997: lxvi–lxvii, 3–104) takes Fission to apply in, inter alia, the Imperfect conjugation in Afro-Asiatic languages (e.g., Classical Hebrew, Egyptian Arabic); see also Halle 1997: 435–441. Harley and Noyer (1999: 5) discuss a Tamazight Berber AGR morpheme which, although a single head in the syntax, can be spelled-out with up to three distinct affixes—for person, number, and gender. Halle (1997: 441–446) argues that "Walbiri *Agr morphemes are subject to fission*" (p. 442; emphasis in original). If Noyer, Noyer and Harley, and Halle are right about the (INFL-related) syntax-morphology mismatches induced by Fission and if—and this seems a big "if"—there is no principled way to preclude Fission from applying to the cases at hand here, then DM cannot exclude the (marked) possibility of V-in-situ languages with "rich," but *Fissioned*, verbal inflection. The multiplicity of affixes resulting from Fission is effectively not visible in the syntax and should have no effect on verb placement, if the latter is, as in Bobaljik's proposal, a property of the narrow syntax and not a strictly PF phenomenon.

Perhaps a solution can be found by investigating learnability-based markedness (see note 20; cf Ackema 2001). If Fission exists, then what may disfavor a V-in-situ language with multiple (fissioned) inflection morphemes on the verb are the learnability difficulties—the markedness—entailed by Fission. Recall that Fission is one of "these departures [from the default situation that] are considered marked options within a grammar, and therefore are assumed to require (substantial) positive evidence during acquisition" (Harley and Noyer 1999: sec. 4.2). So, assuming Bobaljik's treatment, the "mismatched" V-in-situ/rich-inflection correlation is indeed possible, although marked, perhaps as marked as the inverse "mismatch"—namely, the V-to-I/poor-inflection correlation. The latter presumably arises because of some combination of zero-affixation, Impoverishment, and Fusion. Now, if the V-in-situ/rich-inflection combination is rarer than the

V-to-I/no-inflection combination or is altogether nonexistent (cf. Ackema 2001: 253–255), then this may count as evidence that Fission is more marked than Fusion, Impoverishment, and/or zero-affixation—and perhaps specially so in the domain of INFL morphemes—even though all operations that introduce morphology-syntax mismatches are "marked options" (Noyer 1997: xxi, lxvi; Harley & Noyer 1999: §§3.3, 4.2).

19. Dejean (1992: 1, 4, 8, 16–18) mentions the occasional appearance of verb–adverb word order in certain HC dialects and relates these cases to a well-documented sociolinguistic confound—namely, the influence of Fr grammar on the Creole speech of certain Creolophone-Francophone bilinguals. This is not strictly decreolization: the lexifier's V-to-I influence must have played a role from Creole genesis onward and may have been particularly strong in early HC; see for example, Dejean's (1992: 16f.) eighteenth-and nineteenth-century examples. Such influence is also manifested in modern Fr-to-HC translations (see Dejean 1992: 16f.). More generally, the calquing of Fr patterns in Creole speech and the ensuing production of "Frenchified" Creole utterances is often a tacit or deliberate choice on the part of Creole speakers. Frenchification of Creole speech, when possible, often seems to function as a register shift that raises Creole speakers' symbolic capital, according to the dictates of Haiti's linguistic market. Here it can be quipped that V's upward mobility in the INFL layers may diagnose the HC speaker's upward mobility in the socioeconomic layers.

See note 59 for possible analogs related to the diachrony of V-to-I in Capeverdean Creole, a Creole with a Portuguese lexifier. Also see DeGraff (1997: 81, 88, nn28, 33, and the references cited there in) for yet another possible analog in the diachrony of V-to-I in Louisiana Creole under the influence of Cajun French.

DeGraff (1992a, 1994a, 1994b, 1997, 1999b, 2000), Veenstra (1996), Baptista (1997), Vrzić (1997), Déprez (1999), and Roberts (1999) document various domains in Creole morphosyntax where inflectional morphology seems to interact with movement (e.g., within IP and DP).

20. The morphology-syntax mismatches discussed in note 18 regarding Bobaljik's (2001) proposal bear implications for the acquisition of verb placement. Let's consider Bobaljik's (2001: 5, 25) claim that "armed with UG, . . . the child presented with a finite verb bearing more than one overt inflectional morpheme is clearly licensed to conclude that their target grammar has . . . multiple functional heads between CP and VP"—that is, "[such] child . . . is clearly licensed to conclude that the target grammar must contain adequate functional heads to host the form"; thus V-to-I. If one assumes DM *with Fission* as a framework, this can be *clearly* so only in the "*default* situation." In the nondefault situation, as in, for example, Noyer's (1997: lxvi–lxvii, 3–104) Fission-based analysis of INFL in Afro-Asiatic languages such as Tamazight Berber, multiple affixes—the AGR prefixes and suffixes in the Imperfect conjugation—are not licensed by distinct functional heads but are (arguably) induced via Fission, which is driven by postsyntactic and autonomous "constraints on morphological well-formedess" (Noyer 1997: lxvi). If this is correct, the child learning Tamazight Berber is not a priori licensed to postulate multiple functional heads as hosts for the multiple AGR affixes.

The tension between Bobaljik (2001) and various DM assumptions is a constructive one: if Bobaljik is right, then all the INFL-related cases currently treated as Fission must be reanalyzed sans Fission. At any rate, a Fission-less reanalysis of the relevant cases would also tell a story about learnability: How would the learner, given much less evidence than the linguist, resist postulating affix-stacking in the presence of multiple inflectional affixes on the verb stem? (Cf. the Berber case here or the Faroese case discussed in Bobaljik 2001: 13–15.) And, if Fission does exist as a "marked option" and if it does apply to INFL morphemes, what kind of "(substantial) positive evidence" (Harley and Noyer 1999: sec. 4.2) would the child require in order to postulate Fission instead of distinct syntactic heads? Not an easy question—neither for the child nor the linguist. The right answer, for both child and linguist, seems to require a certain amount of inspection and comparison of verbal forms—specially their inflectional combinations—in order to decide whether, and which, particular instances of affix-stacking, if any, result from Fission or from multiple INFL heads (or both). This kind of inspection may well be as computationally expensive as the inspection of paradigms in the scenarios advocated by, for example, Rohrbacher (1994) and Vikner (1997), which Bobaljik argues against.

That verb placement both through acquisition and in the postacquisition steady-state grammar can in principle be driven by other factors besides those related to verbal inflection, is suggested by, for example, Fongbè (see note 33). If Aboh (1999 and chapter 4 in this volume) is right, Fongbè is a V-to-I language, even in absence of a "rich" system of verbal inflection. Outside of verbal inflection per se, there are other morphosyntax-related cues that may suggest a V-to-I setting to both the language learner and the linguist, once certain assumptions are adopted (cf. note 58).

I don't understand what exact factors drive V-to-I in Fongbè, as compared to V-to-I in Romance and Germanic. But it seems to me that the nature of Fongbè V-to-I, especially with respect to the reduplication facts noted in, for example, section 3.3, is quite distinct from V-to-I in Romance and Germanic. V-to-I, when properly investigated across a wider range of languages, may not be a unitary phenomenon. There may thus be other parameters at play in explaining the similarities and dissimilarities in verb syntax between Fongbè, on the one hand, and Romance and Germanic, on the other hand. For example, there is nothing in Romance and Germanic that looks like the aforementioned Fongbè verbal reduplication phenomena. In other words, the Fongbè-versus-Romance/Germanic comparison may not be of the same microparametric type. But at this point I seem far out on a limb, with no fruit in sight (yet).

21. It may be tempting to relate the distributional uniformity of HC postverbal objects to the morphological uniformity of HC pronouns and to postulate some general syntax–morphology correlation vis-à-vis object placement and overt case marking. But, as Holmberg (1999: 24) observes, "the correlation is extremely weak" (cf. Cinque 1999: 217 n18 and Thráinsson 2001: 167f., 185–188). For example, object placement in Norwegian is much "freer" than in English (see, e.g., Nilsen 1997; Cinque 1999: 217 n18; Thráinsson 2001: 199 n17), even though nominal case in Norwegian is not (appreciably) richer than in English. (Also see notes 53 and 54.)

22. The following discussion does not provide an exhaustive overview or analysis of the cross-linguistic syntax of object placement. Neither do I try to survey all the analyses that have been offered to account for object movement. In fact, I am being quite selective here, putting aside a number of interesting analyses of cliticization (e.g., those that do *not* posit object movement). My goal is only to explore the theoretical tools whereby the VP-related HC/Fr object-placement contrasts can be connected to the HC/Fr inflectional differentials, with an eye toward a larger sample of diachronic and cross-linguistic word-order patterns.

23. The term "object cliticization" is used throughout to refer exclusively to *syntac-

tic cliticization, whereby an object pronoun undergoes leftward movement to some VP-external position, from which the pronoun attaches to its host, typically a verb. Syntactic cliticization is distinct from *phonological* cliticization, which applies to HC atonic pronouns and to a host of other morphemes, independently of syntactic cliticization. For example, *li* in (1b) phonologically cliticizes onto the preceding verb, giving *Bouki konnen-l*; see Cadely (1994) for discussion of the conditions under which phonological cliticization takes place in HC.

Passives, Scrambling, and unbounded object movements such as *wh*-movement and topicalization are not discussed here. Presumably such movements have different theoretical bases (e.g., different Case- and binding-properties) and do not proceed along the same paths as object cliticization; see, for example, Déprez (1989) (but see Sportiche 1995 for an approach where cliticization is likened to *wh*-movement and to Dutch-type Scrambling; compare, e.g., Sportiche's extension of the "*wh*-criterion," the "doubly-filled COMP filter," and LF-movement to clitic constructions).

24. More cautiously, it should be said that V-to-I and OS in English (if any) have lower landing sites than in Icelandic. Lasnik (1999) surveys various arguments in favor of overt OS in English.

25. Subsuming object cliticization under OS is far from uncontroversial; see Déprez (1989: 239–241), Holmberg and Platzack (1995: ch. 6), and Thráinsson (2001), and references cited there in for similarities and dissimilarities between object cliticization and canonical Object Shift. One of the more obvious dissimilarities is the height of Object Shift (to the right and below the main verb in (23)) versus that of (Romance) cliticization (often to the left and higher than the main verb (see, e.g., 8b)). I will tentatively abstract away from these differences. It will suffice to assume that object cliticization, as an instantiation of OS, involves leftward object movement to a position outside of VP and within IP (see, e.g., Déprez 1989: ch. 3 for such an implementation, with OS as XP-movement to Spec(Agr$_o$) and object cliticization as head-movement to, or via, Agr$_o$; see also Sportiche (1995) and references therein for an approach where object cliticization involves overt or covert movement, possibly through a Case-checking projection, of some XP$_i$, possibly *pro$_i$*, to the Spec of a phrase headed by clitic$_i$.

26. For technical implementations of (24) in a number of frameworks, see, for instance, Déprez (1989), Kayne (1989a, 1991), Chomsky (1993), Roberts (1997), Bobaljik and Jonas (1996), Holmberg (1999), and Bobaljik (1995, 2002). For counterarguments against Holmberg's Generalization, see Lasnik (1999: 149 n36 and the references cited therein). See also note 28. Thráinsson (2001) provides a critical overview.

27. As remarked by Pollock (1989) and Kayne (1991), Fr participles and infinitives must be able to overtly move out of their VPs (see Pollock's "short movement," which is optional; i.e., the adverb *souvent* in (i)–(ii) can also precede the main verb *mangé/manger*):

(i) Jean a   mangé souvent des   pommes.
     Jean has   eaten often   INDEF-PL apples
     'Jean has often eaten apples'

(ii) Manger souvent des   pommes, . . .
     to eat often   INDEF-PL apples
     'to often eat apples . . .'

(iii) Jean les   a   mangées.
       Jean them   has   eaten
       'Jean has eaten them.'

(iv)   Jean veut   les   manger.
       Jean wants them to-eat
       'Jean wants to eat them.

In Fr, both infinitives and participles may precede VP-adjoined adverbs (indicating verb movement), and both permit object cliticization. (See Kayne 1991 for further evidence for, and theoretical implications of, such short movement and for a rich array of comparative data on, inter alia, adverb and clitic placement in Romance.)

28. Liliane Haegeman (pers. comm., July 31, 1995) notes that West Flemish allows leftward movement of object clitics with nonfinite verbs, which arguably do not move (but see note 27), thus constituting one exception to Holmberg's Generalization. Bobaljik (1995, 2002) offers one explanation for why SOV languages generally escape Holmberg's Generalization, unlike SVO languages. Note that all the languages concerned here are SVO.

If the discussion in the main text is right, Object Shift in verb-second clauses cannot be taken as a trigger for independent V-to-I, contra Bobaljik (2001: 20). That OS does not strictly presuppose independent V-to-I (cf. notes 14 and 34) is suggested by Mainland Scandinavian data, where object cliticization is possible in verb-second environments only. Furthermore, Norwegian, as described in Nilsen (1997), has OS of full NPs in verb-second (e.g., matrix) clauses, in addition to the sort of object cliticization that exists in the other Mainland Scandinavian languages (see Cinque 1999: 217 n18, but see also Thráinsson 2001: 199 n17 for some complicating factors). Yet Norwegian does not seem to have Icelandic-type independent V-to-I. Thus, a child learning Norwegian could not use (apparent?) evidence for OS as a reliable cue for independent V-to-I.

29. A bidirectional implication would make the wrong generalization regarding the English diachronic facts discussed in section 6: the loss of cliticization started in English *before* the loss of overt V-to-I. According to van Kemenade (1987) and Roberts (1997), the demise of English cliticization took place, roughly, between 1100 and 1400, while Kroch (1989) estimates loss of main-verb movement to have been completed by the middle of the sixteenth century. Thus, V-to-I is a necessary, not sufficient, condition for OS (but see notes 26 and 28). In the case of English diachrony, the loss of V2 and of morphological Case may have also had a role in the demise of English cliticization, as argued by van Kemenade. (See also note 53.)

30. The arguments in sections 6 and 7 are expanded on in DeGraff 2003.

31. The effect of L2A on morphological change is presumably linked to the degree and nature of language contact. On one hand, low-contact situations (i.e., with relatively few nonnative speakers) may seem particularly favorable for the maintenance of morphological paradigms; on the other (extremely opposite) hand, abrupt and massive language contact (i.e., with relatively high numbers of adult learners in learner-unfriendly situations) may seem to accelerate inflectional erosion (see, e.g., the "Insular" vs. "Mainland" Scandinavian contrasts alluded to in section 4.2; see also DeGraff 2001b: 219 n5, 281f. 288). Yet, in all cases, the cognitive and linguistic factors that underlie, and constrain, the corresponding developmental patterns and any differences therein are ultimately rooted in individual-level properties of L1A and L2A. In the main, language-

acquisition mechanisms can be assumed to be species-uniform, even though the external (e.g., sociohistorical) factors that determine their specific effects and specific outcomes are necessarily particular and contingent (for some further discussion and references, see DeGraff 1999a: 37, 1999b: 528.

32. There may seem to be a potential contradiction between viewing preverbal object clitics as a V-to-I cue (in light of, e.g., Holmberg's Generalization in section 5.2) and my claim here that the linguistic ecology during HC's genesis became weak in V-to-I triggers. After all, and as Richard Kayne (pers. comm.) reminds me, even if verbal inflections were eroding, every Fr sentence with a preverbal object clitic (e.g., *Elle nous voit*; lit. 'She us sees') would count as a V-to-I trigger, and such sentences seem pervasive.

Two empirical-cum-theoretical questions arise, which I will (too briefly) address here and in section 6.4: What is the status of (Standard) French object placement in the early interlanguages of adult learners learning French in learner-unfriendly contact situations? If, as argued by Meillet (1920), Brunot and Bruneau (1949), Sportiche (1995), and others (object) clitics really belong, alongside verbal inflectional affixes, to verbal inflectional morphology, then such clitics qua "agreement" markers would, like inflectional affixes, be hard to acquire in the *initial* stages of second-language acquisition, especially for learners whose L1s, like Fongbè, do not have object proclitics on the verb. One such case of learners doing away with object proclitics in *early* L2A is documented by Véronique's (1990, 2000) study of Moroccan adults learning French; these data are available from the European Science Foundation (ESF) bilingual database in the CHILDES System (see MacWhinney 2000). The Moroccan learners produce utterances like *la dame / frape / lui* (ESF file lafza32h.1.cha) with the postverbal pronoun *lui*. Compare the target-like utterance *la dame l'a frappé* with the proclitic object *l'* (see note 57). We also find the Fr preverbal clitic *le* in postverbal position in the Moroccans' interlanguages (Klein and Perdue 1992: 254). More generally and perhaps controversially (see, again, note 57), Klein and Perdue (1992: 284f., 297, 325f.) claim that Fr preverbal objects are usually avoided in the initial ("basic variety") interlanguages of adult learners, independently of the learners' respective native languages.

Such a developmental pattern may seem all the more likely given the facts mentioned by Meillet and Brunot and Bruneau (and others) about the use of the more-salient tonic pronouns alongside, or instead of the less salient atonic pronouns. In the same vein, nonstandard "popular" varieties of French, as noted by, for example, Frei (1929:164–166), Gadet (1997: 65), and Fattier (1995: 140–142), often show a preference for postverbal tonic pronouns in context where Standard French uses verbal enclitics (cf. (43)-versus-(44)).

A related empirical question is this: What sorts of object-pronoun placement *did* obtain in the French varieties involved in the genesis of HC? These French varieties could well have been like Cajun French and Missouri French, as illustrated in (43), where we get, for example, *I v'nont voir moi* with a postverbal tonic pronoun *moi* (cf. HC postverbal *mwen*) instead of *Ils me verront*, in (43a), with a preverbal clitic *me*; the latter has no counterpart in HC.

If the actual French varieties in colonial Haiti were anything like Cajun French and Missouri French, and if learners of French do favor tonic over atonic pronouns in their initial interlanguages, then preverbal object clitics were perhaps not as pervasive in the ecology of HC genesis than they are among, say, contemporary Standard French speakers. Be that as it may, the fact remains that preverbal object clitics did not make it into HC grammar. (I return to this question in section 6.4.)

33. For more nuanced details, important empirical and theoretical caveats, and counterexamples and counterarguments, see, for example, Rohrbacher (1994); Vikner (1997); Roberts (1993, 1999); Thráinsson (2001); Kroch and Taylor (1997); Kroch et al. (2000); Sprouse (1998); Lightfoot (1999); Bobaljik (2001).

That other factors besides inflectional morphology trigger V-to-I is suggested by a comparison of, for example, past participles across French and Icelandic. As noted by Richard Kayne (pers. comm.), even in varieties of French that lack past participle agreement, past participles must move to allow object cliticization to their left. There is no such movement with Icelandic past participles, notwithstanding the similar morphology (i.e., no agreement) across the relevant French and Icelandic varieties. In a related vein, Icelandic and mainland Scandinavian infinitives are unlike each other in movement, even though their infinitival suffixes are similar. We also find language-internal movement differences without any (apparent) morphological correlate: Kayne notes that Icelandic infinitives seemingly move in control constructions only, though the morphology of the infinitive is uniform throughout (cf. Bobaljik 2001 for related caveats). (See also notes 18, 20, 21, 49, 53, and 54.)

34. I use V-to-I for independent verb-movement to INFL, with the restrictions identified in note 14. Mainland Scandinavian languages, unlike English and HC, are verb-second (V2) with the verb moving to COMP in the appropriate environments (e.g., in main clauses and a restricted set of embedded clauses). These languages do not seem to have independent verb-movement with INFL as the final landing site (see Vikner 1995: 142–147). HC, a language without V-to-I movement, allows a copy of the verb to occur in the CP layer in appropriate environments, such as the predicate-cleft construction, with a copy of the verb also occurring in situ (see DeGraff 1995b and references therein).

35. Advocating a population-genetics perspective, Mufwene (1996, 2001) offers a competition-and-selection model that takes into account an array of internal and external factors, including markedness, typological, socioeconomic structures, and demography (e.g., the "Founder principle"). Some crucial differences between my and Mufwene's perspectives concern the role or nonrole of children in Creole genesis (contrast, in particular, DeGraff 1999b: 476, 478–495, 524–527, 2002b, 2002c, and Mufwene 2001: 131).

36. Conveniently enough, Ducœurjoly's (1802) Creole manual gives model French sentences and their Creole translations side by side, with the Creole translations written in the French-born author's etymologizing orthography.

Archival texts must be treated with great caution, however, as is the norm in historical linguistics. And extra caution seems warranted vis-à-vis early Creole texts: most of them were transcribed by nonnative speakers—colonial observers who often felt great condescension toward Creole varieties, as discussed in DeGraff 1993: 90 n56 and 2001a: 92–98, 110 n22, for example.

As it turns out, the basic TMA patterns in Ducœurjoly (1802) are by and large corroborated by similar data in a variety of eighteenth- and nineteenth-century Creole samples, from a variety of native and nonnative idiolects (see, e.g., Descourtilz 1809 v3: 135f., 212, 260f., 264, 270f., 277 n1, 279–282, 304f., 353f., 359f., etc.; *Idylles et chansons* (1811); Rosiers (1818); Thomas (1869: 134); and Denis (1935: 346–359); see also references in note 44).

Descourtilz's Early Creole samples include reported speech from two famous Creole ex-slaves, both born of African parents: (i) Toussaint L'Ouverture, Haiti's best known eighteenth-century freedom fighter, born into slavery in colonial Haiti (then known as Saint-Domingue) in 1743; and (ii) Jean-Jacques Dessalines, also a freedom fighter, born into slavery in Saint-Domingue in 1758 and Haiti's first president and first emperor.

37. Gougenheim 1929 gives a comprehensive inventory of verbal periphrases through Fr diachrony. He explicitly notes that many such periphrases, of the sort illustrated in (33)–(36), were explicitly frowned upon as *prononciations vicieuses* 'vicious pronunciations' by eighteenth-and nineteenth-century purists (p. 59f., 104, 120, and passim). This makes it even more likely that such *prononciations vicieuses* were widespread in the 'vicious' environments of French Caribbean colonies, the birthplace of Caribbean French-lexicon Creoles (Gougenheim 1929: 378).

Taken together, Sylvain (1936: 79–105, 136–139), Goodman (1964: 78–90), Chaudenson (1992: 162–167), Chaudenson et al. (1993), Chaudenson and Mufwene (2001: 177–182), and Fattier (1998: 863–888) offer valuable data on the VP-related similarities and dissimilarities across Fr-lexicon Creoles, including HC. Chaudenson (1974, 1992, 1995), Chaudenson et al. (1993), and Mufwene (2001) stress the relevance of diachronic and dialectal (vernacular) data to the geneses of Creoles; also see section 2.

38. Date: November 13, 1982. File: lafae11a.2ch from European Science Foundation (ESF) bilingual database in the CHILDES System. (See MacWhinney 2000).

39. From Alfonso. Date: March 20, 1983. File: lsfal13a.1.cha from European Science Foundation database in the CHILDES System (see Klein and Perdue 1992 and MacWhinney 2000); see also Perdue (1995: 91) for similar data from another Hispanophone learner.

40. The sequence *pa va* to negate an IRREALIS event is ungrammatical in HC, Réunion Creole, other French-lexicon Creoles, and certain regional varieties of French. See Fattier (1998: 870, 883) for some speculations, further data, and relevant bibliographical pointers.

41. Tellingly, Ducœurjoly, in his etymologizing orthography, transcribes the eighteenth-century Creole negation marker / *napa* / as *n'a pa(s)*, on a par with French *n'a pas* 'does not have'. But, in fact, Early HC /*napa*/ is monomorphemic. Ducœurjoly himself indicates that French *ne/n'* is never pronounced in the Creole, where it is replaced by *pa(s)* (p. 335). Besides we don't seem to have *a(s)* as an auxiliary anywhere in Ducœurjoly's Early Creole text. As for French *avoir* as a main verb expressing possession, Ducœurjoly (1802: 293) notes that its Creole equivalent is *gagné* as in *mo pa gagné temps* 'I don't have time' (p. 331). Early HC *gagné* is now, in modern HC, *gen(yen)* as in *Mwen pa gen tan* 'I don't have time' and *Mwen pa genyen li* 'I don't have it'. (The apocope facts in *gen* vs. *genyen* are still not fully understood; see note 7.)

42. Whatever his actual name, the chansonnier was probably an upper-class Creole speaker. If so, *Lisette*'s lyrics would be more symptomatic of the less-restructured Creole varieties, those closer to French (i.e., the ACROLECTAL and MESOLECTAL varieties), than they would be of the more restructured (i.e., BASILECTAL) varieties. Such lyrics give us only a partial representation of the Creole continuum in colonial Haiti. These and related empirical limitations apply to all archival Creole texts: basilectal Creole speakers—usually from the lower social castes—would have had little opportunity for literature and other sorts of literate activities. (See the caveats in note 36.)

43. As can be expected, reanalysis paths are not uniform across all French-lexicon

Creoles. For example, the reanalysis trajectories of French NEG into HC *pa* and LC *pa* ended up at different heights in their respective inflectional layers—higher in HC and lower in Louisiana Creole (LC). HC has *pa te* 'NEG ANT' (cf. Fr *pas été*), whereas LC, as described in, for example, Neumann (1985: 322) and Rottet (1992: 272), has *te pa* (cf. Fr *étais/était pas*). In the diachrony of the French-lexicon Creole of Guyane, the now-archaic *te pa* was, through the nineteenth century, in competition with, before eventually giving way to, *pa te* (Schlupp 1997: 123–126).

Cinque (1999: 120–126) documents various positions of NegP across and within languages, within a framework that upholds a universal hierarchy of INFL heads; cf. note 14.

44. Baissac (1880: 57f.) argues that Fr synthetic forms like *j'irai* 'I go+FUT+1sg' are not as common in vernacular French as they are in literary French and would not be necessarily included in the "complications that Creole must necessarily avoid." In other words, invariant verbal forms (i.e., infinitivals and participials in verbal periphrases) were robustly represented in the input. Furthermore, Baissac (1880: 49–55) notes that, along with frequency, phonological invariance would have made Fr verbal periphrases particularly influential in the genesis of the Creole verbal system. Similar arguments are found in Van Name (1870: 139–149). Also see J. J. Thomas (1869: 50–65); Denis (1935: 346 n4, 347 n25, 348 n37, 351 nn64–66, 352 n73, 355 n4, 357 nn3, 9, 358 nn33, 37, etc.); Mufwene (1991: 131–138); Fattier (1998: 866f.), and others.

I agree with Baissac that Fr verbal periphrases are etymologically related to the Creole TMA+verb patterns. Yet the latter are now autonomous systems with their own morphosyntactic and interpretive complex calculus. Creole TMA systems are by no means the sort of simple systems that would straightforwardly result from what Baissac calls "necessary avoidance of complications" from Fr. As noted by Gougenheim (1929: 379), French verbal periphrases—the ancestors of Creole TMA systems—often express *nuances delicates, des nuances d'une richesse singulière*, with no synthetic counterpart. See Fattier (1998: 863–997) and Howe (2000) for thorough descriptions of the morphosyntactic, semantic, and pragmatic "complications" in the TMA system of HC.

45. With respect to object placement, the empirical and theoretical grounding of the similarities between HC and English diachrony is more tenuous than in the verb-placement case, especially because of current limitations on my understanding of the mechanics of object shift and cliticization (see section 5.2) and because of the complexity of the Old and Middle English diachronic and dialectal facts (see, e.g., Kroch et al. 2000). The parallels are worth noting anyway.

46. Here I focus on the behavior of object pronouns, as these are most relevant to the Fr and HC contrasts. Interesting issues also arise with respect to subject pronouns in both HC and English diachrony, but these issues would take us too far afield (see, e.g., DeGraff 1992a, 1992b, 1992c, and Déprez 1994 for HC and van Kemenade 1987 for English). For similar reasons, I do not discuss placement of full NP objects, except where directly relevant.

47. The full details of (the theoretical debates about) OE word order, with both medial and final INFL and with both VO and OV, are well beyond the scope of this chapter. Suffice it to note that V2 in OE manifests apparent exceptions, as in (40a), with no counterpart in robust V2 languages such as non-English Germanic. See van Kemenade (1987, 1997), Kroch and Taylor (1997), and Kroch et al. (2000) for analyses and references.

48. Van Kemenade (1987: 195) considers the possibility that object cliticization in (40c) is a relic from the earlier OV stage. Postverbal object pronouns were actually more common around 1340, alongside the less-common preverbal object pronouns. This would be characteristic of a change in progress or just completed and of a certain degree of conservatism in the relevant written texts. Van Kemenade also mentions possible dialectal variations in which IP-internal cliticization *and* paradigms of nominal case morphology were preserved longer in the south than in the north of England. The details of these variations are further fleshed out, along with competing analyses, in van Kemenade (1997), Kroch and Taylor (1997), and Kroch et al. (2000).

49. Unlike in French, there are no preverbal object clitics in Icelandic, even though Icelandic, unlike French, has morphological case on both pronouns and nouns (Richard Kayne, pers. comm.). This contrast in object-placement is perhaps due to the Icelandic verb moving higher in the inflectional layer than its French counterpart. At any rate, given their respective morphological profile, the French and Icelandic object-placement contrasts suggest that inflectional morphology cannot by itself "drive" word order. (See note 33.)

50. Van Kemenade assumes that clause-internal cliticization is VP-internal, within the projection of the verb. In her framework, OE's strongly inflected verbs remain in VP (see, e.g., p. 189). Given my assumptions in section 4, OE finite verbs are outside of VP. I thus use the term "IP-internal cliticization" for examples like (40c). This is also consistent with arguments that cliticization is adjunction to a functional head higher than VP (see section 5).

51. There is yet a third, and lower, type of object cliticization that lasted through Early Modern English in the sixteenth century, as in *They tell vs not the worde of God.* That, too, is dependent on verb movement, here to the left of *not*. (See, e.g., Roberts 1997: 424 n7.)

52. Actually, according to Roberts (1997), what was lost in ME, due to the collapse of the morphological case system, is the general capacity for a whole range of leftward movements from under VP, of which object cliticization is only one instance. Roberts's central claim is that OE was uniformly head-initial; thus, underlying VX, with cases of (non-*wh*) X . . . V surface order (e.g., Scrambling and Object Shift, including cliticization) derived by leftward movement via Agr$_o$P. See Kroch and Taylor (1997, 2000) for detailed evidence of dialectal variations affecting some of the relevant VX and XV word-order throughout OE and Early ME.

53. As discussed in note 21, the correlation between nominal and pronominal case markings and object cliticization is controversial: (i) Fr shows morphological case (only) on pronouns (like NE), yet allows cliticization (unlike NE) and even *preverbal* object clitics (unlike Icelandic; see note 49); (ii) Louisiana Creole (LC) first-person and second-person singular pronouns are morphologically distinguished for nominative versus nonnominative case, yet do not cliticize (Neumann 1985: 166–173, 187, 256). However, unlike NE and HC, Fr manifests V-to-I with main verbs, and Fr pronouns manifest more morphological case distinctions than English pronouns (e.g., dative vs. accusative). Furthermore, like NE and HC, and unlike Fr, basilectal LC has no V-to-I and shows fewer morphological case distinctions than Fr; the split is basically between nominatives and nonnominatives in first-person and second-person singular—thus LC morphological case is even poorer than in English. (See Rottet 1992 and DeGraff 1997 for further discussion of V-in-situ vs. V-to-I in the diachrony of LC.)

Other puzzles are posed by comparing Icelandic, German, and Dutch: they all allow Object Shift, but they manifest varying degrees of (pro)nominal case morphology. What is not fully understood includes (i) the threshold of verbal inflectional paradigms above which V-to-I obtains (see notes 18 and 54 and DeGraff 1997: 89); (ii) once V-to-I obtains, the threshold of case-marking paradigms above which overt object cliticization and NP object-shift obtain (does it even make sense to hypothesize such a threshhold given the aforementioned difficulties in connecting OS with case?); (iii) once both V and objects move outside of VP into the inflectional layer, the ordering restrictions between verb and objects. In any case, verb movement seems a necessary, but not sufficient, condition for object cliticization, as attested in the history of English and HC. (See the discussion in section 7, especially note 62, regarding verb and object movement in Capeverdean Creole and Palenquero.)

54. This section has glossed over many interesting details on the cross-linguistic placement of object clitics. The point here is rather broad: the HC–NE pair and the Fr–OE/ME pair oppose each other across the divide between the inflectional "haves" and "have-nots"; this divide corresponds to distinct syntactic effects—namely, movements out of VP versus the absence thereof. In the cases under study here, the distinctions can be made in a simplistic binary fashion: absence versus presence of V-movement, and "poor" versus "rich" inflection. But there are many languages (e.g., Romance languages and various Scandinavian dialects; also Capeverdean Creole and Palenquero Creole, as discussed in section 7) that are located on closer points on the inflectional and verb-movement continua, with much more subtle effects vis-à-vis the landing sites of verb and object placement. Furthermore, there are certainly other factors at play in verb and object placement that I have not considered here. (See notes 18 and 33 for additional caveats.)

55. Neither does the evidence support the claim that HC's object placement was arrived at via the sort of strict relexification whereby Creole syntax is virtually isomorphic to substratum syntax modulo reanalysis and dialect-leveling (see Lefebvre 1998 and its early antecedent in Adam 1883; cf. sections 2.2, 2.3, 3.3 and the critiques in DeGraff 2002b, 2002c and references therein).

56. At least one other, and more speculative, link can be established between HC object-pronoun morphosyntax and certain Fr patterns. In DeGraff (2000: 104f.), I extrapolate from observations in Bruyn et al. (1999), and I tentatively explore the potential role that Fr positive imperatives may have had in the emergence of HC's uniformly postverbal objects. This suggests another reanalysis scenario where imperatives, once again, have a crucial role as the terminus a quo of reanalysis (cf. section 6.2). The key observation here is that Fr positive imperatives (e.g., *Aimez les* 'Love them'), unlike negative imperatives (e.g., *Ne les aimez pas* 'Don't love them') and unlike declaratives (in, e.g., (8)–(9)), have their objects uniformly to the right of the verb, whether or not the object is pronominal. HC imperatives—both positive and negative—have their objects uniformly to the right of the verb, whether or not the object is pronominal (e.g., *Renmen yo*). This (superficial) word-order parallel suggests—and this is admittedly a weak suggestion—that Fr positive imperatives may have contributed additional triggers to the emergence of HC's uniform V-Obj word order.

57. One telling contrast in the development of pronoun placement in the L2A of French is provided by the comparison of Arabophone and Hispanophone adult learners, whose data are publicly available from the CHILDES System (MacWhinney 2000). The

Hispanophone learners seem to produce targetlike object clitics with shorter delays and fewer "discrepancies" than their Arabophone counterparts. As suggested by Véronique (1990: 188), Klein and Perdue (1992: 325f.), and Perdue (1995: 164f.), among others, this differential may be due to the learners' respective L1s: Arabic, unlike Spanish, lacks preverbal object clitics (cf. note 32). Véronique (1990) documents other word-order aspects of Arabophone learners' interlanguage that are influenced by the L1 (e.g., verb-initial orders; p. 190) while taking pains to indicate the limits of L1 transfer (p. 197f.); see also Véronique (2000). In sections 3.3 and 6.2, I offer additional caveats regarding the extent of substrate influence in Creole genesis, and in DeGraff (2002b, 2002c), I offer an extended argument against the relexification hypothesis.

58. Aboh's treatment of OS in (Gun) Gbe also conforms to Holmberg's Generalization: in his analysis (Gun) Gbe has both Object Shift and V-to-I—more precisely verb movement to Aspect (see, e.g., Aboh 1999: 59f., 205–222, and chapter 4 in this volume).

Unlike Aboh's, Ndayiragije's (2000) treatment does not assume V-to-I for Fongbè, at least not of the sort envisaged by Aboh. Yet Ndayiragije, to account for Gbe reduplication, postulates verb-copying to Tense and T-to-C raising, both at PF. Ndayiragije's treatment suffers from a couple of theory-internal inconsistencies:

Ndayiragije assumes that T in Fongbè has an [affix] feature that must be checked. This is supposed to explain certain cases of verb-doubling—namely, when there is no overt (shifted) object in Spec(TP) to provide phonological support to T. For example:

> After *wh*-movement of the shifted object . . . the [affix] feature of T, an uninterpretable PF feature, requires a phonological host in order to be "visible" in the Morphology component of PF . . . Therefore, [verb doubling]. (Ndayiragije 2000: 501)

Elsewhere, T's [affix] feature can be checked without verb doubling. In one such case—namely, subject-less infinitival complements with overtly realized complementizers—"two options arise":

> T's [affix] feature raises to the lexicalized C [this is T-to-C raising]; or it attracts the phonological features of V [this is verb-doubling]. The first option [i.e., T-to-C raising] is arguably better on economy grounds. Indeed, attracting the phonological features of V [i.e., verb-doubling] would involve a second operation: copying these features in the base position of V. . . . This analysis [with other details omitted here] correctly predicts the absence of object shift and verb doubling in nonfinite CP headed by an overt C. (Ndayiragije 2000: 508)

The problem here is that the T-to-C option seems to *incorrectly* rule out verb doubling elsewhere, including certain prospective and progressive constructions where verb doubling does take place (see (20) in section 3.3; see also Aboh 1999: 188–218 and chapter 4 in this volume and Ndayiragije 2000: 498f.). In these constructions, there is a c-commanding lexicalized head that governs T with the [afix] feature and is available as a phonological host to T. If the more economical T-raising option was taken in the prospective and progressive constructions, then there would be no V doubling there, contra the data. As it turns out, Ndayiragije (2000: 502 n16) explicitly allows T to "move to [some higher] head to find phonological support"—in this case, the higher F(inite) head which *also* had the [affix] feature (p. 500). This kind of T-raising to a higher lexicalized head, which may or may not have [affix] features, undermines Ndayiragije's analysis: The option to check the relevant [affix] feature by T- or C-raising to a higher lexicalized head qua phonological host is more economical than, and incorrectly prevents, the (more costly) option of verb doubling to apply where it does apply.

Another apparent flaw in Ndayiragije's treatment is the very mechanics of PF verb movement as verb doubling. Recall that the latter takes place for checking T's [affix] feature when T is not lexicalized. Yet we also have cases when both C and T have [affix] features, while both C and T are not lexicalized, which would then seem to entail verb tripling. Ndayiragije claims that T-to-C, subsequent to V-to-T qua verb doubling, checks C's [affix] feature and that "this T-to-C does not trigger further verb-doubling since what has raised in T is nothing but the pure phonological features of V, categorical features being stranded in the base position of V." I am not sure I understand this, but what seems left unexplained is the absence of verb tripling, given that it is also assumed that "the [affix] feature of T, an uninterpretable PF feature, requires a phonological host in order to be 'visible' in the Morphology component of PF" (p. 501). After T-to-C raises V's "phonetic shell" from T up to C, T is left without a phonetic matrix, which should make T uninterpretable at PF, given Ndayiragije's own assumptions about the checking of [affix] features: absence of phonetic material in either T or C should make the corresponding [affix] feature uninterpretable at PF. Here, we seem to have one [affix] feature too many; without verb "tripling," there should be ungrammaticality, yet there is no verb tripling in the relevant Fongbè examples.

59. Furthermore, CVC manifests subject-verb inversion in conditionals (Baptista 1997: 132). But this is complicated by the occurrence of auxiliary+verb sequences in the "inverted" pre-subject position (Baptista, pers. comm., October 11, 2000). At any rate, HC manifests no such inversion. Baptista cautiously notes that the data in (47) are from her own dialect. She is concerned that such patterns, with these particular adverbs, may reflect V-to-I in the Portuguese spoken by speakers who are bilingual in CVC and Portuguese—such V-to-I patterns may not be "representative." See also note 60. Note 19 mentions a possibly analogous phenomenon vis-à-vis occasional V-to-I patterns in HC.)

60. One could reasonably argue that, in (48), the adverb is right-adjoined to VP, while the direct object is right-dislocated outside of VP, in some (focus?) position. If this is correct, the word order in (48) would not automatically count as evidence for V-to-I in PL. However, Armin Schwegler (pers. comm., October 11, 2000) informs us that the postadverbial position of the object in (48) is not assigned any special property (e.g., contrastive stress); contrastive stress on the object in (48) is obtained by heavy stress on the first syllable of *ese*. Thus, it can be reasonably assumed that the postadverbial object in (48) is within the VP and not in a focus position outside of VP, thus there is V-to-I in PL, as assumed in the main text; see Suñer 1994 for evidence of V-to-I in Spanish, the lexifier of PL. (I am most grateful to Armin Schwegler for extensive and informative discussion of PL data.)

61. Baptista (1997: 227) speculates on the possibility that *ba*-affixation (alongside, and perhaps as a trigger to, V-to-I) is a recent development in CVC. She notes that *ba* is an unbound morpheme in the neighboring Creole of Guinea-Bissau. The history of *-ba* from unbound to inflectional morpheme looks like a typical case of grammaticalization, somewhat on a par with the progression of Romance TMA markers from auxiliaries in verbal periphrases to inflectional suffixes in synthetic tenses. The latter "was achieved through a process of incorporation of the infinitive to the auxiliary . . . [which]

was then progressively 'grammaticalized' in dialects such as Spanish and French; that is, the auxiliary was completely reanalyzed as a normal tense/agreement verbal inflection" (Raposo 2000: 283f.; see also Duarte and Matos 2000: 134, 138). As discussed by Raposo, this reanalysis had not proceeded uniformly across all Romance dialects, and not even across all Portuguese dialects. In Duarte and Matos's account, Portuguese dialects have both "the 'new' synthetic form" and "a survival of the analytic form." In this light, the morphosyntactic differences vis-à-vis affixal -ba in Cape Verdean and nonaffixal ba in Guinea-Bissau are hardly surprising.

62. Given English verb-placement data (see, e.g., (28)), it must then be argued that English inflectional affixes (-ed, -s, and -ing), unlike their CVC and PL counterparts (see (47)–(48)), do not induce V-to-I. Our account so far does not say anything about this difference between English (V-in-situ) versus CVC and PL (V-to-I). Are there any morphological contrasts to be correlated with this word-order difference? Are there CVC- and PL-specific morphological triggers, in addition to syntactic triggers, that enter into the learner's determination of the verb-placement setting for each specific language? Here I will speculate on some possibilities.

Quint (2000: 225) gives the following paradigm for *kanta* 'to sing,' a typical verb in Cape Verdean Creole (Santiago variety): active-present *kanta*, active-past *kantába*, passive-present *kantádu*, passive-past *kantáda*. Quint lists the following inflectional affixes and their "glosses":

(i)   -∅: active present; -ba: active past; -du: passive present; -da: passive past

One can very well dispute Quint's glosses, especially the uniform attribution of "present" and "past" to specific verbal affixes, independent of the aspectual properties of the verbal stem. Witness the temporal interpretive contrast between *e kanta* '(s)he sang' versus *e ten febri* '(s)he has fever' (cf. Baptista 1997: 65f.). This is the factativity effect, a rather common feature of West-African and Creole languages (see section 3.3; see also Déchaine 1991; Aboh 1999: 223–225 and chapter 4 in this volume; and Ndayiragije 2000: 490f.).

Now, let's bravely abstract away from the "minefield" of dialectal variations in CVC studies. (This "minefield," which Marlyse Baptista warns me about (pers. comm., November 2001), can be glimpsed at by comparing the descriptions of passive morphosyntax in Veiga (1996), Quint (2000), and Baptista (2002).) Then let's assume DISTRIBUTED MORPHOLOGY (Halle and Marantz 1993; Noyer 1997; Halle 1997; Harley and Noyer 1999; keeping in mind the caveats in notes 18 and 20) and let's propose the following analysis for the INFL morphemes in (i) with the following associations between phonological exponents and morphosyntactic specifications:

(ii) a.   -/d/-: the exponent of a *passive* voice head

b.   -/a/: the exponent of an *anterior* tense head in the environment of the *passive* voice

c.   -/u/: the exponent of the tense head in the environment of the *passive* voice

d.   -/ba/: the exponent of an *anterior* tense head (cf. Baptista 1997: 97–99, 116–118);

e.   -∅: to be inserted elsewhere.

One possible correlate of V-to-I in CVC resides in the details of the morphemic decomposition in (ii), independent of interpretive subtleties. For any given INFL-related voice head or tense head that the syntax delivers to the morphophonology with the morphosyntactic features [±passive] and [±anterior], the phonological exponent of the "Vocabulary Item" with the greatest number of matching features is inserted in that head. The crucial point here is that the hypothesized structure of CVC passive forms such as *kantá +d +u* and *kantá +d +a* shows *stacking* of inflectional affixes. Thus, there are CVC verbal forms that, like Fr and ME ones, bear multiple inflectional affixes on the verbal stem. In other words, affixal stacking in CVC passives makes its verbal morphology very much unlike that of Modern English; such stacking may well count as a symptom of CVC "rich" inflection of the sort that triggers V-to-I (see Bobaljik 2001: 6, and notes 18 and 20 earlier).

One brief note on the "minefield" of dialectal variations in CVC and possible methodological confounds: Many CVC dialects, including some of those described in Baptista (1997, 2002), the *-da/-du* alternation appears quite elusive. Furthermore, there are dialects without the *-da/-du* alternation that do manifest instances of V-to-I (Baptista 1997; but see note 59). Nevertheless, my speculations here do invite CVC dialectologists to look for particular patterns—in particular, empirical correlations, or lack thereof, between V-to-I and the morphological profile of verbs—while controlling for Portuguese influence, dialect mixing, abstract (nonovert) residue of erstwhile overt affixes, and so on. Not a small task.

Here's another possible symptom of un-English "rich" inflection CVC. Baptista (1997: 263–266) notes that CVC "displays a ban on clitic clustering": there can't be two clitics following the verb. As it turns out, *-ba* participates in "clitic" clustering: once *-ba* affixes to a verb, the verb can no longer host an object clitic:

(iii)　*João*　odja+m.
　　　　João　saw+me

　　"João saw me."

(iv)　**João*　odja+ba+m
　　　　João　saw+PAST+me

(v)　**João*　odja+m+ba
　　　　João　saw+me+PAST

Once the verb is affixed with *-ba*, it can only take a nonclitic pronoun (e.g., *mi* in (vi)):

(vi)　*João*　odjaba　　mi.
　　　　João　saw+PAST　me

　　"João had seen me."

It thus seems that *-ba* and object clitics are in competition to occupy, in atheoretical terms, an "affixal" slot on the verb. If this is correct, then it can be argued that both the TMA affix *-ba* and the clitic *m* are *syntactic* affixal heads that, in this particular case, compete for support from a verbal stem in the narrow syntax. Whichever analysis is offered for such a competition, its sheer existence distinguishes CVC *-ba* from English *-ed*—to wit, *I liked it* (vs. (iv)). The contrast in (iii)–(vi) may be yet another cue, for the linguist if not for the Cape Verdean child, that differentiates CVC *-ba* from English *-ed* vis-à-vis their respective potential for V-to-I. (I am greatly indebted to Marlyse Baptista for her generous comments on some of the discussion in this section and for sharing some of her results and fieldwork data in advance of publication.)

Similarly, PL -*ba* also shows PL-specific morphological properties that set it apart from English -*ed*—properties of the sort that may lead the learner to endow the relevant PL inflectional head(s) with V-to-I potential. In (53), PL -*ba* (unlike CVC -*ba*; cf. (v)) can be separated from its verbal stem by an object clitic. Like CVC -*ba*, PL -*ba* looks like an affixal head that is active in the narrow syntax, as it can attach to the verb+clitic complex head, which is presumably created in the narrow syntax as well, assuming that -*ba* is merged in a position that precedes and c-commands the base positions of both verb and object clitic. Forms like *miná+lo+ba* in (53) may then be one of the triggers that force the learner to analyze PL -*ba* as an independent, syntactically active head, to which the verb+clitic complex *miná+lo* moves in the syntax to host the syntactically active suffix -*ba*, giving *miná+lo+ba*. This is yet another instance of "affix stacking"—if we can call it that—that correlates with V-to-I. Another, perhaps clearer, instance of affix-stacking in PL is the aforementioned *toká-ndo-ba*, which bears both progressive and past inflectional affixes. Recall that English -*ed*, unlike Pl -*ba*, does not enter into affix stacking of any sort: **like+it+ed* and **play+ing+ed*.

If these speculations are on the right track, then both CVC and PL provide the learner with positive evidence that the relevant inflectional heads above VP are affixal and trigger V-to-I. This line of reasoning also suggests that there is a multiplicity of cues that, in principle, can be used to decide on the setting of the verb-placement parameter (cf. Lightfoot 1999; Roberts 1999; Bobaljik 2001).

REFERENCES

Aboh, Enoch (1999) *From the Syntax of Gungbe to the Grammar of Gbe.* Éditions à la Carte, Sierre.

Ackema, Peter (2001) "On the Relation between V-to-I and the Structure of the Inflectional Paradigm. *Linguistic Review* 18: 233–263.

Adam, Lucien (1883) *Les idiomes négro-aryen et maléo-aryen: Essai d'hybridologie linguistique.* Maisonneuve, Paris.

Alleyne, Mervyn (1971) "Acculturation and the Cultural Matrix of Creolization," in Dell Hymes (ed.) *Pidginization and Creolization of Languages.* Cambridge University Press, Cambridge, 169–186.

Archibald, John (ed.) (2000) *Second Language Acquisition and Linguistic Theory.* Blackwell, Malden, Mass.

Avolonto, Aimé (1992) "De l'étude sémantico-syntaxique des marqueurs pré-verbaux à la structure de phrase en fɔngbé." Ph.D. thesis, University of Derek (1981) *Roots of Language.* Karoma, Ann Arbor, Mich.

Baissac, Charles (1880) *Étude sur le Patois Créole Mauricien.* Nomey: Imprimerie Berger-Levrault et Cie.

Baptista, Marlyse (1997) "*The Morpho-Syntax of Nominal and Verbal Categories in Capeverdean Creole.*" Ph.D. diss., Harvard University, Cambridge.

Baptista, Marlyse (2002) *The Syntax of Cape Verdean Creole: The Sotavento Varieties.* John Benjamins, Amsterdam.

Bickerton, Derek (1981) *Roots of Language.* Karoma, Ann Arbor, Mich.

Bickerton, Derek (1984) "The Language Bioprogram Hypothesis." *Behavioral and Brain Sciences* 7(2): 173–203.

Bickerton, Derek (1988) "Creole languages and the bioprogram," in Frederick Newmeyer (ed.) *Linguistics: The Cambridge Survey.* Vol. 2: *Linguistic Theory: Extensions and Implications.* Cambridge University Press, Cambridge, 268–284.

Bobaljik, Jonathan (1995) "Morphosyntax: The Syntax of Verbal Inflection." Ph.D. diss., MIT, Mass.

Bobaljik, Jonathan (1999) "Adverbs: The Hierarchy Paradox." *Glot International* 4 (9/10): 27–28.

Bobaljik, Jonathan (2001) "The Rich Agreement Hypothesis in Review" ("version 2.0, August 2001," 32 pages). Unpublished ms., McGill University.

Bobaljik, Jonathan (2002) "A-Chains at the PF Interface: Copies and "Covert" Movement." *Natural Language and Linguistic Theory* 20.2: 192–267.

Bobaljik, Jonathan, and Dianne Jonas (1996) "Subject Position and the Roles of TP." *Linguistic Inquiry* 27(2): 195–236.

Brunot, Ferdinand (1966) *Histoire de la langue française des origines à nos jours.* A. Colin, Paris.

Brunot, Ferdinand, and Charles Bruneau (1969 [1949]) *Précis de grammaire historique de la langue française.* Masson, Paris.

Bruyn, Adrienne, Pieter Muysken, and Maaike Verrips (1999) "Double Object Constructions in the Creole Languages: Development and Acquisition," in Michael DeGraff (ed.) *Language Creation and Language Change.* MIT Press, Cambridge, Mass., 329–373.

Bunsen, Christian (1854) "The Icelandic and the Modern Scandinavian, or the Effect of Colonization," in Christian Bunsen (ed.) *Outlines of the Philosophy of Universal History Applied to Language and Religion*, vol. 2. Longman, Brown, Green & Longmans, London, 52–57.

Bybee, Joan, Revere Perkins, and William Pagliuca (1994) *The Evolution of Grammar: Tense, Aspect and Modality in the Languages of the World.* University of Chicago Press, Chicago.

Cadely, Jean-Robert (1994) "Aspects de la Morphologie du Créole Haitien." Ph.D. dissertation, Université du Québec à Montréal.

Cadely, Jean-Robert (1997) "Prosodie et cliticisation en créole haïtien." *Études Créoles* 20(1): 77–88.

Chaudenson, Robert (1974) *Le lexique du parler créole de la Réunion.* Librairie Honoré Champion, Paris.

Chaudenson, Robert (1992) *Des îles, des hommes, des langues.* L'Harmattan, Paris.

Chaudenson, Robert (1995) *Les créoles.* Presses Universitaires de France, Paris.

Chaudenson, Robert, and Salikoko Mufwene (2001) *Creolization of Language and Culture.* [English translation and revision of Chaudenson 1992.] Routledge, London.

Chaudenson, Robert, Raymond Mougeon, and Édouard Beniak (1993). *Vers une approche panlectale de la variation du français.* Institut d'Études Créoles et Francophones, Aix-en-Provence.

Chomsky, Noam (1986) *Knowledge of Language.* Praeger, New York.

Chomsky, Noam (1993) "A Minimalist Program for Linguistic Theory," in Kenneth Hale and Samuel Jay Keyser (eds.) *The View from Building 20.* MIT Press, Cambridge, Mass., 1–52.

Chomsky, Noam (1995) *The Minimalist Program.* MIT Press, Cambridge, Mass.

Cinque, Guglielmo (1999) *Adverbs and Functional Heads: A Cross-Linguistic Perspective.* Oxford University Press, New York.

da Cruz, Maxime (1995) "Aspectual Verbs *fó, vɔ* 'finish' in Fɔngbè." *Linguistic Review* 12(4): 361–380.

Déchaine, Rose-Marie (1991) "Bare Sentences," in Steven Moore and Adam Zachary Wyner (eds.) *Proceedings of the First Semantics and Linguistic Theory Conference.* Cornell University, Ithaca, N.Y., 31–50.

Déchaine, Rose-Marie, and Victor Manfredi (eds.) (1997) *Object Positions in Benue-Kwa.* Holland Academic Graphics, The Hague.

DeGraff, Michel (1992a) "Creole Grammars and Acquistion of Syntax." Ph.D. diss., University of Pennsylvania.

DeGraff, Michel (1992b) "Haitian null subjects revisited," in Claire Lefebvre (ed.) *Travaux de Recherche sur le Créole Haïtien.* University of Quebec, Montreal, 59–74.

DeGraff, Michel (1992c) "Is Haitian a Pro-Drop Language?," in Francis Byrne and John Holm (eds.) *Atlantic Meets Pacific: A Global View of Pidginization and Creolization.* John Benjamins, Amsterdam, 71–90.

DeGraff, Michel (1992d) "The Syntax of Predication in Haitian," in Kimberly Broderick (ed.) *Proceedings of NELS 22.* Amherst, Mass.: Graduate Linguistics Student Association, 103–117.

DeGraff, Michel (1993) "A Riddle on Negation in Haitian." *Probus* 5: 63–93.

DeGraff, Michel (1994a) "The morphology-Syntax Interface in Creolization (and Diachrony). *Studies in the Linguistic Sciences* 24(2): 115–132.

DeGraff, Michel (1994b) "To Move or Not to Move? Placement of Verbs and Object Pronouns in Haitian and in French," in Katharine Beals et al. (eds.) *Papers from the 30th Meeting of the Chicago Linguistic Society.* Chicago Linguistics Society, Chicago, 141–155.

DeGraff, Michel (1995a) "On Certain Differences between Haitian and French Predicative Constructions," in Jon Amastae, Grant Goodall, Mario Montalbetti, and Marianne Phinney (eds.) *Contemporary Research in Romance Linguistics.* John Benjamins, Amsterdam, 237–256.

DeGraff, Michel (1995b) "Predicate-Movement, Quantification, Events and Properties," in Victor Manfredi and Karl Reynolds (eds.) *Niger-Congo Syntax and Semantics 6.* Boston University African Studies Center, Boston, Mass.

DeGraff, Michel (1997) "Verb Syntax in Creolization (and Beyond)," in Liliane Haegeman (ed.) *The New Comparative Syntax.* Longman, London, 64–94.

DeGraff, Michel (1998) "Nominal Predication in Haitian and in Irish," in Emily Curtis, James Lyle, and Gabriel Webster (eds.) *Proceedings of the Sixteenth West Coast Conference on Formal Linguistics.* Center for the Study of Language and Information, Stanford, Calif., 113–128.

DeGraff, Michel (1999a) "Creolization, Language Change and Language Acquisition: A Prolegomenon," in Michel DeGraff (ed.) *Language Creation and Language Change.* MIT Press, Cambridge, Mass., 1–46.

DeGraff, Michel (1999b) "Creolization, Language Change and Language Acquisition: An

Epilogue," in (ed.) *Language Creation and Language Change*. MIT Press, Cambridge, Mass., 473–543.

DeGraff, Michel (ed.) (1999c) *Language Creation and Language Change: Creolization, Diachrony and Development*. MIT Press, Cambridge, Mass.

DeGraff, Michel (1999d) "Parameter-Setting in Language Acquisition and through Diachrony," in Rob Wilson and Frank Keil (eds.) *MIT Encyclopedia of Cognitive Sciences*. MIT Press, Cambridge, Mass., 624–627.

DeGraff, Michel (2000). "A propos des pronoms objets dans le créole d'Haïti: Regards croisés de la morphologie et de la diachronie." *Langages* 138: 89–113.

DeGraff, Michel (2001a). "Morphology in Creole Genesis: Linguistics and Ideology," in Michael Kenstowicz (ed.) *Ken Hale: A Life in Language*. MIT Press, Cambridge, Mass., 53–121.

DeGraff, Michel (2001b) "On the Origin of Creoles: A Cartesian Critique of Neo-Darwinian Linguistics." *Linguistic Typology* 5(2): 213–311.

DeGraff, Michel (2002a) "Linguists' Most Dangerous Myth: The Fallacy of Creole Exceptionalism." Unpublished ms., MIT, Cambridge, Mass.

DeGraff, Michel (2002b) "On Creole Genesis and Language Acquisition: Some Methodological and Theoretical Preliminaries." Unpublished ms., MIT, Cambridge, Mass.

DeGraff, Michel (2002c) "Relexification: A re-evaluation." *Anthropological Linguistics* 44.4: 321–414.

DeGraff, Michel (2003) "Haitian Creole Morpho-Syntax: A Micro-Parametric Approach to Its Structure and Genesis." Unpublished ms.

Dejean, Yves (1992) "Manifestations en créole haïtien du principe d'adjacence stricte." Unpublished ms., Institut de Linguistique Appliquée, Port-au-Prince, Haiti.

Denis, Serge (ed.) (1935) *Nos antilles*. G. Luzeray, Orléans.

Déprez, Viviane (1989) "On the Typology of Syntactic Positions and the Nature of Chains." Ph.D. diss., MIT, Cambridge, Mass.

Déprez, Viviane (1994) "Haitian Creole: A Pro-Drop Language?" *Journal of Pidgin and Creole Languages* 9: 1–24.

Déprez, Viviane (1999) "The Roots of Negative Concord in French and French-Lexicon Creoles," in Michel DeGraff (ed.) *Language Creation and Language Change*. MIT Press, Cambridge, Mass., 375–427.

Descourtilz, Michel Étienne (1809) *Voyages d'un Naturaliste et ses Observations faites sur les Trois Règnes de la Nature, dans Plusieurs Ports de Mer Français, en Espagne, au Continent de l'Amérique Septentrionale . . .* 3 vol. Dufart, Paris.

Duarte, Inês, and Gabriela Matos (2000) "Romance clitics and the Minimalist Program," in Joõ Costa (ed.) *Portuguese Syntax: New Comparative Studies*. Oxford University Press, New York, 116–142.

Ducœurjoly, S. J. (1802) *Manuel des Habitans de Saint-Dominque*. Paris: Lenoir.

Ellegård, Alvar (1953) *The Auxiliary Do: The Establishment and Regulation of Its Use in English*. Almquist and Wiksell, Stockholm.

Fabb, Nigel (1992) "Reduplication and Object Movement in Ewe and Fon." *Journal of African Languages and Linguistics* 13: 1–41.

Falk, Cecilia (1993) *Non-Referential Subjects in the History of Swedish Land*. University of Lund, Department of Scandinavian Languages.

Fattier, Dominique (1995) "Une si proche étrangère (quelques remarques à propos de la genèse du sous-système des pronoms personnels du créole d'Haïti)," in Françoise

Gadet and Dominique Fattier (eds.) *Situations du Français, LINX 33*. Centre de Recherches Linguistiques de l'Université Paris X-Nanterre, Paris.

Fattier, Dominique (1998) "Contribution à l'étude de la genèse d'un créole: L'atlas linguistique d'Haïti, cartes et commentaires." Ph.D. diss., Université de Provence. Distributed by Presses Universitaires du Septentrion, Villeneuve d'Ascq, France.

Frei, Henri (1929) *La grammaire des fautes*. P. Geuthner, Paris.

Gadet, Francoise (1997) *Le français populaire*. Presses Universitaires de France, Paris.

Givón, Talmy (1979) "Prolegomena to Any Sane Creology," in Ian Hancock (ed.) *Readings in Creole Studies*. E. Story-Scientia, Ghent, Belgium, 3–35.

Goodman, Morris (1964) *A Comparative Study of Creole French Dialects*. Mouton, The Hague.

Goodman, Morris (1993) "African Substratum: Some Cautionary Words," in Salikoko Mufwene, (ed.) *Africanisms in Afro-American Language Varieties*. University of Georgia Press. Athens, 64–73.

Gougenheim, Georges (1929) *Etude sur les périphrases verbales de la langue française*. Les Belles Lettres, Paris.

Halle, Morris (1997) "Distributed Morphology: Impoverishment and Fission," in Benjamin Bruening, Yoonjung Kang and Martha McGinnis (eds.) *MIT Working Papers in Linguistics* 30. MIT Linguistics and Philosophy, Cambridge, Mass., 425–449.

Halle, Morris, and Alec Marantz (1993) "Distributed Morphology and the Pieces of Inflection." In Kenneth Hale and Samuel Jay Keyser (eds.) *The View from Building 20: Essays in Honor of Sylvain Bromberger*. MIT Press, Cambridge, Mass.

Harley, Heidi, and Rolf Noyer (1999) "Distributed Morphology." *Glot International* 4(4): 3–9.

Haugen, Einar (1976) *The Scandinavian Languages: An Introduction to Their History*. Faber and Faber, London.

Haugen, Einar (1982) *Scandinavian Language Structures: A Comparative Historical Survey*. University of Minnesota Press, Minneapolis.

Hjelmslev, Louis (1938) "Relation de parenté des langues créoles." *Revue des Études Indo-Européennes* 1: 271–286.

Holmberg, Anders (1985) "Icelandic Word Order and Binary Branching." *Nordic Journal of Linguistics* 9: 161–195.

Holmberg, Anders (1999) "Remarks on Holmberg's Generalization." *Studia Linguistica* 53(1): 1–39.

Holmberg, Anders, and Christer Platzack (1990) "On the Role of Inflection in Scandinavian Syntax," in Werner Abraham, Wim Kosmeijer, and Eric Reuland (eds.) *Issues in Germanic Syntax*. 93–118. Berlin: Mouton de Gruyter.

Holmberg, Anders, and Christer Platzack (1995) *The Role of Inflection in Scandinavian Syntax*. Oxford University Press, New York.

Howe, Kate (2000) "Développement d'une théorie de la temporalité: Les cas du créole haïtien et du papiamento," Ph.D. diss., University of Provence.

Idylles et chansons; ou essais de poésie créole par un habitant d'Hayti. (1811) J. Edwards, Philadelphie.

Ionin, Tania, and Ken Wexler (2002) "Why Is 'Is' Easier Than 's'? Acquisition of Tense/Agreement Morphology by Child L2-English Learners." *Second Language Research* 18(2): 95–136.

Jespersen, Otto (1922) *Language: Its Nature, Development and Origin.* G. Allen and Unwin, London.

Josefsson, Gunlög (1992) "Object Shift and Weak Pronominals in Swedish." *Working Papers in Scandinavian Syntax* 49: 59–94.

Kayne, Richard (1989a) "Null Subjects and Clitic Climbing," in Osvaldo Jaeggli and Kenneth J. Safir (eds.) *The Null-Subject Parameter.* Kluwer, Dordrecht, 239–261.

Kayne, Richard (1989b) "Facets of Romance Past Participle Agreement," in Paola Benincà (ed.) *Dialect Variation and the Theory of Grammar.* Foris, Dordrecht, 85–103.

Kayne, Richard (1991) "Romance Clitics, Verb Movement, and PRO." *Linguistic Inquiry* 22: 647–686.

Kayne, Richard (1994) *The Antisymmetry of Syntax.* MIT Press, Cambridge, Mass.

Kinyalolo, Kasangati (1992) "A Note on Word Order in the Progressive and Prospective in Fɔn." *Journal of West African Languages* 22: 35–51.

Klein, Wolfgang, and Clive Perdue (1992) *Utterance Structure: Developing Grammaras Again.* John Benjamins, Amsterdam.

Kroch, Anthony (1989a) "Function and Grammar in the History of English: Periphrastic *do*," in Ralph Fasold and Deborah Schiffrin (eds.) *Language Change and Variation.* John Benjamins, Amsterdam, 133–172.

Kroch, Anthony (1989b) "Reflexes of Grammar in Patterns of Language Change." *Language Variation and Change,* 1(3): 199–244.

Kroch, Anthony, and Ann Taylor (1997) "The Syntax of Verb Movement in Middle English: Dialect Variation and Language Contact," in Ans van Kemenade and Nigel Vincent (eds.) *Parameters of Morphosyntactic Change.* Cambridge University Press, Cambridge, 297–325.

Kroch, Anthony, and Ann Taylor (2000) "Verb-Object Order in Early Middle English," in Susan Pintzuk, George Tsoulas, and Anthony Warner (eds.) *Diachronic Syntax: Models and Mechanisms.* Oxford University Press, Oxford, 132–187.

Kroch, Anthony, Ann Taylor, and Donald Ringe (2000) "The Middle English Verb-Second Constraint: A Case Study in Language Contact and Language Change," in Susan Herring, Pieter van Reneen, and Lene Schøsler (eds.) *Textual Parameters in Older Languages.* John Benjamins, Amsterdam, 353–391.

Lardiere, Donna (2000) "Mapping Features to Forms in Second Language Acquisition," in John Archibald (ed.) *Second Language Acquisition and Linguistic Theory.* Blackwell, Malden, Mass., 102–129.

Larousse, Pierre (1869) *Grand dictionnaire universel du XIX siècle.* Larousse, Paris.

Lasnik, Howard (1995) "Verbal Morphology: *Syntactic Structures* Meets the *Minimalist Program*," in Hector Campos and Paula Kempchinsky (eds.) *Evolution and Revolution in Linguistic Theory.* Georgetown University Press, Washington, D.C., 251–275.

Lasnik, Howard (1999) *Minimalist Analysis.* Blackwell, Malden, Mass.

Lefebvre, Claire (1998) *Creole Genesis and the Acquisition of Grammar: The Case of Haitian Creole.* Cambridge University Press, Cambridge.

Lightfoot, David (1999) "Creoles and Cues," in Michel DeGraff (ed.) *Language Creation and Language Change.* MIT Press, Cambridge, Mass., 431–452.

Lightfoot, David (2002) "Myths and the Prehistory of Grammars." *Journal of Linguistics* 38(1): 113–136.

MacWhinney, Brian (2000) *The CHILDES Project: Tools for Analyzing Talk.* Erlbaum, Mahwah, N.J.

Marantz, Alec (1991 [2000]) "Case and Licensing," in Germán Westphal, Benjamin Ao, and Hee-Rahk Chae (eds.) *Proceedings of Eight Eastern States Conference on Linguistics.* Ohio State University, Columbus, 234–253.

Mchombo, Sam (ed.) (1993) *Theoretical Aspects of Bantu Grammar.* CSLI Publications, Stanford, Calif.

McWhorter, John (1998) "Identifying the Creole Prototype: Vindicating a Typological Class." *Language* 74(4): 788–818.

Meillet, Antoine (1951 [1929]) "Le développement des langues," in Antoine Meillet. *Linguistique historique et linguistique générale.* Klincksieck, Paris, 2: 71–83.

Meillet, Antoine (1958 [1912]) "L'Évolution des formes grammaticales," In Antoine Meillet, *Linguistique historique et linguistique générale.* Honoré Champion, Paris, 1: 130–148.

Meillet, Antoine (1958 [1919] "Le genre grammaticale et l'élimination de la flexion," in Antoine Meillet, *Linguistique historique et linguistique générale.* Honoré Champion, Paris, 1: 199–210.

Meillet, Antoine (1958 [1920]) "Sur les caractères in Antoine Meillet, *Linguistique historique et linguistique générale.* Honoré Champion, Paris, 1: 175–198.

Moreau de Saint-Méry, M.L.E. (1958 [1797]) *Description topographique, physique, civile, politique et historique de la partie française de l'isle de Saint Domingue.* 3 vols. Société de l'Histoire des Colonies Françaises, Paris.

Mufwene, Salikoko (1986) "Can Creole Languages Be Defined without Reference to Their History?" *Études Creoles* 9(1): 135–150.

Mufwene, Salikoko (1990) "Transfer and the Substrate Hypothesis in Creolistics." *Studies in Second Language Acquisition* 12(1): 1–23.

Mufwene, Salikoko (1991) "Pidgins, Creoles, Typology, and Markedness," in Francis Byrne and Thom Huebner (eds.) *Development and Structures of Creole Languages: Essays in Honor of Derek Bickerton.* John Benjamins, Amsterdam, 123–143.

Mufwene, Salikoko (1996) "The Founder Principle in Creole Genesis." *Diachronica* 13(1): 83–134.

Mufwene, Salikoko (1997) "Jargons, Pidgins, Creoles, and Koines: What Are They?," in Arthur Spears and Donald Winford (eds.) *The Structure and Status of Pidgins and Creoles.* John Benjamins, Amsterdam, 35–70.

Mufwene, Salikoko (2001) *The Ecology of Language Evolution.* Cambridge University Press, Cambridge.

Mufwene, Salikoko (2002) "Grammaticization as Part of the Development of Creoles," unpublished ms., University of Chicago, Chicago IL.

Muysken, Pieter (1988) "Are Creoles a Special Type of Language?" in *Linguistics: The Cambridge Survey.* Vol. 2: *Linguistic Theory: Extensions and Implications.* Cambridge University Press, Cambridge, 285–301.

Ndayiragije, Juvénal (2000) "Strengthening PF." *Linguistic Inquiry* 31(3): 485–512.

Neumann, Ingrid (1985) *Le créole de Breaux Bridge, Louisiane: Étude morphosyntaxe, textes, vocabulaire.* Helmust Buske, Hamburg.

Nilsen, Øystein (1997) "Adverbs and A-shift," *Working Papers in Scandinavian Syntax* 59: 1–31.

Noyer, Rolf (1997) *Features, Positions and Affixes in Autonomous Morphological Structure.* Garland, New York.

Pelleprat, Father Pierre (1965 [1655]) *Relato de las misiones de los padres de la Compañía de Jesús en las islas y en tierra firme de América Meridional*. Fuentes para la Historia Colonial de Venezuela, Caracas.

Perdue, Clive (1995) *L'acquisition du français et de l'anglais par des adultes*. CNRS Editions, Paris.

Pierce, Amy (1992). *Language Acquisition and Syntactic Theory: A Comparative Analysis of French and English Child Grammars*. Kluwer, Dordrecht.

Platzack, Christer, and Anders Holmberg (1989) "The Role of Agr and Finiteness." *Working Papers in Scandinavian Syntax* 43: 51–76.

Pollock, Jean-Yves (1989) "Verb Movement, Universal Grammar and the Structure of IP." *Linguistic Inquiry* 20: 365–424.

Prévost, Philippe, and Lydia White (2000) "Missing Surface Inflection or Impairment in Second Language Acquisition? Evidence from Tense and Agreement." *Second Language Research* 16(2): 103–133.

Quint, Nicolas (2000) *Grammaire de la langue cap-verdienne*. L'Harmattan, Paris.

Raposo, Eduardo (2000) Clitic Positions and Verb Movement," in João Costa (ed.) *Portuguese Syntax: New Comparative Studies*. Oxford University Press, New York, 266–297.

Rivera-Castillo, Yolanda (1992) "Enclitic Pronouns in Caribbean Spanish," in Laura Buszard-Welcher, Lionel Wee, and William Weigel (eds.) *Proceedings of the Eighteenth Annual Meeting of the Berkeley Linguistics Society*. Berkeley Linguistics Society, Berkeley, Calif., 424–434.

Rizzi, Luigi (1999) "Broadening the Empirical Basis of Universal Grammar Models: A Commentary," Michel De Graff (ed.) *Language Creation and Language Change*. MIT Press, Cambridge, Mass., 453–472.

Roberts, Ian (1993) *Verbs and Diachronic Syntax: A Comparative History of English and French*. Kluwer, Dordrecht.

Roberts, Ian (1997) "Directionality and Word Order Change in the History of English," in Ans van Kemenade and Nigel Vincent (eds.) *Parameters of Morphosyntactic Change*. Cambridge University Press, Cambridge, 397–426.

Roberts, Ian (1998) "*Have/Be* Raising, Move F and Procrastinate." *Linguistic Inquiry* 29(1): 113–125.

Roberts, Ian (1999) "Verb Movement and Markedness," in Michel DeGraff (ed.). *Language Creation and Language Change*. MIT Press, Cambridge, Mass., 287–327.

Rohrbacher, Bernhard (1994) "The Germanic VO Languages and the Full Paradigm: A Theory of V to I Raising." Ph.D. diss., University of Massachusetts at Amherst.

Rosiers, comte de (1818) *L'Entrée du roi en sa capitale, en janvier 1818, an 15ème de l'indépendance d'Hayti*. Imprimerie Royale, Sans-Souci, Haiti.

Rottet, Kevin (1992) "Functional Categories and Verb Raising in Louisiana Creole." *Probus* 4: 261–289.

Saint-Quentin, Alfred de (1989 [1872]) *Introduction à l'histoire de Cayenne*, with *Étude sur la grammaire créole* by Auguste de Saint-Quentin. *Cayenne: Comité de la Culture, de l'Éducation et de l'Environnement, Région Guyane*.

Schleicher, August (1852 [1850]) *Die Sprachen Europas in Systematischer Übersicht: Linguistische Untersuchungen*. Trans. Hermann Ewerbeck. *Les Langues de l'Europe Moderne*. Ladrange, Paris.

Schlupp, Daniel (1997) *Modalités predicatives, modalités aspectuelles et auxiliaires en créole à base lexicale française de la Guyane française (XVIIIᵉ–XXᵉ siècles)*. Max Niemeyer, Tübingen.

Schütze, Carson (1997) "INFL in Child and Adult Language: Agreement, Case and Licensing." Ph.D. diss., MIT.

Schwegler, Armin, and Kate Green (In press) "Palenquero (Creole Spanish)," in John Holm and Peter Patrick (eds.) *Comparative Creole Syntax*. Battlebridge, London,–.

Seuren, Pieter (1998) *Western Linguistics: An Historical Introduction*. Blackwell, Oxford.

Seuren, Pieter, and Herman Wekker (1986) "Semantic Transparency as a Factor in Creole Genesis," in Pieter Muysken and Norval Smith (eds.) *Substrata versus Universals in Creole Genesis*. John Benjamins, Amsterdam, 57–70.

Siegel, Jeff (2003) "Substrate Influence in Creoles and the Role of Transfer in Second Language Acquisition." *Studies in Second Language Acquisition* 25: 185–209.

Singler, John (1996) "Theories of Creole Genesis, Sociohistorical Considerations, and the Evaluation of the Evidence: The Case of Haitian Creole and the Relexification Hypothesis." *Journal of Pidgin and Creole Languages* 11: 185–230.

Sportiche, Dominique (1995) "Clitic Constructions," in Johan Rooryck and Laurie Zaring (eds.) *Phrase Structure and the Lexicon*. Kluwer, Dordrecht, 213–276.

Sprouse, Rex (1998) "Some Notes on the Relationship between Inflectional Morphology and Parameter-Setting in First and Second Language Acquisition," in Maria-Luise Beck (ed.) *Morphology and Its Interfaces in Second Language Knowledge*. John Benjamins, Amsterdam, 41–67.

Suñer, Margarita (1994) "V-movement and the Licensing of Argumental *wh*-Phrases in Spanish." *Natural Language and Linguistic Theory* 12: 335–372.

Sylvain, Suzanne (1936) *Le créole haïtien: Morphologie et syntaxe*. Wetteren, Imprimerie de Meester, Brussels.

Thomas, John Jacob (1869) *The Theory and Practice of Creole Grammar*. Chronicle, Port-of-Spain, Haiti.

Thomason, Sarah, and Terrence Kaufman (1988) *Language Contact, Creolization, and Genetic Linguistics*. Berkeley, University of California Press.

Thráinsson, Höskuldur (1994) "Comments on the Paper by Vikner [1994]," in David Lightfoot, and Norbert Hornstein (eds.) (1994) *Verb Movement*. Cambridge University Press, Cambridge, 149–162.

Thráinsson, Höskuldur (2001) "Object Shift and Scrambling," in Mark Baltin and Chris Collins (eds.) *Handbook of Generative Syntax*. Blackwell, Malden, Mass., 148–202.

van Kemenade, Ans (1987) *Syntactic Case and Morphological Case in the History of English* Foris, Dordrecht.

van Kemenade, Ans, (1997) "V2 and embedded topicalization in Old and Middle English," in Ans van Kemenade and Nigel Vincent (eds.) *Parameters of Morphosyntactic Change*. Cambridge University Press, Cambridge, 326–352.

van Kemenade, Ans, and Nigel Vincent (eds.) (1997) *Parameters of Morphosyntactic Change*. Cambridge University Press, Cambridge.

Van Name, Addison (1870) "Contributions to Creole Grammar." *Transactions of the American Philological Association* 1: 123–167.

Veenstra, Tonjes (1996) "Serial Verbs in Saramaccan: Predication and Creole Genesis." Ph.D. diss., University of Amsterdam.

Veiga, Manuel (1996) *Introdução à Gramática do Crioulo de Cabo Verde.* 2nd ed. Instituto Caboverdiano do Livro e do Disco, Cabo Verde.

Véronique, Daniel (1990) "Reference and Discourse Structure in the Learning of French by Adult Moroccans," in Hans Dechert (ed.) *Current Trends in European Second Language Acquisition Research.* Multilingual Matters, Clevedon, England, 171–201.

Véronique, Daniel (2000) "Observations préléminaires sur *li* dans l'interlangue d'Abdelmalek," in Alain Giacomi, Henriette Stoffel, and Daniel Véronique (eds.) *Appropriation du français par des Marocains arabophones à Marseille.* Publications de l'Université de Provence, Aix-en-Provence, 207–323.

Vikner, Sten (1994) "Finite Verb Movement in Scandinavian Embedded Clauses," in David Lightfoot, and Norbert Hornstein (eds.) (1994) *Verb Movement.* Cambridge University Press, Cambridge, 117–147.

Vikner, Sten (1995) *Verb Movement and Expletive Subjects in the Germanic Languages.* Oxford University Press, New York.

Vikner, Sten (1997) "V⁰-to-I⁰ Movement and Inflection for Person in all Tenses," in Liliane Haegeman (ed.) *The New Comparative Syntax.* Longman, London, 189–213.

Vinson, Julien (1889) "Créoles," in Adolphe Bertillon et al. (eds.) *Dictionnaire des Sciences Anthropologiques.* Doin, Paris, 345–347.

Vrzić, Zvjezdana (1997) "A Minimalist Approach to Word Order in Chinook Jargon and the Theory of Creole Genesis." in Benjamin Bruening (ed.) *Proceedings of the Eighth Student Conference in Linguistics.* Working Papers in Linguistics 31. MIT, Cambridge, Mass., 467–478.

Weinreich, U. (1968 [1953]) *Languages in Contact.* Mouton, The Hague.

Wexler, Ken (1994) "Finiteness and Head Movement in Early Child Grammars, in David Lightfoot, and Norbert Hornstein (eds.) (1994) *Verb Movement.* Cambridge University Press, Cambridge, 305–350.

Wexler, Ken (2002) "Lenneberg's Dream: Learning, Normal Language Development and Specific Language Impairment," in Jeannette Schaeffer and Yonata Levy (eds.) *Language Competence across Populations: Towards a Definition of Specific Language Impairment.* Erlbaum, Hillsdale, N.J., 11–61.

CHAPTER 9

THE SLAVIC LANGUAGES

STEVEN FRANKS

1 INTRODUCTION

THE Slavic (or Slavonic) languages represent a fairly homogeneous group of languages spoken in a large territory of central and eastern Europe, as well as Russian Asia. This chapter familiarizes the reader with their general structure and surveys a range of problems in Slavic syntax that have received recent attention from linguists working within various formal frameworks. In selecting problems, my aim has been to present those research areas which, although specifically Slavic, should be of the most interest to general linguists. While space limitations have necessarily caused me to sacrifice some diversity in coverage, I have sought, wherever possible, to indicate the most useful resources for further information.

1.1 Overview of the Chapter

The Slavic languages are traditionally divided into the following groups: East Slavic (ESl), which includes Russian (Ru), Ukrainian (Ukr), and Belorusian (Br); West Slavic (WSl), which includes Polish (Pol), Czech (Cz), and Slovak (Slk), as well as Kashubian and Upper and Lower Sorbian (Sor), minority languages spoken by smaller populations in Baltic coast Poland and southeastern Germany, respectively; and South Slavic (SSl), which includes Slovenian (Slvn), Serbo-Croatian (SC)—now typically referred to as "Serbian/Croatian/Bosnian" or variants thereof—Macedonian (Mac), and Bulgarian (Bg). While ESl is fairly cohesive, in WSl Cz and Slvk form a group that can be opposed both to Polish (and Kashubian, which has been sometimes regarded as a dialect of Polish) and the two Sorbians, and in SSl there is a major structural rift between Slvn and SC, on the one hand, and Bg and Mac, on the other.

In sections 3 and 4 of this chapter, I treat a variety of issues in comparative Slavic morphosyntax. These include case and agreement (3.1), the genitive of negation phenomenon (3.2), numerals (3.3), argument structure and voice (3.4), clitics (3.5), *wh* movement (3.6), negation (3.7), binding (4.1), aspect (4.2), and word order (4.3). In this I highlight the major phenomena, drawing attention to differences among the languages, and sketch proposals for how to analyze these phenomena. Much of this material is drawn from my two books, *Parameters of Slavic Morphosyntax* (Franks 1995) and *A Handbook of Slavic Clitics* (Franks and King 2000).

1.2 Some History and Resources for Further Study

In the past decade, research in Slavic syntax has grown considerably, and there has been a resurgence of interest among general linguists in particular types of Slavic language data that promises to elucidate problems of general linguistic analysis.[1] This resurgence of interest is best evidenced by the appearance of several new conferences in the field of formal Slavic linguistics. Perhaps the most effective has been the annual Formal Approaches to Slavic Linguistics (FASL) conference. FASL began as a small workshop organized in 1992 by Jindřich Toman of the University of Michigan, and it rapidly grew into the foremost annual meeting of Slavic linguists in the United States. The proceedings, available from Michigan Slavic Publications, offer a wide range of current research, predominantly oriented toward generative syntax.

In Europe, two new biennial conferences, both initiated in 1995, are Formal Description of Slavic Languages (FDSL) and Formal Approaches to South Slavic and Balkan Languages (FASSBL). The former proceedings are published as complete volumes, with four having appeared so far,[2] and the proceedings from the latter have appeared as *University of Trondheim Working Papers in Linguistics*; a selection of essays from volume 1 of FASSBL are also published in Dimitrova-Vulchanova and Hellan (1999), and many essays from volume 3 appear as a special journal issue, *Balkanistica* 15, edited by Dimitrova-Vulchanova, et al., (2002). As with FASL, most of the papers presented at these European conferences are concerned with syntax.

A variety of smaller, one-time meetings have also produced useful material. Two hosted by Indiana University were Comparative Slavic Morphosyntax: "The

State of the Art," in 1998, and The Future of Slavic Linguistics in America, in 2000.[3] More recently a group of Polish syntacticians founded Generative Linguistics in Poland (GLiP); they have had five meetings in the 1999–2002 period, four devoted to morphosyntax and one to morphophonology. GLiP-1 proceedings appeared as Bański and Przepiórkowski (2000); GLiP-2 proceedings appeared as Przepiórkowski and Bański (2001); GLiP-5 proceedings appeared as Bański and Przepiórkowski (2003); for further GLiP details, consult the website in (1f). Finally, another important new outlet for research in Slavic linguistics, although much more eclectic in scope, is the *Journal of Slavic Linguistics* (*JSL*) founded in 1993 and published by Slavica, at Indiana University. In addition, there is a burgeoning body of work on Slavic languages, especially Pol, on the part of practitioners of Head-Driven Phrase Structure Grammar. An excellent resource for this work is Borsley and Przepiórkowski (1999).[4]

Web pages for most of these ventures are readily accessible, and some, such as those for the Indiana workshops, offer downloadable versions of papers. Some of these sites, although hardly guaranteed to continue to be accurate, are listed in (1):

(1)   a. www.indiana.edu/~slavconf/

       b. www.lsa.umich.edu/slavic/FASL/

       c. aix1.uottowa.ca/fasl12/

       d. www.slavica.com/jsl/

       e. www.ipipan.waw.pl/mmgroup/HPSG/slavic.html

       f. venus.ci.uw.edu.pl/~glip/

       g. www.uni-leipzig.de/~jungslav/fdsl/fdsl-s/fdsl-s.html

       h. www.uni-potsdam.de/u/slavistik/wsw/fdsl4/index.htm

There is also a useful discussion listserv for Slavic and East European languages, known as SEELANGS, and questions about Slavic syntax can be posted there.[5]

There are, of course, many useful written resources about Slavic languages, as well as some monographs on Slavic syntax. The latter are mentioned at appropriate points in the following sections, but for general information by far the best resource is the compendious volume edited by Comrie and Corbett (1993). This massive reference, with chapters by leading experts about each of the languages, provides, inter alia, in-depth and highly accessible descriptions of morphosyntactic phenomena. A popular older book, although with far less information about syntax, is De Bray (1969).

2 A Brief Sketch of Slavic Typology

Probably the most salient and well-known property of the Slavic languages is their robust case systems. Most of the languages have a six-case system: nominative (nom), accusative (acc), genitive (gen), dative (dat), locative (loc; sometimes known as "prepositional"), and instrumental (inst). Some languages also have special vocative forms, but only on nouns. As one travels south and east across the Slavic territory, however, the case systems become simpler and the verbal systems more complex. Hence Bg and Mac display case systems surprisingly like those of French and Spanish (i.e., impoverished to the point of being essentially limited to nom, acc, and dat pronominal forms); in fact, these are perhaps best analyzed as (object) agreement markers rather than case. Concomitantly, while all the languages have grammaticalized aspect, with most verbs coming as imperfective-perfective pairs, Bg and Mac have highly complex tense systems.[6] It will be seen that many of the topics to be discussed here revolve in one way or another around case.

Another significant property of Slavic languages is their relatively free word order, which generally serves to express functional sentence perspective information rather than grammatical relations. This freedom of word order, however, is more restricted in Bg and Mac,[7] and, of course, breaks down as far as clitics are concerned, since these are required to appear in specific positions. All WSl and SSl languages have rich pronominal and verbal auxiliary clitic systems and are to a large extent null subject languages. The ESl languages, however, show neither property, and these languages similarly lack present-tense copula forms and person marking on past-tense verbs, facts that are surely related.

3 Popular Research Areas

This section, the core of the chapter, presents a selection of those research areas in Slavic syntax which have generated the greatest amount of investigation within recent formal models.

3.1 Case and Agreement

As stated, research into morphosyntactic problems that hinge on case facts has been very productive.[8] Here I mention just one such problem.

In a seminal study, Comrie (1974) drew attention to the phenomenon of the so-called second dative in Ru (and, to a lesser extent, Pol).[9] Ordinary predicate adjectives either agree with their nominal antecedents in case or appear in a "default" instrumental, which is obligatory whenever agreement is impossible (and, in Pol but not Ru, agreement is obligatory whenever possible);[10] within simple clauses, agreement is viable only with subject and direct object antecedents. The two "semipredicatives" *sam* 'alone' and *odin* 'one', however, display a default dative instead, which has a much more limited distribution than the predicate instrumental, since it only occurs in embedded environments.[11] In subject control contexts agreement obtains, a phenomenon I refer to descriptively as "case transmission," as in the following Ru examples:[12]

(2) a. Ivan   xočet   [PRO pojti   na večerinku *sam*].
        Ivan.nom   wants   to-go   to party   alone.mnom

    'Ivan wants to go to the party alone.'

    b. Ljuba   priexala [PRO pokupat' maslo *sama*].
       Lyuba.nom   came   to-buy   butter alone.fnom

    'Lyuba came to buy the butter herself.'

In contexts of nonsubject control, arbitrary control, or whenever there is overt material in COMP (either in C⁰ or SpecCP), the dative appears, as shown in (3):

(3) a. Maša   ugovorila Vanju   [PRO prigotovit' obed
        Masha   persuaded Vanya.acc   to-cook   lunch
        odnomu].
        alone.mdat

    'Masha persuaded Vanya to cook lunch by himself.'

    b. Dlja   nas   utomitel'no [PRO delat' èto *samim*].
       for   us   exhausting   to-do   this alone.pldat

    'It's exhausting for us to do this on our own.'

    c. Nevozmožno [PRO perejti ètot most   *samomu*].
       impossible   to-cross this bridge alone.mdat

    'It is impossible to cross this bridge by oneself.'

    d. Ljuba   priexala [čtoby   [PRO pokupat' maslo
       Lyuba.nom   came   in-order   to-buy   butter
       samoj]].
       alone.fdat

    'Lyuba came in order to buy the butter herself.'

e. Ivan ne   znaet   [kak [PRO tuda   dobrat'sja *odnomu*]].
   Ivan not   knows   how   there to-reach   alone.mdat

'Ivan doesn't know how to get there by himself/oneself.'

As most recently discussed by Moore and Perlmutter (2000), there are essentially two approaches to the second dative. Comrie's original insight about the second dative was that it arises through agreement with a dative subject subsequently deleted under Equi. In Franks (1995) and related work, I rejected this approach because, following the GB paradigm, I did not want PRO to have case when it could not be overt, and so I devised a special mechanism for assigning dative to the semipredicative directly whenever it failed to agree with its overt antecedent.

Checking theory now resolves this dilemma: the semipredicative can be dative regardless of where in the derivation that case is in fact checked. Moreover, PRO can have a "null case" that will resemble dative for purposes of access by the semipredicative but which will not suffice for PRO itself to be overt.

The clinching argument that the PRO subject of infinitives has null dative case comes from a fact recently unearthed by Leonard Babby about contrastive *samomu* in gerundive phrases.[13] Crucial examples are given in Ru (4c) and (5c):

(4) a. Ja   vse   videl, [sam/*samomu   ostavajas'
       I.nom   everything   saw   self.nom/self.dat   remaining
       nezamečennym].
       unseen.inst

    'I saw everything, myself remaining unseen.'

   b. Ja   staralsja [PRO vse   videt', [sam/*samomu
      I.nom   tried   everything   to-see   self.nom/self.dat
      ostavajas'   nezamečennym]].
      remaining   unseen.inst

   'I tried to see everything, myself remaining unseen.'

   c. Ščel'   v   doskax   dala   mne   vozmožnost' [PRO   vse
      crack   in   boards   gave   me   opportunity   everything
      videt', [*sam/**samomu**   ostavajas'   nezamečennym]]
      to-see   self.nom/self.dat   remaining   unseen.inst

   'The crack in the boards gave me the opportunity to see everything, myself remaining unseen.'

(5) a. Ivan   žil   v   dovol'stve,   [sam/*samomu   ne   trevožas'
       Ivan.nom   lived   in   contentment   self.nom/self.dat   not   troubling
       o   trude   bednyx].
       about   burden   poor.gen

    'Ivan lived in contentment, he himself untroubled by the plight of the poor.'

b. Ivan   xotel   [PRO žit'   v   dovol'stve,   [sam/
   Ivan.nom   wanted   to-live   in   contentment   self.nom/
   *samomu   ne   trevožas'   o   trude   bednyx]].
   self.dat   not   troubling   about   burden   poor.gen

'Ivan wanted to live in contentment, himself untroubled by the plight
of the poor.'

c. [PRO Žit'   v   dovol'stve,   [*sam/samomu   ne   trevožas'
         to-live   in   contentment   self.nom/self.dat not   troubling
   o   trude   bednyx]]—užasno.
   about   burden   poor.gen awful

'To live in contentment, oneself untroubled by the plight of the poor, is
awful.'

Contrastive *sam* agrees with the subject of its clause, as in the (a) examples, or
with the controller of that subject, as in the (b) examples. Babby's generalization
is about the (c) examples, which show that contrastive *samomu* appears only on
gerundive phrases inside infinitival clauses with dative PRO subjects—that is,
nonobligatory control ones. His solution to the problem of why they do not
appear elsewhere is that the PRO subject of infinitives is always dative in Ru, but
under obligatory control there is no PRO, just a bare VP. Although Babby's
account is inspired by Williams (1995), it seems to me to have more in common
with the LFG analysis found in Neidle (1988).

Alternatively, more in keeping with the GB tradition, there could always be
a PRO in infinitival clauses. Then, as I proposed in Franks (1998), PRO will need
to come in a variety of null cases. Good evidence for this comes from Icelandic,
where a floated quantifier can agree in case with what the subject *would be* if it
were overt (in a finite clause), rather than PRO (cf., e.g., Sigurðsson 1991). This
suggests that PRO is always present and necessarily has null case, which is itself
some silent version of an otherwise available full case.

There is considerable other work on additional aspects of agreement in Slavic.
One type of puzzle that has received much attention is that of gender (and number) resolution with conjoined structures. Corbett (1983 and in press) provides
the SC example (6a), in which coordination of a neuter and a feminine noun
results in masculine plural agreement, and the Slvn example (6b) in which coordination of two neuters behaves similarly giving the masculine dual:

(6) a. *Znanje   i   intuicija   su   kod   njega   sarađivali*
       knowledge.n   and   intuition.f aux.3pl   in   him   worked.mpl
       i   dopunjavali   se . . .
       and   supplement.mpl   refl

'Knowledge and intuition have worked together and supplemented each other in him . . . '

b. To   *drevo*   in   *gnezdo*   na   njem   mi   bosta
   that   tree.n   and   nest.n   on   it   me.dat fut.du
   ostala   v   spominu.
   remained.mdu   in   memory

'That tree and the nest on it will remain in my memory.'

In these two languages, at least, although coordination of feminines results in a feminine plural, all other variants lead to masculine plural agreement. See especially Corbett (in press) for further details.

Another interesting phenomenon is so-called nearest conjunct agreement, which Babyonyshev (1996) discusses at length. In this construction, the verb optionally agrees with the closest conjunct, as in Ru (7):

(7) a. Na   stole   stojala   pepel'nica   i   stakan.
        on   table   stood.f   ashtray.f   and   glass.m

     'On the table stood an ashtray and glass.'

     b. Na   stole   stojal   stakan   i   pepel'nica.
        on   table   stood.m   glass.m nad   ashtray.f

     'On the table stood a glass and ashtray.'

As noted by Vassilieva (2001),[14] the following conditions typically hold of nearest conjunct agreement: the verb is unaccusative, there is a PP that begins the sentence, and the verb precedes the conjoined subject. One interesting approach to this problem may involve LF feature lowering, in the spirit of Bošković's (1997a) account of the *there*-construction in English. Essentially, the formal features of the expletive subject (which in Ru is silent) would lower in LF to its associate NP. If the shortest downward move is to the higher, first conjunct, then the agreement facts will follow.

3.2 Genitive of Negation

Two phenomena that have received wide attention concern the use of genitive in quantificational contexts. In this section I discuss the "genitive of negation" (gen-NEG), and in the next the genitive with numerals (gen-NUM). In the canonical gen-NEG construction, sentential negation causes a direct object NP that would ordinarily appear in the accusative to be genitive instead. This is illustrated for Ru in (8a) and for Pol in (8b):

(8) a. My   ne   obnaružili (nikakix)   dokumentov.
        we   neg   found   any.gen   documents.gen

     'We did not find any documents.'

     b. Ewa ne   lubi   piwa.
        Eva neg   likes beer.gen

     'Eva does not like beer.'

The gen-NEG construction has been discussed extensively: some of the most important monograph treatments are Babby (1980) and Brown (1999),[15] and two classic dissertations that examine gen-NEG (along with gen-NUM) are Pesetsky (1982) and Neidle (1988).[16] A large number of articles and sections of book-length studies deal with this subject; for the former, see, for example, Bailyn (1995a) and Brown and Franks (1995), and for the latter, see the appropriate sections of Chvany (1975) and Franks (1995). A somewhat dated but impressively comprehensive bibliography of gen-NEG materials can be found in Corbett (1986).

Two hallmark properties of gen-NEG are the focus of many relevant discussions. First, only those direct objects that would otherwise be accusative can appear in the genitive under negation; obliques (i.e., quirky cased direct objects) remain oblique.[17] Compare Ru (9), in which instrumental case is required, with (8a):

(9) Maša   ne   vladeet   (nikakimi)   inostrannymi jazykami.
     Masha neg   command   any.inst   foreign.inst languages.inst

     'Masha does not have command over any foreign languages.'

This fact is usually explained by assuming that the verb *vladet'* 'to speak, to command' requires that its complement be in the instrumental case in order for the θ-role it assigns to be visible at LF. Second, some intransitive subjects, which would otherwise appear in the nominative, can be genitive under negation. Note that the effect of this is to restrict gen-NEG to *structural* case contexts. Two examples from Babby (1980), which offers an invaluable discussion of this phenomenon in Ru, are given in (10):

(10) a. V   supe   ne   plavalo   nikakogo   mjasa.
        in   soup   neg   floated   any.gen   meat.gen

     'There was no meat (floating) in the soup.'

     b. Dokumentov   ne   obnaružilo   -s'/obnaruženo.
        documents.gen   neg   found   refl-/found.pass

     'No documents were found.'

Note that the genitive "subject" appears in existential contexts and, as (10b) shows, can be a derived subject.[18] The verb shows "default" third-singular neuter agreement. A standard treatment of this, following insights in Pesetsky (1982), is that genitive "subjects" are really *objects* of unaccusative verbs, thus allowing a single gen-NEG rule to apply exclusively to direct objects.[19] Pesetsky argued that these are Quantifier Phrases (QPs), further unifying them with gen-NUM, which contains a null quantifier.

Interestingly, as I discuss in Franks (1995), Pol and Slvn do not exhibit the phenomenon in (10), with the exception of negated 'to be'. Since gen-NEG is obligatory in Pol,[20] unlike Ru, I argue that the gen-NEG rule literally changes the ability of a verb to assign accusative to genitive in that language, essentially transforming it into a quirky-case assigning verb. This has the combined effect of rendering gen-NEG in Pol obligatory and of preventing it from applying to unaccusative objects. In Ru, in contrast, it applies blindly to direct objects in the scope of negation; conceivably, the difference is one of whether it is the case-licensing features of AgrO/AspP or those of V itself that are manipulated in the scope of negation; (see Brown 1999 and references therein for relevant structures in terms of AspP).

One final issue of some cross-linguistic import concerns the ability of the gen-NEG rule to apply to nonargument time and distance phrases, as in Ru (11) or Pol (12), from Franks and Dziwirek (1993):

(11)   General   ne   pravil   stranoj   ni   odnogo   goda.
        general   neg   ruled   country.inst   not-even   one.gen   year.gen

        'The general didn't even rule the country for one year.'

(12)   Nie   spałam   godziny.
        neg   slept   hour.gen

        'I didn't even sleep for an hour.'

Since such adjuncts appear in the accusative in affirmative sentences, it is commonly claimed that this, too, is an instance of gen-NEG but accidentally applies to noncomplement object NPs. However, Franks and Dziwirek argue that the genitive on adjunct phrases is really an instance of the partitive use. Thus, even in Pol the genitive on adjunct phrases can apply when the verb lacks the capacity to check accusative, as in (12), and it is, in fact, not obligatory, so that (13) is also acceptable.

(13)   Nie   spałam   godzinę.
        neg   slept   hour.acc

        'I didn't sleep for an hour.'

They point out that, although (12) and (13) both presuppose that the speaker slept, they are not synonymous: (13) means either that the speaker did sleep, but for more than an hour, or that she slept for some shorter time, whereas (12) can only mean that the speaker slept for less than an hour. Franks and Dziwirek go on to argue that, across Slavic, the potential to assign genitive to adjuncts correlates perfectly with the availability of the partitive function of genitive, rather than with the genitive on complements of negated verbs.

3.3 Numerals

Just as with gen-NEG, there is a veritable industry of work on Slavic numerals. These exhibit highly complex government patterns in various Slavic languages, but the essential fact is that numerals above 'five' typically assign genitive to the nominal material that they quantify. Pesetsky (1982) first drew the attention of generative grammarians to this fascinating phenomenon, followed by a series of publications by Babby, most notably Babby (1987), and Franks, most notably Franks (1994, 1995: chs. 4–5). For those who are able to read Ru, two essential monographs are Mel'čuk (1985) and Suprun (1959). The following are some representative examples, from Ru, SC, Cz, and Pol, respectively:[21]

(14)　a. Pjat'　mašin　　pod"exalo　k　vokzalu.
　　　　　five　cars.gen　drove-up.n　to　station
　　　　　'Five cars drove up to the train station.'

　　　b. Deset　žena　　　je　　　kupilo　　　ovu　haljinu.
　　　　　ten　women.gen　aux.3sg　bought.nsg　this　dress
　　　　　'Ten women bought this dress.'

　　　c. Těch　　pět　hezkých　　dívek　　upeklo　　dort.
　　　　　these.gen　five　beautiful.gen　girls.gen　baked.nsg　cake
　　　　　'These five beautiful girls baked a cake.'

　　　d. Tych　　pięć　kobiet　　poszło　do　domu.
　　　　　these.gen　five　women.gen　went.n　to　home
　　　　　'These five women went home.'

Pesetsky argued that these are Q(uantifier) P(hrases)—that is, nominal expressions headed by the numeral—and he further claimed that, like gen-NEG, they can only be VP-internal, hence the nsg agreement on the examples in (14).[22] However, while gen-NUM indeed arises on direct object NPs, as in Ru (15a), they can also appear on subjects of transitive verbs, as in SC (14b) and Cz (14c), and, in Ru at least, agreement is also a possibility, as in Ru (15b), obligatorily when there is a nominative demonstrative, as in (15c):

(15) a. Maša   kupila   pjat'   čajnikov.
          Masha   bought   five   teapots.gen

      b. Pjat'   mašin   pod"exali   k   vokzalu.[23]
          five   cars.gen   drove-up.pl   to   station

      c. Èti   pjat'   mašin   pod"exali/*pod"exalo   k   vokzalu.
          these.nom   five   cars.gen   drove-up.pl/drove-up.n   to   station

On the basis of these and similar facts, I argued in Franks (1994, 1995) that numeral phrases in Ru can be either QPs, which remain in SpecVP, hence the subject is an expletive, leading to nsg agreement, or DPs, which raise to SpecIP, leading to pl agreement.[24] The structure adopted was roughly as follows:

(16) $[_{DP} D [_{QP} Q [_{AP} A [_{NP} N]]]]$

I further argued that the DP part of the projection was optional in ESl but obligatory elsewhere, since the pl agreement is generally unavailable outside ESl, modulo SC.[25]

A fundamental paradox in the syntax of Slavic numeral phrases is that, when they are embedded in oblique case contexts, all parts of these phrases usually appear in the appropriate oblique case. Gen-NUM thus appears to be overridden by the particular quirky case, as in the following Ru, Cz, and Pol examples:

(17) a. s   pjat'ju   knigami
          with   five.inst   books.inst

      b. s   pěti   pány
          with   five.inst   men.inst

      c. o   tych   pięciu   kobietach
          about   these.loc   five.loc   women.loc

As with gen-NEG, this can be treated in terms of θ-theory. However, in SC there is no such effect, as seen in (18):[26]

(18) sa   pet   djevojaka
        with   five   girls.gen

        'with five girls'

It appears as though, in SC, the genitive assigned by the numeral blocks the inst governed by the preposition from reaching its NP complement. Franks (1994, 1995) thus proposes, working within a case feature system loosely based on that of Jakobson (1938, 1956), that gen-NUM is its own case, which is a structural [−oblique] in Ru and Pol but an inherent [+oblique] in SC. In this way, assuming the traditional GB view that structural cases are assigned at S-structure but inherent ones at D-structure, we are able to account for these and other differences among the languages.[27]

While at first glance Pol and Cz would seem comparable to Ru in the featural status of gen-NUM, Franks (1998, 2002) argues that, in fact, in WSl gen-NUM is restricted exclusively to accusative contexts. Strikingly, alongside (14d), Pol also allows (19), in which the demonstrative *te* is morphologically ambiguous between nominative and accusative:

(19) Te   pięć kobiet   poszło   do   domu.
      these.nom/acc   five women.gen   went.n   to   home
      'These five women went home.'

The fact that, unlike Ru (15c), the verb does not show plural agreement leads to the conclusion that *te* in Pol (19) is in fact accusative, not nominative, and to the proposal that gen-NUM can only appear in accusative contexts in WSl. If this is correct, an interesting pattern emerges, which Franks (2002) characterizes in terms of the relative markedness of the case features of the DP in which a QP can occur across Slavic.[28]

3.4 Argument Structure and Voice

In this section, I briefly consider some of the most salient issues relating to the general problem of how arguments are realized in the Slavic clause. Voice and diathesis have been a traditional topic of analysis, and their study has continued also in the generative arena. The two primary voice-altering morphemes encountered in Slavic are the "reflexive" morpheme, which in all languages except (most of) ESl is a clitic, such as Ru -*sja* (and SC, Slvn, Bg, Mac, Cz, LSor *se*; Pol *się*; Slk *sa*; and USor *so*)[29] and the "passive" participial morpheme, which is a verbal suffix with variants in -*n*- and -*t*-. For an overview of voice in Slavic, see Siewierska (1988), as well as Franks (1995: ch. 8) and references therein. For informed discussion of the morphological status of -*sja* in Ru, see Schoorlemmer (1996) and Junghanns (1996), the latter containing a very useful comparison with other Slavic languages. An excellent overview of Slavic voice possibilities can also be found in Růžička (1986, 1988), and Billings and Maling (1995) offers a comprehensive annotated bibliography of the *-no/-to* construction (see later).[30] For early generative treatments of voice in Ru, see Babby (1975a), Chvany (1975), or Babby and Brecht (1975), and for a more recent proposal about how argument structure is mapped onto syntactic structure in Ru and Ukr, see Babby (1989, 1993).

Standard reflexive passive examples are comparable to English, with promotion of the accusative argument to subject position, as in Ru (20):[31]

(20)   a. Ivan   prodaet   knigi.
          nom   sells.3sg   books.acc
          'Ivan sells books.'

       b. *e   Prodaet   -sja   knigi.
               sell.3sg   refl-   books.acc

       c. Knigi   prodajut   -sja.
          books.nom   sell.3pl   -refl
          'Books are being sold / are selling.'

Note that Ru (20c) has either passive or middle interpretation. In Pol (21), however, we see the two voices diverge, so that promotion obtains only in the middle (21c); in true passive (21b), the direct object remains accusative:[32]

(21)   a. Jan   sprzedaje   książki.
          nom   sells.3sg   books.acc
          'Jan sells books.'

       b. *e* Sprzedaje   się   książki.
              sells.3sg   refl   books.acc
          'Books are being sold.'

       c. Książki   się   sprzedają.
          books.nom   refl   sell.3pl
          'Books are selling.'

This "passive + accusative" construction appears in a variety of Slavic languages, with both the reflexive and participial morpheme. In Ukr, for example, as Sobin (1985) points out, the *-no/-to* construction allows both retention of the accusative object (22a) and promotion to nominative (22b), with no apparent difference in meaning:[33]

(22)   a. Z   Vinnyci   pryslano   vistku   sestryceju.
          from   Vinnycja brought.n   news.acc   sister.inst
          'News was brought from Vinnycja by the sister.'

b. Cerkva   bula   zbudovana   robitnykamy.
   church.fnom   aux.f built.f   workers.inst

'The church was built by the workers.'

In Franks (1995), I analyze this in terms of variation in what case(s) the "passive" morphology can absorb—that is, as a lexical fact. See also Lavine (2000) for an in-depth treatment of the Pol and Ukr -no/-to constructions, which he demonstrates have sufficiently different properties to reject the simple "case absorption" type of account.

One curious and very robust construction in Slavic that involves the -sja morpheme is the "dispositional" reflexive. Some examples from Franks (1995: sec. 8.4) follow; see also especially Růžička (1988), who notes that it is found in all the Slavic languages:

(23) a. Mne   ne   rabotaet -sja.
     me.dat neg   work   -refl

'I don't feel like working.'

b. Sestře   se   tam   pracuje   výborně.
   sister.dat refl there work.3sg excellently

'(My) sister is working excellently there.'

c. Plače   mi   se.
   cry.3sg me.dat refl

'I feel like crying.'

d. Ne   radi   mi   se   danas.
   neg work.3sg me.dat refl today

'I don't feel like working today.'

Ru (23a), Cz (23b), Bg (23c), and SC (23d) all seem to behave identically: the experiencer "subject" is expressed in the dative, the verb is third-person singular neuter, and the "reflexive" morpheme is introduced.

Observe, however, that the base verbs in all these examples are intransitive, so that it makes little sense to say accusative is "absorbed." Interestingly, most languages, but not Ru, extend the dispositional construction to transitives as well, so that there is an overt derived subject. Compare ungrammatical Ru (24) with its perfectly acceptable SC counterpart in (25):

(24) *Èta   kniga   mne   ne   čitaet -sja.
     this.nom book.nom me.dat neg read.3sg -refl

(25) Ova   knjiga   mi   se   ne   čita.
      this.nom   book.nom   me.dat refl neg   read.3sg
      'I don't feel like reading this book.'

Expressing a dative experiencer with reflexive middles is similarly possible, as in
Cz (26a) or Pol (26b):

(26) a. Matematika   se   mi   studuje   lehce.
         math.nom   refl me.dat   study.3sg   easily
         'Math studies easily for me.'

      b. Ten   artykuł   nie   pisze   mi   się   dobrze.[34]
         this.nom   article.nom neg   write.3sg   me.dat refl well
         'I just can't write this article well.'

The generalization in Franks (1995) is that Ru allows no internal arguments in
this kind of construction, regardless of case. Thus, neither variation in (27) is
felicitous:

(27) a. *Mne   ne   čitaet   -sja   ni   odnoj   knigi.
          me.dat neg   read.3sg   -refl not   one.gen   book.gen

      b. *Mne   ne   rabotaet   -sja   nad   ètoj   zadačej.
          me.dat neg   work   -refl on   this   problem

     I turn now to the question of null subjects. The Slavic languages exhibit
various types of null subject effects. They all allow expletive null subjects,[35] which
is one reason the dispositional reflexive construction is so pervasive. However,
they vary considerably in the degree to which they tolerate argument (θ-marked)
null subjects. In brief, while they all allow unexpressed pronominal subjects, the
ESl languages are not true null subject languages, whereas the others are, although
under varying conditions; see Franks (1995: ch. 7) for examples and discussion.
The capacity to identify null subjects in Slavic seems to correlate with two other
properties: (i) the language must have full agreement, in the sense that there is
an overt copula in the present tense and that past tense verbs mark person and
number, and (ii) there must be a system of pronominal and verbal auxiliary clitics
(see section 3.5). Compare, for example, Ru (28) with Pol (29):

(28) a. Ja/*e   poexal   v   gorod.
         I.nom   went.m   to   town

      b. Ja student.
         'I am a student.'

(29) a. Ja/*e*   pojechał-em   do   miasta.
         I.nom   went.m-1sg   to   town

     b. Ja/*e*   jest-em   studentem.
         be-1sg   student.inst

Admittedly, the subject can be elided even in Ru, but so can other arguments, as long as they are recoverable from the discourse.[36] However, whereas including an unemphatic pronominal subject is generally stylistically marked in the other languages, this is not true of Ru. Moreover, when one applies null subject diagnostics, such as the ability of overt pronominals to function as bound-variables, the classification is confirmed. Whereas Ru (30a) can admit the bound-variable reading despite the presence of overt *on* 'he', otherwise identical SC (30b) or Cz (30c) cannot:[37]

(30) a. Každyj student dumaet, čto *on* polučit pjaterku.

       'Every student thinks that he will get an A.'

     b. Svaki student misli da će *on* dobiti desetku.

     c. Každý student myslí, že *on* dostane jedničku.

In the SC and Cz examples, overt *on* can only have a deictic interpretation. The bound variable reading thus only obtains in these languages when the subject is phonologically null.[38]

3.5 Clitics

There is a vast literature on Slavic clitics. The most comprehensive survey with extensive references can be found in Franks and King (2000); another very important work is Bošković (2001).[39] While all the Slavic languages have clitics, ESl (with the exception of southwestern Ukr dialects) has only simple clitics, to mark things like emphasis, modality, or interrogativity; ESl has lost the rich paradigmatic systems for pronouns and verbal auxiliaries found in the SSl and WSl languages. The following are some representative sentences, with the clitics in italics, from SSl SC, Slvn, Bg, and Mac in (31) and WSl Cz and Pol in (32), respectively:

(31) a. Da *li*   *ste*   *mi*   *ih*   danas   kupili?
        C   Q   aux.2pl   me.dat   them.acc   today   bought

      'Did you buy me them today?'

     b. Janez *mu*   *ga*   *je*   še   dal.
        Janez him.dat it.acc aux.3sg still gave

        'Janez still gave it to him.'

     c. Ti   *si*   *mu*   *gi*   pokazvala.
        you aux.2sg him.dat them.acc shown.fem

        'You have shown them to him.'

     d. *Mi*   *go*   dade Vera včera.
        me.dat it.acc gave Vera yesterday

        'Vera gave me it yesterday.'

(32)   a. Představila *jsem*   *mu*   *tě*   včera.
        introduced aux.1sg him.dat you.acc yesterday

        'I introduced you to him yesterday.'

     b. Piotrek *mi*   *je*   dał.
        Peter   me.dat them.acc gave

        'Peter gave me them.'

As these examples illustrate, there are essentially two patterns for where the cluster goes: second position, as in SC, Slvn, Cz (and Slvk), or verb-adjacent, as in Bg and Mac. (Pol, as discussed later, is neither.) The clitics must appear in a fixed order, according to a template that varies little across the languages: interrogative *li* precedes auxiliary clitics (usually with the exception of third-person singular *(j)e* in SSl, and the future auxiliary *biti* 'to be' in Slvn), which precedes dative clitics, which, in turn, precede accusative clitics, with third-person singular *(j)e* (and the Slvn future clitics) coming last.

There are, however, some divergences from these patterns worth noting. First, with regard to the clitic cluster, whereas most languages disallow initial clitics, a comparison of Bg (31c) and Mac (31d) reveals an interesting difference: clitics invariably precede the verb in Mac, whereas in Bg they do *unless* this would put them in absolute initial position.[40] Verb-adjacent clitics are thus fundamentally preverbal, although there must be some mechanism to retreat from this to avoid being absolutely initial. Contrary to the common assumption—as for example, in Franks and Bošković (2001)—the prohibition against absolute initial status in Bg does not seem to be phonological, since they can immediately follow an intonational phrase boundary.

Second-position clitics similarly cannot be initial in SC. While this might strike one as following from the fact that they are required to appear in "second" position, the fact that they can appear in initial position in Slvn (and Colloquial Cz) reveals that in this case it is a matter of phonology. Apparently, they can be either enclitic or proclitic in Slvn, but only enclitic in SC; otherwise, the syntax of clitics is essentially the same in the two languages. Thus, if the syntax leaves them after a intonational break (indicated by "#"), in Slvn they cause no problem at the interface with phonology, whereas in SC they cannot be pronounced in this position. Compare SC (33) with otherwise identical Slvn (34):

(33) #Ja#, #tvoja mama#, #obećala *sam*   *ti*   igračku#.
      I   your   mother promised aux.1sg you.dat   toy

'I, your mother, promised you a toy.'

(34) Jaz#, #tvoja mama#, *sem ti* obljubila igračko.

Various approaches to this sort of problem exist in the literature; for a survey, see Franks and King (2000). One popular view, extending work due to Halpern (1995), involves the PF restructuring mechanism of "Prosodic Inversion," whereby a syntactically initial clitic hops to its right in order to meet prosodic exigencies. Alternatively, as suggested in Franks and King and extended in Franks (2000), second-position clitics are functional heads that move to the highest functional head position in the clause; if there is a host available to their left, then they are pronounced there, but if not (in SC, but not Slvn), then the next copy down is pronounced. In this way, prosodic requirements are imposed at the interface with the phonology to police the actual phonological realization of clitics, although they move as *syntactic* entities; see Franks (2000) for details.[41]

Bošković (2000) and Franks and Bošković (2001) adapt this approach to certain puzzles presented by verb-adjacent clitics in Bg, also treated in Franks (2000) and Franks and King (2000). Curiously (and unlike in SC), even *i* 'and' can support the clitics in Bg;[42] compare (35) with the ungrammatical (36a), which must surface as (36b) instead:[43]

(35) I   *mi*   *go*   dade Vera včera.
      and   me.dat   it.acc gave Vera yesterday

'And Vera gave it to me yesterday.'

(36) a. *Mi go* dade Vera včera.

      b. Dade *mi go* Vera včera.

The relevant structures are as follows, with unpronounced copies stricken through:

(35)' I [~IP~ *mi go* dade ~~mi go dade~~ Vera včera]

(36)' [~~IP~~ ~~mi go~~ dade *mi go* ~~dade~~ Vera včera]

When the Yes/No interrogative clitic *li* is included (in C°), Franks and Bošković propose the following derivation:

(37) [~~CP~~ [~~C~~ [~~mi go~~ dade] + li] *mi go* ~~dade~~ Vera včera]

Interestingly, addition of *i* 'and' here has no effect; the correct order in Bg is (38):

(38) I   dade <u>li</u>   ti   go?
      and   gave Q   you.dat   it.acc
      'And did she/he give it to you?'

This fact implies that linearization only makes use of very local information—in particular, that *linearization applies cyclically*, in conformity with the recent "Multiple Spell-Out" proposal that the mapping to PF (and, in a parallel fashion, to LF) only takes place at specific junctures in the derivation.

I turn, finally, to two additional divergences from the patterns noted here. The reflexive clitic *se*, which is historically accusative, exhibits somewhat idiosyncratic behavior. Whereas in SC it goes last in the sequence, so that it appears to resemble other accusative clitics, in Cz it *precedes* the dative clitic. Compare (39) with (32a):

(39) Představila *jsem*   <u>*se*</u>   *mu*   včera.
      introduced   aux.1sg   self.acc   him.dat   yesterday
      'I introduced myself to him yesterday.'

It thus seems that the reflexive clitic needs to be treated as a different kind of functional head than the other pronominal clitics.

Lastly, the clitic system of Pol is strikingly distinct from that of the other languages. Clitics in this language do not need to cluster together, as illustrated by the following examples:

(40) a. Dlaczego *ją*   kupiła   -*ś*?
         why   it.acc   bought   -aux.2sg
         'Why did you buy it?'

      b. Kiedy -*śmy*   *go*   wreszcze   *mu*   odebrali, ...
         when   -aux.1pl it.acc   at-last   him.dat   took-away
         When we at last took it away from him, ... '

In addition, word-order requirements are not absolutely respected: in (40b) we see the accusative clitic *go* preceding the dative *mu*. Another example of this can be constructed on the basis of the fact that, as in many languages including even English, first- or second-person clitic or atonic pronouns cannot follow third-person ones. Thus, instead of saying the extremely awkward (41a), (41b) is produced instead:

(41) a. ??Pokazali *mu*   *cię*   wczoraj.
          showed   him.dat you.acc yesterday.

          ??'I showed him you yesterday.'

    b. Pokazali *cię mu* wczoraj.

This problem cannot be circumvented in the same way in the other Slavic languages, where the "dative precedes accusative" restriction is inviolate. Franks and King (2000) and Franks (in press) thus contend that the pronominal clitics in Pol are actually XPs, not heads.[44]

3.6 *Wh*-movement

Wh-movement in the Slavic languages is another classic problem in the generative literature. Since most studies have focused on the phenomenon of multiple *wh*-movement, that is what I treat in this section.

    Although a variety of earlier papers and dissertations considered the problem to some extent, it was the publication of Rudin (1988) that launched Slavic multiple *wh*-movement as a research area. Rudin pointed out that, unlike English, the Slavic languages require all *wh*-words in a sentence to be fronted. Some simple examples from Bg, SC, and Pol follow, respectively:

(42) a. *Koj*   *kogo*   vižda?
        who   whom   sees

    b. *Ko*   *koga*   vidi?
        who   whom   sees

    c. *Kto*   *co*   robił?
        who   what   did

Rudin argued, however, that beneath this superficial uniformity lay two distinct language types: in Bg (and Romanian) all *wh*-phrases behave as a unit, whereas in the other Slavic languages the first *wh*-phrase is in a privileged position, SpecCP, and the remaining ones are slightly lower in the phrase structure. She argued for this on the basis of a variety of diagnostics, including the fact that in Bg the *wh*-phrases undergo long-distance movement as a unit, cannot be separated by parentheticals or clitics (although this fact has an alternative explanation—namely, that clitics are verb-adjacent in Bg), do not induce island effects, and have a fixed relative order, while none of these properties hold for the other languages. Some of her examples are as follows, where Bg (43) contrasts with SC (44) and Pol (45):

(43) a. *Koj kâde misliš [če e otišâl]?*
   who where think.2sg that aux.3sg gone

   'Who do you think has gone where?'
   (**Koj misliš če e otišâl kâde?*)

   b. *Zavisi ot tova, koj kogo prâv e udaril.*
   depends on this who whom first aux.3sg hit

   'It depends on who hit whom first.'
   (**Zavisi ot tova, koj prâv kogo e udaril.*)

   c. **Kogo koj vižda?*
   who whom sees

(44) a. *Ko šta želite [da vam kupi]?*
   who what want.2pl that you buys

   'Who do you want to buy you what?'
   (*Ko želite da šta vam kupi?*)

   b. *Ko je prvi koga udario?*
   who aux.3sg first whom hit

   'Who hit whom first?'

   c. *Što je ko kome dao?*
   what aux.3sg who whom gave

   'What did who give to whom?'

(45) a. **Co komu Maria chce [żeby Janek kupił]?*
   who whom Maria wants that Janek bought

   'What does Maria want Janek to buy for whom?'

   b. *Kto według ciebie komu co dał?*
   who according you whom what gave

   'Who according to you gave what to whom?'

   c. *Co ko robił?*
   what who did

Indeed, in an example such as SC (44c), all relative orders of *wh*-words are possible. Rudin's account of subject-object asymmetries in Bg was based on the ECP (which at the time similarly served to rule out English *What did who say?*) and required considerable machinery to allow the other languages to avoid its effects. Currently, with this phenomenon more generally understood instead in terms of Superiority, the variation identified by Rudin becomes considerably more intractable.

In a series of articles, most notably Bošković (1997b, 1997c, 1998, 2000, in press), Bošković refined Rudin's data to show that this last point, the claim that SC *wh*-movement does not show Superiority effects while Bg does, is technically incorrect, and that in fact two different forces drive *wh*-fronting, in both types of language.[45] According to the analysis in Bošković (1998, in press) and Stjepanović (1999a), the relevant factors are not only the familiar need to check WH features but also the need to check FOCUS features. It is FOCUS that forces overt fronting of all *wh*-phrases in Slavic (although not in English).

As Bošković (1999) demonstrates, the complex patterns described in the literature can be made to follow from the interplay between these two types of feature. His most striking observation is that the Superiority effect exhibited in Bg (42a) versus (43c) disappears when the highest *wh*-phrase is not involved. Consider the paradigm in (46) and (47):

(46) a. *Kogo   kak   e   celunal Ivan?*
         whom   how   aux.3sg kissed   Ivan
         'How did Ivan kiss whom?'

     b. ?**Kak kogo* e celunal Ivan?*

(47) a. *Koj   kogo   kak   e   celunal?*
         who   whom   how   aux.3sg kissed
         'Who kissed whom how?'

     b. *Koj kak kogo e celunal?*

The contrast in (46) shows that the direct object *kogo* 'whom' is higher than the adverb *kak* 'how', so that Attract will apply to force the highest *wh*-phrase to move first.[46] In (47), however, we see that this concern is irrelevant. Bošković argues that this is because only the first *wh*-phrase moves to check WH features, whereas the second and third move to check FOCUS features. Clearly, WH feature checking and FOCUS feature checking must be subject to different requirements. In Bošković (1998), this is handled by assuming both Attract and Move, and making the WH feature on C° strong, hence subject to Attract, but the FOCUS features on the *wh*-phrases themselves strong, hence subject to Move. Bošković

(1999) eschews Move and argues that WH involves standard Attract, whereas FOCUS in these languages invokes an "Attract All" option. Under either scenario, FOCUS movement, but not WH movement, equally satisfies Shortest Move, regardless of the order in which the various *wh*-phrases are fronted.

In SC, in contrast, Superiority effects, although absent in main clause short-distance questions, reemerge in long-distance questions, embedded questions, and root questions with lexical complementizers. Here is an example of the latter, drawn from Bošković (in press), which should be compared to (49):[47]

(48) a. *Ko* li   *šta*   kupuje?
         who Q   what   buys

         'Who on earth buys what?'

      b. **Šta* li *ko* kupuje?

(49) a. *Ko*   *šta*   kupuje?
         who   what   buys

         'Who buys what?'

      b. *Šta ko* kupuje?

Pursuing this framework, Bošković (1997a) argues that clauses need not project up to CP. Any absence of Superiority effects, as in (49b), is thus due to the failure to project a CP in the syntax—hence, overt movement is driven by FOCUS rather than WH features. Since Bošković makes the standard assumption that the clitic *li* (which in *wh*-questions is a marker of emphasis, rather than Yes/No interrogation, as in, e.g., (31a)), is necessarily a C°, the presence of WH features, which are on C, forces Attract WH to target the highest/closest *wh*-phrase in (48).[48]

4 FUTURE DIRECTIONS

In this final section, I note several classic topics which, I feel, have either been neglected or remain poorly understood within the formalist literature. While I draw particular attention here only to the areas of binding, aspect, and word order, there are clearly many more empirical domains in need of closer investigation.[49]

4.1 Binding

Slavic anaphora add significantly to our understanding of the cross-linguistic diversity of binding possibilities. Timberlake (1979) first drew attention to a range of the problems posed by Ru for the classic cyclic transformation account of reflexivization. Rappaport (1986) subsequently treated the Ru binding facts from the perspective of the account in Chomsky (1981), essentially pointing out differences between Russian and English. Among the facts he observed is that, in certain cases, Ru allows for "long-distance" binding. The reflexive personal pronoun *sebja* and possessive *svoj* can be bound out of infinitival complement clauses (i.e., over a PRO subject) and out of a "specified" NP (i.e., over the SUBJECT of an NP), although they cannot be free within a finite (i.e., tensed) clause, as illustrated in (50):[50]

(50) a. *On* ne razrešaet mne [PRO proizvodit' opyty nad
          he not allow me   to-perform experiments on
          soboj].
          self.inst

          'He does not allow me to perform experiments on himself/myself.'

   b. *Ja* čital [*ego* stat'ju o *svoej* rabote].
       I read   his article about self's work

       'I read his article about my/his work.'

   c. Maša znaet, [čto *Boris* ljubit *svoju* sestru].
      Masha knows that Boris loves self's sister

      'Masha knows that Boris loves his/*her sister.'

They thus must find their antecedents within the domain of tense rather than, as in English, the domain of a SUBJECT.

While many languages display comparable anaphora, the Slavic facts serve to corroborate a set of more general correspondences, which I briefly enumerate. For one thing, long-distance anaphora are subject-oriented, whereas local ones are not. Thus, while (50a, b) are ambiguous, (51) is not:

(51) *Milicioner* rassprašival prostitutku o *sebe*.
       policeman.nom questioned prostitute.acc about self.loc

       'The policeman questioned the prostitute about himself/*herself.'

The Ru reflexives thus differ from the English *himself* series in both respects.

This correspondence has been examined for Slavic and more broadly in Progovac (1992, 1993), Progovac and Franks (1992), and related articles. Inspired in part by the Ru data, Progovac puts forward a theory in which domain and orientation of binding depend on the morphological status of the particular anaphor, so that Ru *sebja/svoj* are heads and sensitive to Agr°, whereas English *himself* is a phrase and sensitive to a SUBJECT XP. This approach is important because it localizes variation in the lexicon rather than in parameters that pervade the grammar. Consequently, different anaphora in the same language are expected to display different properties, and this is indeed borne out. For example, the reciprocal pronoun *drug druga* in Ru is local and not subject oriented, just like its English counterpart. This reciprocal is clearly phrasal; indeed, reciprocals are arguably universally so, explaining why they are never long distance anaphora.

Interestingly, even reciprocals that are superficially simple heads behave as if they were phrasal (in Progovac's system). In Pol the "reflexive" pronoun *siebie* can also function as a reciprocal. As a reflexive, it is long distance and subject-oriented, roughly as in the Ru examples just cited, but as a reciprocal it behaves as a strictly local anaphor only. Consider the following Pol sentence, from Reinders-Machowska (1991):

(52) *Chłopcy*   czytali   [*dziewcząt*   wspomnienia   o   *sobie*].
      boys.nom   read   girls.gen   memories   about   self/each other

'The boys read the girls' memories about themselves.' (*girls* or *boys*)
'The boys read the girls' memories about each other.' (*girls* only)

The reason for this is presumably that reciprocals are invariably phrasal at LF, since they necessarily consist of two parts, a "reciprocator" and a "distributor," following Heim et al. (1991). Although the fact that reciprocals are semantically complex may not be reflected in the morphology, since interpretative principles such as binding apply at LF rather than PF, they behave as if phrasal nonetheless. This account makes a variety of predictions that are yet to be fully investigated for Slavic, and there are some potentially problematic data. One set of issues concerns the extent to which binding domains are nested. According to Toman (1991), Cz reflexives, although otherwise similar to Pol, cannot be bound out of an infinitival clause, even though they can be out of a possessed NP. (SC may be similar, although it is difficult to tell in dialects that eschew infinitives.)

Bg presents another set of problems. The question of binding out of infinitives cannot be resolved, since Bg lacks them entirely. More curious is the fact that reflexives in this language are morphologically complex, as in (53), where the second, *si*, part is a (historically) dative possessive clitic:

(53) a. *Ivan*   popita   Penčo   za   *sebe*   *si*.
         Ivan   asked   Pencho   about   self   self

      'Ivan asked Pencho about himself.' (*Ivan only*)

b. *Ivan* popita Penčo za *nego si.*
   Ivan asked Pencho about him self

'Ivan asked Pencho about himself.' (*Ivan* or *Pencho*)

The morphological structure, however, turns out not to be relevant for binding, supporting the claim that this is an LF matter. That is, (53) is just as simple at LF as its Ru counterpart with *sebja* would be; it is just that in the morphological component, fission of its features into two distinct lexical pieces takes place, so that it becomes morphologically phrasal. Strikingly, the colloquial form *nego si* in (53b), which differs from *sebe si* in (53a) in that it bears pronominal features, seems to look and work just like English *himself*, consistent with the assumption that it must be phrasal at LF as well. Clearly, binding in Slavic is a complex and underexplored area. Although comparable data are surely to be found elsewhere, Slavic presents an especially rich and typologically compact array of problems in anaphora, problems with which any theory of variation will need to contend.

4.2 Aspect

Aspect is a classic and pervasive problem in Slavic morphosyntax. Research on Slavic aspect is vast; the data are extremely complex, and the systems in the various languages diverse.[51] The category of aspect is overarching, permeating other subsystems—most importantly, tense, but in addition case, voice, and mood; aspect also interacts in important ways with phenomena such as transitivity and, broadly construed, quantificational categories of negation and partitivity.

Many scholars have produced valuable research on Slavic aspect.[52] A selection of useful resources includes Forsyth (1970) for a survey of Ru data, the articles in Flier and Timberlake (1985) for varying viewpoints, and Durst-Andersen (1992) for a particular account of Ru aspect.[53] Recent work on aspect in other Slavic languages includes Filip (1996) for Cz, Piñón (1997) for Pol, and Fielder (1993) for Bg. If one reads French, a classic work for Ru is Guiraud-Weber (1988), and an important volume on Bg is Guentchéva (1990); there is also a large literature on Slavic aspect written in German (in addition, of course, to Ru, Polish, and other Slavic languages).

Given the complexity and vastness of the data, in this chapter I shall not even attempt to survey them. I merely present several well-known sets of facts from Ru.

First, whereas the conjugated imperfective in (54a) has present-tense meaning, the conjugated perfective in (54b) has a future meaning (and the imperfective future is periphrastic, as in (54c)).[54]

(54) a. Ivan pišet   pis'mo.
         Ivan writes.impf   letter

      'Ivan is writing a letter.'

      b. Ivan napišet   pis'mo.
         Ivan writes.perf   letter

      'Ivan will write [and finish] a letter.'

      c. Ivan budet   pisat'   pis'mo.
         Ivan will   write.inf   letter

      'Ivan will write [be writing] a letter.'

Whereas (54c) focuses on the action itself, (54b) additionally implies its completion.[55]

A second often noted fact concerns the use of the imperfective to negate the consequences of an action, as in the textbook example (55b):

(55) a. Kto   otkryl   okno?
         who   opened.perf   window

      'Who opened the window?'

      b. Kto   otkryval   okno?
         who   opened.impf   window

      'Who had opened the window [which is now closed]?'

A third contrast that emphasizes the distinction between process and completion is the use of the imperfective, with appropriate verbs, to indicate an attempt to achieve the successful conclusion implied by the verb's perfective counterpart.[56] Some aspectual pairs that display this, drawn from Townsend (1970: 54–55), are cited in (56):

(56) a. rešat' 'try to solve, work on'   rešit' 'solve'

      b. ugovarivat' 'try to convince, persuade'   ugovorit' 'convince'

      c. dokazyvat' 'try to prove, point out'   dokazat' 'prove'

      d. otyskivat' 'try to find, look for'   otyskat' 'find'

      e. učit'sja 'try to learn, study'   naučit'sja 'learn'

An illustration of the interaction between aspect and case can be found in its effect on licensing of the partitive.[57] Compare (57a), which involves a perfective verb and allows either accusative or partitive object, with imperfective (57b), which only allows the accusative:[58]

(57) a. Ivan   vypil   čaj/čaju.
          Ivan   drank.perf   tea.acc/tea.part

      'Ivan drank [up] the tea/some tea.'

      b. Ivan   pil   čaj/*čaju.
          Ivan   drank.impf   tea.acc/tea.part

      'Ivan was drinking tea.'

More generally, perfective aspect is intimately associated with transitivity, as a comparison of (58a) with (58b) reveals:[59]

(58) a. *Včera   Saša   napisal.
          yesterday Sasha   wrote.perf

      'Yesterday, Sasha wrote [and finished].'

      b. Včera   Saša   pisal.
          yesterday Sasha   wrote.impf

      'Yesterday, Sasha was writing/wrote.'

This fact has led some scholars to propose a formal relationship between aspect checking (on the verb) and case licensing (on its complement), in that the same functional category, AspP, is implicated in both operations; see, for example, Yadroff (1996).

4.3 Word Order

The final topic I wish to mention in this overview is even broader than aspect and has at least as rich a tradition of description and analysis. This is the problem of "free" word order in the Slavic languages, which Bailyn (2000) rightly characterizes as "the primary overlapping issue of interest for both syntactic theory and Slavic syntax for the foreseeable future." While (as we saw in sections 3.5 and 3.6) elements such as clitics and *wh*-phrases are quite restricted in distribution, most words in most Slavic languages can appear in a variety of relative orders, depending on complex stylistic, register, and information structure considerations.[60] These varied orders, often characterized as "scrambling" in the generative literature, are traditionally taken to reflect considerations of "functional sentence perspective" such as theme versus rheme, old versus new information, focus versus presupposition, and figure versus ground.

There are many classics on word order in Ru which are written in Ru; the two best known are probably Adamec (1966) and Kovtunova (1976). A good textbook source of data which is written in English (although the Ru examples are all in Cyrillic, untranslated) is Krylova and Khavronina (1976). A long history of research on word order and related topics in Slavic has emanated from the Prague school; some useful references are Firbas (1964), Hajičová (1993), Mathesius (1964), Sgall (1972), and Sgall et al. (1986). Yokoyama (1986) is also a very important work, which any linguist studying Ru word order should consult. Recently, several dissertations have dealt at least in part with scrambling in Ru. These include Bailyn (1995b), Borovikoff (2001), Hoffman (1996), King (1995), and Sekerina (1997), the last presenting experimental research on the processing of scrambled sentences; for SC, two new dissertations that treat scrambling are Stjepanović (1999a) and Godjevac (2000). In addition, numerous articles about word order in Slavic have been published.[61] Here I note only a few: Bailyn (1995c, 2001, in press), Borsley and Rivero (1994), Junghanns and Zybatow (1995), Robblee (1994), Sekerina (1999), and Stjepanović (1999b).

Word order interacts also with intonation in complex ways. Consider the following examples, from Borovikoff (2001):

(59)   a.   Učeniki   prinesli   cvety.
            pupils.nom   brought   flowers.acc
            'The students have brought flowers.'

       b.   Cvety   prinesli   učeniki.
            flowers.acc brought   pupils.nom
            'Students brought the flowers.'

       c.   CVETY   učeniki   prinesli.
            flowers.acc pupils.nom brought
            'It was flowers that the students have brought.'

       d.   UČENIKI   prinesli   cvety.
            pupils.nom   brought   flowers.acc
            'It was students who brought the flowers.'

       e.   Učeniki   PRINESLI   cvety.
            pupils.nom   brought   flowers.acc
            'The students have (already) brought flowers.'

She characterizes the final NP as a focus in examples (59a, b) and, in (59b), regards the fronting of the direct object as topicalization. In these two examples, definiteness is expressed through word order, with the old information topic initial and indefinite, the new information focus final and definite.[62] In (59c–e), in which the focused element is not final, it must receive a special intonation.

Here are a few typical examples of scrambled word orders in Pol. Within simple sentences, Swan (2001) provides examples such as the following, again with the last NP being the focus:[63]

(60) a. Pan   rzucił   psu   piłkę.
         man.nom   threw   dog.dat   ball.acc

      'The man threw the dog a BALL.'

      b. Piłkę   rzucił   pan   psu.
         ball.acc   threw   man.nom   dog.dat

      'The ball was thrown by the man TO THE DOG.'

      c. Psu   rzucił   piłkę   pan.
         dog.dat   threw   ball.acc   man.nom

      'To the dog a ball was thrown BY THE MAN.'

He notes that these answer the questions in (61), respectively:

(61)   a. WHAT did the man throw to the dog?

       b. To WHOM did the man throw the ball?

       c. WHO threw the ball to the dog?

Other types of scrambling are possible. For example, adjectives can be separated from the nouns they modify, as in the variants of (62a) offered by Borovikoff (2001):[64]

(62) a. Ja   čital   včera   [NP [AP interesnuju]   stat'ju].
         I.nom   read   yesterday   interesting.acc   article.acc

      'I read an interesting article yesterday.'

      b. *Interesnuju$_i$ ja čital včera [NP [t_i] stat'ju].

      c. Ja *interesnuju$_i$ čital včera [NP [t_i] stat'ju].

      d. Ja čital *interesnuju$_i$ včera [NP [t_i] stat'ju].

      e. ??Ja čital včera [NP [t_i] stat'ju] [FOC *interesnuju$_i$].

She comments that "the AP *interesnuju* 'interesting' can be scrambled out of the NP anywhere in the sentence," which she proposes to be left-adjunction, although it is severely degraded if it moves rightward, even when marked by a contrastive focus intonation, as in (62e).

In general, left-branch condition violations are acceptable in Slavic, as shown by Pol (63) and (64); note that pied-piping is also possible in these examples:[65]

(63) a. Jaką   czytasz   książkę?
       what-kind.acc read.2sg book.acc
       'What kind of book are you reading?'

   b. Kogo   czytasz   książkę?
      who.gen   read.2sg book.acc
      'Whose book are you reading?'

   c. Czyją   czytasz   książkę?
      whose.acc   read.2sg book.acc
      'Whose book are you reading?'

(64) a. Bardzo ciekawą   czytam   książkę.
       very   interesting.acc read.1sg book.acc
       'I am reading a very interesting book.'

   b. Ewy   czytam   książkę.
      Eve.gen read.1sg book.acc
      'I am reading Eve's book.'

   c. Swoją   czytam   książkę.
      self's.acc read.1sg book.acc
      'I am reading my (own) book.'

The availability of left-branch extraction seems to correlate with the absence of a determiner, so that questions such as (63a, c) are possible in all Slavic languages except Bg and Mac, these being the only two with explicit determiners.[66] Interestingly, (63b)—as well as its response (64b)—are impossible in, for example, Ru, where the adnominal genitive is clearly a right-branch rather than left-branch element (cf. Ru *kniga moego brata* '(the) book (of) my brother' but **moego brata kniga* vs. Pol *książka mojego brata* or *mojego brata książka*'), although the counterparts of (63c and 64c) are perfectly fine, these involving extraction of adjectives rather than complement NPs.

Finally, any work on word order in Slavic will need to explore the complexities associated with long-distance scrambling. As is the case in other scrambling languages, the data are sometimes murky. There have been conflicting claims about such matters as which adjunction sites are possible, what phrases are islands for extraction, and the extent to which scrambling exhibits the hallmarks of A- versus

A'-movement. Of the major languages, Ru probably exhibits the freest range of scrambling possibilities, Pol comes next, then SC, with Cz more restricted, and Bg the most.[67] As with many of the other problems encountered in this survey of Slavic syntax, scrambling is a vast topic, ripe for methodical investigation.

NOTES

I am grateful to Karen Baertsch, Wayles Browne, and Guglielmo Cinque for suggestions on improving the manuscript.

1. For some of the most influential early generative work on Slavic syntax, see Chvany (1975), Babby (1975b), and the chapters in the following edited volumes: Brecht and Chvany (1974), Chvany and Brecht (1980), and Flier and Brecht (1985).

2. Volume 1 was published under the title *Formale Slavistik*, edited by U. Junghanns and G. Zybatow; for details, see my review in Franks (1997). Volume 2 appeared as Kosta and Frasek (2002). The bulk of volume 3 appeared as Zybatow et al. (2001); the remaining essays can be found in volume 75 of *Linguistische Arbeitsberichte* (Leipzig 2000). FDSL 4, Kosta et al. (2003), was printed in two volumes, the latter restricted to syntax and semantics.

3. The contributions by A. Przepiórkowski and J. Bailyn to the February 2000 The Future of Slavic Linguistics meeting have been of particular use to me in writing this review of the field, as they offer excellent surveys of the GB/Minimalism and HPSG Slavic literature; see the website listed—(1a)—in the text.

4. See also the review of Borsley and Przepiórkowski by Rappaport in *JSL* 7.2 (1999). Przepiórkowski et al. (2002) offers a comprehensive HPSG treatment of Pol; it is written in Polish, however.

5. Contact seelangs@listserv.cuny.edu to subscribe. Seelangs archives can also be searched using the linguist list archives facility, at listserv.linguistlist.org/archives/seelangs.html.

6. In addition to the descriptions in Comrie and Corbett (1993), an excellent resource for the Mac verb is Friedman (1977) and, for Bg, see Aronson (1967).

7. In these languages, one frequently finds deviations from SVO order (sometimes even required, as, for example, in interrogatives) but scrambling phenomena—typical of colloquial Ru—such as long-distance scrambling and rampant splitting of constituents, are absent.

8. This is surely due to the Jakobsonian tradition, in that the analyses of Russian case features in Jakobson (1936, 1958) long served as standard fare in U.S. Slavic graduate programs and have inspired among students of Slavic more response than any other single proposal. Some useful discussions of his case features can be found in Neidle (1982/1988), Chvany (1986), Young (1988), and Franks (1995).

9. There is a veritable industry of research on the second dative. The following is a short list of relevant works: Comrie (1974), Chvany (1975), Schein (1982), Neidle (1988), Greenberg (1983), Greenberg and Franks (1991), and Laurençot (1997).

10. Predicate NPs also appear in the instrumental, obligatorily in Pol and optionally (with complex conditioning factors) in Ru.

11. Another difference is that, whereas the instrumental is often optional, the dative, whenever possible, is obligatory. Wayles Browne (pers. comm.) suggests Ru (i) as a matrix example of the second dative:

(i) Nam   pojti   samim   ili   ne . idti?
     we.dat to-go   alone.pldat   or   neg   to-go
     'Should we go alone or (just) not go?'

Alternatively, this may be agreement (with dative subject *nam*), rather than the default use of *samim*, or it could be analyzed as embedding of an infinitival clause after a covert modal (whose subject is *nam*). See also Moore and Perlmutter (2000).

12. Throughout this chapter, all examples are drawn from published works, referred to in the text or notes. I do not cite specific sources. Note that there is agreement in gender/number independent of case. Masculine is the default form, as in, for example, (3c); see also Franks and Schwartz (1994).

13. For discussion, see Babby (1998) or Babby and Franks (1998).

14. Her essay concerns the comitative construction, in which coordination involves the preposition 'with' (*s*, in Ru). See McNally (1993) and Dalrymple et al. (1998) for detailed discussion.

15. For a review of Brown (1999), see Haegeman (1999). An influential monograph which, inter alia, treats negation in SC is Progovac (1994). For issues of negation, scope, and polarity in Slavic in general, see these studies by Brown and Progovac, as well as the essays in Brown and Przepiórkowski (2004).

16. A new dissertation that treats gen-NEG in Ru is Borovikoff (2001).

17. For compelling arguments, such as passivization, that at least some Russian genitive and instrumental object NPs are true complements, see Fowler (1996). Presumably, this can be handled by endowing V with quirky case features which it imparts to the functional head (be it AgrO, Asp, v, or whatever) that checks direct object case. The same is presumably true for other Slavic languages; for example, for SC, Stjepanović (1997) argues that inherent (quirky) case is licensed under the same Spec-head relation as is structural case.

18. A variant of (10b) with nominative subject and full agreement, *Dokumenty ne obnaružilis'/obnaruženy*, would mean "The documents were not found."

19. See, however, Babby (1980) for a treatment in terms of theme-rheme structure, and also Borschev and Partee (1998) for a more recent adaptation of Babby's approach.

20. See, however, Przepiórkowski (2000b) for further discussion.

21. All examples to be discussed in this section are based on Franks (2002). See also Yadroff (1999) for an analysis of numerals in Ru, as well as general discussion of the internal structure of Ru NPs and PPs.

22. Pesetsky couched his account of QP in Ru ostensibly appearing only inside VP in terms of the Empty Category Principle (ECP), which at that time was the primary way of dealing with subject–object asymmetries. The details need not concern us here.

23. One interpretive difference between (14a) and (15b), addressed at some length by Pesetsky (1982), is that the former may have a group reading, whereas the latter has an individuated reading.

24. In (15c) agreement is forced since *èti pjat' mašin* can only be a (nom) DP.

25. For apparent agreement in SC, see Franks (1994, 1995).

26. The details about SC are, however, considerably more complicated; see Franks (2002) for a summary of relevant data and a preliminary analysis.

27. This also explains why the demonstrative can only be nom in Ru, assuming it actually originates as an adjective, in a structure as in (16), and raises to D in the course of the derivation. As pointed out to me by Guglielmo Cinque (pers. comm.), a similar account is argued by Bruge̓ for demonstratives in a variety of languages, including SC.

28. Specifically, I propose a "licensing parameter" with the effect that in WSl QPs cannot occur in a DP with any M (marked case feature), in ESl QPs cannot occur in a DP with more than one M, and in SC QPs cannot occur in a DP with more than one/ ??two M (case features). The reason for the "??" has to do with the particular analysis of case features and syncretism in SC, which, as described by Franks (2002), is a system in flux. With the loss of nominal case, in Mac and Bg numerals may impose a special "count form" on m nouns, but there is nothing comparable to gen-NUM found in the other languages.

29. This is essentially the clitic (short) form of the accusative reflexive pronoun, which some languages also use in genitive contexts. A number of the languages also have dative *si*.

30. This bibliography is downloadable at www.slavica.com/jsl/jsl_3_1.html.

31. Babby (1975a) argues convincingly that *-sja* arises whenever the direct object position becomes empty through some syntactic process, thereby extending its coverage to various nonpassive constructions with *-sja*, such as middles, reciprocals, and implicit direct object intransitives. The same is true of SC, as in the following examples from Progovac (2001):

(i)   Milan   se   brije.
      nom   refl   shaves

      'Milan is shaving.'

(ii) Deca   se   tuku.
      children refl   hit

      'The children are hitting each other.'

(iii) Milan   se   udara.
      nom   refl   hits

      'Milan is hitting (someone/me).'

(iv) Deca   se   grle.
      children refl   hug

      'One hugs children.'

32. Under negation the direct object becomes genitive only in (21b), never (21c). Frank Gladney (pers. comm.) offers the following as a minimal pair:

(i)   Tych   drzwi   się   nie   otwiera.
      these.gen doors.gen   refl   neg   open.3sg

      'This door must not be opened.'

(ii) Te   drzwi   się   nie   otwierają.
      these.nom   doors.nom   refl neg   open.3pl

      'This door does not open.'

Unlike in Ru, Pol *się* constructions never allow explicit agents (expressed with bare instrumentals in Ru and Ukr and *przez* + acc in Pol).

33. Lavine (2000) develops a promising minimalist analysis of this and related constructions. See also Shevelov (1963: 139–146, 1969) for discussion of Ukr.

34. The acceptability of this construction in Pol with the object NP in situ, as in (i) with the acc or even (ii) with gen-NEG, seems to vary among speakers:

(i)   %Dobrze   mi   się   pisze   tę   pracę.
      well   me.dat   refl write.3sg   this.acc   work.acc

      'I can write this work easily.'

(ii) %Nie   pisze   mi   się   dobrze   tej   pracy.
      neg   write.3sg   me.dat   refl well   this.gen   work.gen

      'I can't write this work easily.'

35. But see Lavine (2000) for arguments against null expletives in Slavic.

36. For ellipsis of direct objects in various Slavic languages, see McShane (1999a, 1999b).

37. USor, however, behaves like Ru in this regard.

38. One diagnostic with possibly mixed results is the status of third-person plural arb *pro*, which is found in all the Slavic languages, including ESl Ru; see Franks (1995: sec. 7.5). (The issue for Ru is whether overt *oni* 'they' *disallows* the pro arb reading.)

39. Two important recent dissertations, dealing with the Serbian and Croatian variants of SC, respectively, are Stjepanović (1999a) and Ćavar (1999). Franks (in press), which offers a detailed summary of the essential Slavic facts, can be downloaded at www.indiana.edu/~slavconf/linguistics/download.html. A good overview is also offered in Franks (2000). All examples cited in this section are drawn from these papers.

40. They also follow nonfinite verbs—that is, gerunds and imperatives—displaying a pattern well known from studies of Romance clitics.

41. The "copy and delete" approach is extended in Bošković (2001) to *wh*-phrases; see also Bošković and Franks (2002) for its application in both clitic and *wh*-domains.

42. The reason the SC counterpart to (35) would not be acceptable is because second-position clitics ordinarily require a tonic element to precede them as their host.

43. Recall, however, that this word order is perfect in Mac; cf. (31d). Thus, in this language the higher copy of the clitics would be pronounced in (36)'.

44. The verbal person-number affixes in Pol present a host of problems for analysis, since they exhibit mixed affixal and clitic behavior. See Franks and King (2000), as well as Franks and Bański (1999), for discussion of their mixed status, and see Borsley and Rivero (1994) for one standard analysis.

45. Other recent work on *wh*-movement in Slavic includes Citko (1998), Dornisch (1998), Lambova (1999), Pesetsky (2000), Richards (1997), Stepanov (1998, 2001), Stjepanović (1999a), and Strahov (2001). For an optimality theoretic account that treats, inter alia, Cz and Bg, see Ackema and Neeleman (1998). This chapter employs an approach in which *wh*-phrases cluster together *before* moving to SpecCP; this sort of

analysis is developed in minimalist terms in Grewendorf (2001) and is further defended in Sabel (2001).

46. The direct object is higher, according to Bošković, because it moves first to SpecAgrOP, an A-position above the adverb.

47. See this and other works for further examples and details. There is an essential comparative component to Bošković's analysis of multiple *wh*, which space limitations preclude discussion of here, but one point worth noting is that these same environments are where obligatory *wh*-movement is found in French, with the same general explanation.

48. Since FOCUS features always force overt *wh*-movement in Slavic (with one apparent exception, which involves overt *wh*-movement but pronunciation of a lower copy to avoid contiguous sequences of identical elements, as discussed in Bošković 2001 and Bošković and Franks 2002), these are introduced on a functional head below CP. Bošković's explanation for the absence of Superiority effects in SC and the optionality of *wh*-movement in colloquial French is that, in matrix short-distance questions, in both SC and French, a WH C° can be merged in LF, thereby obviating overt movement to check WH features.

49. For an informative survey of current and future Slavic research topics from the perspectives of GB and minimalism, see Bailyn (2000); for an invaluable presentation of HPSG-oriented approaches to Slavic data, see Przepiórkowski (2000a).

50. Slavic reflexives do not show person-number features and can be bound by any person. For discussion within a more general typological approach to anaphora and markedness, see Franks and Schwartz (1994).

51. The basic contrast is between a process-oriented "imperfective" and a goal-oriented "perfective," but there are numerous semantic subtleties beyond the scope of this chapter. There also exist other possibly aspectual classes; for example, in Ru and Pol many motion verbs have a three-way distinction, with the imperfective split into "determinate" and "indeterminate," and the verbal systems of the Balkan Slavic languages display categories such as "resultative," "indefinite," and "reported/renarrated," alongside additional tense distinctions such as "imperfect" or "aorist."

52. For an excellent general introduction to aspect, with much Slavic material, see Comrie (1976).

53. Roman Jakobson's work on the Ru verb, especially Jakobson (1957), is, of course, an invaluable point of departure for any serious research on the topic. For a study of the history of aspect in Ru, see Bermel (1997); for a recent overview of comparative aspect in Slavic, see Dickey (2000); and for an excellent specialized study of aspect and participial passives, see Schoorlemmer (1995). For an impressive online bibliography of work on tense, aspect, and related areas, see the Web pages designed by Robert Binnick, at www.scar.utoronto.ca/~binnick/TENSE. Finally, volume 9.1 (2001) is a special issue of the *Journal of Slavic Linguistics* devoted to problems of Slavic aspect.

54. Pol is similar in this regard to Ru, except that the periphrastic future can employ either the imperfective infinitive, as does Ru, or an imperfective *l*-participle, with no apparent (nonstylistic) difference in meaning.

55. In section 6.1.3 of Franks (1995), I argue that the future meaning is induced by *budet* in examples such as (54c), since this is technically a conjugated form of the verb *byt'* 'to be', which is morphologically (if not semantically) *perfective*.

56. As Wayles Browne (pers. comm.) points out, "semantic . . . and even idiosyn-

cratic properties of individual lexical items interact heavily with the category of perfective/imperfective."

57. In some but not all Slavic languages, the genitive can have a partitive function. In Ru, for certain nouns, there is a special form of the partitive distinct from the ordinary genitive (which is nonetheless almost always a licit alternative in partitive contexts).

58. Interestingly, when (57b) is negated, the partitive reemerges as a viable option:

(i) Ivan ne   pil   čaj/čaju.
     Ivan neg   drank.impf   tea.acc/tea.part

     'Ivan was not drinking the tea/any tea.'

See Klenin (1978) and Franks (1995: sec. 5.3.1) for discussion.

59. Ru (57a) is, of course, acceptable with a discourse-elided direct object; see Franks (1995: sec. 7.2.2) for discussion of discourse ellipsis, as well as Coats and Dong (1994) and McShane (1999a, 1999b).

60. One unsurprising exception is that prepositions (and postpositions, to the extent these can be found in Slavic) must be immediately adjacent to their complements.

61. The literature on scrambling in general is, of course, also vast; one well-known early edited volume is Corver and van Riemsdijk (1994); a new one is Karimi (2003).

62. Example (59a) could, of course, also be neutral, since Ru is basically SVO—although King (1995) argues for a VSO order—in which case *učeniki* would be neither a topic nor necessarily definite.

63. Swan does not use this term, just indicating focus graphically, with small caps; the translations are his.

64. I have retained her analysis and notations.

65. This is an oft-noted fact, in a variety of contexts and for a variety of languages. For an insightful new analysis, see Bošković (2003). The earliest mention of left-branch condition violations in the generative literature is Ross (1967/1986); for Pol, see especially Borsley (1983).

66. For discussion of postpositive articles in Mac and Bg, see Franks and King (2000: sec. 9.2). See Franks (2001) for further details and comparison with the "dative possessive" clitics found in these languages. In these works, as well as Franks (2000, in press), I argue that (putting ESl aside, which seems to admit multiple possibilities, given the analysis in section 3.5) the maximal projection of N is K(ase)P *except* in Mac and Bg, which have evolved to a DP system. For an alternative perspective, see Progovac (1998), who argues for the DP status of SC nominal phrases. The arguments she adduces are, however, also compatible with my KP approach, since they essentially indicate an additional functional projection above NP, which may (but need not necessarily) be taken to be DP.

67. Interestingly, Slvn seems more comparable to Cz than it is to the genetically closer SC, suggesting the relevance of German *Sprachbund* features. One place this difference is highlighted is in the possibility of clitics splitting up apparent constituents, where this simply correlates with the general viability of scrambling (generally, out of NP); see Franks (2000, in press) and especially Bošković (2001) for relevant comparison of SC and Slvn.

REFERENCES

Ackema, P., and A. Neeleman (1998) "Optimal Questions." *Natural Language and Linguistic Theory* 16: 443–490.

Adamec, P. (1966) *Porjadok slov v sovremennom russkom jazyke*. Prague, Academia.

Aronson, H. (1967) "The Grammatical Categories of the Indicative in the Contemporary Bulgarian Literary Language," in *To Honor Roman Jakobson*. Mouton, The Hague, 82–98.

Babby, L. (1975a) "A Transformational Analysis of Transitive -*sja* Verbs in Russian." *Lingua* 35: 297–332.

Babby, L. (1975b) *A Transformational Analysis of Russian Adjectives*. Mouton, The Hague.

Babby, L. (1980) *Existential Sentences and Negation in Russian*. Karoma, Ann Arbor.

Babby, L. (1987) "Case, Pre-Quantifiers, and Discontinuous Agreement in Russian." *Natural Language and Linguistic Theory* 5: 91–138.

Babby, L. (1989) "Subjectlessness, External Subcategorization, and the Projection Principle." *Zbornik Matice Srpske za filologiju i lingvistiku* 32: 7–40.

Babby, L. (1993) "A Theta-Theoretic Analysis of -*en*- Suffixation in Russian." *Journal of Slavic Linguistics* 1: 13–43.

Babby, L. (1998) "Subject Control as Direct Predication," in Ž. Bošković, S. Franks, and W. Snyder (eds.) *Formal Approaches to Slavic Linguistics: The Connecticut Meeting*. Michigan Slavic Publications, Ann Arbor, 17–37.

Babby, L., and R. Brecht (1975) "The Syntax of Voice in Russian." *Language* 51: 342–367.

Babby, L., and S. Franks (1998) "The Syntax of Adverbial Participles in Russian Revisited." *Slavic and East European Journal* 42: 117–149.

Babyonyshev, M. (1996) "Structural Connections in Syntax and Processing: Studies in Russian and Japanese." Ph.D. diss., MIT, Cambridge, Press.

Bailyn, J. (1995a) "Genitive of Negation Is Obligatory," in W. Browne, E. Dornisch and D. Zec (eds.) *Formal Approaches to Slavic Linguistics: The Cornell Meeting*. Michigan Slavic Publications, Ann Arbor, 84–114.

Bailyn, J. (1995b) "A Configurational Apporoach to Russian 'Free' Word Order." Ph.D. diss., Cornell University, Ithaca, N.Y.

Bailyn, J. (1995c) "Underlying Phrase Structure and 'Short' Verb Movement in Russian." *Journal of Slavic Linguistics* 3: 13–58.

Bailyn, J. (2000) "Slavic Generative Syntax 2000 (GB/Minimalism)." Position paper presented at SLING 2K Workshop, Bloomington, Ind. [Downloadable at: www.iub.edu/~slavconf/SLING2K/pospapers.html]

Bailyn, J. (2001) "On Scrambling: A Reply to Bošković and Takahashi." *Linguistic Inquiry* 32: 635–658.

Bailyn, J. (2003) "Does Russian Scrambling Exist?" In S. Karimi, (ed.), *Word Order and Scrambling*. Blackwell, Oxford, 156–176.

Bański, P., and A. Przepiórkowski (eds.) (2000) *GLiP-1. Proceedings of Generative Linguistics in Poland*. Institute of Computer Science, Polish Academy of Sciences, Warsaw.

Bański, P., and A. Prezpiórkowski (eds.) (2003) *Generative Linguistics in Poland. Morphosyntactic Investigations* (Proceedings of the GLiP-5 Conference held in Warsaw,

Poland, 30 Nov.–1 Dec. 2002). Instytut Podstaw Informatyki, Polskiej Akademii Nauk, Warsaw.

Bermel, N. (1997) *Context and the Lexicon in the Development of Russian Aspect*. University of California Press, Berkeley.

Billings, L., and J. Maling (1995) "Accusative-Assigning Participial -*no*/-*to* Constructions in Ukrainian, Polish, and Neighboring Languages: An Annotated Bibliography. *Journal of Slavic Linguistics* 5: 177–217, 396–430.

Borovikoff, N. (2001) "Unaccusativity and Movement in Russian: Integrating Formal Syntax and Discourse Functions." Ph.D. diss., Indiana University, Bloomington.

Borschev, V., and B. Partee (1998) "Formal and Lexical Semantics and the Genitive in Negated Existential Sentences in Russian," in Ž. Bošković, S. Franks, and W. Snyder (eds.) *Formal Approaches to Slavic Linguistics: The Connecticut Meeting*. Michigan Slavic Publications, Ann Arbor, 75–96.

Borsley, R. (1983) "A Note on the Generalized Left Branch Condition." *Linguistic Inquiry* 14: 169–175.

Borsley, R., and Przepiórkowski, A. (1999) (eds.) *Slavic in Head-Driven Phrase Structure Grammar*. CSLI Publications, Stanford, Calif.

Borsley, R., and M.-L. Rivero (1994) "Clitic Auxiliaries and Incorporation in Polish." *Natural Language and Linguistic Theory* 12: 373–422.

Bošković, Ž. (1997a) *The Syntax of Nonfinite Complementation: An Economy Approach*. MIT Press, Cambridge, Mass.

Bošković, Ž. (1997b) "Superiority Effects with Multiple *wh*-fronting in Serbo-Croatian." *Lingua* 102: 1–20.

Bošković, Ž. (1997c) "On Certain Violations of the Superiority Condition, AgrO, and Economy of Derivation." *Journal of Linguistics* 33: 227–254.

Bošković, Ž. (1998) "Multiple WH-fronting and Economy of Derivation," in E. Curtis, J. Lyle, and G. Webster(eds.) *Proceedings of WCCFL 16*. Stanford Linguistics Association, Stanford, Calif., 49–63.

Bošković, Ž. (1999) "On Multiple Feature Checking: Multiple *wh*-fronting and Multiple Head Movement," in S. Epstein and N. Hornstein, (eds.) *Working Minimalism*. MIT Press, Cambridge, Mass, 159–187.

Bošković, Ž. (2000) "Sometimes in SpecCP, Sometimes *in situ*," in R. Martin, D. Michaels and J. Uriagereka, (eds.) *Step by Step: Essays in Honor of Howard Lasnik*. MIT Press, Cambridge, Mass, 53–87.

Bošković, Ž. (2001) *On the Nature of the Syntax-Phonology Interface: Cliticization and Related Phenomena*. Elsevier Science, Amsterdam.

Bošković, Ž. (2003) "On Left Branch Extraction," in P. Kosta, J. Błaszczak, J. Frasek, L. Geist, and M. Żygis (eds.) (2003) *Investigations into Formal Slavic Linguistics*. Peter Lang, Frankfurt am Main, 543–578.

Bošković, Ž. (in press) "Wh-Phrases and Wh-Movement in Slavic," L. Billings (ed.), *Proceedings of Workshop on Comparative Slavic Morphosyntax*. Slavica, Bloomington, Ind., Slavica. [Downloadable at: www.indiana.edu/~slavconf/linguistics/download.html]

Bošković, Ž., and S. Franks (2002) "Phonology-Syntax Interactions in South Slavic." *Balkanistica* 15: 49–74.

Brecht R., and C. Chvany (eds.), (1974) *Slavic Transformational Syntax*. Michigan Slavic Materials, University of Michigan, Ann Arbor.

Brown, S. (1999) *The Syntax of Negation in Russian: A Minimalist Approach.* Stanford Monographs in Linguistics. CSLI Publications, Stanford, Calif.

Brown, S., and S. Franks (1995) "Asymmetries in the Scope of Russian Negation." *Journal of Slavic Linguistics* 3: 239–287.

Brown, S., and A. Przepiórkowski (eds.) (2004) *Negation in Slavic.* Slavica, Bloomington, Ind.

Brugè, L. (1996) "Demonstrative Movement in Spanish: A Comparative Approach." *University of Venice Working Papers in Linguistics* 6: 1–53.

Ćavar, D. (1999) "Aspects of the Syntax-Phonology Interface: Cliticization and Related Phenomena in Croatian." Ph.D. diss., University of Potsdam.

Chomsky, N. (1981) *Lectures on Government and Binding.* Foris, Dordrecht.

Chvany, C. (1975) *BE-Sentences in Russian.* Slavica: Columbus, Ohio.

Chvany, C. (1986) "Jakobson's Fourth and Fifth Dimensions: On Reconciling the Cube Model of Case Meanings with the Two-Dimensional Matrices for Case Forms," in R. Brecht and J. Levine (eds.) *Case in Slavic.* Slavica, Columbus, Ohio, 107–129.

Chvany, C., and R. Brecht (eds.), (1980) *Morphosyntax in Slavic.* Slavica, Columbus, Ohio.

Citko, B. (1998) "On Multiple WH movement in Slavic," in Ž. Bošković, S. Franks, and W. Snyder (eds.), *Formal Approaches to Slavic Linguistics: The Connecticut Meeting.* Michigan Slavic Publications, Ann Arbor, 97–113.

Coats, H., and Z. Dong (1994) "Ellipsis in Russian." *Russian Linguistics* 18: 281–298.

Comrie, B. (1974) "The Second Dative: A Transformational Approach," in R. Brecht and C. Chvany (eds.), *Slavic Transformational Syntax.* Michigan Slavic Materials, No. 10. University of Michigan, Ann Arbor, 123–150.

Comrie, B. (1976) *Aspect.* Cambridge University Press, Cambridge.

Comrie, B. (1980) "Clause Structure and Movement Constraints in Russian," in C. Chvany and R. Brecht, (eds.), *Morphosyntax in Slavic.* Slavica, Columbus, Ohio, 98–113.

Comrie, B., and G. Corbett (1993) *The Slavonic Languages.* London, Routledge.

Corbett, G. (1983) *Hierarchies, Targets and Controllers: Agreement Patterns in Slavic.* Pennsylvania State University Press, University Park.

Corbett, G. (1986) "The Use of the Genitive or Accusative for the Direct Object of Negated Verbs in Russian: A Bibliography," in R. Brecht and J. Levine (eds.), *Case in Slavic.* Slavica, Columbus, Ohio, 361–372.

Corbett, G. (in press) "Agreement in Slavic," In L. Billings (ed.), *Proceedings of Workshop on Comparative Slavic Morphosyntax.* Slavica: Bloomington, Ind., [Downloadable at: www.indiana.edu/~slavconf/linguistics/download.html]

Corver N., and H. van Riemsdijk (eds.) (1994) *Studies on Scrambling.* Mouton de Gruyter, Berlin.

Dalrymple, M., I. Hayrapetian, and T. H. King (1998) "The Semantics of the Russian Comitative Construction." *Natural Language and Linguistic Theory* 16: 597–631.

De Bray, R. G. A. (1969) *Guide to the Slavonic Languages,* rev. ed. Dent, London.

Dickey, S. (2000) *Parameters of Slavic Aspect: A Cognitive Approach.* CSLI Publications, Stanford, Calif.

Dimitrova-Vulchanova, M., D. Dyer, I. Krapova, and C. Rudin (eds.) (2002) *Balkanistica* 15. *Papers from the Third Conference on Formal Approaches to South Slavic and Balkan Languages.*

Dimitrova-Vulchanova, M., and L. Hellan (eds.) (1999) *Topics in South Slavic Syntax and Semantics*. John Benjamins, Amsterdam.

Dornisch, E. (1998) "Multiple-Wh-Questions in Polish: The Interactions between Wh-Phrases and Clitics." Ph.D. diss., Cornell University, Ithaca, N.Y.

Durst-Andersen, P. (1992) *Mental Grammar: Russian Aspect and Related Issues*. Slavica, Columbus, Ohio.

Fielder, G. (1993) *The Semantics and Pragmatics of Verbal Categories in Bulgarian*. Edwin Mellen Press, Lewiston, Maine.

Filip, H. (1996) "Integrating Telicity, Aspect and NP Semantics: The Role of Thematic Structure," in J. Toman (ed.), *Formal Approaches to Slavic Linguistics: the College Park Meeting*. Michigan Slavic Publications, Ann Arbor, 61–96.

Firbas, J. (1964) "From Comparative Word-Order Studies." *Brno Studies in English* 4: 111–128.

Flier, M., and R. Brecht (eds.) (1985) *Issues in Russian Morphosyntax*. Slavica, Columbus, Ohio.

Flier, M., and A. Timberlake (eds.) (1985) *The Scope of Slavic Aspect*. Slavica, Columbus, Ohio.

Forsyth, J. (1970) *A Grammar of Aspect: Usage and Meaning in the Russian Verb*. Cambridge University Press, Cambridge, Mass.

Fowler, G. (1996) "Oblique Passivization in Russian." *Slavic and East European Journal* 40: 519–546.

Franks, S. (1994) "Parametric Properties of Numeral Phrases in Slavic." *Natural Language and Linguistic Theory* 12: 570–649.

Franks, S. (1995) *Parameters of Slavic Morphosyntax*. Oxford University Press, New York.

Franks, S. (1997) "Review of Junghanns and Zybatow, eds. *Formale Slavistik*." *Journal of Slavic Linguistics* 5: 325–357.

Franks, S. (1998) "*Parameters of Slavic Morphosyntax* Revisited," in Ž. Bošković, S. Franks, and W. Snyder (eds.) *Formal Approaches to Slavic Linguistics: The Connecticut Meeting*. Michigan Slavic Publications, Ann Arbor, 134–165.

Franks, S. (2000) "Clitics at the Interface," in F. Beukema and M. Den Dikken (eds.) *Clitic Systems in European Languages*. John Benjamins, Amsterdam, 1–46.

Franks, S. (2001) "The Internal Structure of Slavic NPs, with Special Reference to Bulgarian," in A. Przepiórkowski and P. Bański (eds.), *Generative Linguistics in Poland: Syntax and Morphosyntax*. Instytut Podstaw Informatyki, PAN, Warsaw, 53–69.

Franks, S. (2002) "A Jakobsonian Feature Based Analysis of the Slavic Numeric Quantifier Genitive." *Journal of Slavic Linguistics*. 10: 145–184.

Franks, S. (in press) "Clitics in Slavic," in L. Billings (ed.) *Proceedings of Workshop on Comparative Slavic Morphosyntax*. Slavica, Bloomington, Ind. [Downloadable at: www.indiana.edu/~slavconf/linguistics/download.html]

Franks, S., and P. Bański (1999) "Approaches to 'Schizophrenic' Polish Person Agreement," in K. Dziwirek et al. (eds.) *Formal Approaches to Slavic Linguistics: The Seattle Meeting*. Michigan Slavic Publications, Ann Arbor, 123–143.

Franks, S., and Ž. Bošković (2001) "An Argument for Multiple Spell-Out." *Linguistic Inquiry* 32: 174–183.

Franks, S., and K. Dziwirek (1993) "Negated Adjunct Phrases Are Really Partitive." *Journal of Slavic Linguistics* 1: 280–305.

Franks, S., and T. H. King (2000) *A Handbook of Slavic Clitics*. Oxford University Press, New York.

Franks, S., and L. Schwartz (1994) "Binding and Non-distinctness: A Reply to Burzio." *Journal of Linguistics* 30: 227–243.

Friedman, V. (1977) *The Grammatical Categories of the Macedonian Indicative*. Slavica, Columbus, Ohio.

Friedman, V. (1997) "Review of Grace Fielder, *The Semantics and Pragmatics of Verbal Categories in Bulgarian*." *Journal of Slavic Linguistics* 2: 333–340.

Godjevac, S. (2000) "Intonation, Word Order, and Focus Projection in Serbo-Croatian." Ph.D. diss., The Ohio State University.

Greenberg, G. (1983) "Another Look at the Second Dative and Dative Subjects." *Linguistic Analysis* 11: 167–218.

Greenberg, G., and S. Franks (1991) "A Parametric Approach to Dative Subjects and Second Datives in Slavic." *Slavic and East European Journal* 35: 71–97.

Grewendorf, G. (2001) "Multiple *wh*-fronting." *Linguistic Inquiry* 32: 87–122.

Guentchéva, Z. (1990) *Temps et aspect: l'exemple du bulgare littéraire contemporain*. Collection "Sciences du Langage." Presses du CNRS, Paris.

Guiraud-Weber, M. (1988) *L'aspect du verbe russe (Essais de présentation)*. Universitè de Provence, Aix-en-Provence.

Haegeman, L. (1999) "Review of Sue Brown, *The Syntax of Negation in Russian. A Minimalist Approach*." *Journal of Slavic Linguistics* 7: 139–165.

Hajičová, E. (1993) *Issues of Sentence Structure and Discourse Patterns*. Charles University Press, Prague.

Halpern, A. (1995) *On the Morphology and Placement of Clitics*. CSLI Publications, Stanford.

Heim, I., H. Lasnik, and R. May (1991) "Reciprocity and Plurality." *Linguistic Inquiry* 22: 63–101.

Hoffman, J. (1996) "Syntactic and Paratactic Word Order Effects." Ph.D. diss., University of Maryland, College Park.

Jakobson, R. (1936) "Beitrag zur allgemeinen Kasuslehre: Gesamtbedeutungen der russischen Kasus," in *Selected Writings*, vol. 2 (1971). Mouton, The Hague, 23–71.

Jakobson, R. (1957) "Shifters, Verbal Categories, and the Russian Verb," in *Selected Writings*, vol. 2 (1971). Mouton, The Hague, 130–147.

Jakobson, R. (1958) "Morfologičeskie nabljudenija nad slavjanskim skloneniem," in *Selected Writings*, vol. 2 (1971). Mouton, The Hague, 154–183.

Junghanns, U. (1996) "SJA-Verbs in Russian: Phonology, Morphology, or Syntax?" in A. Alexiadou, N. Fuhrhop, P. Law, and S. Löhken (eds.) *ZAS Papers in Linguistics 6*. Zentrum für Allgemeine Sprachwissenschaft, Typologie und Universalienforschung, Berlin, 66–80.

Junghanns, U., and G. Zybatow (1995) "Syntax and Information Structure of Russian Clauses," in W. Browne, E. Dornisch, and D. Zec. (eds.), *Formal Approaches to Slavic Linguistics: The Cornell Meeting*. Michigan Slavic Publications, Ann Arbor, 289–319.

Junghanns, U., and G. Zybatow (eds.) (1997) *Formale Slavistik*. Vervuert Verlag, Frankfurt am Main.

Karimi, S. (ed.) (2003) *Word Order and Scrambling*. Blackwell, Oxford.

King, T. H. (1995) *Configuring Topic and Focus in Russian*. CSLI, Stanford, Calif.

Klenin, E. (1978) "Quantification, Partitivity, and the Genitive of Negation in Russian," in B. Comrie (ed.) *Classification of Grammatical Categories*. Linguistic Research, Edmonton, 163–182.

Kosta, P., and J. Frasek (eds.) (2002) *Current Approaches to Formal Slavic Linguistics*. Peter Lang, Frankfurt am Main.

Kosta, P., J. Błaszczak, J. Frasek, L. Geist, and M. Żygis (eds.) (2003) *Investigations into Formal Slavic Linguistics*. Peter Lang, Frankfurt am Main.

Kovtunova, I. I. (1976) *Sovremennyj russkij jazyk: porjadok slov i. aktual'noe členenie predloženija*. Prosveščenie, Moscow.

Krylova, O., and S. Khavronina (1976) *Word Order in Russian Sentences*. Russian Language Publishers, Moscow.

Lambova, M. (1999) "The Typology of Multiple WH-fronting Revisited," in T. H. King and I. Sekerina (eds.), *Formal Approaches to Slavic Linguistics: The Philadephia Meeting*. Michigan Slavic Publications, Ann Arbor, 238–258.

Laurençot, E. (1997) "On Secondary Predication and Null Case," in M. Lindseth and S. Franks (eds.) *Formal Approaches to Slavic Linguistics: The Indiana Meeting*. Michigan Slavic Publications, Ann Arbor, 191–206.

Lavine, J. (2000) "Topics in the Syntax of Nonagreeing Predicates in Slavic." Ph.D diss., Princeton University.

Mathesius, V. (1964) "On Some Problems of the Systematic Analysis of Grammar," in J. Vachek (ed.) *A Prague School Reader in Linguistics*. Indiana University Press, Bloomington, Ind., 306–319.

McNally, L. (1993) "Comitative Coordination: A Case Study in Group Formation." *Natural Language and Linguistic Theory* 11: 347–379.

McShane, M. (1999a) "The Ellipsis of Accusative Direct Objects in Russian, Polish and Czech." *Journal of Slavic Linguistics* 7: 45–88.

McShane, M. (1999b) "Predictive Rules of Direct Object Ellipsis in Russian," in K. Dziwirek et al. (eds.) *Formal Approaches to Slavic Linguistics: The Seattle Meeting*. Michigan Slavic Publications, Ann Arbor, 329–348.

Mel'čuk, I. (1985) *Poverxnostnyj sintaksis russkix čislovyx vyraženij. Wiener Slawischer Almanach Sonderband 16*. Institut für Slawistik der Universität Wien, Vienna.

Moore, J., and D. Perlmutter (2000) "What Does It Take to Be a Dative Subject?" *Natural Language and Linguistic Theory* 18: 373–416.

Neidle, C. (1988) *The Role of Case in Russian Syntax*. Kluwer, Dordrecht.

Pesetsky, D. (1982) "Paths and Categories." Ph.D. diss., MIT, Cambridge, Mass.

Pesetsky, D. (2000) *Phrasal Movement and Its Kin*. MIT Press, Cambridge, Mass.

Piñón, C. (1997) "Verbs of Motion in Polish, I: Parts and Processes," in U. Junghanns and G. Zybatow (eds.) *Formale Slavistik*. Frankfurt am Main, Vervuert Verlag.

Progovac, Lj. (1992) "Relativized SUBJECT: Long Distance Reflexives without Movement." *Linguistic Inquiry* 23: 671–680.

Progovac, Lj. (1993) "Long Distance Reflexives: Movement to INFL versus Relativized SUBJECT." *Linguistic Inquiry* 24: 755–772.

Progovac, Lj. (1994) *Positive and Negative Polarity: A Binding Approach*. Cambridge Studies in Linguistics 38. Cambridge University Press, Cambridge.

Progovac, Lj. (1998) "Determiner Phrase in a Language without Determiners." *Journal of Linguistics* 34: 165–179.

Progovac, Lj. (2001) "Clausal Functional Projections in Serbian," in S. Franks, T. H.

King, and M. Yadroff (eds.) *Formal Approaches to Slavic Linguistics: The Blooming-ton Meeting.* Michigan Slavic Publications, Ann Arbor, 229–256.

Progovac, Lj., and S. Franks (1992) "Relativized SUBJECTs for Reflexives," in K. Broder-ick (ed.) *Proceedings of NELS XXII* Graduate Student Linguistic Publications, Uni-versity of Massachusetts, Amherst, 349–363.

Przepiórkowski, A. (2000a) "Formal Grammar (HPSG)." Position paper presented at SLING 2K Workshop, Bloomington, Ind. [Downloadable at: www.iub.edu/~slavconf/SLING2K/pospapers/html]

Przepiórkowski, A. (2000b) "Long Distance Genitive of Negation in Polish." *Journal of Slavic Linguistics* 8: 119–158.

Przepiórkowski, A., and P. Bański (2001) *Generative Linguistics in Poland: Syntax and Morphosyntax.* Instytut Podstaw Informatyki PAN, Warsaw.

Przepiórkowski, A, A. Kupść, M. Marciniak, and A. Mykowiecka (2002) *Formalny opis języka polskiego: teoria i implementacja.* Instytut Podstaw Informatyki PAN, Warsaw.

Rappaport, G. (1986) "On Anaphor Binding in Russian." *Natural Language and Linguis-tic Theory* 4: 97–120.

Rappaport, G. (1999) "Review of Borsley and Przepiórkowski, eds., *Slavic in Head-Driven Phrase Structure Grammar.*" *Journal of Slavic Linguistics* 7: 331–352.

Reinders-Machowska, E. (1991) "Binding in Polish," in E. Reuland and J. Koster (eds.) *Long Distance Anaphora.* Cambridge University Press, Cambridge, 137–150.

Richards, N. (1997) "What Moves Where When in Which Language?" Ph.D. diss., MIT, Cambridge, Mass.

Robblee, K. (1994) "Russian Word Order and the Lexicon." *Journal of Slavic Linguistics* 2: 238–267.

Ross, J. R. (1967) "Constraints on Variables in Syntax." Ph.D. diss., MIT, Cambridge, Mass.

Rudin, C. (1988) "On Multiple WH Questions and Multiple WH Fronting." *Natural Language and Linguistic Theory* 6: 445–501.

Růžička, R. (1986) "Typologie der Diathese slavischer Sprachen in parametrischen Varia-tionen." *Die Welt der Slaven* 21: 225–274.

Růžička, R. (1988) "On the Array of Arguments in Slavic Languages." *Zeitschrift für Sprachwissenschaft und Kommunikationsforschung* 41: 155–178.

Sabel, J. (2001) "Deriving Multiple Head and Phrasal Movement: The Cluster Hypothe-sis." *Linguistic Inquiry* 32: 532–547.

Schein, B. (1982) "Non-finite Complements in Russian." *MIT Working Papers in Linguis-tics* 4: 217–244.

Schoorlemmer, M. (1995) *Participial Passive and Aspect in Russian.* Utrecht University OTS Dissertations Series, Utrecht.

Schoorlemmer, M. (1996) "The Affix-Clitic Distinction and Russian *SJA*," in A. Alexia-dou, N. Fuhrhop, P. Law, and S. Löhken (eds.), *ZAS Papers in Linguistics* 6. Zen-trum für Allgemeine Sprachwissenschaft, Typologie und Universalienforschung, Ber-lin, 66–80.

Sekerina, I. (1997) "The Syntax and Processing of Scrambling Constructions in Russian." Ph.D. diss., CUNY. [Abstract available at www.cis.upenn.edu/~sekerina/DISS.HTM]

Sekerina, I. (1999) "The Scrambling Complexity Hypothesis and Processing of Split Scrambling Constructions in Russian." *Journal of Slavic Linguistics* 7: 265–304.

Sgall, P. (1972) "Topic, Focus, and the Ordering of Elements of Semantic Representations." *Philologica Pragensia* 15: 1–14.

Sgall, P., E. Hajičová, and J. Panevová (1986) *The Meaning of the Sentence in Its Semantic and Pragmatic Aspects.* Reidel, Dordrecht.

Shevelov, G. (1963) *The Syntax of Modern Literary Ukrainian.* Mouton, The Hague.

Shevelov, G. (1969) "The Vicissitudes of a Syntactic Construction in Eastern Slavic." *Scando-Slavica* 15: 171–186.

Siewierska, A. (1988) "The Passive in Slavic," in M. Shibatani (ed.), *Passive and Voice.* John Benjamins, Amsterdam, 243–289.

Sigurðsson, M. (1991) "Icelandic Case-marked PRO and the Licensing of Lexical Arguments." *Natural Language and Linguistic Theory* 9: 327–363.

Sobin, A. (1985) "On Case Assignment in Ukrainian Morphologically Passive Constructions," *Linguistic Inquiry* 16: 649–662.

Stepanov, A. (1998) "On *Wh*-fronting in Russian," in P. Tamanji and K. Kusumoto (eds.) *Proceedings of the North Eastern Linguistic Society 28.* University of Massachusetts, Amherst, 453–467.

Stepanov, A. (2001) "Cyclic Domains in Syntactic Theory." Ph.D. diss., University of Connecticut, Storrs.

Stjepanović, S. (1997) "Is Inherent Case Structural?" in M. Lindseth and S. Franks (eds.), *Formal Approaches to Slavic Linguistics: The Indiana Meeting.* Michigan Slavic Publications, Ann Arbor, 295–311.

Stjepanović, S. (1999a) "What Do Second Position Cliticization, Scrambling, and Multiple Wh-Fronting Have in Common?" Ph.D. diss., University of Connecticut, Storrs.

Stjepanović, S. (1999b) "Scrambling: Overt Movement or Base Generation and LF Movement?" *Journal of Slavic Linguistics* 7: 305–324.

Strahov, N. (2001) "A Scrambling Analysis of Russian WH-questions," in S. Franks, T. King, and M. Yadroff (eds.), *Formal Approaches to Slavic Linguistics: The Bloomington Meeting.* Michigan Slavic Publications, Ann Arbor, 293–310.

Suprun, A. (1959) *O russkix čislitel'nix.* Kirgizskij Gosudarstvennyj Universitet, Frunze.

Swan, O. (2001) *A Grammar of Contemporary Polish.* Slavica, Bloomington, Ind.

Timberlake, A. (1979) "Reflexivization and the Cycle in Russian." *Linguistic Inquiry* 10: 109–141.

Toman, J. (1991) "Anaphors in Binary Trees: An Analysis of Czech Reflexives," in E. Reuland and J. Koster (eds.) *Long Distance Anaphora.* Cambridge University Press, Cambridge, 151–170.

Townsend, C. (1970) *Continuing with Russian.* McGraw-Hill, New York.

Vassilieva, M. (2001) "On the Typology of Russian Comitatives," in S. Franks, T. H. King, and M. Yadroff (eds.) *Formal Approaches to Slavic Linguistics: The Bloomington Meeting.* Michigan Slavic Publications, Ann Arbor, 327–344.

Williams, E. (1995) *Thematic Structure in Syntax.* MIT Press, Cambridge, Mass.

Yadroff, M. (1996) "SpecAspP and Case Assignment," in J. Toman (ed.), *Formal Approaches to Slavic Linguistics: The College Park Meeting.* Michigan Slavic Publications, Ann Arbor, 313–336.

Yadroff, M. (1999) "Formal Properties of Functional Categories: The Minimalist Syntax of Russian Nominal and Prepositional Expressions." Ph.D. diss., Indiana University, Bloomington.

Yokoyama, O. (1985) "A Diversified Approach to Russian Word Order," in M. Flier and R. Brecht (eds.), *Issues in Russian Morphosyntax*. Slavica, Columbus, Ohio, 187–207.

Yokoyama, O. (1986) *Discourse and Word Order*. John Benjamins, Philadelphia.

Young, K. McCreight (1988) "Multiple Case Assignments." Ph.D. diss., MIT, Cambridge, Mass.

Zybatow, G, U. Junghanns, G. Mehlhorn, and L. Szucsich (2001) *Current Issues in Formal Slavic Linguistics*. Peter Lang, Frankfurt am Main.

CHAPTER 10

THE SCANDINAVIAN LANGUAGES

ANDERS HOLMBERG AND CHRISTER PLATZACK

1 INTRODUCTION

THE Scandinavian languages—Danish, Faroese, Icelandic, Norwegian, and Swedish—are closely related Germanic languages (Indo-European), spoken in the northern part of Europe. To be more precise, Norwegian and Swedish are spoken on the Scandinavian peninsula, Danish is spoken in Jutland and on the Danish islands north of Germany, Icelandic is spoken on Iceland, and Faroese is spoken on the Faroe Islands. Not quite 20 million people have a Scandinavian language as their mother tongue, with Swedish (9 million) as the most widely spoken of them and Faroese (40,000) as the least. Whereas Danish, Icelandic, Norwegian, and Swedish are national languages,[1] Faroese is a provincial language, the Faroe Islands being a semi-independent possession of Denmark. Iceland and the Faroe Islands were colonized by Scandinavians around A.D. 800; at about the same time, Scandinavian Vikings also settled on Orkney and Shetland, where a sixth Scandinavian language developed, known as Norn; it became extinct around 1700.

In the Middle Ages, all Scandinavian languages were mutually comprehensible. Speakers of Mainland Scandinavian (Danish, Norwegian, and Swedish) are still able to make themselves understood to each other when speaking their native tongue, although the rapid morphophonological development of Danish has gradually increased the problems for other Scandinavians in understanding spoken Danish. Icelandic and Faroese have had their own developments, and these languages differ enough from the Mainland Scandinavian ones to require mutual learning for comprehension.

The countries where the Scandinavian languages are spoken constitute a sociocultural area, sharing much of their history and displaying many common culture traits, as well as comparable standards of living. In many respects, the languages are no more different than dialects of a single language may be. However, the fact that the Scandinavian languages are national languages has led to the unusual situation that these highly similar languages are fairly well described, and for the last twenty years an intense research on comparative Scandinavian syntax has taken place. Recently the current grammatical knowledge of Norwegian and Swedish has been codified in two comprehensive grammars, *Norsk referansegrammatik* (c. 1,220 pp., Faarlund, et al. 1997) and *Svenska Akademiens grammatik* (c. 2,700 pp., Teleman et al. 1999), respectively; a grammar of the corresponding size for Danish is almost finished (Hansen and Heltoft in press).

From a syntactic point of view, the Scandinavian languages roughly divide in two groups, which, following a suggestion by Haugen (1976: 23), we refer to as *Insular Scandinavian* (Icelandic, partly Faroese, Old Scandinavian) and *Mainland Scandinavian* (Danish, Norwegian, Swedish), respectively. In general, the Insular Scandinavian languages have a richer inflectional system, which mainly accounts for the syntactic differences observed, as shown in Holmberg and Platzack (1995). Some of these differences are discussed in the bulk of this chapter. However, before proceeding, we point out some important syntactic properties that are common to all Scandinavian languages, both Insular and Mainland Scandinavian.

2 SYNTACTIC PROPERTIES COMMON TO ALL SCANDINAVIAN LANGUAGES

Like all the Germanic languages except English, the Scandinavian languages are *verb-second* languages, meaning that, at most, one constituent may precede the tensed verb of the main clause. Consider the Swedish examples in (1); corresponding examples can be given for all the other Scandinavian languages. In the examples, the tensed verb is underlined, and the constituent in front of it is in italics:

(1) a. *Han* <u>hittade</u> faktiskt pengarna under sängen. (subj + tensed verb)
         he found actually money-the under bed-the
         'He actually found the money under the bed.'

     b. *Under sängen* <u>hittade</u> han faktiskt pengarna. (adverbial + tensed verb)
         under bed-the found he actually money-the

     c. *Faktiskt* <u>hittade</u> han pengarna under sängen. (adverbial + tensed verb)
         actually found he money-the under bed-the

     d. *Pengarna* <u>hittade</u> han faktiskt under sängen. (object + tensed verb)
         money-the found he actually under bed-the

     e. *Sjuk* <u>var</u> han inte. (predicative + tensed verb)
         sick was he not
         'He was not sick.'

     f. *Ut* <u>kastade</u> han bollen. (particle + tensed verb)
         out threw he ball-the
         'He threw the ball out.'

     g. <u>Hittade</u> han faktiskt pengarna under sängen? (tensed verb initial yes/no-
         question)
         found he actually money-the under bed-the
         'Did he actually find the money under the bed?'

     h. *Han* <u>kunde</u> faktiskt ha hittat pengarna under sängen. (subj + tensed
         auxiliary)[2]
         he might actually have found money-the under bed-the
         'He actually might have found the money under the bed.'

The reason for placing a particular phrase in first position is mainly pragmatic; often the choice is an effect of the unmarked distribution of information within a clause where the information flow goes from more thematic to less thematic, where information is thematic when it is shared by speaker and hearer.

A second property at the sentential level that is common to all the Scandinavian languages is the requirement that a referential subject must be overt, even if its reference is easily deduced from the context. This is shown for Swedish in (2); note that the subject pronoun in the second clause (underlined) cannot be left out in the corresponding example in any of the Scandinavian languages:

(2) *Igår köpte Johan en ny cykel. Den ställde *<u>(han)</u> i köket.*
     Yesterday bought Johan a new bike. It put he in kitchen-the
     'Yesterday Johan bought a new bike. He put it in the kitchen.'

A third syntactic property at the sentential level, common to all the Scandinavian languages, is the placement of the object (underlined) after the nonfinite verb and in front of adverbials of time, location, manner, and other content adverbials (in italics); see the Swedish example in (3):

(3)   Han hade hittat <u>pengarna</u> *under sängen igår.*
       he had found money-the under bed-the yesterday
       'He had found the money under the bed yesterday.'

There is no difference between main and embedded clauses in this respect: unless it is in first position, the object always follows the nonfinite verb.[3]

A fourth syntactic property of all the Scandinavian languages is the use of prepositions and not postpositions (cf. *under sängen* 'under the bed' in (3)). In all the languages, the preposition may also govern clauses, finite or infinitival:

(4)   a. efter att ha öppnat brevet
           after to have opened letter-the
           after having opened the letter

       b. efter att hon hade öppnat brevet
           after that she had opened letter-the

All the Scandinavian languages have what has been known as Object Shift, illustrated in (5a): a weak pronominal object (underlined) may occur to the left of sentential adverbials (italics) that otherwise precede the object (5b); compare (5a) and (5c):

(5)   a. Han köpte <u>den</u> *inte.*
           he bought it not
           'He did not buy it.'

       b. Han köpte *inte* boken.
           he bought not book-the
           'He didn't buy the book.'

       c. *Han köpte boken *inte.*[4]
           he bought book-the not

Common to all the Scandinavian languages, furthermore, is the presence of a possessive reflexive *sin* (*Han tvättade <u>sin</u> bil* 'He washed his car', he = his; compare *Han tvättade <u>hans</u> bil* 'he washed his car', he ≠ his), the use of inflectional morphemes on the noun for both number and definiteness (*häst-ar-na* 'horse-s-the'), and the placement of attributive adjectives in front of the noun (*den stora bilen* 'the big car'). Furthermore, while all the Germanic languages except modern English have attributive adjective agreement, the Scandinavian languages differ from the continental Germanic languages in also having predicative adjective agreement: *Studenten är lat* 'The student is lazy', *Studenterna är lata* 'The students are lazy-PL'.

In the rest of this chapter, we highlight cases of syntactic variation between the Scandinavian languages, starting with word-order variation at the sentence level in section 3 and proceeding to word-order variation within the noun phrase in section 4. In these sections we mainly consider differences between Icelandic and Mainland Scandinavian. Faroese often takes an intermediate position, having some word-order properties in common with Icelandic and others in common with the Mainland Scandinavian languages. A short overview is given in section 5. In many respects, the syntax of the Middle Ages versions of Danish, Norwegian, and Swedish has a lot in common with the syntax of modern Icelandic. There are many morphological similarities as well; thus, for example, modern Icelandic, as well as Middle Ages Mainland Scandinavian, has morphological case, subjunctive forms of the verb, and subject-verb agreement in person and number; these inflections have disappeared in modern Mainland Scandinavian. This development is the subject of section 6.

When dealing with the syntactic variation within the Scandinavian languages, we sometimes illustrate only the variation at hand, and at other points we also indicate how this variation can be accounted for in recent Principles and Parameters theory. These accounts are based on the theoretical presupposition of the Minimalist program (Chomsky 1995, 1998, 2001) that there is a universal set of principles common for all human languages, and that variation at the structural level is the result of a combination of this universal set of principles with language-particular lexical properties. Readers not interested in these attempts to explain a particular variation may skip this discussion and still get an understanding of the degree of syntactic variation found within the Scandinavian languages.

3 WORD ORDER AT THE SENTENCE LEVEL

3.1 Introduction

Scandinavian word order at the sentence level is the subject of this section. Generally speaking, the Scandinavian languages are almost identical with respect to sentential word order, although there are some interesting differences, mainly between Icelandic and modern Mainland Scandinavian.

There is wide consensus today that the clause is universally structured as in (6):

(6)

VP is the domain where deep semantic roles are assigned (the Agent and Patient of an event, e.g.); TP is the locus of tense and event structure, including sentence adverbials; and CP is a domain where the clause is anchored to the context and the speaker's point of view, and where sentence force is indicated, distinguishing declarative, interrogative, and so on. For the Scandinavian languages, the structure in (6) is mirrored in the word order of the clause, in the sense that the topic, as well as force indicators, are usually found at the left edge of the clause, and semantic roles not expressed by the subject are usually found at the end of the clause, together with event-modifying content adverbials. In our account of word-order properties, we discuss the domains in the order of Merge; that is, we start with VP.

3.2 The Verb Phrase

3.2.1 *Overview*

The schematic word order of the verb phrase for all the modern Scandinavian languages is outlined in (7a), with examples from Icelandic and Swedish in (7b–c); as we will see, at this level of abstraction, the Scandinavian word order is identical to the English one:

(7)   a. VERB   OBJECT   CONTENT ADVERBIALS

      b. skilja   bílinn eftir   heima á morgun. (Icelandic)

      c. lämna   bilen   hemma i morgon (Swedish)
         leave   car-the   home tomorrow

There is no real understanding of how the content adverbials are represented structurally. However, assuming that the computation of the clause starts with the verb and that it first merges with the internal argument, the adverbials must be in Spec-VP, producing the VP-structure outlined in (8):

(8)

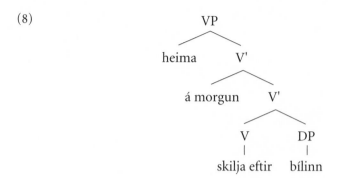

Since both the (nonfinite) verb and the object precede the content adverbials, we conclude that both the verb and the object are raised to higher positions. See Josefsson and Platzack (1998) for further arguments and Johnson (1991) and Koizumi (1993) for a similar account of the English facts.

To determine where the verb and the object are raised, we have to consider also the position of the external argument. There is wide consensus today (Arad 1999; Chomsky 1995, 1999, etc.) that the external argument is merged as a specifier of little *v*, schematically as in (9), where the boldface DP is the external argument and CA represents the content adverbials:

(9)

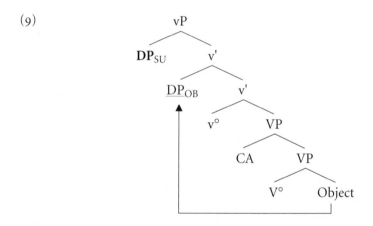

To avoid a violation of the Shortest Move principle, we will assume that the object is attracted to a Spec-vP lower than the external argument, as indicated by the arrow in the diagram; see Chomsky (1998) for a discussion. The verb is presumably attracted by a higher head, outside of vP, using v^0 as an intermediate landing site. We discuss this raising later.

3.2.2 *The Verb Particle*

The main difference between the Scandianvian languages at VP is the order of verb particles and the object. Danish almost always must have the particle after the object, whereas Swedish must have it before the object.[5] Compare the examples in (10), where the particle is in italics, and the object is underlined:

(10)   a. Han tog et lommetørklœde *op*. (Danish)
                he took an handkerchief up

         b. Han tog *upp* en näsduk. (Swedish)
                he took up an handkerchief

Norwegian and Icelandic have both possibilities, as shown by the following examples from Svenonius (1996):

(11)   a. Han spiste tørrfisken *opp*. (Norwegian)
                he ate dry.fish-the up

         b. Han spiste *opp* tørrfisken.
                he ate up dry.fish-the
                'He ate up the dried fish.'

(12)   a. Ég gerði nokkra bíla *upp*. (Icelandic)
                I fixed some cars up

         b. Ég gerði *upp* nokkra bíla.
                I fixed up some cars
                'I fixed up some cars.'

When the object is a weak pronoun, it is placed before the particle in Danish, Norwegian, and Icelandic; in Swedish, it still tends to follow the particle.[6] Evidently, the optionality of particle shift of DPs in Norwegian and Icelandic is similar to that found in English:

(13)   a. Hun har hengt det *opp*. (Norwegian)
                she has hung it up

         b. Hon har hängt *upp* det. (Swedish)
                she has hung up it

Finally, it should be mentioned that the particle and the object, independently of their relative order, always precedes content adverbials (14a, b) and that the verb is always left-adjacent to the particle, except when it is in the verb-second position (14c):

(14)   a. Hun har hengt billedet opp på veggen. (Norwegian)
            she has hung picture-the up on wall-the

      b. Hun har hengt opp billedet på veggen. (Norwegian)
            she has hung up picture-the on wall-the

      c. Till slut åt Kalle verkligen upp torrfisken. (Swedish)
            at last ate Kalle really up dry.fish-the

We abstain from presenting an account of the obligatory pronoun shift around the particle in Danish, Norwegian, and Icelandic and concentrate on discussing some thoughts about the optionality of DP particle shift in Norwegian and Icelandic, the obligatory order object–particle in Danish, and the obligatory order particle–object in Swedish. The account we present is a modification of Svenonius (1996), who does not discuss the obligatory orders in Swedish and Danish and does not consider the placement of the particle and the object in front of the content adverbials.

    Partly following Svenonius (1996), we assume that the particle merges with the object DP and that this combination merges with the verb, yielding (15):

(15) $[_{VP}$ spise $[_{PP}$ opp   tørfisken]]
           eat   up   dry.fish-the

As mentioned, the verb raises to a position outside of vP, passing through v^0, and the object raises to a lower Spec-vP. Since the particle precedes content adverbials, it is assumed that it cliticizes to the verb and raises with the verb as a free rider at least as far as v^0.[7] This gives us object–particle order in case the particle is stranded in v^0, and particle–object order in case the particle follows the verb out of vP, as indicated in (16); we use embedded clauses to avoid verb-second effects:

(16)   a. at han$_{SU}$ tog$_V$ $[_{vP}$ t$_{SU}$ et lommetørklœde $[_{v^0}$ op t$_V$] $[_{VP}$
            that he   took   an handkerchief   up
            fra lommen . . .]] (Danish)
            from pocket-the

      b. att han$_{SU}$ [tog upp]$_V$ $[_{vP}$ t$_{SU}$ en näsduk $[_{v^0}$ t$_V$] $[_{VP}$
            that he   took up   an handkerchief
            från fickan . . .]] (Swedish)
            from pocket-the

As shown in the next section, the difference between Swedish and Danish in (16) provides for a difference with respect to Object Shift in these languages in constructions with the particle.

To account for the optional word order in Icelandic and Norwegian, where the counterparts of both (16a) and (16b) are well-formed, we obviously have to design our description in such a way that stranding the particle either in v^0 or outside of vP is equally costly. We do not provide a discussion of these matters here.

3.3 The Middle Field (TP)

The middle field is built up around the T(ense) P(hrase), presumably containing a number of positions related to mood, tense, and aspect, as suggested in Cinque (1999). In addition, we find different kinds of sentence adverbials here, including the negation. In our presentation, we concentrate on some points of variation between the Scandinavian languages—namely, Object Shift, the position of the verbs that are not in the V2-position, and a middle-field position for the subject.

3.3.1 *Object Shift*

In all the Scandinavian languages, an object may occur in the middle field, preceding the negation and other sentence adverbials, under certain conditions. See Holmberg and Platzack (1995: chap. 6) and Hellan and Platzack (1999) for overviews. In Mainland Scandinavian, only pronominal objects may occur in this position, while in Icelandic any definite DP object may do so. As Holmberg (1999) has shown, Object Shift is prevented across any phonologically visible nonadjunct category that c-commands the object position in vP. Compare the well-formed example in (17) with the ungrammatical ones in (18), where Object Shift is blocked by the presence of a verb (18a), a particle (18b), a preposition (18c), or another argument (18d). As (18e, f) show, the pronominal indirect object alone, or both the indirect and the direct object, may shift:

(17) Jag kysste henne inte t_{OB}. (Swedish)
     I kissed her not

(18)   a. *att jag henne inte kysste t_{OB}. (Swedish)
        that I her not kissed

    b. *Jag skrev det inte upp t_{OB}.
       I wrote it not up

    c. *Jag talade henne inte med t_{OB}.
       I spoke her not with

    d. *Jag gav den inte Elsa t_OB.
       I gave it not Elsa

    e. Jag gav henne inte den.
       I gave her not it

    f. Jag gav henne den inte.
       I gave her it not

In Danish, Icelandic, and Norwegian, where the object may or must be placed in front of the particle, as shown in the previous section, Object Shift in cases like (18b) is well-formed:[8]

(19)   Jeg skrev det måske ikke t_{OB} op. (Danish)
       I wrote it maybe not up

Holmberg (1999) argues that Object Shift is a P(honetic) F(orm) operation and that an important prerequisite is that the shifted object is not a focus. See Josefsson (2001) for an alternative view.

    Icelandic is exceptional among the Scandinavian languages in that Object Shift applies freely to full definite DPs, as well as to weak pronouns, provided the DPs are not focused:

(20)   a. Ég les aldrei þessar bœkur (Icelandic)
         I read never these books
     b. Ég les þessar bœkur aldrei.
         I read these books never

See Holmberg (1999) and Chomsky (2000) for recent attempts to account for this optionality.

3.3.2 Position of the Verb in the Middle Field

In main clauses, the finite verb in Scandinavian is always raised to the C-domain (verb second), as we discuss in the next section. In embedded clauses, the Mainland Scandinavian finite verb usually occupies a lower position within the middle field (21), and the nonfinite verb never moves higher than the middle field (22a), unless it is topicalized, as, for example, in (22b), taken from Holmberg (1999); this is presumably a case of VP fronting.

(21)   att John faktiskt hade köpt boken (Swedish, the same in Danish and Norwegian)[9]
       that John actually had bought book-the

(22)   a. (Han lovade) att inte läsa boken. (Swedish; the same in Danish and
           Norwegian)
           he promised to not read book-the
           'He promised not to read the book.'

        b. Kysst henne har jag inte (bara hållit henne i handen). (Swedish)
           kissed her have I not only held her by hand-the
           'Kissed her I haven't (only held her by the hand).'

As shown in (22a), the nonfinite verb in Mainland Scandinavian control infinitives
is found after the negation and other sentence adverbials.[10] In Icelandic, in contrast, the infinitive precedes the negation in control infinitives but follows the
negation in case it is governed by an auxiliary:

(23)   a. Skúli lofaði að lesa aldrei bókina.
           Skúli promised to read never book-the

        b. Skúli má aldrei lesa bókina.
           Skúli must never read book-the

        c. *Skúli má lesa aldrei bókina.
           Skúli must read never book-the

The difference between Mainland Scandinavian and Icelandic in control infinitives
with respect to the position of the infinitival verb vis-à-vis the negation and other
sentence adverbials can be accounted for if we assume that the Icelandic infinitive
in control infinitives is raised to the C-domain, whereas the Mainland Scandinavian infinitive is stuck in the middle field. Judging from the surface order, the
Mainland Scandinavian infinitive, as well as the tensed verb in embedded clauses,
is raised to a position below NegP, whereas the Icelandic infinitive is raised to a
position above NegP (and other sentence adverbials). We assume the Mainland
Scandinavian position to be T^0 and the Icelandic position to be Fin^0; see section
3.4.[11]

3.3.3 Floating Subjects

With the exception of Danish, all the Scandinavian languages allow for floating
subjects. Because they are verb-second languages, we expect to find the subject
immediately after the finite verb when it is not in first position, as is illustrated
in (24); in this and the following examples, the subject is in italics and the adverbials are underlined:

(24)   Nu borde *Kalle* <u>väl faktiskt inte</u> säga mer. (Swedish)
       now should Kalle probably actually not say more

As we argue in the next section, the position of the subject immediately after the finite verb is a position within the C-domain, presumably Spec-FinP.

However, the subject in (24) may also occur further to the right, as shown in (25a–c):

(25)   a. Nu borde <u>väl</u> *Kalle* <u>faktiskt inte</u> säga mer.
           now should probably Kalle actually not say more

       b. Nu borde <u>väl faktiskt</u> *Kalle* <u>inte</u> säga mer.
           now should probably actually Kalle not say more

       c. Nu borde <u>väl faktiskt inte</u> *Kalle* säga mer.
           now should probably actually not Kalle say more

Since we do not want to have sentence adverbials both in the C-domain and in the middle field, we will assume that the subject has not raised to Spec-FinP in cases like (25) but is stuck in Spec-TP. This assumption is supported by the fact that the relative order of sentence adverbials is the same, whether they precede or follow the subject, as indicated in (24) and (25).

3.4 The Left Periphery

3.4.1 *Introduction*

The initial part of the sentence, constituting the highest part of sentence structure, here called the left periphery, contains several projections of features that regulate the place of the sentence in its context. Following Rizzi (1997) we discern a Force Phrase (ForceP), which is a projection of the sentence type feature, indicating sentence type (declarative, interrogative, imperative), and a Finite Phrase (FinP) projected of the finiteness feature that regulates the subject–predicate relation and anchors the utterance to the time, location, and point of view of the speaker; without this anchoring, a statement cannot be truth evaluated. In many languages, including the Scandinavian ones, FinP also hosts an EPP feature, meaning that it must have a specifier. Encompassed between ForceP and FinP are projections for Topic and Focus, yielding the universal structure of the left periphery outlined in (26):

(26)

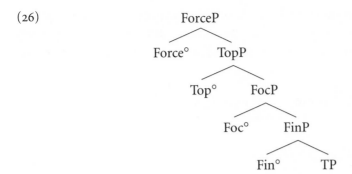

In Rizzi's conception of the left periphery, based on Italian data, there are Topic phrases both above and below the Focus phrase. The structure in (26) is enough for our purposes, however, and furthermore it is not clear that the Scandinavian languages offer support for multiple Topic phrases.

Later we discuss a number of syntactic differences between Mainland Scandinavian and Icelandic which all involve the left periphery. As we will see, these differences are the results of a single inflectional difference between these languages: the finite verb in Icelandic, but not in Mainland Scandinavian, is inflected for person. Building on ideas in Alexiadou and Anagnostopoulou (1998) and Pesetsky and Torrego (2001), we assume that the person inflection hosts an uninterpretable finiteness feature uFin.[12] For Mainland Scandinavian, which does not have person inflection, the feature uFin is contained in the nominative DP.

Two additional assumptions about the left periphery are needed: as mentioned, all the Scandinavian languages are verb-second languages, which means that Fin^0 must be filled; this might be a trivial phonological property, according to Chomsky (1999), with no deeper syntactic implication besides word order, although the consequence in the case of Icelandic is that the uninterpretable feature uFin is raised to Fin^0 as a free rider and thus is eliminated. We also assume that all the Scandinavian languages are alike in that FinP hosts an EPP feature that attracts an element with phonological features.

It follows from the discussion so far that both the head and the specifier of FinP must be filled in a Scandinavian language. The syntactic differences (discussed later) all result from the single parametric difference: the location of uFin in the person inflection of the verb in Icelandic and in the nominative DP in Mainland Scandinavian.

3.4.2 Expletive Subject

Like English, Mainland Scandinavian must have a visible subject in all finite clauses, expletive or real. Icelandic, in contrast, must have a visible element in front of the finite verb, but there is no obligation for this element to be a subject.[13]

Consider the examples in (27) and (28): in (27) the Swedish example is introduced by an expletive subject *det* 'it', whereas the Icelandic example, which apparently has the same structure, is introduced by the filler word *það*. The difference between the expletive subject and the filler is evident when the sentence is introduced by an adverbial or any other constituent that is a nonsubject. In this case the expletive subject in Swedish inverts with the finite verb, whereas the Icelandic filler must be absent:

(27)   a.   Det regnade igår. (Swedish)

     b.   það rigndi í gær. (Icelandic)
        it rained yesterday

(28)   a.   Igår regnade *(det). (Swedish)

     b.   Í gær rigndi (*það). (Icelandic)
        yesterday rained it

This difference follows from the assumptions about the left periphery presented previously. In both Swedish and Icelandic, the finite verb must be in Fin⁰, due to the verb-second requirement. Icelandic has person agreement with the feature uFin, which follows the verb to Fin⁰ as a free rider. In this position uFin is checked by the finite feature and deleted. The EPP feature of FinP forces the insertion of *það* in Spec-FinP, or the fronting of some other element of the clause, like the adverbial in (28b). There is no place or function for *það* when *í gær* is fronted. See Sigurðsson (2001) for a partly different view.

    Consider next the Swedish examples. After raising the finite verb to Fin⁰, the Swedish grammar still has to eliminate the EPP feature of FinP and the uFin feature of the expletive *det*. Placing *det* in Spec-FinP fulfills both demands at the same time. The fronting of the adverbial in (28a) has no consequences for FinP; in particular, the expletive subject is still needed in Spec-FinP.

    It was mentioned in connection with our discussion of the Icelandic example (28b) that the raising of the adverbial *í gær* 'yesterday' to Spec-FinP was triggered by EPP in FinP: if the adverbial is not fronted, a first-position filler *það* must be inserted in Spec-FinP. Since Spec-FinP is filled by the expletive subject in the corresponding Swedish example (28a), we conclude that the fronted adverbial in (28a) must be in a position above Spec-FinP, presumably in Spec-TopP. Whether or not the adverbial in Icelandic is vacuously raised from Spec-FinP to Spec-TopP is a question we do not want to answer here. More important for our discussion is the observation that the finite verb in (28a) cannot remain in Fin⁰, as it presumably does in the Icelandic example (28b), but must raise to a higher head, maybe Top⁰. This raising, which preserves verb second, can be seen as a consequence of Shortest Move: the subject *det* is closer to Spec-TopP than the adverbial *igår*, and hence the raising of the adverbial should be banned. However, the subsequent raising of the finite verb removes the obstacle, according to the Principle of Minimal Compliance (Richards 1998). See Platzack (2004).

3.4.3 *Transitive Expletives*

As is evident from the discussion in the previous section, Swedish (but not Icelandic) has an expletive subject; Icelandic *það*, seemingly corresponding to Swedish *det* in (27), is simply a filler of Spec-FinP, whereas Swedish *det* has nominative Case and thus the uninterpretable feature uFin, making it a real subject. As a consequence, it must be moved to Spec-FinP to eliminate uFin. In Icelandic, where uFin is a part of the verb inflection, no single DP is forced to move to Spec-Fin. In particular, the subject of a transitive verb may remain lower down in the structure, in which case the filler *það* is inserted into Spec-FinP to eliminate the EPP feature of FinP, which will produce sentences like (29a), known as the Transitive Expletive Construction; see Sigurðsson (1989), Vikner (1995), and Bobaljik and Jonas (1996). The corresponding Swedish sentence is ungrammatical, due to the impossibility of eliminating the nominative feature uFin in the "real" subject:

(29)   a. það hefur einhver étið hákarlinn. (Icelandic)

    b. *Det har någon ätit hajen. (Swedish)
       it has someone eaten shark-the

3.4.4 *Stylistic Fronting*

The raising of the adverbial *í gær* 'yesterday' to Spec-FinP in (28b) is available in Icelandic but not in Swedish, as should be obvious from the previous discussion: the EPP feature of FinP must be checked by a subject in Spec-FinP in Swedish, otherwise the feature uFin will remain, ruling out the derivation. This restriction is not found in Icelandic, where uFin is part of the person agreement of the finite verb and hence is deleted when the verb raises to Fin⁰. Since the EPP is satisfied by any phonological material in Spec-FinP, only independent principles like Shortest Move will determine which element is fronted in Icelandic. See Holmberg (2000) for a discussion of these matters. In the general case, the element closest to Spec-FinP must be selected; thus when the subject is available, it is the subject that is raised. In such cases the Icelandic example is identical to the Swedish one. When the subject for some reason is not present, or remains in some lower position of the clause, however, an adverbial, the object, the predicative, or the nonfinite verb is raised to Spec-FinP. This fronting, which is easier to detect in embedded clauses, is known as Stylistic Fronting; see Holmberg (2000) for references, and consider the alternative account in Sigurðsson (2001). Some examples, from Jónsson (1991) and Holmberg (2000), are presented in (30), where the stylistically fronted element is underlined:

(30)   a. þetta er tilboð sem <u>ekki</u> er hœgt að hafna.
          this is offer that not is possible to reject

       b. þeir sem <u>þessa erfiðu ákvörðun</u> verða að taka.
          those that this difficult decision have to take

       c. Hver heldur þú að <u>stolið</u> hafi hjólinu?
          who think you that stolen has the-bike

3.4.5 *Oblique Subjects*

The presence of uFin in the person inflection of the finite verb is also a necessary prerequisite for oblique subjects in Icelandic, and the absence of uFin in the person inflection of the finite verb is one reason that Mainland Scandinavian does not have oblique subjects. The other reason is the absence of an active morphological case system. The possibility to use DPs in dative, genitive, and accusative as subjects in modern Icelandic has been noticed by many scholars. These oblique DPs share most subject properties with nominative DPs; the only subject property they lack, besides nominative case, is the possibility to agree with the tensed verb. See Sigurðsson (1989) for an overview of the relevant properties and Sigurðsson (2001) for a recent account. One of these properties, the placement after the finite verb when the subject is not sentence initial, is illustrated in the following sentences, taken from Sigurðsson (1989); in these examples, the oblique subject is underlined:

(31)   a. Hafði <u>mér</u> því leiðst Haraldur.
          had me.DAT thus bored Harold.NOM

       b. Vantaði <u>þig</u> vinnu?
          lacked you.ACC job.ACC

       c. Gœtti <u>verkjanna</u> mjög lengi?
          noticed pains-the.GEN very long
          'Were the pains noticeable very long?'

The subject properties found with Oblique subjects can all be derived from their position in Spec-FinP. According to the previous discussion, these DPs are not raised to Spec-FinP to check any feature of their own: the uFin feature is part of the verb inflection and is checked in Fin^0 when the verb raises to this position, and we take for granted that the morphological case is checked by the main verb, if checking is necessary in such cases. The mechanism that forces the oblique subject to go to Spec-FinP is the EPP feature of FinP, in combination with the fact that the oblique subject is the highest argument of VP and thus available for raising to FinP without violating Shortest Move. (For some tricky cases where a violation of Shortest Move seems to be involved, see Platzack (1999).

3.4.6 *Embedded Subject Questions*
Consider next the following difference between Swedish and Icelandic:

(32)   a. Hon frågade   vad *(som) låg   i byrån. (Swedish)

      b. Hún spurði   hvað (*sem) lægi   í skúffunni. (Icelandic)
         she asked   what that was-lying in chest-the

Swedish must have the complementizer *som* after the wh-word in embedded subject questions, whereas *sem* is not allowed in Icelandic. As a complementizer, *som* meets the requirement that Fin should be filled. The difference between Swedish and Icelandic follows from the previously stated assumptions about the left periphery. In both Swedish and Icelandic, wh-words must raise to Spec-FocP. Since it is the subject that is raised in (32), we take it for granted that the wh-word checks the EPP-feature in Spec-FinP in both languages. Being the subject, the Swedish wh-word also carries the uFin-feature that is checked in Spec-FinP. In Icelandic, where uFin is in the person inflection of the finite verb, no complementizer is allowed in Fin^0, since that would prevent raising of the finite verb to Fin^0, as is necessary to eliminate uFin. Norwegian is like Swedish in this respect. The counterpart to *som* in Danish embedded subject questions is *der*, which arguably is not a complementizer but the expletive subject *der* (see Taraldsen 1991, Vikner 1991, Holmberg 2000). In terms of the present analysis, *der* would, in that case, be merged in Spec-FinP, checking uFin.

3.4.7 *Embedded Word Order*
In embedded clauses, the relative order of the finite verb and sentence adverbials is different in Mainland Scandinavian and Icelandic: whereas the verb follows the adverbial(s) in Mainland Scandinavian, it precedes the adverbial(s) in Icelandic; in these examples the adverbial is underlined, and the finite verb is in italics:

(33)   a. Jag vet att Maria <u>inte</u> *läste* boken. (Swedish)
        I know that Mary not read book-the

      b. Ég veit að María *las* <u>ekki</u> bókina. (Icelandic)
        I know that Mary read not book-the

The word-order difference in (33) follows immediately from our account: the Swedish complementizer *att* 'that' is merged in Fin⁰, giving this head phonological content, and the subject *Maria* is raised to Spec-FinP to eliminate EPP and uFin. Subsequently, the complementizer is raised to Force⁰ to indicate that we have an embedded declarative. The finite verb is stuck in T⁰, below the negation and other sentence adverbials.

It should be evident by now that a derivation similar to the one just outlined for Swedish would be impossible in Icelandic: with the complementizer *að* inserted in Fin⁰, the requirement that Fin⁰ must be filled is met, but the uninterpretable uFin of person agreement would not be eliminated. The only available way for Icelandic to resolve the situation is to raise the finite verb to Fin⁰, which erases uFin and makes Fin⁰ visible, and later on insert *að* in Force⁰. This will assure that the finite verb precedes the negation and other sentence adverbials in the middle field. The fact that the Mainland Scandinavian complementizer *att* may be omitted or deleted under certain conditions (just like *that* in English), while the Icelandic *að* may not be, may be construed as support for the assumption that the complementizers are merged in different positions.[14]

In Faroese, there is dialectal variation regarding the position of the finite verb. We return briefly to Faroese in a separate section. It should be noted that the order finite verb > adverbial is not obligatory in all embedded clauses in Icelandic, either: in relative clauses and adverbial clauses, it is optional; see Sigurðsson (1989) and note 9.

4 NP-STRUCTURE

As we have tried to show, in the case of sentential syntax and VP-syntax, the variation among the Scandinavian languages mainly follows the division between Mainland and Insular Scandinavian. There is variation within Mainland Scandinavian, but it is relatively minor. In the case of noun phrase internal syntax, the variation does not follow the Mainland-Insular division. There is as much variation between, say, Bokmål Norwegian and Standard Swedish as there is between Bokmål and Icelandic. On the whole, there is a striking amount of variation regarding noun phrase internal syntax among the Scandinavian languages. Not only do the standard languages each have their own distinct ways of combining articles, adjectives, demonstratives, quantifiers, possessives, and head nouns but almost every local dialect appears to have its own NP-syntax. To take an example, there are at least seven distinct ways of saying 'John's book' in Scandinavian, with additional minor variations, such as the choice of preposition in (34g), or dative instead of genitive case on the possessor:

(34) a. Jons bok
         Jon's book

      b. bok Jons
         book Jon's

      c. Jons boken
         Jon's book-the

      d. boken Jons
         book-the Jon's

      e. boken hans Jon(s)
         book-the his Jon('s)

      f. Jon sin bok
         Jon his.REFL book

      g. boken til Jon
         book-the to Jon

See Taraldsen (1990), Delsing (1993), and Holmberg and Sandström (1996a). We do not discuss possessive constructions here, though, but present some views on another controversial topic in Scandinavian NP-syntax—namely, the interplay of attributive adjectives and definiteness marking.

In simple NPs, definiteness is expressed by a suffix on the head noun in all the Scandinavian languages:

(35) a. bók-in (Icelandic)

      b. bok-a (Norwegian)

      c. bog-en (Danish)
         'the book'

The definite suffix is inflected for gender, number, and (in Insular Scandinavian) case. Historically, the definite suffix is assumed to be derived from a postnominal demonstrative *hinn* 'this', and this hypothesis is supported by the observation that the inflectional paradigm of the Old Norse demonstrative *hinn* is exactly the same as the paradigm of the suffixed article. Singular indefiniteness is expressed by a free, prenominal indefinite article (inflected for gender) in Mainland Scandinavian and Faroese, and by the absence of an article in Icelandic and Old Scandinavian. There is no indefinite article in plural:

(36)   a. bók (Icelandic)

       b. en bok (Swedish)
          'a book'

(37)   a. bœkur (Icelandic)

       b. böcker (Swedish)
          'books'

A straightforward analysis of the suffixed definite article—henceforth abbreviated Dx—is that it is a form of D, merged with NP and forming a regular head-initial [D NP], but triggering noun movement, so that it ends up as a suffix on the noun.[15]

   Some initial support for the movement hypothesis is provided by the possessive construction (38a), characteristic of Icelandic, Norwegian, and Northern Swedish. The counterpart in Danish and Standard and Southern Swedish is (38b):

(38)   a. bókin mín (Icelandic)
          book-the my

       b. min bog (Danish)
          my book

The contrast can be described as a difference in the features of the possessive pronoun, as follows: In all the languages, the possessive pronoun is merged in prenominal position. In Icelandic, Norwegian, and Northern Swedish, the possessive pronoun does not itself encode definiteness and therefore allows merge of the definite article, which triggers noun movement. In Danish, Standard, and Southern Swedish, the possessive pronoun itself encodes definiteness and therefore precludes merge of an article.[16]

   Attributive adjectives pose a serious complication: In indefinite NPs the adjectives are prenominal:

(39)   en ny bil
       a new car

In view of (38a), one might expect at least some of the Scandinavian languages to have postnominal attributive adjectives in construction with the definite suffix. This does not occur, however. Instead, we find the following pattern:

(40)   a. nýja bílinn (Icelandic)

     b. den nya bilen (Norwegian, Swedish, Faroese)

     c. den nye bil (Danish)

     d. nybilen (Northern Swedish)
       'the new car'

In Icelandic definite noun phrases, the adjective precedes noun+suffix. In Norwegian, Standard Swedish, and Faroese, the adjective precedes noun+suffix, but, in addition, they have a free definite article preceding the adjective. Danish has a free definite article preceding the adjective and the suffixless noun. Yet another variant is exhibited by Northern Swedish: the adjective is incorporated in the definite form of the noun.

In most recent works on the Scandinavian NP, the Mainland Scandinavian free definite article is seen as a kind of expletive: the adjective blocks movement of the noun to D, triggering insertion of the free article to "license D" in some sense (see Santelmann 1993; see Kester 1996 for a review of the literature). The fact that Icelandic doesn't need the free article would be an effect of the richer morphology of Icelandic (see Vangsnes 1999). This is relatively straightforward in the case of Danish but less so in Faroese, Norwegian, and most varieties of Swedish, where a free and a suffixed article are both required, in construction with attributive adjectives. The double definiteness marking exhibited by this construction is a classical problem in Scandinavian grammar. The question is: Which of the two articles is the interpretable one, encoding definiteness, and which is expletive? Or are they both interpretable but fulfilling different, complementary functions in relation to definiteness, specificity, familiarity, or some such notions?

Within traditional Swedish and Norwegian grammar—for instance, Lundeby (1965)—the free article is sometimes called "the article of the adjective," implying that its function is specifically to license the adjective. Kester (1996) presents a modern version of this idea: Following Higginbotham (1985), she assumes that both the adjective and the noun are predicates that have a θ-role that needs to be discharged. The θ-role is formally an open position in the lexical makeup of the lexical head. In DPs, unlike VPs, this θ-role is generally not discharged by θ-role assignment but by virtue of being bound by a determiner, so called θ-binding. If and only if every predicate is θ-bound by a determiner, the noun phrase is saturated, and only then can the noun phrase function as an argument. The reason

(41) is ungrammatical in Swedish, Norwegian, and Faroese is, according to Kester, that the adjective is not θ-bound, and the noun phrase therefore is not saturated:

(41)   *nya bilen
        new car-the

The suffixed article can θ-bind the noun, but not the adjective. Following Cinque (1994), Kester assumes that attributive adjectives are merged as specifiers of functional heads encoding properties like "size," "age," and "material." We can label these heads 'a'. She also assumes that the suffixed article is a head, called F, situated between D and NP, which attracts the noun out of NP (see also Giusti 1997 and Vangsnes 1999). The structure of (41) is therefore (42), where the adjective is outside the scope of the definite article:

(42) $[_{aP} [_{AP}$ nya$] [_{a'}$ a $[_{FP}$ bil+en $[_{NP}$ t$]]]$

According to Kester, F encodes "familiarity," while D encodes "specificity." See Vangsnes (1999) for a more fine-grained analysis of the semantics of nominal heads.

The adjectival head a is also not capable of binding the predicate variable of its specifier adjective. Therefore, a free definite article must be merged. As for Danish, which has no Dx, but only a free article in construction with attributive adjectives, either it has no F, or F has no morphological realization.

As shown, Icelandic doesn't need a free determiner. Old Scandinavian, too, managed without a free determiner. Plausibly this is linked to some other property that Icelandic and Old Scandinavian have but the other Scandinavian languages do not have. An idea articulated by Holmberg (1994), Holmberg and Sandström (1996a), and Kester (1996) is that the crucial property is morphological Case. In Higginbotham's (1985) terms, morphological Case would be able to θ-bind the adjective, perhaps by virtue of being represented as an abstract head K, c-commanding aP-NP:

(43) $[_{KP}$ K $[_{aP}$ nýja $[_{a'}$ a $[_{FP}$ bílinn$]]]$

An alternative is that morphological Case provides the additional feature needed for the adjectival head a to θ-bind the adjective in its specifier.[17] Vangsnes (1999) argues that the crucial property is gender morphology: in Icelandic and Old Scandinavian, but not in modern Mainland Scandinavian, the attributive adjective is marked for gender.[18]

We still need an explanation why D must be a *free* article in Mainland Scandinavian and Faroese. In other words, why can't D be a suffixed article attracting the noun (or NP) to yield *bilen nya* from $[_{DP}$ -en [nya [(F) [bil]]]], neither in

Danish nor in the other languages?[19] As mentioned, the received view is that the adjective blocks noun movement. In fact, given an appropriate version of Cinque's (1994) theory, the adjective itself will not block noun movement, but the head *a* will, by virtue of the Head Movement Constraint (HMC), unless *a* itself can attract the noun, and then D can attract *a* with an adjoined noun. So, assuming that Scandinavian *a* does not attract the noun, noun movement to D across an adjective is impossible. Within this theory the adjective itself, a specifier of *a*, will block NP-movement to Spec-DP by virtue of some version of Shortest Move or the Minimal Link Condition. Hence the order *bilen nya* cannot be derived by NP-movement, either.

An attractive consequence of this theory (not mentioned by Kester, 1996) is that it explains straightforwardly why the free article is not needed in Faroese and Swedish in those cases where the adjective-noun combination is a name, as in *Vita Huset* 'the White House', and *Döda Havet* 'the Dead Sea': see Delsing (1993: 117f.) and Lockwood (1977). The adjectives in these expressions are not descriptive, but part of a name. Formally, they do not have a θ-role to discharge (in Higginbotham's 1985 terms) and therefore do not need a c-commanding determiner. In Faroese and Swedish, the free determiner is, in fact, frequently left out as soon as a convention has been established between a set of interlocutors to use an adjective-noun combination to refer to a specific object. The determinerless form *nya bilen* can be used when, say, the interlocutors have two cars at their disposal, in which case a convention can be established, more or less ad hoc, to refer to them as *nya bilen* 'the new car' and *gamla bilen* 'the old car', respectively. In this case, too, the adjective is not descriptive, but "identifying," in the manner of a proper name. That is, it doesn't have a θ-role to discharge and therefore doesn't need a free determiner.[20]

The theory also offers an interesting outlook on the incorporated adjectives in Northern Swedish. First, the incorporated adjectives are, or can be, truly descriptive. They can also be stacked:

(44)   Ser du storsvartbilen jänna?
       see you big-black-car-the there
       'Do you see that big, black, car?'

Second, the incorporation takes place only in constructions with the definite form of the noun. Indefinite noun phrases generally have the form (45b) in NSw dialects; the standard form is (45c); and no dialect has the form (45a):

(45)   a. *en storsvartbil

       b. en stor en svart en bil

c. en stor svart bil
   'a big black car'

Plausibly the incorporation is a way of bringing the adjective within the scope of the definite suffix, so that the definite suffix can θ-bind the adjective, as well as the noun, in which case the free determiner is redundant. In the indefinite noun phrase, the article is, and always has been, a free article, which c-commands, and thereby takes scope over the adjective(s) and the noun with no need for movement or incorporation. In definite noun phrases, the article is a suffix attracting a noun or NP, which calls for something special to ensure θ-binding of the adjective.

In terms of language change, the form [Adj N-Dx] was licit as long as there was Case morphology (or adjectival gender morphology, according to Vangsnes 1999). When the Case morphology (or gender morphology) disappeared, perhaps for independent phonological reasons, basically two strategies emerged to compensate for the loss and to ensure θ-binding of the adjective: one was to bring the adjective within the scope of the suffixed article by a form of incorporation or compounding (Northern Swedish); the other was to introduce a free definite article (other Mainland Scandinavian languages and Faroese).[21]

How is the Northern Swedish A+N compound derived? Sandström and Holmberg (1994) have a proposal: they assume that N+Dx is derived by N-movement to D. In Northern Swedish the movement applies across the adjective, analyzed as a head taking NP as complement (following Abney 1987), as in (46a):

(46)   a. $[_{DP}$ [bil-en] $[_{AP}$ ny $[_{NP}$ t]]]
                        car-the   new

       b. $[_{DP}$ [ny-bil-en] $[_{AP}$ t $[_{NP}$ t]]]
                        new-car-the

This movement violates the HMC, but the HMC violation is then repaired by movement and incorporation of the adjective into the N+D head, as in (46b), given that the derived head *nybilen* can have only one index, so that the resulting head chain is (*nybilen, t, t*).

This presupposes a representational view of conditions on movement: A movement may violate a condition—for example, the HMC—if the violation can be repaired by subsequent operations, so that the end result respects all the relevant constraints.

An alternative is that N+Dx is derived by XP-movement to Spec-DP. In the case of adjective incorporation, the phrase that moves is *a*P, made up of a series of adjectives and a noun. In PF, the A+(A)+N+D sequence is spelled out as a word. It follows that the order of adjectives is the same in the synthetic definite DPs as in analytic DPs: namely, the order discussed by Cinque (1994). This was a complication in the theory of Sandström and Holmberg (1994):

(47)   a. en stor svart bil   *en svart stor bil
            a big black car   a black big car

        b. storsvartbilen   *svartstorbilen
            big-black-car-the   black-big-car-the

Still, the fact that Northern Swedish DPs do not make use of a free determiner or any additional inflectional morphology indicates that the adjective incorporation is not just a matter of phonology but is syntactic, with effects at LF as well as at PF: the adjective(s), the noun, and the article undergo a syntactic operation, as a result of which the suffixed definite article θ-binds both the adjective and the noun at LF and is spelled out as a form of compund at PF. We leave the precise nature of this operation for future research.[22]

As an additional comment on θ-binding, we notice that an expression such as *the new car* denotes a single object which is new and is a car. This is ensured if the adjective and the noun have the same θ-binder. This, in turn, suggests that only one of the articles in the Faroese-Norwegian-Swedish double definiteness DPs is a θ-binder. Given the assumptions made here, following Kester (1996) and Cinque (1994), this should be the free determiner. In that case, what is Dx doing there? Either it is just agreement morphology—in other words, it encodes only uninterpretable features (see Giusti 1997 for an elaboration of this hypothesis)—or it encodes some other feature(s), not related to θ-binding.

Support for the contention that the free article alone is the θ-binder, and hence the one that determines the reference of the noun phrase, is provided by the following observation (due to Tarald Taraldsen, pers. comm.). There is a clear contrast between (48a, b): (48a) necessarily denotes only one person, while (48b) preferably denotes two:

(48)   a. den unge professorn och nyblivne fadern
            the young professor-the and recent father-the

        b. den unge professorn och den nyblivne fadern
            the young professor-the and the recent father-the

This follows if the free article alone is the θ-binder. In (48a) there is but one free article; in (48b) there are two. The number of suffixed articles makes no difference.

In contrast, there is conflicting evidence that Dx is interpretable while the free article is, or at least can be, expletive, as discussed by Delsing (1993: 128–129) and Kester (1996: 141ff.). The following example is Delsing's:

(49)   Det finns inte den minsta anledning(*-en) att betvivla detta.
       there is not the smallest reason (-the) to doubt this

In this context, an argument is normally subject to the definiteness effect. The free article is possible in this context, but Dx is not. This effect is seen typically in construction with superlative adjectives. Whatever the explanation, the observation militates against the hypothesis that Dx is expletive.

5 A NOTE ON FAROESE

The Faroe islands are geographically about halfway between Mainland Scandinavia and Iceland. The grammar of Faroese is also in many respects halfway between Mainland Scandinavian and Icelandic.

In terms of inflectional morphology, Faroese is "more Insular than Mainland," as it has both Case and subject-verb agreement morphology. The Case and agreement paradigms are simpler, though, than the Icelandic and Old Scandinavian counterparts. As for Case, the genitive has ceased to be "completely active" in modern spoken Faroese, according to Petersen et al. (1998). As for subject-verb agreement, the most striking difference between Faroese and Icelandic/Old Scandinavian is that there is no person distinction in the plural of finite verbs; see Petersen et al. (1998) and Rohrbacher (1994).

As for the phenomena discussed in sections 3.3 (the middle field) and 3.4 (the left periphery), the broad tendency is that the structures and operations that are obligatory in Icelandic and nonexistent in Mainland Scandinavian are optional or subject to dialectal variation in Faroese. For instance, with regard to the position of the finite verb in relation to the negation and other adverbs in embedded clauses, the most commonly occurring order is Adv–Vfin, as in Mainland Scandinavian, but the Insular Scandinavian order Vfin–Adv occurs as well. According to Petersen et al. (1998), there is considerable variation in the use of Vfin–Adv order in written Faroese, and speakers vary in their acceptance of this order; see Jonas (1996: ch. 4). Recently, Petersen (2000) has shown that Faroese speakers around the age of 20 tend to use only the Adv–Vfin order.

As shown in section 3.4.2, in Icelandic the expletive always precedes the finite verb, while in Mainland Scandinavian it may precede or follow the finite verb; see (27, 28). In Faroese the expletive may optionally follow the finite verb (examples from Petersen et al. 1998):

(50) a. *Tað* eru mys í baðikarinum.
          there are mice in bathtub-the

      b. Eru (*tað*) mys í baðikarinum?

      c. *Tað* regnar ofta í Havn.
          it rains often in Torshavn

      d. Í Havn regnar (*tað*) ofta.

We proposed that the crucial difference between Insular and Mainland Scandinavian is that the Insular Scandinavian person agreement feature in T has a uFin
feature. This triggers movement of T to Fin in all finite clauses in Insular Scandinavian and eliminates the need for an expletive, except to check the EPP-feature
of Fin. The Faroese facts follow if Faroese person agreement has a uFin feature
optionally. When it has the feature, T must move to Fin, together with the verb,
in which case there is no need for an expletive, except to check the EPP-feature
of Fin.

As we might expect, Faroese has transitive expletives (at least some speakers
do; see Jonas 1996), oblique subjects, and Stylistic Fronting—all properties of a
language with uFin in T. It also has deletion of the complementizer *at* 'that',
which we suggested is a characteristic of languages without uFin in T; see Petersen
et al. (1998: 218f.). As predicted, the complementizer *ið* 'as', 'that', the Faroese
counterpart to Swedish and Norwegian *som*, is optional in embedded subject
questions (see Petersen et al. 1998: 221); compare section 3.4.6.

What has been said here predicts certain correlations of properties in Faroese.
For instance, insofar as an oblique subject presupposes person agreement with
uFin, and consequently obligatory movement of T to Fin, the prediction is that
oblique subjects should not be allowed in embedded clauses where the finite verb
follows the negation, indicating that T has not moved to Fin. This prediction is
false (Johan í Lon Jakobsen, pers. comm.). Since we have to allow for a certain
amount of "peripheral grammar," with fixed expressions, archaic forms, semi-
productive rules, and the like, the following is a more interesting formulation of
the prediction: a number of verbs in Faroese take either an oblique or a nominative subject—the former typically in written and the latter in spoken language.
Petersen et al. mention *dáma* 'like', *leingjast* 'long, years', *mangla* 'need', and a
few more. The following is one of their examples:

(51) Honum/hann leingist altíð heimaftur.
      he-DAT/he-NOM longs always back home
      'He is always homesick.'

The prediction is that there should be a preference for using the nominative when T manifestly has not moved to Fin, that is in embedded clauses with Adv–Vfin order. The prediction is hard to test given the stylistic differences between the two alternatives, but presumably it is not impossible.[23]

6 Historical Notes

In the preceding sections, we have occasionally mentioned that the syntax of the Middle Ages versions of Danish, Norwegian, and Swedish has a lot in common with the syntax of modern Icelandic. There are many morphological similarities as well; thus, for example, modern Icelandic, as well as Middle Ages Mainland Scandinavian, has morphological case, subjunctive forms of the verb, and subject-verb agreement in person and number; these inflections have disappeared in modern Mainland Scandinavian. Generally speaking, the change from an Icelandic type of grammar to a Mainland Scandinavian type of grammar seems to coincide with the loss of person inflection on the tensed verb; see Falk (1993) for a thorough demonstration of this correlation for Swedish, where the loss of agreement took place during the sixteenth century. See also Holmberg and Platzack (1995: 121–123). We will here exemplify some of the Icelandic type of properties of Old Swedish prior to the loss of person agreement.

Like modern Icelandic, Old Swedish has the finite verb in front of sentence adverbials in embedded clauses, as shown in (52); compare section 3.4.7:

(52)   hvi kristne män räddos ei pino (1385)
       why Christian men feared not pain

Stylistic fronting—that is, the satisfying of EPP in Spec-FinP by the raising of the closest phonological realized element in cases where the subject is not clause initial (see section 3.4.4)—is also found in Old Swedish:

(53)   ok vppinbaradhe hwat hanum hafdhe hänt (1375)
       and revealed what him had happened

Old Swedish has Oblique subjects, like modern Icelandic (see section 3.4.5):

(54)   tha hungradhe varom herra (end of 14th century)
       then starved our lord (dative)

In Old Swedish it is not necessary to express the subject overtly. Thus, as in modern Icelandic, an expletive subject is not obligatory (see section 3.4.2):

(55) är grauit vndir syll (13th century)
      is dug under sill

This list can be enlarged. However, there are also some diachronic changes at the sentence level that are not related to the loss of person agreement and do not lead to a syntactic difference between Insular and Mainland Scandinavian. A case at hand is the concurrent occurrence of both *finite verb > object > nonfinite verb* and *finite verb > nonfinite verb > object*, in all the medieval variants of the Scandinavic languages; this has been observed at least since Wenning (1930) and Larsson (1931), and it has been discussed recently for Old Icelandic by Sigurðsson (1988), Rögnvaldsson (1996), and Hróarsdóttir (1996, 1998, 2000) and for Old Swedish by Delsing (1999, 2001). See also Pintzuk (1991) for a similar situation in Old English. As Hróarsdóttir has shown, this variation disappears in Icelandic during the nineteenth century, whereas it is lost in Mainland Scandinavian already at the end of the Middle Ages.

The following examples illustrate the variation at hand; the Old Icelandic sentences are from Sigurðsson (1988), the Old Swedish ones from Delsing (1999):

(56) a. Móðir mín skal því ráða. (Old Icelandic: OV)
         mother my shall that decide
         'My mother will decide.'

      b. Skalt þú jafnan þessu sœti halda. (Old Icelandic: OV)
         shall you always this seat keep
         'You will always keep this seat.'

      c. þa let herodes taka ioan. (Old Icelandic: VO)
         then let Herodes take John
         'Then Herodes took John prisoner.'

      d. hvárt hon vill eiga hann. (Old Icelandic: VO)
         whether she wants to own him
         'if she wants to own him'

(57) a. at han skulde ekke seger fa (Old Swedish: OV)
         that he should not victory get
         'that he won't get a victory'

    b. at hon aldrig skulde thz nakrom sighia (Old Swedish: OV)
       that she never should it someone-DAT say

       'that she would never tell it to somebody'

    c. ok scende mik at løsa thin band (Old Swedish: VO)
       and sent me to open your fetters

       'and sent me to open your fetters'

    d. celler han wildi radhce hcenni ok cei drcepa hance (Old Swedish: VO)
       or he wanted to advise her and not kill her

       'and he wanted to give her advice and didn't want to kill her'

Delsing (1999, 2001) has made the interesting observation that only a subset of all objects may occur in preverbal position. Objects containing proper names, definite or indefinite articles, genitive attributes, and cardinal numerals almost always occur after the nonfinite verb, whereas objects containing demonstrative pronouns, possessive pronouns, and indefinite pronouns may be placed either in front of or after the nonfinite verb. Although his study is not as detailed as Delsing's, the data in Rögnvaldsson (1996) indicate that the same situation probably existed in Old Icelandic. Observing that the two types of objects may be analyzed in terms of filled or activated D, Delsing (1999, 2001) suggests that objects with filled/activated D are licensed in postverbal position, whereas objects where D is not filled or activated have to move to preverbal position to be licensed.

    The loss of OV in Icelandic is the subject of a paper by Hróarsdóttir (1996), and see also Hróarsdóttir (1998); the main results are that in the course of approximately 60 years around the year 1800, the frequency of OV order dropped rapidly.

7 SUMMARY AND CONCLUSION

In this chapter we have given an overview of the syntax of the modern Scandinavian languages—that is, Danish, Faroese, Icelandic, Norwegian, and Swedish; we have also added some remarks on earlier stages of these languages. Generally speaking, the Mainland Scandinavian languages have almost identical syntactic properties on the sentential level and differ in some respects profoundly from Icelandic, where person agreement on the finite verb and case marking on nouns trigger verb movement and make available syntactic properties like stylistic fronting, transitive expletive constructions, and oblique subjects not available to present-day Mainland Scandinavian. Faroese seems to be in the process of changing from a syntax closely related to the Icelandic one to a Mainland Scandinavian syntax.

As we have mentioned, noun phrase syntax does not group the Scandinavian languages in the same way as sentential syntax: with respect to the internal syntax of the noun phrase, the Scandinavian languages display great variation, especially if dialectal variants are considered.

NOTES

1. Besides being the national language of Sweden, Swedish is also an official language of Finland, together with Finnish (a Uralic language, not included among the Scandinavian languages). There are two Norwegian variants with official status as national languages: Bokmål and Nynorsk. Syntactically, these languages are almost identical (cf. Faarlund et al. 1997: 2), and we will therefore usually subsume them under the label "Norwegian."

2. This example is included to show that verb-second pertains to the tensed (finite) verb, irrespective of its status as main verb or auxiliary. Another property, common to all the Scandinavian languages, that is illustrated by this example is that the auxiliaries, both finite and nonfinite ones, precede the main verb. This holds true for main clauses as well as for embedded clauses:

(i)   Han undrade om jag faktiskt kunde ha hittat pengarna under sängen.
      he wondered if I actually might have found money-the under bed-the

3. Negated objects are exceptional in this respect, since they occur before the nonfinite verb, in the position of the negation, with some cross-Scandinavian variation. See Koch-Christensen (1986) and Kayne (1998) for a recent discussion. The object is underlined in the following Swedish examples:

(i)   a. Han hade inte köpt <u>något</u>.
         he had not bought anything

      b. Han hade <u>ingenting</u> köpt.
         he had nothing bought

(ii) a. Han hade inte träffat <u>någon</u>.
         he had not met anyone

      b. *Han hade <u>ingen</u> träffat.
         he had noone met

The Norwegian counterpart to (iib) is well-formed.

4. Note that the Icelandic counterpart to (5c) is well-formed. An indefinite object may not precede the adverbial:

(i)   *Hann keypti bœkur ekki.
      he bought books not

5. Some Swedish dialects, like Fenno-Swedish, put the particle after the object when the particle has a locative reading. In fact, this is not impossible in the standard language, either, as shown in (i), especially when the object is a weak pronoun:

(i)   %Han kastade <u>den</u> *ut* (genom fönstret).
       he throw it out through window-the

The Swedish Academy grammar (Teleman et al. 1999) analyzes *ut* 'out' as a locative adverbial in cases like this.

6. Reflexive pronouns may precede the particle in Swedish.

7. Consider in this connection the fact that the particle may also overtly occur left-adjoined to the verb, as in (i); such cases are not discussed here:

(i)   Fisken blev *upp*äten.
       fish-the became upeaten

       'The fish was eaten up.'

8. For the same reason, a Swedish example corresponding to (18d) but with a PP instead of an indirect object is well-formed:

(i)   Jag gav den$_{OB}$ inte t$_{OB}$ till Elsa.
       I gave it not to Elsa

9. The corresponding Icelandic word order is given in (i):

(i)   að Jón hafði raunverulega keypt bókina (Icelandic)
       that John had actually bought book-the

We argue in the next section that the finite verb in embedded Icelandic clauses of the type in (i) is in the C-domain; this is thus a clear difference between Mainland Scandinavian and Icelandic. There are, however, also embedded clauses in Icelandic with the finite verb after a sentence adverbial, presumably in a middle-field position (Maling 1980):

(ii)   þegar ég loksins fann lagið.
       when I finally found the tune

This word order is mainly found in adverbial clauses and is not discussed further in this chapter. See Angantýrsson (2001) for a recent discussion.

10. The sentential negation is usually classified as an adverb in Scandinavian. More precisely, we assume that the negation word is the specifier of a NegP, which has its place in the sentential hierarchy of adverbs described by Cinque (1999). In Danish the negation is more "head-like." In particular, it cannot be moved to spec-CP, the way it can in the other Scandinavian languages.

11. The theory is thus consistent with a syntactic derivational view of verb inflection: what is merged in VP is the verb stem. The tensed form is a result of verb movement to T. See Julien (2000).

12. Following Chomsky (1995: ch. 4, 1998, 2001), we assume that syntactic features come in two varieties, interpretable and uninterpretable. The latter ones have to be eliminated in the course of the syntactic derivation. This is what drives syntactic operations, including movement.

13. With varying degree of acceptance, all the Scandinavian languages can have de-

claratives, which apparently are introduced by the finite verb. This is often found in oral tellings and is known as Narrative inversion; a Swedish example is given in (i), taken from Dahlbäck and Vamling (1983). See Mörnsjö (2002) for a detailed account.

(i)   Så låg han bara där. Kommer hon in där, kände han igen henne, började han darra.
      so lay he just there comes she in there recognized he her began he tremble

14. See Branigan (1996) for a theory that is close to the one presented here. See Koeneman (2000) for another recent account of verb placement in Scandinavian.

15. Another possibility is that the order N–Dx is the result of NP-movement to Spec-DP. The word order of (i) is a complication for the NP-movement hypothesis:

(i)   bilden av kungen
      picture-the of king-the

      'the picture of the king'

It can still be derived on the assumption that *av kungen*, the complement of N, first moves to a position between D and N (assuming that all phrases are underlyingly head-initial and that all movement is leftward), before the remnant NP moves to Spec-DP. Later we suggest that there is at least one case where N–Dx order is derived by NP-movement.

16. See Taraldsen (1990), Delsing (1993), Holmberg and Sandström (1996a), and Vangsnes (1999). At first, the possessive pronoun looks to be the same in (38a, b), but a closer look reveals that, while the prenominal pronoun is unrestricted, the postnominal pronoun is obligatorily weak (in the sense of Cardinaletti and Starke 1999). For example, the prenominal pronoun can be coordinated, the postnominal pronoun cannot:

(i)   min og din bok (Norwegian)
      my and your book

(ii) *boka min og din
      book-the my and your

17. As discussed in Holmberg (1994), at least among the languages in Europe, languages without articles all have fairly rich Case morphology; conversely, languages without Case morphology all have articles.

18. In Vangsnes's terms, the gender feature makes the adjective capable of licensing D (to put it simply), by actually moving covertly to D. It could be mentioned that, although the Case-morphology of nouns and pronouns is rich enough in Icelandic and Old Scandinavian, morphological Case-marking on attributive adjectives is minimal, distinguishing only between nominative and oblique. Faroese is a potential counterexample to both the Case hypothesis and the gender hypothesis, since Faroese has morphological Case and has gender marked on attributive adjectives, yet requires a free determiner. Holmberg (1994), Holmberg and Platzack (1995), and Vangsnes (1999) all point to the fact that Case, as well as gender marking, is lower in Faroese than in Icelandic or Old Scandinavian.

19. Kester (1996) has an explanation in terms of checking theory: If the noun moved to D, it would check and thereby eliminate the feature required to θ-bind the

adjective. However, this presupposes that checking eliminates interpretable features, which is impossible, as discussed in Chomsky (1995: ch. 4).

20. As mentioned, Danish doesn't have Dx in construction with descriptive attributive adjectives and also does not do so in names: *Det Hvide Hus* "The White House', *Det Døde Hav* 'The Dead Sea'. Norwegian, for some reason, either behaves like Danish or employs a form of compounding: *Det Hvite Hus* but *Døde Havet*, the latter with compound intonation. The generalization is that proper names never show double definiteness. The question is why proper names have an article at all, given that there is no need for θ-binding. Possibly it is just a segment of the name with no syntactic function, as in, say, *The Hague*. Still, there are languages that consistently use articles with proper names, including, in fact, many Scandinavian dialects; see Delsing (1993).

21. A factor that we have ignored entirely here is the "weak-strong" or definite-indefinite inflection on adjectives, found in all the Scandinavian languages. The question is, does it realize an uninterpretable feature, or does it play a more active role somehow? It might perhaps be a realization of *a*, but in the absence of a more thorough investigation, this suggestion must be taken with great care.

22. As discussed by Holmberg and Sandström (1996b), it is characteristic of Northern Swedish that definite noun phrases always exhibit an overt definite article—namely, the definite suffix. This includes possessive constructions. Out of the possessive constructions listed under (34), all and only those that employ Dx (that is c, d, e, and g) are characteristic of Northern Swedish dialects. It also includes generic noun phrases; compare the following:

(i)   Koen je klook. (Northern Swedish)
       cows-the are clever

(ii)   Kor är kloka. (Standard Swedish)
       cows are clever.

       'Cows are clever.'

As they note, in this respect Northern Swedish is closer to Romance than to Germanic languages, in terms of the typology of Longobardi (1994).

23. Jonas (1996) reports some correlations of the expected kind. In particular, among the speakers she consulted, those who accepted transitive expletives were the ones who also accepted the order Vfin–Adv in nonbridge-embedded clauses.

REFERENCES

Abney, Steven (1987) "The English Noun Phrase in Its Sentential Aspect." PhD diss., MIT, Cambridge, Mass.

Alexiadou, Artemis, and Elena Anagnostopoulou (1998) "Parametrizing AGR: Word Order, V-movement and EPP-checking." *Natural Language and Linguistic Theory* 16: 491–539.

Angantýrsson, Ásgrimur (2001) "Skandinavísk orðaröð í íslenskum aukasetningum." *Íslensk mál og almenn málfræði* 23: 95–122.

Bobaljik, Jonathan, and Dianne Jonas (1996) "Subject Positions and the Roles of TP." *Linguistic Inquiry* 27: 195–236.

Branigan, Philip (1996) "Verb-Second and the A-bar Syntax of Subjects." *Studia Linguistica* 50: 50–79.

Cardinaletti, Anna, and Michal Starke (1999) "The Typology of Structural Deficiency," in Henk van Riemsdijk (ed.) *Clitics in the Languages of Europe.* Mouton de Gruyter, Berlin, 145–233.

Chomsky, Noam (1995) *The Minimalist Program.* MIT Press, Cambridge, Mass.

Chomsky, Noam (1998) *Minimalist Inquiries: The Framework.* MIT Occasional Papers in Linguistics, no. 15. Department of Linguistics and Philosophy, MIT, Cambridge, Mass.

Chomsky, Noam (2001) "Derivation by Phase," in Michael Kenstowicz (ed.), *Ken Hale. A Life in Language.* MIT Press, Cambridge, Mass., 7–52.

Cinque, Guglielmo (1994) "On the evidence for Partial N-movement in the Romance DP," in Guglielmo Cinque, Jan Koster, Jean-Yves Pollock, Luigi Rizzi, and Rafaella Zanuttini (eds.) *Paths towards Universal Grammar.* Georgetown University Press, Washington D.C., 85–110.

Cinque, Guglielmo (1999) *Adverbs and Functional Heads.* Oxford University Press, New York.

Dahlbäck, Hans, and Karina Vamling (1983) "Tog han då foto': ett syntaktiskt fenomen i malmöitiskt talspråk." Unpublished ms., Department of Linguistics, Lund University.

Delsing, Lars-Olof (1993) "The Internal Structure of Noun Phrases in the Scandinavian Languages." Ph.D. diss., Department of Scandinavian Languages, Lund University.

Delsing, Lars-Olof (1999) "Från OV-ordföljd till VO-ordföljd: En språkförändring med förhinder [From OV to VO: A prevented linguistic change]." *Arkiv för nordisk filologi* 114: 151–232.

Delsing, Lars-Olof (2001) "From OV to VO in Swedish," in S. Pintzuk, G. Tsoulas, and A. Warner (eds.) *Diachronic Syntax: Models and Mechanisms.* Oxford University Press, New York, 255–274.

Faarlund, Jan Terje, Svein Lie, and Kjell Ivar Vannebo (1997) *Norsk Referansegrammatikk.* Universitetsforlaget, Oslo.

Giusti, Giuliana (1997) "The Categorial Status of Determiners," in L. Haegeman (ed.) *The New Comparative Syntax.* Longman, London, 95–123.

Hansen, Erik, and Lars Heltoft (in press) *Dansk referansegrammatik.*

Haugen, Einar (1976) *The Scandinavian Languages: An Introduction to Their History.* Faber and Faber, London.

Hellan, Lars, and Christer Platzack (1999) "Pronouns in Scandinavian Languages: An Overview," in Henk van Riemsdijk (ed.) *Clitics in the Languages of Europe.* Mouton de Gruyter, Berlin, 123–142.

Higginbotham, James (1985) "On Semantics." *Linguistic Inquiry* 16: 547–593.

Holmberg, Anders (1994) "Morphological Parameters in Syntax: The Case of Faroese." *Reports* 35. Department of General Linguistics, University of Umeå.

Holmberg, Anders (1999) "Remarks on Holmberg's Generalization." *Studia Linguistica* 53: 1–39.

Holmberg, Anders (2000) "Scandinavian Stylistic Fronting: How Any Category Can Become an Expletive." *Linguistic Inquiry* 31: 445–484.

Holmberg, Anders, and Christer Platzack (1995) *The Role of Inflection in Scandinavian Syntax*. Oxford University Press, New York.

Holmberg, Anders, and Görel Sandström (1996a) "Scandinavian Possessive Constructions from a Northern Swedish Viewpoint," in James Black and Virginia Motapanyane (eds.) *Microparametric Syntax and Dialect Variation*. John Benjamins, Amsterdam; 95–120.

Holmberg, Anders, and Görel Sandström (1996b) "Vad är det för särskilt med nordsvenska nominalfraser? [What is special about Northern Swedish noun phrases?]" *Nordica Bergensia* (University of Bergen) 9: 75–89.

Hróarsdóttir, Thorbjörg (1996) "The Decline of OV Word Order in the Icelandic VP: A Diachronic Study." *Working Papers in Scandinavian Syntax* (Lund University) 57: 92–141.

Hróarsdóttir, Thorbjörg (1998) "Verb Phrase Syntax in the History of Icelandic." Ph.D. diss., University of Tromsø.

Hróarsdóttir, Thorbjörg (2000) "Parameter Change in Icelandic," in P. Svenonius (ed.) *The Derivation of VO and OV*. John Benjamins, Amsterdam, 153–179.

Johnson, Kyle (1991) "Object Positions." *Natural Language and Linguistic Theory* 9: 577–636.

Jonas, Dianne (1996) "Clausal Structure and Verbal Syntax of Scandinavian and English." Ph.D. diss., Harvard University.

Jónsson, Jóhannes Gísli (1991) "Stylistic Fronting in Icelandic." *Working Papers in Scandinavian Syntax* (Lund University) 48: 1–43.

Josefsson, Gunlög (2001) "The True Nature of Holmberg's Generalization Revisited: Once Again." *Working Papers in Scandinavian Syntax* (Lund University) 67: 85–102.

Josefsson, Gunlög, and Christer Platzack (1998) "Short Raising of V and N in Mainland Scandinavian." *Working Papers in Scandinavian Syntax* (Lund University) 61: 23–52.

Julien, Marit (2000) "Syntactic Heads and Word Formation." Ph.D. diss., University of Tromsø.

Kayne, Richard (1998) "Overt vs. Covert Movements." *Syntax* 1: 128–191.

Kester, Ellen-Petra (1996) "The Nature of Adjectival Inflection." Ph.D. diss., University of Utrecht.

Koch-Christensen, Kirsti (1986) "Norwegian *ingen*: A Case of Postsyntactic Lexicalization, in Ö. Dahl and A. Holmberg (eds.) *Scandinavian Syntax*. Institute of Linguistics, University of Stockholm, Stockholm, 21–35.

Koeneman, Olaf (2000) "The Flexible Nature of Verb Movement." Ph.D. diss., University of Utrecht.

Larsson, Carl (1931) *Ordföljdsstudier över det finita verbet i de nordiska fornspråken* [Word order studies of the finite verb in Old Scandinavian]. Lundequistska, Uppsala.

Lockwood, W. B. (1977) *An Introduction to Modern Faroese*. Føroya Skúlabókagrunnur, Tórshavn.

Longobardi, Giuseppe (1994) Reference and Proper Names. *Linguistic Inquiry* 25: 609–666.

Lundeby, Einar (1965) *Overbestemt substantiv i norsk og de andre nordiske sprog*. Universitetsforlaget, Oslo.

Maling, Joan (1980) "Inversion in Embedded Clauses in Modern Icelandic." *Íslenskt mál og almenn málfræði* 2: 175–193.

Mörnsjö, Maria (2002) "Declarative VI-Constructions in Spoken Swedish: Syntax, Information Structure, and Prosodic Pattern." Ph.D. diss., Lund University.

Pesetsky, David, and Esther Torrego (2001) "T-to-C Movement: causes and consequences," in Michael Kenstowicz (ed.). *Ken Hale: A Life in Language.* MIT Press, Cambridge, Mass., 355–426.

Petersen, Hjalmar (2000) "IP or TP in Modern Faroese." *Working Papers in Scandinavian Syntax* (Lund University) 66: 75–83.

Petersen, Hjalmar, Jógvan í Lon Jacobsen, Zakaris Hansen, and Höskuldur Thráinsson (1998) "Faroese: An Overview for Students and Researchers." Unpublished ms. Torshavn and Reykjavik.

Pintzuk, Susan (1991) "Phrase Structures in Competition: Variation and Change in Old English Word Order." Ph.D. diss., University of Pennsylvania.

Platzack, Christer (1999) "The Subject of Icelandic Psych-Verbs: A Minimalist Account." *Working Papers in Scandinavian Syntax* (Lund University) 64: 103–115.

Platzack, Christer (2004) "Cross-linguistic Word Order Variation at the Left Periphery: The Case of Object First Main Clauses," in David Adger, Cécile de Cat, and George Tsoulas (eds.) *Peripheries: Syntactic Edges and Their Effects.* Kluwer, Dordrecht, Boston, London, 191–210.

Richards, Norvin (1998) "The Principle of Minimal Compliance." *Linguistic Inquiry* 29: 599–629.

Rizzi, Luigi (1997) "The Fine Structure of the Left Periphery," in Liliane Haegeman (ed.) *Elements of Grammar: Handbook in Generative Syntax.* Dordrecht, Kluwer, 281–337.

Rögnvaldsson, Eiríkur (1996) "Word Order Variation in the VP in Old Icelandic." *Working Papers in Scandinavian Syntax* (Lund University) 58: 55–86.

Rohrbacher, Bernhard (1994) "The Germanic Languages and the Full Paradigm: A Theory of V-to-I Raising." Ph.D. diss., University of Massachusetts at Amherst.

Sandström, Görel, and Anders Holmberg (1994) "Adjective Incorporation and the Syntax of the Scandinavian Noun Phrase." *Report 35.* Department of General Linguistics, University of Umeå.

Santelmann, Lynn (1993) "The Distribution of Double Determiners in Swedish: *Den* Support in D." *Studia Linguistica* 47: 154–176.

Sigurðsson, Halldór. Á. (1988) "From OV to VO: Evidence from Old Icelandic." *Working Papers in Scandinavian Syntax* (Lund University), 34.

Sigurðsson, Halldór. Á (1989) "Verbal Syntax and Case in Icelandic." Ph.D. diss., Department of Scandinavian Languages, Lund University.

Sigurðsson, Halldór Á. (1991) "Icelandic Case-Marked PRO and the Licensing of Lexical Arguments." *Natural Language and Linguistic Theory* 9: 327–363.

Sigurðsson, Halldór Á. (2001) "Case: Abstract vs. Morphological." *Working Papers in Scandinavian Syntax* (Lund University) 67: 103–151.

Svenonius, Peter (1996) "The Optionality of Particle Shift." *Working Papers in Scandinavian Syntax* (Lund University) 57: 47–75.

Taraldsen, K. Tarald (1990) "D-projections and N-projections in Norwegian," in Juan Mascaro and Martina Nespor (eds.) *Grammar in Progress.* Foris, Dordrecht, 419–431.

Taraldsen, K. Tarald (1991) "Two Arguments for Functional Heads." *Lingua* 84: 85–108.

Teleman, Ulf, Staffan Hellberg, and Erik Andersson (1999) *Svenska Akademiens grammatik* [The Swedish Academy grammar]. NorstedtsOrdbok, Stockholm.

Vangsnes, Øystein (1999) "The Identification of Functional Architecture." Ph.D. diss., University of Bergen.

Vikner, Sten (1991) "Relative *der* and Other C-elements in Danish." *Lingua* 84: 109–136.

Vikner, Sten (1995) *Verb Movement and Expletive Subjects in the Germanic Languages.* Oxford University Press, New York.

Wenning, Alf (1930) *Studier över ordföljden i fornsvenskan: predikatets bestämningar i äldre och yngre fornsvenska* [Studies of word order in Old Swedish: the modifiers of the predicate in Early and Late Old Swedish]. Lindstedts, Lund.

....

CHAPTER 11

NOUN CLASS, GENDER, AND THE LEXICON-SYNTAX-MORPHOLOGY INTERFACES

A Comparative Study of Niger-Congo and Romance Languages

....

ALAIN KIHM

1 INTRODUCTION

....

Not all grammatical categories are created equal, as far as universality is concerned. For instance, Number—that is, the formal indication of whether one or more than one token of a given entity concept is being referred to—is an excellent candidate for universality, inasmuch as no natural language seems to be devoid of the category, even though there is variation as to its applicability (on this, see Chierchia 1998). Gender, on the other hand, appears a poor candidate. Consider a rudimentary gender system like that of English: noun phrases denoting interestingly sexed organisms (i.e., human beings and pets) are masculine or feminine;

all others are neuter.[1] The allotment is made perceivable only by the choice of a coreferential singular pronoun, *he, she,* or *it*. Even such a cognitively simplistic (and realistic) system is entirely absent in a language like Turkish, where all noun phrases are pronominalized as *o* 'she/he/it', irrespective of their denotation. And Turkish is by no means an isolate: many languages all over the world are like it in this respect.

Traditional lore about gender has long reflected this state of affairs: when marked in any way, gender was either considered to be as in English—that is, the linguistic expression of the obvious and obviously vital sexual division of the animate and, through mythology, part of the inanimate world as female, male, or nil—or it was as in French: arbitrary, not to say absurd (why *la table*, but *le cable*?) but for that portion of the vocabulary denoting sex-relevant entities.[2] In both cases, it was uninteresting from the serious linguist's point of view, except for the agreement phenomena it may trigger (on this and much more, see Corbett 1996). The cognitive trivialness or arbitrariness of gender was taken as the reason that so many languages do without it altogether.

In recent years, a shift away from this tradition has occurred. Numerous studies deal seriously with gender and related categories as a classification device that necessarily reflects some central property of human cognition as it expresses itself in the language faculty (see, e.g., Allan 1977, Serzisko 1982, Craig 1986, Aronoff 1994, Croft 1994). Most recently (to my present knowledge), Aikhenvald (2000) gave us a thorough typological review of "noun categorization devices" in a vast array of languages, including a host of references to little accessible works, because of their age or the language in which they were written, namely, Russian or German. In the work presented here, I wish to contribute to this revival, albeit from a somewhat different perspective, as will appear.

Motives for doubting the old vulgate are indeed easy to find. Sex-based gender systems, of the English "rational" or French "arbitrary" type, are certainly not the only ones in existence. In many languages in various families (Niger-Congo, Caucasic, Sino-Tibetan, Oceanic, Australian, Amerindian of all families, etc.), nominal items are formally divided by diverse means, according to criteria that have to do either with "natural" categories such as being a human (of either sex), a plant, an animal, or a dangerous thing or with descriptive properties of the denoted object, like being elongated, flat, or liquid, and so forth.[3] Noun classes and classifiers are the names for what these languages present. And, exactly as in sex-based systems, irrelevancies—that is, currently incomprehensible allotments—are widespread, although never to the point of entirely obscuring some rationale for the division.

There seems to be no good reason, therefore, for not considering gender, noun classes, and classifiers as diverse expressions of a fundamental faculty of the human mind, namely, classification, understood as the spontaneous and irrepressible need we have of pigeonholing all things in the world in order simply to *see* them, what Aronoff (1994: 181, n. 3) describes as the "inherent human desire for order, however ungrounded the particular order may be" (see also Lakoff 1986).

It is not my intention, however, to speculate more than has already been done on the cultural and biological foundations of the classificatory faculty and activity. All I want to suggest by the preceding remarks is that a linguistic phenomenon so rooted in such a basic faculty of mind is hardly likely to be uninteresting to linguists who view language as a mental organ whose design is supposed to be driven by the need to optimally interface with cognitive faculties (see Chomsky 1998).

What really interests me is the *grammatical* function of "Class," as I will designate the global expression of classification however it is realized. This is a sorely neglected subject, I feel, due perhaps to too much focusing on the extra-linguistic correlates. Such neglect is all the more deplorable as Class is a particularly apt topic for comparative grammar, precisely because of its uncertain status as far as universality is concerned. Why should so many grammars avail themselves of such an often cumbersome system, while many others apparently ignore it? Does it mean that Class as a category is indeed different from universal Number (or Tense), or is it that we do not know yet what purpose it really serves and that, as a consequence, Class's nonuniversality is only an appearance?

In one of the most extensive surveys of the issue to date, Corbett (1996) assumes the widespread view that Class (what he calls Gender) qua grammatical category exists only as agreement. Portuguese and Swahili have Class because, for example, attributive and predicative adjectives must agree for it with the noun they modify or are predicated of. Therefore, a language that formally divides its nominals according to Class criteria without triggering agreement of any sort does not have Class. Interestingly enough, such a language does not seem to exist: I know of no language where Class is overtly marked *on the noun itself* without some agreement ensuing, whereas languages where Number is marked and does not trigger agreement are easy to find.[4] Of itself, this is an interesting observation. Furthermore, it seems to me, the fact (let's assume it is one) that the theoretically conceivable Class-without-agreement type of language is not attested shows that agreement cannot be used to define or explain Class, precisely because it is a necessary correlate of it. To conclude from entailment to identity is a logical fallacy typical of structuralist views that hold that relations (here, agreement) are more real than what they relate. Generative grammar takes the opposite view: namely, that elements or features are real, and relations such as agreement are abstractions on feature matching or nonmatching.[5]

In this chapter I follow a rather narrow path but one that takes us, hopefully, onto wider grounds. As mentioned earlier, Class systems can be considered to fall out into three types: (sex-based) gender systems consisting in two or three genders, with Romance as a typical representative; noun class or multiple (more than three) gender systems, as exemplified by many Niger-Congo languages; and numeral classifier systems, as in Chinese (see Aikhenvald 2000 for a different taxonomy which the present one crosscuts and simplifies but does not contradict).[6] I leave the latter mostly out of consideration. What I intend to do is to compare the first two systems in order to try to make sense of two empirical generalizations that I find significant, even though they have been given little notice so far.

First, there is the observation that Class exponents of gender systems are suffixes, whereas those of noun class systems may be suffixes or prefixes.[7] Actually, the distinction one must draw is more subtle: languages with gender systems belong to the inflectional type where functional morphemes are suffixed to and fused with the roots. In contrast, noun class languages manifest the agglutinative typology where functional morphemes are merged with the roots that they may either precede or follow;[8] in either case, they look more like proclitics or enclitics than affixes.[9] This seems to be the true generalization that stands in need of an explanation (see Dixon 1986 for a study of typological correlates that largely anticipates my own efforts).[10]

The second empirical generalization is better known but just as unexplained as the first one (but see Renault 1987). It is that Class exponents, both gender and noun class, are always combined with Number morphemes when overt—that is, nonsingular. For gender languages, we can take Italian *case* /cas-e/ 'houses' as an exemplar, and Manjaku *ito* /i-to/ 'houses' for noun class languages.[11] Both /-e/ and /i-/ are syncretic morphemes where Class (respectively, feminine gender and noun class 7; see later) and Number (plural) cannot be told apart. As for the corresponding singulars, *casa* and *kato*, it seems we may assume that /-a/ and /ka-/ are pure Class exponents without a Number feature. I return to all this at length, as it raises many questions.[12]

Those are genuine grammatical generalizations insofar as none of the semantic or conceptual properties that may be associated with Class forces them into existence. Therefore, they must proceed from a grammatical property of Class. This property, I argue, ought to be deduced from the basic fact—all too often held to be so self-evident as to hardly merit discussion—that Class is a property of nouns as opposed to verbs, to a degree that sets it apart from the other so-called ϕ-features, Number and Person.[13] The hypothesis I try to support, then, is that Class's grammatical function is as a nominalizer, an *n* category similar to verbalizing *v*. More precisely, I argue that Class is the one possible content of the *n* head already proposed in the literature (see, e.g., Marantz 1997) and that the differences observed as to its position and degree of fusion with the root are related to how contentful that head is. Whether several *n*s should be assumed, as is being currently envisaged for *v* (see Arad 1999, Doron 2000), is a related issue I also consider.

The discussion is reported within the global framework of Distributed Morphology (see Halle and Marantz 1993, Noyer 1997, Marantz 1997, Embick and

Noyer 1999): I adopt the notion that syntax operates on abstract feature bundles (roots) drawn from the lexicon, then delivering the outcome of its operations to the autonomous morphological component where vocabulary items—namely, overt realizations of the feature bundles—are inserted and further worked upon (also see Aronoff 1994 for a different but compatible architecture). However, contra Embick and Noyer (1999), I keep to the assumption that Kayne's (1994) Linear Correspondence Axiom (LCA) is fully valid, crucially implying that lowering (rightward movement) is disallowed and adjunction is to the left across the board. It is not my purpose to make a general argument against these particular proposals of Embick and Noyer, who accept lowering and rightward adjunction in both syntax and morphology. I will be satisfied with showing that such anti-LCA operations are not needed to account for the empirical generalizations just stated.

These generalizations come from comparing gender systems like those of the Romance languages with noun class systems as examplified by Manjaku. Since the latter is in all probability much less well known than the former, I present it first in some detail.

2 MANJAKU NOUN CLASSES

I chose Manjaku rather than the Bantu languages usually adduced when it comes to noun classes for two reasons. First, it is a language for which I have firsthand data (see Kihm and Gomes 1988, Kihm 1998). Second, the syntactic correlate of having noun classes—namely, agreement—is limited to the DP in this language, which simplifies the presentation. In addition to my own data, I rely on that of Doneux (1967, 1975) and Buis (1990).

As noted already (see n. 11), Manjaku belongs to the Atlantic subfamily of the Niger-Congo family, more precisely to the Bak subgroup of this subfamily (see Doneux 1975).[14] Actually, Manjaku is a cluster of closely related languages that include, inter alia, Mankanya (see Trifkovic 1969), Pepel, Cur, and Bok. The variety I deal with is Bok, spoken to the north of Bissau, which has vehicular currency among all (ethnic) Manjakus, although not among Mankanyas, the latters' language being markedly different, at least in vocabulary. I will continue to use "Manjaku" as a convenient denominator, however.

Manjaku used to be dubbed Bantoid because its noun class system looks very much like that of Bantu languages. It can be schematized as follows, adapting Bantuist traditional presentation:

(1)   1 na-   2 ba-
      1a a-
      3 u-   4 ngë-
      5 bë-   6 m-
      7 ka-   8 i-
      9 pë-   10 kë-
      11 ndë-
      12 tsë-
      13 dë-

In principle, each row represents a singular–plural pair. Entry 1a is a subset of 1 that includes only kinship terms and is paired with 2 as well; entry 11 is used to derive diminutives from roots of any other noun class, and it has no plural. Similarly, 12 and 13, locative in meaning and extremely limited in use, have no associated plural noun classes. I now give examples for each noun class and its paired plural: *na-kiëj* (1) / *ba-kiëj* (2) 'thieve(s)'; *a-nin* (1a) / *ba-nin* (2) 'mother(s)'; *u-ndali* (3) / *ngë-ndali* (4) 'cat(s)'; *bë-calam* (5) / *m-calam* (6) 'wild mango tree(s)'; *ka-to* (7) / *i-to* (8) 'house(s)'; *pë-kës* (9) / *kë-kës* (10) 'eye(s)'; *ndë-bus* (11) 'little dog'; *tsë-ko* (12) 'place'; *d-i* (13) 'in, at'.[15]

These examples show an idealized view of the system where each pluralizable noun class is paired with one and the same plural noun class and the semantic correlates are fairly transparent: 1(a)/2 are for human beings; 3/4 for animals; 5/6 for plants; 7/8 for artifacts; and 9/10 for body organs. These correlations hold for a great number of nouns, but it is also a fact, and a well-known one, that they do not hold for another great number of nouns.[16] To take but a few examples, we find nouns denoting instruments in 3/4 (e.g., *u-ndink/ngë-ndink* 'machete(s)'; *u-mbanj/ngë-mbanj* 'knife/knives'); many nouns denoting natural phenomena in 3 or 5 (e.g., *u-ru* 'smoke', *u-futs* 'wind', *u-nu* 'day', *bë-rëm* 'night,' *bë-ruä* 'fire') or even 7 (e.g., *ka-nkuël* 'twilight', *ka-borar* 'dew', *ka-mpalambamb* 'thunder'); and many nouns denoting artifacts in 9 (e.g., *pë-caa* 'basket', *pë-bank* 'dike'). In addition, 3 hosts a number of nouns referring to abstract entities (e.g., *u-bon* 'hunger', *u-lemp* 'work), as well as language names (e.g., *u-jakin* 'Wolof language'), including the word for 'language' itself (*u-jipan/ngë-jipan*).

The pairings indicated in (1) are not fully regular, either. For instance, 1 *na-päts* 'child' has a 3 plural *u-päts* 'children', not 2 /*ba-päts/. Nouns in 9 denoting artifacts regularly have plurals in 8 rather than 10 (e.g., *i-bank* 'dikes', *i-caa* 'baskets', *pë-ndog/i-ndog* 'stick(s)', *pë-ngare/i-ngare* 'gun(s)').[17] Mass nouns, which normally have no plural, appear in several noun classes, as shown by *bë-ruä* (5) 'fire', *i-tuj* (8) 'saliva', *m-lik* (6) 'water'—although the latter's membership is probably due to the fact that 6 seems to be the preferred noun class for liquids (see *m-cäm* 'palm oil', *m-kër* 'oil', *m-ne* 'pus', *m-taw* 'milk'—but *pë-ñaak* 'blood' is in 9).

Unique (or "lexical") class membership is a property of nouns.[18] This means that verbs, prepositions, and adverbs lie outside the noun class system. This proposition is straightforwardly true for the first named: since agreement in Manjaku does not exceed the boundaries of the DP, as we shall see presently, verbs in this language never bear any marking as to the noun class of their arguments—and verbs as such are immune to Class categorization, for reasons I try to clarify later on. It must be qualified, however, for prepositions and adverbs. For one thing, basic prepositions are few in Manjaku, perhaps limited to *di* 'in, at' and *ni* 'with' (also 'and')—and even the first item may be analyzed as /d+i/—that is, noun class 13 plus a deictic morpheme (see later).[19] Other relations for which English uses simple prepositions are expressed through PPs consisting of *di* and various nouns (e.g., *di bë-run* 'in front, before'; *di u-fets* 'at the back, behind'; *di ruäts* 'on top, on'). As shown, those nouns may pertain to noun classes 5, 3, or 13 and perhaps others.[20] Likewise, adverbs fall out into two categories, depending on whether they exhibit no noun class membership (e.g., *takël* 'yesterday', *ntsäri* 'today', *faan* 'tomorrow, *kotiës* 'a little') or whether they are nouns generally pertaining to noun class 3 (e.g., *u-cäk* 'firstly').[21]

Besides nouns, whose noun class is fixed, and classless items, there is a third category; namely, agreeing items that include adjectives, some numerals, determiners, and a particular type of pronominals. Since this section aims only to description, I will content myself with giving examples for each type. Adjectives in Manjaku do not constitute a unified syntactic category, as they are represented by agreeing items when in attributive function but by (stative or quality) verbs when predicative:

(2) ka-to   ka-mak
     7-house 7-big
     'the/a big house'

(2a) i-to   i-mak
     8-house 8-big
     '(the) big houses'

(3) Ka-to   a   mak.
     7-house Pro be-big
     'The house is big.'

(3a) I-to   a   mak.
     8-house Pro be-big
     'The houses are big.'

As evidenced in (2) and (2a), attributive adjectives follow the head noun they modify and agree with it in noun class (and number).[22] Entries (3) and (3a) illustrate an already mentioned feature—namely, absence of agreement beyond the DP. The *a* morpheme glossed Pro is a kind of predicate marker that is obligatorily present with third-person subjects (compare *M mak* /you(sg) be-big/ 'You are big'), although it does not agree with them. I have more to say about it in the following.

Numerals from 'one' to 'ten' are also split. From 'one' to 'four' they behave like adjectives:

(4)   ka-to   ka-lole
       7-house   7-one

       'one house'

(4a)   i-to   i-tëb /   i-wants /   i-bakër
       8-house   8-two   8-three   8-four

       'two/three/four houses'

From 'five' to 'ten', in contrast, they are nouns with their own class membership, although they still follow the noun they quantify, as if they were in some kind of apposition to it:

(5)   i-to   kà-ñän /   p(ë)-aaj /   k(ë)-uäs /   u-ntaja[23]
       8-house   7a-five   9-six   10-eight   3-ten

       'five/six/eight/ten houses'

Determiners are /-i/ 'this', /-un/ 'that', and /-lon/ 'some, a certain', and they appear rightmost in the DP:

(6)   ka-to   ka-mak k-i /   k-un/   ka-lon[24]
       7-house   7-big 7-this   7-that   7-some

       'this/that/some big house'

Finally, there is the intriguing root /ko/, probably to be analyzed as a fully unspecified nominal or pronominal. I use this label because /ko/ is able to enter all noun classes, thus giving rise to items that function either as kind terms or as anaphoric, classified pronouns. For instance, *na-ko* (1) means 'he/she' with specific reference to the person designated as the Topic;[25] similarly, *u-ko/ngë-ko* (3/4) 'it/ they', if the Topic is an animal or a nonmaterial entity; *ka-ko/i-ko* (7/8) if it is a concrete object. In contrast, *u-ko/ngë-ko* may be used as a noun with the meaning 'animal' (e.g., *u-ko w-i* 'this animal'); likewise, *ka-ko k-i* 'this thing' (also 'this piece') and the diminutive (class 11) *ndë-ko nd-i* 'this small thing'. The latter, however, cannot be used as an anaphoric pronoun referring back to anything being described as small, nor can, it seems, *bë-ko/m-ko* (5/6), *pë-ko* (9), and *tsë-ko* (12), which are only kind terms meaning, respectively, 'tree(s)', 'fruit' (a mass noun), and 'place'. I hedge this claim, because there might be some, as yet unexplored, variation or special conditions in this area. Perhaps idealizing somewhat, then, noun class distinctions for anaphoric Topic pronouns seem to reduce to three: 1/2 for humans, 3/4 for animals and nonmaterial entities (and perhaps more if 3/4 is indeed the less specified noun class), and 7/8 for concrete objects. Naturally, given a felicitous discourse context, determined kind terms may always be used to refer to Topic entities for which there is no specific *-ko* pronoun:

(7) Man   win bë-mango.   Bë-ko   b-i   a   mak.
     I   see 5-mango   5-KO   5-this   Pro   be-big

     'I saw a mango tree. This tree/it is big.'

(7a) Man   ya   ka-to   Jon.   Tsë-ko   ts-un   a   wara.
     I   go   7-house   Jon   12-KO   12-that   Pro   be-nice

     'I went to Jon's house. That place/it is nice.'

Ko-pronouns only fulfill the subject function and they do not cooccur with *a*:

(8) Man   me   Jon.   Na-ko   (*a)   wara.
     I   know   Jon   1-KO   (*Pro)   be-nice

     'I know Jon. He is nice.'

This suggests they compete for the same position (say Spec vP). This accords with the fact that, even though *ko*-pronouns are discourse-linked with a current topic, their use does not imply explicit topicalization. What must be considered here is that *a* is sufficient by itself to provide a sentence with its necessary overt subject (Manjaku not being a null subject language), so that *A wara* 'She/he/it is nice' is a perfect sentence. In that case, however, the noun class of the intended subject is grammatically irretrievable; all one knows is that it is third person and singular or generic. *Ko*-pronouns' main (or sole) function, therefore, seems to be disambiguation. Perhaps they can be defined as antiobviative, insofar as they signal that a previously introduced topic has not been switched.

For explicit topicalization (involving left-dislocation) as well as for nonsubject functions, another set of third-person pronouns is used, based on the root /-ul/: *n-ul/buk-ul* (1/2); *w-ul/ng-ul* (3/4); *k-ul/y-ul* (7/8); *nd-ul* (11); *d-ul* (13).[26] Here is an example showing both uses:

(9) N-ul,   na-ko   me   ul.[27]
     1-3SG   1-KO   know   1a-3SG

'As for her/him, she/he knows her/him.'

It is noteworthy that the same restrictions as to noun class combinability seem to hold with *ul* as with *ko*.

3 The Function of Noun Classes

The semantic and number pairing vagaries just reviewed, for which Manjaku is far from being a signal case, led many authors, especially in the Africanist tradition, to conclude that noun classes as such do not serve any purpose (but see Denny and Creider 1986 for a welcome exception). A function that is often granted them, however, but not "as such," is that of marking Number. Indeed, the class prefix alternation of, for example, *ka-to/i-to* expresses whether one or a plurality of the denoted object is implied—just as the /-s/ of *houses* does—and since linguists do not know and native speakers cannot tell what *ka-/i-* "means" as a classifying device, it may be good method to assume that the understandable function is the only active one, at least in the present state of the language.

Actually, it is not entirely true that native speakers cannot tell. They have a clear awareness of the blueprint of the system, so to speak, in the sense that if the prefix is *na-/ba-*, then it's a human being, if it is *u-/ngë-*, then it is likely to be an animal, and so on. Borrowings demonstrate it; they are infallibly assigned to the noun classes that best suit their denotations. For instance, /mango/, a borrowing from Portuguese, is entered into 5/6 (*bë-mango/m-mango*) if it refers to the tree or into 9 if it refers to the fruit (*pë-mango*), following a regular pattern according to which fruits or parts of trees are in 9 (see *bë-jaak/m-jaak* 'palm tree' vs. *pë-jaak* 'palm'; *bë-jaam/m-jaam* 'bamboo tree' vs. *pë-jaam* 'bamboo piece'). It is that knowledge, moreover, that allows language users, upon hearing, say, *Man win k-ul* 'I saw it', to infer that the object of seeing allusively referred to by means of the pronoun *k-ul* is most probably one concrete inorganic thing, even if they may know nothing more about it.

The problem, as is well known, is that it is no more than a blueprint, valid at a certain level of abstraction, but replete with inconsistencies when one comes down to particulars. For instance, the plural of *pë-mango* (9) 'mango' is *m-mango* (6) 'mangoes' (and similarly for *pë-jaak*, *pë-jaam*, etc.), so that the distinction of the tree and its fruit or part is erased in the plural. Worse, there are exceptions to the rule of thumb that fruits are in 9, as shown by *bë-kuäle/m-kuäle* 'cola tree(s)' (5/6) versus *ka-kuäle/i-kuäle* 'cola nut(s)' (7/8). In still other cases, the distinction cuts along different lines, as in *bë-rungäl/m-dungäl* (5/6) 'baobab' versus *m-dungäl* (6) 'baobab fruit' versus *pë-rungäl* (9) 'baobab fruit seed'. Similarly, as already noted, it is not predictable whether a noun denoting a concrete object belongs to 7/8 or to 9 with a plural that is generally in 8 rather than 10.

Examples could be multiplied, but they would add nothing to the unescapable verdict: noun classes work poorly as a classifying device. Now, this should not be taken to mean that noun class systems do not express some classificatory faculty of the mind, as they do achieve some reliable classification (insofar as, e.g., Manjaku 1/2 nouns *always* denote humans). But they do so in an unsystematic, far from optimal, fashion. The conclusion we draw from this observation, however, is not that noun classes are useless hindrances—the linguistic equivalent of the appendix in a human body—but rather that their *grammatical* function is distinct from classification as such, although not disconnected from it, as will be seen.

That this function could be Number marking seems highly unlikely, though. Indeed, if it were merely that, why should Number features be required to associate with other, grammatically otiose features? Or, if noun class is not considered a feature at all, why should Number multiply its exponents so unaccountably? An interesting standard of comparison in this respect is given by Wolof, a neighboring language, genetically related to Manjaku.[28] In Wolof, noun class exponents are consonants merged with determiners postposed to the head noun (e.g., *kër g-i* /house G-Det/ 'the house', where /g/ is the noun class exponent). In Standard Wolof, there are eight noun classes for singular DPs but only two for plural DPs, one of which is limited to basic nouns denoting humans (e.g., *jigéen j-i/ñ-i* 'the woman/women', but *kër g-i/y-i* 'the house(s)' like *fas w-i/y-i* 'the horse(s)'). In Dakar Wolof, however, noun class contrasts are definitely on the wane, so that for many speakers, with of course a lot of variation, the tendency is to use only one noun class in the singular (*b-*) and one in the plural (*y-*). If this tendency goes to completion, then clearly *b-i/y-i* will reanalyze as a postposed determiner, with the consonant alternation uniquely expressing the Number contrast. What this will amount to, then, is for a complex noun class plus Number distinction to be *replaced* by a simple singular versus plural contrast. Such seems indeed to be the general direction of this type of historical changes (see, e.g., the evolution from Old to Modern English), which proves *a contrario* the grammatical significance of noun class (or Class) contrasts as long as they are represented.

I now introduce more facts about the Manjaku system that should help us asseverate the basic function of noun classes and, by extension, of Class. We saw that noun class 9 (*pë-*) includes nouns of rather various semantics: fruits or parts of trees (e.g., *pë-mango* 'mango', *pë-jaak* 'palm') and artifacts (e.g., *pë-caa* 'basket', *pë-ngare* 'shotgun') but also body parts (e.g., *pë-konj* 'finger', *pë-kaba* 'buttock', *pë-kës* 'eye') and natural formations (e.g., *pë-bos* 'sandy hill'). Concerning body part nouns, something must be noted that is not entirely an aside: the Number contrast associated with noun class pairing may be actually more complex than a mere singular versus plural distinction. Take 'fingers', for instance: if the plural refers to a discrete number of fingers that does not usually exceed ten, the normal number a human being is endowed with, then it is expressed in noun class 10 (e.g., *kë-konj kë-wants* 'three fingers');[29] if it refers to an unknown or an indefinite number, generic interpretation (fingers in general) included, it is expressed in noun class 8 (*i-konj* 'fingers'). This shows, at the very least, how inadequate it is to consider 8 as simply being "the plural" of 7. Not only can it be paired with other noun classes (9 and also 5; see *bë-rëk/-rëk* 'river(s)'), but its precise meaning depends on the root it is merged with, since *i-to*, for instance, in contrast with *i-konj*, refers to any plurality of houses.

Another important function of noun class 9 is to nominalize verbs to produce the equivalent of English infinitives in Control constructions:

(10) Na-kiëj   a   ngal   pë-fäm   pë-lëman.[30]
      1-thief   Pro   want   9-break   9-door

'The thief wants to break the door.'

Notice that *pë-fäm* 'to break' keeps its ability to θ- and Case-mark an object.[31] On the one hand, noun class 9 "infinitives" enter a construction that is syntactically and semantically similar to the English *be- -ing* construction:

(11) A   ci   tsi   pë-ji.
      Pro   be   in   9-laugh

'She/He is laughing.'

On the other hand, phrases like *pë-fäm pë-lëman* may be used as argument DPs in sentences like (12):

(12) Pë-fäm   pë-lëman   wara-ts.[32]
      9-break   9-door   be-nice-Neg

'Breaking the/a door is not nice.'

It is impossible, however, to pluralize *pë-fäm* to denote, say, repeated breakings of the same or several doors.

Such a collection of properties suggests that noun class 9 items derived from verbal roots (or rather roots used in a verbal capacity; see later) constitute a mixed category of nominalized verbs, sharing features with English infinitives and gerunds. The main value for my purpose of this observation about noun class 9, however, is to draw attention to what I claim is the basic function of noun classes—namely, noun formation.

This function appears very clearly, when we look at the two arguments in sentence (10). It then appears that *pë-lëman* 'door' is built on a root /lëm/ meaning 'to cover' when used verbally (e.g., *A lëm pë-lik* 'She/He covered the well').[33] Likewise, *na-kiëj* 'thief' derives from /kiëj/ that shows up as a verb in, for example, *A kiëj pë-lëman* 'She/He stole the door'. Such a use of noun class 1/2 as an agentive morpheme is fully productive; other examples are *lam* 'to swim' versus *na-lam/ ba-lam* 'swimmer(s)', *lemp* 'to work' versus *na-lemp/ba-lemp* 'worker(s)', and so on. Actually, "agentive" is too precise a label, as evidenced by such formations as *na-cën/ba-cën* 'neighbor' related to *cën* 'to be neighbors', itself associated with *pë-cën* 'fact of being neighbors, neighborhood'; or *na-fur/ba-fur* 'madman/madmen' related to *fur* 'to be mad'; or *a-buk* (1a) / *ba-buk* 'child(ren)' related to *buk* 'to give birth'. The real meaning of noun class 1/2 would then rather be "person involved in the event or state implied in the meaning of the root," with much indetermination as to the thematic relation of that person with respect to the event or state—insofar as *a-buk* denotes the result of the event, the child, rather than its agent, the mother.

Another thing worthy of note is that, despite appearances, /pë-/ formations as in (10) and (11) cannot readily be analyzed as inflectional, in the sense that an English gerund is inflectional. For one thing, noun class 9 is not the only one to form infinitive-like items, as shown by the following Mankanya examples (Trifkovic 1969: 117, 118, 121):

(13)   U-ñiing   wo   tsi   u-pay.
       3-hyena   be   in   3-climb

       'The hyena is climbing.'

(14)   I   wo   tsi   ngë-tsiilën.
       you   be   in   4-lie

       'You are lying.'

(15)   Dë   bi   yitir   ba-jaar   ba-wajents   du   ka-tiiban
       I   Past   meet   2-farmer   2-three   in   7-clear the ground

       'I had met three farmers clearing the ground.'

In (13), the root /pay/, with the general meaning of 'climbing, going up', is nominalized in noun class 3 which, apart from including most animals, language names, and still other things, is also the class for abstractions in the dual sense of abstract notions (e.g., *u-wejëts* 'thought' next to *wejëts* 'to think') and of logical abstraction over the extension of a concept (e.g., *u-bon* 'hunger, famine' next to *bon* 'to be hungry' and *u-lemp* 'work' next to *lemp* 'to work'). Apparently, there is no referential difference between (13) and the equally possible . . . *wo tsi pë-pay*, in the sense that both describe the same event. In (14), *ngë-tsiilën* is a plural meaning 'lies', with a paired singular *m-tsiilën* (5), so that a more literal translation might be something like 'You are (deep) in lies'. Again, the same state of affairs could be described, with perhaps some difference in expressivity, as *I wo tsi pë-tsiilën*. Finally, *ka-tiiban*'s closest equivalent is probably French *défrichage*.[34] An important function of noun class 7 in all Manjaku languages is thus highlighted, which consists in building "action nouns" comparable to Arabic *maSdar*'s (e.g., *'ilm* 'fact of knowing, knowledge' on the root *'lm*), whose semantic (and syntactic) difference from /pë-/ infinitive-like formations, although certainly real, is not easy to assess.[35] This point is taken up again later on.

On the other hand, "infinitivization," if it may be so called, is not the only function of 9. We already met with several nouns in that noun class denoting fruits (e.g., *pë-mango* 'mango'), body parts (e.g., *pë-kës* 'eye'), artifacts (e.g., *pë-caa* 'basket'), or natural objects (e.g., *pë-bos* 'sandy hill' next to *m-bos* 'sand') which are obviously not built on roots that have a verbal capacity. Even when the root does have this capacity, the result is not always something we want to describe as an infinitive: see, for instance, *pë-lik/i-lik* 'well(s)' versus (*pë-)lik* 'to draw water'. (Other formations on the same root are *m-lik* (5) 'water' and *ka-lik* (7) 'fruit juice'.) Shall we consider those instances of /pë-/ different morphemes than the one in (10)? There seems to be no compelling reason for such a move. A more interesting solution is to view /pë-/ as the same noun-forming morpheme in all cases, for whose general meaning I won't try to devise a formula at this point. Only consider that a well is indeed something water is drawn from, thus manifesting the same thematic indetermination we already observed with noun class 1/2 (see *a-buk* with respect to *buk* as discussed previously).[36] That an associated verb cannot always be found out may be either one of those accidents customary in languages, or it may be simply due to the not fully explored state of the Manjaku vocabulary. What we have to explain, then, is the apparently more verblike character of /pë-/ formations in examples like (10). The issue is tackled in the next section.

Before we come to that, however, there are two more facts I wish to point out, as they clearly demonstrate the inherent noun-forming potential of noun class exponents. One has to do with numerals: as mentioned, some agree with the noun they quantify; and some do not. When counting from one to ten, the agreeing numerals are assigned to class 3 for 'one' (*u-lole* '1') to class 4 for the remainder (*ngë-tëb* '2', *ngë-wants* '3', *ngë-bakër* '4'), thus quantifying over all possible nominals in accordance with the abstracting meaning of noun class 3/4 (see (5) and n. 23 for the numerals from five to ten).

The other significant fact is the pronominal use of noun class exponents. In Manjaku (i.e., Bok), as we saw, noun class exponents in this function are merged

with /-ko/ when they are subjects and with /-ul/ when they are objects. In Mankanya, however, they appear as such in the position where Bok has *a* for all
subjects, the latter being restricted to human subjects of noun class 1(a) in Mankanya. We thus find (Trifkovic 1969: 102):

(16) Ba   daan.
      2   drink

      'They (humans) drink.'

(17) Ka-toh   ka   joot-i.
      7-house   7   crumble-Perf

      'The/a house crumbled.'

and so forth.[37] They also appear in object position, as in (18) (Trifkovic 1969: 105):

(18) Dë thuuman ka
      I fill 7

      I fill it

where *ka* refers to, for instance, *ka-kana* 'calabash' (Bok equivalent: *Man cuman
k-ul*). Something similar is observed in Manjaku (Bok) but only in the subject
position of embedded clauses; see *Man ngal u-bus w-i u tsëp* /I want 3-dog 3-this
3 leave/ 'I want this dog to leave' (lit., 'I want this dog it leaves'). In the following,
I make full use of this property of noun class exponents.

    To sum up this section, evidence was presented to show that the basic func-
tion of noun classes beyond classification itself—imperfectly ensured in any case—
is to form nouns. That noun classes play a part in derivation has naturally been
recognized in all studies on the subject (see in particular Mufwene 1980, whose
conclusions largely foreshadow my own; see also Katamba 1993:211ff.). My claim,
as I hope to show later, goes further than that, however, and, if correct, will
enable us to connect what can be observed in Manjaku with a more general theory
of Class. Let me just indicate for the present that there is nothing surprising in
the fact that noun formation (in the sense to be clarified presently) and classification should go hand in hand. Indeed, it belongs to the inherent properties of
nouns that they denote entities that can (perhaps must) be allotted to different
classes of *things*, by virtue of innate and culturally informed cognitive processes,
diversely expressed in languages. Events and states, in contrast, seem never to be
classified in the same way—for instance, we find languages where nouns denoting
dangerous objects belong to a given noun class (see Lakoff 1987)—but I know of
no description of a language where verbs referring to dangerous actions or events
(e.g., 'to wound', 'to climb', 'to fight') bear some specific morpheme marking this

character. Verbs are categorized, sometimes overtly, according to stage-setting properties of the denoted processes (whether they are open-ended or not, continuous or not, stative or dynamic, which participant they affect, and so forth) but never, it seems, according to "real" descriptive properties such as being perilous or harmless or typical of this or that entity.[38] I will refrain from speculating about why it is so, but it seems to be a true and significant generalization related to what deeply separates nouns from verbs—namely, Class (see Aronoff 1994: 66, who asks the same question in more or less my terms).

4 Noun-Forming Class

My purpose in this section is to account for the Manjaku evidence by using the framework of Distributed Morphology (DM) and then try to generalize it at least to gender languages such as Romance (and secondarily Semitic). In so doing, I also attempt to make sense of the empirical generalizations stated in the introductive section.

As already indicated, one of the basic tenets of DM is that the lexicon consists in roots that lack category, as well as a phonological form and that may be semantically underspecified to varying degrees (see, e.g., Marantz 1997). Roots acquire a category by being inserted in particular syntactic configurations, thus becoming morphemes; morphemes are associated with phonological features in the vocabulary component of morphology and may then be called "exponents" (see Embick and Noyer 1999).

Manjaku supports these assumptions rather straightforwardly. Take, for instance, the series *lik* 'to draw water', *pë-lik/i-lik* 'well(s)', *m-lik* 'water', *ka-lik* 'fruit juice'. We might content ourselves with observing we have here four (or five) words that share a root and have some meaning in common but are not related to each other in any meaningful way—just four (or five) separate "lexical items" among thousands.[39] If that is the truth, it is a dead end, and a dull one, and we should bow to it only if nothing else works. Let us try something else, then.

Assume that √lik is a root in the Manjaku lexicon. (The square root sign is there to indicate that the letters or phonemes it flanks are intended as no more than a label.) On the semantic side—that is, at the interface of the lexicon with language-external cognitive faculties—it seems to be related to the global concept of "water," meaning a set of entities and events that are conceived of as bearing a direct relation to "water," in the same way that the Arabic root √ktb is related to the global concept of "writing," surfacing sometimes as a verb (e.g., *kataba* 'he wrote') and other times as a noun (e.g., *kitaab* 'book', i.e., object produced by writing). This is a very vague characterization, to be sure, but one we have to be content with since we cannot probably do much better in the present state of our knowledge of how concepts are represented in the mind.

Although vague, such a characterization must at least aim to be correct. In this respect, there is a question that cannot be eschewed, given the constituency of the √lik series: why choose "water" as a semantic correlate rather than "well"? Why, in other terms, assume an implicit definition of "well" as something water is drawn from, rather than of "water" as something drawn from wells? Numerous, more or less speculative, answers can be given to justify the present choice, including, for instance, the greater pregnancy and universality of natural kinds such as "water" over unnecessary artifacts such as wells. A more concrete and, I think, more convincing reason, though, is the presence of *ka-lik* 'fruit juice' in the series. A cognitive connection from "water" to "fruit juice," on the one hand, and to "well," on the other, seems indeed natural enough, whereas if we proceeded from "well" to "water," then we would need an independent connection from the latter to "fruit juice." That is to say, selecting "water" as the semantic pivot allows us to build a more tight-knit network than had we chosen "well" in this function.

The real point of this discussion, I think, is to show that roots are indeed *roots* in a very concrete sense and that the property and its content can be empirically validated by such evidence as the Manjaku √lik series (or paradigm). Later on, I attempt to be more precise about what roots are the root of, for which the notion "encyclopedia" will have to be introduced.

Let us now return to more language-internal issues. Roots are selected from the lexicon to be inserted into syntactic structures, thus becoming heads as shown in (19), where XP is the (obligatory) complement of the head:

(19) $[_{\sqrt{P}} \sqrt{^0} [_{XP}]]$

Clearly, (19) is not a well-formed syntactic object, as it has no category allowing it to function as a predicate or an argument. Suppose we want (19) to be a predicate. We can assign it the required category by merging it with a functional projection headed by the functional head *v* also selected from the lexicon. Assuming *v* to be of the causative variety (see Arad 1999) and the root to be √lik, we turn (19) into (20), where YP is a subject in Spec *v*P:

(20) $[_{vP} [_{YP}] v^0 [_{\sqrt{P}} [_{\sqrt{^0}} lik][_{XP}]]]]$

The root head then raises-adjoins to v^0, thereby acquiring verbal features:

(21) $[_{vP} [_{YP}] lik{+}v^0 [_{\sqrt{P}} [_{\sqrt{^0}} t][_{XP}]]]]$

Since *v* is not associated with a morphological exponent, the final form is *lik*—that is, the exponent (or vocabulary item) associated with the root.

The question we have to ask now is: Does (21) account entirely for the meaning of *lik*, (namely, 'to draw water from a well') and the fact that it can be used intransitively or with a complement that looks very much like a cognate object (namely, *m-lik* 'water')?[40] The answer seems to be "no". Given the global meaning we assumed for the root √lik, (21) yields a verb analogous to the English *to water*. Now, there is no necessary reason why *to water* should have the meaning it has in English, "to pour water on (plants)", rather than the one it has in Majaku, "to draw water from (wells)". Yet, we should be able, if not to predict, at least to formalize such diverse meanings in different languages.

A possible formalization consists, following Hale and Keyser (1993), to derive *lik* from a lexical relational structure (LRS) like (22) (I use English words for convenience):

(22)   [$_{VP}$ V [$_{VP}$ water [$_{PP}$ from well]]]

Incorporating the PP into the abstract verb yields a verb that has the semantics of *lik*. Notice by the way that (22) also accounts for French *puiser (de l'eau)*, related to *puits* 'well', which happens to match *lik*'s semantic and syntactic properties quite closely.

The problem, however, is that Hale and Keyser's theory is not prima facie compatible with a view of the lexicon including globally underspecified roots.[41] Neither does there seem to be room in DM for the lexical syntax Hale and Keyser assume (see, e.g., Harris's 1999 flow chart of the grammatical organization generally assumed in DM). Moreover, (22) clearly predicts that the final form of the verb must be derived from *well* (as it indeed is in French), not from *water*, as it appears to be in Manjaku. The two theories, then, seem hardly gearable to one another (but see Bouchard 1995 for an approach to the relations of semantics to syntax that might be more immediately congenial to the present attempt).

It is not necessarily so, however. DM's model of grammar provides for a component distinct from the lexicon and the vocabulary, called the "encyclopedia." As the name suggests, it is the component where terms (to use a neutral label) having a denotational relation with language-external reality are given their effective meaning (e.g., that *cat*, in addition to being a noun and a CVC syllable, refers to a purring mammal, or that you water aspidistras but you don't water your own body when you take a shower), thus ensuring that they are used not only grammatically but also felicitously. In the usual model, the encyclopedia steps in at the output of PF and LF, and it feeds semantic interpretation at the interface of language proper and "external" faculties (see Harris 1999). The assumption, then, is that only fully derived items (exponents) are susceptible to possess encyclopedic meaning. Intuitively, that is true: only *kitaab* 'book' refers to something; the root √ktb does not (in Fregean terms, it has meaning but no denotation). That truth, however, does not necessarily imply that the encyclopedia must be ordered after all other grammatical operations. In a strictly derivational view of grammar, it does, but if we adopt a grammatical organization more in terms of parallel processing (in line with, e.g., Brody 1995 and Jackendoff 1997, and perhaps Chomsky 2001), the encyclopedia may be considered an autonomous component, along with the lexicon and morphology.[42] Under such a conception, what the grammar produces are signs (in the Saussurean sense; see also Sag and Wasow 1999: 356ff.) which are the embodiment of three interfaced processings: categorization and merger of roots in the syntax, morphophonological operations on morphemes, and semantic characterization. Provided that each component has access to the others—that is, that the expression of the sign in one component is linked to its expressions in the other components—no ordering is required.

The inner organization of the encyclopedia has not really been explored, as far as I know. Yet, as it is a grammatical component, we should expect it to house the same kinds of structures and operations we find in the other components. My proposal, then, is that insofar as LRSs such as (22) are formal explicitations of semantic representations, the encyclopedia is their proper location, provided it is related to lexicon and syntax in the way just sketched. What Hale and Keyser call lexical syntax (l-syntax), I therefore call encyclopedic syntax (e-syntax), parallel to and interfaced with syntax *tout court* (s-syntax or narrow syntax). My difference with these authors is thus that, for independent reasons, I assume the lexicon to be made up of roots rather than full-fledged lexical items and that it is these roots that are manipulated by s-syntax. Moreover, the encyclopedia must be geared to the fact that the developed representations it includes may correspond to simple roots (such as √lik or √shelve, to use one of Hale and Keyser's staple examples) and to simple exponents (*lik, shelve*)—hence the justification of e-syntax (e.g., incorporation into V in (22) resulting in compacting the whole phrase into one position) to allow for one-to-one association between the components.

Concretely, this means that at the same time that √lik (the root) is projected into syntax as shown in (20) and (21), it is linked to an encyclopedic representation like (22) that tells us that behind the verbal morpheme (sign) *lik* that we hear, there is water, a well, and a drawing of the former from the latter. But what about the remark that the surfacing exponent ought to be that of "well" (as in French)? Actually, that would be a problem only if e-syntax fed s-syntax, as Hale and Keyser's l-syntax does. But it does not, being a parallel depiction of the relations associated with the meanings of particular instantiations of the root. Moreover, this is where the global underspecification of roots in a language like Manjaku (perhaps more extreme in this regard than English or French) comes into play. Indeed, given the series that grows from $\sqrt{}$lik, all the elements that enter the encyclopedic representation of *lik* 'to draw water (from a well)' turn out to proceed from the same root.

The foregoing discussion seems to have veered somewhat from the issue of noun classes. It hasn't really, however, since its purpose was mainly to present some plausible (I hope) concepts I intend to use in order to tackle that issue.

As we just saw, merging the root $\sqrt{}$lik with a *v* projection in syntax and associating the resulting verbal [lik+v] morpheme with an exponent (/lik/) in morphology, on one hand, and an encyclopedic structure, on the other hand, gives us a full representation of the Manjaku verb *lik* 'to draw water (from a well)'. Our next task, then, is to account for the other members of the $\sqrt{}$lik paradigm, such as *pë-lik/i-lik* 'well(s)'. In fact, we have no choice of the analysis, given our assumptions: since $\sqrt{}$lik is uncategorized, it must be merged with a noun-forming functional category, call it *n*, if it is to be used as an argument, just as it must be merged with verb-forming *v* when a predicate head; /pë-/ is one exponent of *n*; noun class morphemes in general are exponents of *n*.[43]

Basically, this is the solution I will adopt (see Lecarme 1999 for a similar treatment of Somali gender). A number of issues have to be dealt with, though, before we can feel confident it is at least a plausible solution. The first one is that of the exact definition of the {*n* ↔ /pë-/} (or any other noun class prefix) item.[44] Embick and Noyer (1999) distinguish crucially between what they call "functional morphemes" (f-morphemes) and "roots" (lexical items, in more familiar terms). The rationale for the distinction is the notion that for f-morphemes "vocabulary Insertion is deterministic and only one choice is possible in any given context" (p. 267); root insertion, in contrast, is free, depending on the speaker's choice.[45] The question, then, is whether {*n* ↔ /pë-/}, (or *pë-*, for short) is an f-morpheme or a root.

Considering that *v* is generally defined as a functional category, the answer seems straightforward: *n* is an f-morpheme. Yet, given our characterization of roots and a mere examination of the Manjaku vocabulary, there can be little doubt that *pë-* is the only element uniquely associated with the meaning 'well' in *pë-lik* as compared with *m-lik* 'water' and *ka-lik* 'fruit juice', even if the content of the association is far from clear. It follows that, in the context of $\sqrt{}$lik being selected, the choice of *pë-* rather than of *m-* or *ka-* is free, depending on whether the speaker intends to talk about a well, water, or fruit juice. Therefore, *pë-* does not lack descriptive content, and it is a root, as are *m-*, *ka-*, and so on.

Actually, to be accurate, what we must say is that *n* is a root (that is, a member of the lexicon) and that to the difference of all other roots, except *v*, it is endowed with a category, namely, N. In other words, *n* is *the* noun in the lexicon (and *v* *the* verb). And we must add that *n* is a label for a set of prototypical nouns, or protonouns, each having its own meaning and exponent (and perhaps assuming a theory of prototypes as in Lakoff 1987 and Posner 1986). This points to an important property of noun class systems, evidence for which was given in the preceding section: {n}, the set of protonouns, not only forms nouns from roots but also imparts the nouns so formed with particular meanings, such as Agent (or rather "person involved") as in *na-lam* 'swimmer'. That is, {n} also fulfills the function of derivational morphemes such as /-er/ in English. Actually, rather than with /-er/, the significant comparison is with *man* in such forms as *madman* (*na-fur*). Each member of {n} is thus associated with a general concept.

The practical difficulty for the analysis is that this concept is not always clearly recognizable in the present state of the language. It is obvious for the *n* whose exponent is /na-/—that is, "human being" or for the *n* realized as /ts-/, meaning "place, location" (except, probably, in the one exception *tsë-mak* 'big brother'). In other cases, we have to acknowledge the fact that only part of the mergers of a particular member of {n} with a particular root reveals what we may consider to be the concept inherently linked to that *n*. Here, I am merely repeating what I pointed out earlier—that noun class systems lost their optimality in the course of time, if they ever were optimal to begin with. Nevertheless, the fact that meanings must be assigned, even if imperfectly, to the members of {n} confirms their lexical status as protonouns.

To sum up, the following overall characterization of an *n* may be given:

(23) Lexicon: [N, human]
       ↔ Vocabulary: /na-/ ∼ /a-/
       ↔ Encyclopaedia: $((\sqrt{}_x)(N \text{ human}))$
       ↔ Syntax: $[_{nP} n^0 [_{\sqrt{}P} \sqrt{}_x]]$

I take (23) to be the representation of what I called a "sign," that is the summation of all dimensions that define a given linguistic unit. The encyclopedic tier of (23) is an informal notation of the fact that the lexical item (root) consisting in the features N and [human] must enter into some semantic relation with another root. The relation is underspecified (Agent with *na-lam* 'swimmer', but Theme with *a-buk* 'child', given the meaning of √buk 'concept of giving birth' as discussed previously). The basic meaning of the *n* defined in (23), resulting from the interfacing of lexical features and encyclopedic representation (e-syntax), is thus "person involved in some event or state of affairs." At the same time, the syntactic specification states that this lexical item is the head of a projection taking the same root targeted in e-syntax as its complement, and the vocabulary shows its exponent to be /na-/ or /a-/, with the morphological property of being a prefix.[46] As we shall see, this property, far from being idiosyncratic, can be deduced from the characterization.

Finally, the mixed (verbal and nominal) character of /pë/-infinitives (but not, it seems, of /ka/ or /u/ verbal nouns) is easily accounted for in this framework by assuming the root to be successively merged with *v* and then *n* (see Marantz

1997 for a similar derivation of English *destruction*-type nominalizations, an issue that will be taken up later on). The first merger accounts for the verbal properties of the item (θ- and Case-marking), the second for its NP type.

5 NOUN CLASS, GENDER, AND CLASS

We are now equipped to embark on a comparison of noun class systems with gender systems as represented in, for example, the Romance languages. If the basic function of what surfaces as noun class markers is indeed to make nouns out of uncategorized roots, and given the undeniable relatedness of noun class to gender, as well as the conceptual necessity of finding a function for the latter, a generalization suggests itself: gender is also basically a noun-forming device. This means that the Romance lexicon is a set of uncategorized roots plus the two categorized n and v elements, just like the lexicons of Manjaku or the Semitic languages (or all languages, we assume). The /-a/ morpheme of Spanish *gata* 'she-cat', for instance, thus represents the morphological exponent of one member of the lexical set {n}, syntactically realized as the n^0 head taking the $\sqrt{gat}$ root as its complement. Only through that merger can the root gain actual denotation and enter a proposition about some possible world.

To that extent, then, noun class and gender systems are alike: parallel instantiations of the classificatory faculty that requires entity-denoting signs (as opposed to event-denoting signs) to be stacked on this or that shelf in the library of the mind. But the two types of systems are markedly different on a number of counts, as we saw. My task, therefore, is to account for these differences in an illuminating way, if I can, by showing them to proceed from minimal variations in the initial, globally common, conditions.

The most striking difference is revealed by the foregoing analysis of Manjaku, and it is that noun class signs, such as the one represented in (23), are not only classificatory but also derivational. Gender morphemes never have such a role: in Spanish *nadador* 'swimmer' (compare Manjaku *na-lam*), Agent is the exclusive meaning of /-dor/ and the noun is masculine by virtue of not bearing an explicit gender morpheme: if the swimmer is a woman, *nadadora* is used. Moreover, it never happens that /-dor/ fails to have the Agent (or some related) meaning, whereas there are many cases where /na-/ (or rather $\sqrt{na}$) does.

This points to somewhat distinct organizations of the lexicons. Actually, the apparent derivational function of noun class signs is a by-product of their being meaningful roots: as already suggested, *na-lam* is not the exact equivalent of *swimmer*, but it designates a human being ($\sqrt{na}$) involved in the event of swimming ($\sqrt{}$lam). Similarly, *pë-lik* is a thing ($\sqrt{}$pë) associated with the concept of water ($\sqrt{}$lik), and it is the encyclopedia's role to apprise us of the fact that this particular collocation is to be understood as 'well'. In addition, *tsë-ko* means a location ($\sqrt{}$tsë) associated with a very general concept ($\sqrt{}$ko) perhaps translatable as 'being', hence 'place'; and so forth. Classification, on the other hand, falls out directly from meaningfulness, even though, as noted, in an imperfect fashion, because of the fuzzy or multivalued character of the semantics of noun class signs.

Such a conflation of classification and derivation does not occur in languages like Spanish. On the one hand, we find signs such as Spanish /-dor/ or Italian /-ata/ (e.g., *ombrellata* 'hit with an umbrella'; see Ippolito 1999), which seem to be endowed with fairly precise meanings but do not of themselves partition the noun set into several classes (for a reason to be soon made clear). On the other hand, there are the morphemes /-o/, /-a/, /-e/, and /∅/ acting as word class markers (see Harris 1992, 1999) that do perform such partitioning, since every noun in a Romance language (to the possible exception of French) must overtly belong to one of those classes. The question we must ask to further our comparative task, then, is whether these morphemes have meaning and ought to be considered roots as are Manjaku noun class signs.

This is a complex and disputed issue. In a significant number of cases where sex of the *denotatum* is relevant, /-a/ plainly refers to the female (e.g., *gata* 'she-cat', *jefa* 'woman chief', *nadadora* 'woman swimmer'), whereas one of the other morphemes refers to the male or is ambivalent (*gato* 'tomcat, cat', *jefe* 'chief', *nadador* 'swimmer'). When sex is not relevant, the same morphemes seem to play no other role than defining word classes (*libro* 'book,' *puerta* 'door', *coche* 'car', *pared* 'wall'). Harris (1999) thus defines three major classes labeled I (/-o/), II (/-a/), and III (all the rest), plus a fourth class (IV) for exceptional items, making it very clear that the binary feature masculine versus feminine (M/F) cannot simply overlay this division, since all classes include M and F nouns, although the information about (sex-based) gender must be available in order to select the proper word class from when there is a choice (e.g., *gato* or *gata*). A further complexity stems from the possible interaction of derivational morphemes with word classes and the M/F feature: for instance, all nouns showing the suffix /-ist/ belong to class II (e.g., *linguista* 'linguist') irrespective of whether the denoted individual is a man or a woman (this is decided by the choice of the determiner *el* or *la*, *un* or *una*, which thus expresses the M/F feature). In Portuguese, in contrast, nouns in /-(a)gem/, while belonging to class III and denoting sexless entities, are all feminine, as far as determiner selection and agreement are concerned (e.g., *A linguagem é complicada* "Language is complicated").

Insofar as Romance word classes classify entities, then, they do so according to the criterion of sex or, as I will continue to call it, gender. Perforce such a criterion is applicable only to a subset of actually or mentally existing entities. The consequence of this state of affairs, I will assume, is therefore that in Romance, contrary to Manjaku, the classificatory feature (M/F) is divorced from the categorical feature N. The latter is inherent to the word class morpheme, being its grammatical raison d'être: word class morphemes form nouns from roots, just like noun class signs do. The former, in contrast, is linked only when gender is relevant, given the meaning of the root to which the word class morpheme is attached. Thus, *gata* 'she-cat' and *puerta* 'door' receive the following representations:

(24)   √gat-a   √puert-a
           N(II) F   N(II)

Gata is indeed feminine (classificatorily feminine); *puerta*, however, is only class II. The same is true for *gato* when it denotes a tomcat (N(I)M) and *libro* (N(I)). What remains is an entailment to the effect that class I and II nouns whose roots denote relevantly sexed kinds refer to the masculine and feminine members of that kind respectively.[47] The entailment does not go the other way, however, since not all nouns referring to classificatorily feminine or masculine entities belong to class II or I; see *mujer* 'woman' (N(III) F) and *jefe* 'chief' (N(III) M).

What about nouns like *linguista* or *acrobata* 'acrobat', which seem to run afoul of the entailment, as they are class II and may refer to masculine members of the kind, or *modelo* 'model', which is class I and able to refer to a woman model, as in *esa modelo finlandesa* 'this(F) Finnish(F) model(I)'? (All examples in this discussion are from Harris 1999.) There is a ready explanation for the first one, and it is to assume that the word class morpheme is attached not to the root but to the derivational morpheme /ist/. Not being a denoting root, this morpheme cannot be gender relevant. Therefore, *linguista* is actually like *puerta* (that is only class II), not like *gata*. The same account probably extends to *acrobata* with class II also preempted by the /ata/ ending (also see *pirata* 'pirate'). As for *modelo*, the human denotation of 'fashion model' is a fairly recent development from the basic, gender-irrelevant meaning of 'model' as an object or a notion. Therefore, *modelo* is like *libro*. But nothing says that class I is incompatible with the F feature, should it be relevant, beyond the word, because the entailment is only valid of the primary combination of a root with a word class morpheme, and the compatibility we observe in *esa modelo* 'this (woman) model' is a direct consequence of the global mutual independence of word class and gender.

It follows from this that whenever gender is relevant, but word class of the noun is preempted for some reason (special suffix or ending, metaphorical usage, etc.) so the entailments I → M and II → F cannot hold, then the M/F feature shows up only on modifiers of the noun, being then divorced from the noun-forming word class morpheme. *El linguista* 'the (man) linguist' may thus be represented as follows.

(25) el   √lingw [-ist- a]
     M   N(II)

The determiner in (25) includes a gender feature, and so it does whenever gender is relevant, whatever the word class of the noun (*la gata* 'the she-cat', *la madre* 'the mother', and so forth). When gender is not relevant, however, the logic of the explanation forces us to assume that no gender feature is present in the determiner and other modifiers, so that *el* is merely class III, not M, in *el libro* 'the book' and *la* is merely class II, not F, in *la puerta* 'the door'.[48] This raises a question as, here as well, there is a measure of mutual independence, this time between the word class of the noun and that of the modifiers: class III nouns, with word class exponent /e/ or /∅/, have modifiers in class III (e.g., *un mar frío* 'a cold sea') or II (e.g., *una pared alta* 'a high wall); and there is also the case of *la mano derecha* 'the(II) right(II) hand(I)'. I do not feel bound to integrate these data into my account, however, as they do not seem to me to be crucial for the point I am trying to make. After all, since there are three (of four) distinct classes for nouns but only two for modifiers, we expect an amount of shifting around in the distribution, sometimes due to discernible factors (e.g., class III nouns ending in /-ed/ are usually feminine, to use the received terminology) but sometimes unaccountable (and *la mano* is a genuine exception).

Important for my purpose is the proposal I am making that, in order to make sense of the Spanish system, the classificatorily (i.e., semantically) valued M/F feature must be firmly dissociated from the solely grammatical word class morphemes, even though they may be morphologically fused at the exponence level, and there is a limited entailment from the one to the others. Actually, this dissociation should make us wonder whether M/F is a lexical feature at all. Since it is linked only when gender is relevant, and gender is determined on the basis of the denotation of the whole sign (see *el linguista, la modelo*), it seems more coherent to assume that M/F is in fact an encyclopedic feature, assigned in this interface component with semantics and not at all in the lexicon.

If this is true, word class becomes a purely functional feature indeed, whose sole function is to form nouns from roots. Let me give a broad outline of the system thus reached: the Spanish lexicon (not special in this respect) includes roots like √gat or √puert and the functional set {n}. This set consists in four members, call them nI, nII, nIII, and nIIIa, the exponents of which are /o/, /a/, /e/, and /∅/.[49] Suppose √puert is chosen. To be usable as a syntactic noun, it has to be merged with an nP projection having nII as its head. Here there is no choice: it is simply a fact of Spanish that √puert "goes with" nII (recall Embick and Noyer's 1999 definition of functional items).[50] In the encyclopedia, nothing happens as far as gender is concerned: a door is not a gender-relevant entity; therefore, the M/F feature is not associated with the encyclopedic representation of √puert. In morphology, nII is spelled out as /a/ and √puert as /pwert/, hence the final exponent /'pwerta/ (I will return to what happens between initial syntax and morphology). Should [nII + √puert] be further merged with a DP projection, then word class agreement takes place to the effect that D spells out as /la/.

Now suppose that √gat is chosen. Cats being sexed entities, the M/F feature links to its encyclopedic representation, and a choice has to be made. Let us assume the speaker wants to talk about a she-cat and F is selected.[51] We can now think of the entailment previously stated as of a specific connection between encyclopedia and lexicon, such that if F is selected in the former, then nII is activated in the latter, unless some factor more specific than the entailment prevents it. No such factor is present with √gat, so the ultimate result is *gata*—an ordinary class II feminine noun.

It is present, in contrast, in the case of *linguista*, inasmuch as nII associates with the derivational morpheme /ist/ rather than with the primary root √lingw. This is not problematic in the account presented here since we concluded earlier that, in Spanish, to the difference of Manjaku, derivation is distinct from Class. We can therefore consider derivational morphemes to be functional roots that, because of their functional character, must combine with a nonfunctional root when they are taken from the lexicon.[52] Given Williams's (1981) Righthand Head Rule and our assumptions about the syntax of word derivation, we then expect word class to attach to the derivational morpheme (the noun's head) rather than to the nonfunctional root, as shown in the following initial representation of *linguista*:

(26)   [$_{nP}$ nII [$_{√P}$ √ist [$_{√P}$ √lingw]]]

Noun-forming nII attracts the closest root, which adjoins to its left—hence, [ist+nII]; the complex functional head thus formed then attracts the nonfunctional root—hence, [lingw + [ist+nII]].[53]

A further distinction has now to be made: among derivational roots, some like √dor are contentful enough that they have encyclopedic representations. In its meaning "human agent," √dor is thus gender-relevant, and a decision has to be taken as to whether M or F is attached to it.[54] If F, as in *nadadora* 'woman swimmer', the encyclopedia-lexicon special connection (or entailment) ensures that nII associates with √dor, winning over nIIIa by the Elsewhere Principle, since it is more specified as it is connected to an encyclopedic feature, which nIIIa is not (see n. 54). In contrast, if M is chosen as in *nadador* 'swimmer (male or unspecified)', the M → nI entailment (yielding ungrammatical **nadadoro*) cannot prevail, because √dor is globally associated with nIIIa (a fact to be learned) and nI is not more specified than nIIIa, as both may refer to males or to the whole kind (see *gato*).

If the foregoing argument holds, then it implies, *a contrario*, that √ist has no encyclopedic representation—or at least it is not valued as gender-relevant there. It is only associated with nII, as shown in (26). What must have an encyclopedic representation, in contrast, is the whole sign realized as *linguista* after derivation through syntax and morphology. Recall we assume all components to be interfaced, so syntax *may* not only feed the encyclopedia but also *must* do so since the meaning of derived nouns is rarely, if ever, fully compositional.[55] Because *linguista* is gender-relevant whereas neither $\sqrt{}$lingw nor $\sqrt{}$ist is—the M/F feature links to it. The problem now is that, whatever feature value is chosen, it cannot mark the sign since word class is already assigned.[56] Therefore, it is merely appended to the sign (hence something like [linguista]M/F), manifesting itself only through agreement (as in *un linguista americano* 'an American linguist'). With a few slight adjustments, the same account holds for *modelo*.

We are now in a position to appraise the full extent of the difference between Spanish (or Romance) and Manjaku. In Spanish, as we just saw, classificatory gender (M/F) and word class are divorced, the former being (possibly) an encyclopedic feature and the latter a purely grammatical (or functional) noun-forming feature. In Manjaku, on the contrary, classification and noun class are not separate, but both are represented in the lexicon as features of particular roots ($\sqrt{}$na, $\sqrt{}$ka, etc.).[57] Moreover, the classificatory criteria differ in both intension and extension. Whereas Romance resorts to the masculine versus feminine contrast, only applicable to a subset of entities, Manjaku supports its classification on representations of natural-conceptual kinds such as humans, animals, plants, and abstractions, which are potentially applicable to all conceivable entities. The non-separability of classificatory meaning and functional noun class, I submit, follows precisely from this. That is: members of the {n} set in Manjaku are endowed with the inherent capacity to not only nominalize roots, as they do in Romance as well, but also address them to delineated sectors in semantic space. Encyclopedic representations of such presorted signs (i.e., subsequent to syntactic merger of some member of {n} with a given root) then come as a further narrowing of the signs' partly defined meanings, and also as a check.

I add the latter provision because, as we saw, mismatches occur. To give just one more striking example: whereas it seems to be the case that all class 1/2 nouns refer to humans, the reverse is not entirely true, and there are at least two exceptions, one in class 5, *bë-fetsar* 'friend', and the other in class 12 (which is otherwise reserved for locative words), *tsë-mak* 'big brother'. To make matters worse, *bë-fetsar*'s plural is in class 8 (*i-fetsar* 'friends').[58] Sensibly enough, *tsë-mak*'s plural is in class 2 (*ba-mak*). Yet, such discrepancies are of a different order than those we observed in Spanish. In the latter, it is simply the case that the classificatory criterion associated with (but distinct from) noun class does not apply at all to a vast number of roots and derived nouns. In Manjaku, in contrast, the classificatory dimensions inherently linked to noun classes have the potential of always matching the meaning or one of the meanings of the roots they combine with.

Sometimes they do not: a friend is not a plant (see prior discussion for what may be the basic meaning of class 5), and several friends are not artifacts (if that is the meaning of class 8, besides plural). Then we have a mismatch, which encyclopedia checks when it tells us that, despite being merged with class 5, bë-fetsar means 'friend', not some plant like bë-ko 'tree' or bë-mango 'mango tree'.

Mismatches, however numerous, do not call the overall classificatory value of the system into question, though. They merely draw attention to the fact that, as already emphasized, the system is imperfect, from various mostly irretrievable and probably accidental causes, and also, at a deeper level, that the meanings of noun classes like those of Manjaku (or Bantu or Dyirbal) and their combinations with roots are not something that can be defined from mere observation of the language as we hear it. It would require full knowledge of the representational system shared by the native speakers of the language or by those who bequeathed it to them along generations.[59] Since such knowledge is unattainable, we must satisfy ourselves with acknowledging that noun classes have meaning, because assuming so much is the best and perhaps only way to make sense of the system, and proposing tentative and no doubt hopelessly partial interpretations on the basis of what we observe.

The basic difference between Manjaku and Romance appears thus to be at the same time limited and profound: limited because both language (UG) varieties share the category I term Class, that is, the linguistic expression of the mental classificatory faculty that gives rise to the grammatical objects called "nouns," and profound because the *lexical* expressions of the said category are meaningful roots in Manjaku but semantically empty functional items in Romance. In other terms, Class morphemes in Romance are indeed *inflectional class* morphemes in the sense of Aronoff (1994)—that is, creatures of autonomous morphology that are linked to gender proper only through particular entailments (or implicational rules) with encyclopedic knowledge and to the classificational faculty insofar as they nevertheless impose an order on the entity-denoting (nominal) vocabulary, albeit a largely meaningless one.[60] Manjaku Class morphemes, in contrast, are direct, even though often obscure, expressions of encyclopedic knowledge. The typological generalizations pointed to previously follow from this, as I now try to show.

6 THE MORPHOSYNTAX OF CLASS EXPONENTS

In this section, I examine the position of Class exponents relative to the (main) root and also with respect to other elements that may attach to the root, an issue that, although somewhat tangential at first sight, may have far-reaching theoretical consequences, as we shall see. Then I deal with the fusion of Class and Number.

6.1 The Position of Class Exponents

Let us return to the syntactic representation of Spanish *gata* 'she-cat':

(27)   [$_{nP}$ nII [$_{\sqrt{P}}$ $\sqrt{}$gat]]

To derive the surface form /gata/ from it, we need only the minimal assumptions that (1) functional lexical items inserted into syntax are morphologically illegible unless they attach to the nonfunctional roots over which they have local scope and (2) attachment proceeds through attraction of the root by the functional item, so that the former left-adjoins to the latter in accordance with Kayne's (1994) LCA. From (27), we thus derive (28):

(28)   [$_{nP}$ $\sqrt{}$gat+nII [$_{\sqrt{P}}$ t]]

Stripped of all unpronounceable, (28)—or rather [$\sqrt{}$gat+nII]—is then delivered over to morphology where $\sqrt{}$gat and nII are associated with their respective exponents, /gat/ and /a/. In this account there is no need to specify /a/ as being a suffix (representing it as, say, /-a/). Suffixation follows directly from the syntactic processing required to build an object fit for morphological treatment, as a consequence of the functional nature of nII. Actually, (28) makes the very strong prediction that functional morphemes may only suffix and that suffixes can only spell out functional morphemes. Whether this is a true prediction obviously could not be tested in the study presented here. Counterexamples come readily to mind, such as the Classical Arabic contrast of *'aktabu* 'I (will) write' versus *katabtu* 'I wrote' where the same feature bundle [1SG] seems to be expressed sometimes as a prefix (/'a-/) and sometimes as a suffix (/-tu/). To dispel it, one needs to prove that these elements have different lexical statuses—that, for example, /'a-/ is a clitic pronoun, the reduced form of the strong pronoun *'ana* 'I', whereas /-tu/ is a functional complex including Tense.[61] For my present purposes, however, it is enough to accept the weaker claim that the suffixal property of gender exponents in Romance follows directly from their functional character.

Conversely, therefore, the prefixal property of Manjaku noun class exponents must follow from the fact that they are roots, fundamentally no different from the roots they attach to but for their being categorized as N. Crucial here is the observation that noun class morphemes may be inserted as such, functioning then as pronouns, without restriction in the Mankanya dialect (see (17) *ka joot-i* 'it (e.g., the house) crumbled'), in embedded clauses in Manjaku. This implies that the syntactic structure associated with *ka* in (17) is probably the following:

(29) $[_{nP} \sqrt{ka} [_{\sqrt{P}} \varnothing]]$

That is to say, no particular root is selected to merge with the chosen member of {n}.[62] The structure of, for example, *ka-lik* 'fruit juice' is the same:

(30) $[_{nP} \sqrt{ka} [_{\sqrt{P}} \sqrt{lik}]]$

Obviously, (30) is just like (27). What distinguishes them is not structural but substantial: $\sqrt{ka}$ is a root, whereas nII is functional. Only functional elements have the property Attract. (I take this as a self-evident generalization supported by all theoretical developments since the very inception of generative grammar.) Therefore, no syntactic operation applies to (30), which is delivered as such to morphology.[63]

Naturally, the foregoing account would be circular, had we no independent grounds for our analysis of $\sqrt{ka}$ and nII. This is why I took pains to demonstrate at length the root character of noun class signs in Manjaku, basing my demonstration on semantic criteria: noun class signs in Manjaku are endowed with a denotational potential that Romance gender morphemes lack entirely. If the conclusion is accepted, there is no circularity.

The question we want to ask now is what happens to (27) and (30) once they enter the morphological component. The answer, apparently, is "next to nothing." What morphology receives from syntax, apart from the feature bundles to which exponents get associated (e.g., /gat/ and /a/, /ka/ and /lik/), is the specification that this particular collocation of features constitutes one projection. That is: inner brackets are erased (or not read), and outer brackets are interpreted as word boundaries.[64] Examples (27) and (30) are thus converted to #gat+a# and #ka+lik#, respectively, and submitted to whatever word-forming and phonological processes are required by the language—not many in the present case.[65]

In fact, given the root character of the constituents, the morphological formation of *ka-lik* does not look essentially different from that of compounds such as *pez-espada* 'swordfish' (lit. 'fish sword') in Spanish, where the first root indicates the general category of the entity, more or less as *ka* does in Manjaku, while the second root specifies the identity. Of course, there are differences inasmuch as (1) $\sqrt{pez}$ is semantically richer than $\sqrt{ka}$ and (2) *ka-lik* is more wordlike than *pez-espada* because *ka* has a clitic property that *pez* has not. Now, clitichood may be a phonological property related to the availability of a CV slot to the left of any root *qua* CV sequence (see Lowenstamm 1996, who presents empirical and theoretical arguments in favor of such a slot as a universal feature of phonological form). *Ka* and all other noun class exponents, being CV objects, will naturally "slide" into this slot.[66]

The "agglutinative" typology of noun class exponence as opposed to the "inflectional" character of Romance gender marking also falls out rather naturally from these considerations. Because they are nonfunctional roots that trivially merge with other roots to which they then cliticize by virtue of general phonological properties, noun class exponents cannot but keep their distinctivity. Moreover, both types of roots exist autonomously. Romance gender morphemes, in contrast, because they are functional roots, must fuse with nonfunctional roots that may not be associated with legitimate word forms in the language (as is the case with Spanish $\sqrt{}$gat, which cannot surface unless it is combined with something else).[67]

Finally, something must be said of an issue that was mentioned earlier in passing (see n. 58). It has to do with the existence in Manjaku of nouns such as *bë-fetsar* 'friend', showing that noun class roots may combine not only with simple roots, as in *ka-lik*, but also with derived ones, since *fetsar* is the applicative derivation of a root whose associated vocabulary item *fets* means 'to follow'. Other examples are *pë-lëman* 'door', *lëman* 'cause *x* to be covered' (a causative of *lëm* 'to cover'), *na-rukand* 'heir', *dukand* 'to bequeath' (a causative of *duk* 'to leave'), and so on. Forms like /-ar/, /-an/, and /-and/ are members of a rich paradigm of verbal derivational morphemes with meanings such as causative, applicative, directional (e.g., *pëni* 'to come out' from *pën* 'to go out'), reciprocal (e.g., *telar* 'to understand each other' from *te* 'to hear'), and so forth (see Buis 1990: 46–49). They are all suffixes in accordance with the functional character of the roots they spell out, and, as mentioned, they are uniquely verb-forming (perhaps members of ({v}), as the derivational function for nouns is entirely taken over by noun classes. Given this, a possible syntactic representation of, for example, *fetsar* 'to follow for / in favor of *x*', is (31):

(31) $[_{vP} \sqrt{}\text{ar} [_{\sqrt{P}} \sqrt{}\text{fets}]]$

from which we derive (32):

(32) $[_{vP} \sqrt{}\text{fets} + \sqrt{}\text{ar} [_{\sqrt{P}} \text{t}]]$

Merging (32) with an nP projection headed by n^0 = Class 5 would then yield *bë-fetsar* 'friend'. Given the absence of verbal derivation of this type in Romance, the nearest equivalent seems to be nominalizations similar to English *destruction* (Spanish *destrucción*). Following Marantz (1997; see also Pesetsky 1995: 69ff.), such forms are syntactically built on a structure like (33):

(33) $[_{nP} \sqrt{}\text{tion} [_{vP} \text{v} [_{\sqrt{P}} \sqrt{}\text{DESTROY}]]]$

The inclusion of *v* in the representation captures the fact that these forms, despite being nouns, have the argument structure of the verb they nominalize (see *the enemy's destruction of the city, la destrucción de la ciudad por el enemigo*, and recall our analysis of /pë/ infinitives). At the same time, it shows how different Manjaku *bë-fetsar* and like forms are, since they inherit nothing of the argument structure of the corresponding verb. For instance, *fetsar* as an applicative verb requires a beneficiary and a direct object in a Double Object Construction (see *Man fetsar ul u-ndali* /I follow+Appl her/him 3-cat/ 'I followed the cat for her/him'); *bë-fetsar* 'friend' requires nothing of the sort. To put it tersely, *bë-fetsar* is a noun; it is not a nominalization. The derivation sketched here cannot therefore be the right one.

We are thus led to assume a rather strong version of our interfacing model: not only is the lexicon connected to syntax, but also syntax, in its turn, may feed the lexicon by returning to it the complex roots that it builds, such as $\sqrt{}\sqrt{}$fets$\sqrt{}$ar. As a complex root, $\sqrt{}$fetsar (for short) is voided of the categorical features syntax assigns it and is therefore available for insertion (or reinsertion) into syntax, this time under an nP projection—hence, *bë-fetsar* 'friend', where the verbal character of the main root is entirely erased from memory, so to speak.

That said, I am quite willing to admit that such an explanation is certainly not the last word on the subject, if only because the doing-undoing mechanism it involves has something definitely awkward to it. Perhaps the Manjaku data should be taken as support to the notion that the function that syntactic head movement fulfills would be better entrusted to some intralexical root-combining operation. There would be no contradiction between such a move and the overall view of the lexicon defended here (see n. 63). Alternatively, nominalizations such as (33), the end results of which keep the memory of their formative process, show that we cannot dispense altogether with a syntactic component or, more accurately, with a component that manipulates and categorizes heads according to syntactic principles such as the LCA and the V versus N feature contrast (for an early extension of Move-α to the lexicon, see Keyser and Roeper 1984; see also Roeper 1993). How this component is to be called and where exactly it is located (inside or outside the lexicon or as an interface of the lexicon with morphology) are relatively secondary matters. I will say no more on the subject, however.

To return to our main topic, it seems, therefore, that the opposed linearizations (and distinct "visibilities") of Class exponents in Manjaku and in Romance can be completely deduced from their different lexical statuses. Let us now proceed to the Class-Number issue.

6.2 The Fusion of Class and Number

The empirical generalization that Class and Number (i.e., plural) morphemes combine to be spelled out as syncretic exponents seems quite solid. Typical examples are Italian *gatta* /√gatt+nII/ versus *gatte* /√gatt+nII.Pl/ 'she-cat(s)', Modern Hebrew *tmuna* /√tmun+F/ versus *tmunot* /√tmun+F.pl/ 'picture(s)', and of course Manjaku *ka-to* versus *i-to* 'house(s)'. To the difference of Class, Number is a functional element unequivocally, at least in those languages where it is obligatorily expressed as a bound morpheme.[68] A plausible assumption within the present framework, then, is that Number is a functional root meaning "Plurality" ($1 < x$).[69] Singularity has no grammatical representative in this view: it is the interpretative result of not combining Plurality with a root denoting a countable entity. (If the denoted entity is noncountable, the result is massivity.) Plurality is syntactically expressed as a head (Num^0) c-commanding the noun (see Ritter 1991). The syntactic representation of *gatte* 'she-cats' is thus the following:

(34) $[_{NumP} Num^0 [_{nP} nII [_{\sqrt{P}} \sqrt{gatt}]]]$

It is easy to see that, given our basic assumptions, Number-Class syncretism follows straightforwardly from such a representation: nII attracts the root as already explained, hence:

(35) $[_{NumP} Num^0 [_{nP} \sqrt{gatt}+nII [_{\sqrt{P}} t]]]$

(This, note, must indeed be the first step, because, under the assumption that Attract is local, Num^0 could only target nII, but it would "gain" nothing by so doing since nII is also functional.) Then Num^0 attracts the complex (nonfunctional) head √gatt+nII—hence:

(36) $[_{NumP} \sqrt{gatt}+nII+Num^0 [_{nP} t [_{\sqrt{P}} t]]]$

Class and Number are thus necessarily adjoined, and in that order. It is precisely this that my analysis of Class and Number predicts. The outcome of the adjunction then depends on the morphophonological form of the exponents. In Italian, we may assume the exponent of Plurality to be /I/—a high vowel that gives an /e/ when fused with the /a/ exponent of nII.[70] In Spanish, on the other hand, Plurality spells out as /s/, a consonant that can only be merged (in the sense of added to, not fused) with the Class exponent, hence *gatas* 'she-cats'.[71]

　　Can this analysis be extended to Manjaku? Let us take (34) as also representing what surfaces as *i-to* 'houses':

(37) $[_{NumP} Num^0 [_{nP} n^0 [_{\sqrt{P}} \sqrt{to}]]]$

Here, functional attraction is a property of Num⁰ only, and it targets the closest nonfunctional category—n⁰. What enters morphology is therefore:

(38) $[_{\text{NumP}} \, n^0 + \text{Num}^0 \, [_{nP} \, t \, [_{\sqrt{P}} \, \sqrt{\text{to}}]]]$

Class-Number adjunction is again predicted, plus the fact that the resulting complex will appear as a prefix to the root. Accounting for the form of this complex is not so obvious, however; it depends crucially on the choice we make for the identity of n⁰ in (37)–(38). Suppose we consider it to be the syntactic projection of Class 7—that is, the noun class lexically associated with the root √to when Plurality is not activated. Since the exponent of Class 7 is /ka/, and it is not morphophonologically related to /i/ as the exponent of /n⁰ = 7 + Num/, we are led to assume generalized suppletion: /ka + Num/ = /i/, /na + Num/ = /ba/, /u + Num/ = /ngë/, and so on. In fact, it is the assumption underlying the common notion that *i-to* "is the plural of" *ka-to*. Nor is suppletive pluralization an unheard-of phenomenon (see French *œil* vs. *yeux* 'eye(s)', Modern Hebrew *iša* vs. *našim* 'woman/women', Xârâcùù *kâmûrû* vs. *pââdo* 'man/men').[72]

The problem with this account is thus not suppletion per se but, rather, the usual conundrums of noun class systems—namely, that singular–plural pairings are not one to one, as in the idealized chart (1), in a significant number of cases— see *pë-bank/i-bank* (not * *kë-bank*) 'dike(s)', *bë-fetsar/i-fetsar* (not **m-fetsar*) 'friend(s)'—and that it is even possible for a root to be pluralized in a class that is not normally associated with Plurality; see *na-päts/u-päts* 'child/children' (compare *u-ndali* 'cat'). In other words, the form of the "plural" exponent is not predictable from that of the nonplural exponent through simple suppletive equations such as the ones given before, and it also depends on the identity of the root in the sense that speakers must know that, if they choose to refer to 'children', then the proper exponent to prefix to the denoting root is the one that spells out *n* = Class 3.

Therefore, an explanation involving the syntactic steps (37) and (38), followed by suppletive exponence, although it works in a fair number of cases, does not seem adequate for Manjaku. True, we could repair it by postulating multiple suppletion, that is, by positing disjunctive sets of suppletive equations such as {/pë+Num/ = /kë/ ∨ /pë+Num/ = /i/} and indexing roots for the member of the disjunction they merge with (e.g., √bank ⊃ /pë+Num/ = /i/). This is quite an ad hoc solution, however, which is not even descriptively adequate since, as we saw, more than one type of plural must be accommodated for some roots (e.g., *pë-konj* 'finger', *kë-konj kë-wants* 'three fingers', *i-konj* 'fingers').

In fact, the difficulty with explaining Manjaku plural formation comes from the need to provide for two different aspects at the same time: on one hand, it seems to be the case that the lexical association between a root and a Class root varies independently, according to whether the association denotes one or several tokens of the referred entity. In other words, the association $\{Class_i + \sqrt{x}\}$ with singular denotation is independent from the association $\{Class_j + \sqrt{x}\}$ with plural denotation. Nonpredictability of plural Class membership with respect to the singular (and the other way around) depends on this. On the other hand, it is also true that Class signs (i.e., Class roots and their exponents) are inherently specified for Number, as it is never the case that $ka\text{-}\sqrt{x}$, for instance, may refer to several tokens of the entity denoted by $\sqrt{x}$, or $i\text{-}\sqrt{x}$ to one token of the same entity.[73] Because of the former fact, as already mentioned, we cannot simply derive *i-bank* from *pë-bank* as we do *gatas* from *gata*.[74] The latter fact, for its part, is what prevents us from adopting another a priori plausible solution by assuming that roots merge with Plurality first,—that is, reversing the order of nP and NumP in (37). If we did that (and only that), and since singular and plural lexical associations are independent from one another, how could we make sure that pluralized roots do not combine with *any* Class roots rather than with the subset they actually associate with?[75]

Recall now that we entertained the minimal possibility (minimal in term of changes in the model) that what is attained through syntactic head movement as in (37)–(38) may also be realized through intralexical combination. I can then make the following proposal: in Manjaku-type languages, the functional lexical item Plurality is not mapped into syntax, but it merges with Class roots within the lexicon.[76] To put it more formally: to each member of $\{n\}$ (that is, to each $\{\{n_i\}\}$), there corresponds another singleton set consisting of the intersection of $\{\{n_i\}\}$ with $\{Plurality\}$, namely, $\{\{n_i\} \cap \{Plurality\}\}$. Members of both sets have different exponents (e.g., /na/ and /ba/). Given a particular root not belonging to these sets (e.g., $\sqrt{bank}$), there must be a statement of the fact that this root can associate with a particular member of $\{n\}$—that is, a piece of knowledge that language learners have to acquire and that is inherently part of what it means to know that root. And there must be another independent, statement of the fact that the same root can associate with a particular member of $\{\{n\} \cap \{Plurality\}\}$. As a consequence, there is no NumP projection in syntax, and the n^0 head includes both Class and Number features.

Because roots and Class roots have meaning, and associations are not haphazard semantically, the same n_i will be mentioned in both statements in a fair number of cases, so that deductive generalizations can indeed be drawn, such as "if a root denotes a human being, then it associates with $\{n_i = /na/\}$, on the one hand, and with $\{n_i \cap Plurality = /ba/\}$, on the other hand."[77] But, and that is the gist of the proposal, those are no more than factual generalizations, as nothing in the system forces the same n_i to be targeted in the two statements. In other words, because the selections are independent, there is no necessary connection (just a frequent one) between the semantic contents of the n_i's that associate with a root in or out of intersection with Plurality—just as no connection is observed in a significant number of cases between the basic semantics of the Class signs and the meanings of the roots they attach to.

Actually, the deep implication of the present account is that, in languages like Manjaku, Plurality's primary association is not with denoting roots, as in English or Romance, but with Class roots understood as protonouns (as discussed previously). It is Class roots that are pluralized *and* associated with denoting roots which, of themselves, have no specification for Number. And it is the global mutual independence (not precluding significant predictability) of {n} and {n ∩ Plurality } selection that justifies conceiving of the association as a set-theoretic operation within the lexicon rather than as syntactic merger. In Romance-type languages, roots are unspecified for Number as well, but Plurality does not gravitate toward Class. It is autonomously mapped into syntax as a Num^0 head, and Number-Class merger is a morphological operation. In other words, Manjaku *ngë-ndali* 'cats' is not the plural of *u-ndali* in the sense that Spanish *gatas* is the plural of *gata*; rather, {{n} ∩ {Plurality}} = /ngë/ is an inherently plural Class sign semantically paired with {{n}} = /u/, that may (because of this pairing) but need not be associated with the same denoting roots {{n}} = /u/ attaches to (see *ngë-nana* as the numbered plural paired with *bë-nana* 'banana tree').

Admittedly, such a conclusion does not wander far from what has long been received wisdom in noun class studies of Bantu and so-called Bantoid languages. What I claim to contribute, beyond formalization, is the discovery of a basic relation between this state of affairs and the root character of Class signs in these languages, as opposed to the purely functional nature of gender morphemes in Romance languages. I will refrain from further predictions at this stage, however, because Class systems are complicated, and I prefer not to overstep the comparative domain I chose. Let me just underline a few points in connection with the preceding considerations.

First, this account is fully compatible with the existence of systems such as that of Standard Wolof, outlined previously, where the number of distinguished classes in the plural is drastically reduced relative to the singular. My interpretation of this fact is simply that, whereas {n} consists of eight members, {{n} ∩ {Plurality}} includes only two—one for some humans and one for all the rest, including humans—a dramatic illustration of the possible unconnectedness of *n*'s semantic contents in the two sets. (The limiting case where {{n} ∩ {Plurality}} is further reduced to one member implies that *n* is semantically void in this set; i.e., it has no features except N.[78])

Second, and this is to be taken as a tentative opening onto further research, it might be that the contrast root versus functional element, clearly exposed by the comparison of Manjaku with Romance, admits of intermediate cases. One such case would be Modern Hebrew. It is well known that in this language the intersection of gender and plural marking yields a number of idiosyncratic formations: masculine nouns (as shown by agreement) may take the feminine plural ending (e.g., *šulxan/šulxanot* 'table(s)'), while some feminine nouns take the masculine plural ending (e.g., *dvora/dvorim* 'bee(s)', *šibolet/šibolim* '(corn) ear').[79] Moreover, the true assertion that masculine nouns never bear an overt gender morpheme is not reversible, as a number of feminine nouns are also unmarked (e.g., *kos mala* 'a full cup' / *kosot malot* 'full cups').[80] Such facts led Ritter (1991) to assume that Hebrew gender, in addition to being an inherent lexical property of nouns, is morphologically derivational (see Ritter 1991: 50ff. for evidence to that effect, based on work by Bat-El 1986), whereas Number is inflectional—carried by a functional projection NumP that is unspecified for gender. Agreement facts such as *šulxanot ktanim* 'small tables', showing that the adjective agrees in gender with the (masculine) base rather than with the (theoretically feminine) plural ending, bear out the latter claim.

Yet, the fact that *šulxan* has *šulxanot* for a plural instead of expected * /šulxanim/ (and *dvora, dvorim* instead of */dvorot/) receives no explanation in Ritter's account. Her observation that gender fulfills clearly derivational functions in Hebrew (as in her example of *amud* 'page' vs. *amuda* 'column', p. 51) makes Hebrew gender look similar, in this respect at least, to Manjaku noun classes, whose derivational potential was shown to be crucial for their analysis. Hence, there is a suggestion that the complexities of Hebrew gender-number marking might at least be sorted out, if not fully disentangled or clarified, by means of the same analytical tools as we used for Manjaku (and for Romance).

A first necessary step, I think, is to rid ourselves of the traditional but obscuring categories "masculine" and "feminine" in favor of word classes, as in Harris's analysis of Spanish, keeping them only as an encyclopedic classificational criterion applicable to a small subset of the total lexicon (as noted before). Assume then that Hebrew roots are nominalized into four word classes, which I shall designate as nI (corresponding to old masculine), nII, nIII, and nIV (these latter three corresponding to old feminine). The exponents are as follows: nI = /∅/ (e.g., *xatul* 'cat'); nII = /a/ (e.g., *xatula* 'she-cat'); nIII = /Vt/ (e.g., *igeret* 'letter', *balšanut* 'linguistics', *mexonit* 'car'); nIV = /∅/ (e.g., *kos* 'cup').[81] These four (or three) elements constitute the membership of the {n} set in Hebrew. I will not speculate about their semantics.

Assume further than in Hebrew as in Manjaku there is a second, disjoint set formed by intersecting {n} with Plurality. (For simplicity, I will use nXPL as a notation, and I abstract from Dual.) One member of this set is nIPL = /im/ (e.g., *xatulim* 'cats'). Another member is nIPLa = /ot/ (e.g., *šulxanot* 'tables'). Empirical evidence shows that the roots lexically associated with this class must be listed, since they are in finite number (no new nouns enter this class) and no natural generalization over them, touching their form or meaning, seems feasible (see

Cohen and Zafrani 1968: 172ff.). By a simple application of the Elsewhere Principle, all roots not in the list are associated with class nIPL if they are also associated with class nI. Similarly, we have classes nIIPL = /ot/ (e.g., *xatulot* 'she-cats', *igarot* 'letters', *mexoniyot* 'cars') and nIIPLa = /im/ (e.g., *dvorim* 'bees', *šibolim* '(corn) ears') where roots associated with nIIPLa also have to be listed. Note that classes nII, nIII, and nIV can be collapsed when intersected with Plurality, even though it seems to be the case that no noun in class nIV (e.g., *kos* 'cup') has its plural in class nIIPLa.[82] Four plural classes have thus to be distinguished as well.

What we see, then, is that {n} and {nPL} are not independent in Hebrew in the sense they are in Manjaku, since all nI-associated roots associate with nIPL or nIPLa, and all nII/III/IV-associated roots associate with nIIPL or nIIPLa. There is a measure of unpredictability unknown in Romance, however, insofar as given an nI root, for instance, learners of the language cannot associate it with nIPL or nIPLa "before consulting the list." It is in that sense that Hebrew may be said to have no inflectional classes as argued by Aronoff (1994: 75ff.). Moreover, it is possible for a root to be associated with {nPL} without being associated with {n} (so-called *pluralia tantum*; e.g., *mayim* 'water', *šulayim* 'margin'). Because of these complexifying factors, therefore, a Manjaku-like solution, with Class and Plurality lexically combined rather than syntactically merged, seems adequate—all the more so since, as we saw, Hebrew gender has derivational features like Manjaku noun classes, although to a much lesser extent.

Nevertheless, Hebrew gender or gender-number morphemes are suffixes like their Romance equivalents. In our terms, this means that members of {n} and {nPL} in Hebrew are not denoting roots but functional roots, in correlation with the semantic narrowness of the classificational criterion they invoke, as well as their limited derivational role as compared with Manjaku noun classes. In this way, then, Hebrew does represent an intermediate case between Manjaku and Romance: it is like the former insofar as Class and Plurality combine in the lexicon, thus precluding the syntactic insertion of a Num⁰ head below DP contra Ritter (1991), an option that UG must allow, I submit. It is like Romance, on the other hand, because Class, being only weakly derivational and limited in terms of classificatory relevance, is functional, with the consequence that the n(PL)⁰ head that expresses it in syntax must attract the root it nominalizes, therefore appearing as a suffix at the output of morphology.[83]

7 Conclusion (With an Outlook on Classifiers beyond Gender and Noun Classes)

If all the foregoing makes some kind of sense, there is in the universal lexicon an element I call Class, the unvarying property of which is to convert roots into nouns. Correlated to this grammatical property, Class is endowed with a classificatory (i.e., semantic) content of varying richness or relevance with respect to the universe of concepts each language's particular lexicon expresses. The lexical status of Class items as denoting or functional roots, and the morphosyntactic effects that ensue, depends on this content. This is, I claim, the significant result of the present enquiry. I next mention a few issues that follow from or are connected with it and have not been dealt with so far.

Given such a universality assumption, what about languages like Turkish, where Class has no overt manifestation whatsoever, or classifier languages such as Chinese? As for the former, the simplest assumption is that they represent the limiting case where Class, or {n}, has no content at all, being purely noun forming (and functional).[84] Note the existence of such a case is expected in principle, since Class's content is a gradient by definition, and there are numerous examples showing how a contentful Class system, of the Romance or Bantu/Bantoid type, may evolve into a less contentful or a contentless Class system analogous to Turkish; see, for example, the cases of Wolof or Turkana mentioned previously and the Romance or Bantu-based creole or pidgin languages (e.g., Manessy 1977).

It is not possible, however, to do justice to numeral or possessive classifier systems, to use Aikhenvald's (2000) characterizations, in such a cursory fashion, and examining them in detail would inflate this article out of all proportion. Let me just suggest a few directions.

As their name indicates, numeral classifiers occur only in conjunction with quantifying expressions, typically numerals. The most widely known such system is that of Chinese, but I will rather give an example from Ejagham, a Benue-Congo, Southern Bantoid language (see Watters 1981: 310, quoted in Aikhenvald 2000: 99):[85]

(39) à-məgɛ   í-čɔkúd   á-bá'ɛ
      6-CL:SMALL.ROUND Gen6   19-orange.seed 6-two

      two orange seeds

Ejagham, by no means exceptional in this respect, is especially interesting as it shows that a language may have recourse to more than one Class system, as here where noun classes are concurrent with numeral classifiers. Moreover, it dramatically demonstrates the nonfunctional, root nature of numeral classifiers, since the classifier *à-mɔgɛ* is marked for noun class (6, a plural class) like any noun, and the numeral meaning 'two' agrees with it. The discontinuous noun phrase [à-mɔgɛ . . . á-bá'ɛ] then forms a genitive construction (whose marker is the floating low tone glossed Gen, also associated with class 6) with the noun *í-čɔkúd*, which belongs to a different noun class than the classifier, namely, 19, a *singular* class.[86] It seems we have every reason, therefore, to consider /mɔgɛ/ a protonoun with the meaning "small round object" morphologically realized as a free form—and likewise Vietnamese *hòn* 'rock', *búc* 'flat, rectangular object', and so forth (see Thompson 1987). What will be the difference, then, between such a free protonoun and a full noun such as *í-čɔkúd* 'orange seed', on one hand, and a bound protonoun as noun class markers are, on the other hand?

With respect to the latter difference, it clearly lies in the fact that bound protonouns such as Manjaku /na/ and /ka/ *are* instantiations of {n}, whereas free protonouns must combine with (members of) {n}, either visibly as in Ejagham or invisibly as in Vietnamese. Ejagham *n-mɔgɛ* (the class 1 singular correspondent of *à-mɔgɛ*) and Vietnamese *hòn* are thus independent lexemes, which do not form one projection with the noun they bear on, to the difference of Manjaku /na/, /ka/, and so on, which, despite being denoting roots, must merge with another root because of the noun-forming property of {n} that they spell out. This is enough to preclude agreement from NP in languages with numeral classifiers of such a sort. In the best of worlds, we should be able to correlate this morphological difference with the varying semantic richness of the items, since Ejagham *n-mɔgɛ* or Vietnamese *hòn* clearly have more specific meanings than Manjaku /na/ or /ka/. We are not allowed such a move, though, because of the existence of languages like the Papuan language Nasioi (see Foley 1986), the lexicon of which contains more than a hundred Class elements as specific semantically as the numeral classifiers of Ejagham or Vietnamese, but with agreement within the DP as the exponent of the chosen element, an enclitic attached to the head noun, is copied onto each component (also as an enclitic).[87]

It does not mean there is no correlation between semantic content—that is, classificatory potential—and morphological status, but it is a complex correlation. What we have, indeed, is a classificatory potential continuum that goes from poor (genders) to general (noun classes of the Manjaku type) to specific (numeral classifiers or noun classes of the Nasioi type) and that projects onto a three-way alternative for exponence: suffix, clitic, or free form, corresponding to the three options of fusion, merger, or no operation, in a hierarchy of increasing morphological freeness. From this, it seems we can draw the following observational generalizations: poor classificatory potential is never expressed as free forms, although it may be realized as clitics as in Turkana; that is to say, it is always a value of {n}, whose contentfulness varies (and may become impoverished). At the other end of the continuum, specific classification can be realized as free forms or clitics but never, it seems, as suffixes, meaning that the rich content of {n} then required prevents it from being fully functional. Finally, there do not seem to be cases where general classification of the Manjaku type, in the middle of the continuum, is realized as either suffixes or free forms. All this seems to be consistent with our basic assumptions, although, I repeat, it is no more than generalizations still far from real explanations (see Aikhenvald 2000 for more facts and for the grammaticalization issues involved).

As for the difference between numeral classifiers and "ordinary" nouns, there does not seem to be anything intrinsic in it, if only because in many languages numeral classifiers are open lexical classes, and one and the same item may be used both as a numeral classifier, and as an ordinary noun (see English *head*, with the intriguing property that it does not pluralize when used as a classifier).[88] The crucial property would rather be external to Class proper, and it would have to do with the fact that all nouns in numeral classifier languages are basically Mass nouns that need the classifier to be quantified (see Chierchia 1998). This would be the case of Vietnamese, for instance. In Ejagham, it is noteworthy that the quantified noun in examples like (39) is singular, probably interpreted as generic.[89]

To conclude, I would like to say a few words about agreement, which, as a matter of fact, has been almost entirely left out of this study. This apparent oversight reflects to some extent my initial reaction against treatments that consider agreement the be-all and end-all of Class phenomena. But it is also due to the fact that agreement is not really problematic for my account and is largely tangential to it. Take noun-adjective agreement, the only form Romance and Manjaku have in common. For Romance, we have Cinque's (1994) theory, according to which adjectives are generated prenominally in the specifiers of dedicated functional projections, and N^0 raises over them through the heads of these functional projections, thereby creating the necessary Spec-Head configuration for agreement. According to the present analysis, N^0 is not basically present in the syntax, but there is a maximal projection $[_{nP} n^0 [_{\sqrt{P}} \sqrt{^0}]]$. Once n^0 has attracted the root head, however, a complex head $[\sqrt{^0}+n^0]$ is created, which is no more (and no less) than the decomposition of N^0. The derivation can then proceed unaltered.

Cinque's account can probably be extended to Manjaku, where attributive adjectives also follow the head superficially (see *u-ndali u-faacal* /3-cat 3-white/ 'white cat').[90] A problem, though, is that root heads do not adjoin to n^0 in Manjaku, so that syntax has to deal with a maximal nP projection until Spell Out (i.e., delivery to morphology). This certainly stands in the way of N^0 passing through intermediate functional heads. A possible solution is to adopt (and adapt) Cinque's suggestion (p. 106) for prenominal adjectives in Romance: that is, to assume that nP raises overtly to a higher position whereas the root head raises at LF (perhaps to D if it is projected in Manjaku). Spec-Head agreement would ensue, since roots are lexically associated with noun classes. Number would still be a problem, however, under our assumption that Plurality and Class combine lexically in {n} and there is no NumP projection, with the consequence that, if the root head moves by itself, LF may "know" that it belongs to noun class 3, but it may not know whether it is pluralized. Moreover, justifying nP raising is no easy task.

A much simpler solution is available, however. Consider that so-called adjectives are not different from nouns in Manjaku except for the fact that their class membership is not lexically specified. It means that /x-faacal/ 'white' (x = any noun class) has the same basic structure as *u-ndali* 'cat', namely $[_{nP}$ n^0 $[_{\sqrt P}$ $\sqrt{}^0]]$, but for the fact that n^0 is unspecified (beyond the N feature). In the spirit of Cinque's analysis, the basic structure of what surfaces as *u-ndali u-faacal* 'white cat' is therefore the following, with the ellipsis indicating whatever structure may be present between the two nPs (perhaps none):

(40) $[_{nP}$ n^0 $_x$ $[_{\sqrt P}$ $\sqrt{}^0$ = faacal ... $[_{nP}$ n^0 $_3$ $[_{\sqrt P}$ $\sqrt{}^0$ = ndali]]]]

In fact, such a configuration is strikingly similar to that of Semitic genitive phrases (so-called Construct States) headed by an adjective (see Standard Arabic *Hasanu l-wajhi* /handsome the-face/ 'handsome of face'). Given the form of Manjaku genitive phrases (see *u-ndali na-cën* /3-cat 1-neighbor/ 'the cat of the neighbor') and the noun-adjective indistinction just mentioned, such a parallel appears quite sound. The main point of (40), however, is that it provides us with a reason why the lower nP must raise—namely, that the higher nP's head n^0$_x$ is unspecified and must get a class value before it may pass the morphological threshold. Therefore, the lower nP raises to the specifier of the higher one, thus creating an agreement configuration such that n^0$_x$ gets the class value of n^0$_3$.[91]

That said, there is a still simpler solution, and that is to assume that nothing particular happens in the syntax and that Agree (in the sense of Chomsky 1999) is an operation of the interface, either between the lexicon and syntax or even between the lexicon and morphology (if word order is taken care of by the latter, and syntax is pure LF). That would be a really minimal account. My proposal that Class and Plurality combine lexicon-internally in Manjaku certainly points toward that direction. Alternatively, as also mentioned, *destruction*-type nominalizations seem to indicate that not all morphology-relevant operations can be done "in the privacy of your own lexicon," to use Marantz's expression (but see Roeper 1993). As such speculations open some sort of a Pandora's box, the contents of which far exceed the aims of this work, I leave them at that for the moment.

NOTES

1. There is the well-known exception of noble vehicles like ships, cars, and locomotives and country names, all optionally feminine. As a matter of fact, neuter is always an option for nouns denoting nonhumans.

2. Even there irrelevancies abound, such as French *sentinelle* 'sentry', feminine, despite the fact that, up to a recent period, sentries were obligatorily male.

3. The classic studies for such systems are Dixon (1972) and Lakoff (1987). See Miller and Johnson-Laird (1976) for arguments to the effect that shape is the most basic and stable descriptive property (see also Grandi 2002).

4. Here I am talking about subject-predicate and DP-internal agreement. Pronoun concord (i.e., the fact that *girl* is coreferred to by *she*, but *syntax* by *it*) is quite probably a different matter, which is why English is such a tricky object for reflecting on Class. The fact is that Class in English is an overt grammatical category for pronouns only, and the relation of *she* to *girl* (or to *ship*)—that is, of the form *she* rather than *he* or *it* to that particular word—is not a matter for syntax (*I know him* preferred when referring to a girl is not ungrammatical, but inappropriate or even mean). Since English pronouns are DPs to themselves and cannot be modified (see **nice she,* *nice who), and subject-predicate agreement is much less of a criterion than DP-internal agreement, the English state of affairs does not contradict the claim just made; it merely voids it of its relevance in the particular case. Numeral classifier systems of the Chinese type (see Aikhenvald 2000: ch. 4), which do not involve agreement, are no counterevidence, as we shall see.

5. Even more so if agreement is viewed as a relation ("Agree") motivated by the need to remove uninterpretable features from syntax (see Chomsky 1999, 2001).

6. Aikhenvald collapses gender and noun class systems, contrasting them with numeral classifiers, classifiers in possessive constructions, and so-called verbal classifiers (see later). Given her typological-cognitive perspective, she is quite right to do so. For my own purposes, however, gender and noun class must be kept distinct at the grammatical level.

7. By "Class exponents" I mean *overt* Class morphemes in whatever system.

8. I am giving "fusion" and "merger" the sense they have in Distributed Morphology as presented in Halle and Marantz (1993).

9. A clear example of a language with enclitic noun class morphemes is Fulfulde (see Sylla 1982). Wolof, to which I will return, where noun class morphemes also seem to be enclitics, is actually a more complex case. Turkana, an East-Nilotic language with three genders—masculine, feminine, and neuter—marked with prefixes would seem to ruin the generalization (see Dimmendaal 1983). Yet, considering the way it functions, the Turkana gender system looks more like a very reduced noun class system than a gender system of the Indo-European or Semitic type. Moreover, we know that gender and noun class are not separate categories, as shown by Aikhenvald (2000), so the generalizations I am trying to make can be fully valid for only the ends of the continuum, although perhaps not for midway cases like Turkana.

10. At least, it does look true in the language families of which I have some first-hand knowledge (Indo-European, Niger-Congo, and Afroasiatic), and I am not aware of

any evidence from other families that would contradict it. Needless to say, I am expecting such evidence any minute (but see preceding note). I also want to make it clear that the generalization is intended only for Class exponents: that is, I am not implying that noun class languages, for instance, are globally agglutinative (if that makes sense) but only that noun class morphemes are always attached to roots agglutinatively rather than inflectionally, and the reverse for gender morphemes, which, if true, is unexpected and therefore interesting.

11. Manjaku, a Niger-Congo language of the Atlantic subfamily spoken in Guinea-Bissau and South Senegal, is presented in more detail later, in this chapter.

12. For instance, the obvious apparent counterexample of Iberian Romance *casas* 'houses', where Class and Number seem indeed to be expressed through separate morphemes (see Harris 1992).

13. Highly relevant here is Bybee's (1985) observation that Class agreement on verbs is far less frequent than Number and Person agreement.

14. *Bak* is from the protoform of the class 2 prefix in all these languages.

15. For clarity's sake, I separate the noun class prefix from the root with a hyphen. Note that a Manjaku dictionary (e.g., Doneux 1975) is best organized according to the alphabetical order of roots. As for transcription, /ë/ is a schwa, that can be deleted under certain conditions; /ä/ is a centralized /a/; /c/ and /j/ are palatal obstruents. For simplicity, I ignore the contrast of [+ATR] and [−ATR] (or tense and lax) vowels.

16. Whether actually greater or not is something I do not try to assess here, if only because no complete dictionary of Manjaku is available. For an overview of noun class systems in the Atlantic languages, see Pozdnjakov (1993).

17. The latter item is probably a borrowing of Portuguese *espingarda* 'gun', the [p] being reanalyzed as the noun class 9 prefix /p(ë)-/. This shows the productivity of the pattern.

18. A few nouns belong to more than one noun class without change in reference (e.g., besides *pë-ndog* (9) / *i-ndog* (8) 'stick(s)', there is *u-ndog* (3) / *ngë-ndog* (4) with the same meaning). This seems rather exceptional, however.

19. *Te* 'until' is a borrowing of Portuguese Creole *te*, itself from Portuguese *até*.

20. Both [d] and [r] are allophones in Manjaku, [d] being found word-initially and after a nasal, [r] elsewhere. Interestingly, the fact that [r] shows up in *di ruäts* (underlyingly /Di D-uäts/) demonstrates that the phrase is treated as a phonological word (a morphosyntactic word, or M-word, in Embick and Noyer's 1999 terminology).

21. *Kotiës* actually is a fused NP consisting of *ko* 'entity', an item to which we shall return, and *tiës* 'small.' Here again, what English expresses through adverbials is often expressed by other means in Manjaku—in particular, modal verbs such as *kak* 'do again' (as in, e.g., *Jon a kak pë-ro w-ul*/Jon Pro do-again 9-do 3-3SG/'Jon did it again'; see later for *a* glossed Pro, *pë-ro*, and *w-ul*).

22. Failure to agree of course is, not sufficient to assign adjective predicates to a different category than attributive adjectives (see, e.g., German). More convincing is the fact that adjective predicates do not include a copula, although Manjaku is equipped with such an element, that is obligatorily used when the predicate is a noun: compare *A (*ci) mak* 'She/he/it is big' with *A *(ci) nasiën* 'He is the/a chief'. Actually, as noted in Buis (1990: 23), agreeing adjectives may be used as predicates as a "less common" alternative to using quality verbs (e.g., *A ci na-war*/Pro Cop 1-good/'She/He is good' vs. *A wara* 'She/He (is) good'). The fact that copula *ci* is then obligatory suggests that *A ci na-*

war ought rather to be translated as 'She/He is a good person', which, if true, would come as support for the analysis of noun class prefixes I will propose later. As shown by this example, quality verbs are sometimes morphologically distinct from the corresponding adjective (but the status of final /a/ in *wara* is unclear). In addition, attributive adjectives may be derived from quality verbs through a suffix /-al/ (see *U-ndali a faac* 'The cat is white' vs. *u-ndali u-faacal* 'the/a white cat'). Also shown is the absence of overt "simple" determiners in Manjaku, such that, out of context, (2) and (2a) can be interpreted as either definite, indefinite, or generic.

23. *Kà-ñän* 'five' belongs to a "derived" noun class in which the prefix is followed by a low tone /à/ morpheme (perhaps the same as shows up in 1a). Morphophonological processes then apply so that /ka+à/, /ngë+à/, /bë+à/, /m+à/, /pë+à/, and /kë+à/ are realized as /kà/, /ngà/, /bà/, /màn/, /pà/, and /kà/, respectively (see Doneux 1975 for the analysis; also Pozdnjakov 1993). Only noun classes 3, 5, 6, 7, 9, and 10 seem to be accompanied with derived classes. Their origin, distribution, and function are unclear. (Note that *kà-ñän* (7) / *i-ñän* (8) means 'hand'.) The numerals for 'six' and 'eight' are always pronounced /paaj/ and /kuäs/. Since the supposed roots ?/aaj/ and ?/uäs/ are, in fact, unindentifiable, noun class membership is only hypothetical (whereas *u-ntaja* has a plural *ngë-ntaja* meaning 'tens'). There are no simple numerals for 'seven' and 'nine', which are expressed respectively as 'six and one' and 'eight and one' (see *ngë-pi paaj ni u-lole* /4-goat six and 3-one/ 'seven goats', *ba-ñan kuäs ni na-lole* /2-man eight and 1-one/ 'nine men').

24. With noun class 2 there is a special form *bik-i* and *buk-un* (*ba-kiëj bik-i* 'these thieves', *ba-kiëj buk-un* 'those thieves') where /bi/uk-/ is probably the same morpheme as appears in the pronoun *bukul* 'they' (see later). There is vowel harmony in Manjaku.

25. *Na-ko*'s irregular plural is *buk-ul* 'they' (humans only), consisting in the /bi/uk/ allomorph of the noun class 2 prefix /ba-/ (see note 24) and the third-person singular clitic pronoun /-ul/ (for which, see later).

26. *Buk-ul* is thus ambiguous, serving both as the plural of *na-ko* and of *n-ul*. Noun class 3 *w-ul* is actually realized as [wël]. Noun class 13 *d-ul* is a locative pronoun similar to French *y* (see *Man ya d-ul* 'I went there / J'y suis allé'). Noun class 12 does not combine with /ul/, but it does with the determiners /i/ and /un/ to build the locative adverbials *ts-i* 'here' and *ts-un* 'there'.

27. In object function, *n-ul* generally (always?) takes on the form *ul*, which I propose to explain by assuming it is then assigned to noun class 1a, whose exponent /a-/ would normally coalesce with the initial vowel. In (9), *na-ko* may of course be replaced by *a* or any third-person DP denoting humans without modifying the intended reference.

28. Wolof, the main language of Senegal spoken by several millions, is also classified as Atlantic, but the structural differences with Manjaku are rather enormous. On Wolof in general, see Sauvageot (1965); see Kihm (1999) for a particular study of the noun phrase.

29. I say "usually" because the criterion is not so much anatomy as the fact that the number be determined, explicitly or not. Doneux's (1975) term for this is *pluriel dénombré* 'numbered plural'.

30. Compare *Na-kiëj a fäm pë-lëman* 'The thief broke the door'.

31. Whether the Case is accusative or genitive may be in debate, since Manjaku genitive phrases are overtly similar to verb-object constructions (see *pë-lëman na-kiëj*

'the/a door (of) the/a thief'). The issue may be decided by looking at the Mankanya dialect where, next to the "direct" genitive construction of Manjaku, there is a construction implying an intermediate determiner agreeing in noun class with the head noun, as in *ka-bats k-i na-pots* /7-ear 7-Det 1-child/ 'the child's ear' (Trifkovic 1969: 88; I modify her transcription somewhat). This construction, however, seems never to be used when the head is a noun class 9 "infinitive", as in *nga bi tsiñan pëjaar u-lugar* /4 Past decide 9-cultivate 3-field/ 'they (the animals) had decided to cultivate a field' (p. 121)—not **pëjaar p-i-u-lugar*.

32. Pro does not appear before negative predicates (see Kihm and Gomes 1988). Unfortunately, I lack data on whether equivalents of "his breaking the door" are constructible in Manjaku. I guess not, as "His breaking my door was not nice" would most certainly be expressed as "He broke my door (and) that was not nice." More research is clearly necessary, though.

33. The /-an/ suffix is a causative morpheme (see *col* 'to stand' vs. *colan.* 'to put in an upright position' from Buis 1990: 46).

34. Although Trifkovic translates *J'avais rencontré trois cultivateurs (qui étaient) en train de défricher,* . . . *trois cultivateurs en plein défrichage* conveys exactly the same idea of the situation.

35. Also worthy of note are the "adverbial" usage of reduplicating /kë/-prefixed verbal roots (e.g., *man par kë-par* /I pass 10-pass/ 'I'm just passing by' from Buis 1990: 46) and expressions like *u-bandi inji* /3-arrive me/ '(on) my arrival, when I arrive(d)'.

36. The indetermination is dramatically exposed by the correspondence of *u-kas/ngë-kas* 'male animal(s)' with *kas* 'to castrate'!

37. Recall that *Ka jooti* means 'It crumbled', with a noun class 7 unmentioned subject.

38. Possible counterexamples are verbs like French *mettre bas* 'to whelp', normally said only of animals, whereas *accoucher* 'to give birth' is only for women. However, it is always possible to be gross and apply the former to women, and few pet lovers have qualms saying 'Ma chatte a accouché'. Such things are therefore a matter of social convention, not of inherent categorization. As for the so-called verbal classifiers studied at length by Aikhenvald (2000:ch. 6), they are actually verb-internal agreement morphemes cross-referencing the Class of the verb's *arguments.* "Verbal classifiers" is thus something of a misnomer, since they do not classify the verb itself.

39. In a strictly lexicalist model, even *pë-lik* and *i-lik* should count as two separate lexical items.

40. I assume the intransitive (unergative) use of *lik* to result from incorporation of the cognate object (see Hale and Keyser 1993).

41. Such a view is not a necessary tenet of DM. Marantz (1997), for instance, assumes otherwise. It seems to me, however, to be both empirically justified and a natural extension of DM's basic hypotheses, in particular, the notion that *all* lexical items are actually constructs.

42. For a distinct, but compatible, view of the encyclopedia, see Borer (2001).

43. Having exponents thus sets *n* apart from *v* in Manjaku. Yet a rich array of derivational verbal morphemes exist in the language, with meanings such as causative, reciprocal, applicative, and illative, which may be viewed as being exponents of *v* plus special meanings. The fact that these (suffixal) morphemes attach only to stems that are already verbs by themselves make the identification doubtful, however. I must leave this

issue unsettled here. Note that in the Romance languages the theme vowels of verbs could be considered exponents of *v* (see Aronoff 1994: 45).

44. I abstract away the issue of Number for the moment.

45. Embick and Noyer's definition of functional categories continues Abney's (1987) crucial notion that functional categories are devoid of "descriptive content" (also see Chametzky 2000: 17ff.). As we shall see, however, such a two-way contrast may not be sufficient.

46. As indicated in the text, (23) does not constitute a "package," as traditional lexical matrices do, but it represents the interfacing of the several analytical dimensions that contribute to defining the sign. The fact that the syntactic specification is the same for all members of {n} thus raises no economy of representation issue.

47. What I call "entailment" is what Aronoff (1994: 63) calls "implicational rules."

48. I assign *el* to class III since it does not include an overt class morpheme, contrary to *la* (/l+a/). The plural counterpart *los* (/l+o+s/), in contrast, is class I. I abstract from "neutral" *lo*, which does not precede nouns in Spanish, as well as from phonological alternations such as *el agua* 'the water', where selection of *el* rather than *la* seems to be due to hiatus avoidance (but see Baker 1992).

49. I follow Harris (1999) in considering /e/ and /Ø/ allomorphs for class III— hence, my labels nIII and nIIIa (avowedly inspired from Bantuist descriptive practice).

50. Naturally, the root $\sqrt{}$puert that appears in *puerto* 'port' has to be counted as a homonym, etymology notwithstanding.

51. I leave it as a moot point whether, when one does not wish to specify the cat's sex or does not know it, M is selected, having the whole kind as a submeaning, or M/F is not associated at all, $\sqrt{}$gat being then assigned to class I by default. Somehow, the first alternative strikes me as more plausible and more in line with the present model.

52. Naturally, derivational morphemes may link to each other as in Italian *linguis-tucolo* 'poor linguist' (I am grateful to Guglielmo Cinque, pers. comm., for this example), and that is even one of the (relatively) distinguishing criteria between derivational and inflectional morphology (see Scalise 1988 and Dressler 1989). For this, we may content ourselves with the standard explanation,—namely, that $\sqrt{}$ist (the first morpheme generally) having attached to the nonfunctional root, a new nonfunctional root $\sqrt{}$lingw-ist is created to which further derivational morphemes may attach.

53. Interpreting movement in terms of attraction is crucial here. Otherwise, moving first $\sqrt{}$ist to nII would be countercyclic, and to comply with cyclicity we would have first to raise $\sqrt{}$lingw to $\sqrt{}$ist, and then the complex $\sqrt{}$lingw+ist to nII, thus distorting the, I think, important notion that *linguista's* gender is /-ist/'s gender. If $\sqrt{}$ist and nII pertain to different cycles (or constitute distinct phases in Chomsky's 1999 terminology), however, then the attract versus raise distinction might indeed be moot. (I thank Guglielmo Cinque, pers. comm., for drawing my attention to this issue.) See Harris (1992: 74–75) for a discussion concerning the nonsyllabicity of /u/ in the root I note as $\sqrt{}$lingw.

54. This is obviously not the case when the meaning is "instrument" as in *colador* 'strainer'. /dor/ is then only associated with nIIIa in the lexicon.

55. "Language specialist," as the compositional meaning of $\sqrt{}$lingw plus $\sqrt{}$ist would sound, does not suffice by far to understand what a linguist is. In seventeenth-century Portuguese (perhaps Spanish as well) a language specialist, a *linguista*, was an interpreter.

56. "Piling up" leading, for example, to the ungrammatical (but sensible) *linguis-taa* for 'woman linguist' is probably made impossible in morphology.

57. Naturally, classification is also represented in the encyclopedia because the lexical features of, for instances, √ka, are not enough to determine the meaning of, say, *ka-lik* 'fruit juice'.

58. *Fetsar* is an applicative derivation on the root √fets 'follow', thus meaning 'follow for / in favor of'. This raises an issue to which I will return.

59. A similar argument has sometimes been made for gender, saying that perhaps at some time a door was conceived of as a feminine entity (metaphors can be imagined) or that what is now the privileged exponent of feminine gender (viz. /-a/) was not so at earlier stages. The latter is true, as Indo-European studies revealed long ago; the former is at best conceivable in a few cases, hopeless in many more, given the narrowness of the classification compared with what Manjaku and similar languages achieve. In any case, the difference between modern Romance languages and modern Manjaku in terms of applicability of the classificatory criteria remains in its entirety.

60. This relative divorce is what makes it possible for membership in a given inflectional class or gender to be a function of purely formal properties such as phonological form, as in the Papuan languages Arapesh and Yimas (see Aronoff 1992, 1994) or perhaps French (see Corbett 1996: 57ff.).

61. A clue in that direction is given by the contrast between *taktubiina* 'you(Fsg) write' and *katabti* 'you(Fsg) wrote': in the former, second person (i.e., the purely pronominal component of meaning) is spelled out through the prefix /ta-/ (compare *taktubu* 'you(Msg) write'), while marked gender (F) and Number are expressed by the suffix /-iina/ (compare *taktubuuna* 'you(Mpl) write' and *taktubna* 'you(Fpl) write'); in the latter, in contrast, person, gender, and Number—and presumably Tense as well—are all bundled together in the suffix /-ti/ (compare *katabta* 'you(Msg) wrote', *katabtum* 'you(Mpl) wrote', and *katabtunna* 'you(Fpl) wrote'). See Benmamoun (2000) and Halefom and Lumsden (2000).

62. We might assume (29) to be the basic structure of third-person pronouns in a language like English as well, with *he/she/it* the lexical expressions of *n* (thus accounting for *she-cat* and similar forms). I won't pursue this matter.

63. I do not consider here recent proposals by Chomsky (1999) to the effect that head movement (or Attract Head) should be entirely eliminated from syntax. If Chomsky's arguments bear weight, and we wish to stand by our notion of the lexicon and its relationships to the other components of grammar, then we will have to enrich the lexicon with processes that mimic what head movement does in syntax. I am not sure it would be such a sweeping change in the model.

64. Recall that "word" is a morphological unit that has no relevance outside morphology.

65. The '+' signs are mere indications of the fact that different exponents are merged or fused together. They do not necessarily correspond to syntactic brackets.

66. It is remarkable that, not taking various "expansions" into account, prefixed noun class exponents in Niger-Congo always consist of one CV syllable. A further argument in favor of that solution is that noun class signs, although derivational, cannot stack: there is no such word as */na-pë-lik/ meaning 'someone having to do with wells' ('well-digger', for instance). Yet, no general constraint on derivation prevents it (see, e.g., Matthews 1974: 164ff.).

67. Whatever explains it, word-form legitimacy seems to be a parochial property (compare, e.g., Spanish *gato/gata* with Catalan *gat/gata*).

68. That is, to the exception of Chinese and similar languages where Number is not a necessary category within DP (see Chierchia 1998).

69. As a minimum. There may also be a functional root meaning "Duality" and, in some grammars, still another one meaning "Triality."

70. See Kaye, et al. (1985) for the underlying theory of the phonological segments that I am assuming here. If Class is nI (e.g., *gatto* 'cat') or nIII (e.g., *cane* 'dog'), /I/ does not fuse with the Class exponent, but replaces it (*gatti, cani*). I leave this problem pending.

71. I assume the /e/ of *paredes* 'walls' (from *pared* 'wall') to be epenthetical.

72. Xârâcùù is a New Caledonian language (see Moyse-Faurie 1995). Historically, there is a phonological relation between *æıl* (Latin *oculum*) and *yeux* (Latin *oculos*). For present-day French speakers, however, the two roots are not phonologically related.

73. The isolated case of *u-päts* 'children' ceases to be a problem if we view it as a collective (see French *marmaille* 'gang of kids, brood'), which accords well with the abstracting meaning of /u/.

74. We can, actually, but to a price: namely, having to perform meaningless morphological tricks.

75. Indeed, knowing that *ka-√* has plural meaning with such and such roots would not be more complex than knowing that *bë-fetsar* denotes a human despite /bë/'s basic meaning(s).

76. I abstract from the distinction between numbered and unnumbered Plurality because it is not well explored enough. Taking this distinction into account, I trust, would not modify the reasoning significantly.

77. Such generalizations are exploited, for instance, for integrating loanwords.

78. The most widespread dialect of present-day Wolof seems to be one where class distinctions are fairly well preserved in the singular, whereas plural presents us with the contrast of one root associated with the Class sign {n ∩ Plurality} = /ñ/ (*nit ñ-i* 'the persons') versus all others associated with {n ∩ Plurality} = /y/.

79. In both cases, agreeing items preserve the "real" gender (see *šulxanot ktanim* 'small tables', *dvorim yafot* 'nice bees').

80. Compare masculine *bakbuk male / bakbukim malim* 'full bottle(s)'.

81. Actually, nII and nIII have the same exponent /Vt/, except that /t/ is only realized in the so-called Construct State in nII (i.e., when V is /a/—see *xatulat ha-šaxen* 'the neighbor's she-cat'), whereas it is stable in nIII (i.e., when V is another vowel than /a/). The two classes could therefore perhaps be united (but see Aronoff 1994: 184, n. 32 for a skeptical assessment). I also assume that nouns (not numerous) like *sade/sadot* 'field(s)' constitute a subset of nII. Let me emphasize again the tentative nature of all this.

82. Meaning simply that no nIV noun stands in the list (supposing it to be true).

83. It is important not to lose sight of the fact that we are here operating at the infra-D level. The present analysis has thus no bearing on the discussion of whether N or (remnant) NP raises to D in the Semitic and Romance languages, except insofar as it shows that what moves to D, if anything, must be a maximal projection at some level. For recent developments, see Cinque (2000) and Shlonsky (2000).

84. English, as already noted, is a somewhat complex case where Class is contentful

(taking the form of gender) but is only manifest on singular third-person pronouns. What we might say, then, is that English is like Spanish, but Class has a null (/∅/) exponent across the board, except when the merged root is pronominal and Number does not intersect, in which case there is suppletion: /she/ or /he/ if sex is relevant (encyclopedically potent), /it/ otherwise.

85. I am grateful to Jacqueline Leroy for putting Watter's dissertation at my disposal and discussing the data with me.

86. Statement (39) may thus be compared with, for example, Portuguese *duas cabeças de gado* 'two head of cattle', where the numeral agrees in gender with the "classifier" *cabeça(s)*. Naturally, differences are at least as important as similarities, hence my use of scare quotes in "classifier."

87. While the present framework explains why fully functional Class elements such as Spanish word classes must surface as suffixes, it merely predicts that denoting Class elements can be proclitics or enclitics, but it does not explain why they are the one or the other in particular languages. More research is obviously required.

88. According to Foley (1986), this is also the case in Naisioi, implying that the same root may function as either a value of {n} or an argument of {n}.

89. I have little to say about classifiers in possessive constructions, except to remark that they rather look like the misnomed "verbal classifiers" in that they cross-reference features of one argument in the construction, generally the possessed noun (as in the one language in Africa having that type of object, viz. the Mba, Ubangi language 'Dongo-ko; see Pasch 1985; Aikhenvald 2000: ch. 5).

90. To the difference of Romance, attributive adjectives *never* precede the noun in Manjaku, and recall there are no predicative adjectives, but quality verbs, sometimes formally different from the corresponding adjectives (see *U-ndali a fac* /3-cat Pro be-white/ 'The cat is white'). As for the derived status of *faacal*, see the prior discussion about *bë-fetsar*.

91. Lest readers should resent it that this account offends Greed (see Chomsky 1995: 201ff.), it can easily be recast in the following terms: n^0_x needs a Class feature; it targets the closest one namely, n^0_3,—and attracts it, pied-piping the whole nP (for some reason). In the Arabic example, the adjective (*Hasan*) does not agree with the noun *wajh*, but with the noun *Hasanu l-wajhi* is predicated of. That is, the Arabic phrase spells out a derived structure, whereas (39) is basic.

REFERENCES

Abney, Steven (1987) "The English Noun Phrase in its Sentential Aspects." Ph.D.diss., MIT, Cambridge, Mass.

Aikhenvald, Alexandra Y, (2000) *Classifiers: A Typology of Noun Categorization Devices.* Oxford University Press, Oxford.

Allan, K. (1977) "Classifiers." *Language* 53: 284–310.

Arad, Maya (1999) "On 'little v,' " in Karlos Arregi et al. (eds.) *Papers on Morphology and Syntax, Cycle One.* MIT Working Papers in Linguistics 33. MIT, Cambridge, Mass., 1–25.

Aronoff, Mark (1992) "Noun Classes in Arapesh," in Geert Booij and Jaap van Marle (eds.) *Yearbook of Morphology 1991.* Kluwer, Dordrecht, 21–32.

Aronoff, Mark (1994) *Morphology by Itself: Stems and Inflectional Classes.* MIT Press, Cambridge, Mass.

Baker, Mark C. (1992) "Morphological Classes and Grammatical Organization," in Geert Booij and Jaap van Marle (eds.) *Yearbook of Morphology 1991.* Kluwer, Dordrecht, 89–106.

Bat-El, Outi (1986) "Extraction in Modern Hebrew Morphology." M.A. diss., UCLA.

Benmamoun, Abbas (2000) "Lexical Relations and the Role of the Imperfective Template in Arabic Morphology." Unpublished ms., University of Illinois, Urbana-Champaign.

Borer, Hagit (2001) "One Is the Loneliest Number." Paper presented to the Conference on the Syntax and Semantics of Semitic Languages, University of Southern California, Los Angeles, May 4–5, 2001.

Bouchard, Denis (1995) *The Semantics of Syntax: A Minimalist Approach to Grammar.* University of Chicago Press, Chicago.

Brody, Michael (1995) *Lexico-Logical Form: A Radically Minimalist Theory.* MIT Press, Cambridge, Mass.

Buis, Pierre (1990) *Essai sur la langue manjako de la zone de Bassarel.* Instituto nacional de Estudos e Pesquisas, Bissau.

Bybee, Joan L. (1985) *Morphology: A Study of the Relation between Meaning and Form.* John Benjamins, Amsterdam.

Chametzky, Robert A. (2000) *Phrase Structure: From GB to Minimalism.* Blackwell, Oxford.

Chierchia, Gennaro (1998) "Plurality of Mass Nouns and the Notion of 'Semantic Parameter'," in Susan Rothstein (ed.) *Events and Grammar.* Kluwer, Dordrecht, 53–103.

Chomsky, Noam (1995) *The Minimalist Program.* MIT Press, Cambridge, Mass.

Chomsky, Noam (1998) *Minimalist Inquiries: The Framework.* MIT Occasional Papers in Linguistics 15. MIT Press, Cambridge, Mass.

Chomsky, Noam (1999) "Derivation by Phase." Unpublished ms., MIT, Cambridge, Mass.

Chomsky, Noam (2001) "Beyond Explanatory Adequacy." Unpublished ms., MIT, Cambridge, Mass.

Cinque, Guglielmo (1994) "On the Evidence for Partial N-Movement in the Romance DP," in Guglielmo Cinque et al. (eds.) *Paths towards Universal Grammar: Studies in Honor of Richard S. Kayne.* Georgetown University Press, Washington, D.C., 85–110.

Cinque, Guglielmo (2000) "On Greenberg's Universal 20 and the Semitic DP." *University of Venice Working Papers in Linguistics,* 10(2): 45–61.

Cohen, David, and Haïm Zafrani (1968) *Grammaire de l'hébreu vivant.* Presses Universitaires de France, Paris.

Corbett, Grenville (1996) *Gender.* Cambridge University Press, Cambridge.

Craig, Colette (ed.) (1986) *Noun Classes and Categorization.* John Benjamins, Amsterdam.

Croft, W. (1994) "Semantic Universals in Classifier Systems." *Word* 45: 145–171.

Denny, J. Peter, and Chet A. Creider (1986) "The Semantics of Noun Classes in Proto

Bantu," in Colette Craig, (ed.) *Noun Classes and Categorization*. John Benjamins, Amsterdam, 217–239.

Dimmendaal, Geert I. (1983) *The Turkana Language*. Foris, Dordrecht.

Dixon, R. M. W. (1972) *The Dyirbal Language of North Queensland*. Cambridge University Press, Cambridge.

Dixon, R. M. W. (1986) "Noun Classes and Noun Classification in Typological Perspective," in Colette Craig, (ed.) *Noun Classes and Categorization*. John Benjamins, Amsterdam, 105–112.

Doneux, Jean-Léonce (1967) "Le manjaku, classes nominales et questions sur l'alternance consonantique," in Gabriel Manessy (ed.) *La classification nominale dans les langues négro-africaines*. CNRS Editions, Paris, 261–276.

Doneux, Jean-Léonce (1975) *Lexique manjaku*. Centre de Linguistique appliquée de Dakar, Dakar.

Doron, Edit (2000) "Transitivity Alternations in the Semitic Template System." Unpublished ms., The Hebrew University of Jerusalem.

Dressler, Wolfgang U. (1989) "Prototypical Differences between Inflection and Derivation." *Zeitschrift für Phonetik, Sprachwissenschaft und Kommunikationsforschung* 42: 3–10.

Embick, David, and Rolf Noyer (1999) "Locality in Post-Syntactic Operations," in Vivian Lin et al. (eds.) *Papers on Morphology and Syntax, Cycle Two*. MIT Working Papers in Linguistics 34. MIT, Cambridge, Mass., 265–317.

Foley, William A. (1986) *The Papuan Languages of New Guinea*. Cambridge University Press, Cambridge.

Grandi, Nicola (2002) *Morfologie in contatto: le costruzioni valutative nelle lingue del Mediterraneo*. Franco Angeli, Pavia.

Hale, Kenneth, and Samuel J. Keyser (1993) "On Argument Structure and the Lexical Expression of Syntactic Relations," in Kenneth Hale and Samuel J. Keyser (eds.) *The View from Building 20: Essays in Linguistics in Honor of Sylvain Bromberger*. MIT Press, Cambridge, Mass., 53–109.

Halefom, Girma, and John S. Lumsden (2000) "Decomposing the Perfective Conjugation." Unpublished ms., Université du Québec à Montreal.

Halle, Morris, and Alec Marantz (1993) "Distributed Morphology and the Pieces of Inflection," in Kenneth Hale and Samuel J. Keyser (eds.) *The View from Building 20: Essays in Linguistics in Honor of Sylvain Bromberger*. MIT Press, Cambridge, Mass., 111–176.

Harris, James (1992) "The Form Classes of Spanish Substantives," in Geert Booij and Jaap van Marle (eds.) *Yearbook of Morphology 1991*. Kluwer, Dordrecht, 65–88.

Harris, James (1999) "Nasal Depalatization *no*, Morphological Wellformedness *sí*: The Structure of Spanish Word Classes," in Karlos Arregi et al. (eds.), *Papers on Morphology and Syntax, Cycle One*. MIT Working Papers in Linguistics 33. MIT, Cambridge, Mass., 47–82.

Ippolito, Michela M. (1999) "On the Past Participle Morphology in Italian," in Karlos Arregi et al. (eds.) *Papers on Morphology and Syntax, Cycle One*. MIT Working Papers in Linguistics 33. MIT, Cambridge, Mass., 111–137.

Jackendoff, Ray (1997) *The Architecture of the Language Faculty*. MIT Press, Cambridge, Mass.

Katamba, Francis (1993) *Morphology*. Macmillan, London.

Kaye, Jonathan, Jean Lowenstamm, and Jean-Roger Vergnaud (1985) "The Internal Structure of Phonological Elements: A Theory of Charm and Government." *Phonology Yearbook* 2: 305–328.

Kayne, Richard S. (1994) *The Antisymmetry of Syntax*. MIT Press, Cambridge, Mass.

Keyser, Samuel J., and Thomas Roeper (1984) "On the Middle and Ergative Constructions in English." *Linguistic Inquiry* 15: 381–416.

Kihm, Alain (1998) "Propositions relatives en manjaku et théorie du déplacement comme copie." *Linguistique africaine* 20: 75–99.

Kihm, Alain (1999) "Wolof NP and the Fusion vs. Merger Contrast." *Actes du Colloque Langues et Grammaires, II Syntaxe*. Presses Universitaires de Vincennes, Saint-Denis.

Kihm, Alain, and Aristide Gomes (1988) "Quelques points de syntaxe du manjaku." *Langues et grammaire* 1: 21–56.

Lakoff, George. (1986) "Classifiers as a Reflection of Mind," in Colette Craig (ed.) *Noun Classes and Categorization*. John Benjamins, Amsterdam, 13–51.

Lakoff, George (1987) *Women, Fire, and Dangerous Things: What Categories Reveal about the Mind*. University of Chicago Press, Chicago.

Lecarme, Jacqueline (1999) "Gender 'Polarity': Theoretical Aspects of Somali Nominal Morphology." Unpublished ms., CNRS Editions, Paris.

Lowenstamm, Jean (1996) "CV as the Only Syllable Type." *Current Trends in Phonology* 419–441.

Manessy, Gabriel (1977) "Processes of Pidginization in African Languages," in Albert Valdman (ed.) *Pidgin and Creole Linguistics*. Indiana University Press, Bloomington, 129–154.

Marantz, Alec (1997) "No Escape from Syntax: Don't Try Morphological Analysis in the Privacy of Your Own Lexicon," in A. Dimitriadis et al. (eds.) *Proceedings of the 21st Penn Linguistics Colloquium*. UPenn Working Papers in Linguistics. University of Pennsylvania, Philadelphia, 201–225.

Matthews, P. H. (1974) *Morphology: An Introduction to the Theory of Word-Structure*. Cambridge University Press, Cambridge.

Miller, G. A., and P. N. Johnson-Laird (1976) *Language and Perception*. Cambridge University Press, Cambridge.

Moyse-Faurie, Claire (1995) *Le xârâcùù, langue de Thio-Canala (Nouvelle-Calédonie): éléments de syntaxe*. Peeters-SELAF, Paris.

Mufwene, Salikoko S. (1980) "Bantu Class Prefixes: Inflectional or Derivational?" in Jody Kreiman and Almerindo E. Ojeda (eds.), *Papers from the Sixteenth Regional Meeting of the Chicago Linguistic Society*. Chicago Linguistic Society, Chicago, 246–258.

Noyer, Rolf (1997) *Features, Positions, and Affixes in Autonomous Morphological Structure*. Garland, New York.

Pasch, Helma (1985) "Possession and Possessive Classifiers in 'Dongo-ko." *Afrika und Übersee* 68: 69–85.

Pesetsky, David (1995) *Zero Syntax: Experiencers and Cascades*. MIT Press, Cambridge, Mass.

Posner, Michael (1986) "Empirical Studies of Prototypes," in Colette Craig, (ed.) *Noun Classes and Categorization*. John Benjamins, Amsterdam, 53–61.

Pozdnjakov, Konstantin I. (1993) *Sravnitel'naja grammatika atlanticeskix jazykov: imennye klassy i fono-morfologija* [A comparative grammar of the Atlantic languages: noun classes and morphophonology] Nauka, Moscow.

Renault, Richard (1987) "Genre grammatical et typologie linguistique." *Bulletin de la So-ciété de Linguistique de Paris* 82: 69–117.

Ritter, Elizabeth (1991) "Two Functional Categories in Noun Phrases: Evidence from Modern Hebrew," in Susan D. Rothstein (ed.) *Perspectives on Phrase Structure: Heads and Licensing.* Vol. 25 of *Syntax and Semantics.* Academic Press, New York, 37–62.

Roeper, Thomas (1993) "Explicit Syntax in the Lexicon: The Representation of Nominal-izations," in James Pustejovsky (ed.) *Semantics and the Lexicon.* Kluwer, Dordrecht, 185–220.

Sag, Ivan, and Thomas Wasow (1999) *Syntactic Theory: A Formal Introduction.* CSLI Publications, Stanford.

Sauvageot, Serge (1965) *Description synchronique d'un dialecte wolof: le parler du Dyolof.* Institut Fondamental d'Afrique Noire, Dakar.

Scalise, Sergio (1988) "Inflection and Derivation." *Linguistics* 26: 561–581.

Serzisko, F. (1982) "Gender, Noun Class and Numeral Classification: A Scale of Classifi-catory Techniques," in R. Dirven and G. Radden (eds.) *Issues in the Theory of Uni-versal Grammar.* Tübingen, Gunther Narr, 95–123.

Shlonsky, Ur (2000) "The Form of Semitic Noun Phrases: An Antisymmetric, non N-Movement Approach." Unpublished ms., University of Geneva.

Sylla, Yèro (1982) *Grammaire moderne du pulaar.* Les Nouvelles Editions Africaines, Da-kar.

Thompson, Laurence C. (1987) *A Vietnamese Reference Grammar.* University of Hawai'i Press, Honolulu.

Trifkovic, Mirjana (1969) *Le mancagne: étude phonologique et morphologique.* Institut Fondamental d'Afrique Noire, Dakar.

Watters, J. (1981) "A Phonology and Morphology of Ejagham: With Notes on Dialect Variation. Ph.D. diss., University of California, Los Angeles.

Williams, Edwin (1981) "On the Notions 'Lexically Related' and 'Head of a Word'." *Lin-guistic Inquiry* 12: 234–274.

CHAPTER 12

AGREEMENT AND ITS PLACEMENT IN TURKIC NONSUBJECT RELATIVE CLAUSES

JAKLIN KORNFILT

1 INTRODUCTION

THE most productive type of relative clauses (RCs) in Turkic languages is a right-headed construction whose modifier clause has a gap in the position of the target and whose predicate is nonfinite. Such constructions appear to be typologically typical for head-final languages, and Turkic languages are indeed head-final in general, with the exception of some, such as Karaim and Gagauz, which have been heavily influenced by surrounding Indo-European (mainly Slavic) languages that are predominantly head-initial and which have, as a consequence, become essentially head-initial themselves (and thus also exhibit head-initial RCs).

While even head-final Turkic languages do exhibit some instances of head-initial (and usually finite) RCs, I concentrate in this chapter on the more typical and productive head-final type of RC.

The focus here are RCs whose target is a nonsubject. This type of RC is interesting because there are essentially three types of such RCs in the Turkic languages, and it is challenging to find an economical account that would cover all of them. These three types differ according to the presence versus the absence of overt (person and number) agreement with the subject of the modifying clause and, where such overt agreement is present, according to the placement of the agreement marker: while that marker shows up on the predicate of the modifying clause in some languages, it shows up on the head of the RC on some others.

I argue here that such an account—that is, one that can capture the common as well as the different properties of such "nonsubject" RCs—can be based on Kayne's (1994) approach to such constructions. This might be a surprising result, given the complexity of Kayne's derivations of such constructions in head-final languages and his proposal for a universal phrase structure with Specifier–Head–Complement order. Therefore, such an account is particularly welcome, as it comes from a direction that is not immediately anticipated.

Due to space considerations, I do not address RCs with subject targets and their differences across the Turkic languages. However, full consideration of those RCs does throw some interesting light on nonsubject RCs; future work will address similarities and differences between subject and nonsubject RCs in the Turkic languages.[1]

This chapter is structured as follows: section 2 presents the three main types of nonsubject RCs in Turkic, with examples and brief discussion. Section 3 presents the approach taken to their derivation: a Kayneian derivation is assumed to be common to all three types and accounts for the common properties of all three types. Proposals are made to account for the differences among these types, especially for type 3, which is remarkable because it appears to exhibit a nonlocal agreement relation; a proposal is made about how this type can be insightfully accounted for within a Kayneian approach. Section 4 presents a rival derivation for type 3 RCs, based on raising of the subject of the modifier clause to a "possessor" position—that is, a specifier position of a higher DP. Section 5 presents counterarguments and counterevidence against the raising analysis. Section 6, in conclusion, raises some questions, mainly concerning the nature of the Agr and Case morphemes involved, and points toward the kind of future research that would be needed to resolve them.

The chapter is written within a rather loose theoretical model, so as to make the material and discussion accessible to a wide readership. The analyses proposed can be "tightened up" and formulated within a Principles-and-Parameters version of Government and Binding Theory, as well as within the more recent Minimalist Program.

The data used for this chapter comes from a variety of sources: the Modern Standard Turkish [MST] facts are based on my own native intuitions; the data on the other Turkic languages were taken from published grammars and readers (wherever possible, I tried to use readers rather than grammars, so as to be influenced as little as possible by existing views on the nature of the constructions at hand), as well as from transcriptions of elicitation sessions conducted by Phil LeSourd on Modern Uigur and by myself on Sakha.[2]

2 Facts: the Main Construction Types

I start with the type of "nonsubject RC" that we find in Modern Standard Turkish, exemplified here:

(1) [Oya-nın   kütüphane-den e$_i$ çal-dığ-ı]$_{IP=AgrP}$ bu
     Oya-Gen.   library-Abl.   steal-F(active)N(onimalization)-3.sg.   this
     eski kitap$_i$
     old book

     'this old book that Oya stole from the library'

(2) [var-dığ-ımız]$_{IP=AgrP}$ yer
     arrive-FN-1.pl.   place

     'the place where we arrive(d)'

   The main characteristics of this construction are the following: it is right-headed, the subject is in the Genitive case, and the (subject) Agr(eement) morpheme is located on the predicate of the modifier clause. This agreement morpheme is of the "nominal" type; note that the third-person singular morpheme is -(s)I in the nominal paradigm, while it is null in the verbal paradigm.[3] As we shall see later, these nominal agreement forms are the same ones as those found on the heads of possessive nominal phrases, where the possessee overtly agrees in person and number with the possessor. Following Kornfilt (1984), I characterize modifier phrases with these characteristics as (nominal) Agreement Phrases [AgrPs].
   A second type of construction is illustrated by (3) from Uzbek and by (4) from Azeri:

(3) [men   qil-gan]$_{IP=Asp}$ isloh
     I   do-P(=[Aspectual] Participle)   reform(s)

     (the) reforms which I have made' (Schönig 1992–93: 329)

(4) [sen   iste-yen]$_{IP=AspP}$ šey[4]
     you   want-P   thing

     'the thing that you want' (Slobin 1986: 287)

In this construction, which was the predominant one historically, as found in the documents from the Old Turkic [OT] period[5] and is currently found in many languages of the areal periphery of the Turkic languages, that is, in the western and eastern parts of the area in which Turkic languages are spoken, we do find the right-headedness just mentioned for the first type of relative clause. However, note that the modifier clause differs in two respects: the subject is not in the Genitive,[6] and there is no overt Agreement element. I propose that such modifier clauses be characterized as Aspect Phrases [AspPs]. I shall return to this point.

A third construction exhibits characteristics of either or both types, with a surprising property of its own. The properties it shares with the other types are as follows:

1. The right-headedness that is common to all three
2. The Genitive marking on the subject of the modifier clause (as in the first type; however, in some other Turkic languages, the subject is bare, i.e., syntactically Nominative, as in the second type; these appear to be languages where the subject in embedded clauses are bare, i.e., Nominative, rather than Genitive in general)
3. The lack of Agreement marking on the predicate of the modifier clause, as in the second type, and in contrast with the first type.

The distinctive and surprising property of this third type of (nonsubject) RC is its fourth characteristic:

4. The construction does exhibit an Agr morpheme (as in the first type), but this morpheme is placed on the head of the relative clause (rather than on the predicate of the modifier, as in the first type).

In other words, the structural relationship between the subject of the modifier clause and the Agr morpheme that realizes the person and number features of that subject is not a local one, in contrast with the corresponding relationship in type 1 where the subject and its Agr are within a local domain; that is, they are both within the same clause.

This third construction is found in many contemporary Central Asian languages (e.g., Tuvan, Uzbek, Turkmen, Kazakh). The following Uzbek and Turkmen examples illustrate this type:

(5) a. [men-iŋ   gapir-gan]$_{\text{IP=AspP}}$ gap-**im**
         I-Gen.   say-P   word-**1.sg.**

     'the word(s) I said' (Uzbek; Raun 1969: 199)

     b. Yašulu-lar   [šeyle   pis   adam-lar-ïŋ   gel-en]$_{\text{IP=AspP}}$
        elder-pl.   these   bad   person-pl.-Gen.   come-P
        öy-ler-**in-i**   yüze çïkar-malï-dïrlar.
        house-pl.-**3.Agr.**[7]-Acc.   point out-Necc.-3.pl.

'Elders must point out the houses which these bad people visited.'
(Turkmen; Frank 1995: 100)

The boldface agreement element agrees with the subject of the modifier clause, rather than with a possessor, as would necessarily be the case in a language like MST if the head of a RC were to exhibit an agreement element. This observation is important for any insight into the nature of this construction, for the following reasons:

1. The nominal agreement morphemes that are found on the predicates of nominalized embedded clauses and that agree with the φ-features of the local subject are the same ones that mark possession on the head of a possessive phrase.
2. Agreement between possessor and possessee in terms of φ-features is obligatory in Turkish, as well as in the other Turkic languages.[8]

Thus, if the overt Agr on the head of the RC were interpreted as a possessive marker rather than an agreement marker with the subject, the relationship between Agr and the DP it agrees with—that is, the possessor—would be a local relationship and therefore not a particularly remarkable or interesting one. In fact, this relationship was analyzed, for MST, as a regular Head-Spec relationship in Kornfilt (1984), where the Agr morpheme on the head of the possessive phrase was analyzed as the syntactic head of a nominal AgrP, and its agreeing possessor was analyzed as the specifier of that AgrP—a straightforward local relation between the agreement elements.[9] Let me illustrate this with a corresponding example in MST:

(6) Yaşlı-lar$_j$[**şu kötü adam-lar-ın$_i$**   [*pro*$_{i/j}$git-tik-leri]$_{IP}$
    old-pl.   these bad man-pl.-Gen. go-FN-e.pl.
    ev-ler-**in**-i]$_{DP}$göster-meli-dirler.
    house-pl.-**3.Agr**-Acc.show-Necc.-3.pl.

    'The elders$_j$ should point out [*these bad men's*]$_i$ houses which (they$_{i/j}$) visited.'

Or, with the same phonological sequence, but with a different structural analysis:

(7) Yaşlı-lar$_j$ [***pro*$_j$** [şu kötü adam-lar-ın   git-tik-leri]$_{IP}$
    old-pl.   these bad man-pl.-Gen. go-FN-3.pl.
    ev-**lerin**-i]$_{DP}$ göster-meli-dirler.
    house-**3.pl.**[10]-Acc.   show-Necc.-3.pl.

    'The elders$_j$ should point out *their$_j$* house(s) which these bad men visited.'

Under either analysis, the boldface Agr marker on the head noun of the RC agrees *locally* with the (boldface) DP possessor, rather than with the subject of the modifier clause (while in the embedded clause itself, the nominal agreement on the nominalized predicate agrees, also locally, with the subject). The interpretation calls for a possessive interpretation, pointed out by an italicized possessor in the translations. I don't know whether the Turkmen example allows for such possessive interpretations; some of these possessive interpretations are pragmatically unlikely or even non-sensical. What is important here is that the translation as given for the Turkmen example is the one stated in the source. Furthermore, this reading makes the most sense pragmatically. Most important, this translation does not carry over to MST, where this reading is completely impossible. While in Turkmen, the overt Agr marker on the head of the RC does, or at least can, agree with the subject of the modifier clause, it cannot do so in Turkish.

As a matter of fact, in descriptive or reference grammars of Turkic languages that have this third construction and which are written in MST, the existence of this construction is not mentioned, and examples of this kind, if at all listed, are translated as though they were Turkish—namely, with a possessive reading. This is a telling fact. In MST, and in other Turkic languages like it (e.g., Azeri), where constructions of this "third kind" do not exist, an overt Agr marker can only agree with a *local* antecedent (and this restriction is so strong that it blinds even scholars to other possibilities); in languages like Turkmen, in contrast, which do have these constructions, the syntactic relation between an overt Agr marker and the DP whose ϕ-features the marker expresses may be a nonlocal one.

Clearly, nonlocal agreement is universally an extremely marked phenomenon; there is a strong possibility that it does not exist. In a number of instances where such nonlocal agreement appears to hold, analyses based on reanalysis or restructuring have been proposed in the literature, thus resulting in locality of agreement. Here, such an approach is not likely to succeed; given that readings without possessivity are possible, or are even the primary ones, as in the Turkmen example we just saw, it is hard to see what the structure of any reanalysis in this construction would be.

I would like to claim that agreement is, in fact, universally a local relationship, at least at relevant levels of representation. In the next section, I present an approach to deriving RCs of the third kind, where such locality does hold at some point in the derivation of these constructions.

3 THE BASIC DERIVATION OF RIGHT-HEADED RCs

Kayne (1994) proposes a universal syntactic phrase structure, where heads follow their specifiers and precede their complements. Movement is leftward. A complement or adjunct that precedes a head has landed in its position as a result of leftward movement.

Relative clauses involve leftward movement of the "target" of relativization into Spec/CP; the CP (= "Complementizer Phrase," the modifying clause in the construction), in turn, is the complement of the D in a DP (= Determiner Phrase). This is, essentially, all that is needed for the derivation of relative clauses in head-initial languages like English:

(8) $[_{DP} [_{D}^{0}$ the$] [_{CP} [_{NP}$ book$]_i [_{C'}[_{C}^{0}$ that$] [_{IP}$ Jane stole [e $]_i]]]]$

The same derivation is involved in the relative clauses of (superficially) right-headed languages like the Turkic languages, but an additional step is necessary: the IP-complement (IP = Inflectional Phrase) of C moves to the specifier position of the higher DP. The last movement yields prenominal modification; the structure would be as follows (with English morphemes):

(9) $[_{DP} [_{IP}$ Jane stole $[e]_i]_j [_{D}^{0}$ the$] [_{CP} [_{NP}$ book$]_i [_{C'}[_{C}^{0}$ that$] [e]_j]]]$

An additional assumption is that an overt C cannot be stranded; thus, in such languages, the C cannot be overt:

(10) $[_{DP} [_{IP}$ Jane stole $[e]_i]_j [_{D}^{0}$ the$] [_{CP} [_{NP}$ book$]_i [_{C'}[_{C}^{0}$ e$] [e]_j]]]$

There is some evidence in favor of this derivation. Thus, in right-headed languages, the C is indeed not overt in relative clauses. Furthermore, the determiner tends to be placed between the modifier clause and the head—a very surprising sequential order from the perspective of non-head-final languages. Example (1) illustrates these properties and is repeated here as (11a) for the readers' convenience:

(11)   a. [Oya-nın   kütüphane-den $\mathbf{e_i}$ çal-dığ-ı$]_{IP=AgrP}$ **bu**   eski kitap$_i$
           Oya-Gen.   library-Abl.   steal-FN-3.sg.   **this**   old book

          'this old book that Oya stole from the library'

This unexpected order of the determiner with respect to the modifier clause is a natural consequence of a Kayneian derivation.[11]

I now sketch the following parametric approach to a description of all the Turkic RC types:

1. In Turkish and other Turkic languages closely related to it (e.g., Azeri), the IP that moves to Spec/DP is an AgrP. This yields familiar examples like (1) (= 11), with the expected *local* relationship between overt Agr and the DP that "triggers" agreement: predicate agreement (verbal as well as nominal) with the local subject; possessive agreement between the possessee and the possessor. The agreement element is a suffix morphologically; it shows up on participles (i.e., the nominalized predicates of the modifier clause in RCs) just as it does on other kinds of predicates in the language:

(11)   b. [[Oya-nın   kütüphane-den bu   eski kitab-ı
          Oya-Gen.   library-Abl.   this old book-Acc.
          çal-dığ-ın]$_{IP=AgrP}$-ı]$_{KP}$ duy-du-m.
          steal-FN-3.sg.-Acc.   hear-Past-1.sg.

       'I heard that Oya stole this old book from the library.'

The Agr morpheme has a syntactic presence as the head of a phrase; therefore, the modifier phrase is an AgrP.

2. In the many languages of the areal periphery where there is no subject agreement in relative clauses, the modifier "clause" that moves to Spec/DP is a bare Aspect or Mood Phrase. (Azeri has both type 1 and 2.)

3. For the Central Asian languages where the subject agreement element shows up on the head noun rather than on the nominalized predicate of the modifier clause, I claim that overt agreement is not the head of the modifier clause even underlyingly.

Furthermore, I claim that in subordinate nominalized clauses in those languages with type 3 RCs, the subject agreement marker that shows up on the nominalized predicate of an argument or adjunct clause in general—that is, not just in RCs—is there just to overtly express the subject's φ-features, but that this marker is not the syntactic head of that clause. Rather, the head of that clause is the nominal Aspect/Mood (whose morphological expression precedes the agreement marker in the sequence of morphemes in the word). Consequently, what moves to the specifier position of the DP (or of a higher functional projection) is a bare Aspect or Mood phrase, just like in the areally peripheral languages of type 2. The agreement morpheme is stranded and cliticizes to the head of the relative clause, thus giving rise to constructions with the unexpected placement of the subject agreement morpheme on the head of the relative clause rather than, as expected, on the IP. This results in examples like (5).

Illustrative examples from Yakut/Sakha[12] follow. This is a language whose nonsubject RCs are of type 3, with subject agreement on the head, and with the subject in the Nominative (i.e., the morphologically bare form) rather than in the Genitive:

(12) [ït   ih-iex-teex]   üüt-**e**
      dog   drink-Fut.-Mood   milk-**3.sg.**

      'the milk the dog should drink' (Kornfilt and Vinokurova 2001)

It is telling that in corresponding embedded argument clauses, the subject is in the Nominative, as well—thus strongly suggesting that the modifier clause of type 3 RCs is directly related to such argument clauses and therefore exhibits similar properties; note that the Agr marker is on the predicate—that is, is in a local relation with the subject (and that this is the only difference between the nominalized argument clause and the modifier clause of the type 3 RC):

(13) [$_{KP}$ [$_{MdP}$ ït   üüt-ü   ih-iex-teeq+i]-n]   bil-e-bin.
            dog   milk-Acc.   drink-Fut.-Mood+**3.sg.**[13]-Acc   know-Aor.-1.sg.

      'I know that the dog should drink the milk.' (Kornfilt and Vinokurova 2001)

I assume that the Accusative complement of the matrix verb *bil* 'know' is a Case Phrase [CP] whose complement is a nominal Mood Phrase [MdP]. The agreement marker is cliticized to the predicate of that MdP and is thus in a local relation to its subject. I assume that the Case of the subject is licensed by the nominal Mood head of the clause, as Agr does not have syntactic head status here—as opposed to languages that have type 1 RCs, where Agr does have that status in argument embedded clauses, as well as in the modifier clauses of RCs. This is a reasonable analysis, as we find the same morphologically unmarked Case on the subjects of embedded clauses that lack Agr altogether—in argument clauses, as well as in RCs of type 2.

Turning to the corresponding nonsubject RC, which I claim is derived from the structure of (13), this means that, while the relationship between the subject and the agreement element on the head of the RC is not local on the surface or at Spell-Out, it is local underlyingly. Furthermore, at the surface or at Spell-Out level this relationship is local indirectly, via the trace left behind by the moved (or, in minimalistic terms, copied[14]) AspP on the one hand and the trace of the moved/copied Agr element, on the other hand.

The structure of (12), renumbered as (14), would then be as follows:

(14) $[_{DP} [_{MdP}$ it $[e]_i$ ih-iex-teex$]_j$
              dog   drink-Fut.-Mood
      $[_{D^0} e] [_{CP} [_{NP}$ üüt$]_i + e_k [_{C'} [_{C^0} e] [_{MdP} e_j + e_k]]]]^{15}$
                      milk+3.sg.

'the milk the dog should drink'

Although the Agr marker -e and the subject it are not in a local relationship, they were in such a relationship at an earlier point in derivation, as we saw in (13), and this locality is encoded in this representation. (Cliticization sites are marked by + in these examples.)

A possible objection that might be raised to this derivation is that the Agr clitic is part of the MdP; since only constituents move, the clitic should have moved along with the MdP to Spec/DP. This is not a serious problem, however. I propose that the relevant syntactic constituent is bounded overtly by the Mood morpheme,[16] since that morpheme is the head; therefore, even though the Agr clitic is part of the embedded predicate in terms of the phonological word, it is not part of the syntactic projection. Therefore, while it can overtly express the φ-features of the subject, it can be left behind when the MdP moves.

It might seem paradoxical to claim that part of a phonological word is outside of the syntactic projection of another part of the same word. However, I have argued elsewhere (Kornfilt 1996) that complex phonological words in MST may consist of smaller domains with different syntactic status. Kayne (1994) proposes something akin to this idea for agglutinative languages in general, as subdomains of certain phonological words would need to contain empty categories between subdomains of the word, due to the leftward movement of phrasal remnants. Therefore, the derivation I just proposed for type 3 RCs is consistent with these ideas for agglutinative and syntactically (surface-)head final languages.

The same derivation for type 3 RCs carries over to similar constructions in related languages where the subject is in the Genitive rather than in the Nominative. In such languages, the nominal Agr marker that is cliticized to the nominal Mood Phrase in embedded clauses in general—that is, in clauses corresponding to the Sakha example in (13)—participates in checking the Case of the clause. I illustrate with examples from (Modern)[17] Uigur; these data ((15)–(20)) are taken from LeSourd's (1989) transcriptions of his four elicitation sessions with a native informant:

(15) Sen   [bïz-**nïŋ**   ürümči-dε   yaša-ydïɣanlïɣ-**imïz**-ni]
      you (sg.) we-**Gen**. Ürümçi-Loc. live-PresN-**1.pl.**-Acc.
      bil-i-sεn.
      know-Aor.-2.sg.

'You (sg.) know that we live in Ürümçi.'

(16)   Sen   [min-**iŋ**   ürümči-dɛ   yašï-γanlïγ-**ïm**-ni]
        you (sg.)   I-**Gen.**   Ürümçi-Loc.   live-PastN-**1.sg.**-Acc.
        bil-i-sɛn.
        know-Aor.-2.sg.

        'You (sg.) know that I lived in Ürümçi.'

At first, such embeddings look just like their counterparts in languages like MST:
that is, those whose nonsubject RCs are of type 1; this can be seen by comparing
the last two examples with (11)b. However, Modern Uigur does not have nonsubject RCs of type 1. While it does have type 2 RCs, the most typical nonsubject
RC pattern appears to be type 3:

(17)   Min-**ïŋ**   tut-ïdïγan /   tut-qan   at-**ïm.**
        I-Gen.   catch-FutN[18]   catch-PN   horse-**1.sg.**

        'The horse I will catch/have caught.'

(18)   Sïn-**ïŋ**   kör-ïdïγan adɛm-**ïŋ**   ürümči-dɛ   yaša-ydu.
        you (sg.)-Gen.   see-FutN   man-**2.sg.**   Ürümçi-Loc.   live-Pres.

        'The man you will see lives in Ürümçi.'

This shows, then, that the status of the Agr morpheme is that of a clitic, just like
the corresponding morpheme in Yakut/Sakha, rather than that of a genuine suffix
with syntactic head status, as in MST. A possible criticism at this juncture might
be to question the clitic nature of the nominal Agr marker; if that marker is not
a syntactic head and if the subject is not its specifier, how can it participate in
the checking of the Genitive Case on the subject?
    It has to be pointed out here that in Modern Uigur, the Agr marker does,
indeed, contribute to the Genitive. The nominal Tense/Aspect/Mood [TAM]
markers on the embedded predicate cannot be solely responsible for that marking.
This can be seen clearly from the fact just mentioned that this language also has
the option of type 2 RCs for nonsubject targets. In those RCs the subject is in
the Nominative (bare) Case, and there is no overt Agr marking at all—neither
on the predicate nor on the head of the RC. At least some of these nominal TAM
markers can show up in either type 2 or type 3 RCs. Thus, along with (18), which
is clearly of type 3, we also have (19), which is obviously of type 2, and where the
same nominal TAM marker shows up on the embedded predicate:

(19)   Sïn   kör-ïdïγan adɛm   ürümči-dɛ   yaša-ydu.
        you (sg.)   see-FutN   man   Ürümçi-Loc.   live-Pres.

        'The man you will see lives in Ürümçi.'

Example (19) has no overt Agr marker at all; the embedded subject is not in the Genitive, but in the bare (= Nominative) Case.

These elicited examples might not be quite sufficient to show that the nominal TAM marker cannot check for a Genitive subject by itself—that is, without nominal Agr—as Genitive subjects in the absence of nominal Agr might be rare (and thus not offered by the informant without explicit mention) but still possible. However, LeSourd's material includes at least one item where this constellation was checked in particular and was rejected by the informant:

(20)   *Min-iŋ   tut-ïdïɣan   at   qaš-maxçi
       I-Gen.   catch-FutN   horse   run away-Mood[19]

       Intended reading: 'The horse I will catch tries to run away.'

Instead, either one of the following two possibilities were stated as well-formed for the intended reading:

(21)   mɛn-**iŋ**   tut-ïdïɣan   at-**ïm**   qaš-maxči
       I-**Gen.**   catch-FutN   horse-**1.sg.** run away-Mood

       This is an RC of type 3, with the nominal Agr marker on the head of the RC.

The other possibility is an RC of type 2, with a "bare" subject and complete lack of overt agreement:

(22)   mɛn tut-ïdïɣan at qaš-maxči

Given these two options, a question arises as to whether these are completely synonymous and equivalent. According to the informant, there is indeed a discourse-related difference; the Genitive subject is felt to be more of a topic.[20] For our purposes, however, this is a peripheral concern. What's important for us is the correlation between the Genitive Case of the subject in the modifier clause and the overt nominal Agr on the RC's head. Incidentally, the same correlation holds for the Genitive subject and the agreeing nominal predicate in nominalized argument clauses, as we saw in (15) and (16).[21]

These observations bring us back to our original question: How can an Agr marker which is not the head of an AgrP, but is "only" a clitic on the predicate, participate in the licensing of Genitive (or of any Case, for that matter) on the subject?

Actually, this question is not really different from the more general one that we posed with respect to the Yakut/Sakha examples, even though the subject there was "bare" and not Genitive. The question is: In what sense is a morphological element which is not genuinely part of a syntactic projection able to express agreement with the specifier of that projection? The answer there had been to simply say: by virtue of being within the same phonological word as the syntactic head of that projection—namely, the nominal TAM marker on the predicate. Here, then, we have the same question, only with the additional query about Case licensing. I will then say that whatever enables the clitic Agr to "agree" with the subject also enables it to participate in licensing the Case of the subject; that is, the Agr imparts its features to the nominal predicate by virtue of being within the same phonological word, and Case checking proceeds as usual within the nominal TAM-projection—and, most importantly, in a *local* fashion.

Summarizing this section, we have seen that a Kayneian derivation is able to capture insightfully and very economically the "microparametric" variation among the Turkic languages with respect to the nonsubject RCs they exhibit. The three types (i.e., [1] Genitive subject and nominal Agr on the predicate of the modifying clause, [2] Nominative (or bare) subject and no Agr anywhere, and [3] Genitive or Nominative/bare subject and Agr on the head of the RC) have been claimed to all be derived in accordance with Kayne's (1994) approach: a first step of moving the target NP to Spec/CP, and a second step of moving the remnant IP to Spec of the large DP (or DemP). The variation among the languages was said to depend on the nature of the moving IP: a (nominal) AgrP for type 1, and an Agr-less, bare nominal TAM-P for types 2 and 3. The difference in status between these two types of IP was claimed to follow from a difference in status of the Agr element, in those instances where an Agr exists: Agr as a genuine suffix and as the syntactic head of the "IP" in type 1; Agr as a clitic (and not as a syntactic head) in type 3. The impossibility of the IP to be an AgrP in type 2 is a trivial consequence of the fact that there is no Agr in these constructions at all.

The next section is devoted to a different account of type 3 RCs in Mongolian.

4 A Rival Account: Subject Raising

To my knowledge, there is no other treatment in the literature of these Turkic nonsubject RCs, in the sense of offering any other analysis for their derivation and for the variation among them. Descriptive accounts in Turkological literature do exist (e.g., Csató 1996, Schönig 1992–93), but no attempt at a general account or at a derivation is made there, given the nature of that philological field.

However, there does exist an interesting analysis of the type 3 pattern in Mongolian.

A number of modern Mongolian languages and dialects have type 3 in relative clauses whose target is a nonsubject. The following example, discussed in Hale (2002) (and also reported, in a slightly different form, in Hale and Ning 1996 and elicited by Hale and Ning in the context of their fieldwork on Dagur, a Mongolian language primarily spoken in China, mainly in the Manchurian region), illustrates this point:

(23) [**Mini**   au-sen]   mer^y-**min^y**]   sain.
       1.sg.GEN   buy-PERF   horse-**1.sg.GEN**   good

      'The horse I bought is good.' (Hale 2002: ex. 1)

Under Hale's (as well as Hale and Ning's) analysis, the agreement morpheme is base-generated on the head of the RC. The subject is raised from its original position within the modifier clause to the specifier position of the possessive DP (i.e., what I have called earlier in this chapter a nominal AgrP for corresponding possessive phrases in MST).

This movement is motivated by referring to the Case Filter. It is claimed that, due to the absence of overt Agr on the participle, that is, of the nominalized predicate, in examples like (23), the subject is in danger of violating the Case Filter and therefore must move to a possessor position (i.e., the specifier position of the higher DP). In that position, the original subject would receive Case (i.e., the Genitive) from the nominal agreement on the head of the relative clause. The representation of the relative clause in (23) would be as in (24):

(24) mini$_i$ [t$_i$ au-sen]   mer^y-**min^y**
       1.sg.GEN   buy-PERF   horse-**1.sg.GEN**

      'the horse I bought'

In this chapter, I don't want to take issue with this rival analysis with respect to the Mongolian languages. My question will be: whether this analysis can carry over to type 3 RCs in Turkic. My answer is in the negative. I now turn to discussing arguments that substantiate this answer.

5 ARGUMENTS AGAINST SUBJECT RAISING TURKIC RCs OF TYPE 3

5.1 First Argument

The first problem with raising of subject to possessor position is the (possibility of) possessive interpretation, pointed out earlier in this essay. Hale and Ning recognize this problem and state, essentially, that in Dagur, formally possessive phrases (i.e., DPs with a Genitive possessor and an agreeing possessee head) do not have to have possessive interpretation; in other words, the nominal head (with its agreement marker) does not assign a possessive θ-role to the DP in its specifier position. Rather, there is some vague relationship of relevance between head + Agr and the specifier, and, formally, no θ-role is assigned to the DP-specifier of the "large" DP. Thus, in the RCs in question, the raised subject (which receives a θ-role from its predicate) may raise to "possessor" position without violating the θ-Criterion and does not assume a reading of possessor.

This reasoning is only as convincing as the putative lack of strong possessive interpretation in regular "possessive phrases" does indeed hold. Otherwise, if lack of possessive readings must be posited only for type 3 RCs, but not for possessive phrases in general, there is no independent justification for the placement of the embedded subject into the specifier position of the "possessive phrase" at Spell-Out.

In MST "possessive phrases," a reading of possession or very tight relationship between the Genitive "possessor" and the agreeing "possessee" is obligatory. Vaguer readings of the sort allowed by, say, English are not possible. For example,

(25)   I found [**your book**] in a bookstore.

might be fine, under a reading where the book neither belongs to nor was written by the hearer of the utterance, but rather where that hearer had spoken at great length about a particular book. Such a reading would be impossible in the corresponding MST utterance:

(26)   [(**Sen-in**)   kitab-ın-ı]   bir   kitapçı-da   bul-du-m
       you (sg.)-Gen.   book-**2.sg.**-Acc.   a   bookstore-Loc.   find-Past-1.sg.
       'I found your book in a bookstore.'

The bracketed possessive phrase is acceptable only if "you" is the possessor or author of the book. To achieve a reading alluded to for the previous English example, one would have to modify the "possessee" overtly (e.g., with a relative clause, expressing the vague relationship of previous mention), and, most important, the Agr marker would need to be omitted.

With respect to other Turkic languages, a survey of descriptions of "possessive phrases" strongly implies that similar facts hold for them, as well.

In addition, my own elicitation of Yakut/Sakha, as well as LeSourd's fieldwork in Modern Uigur, shows more clearly than the general remarks in the literature about this topic that the "possession" or "strong relationship" reading in "possessive phrases" with overt nominal Agr markers on the head is a real fact in those languages, as well, and cannot be captured by imputing an interpretation of a vague relation between head and specifier in such instances.

Thus, given that Yakut/Sakha and Modern Uigur do have type 3 RCs, a derivation that relies crucially on raising of the subject out of the modifier clause to a higher possessor (or Spec/AgrP) position is not viable.

5.2 Second Argument

The second problem is probably even more serious, as it has to do with the motivation of the raising. In more recent models of generative syntax, movement has to be motivated. Indeed, Hale and Ning do formulate such a motivation, as mentioned previously: the subject DP needs Case; given that no Case can be licensed within its local domain—that is, within the modifier clause of the RC, the subject raises to the specifier position of the higher DP, where Genitive Case can be checked by the nominal Agr morphology on the head.

While this motivation might work for Mongolian, it does not carry over to type 3 RCs in the Turkic languages that have that construction.

First, note that UG must have some way of licensing the Case on the subjects of all clauses (i.e., not just in RCs) that don't have overt Agr (or even other inflectional morphology). A default Case assignment possibility has often been mentioned in this regard for languages like Chinese and Japanese that lack overt Agr morphology. In the Turkic languages it would make sense to assume the existence of such a mechanism for type 2 RCs, under the assumption that the default Case is the morphologically unmarked Nominative. Alternatively, one can posit unmarked/Nominative Case licensing by the TAM morphology. Either way, it is clear that for many of the Turkic languages the absence of an overt Agr element on the embedded predicate is not an obstacle for the related subject DP to receive Case. Thus, there would be no Case-based need for the subject to move out of its original position.

It is possible to object here that languages that have type 2 RCs might indeed not need overt Agr to license Case on subjects, but that languages that have type 3 RCs do need such Agr; therefore, given that such RCs don't have Agr on their modifier clauses, the subject would need Case in such languages. But this objection is not convincing: some of the languages with type 3 RCs also have RCs of type 2. As we saw earlier, Modern Uigur is one such language. This means that, beyond possibilities allowed for in UG and in the grammars of cognate languages, the grammar of Modern Uigur itself has a way of licensing Case on the subject of Agr-less clauses, thus making the raising of such subjects unmotivated.

Yet another objection could be raised against this argument: the subject of type 2 RCs is "bare" or Nominative; in Modern Uigur, the subject of the modifier clause in a type 3 RC is Genitive. As a matter of fact, we have seen examples of a correlation between Genitive subjects and overt Agr in Modern Uigur. Therefore, supposing that overt Agr cannot show up on the predicate of such a modifier clause in Modern Uigur, and supposing that discourse reasons of the sort mentioned earlier (e.g., the need to mark the subject as a topic) necessitate Genitive marking on the subject, raising of such a subject to a domain that provides a local licensing Agr would still be necessary.

But there is a counterargument to this objection as well. Note that the derivation of RCs—not just of type 3 but of all RCs—proposed in this chapter links the modifier clause of RCs intimately to embedded nominalized clauses in general.[22] The fact that, given any particular Turkic language, essentially the same nominal TAM markers are found on the modifier clauses of RCs and on nominalized embedded clauses in general strongly suggests that this is the right approach to deriving RCs.

We saw previously that exactly this observation holds for Modern Uigur argument clauses and type 3 RCs. In addition to the same nominal TAM morphemes, these two constructions were also similar in exhibiting Genitive subjects. Most important, the argument clauses do have overt Agr on the nominal predicate (cf. examples (15) and (16)). Thus, the Genitive subject does have a local licenser in its own clause (i.e., the overt Agr, together with the nominal TAM morphology, as was said earlier) and would not need to raise out of its clause to have its Genitive Case checked in the higher DP.

Under this approach, lack of Agr on the modifier clause in the corresponding type 3 RCs—(for Modern Uigur, these would be examples (17) and (18)—is a later effect of the derivation, namely, of the leftward movement of the nominal IP (or TAM-Phrase), leaving behind the clitic Agr, and not of an underlying lack of Agr on the embedded clause.

Similar facts also hold for other Turkic languages, such as Turkmen and Uzbek, that have type 3 RCs with Genitive subjects: their embedded clauses have Genitive subjects, too, with nominal TAM markers on the predicates that are similar to those on the embedded predicates of the RCs, and, crucially, with overt Agr markers on those predicates. One example per language should suffice for our purposes.

(27) Mïrat [on-non   nä:č-inǰi   klaθ-θa   oko-n-un-ï]
      Mïrat   he-Gen.   what-ordinal   class-Loc.   study-P-3.sg.-Acc.
      θo:r-odï. (Turkmen)
      ask-Past

      '[Then] M. asked in which class he studied.' (Hanser 1977: 190)

(28) Men   bu   ɔdam-niŋ   jǒja-ni   oɣirla-gan-i-ni
      I   this man-Gen.   chicken-Acc steal-P-3.sg.-Acc.
      bil-a-man. (Uzbek)
      know-Aor.-1.sg.

      'I know that this man stole the chicken.' (Noonan 1985: 85, ex. 186)

In summary, we have seen that in Turkic languages that have type 3 RCs, there is no clear motivation based on Case for raising the subject out of its original position in the modifier clause.

While the examples we saw in this context involved Genitive subjects, the same is, of course, also true for type 3 RCs that have bare/Nominative subjects, such as the ones we saw for Sakha (cf. example (12)). In Sakha, too, the nominal TAM marker on embedded clauses is essentially the same as the markers found on the embedded predicates of RCs; an illustrative pair was given in (12), illustrating type 3 RCs, and (13), illustrating what I claim is the related construction—namely, a nominalized embedded argument clause. We also saw in the latter example that the embedded predicate of an argument clause can—and does—exhibit overt Agr. Thus, no matter whether we attribute any participatory relevance to the Agr in the checking of the bare Case on the subject, or whether we say that it is the TAM marker that licenses the Case on the subject, or, as yet another possibility, whether we claim that the bare subject is licensed for its Case by a default licensing mechanism, it is clear that the subject of an embedded clause like the one in (13) gets its Case checked locally, within its clause, and does not need to raise for Case reasons in the corresponding RC, where the subject's Case is bare (rather than Genitive).

Having thus argued that the putative subject-to-possessor raising would be unmotivated for Turkic languages that have type 3 RCs, I now turn to some evidence that very strongly argues against the structure that would result from such a raising—evidence that argues that the subject of a type 3 RC is still within the modifier clause. I first present such evidence for Sakha and then turn to Modern Uigur.

5.3 Third Argument

It would be interesting to find a language with type 3 RCs where the Case on the subject of the modifier clause is different from the Case on possessors. This would show convincingly that the subject has not risen to possessor position.

Since (agreeing) possessors are typically Genitive, one would look for bare/Nominative subjects in a type 3 RC. As I said earlier, such subjects are typically Genitive as well. However, there are some languages, though few in number, that do have bare subjects. We saw such examples earlier in the chapter. Those were from Sakha, and given my own elicitation of some relevant Sakha data (Kornfilt and Vinokurova 2001), I shall offer Sakha examples in this context.

The "conventional wisdom" on the Genitive in Sakha is that it does not exist (cf. Johanson 1998: 49, Stachowski and Menz 1998: 421). This appears to be correct, as it is indeed very difficult to find any evidence for a Genitive marker. Possessors are typically "bare"—that is, are said to be in the Nominative Case—while the head of the possessive phrase does bear overt Agr that agrees in person and number with the possessor. (All of the following Sakha examples ((29)–(33)) are from Kornfilt and Vinokurova 2001.)

(29) k ï ï s   oquh-a
      girl (Nom.)   ox-3.sg.
      'the girl's ox'

However, when the specifier of a possessive phrase is a possessive phrase itself, and if that complex specifier has a head which is a third person, then that complex specifier does get marked with a Genitive:

(30) [k ï ï s   oquh-u]-**n**   kuturug-**a**
      girl (Nom.)   ox-3.sg.-**Gen.**   tail-**3.sg.**
      'the girl's ox's tail'

This is a productive pattern; further embeddings of the same kind will also be marked with the Genitive:

(31) [k ï ï s   oquh-u]-**n**   kuturug-**u**]-**n**   tüü-**te**
      girl (Nom.)   ox-3.sg.-**Gen.**   tail-**3.sg.-Gen.**   fur-**3.sg.**
      'the girl's ox's tail's fur'

What we now need is a type 3 RC with a possessive phrase (whose head is a third person) as a subject. If that complex subject is marked with Genitive Case, this might be taken as evidence that the subject has undergone raising. However, interestingly, such examples are ill-formed; the complex subject has to be in the bare/Nominative Case:

(32) a. [[kini   aqa-ta]   öl-ör-büt]   oquh-**a**
          he(Nom.)   father-3.sg.(**Nom.**)   die-CAUS-P   ox-**3.sg.**
          'the ox which his father killed'

      b. *[[kini   aqa-tï]-**n**   öl-ör-büt]   oquh-**a**
          he(Nom.)   father-3.sg.-**Gen.**   die-CAUS-P   ox-**3.sg.**
      Intended reading: Same as in the previous example.

The Genitive marking does show up on such a possessive phrase when it is not a subject but is itself a possessor:

(33) [[kini   aqa-tï]-**n**   oquh-**a**
        he(Nom.) father-3.sg.-**Gen.** ox-**3.sg.**

      'his father's ox'

Thus, if the subject of a type 3 RC as the one in (32) were indeed raised to the specifier position of a higher nominal AgrP, it should be marked with the Genitive, as it is in (33), when it is indeed in such a position. The fact that such Genitive marking is ill-formed, as shown in (32b), strongly argues that the subject in such RCs is still in its own clause, where its Case is licensed as the bare or Nominative Subject Case, in line with the Case in all embedded clauses.

5.4 Fourth Argument

Modern Uigur offers a different type of counterevidence to the raising analysis for type 3 RCs. This evidence is based on word order:

(34) [[Tünögün min-ïŋ tut-qan] at-ïm]   εtε
        yesterday I-Gen. catch-P horse-1.sg. tomorrow
      qaš-maxči.
      run away-Mood

      'The horse that I caught yesterday will run away tomorrow.' (LeSourd 1989)

Here the adverb *tünögün* 'yesterday' precedes the Genitive subject of the RC's modifier clause. If the subject had risen out of the modifier clause and had landed in the specifier position of the higher nominal AgrP, this would mean that the adverb, which is interpreted as belonging to the modifier clause, had risen to an even higher position, so as to end up sequentially to the left of the subject.

However, while topicalization does indeed place topics in structurally high and sequentially initial positions, it appears to be very local. The most unmarked position for adverbs is to the left of the VP. Thus, I assume that (34) is derived from (35) via local topicalization of the adverb *tünögün* 'yesterday':

(35) [[Min-ïŋ tünögün tut-qan] at-ïm]   εtε   qaš-maxči.
        I-Gen. yesterday catch-P horse-1.sg. tomorrow run away-Mood

      'The horse that I caught yesterday will run away tomorrow.' (LeSourd 1989)

Likewise, the matrix adverb *ɛtɛ* 'tomorrow' can be topicalized locally, within the matrix clause:

(36) ɛtɛ   [[tünögün   min-iŋ   tut-qan]   at-ïm]   qaš-maxči.
      tomorrow   yesterday I-Gen.   catch-P   horse-1.sg. run away-Mood

      'Tomorrow, the horse that I caught yesterday will run away.' (LeSourd
      1989)

However, the embedded adverb cannot topicalize into the matrix clause:

(37) *Tünögün ɛtɛ   [[min-iŋ   tut-qan]   at-ïm]
      yesterday   tomorrow   I-Gen.   catch-P   horse-1.sg.
      qaš-maxči
      run away-Mood (LeSourd 1989)

The last example shows that a constituent of the embedded clause cannot topicalize to the left of a matrix constituent. Thus, the fact that the same adverb can successfully precede the Genitive subject in (34) shows that the subject is still in the embedded clause and has not undergone raising.

6 CONCLUSIONS AND SOME OPEN QUESTIONS

I hope to have shown that all three types of nonsubject RCs in Turkish are amenable to a Kayneian derivation, in which the target of the RC moves to Spec/CP, and where the clause remnant, that is, the IP, moves leftward to Spec/DP or Spec/DemP. While this derivation captures the common properties of all three types (e.g., right-headedness, placement of articles, and demonstratives between the modifier clause and the head of the RC), it also leaves room for explaining the differences among these three types. This was done by attributing different status to the overt nominal Agr element where it does occur (i.e., as a syntactic head of the moving IP in type 1 and as a clitic in type 3) and also to the moving IP (i.e., as a functional projection of Agr in type 1 and as a projection of nominal TAM in types 2 and 3).

Perhaps the most interesting type of nonsubject RCs is type 3, given the nonlocal relationship between the subject of the modifier clause and the Agr element which is placed on the head (rather than the predicate) of the RC, and thus appears to agree with the subject in a nonlocal way. I proposed an account for this type of RC, where this nonlocal relationship actually derives from a local one, still using a Kayneian derivation.

I also hope to have shown that a rival analysis for type 3—a logical possibility for the Turkic languages and an actually proposed account for a similar construction in some Mongolian languages—is unmotivated and runs into problems concerning facts of word order and Case marking. This was an analysis based on raising the subject out of the modifier clause and into the specifier position of a putative higher nominal Agr phrase, headed by either the head of the RC or by the Agr placed on that head.

Two questions arise here. First, is there any independent evidence to show that the Agr marker in type 3 RCs is a clitic, as opposed to the Agr marker in type 1 RCs, which, I claimed, is a genuine suffix? Second, if the Agr marker in type 3 RCs is indeed a clitic, and it cliticizes onto the head of the RC as a result of the derivation I proposed, wouldn't one expect to find it after the Case marker on that head, rather than before it? Note that the head of such RCs, just like the heads of *all* the types of RCs, bears the Case marker which is checked within the higher clause. If words enter the syntactic derivation fully formed, as is assumed in the Minimalist Program, and have their features checked off during the syntactic derivation, one would expect the head to enter the derivation together with its Case marker. Therefore, the Agr marker should cliticize to that fully formed word and thus follow the Case marker. Yet, as illustrated in (5b), the Agr marker follows the head but precedes the Case marker in these type 3 RCs. I have only tentative remarks to make in response to these questions, pointing the way toward future field work to resolve them.

To address the first question, one needs to show that in languages that have RCs of type 3, the Agr elements are, phonologically and morphologically, different from their counterparts in languages that have RCs of type 1, as well as different from straightforward suffixes in the same language. Such differences can be properties like different stress patterns (i.e., showing that the word, minus the Agr element, is being treated like a primary domain of stress assignment), exceptional behavior with respect to vowel harmony (again showing that the Agr element does not, or at least not fully, undergo harmony with respect to the relevant harmony features of the preceding harmony domain), and exceptional sandhi phenomena at the boundary between the Agr element and the preceding domain.

As a matter of fact, some historical evidence points in the right direction. Some of the older Turkic languages (e.g., Khorezmian, a language of the Middle Turkic period) appear to have had nonsubject RCs of type 2 and 3 but not of type 1. Furthermore, the oldest documented Turkic languages appear to have had nonsubject RCs of type 2, but not of type 3 or 1 (some claims notwithstanding that type 1 did exist). At the same time, there is evidence of just the sort mentioned in the previous paragraph to suggest that the oldest stages of the language did not have real Agr elements but rather duplicated subject pronouns, which became clitics, which, in turn, became genuine suffixes. There does seem to be a correlation, then, between type 2 RCs and no Agr, between type 3 RCs and clitic Agr, and finally between type 1 RCs and genuine, suffixal Agr.[23]

The historical evidence just mentioned is rather sketchy. Still, it is suggestive. A good deal of work needs to be done, both on the available historical material and even more interestingly on contemporary languages, before clear conclusions on correlations between morphology and syntax can be drawn. The phonology and morphology of the contemporary Turkic languages is very complex, making quick conclusions impossible. But at least we know where to look, and how, in order to move along toward the answers we need.

As for the second question, the one about the unexpected order between the Agr and Case morphemes on the head of type 3 RCs, there are a number of directions to investigate. One might be to say that the order we do find—Agr before Case—is not the result of the syntactic derivation, which would yield the result of Agr *after* Case (if the head plus Case were a preformed word), but rather the result of some later morphological reordering of morphemes, due to a morphological template that enforces orders of Agr before Case sequentially, irrespective of syntactic structure. This type of solution would be possible in a framework where morphology, or at least part of morphology, "takes place" after syntax (e.g., as in Halle and Marantz's 1993 framework of Distributed Morphology).

That this might be a viable solution is shown by the fact that type 3 RCs in the Mongolian languages do in fact show Agr *after* Case on the head of the RC. Under this analysis, then, one could say that the Mongolian pattern reflects the syntactic derivation and that the Turkic pattern is the result of the same derivation, with an additional morphological operation to satisfy a morphological, Turkic-internal template.

A second solution might be to say that words don't in fact come preformed and that a good deal of inflection (as well as derivation) is the result of syntax. In such an approach, the cliticization of the Agr to the RC head would be dealt with in the syntax, on the cycle (or within the phase) that deals with the RC construction as a DP. It would be only after that cycle or phase, at the level of the matrix, that the appropriate Case would be licensed, thus explaining the fact that it is the last morpheme of the word.[24]

Akin to this second solution is a third one that would treat Case morphemes in the languages that have type 3 RCs as clitics, too, and thus able to follow another clitic, the Agr marker. To substantiate such an analysis, one would need to subject the phonological and morphological properties of the Case morphemes in these languages to the same kind of scrutiny that was suggested for the evaluation of Agr elements.

There are some examples in LeSourd's Modern Uigur materials which are very interesting in this regard, as they are amenable to an analysis of Case morphemes as clitics and seem to show Case morphemes that "survive" the movement of the target NP to Spec/CP in Free Relatives and attach to the closest, overtly headed DP host. But these examples are so few, and thus any analysis based on them would have to be so tentative, that I have decided not to include them here and only mention their existence as a basis of future fieldwork in this direction.

In conclusion, we have seen that an apparent problem with the approach proposed for all RCs in general, and for type 3 nonsubject RCs in particular, can be dealt with in a variety of ways that are promising.

NOTES

The very beginnings of the analysis proposed in this chapter were presented at a plenary lecture of the German Summer School in Linguistics, held in September 1998, at Mainz University. However, that presentation was primarily historical. All of the data on the contemporary Turkic languages are new, with the exception of the Azeri example from Slobin (1986) and the Turkmen example from Frank (1995). The discussion of the contemporary Turkic languages is new as well. I am grateful to Guglielmo Cinque and to Richard Kayne for helpful comments on a preliminary version of this chapter, to Guglielmo Cinque for discussion after the plenary lecture just mentioned, and to Claus Schönig for discussion of the historical material; while not used in this chapter, that material gave me a proper perspective for viewing the contemporary data. I also thank Elena Skribnik, for information on the southern Siberian languages and for generously sharing her notes on those languages. Again, although I did not use that material directly, it helped me in viewing the data from related languages, which I did use with an informed mind. I am particularly grateful to Nadya Vinokurova, who generously gave of her time during one elicitation session and also discussed aspects of Sakha syntax, phonology, and morphology with me. Likewise, I am immensely indebted to Phil LeSourd, who generously provided his transcriptions of four informant sessions he conducted with a native informant of Modern Uigur in 1989. Ken Hale was very helpful in discussions on Dagur in general and type 3 RCs in particular. I am grateful to Aditi Lahiri and to Frans Plank, who provided financial support of various sorts used during visits to Konstanz University in the summer and fall of 1999, during which time I found and sifted through published material on the Turkic languages. I further would like to thank the Fulbright Commission of Germany for the award of a fellowship during the fall of 1999 and Marcel Erdal, who hosted me at the Turkology Department of Frankfurt University; I benefited from the materials of the department and of the university library in putting the data together which I used, in part, for this chapter. Any mistakes and shortcomings are my own responsibility.

This chapter is dedicated to the memory of Ken Hale, who, at different stages of my life, was a teacher, a mentor, and a friend to me. His work on and interest in Dagur motivated important aspects of this study, although his analysis of Dagur relative clauses is different from my analysis of the corresponding construction in the Turkic languages.

1. For a study of subject as well as nonsubject RCs in MST, consult Kornfilt (2000), although some aspects of that approach is outdated.

2. My native informant, Nadya Vinokurova, is a doctoral student of linguistics at Utrecht University; consequently, her participation in our elicitation session went further than merely offering data. She also helped with morphological analysis and phonological explanations. The inclusion of her name in the references reflects her involvement and my gratitude.

3. I follow general Turkological tradition in using capital letters to signal sounds that undergo predictable phonological changes. Where a capital letter denotes a vowel, that vowel undergoes vowel harmony; where such a letter stands for a consonant, the consonant undergoes voicing assimilation. Segments in parentheses alternate with null in certain environments; usually, these are consonants that are deleted after another consonant, as is the case with the third-person singular agreement marker in the text.

4. The examples in this chapter are presented in the following way: For MST, I have used regular Turkish orthography, since it is Latin based and has, essentially, the character of a broad phonetic transcription. The few diacritics that are Turkish-specific can be looked up in any Turkish dictionary or grammar—and, after all, examples from languages with Latin-based writing systems (e.g. English, French, and German) are also usually presented in their original orthographies. For examples in the other Turkic languages, I have used transliterations for the original Cyrillic or Arabic writing systems. I have used a broad phonetic transcription for those, with the exception of the symbol ï, which is widely used in Turkological literature for the barred-i, that is, for ɨ. (Please note that the MST equivalent of this symbol is the dotless i, i.e., ı.)

5. The exact timing and duration of this period is not completely clear. However, the literature usually covers, under this term, the language of the so-called Orkun inscriptions (runic inscriptions on stone monuments) of the seventh century AD, and the language of the Old Uigur manuscripts, mainly of the eighth century AD.

6. While absence of Genitive marking clearly shows that the subject is not in the Genitive Case, it is not clear what the Case of the subject is. There is no Case marking on the subject of these RCs; given that the Nominative (i.e., the Case of subjects in fully finite clauses) is not morphologically marked, it makes sense to analyze these subjects of nonfinite clauses as being Nominative as well. I shall return to this issue later in the chapter.

7. We have here a general third-person marker, rather than the fully spelled-out third-person plural marker *-lArIn*. This is because the preceding plural suffix *-lAr* is identical to the plural part of the third-person agreement marker; therefore, the abbreviated agreement form without overt plurality is used. Similar facts hold for the examples from MST that follow this example in the text.

8. This statement is true for written or otherwise formal language styles. In colloquial spoken styles, it is possible to leave out the agreement morpheme on the possessee; however, the resulting phrases are not completely synonymous with their agreeing counterparts and have a flavor of familiarity; for example, MST:

(i)   biz-im   köy-ümüz
       we-Gen.   village-1.pl.

       'our village'

(ii) biz-im   köy
      we-Gen.   village

      'our [good old, dear] village'

Incidentally, while it is possible to "drop" the possessor in examples like (i), this is impossible in (ii). It has been shown previously that, at least in MST, which is a Null Subject Language, *pro* subjects are licensed and identified by overt, rich agreement on the predicate (cf. Kornfilt 1984, 1996, 2000, and related work; Erguvanlı-Taylan 1986, and others). This is true both for verbal and nominal agreement. The latter licenses *pro* not only as the subject of a nominalized embedded clause but also as a possessor in a possessive phrase. Where there is no such overt agreement, as in (ii), it becomes impossible to have a *pro* possessor. Similar facts obtain in other Turkic languages, as well, but I am not sure whether this is true in all Turkic languages; future fieldwork will address this issue.

9. It does not matter at this point whether the possessor is base generated (i.e., merged) in the Spec/AgrP, as assumed in Kornfilt (1984), or whether it reaches that position via movement. The important point is the *local* relationship between the DP (which is interpreted as the possessor) and the Agr element (which is placed on the possessee).

10. I assume here that we have the full form of the third-person plural agreement marker, rather than a sequence of the plural marker and of the abbreviated third-person Agr marker, as in the previous examples. This is because the possessor here is *pro*, rather than a regular, referential DP. For *pro* to be not only formally licensed but also fully identified in all its relevant features, the licensing Agr marker must be fully realized (as well as being in a syntactically local relationship to *pro*). It would take us too far afield to provide independent evidence for this claim; Kornfilt (1996: 114) is one source where the interested reader may find such evidence.

11. Actually, there is some evidence that the modifier IP moves to the specifier position of a functional projection that is higher than the DP; this might be a Dem(onstrative)P. Where a head is modified by both a relative clause and an adjective, and where there is both a demonstrative and a (nonspecific, as the only overt article) determiner, the unmarked order is as follows: modifier clause–demonstrative–adjective–(nonspecific) article–head. Thus, if we assume, again following Kayne (1994), that prenominal adjectival modifiers originate postnominally and move leftward to a specifier position, it would make sense to analyze such sequences as the result of moving the adjective to the specifier position of the DP, and the modifier clause to the specifier position of a higher functional projection—a DemP, as previously proposed.

12. The name for this language as most often found in (older) literature is *Yakut*. This still is the term used for the language and its speakers by other nationalities, especially in Russian. The corresponding term in this language itself is Sakha/Saxa/Saha (depending on the transliteration conventions).

13. The differences between the Agr and the Modality markers in this and the previous example are due to phonologically motivated alternations.

14. In syntactic approaches that treat movement as copy + deletion, the position of the "traditional" movement trace would be the site of deletion, or the original position of the copied element.

15. The traces and other phonologically empty elements (e.g. the determiner head

of the "large" DP and the C) are represented here by boldface **e**, while the third-person singular Agr element, which happens to be realized phonologically as *-e*, is not boldface.

16. While it is bounded covertly by the trace of the VP, which has been moved to the left of the Mood marker.

17. I qualify the language as "modern" because the name *Uigur* is often used for a Turkic language that falls under the period of Old Turkic, the language of manuscripts written in the eighth and ninth centuries AD.

18. This nominal future marker can also function as a nominal present-tense marker. Thus, the first form in this example can also mean 'The horse I am catching'. The same is true for the next example, whose alternative translation would be 'The man you see lives in Ürümçi'. The same nominalized predicate form shows up in (15), on an embedded argument clause, and with a gloss and translation for a (nominalized) present tense.

19. The *-maxči* Mood marker expresses desire for an action.

20. The same seems to be the case for those South Siberian Turkic languages that also have an option of exhibiting either "bare" or Genitive subjects in their nonsubject RCs, in particular for Altai. I am indebted to Elena Skribnik (pers. comm.) for this information.

21. This correlation holds in many other Turkic languages, as well, especially in those where either a Genitive or a Nominative subject can be found in RCs. However, some South Siberian languages—most notably, Altai and Shor—can, apparently, also have Genitive subjects in absence of overt Agr and bare Nominative subjects in the presence of overt Agr. I am indebted to Elena Skribnik for this information. Skribnik (1999) has some illustrative examples that are strongly suggestive but not completely clear. I have therefore not included them here. However, I hope that future fieldwork will resolve these unclarities.

22. Of course, deriving relative clauses from regular embedded clauses is a type of analysis that is taken for granted in generative studies, especially for languages that have finite relative clauses. In traditional studies, however, and especially in those of languages with nonfinite embeddings, this is not usually done. At least in Turkological studies, one often finds characterizations of the nominalized predicates in modifying clauses of RCs as participles, while corresponding predicates of general embeddings are referred to as gerunds, or verbal nouns. However, when one looks at any given Turkic language, the so-called participles are typically the same as, or are a subset of, the so-called gerunds or verbal nouns (in that same language, of course, as the nominalization forms across cognate languages are typically related to each other, but are not always identical or even clearly cognate to each other).

23. For philological studies of historical material, see von Gabain (1941) and Tekin (1968).

24. I am grateful to Guglielmo Cinque for pointing out that the second solution is possibly more plausible and more in the spirit of the approach adopted in this chapter, as well as in Kornfilt (1996).

REFERENCES

Csató, É. (1996) "A Typological Review of Relative Clause Constructions in Some Turkic Languages," in B. Rona (ed.) *Current Issues in Turkish linguistics: Proceedings of the Fifth International Conference on Turkish Linguistics*, Vol. 1. Hitit Yayınevi, Ankara, 28–32.

Erguvanlı-Taylan, E. (1986) "Pronominal versus Zero Representation of Anaphora in Turkish," in D. I. Slobin and K. Zimmer (eds.) *Studies in Turkish Linguistics*. John Benjamins, Amsterdam, 209–232.

Frank, A. J. (1995) *Turkmen Reader*. Dunwoody Press, Kensington, Md.

Gabain, A. von (1941) *Alttürkische Grammatik*. Otto Harrassowitz, Wiesbaden.

Hale, K. (2002) "On the Dagur Object Relative: Some Comparative Notes." *Journal of East Asian Linguistics* 11(2): 109–122.

Hale, K., and C. Ning (1996) "Raising in Dagur Relative Clauses," in B. Aghayani, K. Takeda, and S.-W. Tang (eds.) *UCI Working Papers in Linguistics* 1: 35–38.

Halle, M., and A. Marantz (1993) "Distributed Morphology and the Pieces of Inflection," in K. Hale and S. J. Keyser (eds.) *View from Building 20: Essays in Linguistics in Honor of Sylvain Bromberger*. MIT Press, Cambridge, Mass., 111–176.

Hanser, Oskar (1977) *Turkmen Manual: Descriptive Grammar of Contemporary Literary Turkmen*. Verlag des Verbandes der Wissenschaftlichen Gesellschaften Österreichs, Vienna.

Johanson, L. (1998) "The Structure of Turkic," in L. Johanson and É. Csató (eds.) *The Turkic Languages*. Routledge, London, 30–66.

Kayne, R. (1994) *The Antisymmetry of Syntax*. MIT Press, Cambridge, Mass.

Kornfilt, J. (1984) "Case Marking, Agreement, and Empty Categories in Turkish." Ph.D. diss., Harvard University.

Kornfilt, J. (1996) "On Copular Clitic Forms in Turkish," in A. Alexiadou, N. Fuhrhop, P. Law, and S. Löhken (eds.) *ZAS Papers in Linguistics* 6, ZAS, Berlin, 96–114.

Kornfilt, J. (2000) "Some Syntactic and Morphological Properties of Relative Clauses in Turkish." in A. Alexiadou, P. Law, A. Meinunger, and C. Wilder (eds.) *The Syntax of Relative Clauses*. John Benjamins, Amsterdam, 121–159.

Kornfilt, J., and N. Vinokurova (2001). "Transcriptions and Notes of One Field Work Session on Sakha." Unpublished ms., Syracuse University and University of Utrecht.

LeSourd, P. (1989) "Transcriptions of Four Informant Sessions on Modern Uigur." Unpublished ms., Indiana University.

Noonan, M. (1985) "Complementation." In T. Shopen (ed.) *Language Typology and Syntactic Description*. Vol. 2: *Complex Constructions*. Cambridge University Press, Cambridge, 42–140.

Raun, A. (1969) *Basic Course in Uzbek*. Uralic and Altaic Series 59. Indiana University Publications, Bloomington.

Schönig, C. (1992–93) "Relativsatzbautypen in den sogenannten altaischen Sprachen." *Acta Orientalia Academiae Scientiarum Hung.* 46(2–3): 327–338.

Skribnik, E. (1999) "Notes on Relative Clauses in the Turkic Languages of Southern Siberia." Unpublished ms., University of Munich.

Slobin, D. I. (1986) "The Acquisition and Use of Relative Clauses in Turkic and Indo-European Languages." in D. I. Slobin and K. Zimmer (eds.) *Studies in Turkish Linguistics*. John Benjamins, Amsterdam, 273–294.

Stachowski, M., and A. Menz (1998) "Yakut," in L. Johanson and É. Csató (eds.) *The Turkic Languages*. Routledge, London, 417–433.

Tekin, T. (1968) *A Grammar of Orkhon Turkic* Uralic and Altaic Series 69. Bloomington: Indiana University Publications.

CHAPTER 13

....

QU'EST-CE-QUE (QU)-EST-CE-QUE?

A Case Study in Comparative Romance Interrogative Syntax

....

NICOLA MUNARO AND
JEAN-YVES POLLOCK

1 INTRODUCTION

....

THE main goal of this chapter is to shed light on the syntax of the extremely common, though rarely studied, *(que)est-ce que/qui* questions of Modern French and Northern Italian dialects (NIDs). The French, Valle Camonica[1], Mendrisiotto,[2] and Bellunese[3] examples in (1), (2), (3), and (4) illustrate some of the constructions we have in mind:[4]

(1)   a. Qui est-ce qui porte le pain?
         (Who is it that is bringing the bread?)

      b. Qu'est-ce que tu as fait?
         (What is it that you have done?)

(2)   a. Ch'è-l chi che maja la patate?
          (Who is-l who that eats the potatoes?)

       b. Ch'è-l chi che vè al to post?
          (Who is-l who that comes in your stead?)

(3)   a. Chi l'è che l'a parlaa da mi?
          (Who it is that scl has spoken of me?)

       b. Cusa l'è che t'e mia fai?
          (What it is that you have not done?)

(4)   a. E-lo che che te disturba?
          (is-*lo* what that disturbs you = What is it that disturbs you?)

       b. E-lo che che no te-à parecià?
          (is-*lo* what that no you have prepared? = What is it that you haven't
          prepared?)

The empirical properties of (some of) (1)–(4), henceforth "Wh-est-ce
Q(uestions),"[5] to be explained in this chapter are listed and illustrated under A,
B, C, and D (sections 1.1–1.4).

1.1 A:

When the bare wh-word *que* 'what' is extracted from subject position in French
root questions, Wh-est-ce Q *must* typically be used, as (5a) versus (5b) shows;
subject extraction of *qui* 'who' in contrast, can but need not—see (5c) and (5d)—
make use of that strategy:

(5)   a. *Que {tombe, surprend Marie, arrive}?
          (What falls, surprises Marie, happens?)

       b. Qu'est-ce qui {tombe, surprend Marie, arrive}?
          (What is it that+i falls, surprises Marie, happens?)

       c. Qui {tombe, surprend Marie, arrive}?
          (Who falls, surprises Marie, arrives?)

       d. Qui est-ce qui {tombe, surprend Marie, arrive}?
          (Who is it that+i falls, surprises Marie, arrive?)

More generally, many NIDs show an extremely strong tendency to make systematic use of (Wh-)est-ce Q when subjects are questioned; this is true of both *che* and *chi* in Bellunese; compare (6a, b) with (6c, d):

(6)   a. *Che te disturba?
         (What disturbs you?)

      b. *Chi te disturba?
         (Who disturbs you?)

      c. E-lo che che te disturba?
         (is-lo what that disturbs you = What is it that disturbs you?)

      d. E-lo chi che te disturba?
         (is-lo who that disturbs you = Who is it that disturbs you?)

In partially similar fashion, the Northern Veneto dialects require (Wh-)est-ce Q when, as in (4b), the corresponding affirmative sentence is negative; in that respect, French is very different since both (7a) and (7b) are fine, unlike (7c) in Bellunese:

(7)   a. Que n'as-tu pas préparé?
         (What haven't you prepared?)

      b. Qu'est-ce que tu n'as pas préparé?
         (What is it that you haven't prepared?)

      c. *No à-tu parecià che?
         (No have you prepared what? = What haven't you prepared?)

      d. E-lo che che no te-à parecià?
         (is-*lo* what that *no* you have prepared?)

Why should that be so?

1.2 B:

French Wh-est-ce Q is fine in embedded contexts, while subject clitic inversion (SCLI) isn't (cf. Kayne (1972: 106), Langacker (1972: 54), Obenauer (1981: 102)); (8b, c, d) thus contrast with (9):[6]

(8)   a. Je ne sais pas {qui, qu'} est-ce qui a surpris Marie.
         (I *ne* know not {who, what} is it that has surprised Marie)

b. Dis moi où est-ce qu'elle est allée.
   (Tell me where is it that she is gone)

c. Elle ne sait plus à qui est-ce que tu avais promis ce livre.
   (She *ne* knows no longer to whom is it that you had promised the book)

d. Max ne sait pas qui est-ce qu'ils veulent inviter.
   (Max *ne* know not who is it that they want to invite)

(9) a. ?*Dis moi où est-elle allée.
        (Tell me where is she gone)

     b. *Elle ne sait plus à qui avais-tu promis ce livre.
        (She *ne* knows no longer to whom had you promised the book)

     e. *Max ne sait pas qui veulent-ils inviter.
        (Max *ne* knows not who want they to invite)

Yet the word order Wh+est+ce is otherwise banned in embedded contexts, as shown in (10b). What distinguishes sentences like (8) and (10)?

(10) a. Qui était-ce donc qu'il voulait inviter?
         (Who was it then that he wanted to invite?)

      b. *Je ne sais plus qui était-ce donc qu'ils voulaient inviter.
         (I know no longer who was it then that he wanted to invite.)

1.3 C:

Wh-est-ce Q shows a Subject versus Object asymmetry tied to a bare versus complex wh-phrase contrast; while it is possible, in fact sometimes mandatory, to use Wh-est-ce Q when a bare wh-word is extracted from subject position, as in (5), this option is banned if the wh-phrase is complex (cf. Obenauer 1981), but using Wh-est-ce Q and extracting a complex wh-phrase from nonsubject position is fine; compare (11) and (12):

(11) a. *Quelles nouvelles promesses est-ce qui vont encore tromper les électeurs?
         (What new promises is it that will again deceive the voters?)

      b. *Quel joueur est-ce qui a pris le chapeau de Paul? (= Obenauer's 1981: (27))
         (What player is it that has taken Paul's hat?)

c. *Quel autobus est-ce qui a embouti ma voiture?
(Which bus is it that has bumped into my car?)

(12)   a. Quelles nouvelles promesses est-ce que ce politicien va encore faire?
(What new promises is it that this politician will again deceive the voters?)

b. Quel escroc est-ce que la police a arrêté?
(What crook is it that the police have arrested?)

c. Quel autobus est-ce que tu as embouti?
(Which bus is it that you have bumped into?)

Sentences deceptively similar to (11a, b, c) are acceptable if the est-ce-que string is a "real" cleft; stressing *est* and *ce* and giving them the proper intonation contour is then required:

(13)   a. Quelles nouvelles promesses EST-CE qui vont encore tromper les électeurs?
(What new promises is it that will again deceive the voters?)

b. Quel joueur EST-CE qui a pris le chapeau de Paul?
(What player is it that has taken Paul's hat?)

c. Quel autobus EST-CE qui a embouti ma voiture?
(Which bus is it that has bumped into my car?)

The (11) versus (12) contrast seems like a familiar example of the pervasive subject versus object asymmetry which motivated the ECP principle in the 1980s; the (5) versus (11) and (11) versus (13) pairs, however, are unexpected in that perspective. How can one account for them?

1.4 D:

"Wh-est-ce Q" is fine in (colloquial) French in questions like (14) which contain two occurrences of *est* and *ce*.[7] Example (14), however, only accepts (some)[8] *bare* qu-words and so contrasts significantly with (15) for a number of speakers:

(14)   a. Qu'est-ce que c'est qu'il a dit?
(What is it that it is that he has come up with?)

b. Où est-ce que c'est qu'il va?
(Where is it that it is that he goes?)

    c. Quand est-ce que c'est qu'il prend ses vacances?
      (When is it that it is that he goes on holiday?)

(15)   a. ?*Quelle bêtise est-ce que c'est qu'il a dit?
       (What stupidity is it that it is that he has come up with?)

    b. ?*À quel endroit est-ce que c'est qu'il va?
      (To what resort is it that it is that he goes?)

    c. ?*Pendant quelle période est-ce que c'est qu'il prend ses vacances?
      (During what period is it that it is that he goes on holiday?)

Example (15) has the flavor of subjacency violations, but subjacency effects in Romance and Germanic have seldom, if ever, been tied to different types of wh-phrase, as would seem to be required by pairs like (14) versus (15).[9] How can one make sense of this surprising correlation? To make the final picture concerning Wh-est-ce Q a little more puzzling and thorough, it must be noted that (embedded) Wh-est-ce Q shows no significant[10] bare versus nonbare asymmetry when nonsubjects are extracted and when no *est+ce* reduplication is involved:

(16)   a. (Dis moi) qu'est-ce qu'il a dit.
      (Tell me) what is it that he has said.)

    b. (Je ne sais plus) où est-ce qu'il va.
      (I *ne* know no longer) where is it that he goes.)

    c. (J'ai oublié) quand est-ce qu'il prend ses vacances.
      (I have forgotten) when is it that he goes on holiday.)

(17)   a. (Dis moi) quelle nouvelle bêtise est-ce qu'il a dit.
      (Tell me) what new stupidity is it that he has come up with.)

    b. (Je ne sais plus) à quel endroit est-ce qu'il va.
      (I *ne* know no longer) in what resort is it that he goes.)

    c. (J'ai oublié) pendant quelle période est-ce qu'il prend ses vacances.
      (I have forgotten) during what period is it that he goes on holiday.)

1.5 Summary of A–D

The problems under A, B, C, and D have rarely been noted before or have not been discussed at any length in the (generative) literature on French and Romance.[11] We shall show that they follow from UG and the invariant left periphery of Romance questions once the proper formal characterization of the various wh-words in French and the NIDs is identified; because linguists, unlike children, have no direct access to UG, a comparative approach is of invaluable support: French helps us understand the NIDs, and the NIDs help us understand French. The article is organized as follows: Section 2 briefly recapitulates some of the arguments that have recently been adduced in favor of a highly "split" left periphery for Romance questions; sections 3 and 4 lay the groundwork by showing in what way bare wh-words and complex wh-phrases differ syntactically and semantically (section 3) and introduce the notion of wh-clitic (section 4); section 5 then moves on to deal with problem A; section 6 tackles problem B; section 7 concerns itself with the subject versus nonsubject and bare versus nonbare asymmetries of problem C and with the subjacency effects of problem D; and section 8 concludes the chapter on a speculative note.

2 ON THE LEFT PERIPHERY OF ROMANCE QUESTIONS

Let us begin by summarizing some of the arguments given in Kayne and Pollock (2001), Poletto and Pollock (2000a), Munaro et al. (2001), and Pollock (2000, 2003) in favor of the idea that the left periphery of Romance wh-questions should countenance at least two different positions for wh-words and a variety of layers attracting (different types of Remnant) IP in between; some of those stem from a comparison between French and Bellunese; French, as is well known, has a variety of nonecho questions like *Tu vas où?* 'You're going where?' and *Tu as parlé à qui?* 'You've spoken to whom?' in which the qu-words and phrases occur at the right edge of the sentence. *Que*, however, cannot occur in such contexts: **Jean a acheté que?* 'Jean has bought what?' is sharply umgrammatical.

Seen in this light, Bellunese behaves quite unexpectedly: *che*, the counterpart of *que*, and the other bare wh-words *andé* 'where', *chi* 'who', and *comé* 'how' *must* all occur in postverbal position (cf. Munaro 1999):[12]

(18)   a. A-tu magnà che?
          (Have you eaten what?)

        b. *Che a-tu magnà?
          (What have you eaten?)

    c. Sé-tu 'ndat andé?
       (Are you gone where?)

    d. *Andé sé-tu 'ndat?
       (Where are you gone?)

Example (18) and their French analogs *tu as mangé quoi?* and *tu vas où?* must be carefully distinguished since the former show obligatory subject verb inversion, which French "in situ"[13] questions ban totally, as the sharply ungrammatical *Vas-tu où?* (Go you where?) shows.

Modulo that important difference—on which see Munaro and Poletto (2002), Munaro et al. (2001), and Poletto and Pollock (2000b)—the distribution of *che* and *que* is puzzling; if one took things at their face value and held that Bellunese *che* was IP internal, one would be hard put to explain why its French counterpart *que*, which does not appear to be any more or less "defective" morphologically or semantically than *che*,[14] has to move to the left periphery. Everything else being equal, the morphological similarity of *que* and *che* should trigger similar syntactic behavior, but pairs like *A-tu magnà che?* versus *Tu as mangé que* seem to falsify that reasonable expectation. As Munaro et al. (2001) show, appearances are deceptive; Bellunese and French wh-syntax can be reconciled if one assumes that *che* in (18a) and *andé* in (18c) have indeed moved to the Comp field, just as French *que* must in (19):

(19)   a. Qu'a acheté Jean?
        (What has bought Jean?)

       b. Qu'a-t-il acheté?
        (What has-t-he bought?)

This is independently supported by the fact that (18a, c) and (20) are sensitive to strong and weak island effects, as (21) from Munaro et al. (2001) shows:

(20)   a. À-tu parecia che?
        (Have you prepared what?)

       b. Va-lo 'ndé?
        (Goes-*lo* where?)

       c. Se ciàme-lo comé?
        (himself call-*lo* how?' = What's his name?')

(21)   Strong island effects:
       a. *Te a-li dit che Piero l'à comprà an libro che parla de che?

(you have-scl told that Piero scl-has bought a book that speaks of what?)

'What have they told you that Piero bought a book about?'

b. *Te à-li dit che i parenti de chi no i-é vegnesti?

(you have-scl told that the relatives of whom not scl-have come?)

'Who have they told you that the parents of haven't come?'

Weak island effects:

c. *Te à-li domandà andé che te se 'ndàt quando?

(you have-scl asked where that scl-are gone when?)

'They asked you where you went when?'

d. *Ò-e da telefonarte inveze de 'ndar andé?

(have-scl to phone you instead of going where?)

'Where do I have to phone you instead of going?'

That Bellunese *che* in (18a)–(20a) is *not* in its IP internal argument position is also suggested by ordering and prosodic factors: the wh-counterpart to a sentence-final argument like *a so fradel* in (22a) cannot appear in sentence-final position, as the deviance of (22b), the interrogative counterpart of (22a), shows; all such must surface to the left of the right-dislocated direct object, as in (22c), where the wh-item and the following constituent are separated by a clear intonational break:

(22)   a. Al ghe à dat al libro a so fradel.

(He to him has given his book to his brother)

'He gave the book to his brother.'.

b. ?*Ghe à-lo dat al libro a chi?

(To him has he given the book to whom?)

c. Ghe (lo) à-lo dat a chi, al libro?

(To him it has he given to whom, the book?)

'To whom has he given the book?'

If *che* in (18a) was in the ordinary sentence-internal object position in which *al libro* in (22a) is standing, such facts would be difficult to understand; pairs like (22b) versus (22c) thus give further support to an *overt* movement analysis of all wh-questions in Bellunese.[15]

Accepting the conclusion that *che, andé,* and *comé* in (18)–(20) *have* moved to the CP field, we are evidently forced to hold that the rest of the clause has itself crossed over the position in which the bare wh-words stand. Such sentences therefore involve wh-movement of the ordinary kind and Remnant Movement of (some layer(s) of) IP to the left periphery. The much-simplified derivation of a sentence like (20a) must thus look something like (23):

(23) Input: [$_{IP}$ tu à parecia che]

    (a) Wh-movement $\Rightarrow$ [$_{XP}$ che$_i$ X^0 [$_{IP}$ tu à parecia t$_i$]]

    (b) Remnant IP Movement and further displacement $\Rightarrow$ [$_{YP}$ [$_{IP}$ à-tu parecia t$_i$]$_j$ Y [$_{XP}$ che $_i$ X^0 t$_j$]

Example (23b) lumps together computations and landing sites that are analyzed at length in Munaro et al. (2001) and Poletto and Pollock (2000a, b) and are described in more detail here later.

Moreover, the Comp domain of wh-questions in those languages must contain (at least) two different wh-positions; this follows from our discussion of (24):

(24) a. Sé-tu 'ndat andé?
    (Are you gone where?)

    b. Où est-il allé?

If, as we have said, both sentences involve (Remnant IP) Movement of *Sé-tu 'ndat* and *Est-il allé* to some layer(s) of the left periphery, then one major difference between Bellunese and French must lie in the fact that *andé* in (24a) is standing "low" in the structure, while *où* has moved on and crossed over the position(s) to which *Est-il allé* has been attracted. That there should be two such wh-positions in Romance[16] is shown quite clearly in various NIDs; Bellunese, in addition to (24a), (25a), and the like, also has "doubling structures" like (25b):[17]

(25) a. À-lo fat che?
    (Has-*lo* done what?)

    b. Cossa à-lo fat che?
    (What has *lo* done what?)

The same is true in the Val Camonica dialects spoken in the north, in which examples like (26) alternate with (27),[18] whose leftmost position remains empty:

(26) a. Ch'è-l chi che maja la patate?
    (Who is-l who that eats the potatoes?)

    b. Ch'è-l chi che vè al to post?
    (Who is-l who that comes in your stead?)

(27)   a. É-l chi che porta al pa?
           (Is-l who that brings the bread?)

        b. É-l chi ch'è 'ndà a ca?
           (Is-l who that is gone home?)

Monnese[19] doubling wh-questions like (28a) can also alternate with nondou-
bling ones like (28b) and (28c), in which either the *rightmost* ((28b)) or the
leftmost ((28c)) wh-word remains empty:

(28)   a. Ch'et fat què?
           (What have-Scl done what?)

        b. Ch'et fat?
           (What have-Scl done?)

        c. Fet fà què?
           (Do-Scl do what?)

The wh-position filled by bare wh-words in (25a) and (27) cannot host complex wh-phrases at spell-out, as the Bellunese examples in (29) show:

(29)   a. Quanti libri à-tu ledest?
           (How many books have-you read?)

        b. Che vestito à-la comprà?
           (What dress has she bought?)

        c. Con che tozàt à-tu parlà?
           (With what boy have you spoken?)

        d. *À-tu ledest quanti libri?
           (Have-you read how many books?)

        e. *À-la comprà che vestito?
           (Has she bought what dress?)

        f. *À-tu parlà con che tozàt?
           (Have you spoken with what boy?)

Examples (29d, e, f) should, we believe, be grouped with (30a, b, c):

(30)   a. *À-la comprà che vestito?
           (Has she bought what dress?)

b. *Cossa à-la comprà che vestito?
(What has she bought what dress?)

c. *Che à-la comprà vestito?
(Which has she bought dress?)

d. Che vestito à-la comprà?
(What dress has she bought?)

The descriptive generalization that these facts suggest is as follows:[20] In Northern Eastern (NE) Romance a wh-word can stay "low" in the left periphery if it can be doubled by a lexical or nonlexical wh-word that is "higher" in the left periphery.

3 COMPLEX WH-PHRASES, BARE WH-WORDS, AND THE LEFT PERIPHERY

Let us try to derive the generalization from deeper principles of grammar; consider (31), (32), and (33) in this light:

(31) There are two positions for wh-words in the left periphery of NE Romance questions—one structurally low, the other high; other layers stand between them, attracting various types of Remnant IP.

(32) A. Bare qu-words are to be analyzed as existential quantifiers in the scope of a disjunction operator.

B. Complex qu-phrases or D-linked bare qu-words are not existential quantifiers and contain only a disjunction operator.

(33) A. The "low" wh-position—henceforth Op1P—is checked by existential quantifiers.

B. The "high" wh-position—henceforth Op2P—is checked by disjunction operators.

As pointed out in the preceding section, (31) is transparently required by (25)–(28); as for (32A), it merely rephrases an idea that goes back to at least Katz and Postal (1964), according to which bare wh-words like *who, what, when, where, qui, que, quand, où, che, chi, comé,* and *andé,* should be analyzed as wh+some {one, thing, time, place, etc.}, where 'someone', 'something', or the like spells out the existential quantifier '#' and where the disjunction operators such as 'wh-', 'qu-', and 'ch-' are morphologically marked with restrictor features (thing, place, human, etc.) which define the 'space' where the infinite disjunction is defined. In those terms, 'who' means something like "in the set of humans {x, y, z, . . . } either $\exists$x or $\exists$y or $\exists$z or . . .), 'what' means "in the set of objects {x, y, z, . . . } either $\exists$x or $\exists$y or $\exists$z or . . .)," and so on.[21]

Statement (32B) is that the disjunction operator of complex wh-phrases like *which man, which place, what man, quel homme, quel endroit,* and *quels livres* has either a definite DP in its scope—such as [wh-(l'homme)], [wh-(l'endroit)], [wh-(les livres)]—as the morphology of *quel(s)* (= *que+l(e)s*) indicates in French, or a presupositional indefinite as in, for instance, *che libro, what book.*[22]

Granted this, suppose (33) holds; if so, complex wh-phrases cannot be attracted to the low wh-position since they have no existential import and, hence, no existential feature to check there. This derives (29) and (30a, b). Assuming further that the disjunction operator "strands" the elements in its scope if they have checked some left periphery feature, (30c) also follows. The following parameters now suggest themselves:

(34)   A. In L the disjunction operator either is or is not spelled out at PF.

B. In L the existential quantifier either is or is not spelled out at PF.

Consider the Val Camonica and Monnese facts in the light of (34); in (35) and (36), the B parameter has positive value:

(35)   a. Ch'è-l chi che maja la patate?
(Who is-l who that eats the potatoes?)

b. Ch'è-l chi che vè al to post?
(Who is-l who that comes in your stead?)

(36)   a. É-l chi che porta al pa?
(Is-l who that brings the bread?)

b. É-l chi ch'è 'ndà a ca?
(Is-l who that is gone home?)

In (38), parameter (34A) has negative value, but it has positive value in (35), just as in (37a) in Monnese:

(37) a. Ch'et fat què?
         (What have-you done what?)

     b. Ch'et fat?
         (What have-you done?)

In (37b), in contrast, (34B) has negative value, while the Bellunese (38), has the positive value for (34B) and the negative one for (34A):

(38) a. Sé-tu 'ndat andé?
         (Are-you gone where?)

     b. À-lo fat che?
         (Has-*lo* done what?)

As for (39), it has positive value for both:

(39) Cossa à-lo fat che?
      (What has he done what?)

In sum, we have argued that there is a fundamental difference between bare wh-words and complex wh-phrases (in (NE) Romance), transparently manifested in the syntax of wh-questions in a language like Bellunese.[23] Bare wh-words check the uninterpretable features of two distinct left periphery positions, a "low" (existential) position and a "high" (disjunction) position; complex wh-phrases and D-linked bare wh-words check only the high feature. Languages vary as to whether their bare wh-words lexicalize the existential quantifier (that is, Valle Camonica (36) or Bellunese (38)), the disjunction operator (that is, French, or Italian) or both, (that is, Valle Camonica (37) or Bellunese (39)). Put another way, granted the invariant structure of the left periphery argued for here and given the relative opacity of the wh-words morphology in Romance, the language learner has to figure out which of the existential or disjunction features the wh-words in his or her language lexicalize; (34) is a template for what must be identified.

4 CLITIC WH-WORDS

One additional ingredient[24] is needed to make sense of the syntax of Wh-est-ce Q: the *clitic* character of some bare wh-phrases in NE Romance, already argued for in Poletto (2000: sec. 3.3.5) concerning Friulian *do* and Bouchard and Hirschbühler (1986) concerning French *que*. That French *que* and Friulian *do*—traditionally seen as the "weak" forms of *quoi* 'what' in French and *dulà* 'where' in S. Michele al Tagliamento—compare Poletto (2000: 74)—should be seen as *clitics* is strongly suggested by facts like the following:

(40)   French:
    a.   *Que, d'après toi, a vu Jean?
       (What, according to you, has Jean seen?)

    b.   Qui, d'après toi, a vu Jean?
       (Who, according to you, has John seen?)

    c.   *Que? Qui? Quoi?
       (What? Who? What?)

    d.   À {*que, qui, quoi} elle pense?
       (To what, whom, what she thinks? = What, whom, what is she thinking of?)

    e.   *Que et qui a-t-elle vu?
       (What and who has she seen?)

    f.   À quoi et à qui a-t-elle pensé?
       (Of what and of whom has she thought?)

(41)   San Michele (Poletto 2000: sect. 3.3.5):
    a.   *Do, seconde tu, van-u?
       (Where, according to you, go they?)

    b.   Dulà, seconde tu, van-u?
       (Where, according to you, go they?)

    c.   *Do? Dulà?
       (Where? Where?)

    d.   Di {*do, dulà)} al vegna?
       (From where he comes?)

    e.   *Do e quant van-u?
       (Where and when go they?)

    f.   Dulà e quant van-u?
       (Where and when go they?)

Examples (40–(41) show that *que* and *do*, unlike the other French and San Michele wh-words, cannot be separated from their (prosodic) host by parentheticals, cannot occur in isolation, cannot be preceded by a preposition, and cannot be coordinated. In that respect, *que* and *do* are strikingly similar to pronominal clitics like *le* and *y*, which share the same properties.[25]

Let us take this similarity seriously and say that *que* and *do*, like *le* and *y*, are indeed clitics; we now expect them to behave as other clitics do, hence to be attracted to a (wh-specific) IP-internal clitic projection. Once they have "cliticized," they should only move to higher targets as clitics—namely, as *heads*—just like their pronominal counterparts (cf. Sportiche 1996). If this occurs, Travis's (1984) head movement constraint, or some minimalist version thereof, should block movement of *que* and *do* to their wh-disjunction targets in left periphery if other heads stand in the way. It is in this light, we believe, that (40a)–(41a) should be looked at: *selon toi* and *seconde tu* are in the specifier position of a head position in the CP field standing between the clitic projection in which *que* and *do* are standing and their ultimate target, the high disjunction position discussed in the previous section; this blocks movement and causes the derivation to crash.

Of course, wh-clitics differ crucially from their pronominal counterparts in that they can be separated from their input position by any number of sentence boundaries, as (42) illustrates:

(42)   Qu'as-tu dit que Marie pensait que Jacques dirait que Paul avait fait?
       (What have you said that Marie thought that Jacques would say that Paul had done?)

Romance pronominal clitics like *le* and *y* can cross over only a very limited set of cyclic nodes in restructuring contexts, as in the "clitic climbing" cases discussed in, for instance, Rizzi (1976) and Cinque (2004). This major difference arguably follows from the fact that wh-clitics, like other bare wh-words, enter the numeration as the complex wh-phrase in (43):

(43)   a. <que, O>

       b. <do, O>

Clitic *que* and *do* have a high (see previous section) disjunction feature to check in Op2P while "O" is the nonlexical existential quantifier discussed in section 3. In sentences like (42), the complex in (43a) is merged in the object position of *faire* and moves cyclically as a whole to the various (noninterrogative) slots in the Comp domains of the declaratives embedded under *dirait*, *pensait*, and *dit*. If pronominal clitics have no such landing site in CP, the essential clause-boundedness of clitic movement in Romance follows.

From its position in the Comp area, the null existential quantifier "O" in (43) moves on to the Op1P in the left periphery of the root question for checking purposes; clitic *que* must in addition adjoin to a clitic position within IP. In SCLI sentences like (42) we know that I(P)[26] itself is attracted to an intermediate layer of the left periphery, ForceP, and it can therefore "drag along" clitic *que*, just as negative and pronominal clitics are pied piped in SCLI sentences like (44):

(44)   Ne le lui as-tu pas donné?
       (neg it to him have you not given?)

From its new position in (the specifier of) Force, *que* can then move as a head to the disjunction position Op2P; if no intervening head blocks *que*'s final movement, a converging derivation will obtain, as in (42) and simpler cases, as in (45):

(45)   Qu'as-tu dit?
       (What have you said?)

(46)   Input: $[_{IP}$ tu as dit [que, O]]
       a. Clitic *que* to Wh clitic phrase within IP $\Rightarrow$
          $[_{IP}$ tu $[_{CIP}$ que$_i$ [as] dit $[t_i, O]]$

       b. Merge T(op) and IP and attract participle phrase to Spec TopP $\Rightarrow$
          $[_{TopP}$ [dit $[t_i, O]]_j$ Top$^0[_{IP}$ tu$[_{CIP}$ que$_i$ [as]$t_j]]$

       c. Merge Op1^0 and TopP and attract O to spec OP1P $\Rightarrow$
          $[_{Op1P}$ O$_k$ Op1$[_{TopP}$ [dit$[t_i, t_k]]_j$ Top$^0[_{IP}$ tu $[_{CIP}$ que$_i$ [as] t$_j$]]]$

       d. Merge G(round) and attract *tu* to Spec GP $\Rightarrow$
          $[_{GP}$ tu$_l$ G^0 $[_{Op1P}$ O$_k$ OP1[TopP [dit $[t_i, t_k]]_j$ Top$^0[_{IP}$ t$_l$ $[_{CIP}$ que$_i$ [as] t$_j$]]]$

       d.' Merge Force and GP and attract Remnant IP to Spec Force $\Rightarrow$
          $[_{ForceP}$ $[_{IP}$ t$_l$ $[_{CIP}$ que$_i$ [as] t$_j$]]_m$ Force^0 $[_{GP}$ tu$_l$ G^0 $[_{Op1P}$ O$_k$ Op1$[_{TopP}$ [dit $[t_i, t_k]]_j$ Top^0 t$_m$]]]$

       e. Merge Op2 and ForceP and attract *que* to Op2P $\Rightarrow$
          $[_{Op2P}$ que$_i$ Op2^0 $[_{ForceP}$ $[_{IP}$ t$_l$ $[_{CIP}$ t$_i$ [as] t$_j$]]_m$ Force^0 $[_{GP}$ tu$_l$ G^0 $[_{Op1p}$ O$_k$ Op1 $[_{TopP}$ [dit $[t_i, t_k]]_j$ Top^0 t$_m$]]]$

A stylistic inversion sentence like (47), in addition to the computations argued for at length in Kayne and Pollock (2001), also involves *que* cliticization and pied-piping of *que* to the Force layer of the left periphery, as shown in (48):

(47)   Qu'a fait Marie?
       (What has done Marie?)

(48) Input [$_{IP}$ Marie a fait [que, O]]

    a. Attract *que* to Wh-clitic phrase within IP ⇒

       [$_{IP}$ Marie que$_i$ a fait [t$_i$, O]]

    b. Merge Op1 and IP and attract O to Op1P ⇒

       [$_{Op1P}$ O$_j$ Op1 [$_{IP}$ Marie [que$_i$ [a fait [t$_i$, t$_j$]]]

    c. Merge T(op) and Op1P and attract *Marie* to Spec Top ⇒

       [$_{TopP}$ Marie$_k$ Top^0 [$_{Op1p}$ O$_j$ Op1 [$_{IP}$ t$_k$ [que$_i$ [a fait [t$_i$, t$_j$]]]]

    d. Merge G(round) and TopP and attract the participle phrase *fait* to GroundP ⇒

       [$_{GP}$ fait$_k$ G[$_{TopP}$ Marie$_k$ Top^0 [$_{Op1P}$ O$_j$ Op1 [$_{IP}$ t$_k$ [que$_i$ [a t$_1$ [t$_i$, t$_j$]]]]]

    e. Merge Force and GP and attract remnant IP to Spec Force ⇒

       [$_{ForceP}$ [$_{IP}$ t$_k$ [que$_i$ [a t$_1$ [t$_i$, t$_j$]]]$_m$ Force^0 [$_{GP}$ fait$_k$ G^0[$_{TopP}$ Marie$_k$ Top^0 [$_{Op1P}$ O$_j$ Op1t$_m$]

    f. Merge Op2P and ForceP and attract *que* to Force ⇒

       [$_{Op2P}$ que$_i$+Op2^0[$_{ForceP}$ [$_{IP}$ t$_k$ [t$_i$ [a t$_1$ [t$_i$, t$_j$]]]$_m$ Force^0 [$_{GP}$ fait$_k$ G^0[$_{TopP}$ Marie$_k$ Top^0 [$_{Op1P}$ O$_j$ Op1t$_m$]

We are now in a position to tackle the other properties of French *que* that single it out from *qui*, *quand*, *où*, and *comment*; compare, for example, (49) and (50):

(49) a. *Qu'il a vu?
      (What he has seen?)

    b. *Que Pierre a-t-il vu?
      (What Pierre has he seen?)

    c. *Il a vu que?
      (He saw what?)

    d. *Qu'a éberlué Jean?
      (What has stunned Jean?)

(50) a. Qu il a vu?
      (Who he has seen?)

    b. Qui Pierre a-t-il vu?'
      (Who Pierre has he seen?)

    c. Il a vu qui?
      (He has seen who?)

d. Qui a éberlué Jean?
   (Who has stunned Jean?)

Examples (49a) versus (50a) shows that *que*, unlike *qui*, requires SCLI; in our perspective, this follows from the clitic nature of *que*: if (Remnant) IP to Force does not take place, *que* is left to its own devices to check the high disjunction feature in Op2P, but that would require it to cross over the I^0 head in (the specifier of) which *il* is standing, as well as, at least, the low Op1 head to which the null existential quantifier O has moved. This will prevent *que* from checking its disjunction feature, whence the unacceptability of (49a); everything else being equal, the fact that *qui* in (50a) is *not* a clitic head allows the corresponding derivation to converge.

Essentially the same account goes through for the Complex Inversion cases in (49b) versus (50b). Here, too, the wh-word has to cross over at least the head in the specifier of which *Pierre* is standing. The clitic nature of *que* makes that impossible, but *qui* is not affected, whence the contrast.[27] Similarly, whatever analysis one may suggest for 'in situ' wh-questions like (49c) and (50c),[28] one thing is clear: *que* is not in a clitic position, which is enough to exclude them.[29]

Finally the striking pair in (49d) versus (50d) shows that *que*, unlike *qui*, cannot be extracted from subject position; this again follows from our version[30] of the idea that *que* is a clitic. For one thing, its input position in Spec IP is too "high" for it to move to a cliticization site since this would require lowering— that is, movement to a non-c-commanding position. In addition, even if it did somehow cliticize to some IP internal clitic position, *que* would still fail to get a free ride to ForceP because, as is well known, no SCLI/Subject Aux Inversion may take place in subject extraction cases (cf., e.g., *Who did see Mary?*). As a consequence, *que* would still have to cross over at least the low $Op1^0$ in the left periphery, which it can't do; on the other hand, *qui* in (50d) is not a clitic, so it does not violate (any minimalist version of) the head to head constraint in its displacement, whence the contrast.

In sum, this section has adopted a fairly literal execution of the idea that French *que*, like San Michele *do*, is a (wh-)clitic; if this is true, *que* can reach its (high) target position in the CP field only if it can get a "free ride" to the Force layer via I(P) to Force(P).[31] Among other properties, this allows for an explanation of the ban on *que* extraction from subject position. It is worth noting that although our analysis of *que* supports the traditional intuition that *que* is a clitic wh-word, contra some of Obenauer's early work (e.g., 1976), which analyzed it as a complementizer, it also integrates and generalizes to all bare wh-words one major aspect of his analysis of interrogative *que*: namely, the idea that *que* questions make crucial use of a null operator moving to the left periphery. This is the part our (null) existential quantifier plays in the derivations we have suggested for *all* bare wh-word questions.

5 WH-EST-CE QUESTIONS, SUBJECT EXTRACTION, AND NEGATION IN NE ROMANCE

5.1 French

The chief ingredients needed to make sense of pairs like (51a) versus (51c) in French have now been introduced:

(51)   a.   *Que {est tombé, a surpris Marie, est arrivé}?
             (What {is fallen, has surprised Marie, is happened}?)

        b.   Que dis-tu qui {est tombé, a surpris Marie, est arrivé}?
             (What do you say that+i is fallen, has surprised Marie, is happened?)

        c.   Qu'est-ce qui {est tombé, a surpris Marie, est arrivé}?
             (What is it that+i {is fallen, has surprised Marie, is happened}?)

In fact, we already know why (51a) is excluded: there cannot be any clitic position for subject *que* in the left periphery of a root question, nor is there an accessible one within IP, since that would require lowering subject *que* to a non-c-commanding IP, internal clitic layer. Even assuming *que* did somehow cliticize within IP via "sideward" movement, it would still fail to reach its target in the high Op2P because, as a clitic head, it couldn't cross over to $Op1^0$ and $force^0$ heads of the left periphery. In sum, there's no way (51a) can be generated.

The acceptability of (51b) in fact demonstrates that what bans (51a) is not extraction from subject position per se but, rather, the fact that a clitic wh-word extracted from the subject position of a root sentence does not have a proper cliticization site to its left. In (51b), however, the matrix clause *tu dis* provides one; therefore, upon further I(P) movement to the left periphery, clitic *que* in (51b) will get a free ride to a position adjacent to its target, whence pairs like (51a) versus (51b).

Now, evidently, French needs to express the perfectly fine meaning associated with (51a); clearly, "est+ce (que)" in (51c) must allow it to do so at a minimal cost; we claim that it does in a way that resembles what obtains in (51b), by providing within the left periphery a licit cliticization site for *que*.

To turn that guiding intuition into a real analysis, let us begin by investigating the structure of "est+ce (que)" in (51c). Related things occur elsewhere in French, in (52), for example, whose input structure is (53):

(52)   Pierre est {cela, là}.
       (Pierre is {this, there})

(53)   [$_{CopP}$ est [$_{SC}$ Pierre {cela, là}]]

Cela and *là* are the demonstrative and locative predicates of a small clause em-
bedded under the copula *est*, forming a Copulative Phrase;[32] I⁰ then merges with
CopP, and *Pierre* and *est* move to Spec IP and I⁰, respectively, deriving (52).
Consider (54) now:

(54)   a.   [$_{CopP}$ est [$_{SC}$ <que, O> ce]]

       b.   %Qu'est-ce?
            (What is this/it?)

       c.   *Qu'est la?
            (What is it?)

Example (54a) differs from (53) only in having disjunctive *que* and its associate
null existential quantifier in the subject position of the small clause whose predicate is *ce*. In Middle and classical French, this ultimately yielded well-formed
questions like (54b, c)—(54b), unlike (54c), is preserved as an archaic-sounding
joke (whence the "%") in the speech of some Modern French speakers—after
merger of I⁰ and merger of, and attraction to, Op1P and Op2P. In earlier stages,
this was allowed because *que* had not yet been obligatorily analyzed as a clitic,
and it could thus cross over the Op1P head without violating any locality constraint; (54b) thus had the status of the perfectly ordinary (55b, c), which are
arguably derived in the same manner from (55a):

(55)   a.   [$_{CopP}$ est [$_{SC}$ <qui, O> {ce, là}]]

       b.   Qui est-ce?
            (Who is this/he?)

       c.   Qui est là?
            (Who is it?)

Suppose now we allowed a structure closely related to (54a) to merge in the
Specifier of interrogative Force in the left periphery of questions; if this were so,
Modern French clitic *que* would be able to reach its Op2P target without crossing
over the Op1 head since it would be first merged *above* Op1. Let us indeed take
that tack and suggest that one of the possible realizations of the left periphery of
questions in Modern French is (56):

(56) $[_{\text{ForceP}} [_{\text{CopP}} \text{ est } [_{\text{SC}} \text{ que ce}]] \text{ F}^0[_{\text{Op1P}} \text{ O}_i \text{ que}] [_{\text{IP}} \text{ t}_i \text{ (i) } [_{\text{vP}} \text{ t}_i \text{ V (DP)}]]]$

In (56) the *clitic* disjunction operator *que* is merged in the subject position of the SC whose predicate is *ce*. Let us say further that CopP is a possible cliticization site for *que*: this simply extends to our Wh-clitic phrase what is true of pronominal clitics, as shown by sentences like *Jean l'est* (Jean it is). Once merged with CopP, that Wh-clitic layer will attract *que* from its SC subject position and check its clitic feature, as it must. So (56), *qua* VP, provides a cliticization site for *que* within the left periphery of a root clause, as required; further merging of Op2⁰ will allow *que* to move (string vacuously) to its target to check its wh-disjunctive feature. This will yield the parses in (57):

(57) a. $[_{\text{ForceP}} [_{\text{CLP}} \text{ que}_i [_{\text{CopP}} \text{ est } [_{\text{SC}} \text{ t}_i \text{ ce}]]]] \text{ F}^0[_{\text{Op1P}} \text{ O}_i \text{ que}] [_{\text{IP}} \text{ t}_i \text{ i } [_{\text{vP}} \text{ t}_i \text{ tombe}]]$

   b. $[_{\text{Op2P}} \text{ que}_i \text{ Op2}^0[_{\text{ForceP}} [_{\text{CLP}} \text{ t}_i [_{\text{CopP}} \text{ est } [_{\text{SC}} \text{ t}_i \text{ ce}]]]] \text{ F}^0[_{\text{Op1P}} \text{ O}_i \text{ que}] [_{\text{IP}} \text{ t}_i \text{ i } [_{\text{vP}}$
   $\text{t}_i \text{ tombe}]]]$

Example (57b) obeys all the requirements on the left periphery of questions identified so far: the low Op1P hosts an existential operator, as it must. "O" has moved from the specifier of vP, via the spec IP position, whose head "i" cliticizes at PF on the "complementizer" *que*, the head of Op1P.[33] The disjunction clitic operator *que* itself has moved from the SC subject position to its cliticization site and from there to Op2P locally, without crossing over any intervening head, and it can therefore check its disjunction feature. Example (57b) thus converges and yields the fine sentences in (51b)—*Qu'est-ce qui {tombe, surprend Marie, arrive}?*—although, as we have already seen, adding an intervening parenthetical (head) between ForceP and Op2P blocks movement of *que* and, hence, yields ungrammatical sentences like **Que, à ton avis, est-ce qui {tombe, surprend Marie, arrive}?*

Several aspects of (56)–(57) require immediate comment.

First, these structures and derivations claim that *ce* in Modern French Wh-est-ce Q is a "living fossil," the demonstrative predicate of Old and Middle French V2 assertions like *Ce suis je* ('this am I'), *ce es tu* ('this are you'), and *ce sommes nous* ('this are we'). (See, e.g., Foulet 1974: 331–332, Zink 1997: 156–171, Pollock 1983.) The "fossil" *ce* is also alive and kicking in phrases like *sur ce* (whereupon). Note that (56)–(57) say that the Wh+est+ce sequence does *not* result from any form of subject/verb inversion; living fossil *ce* should not be confused with the Modern French nominative clitic *ce* of, say, *c'est bien* 'that's fine, *c'est lui* 'that's him' and *c'est moi* 'that's me' whose nonclitic version is *cela*, used in all contexts except the subject position of *être*. As we shall see in the next section, it is nominative *ce* that occurs in real clefts like *C'est Paul qui est venu*, and the questions these can yield do involve subject clitic inversion. In the rest of this section, we do not take a stand as to whether the Wh-est+ce Q at work in the NIDs is of the former or latter type; we come back to that question in section 6.2.

Second, section 4 treated *que* as well as *qui, quand, où, comment,* and *pourquoi* and the null existential quantifier O as making up complex lexical items; compare (44a) and (55a). Their two subparts, the existential quantifier and the disjunction operator, were therefore merged as a unit in a single argument position, although each moved independently to its own target in the Comp domain, as in (54) and (55). Then (56)–(57) claim that this can be relaxed and that the two elements, though obligatorily present in the numeration of bare wh-questions, can be first merged in two different positions: the null existential quantifier O is merged in argument position, and the (clitic) disjunction operator *que* is merged as the subject of the SC embedded under *être* in ForceP. In short, *que* and O form a discontinuous lexical item, a chain, as their coindexation in (56) indicates informally. Note that coindexation is introduced only for readability's sake since it follows from the (universal) definition of bare wh-questions adopted previously, namely, an existential quantifier in the scope of the disjunction operator.

Third, (56)–(57) say that such questions are monoclausal and thus raise the obvious question of what it is that allows a copulative phrase and its small clause complement to merge and stay in ForceP. We shall hold it in abeyance till section 6. What we do in the remainder of section 5, rather, is show that the strategy at work in (56)–(57) is a general one; in Modern French, it is restricted neither to (subject) *que* nor to subject extraction:

(58) a. Qui est-ce qui est tombé?
          (Who is it that+i is fallen?)

      b. Qu'est-ce que Paul a raconté?
          (What is it that Paul has said?)

      c. Où est-ce que Pierre a passé ses vacances?
          (Where is it that Pierre has spent his holidays?)

      d. Quand est-ce que tu pars?
          (When is it that you're going?)

      e. Pourquoi est-ce qu'il a dit ça?
          (Why is it that he has said that?)

All such are amenable to a very similar analysis. They differ from the simpler (59),

(59) a. Qui est tombé?
          (Who is fallen?)

b. *Que Paul a-t-il raconté?
(What Paul has said?)

c. Où Pierre a-t-il passé ses vacances?
(Where Pierre has he spent his holidays?)

d. Quand pars-tu?
(When go you?)

e. Pourquoi a-t-il dit ça?
(Why has he said that?)

in having "split" the lexical entry of the various bare wh-words into a null existential quantifier merged in argument (or adjunct) position—ultimately attracted to Op1P—and a lexical item spelling out the disjunction operator and its various ranges of variation; *que, qui, où, quand, comment,* and even *pourquoi* are all merged in the subject position of the SC under *être* in Spec F⁰ despite the fact that except for *que* none of these is a clitic (cf., e.g., the perfectly fine *Où, a ton avis, est-ce que Pierre a passé ses vacances? Pourquoi, à ton avis, est-ce qu'il a dit cela?*). This is expected since the Copulative phrase merged in Spec Force can, but need not, be merged with a clitic phrase at a later stage.

5.2 Northern Italian Dialects

Some important features of this analysis carry over to Northern Veneto and East Lombard dialects and explain puzzling properties of wh-questions in those languages as well. Starting with Northern Veneto, we begin with Munaro's (1999) observation that all varieties disallow "simple" subject extractions, which obligatorily come out as (61):³⁴

(60) a. *Che te disturba?
(What disturbs you?)

b. *Chi laora de pì?
(Who works the most?)

c. *Chi à magnà la torta?
(Who has eaten the cake?)

(61) a. É-lo che che te disturba?
(Is-*lo* what that disturbs you? = What is it that disturbs you?)

    b. É-lo chi che laora di pì?
       (Is-*lo* who that works the most?)

    c. É-lo chi che à magnà la torta?
       (Is-*lo* who that has eaten the cake?)

Section 3 argued that (61) and the like contain a null disjunction operator standing to the left of *élo* in Op2P; this is reinforced by the fact that in Agordino and more systematically in the Valbelluna varieties, (61) can either surface (as shown) or have their wh-word in initial position; in those dialects (62a) and (62b) alternate:

(62)   Agordino:
    a. Chi é-lo che porta al pan?
       (Who is-*lo* that is carrying the bread?)

    b. É-lo chi che porta al pan?
       (Is-*lo* who that is carrying the bread?)

As before, we hold that *chi* in (62a) is the spell-out of the disjunction operator, just like the topmost *qui* in French questions like (63):

(63)   Qui est-ce qui porte le pain?
      (Who is it that+i is carrying the bread?)

In (62b), in contrast, *chi* is the existential quantifier, and it is standing in the low existential position Op1P. In assuming a nonlexical disjunction operator is present in (61), we simply extend to (Wh-)est-ce Q the conclusion we adopted for (64) in Bellunese:

(64)   a. A-tu magnà che?
       (Have you eaten what?)

    b. Sé-tu 'ndat andé?
       (Are you gone where?)

If the left periphery of (NE) Romance is invariant, a null disjunction operator in (64) must have been attracted to Op2P.[35] Why should that be impossible in (60)? (60) versus (64) must, we believe, be seen in the light of pairs like (65) in French:

(65)   a. Qu'as-tu mangé?
       (What have you eaten?)

    b. *Que te dérange?
      (What disturbs you?)

This desirable generalization can be expressed very simply if we posit that the disjunction operator of Northern Veneto is a (null) clitic just like French *que*; since wh-clitics, null or lexical, can reach their high Op2P target only if they can get a free ride via SCLI, and since no SCLI is possible in subject extraction— recall *Who did disturb you?*—the disjunction feature cannot have been checked in (60), whence its ungrammaticality; since SCLI has on the contrary applied in (64), Bellunese null *que* has reached its target without violating the constraint that regulates head movement.

    This predicts that if some cases of subject extraction allowed for SCLI, the "simple" (64) should coexist with its '(Wh)-est-ce-Q' analog. As (66) and (67) show, French and Northern Veneto meet our expectations:

(66)   a. Qu'est-il arrivé?
       (What is it happened?)

       b. Qu'est-ce qui est arrivé?
        (What is it that is happened?)

(67)   a. Vien-lo chi?
       (Comes-*lo* who?)

       b. É-lo chi che vien?
        (Is-*lo* who that comes?)

    In (66a)–(67a), SCLI has applied because the unaccusative verb allows its argument to stay 'low' in the vP. When this obtains, converging derivations like (68) yield fine sentences:[36]

(68)   Input [{il, lo} [{arrive, vien} {<que, ø>, <ø, chi>}]
     a. Cliticize {que, ø} $\Rightarrow$
       [$_{IP}$ {il, lo} [{que, ø}$_i$[{arrive, vien} {<t$_i$, ø>, <t$_i$, chi>}]]]

     b. Merge Op1^0 and IP and attract {ø, chi} to Spec Op1P $\Rightarrow$
       [$_{Op1P}$ {ø, chi}$_j$ Op1^0 [$_{IP}${il, lo} {que, ø}$_i$ {arrive, vien} {<$_i$, t$_j$>, <t$_i$, t$_j$>}]]]

     c. Move {il, lo} to G(round)P $\Rightarrow$
       [$_{GP}$ {il, lo}$_k$ G^0[$_{Op1P}$ {ø, chi}$_j$ Op1^0 [$_{IP}$ t$_k${que, ø}$_i${arrive, vien} {<t$_i$, t$_j$>, <t$_i$, t$_j$>}]]]]

d. SCLI (i.e. Remnant IP Movement to ForceP) $\Rightarrow$

[$_{ForceP}$ [$_{IP}$ t$_k$ {que, ø}$_i${arrive, vien} {<t$_i$, t$_j$>}]$_1$ Force^0[$_{GP}$ {il, lo} $_k$ G^0[$_{Op1P}$ {ø, chi}$_j$ Op1^0 t$_1$]]

e. Merge Op2^0 and ForceP and attract clitics {que, ø} $_i$ to Op2P $\Rightarrow$

[$_{Op2P}$ {que, ø}$_i$ Op2^0[$_{ForceP}$ [$_{IP}$ t$_k$ t$_i$ {arrive, vien} {<t$_i$, t $_j$ >, <t$_i$, t$_j$>}]$_1$ Force^0[$_{GP}$ {il, lo{$_k$ G^0[$_{Op1P}$ {ø, chi} $_j$ Op1^0 t$_1$]] $\Rightarrow$ Qu'arrive-t-il?, vien-lo chi?

If the subject of the inaccusatives *arrive* and *vien* is attracted to Spec IP, however, speakers must fall back on Wh-est-ce Q derivations like (57) since no local (head-to-head) movement of the clitics *que* or *ø* from Spec IP can reach Op2P without incorrectly crossing over at least the lexical subjects *il* and *lo* and the Op1^0 head in the left periphery.

Eastern Lombard dialects provide additional support for the idea that the null disjunction operator of Northern Veneto is a clitic, like French *que*. The dialects spoken in the northern part of Valle Camonica differ from the southern ones in having a weak form of *kwe* (what) and *chi, ch'*, in precopula position; sentences like (69) can thus surface as (70) in the North:

(69) a. É-l chi che porta al pan?
         (Is-l who that brings the bread?)

      b. É-l chi ch'è 'nda a ca?
         (Is-l who that is gone home?)

(70) a. Ch'é-l chi che porta al pan?
         (wh is-l who that brings the bread?)

      b. Ch'é-l chi ch'è 'nda a ca?
         (wh is-l who that is gone home?)

Examples (69) and (70) are used obligatorily when questioning a subject, as in the Northern Veneto cases just discussed, but *Ch'* in (70) wears its weak nature on its sleeves, which makes our hypothesis that (69), (67), and (61) have null clitic wh-words in Op2P all the more plausible. Just as the corresponding structures in Northern Veneto, (69) and (70) can, but need not, be used to question objects, as in (71), which alternate with the "simpler" (72):

(71) a. (Ch')è-l chi che te'ncuntret semper?
         (Wh) is-l who that you meet always?)

      b. (Ch')è-l chi che ò desmentegà?
         (Wh-) is-l who that (I) have forgotten?)

(72)   a. (Ch') 'ncuntre-t chi semper?
       (Wh-) meet-you who always?)

       b. (Ch') ò-i desmentegà chi?
       (Wh-) have I forgotten who?)

Just as in Northern Veneto and French, unaccusative cases like (66) and (67), the North and South Valle Camonica dialects can use the "simpler" questions in (73):

(73)   a. Ch'é-l vignì chi?
       ('Wh-is-l come who?)

       b. É-l vignì chi?
       (Is-l come who?)

5.3 French versus the NIDs

Having solved the first half of puzzle A in the introduction, we now briefly discuss the second half, which (74) will bring back to the reader's mind:

(74)   a. Que n'as-tu pas préparé?
       (What haven't you prepared?)

       b. Qu'est-ce que tu n'as pas préparé?
       (What is it that you haven't prepared?)

       c. *No à-tu parecià che?
       (*no* have you prepared what? = What haven't you prepared?)

       d. É-lo che che no te-à parecià?
       (Is-it what that *no* you have prepared?

Example (74) shows that Northern Veneto[37] requires (Wh-) est-ce Q when the input sentence is negative, while French allows both the simple wh-question (74a) and Wh-est-ce Q (74b). Note it is not just bare wh-words that simple negative interrogatives like (74c) exclude; (75) does not have well-formed *questions* either, and they are acceptable only as exclamatives, unlike (76), which can be both:

(75)   a. Con che tosat no à-tu parlà!
       (With what boy hasn't he spoken!)

570 THE OXFORD HANDBOOK OF COMPARATIVE SYNTAX

b. Quanti libri no à-lo ledest!
(How many books hasn't he read!)

(76) a. Avec quel garçon n'as-tu pas parlé?
(With what boy haven't you spoken?)

b. Combien de livres n'a-t-il pas lu?
(How many books hasn't he read?)

Only (77) can render the meaning of (76), although (78) does translate as (79):

(77) a. Con che tosat é-lo che no t'à parlà?
(With what boy is-*lo* that not you have spoken?)

b. Quanti libri é-lo che no l'à ledest?
(How many books it-*lo* that not he has read?)

(78) a. Avec quel garçon as-tu parlé?
(With what boy have you spoken?)

b. Combien de livres a-t-il lu?
(How many books has he read?)

(79) a. Con che tosat à-tu parlà?
(With what boy have you spoken?)

b. Quanti libri à-lo ledest?
(How many books has-*lo* read?)

The fact that (75) has ill-formed questions is enough to show that any account of (74c) relying on the clitic nature of the null *que* present in such sentences would be insufficiently general. Zanuttini (1997: 40–59) offers an elegant solution to our puzzle; it relies on her well-supported claim that negation in French and Northern Veneto do not stand in the same layer of the IP domain. In Northern Veneto, *no* is merged "high," say, in a NegP taking IP as its complement, while *ne pas* in French is merged within IP, maybe as the low NegP discussed in Pollock (1989: sec. 6.3) and Zanuttini (1997), whose head *ne* cliticizes to an IP internal projection above the other pronominal clitic projections and the finite verb.

As a consequence, on the Remnant movement derivations for SCLI adopted previously (cf., e.g., (68)), Northern Veneto negative inputs like (80) will yield the much simplified parses in (81),

(80) a. [$_{\text{NegP}}$no [$_{\text{IP}}$ tu a parecia <ø che>]] ⇒ *No à-tu parecià che? (= (73c))

     b. [$_{\text{NegP}}$ no [$_{\text{IP}}$ tu a parlà con che tosat]] ⇒ *Con che tosat no a-tu parlà? (= (74a))

(81) a. [$_{\text{Op2P}}$ ø Op2^0[$_{\text{ForceP}}$ [$_{\text{NegP}}$ no a]$_i$ Force^0[$_{\text{GP}}$ tu G^0[$_{\text{TopP}}$ [parecià] [$_{\text{Op1P}}$ che Op1^0 t$_i$]]]

     b. [$_{\text{Op2P}}$ Con che tosat Op2^0[$_{\text{ForceP}}$ [$_{\text{NegP}}$ no a]$_i$ Force^0 [$_{\text{GP}}$ tu G^0 [$_{\text{TopP}}$[parlà] Top^0] t$_i$]]]

in which the (remnant) NegP *no a* in Spec Force *cannot* check the interrogative force feature it should check, as Zanuttini (1997: 47) already argued.[38] Adopting the Wh-est-ce Q strategy, on the other hand, will result in copula+lo in Spec Force, which is fine, whence pairs like (75) versus (77). The Northern Veneto versus French contrasts follow as well: since *ne* is a (clitic) subconstituent of the (remnant) IP *n'a*, nothing blocks the checking of interrogative Force and (83) converges:

(82) Avec quel garçon n'as-tu pas parlé? (= (75a))

(83) [$_{\text{Op2P}}$ Avec quel garçon Op2^0[$_{\text{ForceP}}$ [$_{\text{IP}}$ n'a]$_i$ Force^0[$_{\text{GP}}$ tu G^0 [$_{\text{TopP}}$ [pas parlé] Top^0] t$_i$]]]

In sum, we have shown in this section that the obligatory uses of (Wh-) est-ce Q in French, Northern Veneto, and East Lombard follow from:

1. The invariant structure of the left periphery of (NE) Romance which contains two checking positions for bare wh-words: a "low" existential quantifier position and a "high" disjunction operator position
2. The clitic nature of some disjunction operators, in particular, French *que* and its null analogs in Northern Veneto and East Lombard
3. Parameter (34A)—that is, in L the disjunction operator is or is not spelled out at PF
4. Zanuttini's (1997) parameter,—that is, NegP is merged high or low in the IP domain
5. The fact that the computations yielding SCLI in NE Romance drag along ((null) wh) clitics to a position from which they can reach their target without violating some suitably reformulated version of the Head-to-Head constraint.

Elsewhere 1, 2, and 4 have received ample empirical support; (5) is a fact that any theory of SCLI and CI must express; and 3 is added to the syntax and interpretation of questions (in Romance), but it capitalizes on a notion that seems to be of virtual conceptual necessity and that has been developed and supported independently.

6 On Subordination

6.1 French 'Wh-est-ce Q' and Pseudosubordination

Naturally, these results crucially hinge on the idea that merging a copulative phrase in Spec Force and leaving it there is an option of U(niversal) G(rammar). Our task is now to derive this surprising configuration of data from better understood properties of UG.

We approach the problem by taking a fresh look at the well-known root versus embedded asymmetries with which Romance and Germanic have made us familiar, such as (84):

(84)   a. Qui a-t-il vu?

    b. *Je ne sais plus qui a-t-il vu.

    c. Je ne sais plus qui il a vu.

    d. Who has he seen?

    e. *I don't remember who has he seen.

    f. I don't remember who he has seen.

The usual account goes something like this: all six sentences have a left periphery whose force layer contains an interrogative feature to be checked; in root clauses like (84a, d), Infl(P) movement to Force makes that possible because I(P) bears the appropriate [+Q] feature. Checking of the [+Q] Force under Specifier head agreement thus obtains, whence (84a, d). In embedded contexts, however, the matrix verb or predicate can in itself check the interrogative feature of the embedded interrogative, whence (84d, f).

These ideas can be formally implemented in representational theories if, in addition to Specifier head configurations, checking can be done via some form of (chain) government. In a derivational framework like the one we have been adopting here, however, this account is extremely problematic since it requires countercyclic checking under government into a lower domain (cf. Chomsky

2001). In addition, this is not only possible, an oddity in itself, but even *necessary*, since the perfectly ordinary cyclic movement that ensures appropriate checking in (84a, d) must be blocked if (84b, e) are to be excluded.

These problems arise because of the seldom challenged assumption that the matrix verb or predicate that "types" the subordinate clause as a question are merged high, as complements or specifers of some heads in the split matrix Infl. We now deny it and assume instead that they are merged in the Specifier of Force of the embedded clause; they will thus "type" Force and its IP complement as a question—in checking terms their selectional [+Q] feature will check [+Q] Force—in the usual Specifier head configuration;[39] such low merger will now also easily block Infl(P) attraction to Force in the proper "phase" on the standard view that merge is favored over move.

Of course, most selecting predicates must ultimately raise from the Force layer, because of various checking requirements their elements must meet: a finite V(P) must check its tense and agreement features against appropriate functional heads; its arguments must also check their case and EPP features, which require them to move to another dominating IP domain as well; so, almost invariably, other functional projections must be merged higher and attract the selecting predicate and its arguments, which must therefore vacate the specifier of interrogative Force and end up in various layers of an immediately dominating IP.[40]

Our claim is that the est+ce substring of Wh-est-ce Q does *not* move out of Force because *est* and *ce* are 'inert' and, hence, have no need for functional heads above the left periphery in which they occur. French has preserved that option instead of weeding it out because, for the last 500 years at least, it has reconciled *que*'s requirements as a disjunction operator and its morphosyntactic identity as a clitic. French also has genuine interrogative clefts, however, which exclude *que*, *pourquoi*, and *comment*; in those, both *être* and *ce do* vacate the Spec Force position to move to appropriate functional projections in the matrix IP.

Let us tease those two structures apart. The first point to make, with Ambar et al. (1986), is that in (85) the copula *être* can only surface in its present-tense form:

(85) a. Qu'est-ce que Paul lisait?
          (What is it that Paul was reading?)

      b. *Qu'était-ce que Paul lisait?
          (What was it that Paul was reading?)

      c. Pourquoi est-ce qu'il chantait?)
          (Why is it that he was singing?)

      d. *Pourquoi était-ce qu'il chantait?
          (Why was it that he was singing?)

e. Comment est-ce qu'il parlait?
(How is it that he spoke?)

f. *Comment était-ce qu'il parlait?
(How was it that he spoke?)

The same is not true of (86):

(86) a. Quel homme était/est-ce que Marie voulait rencontrer?
(What man was/is it that Marie wanted to meet?)

b. C'était/est quel homme que Marie voulait rencontrer?
(It was/is what man that Marie wanted to meet?)

c. C'était/est Jean qu'elle voulait rencontrer.
(It was/is Jean that she wanted to meet.)

As Obenauer (1981) observes, the questions in (86) are unambiguous cleft questions, just like their English glosses, and correspondingly *est* in (86) can appear in the "imparfait" tense form *était*.[41] The imparfait, then, can only be used in real cleft questions and (85b, d, e) show that it is incompatible with *que, pourquoi,* and *comment*; the reason *pourquoi* and *comment* are excluded is not specific to French since their counterparts are banned in English cleft questions as well, as shown by the fact that the glosses to (85d, e) are not felicitous if *how* and *why* are interpreted as modifiers of *sing* and *speak*.[42] As for the ungrammaticality of (85b), we evidently need to tie it to the clitic nature of *que*. We do so by asserting that an input structure like (87),

(87) $[_{IP}ce_j \ [_{I°} \ \hat{e}tre_i \ I° \ [C_{CoPP}t_i \ [_{SC}t_j \ que]]] \dots$

which would yield (88a),

(88) a. *C'était que (que Paul lisait)?
(It was what that Paul was reading?)

b. C'était quoi (que Paul lisait)?

is excluded for the same reason (89a) is,

(89) a. *C'est le.
(That is *le*.)

b. C'est lui.
(That is him.)

although, of course, merging nonclitic (wh-) forms like *quoi* and *lui* is fine in (88b) and (89b).

Suppose now, in line with the ideas about subordination just sketched, that cleft Copulative Phrases like (87) are first merged in Spec Force in a well-formed sentence like (86a). If so, at the relevant point in the derivation we have something like (90),

(90) $[_{ForceP} [_{CopP}$était $[_{SC}$ce quel homme]]$F^0 [_{Op1P}O_i$ que $[_{IP}$Marie voulait rencontrer $t_i]]]$

where Op1P is occupied by the null (definite) operator involved in (free) relatives; if nothing happens (90) will crash: *quel homme, ce,* and *était* have disjunction, EPP/case, and tense features to check, respectively; the relevant functional projections must therefore be merged, ultimately yielding a biclausal interrogative whose parse is (91):[43]

(91) $[_{Op2P}$ Quel homme$_j$ Op2P $[_{ForceP} [_{IP} t_k$ était $t_j]_1$ F^0 $[$ $[_{GrounP}$ ce$_k$ $G^0[_{TopP} [_{ForceP}$ $[_{CopP} t_j [_{SC} t_k t_j$ $]]$ O_j que $[_{IP}$ Marie voulait rencontrer t_j $]]]_i$ Top^0 $[_{IP}t_1t_i]]]]$

Going back to (85a, c, e) now, it must be the case that none of the elements in the noncleft copulative phrase merged in Spec Force in (92) needs to vacate its input position:

(92) $[_{ForceP} [_{CopP}$ est $[_{SC}$ que ce]]$F^0 [_{Op1P}$ O_i que$[_{IP}$ Marie voulait rencontrer $t_i]]]$

Why should that be so?

Ce is morphologically caseless and a predicate here, so that whatever case feature it may have or need, we shall say it is checked or assigned under specifier head agreement with its subject *que,* which binds the existential quantifier in OP1P. We have already made crucial use of the idea that CopP is further merged with a Wh-clitic phrase, and we now state explicitly that that clitic position allows for case checking of *que,* just as the pronominal clitic phrase checks the (objective) case of *le* in *Jean l'est.* Therefore, neither *que* nor *ce* requires the merging of higher functional projections for case checking or assignment purposes; as for the tense feature of *est,* we hold it is invisible because, as we saw before, the copula cannot alternate in tense or mood in these constructions: *est* is indeed "inert" tensewise. Finally, the third-person morphology of *est* we say is *default* morphology—that is, it instantiates a [0 person] feature—and we hold that default features are invisible at LF, hence in no need of checking or deleting. All the elements merged in the ForceP layer of (92) can therefore stay put.

Suppose, finally, that the Copulative Phrases in ForceP *may* check an interrogative feature; we know that it does not *have to* because in various regional dialects or sociolects it can also be merged in the Force layer of other types of finite (subordinate) clauses, as in the relatives and exclamatives in (93):[44]

(93) a. La ville où est-ce qu'il vit c'est Paris
          (The city where is that that he lives, it's Paris = 'The city where he lives is Paris'.)

      b. Qu'est-ce qu'il est grand!
          ('What is it that he is tall! = 'How tall he is'!)

Thus the copulative phrase in (92) may be [+Q]; therefore, it may—here, must—"type" the clause as a question. Op2P ultimately merges with force, and *que* is attracted there, yielding converging structures like (94),

(94) $[_{Op2P}$ que$_i$ Op2^0 $[_{ForceP}$ $[_{CLP}$ t$_i$ $[_{CopP}$ est [SC t$_i$ ce]]] F^0 $[_{Op1P}$ O$_i$ que $[_{IP}$ Marie voulait rencontrer t$_i$]]]

in which the disjunction feature of wh-questions has been checked by (clitic) *que*, the existential feature by the null existential operator in Op1P, and the [+Q] feature of Force^0 was checked upon merging with the Copulative Phrase.

In short, unlike (91), (94) is a monoclausal root wh-question, similar in that respect to simple SCLI sentences. What this is saying, then, is that est+ce in (94) and the like have been "reanalyzed," as many traditional grammarians claimed; in our terms, they have become mere (interrogative) force indicators, and "reanalysis" only means that, because *ce* and *est* have no functional features to check, they can remain in the position where all matrix predicates are merged: Spec, Force. If this is right, Wh-est-ce Q serves as an indirect probe into the structural configuration of interrogative subordination, and the sheer existence of noncleft Wh-est-ce Q in French offers interesting, if indirect, support for the derivational analysis of the data in (84) we started off with.

Let us now go back to questions like (95), which we know from the above are interrogative clefts because of the "imparfait" *était*:[45]

(95) À qui était-ce donc que tu avais promis ce livre?
      (To whom was it, then, that you had promised this book?)

Under the analysis just adopted, (95) is a SCLI sentence (cf. (92)), and it is therefore restricted to root contexts just like (96):[46]

(96) a. *Elle ne sait plus à qui était-ce donc que tu avais promis ce livre.
          (She *ne* knows no longer to whom was it then that you had promised this book.)

b. *Elle ne sais pas à qui avais-tu donc promis ce livre.
(She *ne* knows not to whom had you then promised this book.)

We in fact know why: the Force layer of the embedded interrogative has two specifiers, but there is only one interrogative Force feature to check, so one of the two specifiers will not "discharge" its [+Q] feature; moreover, there is no way the unique functional Tense projection merged later in the matrix IP can check the tense features of both *sais* and *avais*. If only for that reason, no converging derivation can yield (96) or other cases of SCLI like (97) (=(9)):[47]

(97) a. ?*Dis moi où est-elle allée.
(Tell me where is she gone.)

b. *Elle ne sait plus à qui avais-tu promis ce livre.
(She *ne* knows no longer to whom had you promised the book.)

c. *Max ne sait pas qui veulent-ils inviter
(Max *ne* know not who want they to invite.)

Let us now at long last go back to fine sentences like (98) (=(8)):

(98) a. Dis moi où est-ce qu'elle est allée.
(Tell me where is it that she is gone.)

b. Elle ne sait plus à qui est-ce que tu avais promis ce livre.
(She *ne* knows no longer to whom is it that you had promised the book.)

c. Max ne sait pas qui est-ce qu'ils veulent inviter.
(Max *ne* know not who is it that they want to invite.)

d. Je ne sais pas {qui, qu'} est-ce qui a surpris Marie.
(I *ne* know not {who, what} is it that has surprised Marie.)

We naturally tie their acceptability to the fact that *est* and *ce* do *not* have to be attracted to any functional layer in the matrix IP: Suppose—in partial disagreement with Kayne (1994)—that having multiple specifiers in the Force layer of embedded questions is not banned in and of itself but, rather, because it would mean that one or more of the selecting predicates merged there have their functional features unchecked. From that point of view, nothing excludes (98) since by hypothesis *est-ce* in the lower of the two specifier positions is functionally "inert" and so does not have any functional feature to check. If furthermore in such cases, the two specifiers of the embedded interrogative Force—*ne sais pas/ plus*, imperative *dis*, and the lower inert *est-ce*—do not compete for checking the

unique [+Q] Force, the derivations of (98) should converge; we already know
est-ce is only optionally [+Q], because of relatives and exclamatives like (93).
Therefore, our analysis of Wh-est-ce Q does permit the derivation of sentences
like (98), as it must.

6.2 Wh-est-ce Q in the NIDs

Before we move on to the remaining two problems with French Wh-est-ce Q, let
us briefly go back to the NIDs. Our section 5 analysis of the Northern Veneto
pairs in (99) and Eastern Lombard (100),

(99)   a. *Che te disturba?
            (What disturbs you?)

        b. *Chi laora de pì?
            (Who works the most?)

        c. *Chi à magnà la torta?
            (Who has eaten the cake?)

        d. É-lo che che te disturba?
            (Is-*lo* what that disturbs you?)

        e. É-lo chi che laora de pì?
            (Is-*lo* who that works the most?)

        f. É-lo chi che a magnà la torta?
            (Is-*lo* who that has eaten the cake?)

(100)   a. É-l chi che porta al pan?
            (Is-l who that brings the bread?)

        b. É-l chi ch'è 'nda a ca?
            (Is-l who that is gone home?)

        c. Ch'é-l chi che porta al pan?
            (wh is-l who that brings the bread?)

        d. Ch'é-l chi ch'è 'nda a ca?
            (wh is-l who that is gone home?)

rests on the following two claims:

   1. There is a (null) clitic disjunction operator in the leftmost Operator po-
      sition in *(Ch')É-l chi, É-lo che* strings.

2. No clitic element can be merged in the object position of a genuine cleft.

It follows that 'é+lo' and 'é+l' in Northern Veneto and Eastern Lombard (99)–(100) should have an input of the noncleft variety; (98–99a), for example, would start off as (101):

(101)   a. [$_{ForceP}$ [$_{CopP}$ é [$_{SC}$ ø$_i$ lo]]]F⁰ [$_{Op1P}$ che$_i$ che [$_{IP}$ t$_i$ te disturba]]]]

    b. [$_{ForceP}$ [$_{CopP}$é [$_{SC}$ Ch/;ø$_i$ l']]]F⁰ [$_{Op1P}$ chi$_i$ che[$_{IP}$ t$_i$ porta . . .]]]]

where *lo* and *l'* are predicates and the (null) clitic disjunction operators ø and *ch'* are merged in the subject position of the SC embedded under the copula and where the embedded clause is a free relative. In the best of all possible worlds, *lo* and *l'* in (101) would be of the same ilk as *ce*; this would receive some support if they were historically derived from a demonstrative, say, from *quello* in examples like (102), from the sixteenth-century Northern Veneto "Rime" by Cavassico (cf. Munaro 1999:87):

(102)   Chi è quel che vien?
    (Who is that one that comes?)

Although this may sound plausible, it is rather unlikely, in part because of eighteenth-century questions like (103), where *lo* and *la* cooccur with demonstratives:

(103)   a. Chi é-lo quel doen, che gnen in qua?
        (Who is-*lo* that young, that comes in here?)
        'Who is that young guy, who comes in here?' (Villabruna, "Fioretta," act 2, scene 1)

    b. Chi é-la quéla là entre che rit?
        (Who is-she that there inside that laughs?) (ibidem)
        'Who is the woman inside there, who is laughing?'

It seems, then, that North Veneto *lo* and *la* and Valle Camonica *l'* are indeed what they appear to be: pronominals. If this is correct, we must analyze them as predicates of the *le* type in French examples like *Il l'est* ('He it is'), except, of course, that they are morphologically nominative rather than accusative. If this is correct, there is no way for *lo* in (101) to check its nominative case feature within the ForceP layer proper; as a consequence, a c-commanding IP will have to merge with (101), and *lo* will be attracted to a nominative checking position, in a way that is reminiscent of inverse copulative sentences like *the cause of the riot is the painting*.

In short, the case feature of the predicative pronoun in (Wh-) est-ce Q constructions in the Northern Veneto and Eastern Lombard dialects prevents them from being "fossilized" the way they are in French. The further fact that in Modern North Veneto and East Lombard the copula in (Wh-) est-ce Q constructions inflects for tense, just as it did in earlier stages, makes that conclusion unavoidable:[48]

(104)   a.   . . . chi é-lo stà el prin che à més el mondo a la rason . . . ?
             (. . . who is-scl been the first that has put the world to the reason . . . ?)
             '. . . and who was the first that made the world see reason . . . ?' (Zuppani, "Sfogo de barba Toni," 1880)

        b.   . . . chi sarà-lo mai chél?
             (. . . who will-be-scl ever that?')
             '. . . whoever may that guy be?' (Anonymous, "L'orazion de la cros," 19th c.)

        c.   Chi sarà-lo che la fala?
             (Who is-scl that it misses?
             'Who will miss it?' (Zanella, "Poesie," 19th–20th c.)

        d.   Ére-lo chi che magna / à magnà la torta?
             (Is-scl who that eats / has eaten the cake?)

        d.   È-lo chi che magnéa / avéa magnà la torta?
             (Was-scl who that ate / had eaten the cake?)

        f.   Sarà-lo chi che magnarà / avarà magnà la torta?
             (Will-be-scl who that will-eat / will-have eaten the cake?)

We therefore expect *é-lo* structures to be banned in embedded contexts, which they indeed are, as the ungrammaticality of (105), the two possible Bellunese translations of French (98), repeated next, shows:

(98)   a.   Dis moi où est-ce qu'elle est allée.
             (Tell me where is it that she is gone.)

        b.   Elle ne sait plus à qui est-ce que tu avais promis ce livre.
             (She *ne* knows no longer to whom is it that you had promised the book.)

        c.   Max ne sait pas qui est-ce qu'ils veulent inviter.
             (Max *ne* know not who is it that they want to invite.)

(105)   a.   *Dime é-lo andé che la é 'ndada.

a'. *Dime andé é-lo che la é 'ndada.

b. *No la sa pì é-lo a chi che te ghe à proméss al libro.

b'. *No la sa pì a chi é-lo che te ghe à proméss al libro.

c. *Mario no'l sa chi élo che i ol invidar.

c'. *Mario no'l sa élo chi che i ol invidar.

This is a straightforward consequence of the fact that all of (105) are cases of SCLI, a configuration we know cannot obtain in embedded contexts (see prior discussion of (90)–(91)); the same facts and conclusion hold for East Lombard.

In sum, the only possible derivation of say, (104f), would go roughly as follows:

(106)   Input: $[_{ForceP} [_{CopP}$ sarà $[_{SC}$ ø$_i$ lo$]]]$ Force^0 $[_{Op1P}$ chi$_i$ che $[_{IP}$ t$_i$ magnarà la torta$]]]$

    a. Merge Infl, attract *lo* to Spec Infl and *sarà* to I^0 and cliticize ø $\Rightarrow$
       $[_{IP}$ lo$_k$ $[_{CLP}$ ø$_i$ $[$sarà$_j$ Infl^0 $[_{ForceP} [_{CopP}$ t$_j$ $[_{SC}$ t$_i$ t$_k]]]$ Force^0 $[_{Op1P}$ chi$_i$ che $[_{IP}$ t$_i$ magnarà la torta$]]]]]$

    b. Merge Top and attract the Remnant subordinate clause (i.e., ForceP) to Spec Top $\Rightarrow$
       $[_{TopP} [_{ForceP} [_{CopP}$ t$_j$ $[_{SC}$ t$_i$ t$_k]]]$ Force^0 $[_{Op1P}$ chi$_i$ che $[_{IP}$ t$_i$ magnarà la torta$]]]_1$ Top $[_{IP}$ lo$_k$ $[_{CLP}$ ø$_i$ $[$sarà$_j$ Infl^0 t$_1[[[$

    c. Merge G(round) and TopP and attract *lo* to Spec GP $\Rightarrow$
       $[_{GP}$ lo$_k$ Ground^0 $[_{TopP} [_{ForceP} [_{CopP}$ t$_j$ $[_{SC}$ t$_i$ t$_k]]]$ Force^0 $[_{Op1P}$ chi$_i$ che $[_{IP}$ t$_i$ magnarà la torta$]]]_1$ Top $[_{IP}$ t$_k$ $[$CLPø$_i$ $[$sarà$_j$ Infl^0 t$_1]]]]$

    d. Merge Force and GP and attract (Remnant) IP to Spec Force $\Rightarrow$
       $[_{ForceP}[_{IP}$ t$_k$ $[_{CLP}$ ø$_i$ $[$sarà$_j$ Infl^0 t$_1]]]]_m$ Force^0 $[_{GP}$ lo$_k$ Ground^0 $[_{TopP} [_{ForceP} [_{CopP}$ t$_j$ $[_{SC}$ t$_i$ t$_k]]]$ Force^0 $[_{Op1P}$ chi$_1$ che $[_{IP}$ t$_i$ magnarà la torta$]]]_1$ Top^0 t$_m]$

    e. Merge Op2P and attract the null clitic disjunction operator ø to Op2P $\Rightarrow$
       $[_{Op2P}$ ø$_i$ Op2P $[_{ForceP} [_{IP}$ t$_k$ $[_{CLP}$ ø$_i$ $[$sarà$_j$ Infl^0 t$_1]]]]_m$ Force^0 $[_{GP}$ lo$_k$ Ground^0 $[_{TopP} [_{ForceP} [_{CopP}$ t$_j$ $[_{SC}$ t$_i$ t$_k]]]_m$ Force^0 $[_{Op1P}$ chi$_i$ che $[_{IP}$ t$_i$ magnarà la torta$]_1$ Top^0 t$_m]]$
       $\Rightarrow$ *Sarà-lo chi che magnarà la torta?*

Clearly the biclausal (106) differs drastically from its French analogs (92)–(94), which remain monoclausal, because of the fossilized character of *est* and *ce*. Despite their different case features, Northern Veneto *lo*, East Lombard *l'*, and

French *ce* do share one important property: they can be either predicates or arguments. We have just illustrated the predicative use of *lo/l'*: as arguments they would be merged as subjects in the Copulative SC of a genuine cleft, and a wh-phrase would occupy the focus (object) position; only a restricted subset of wh-elements would qualify; the null clitic wh-word ø would be excluded for the same reason *que* was in the corresponding structures in French; the same is true of the weak or clitic *ch'* of East Lombard. Merging bare wh-words is arguably excluded as well: bare wh-words, recall, only have an existential feature to check; consider the derivation of a cleft like (107) in which bare *chi* is merged in the focus position of the cleft:

(107)   Input: [$_{ForceP}$ [$_{CopP}$ sarà [$_{SC}$ lo chi]]] Force^0 [$_{Op1P}$ O$_i$ che [$_{IP}$ t$_i$ magnarà la torta]]]

    a. Merge Infl, attract *lo* to Spec Infl and *sarà* to I^0 and case checking of *chi* $\Rightarrow$
      [$_{IP}$ lo$_k$ [sarà$_j$ Infl^0 chi$_k$ [$_{ForceP}$ [$_{CopP}$ t$_j$ [$_{SC}$ t$_i$ t$_k$]]] Force^0 [$_{Op1P}$ O$_i$ che [$_{IP}$ t$_i$ magnarà la torta]]]]]

    b. Merge Top and attract the Remnant free relative (i.e. ForceP) to Spec Top $\Rightarrow$
      [$_{TopP}$ [$_{ForceP}$ [$_{CopP}$ t$_j$ [$_{SC}$ t$_i$ t$_k$]]] Force^0 [$_{Op1P}$ O$_i$ che [$_{IP}$ t$_i$ magnarà la torta]]]$_1$ Top [$_{IP}$ lo$_k$ [sarà$_j$ Infl^0 chi$_k$ t$_1$]]]

    c. Merge G(round) and TopP and attract *lo* to Spec GP$\Rightarrow$
      [$_{GP}$ lo$_k$ Ground^0 [$_{TopP}$ [$_{ForceP}$ [$_{CopP}$ t$_j$ [$_{SC}$ t$_i$ t$_k$]]] Force^0 [$_{Op1P}$ O$_i$ che [$_{IP}$ t$_i$ magnarà la torta]]]$_1$ Top [$_{IP}$ t$_k$ [sarà$_j$ Infl^0 chi$_k$ t$_1$]]]]

    d. Merge Force and GP and attract (Remnant) IP to Spec Force $\Rightarrow$
      [$_{ForceP}$[$_{IP}$ t$_k$ [sarà$_j$ Infl^0 chi$_k$ t$_1$]]]$_m$ Force^0 [$_{GP}$ lo$_k$ Ground^0 [$_{TopP}$ [$_{ForceP}$ [$_{CopP}$ t$_j$ [$_{SC}$ t$_i$ t$_k$]]] Force^0 [$_{Op1P}$ O$_i$ che [$_{IP}$ t$_i$ magnarà la torta]]]$_1$ Top^0 t$_m$]

    e. Merge Op2P and attract a disjunction operator to Op2P $\Rightarrow$ *
      $\Rightarrow$ *Sarà chi lo che magnarà la torta? *Chi sarà lo che magnarà la torta?

The whole point of such derivations is that they allow pied-piping of a wh-phrase to a position adjacent to Op2P and subsequent (local) checking of the disjunction feature. But, as we saw in section 3, (Modern) Northern Veneto bare wh-words are only existential quantifiers, so the derivation crashes at step (e), and the resulting string is ill-formed. Granted this, it appears that only complex wh-phrases can merge in the focus position of cleft questions and yield converging derivations, which is how (108) and the like would be derived:

(108)   a. Che sòci é-lo che à telefonà
       (What colleagues is-*lo* that have phoned?)

b. Con che tosàt é-lo che t'a parlà?
(With what boy is it that you've spoken?)

As we see in 7.1, there are empirical facts that show that complex wh-phrases like *quel collègue*, (hence also presumably *che sòci* and the like) cannot be merged in the subject position of noncleft *est-ce* (*è-lo*) structures. If this is correct, Northern Veneto wh-words and phrases are close[49] to being in complementary distribution: lexical wh-words are only merged in argument position and invariably surface in the existential quantifier position Op1P; (null) clitic wh-words merge only in the subject position of noncleft *est-ce* (*è-lo*) structures, and complex wh-phrases are only merged in the focus position of genuine clefts.

Let us finally go back to Mendrisiotto and French questions like (109):

(109)   a. Chi l'è che l'a parlaa da mi?
            (Who it is that scl has spoken of me?)

        b. Cusa l'è che t'e mia fai?
            (What it is that you have not done?)

        c. Qui c'est qui a parlé de moi?
            (Who it is that scl has spoken of me?)

In French, sentences like (109c) and their SCLI counterparts in (85b, d, f) exclude *que, pourquoi,* and *combien*:[50]

(110)   a. *Que c'était que Paul lisait?
            (What it was that Paul read?)

        b. *Pourquoi c'était qu'il chantait?
            (Why was was that he was singing?)

        c. *Comment c'est qu'il parlait?
            (How it is that he spoke?)

A common account is clearly needed and will treat (85), (109), and (110) as genuine clefts in which *ce* is merged in subject position, the displaced wh-word or phrases are merged in the focus position, and the subordinate *que/che* sentences are free relatives in which a null quantifier stands in their left periphery—Op1P, presumably. Mendrisiotto *chi, cusa,* and so on must consequently be of the same type as French *qui* but different from clitic *que*; indeed, one does *not* find in Mendrisiotto the counterpart of a (neutral) clitic wh-word corresponding to *ch'* in East Lombard; although this barely scratches the surface of the rich body of facts in Mendrisiotto Wh-est-ce Q, it will have to suffice here.[51]

In sum, the main thrust of our account of French Wh-est-ce Q does seem to carry over nicely to Northern Veneto and Eastern Lombard; we have also argued, however, that the case and tense features of the NID counterparts of French *est* and *ce* require merging of higher functional layers—vP, IP, and the like—and subsequent movement of *é, lo/la* to IP and further wh- and Remnant IP movement to the various positions of the matrix left periphery. Comparative analysis thus shows that French pushes the use of Wh-est-ce Q structures to monoclausal extremes, out of reach or the NIDs, for principled reasons.

7 FRENCH WH-EST-CE Q, ECP, AND SUBJACENCY EFFECTS

7.1 ECP

Let us now move on to problems C and D in section 1; we start with pairs like (111a, b, c) versus (111c, d, e) and note that (111) itself contrasts minimally with (112) and (113):

(111)   a. Qu'est-ce qui va encore tromper les électeurs?
            (What is it that will again deceive the voters?)

        b. Qui est-ce qui a pris le chapeau de Paul?
            (Who is it that has taken Paul's hat?)

        c. Qui est-ce qui a embouti ma voiture?
            (Who is it that has bumped into my car?)

        d. *Quelles nouvelles promesses est-ce qui vont encore tromper les électeurs?
            (What new promises is it that will again deceive the voters?)

        e. *Quel joueur est-ce qui a pris le chapeau de Paul? (= Obenauer's 1981: (27))
            (What player is it that has taken Paul's hat?)

        f. *Quel autobus est-ce qui a embouti ma voiture?
            (Which bus is it that has bumped into my car?)

(112)   a. Quelles nouvelles promesses est-ce que ce politicien va encore faire?
            (What new promises is it that this politician will again deceive the voters?)

    b. Quel escroc est-ce que la police a arrêté?
      (What crook is it that the police have arrested?)

    c. Quel autobus est-ce que tu as embouti?
      (Which bus is it that you have bumped into?)

(113)   a. Quelles nouvelles promesses EST-CE qui vont encore tromper les élec-
       teurs?
       (What new promises is it that will again deceive the voters?)

    b. Quel joueur EST-CE qui a pris le chapeau de Paul?
      (What player is it that has taken Paul's hat?)

    c. Quel autobus EST-CE qui a embouti ma voiture?
      (Which bus is it that has bumped into my car?)

We know that (113) are "real" clefts, because of the stress and intonation on *est-ce*; putting these aside for the moment, it is evidently tempting to deal with subject versus object asymmetries like (111) versus (112) in terms of some revised version of the ECP, as Obenauer (1981) did.

    Taking that tack raises two problems. The first is technical: the ECP crucially rests on the notion of head or antecedent government (or both), which is hard to integrate within a more "minimalist" framework (cf. Chomsky 1995, 2001). The second is conceptual: any such approach would somehow state that bare wh-words like *que* or *qui* antecedent govern a subject trace in (111a) but that wh-phrases like *quel joueur* or *quel autobus* do not in (111d). The question immediately arises of why that should be true, rather than the other way round.

    We shall answer the second question, though we will not attempt to solve the first problem. To do so, we capitalize on the fact that bare wh-words—that is, disjunction operators—can be merged as subjects of copulative SCs in structures like (114),

(114) $[_{Op2P}$ qui$_i$ Op2^0][$_{ForceP}$ $[_{CopP}$ est $[_{SC}$ t$_i$ ce]]] F^0[$_{Op1P}$ O$_i$ que] $[_{IP}$ t$_i$ i a embouti ma voiture]]]

but that complex wh-phrases cannot. Modern French has a construction that shows this quite clearly, illustrated in dialogues like (115), (116), (117), and (118):

(115)   A. Elle a rencontré Jean.
       (She has met Jean.)

    B. Qui ça/cela? vs. Quel homme (*ça/cela)?
      (Who that? vs. What man that?)

(116)   A. Elle passe ses vacances à Paris.
              (She spends her holidays in Paris.)

         B. Où ça/cela? vs. Dans quelle ville (*ça/cela)?
              (Where that? vs. In what city that?)

(117)   A. Elle prend ses vacances en septembre.
              (She goes on holiday in September.)

         B. Quand ça/cela? vs. À quel moment (*ça/cela)?
              (When that? vs. At what period that?)

(118)   A. Elle a dit cela à Paul.
              (She's said that to Paul)

         B. À qui ça/cela? vs. À quel homme (*ça/cela)?
              (To whom that? vs. To what man that?)

Qui ça/cela, où ça/cela, and so on in these examples should, we believe, be seen as absolute copulative small clauses in which *ça* and *cela* are the strong forms of the (weak) demonstrative predicate *ce* in (114). The dramatic unacceptability of **Quel homme ça/cela?* and **Dans quelle ville ça/cela?* shows that complex wh-phrases cannot be the subjects of *ça/cela* predicates, conceivably because *ça* and *cela* can only be predicated of the existential quantifiers associated with bare wh-words (see sections, 3, 4, and 5); we conclude that *ce*, the weak form of *ça/cela*, cannot be predicated of complex wh-phrases in (113), either. Thus, pairs like (111a) versus (111d) can in principle be tied to the fact that bare wh-words alone can be merged in the subject position of the copulative SC and yield an acceptable predication.

This is the first ingredient in our explanation of such pairs. We still need another one, which an analysis of (112) provides. We have just shown that in all such sentences, the complex Wh-phrases in sentences-initial position can't have been merged in the subject position of the predicative small clause in ForceP; they must therefore originate in the object position of *faire, arrêter*, and *ambouti*, uncontroversially. But this, in turn, raises the problem of what stands in the subject position of the SC under *est* in such questions.

Section 6 excludes certain a priori conceivable solutions; for many speakers, embedded questions like (119) are perfectly fine,

(119)   a. Dis mois quelles nouvelles promesses est-ce que ce politicien va encore
              faire.
              (Tell me what new promises is it that this politician will again make?)

    b. Je ne sais plus quel escroc est-ce que la police a arrêté.
      (I don't remember what crook is it that the police have arrested.)

    c. On se demande quel autobus est-ce que tu vas emboutir la prochaine
      fois.
      (One wonders what bus is it that you will bump into next.)

therefore *ce* itself cannot be the subject of a SC whose predicate would be a null
analog of *vrai* or *un fait* in (120),

(120)   a. Est-ce vrai que tu as embouti un autobus?
        (Is it true that you have bumped into a bus?)

       b. Est-ce un fait que tu as embouti un autobus?
        (Is it a fact that you have bumped into a bus?)

since that would imply that *ce* in est+ce is a nominative subject and that (119)
results from "true" SCLI, which would incorrectly exclude them.[52] On the other
hand, something like (120) might well underlie est-ce que yes-no questions like
(121a) since, as the fairly sharp ungrammaticality of (121b) shows, those are indeed
excluded in embedded contexts:

(121)   a. Est-ce que la police a arrêté un escroc?
        (Is it that the police have arrested a crook?)

       b. *Je ne sais plus est-ce que la police a arrêté un escroc.
        (I no longer know the police have arrested a crook.)

    We would like to claim, rather, that for the many speakers who find (118)
perfect, the subject is a null expletive associated with the embedded clause itself,
as sketched in (122):

(122)   [$_{ForceP}$ [$_{CopP}$ est [$_{SC}$ pro ce] [$_{TopP}$ [$_{Op1P}$ que [$_{IP}$ tu as embouti quel autobus]]]

    Granted this, the proper spell-out parse for (112c) is (123):

(123)   [$_{Op2P}$ Quel autobus$_i$ Op2^0 [$_{ForceP}$ [$_{CopP}$ est [$_{SC}$ pro ce [$_{Op1P}$ que [$_{IP}$ tu as embouti
       t$_i$]]]]]

    By the same token, that of the ill-formed (110c)—*Quel autobus est-ce qui a
embouti ma voiture?*—would be (124a), which contrasts with (124b), the structure
of the well-formed (110c), *Qui est-ce qui a embouti ma voiture?*

(124)   a. $[_{Op2P}$ Quel autobus$_i$ Op2^0 $[$ $_{ForceP}$ $[_{CopP}$ est $[_{SC}$ pro ce $[_{Op1P}$ que $[_{IP}$ t$_i$+i a embouti ma voiture$]]]]]$

b. $[_{Op2P}$ Qui$_j$ Op2^0 $[_{ForceP}$ $[_{CopP}$ est $[_{SC}$ t$_j$ ce$]]]$ Force^0 $[_{Op1P}$ O$_j$ que $[_{IP}$ t$_j$+i a embouti ma voiture$]]]]]$

All displacements in (124b) are local: the null quantifier hops from the subject position to the immediately c-commanding Op1P, and the disjunction operator *qui* hops from its subject position in the copulative SC to the immediately c-commanding Op2P. In (124a), in contrast, *quel autobus* has to move in one swoop from its subject position in IP, a left branch, to Op2P, crossing over the Op1P and Force layers; this target we shall say is "too far" for an element starting off on a left branch. In (123), however, *quel autobus* starts out on a right branch, which allows it to reach more distant targets, whence the contrast. This, then, is our account of (110) versus (111), which is in the same spirit as Obenaeur (1981), though it is evidently very different technically.

The fact that genuine cleft questions like (112), repeated in (125),

(125)   a. Quelles nouvelles promesses EST-CE qui vont encore tromper les élec-teurs?
(What new promises is it that will again deceive the voters?)

b. Quel joueur EST-CE qui a pris le chapeau de Paul?
(What player is it that has taken Paul's hat?)

c. Quel autobus EST-CE qui a embouti ma voiture?
(Which bus is it that has bumped into my car?)

are acceptable is now easily explained; the parse of (125c), for example, would be (126)—see (91) and its discussion for a description of the computations yielding such structures

(126) $[_{Op2P}$ Quel autobus$_j$ Op2P $[_{ForceP}$ $[_{IP}$ t$_k$ est t$_j]_l$ F^0 $[$ $[_{GrounP}$ ce$_k$ G$^0[_{TopP}$ $[_{ForceP}$ $[_{CopP}$ t$_j$ $[_{SC}$ t$_k$ t$_j$ $]]$ O$_j$ que $[_{IP}$ t i a embouti ma voiture $]]]_i$ Top^0 $[_{IP}$ t$_l$ t$_i$ $]]]]$

—a banal SCLI configuration in which *quel autobus* is merged as an object of the copulative sentence whose (displaced) subject is *ce*; as discussed in section 6.1, the copulative sentence is first merged in the Force layer of the embedded relative, and its elements move to the matrix IP domain. *Quel autobus* is pied piped to Spec Force, along with the (remnant) IP whose head is the copula *est*. From there, it moves a short distance to Spec, Op2; the null definite operator O of free relatives moves locally from the subject position of embedded IP to Op1P. In short, the

Wh-displacements in (126) are as local as they are in (124), despite otherwise major structural differences, whence their common acceptability.

7.2 Subjacency

Let us finally consider the much more enigmatic subjacency effect of pairs like (127) versus (128) (=(14) versus (15)):

(127)　a.　Qu'est-ce que c'est qu'il a dit?
　　　　　(What is it that it is that he has said?)

　　　　b.　Où est-ce que c'est qu'il va?
　　　　　(Where is it that it is that he goes?)

　　　　c.　Quand est-ce que c'est qu'il part en vacances?
　　　　　(When is it that it is that he goes on holiday?)

(128)　a.　?*Quelle nouvelle bêtise est-ce que c'est qu'il a dit(e)?
　　　　　(What new stupidity is it that it is that he has come up with again?)

　　　　b.　?*À quel endroit est-ce que c'est qu'il va?
　　　　　(To what resort is it that it is that he goes?)

　　　　c.　?*Pendant quelle période est-ce que c'est qu'il prend ses vacances?
　　　　　(During what period is it that it is that he goes on holiday?)

　　　　The topmost est+ce in (127) is a noncleft CopP, merged in the matrix ForceP, and *où, quand,* and clitic *que* typically move from the subject position of the SC to check a disjunction feature. We also know that the lower ce+est is a genuine cleft in which *ce* is a nominative subject. It is in the focus position of such clefts that wh-elements are standardly assumed to be merged. As for the most embedded clause, a free relative, its left periphery hosts a null operator attracted from an argument position. But clearly *que, où,* and *quand* in (127) cannot have been merged in the subject of the topmost CopP and in the focus position of the lower cleft at the same time. Our discussion of (86), (88), and (89) in section 6.1 has shown that clitic *que* cannot be merged in the focus position of a cleft. We conclude, then, that in (127) the wh-words are merged as subjects of CopP in the matrix ForceP. If this is correct, the question again arises of what element stands in the focus position of the real cleft. Assuming that focused elements cannot be null, we have only one option left: the embedded clause itself must be the focused element in the cleft. We further assume that the null operator in the most embedded clause has moved to Operator position in the subordinate clause and from there to the immediately c-commanding Op1P in the matrix left periphery. The spell-out parse of (127) is thus (129),

(129) $[_{Op2P}$ Que$_i$ Op2^0 $[_{ForceP}$ $[_{CLP}$ t$_i$ $[_{CopP}$ est $[_{SC}$ t$_i$ ce]]] Force^0 $[_{Op1P}$ O$_i$ que $[_{IP}$ ce est $[_{Op1P}$ t$_i$ que $[_{IP}$ il a dit t$_i$]]]]]

where, as discussed in section 5—see text to example (57)—all the elements in the various Comp domains form a chain. All wh-displacements in (129) are local: the lowest nonlexical existential quantifier moves from the object position to the closest c-commanding operator position Op1P; the other null operator O merged in the object position of the cleft similarly moves locally to its immediately c-commanding Op1P; the clitic disjunction operator *que* itself moves as a head to the immediately c-commanding Op2P from its clitic position CLP.

Examples (115)–(118) established that complex wh-phrases cannot be merged in the topmost copulative phrase; as a consequence, the (simplified) input parse to the unacceptable (129) must be (130), where, as before, pro in the subject position of SC is a null sentential expletive:

(130) $[_{Op2P}$ Op2^0 $[_{ForceP}$ $[_{CopP}$ est $[_{SC}$ pro ce] $[_{Op1P}$ que $[_{IP}$ ce est [[quelle nouvelle bêtise]$_i$ $[_{Op1P}$ t$_i$ que $[_{IP}$ il a dit t$_i$]]]]]]

Quelle nouvelle bêtise must therefore move from the object position of the cleft to the topmost Op2P in one swoop crossing over Op1P and ForceP; this is very clearly nonlocal movement. Still, in cases like (112)—such as *Quelles nouvelles promesses est-ce que ce politicien va encore faire?*—complex wh-phrases also move to the topmost Op2P crossing over Op1P and Force without adverse consequences; similarly, the minimally different (131a) is fine, and the derivation sketched in (131b) must therefore converge:

(131)   a. Quelle nouvelle bêtise est-ce qu'il a dit?

      b. $[_{Op2P}$ Quelle nouvelle bêtise$_i$ Op2^0 $[_{ForceP}$ $[_{CopP}$ est $[_{SC}$ pro ce] $[_{Op1P}$ que $[_{IP}$ il a dit t$_i$]]]]]

What distinguishes (130) and (131a) is evidently the extra subordinate cleft in (130); the fact that (132) is acceptable

(132)   Quelle nouvelle bêtise est-ce que tu crois qu'il va encore dire?
      (What new stupidity is it that you believe that he has come up with again?)

shows that it's not the extra embedding in itself that is responsible for the degradation but, rather, the fact that the extra embedded sentence is a *cleft*.

Why should that matter? It wouldn't be enlightening to simply stipulate that clefts are absolute barriers to movement, so let us make a conjecture: the null expletive's associate in (131) is the free relative *qu'il a dit*. Suppose now that in (130) the expletive's associate is *also* the lowest free relative *qu'il a dit*, not the cleft itself. To make the dependency between the two occurrences of the null expletive and their respective associates more transparent, let us coindex them, as follows:

(130') $[_{Op2P}$ Quelle nouvelle bêtise$_i$ Op2^0 $[$ $_{ForceP}$ $[_{CopP}$ est $[_{SC}$ pro$_j$ ce$]$ $[_{Op1P}$ que $[_{IP}$ ce est $[t_i$ $[_{Op1Pj}$ t_i que $[_{IP}$ il a dit $t_i]]]]]$

(131') $[_{Op2P}$ Quelle nouvelle bêtise$_i$ Op2^0 $[_{ForceP}$ $[_{CopP}$ est $[_{SC}$ pro$_j$ ce$]$ $[_{Op1Pj}$ que $[_{IP}$ il a dit $t_i]]]]]$

As is now clear, the dependencies between the null expletive and its associate and the wh-phrase and its trace are nested in (131) but crossing in (130), which, following and extending Petsetsky (1982), might be the reason (130) is degraded in a way (131) is not. If, as we have implied, the ban on the expletive-cleft association depends on the presence of a lower subordinate clause, we would have an account of the fact that (133), unlike (128b), is fine under the parse shown in (134):

(133)   A quel endroit est-ce que c'est?
         (In what place is-it that it is?)

(134) $[_{Op2P}$ À quel endroit$_i$ Op2^0 $[_{ForceP}$ $[_{CopP}$ est $[_{SC}$ pro$_j$ ce$]$ $[_{Op1Pj}$ que $[_{IP}$ ce est $t_i]]]]$

8 CONCLUDING REMARKS AND FURTHER SPECULATIONS

More than 30 years ago, E. Bach and R. Harms published "How Do Languages Get Crazy Rules?" an article whose title certainly expressed our puzzlement when we started working on the topic discussed in this chapter. If the analyses developed here are on the right track, our puzzlement was misplaced: there's nothing "crazy" about Wh-est-ce Q syntax in French or the NIDs; as argued in the first five sections it is a consequence of the following elements:

1. The invariant structure of the left periphery of (NE) Romance, which contains two checking positions for bare wh-words: a "low" existential quantifier position and a "high" disjunction operator position
2. The clitic nature of some disjunction operators, in particular, French *que* and its null analogs in Northern Veneto and East Lombard
3. Parameter (34A)—that is, in L the disjunction operator either is or is not spelled out at P-F
4. Zanuttini's (1997) parameter—that is, NegP is merged high or low in the IP domain
5. The fact that the computations yielding SCLI in NE Romance drag along ((null) wh) clitics to a position from which they can reach their target without violating some suitably reformulated version of the Head-to-Head constraint.

In addition, section 6 has argued that the fact that a noncleft CopP can be merged in the Force layer of a matrix clause and stay there in French, though not in the NIDs, is a side effect of the featurelessness of the copula and *ce*, given our interpretation of what it formally means for a predicate to select an interrogative sentential complement. Finally, section 7 has outlined an analysis of the ECP and subjacency phenomena at work in French Wh-est-ce Q in terms of a general "shortest move" approach to the displacements to the left periphery that we hope will eventually be integrated into a truly explanatory theory of the locality constraints on wh-movement.

One of the main empirical claims of this chapter is that the *est-ce* string in questions like (135) in French

(135)   a. Qu'est-ce que Paul a dit?
            (What is it that Paul has said?)

        b. Qu'est-ce qui a surpris Paul?
            (What is it that has surprised Paul?)

is *not* to be analyzed as a cleft, contrary to what the word-for-word English gloss might lead one to believe.[53] If we are right, in all such *ce* is merged as the predicate of a small clause embedded under the copula, and (clitic) *que* is merged as the subject of that SC before it moves on to its disjunction position in the complementizer area.

To end on an empirical note, we shall try to refine this analysis somewhat and provide one extra argument in its favor; we do so by raising the question of how the title of this chapter "Qu'est-ce que *est-ce que*" or other questions like (136) should be analyzed:

(136)   a. Qu'est-ce qu'un homme?
            (What is it that a man? = 'What's a man?')

        b. Qu'est-ce que c'est qu'un homme?
            (What is it that it is that a man? = 'A man, what is it?')

What is intriguing in (136) is the obligatory presence of what looks like complementizer *que* to the left of *un homme*; omitting *que*, as in (137),

(137)   a. *Qu'est-ce un homme?

        b. *Qu'est-ce que c'est un homme?

yields an ill-formed sentence if pronounced on a flat intonation; omitting *un homme* or making it a right dislocation yields the fine Middle French question in (138a) or the fine Modern French question in (138b):

(138)   a. %Qu'est-ce(, un homme)?

        b. Qu'est-ce que c'est(, un homme)?

We know why questions like (137) are excluded: they contain one argument or predicate too many, since *que, ce,* and *un homme* would all have to be arguments or predicates in a *binary* copulative SC. Making *un homme* a right or left dislocation makes coreference with predicate *ce* possible, whence (138). We also know, of course, why (138a) is not well-formed in Modern French: (wh-) *que* is a clitic (see section 4).

Granted this, *un homme* in acceptable (136) must be the argument of a hidden predicate. If that hidden predicate is finite, the obligatory presence of *que* follows: *que* would be the ordinary complementizer of French finite subordinate clauses. Suppose the missing finite predicate is a null copula; if so, the analysis we have argued for in this chapter would associate with (136a) and (136b) the spell-out parses sketched in (139) and (140), where 'ø' is the null copula just hypothesized:

(139) $[_{Op2P}$ Que$_i$ Op2^0 $[$ $_{ForceP}$ $[_{CLP}$ t$_i$ $[_{CopP}$ est $[_{SC}$ t$_i$ ce$]]]$ Force^0 $[_{Op1P}$ O$_i$ que $[_{IP}$ $[_{CopP}$ ø $[_{SC}$ un homme t$_i]]]]$

(140) $[_{Op2P}$ Que$_i$ Op2^0 $[_{ForceP}$ $[_{CLP}$ t$_i$ $[_{CopP}$ est $[_{SC}$ t$_i$ ce$]]]$ Force^0 $[_{Op1P}$ O$_i$ que $[_{IP}$ ce est t$_i$ $[_{Op1P}$ O$_i$ que $[[_{IP}$ $[_{CopP}$ ø $[_{SC}$ un homme t$_i]]]]]$

That null copula shows up in other constructions as well; all involve predicate raising to the Comp area. This is illustrated in (141), which also alternates with right dislocation analogs, as in (142):

(141)   a.   C'{est, était} un idiot *(que) ce type!
             (It {is, was} an idiot that this guy!)

        b.   Quel idiot *(que) ce type!
             (What a fool that that guy!)

(142)   a.   C'{est, était} un idiot, ce type!
             (It {is, was} an idiot that this guy!)

        b.   Quel idiot, ce type!
             (What a fool, that guy!)

In (141a), the phrase in the focus position of the matrix cleft is clearly a raised predicate—or binds a null predicative operator in Op1P.

(143) $[_{IP}$ ce$_j$ $[_{CopP}$ est $[_{SC}$ t$_j$ un idiot$_i$]] $[_{Op1P}$ O$_i$ que $[[_{IP}$ $[_{CopP}$ ø $[_{SC}$ ce type t$_i$]]]]$

As for (141b), it is an exclamative whose wh-phrase is also a raised predicate:

(144) $[_{Exc1P}$ Quel idiot$_i$] Excl . . . $[_{Op1P}$ O$_i$ que $[[_{IP}$ $[_{CopP}$ ø $[_{SC}$ ce type t$_i$]]]]$

Alternatively, there are other types of copulative sentences in which no "être deletion" can take place in a finite subordinate clause:

(145)   Pierre n' {est, était} pas l'idiot que Jean *({est, était})
        (Pierre {is, was} not the fool that John *({is, was}))

Why should that be so? What is it that makes the occurrence of the null copula licit, indeed, obligatory, in (136) and (141) and bans it in (145)?

Our conjecture is that the relevant property is to be tied to the fact that in the former cases the raised predicate first moves to the Specifier positions of the copulative phrase and IP before moving to its target in the left periphery. In short, (136)–(141) are *inverse* copulative sentences in Moro's (1997) sense, while (145) is an ordinary noninverse copulative sentence.

There are several ways of implementing that idea; let us choose one somewhat arbitrarily and say that in all of (146), the fully fledged parses of (136)–(141),

(146)   a. $[_{Op2P}$ Que$_i$ Op2^0 $[$ $_{ForceP}$ $[_{CLP}$ t$_i$ $[_{CopP}$ est $[_{SC}$ t$_i$ ce]]] Force^0 $[_{Op1P}$ O$_i$ que $[_{IP}$ t$_i$ $[_{CopP}$ t$_i$ ø $[_{SC}$ un homme t$_i$]]]]]]$

b. [$_{Op2P}$ Que$_i$ Op2^0 [$_{ForceP}$ [$_{CLP}$ t$_i$ [$_{CopP}$ est [$_{SC}$ t$_i$ ce]]] Force^0 [$_{Op1P}$ O$_i$ que [$_{IP}$ c'est t$_i$ [$_{Op1P}$ O$_i$ que [[$_{IP}$ t$_i$ [$_{CopP}$ t$_i$ ø [$_{SC}$ un homme t$_i$]]]]]

c. [$_{IP}$ ce$_j$ [$_{CopP}$ est [$_{SC}$ t$_j$ un idiot$_i$]] [$_{Op1P}$ O$_i$ que [$_{IP}$ t$_i$ [$_{CopP}$ t$_i$ ø [$_{SC}$ ce type t$_i$]]]]]

d. [$_{ExcIP}$ Quel idiot$_i$] Excl . . . [$_{Op1P}$ O$_i$ que [$_{IP}$ t$_i$ [$_{CopP}$ t$_i$ ø [$_{SC}$ ce type t$_i$]]]]]

the copula may[54] remain lexically null because there is a stage in the derivation at which it "agrees" (i.e., is in a Spec-head configuration with) the raised predicate that winds up in Op1P at spell out. On the other hand, the parse of (145) would be (147),

(147) [$_{IP}$ Pierre$_k$ ne [$_{CopP}$ t$_k$ est pas [$_{SC}$ t$_k$ l'idiot$_j$]] [$_{Op1P}$ O$_j$ que [[$_{IP}$ Jean$_i$ [$_{CopP}$ t$_i$ était [$_{SC}$ t$_i$ t$_j$]]]]]

in which O$_j$, the raised predicate of the embedded relative, never finds itself in the specifier-head relationship with the copula *était*, which would allow for a nonlexical duplicate.[55]

In sum, the fact that *Qu'est-ce que* questions share one major syntactic property with structures like (141), which must plainly be analyzed as predicate raising constructions, gives further support to one of the chief descriptive claims in this article.

NOTES

Many of the ideas developed here first arose during the extremely close intellectual exchanges that each author has had over the years with Cecilia Poletto. Without this constant stimulation, this chapter would not exist in its present form and would probably have missed some of the generalizations we hope it expresses. Thanking her here is thus a very inadequate acknowledgment of our debt to Cecilia, although, of course, she cannot be blamed for any mistake, misconception, or shortcoming the reader might find here. Many thanks also to Željko Bošković and Richard Kayne for their comments on an earlier draft of this chapter. Although each of us has contributed to each part of this essay, for administrative reasons in Italy, Nicola Munaro takes responsibility for 1, 2, 5.2, 5.3, and 6.2, and Jean-Yves Pollock for 3, 4, 5.1, 6.1, 7, and 8.

1. The dialects grouped under this name are spoken in and around the towns of Edolo, Malonno, and Vione.
2. A group of Italian dialects spoken in Switzerland in and near the town of Mendrisio. Mendrisiotto is spoken in an area standing to the northwest of the Camonica Valley; the word order contrast illustrated in (2) versus (3) is a general fact about those

dialects, not just the cleft interrogatives. Modern French speakers often fail to "invert" *ce*, just as Mendrisiotto speakers do; (1a) thus alternates with (i):

> (i)   Qui c'est qui porte le pain?
>
>   'Who is it that is bringing the bread?'

Example (i) is more colloquial than (1) in Modern French. On the structure of (i) and its incompatibility with *que* (what), *pourquoi* (why), and *comment* (how), see sections 5 and 6.

3. Bellunese is a group of dialects spoken in and around Belluno, a city in Northern Veneto. See Munaro (1999) and Munaro et al. (2001).

4. Throughout the English glosses are only meant to give a word-for-word analog of the original sentences but in the majority of cases they do *not* convey their meaning; so, for example, the meaning of (1a) and (1b) is really that of the simple, noncleft questions *Who's bringing the bread?* and *What are you doing?* respectively. Sections 5 and 6 explain why this is so.

5. In our informal "Wh-est-ce Q" label, 'ce' is meant to cover not only *ce* but also *lo, l'*, and other pronominals in the NIDs; we are thus lumping together very different entities and structures to be teased apart as we proceed.

6. As Obenauer (1981: note 6) notes, quoting Renchon and other traditional grammarians, "Wh-est-ce Q" in embedded contexts is often considered more "colloquial" than in main clauses; French children used to be taught at school, and some probably still are, that embedded "Wh-est-ce Q" should be avoided. Maybe because of that normative teaching, some speakers do not like (8), but most still perceive a robust contrast with (9), judging the latter to be (much) worse than the former; to our knowledge, the reverse judgments do not exist; the SCLI analog of (8a) is excluded for more general reasons since SCLI is typically banned with subject extraction as *Qui a (*-t-il) surpris Marie?* (Who has (*he) surprised Marie?) shows.

7. Just like Wh-est-ce Q in embedded contexts (see previous note), these sentences used to be banned in written French in primary school and are thus often considered somewhat substandard, although they are extremely common in ordinary conversation and fail to attract any attention, let alone disapproval, in spoken French.

8. As shown in section 6, the second occurrence of *ce +est* in (14) is a genuine cleft; consequently, only those bare qu-words that can appear in the focus position of clefts can appear in such examples; this accounts for why the bare qu-words *pourquoi* and *combien* are excluded in (i) (compare (ii)):

> (i)   a. *Pourquoi est-ce que c'est qu'il est parti? (Why is it that it is that he left?)
>
>   b. ??Combien est-ce que c'est qu'il a payé? (How much is it that it is that he paid?)
>
> (ii)   a. *C'est pourquoi qu'il est parti? (It is why that he left?)
>
>   b. ??C'est combien qu'il a payé? (It is how much that he paid?)

Example (ii) is from Obenauer (1981) and should not be confused with examples like (iii) (from Philippe Delerm's *La Sieste assassinée*, éditions de l'arpenteur, p. 58):

> (iii)   a. C'était pourquoi exactement? Je peux peut-être vous aider?
>   (That was why exactly? Maybe I can help you = What was it you wanted? Maybe I can help.)

b. C'était combien? (That was how much?)

In (iii) *pourquoi* and *combien* are arguments of a copulative small clause whose underlying form is (iv), in which the predicate 'ce' denotes something like 'your being here' or 'your paying'.

(iv) était [$_{SC}$ {pourquoi, combien} ce]

On (iv) in (one type of) 'Wh-est-ce Q,' see section 5.

9. As Željko Bošković reminds us (pers. comm.), there actually have been a few suggestions in the literature on the Slavic languages that wh-island/subjacency effects depend on the D-linking dimension of the wh-phrases; see, for example, Rudin (1988) and her references.

10. Jean-Yves Pollock systematically contrasts (16), which has fine examples, and (17), which he finds less than perfect; other speakers don't seem to make any such distinction. He finds (15) worse than (17), however; on the raison d'être of these variations across speakers, see section 7.

11. The only exception is Obenauer (1981), to which we shall return.

12. As (18b, d) show very clearly, wh-fronting is excluded in standard wh-interrogatives in Bellunese, but it is required in the peculiar "reproach" reading described at length in Munaro and Obenauer (1999), in which the wh-word moves to a further, "higher" position in the left periphery.

13. That terminology is misleading since we have claimed elsewhere that these also involve (Remnant) IP movement to a (truncated) left periphery. See Munaro et al. (2001) and Poletto and Pollock (2004). Nothing hinges on the proper analysis of French in situ questions here. See also Cheng and Rooryck (2000).

14. On "defective" wh-words, see Munaro and Obenauer (1999), Poletto and Pollock (2004).

15. On a remnant movement approach to the Spanish and Portuguese counterparts of (7), see Ambar (2002), Etxepare and Uribe-Etxebarria (2000); see also Poletto and Pollock (2004).

16. Obenauer and Poletto (2000) argue that in rhetorical questions a still higher third position must be countenanced in the Comp area.

17. Example (25b) is used only when the "special" semantics described in Munaro and Obenauer (1999) obtains. Note that the "doubling" structures (and wh-in situ) we discuss here all involve Subject clitic inversion (SCLI) and thus stand in fairly sharp contrast with many cases of wh-doubling reported in the literature in which SCLI or subject aux inversion cannot take place.

18. In Val Camonica and the South-Eastern Lombard dialects in general, it appears that (27) is preferably associated with a D-linked interpretation for the wh-word.

19. Monnese belongs to the North-Eastern Lombard group of dialects; in questions without an auxiliary, Monnese shows "fà-support" for independent reasons; see Benincà and Poletto (1998).

20. This generalization holds only in those languages and dialects that display SCLI.

21. That wh-questions involve infinite disjunction is argued for at length in Jayaseelan (2001).

22. Our (32B) incorporates David Pesetsky's (1987: (34)), repeated in (i):

(i) D-linked wh-phrases are not quantifiers.

The extension of (i) to all complex wh-phrases, including indefinites like *what book* and *che libro*, also assumed in Petsetsky (1987), raises nontrivial questions since, everything else being equal, we might expect, incorrectly, such complex wh-indefinites to behave like bare *what* or *che*. In the spirit of Heim (1987: 30–33), we would like to suggest that *what* and *che* in [{what, che} + NP], unlike bare *what* and *che* in non D-linked contexts (on which see Pesetsky 1987: 108–109), are always presuppositional because they are the wh-counterparts of 'such' in DPs like *such books* and *such a book*. Thus, *what book(s)* is the interrogative analog of 'books of that kind' or 'a book of kind x', where "x is understood as referring to some contextually salient kind or introduced in immediately preceding discourse" (Heim 1987: 31). On the other hand, as stated in the text, bare *what* and *che* are existential quantifiers bound by the disjunction operator—as Heim (1987: 32) puts it, "variables bound by an interrogative operator in Comp."

23. In the Germanic languages in general and English in particular, the syntactic relevance of the bare versus complex wh-phrase distinction, more generally that of the existential versus nonexistential dimension, is harder to detect. Richard Kayne (pers. comm.) notes, however, at least one syntactic environment in which it shows up. Compare:

(i) a. John is trying to repair the radio, but I am not sure what with.

   b. Mary is trying to elope, but I am not sure who with.

(ii) a. *John is trying to repair the radio with the screwdriver or the pliers, but I am not sure which with.

   b. *Mary is trying to elope with John or Peter, but I am not sure {who, which of them} with.

   c. *John is trying to repair the radio, but I am not sure what tool with.

Similarly, a clear contrast exists between (iiia) and (iiib, c):

   a. What in the world is he going to buy?

   b. *What in the world book is he going to buy?

   c. *What book in the world is he going to buy?

We shall not try to say here whether (i) versus (ii) should be analyzed along Bellunese lines, for example, as an elided sentence with a left periphery in which only the "lower" (existential) wh-position would be available.

24. This section incorporates many ideas first developed in Poletto (2000) and extended in Poletto and Pollock's talk in Cortona; it thus owes even more to Cecilia's ideas than the other parts of the article.

25. See for example (i):

(i) a. *Il, paraît-il, aime la linguistique. (He, it appears likes linguistics.)

   b. Qui est venu? *Il, lui. (Who came? He, him.)

   c. Il parle à {*le, lui}. (He speaks to {he, him}.)

   d. Je *{la et le} rencontre souvent. (I her and he meet often.)

Pollock (2000) shows, in line with much previous work, that these properties follow from the fact that clitics are heads.

26. In standard approaches (e.g., Rizzi and Roberts 1989), SCLI configurations result from head movement of I^0 to C^0 (i.e., Force^0 in Rizzi's 1997 terminology); I^0 moves with the finite verb and the clitics adjoined to it; Pollock (2000), Poletto and Pollock (2000a, b), and Pollock (2001) argue that SCLI and Complex Inversion, just like SI under Kayne and Pollock's (2001) analysis, are cases of Remnant IP movement; for our immediate purpose, the question of which of the two lines is correct is irrelevant since (44) shows that clitics are carried along with the verb in SCLI, which is all our analysis of *que* needs; however, we shall adopt Remnant movement derivations for SCLI in the following sections.

27. As Obenauer (1976, 1981, 1994) has often stressed, when *diable* (devil) is added to *que* sentences like (i) and (ii), they become noticeably less deviant than their bare *que* counterparts:

(i)   ??Que diable il a bien pu voir?
      (What the hell she may have seen?)

(ii) Que diable Pierre a-t-il vu?
      (What the hell Pierre has he seen?)

This follows in part from the text analysis on the view that adding *diable* to *que* makes it "less of a clitic." The fact that (i) is worse than the almost perfect (ii) also follows from the text analysis: in Complex Inversion (CI) cases like (ii) *que diable* gets a free ride to Spec Force, just as it does in simple SCLI cases. (On the common treatment of SCLI and CI, see, e.g., Kayne 1972, Rizzi and Roberts 1989, and Pollock 2000, 2003.) From that position, it need only cross over *Pierre*. In (i), on the other hand, *que diable* has to cross over both the IP internal subject *il* and the lower Op1^0 head, a difference that may be tied to their respective status. One should probably consider the fact that some speakers find (49b̄) (almost) acceptable, unlike the other three examples, in the same light. Perhaps such speakers allow *que* to remain in the ForceP layer. *Que diable* being aggressively non-D-linked in the terminology of Pesetsky (1987), no improvement results from adding *diable* to (49c):

(iii) *Il a vu que diable?
       (He's seen what the hell?)

Simple SCLI cases like (iv) are perfect:

(iv)   Qu'a-t-il fait?
       (What has he done?)

On the Remnant movement analysis of SCLI argued for in Pollock (2000, 2003) and Poletto and Pollock (2000a, b), clitic *que* must be blind to the trace of *il*. This would follow from Kayne's (2001: 324) view that "syntax must be derivational but without traces and thus with cyclic interpretation and no reconstruction."

28. See Cheng and Rooryck (2000), Munaro et al. (2001), and Poletto and Pollock (2004) for conflicting analyses.

29. The fact that *Il que a vu?* in which cliticization has taken place, is also crashingly bad shows that wh-in situ cannot be licensing *que* in its IP internal position, con-

trary to the approach taken in Cheng and Rooryck (2000); see Poletto and Pollock (2004).

30. Note in passing that saying that *que* is a morphophonological clitic that must be left adjacent to a finite verb at spell out would not suffice since that requirement is met in (49d). Adding *diable* to *que* in (49d) makes things better (see note 27):

(i)   ?Que diable peut bien avoir éberlué Jean?
      (What the hell may have stunned Jean so?)

31. If this analysis of *que* and its null analog in Northern Veneto and val Camonica (see later) is correct, it casts serious doubts on various attempts to formulate a "freezing principle" banning extraction out of moved constituents; consequently, the unacceptability of cases like (i) should be rethought:

(i)   *When$_i$ do you wonder [how likely to fix the car t$_i$] John is?

32. Another obvious candidate would be a cleft of the type *C'est {Jean, qui, *que}*; this would be very unlikely, however, since clitics are banned from the focus position of clefts, which would exclude (51c). We come back to genuine clefts in Wh-est-ce Q later.

33. On the analysis of the *que* to *qui* alternation presupposed here, see Taraldsen (2001). Nothing in what we have seen so far requires complementizer *que* to lexicalize Op1P; it could just as well lexicalize Force⁰. Bellunese wh-est-ce Q provides an empirical argument in favor of the text analysis, and so does the fact that parentheticals can occur in between *est-ce* and *que*, as in (i):

(i)   a. Qui est-ce, à ton avis, qui a dit cela?
          (Who is it, in your opinion, that has said that?)

      b. Qù est-ce, à ton avis, que Pierre est allé?
          (Where is it, in your opinion that Pierre is gone?)

In addition, the fact that *que* never occurs in matrix yes/no questions would be unexpected if *que* lexicalized interrogative Force.

34. The SCLI counterparts (i) of the ill-formed (60) are equally ungrammatical,

(i)   a. *Che te disturbe-lo.

      b. *Chi laore-lo de pì.

      c. *Chi à-lo magnà la torta.

because, as already stressed, no SCLI can take place in case of subject extraction (cf. *Who did come?*), in our terms, no Remnant IP movement to Force can take place in subject extraction cases, for reasons we shall not discuss here (see Poletto and Pollock 2004).

35. The diachronic facts concerning Bellunese support the general line taken here; *chi* originally surfaced in the high Op2P disjunction position and was thus followed by the copula:

(i)   a. Chi é-lo che se ricorda pì che mi sie stata?
          (Who is-it that himself remembers more that I be been?)

          'Who is it that remembers that I have existed?'

   b. Chi é-lo che no se sente a repelir . . . ?
     (Who is it that not himself feels to recover?)

     'Who is it that does not feel better?' (Zuppani, "Benefizi de la campagna,"
     1877)

In a less richly attested intermediate stage, *chi* appeared twice both before and after the copula:

(ii)   *Chi é-lo chi* che dit aree che de quei bisogn se aree?
      (Who is-*lo* who that said would-have that of those need we would-have

      'Who is it that would have said that we would need them?' (Zanella, "Poesie,"
      1901)

In our terms, the high *chi* at that stage was the disjunction operator, and the low one the existential quantifier; finally in Modern Bellunese *chi* appears only in the low position and a null wh-element stands in the high one:

(iii)   Sarà-lo mai *chi* 'sta sort de strambèl che a far da oroloio l'à més an osèl?
      (Will-be-*lo* ever who this kind of silly person that to do as clock scl-has put a
      bird?) (Chiarelli, "An oroloio," 1955)

      'Who will ever be this sort of silly person that has put a bird to work as a
      clock?'

The following example is particularly significant as it shows extreme variability at the intermediate stage, with *chi* in one sentence preceding, and in the other following, the copula:

(iv)   *Chi é-lo?* Son mì! *É-lo chi* sto mì?
      ('Who is-it? am I! is-scl who this I?')

      'Who is it? It's me! Who is this me?' (Luciani, "I griff," twentieth century)

   36. On the fact that the trace of the moved pronoun does not block movement of the clitic wh-word at step (68e), see note 27.

   37. Including Paduan; cf. Zanuttini (1997: sec. 2.4).

   38. Zanuttini (1997: 47) writes: "Because of feature mismatch the derivation will either converge as gibberish or will terminate." Zanuttini's analysis of SCLI relies on head movement, but the insight is exactly the same. The text analysis presupposes that *no* cannot topicalize prior to Remnant IP movement—yielding gibberish like **vien no lo chi?* or **vien lo no chi?*; this, we believe, should be seen in the same light as the fact that English *not*, unlike negative adverbs like *never* and *hardly*, can never move to the Comp field: *Never have I seen such a thing* versus **Not have I seen such a thing* (cf. Pollock 1989: note 8).

   39. A selecting predicate has its object sentence in its complement position. In the configuration suggested here, this is not true. To solve the problem, we adopt an idea first expressed in generative grammar in Rosenbaum (1964) and claim that the selecting predicate in Spec Force has a (null) *it/ce* in its complement position, thereby "doubling" the selected IP. The *ce* in *est-ce que* questions plays the same role, in addition to being the predicate that we claim it is.

   40. In the rest of this chapter, we remain somewhat vague concerning the proper

characterization of the computations that attract the various elements of the selecting predicate to the IP field from their input position in the Force layer of the embedded clause. In French, in cases like *Je ne lui dirai pas à qui Jean a téléphoné* (I won't tell him to whom Jean has phoned), for example, *pas* must adjoin to the low (cf. Zanuttini 1997) negative phrase headed by *ne* (see also Pollock 1989); the verb itself and its dative argument could either move as a phrase and adjoin to vP and from there move on to their various checking positions or, alternatively, move individually in one swoop to these checking positions.

41. In genuine (interrogative) clefts like (86), the possible use of the present-tense form is somewhat unexpected, as shown by the fact that the corresponding English glosses are not perfectly idiomatic. That English clefts, unlike French ones, require tense concord with the embedded verb is brought out more clearly in pairs like (ia, b), which contrast fairly sharply with the French (ic) and (id), both fine:

(i)   a.   Wasn't that Chomsky the person you were talking to?

       b.   *Isn't that Chomsky the person you were talking to?

       c.   C'était pas Chomsky la personne à qui tu parlais?

       d.   C'est pas Chomsky la personne à qui tu parlais?

So, in Wh-est-ce Q questions like (85), the copula *must* be noninflected for the reasons discussed in the text; in genuine cleft questions, *être* can inflect for present and "imparfait," but, unlike its counterpart in English, it need not "agree" in tense with the embedded verb. It is tempting to say that this difference is to be tied to the existence of the "inert" copula of genuine Wh-est-ce Q in French, which English lacks; we do not try to give this idea a formal execution here.

42. When scoping on the matrix cleft, they are fine, as in *How could it be that he left?*

43. The full derivation of (91) would involve (a) merging the IP layers in (87) and attracting *ce* and *était* to Spec Infl and Infl⁰, as discussed before (see also note 39); (b) merging TopP and attracting the whole embedded (affirmative) ForceP—namely, the whole free relative—to Spec Top; (c) merging of Ground and TopP and attracting *ce* to Spec Ground; (d) merging of interrogative Force and attracting Remnant IP to Spec Force, thus typing the clause as a question; and finally (e) merging of Op2 and attracting *quel homme* from the force layer of the relative to Spec Op2P of the matrix question. That embedded sentences are attracted to the left periphery in cases like (91) and more generally in questions where the wh-word is extracted from an embedded affirmative is shown by cases like (i) in Bellunese (cf. Munaro 1999: 71–73):

(i)   a.   À-tu dit che l'à comprà che?
            (Have you said that he has bought what? = 'What have you said he's bought?')

       b.   À-tu dit che l'é 'ndat andé?
            (Have you said that he is gone where? = 'Where have you said he's gone?')

Since *che* and *andé* have moved to the Op1 layer in all such (see section 1), it must be the case that the embedded *che l'à compra* and *che l'é 'ndat* have themselves undergone (Remnant) movement to the left periphery of the matrix question.

44. Many thanks to Jean-Charles Khalifa for pointing out relatives like (93a), which

according to him were very common in the Pied noir French of older generations. Exclamatives like (93b) are fine in standard French and do not differ stylistically from the synonyms in (i):

(i) a. Comme il est grand!

  b. Qu'il est grand!

45. And because *donc* makes the simple Wh-est-ce Q pragmatically implausible (see Obenauer 1994).

46. This comes with the usual provisos concerning the marked possibility to interpret the embedded CP as a direct quote. This seems easier with *dis moi* than with *je ne sais pas/plus*, for unclear reasons, whence the (weak) contrasts for some speakers between, for example, (97a) versus (97b) later. See also next note.

47. There are well-known cases of languages and dialects allowing SCLI/Subject/ Aux inversion in embedded sentences. The Belfast English (i) sentences—from Henry (1995: 105)—for example, are fine:

(i) a. I wondered was Bill going.

  b. They asked them what had they done.

A variety of possible analyses would make such facts compatible with our framework, such as multiple Force layers, selection of question clauses as if they were DPs—which would treat (ib) as parallel to 'they asked them the time'—and many other approaches advocated over the years. Space does not permit taking up the subject here.

48. In Modern Bellunese, there is obligatory tense concord between the copula and the embedded verb, which in our system would be a further reflex of the fact that the *e-lo* substring starts off in the same syntactic domain as the tensed main verb since they belong in the same CP domain.

49. Only close, because of "simple" SCLI cases like (i) and (ii)

(i) Quanti libri à-tu ledést?
  (How many books have you read?)

(ii) À-tu ledést che?
  (Have you read what? = 'What have you read?')

in which both the complex bare wh-word {ø, che} and the full wh-phrase *quanti libri* are merged in the object position of *ledést*.

50. As already observed in Obenauer (1981), for some speakers *combien* in (110c) is less crashingly bad than *pourquoi* and *que*, for reasons that still need to be understood. The same contrast obtains in Bellunese sentences like (i), in which *come* 'how' is less deviant than *parché* 'why':

(i) a. ?(?) Come é-lo che'l se à comportà?
  ((How) is it that he behaved?)

  b. *Parché é-lo che te-va anca ti?
  (Why is it that you go you too?)

51. See Munaro (1999) and Poletto and Pollock (2004).

52. It could be Jean-Yves Pollock, who dislikes (118) and the like, does have a (re-

sidual) analysis of that sort; our analysis of (121a) predicts that *est* can inflect for tense and mood, which it does, as the acceptability of (i) shows:

(i) a. Serait-ce que la police a arrêté le coupable?
         (Could it be that the police have arrested the criminal?)

     b. Est-ce donc que Pierre a téléphoné?
         (Is it then that Pierre has phoned?)

53. We share that claim with Obenauer (1981), although he formulated it very differently; for him, the input of Wh-est-ce Q was indeed a cleft, but a late deletion rule erased the equative part of the LF form, as in (i):

(i)   What is the x such that x = y & P(y)? ↔ What is the x & P(x)?

Clearly, we have no need for this process, which in any case could not be formulated in our more minimalist framework.

54. Choosing to lexicalize the copula often yields sentences that feel more awkward than downright ungrammatical; to Jean-Yves Pollock's ear *Qu'est-ce qu'est un homme?* and *Qu est-ce que c'est qu'est un homme?* are almost fine. Their non SI counterparts—*Qu'est-ce qu'un homme est?* and *Qu'est-ce que c'est qu'un homme est?*—are less felicitous, though they again feel more infelicitous than ungrammatical. However, Pollock finds *C'est un idiot qu'est ce type*, *C'est un idiot que ce type est*, *Quel idiot qu'est ce type*, and *Quel idiot que ce type est* far worse; the reason for these variations in relative (un)acceptability still have to be fully understood.

55. If this is right in comparatives like *Pierre est plus grand que Jean* (Pierre is taller than Jean), *que* cannot be a complementizer but, as standardly assumed, a preposition of the *di/than* type in Italian/English.

REFERENCES

Ambar, M. (2002) "Wh-questions and Wh-exclamatives: Unifying Mirror Effects," in C. Beyssade et al. (eds.) *Romance Languages and Linguistic Theory*. Benjamins, Amsterdam, 15–40.

Ambar, M., J. Luis, and H. Obenauer (1986) Talk given at the GLOW conference, Girona.

Bach, E., and R. T. Harms (1972) "How Do Languages Get Crazy Rules?" in R. Stockwell and R. K. S. Macaulay (eds.) *Linguistic Change and Generative Theory*. Indiana University Press, Bloomington.

Benincà, P., and C. Poletto (1998) "A Case of 'do Support' in Romance." *University of Venice Working Papers in Linguistics* 8(1): 27–63.

Bouchard, D., and P. Hirschbühler (1986) "French *Quoi* and Its Clitic Allomorph *QUE*," in C. Neidle and R. A. Nuñez Cedenao (eds.) *Studies in Romance Languages*. Foris, Dordrecht, 39–60.

Cheng L. S., and J. Rooryck (2000) "Licensing Wh-in-Situ." *Syntax* 3(1): 1–19.

Chomsky, N. (1995) *The Minimalist Program*. MIT Press, Cambridge, Mass.

Chomsky, N. (1999) "Derivations by Phase." Unpublished ms., MIT, Cambridge, Mass.

Chomsky, N. (2001) "Beyond Explanatory Adequacy." Unpublished ms., MIT, Cambridge, Mass.

Cinque, M. (2004) "Restructuring and Functional Structure," in A. Belletti (ed.) *Structures and Beyond*. Oxford University Press, New York.

Etxepare, R., and M. Uribe-Etxebarria (2000) "On the Properties of In Situ Wh-Questions in Spanish." Talk delivered at the Minimal Elements of Linguistic Variation Workshop, Paris 15–16 December.

Foulet, L. (1974) *Petite syntaxe de l'ancien français*. Champion, Paris.

Heim, I. 1987 "Where Does the Definiteness Restriction Apply? Evidence from the Definiteness of Variables," in E. Reuland and A. ter Meulen (eds.) *The Representation of Indefinites*. MIT Press, Cambridge, Mass., 21–42.

Henry, A. (1995) *Belfast English and Standard English*. Oxford University Press, New York.

Jayaseelan, K. A. (2001) "Questions and Question Words Incorporating Quantifiers in Malayalam." *Syntax* 4(2): 63–94.

Katz, J., and P.-M. Postal (1964) *An Integrated Theory of Linguistic Descriptions*. MIT Press, Cambridge, Mass.

Kayne, R. S. (1972) "Subject Inversion in French Interrogatives," in J. Casagrande and B. Saciuk (eds.) *Studies in Romance Languages*. Newbury House, Rowley, Mass., 70–126.

Kayne, R. S. (1994) *The Antisymmetry of Syntax*. MIT Press, Cambridge, Mass.

Kayne, R. S. (2001) *Parameters and Universals*. Oxford University Press, New York.

Kayne, R. S., and J.-Y. Pollock (2001) "New Thoughts on Stylistic Inversion," in A. Hulk and J-Y. Pollock (eds.) *Subject Inversion and the Theory of Universal Grammar*. Oxford University Press, New York, 107–162.

Langacker, R. W. (1972) "French Interrogatives Revisited," in J. Casagrande and B. Saciuk (eds.) *Generative Studies in Romance Languages*. Newbury House, Rowley, Mass., 36–70.

Moro, A. (1997) *The Raising of Predicates, Predicative NPs and the Theory of Clause Structure*. Cambridge University Press, Cambridge.

Munaro, N. (1999) *Sintagmi interrogativi nei dialetti italiani settentrionali*. Unipress, Padua.

Munaro, N., and H.-G. Obenauer (1999) "On Underspecified wh-Elements in Pseudo-Interrogatives." *Venice Working Papers in Linguistics* 9(1–2): 181–253.

Munaro, N., and C. Poletto (2002) "La tipologia dei wh-in-situ nelle varietà alto italiane." *Quaderni Patavini di Linguistica* 18: 79–91.

Munaro, N., C. Poletto, and J.-Y. Pollock (2001) "Eppur si muove! On Comparing French and Bellunese Wh-Movement," in P. Pica & J. Rooryck (eds.) *Linguistic Variation Yearbook* 1, Benjamins, Amsterdam, 167–180.

Obenauer, H.-G. (1976) *Etudes de syntaxe interrogatives du français*. Niemeyer, Tübingen.

Obenauer, H.-G. (1981) "Le principe des catégories vides et la syntaxe des interrogatives complexes." *Langue Française* 52: 100–118.

Obenauer, H.-G. (1994) "Aspects de la syntaxe A-barre: effets d'intervention et mouvements des quantifieurs." Thesis, University of Paris VIII.

Obenauer, H.-G., and C. Poletto (2000) "Rhetorical Wh-Phrases in the Left Periphery of the Sentence." *Venice Working Papers in Linguistics* 10(1): 121–151.

Pesetsky, D. (1982) "Paths and Categories." Ph.D. diss., MIT, Cambridge, Mass.

Pesetsky, D. (1987) "Wh-In Situ: Movement and Unselective Binding," in E. Reuland and A. ter Meulen (eds.) *The Representation of Indefinites*. MIT Press, Cambridge, Mass.

Poletto, C. (2000) *The Higher Functional Field in the Northern Italian Dialects*. Oxford Studies in Comparative Syntax. Oxford University Press, New York.

Poletto, C., and J.-Y. Pollock (2000a) Talk delivered at the Cortona conference, Cortona, May.

Poletto C., and J.-Y. Pollock (2000b) "On the Left Periphery of Some Romance Wh-questions." Unpublished ms., Padua and Amiens.

Poletto C., and J.-Y. Pollock (2004) "On Romance Interrogatives." Unpublished ms.

Pollock, J.-Y. (1983) "Sur quelques propriétés de phrases copulatives." in H. Obenauer and J.-Y. Pollock (eds.) *Français et Grammaire Universelle* Larousse, Paris, 89–125.

Pollock, J.-Y. (1989) "Verb Movement, Universal Grammar and the Structure of IP." *Linguistic Inquiry* 20: 365–424.

Pollock, J-.Y. (2000) "Subject Clitics, Subject Clitic Inversion and Complex Inversion: Generalizing Remnant Movement to the Comp Area." Unpublished ms., Amiens.

Pollock, J.-Y. (2003) "Three Arguments for Remnant IP Movement in Romance," in A. M. DiSciullo (ed.) (2003) *Asymmetry in Grammar* vol. 1, John Benjamins, Amsterdam, 251–277.

Rizzi, L. (1976) *Issues in Italian Syntax*. Foris, Dordrecht.

Rizzi, L. (1997) "The Fine Structure of the Left Periphery," in L. Haegeman (ed.) *Elements of Grammar*. Kluwer, Dordrecht, 281–337.

Rizzi, L., and I. Roberts (1989) "Complex Inversion in French." *Probus* 1: 1–30.

Rudin, C. (1988) "On Multiple Questions and Multiple WH Fronting." *Natural Language and Linguistic Theory* 6(4): 445–502.

Sportiche, D. (1996) "Clitic Constructions," in J. Rooryck and L. Zaring (eds.) *Phrase Structure and the Lexicon*. Kluwer, Dordrecht, 213–276.

Taraldsen, K. T. (2001) "Subject Extraction, The Distribution of Expletives and Stylistic Inversion," in A. Hulk and J.-Y. Pollock (eds.) *Subject Inversion and the Theory of Universal Grammar*. Oxford University Press, New York, 163–182.

Travis, L. (1984) "Parameters and Effects of Word Order Variation." Ph.D. diss., MIT, Cambridge Mass.

Zanuttini, R. (1997) *Negation and Clausal Structure*. Oxford University Press, New York.

Zink, G. (1997) *Morphosyntaxe du pronom personnel en moyen français*. Droz, Geneva.

CHAPTER 14

CLITIC PLACEMENT, GRAMMATICALIZATION, AND REANALYSIS IN BERBER

JAMAL OUHALLA

1 INTRODUCTION

BERBER[1] clitics (CLs) can occur in either of the two positions shown in (1a, b) in the clause: postverbal (1a) and preverbal (1b):

(1)   a. V=**CL**

    b. F=**CL** V

   F in (1a, b) is an overt functional category that can correspond to any member of the core class of functional categories in the clause, Tense (T), Negation (Neg), or Complementizer (C). The latter can have one of a number of clause-typing values, including C_Q (yes-no-questions), C_{WH} (wh-questions), C_{FOC} (focus constructions), C_{REL} (relative clauses), C_{COND} (conditional clauses) or C_{THAT} (finite declarative clauses) (see later for examples). The symbol "=" on the left side of

CL encodes the information that Berber clitics generally appear to the right of their host. This property, which has interesting theoretical implications explored in this chapter, arguably distinguishes Berber clitics from their counterparts in some other languages.

CL in (1a, b) can be a single clitic or a cluster of up to five different clitics in a single clause (see Dell and Elmedlaoui 1989). Traditionally, it is thought that Berber clitics can be pronominal (CL_{PRON}), directional (CL_{DIR}), adverbial (CL_{ADV}), or prepositional, in which case they can consist of either a bare preposition (CL_P) or a complex consisting of P and a pronominal clitic (CL_{PP}). In this chapter, at least two additional types of clitic are identified: one corresponds to a Tense-element (CL_T) and another to demonstrative determiners (CL_{DEM}).[2] The variety of categories that can be clitics in Berber is such that one gets the distinct impression that virtually any functional category can be a clitic. Although no attempt is made in this chapter to provide a definition of clitics, there is a clear sense in which clitics are easily identifiable in Berber on distributional grounds. The position between overt F and V in (1b) is exclusively reserved for clitics such that any element that appears in it is a clitic: in the context [F-X-V], X = CL. It is usually sufficient for a given element to occupy this unique CL position for it to be identified as a clitic, but one can also appeal, by way of confirmation, to non-CL positions, such that if a given element can occur in the CL position and is excluded from non-CL positions, then it is a clitic. In Berber, non-CL positions include, in addition to the non-CL positions found across CL languages, for example, non-V-adjacent positions: V DP *CL, the so-called first position discussed shortly.

Context (1a), where V is not preceded by an overt functional category, is not subject to variation. There is no known Berber variety where CL appears before the verb in the absence of an overt functional category to the left of the verb. This is due to the constraint stated in (2), which Berber shares with the group of languages loosely called "second-position clitic languages." A possible account of (2) is entertained in this chapter, which locates it at the PF level (Prosodic Structure) on the ground that it is motivated by prosodic considerations:

(2)   CL cannot be the 'first word' in the clause that includes it.

In contrast, context (1b) is subject to considerable variation, all of which is determined by the value and peculiar properties of F. Although CL appears before the verb in most varieties when overt F has the value Neg, C_Q, C_{WH}, C_{FOC}, or C_{REL} (see section 3 for an explanation), this is not the case when overt F has the value T or C_{THAT}. In some varieties, CL appears after the verb in the presence of what seems to be an overt T or C_{THAT} to the left of the verb. One of the major aims of this chapter is to show that, despite the attested variation, the distribution of

CL in all Berber varieties discussed is consistent with the simple generalization in (3):

(3)   CL is attracted (to the preverbal position) by functional categories.

Variation across varieties, as well as contexts that superficially appear to be inconsistent with (3), is shown to be determined by well-known processes of language change—in particular, grammaticalization (the process through which a lexical category gradually transforms into a functional category) and reanalysis (the process that involves a change in underlying structure). A category that is at different stages of grammaticalization in different varieties may behave differently with respect to its ability to attract CL in those varieties, and may do this in some but not in others. Reanalysis, in contrast, affects the distance over which CL can move, so that it can appear either lower or higher in a given domain, depending on whether the domain has undergone reanalysis in a given variety. The instances of grammaticalization discussed involve T-elements that derive from the (semantically light) verb BE, along with Kinship Terms that derive from (semantically light) relational nouns. The instances of reanalysis involve the change from a biclausal to a monoclausal structure, as a result of the grammaticalization of BE and the change from an analytic to a synthetic structure of possessive DPs.

The statements in (2) and (3) together confirm the long-standing view that CL placement is determined by factors that are partly syntactic and partly prosodic (see Klavans 1980, 1985). Attraction to or by functional categories is a property of movement at the syntactic level in general, which in Minimalism (Chomsky 1995), for example, is accounted for in terms of the mechanism of feature matching and deletion within local domains (Spec, Head, or Head-adjunction relations). The prosodic aspect of the distribution of clitics follows, arguably inevitably, from the fact that CL elements are not prosodic constituents. As such, they are required to be associated with a neighboring overt category that is capable of serving as a prosodic host for them. Another major aim of this chapter is to show that prosodic association of clitics may, in a well-defined set of contexts, involve a local reordering rule that affects CL and its host, called here CL-Host Inversion (CL-H Inversion).

Although (3) is based on the facts of Berber, there are indications that it describes a property of clitics in general. Kayne (1994: 45) points out: "Romance clitics are never adjoined to any form of V, but only to an abstract functional head." To the extent that (3), or a more appropriate version of it, describes the syntactic aspect of CL-placement, it seems to be common to all languages, with variation arguably determined by prosodic considerations at PF (Prosodic Structure).

The rest of the chapter is organized as follows. Section 2 discusses examples from certain varieties of Berber where CL appears after the verb in the presence of what seems to be an overt T or C_{THAT} to the left of the verb. On closer inspection, these examples turn out to be consistent with generalization (3) in a way that reveals its rather absolute nature. The discussion in this section sheds light on how the processes of grammaticalization and reanalysis interact with the mechanisms that determine CL placement.

Section 3 deals with contexts where CL appears associated with V (1a). These contexts, too, are shown to be consistent with generalization (3), once a distinction is made between the syntactic process that displaces CL to a functional head, including a null or abstract head, and the prosodic process that associates the displaced CL with an adjacent prosodic constituent. Although the syntactic host and the prosodic host of CL are the same category in many contexts, there are contexts where they may be two different categories (see Klavans 1985, Nespor 1999). Examples with the V=CL order are precisely such contexts. Moreover, when these examples are considered in the light of the ban on first-position clitics, they make evident the probable involvement in CL placement of a local reordering process that inverts the order of CL and an adjacent prosodic constituent (CL-H Inversion).

Section 4 discusses a different set of examples that arguably provide more direct evidence for CL-H Inversion. These involve certain negative sentences in a particular dialect of the Tashl*h*it variety where CL appears to the left of Neg, an unusual order that appears inconsistent with the widely supported generalization that Neg blocks CL movement across it in Berber (see Ouhalla 1988, 1989). These examples are argued to reflect directly the effect of the syntactic process that displaces CL to its attractor, whereby CL is left-adjoined to its attractor. The fact that CL appears to the right of its syntactic attractor in general is due to CL-H Inversion.

Finally, section 5 looks at the distribution of CL in other (nonclausal) domains, in particular, PPs and DPs. Here again, most of the data seem to be consistent with the generalization that CL is attracted to functional categories and never to lexical categories in Berber. Three different sets of data that initially appear to be inconsistent with this generalization—that is, DPs where CL is directly associated with N rather than with an intervening functional category—are examined in detail. One set involves DPs where N belongs to a small class of Kinship Terms with peculiar properties that set them apart from nouns in the language. Another set involves demonstrative DPs, where the demonstrative elements are clitics. The third set involves possessive DPs in a variety of Berber where a possessor clitic can appear directly on N instead of on an intervening preposition OF. This peculiar distribution is argued to be the consequence of a process of reanalysis that has transformed an analytic structure that includes OF (and its phrase structure projections), typical of Berber possessive DPs, to an innovative synthetic structure that lacks OF more typical of the type of possessive DPs found in the Semitic languages and others.

2 CLITICS AND FUNCTIONAL CATEGORIES

The Tamazight examples (4a, b) both include the element *LLA*, which is responsible for the present tense progressive (or habitual) reading of the sentences, along with the imperfective (IMPER) form of the verb. The element *LLA* is glossed as $T_{PRES(ENT)}$ in (4a) and merely as PRESENT in (4b) for reasons that will become clear shortly:

(4) a. Lla   =**t**   i-ssa. (M. Guerssel, pers. comm., 2000)
      T_{PRES} =it$_{ACC}$ 3MS-drink$_{IMPERF}$

     'He is drinking it / He drinks it.'

    b. Lla   i-ssa   =**t**.
       PRES   3MS-drink$_{IMPERF}$ =it$_{ACC}$

Example (4a) is consistent with generalization (3) since CL is associated with a functional category to the left of the verb. Example (4b), however, apparently is not. CL is associated with the verb in the presence of what seems to be an overt functional category to the left of the verb. M. Guerssel (pers. comm., 2000) points out that the two orders in (4a, b) are subject to dialectal variation within Tamazight. In one dialect, Ait A'yyash Tamazight, only the order in (4a) is possible. In another dialect, Ait Seghroushn Tamazight, both orders are possible.

To understand the apparently inconsistent behavior of CL or, for that matter, the present-tense element *LLA*, in Tamazight, some related facts of Tarifit need to be explored. Tarifit (along with a number of other varieties—e.g., Taqbaylit and Tamahaght Tuareg) does not have an equivalent of the Tamazight present-tense *LLA*. Parallel sentences in Tarifit (i.e., sentences with a present-tense habitual or progressive reading) include only the bare imperfective form of the verb, with consequences for the order of CL discussed in section 3. However, Tarifit has a past-tense version, *ILA*, seen in examples (5a, b) from the Ait Waryaghl dialect. Interestingly, the Tarifit past tense *ILA* never attracts CL (to the preverbal position):

(5) a. Ila   ttari-n   =**t.**
        PAST   write$_{\text{IMPERF}}$-3PL   =it$_{\text{ACC}}$

     'They were writing it.'

     b. Ila   ttessnenna-n   =**t.**
        PAST   cook$_{\text{IMPERF}}$-3PL   =it$_{\text{ACC}}$

     'They were cooking it.'

There are now three different types of tense elements with different properties in different varieties. One type invariably attracts CL (the Ait A'yyash Tamazight present-tense *LLA*). Another type attracts CL only optionally (the Ait Seghroushn Tamazight present-tense *LLA*). A third type does not attract CL at all (the Tarifit past-tense *ILA*). The Tarifit facts, while appearing to complicate the situation, also point to the source of the apparent inconsistency. The obvious similarity in form between the Tamazight present-tense *LLA* and the Tarifit past-tense *ILA* suggests they both derive from the same root. Once this link is made, another link becomes obvious—namely, that both elements are related to the verb BE. The Tamazight present-tense *LLA* corresponds to the imperfective form of BE, which is normally associated with the present tense reading. The Tarifit past-tense *ILA*, in contrast, corresponds to the perfective (PERF) form of BE, which is normally associated with the past-tense reading. In Tarifit, the imperfective LLA can still be used as a main verb, as shown in the Ait Waryaghl example (6). In contrast, the pefective ILA can no longer be used as a main verb for reasons partly explained in what follows:

(6) a. (Lla-n)   ifruxn   g-uxxam.
        be$_{\text{IMPERF}}$-3PL   boys   in-room

     'The boys are in the room.'

     b. ILA Ila-n   ifruxn   g-uxxam.
        PAST be-3PL   children in-room

     'The boys were in the room.'

The tense elements differ from the corresponding forms of the verb BE only in that they lack the subject agreement inflection that normally characterizes verbs in Berber. It is clear that these elements have evolved from the corresponding aspectual forms of the verb BE, an instance of grammaticalization. As is well known, the process of grammaticalization of a given category is not uniform across varieties of the language that have it. It may be more (or less) advanced in some varieties than it is in others along a given continuum of grammaticalization. This appears to be the case with *LLA* and *ILA*. At the extreme end of the continuum, we find the present-tense *LLA* of Ait A'yyash Tamazight, which has been completely transformed into a T-element. In structural terms, this means that the Ait A'yyash *LLA* projects a T(P), as shown in (7b). The fact that CL invariably gets attracted to it follows in a straightforward way:

(7) a. Lla   =**t**   i-ssa.

    T$_{PRES}$ =it$_{ACC}$ 3MS-drink$_{IMPERF}$

    'He is drinking it.'

    b. [$_{TP}$ *LLA* =**CL** [$_{VP}$ V$_{IMPERF}$ $\cdots$

At the opposite end (i.e., the beginning) of the continuum, we find the Tarifit past-tense *ILA*. That this element has already embarked on the process of grammaticalization is shown by the fact that it has already shed the subject agreement inflection typical of verbs in Berber in all contexts. However, it appears that this element has not yet shed its verbal properties completely. In structural terms, this means that the Tarifit *ILA* projects a V(P) rather than a T(P), as shown in (8b). Like all verbs in the perfective form in the language (see later), *ILA* is selected by a null T category with past-tense value, with the two together forming an independent clause. The status of Tarifit *ILA* as a verb (i.e., a lexical category) explains why CL is never attracted to it, although a full explanation of CL placement in this context also involves the distance between the underlying position of CL and its potential attractors, as we will see later:

(8) a. Ila   ttari-n   =**t.**

    be$_{PERF}$ write$_{IMPERF}$-3PL   =it$_{ACC}$

    'They were writing it.'

    b. [$_{TP}$ T$_{\varnothing}$ [$_{VP}$ *ILA* [$_{TP/VP}$ V$_{IMPERF}$ =**CL** $\cdots$

At the intermediate stage, we find the present-tense *LLA* of Ait Seghroushn Tamazight. Not unusually, this element displays both its original properties (as a verb) and the properties of what it is turning into (i.e., a T-element). Formally, this means that Ait Seghroushn Tamazight *LLA* has an ambiguous status. It can either be a T-element, in which case it is included in a structure along the lines of (7b), which corresponds to the order where CL precedes the main verb. Alternatively, it can be a V, in which case it is included in a structure along the lines of (8b), which corresponds to the order where CL appears following the main verb. Thus, what originally appeared to be optional CL movement (or optional attraction of CL) turns out merely to reflect the ambiguous status of *LLA* in Ait Seghroushn Tamazight.

In all examples discussed, the distribution of CL is consistent with generalization (3). The reason CL appears after the main verb in the embedded TP/VP in (8) is explained in section 3, which deals with the derivation of the V=CL order. The null T in the embedded TP corresponds to the null T that cooccurs with the imperfective form of the verb in Tarifit and other varieties (see section 3). The presence of two separate Ts in (8), each of which selects a different VP, implies a biclausal structure. In contrast, (7b) clearly has a monoclausal structure, with a single T selecting a VP. This difference is the result of the grammaticalization of the verb BE as T and is an instance of the well-known process of reanalysis that reduces biclausal structures to monoclausal structures:

(9)   a. $[_{CP}$ C $[_{TP}$ T $[_{VP}$ V $([_{CP}$ C$)$ $[_{TP}$ T $[_{VP}$ V . . . $\rightarrow$ (reanalysis)

      b. $[_{CP}$ C $[_{TP}$ T $[_{VP}$ V . . .

This instance of reanalysis has an inevitable consequence for CL placement. In the biclausal structure (8b, 9a),) the local domain of CL is the embedded clause that includes it, and hence the fact it appears within this clause.[3] In the monoclausal structure (7b/9b), however, the local domain of CL is the root clause, resulting in the fact that CL appears associated with the T of the root clause.

We now turn to a context that involves C_{THAT}. Example (10) shows that the Imadlawn Tashlhit C_{THAT} element *IS* attracts CL to it, a property not necessarily shared by its counterparts in other dialects of Tashlhit:

(10)   Ur   i-ssin   is   =**ghid**   lla-n. (Elmedlaoui 1999: 71)
       Neg   3MS-know$_{NEG}$ that   =there   be$_{IMP}$-3PL
       'He does not know that they are there.'

There is a whole group of C_{THAT} elements across Berber varieties that consistently never attract CL (see Ouhalla 2000).[4] Here, the discussion is limited to the C_{THAT}-element of the Tamahaght dialect of Tuareg (Tamahaght Tuareg), which has the form *INNIN* seen in (11a, b):

(11)   a. T-nna   innin   i-uri   =**t**
           3FS-say$_{PERF}$ that   3MS-open$_{PERF}$ =it$_{ACC}$
           arrau. (Mohammed Ali 1992:47)
           boy
           'She said that the boy opened it.'

       b. I-ghil   innin   i-rms   =**tn**   amnokal.
           3MS-think   that   3MS-seize$_{PERF}$ =them$_{ACC}$ president
           'He thinks that the president seized them.'

Once again, this is a context where CL appears to prefer to associate itself with the verb in the presence of what seems to be a functional category to the left of the verb. This situation is similar to the situation in Tamazight and Tarifit discussed earlier involving the tense elements *LLA* and *ILA*. As in that situation, too, what appears to be a functional category to the left of the verb turns out, on closer inspection, to be a lexical category. The Tamahaght Tuareg *INNIN* corresponds to one of the participial forms of the verb SAY—in particular, the negative participial form. The verb SAY has the consonantal root √NN, from which the perfective form in (11a) and the negative participial form *I-NNI-N* are derived. The perfective form is derived by mapping of the consonantal root onto the aspectual (or theme) vowel, followed by affixation of agreement inflection. The participial form is derived in roughly the same way, except that the affixation part of the derivation involves the suffixation of the so-called participial affix (PART) *-N*.[5]

Tamahaght Tuareg is not unique in using a form of the verb SAY as a declarative complementizer (see Lord 1976). To the extent that the Tamahaght Tuareg *INNIN* is in the process of being grammaticalized as a functional category of the type C_{THAT}, it seems that this process so far has affected only its meaning ("semantic bleaching"). Its status as a lexical category persists, and this is the reason CL is not attracted to it. Exactly what structure Tamahaght Tuareg *INNIN* clauses have is an interesting but complex question that falls outside the main scope of this chapter. Example (12) includes a rough representation, where C is filled with a participle with the mixed internal verbal properties and external nonverbal properties usually associated with participles across languages:

(12)   ... [$_{CP}$ [$_{PART}$ SAY-PART] [$_{TP}$ ... [V]=**CL** ...

To conclude this section, the fact that CL follows the verb in the presence of what seems to be an overt T or C_{THAT} to the left of the verb in some varieties is not necessarily inconsistent with the generalization that CL is attracted to functional categories but never to lexical categories in Berber. On closer inspection, the elements preceding the verb turn out to be lexical categories, albeit with a function normally associated with the functional categories T and C_{THAT}.

3 CLITICS AND LEXICAL CATEGORIES

The V=CL order is found in numerous contexts. One such context involves nonnegative imperatives, illustrated with the Ait Waryaghl Tarifit example (13a). Another context involves sentences with a bare perfective form of verb and a past-tense reading, illustrated with the Ait Waryaghl Tarifit example (13b):

(13) a. Sqad   =**as**   tabratt!
         send$_{IMP}$ =him$_{DAT}$ letter

      'Send him the letter!'

      b. T-sqad   =**as**   tfruxt   tabratt.
         3FS-send$_{PERF}$ =him$_{DAT}$ girl   letter

      'The girl (has) sent him the letter.'

Both examples include a double object verb and a dative CL, so that the dative CL must have moved across at least the direct object in (13a), and across both the direct object and the postverbal subject in (13b). The fact that this movement appears to target the verb is what makes these examples potentially inconsistent with generalization (3).

The contexts illustrated in (13a, b) and the orders they exhibit are uniform across Berber varieties. However, there are contexts in which the V=CL order is found in some varieties but not in others, the determining factor, as usual, being whether the verb is preceded by an overt functional category. One such context involves sentences with a verb in the imperfective form and a present-tense (or habitual) reading. In Tamazight (as well as Tashlḥit), such sentences include an overt T-element to the left of the verb that attracts CL to it (see discussion in the previous section). The Tamazight example (14a) is repeated from the previous section. In Tarifit (as well as Taqbaylit and Tamahaght Tuareg), the corresponding sentences do not include an overt T-element. They include only the bare imperfective form of the verb, with the consequence that CL appears following the verb rather than preceding it. This is shown in the Ait Waryaghl Tarifit example (14b):

(14) a. Lla   =**t**   i-ssa.
         T$_{PRES}$ =it$_{ACC}$ 3MS-drink$_{IMPERF}$

      'He is drinking it.'

      b. I-tessnenn   =**as**   seçsu.
         3MS-cook$_{IMPERF}$ =her$_{DAT}$ couscous

      'He is cooking / he cooks couscous for her.'

Another context in which there appears to be variation across varieties involves root yes-no questions. In Tashlḥit (as well as Tamazight), root yes-no questions include an overt Q-element that attracts CL, as shown in example (15a) from the Agadir/Inzggan dialect of Tashlḥit. In Tarifit (as well as in Taqbaylit and Tamahaght Tuareg), root yes-no questions do not include an overt Q-element; they merely rely on rising intonation applied to the usual VSO order. Consequently, CL appears following the verb rather than preceding it in the equivalent examples in these varieties. This is shown in the Ait Waryaghl Tarifit example (15b):

(15) a. Is   =**t**   i-zra   ufrux? (L. Alami, pers. comm., 2000)
         C_Q =her$_{ACC}$ 3MS-see$_{PERF}$ boy

     'Did the boy see her?'

     b. T-sqad   =**as**   tabratt?
         3FS-send$_{PERF}$ =him$_{DAT}$ letter

     'Did she send him the letter.'

Presumably, Tarifit root yes-no questions resemble their Tashlhit counterparts in that they, too, have a C marked with the feature [Q] (C_Q) necessary for interpretation. The difference reduces to whether C_Q is spelled out (Tashlhit) or remains null (Tarifit). This reasoning extends to the sentences in (14a, b). The Tarifit example (14b) also includes a T-category marked with the tense feature [PRES]; it differs from its Tamazight counterpart (14a) in that this T-category is not spelled out. As for sentences such as (13b), postulating the presence of a null T with the feature [PAST] for them may look implausible in view of the fact that there are no known Berber varieties that overtly realize T in such contexts. However, a case can plausibly be made on numerous grounds (see Ouhalla 1988). For the purposes of the current discussion, it is perhaps sufficient to point out that a distinctive property of Berber grammar is that the various aspectual forms of the verb usually occur in strict correlation with a functional category that selects for them. It is not unreasonable, therefore, to assume that the perfective form of the verb in sentences such as (13b) co occurs with a null T-category that selects for it. There are no reasons why a similar case cannot be made for nonnegative imperatives such as (13a), with the null functional category that selects for the imperative form of the verb being C/I with the feature [IMP(erative)] (C/I_{IMP}).

In view of this, it appears as though whether a given functional category is overt or null plays a crucial role in whether it attracts CL (to the preverbal position). The previous paradigm suggests that only overt functional categories attract CL. However, it is possible to assign to sentences with the V=CL order an analysis that is consistent with generalization (3) but which does not require a distinction between overt and null functional categories in syntax. To the extent that the null/overt distinction plays a role, it must be at a later level where representations are assigned phonetic content (PF).

The analysis rests on the idea that sentences with the V=CL order have basically the same representation as sentences with the F=CL^V order in syntax. The representation in question has the form $[_{FP} F_\varnothing = CL [_{XP} V \dots]]$, where $F_\varnothing$ is a null functional category that can have the values C_Q (15b), T_{PRES} (14b), T_{PAST} (13b), or C_{IMP} (13a). This representation is clearly consistent with the generalization that CL is attracted to functional categories and never to lexical categories. However, the representation is equally clearly inconsistent with the constraint that CL can never be the "first word" in the clause in Berber. Presumably, the constraint in question is prosodic in nature, in the sense that it must have to do, at least in part, with the fact that clitics are not prosodic constituents. As such, clitics are therefore required, for example, by the principle of Exhaustivity (Selkirk 1986), to be associated with a prosodic host at the level of Prosodic Structure. Representation $[_{FP} F_\emptyset = CL [_{XP} V \ldots]]$ includes a prosodic constituent, namely, the verb, but the verb is on the wrong side of CL in a sense to be made clear shortly.

There is a tradition in work on prosody that assumes a difference between languages in the directionality of prosodic parsing, such as the choice between left-edge and right-edge alignment assumed in Selkirk (1986) and Selkirk and Shen (1990). In view of this, it is arguably plausible to assume a parametrized constraint on the directionality of prosodic association of CL (see Halpern 1995), such that in some languages it can operate only leftward (see Nespor and Vogel 1986 on directional clitics). Whether this constraint is true of all so-called second-position clitic languages remains to be seen. What is reasonably clear is that it rings very true for Berber, where clitics invariably appear associated with the overt category immediately to their left, irrespective of what appears to their right.

Assuming this to be the case, what needs to happen to the syntactic representation $[_{FP} F_\emptyset = CL [_{XP} V \ldots]]$ is for V to be placed to the left of CL, essentially Kayne's (1991) analysis of the $V_{INF}=CL$ order in Romance. There are two ways this order can be derived, both of which have been suggested in the literature. One way would be simple linear inversion of CL and V. However, while this may be compatible with languages where CL can be prosodically associated with any phonological material in the first position (see Halpern 1995), it is arguably incompatible with Berber, where CL appears to be particularly selective about its prosodic host. Basically, Berber CL can be prosodically associated only with head categories, including V. This can be seen more clearly in the Ait Waryaghl Tarifit examples (16a, b), which are instances of CLLD and PP Topicalization, respectively.[6] Even though both constructions involve phonological material to the left of the verb, CL cannot appear associated with them. Placement of the verb to the left of CL is still necessary:

(16) a. Gi ssnduq(,)   (*=**asn**)   t-sqad   =**asn**   tabratt.
         in box   =them$_{DAT}$ 3FS-send$_{PERF}$ =them$_{DAT}$ letter
      'In the box, she sent them the letter.'

      b. Tabratt,   (*=**t**)   t-sqad   =**t**   gi ssnduq.
         letter   =it$_{ACC}$ 3FS-send$_{PERF}$ =it$_{ACC}$ in box
      'The letter, she sent it in the box.'

Examples (16a, b) and others discussed later suggest that the constraint in (2) should be strengthened along the lines in (2'), where the expression "first word" is replaced with the more accurate expression "first head constituent." The effect of (2') on clitics included in the DP and PP domains is discussed in section 5:

(2')   CL cannot be the first head constituent in the minimal domain (CP, DP, or PP) that includes it.

On a more formal level, examples (16a, b) suggest that the process that places the verb to the left of CL in the V=CL order—in particular, the fact that it is sensitive to heads but not to nonheads—takes the form of head raising. Assuming representation $[_{FP} F_\emptyset = CL [_{XP} V \dots]]$, head raising of V can, in principle, target a null functional category above $F_\emptyset$. However, at least in sentences where $F_\emptyset$ has the value C_Q (15b) or C_{IMP} (13a) (the highest functional head in the clause), it is not clear what this additional null functional category could be. The other options depend on the structural relation of CL to its attractor, which is yet to be made specific.

The order of CL and its attractor in the representation $[_{FP} F_\emptyset = CL [_{XP} V]]$ reflects the fact pointed out earlier in this chapter that Berber CL normally appears to the right (rather than to the left) of its attractor. This is the reason Berber CL was assumed to right-adjoin to its attractor in Ouhalla (1988, 1989), who was mainly concerned with the facts of Tarifit. However, there are now reasons—one internal to Berber and the other external—to believe that this is unlikely to be the right analysis. The internal reason has to do with the fact that there are contexts in a specific dialect of Tashlhit (Imdlawn Tashlhit) where CL appears to the left of its attractor. Because these contexts involve Neg, their discussion is postponed to the next section. The external reason has to do with the widely held view, supported with data from across languages, that CL left-adjoins to its host (see Kayne 1991, 1994 and Halpern 1995, among others). Considering these factors, the assumed representation now has the more accurate form $[_{FP} [=CL] F_\emptyset [_{XP}$ $V \dots]]$, with CL left-adjoined to its attractor $F_\emptyset$. This representation still leaves two options for the V-raising process that derives the V=CL order. One is further adjunction to complex $F_\emptyset$, and the other is adjunction to CL itself. As far as the data discussed here are concerned, the choice between these two options seems to be mainly theoretical. For example, the first option (adjunction to complex $F_\emptyset$) is excluded in the Antisymmetry theory of phrase structure (Kayne 1994), which rules out multiple adjunction in general.[7]

According to the analysis outlined, the V=CL order is derived by left-adjunction of CL to a null F, followed by raising of the verb to the left of CL, which I assume here takes the form of left-adjunction of V to CL. This second step is necessitated by the need for CL to be prosodically associated with an overt head constituent situated to its left. As noted earlier, the rule that raises V to the left of CL is called CL-H Inversion:

(17) a. $[_{FP}$ F $[_{XP}$ V . . . CL . . .

    b. $[_{FP}$ [[CL] $F_{\varnothing}]$ $[_{XP}$ V . . .   (Left-adjunction of CL to $F_{\varnothing}]$

    c. $[_{FP}$ [[V] =CL] $F_{\varnothing}$ $[_{XP}$ . . .   (CL-V Inversion)

Whether the rule that places V to the left of CL applies in syntax or at PF (see Chomsky 1995 on head raising at PF) will remain an open question. If it is indeed the case that the rule is motivated merely by the need to provide a prosodic host for CL, and if syntactic rules are not expected to anticipate prosodic considerations applying at PF, there is perhaps a case for concluding that it applies at PF. At any rate, there seems to be considerable additional evidence for such a rule, and this is discussed in the remaining sections.

For the moment, note that the proposed analysis—in particular, the idea that CL left-adjoins to the functional head that attracts it—has major implications for the derivation of the F=CL^V order. It implies a syntactic representation (that feeds CL-H Inversion) of the form $[_{FP}$ [[CL] F] $[_{XP}$ V . . .]], with CL left-adjoined to the overt functional head F. It follows that the F=CL^V order is derived by CL-H Inversion at a later level (Prosodic Structure). In other words, the claim implies a derivation along the lines in (18):

(18) a. $[_{FP}$ F $[_{XP}$ V . . . CL . . .

    b. $[_{FP}$ [[CL] F] $[_{XP}$ V . . .   (Left-adjunction of CL to F)

    c. $[_{FP}$ [[F] [=CL]] $[_{XP}$ V . . .   (CL-F Inversion)

The next section discusses a group of constructions in Imdlawn Tashlḥit that appear to confirm that CL left-adjoins to its functional attractor and is forced into the second head position only in contexts where there is no head category to its left that could function as a prosodic host for it.

To conclude this section, the V=CL order is not necessarily inconsistent with the generalization that CL is attracted to functional categories and never to lexical categories in Berber. The contexts that display this order are consistent with an analysis in which CL is attracted to a null functional category to the left of the verb, with the surface V=CL order derived by a head-raising process, called CL-H Inversion, which places the verb to the left of CL.

4 CLITICS AND NEGATION

Berber sentence negation is encoded at two levels: the functional level and the lexical (or verb) level. At the functional level, it is encoded in terms of the functional category *UR* that appears to the left of the verb.[8] At the lexical level, sentence negation is expressed in terms of a distinctive form of the verb known in the Berber linguistic tradition as the NEG(ATIVE) (or irrealis) form. The latter differs from the derivationally related perfective form by a change in the internal vowel (usually from /a/ to /i/) in the third-person members of the paradigm. For example, the third-person nonnegative perfective form of the verb 'send' has the form *sqad*, whereas its negative counterpart has the slightly different form *sqid* seen in the Ait Waryaghl Tarifit example (19b):

(19) a. Ur   =**tn**   tjj   diha!
          Neg   =them$_{ACC}$ leave   there

          'Don't leave them there!'

      b. Ur   =**(d)asn**   i-sqid   tabratt.
          Neg   =them$_{DAT}$ 3MS-send$_{NEG}$ letter

          'He has not sent them the letter.'

It is clear from examples (19a, b) that Neg attracts CL, which is trivially consistent with generalization (3). Besides attracting CL, Neg also blocks CL movement across it to a higher functional head, on a par with its counterparts in Romance (see Kayne 1989). These properties of Berber Neg are discussed in Ouhalla (1988, 1989) in relation to Tarifit. The same situation is found in Tamazight, as shown in examples (20a–d) from the Zemmour or Khmisset dialect (see Boukhris 1998). Examples (20a) and (20b) show that C_Q and Neg can each attract CL. When both categories are present in a clause, with the expected order $C_Q \wedge$Neg, CL appears to the right of Neg (20c) ($C_Q \wedge$Neg=CL):

(20) a. Is   =**tn**   'li-x? (Boukhris 1998: 318)
          C_Q =them$_{ACC}$ see$_{PERF}$-1S

          'Have I seen them?'

      b. Ur   =**tn**   'li-x.
          Neg   =them$_{ACC}$ see$_{PERF}$-1S

          'I have not seen them.'

c. Is   ur   =**tn**   'li-x?
  C_Q Neg   =them$_{ACC}$ see$_{PERF}$-1S

'Have I not seen them?'

The pattern seen in (20c) appears to be characteristic of most varieties. However, Tashlhit allows a limited degree of variation on this pattern that looks untypical and somewhat bizarre. This variation is discussed in Dell and Elmedlaoui (1989) in relation to examples from the Imdlawn dialect, some of which are repeated next:

(21)   a. Waxxa   ur   =**iyi**   zri-n. (Dell and Elmedlaoui 1989: 173)
       even-if   Neg   =me$_{ACC}$ see$_{NEG}$-3PL

      'Even if they did not see me.'

  b. Waxxa   =**iyi**   ur   zri-n.
       even-if   =me$_{ACC}$ Neg   see$_{NEG}$-3PL

      'Even if they did not see me.'

Example (21a) exhibits the expected order in which CL is to the right of Neg, whereas Example (21b) exhibits an alternative possible order in which CL is to the left of Neg. This particular order not only is unusual from the comparative perspective but also appears to undermine the otherwise widely attested fact, that in Berber, Neg blocks CL movement across it.

Dell and Elmedlaoui (1989: 173) deal with the unusual order in (21b) by postulating an (*Aspects*-style) transformational rule called *UR*-shift. The latter applies to the order in (21a) and shifts the Neg-element *UR* to the position immediately preceding the verb, thereby deriving the order seen in (21b). The rule has the form $1_{IP}2_{UR}3_X4_V \rightarrow 1_{IP}3_X2_{UR}4_V$ (IP = Initial Preverbal element), which easily translates as CL-H Inversion in the analysis proposed in this chapter, but with an interesting twist. It has the consequence of treating the (unusual) order in (21b) as the more basic order, in the precise sense that it is the order derived by left-adjunction of CL to Neg in syntax. The (more usual) order in (21b) is derived by CL-H Inversion, which places Neg to the left of CL. CL-H Inversion applies optionally in (21) because CL/Neg is preceded by a category that can host CL, the conditional C-element *waxxa* 'even if' (C_{COND}).

According to this analysis, the (unusual) order in (21b) is not due to some peculiar property of the Neg-element *UR* in Imdlawn Tashlhit that makes it more permissive with respect to CL-movement. This would not make sense, particularly in view of the fact that the Neg-element of Imdlawn Tashlhit is the same element found in other varieties. Rather, it reflects directly the effect of the syntactic rule of CL movement to Neg, which left-adjoins CL to Neg. In (21a) and (19a, b), the order derived by CL movement is subsequently distorted by the effect of CL-H Inversion.

The same effect can be seen in other contexts. The pair (22a, b) is among the examples discussed by Dell and Elmedlaoui in relation to *UR* shift, although the interpretation given to the examples in the gloss is slightly different (Elmedlaoui, pers. comm., 2000). In Tashlhit (as well as Tamazight), the C-element *IS* can function either as a Q-morpheme (C_Q) or, somewhat surprisingly, as a declarative complementizer (C_{THAT}) in both root and embedded domains:[9]

(22) a. Is   ur   a   =**dis**   i-shtta.
          that   Neg T_{PRES} =with-her   3MS-eat$_{IMPERF}$
          (Dell and Elmedlaoui 1989: 173)

          'It is indeed the case that he eats with her.'

      b. Is   a   =**dis**   ur   i-shtta.
          C_Q T_{PRES} =with-her   Neg   3MS-eat$_{IMPERF}$

          'It is indeed the case that he eats with her.'

Besides the C_{THAT}-element *IS*, examples (22a) and (22b) both include the present T-element *A*, the Neg-element *UR*, and the CL_{PP} *DIS* 'with her', in addition to the imperfective form of the verb. The two examples, however, differ in the order of the functional elements preceding the verb. Example (22a) displays the (more usual) order $C\wedge Neg\wedge T\wedge =CL_{PP}\wedge V$, with Neg to the left of T and CL_{PP}. In contrast, example (34b) displays the (unusual) order $C\wedge T\wedge =CL_{PP}\wedge Neg\wedge V$, with Neg to the right of both T and CL_{PP}. In the analysis outlined by Dell and Elmedlaoui (1989), *UR*-shift applies to the order in (22a) and places Neg rightward, to the position immediately to the left of the verb and deriving the order in (22b).

To appreciate the variation in (22a, b) two crucial facts have to be understood and taken into consideration. First, in Tashlhit—and indeed Berber in general— Neg normally appears to the left of T rather than following it. In other words, the normal order is $C\wedge Neg\wedge T\wedge V$, which corresponds to the order in (22a). It follows that the different $C\wedge T\wedge Neg\wedge V$ order in (22b) is derived somehow. Second, the T-element *A* is a reduced form of the present-tense element *AR* seen (in its full glory) in (23):

(23) Ar   =**ghinn**   ili-n. (Dell and Elmedlaoui 1989: 171)
      T_{PRES} =there   be$_{IMPER}$-3PL

      'They are usually there.'

A consequence of the reduced nature of the T-element *A* is that it itself is a CL (CL_T). This particular property of the reduced T-element *A* can be seen clearly in the pair (24a, b), compared with (23). The only conceivable reason that (24b) is excluded is because it violates the constraint that CL cannot be the "first head-constituent" in the clause:

(24) a. Ur   a   =dis   i-shtta? (Dell and Elmedlaoui 1989: 173)
         Neg T$_{PRES}$ =with-her   3MS-eat$_{IMPERF}$

      'He does not eat with her.'

      b. *A   =dis   ur   i-shtta?
         T$_{PRES}$ =with-her   Neg 3MS-eat$_{IMPERF}$

The CL status of the reduced T-element provides an obvious clue as to how the (unusual) order C∧=CL$_T$∧=CL$_{PP}$∧Neg∧V in (22b) is derived. It is derived by adjunction of CL$_{PP}$ to Neg, followed by adjunction of CL$_T$ to CL$_{PP}$, as would be required in the context of Antisymmetry (see Kayne 1994 on the representation of clitic clusters). The more usual order, C∧Neg∧=CL$_T$∧=CL$_{PP}$∧V in (22a) is derived by CL-H Inversion, which places Neg to the left of the CL cluster. In this particular context, CL-H Inversion applies optionally because CL/Neg is preceded by a head category that is capable of functioning as the prosodic host for CL. CL-H Inversion also applies in the derivation of example (24a), with an identical effect on the order of the same categories. In (24), though, CL-H Inversion applies obligatorily, due to the fact that CL is the first head-constituent in the clause. Example (24b) is basically the representation of (24a) prior to (or minus) CL-H Inversion.

In conclusion, the unusual orders found in the Imdlawn Tashlḥit negative examples discussed offer both direct evidence for the claim that CL left-adjoins to its attractor in syntax and indirect evidence for the claim that the order of CL in relation to its host involves a local reordering operation that places the overt attractor or host to the left of CL (CL-H Inversion). The proposed analysis of these examples is consistent with the general fact that Neg both attracts CL and blocks CL movement across it in Berber.

5 CLITICS IN PPS AND DPS

The Ait Waryaghl Tarifit examples (25a–c) include a few representative prepositions with a pronominal CL object:

(25) a. I-ssas   tabratt   x(f)e=**s.**
          3MS-place_PERF   letter   on=it_DAT

      'He put the letter on it / beside him.'

      b. I-gga   tabratt   ge=**s.**
          3MS-put_PERF   letter   in=it_DAT

      'He put the letter in/on it.'

      c. I-ssufgh   tabratt   zge=**s.**
          3MS-pull_PERF   letter   from=it_DAT

      'He pulled the letter from it.'

The P=CL order is consistent with generalization (3) on the arguably uncontroversial view that prepositions are functional categories. Unlike lexical categories (verbs and nouns), prepositions do not carry any inflection at all and therefore have the form typical of functional categories in Berber.[10] According to the analysis whereby CL left-adjoins to its attractor in syntax, the P=CL order must be the result of CL-H Inversion. As in all other contexts where it applies, this rule is motivated by the need to provide CL with a prosodic host to its left within the minimal domain that includes CL—PP in this case.

One of the interesting properties of prepositions is that they not only can attract or host CL but also can themselves be CL, meaning they can occupy CL positions. Berber prepositional clitics can have one of two forms shown in the Imdlawn Tashlḥit examples (26a, b). They can consist of the bare preposition (CL_P), or they can have a complex form consisting of the preposition and a pronominal dative CL (CL_PP). The first type is found in contexts where the preposition is stranded by extraction of its object (26a). The second type is not restricted to any specific contexts:

(26) a. Man tfruxt   a   =**f**   ra   sawl-x?
          which girl   C_WH   =on   FUT   talk_AOR-1S
          (Dell and Elmedlaoui 1989: 185–168)

      'Which girl shall I talk to you about?

      b. Is   =tn   =**gis**   i-ga   ufrux?
          C_Q   =them_ACC   =in-it   3MS-put_PERF   boy

      'Did the boy put them in it?'

The fact that prepositions can both host CL and be CL raises significant but fairly complex questions not all of which can be explored here. Of particular importance is the fact that CL_PP can occur in both non-CL positions, such as the final position in (25a–c) where it is separated from the verb by the direct object, and in CL positions (26b). Presumably, the fact that CL_{PP} can occupy the final position following the direct object (25a–c) implies that it is able to receive primary stress. If this is correct, then CL_{PP} is perhaps an instance of a category that is not a "phonological clitic" but at the same time is a "syntactic clitic" by virtue of the fact that it can occupy CL positions (see Nespor 1999 on the distinction between phonological and syntactic clitics). However, if being a "syntactic clitic" implies having a property relevant to syntax, an issue not addressed in this chapter, then CL_{PP} must have this property optionally.[11]

Turning now to CL in DPs, there is a sense in which the N=CL pattern, with CL directly associated with N, is rather untypical in Berber. The more typical pattern is for CL to be associated with an intervening functional head, at least in contexts where this is possible. For example, when CL is a possessor (CL_{POSS}), what is found in most varieties is a situation where CL is associated with the semantically vacuous preposition OF (N^OF=CL_{POSS}) rather than directly with N. This is the case, for example, in Tarifit illustrated with the Ait Waryaghl examples (27a, b) compared with examples (28a, b), which include a non-CL DP possessor:

(27) a. axxam   *(nn)   =**s**
         room   of   =him$_{DAT}$

         'his room'

      b. afrux   *(nn)   =**s**
         boy   of   =him$_{DAT}$

         'his boy'

(28) a. axxam   (n)   wargaz
         room   of   man

         'the man's room'

      b. afrux   (n)   wargaz
         boy   of   man

         'the man's child'

Examples (28a, b) show that when the possessor is a non-CL DP, the presence of the preposition OF is only optional. This leads to the conclusion that the only reason for the obligatory appearance of the preposition OF in (27a, b) is to provide a host for CL that is not a lexical category. If so, the distribution of CL in DPs in Tarifit and similar varieties appears to reinforce the part of generalization (3) that states that CL is never attracted to or by lexical categories in Berber.

Two types of DP initially appear to be inconsistent with the generalization that the N=C pattern is generally not readily available in Berber. The first type is illustrated with the Ait Waryaghl Tarifit examples (29a–f), which include Kinship Terms (KT):

(29) a. mmi=**s**   b. yilli=**s**
          son=her/him$_{DAT}$ daughter=her/him$_{DAT}$

          'his/her son'   'his/her daughter'

      c. aba=(d)**sn**   d. yemma=(d)**sn**
          father=them$_{DAT}$ mother=them$_{DAT}$

          'their father'   'their mother'

      e. um=**as**   f. wtchm=**as**
          brother=her/him$_{DAT}$ sister-her/him$_{DAT}$

          'her/his brother'   'her/his sister'

The KTs in (29a–f) have a number of properties that distinguish them from nouns, nearly all of which follow from the general property stated in (30). (State inflection corresponds, roughly, to Case inflection):

(30)   KTs lack the Number, Gender, and State inflection that normally characterizes Nouns in Berber.

The property described in (30) implies that the KTs in question are basically "relational terms" more akin to prepositions than to nouns. There is a significant similarity between KTs and the T-elements that have evolved from auxiliary BE discussed earlier. Just as BE is a (semantically) light verb and therefore susceptible to grammaticalization, KTs are also (semantically) light nouns (by virtue of being relational terms) and therefore susceptible to grammaticalization. Although it is not clear if the Berber KTs in (29a–f) have evolved from fully inflected nouns, the fact that they lack nominal inflection means that they belong to the class of functional categories rather than to the class of nouns. This is the reason they can host CL.[12]

On the view that the KTs in (29a–f) are functional categories, the KT=CL sequence is consistent with the claim that CL is never attracted to lexical categories in Berber. Examples (30a–f) have the derivation roughly outlined in (31a, b). KT is located under D, possibly as a result of raising from a lower functional position. CL originates in a lower subject or possessor position and left-adjoins to KT in syntax. The KT=CL order is derived by CL-H Inversion, which places KT to the left of CL (31b):

(31) a. [$_{DP}$[[CL] KT][$_{XP}$ ... (Left-adjunction of CL to KT)

      b. [$_{DP}$ [[KT] [=CL]] [$_{XP}$ ... (CL-KT Inversion)

The second type of DPs that exhibit the N=CL pattern is illustrated in (32a–d), which are all demonstrative DPs. The form of the demonstrative elements given in (32a, b) is the basic, underlying form, the realization of which may differ from one variety to another:

(32) a. afrux =**ad**   b. ifruxn =**ad**
         'boy'   =this   'boys'   =this

         'this boy'   'these boys'

      c. afrux =**ann**   d. ifruxn =**ann**
         'boy'   =that   'boys'   =that

         'that boy'   'those boys'

In a language that is otherwise strictly head-initial, the N∧Dem order is unusual on the assumption that Dem is a D-element (i.e., the head of DP). The demonstrative elements in (32a–d) do not bear any agreement inflection (i.e., they do not agree with N) and therefore are consistent with the broader class of functional categories in the language. The fact that the demonstrative elements appear following N rather than preceding it ceases to be a mystery when one realizes that they actually are clitics (CL_{DEM}). Consequently, they are subject to the constraint that they can never be the first head constituent in the minimal domain that includes them, DP in this case. Assuming that CL_{DEM} originates under D, the N=CL_{DEM} order is derived by N raising to the left of CL_{DEM}. The details of the derivation are given later, once the exact status of the demonstrative elements is further explicated.

According to this analysis, the N=CL_{DEM} order is derived in basically the same way as the V=CL sequence in clauses previously discussed. In both situations, it is the lexical category that moves to CL rather than the other way around. The absence of an intervening overt functional head that could serve as the host for CL leads to the default situation, whereby the nearest lexical head is raised to CL. A closer look reveals that the parallelism between the two situations goes even deeper. It turns out that the demonstrative elements also cooccur with a small class of motion verbs in clauses giving rise to a V=CL_{DEM} sequence that is superficially the exact parallel of the N=CL_{DEM} sequence in demonstrative DPs.

The instances of demonstrative clitics that appear with verbs in clauses are traditionally identified as "directionality clitics" that convey meanings roughly translatable as 'toward the speaker' (proximitive) and 'away from the speaker' (distant). Their function is to specify the directionality of motion for a small class of motion verbs that are otherwise inherently unspecified for directionality of motion. In isolation, these verbs are ambiguous between pairs of meanings such as GO/COME and TAKE/BRING. The meanings in each pair are disambiguated with the use of the directionality/demonstrative clitics, such that the proximitive clitic yields the meanings COME and BRING, and the distant clitic yields the meanings GO and TAKE. In Ait Waryaghl Tarifit, the distant clitic has largely fallen out of use, and the meanings GO and TAKE, for example, are conveyed by the absence of a directionality/demonstrative clitic (by default). The proximitive clitic, in contrast, is comparatively better preserved. In (33), the verb *AW* has the meaning TAKE by default. In (34a, b), the same verb has the meaning BRING because of the proximitive clitic =*D*. Example (34b) is intended to show that directionality/demonstrative clitics have the same distribution as other clitics within the clause; that is, they are subject to the "second head position effect" as defined previously:

(33) I-awi   (=**n**)   afrux.
      3MS-move$_{PERF}$ =there   boy

      'He took the boy.'

(34) a. I-awi   =**d**   afrux.
         3MS-move$_{PERF}$ =here   boy

         'He brought the boy.'

      b. Ur   =**d**   i-awi   afrux.
         Neg   =here   3MS-move$_{NEG}$ boy

         'He did not bring the boy.'

As with other clitics in clauses, directionality/demonstrative clitics presumably do not originate together with the verbs they cooccur with. The category "direction of motion" is not easy to classify, but it is perhaps not unreasonable to group directionality/demonstrative clitics together with adverbs and adverbial clitics (CL_{ADV}), such as those seen in the Imdlawn Tashlhit examples (35a–c):

(35) a. Ur   =**ghinn**   lli-n. (Dell and Elmedlaoui 1989: 1172–1173)
         Neg   =there   be$_{NEG}$-3PL

         'They are not there.'

      b. Rad   =as   =t   =**ghid**   i-fk.
         T$_{FUT}$ =her$_{DAT}$ =it$_{ACC}$ =here   3MS-give$_{AOR}$

         'He will give it to her here.'

      c. Is   =t   =inn   =**sul**   =gis   i-srs?
         C$_Q$ =it$_{ACC}$ =dct   =finally   =in-it   3MS-put$_{PERF}$

         'Did he finally put it into it?'

As adverbial elements, directionality/demonstrative clitics either originate in a complement position of a complex V (see Larson 1988) or in the Spec position of an appropriate functional head (see Cinque 1999). The V=$CL_{DIR/DEM}$ order is derived in exactly the same way as the more general V=CL order discussed before, by left-adjunction of CL to a null Tø in syntax, followed by raising of V to the left of CL (CL-H Inversion) at PF.

(36)   a. $[_{TP}$ Tø $[_{VP}$ V . . . =CL . . .

   b. $[_{TP}$ [[CL] Tø] $[_{VP}$ V . . . (Left-adjunction of CL to Tø)

   c. $[_{TP}$ [[V] [=CL]] Tø $[_{VP}$ . . . (CL-V Inversion)

Attempting a uniform analysis for directionality/demonstrative clitics in both clauses and DPs would amount to the derivation outlined in (37a, b) for the N=CL_{DEM} order in demonstrative DPs. CL_{DEM} originates in a lower position that parallels the position of adverbs in clauses and left-adjoins to a null Dø in syntax. This is then followed by raising of N to the left of CL_{DEM} (CL-H Inversion):

(37)   a. $[_{DP}$ Dø . . . [(=CL_{DEM}) $[_{NP}$ N (=CL_{DEM}) . . .

   b. $[_{DP}$ [=CL_{DEM}] Dø $[_{NP}$ N . . . (Left-adjunction of CL_{DEM} to Dø)

   c. $[_{DP}$ [N] [=CL_{DEM}] Dø $[_{NP}$ . . . (CL-N Inversion)

A more orthodox analysis would be one where CL_{DEM} originates directly under D (rather than in a lower position). There seems to be no empirical considerations to decide between the two competing analyses, more precisely, to determine whether CL_{DEM} originates under D or in a lower position from which it moves to a null Dø. The derivation outlined in (37a–c) is motivated purely by considerations of uniformity of analysis.

To the extent that the derivation outlined in (37a–c) is possible, the question arises as to why DPs that include a CL_{POSS} cannot have the same derivation in Tarifit and similar varieties, which would yield the nonattested sequence N=CL_{POSS} instead of the attested sequence N^OF=CL_{POSS}. The reason has to do with the structure of possessive DPs compared with that of demonstrative DPs. It was pointed out earlier that when the possessor is a non-CL DP, the presence of the preposition OF is optional: $[_{DP}$ N (OF) DP]. However, there is evidence that the preposition OF is present, in the form of an assimilated sound, even when it superficially appears to be absent (see El Moujahid 1993 for evidence). This evidence points to the conclusion that possessive DPs invariably have the so-called analytic structure $[_{DP}$ N [OF [CL/DP_{POSS}]]], which includes the preposition OF and its phrase structure projections, in the varieties in question (as in Romance). Whatever the reasons that make its presence obligatory, the preposition

OF defines the local domain within which CL_{POSS} appears, as is generally the case with all contexts that involve CL inside PP. This explains why CL appears associated with OF (i.e., within PP) instead of directly with N in possessive DPs. In contrast, demonstrative DPs do not include a parallel preposition, with the consequence that N is the only overt head category within the DP domain that includes CL_{DEM}. This is the reason they exhibit the $N=CL_{DEM}$ sequence, unlike possessive DPs.

The (analytic) type of possessive DP discussed is characteristic of most Berber varieties and seems to be the basic pattern. However, there is (at least) one variety, Taqbaylit, where one finds examples such as (38a, b), which exhibit the $N=CL_{POSS}$ sequence that is otherwise not attested in the other varieties:

(38)   a. axxam=**iw** (—. K. Achab, pers. comm., 2000)
           room/tent=me$_{DAT}$

           'my room/tent'

       b. axxam=**ik**
           room/tent=you$_{DAT}$

           'your room/tent'

The pattern in (38a, b) is more typical of the N-initial analytic possessives found in the Semitic languages, for example. In view of this, it is conceivable that their appearance in Taqbaylit is due to a process of reanalysis that has transformed an originally analytic structure of the form $[_{DP}$ D $[$N $[_{PP}$ P $[CL/DP_{POSS}]]]]$, which includes the preposition OF (and its phrase structure projections), into a synthetic structure of the form $[_{DP}$ D $[$N $[CL/DP_{POSS}]]]$, which does not include the preposition OF. This would explain why CL_{POSS} appears on N in Taqbaylit possessive DPs.

To what extent this is indeed the case remains to be seen and would require a close look at all types of DP in Taqbaylit. What is clear, though, is that the proposed instance of reanalysis is not uncommon, although it appears to differ from the other instances of reanalysis discussed previously in that it does not result from grammaticalization (unless, of course, extinction can be considered as the final stage of a hypothesized continuum of the grammaticalization of OF). Although grammaticalization and reanalysis are often assumed to be intricately linked (see Hopper and Traugott 1993 and Heine, et al. 1991), there is evidence that reanalysis can occur without necessarily being accompanied by grammaticalization (see Haspelmath 1998 for discussion).

To conclude this section, the P=CL sequence is consistent with the generalization that CL targets functional categories, on the view that prepositions are functional categories. The absence of the $N=CL_{POSS}$ sequence in varieties such as Tarifit, which require instead the more complex sequence $N{\wedge}OF=CL_{POSS}$, confirms the claim that CL never targets lexical categories in Berber. The KT=CL sequence found in DPs that include a Kinship Term is also consistent with the generalization on the view that the KTs in question have undergone a process of grammaticalization that has transformed them (from nouns with the usual characteristic inflection) to preposition-like functional categories (with no inflection). Likewise, the N=CL$_{DEM}$ sequence found in demonstrative DPs is consistent with an analysis whereby CL$_{DEM}$ either originates under or is attracted to a null D to the left of N, with the surface order derived by CL-N Inversion. Finally, the existence of the untypical sequence N=CL$_{POSS}$ in Taqbaylit arguably suggests the involvement of a process of reanalysis affecting possessive DPs that has converted an essentially analytic structure that includes OF characteristic of Berber DPs into an innovative synthetic structure that does not include OF.

6 CONCLUSION

This chapter examined differences in the distribution of clitics in selected contexts from various Berber varieties. A number of conclusions were reached. First, despite appearances to the contrary in some contexts, the distribution of clitics in Berber is consistent with the generalization that they are attracted to functional categories and never to lexical categories. Not surprisingly, Berber clitics share this property with their counterparts in other languages (see Kayne 1994 on Romance) and are arguably a manifestation of the broader fact that syntactic movement in general, including CL movement, targets functional categories.

Second, although CL placement is determined to a large extent by syntactic considerations, there is evidence for the involvement of prosodic factors applying at PF, which is not unexpected in view of the fact that clitics are not prosodic constituents. The prosodic factors involve a local rule, called here CL-Host Inversion, which inverts the order of CL and the nearest overt head to it in contexts where CL is placed (via CL movement) in a position where it is the "first head constituent." The so-called ban on first-position clitics was shown to be blind to nonhead constituents in the initial position in Berber. This is the reason CL-H Inversion was concluded essentially to be an instance of head movement that involves left-adjunction of the host to CL.

Third, all cases of variation across varieties, and all contexts that superficially appear to be inconsistent with the generalization that CL is attracted only to functional categories, can be consistently explained in terms of the two main processes of language change: grammaticalization and reanalysis. A category that is at different stages of grammaticalization in different varieties may behave differently with respect to its ability to attract CL in those varieties, such that it may do in some but not in others. Reanalysis, however, affects the distance over which CL can move, such that CL can appear either lower or higher in a given domain, depending on whether the domain has undergone analysis in a given variety.

NOTES

I am grateful to Karim Achab, Lahcen Alami, Joseph Aoun, Dirk Bury, Guglielmo Cinque, Lina Choueiri, Mohamed Elmedlaoui, Mohamed Guerssel, Richie Kayne, Ur Shlonsky, and Vina Tsakali for their help with data, analysis, and presentation.

1. Berber is a branch of the Afroasiatic family, along with Ancient Egyptian, Chadic, Cushitic, Omotic, and Semitic. Berber has a few major varieties associated with specific geographical areas in North Africa, such as Tuareg (Sahara), Tamazight (Middle and High Atlas), Taqbaylit (Kabylie), Tarifit (Rif), and Tashlhit (Anti Atlas and Souss Valley). Each variety has numerous dialects, mostly associated with specific tribes, such as Ait Waryaghl Tarifit and Imdlawn Tashlhit, and increasingly with major urban centers and cities, such as Zemmour/Khmisset Tamazight and Agadir/Inzggan Tashlhit. All known Berber varieties are strictly VSO and head-initial. Tarifit has the peculiar phonological property of realizing the lateral sound /l/ as [r] and its geminate counterpart /ll/ as [ʤ] (see Ouhalla 1984). Tarifit data presented in this chapter abstract away from these phonological peculiarities. The so-called fake [r] and fake [ʤ] are transcribed as /l/ and /ll/, respectively.

On the basis of what is currently known about the Afroasiatic languages (not much, on the whole), Berber seems to have the richest and most variable system of clitics, in terms of the range of clitics it includes and their variable distribution. The better-known clitic system of the Semitic languages, Amharic (see Halefom 1994 and Mullen 1986, among others) and Arabic and Hebrew (see overview and cited references in Ouhalla & Shlonsky's 1992 reference volume on Arabic and Hebrew syntax), mainly consists of pronominal clitics, which, moreover, have a fixed distribution.

2. There seem to be less-known types of CL besides the ones identified here. For example, some dialects of Tamazight and Tashlhit have a clitic that corresponds to wh-words (CL_{WH}) found in constructions that involve local extraction of the indirect object. These constructions include, in addition to the Operator immediately to the left of the $C_{FOC/REL/WH}$-head (Spec, C), a wh-element situated in the CL position immediately to the right of $C_{FOC/REL/WH}$-head. When the Operator is a wh-word, as in the wh-question (iii), two instances (copies) of the wh-word *M(i)* appear, one in the Operator position and the other in the CL-position:

> (i) argaz da=**mi**   i-fa   Hmad lktab (Sadiqi 1986: 44)
>   man C_{REL}=CL_{WH} 3MS-send$_{PERF}$ Hmad book
>
>   'the man to whom Hmad sent the book'

(ii)   ARGAZ   a(y)=**mi**   i-fa   Hmad lktab.
       man   C$_{FOC}$=CL$_{WH}$ 3MS-send$_{PERF}$ Hmad book

'It's to the man that Hamd sent the book.'

(iii)   M-a(y)=**mi**   i-fa   Hmad lktab.
        who-C$_{WH}$=CL$_{WH}$ 3MS-send$_{PERF}$ Hmad book

'To whom did Hmad send the book?'

3. Berber lacks CL climbing of the type found in Romance and other languages, as shown in the Ait Waryaghl Tarifit examples (i) and (ii):

(i)   Ur   i-tush   ad=**tn**   i-segh.
      Neg   3MS-want$_{IMPERF}$ to=them   3MS-buy$_{NEUT}$

'He does not want to buy them.'

(ii)   *Ur=**tn**   i-tush   ad   i-sgh.
       Neg=them   3MS-want$_{IMPERF}$ to   3MS-buy$_{NEUT}$

4. The group includes *belli*, found in Taqbaylit and some dialects of Tamazight; *hati*, found in some dialects of Tashlhit; and *qa*, found in most varieties of Tarifit, and illustrated with the Ait Waryaghl Tarifit examples (i) and (ii):

(i)   Ur   i-ssin   qa   (*=**tn**)   t-sgha   =**tn**.
      Neg   3MS-know$_{NEG}$ that   (=them$_{ACC}$)   3FS-buy$_{PERF}$ =them$_{ACC}$

'He doesn't know that she has bought them.'

(ii)   Nna-n   qa   (*=**as**)   mml-n   =**as**   abrid.
       sayPERF-3PL   that   (=him$_{DAT}$)   show$_{PERF}$-3PL   =him$_{DAT}$ way

'They say/claim that they have shown him the way.'

5. For a discussion of the form and distribution of the participle in Berber, see Dell and Elmedlaoui (1989) and El Moujahid (1993), among others. The Tamahaght Tuareg examples (i) and (ii) illustrate the participial form of two other verbs, *RWL* 'escape' and *FK* 'give':

(i)   Isu   ay   **i-rwl-n**   s- ghzer. (Mohammed Ali 1992: 105–106)
      ox   C$_{FOC}$ 3MS-escape$_{PERF}$-PART   to valley

'It was the ox that escaped to the valley.'

(ii)   Tarraut   ay   **i-fk-n**   timzin   i-ulli.
       girl   C$_{FOC}$ 3MS-give$_{PERF}$-PART   barley   to goats

'It was the girl that gave the barley to the goats.'

6. The terms CLLD and Topicalization are used here purely descriptively and do not take into consideration the possibility that (16a) may also be an instance of CLLD, on par with its counterpart in Italian (Cinque 1990 and pers. comm.).

7. Kayne (1994: 139, n.19) briefly entertains two options for the derivation of the V=CL order that are consistent with the theory of Antisymmetry. One option is V-raising to a higher null head, which has already been entertained and discounted. The

other option is adjunction of V to CL itself, which he points out was originally suggested in Benincá and Cinque (1990).

8. In some varieties, the preverbal negation element is accompanied with a postverbal correlate, obligatorily in Taqbaylit (see Chaker 1983) and optionally in Tarifit (see Ouhalla 1988). The Tarifit negative sentences discussed here do not include the postverbal correlate, as it has no bearing on the distribution of clitics.

9. See Sadiqi (1990) for discussion of this rather bizarre dual function of the Tamazight and Tashlhit complementizer *IS*.

10. In Berber, an arguably clear distinction can be drawn between lexical and functional categories in terms of inflection. Lexical categories, which include verbs and nouns (there is no distinct class of adjectives in the language), carry distinctive inflection that is obligatory in all contexts (including Control contexts for verbs). In contrast, functional elements do not carry any inflection—distinctive or otherwise. Moreover, grammaticalization typically involves, in the first stage, the shedding of the distinctive inflection of lexical categories. We have already seen this process in relation to the grammaticalization of the verb BE in the varieties mentioned. In this section, we see the same process in relation to the grammaticalization of some nouns into preposition-like functional elements.

11. In addition to the complex P+Pro elements, there are other apparently non-complex elements that seem to have similar properties. For example, in Iql'iyin Tarifit the second-person feminine singular pronoun *shem* can appear in both non-CL positions (i) and CL positions (ii). The CL version of the pronoun in other Tarifit dialects, such as Ait Waryaghl, is necessarily a reduced form (*-m*) of the strong pronoun (*shem*). The existence of such ambiguous elements arguably appears to make it difficult to draw a link between morphological complexity or lack of it and the ability to be a clitic.

(i) **Shem** ay(d)=ay   izra-n.
     you C_{FOC}=me$_{ACC}$ see-PART
     'You are the one who saw me.'

(ii) Nesh   ay=**shem**   izra-n.
     I C_{FOC}=you$_{ACC}$ see-PART
     'I am the one who saw you.'

12. Not all items in the language that express kinship relationships appear to behave the same way. For example, the items that correspond to WIFE and HUSBAND have the full inflection associated with nouns in general and, consequently, trigger the obligatory appearance of the preposition OF when related to a possessor CL, at least in Ait Waryaghl Tarifit:

(i) tamghart *(nn)=s   (ii) argaz   *(nn)=s
     woman   of=him$_{DAT}$ man   of=her$_{DAT}$

     'his wife'   'her husband'

To the extent the items in (i) and (ii) are KTs, their behavior seems to confirm the proposed analysis, whereby only nouns that undergo grammaticalization can be directly

associated with CL. However, the fact that the items
in (i) and (ii) have the basic mean-
ings of MAN and WOMAN suggests they may not be (necessarily) relational and
therefore are not genuine examples of KTs.

REFERENCES

Benincá, Paola, and Guglielmo Cinque (1990) "On Certain Differences between Enclisis
and Proclisis." Paper presented at the University of Geneva.

Boukhris, Fatima (1998) "Les Clitiques en Berbère Tamazight: Approche minimaliste
(Parler Zemmour, Khémisset)." Doctorat d'Etat, University of Mohammed V, Rabat.

Chaker, Salem (1983) *Un Parler Berbère d'Algérie (Kabylie): Syntaxe*. Publications Université de Provence, Provence.

Chaker, Salem (1995) *Linguistique berbère: études de syntaxe et de diachronie*. Peeters,
Paris-Louvain.

Chomsky, Noam (1995) *The Minimalist Program*. MIT Press, Cambridge, Mass.

Cinque, Guglielmo (1990) *Types of A'-Dependencies*. MIT Press, Cambridge, Mass.

Cinque, Guglielmo (1999) *Adverbs and Functional Heads: A Cross-linguistic Perspective*.
Oxford: Oxford University Press, New York.

Dell, François, and Mohamed Elmedlaoui (1989) "Clitic-Ordering, Morphology and
Phonology in the Verbal Complex of Imdlawn Tashelhiyt Berber." *Langues orientales
anciennes: philologie et linguistique*. Peeters, Louvain, 165–194.

Elmedlaoui, Mohamed (1999) *Principes d'Orthographe Berbère*. Serie Etudes et Monogra-
phies 6. Publications du Faculté des Lettres et des Sciences Humaines. University of
Mahammed I, Oujda.

Elmedlaoui, Mohamed (2000) "On Clitic-Movement in Imdlawn Tashehiyt Berber." Unpublished ms., University of Mohammed I, Oujda.

El Moujahid, El Houssain (1993) "Syntaxe du Groupe Nominal en Berbère Tachelhiyt
(Parler d'Igherm, Sous, Maroc)." Doctorat d'Etat, University of Mohammed V, Rabat.

Guerssel, Mohamed (1995) "Berber Clitic Doubling and Syntactic Extraction." *Revue
quebecoise de linguistique* 24: 111–133.

Guerssel, Mohamed, and Ken Hale (1987) *Studies in Berber Syntax*. Lexicon Project
Working Papers 14. Center for Cognitive Science, MIT, Cambridge, Mass.

Halefom, Girma (1994) "The Syntax of Functional Categories: A Study of Amharic."
Ph.D. diss., University of Quebec, Montreal.

Halpern, Aaron (1995) *On the Placement and Morphology of Clitics*. CSLI Publications.
Center for the Study of Language and Information, Stanford, Calif.

Harris, Alice C., and Lyle Campbell (1995) *Historical Syntax in Cross-Linguistic Perspective*. Cambridge University Press, Cambridge.

Haspelmath, Martin (1998) "Does Grammaticalization Need Reanalysis?" *Studies in Language* 22: 49–85.

Heine, Bernd, Ulrike Claudi, and Friederike Hunnemeyer (1991) *Grammaticalization: A Conceptual Framework*. University of Chicagor Press, Chicago.

Heine, Bernd, and Mechthild Reh (1984) *Grammaticalization and Reanalysis in African Languages*. Buske, Hamburg.

Hopper, Paul J., and Elizabeth C. Traugott (1993) *Grammaticalization*. Cambridge University Press, Cambridge.

Kayne, Richard (1989) "Null Subjects and Clitic-Climbing," in Osvaldo Jaeggli and Ken J. Safir (eds.) *The Null Subject Parameter*. Kluwer, Dordrecht, 239–261.

Kayne, Richard (1991) "Romance Clitics, Verb-Movement and PRO." *Linguistic Inquiry* 22: 647–686.

Kayne, Richard (1994) *The Antisymmetry of Syntax*. MIT Press, Cambridge, Mass.

Klavans, Judith (1980) "Some Problems in a Theory of Clitics." Ph.D. diss. University College London.

Klavans, Judith (1985) "The Independence of Syntax and Phonology in Cliticization." *Language* 61: 95–120.

Larson, Richard K. (1988) "On the Double Object Construction." *Linguistic Inquiry* 19: 589–632.

Lord, Carol (1976) "Evidence for Syntactic Reanalysis: From Verb to Complementizer in Kwa," in Sanford B. Steever, Carol A. Walker, and Salikoko S. Mufwene (eds.) *Papers from the Parassession on Diachronic Syntax*. Chicago Linguistic Society, Chicago, 179–191.

Mohammed Ali, Aoussouk (1992) "Tuareg Clause Structure." MA diss. University of North Wales, Bangor.

Mullen, Dana (1986) "Issues in the Morphology and Phonology of Amharic: The Lexical Generation of Pronominal Clitics." Ph.D. diss. University of Ottawa, Ottawa, Ontario.

Nespor, Marina (1999) "The Phonology of Clitic Groups," in Henk van Riemsdijk (ed.) *Clitics in the Languages of Europe*. Mouton de Gruyter, New York, 865–890.

Nespor, Marina, and Irene Vogel (1986) *Prosodic Phonology*. Foris, Dordrecht.

Ouhalla, Jamal (1984) "Some Phonological Issues of Tarifit Berber." Unpublished ms., University of Mohammed V, Rabat.

Ouhalla, Jamal (1988) "The Syntax of Head Movement: A Study of Berber." Ph.D. diss. University College London.

Ouhalla, Jamal (1989) "Clitic-movement and the ECP." *Lingua* 79: 165–231.

Ouhalla, Jamal (2000) "Complementizers and CL2 in Berber." Paper presented at the fifth Conference on Afroasiatic Languages, Denis Diderot, Paris.

Ouhalla, Jamal, and Ur Shlonsky (2002) *Themes in Arabic and Hebrew Syntax*. Kluwer, Dordrecht.

Rizzi, Luigi (1990) *Relativized Minimality*. MIT Press, Cambridge.

Sadiqi, Fatima (1986) *Studies in Berber Syntax: The Complex Sentence*. Konigshausen and Neumann, Würtzburg.

Sadiqi, Fatima (1990) "On the Notion of Comp in Berber," in J. Pleines (ed.) *Linguistique au Maghreb*. Okad, Rabat, 329–343.

Selkirk, Elisabeth (1986) "On Derived Domains in Sentence Phonology." *Phonology Yearbook* 3: 371–405.

Selkirk, Elisabeth (1995) "The Prosodic Structure of Function Words," in *University of*

Massachusetts Occasional Papers 18: Papers in Optimality Theory. University of Massachusetts, Amherst, 439–469

Selkirk, Elisabeth, and Tong Shen (1990) "Prosodic domains in Shanghai Chinese," in Sharon Inkelas and Draga Zec (eds.) *The Phonology-Syntax Connection.* Chicago University Press, Chicago, 313–337.

CHAPTER 15

....

CLITIC PLACEMENT IN WESTERN IBERIAN

A Minimalist View

....

EDUARDO P. RAPOSO AND

JUAN URIAGEREKA

1 INTRODUCTION AND BASIC DESCRIPTION

....

IN Central and Eastern Iberian (henceforth C/EI) languages like Spanish and Catalan, clitic placement is sensitive to the finiteness of the clause that hosts the clitic: proclisis is obligatory in finite clauses, enclisis in infinitival ones. This is illustrated for Spanish in (1)–(2), respectively (in this and in subsequent examples, the material in parentheses represents possible or impossible verb-clitic/clitic-verb alternatives to the ones in the main example-sentence; impossible alternatives are signaled in the usual way, with an asterisk):

(1)   a. **La**   vi   ayer. (***vila**).
         her-cl (I-)saw yesterday
         'I saw her yesterday.'

    b. Quién **la**   vio   ayer? (***viola**)
       who   her-cl saw yesterday

       'Who saw her yesterday?'

    c. Pienso   que **la**   vi   ayer. (***vila**)
       (I-)think that her-cl (I-)saw yesterday

       'I think that I saw her yesterday.'

(2)   Después de ver**la**,   lloré. (***la** ver)
      after   of to-see-her-cl (I-)cried

      'After seeing her, I cried.'

In Western Iberian (henceforth WI), variants like European Portuguese (henceforth EP) and Galician, the pattern is more complex. Enclisis and proclisis are complementary in root finite clauses, proclisis occurring after negation or after a displaced *wh-* 'or affective' phrase (see section 2) and enclisis elsewhere (e.g., in simple declarative root clauses). This is illustrated in (3):[1]

(3) a. Quem **a**   viu   ontem? (***viu-a**)
       who   her-cl saw yesterday

       'Who saw her yesterday?'

    b. Não **a**   vi   ontem. (***vi-a**)
       not her-cl (I-)saw yesterday

       'I didn't see her yesterday.'

    c. (Eu) vi-**a**   ontem. (***a** vi)
       (I)   saw-her-cl yesterday

       'I saw her yesterday.'

In most subordinate finite contexts of WI, proclisis is the unmarked case, as in (4a); however, enclisis occurs in contexts where a topic intervenes between the complementizer and the verb, as in (4b):

(4) a. Ele disse que **a**   viu   ontem. (***viu-a.**)
       he   said that her-cl (he-)saw yesterday

       'He said that he saw her yesterday.'

    b. Dizem   que esses panfletos, distribuiu-**os**   (o
       (they-)say that those pamphlets distributed-them-cl the
       partido) ontem. (***os** distribuiu)
       party   yesterday

       'they say that those pamphlets, the party distributed them yesterday'

In contrast, proclisis and enclisis in infinitival clauses are not in complementary distribution. Thus, while there are contexts that allow only enclisis, there are others in which both patterns appear in free variation. One such context involves adverbial clauses introduced by prepositions such as *sem* 'without', *depois de* 'after', and *para* 'for'. This is illustrated in (5):

(5) Depois de **a**   ver, chorei. (vê-**la**)
     after   of her-cl see   (I-)cried

     'After seeing her, I cried.'

With their bizarre pattern of clitic placement, infinitival clauses have defied successful analysis in the literature on WI clitics. Familiar studies on EP and Galician cliticization normally omit infinitival contexts, and analyses that may be arrived at based on finite clause proposals often do not fare well when applied to infinitivals. One novelty of our study is its explicit attempt to cover infinitival contexts.

We will argue that a morphophonological property of the peripheral functional category F, proposed in Uriagereka (1995b), accounts for the complex pattern of WI clitic placement versus its more homogeneous pattern in C/EI variants (see also Martins 1994a and 1994b and Uriagereka 1995a for different approaches exploring the same or a similar idea). One aspect that sets this study apart from many others is that we do not rely on peculiar morphophonological differences between WI pronominal clitics and those of the C/EI variants as a basis for the difference in clitic placement. Moreover, appropriately idealized, fundamental aspects of the parametric differences observed in Iberian can be witnessed elsewhere in Romance (e.g., seventeenth-century Neapolitan vs. modern varieties), Greek (e.g., Cypriot vs. standard variant), or Slavic (e.g., Bulgarian vs. other varieties), as a growing literature attests (see, e.g., Maurer 1968 for Neapolitan; Anagnostopoulou 1994 and Terzi 1999 for Greek; Izvorski 1995 and Bošković 2001 for Slavic). This suggests that relevant differences must be deep, not ad hoc, properties of peculiar dialects. Moreover, our analysis does not rely on differences in the parameterized geometry of clitic placement (e.g., left-adjunction vs. right-adjunction). In these and other respects, this study owes much to Kayne (1991).

The remainder of the chapter is organized as follows: section 2 is about our general assumptions regarding clausal structure and the FP projection. Section 3 discusses general issues regarding determiner clitics—in particular, why they appear in displaced positions and what these positions are. We propose a Phonetic Form (PF) approach to these questions, and we make a crucial distinction between two operations that apply to determiner clitics: *fusion* and *clitic placement*. In section 4, we discuss the Tobler-Mussafia property of WI, providing a solution in terms of properties of the functional category F in these variants. In section 5, we discuss in more detail the rule of fusion, showing that it obeys somewhat different constraints, depending on the directionality of attachment. We also present a condensed summary of the system set in place up to this point. In section 6, we address clitic placement in plain (noninflected) infinitival clauses of Spanish and of WI. We introduce a new important constraint on fusion and discuss the role of Object Shift in the derivation of several examples with determiner clitics. Section 7 takes up clitic placement in inflected infinitives of WI. Section 8 concludes our work. Finally, in an appendix, we briefly take up the matter of clitic placement in French infinitival clauses.

2 Clause Structure and the F Projection

2.1 The F Projection

A considerable amount of work initiated in the 1980s has converged on the idea that there is a functional category in the left periphery of the clause, between C and T. Following our own work on this category (see Raposo and Uriagereka 1996: 766–768) and without attaching significance to this name, we call it F, presupposing the following clausal structure:

(6) $[_{CP} \dots C [_{FP} \dots F [_{TP} \dots T [_{vP} \dots v [_{VP} \dots V \dots]]]]]$

Although proposals concerning F's function vary, there is a general consensus that it serves as an interface between syntax and discourse. More concretely, it provides a configuration where semantic properties with a pragmatic import, often "discourse-oriented" and encoding the speaker's or the matrix subject's "point of view" (in main and subordinate clauses, respectively) are realized by merging or moving appropriate elements into its projection (see Uriagereka 1995b).

A class of elements that are realized in FP are so-called affective operators (Raposo 1994, Raposo and Uriagereka 1996). These elements typically involve a value judgment by a speaker or a perspective-bearing subject and include some quantifier phrases, phrases with overt focus operators, and elements encoding the polarity of a proposition, such as aspectual adverbs like *já* 'already', *ainda* 'yet', *também* 'also', the negative morpheme *não* 'not', and other negative expressions, as well as questions and emphatic expressions (see (7a), for an example with an overt focus operator).

In turn, it is not immediately obvious whether there are phrases which, not being affective (i.e., not involving value judgments), nonetheless target the F position—for example, a class of topics and left-dislocated elements, as in (7b). Semantically, these elements, too, are point-of-view dependent, in that, for instance, they set up a context for a given speaker to comment on. Nonetheless, it is very clear that, with regard to associated clitic placement, elements of this sort behave very differently from "affective" elements. Thus, while displaced affective phrases "trigger" proclisis (7a), topics and "left-dislocated" phrases "trigger" enclisis (7b); if both are present, proclisis obtains (7c):

(7) a. Só   um   whisky **lhe**   demos (*demos-**lhe**)
        only one whisky to-him-cl   (we-)gave

   'Only one whisky did we give him.'

   b. Esse whisky,   demos-**lhe**. (***lhe** demos)
      this   whisky   (we-)gave-him-cl

   'This whisky, we gave him.'

   c. Ao   capitão, só   um   whisky **lhe**
      to-the captain   only one whisky to-him-cl
      demos. (*demos-**lhe**)
      (we-)gave

   'To the captain, only one whisky did we give him.'

Following our earlier work in Raposo and Uriagereka (1996), we tentatively assume that topics and other left-dislocated elements target the F projection, adjoining to FP, thus occurring to the left of dislocated affective phrases.[2] In any case, the conclusion is clear: 'affective' spec of F is crucial in determining a proclisis pattern in WI dialects.

Let us now turn to a discussion of the nature and constitution of F. One early attempt to address the question is Uriagereka (1995b), in terms of what he calls a "syntactic" and a "morphological" parameter associated with F (see the hierarchical schema in (8)). The syntactic parameter expresses whether F is projected in the overt or only the covert component (at LF), depending on whether the language has or lacks generalized left-peripheral "affective" constructions such as (7a) (types A and B versus type C, in (8)). With Uriagereka (1995b), we call languages of type C (such as French) "radical." In turn, the morphological parameter provides a PF representation for a syntactically active F; this is meant to distinguish "conservative" languages (type A languages like WI, baroque Neapolitan, and medieval Romance) with overt focus heads, inflected infinitivals, recomplementation, and the EP pattern of clitic placement, from "standard" languages (type B languages such as E/CI and most of the rest) that lack these properties. The division among conservative, standard, and radical variants are the logically possible in this view, as it makes no sense to have morphological options for a syntactically inactive head. This hierarchy is illustrated in (8):

(8)

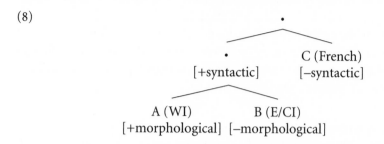

$$
\begin{array}{ccc}
 & \bullet & \\
 & \diagup\diagdown & \\
\bullet & & \text{C (French)} \\
\text{[+syntactic]} & & \text{[-syntactic]} \\
\diagup\diagdown & & \\
\text{A (WI)} & \text{B (E/CI)} & \\
\text{[+morphological]} & \text{[-morphological]} &
\end{array}
$$

With the development of minimalist proposals such as those of Chomsky (2000, 2001), this early attempt at distinguishing between different types of F heads in terms of "realization parameters" calls for some clarification and reformulation. In particular, the syntactic parameter is not easily expressed within such a framework. One of Chomsky's proposals is that there is no distinction between overt and covert cycles. Thus, we cannot claim that F is introduced sooner or later in the derivation. However, suppose that (universal) F involves a putative feature [affective], associated with what we have been calling "affective fronting." Crucially, [affective] can be strong or weak, in roughly Chomsky's (2001) sense. Strong [affective] (we mean the underlining to code strength) entails the displacement of affective phrases and can thus be seen as a peripheral feature that is added optionally in the numeration to trigger overt displacement of the relevant items. In contrast, weak [affective] does not entail (and hence prevents, given Last Resort) any sort of displacement of affective phrases to its domain, resulting in what might be called "affective-in-situ"[3] Clearly, these are not parametric options, as the two outputs may arise in a single language: for example, both EP and Spanish may instantiate (strong) [affective] or (weak) [affective], as they allow both displaced and in situ affective operators. This is illustrated in (9a, b), respectively:

(9)   a. *Só   um   whisky* lhe   demos.
         only   one   whisky   to-him-cl (we-)gave
         'Only one whisky did we give him.'

      b. Demos-lhe *só um whisky.*
         'We gave him only one whisky.'

This situation is parallel to what we find with *wh*-movement, where there are languages with both displacement and *wh*-in situ, alongside languages that do not tolerate and languages that force displacement of *wh*-phrases. So, too, with the [affective] feature we find languages that tolerate displacement alongside affective-in situ (such as Spanish or EP) and languages that do not tolerate displacement (such as French).[4]

Consider now the morphological parameter. Our proposal is that this involves the possibility of F being endowed with φ-features, participating in the Case/Agreement system (see Raposo and Uriagereka 1996). We thus have the following four logical possibilities for F:

(10)   a. [affective, +φ]

        b. [affective, +φ]

        c. [affective, −φ]

        d. [affective, −φ]

Example (10a–b) appear in the conservative WI case (A in (8)) that concerns us here. We will use a lowercase, italic *f* to represent these two types of F: that is, F endowed with φ-features. Example (10d) is the F of the radical dialects such as French (C in (8)), with no displacement of affective phrases and no agreement activity in this category either. Finally, (10c) is a possible realization of F in the standard variants such as Spanish (B in (8)), which allow displacement of affective phrases but have no agreement activity in the category.

Diachronic changes in Romance were from languages with *f* (the A languages of (8), covering (10a, b)), to languages of the (10d) sort, presumably with an intermediate step in languages allowing the F of (10c). In other words, we have a diachronic hierarchy (10a, b)>(10c)>(10d) from conservative to standard to radical languages (A>B>C in terms of (8)). Synchronically, this hierarchy sets up different cutting points, with the different language types of (8) settling on a particular state. Recall that the strength of the [affective] feature is strictly not a parametric choice: the Iberian standard and conservative dialects manifest both [affective] and [affective] features. Likewise, we speculate that the choice between *f* and standard F is also not parametric; that is, it is possible that languages of the conservative type may instantiate either F or *f* (the choice being perhaps context-dependent). If this is correct, WI variants would allow all four types.

Consider, finally, whether categories like infinitivals, which do not involve topicalization, focus fronting, or similar left-peripheral phenomena, even have an F projection to start with. One possibility is that F is blindly projected between C and T but for some reason must involve weak [affective] or [topic] features (see note 4) in infinitival contexts, thus allowing no displacement that would make F obvious. A second possibility is that F is not even present in these contexts. The former possibility has two advantages. One is that having F in infinitival clauses allows for the possibility of *f* (i.e., of φ-features in F), which may translate in these contexts as inflected infinitivals, present in languages of the conservative type. The other advantage has to do with the fact that the conservative dialects have a special pattern of clitic placement not only in finite clauses but also in infinitival ones. By postulating F (and thus the possibility of *f*) in infinitival contexts, and to the extent that we are able to use it successfully in building a plausible account of this special clitic pattern, we provide an explanation for why this pattern is found in the WI conservative dialects together with inflected infinitives. This is the route that we pursue next.

2.2 On the Existence of an Autonomous F Projection

With the advent of "bare" phrase-structure (Chomsky 1994), and with it the possibility of multiple specifiers, mere presence of *n* phrases in the left periphery of a clause does not constitute immediate evidence for *n*-peripheral functional categories. From a semantic perspective, there are two possible situations. If these phrases have different semantic import, it is at least plausible that they could involve the domains of different projecting heads. A limiting version of this proposal is the so-called cartographic project of Cinque, Rizzi, and others (see, e.g., Cinque 1999, Rizzi 1997). From this perspective, each difference in semantic import corresponds to a separate head. Alternatively, it is possible that an already assumed head hosts multiple specifiers for specific phrases, each semantic difference being coded as a mere feature of the same head. With respect to F, these considerations raise the following two questions: (i) Is F just a convenient coding for separate heads? (ii) Alternatively, could it be that F does not really exist as a separate head and is merely a feature of C?

Consider question (ii) first. One relevant factor is whether a given language presents separate, pronounced peripheral heads. At the time Uriagereka wrote his 1995 article (1995b), presence of agreement morphemes (e.g., as in inflected infinitivals) was considered a sufficient argument for a separate (Agr type) head. However, Chomsky (1995: ch. 4) suggestively argues for interpreting Agr elements as mere features, in which case this sort of fact leaves open which limiting situation (multiple heads vs. multiple features of a single head) should be pursued. More directly relevant is the presence of sheer heads, separated by phrases that presumably occupy their specifiers. Uriagereka provided examples of that sort in Galician. A striking one is based on "recomplementation," illustrated in (11):

(11) Dixeron **que** a   este home **que** non o   maltratemos.
      said   that to this man   that not him-cl (we-)mistreat
      'They said that, this man, we shouldn't mistreat.'

In (11) we have two different *que* heads (with a "sandwiched" topic in between). These sentences are common in colloquial registers of type A languages but are (getting) lost in many modern (type B and C) variants. Occasionally, examples of this type have been analyzed as involving 'CP recursion.' But it is not clear why recursion ought to be restricted to a given number of occurrences (typically two, putting aside speech errors). It is more natural to analyze the relevant phenomena as involving two distinct functional categories: C and F.

Another argument for F as a distinct head separate from C is the fact that the existence of *wh*-movement has not been affected in the radical C dialects, which, however, have lost affective movement of the sort illustrated in (7a). This makes sense if *wh*-movement is ultimately triggered and realized in the CP projection (even if it targets F as an intermediate step, as argued by Raposo 1994 and Raposo and Uriagereka 1996), while affective movement is triggered and realized in the separate FP projection.

One important consideration pertaining to the existence of F is how to rationalize the diachronic change, which, as mentioned, goes historically from the conservative A setting to the radical C setting, presumably through the standard B one. Minimally then, the correct analysis must postulate something morphologically "strong" for some functional element in the left periphery of these languages, which gets "weakened" in history. Let us continue to use the name *f* for this property (see the discussion after (10)), and let us think of it in the terms suggested in Raposo (2000), as a sort of more or less abstract clitic element. From the perspective in which C and F are independent, the head of F itself can be *f*. In contrast, from the perspective of the C-F approach, *f* must be C. The problem, then, is that it is unclear how to distinguish the three types of languages. For example, in most Romance variants, C is pronounced [*ke*] in embedded clauses, and it is silent in matrix clauses. Clearly, then, either *f* is not [*ke*], or else *f* is some property of [*ke*], present in conservative dialects but not elsewhere. The latter option, though, begs the question of what *f* is: in this view, it is just a property that conservative Romance has, but other variants lack, and which has nothing to do with the morphophonemics of [*ke*] and its "strength." Similar considerations apply to matrix C, if *f* appears in matrix contexts, too, as it does. Once again, in practically all of Romance, as well as most other languages, matrix C is not pronounced. So the behavior we witness in EP can have nothing to do with the putative strength of C, unless we again beg the question: that (null) matrix C is different across Romance languages, in mysterious ways.

In contrast, treating *f* as the head of F is sensible, synchronically, as it can be shown to rationalize the position of clitics in EP, as discussed later. Diachronically, too, the idea makes sense. Medieval forms of Romance had a clitic element—in fact, it was pronounced in some instances (the *er* particle of thirteenth-century Galician-Portuguese, according to Uriagereka 1995b). Historically, this element weakened phonologically in the conservative WI dialects, but it is still present in an abstract clitic guise, in our coding *f*, inducing the WI phenomenology. In the standard dialects, in turn, the head of F ceases to have any morphophonemic representation, inducing the more "modern" Romance phenomenology of type B dialects (and of type C, once F ceases to be syntactically "active," as well). Complementizers are never involved in the process, and as far as one can determine, they remain constant since the Middle Ages, at least in Western Romance (as opposed to Eastern Romance, where, for instance, in Romanian and some Northern Italian dialects, they vary according to mood, as in Latin—a different parameter unrelated to clitic placement).

Consider finally question (i): Is F just a convenient coding for separate heads? If each observed semantic or syntactic property of the conservative dialects corresponded to a different functional category, it is unclear why we have the rational course of diachronic change described previously (from A to B to C type languages), with various properties swinging in tandem. If different heads were involved, we would rather expect different diachronic phenomenology for focus fronting, recomplementation, the clitic pattern, and so on, but not for all those "left peripheral" traits as a group. Suppose that learnability considerations demand that parameters target only easily observable entire heads (thus entire feature bags within them); then we must have a single head to host the pertinent features that are to be weakened; that is, we must postulate a homogeneous head F, not multiple separate heads (see Lambova 2001).

3 Some Assumptions about Clitic Placement

Two of the most debated issues in the literature in Romance grammar are why clitics move and where they move. We address each of these issues in turn.

3.1 Why Do Clitics Move?

Since standard clitics to a large extent correspond to DP arguments, which enter into checking relations in the general sense of the Minimalist Program, one theory of why clitics move appeals directly to checking considerations (Rizzi 1993, Duarte and Matos 2000). Under this view, clitics move because they have to check their Case and ϕ-features against the uninterpretable matching features of some functional category.

The checking theory solution ties up the *why* and the *where* questions, providing a unified answer to both: clitics move to the functional category that checks their features. For instance, since direct objects (DO) check their Case and φ-features against those of v, DO clitics target the v projection, either as heads under head-to-head movement or as maximal projections to [spec, v], or both.

Despite that advantage, there are some problems facing the checking theory solution. One is that Romance clitics often (or always, depending on the language) end up in a projection which is clearly higher than v, as illustrated in the Galician example (12), involving subject "interpolation":

(12) A   bon   fado   **a**   Deus   encomende!
      to   good   fate   her-cl   God   entrust
      'May God entrust her to a good fate!'

In this instance, clitic a 'her' is clearly placed above the subject *Deus* 'God', hence could not be in v. Indeed, the clitic in (12) appears so high up in the clause (possibly in F) that it seems unlikely the placement in (12) is a mere consequence of v itself, with the clitic attached, moving (so) high up. Thus, further stipulations are required to justify the subsequent movement of the clitic from v onward, and the proposal is weakened.

Two additional, and related, conceptual difficulties face the checking theory solution. First, since there is no overt object raising of full DPs in Romance for checking purposes, the proposal must ascribe to clitics some special property *related to checking* that forces overt rather than covert movement (morphologically heavy or strong φ-features, for instance).[5] Besides being ad hoc (especially from the perspective that clitics are just ordinary determiners), this solution is not consistent with the idea within the Minimalist Program (assumed since Chomsky 1995: ch. 4) that feature-driven movement is triggered by some property of the target rather than the element that moves. Second, and in the same vein, this solution for why clitics move does not fare well with Chomsky's (2000, 2001) reinterpretation of checking theory as involving an Agree relation rather than actual movement (of a category or of formal features). If checking reduces to Agree, one wonders why, for the specific purposes of checking, clitics would have to move to the functional category that contains their probe (in Chomsky's 2000 sense), rather than Agreeing in situ like full DPs.

Another account of clitic movement invokes some interface condition not related to φ-feature checking, which would be violated if clitics did not move. In this view, clitic movement becomes a "last-resort" operation to avoid crash (though the analysis is not last resort in the technical sense of involving checking theory). This is the route we pursue, exploiting the role of an interface condition at PF involving determiner clitics (see also Bošković 2001 for a similar approach). Following Postal (1969), the main idea is (13a), to be coupled with assumption (13b) (see Raposo 1973, 1999; Uriagereka 1995a):

(13) a. Romance pronominal clitics are normal Ds heading a DP.

   b. Romance determiners (special clitics or regular articles) are phonolog-
      ical clitics that must find themselves within a well-formed prosodic word
      at PF.

The demand in (13b) is normally achieved in D's base position by essentially
"fusing" D to an adjacent phonological host in its immediate c-command domain
within DP; this entails, given X-bar architecture, "leaning" to the right, directly
deriving the fact that most Romance Ds are proclitic within DP. We take fusion
to be a morphological operation of the PF component, applying within the phonological cycle. In turn, we assume (with Chomsky 2000, 2001) that this cycle
proceeds in parallel with the narrow-syntactic cycle in a phase-based derivation.
Fusion is illustrated in the Spanish examples (14) with the definite determiner *la*
'the' (henceforth in our representations, we use '+' to signal morphological fusion
and '-' to signal head-adjunction):

(14) a. No   compré   [$_{DP}$ la   aspirina   corriente]. > la + aspirina
         not (I-)bought   the aspirin   normal
         'I didn't buy the normal aspirin.'

   b. Pero compré   [$_{DP}$ la   N   efervescente]. > la + efervescente
      but   (I-)bought   the   effervescent
      'But I bought the effervescent one.'

Suppose now that the object DP consists of just a determiner; that is, there are
no overt modifiers within DP:[6]

(15) No   compré [$_{DP}$ la   N]
      not (I-)bought   the

In (15), the determiner does not have a fusion host within DP, and the derivation
containing it crashes at PF. There is, however, a last resort, alternative derivation,
that does converge: D is overtly displaced to a position (containing the verb)
where it can find an appropriate fusion host, avoiding a PF crash. For reasons
that we discuss later, that position varies in different Romance languages, so, for
the moment, we just call it "X." There, the clitic and the verb can be mapped by
fusion into a well-formed prosodic word, as illustrated in (16):

(16) [$_x$ **la**-[$_x$ compré-X]] > **la**+[$_x$ compré-X]

Under this approach, the answer to the *why* question of clitic placement is that determiner clitics move whenever their phonological deficiency cannot be remedied within DP. This pattern of explanation, in turn, implies that clitic placement ought to take place early enough to appropriately feed the PF component, or else be a matter of PF displacement, depending on one's assumptions about "stylistic" processes. To be sure, our analysis crucially distinguishes *clitic placement*, a movement operation at work in (15)–(16), from the morphological process of *fusion*, at work in (14) as well as in (16), in the latter example after clitic placement.

3.2 Where Do Clitics Move?

The logic of the previous account requires the determiner clitic to move to a position where its prosodic demands are met. That position and that movement ought to be optimal. To study what the optimal options may be, consider a language with verb raising to T, as is the general case in Romance. In the abstract structure (17), the only way that the determiner clitic *o* 'him, it' can find a fusion host is by adjoining to the complex T that contains the verb:[7]

(17)

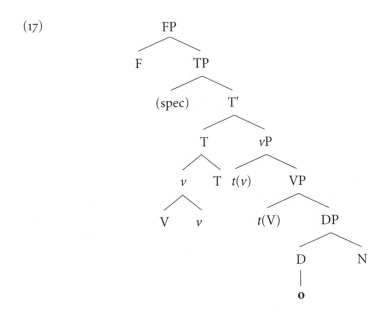

Thus, the output representation (after clitic placement) must be as in (18), a widespread Romance pattern (see Kayne (1991) for an identical structure, setting F aside):

(18)

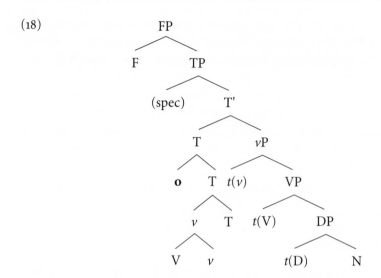

If the structure involves *f*, which we take to be the case in the conservative setting of WI, the question is how this element affects the way in which D survives PF. To elucidate this matter, we make three further restricting assumptions concerning clitic placement.

First, we assume (19) as a way of cutting derivational options:

(19)   Adjunction is universally left-adjunction.

This follows if we accept the theory in Kayne (1994), but regardless, we presuppose it. Condition (19) rules out an account of the enclisis–proclisis alternation by stipulating a linear variation in the adjunction of clitics.

Second, we assume (20):

(20)   Clitics are the last elements to adjoin to their target head.

This may be due to a morphological requirement forcing clitics to appear at the edge of the head that contains them (see Anderson 1992), or it could be a consequence of clitics being placed late wherever they meet their PF demands.

Third, there is ample evidence across Romance and other languages for a condition like (21):

(21)   Clitics within a given derivational phase cluster around one another.

For example, in "climbing" scenarios, speakers cannot choose to climb indirect object *lhe* 'to him' leaving behind direct object *o* 'him', as in (22c). The clitics must cluster, either in the complement (22a) or in the matrix (22b):

(22) a. Tentaram   dar-**lho**.
          (they-)tried   to-give-him-it

          'They tried to give it to him.'

      b. Tentaram-**lho**   dar.
          (they-)tried-him-it   to-give

      c. *Tentaram-**lhe**   dá-**lo**.
          (they-)tried-him   to-give-it

Next, following Raposo (2000), we assume (23) about *f*:

(23) *f* is a clitic-like element.

The combination of (21) and (23) implies that when F = *f*, determiner clitics in WI raise to F (making the standard assumption that movement is always upward in the phrase marker) in order to cluster with it. This is illustrated in (24a–b), depending on whether the verb raises to T, or further to *f* (via T) (compare with (18)).[8]

(24) a.

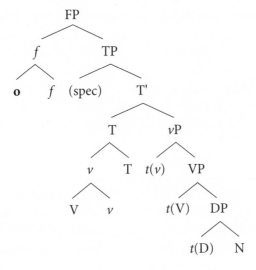

b.

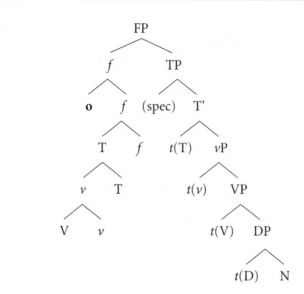

Consider why we take the determiner clitic to move to *f* in one fell swoop in (24). The output of this movement straightforwardly satisfies (21) (we assume that clitics within a cluster must be adjacent). If the clitic had moved to T as in (18) (prior to moving to *f*), there are two logically possible ways whereby it could cluster with *f*, but they are both illegitimate. The first would be by excorporating from the T complex. With Chomsky (1995: ch. 4), however, we take excorporation to be ruled out. The second is if the entire T complex moved to *f* by right-adjunction, so that the determiner clitic in T and *f* could be adjacent in order to form a cluster, as the reader can verify easily. This, however, violates our assumption (19).

As presented, the derivations in (24) are not sensitive to phases, in the sense of Chomsky (2000, 2001), since the clitic moves in one fell swoop from the D position inside the *v*P phase to *f* in the CP phase, without taking an intermediate step on a phase "edge." This issue, of course, arises even for the derivation in (18) which targets T, also within the CP phase. We raise the question at this point, suggesting that, in principle, two possible avenues exist to address it. One is that clitic placement is a late process that is not sensitive to syntactic phases. Another is that clitic placement involves an intermediate step of object shift. We pursue the second alternative in section 6, where we return to this issue. For now, we leave the matter aside.

If (24) is correct for the WI dialects, then clitic placement to a given site cannot be determined absolutely in Romance: it follows the optimal course, given other derivational details. As it turns out, (24) is incomplete; for instance, it does not prevent clitic initial structures in WI. We return to this in the next section.

4 CLITIC PLACEMENT IN SIMPLE FINITE ROOT CLAUSES

4.1 Enclisis Is Phonologically Motivated

Descriptively, clitic placement in root WI finite clauses can be summarized as follows:

(25)   a. If there is an overt "affective" element in FP, proclisis results.

      b. Otherwise, enclisis results.

This is illustrated in (26a–b), respectively:

(26)   a. A muito mestre   **o**   enviaram!   (*enviaram-**no**)
          to many teacher   him-cl   (they-)sent

          'Many teachers have they sent him to!'

      b. Enviaram-**no**   aos   Jesuitas.   (***o** enviaram)
          (they-)sent-him-cl   to-the   Jesuits

          'They sent him to the Jesuits.'

A traditional way of describing this pattern is embodied in (27), the Tobler-Mussafia law:

(27)   Where the sequence clitic-verb would normally start a sentence, we have enclisis rather than proclisis.

Preverbal subjects and topics "do not count" for the Tobler-Mussafia effect, as we find enclisis with them, too:

(28)   a. Os   meninos   viram-**no**. (***o** viram)
          the   children   saw-it-cl

          'The children saw it.'

      b. Esse   livro,   dei-**o**   ao   meu   amigo. (***o** dei)
          that   book   (I-)gave-it-cl   to-the   my   friend

          'That book, I gave it to my friend.'

Putting aside (28) for the moment, the overall pattern suggests that a phonological factor is at stake, apparently affecting the clitic's capacity to appear in initial position. Under this view, WI clitics are enclitic elements; that is, they lack prosodic independence and need a phonological host to their left. This general line of reasoning was first explored, in some form, by Anderson (1992), and in these very terms by Halpern (1992), for so-called second-position clitics (see also Barbosa 1996, 2000).

Although we will not follow the specifics of that approach, the idea could certainly be recast in the minimalist terms assumed here. In the unmarked situation, clitics left-adjoin to their functional host, for reasons of the sort already discussed in section 3. In addition, suppose that determiner clitics of WI are second-position clitics and that an extra condition like (29) holds of these clitics:

(29)   Second-position clitics must have phonological material to their left (i.e., they are "enclitic").

If in a given context there is indeed adequate material to the left of a second-position clitic, then that material can satisfy (29), and the derivation converges, as in (26a). If the output of left-adjunction leaves the clitic in initial position, however, the derivation crashes. In this case, the derivation backtracks, and a last-resort operation applies that avoids crash, as in (26b). The concrete implementations of this analysis may vary. In Barbosa's (1996, 2000) approach (based on Halpern's and inspired by Chomsky 1995, whereby crash of a derivation frees alternative ones), the problematic derivation takes a different route so that the clitic right-adjoins to an Infl-type head and the verb moves through it (by left-adjunction) as it raises.

In those terms, the pattern in (28) suggests that the host for the clitic must be found within a specified prosodic domain containing the clitic, and that, for some reason, a topic or a subject is outside such a domain, not counting as valid hosts (see Barbosa 2000: sec. 2.1.6). The last resort operation is thus induced, just as in (26b).

In this work, we adopt some aspects of the Halpern-Barbosa approach: namely, that the factor involved in enclisis is ultimately phonological, and that (as in Barbosa's analysis) the derivation involves a last-resort "fix," though not the one she proposes. Rather, we propose that the fix involves a more marked way in which verb raising applies (see section 4.3). Independently of that, we agree with these authors (contra Duarte and Matos 2000) that proclisis of the determiner clitic is the basic, unmarked pattern that results from clitic placement. Enclisis requires an extra, more costly step to "fix" the derivation.[9]

That is very consistent with both the typological and the diachronic Romance data. In finite clauses, there are languages with only proclisis and languages with both proclisis and enclisis, but no languages with only enclisis and no proclisis, suggesting that these phenomena stand in a subset–superset relation, enclisis requiring positive evidence by the learner. Historically, enclisis (marked) is lost in favor of proclisis (the unmarked option), but not the other way around.

However, we disagree with the Halpern-Barbosa line on a major point: in our view, the PF crash of sentence-initial proclitic elements in WI is not induced by properties of the determiner clitic.

4.2 Against an Analysis Based on Properties of Determiner Clitics

The idea expressed in (29) that properties of the WI determiner clitics themselves are at stake in crashing the derivations that lead to further V movement is suspicious. This view would force us to abandon the simple reasoning that the pronominal clitic is the determiner (Postal's hypothesis), moved from its base position. If we are dealing with one and the same element, it obviously has unique properties, specified in its lexical entry. These cannot include the property [enclitic], since determiner clitics can initiate a clause, as articles:

(30) [O   livro] é   meu.
      the book   is mine

      'The book is mine.'

Within a restrictive minimalist framework containing the Inclusiveness Condition (Chomsky 1995: ch 4), we cannot likewise appeal to the idea that lexical items may change their properties during the course of a derivation, according to the contexts in which they find themselves (thus allowing the determiner clitic to somehow "become" enclitic once it is raised out of the DP).

Ultimately, of course, our line of argument here depends on the validity of Postal's hypothesis. To the extent that it is successful in attaining both descriptive and explanatory adequacy, keeping it outweighs the loss of the particular instantiation of the Halpern-Barbosa analysis, especially when there is an alternative (and we believe more natural) analysis available that we discuss shortly.

Moreover, we saw that there are infinitival constructions with "free" alternation in clitic ordering, where the prima facie leftward prosodic context of the (pro-)clitic is enough to satisfy its prosodic properties. One such context is illustrated in (31):

(31) O   medo de **o**   ver   (vê-**lo**)
      the fear of him-cl   to-see

      'the fear of seeing him'

The idea that enclisis is triggered by an inadequate phonological left context for the clitic is difficult to reconcile with the possibility of proclisis here.

Finally, the suggestion that a special prosodic property of WI clitics (such as (29)) is at work in the proclisis–enclisis alternation does not fare well cross-linguistically. Determiner clitics in C/EI and WI are practically identical, segmentally and prosodically. There simply are no systematic, learnable morphophonological differences between the two paradigms that could motivate the drastically different behavior observed in each group of languages, nor is there a way to rationalize in these terms the diachronic tendency throughout Romance to move from conservative dialects in the unmarked direction of standard systematic proclisis.

4.3 Deriving the Tobler-Mussafia Law from a Property of f

Consider again (26b), repeated here as (32):

(32)　Enviaram-**no**　　　aos　　Jesuitas.　(*o enviaram)
　　　(they-)sent-him-cl　to-the　Jesuits

　　　'They sent him to the Jesuits.'

We want to propose that sentence-initial proclisis in WI crashes not because of requirements against initial position for the determiner clitic but, rather, because of conditions affecting the f element hypothesized for conservative dialects (F with ϕ-features, as in (10a–b)).

The fundamental assumption we are making is (23)—that f is a cliticlike element. We assume that as a clitic, f (or the clitic cluster containing it) needs to fuse with an appropriate phonological host. Our analysis of determiner clitics in (14) assumed that the unmarked option for fusion is to seek a host within the immediate domain of the prosodically defective head (thus, given X-bar architecture, to its right). Note now that f has phonological material to its right—namely, the verb raised in T. Therefore, f in (32) ought to take that path, as illustrated in the derivation (33) (recall that we use + to signal morphological fusion and − to signal head-adjunction; in this and subsequent representations, we omit the trace of the subject in [spec, v]):

(33)　a.　$[_{CP} [_{FP} f [_{TP} pro [_{T} [_{v} \text{ enviaram-}v]\text{-T}] [_{vP} t(v) [_{vP} t(V) [_{DP} \mathbf{o} \text{ N}] \text{ aos}$
　　　　Jesuitas$]]]]]$

　　　b.　$[_{CP} [_{FP} [_{f}\mathbf{o}\text{-}f] [_{TP} pro [_{T} [_{v} \text{ enviaram-}v]\text{-T}] [_{vP} t(v) [_{vP} t(V) [_{DP} t(D) \text{ N}] \text{ aos}$
　　　　Jesuitas$]]]]] > {}^{*}[_{f}\mathbf{o}\text{-}f] + [_{T} [_{v} \text{ enviaram-}v]\text{-T}]$

This, however, cannot be the correct way of licensing *f*, since it yields the ungrammatical pattern of enclisis. The fusion operation in (33) must therefore be prevented.

Suppose that, in the spirit of Lasnik (1999) (see also Bobaljik 1995 for a broader perspective), fusion is possible only across adjacent heads, where the relevant notion of adjacency is predicated of terminal elements (i.e., only strictly adjacent formatives can undergo fusion). In (33), *pro* intervenes between *f* and T, breaking the adjacency for rightward fusion of *f* into T. This is an important difference with (14), where at no point in the derivation is there a specifier or any other grammatical formative between *o* and its host (see note 6).[10]

At that point, a derivation involving *f* ought to crash, unless an alternative route is taken. We have assumed that determiner clitics may meet their PF requirements by going up in the phrase marker. Unlike D, though, *f* in a simple root clause (with a silent complementizer) doesn't have a place to go upward (recall that the host for a clitic must be phonologically realized).[11] But before crashing, the derivation takes a final stab at convergence: displacement of the verb to host the otherwise stranded clitic. Surely that option, whatever its details, ought to be as costly as clitic placement (see (15)–(16)), as both involve syntactic transformations.

That is not implausible if the grammar literally seeks this option as a very last resort: the derivation has reached F and detects, within the FP projection, a problem. There is no way to meet the PF demands of *f* (or the clitic cluster which includes it), to the right, to the left, or even with further placement upward in the phrase marker; it is stuck. At this point the "desperate move" of the derivation is to seek the closest accessible element within the active phase and bring it to the clitic rescue.

In principle, the displaced verb that ends up hosting the clitic could move to the C projection or to the F projection. Our claim is that the verb (or T containing the verb) moves to the F projection, in a way that provides an appropriate host for late (leftward) fusion of *f* or the clitic cluster which includes it. This is illustrated in (34) (compare with (33)):[12]

(34) $[_{CP} [_{FP} [_T [_v$ enviaram-*v*]-T] $[_f \mathbf{o}\text{-}f] [_{TP} pro \ t(T) [_{vP} t(v) [_{VP} t(V) [_{DP} t(D) \ N]$
      aos Jesuitas]]]]]] $> [_T [_v$ enviaram-*v*]-T] $+ [_f \mathbf{o}\text{-}f] =$ enviaram-no

We do not completely specify in (34) the position of the verb within the F projection. There are two possibilities, and each one is "costly" in its own way: either the verb (or T with the verb) raises to a "spec position" as in (35a), or it adjoins to *f* last—namely, after the clitic itself, as in (35b). Whichever configuration is the correct one is not terribly important for our purposes, though, and in the following discussion we refer in a general way to "configuration (35)," without any implied choice:[13]

(35)   a.

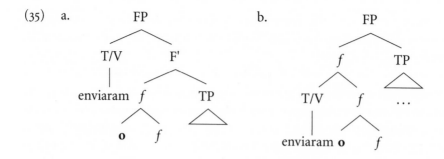

Clitic placement has in common with the "salvaging" route taken in (35) the fact that both are "costly" transformations, but aside from that the two are quite different. In the former, the clitic takes a syntactic tour until it finds a suitable host, whereas in the latter the clitic itself searches locally for a suitable host and brings it to its needy site. This is why we have chosen the metaphorical expression "verb swallowing" (which we use henceforth) to refer to the verb raising to FP resulting in configuration (35).

As Anderson (1993) has noted, when Wackernagel first studied the position of clitics in Germanic, he aptly observed that auxiliary elements in these languages act as if they were themselves clitics. The Tobler-Mussafia effect has a family resemblance with that behavior, in that the verb closest to f (either an auxiliary or a main verb) joins the clitic cluster in this category. If we assume with Chomsky (2001) that these last-minute adjustments are possible only within the confines of an active phase, this general solution will be possible only in a language where verbs are raised (or base-generated) outside of the vP phase. This seems very consistent with the facts, as to our knowledge there are no languages of the Tobler-Mussafia sort that do not allow pro-drop, which is arguably a sign of verb movement to T, at least within Romance.[14]

Finally, it is important to note that the more standard configuration (36) *must also* be allowed in WI:

(36)

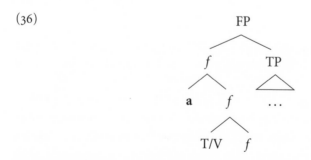

This configuration possibly underlies perfectly grammatical examples, such as (37):

(37) Muitas vezes *a*   *tinha* ele beijado.
      many   times she-cl had   he   kissed

'Many times had he kissed her.'

In (37), both the clitic *a* and the auxiliary finite verb *tinha* 'had' are arguably
adjoined to *f*, as they are "sandwiched" between the affective operator *muitas vezes*
'many times' in [spec, *f*] and the subject *ele* 'he' in [spec, T]. In other words,
normal adjunction of a verb (or T with a verb) to *f* followed by clitic placement
in *f* in the unmarked way prescribed by (20) independently exists in WI. Of
course, such a configuration requires an alternative fusion host for (the clitic
cluster including) *f*, such as a complementizer (see section 5.1), a displaced affective phrase (as in (37); see also section 5.2), or the negative morpheme (see section
6.3).[15]

5 Fusion Reconsidered

In this section, we reconsider the process of fusion and its relation to standard
clitic placement. For this, we need to discuss the contexts in which proclisis arises
in the WI variants. We have seen that in simple root clauses such as (32) *f* does
not have a phonological host c-commanding it, forcing the derivation to a last-
resort operation, whereby the verb raises to FP under verb swallowing (35). There
are cases, however, where such a host exists: in embedded finite clauses introduced
by the complementizer *que* 'that' and in sentences with affective operators in
[spec, *f*]. We consider these in turn, starting with embedded clauses.

5.1 Leftward Fusion: Clitic Placement in Embedded Finite Clauses

Consider a typical example such as (38):

(38) Ela disse que **o**   tinha   visto ontem.   (*tinha-**o**).
      she said   that him-cl   (she-)had seen   yesterday

'She said that she had seen him yesterday.'

Let us assume that the clitic *o* has been placed in *f*, forming the cluster $[_f \mathbf{o}\text{-}f]$ (see
(24)). In (38), there is a putative host for the clitic cluster—namely, the overt

complementizer *que* 'that'. This is in satisfaction of a phase-based theory of derivations, together with Chomsky's (2000, 2001) proposal that *v*P and CP are the
(strong) phases relevant for derivational purposes. Thus, the derivation does not
have to (and by minimalist reasoning, cannot) take the costly route of verb swallowing, and the ungrammatical output with enclisis is ruled out. We claim that
in (38) the cluster leans into *que* by leftward fusion. There are two possible inputs
to this operation, depending on whether the verb is adjoined to T (24a) or to *f*
(as in (24b) and (36)). This is illustrated in (39):

(39)   a. [$_{CP}$ que [$_{FP}$ [$_f$ **o**-*f*] [$_{TP}$*pro* [$_T$ tinha-T] visto ontem]]] > que + [$_f$ **o**-*f*]

       b. [$_{CP}$ que [$_{FP}$ [$_f$ **o**-[$_f$ [$_T$ tinha-T]-*f*]] [$_{TP}$*pro* *t*(T) visto ontem]]] > que +
           [$_f$ **o**-[$_f$[$_T$ tinha-T]-*f*]]

A striking piece of evidence for this analysis (and especially for the role of the
complementizer *que*) is provided by examples in which a topic is adjoined to FP,
intervening between *que* and *f* (and with no affective operator that could provide
an independent licenser for *f*). In this configuration, the topic breaks the adjacency
between *que* and *f*, disrupting the context for leftward fusion of *f* to *que*. As in
root clauses, the derivation is then forced to take the more costly alternative of
verb swallowing, yielding enclisis. This is illustrated in (40), with the topic *esses
panfletos* 'those pamphlets':[16]

(40)   Dizem   que   esses   panfletos,   distribuiu-**os**   (o   partido)
       (they-)say that   those   pamphlets   distributed-them-cl   the   party
       ontem. (*__os__ distribuiu)
       yesterday
       'They say that those pamphlets, the party distributed them yesterday.'

The word order in (40) also provides an argument that the landing site of verb
swallowing (35) is the FP projection, rather than the CP projection, since the verb
is to the right of both the complementizer *que* and the topic adjoined to FP, and
to the left of the subject arguably in [spec, T].

In (39), the clitic cluster does not undergo *clitic placement* to *que*. If it did,
the cluster would *left*-adjoin to *que* (in satisfaction of (19)), yielding after fusion
one of the ungrammatical outputs in (41), for (39a) and (39b), respectively:

(41)   a. *Ela disse o que tinha visto ontem   [$_f$**o**-*f*] + que

       b. *Ela disse o tinha que visto ontem   [$_f$**o**-[$_f$ [$_T$ tinha-T]-*f*]] + que

We thus have to provide a rationale as to why the clitic cluster is salvaged by (leftward) fusion to *que* (yielding (39)) rather than clitic placement (followed by rightward fusion) to *que*. We have seen already that some form of adjacency holds for fused elements. Let us formulate this requirement more specifically as in (42):

(42)   Fusion of a clitic is to the closest adjacent head.

The key is going to be what counts as "closest" and the relative cost between the various options to license a clitic or clitic cluster. With the data seen so far, the phenomenology is clear:

(43)   a. If there is a right-adjacent head, that is the target for fusion of the clitic.

      b. Otherwise, a left-adjacent head is the target for fusion of the clitic.

      c. Otherwise, either optimal clitic placement or displacement of an appropriate host provides a target for fusion of the clitic.

For convenience, we refer to (43a) as rightward fusion, to (43b) as leftward fusion, to the first half of (43c) as standard clitic placement, and to the second half of (43c) as verb-swallowing. The two options of (43c) have already been studied, and they are the least desirable, in that they must involve a standard syntactic movement operation in addition to—and before—fusion. In these terms, the derivations of (39) block those of (41), as desired. But why is (43a) more optimal than (43b)? If it were not, we would be seeing determiners systematically fusing to a left-adjacent head (to a verb or a preposition) instead of to a right-adjacent one inside NP, contrary to fact.

We suggest that the asymmetry between (43a) and (43b) reflects the cyclic nature of the derivation. Certainly fusion of a given head to one to its right basically involves existing structure, whereas fusion of the head in question to its left presupposes looking for new structure—perhaps not finding it, perhaps needing to go into more elaborate climbing. In this spirit, preference for (43a) over 43(b) would be very much in the spirit of Pesetsky's (2000) Earliness Condition:

(44)   Fuse early (to an already established structure, i.e., rightward).

Evidently, this cannot be a convergence criterion; if early fusion is impossible, a late one will do.

5.2 Early versus Late Fusion: Clitic Placement with Affective Operators

One issue that we have not fully addressed yet concerns the question whether an *entire phrase* can serve as the host for fusion. As our brief discussion in note 10 already indicated, this is not possible for rightward fusion. Consider again the example presented there, the derivation of which we give in (45):

(45) a. $[_{CP} [_{FP} f [_{TP} [$ seus   pais$] [_T [_v$ enviaram-$v]$-T$] [_{vP} t(v)$
              his   parents   sent
        $[_{VP} t(V) [_{DP}$ **o** N$]$ aos   Jesuítas$]]]]]$
              him   to-the   Jesuits

      b. $[_{CP} [_{FP} [_f$**o**-$f] [_{TP}$ [seus pais] $[_T [_v$ enviaram-v$]$-T$] [_{vP} t(v) [_{VP} t(V) [_{DP}$
          $t(D)$ N$]$ aos Jesuítas$]]]]] > *[_f$**o**-$f]+$[seus pais]

In (45), the clitic cluster is adjacent to the entire phrase *seus pais* 'his parents'. Still, fusion of the cluster with this phrase must be blocked, since it yields the incorrect output **o seus pais enviaram aos Jesuítas* 'him his parents sent to the Jesuits' (rather than the correct *enviaram-no os seus pais aos Jesuítas* 'sent him his parents to the Jesuits', with enclisis and involving verb swallowing).

A complex spec is arguably an independently spelled-out "derivational cascade," in the sense of Uriagereka (1999). Capitalizing on this, we assume that rightward fusion of the clitic requires that the host belongs to the same derivational cascade as the clitic. The fusion operation in (45b) is thus correctly blocked. We return later to some considerations why this should be the case.

Leftward fusion, however, is less restrictive. To see this, observe that a late alternative must be involved in the derivation of (26a), with a dislocated affective operator in [spec, *f*] (repeated in (46) with structure added):

(46) a. $[_{FP} [_f$ **o**-$f] [_{TP}pro [_T[_v$ enviaram-v$]$-T$] [_{vP} t(v) [_{VP} t(V) [_{DP} t(D)$ N$]$
              him-cl   send
        a muito mestre$]]]]]$
        to many teacher

      b. $[_{CP}$ C $[_{FP}$ [a muito mestre] $[_f$**o**-$f] [_{TP} pro [_T [_v$ enviaram-v$]$-T$] [_{vP} t(v)$
          $[_{VP} t(V) [_{DP} t(D)$ N$]$ t(affective operator)$)]]]]] >$ [a-muito-mestre]$+$
          $[_f$**o**-$f]$

        'Many teachers have they sent him to!'

First, consider the determiner-clitic *o* 'him'. Not having a fusion host within its immediate DP domain, it cannot be licensed by (43a). Clitic placement in *f* (43c) is the only option.[17] Consider now the cluster $[_f\mathbf{o}\text{-}f]$ in (46a). Is (43a) an option? No, since *pro* intervenes between the clitic cluster and its target T (see the text immediately after (33)). The cluster must thus use strategy (43b). This is arguably possible, given the movement of *a muito mestre* to the specifier of FP within the same CP phase.

The Galician example (47) confirms that [spec, *f*] is indeed the cliticization target:

(47) Deu-**lo**   tenha na   Gloria!
      God-him-cl have   in-the Glory

      'May God have him in Heaven!'

In this emphatic (affective) context, there is no doubt that the clitic is phonologically attached to the element *Deu* 'God' in [spec,*f*], since the last consonant of this element truncates (*Deus* > *Deu*) and the underlying onset [*l*] of the determiner clitic surfaces, yielding *Deu-lo* 'God+him'.

Dependency on an entire phrase thus appears to be an option for late leftward fusion, but not for early rightward fusion (see (44)). That ought to be a consequence of an architecture as in (48):

(48)   a. Early rightward fusion obeys morphological constraints.

       b. Late leftward fusion obeys prosodic constraints.

The idea is that strict head-to-head relations, in the morphological sense, are witnessed in the earliest, unmarked form of fusion. If that optimal path is not taken and as the derivation advances, things change. After multiple spell-out proceeds and prosody is accessed, what matters are no longer lexical heads but, rather, entire derivational cascades that constitute the input to prosodical requirements. For the purposes of the derivation at the stage where fusion of $[_f\mathbf{o}\text{-}f]$ in (46) and (47) takes place, the specifier of FP is a giant compound behaving as a unit, to which the clitic cluster can appropriately attach (see Uriagereka 1999 and Guimarães 1998 for extensive discussion and refinements of these ideas).[18]

5.3 Summary

Before we turn to infinitival contexts, we present a condensed summary of our system up to this point:

(49)   *Assumptions about clitic placement*
       a. Adjunction is universally left-adjunction (= (19))

b. Clitics are the last elements to adjoin to their target head (= (20))

c. Clitics within a given derivational phase cluster around one another (= (21))

The basic requirement for clitics is *fusion* (42), reformulated here as (50) in light of our previous discussion in section 5.2. Fusion is constrained by the optimality strategy (44) and the architectural principles (48), repeated here, respectively, as (51) and (52) (the latter now with additional specification):

(50)   Fusion of a clitic is to the closest adjacent relevant unit.

(51)   Fuse early (to an already established structure, that is, rightward).

(52)   *Consequences of timing in cliticization*
       a. Early rightward fusion obeys morphological constraints (it can target only a head).

       b. Late leftward fusion obeys prosodic constraints (it can target a head or a phrase).

This system, in turn, entails that the typology in (43) ought to be modified as in (53):

(53)   a. If there is a right-adjacent head, that is the target for fusion of the clitic.

       b. Otherwise, a left-adjacent unit (phrase or head) is the target for fusion of the clitic.

       c. Otherwise, either optimal clitic placement or displacement of an appropriate host provides a target for fusion of the clitic.

This typology seems essentially correct, although it is certainly not primitive. We have also suggested that the ranking between (53a) and (53b) follows from the optimality strategy in (51) and that the ranking between (53b) and (53c) follows from standard economy considerations: a syntactic displacement is more costly than a PF fusion (and since it involves a subsequent PF fusion, it is also a matter of "more vs. less"). More subtle is the way in which rightward or leftward fusion affects the possible clitic hosts. We have suggested that this follows from (52).

Aside from these general assumptions about clitics, fusion, and clitic placement (which will remain solid and sound only inasmuch as our generalizations can be replicated in other languages), we have made the following specific assumptions for Romance ((13) and (23), respectively):

(54)   a. Romance pronominal clitics are normal Ds heading a DP.

       b. Romance determiners (special clitics or regular articles) are phonolog-
           ical clitics that must find themselves within a well-formed prosodic word
           at PF.

(55)   *f* is a clitic-like element.

The gist of our proposal is this: clitic *f*, for which there is ample diachronic
and synchronic evidence, creates a mini-chaos inside the WI clause. Ideally, its
clitic properties are satisfied locally by phonological material that provides the
appropriate prosodic support—either an adjacent c-commanding (overt) complementizer or a phrase in its spec position. Otherwise, it forces the displacement
of a nearby verb to it (basically because that is the closest head that can do the
trick), but this is a more costly alternative that we referred to as "verb swallowing."
A minimal pair that illustrates this basic difference involves exclamative idiomatic
sentences with subjunctive mood, where a "root" overt complementizer *que* 'that'
is optional. In the presence of *que*, proclisis is obligatory; otherwise, enclisis is the
only possible output:

(56)   a. Que   **me**   valha   Deus!   (*valha-**me**)
           that   to-me   may-help   God

           'May God help me!'

       b. Valha-**me** Deus! (***me** valha Deus)

In (56a), *que* hosts *f*. When absent, as in (56b), the grammar has to go into a
roundabout, bringing the verb to *f* in order to salvage the derivation.[19]

6 CLITIC PLACEMENT IN NONINFLECTED INFINITIVAL CLAUSES: THE ROLE OF FUSION AND OF OBJECT SHIFT

In this section we discuss the patterns of cliticization in plain infinitival clauses
of the standard languages and of WI, again focusing on Spanish and EP. We
consider how contextual factors, both clause-internal (such as negation) and
clause-external (such as the grammatical function of the infinitival in the overall
structure), affect this pattern in WI variants but not at all in the standard variants.

From a theoretic perspective, we introduce an important constraint on fusion, and we address a question left open at the end of section 3.2—namely, the role of Object Shift in those derivations that involve clitic placement in the CP cycle in the sense of (53c).

6.1 Patterns of Infinitival Clitic Placement in Standard versus Conservative Dialects

In plain (noninflected) infinitival clauses, there is generalized enclisis in standard variants such as Spanish. This pattern is completely insensitive to contextual factors, either clause-internal or clause-external. Negation, for example, will not disrupt the pattern, nor will the grammatical function of the clause in the overall structure. This is illustrated in (57) with, respectively, a subject clause, a subcategorized clause, and a nonsubcategorized adverbial clause introduced by a preposition:

(57)   a. [(No)   invitar**la**   a   nuestra   fiesta]   sería   una   buena
            (not)   to-invite-her   to   our   party   would-be   a   good
            idea.   *((no) **la** invitar)
            idea

      '(Not) to invite her to our party would be a good idea.'

      b. Intenté   [(no)   invitar**la**   a   la   fiesta].
            (I-) tried   (not)   to-invite-her-cl   to   the   party
            *((no) **la** invitar)

      'I tried (not) to invite her to the party.'

      c. [Para   (no)   ver**la**   más],   haría   de   todo.
            for   (not)   to-see-her   anymore   (I-)would-do   of   everything
            *((no) **la** ver)

      'In order (not) to see her anymore, I would do everything.'

In contrast, clitic placement in plain WI infinitives is highly sensitive to contextual details, both clause-external and clause-internal. Consider, for example, the effect of internal negation. Only enclisis is possible in affirmative subject clauses, as shown in (58):

(58)   [Convidá-**la**   para   a   nossa   festa]   seria   uma   boa
         to-invite-her-cl   for   the   our   party   would-be   a   good
         ideia. (*a convidar)
         idea

      'To invite her to our party would be a good idea.'

However, this is not the case in their negative counterpart, as shown in (59a), a pattern that apparently mimics what happens in finite clauses (compare with (3b)). The similarity with finite clauses, however, is not complete. Contrary to finite clauses, enclisis is also possible with negation in infinitival sentences, irrespective of the grammatical function of the clause. This is illustrated in (59):

(59) a. [Não   **a**   convidar para a   nossa festa] seria   uma
         not   her-cl to-invite for   the   our   party would-be a
         boa   ideia. (não convidá-**la**)
         good idea

       'Not to invite her to our party would be a good idea.'

    b. Tentei   [não **a**   convidar para a   festa].
        (I-)tried   not her-cl to-invite for   the party
        (não convidá-**la**)

       'I tried not to invite her to the party.'

    c. [Para não **a**   ver   mais],   faria   tudo.
        for   not her-cl to-see anymore (I-)would-do everything
        (não vê-**la**)

       'In order (not) to see her anymore, I would do everything.'

Clause-external contextual factors also interfere with the pattern of clitic placement. While affirmative subject clauses and affirmative subcategorized clauses disallow proclisis, affirmative nonsubcategorized adverbial clauses introduced by a preposition do allow it. This is illustrated in (60) ((60a) = (58)):

(60) a. [Convidá-**la** para a nossa festa] seria uma boa ideia. (***a** convidar)

    b. Tentei   [convidá-**la**   para a   festa].   (***a** convidar)
        (I-)tried to-invite-her-cl for   the party

       'I tried to invite her to the party.'

    c. [Para vê-**la**   outra   vez], faria   tudo.
        for   to-see-her-cl another time (I-)would-do everything
        (**a** ver)

       'In order to see her one more time, I would do everything.'

We turn in the next subsections to an analysis of the factors involved in these series of complex contrasts.

6.2 Infinitival Enclisis in the Standard Variants: The Role of Fusion

Let us start with the uniformity of enclisis in the infinitival clauses of the standard variants such as Spanish. The generality of this pattern suggests that clitic placement (in the specific sense of (53c)) is not involved in deriving this pattern.[20] Our proposal is that in these contexts, the clitic is directly (leftward) fused with the verb within the vP phase (option (53b)), without needing to be syntactically placed in the CP cycle first (we refer to a vP-internal fusion process as "low fusion"). Taking (57a) as a representative example, the relevant step in this derivation is shown in (61):[21]

(61) $[_{CP} [_{FP} F [_{TP} \dots T [_{vP} [_v \text{invitar-}v] [_{VP} t(V) [_{DP} \textbf{la} N]]]]]] > [_v \text{invitar-}v]+\textbf{la}$
       $= \text{invitar}\textbf{la}$

In turn, the availability of low leftward fusion for the determiner-clitic in (61), together with the ranking in (53), blocks the more costly derivation involving clitic-placement to T. This is certainly the correct result since clitic placement in T yields the ungrammatical proclitic outcome (see (18)).[22]

   Subsequently to (61), the whole verbal complex *invitarla* raises to T at the CP-phase (i.e., after low fusion of the clitic). In fact, the complex can raise still higher in Spanish, as in "personal" infinitives with an overt subject such as (62):

(62)   [Invitar**la**   nosotros   a   la   fiesta]   seria   una   buena
       to-invite-her   we   to   the   party   would-be   a   good
       idea.
       idea

       'For us to invite her to the party would be a good idea.'

In this example, the infinitival verb (with the clitic) is fronted over the subject, appearing as if the WI route has been taken. This is not inconsistent with anything we have said, as the standard Romance variants involve F. Assume that in personal infinitives of standard dialects the verb raises to infinitival F for some reason. Crucially, though, F is not a clitic, and therefore neither does **la** have to cluster with it, nor does the verb need to move to the exact same "leftward" position (35) of verb swallowing as in EP. In sum, despite appearances, the enclisis in (62) is derived quite low in the structure, at the vP phase, as illustrated in (61).

   The low derivation of enclisis at the vP level in the standard dialects has one immediate consequence. Grammatical factors at the higher CP phase (such as negation) or external to the clause (e.g., whether the clause is subcategorized and whether it is introduced by a preposition) will not affect this pattern, since they do not interfere with the derivation of the lower *v*P cycle.

At this point, our analysis raises a serious issue: Why can't this very same route be taken in *finite* clauses? We know that this is not the case, because otherwise generalized enclisis would extend to these domains, too, but this, obviously, would be an incorrect result (i.e., with the pattern of (1a) reversed).

To answer this, consider the clitic placement patterns of other tenseless forms such as gerunds and participles. With gerunds, the pattern in the standard dialects is similar to infinitives; that is, we have generalized enclisis, as illustrated in (63):

(63) a. Enviando**te**   este   regalo,   te   doy   una   prueba
         sending-to-you-cl this   present   to-you   (I-)give   a   proof
         de   mi   amor. (*te enviando)
         of   my   love

         'By sending this present to you, I give you proof of my love.'

      b. No   enviando**te**   este   regalo,   te   doy
         not   sending-to-you-cl   this   present   to-you   (I-)give
         una   prueba   de   mi   odio. (*no **te** enviando)
         a   proof   of   my   hatred

         'By not sending you this present, I give you proof of my hatred.'

With participles, however, the pattern is different. Clitics do not attach easily to the righthand side of participles, as has been often noticed in the Romance literature (see Kayne 1991: 657–660 and references therein).[23] This is illustrated in (64):

(64) a. Enviados   los   regalos   a   Maria,   fuimos   a   casa.
         sent-3pl   the   presents to   Maria   we-went   to   house

         'Once the presents were sent to Maria, we went home.'

      b. *Enviado(s)**los**   a   Maria,   fuimos   a   casa.
         sent-(3pl)-them-cl   to   Maria   we-went   to   house

Generalized enclisis with gerunds in standard dialects suggests that, as with infinitives, placement of the clitic is by a simple process of phonological leftward fusion within the lowest phase that contains both the gerund and the determiner clitic. But why would participles be different from gerunds in this respect?

We suggest that the relevant difference has to do with the fact that participles are agreeing forms while gerunds are not, and we propose the following morphological condition on determiner clitic fusion:

(65)   *Condition on determiner clitic fusion*
       A determiner clitic cannot fuse to the "agreeing edge" (i.e., the right edge,
       in Romance) of a verbal form displaying agreement.

We assume that (65) is not a primitive principle but, rather, derives from morphological conditions on verbal checking. The intuitive idea is that direct fusion
of the clitic to the agreeing edge interferes with the checking of verbal (subject)-
agreement features, these features being now "buried" inside the resulting form.[24]
Since ordinary finite forms obligatorily display agreement in Romance, low leftward fusion of determiner clitics to a finite verbal form in the vP phase is also
ruled out, as desired.[25] In other words, finite forms must take the more costly
route of (53c), involving either long-distance clitic placement to T followed by
rightward fusion to the verb, or clitic clustering with f.[26]

6.3 Clitic Placement in Negative Infinitival Clauses of WI and the Role of Object Shift

We start our discussion of WI with negative infinitival clauses, which display a
pattern of free variation between enclisis and proclisis (see (59)). As a representative example, consider (59a), repeated here as (66) (compare with (57a)):

(66)   [Não **a**   convidar para a   nossa festa] seria   uma
        not   her-cl   to-invite for   the   our   party   would-be   a
        boa   ideia. (não convidá-**la**)
        good idea

       'Not to invite her to our party would be a good idea.'

There must be some additional factor not present in the standard variants which
is responsible for the different pattern of (66) in WI. That ought to be clitic f,
which we thus take to be present in these contexts. As discussed, f needs an
adjacent element capable of hosting it. We assume that in (66) the negative morpheme *não* is within the FP projection, providing a host for leftward fusion of f,
as illustrated in (67):[27]

(67) $[_{CP} [_{FP} \text{não } f [_{TP} \ldots \text{T } [_{vP} [_{v} \text{convidar-}v] [_{VP} t(\text{V}) [_{DP} \text{a N}]]]]]]$

As for the determiner clitic, it can fuse leftward with the verb within vP, prior to
verb raising to T, in the manner discussed in section 6.2. Note that condition
(49c) on clitic clusters holds only if the clitics belong to the same phase. Thus,
in (67) nothing requires a and f to cluster, since they are in distinct phases (vP

and CP, respectively). The lower vP in (67) thus provides the direct input for the relevant fusion of the determiner clitic, as illustrated in (68a). Subsequently, verb raising to T applies to the output of fusion, yielding (68b):

(68) a. $[_{CP} [_{FP}$ não $f [_{TP} \ldots$ T $[_{vP}$ convidar-v $[_{VP}$ t(V) $[_{DP}$ **a** N$]]]]]]$
$> [_v$ convidar-$v] +$**a** $=$ convidá-**la**

   b. $[_{CP} [_{FP}$ não $f [_{TP} \ldots [_T [_v [_v$ convidar-$v]+$**a**$]$-T$] [_{vP}$ t(v) $[_{VP}$ t(V)
$[_{DP}$ t(D) N$]]]]]]]$
$>$ não$+f$ $(> [_v$ convidar-$v]+$**a** $=$ convidá-**la**$)$

In the CP-phase, finally, f fuses to the negative morpheme *não*. Verb raising in (68b) carries the *whole form* $[_v [_v$ convidar-v$]+$**a**$]$ without changing the linear order within the complex. In particular, condition (49c) on clitic clusters is not applicable anymore at that phase. Once fusion has applied, the licensed determiner-clitic is "buried" inside the verbal form and ceases to be visible as a unit to the computational system. In other words, when the verb complex raises to the higher CP cycle containing f, *a* is already licensed, stuck within the complex, and not there anymore for f to cluster with. Derivation (68) yields the case of (66) with enclisis.

Let us now consider the equally grammatical case of (66) with proclisis. This output seems to involve an extra movement of the determiner clitic to f. Prima facie, however, this move seems to be more costly than the fusion operations in (68). The question then arises whether it should not be ruled out according to the ranking in (53).

In the spirit of a proposal systematically explored in Sportiche (1996) and going back to ideas of Rivero (1986), suppose it is possible for the DP object in EP to undergo object shift (henceforth OS) to [spec, v], yielding (69) from (67):[28]

(69) $[_{CP} [_{FP}$ não $f [_{TP} \ldots$ T $[_{vP} [_{DP}$ **a** N$] [_v$ convidar-$v] [_{VP}$ t(V) t(DP)$]]]]]]$

Consider now assumption (49c). We have just concluded that, in (67), *a* and f do not cluster since they are independently licensed in distinct phases. But after OS in (69), the displaced DP is now plausibly within the active window of the CP phase (at the edge of the vP phase, in Chomsky's 2001 terms), the determiner clitic in that DP is still not licensed, and therefore condition (49c) is now in full force. This means that the determiner clitic must be placed in f, in the way discussed in section 3.2 (see (24)). This yields (70), where the negative morpheme now salvages the cluster *a-f*, yielding proclisis:[29]

(70) $[_{CP} [_{FP}$ não $[_f$**a**-$f] [_{TP} \ldots$ T $[_{vP} [_{DP}$ t(D) N$] [_v$ convidar-$v] [_{VP}$ t(V) t(DP)$]]]]]]$
$>$ não $+ [_f$**a**-$f]$

Is the derivation (69)–(70) competing with (68)? Our answer is no, because they are based on different numerations. The crucial difference is based on lack versus presence of OS. Following Chomsky's (2001:34–35) analysis of OS, we assume that *v* has an EPP feature in the numeration underlying the latter derivation, whereas it lacks it in the numeration underlying the former. The two derivations are thus not comparable for economy purposes.[30]

This analysis, in turn, raises an important issue. What allows assignment of an EPP feature in the derivation (69)–(70)? With Chomsky (2001), we assume that (71) is an invariant principle of UG:

(71)   *v* is assigned an EPP feature only if that has an effect on outcome.

Principle (71) works in tandem with another phase-theoretical condition, the Phase Impenetrability Condition (72), which rules computational interactions between (strong) phases (from Chomsky 2001: 13):

(72)   *Phase Impenetrability Condition*
       For strong phase HP with head H, the domain of H is not accessible to operations outside HP; only H and its edge are accessible to such operations.

The edge is what Chomsky calls the residue outside of H': either specs or elements adjoined to HP.

A consequence of (72) is that if an element from a *v*P phase α immediately subjacent to a CP phase β is to be extracted from α (say, a complement *wh*-phrase in its way to spec of higher C), then an EPP feature may (and must) be assigned to *v*, so that extraction takes place without violating the PIC (72). This is a case in which assignment of the EPP feature has an effect on outcome, since otherwise the *wh*-phrase could not check the strong feature of higher C, and the derivation would crash.[31]

Consider now the derivation (69)–(70). Are we allowing a different outcome by assigning an EPP feature to *v*, one that would have not been obtained if the feature were not assigned? The answer is yes. Derivation (68), with neither an EPP feature nor OS, has the fusion outcomes *não+f* and $[_v$ convidar-*v*$]+$**a**; in addition, its linear PF output is the sequence *não convidá-la para a festa*. Derivation (69)–(70), with an EPP feature on *v* and with OS, has the different fusion outcome *não+*$[_v$**a**-*f*$]$, as well as the different linear PF output *não a convidar para a festa*. Whether we take the "distinctness" relevant for (71) to be predicated over simple linear PF outputs or over the slightly more abstract fusion outcomes, an EPP feature is therefore allowed in (69)–(70).

As the reader can easily verify, the derivation of enclisis and proclisis in negative subcategorized (59b) or negative adverbial clauses (59c) follows exactly the same paths as for subject clauses. We thus omit discussion of these two cases here.

A question that can be raised at this point concerns the role of OS in the derivation of Spanish infinitival clauses with clitics—to be precise, whether (71) allows a derivation with OS in addition to (61), possibly with incorrect results. We leave this matter aside for now, returning to it in section 6.5.

To conclude this section, note that the logic of our system forces us to revise our analysis of the derivations involved in those cases where strategy (53c) (clitic placement from the vP phase to the CP phase) is taken by the determiner clitic. Recall that condition (65) forces determiner clitics in finite clauses to exit the vP, since they cannot undergo low (leftward) fusion to the right edge of the verbal complex. Then, given the PIC (72), the determiner clitic is forced to exit the vP through [spec, v]—that is, by an application of OS. This adjustment in the derivations presented here does not have any further consequences.[32]

6.4 Clitic Placement in Affirmative Infinitival Clauses of WI

As stated, with affirmative clauses, the pattern of clitic placement varies according to the external context of the infinitival clause (see (60)). While enclisis is generally possible, proclisis is allowed in adverbial clauses introduced by a preposition, but not in subject or subcategorized clauses. Given these differences, each case deserves independent scrutiny. We start with subject clauses, then turn to adverbial clauses, leaving the discussion of subcategorized clauses for last.

6.4.1 *Subject Clauses*

Consider (60a), repeated here as (73) with structure (74) (see note 21):

(73) [Convida-**lá**   para   a   nossa festa] seria   uma boa
      to-invite-her-cl for   the our   party   would-be   a   good
      ideia. (*__a__ convidar)
      idea

      'To invite her to our party would be a good idea.'

(74) $[_{\text{CP}} [_{\text{FP}} f [_{\text{TP}} \ldots \text{T} [_{v\text{P}} [_v \text{convidar-}v] [_{v\text{P}} t(\text{V}) [_{\text{DP}} \textbf{a} \text{ N}]]]]]]$

Two points about this structure are worth noting. First, f has no element within the CP phase that can host it; second, since the determiner clitic a and f are *not* within the same phase, they are not forced to cluster, if a finds a way to fuse low within its own phase. One possible derivation then proceeds as follows: in the lower vP phase, the determiner clitic fuses leftward with $[_v \textit{convidar}+v]$, yielding (75a); subsequently, the complex verb (with the clitic attached to it) raises to f (via T) in the swallowing configuration (35), yielding (75b) (after fusing, the determiner clitic within the verbal form is invisible to (49c)):

(75)   a. $[_{CP} [_{FP} f [_{TP} \dots T [_{vP} [_v [_v \text{convidar-}v]+\textbf{a} [_{VP} t(V) [_{DP} t(D) N]]]]]]]$

       b. $[_{CP} [_{FP} f [_T [_v [_v \text{convidar-}v]+\textbf{a}]\text{-}T] f [_{TP} t(T) [_{vP} t(v) [_{VP} t(V) [_{DP} t(D) N]]]]]]] > [_T [_v [_v \text{convidar-}v]+\textbf{a}]\text{-}T]+f = \text{convidá-}\textbf{la}$

The step in (75b) is costly, but without it f would not be licensed, and the derivation would crash; therefore, it is allowed. Note that this derivation is very similar to the derivation (61) of the equivalent Spanish example (57a), modulo the raising of the infinitival verb+clitic sequence to f in WI (vs. T in Spanish).

Another possible derivation involves OS. Let us see how this derivation proceeds and whether it should be allowed by (71). The output of OS is illustrated in (76a). Because the unlicensed determiner clitic at the edge of vP is now within the active CP phase, it must cluster with f, according to (49c), yielding (76b); the infinitival verb then raises to f (via T) by swallowing, yielding (76c):

(76)   a. $[_{CP} [_{FP} f [_{TP} \dots T [_{vP} [_{DP} \textbf{a} N] [_v \text{convidar-}v] [_{VP} t(V) t(DP)]]]]] \dots$

       b. $[_{CP} [_{FP} [_f \textbf{a-}f] [_{TP} T [_{vP} [_{DP} t(D) N] [_v \text{convidar-}v] [_{VP} t(V) t(DP)]]]]] \dots$

       c. $[_{CP} C [_{FP} [_T [_v \text{convidar-}v]\text{-}T] [_f\textbf{a-}f] [_{TP} t(T) [_{vP} [_{DP} t(D) N] t(v) [_{VP} t(V) t(DP)]]]]] \dots > [_T [_v \text{convidar-}v]\text{-}T+[_f\textbf{a-}f] = \text{convidá-}\textbf{la}$

The linear PF outcome of this derivation is identical to the linear PF outcome of derivation (75) without OS. However, the fusion outcomes are different: $[_T [_v [_v \text{convidar-v}]+\textbf{a}]\text{-}T]+f$ in (75) versus $[_T [_v \text{convidar-v}]\text{-}T]+[_f \textbf{a-}f]$ in (76). If (71) requires strict linear PF distinctness, then derivation (76), with its extra EPP feature, is not allowed. However, if distinctness in the fusion outcomes is sufficient for the purposes of (71), (76) is allowed. We leave this matter open here. In any case, there is at least a legitimate derivation for the output with enclisis— that of (75). Finally, there is no possible derivation yielding proclisis, since that would require a (nonexisting) independent host for f within the CP cycle in order to avoid verb swallowing.

6.4.2 Adverbial Clauses

We turn next to adverbial clauses introduced by a preposition. Contrary to subject clauses, these allow proclisis as well as enclisis, as illustrated in (77):

(77) [Para vê-**la**   outra   vez],   faria   tudo. (**a** ver)
      for   to-see-her-cl another time (I)-would-do everything

'In order to see her one more time, I would do everything.'

Recall that in (73) the absence of an independent host for f forces verb swallowing, yielding enclisis and disallowing the proclitic pattern (cf. the last step of both (75) and (76)). In (77), however, the preposition introducing the clause is a potential host for f. We thus propose that f fuses leftward to the preposition (very much like f fuses leftward to the complementizer *que* 'that' in finite clauses), blocking the more costly route with verb swallowing. Let us now see how this way of licensing f is compatible with *both* enclisis and proclisis. Consider first a derivation *without* OS, as in (78):

(78)   para $[_{FP} f [_{TP} \ldots T [_{vP} [_v \text{ver-}v] [_{VP} t(V) [_{DP} \textbf{a} N]]]]]]$
        >**para**+f >$[_v \text{ver-}v]$+**a** = vê-**la**

In (78), the determiner clitic fuses leftward with the verb within vP; in turn, f fuses with the preposition, yielding the enclitic pattern. Again, note that f and **a** do not have to cluster, since each is licensed in its own phase. Raising of the verbal complex (including the clitic) to T or to f (in a configuration like (36)) does not disrupt the pattern (see note 29).

Consider now a derivation involving OS, illustrated in (79):

(79)   a. para $[_{FP} f [_{TP} \ldots T [_{vP} [_v \text{ver-}v] [_{VP} t(V) [_{DP} \textbf{a} N]]]]]] \ldots$

        b. para $[_{FP} f [_{TP} \ldots T [_{vP} [_{DP} \textbf{a} N] [_v \text{ver-}v] [_{VP} t(V) t(DP)]]]]]] \ldots$

        c. para $[_{FP} [_f \textbf{a}\text{-}f] [_{TP} \ldots T [_{vP} [_{DP} t(D) N] [_v \text{ver-}v] [_{VP} t(V) t(DP)]]]]]] \ldots$
            > para+$[_f \textbf{a}\text{-}f]$

Here, after OS, the determiner clitic must be placed in f by virtue of condition (49c). Thus, it is now *the cluster* $[_f \textbf{a}\text{-}f]$ which fuses leftward with the preposition, yielding the desired pattern of proclisis to the infinitive (or, perhaps more accurately, of enclisis to the preposition). Finally, whether we take "distinctness" for the purpose of (71) to involve simple PF linear order or fusion outcomes, the two derivations have different outputs, thus allowing the EPP feature that makes (79) possible.

6.4.3 Subcategorized Clauses

As discussed, in the case of adverbial clauses, a derivation yielding proclisis is possible because there is an independent host for leftward fusion of f (see (79), with the OS option). In this respect, subcategorized clauses present an interesting wrinkle: even though there is phonological material to the left of the clause, which could serve as a potential host for f, proclisis to the infinitive is not an option, as shown in (80):

(80) Tentei   [convidá-**la**   para   a   festa].   (*a convidar)
      (I−)tried to-invite-her-cl for   the   party

      'I tried to invite her to the party.'

In other words, we get the pattern of affirmative *subject* clauses (cf. (73)) rather than the expected pattern of affirmative *adverbial* clauses (cf. (77)). The issue then is why we cannot have a derivation for (80) in which the finite matrix verb plays the same role for f as the preposition *para* in (79), yielding proclisis to the infinitival form. Consider how such a derivation, illustrated in (81), would proceed (compare with (79)):

(81) a. Tentei $[_{FP} f [_{TP} \ldots T [_{vP} [_{v}$ convidar-$v] [_{VP} t(V) [_{DP}$ **a** N] para a festa$]]]]]$

      b. Tentei $[_{FP} f [_{TP} \ldots T [_{vP} [_{DP}$ **a** N$] [_{v}$ convidar-$v] [_{VP} t(V) t(DP)$ para a festa$]]]]]$

      c. Tentei $[_{FP} [_{f}$ **a**-$f] [_{TP} \ldots T [_{vP} [_{DP} t(D)$ N$] [_{v}$ convidar-$v] [_{VP} t(V) t(DP)$ para a festa$]]]]] > $ *tentei$+[_{f}$**a**-$f]$

After OS (81b), the determiner clitic is placed in f (81c), and, in turn, the cluster $[_{f}$ **a**-$f]$ leftward fuses to the matrix verb *tentei* '(I)-tried', yielding the (ungrammatical) pattern of infinitival proclisis (more accurately, enclisis to the matrix finite form).[33]

Neither (79) nor (81) seems to violate any constraints, yet the result is unacceptable in (81), indicating that there is a crucial difference between the examples. Our proposal is the following. Whereas in (79) leftward fusion of the clitic cluster to the preposition is resolved within the CP phase, in (81) it crosses the boundary of that phase, to join the phonological material of the selecting verb *tentei* '(I-)tried'. In other words, (79) and (81) must be further analyzed as in (82a–b), respectively (we give only the last step of each derivation):[34]

(82) a. $[_{CP}$ para $[_{FP} [_{f}$ **a**-$f] [_{TP} \ldots T [_{vP} [_{DP} t(D)$ N$] [_{v}$ ver-$v] [_{VP} t(V) t(DP)]]]]]$
         $\ldots > $ para$+[_{f}$**a**-$f]$

      b. Tentei $[_{CP} [_{FP} [_{f}$ **a**-$f] [_{TP} \ldots T [_{vP} [_{DP} t(D)$ N$] [_{v}$ convidar-$v] [_{VP} t(V) t(DP)$ para a festa$]]]]] > $ *tentei$+[_{f}$**a**-$f]$

The resolution of phonological demands requires that the clitic be licensed within the CP phase. This is satisfied in (82a) but not in (82b), arguing yet again for a strict cyclic interpretation of derivational processes, even in these late phonological adjustments. In addition, we also have an argument for the unification of the narrow-syntactic and the PF cycles, the latter proceeding in parallel with the former.

As is by now familiar, the only way to salvage derivation (81) is by applying the costly step of verb swallowing, yielding the desired pattern of enclisis, as shown in (83):

(83)   Tentei $[_{CP} [_{FP} [_T [_v$ convidar-$v]$-T$]$ $[_f \mathbf{a}\text{-}f]$ $_{TP} \ldots t(T) [_{vP} [_{DP} t(D)$ N$]$ $t(v) [_{VP}$
       $t(V) t(DP)$ para a festa$]]]]] > [_T [_v$ convidar-$v]$-T$] + [_f\mathbf{a}\text{-}f]$ = convidá-**la**

6.4.4 A Correlation between Proclisis and Agreement Inflection in Infinitives

Inflected infinitives are impossible in infinitival clauses subcategorized by verbs like *tentar* 'to try' (Raposo 1987), as ilustrated in (84):

(84)   *Tentámos convidar*mos*   a   Maria   para   a   festa.
       (we-)tried to-invite-1pl   the   Maria   for   the   party

       'We tried to invite Mary to the party.'

As indicated in section 6.4.3, proclisis to the infinitive form (or enclisis to the matrix finite form) is likewise impossible in this context (see (80)). Conversely, infinitival domains that allow proclisis to the infinitive form, such as (77), also allow for inflected infinitives, as illustrated in (85):

(85)   [Para ver*mos*   a   Maria],   faríamos   tudo.
       for   to-see-1pl the   Maria,   (we-)would-do   everything

       'In order to see Maria, we would do everything.'

The issue thus arises whether there is any correlation between the availability or unavailability of proclisis and that of inflection in these two infinitival contexts.

Raposo (1987) argues that an infinitival Agr assigns Case if it is itself specified for Case. This implies that Agr has to be in the domain of an external Case assigner, which cannot be too far away from it. We have suggested elsewhere that Raposo's analysis should be reinterpreted (and perhaps modified in key points) in terms of *f* (see Uriagereka 1995b, Raposo and Uriagereka 1996). Plausibly, *f* is involved in the Case/Agreement system of the WI clause, providing a Case that licenses the morphologically visible agreement in infinitivals (and indirectly, a lexical subject). This reanalysis, however, still leaves an open question: Does *f* itself need a licensor of some sort in order to participate in the Case/Agreement system (the way Raposo thought Agr did)? The question is complex. One tentative answer is that root f (i.e., the f in main and "paratactic" clauses, in the sense of Torrego and Uriagereka 1995; see also Hooper and Thompson 1973) activates the Case/Agreement system autonomously, in what has been called traditionally *nominativus pendens*; in contrast, f in true subordination (or "hypotactic") contexts does not.

The distinction just mentioned is also the one found for the licensing of affective quantifier phrases in the F projection, for reasons that do not concern us here. We can use that as a diagnostic to determine whether adverbial clauses involve "hypotaxis." In this respect, consider (86):

(86)   *Antes   de   *tanto*   *vinho*   te   dar(*mos*),   oferecemos-te
        before   of   so-much   wine   to-you-cl to-give(-3pl)   (we-)gave-you
        algum   pão.
        some   bread

'Before giving you so much wine, we offered you some bread.'

Affective fronting in these domains is excluded, which directly suggests that these infinitival domains do not tolerate root f, and that f in this context must be licensed by a Case-assigner.

In turn, that conclusion entails that f in adverbial clauses introduced by a preposition must be structurally close to the preposition/Case-assigner, for familiar reasons having to do with the Case phenomenology, in whichever terms we care to characterize it (assignment, checking, realization). An intervening CP boundary arguably puts the licensor of f too far away from it. We can thus successfully distinguish in a minimal way the contexts allowing inflected infinitives (87a) from those that do not (87b):

(87)   a. $[_{CP}$ para $[_{FP}$ f $[_{TP}$ . . .   vermos . . .]]]
                      for   to-see-1pl

       b. Tentámos $[_{CP}$ $[_{FP}$ f $[_{TP}$ . . . convidar(*mos)]]]
           (we-)tried   to-invite-(*1pl)

In (87a) the prepositional Case-assigner within CP is close to f, while in (87b) the matrix verb, being outside the embedded CP projection, is arguably too far away to assign Case to f. In all this, derivation by phase seems again crucial: infinitival agreement is possible if there is a Case-assigner for f within the CP-phase, but not otherwise.[35] But these are the exact same configurations that play a role in independently licensing f as a clitic: availability of a phase-internal host in (82a) but not in (82b), with the concomitant possibility of infinitival proclisis in (77) but not in (80). If these considerations are on the right track, they constitute an interesting account of the connection between the impossibility of proclisis (to the infinitive form) and inflection in nonroot affirmative infinitival clauses; in particular, why they are both present in nonsubcategorized contexts headed by a preposition such as (77) and (85) and why they are both absent in subcategorized contexts such as (80) and (84) (see also Pires 2001 for related discussion).

6.5 Spanish Infinitival Clitic Placement and the Applicability of OS

We now return to some issues concerning the applicability of OS that were left unresolved at the end of section 6.3; namely, we discuss whether the availability of OS under condition (71) will not open a Pandora's box for Spanish clitic placement in infinitival clauses, incorrectly allowing a proclitic pattern. Consider again the Spanish example (57a), repeated here as (88a), together with structure (61), repeated here as (88b):

(88) a. [Invitar**la**   a   nuestra fiesta] sería   una   buena idea.
          to-invite-her   to   our   party   would-be a   good   idea
          (***la** invitar)

          'To invite her to our party would be a good idea.'

      b. $[_{CP} [_{FP} F [_{TP} \ldots T [_{vP} [_v \text{invitar-}v] [_{VP} t(V) [_{DP} \textbf{la} N]]]]]] > [_v \text{invitar-}v]$
          $+\textbf{la} = \text{invitarla}$

In section 6.2 we suggested that the incorrect output with proclisis in (88a) is not generated in our system because the availability of low fusion blocks clitic placement of the determiner clitic in T (see the discussion immediately after (61)). However, in the analysis developed in section 6.3, clitic placement is mediated by OS, and OS, in turn, is allowed if it has an effect on outcome. But if the outcome of clitic placement in T is proclisis (see (18)), then this derivation would be after all legitimate in our system, since this outcome is different from the low enclitic outcome of (88b) (both linearly and with respect to fusion outputs). This would be an incorrect result.

The key point lies precisely in the application of OS. After OS, clitic placement in T is still blocked for the determiner clitic. Consider the relevant derivation, given in (89):

(89) a. $[_{CP} [_{FP} F [_{TP} \ldots T [_{vP} [_v \text{invitar-}v] [_{VP} t(V) [_{DP} \textbf{la} N]]]]]]$

      b. $[_{CP} [_{FP} F [_{TP} \ldots T [_{vP} [_{DP} \textbf{la} N] [_v \text{invitar-}v] [_{VP} t(V) t(DP)]]]]]]$

c. $[_{CP}\ [_{FP}\ F\ [_{TP} \ldots [_T\ [_v\ \text{invitar-}v]\text{-T}]\ [_{vP}\ [_{DP}\ \textbf{la}\ \text{N}]\ t(v)\ [_{VP}\ t(\text{V})\ t(\text{DP})]]]]]]$

Subsequently to OS (89b), the verb raises to T in the CP phase (89c). Consider now the options open to the determiner clitic. Although rightward fusion is impossible because there is no available host, leftward fusion to $[_T\ [_v\ \textit{invitar-}v]\text{-T}]$ (yielding enclisis) is available, since the verbal complex is adjacent to the clitic and, crucially, condition (65) is not violated. This outcome is shown in (90):

(90) $>[_T\ [_v\ \text{invitar-}v]\text{-T}]+\textbf{la}$

In other words, clitic placement is blocked by the availability of (leftward) fusion, *even after OS*. A related question is whether OS is actually legitimate in the first place, given that the PF linear output is the same, whether or not it applies. Again, this depends on how exactly "distinctness of outcome" should be interpreted for condition (71). If this is predicated on fusion outcomes, then, strictly speaking, an application of OS should be allowed, since the outputs are different. Notice, however, how subtle the issue is here. In (88b), the fusion outcome is $[_v\ \text{invitar-}v]+\textbf{la}$; in (89)–(90), the fusion outcome is $[_T\ [_v\ \text{invitar-}v]\text{-T}]+\textbf{la}$. Again, we leave the matter open.[36]

There is still another potentially problematic derivation based on the same numeration that underlies (89). In (89b), subsequently to OS, but *before verb raising to T*, what prevents the determiner clitic from fusing rightward to the verb *still in v*, yielding the *proclitic* output (91)?

(91) $>^*\textbf{la}+[_v\text{invitar-}v]$

Our claim is that the fusion in (91) is ruled out by general constraints on "phase-based" derivations. At the derivational stage (89b) following OS, the determiner clitic in [spec, v] belongs now to the higher CP phase. If fusion is a morphological operation of the PF component, and if the PF cycle proceeds in parallel with the narrow syntactic cycle, as we assume here, the only point where it becomes available for an object displaced by OS is at the higher CP cycle. But at that stage, V-raising to T will have applied, destroying the configuration which serves as the input for (91). In other words, only leftward fusion (to the verb in T) is now applicable, with its enclitic pattern.[37] This analysis predicts that in a language (or context) with no V-raising to T, rightward fusion of the determiner clitic in [spec, v] (after OS) to the verb in v might be possible, even at the higher CP cycle, yielding an output like (91). We speculate that this is the correct account for French generalized proclisis in infinitival cases, and we briefly address this issue in the appendix (another possible case is proclisis to participles in BP, see note 23).

7 CLITIC PLACEMENT IN INFLECTED INFINITIVAL CLAUSES

Let us examine now clitic placement in inflected infinitival clauses of WI. Again, we have special patterns, highly dependent on context, which differ in interesting ways from the pattern(s) of plain infinitival clauses.

We start with nonsubcategorized adverbial clauses introduced by a preposition within the CP projection, the inflected equivalent of (77). Contrary to plain infinitivals, where both enclisis and proclisis obtain, only proclisis is possible now. This is illustrated in (92):

(92) [Para **a**   vermos   outra   vez],   faríamos
      for   her-cl   to-see-lpl another   time   (we-)would-do
      tudo. (*vermo-**la**)
      everything

      'In order for us to see her one more time, we would do everything.'

Example (93) is the structure of the bracketed clause of (92), before any material moves out of the vP (see note 21):

(93) $[_{CP}$ **para** $[_{FP}f$ $[_{TP} \ldots$ T $[_{vP}$ $[_{v}$ vermos-$v]$ $[_{VP}$ $t(V)$ $[_{DP}$ **a** N$]]]]]]$

In (93), condition (65) precludes leftward fusion of the determiner clitic to the verbal complex in v (since this is an agreeing form). Thus, like in finite clauses, the clitic is forced to leave the vP (we now assume, via OS, see section 6.3) in order to fuse. The output of OS is illustrated in (94a). Condition (49c) on clitic clusters is now applicable, since the still unlicensed determiner clitic in [spec, v] belongs to the higher CP phase. This forces clitic placement in f (94b). Since f has a prepositional host, verb swallowing cannot apply. The relevant fusion operation is thus the one illustrated in (94b), which yields proclisis (see note 29):

(94) a. $[_{CP}$ **para** $[_{FP}f$ $[_{TP} \ldots$ T $[_{vP}$ $[_{DP}$ **a** N$]$ $[_{v}$ vermos-$v]$ $[_{VP}$ $t(V)$ $t(DP)]]]]]]$

      b. $[_{CP}$ **para** $[_{FP}$ $[_{f}$ **a**-$f]$ $[_{TP} \ldots$ T $[_{vP}$ $[_{DP}$ $t(D)$ N$]$ $[_{v}$ vermos-$v]$ $[_{VP}$ $t(V)$ $t(DP)]]]]]]$
          $>$ para$+$ $[_{f}$ **a**-$f]$

In the system argued for here, enclisis arises in two possible ways: first, via low leftward fusion to a nonagreeing verbal form, and second, by verb swallowing, when f does not have an independent host. With adverbial inflected infinitivals, as we have just seen, enclisis is excluded on both counts. These two factors thus conspire to force the single outcome with proclisis.

The second way just mentioned for enclisis to arise depends on contextual factors, such as presence or absence of an overt complementizer, or overt negation. Suppose, then, that the inflected infinitival occurs in a context lacking these elements, which could have hosted *f*. We then predict that the pattern reverts to obligatory enclisis, since verb swallowing will now have to apply. This is precisely what happens in the cases illustrated in (95):

(95) a. Tu,   dizeres-**me**   a   verdade...! (***me** dizeres)
          you   to-tell-2sg-me-cl   the   truth

          'You, telling me the truth...!'

      b. A   Maria   disse   [terem-**no**   visto   ontem]. (***o** terem)
          the   Mary   said   to-have-3pl-him-cl   seen   yesterday

          'Mary said that they saw him yesterday.'

      c. [Convidarmos-**te**   para   a   festa]   seria   uma   boa
          to-invite-3pl-you-cl   for   the   party   would-be   a   good
          ideia. (***te** convidarmos)
          idea

          'To invite you to the party would be a good idea.'

The bracketed clauses of (95) illustrate the "root" contexts mentioned in note 35. Example (95a) is a (matrix) inflected infinitival expressing surprise about an event, (95b) is a complement to an epistemic verb, and (95c) is a subject clause (see Ambar 1992, Raposo 1987, Raposo and Uriagereka (1996). Our claim is that in these cases the bracketed infinitival clauses are CPs with a null complementizer (contrary to Raposo's 1987 analysis for (95c)). Thus, *f* cannot be licensed within the CP phase, and the derivation has to resort to the familiar verb swallowing. We illustrate this here with the derivation (96) for (95c)):

(96) a. $[_{CP}$ C $[_{FP}f\,[_{TP}pro$ T $[_{vP}\,[_{v}$ convidarmos-$v]\,[_{VP}\,t(V)\,[_{DP}$ **te**$]$ para a festa$]]]]]$

      b. $[_{CP}$ C $[_{FP}f\,[_{TP}pro$ T $[_{vP}\,[_{DP}$ **te**$]\,[_{v}$ convidarmos-$v]\,[_{VP}\,t(V)\,t(DP)]$ para a festa$]]]]$

      c. $[_{CP}$ C $[_{FP}\,[_{f}$ **te**-$f]\,[_{TP}$ *pro* T $[_{vP}\,t(DP)\,[_{v}$ convidarmos-$v]\,[_{VP}\,t(V)\,t(DP)]$ para a festa$]]]]$

      d. $_{CP}$ C $[_{FP}\,[_{T}\,[_{v}$ convidarmos-$v]$-T$]\,[_{f}$ **te**-$f]\,[_{TP}$ *pro* $t(T)\,[_{vP}\,t(DP)\,t(v)\,[_{VP}$ $t(V)\,t(DP)]$ para a festa$]]]] > [_{T}\,[_{v}$ convidarmos-$v]$-T$]\,+\,[_{f}$ **te**-$f]\,=$ convidarmos-**te**

Since condition (65) is relevant here, the determiner clitic cannot fuse to the verb on its left (doubly so in (95b), where both the participle and the infinitival auxiliary are agreeing forms); it is thus forced to exit the *v*P via OS (96b); by condition (49c), it must be placed in *f* (96c); finally, since there is no licenser for *f*, verb swallowing applies, yielding (96d), where the fusion outcome yields enclisis. No other derivation is possible in this case. Similar derivations underly (95a–b).

Finally, as predicted by our analysis, if a clause-internal host such as negation or a displaced affective phrase becomes available, the pattern reverts to proclisis, since the swallowing configuration is not needed, and thus, in minimalist terms, not permissible either. This is illustrated in (97a–c) for the three constructions, respectively:

(97) a. Tu,   não **me**   dizeres   a   verdade . . . ! (*não dizeres-**me**)
         you   not to-me-cl   to-tell-2sg   the   truth

      'You, not telling me the truth . . . !'

      b. A   Maria   disse   [só   ontem   **o**   terem
         the   Mary   said   only   yesterday   him-cl   to-have-3pl
         visto]. (*terem-**no**)
         seen

      'Mary said that only yesterday did they see him.'

      c. [Não   **te**   convidarmos   para   a   festa]   seria   uma
         not   you-cl   to-invite-3pl   for   the   party   would-be   a
         boa   ideia. (*não convidarmos-**te**)
         good   idea

      'Not to invite you to the party would be a good idea.'

8 CONCLUSION

The main result of this chapter is that the complex pattern of pronominal clitic placement in WI, whether in finite or infinitival contexts, is an epiphenomenon. It results from the special requirements of a morphologically heavy, clitic-like functional category *f* in the periphery of the clause, c-commanding T but c-commanded by C. Pronominal clitics have a uniform syntax as determiners, irrespective of their ultimate fate as proclitics or enclitics. The question of which of these options arises has to do with what is the optimal route for a determiner clitic to find morphoprosodic support (given parametric variations) and in particular whether f is present, demanding both its own host and, if determiner clitics are in the same phase, a characteristic, appropriate clustering.

We also have proposed a different way of looking at the licensing of determiner clitics. The basic requirement for these elements is "fusing" with an appropriate phonological host. "Clitic placement," in this respect, is just a complex and costly route whereby a determiner clitic reaches its fusion host, if it cannot find it in its immediate adjacency. This way of looking at clitic placement allowed us to have a simple analysis of the generalized enclitic pattern in infinitival clauses of the standard variants and why this deviates in interesting ways from the conservative variants once an element like f gets in the picture.

Throughout this work, we have raised a number of questions that are relevant to the minimalist program. The system uncovered argues both for the need to take optimal operations within comparative sets and for the idea that operations apply only when necessary in order to derive a convergent interface. This is a generous interpretation of "last resort," however, much in the spirit of stylistic movements recently studied by Chomsky and others, which are not self-serving as such but contribute to salvage the derivation. The system also relies crucially on the notion of "phase," and the idea that within active phase domains (a phase and the edge of the subjacent one) operations can "look ahead"; for instance, we have allowed verbs to raise in order to avoid a later PF crash, but only within strictly cyclic confines.

APPENDIX: CLITIC PLACEMENT IN FRENCH INFINITIVAL CLAUSES

Consider again the derivation (89) with OS of the infinitival clause of example (88a) *invitarla a nuestra fiesta sería una buena idea* 'to invite her to our party would be a good idea'. We repeat this derivation here as (98):

(98)   a. $[_{CP} [_{FP} F [_{TP} \ldots T [_{\nu P} [_{\nu} \text{invitar-}\nu] [_{VP} t(V) [_{DP} \textbf{la } N]]]]]]$

     b. $[_{CP} [_{FP} F [_{TP} \ldots T [_{\nu P} [_{DP} \textbf{la } N] [_{\nu} \text{invitar-}\nu] [_{VP} t(V) \, t(DP)]]]]]]$

     c. $[_{CP} [_{FP} F [_{TP} \ldots [_{T} [_{\nu} \text{invitar-}\nu]\text{-T}] [_{\nu P} [_{DP} \textbf{la } N] \, t(\nu) [_{VP} t(V) \, t(DP)]]]]]]$

At the end of section 6.5, we asked the following question: What prevents the determiner clitic from fusing rightward to the verb *still in v* in (98b), thus yielding the *proclitic* output (99) (= (91))?

(99)   > ***la** + [$_v$ invitar-v]

For Spanish, the answer was that verb raising to T, interacting with a phase-based, cyclic derivational system ensured that (98b) is not a possible input for fusion (i.e., fusion is only applicable at (98c), *after* verb raising). However, we then suggested that in a language (or context) with no V-raising to T, rightward fusion of the determiner clitic in [spec, v] (after OS) to the verb in v might be possible, even at the higher CP cycle, yielding a fusion output like (99). This is what we claim happens in French infinitival clauses.

French has generalized proclisis in infinitival clauses (see, e.g., Kayne 1991), as illustrated in (100):

(100) a. [L'inviter]   serait   une bonne idée.   (*inviter-**la**)
           her-to-invite   would-be   a   good   idea

           'To invite her would be a good idea.'

       b. [Ne pas l'inviter]   serait   une   bonne
           neg   not   her-to-invite   would-be   a   good
           idée. (*ne pas inviter-**la**)
           idea

           'Not to invite her would be a good idea.'

Consider now structure (101) underlying the bracketed clause of (100a) after V-to-v raising but before any displacement of the object determiner clitic:

(101)   [$_{CP}$ [$_{FP}$ [$_{TP}$ ... T [$_{vP}$ [$_v$ inviter-v] [$_{VP}$ t(V) [$_{DP}$ **la** N]]]]]]

Suppose that v in (101) is not assigned an EPP feature. Our system then predicts that low *leftward* fusion should apply to (101), yielding an enclitic pattern, just as in similar derivations of the standard and radical variants discussed previously. According to (53), this is the less costly route that can be taken, so other options should be blocked (in addition, condition (65) is not violated). This is the incorrect result for French.

It is well known that French is different from WI and other C/EI variants in that it has a form of nominal displacement with pronominal-quantifiers such as *tous* 'all', *tout* 'everything', and *rien* 'nothing' (see Kayne 1975). This is illustrated in (102):

(102) a. Je ne   peux rien   promettre.
          I   neg can   nothing to-promise

       'I can't promise anything.'

       b. J'ai   tout   mangé
          I-have everything eaten

       'I have eaten everything.'

Visibly, French has retained a form of "systematic" OS for these elements that Spanish and many other Romance languages have lost. In addition, the word order in (102) suggests that the nonfinite participles remain quite "low" in the structure, plausibly in the v position. This is also then expected of "pure" infinitival forms.[38]

Suppose now that we extend this systematic OS of French to determiner clitics.[39] Then, OS applies obligatorily to (101), deriving (103):

(103) $[_{CP} [_{FP} [_{TP} \ldots T [_{vP} [_{DP} \textbf{la } N] [_v \text{ inviter-}v] [_{VP} t(V) \ t(DP)]]]]]$

The derivation now proceeds to the CP cycle, and the question now is whether there are any factors forcing the determiner clitic to exit the vP. Consider, first, clitic placement in F. Since French, one of the "radical" variants, lacks f (see section 2.1), condition (49c) on clitic clusters is void. The only reason the determiner clitic would be forced to leave the vP would be to satisfy its own prosodical properties—that is, to find an appropriate host for fusion by adjoining to T. However, we have just suggested that there is no verb raising to T in French infinitivals. Then, (103) itself offers the context for application of rightward fusion of the determiner clitic to the infinitive. This yields (104), with the desired proclitic outcome:

(104) $> \textbf{la}+[_v \text{ inviter-}v]$

In addition, note that we cannot invoke an EPP feature to get the determiner clitic into the CP cycle (i.e., for standard clitic placement, followed by rightward fusion to the verb in v). The reason is that the derivation that leads to (104) *already has an EPP feature on v and is convergent*. This makes that derivation and the one with clitic placement in T actually comparable for economy purposes, with the former blocking the latter in terms of (53).[40] In sum, determiner clitics in French infinitivals will be stuck within vP.

We suggest that one factor involved in the absence of "clitic climbing" in French is this sheer impossibility of getting clitics to exit the vP in infinitival clauses. Given this, we have an account of the contrast between the French (105a) and its Spanish version in (105b) (see Kayne 1975, Uriagereka 1988):

(105) a. *J'ai   essayé   de **le** promettre   et   jurer.
            I-have   tried   of it   to-promise   and   to-swear

       'I tried to promise and swear it.'
       (cf. J'ai essayé de **le** prometter et **le** jurer.)

       b. **Lo** intenté   prometer   y   jurar.
           it   (I)-tried   to-promise and to-swear

In the Spanish (105b), the clitic is scoped out of the lower infinitival verb phrase, so that the remaining material can be conjoined with the clitic ranging over both conjuncts. Assuming our account of French infinitival cliticization, the clitic does not succeed in the task in (105a), as it is stuck in the *v* projection.

NOTES

1. Our examples of WI are from European Portuguese (EP) unless noted otherwise.

2. An alternative to adjunction to FP would be that topics raise to a "second spec" of F. In the framework of Rizzi (1997), topics occur in a functional projection distinct from F. Still a more drastic alternative is proposed in Raposo (1996) (developing ideas in Chomsky 1995: sec. 4.7.3): that topics are generated as independent phrase markers and are later "merged" in some performance or discourse component outside of the computational system. This would provide a straightforward account of why topics do not affect the standard pattern of enclisis in simple root clauses: they simply are not there during the derivation of a sentence.

3. If this is correct, the relevant relation between such a "weak" F probe (in the sense of Chomsky 2000) and a given affective "goal" down the clause must be established in this instance via a long-distance "agreement" relation.

4. If the realization of topics and other left-dislocated elements of the type displayed in (7b) also involves the FP projection (see the prior discussion), we could postulate a [topic] feature in F which likewise could be either strong or weak, yielding respectively sentences with topicalization (such as (7b)) and normal declarative sentences. We leave the matter open.

5. The italicized phrase *related to checking* is important, since we propose in section 6 that clitics do raise in some circumstances as maximal projections to [spec, *v*], though not because of checking considerations.

6. See Raposo (2002) for discussion of fusion and its sensitivity to phase boundaries. We are not concerned here with the internal structure of DPs headed by determiner-clitics. This structure may actually vary for different types of "pronominal" determiner clitics (see Raposo 1999, 2002 for some remarks on this matter). We only mention here that in Raposo (2002) it is argued that the nominal "gap" in examples like (14b) is the result of deletion of a full Noun in the PF component. If so, there is literally nothing in this position at PF. Likewise, the pronominal DP in (15) is arguably a minimal-maximal projection in the sense of Chomsky (1995). Under this view, there is no nominal empty

category *pro* in these DPs. This being so, *la* and *efervescente* are literally adjacent in the terminal string of (14b). In this and subsequent examples, we use the categorial symbol "N" to indicate the position of the missing noun, but this should be viewed just as a convenient device.

7. There is a wrinkle in this analysis: we have to block (left) fusion of the determiner clitic to the verb within *v*P, before verb raising to T. For the time being, we assume that this choice is ruled out. We return to a detailed discussion of this matter in section 6.

8. If our remarks at the end of section 2.1 to the effect that WI dialects may also instantiate standard F are correct, then a derivation like that of (18) is also available in these dialects. We return briefly to this issue in note 19.

9. But see section 6, where we discuss a different sort of derivation for infinitival enclisis in the standard languages and in (some cases of) WI.

10. This provides evidence that *pro*, whatever its internal constitution, is a (featural or categorial) formative occupying [spec, T]. Note that *f* cannot obviously fuse to *pro* itself since this element is not phonological. If [spec, T] is lexically filled rather than *pro* (for instance, with the subject *seus pais* 'his parents'), fusion of *f* or a cluster including *f* to that spec or to material inside that spec is still not possible, as shown by the ungrammaticality of **o seus pais enviaram*, lit. 'him his parents sent', 'his parents sent him', which would be the output resulting from fusion of [o-*f*] to [*seus pais*] (or to *seus*). We return to this matter in section 5.2.

11. The situation is, of course, different in simple clauses with an affective operator such as (26a) or in embedded finite clauses introduced by the complementizer *que* 'that'. These are discussed in section 5.

12. Our discussion of example (40) provides a direct argument that the verb raises to the F projection. The underlying lateral onset of the third-person singular masculine, clitic (*lo*) nasalizes (instead of dropping) due to assimilation with the preceding final nasal segment of the verb. We further discuss leftward fusion in section 5. This analysis forces us to the claim that in *seus pais enviaram-no aos jesuitas* 'his parents sent him to the Jesuits' the lexical subject *seus pais* 'his parents' is in a left-peripheral or topic position. For discussion of this matter, see Raposo (2000: note 4 and references therein).

13. T/V codes the T complex containing the verb. Both options are "marked" in some way: in (35a), a head raises to a spec position and in (35b), the verb adjoins to *f* after the determiner clitic, in violation of condition (20). Raposo (2000) assumes (35a), providing a rationale in terms of May's (1985) theory of segments and motivating the "head in spec" configuration in terms of ideas of Nunes (1998). In turn, (35b) requires formulating (20) as an economy condition that may be violated to avoid crash (in the sense of Chomsky 1995) rather than as a convergence requirement.

14. "Swallowing" by a clitic presumably also takes place in Romanian in order to salvage determiner clitics within DP. Consider the following examples:

(i) a. prinţul   viteaz (*prinţ viteazul)
         prince-the   valiant

         'the prince valiant'

     b. viteazul   prinţ (*viteazu prinţul)
         valiant-the prince

         'the valiant prince'

The determiner *-ul* here is enclitic on the first element within the NP complement of the DP. This would follow if, for some reason, Romanian disallows simple rightward fusion of the determiner to an immediately adjacent element within NP (the unmarked Romance option). Then, rather than having the determiner displaced to a higher site within the *v*P phase, it is the clitic host (a noun or an adjective) that is raised to the left of the determiner, very much in the same way the verb is raised to *f* in (35).

15. We leave open the exact reason why the verb in the configuration (36) does not license the clitic cluster by fusion. Notice that the verb in (36) is contained within the clitic cluster [a-*f*] that must be licensed. This is arguably an illegitimate configuration if licensing of a clitic (cluster) requires its phonological host to (strictly) precede the clitic (cluster).

16. For the position of topics, see the text immediately after (7). Recall that topics are not appropriate hosts for clitics (see the discussion of (28) in section 4.1). The analysis of (40) in the text extends to the grammatical *ela disse que o Luis telefonou-te* 'she said that Luis called you' with enclisis, if the subject is itself in topic position, preventing the clitic cluster [**te**-*f*] from fusing with *que*. See note 19 for an analysis of *ela disse que o Luis **te** telefonou* (with proclisis).

17. In section 6.2, we discuss why the determiner clitic cannot leftward-fuse directly with the verb, either in *v* or in T—that is, without the intermediate operation of clitic placement.

18. After spell-out of a cascade, its internal units cease to be accessible to the computation (Uriagereka 1999). This entails that they cannot be the target of fusion, either leftward or rightward. For instance, neither *seus* in (45) nor *mestre* in (46) is an appropriate target of fusion.

19. We have not discussed clitic placement in examples where the subject appears sandwiched between a complementizer or an affective phrase to its left, and the sequence clitic-verb to its right, as in (i), where we italicize the subject:

(i) a. Muitos livros *os*   *meus* *pais*   **me**   deram.
        many   books the   my   parents to-me-cl gave

   'Many books did my parents give to me.'

   b. Ela   disse que *o*   *Luis* **te**   telefonou.
      she   said   that the   Luis   to-you-cl called

   'She said that Luis called you.'

One possibility is that the subject is in [spec, T], and the clitic-verb sequence is in T with a standard instantiation of F, that is, *not f* (see the discussion at the end of section 2.1, and Raposo 2000 for arguments in favor of this analysis). If this is correct, then the determiner clitics take the standard route illustrated in (18); that is, they left-adjoin to T since there is no *f* to cluster with. Alternatively, *f* is instantiated, the clitic-verb sequence is adjoined to *f* in the manner of (36), and the nonaffective subject raises to [spec, *f*], providing phrasal support for the clitic cluster. In this case, nonaffective elements in [spec, *f*] must be restricted to embedded clauses, since proclisis is impossible in root clauses with preverbal subjects, as we have discussed. We are unable to tease out these two analyses further; therefore, we leave the matter open.

20. Contrary to Kayne (1991), whose analysis of standard infinitival enclisis requires the clitic to raise to T and the verb to raise to a category higher than **T** *and* to skip T

in doing so. However, his rationale for which heads can be skipped by the verb (such as infinitival T) bears some resemblance to our proposal in (65), in that it appeals to lack of agreement features (in the skipped functional head, for Kayne; in the verbal form itself, for us).

21. In the strictly cyclical, bottom to top derivation assumed in minimalist work since Chomsky (1995), at the point where the vP-cycle is processed, the higher categories T, F, and C have not been merged yet. In this and subsequent examples, we include them just for expository purposes.

22. We tentatively assume that low fusion takes place between the determiner clitic and the verbal complex V-v—that is, after V-raising to v. Traces do not block adjacency, presumably because at the point where fusion applies they will already have been eliminated within the PF component. Since we take fusion to be a morphogical operation of the PF component, this entails that v must be available to the PF cycle at the vP-phase, a conclusion not completely within the spirit of Chomsky's (2000, 2001) system, in which the head and the edge of a strong phase are sent to spell-out (and thus to the PF cycle) only at the next higher phase (i.e., at the CP phase, for v). This can be overcome by having low leftward fusion of the determiner clitic be directly to V within VP—that is, before it raises to v. We leave this matter open. See section 6.5 for additional discussion of these matters.

23. However, the same is not true of the lefthand side of participles. Although it is not common in most Romance variants, it is standard in Brazilian Portuguese (BP), where the clitic in (i) can be shown to be rightward fused to the participle rather than leftward fused to the finite auxiliary verb:

(i) Maria tinha **te**   dado   o   livro. > **te**+dado
     Maria had   to-you-cl given the   book

     'Mary had given the book to you.'

One possibility is that in BP the determiner clitic undergoes Object Shift to [spec, v] and subsequently fuses rightward with the participle in v, rather than being clitic-placed in T. Alternatively, if the participle is outside vP, it is a legitimate target for clitic placement in BP, though not in other Romance variants, where the clitic is forced to seek T as its target. Unfortunately, the complex and changing patterns of BP clitic placement are outside the scope of this essay (see Pagotto 1992 and Galves 2001, among others). For the role of Object Shift in standard and WI dialects, see section 6.3.

24. This is perhaps related to the considerations discussed in Uriagereka (1996b), that the checking process may not be able to overcome ambiguity created by the presence of multiple sets of φ-features on the same side of a single verbal form. (65) forces us to analyze superficial righthand attachments of clitics to participial forms (as in the Italian *ogni persona presentataci* 'every person presented to us', and see Kayne 1991 for additional examples) as "indirect fusion" involving an additional "clitic-like" functional category to which the determiner clitic adjoins, followed by participle movement in the manner of (35) (see also note 25). The same holds of leftward cliticization of determiners to finite verbal forms in Galician, discussed in Uriagereka (1996a), contra Otero (1996); that is in turn in contradiction with Uriagereka (1999), which agrees with the essentials of Otero's challenge. Alternatively, these types of clitic placement might result from a postcyclic and very late process of phonological fusion (i.e., unmediated by clitic

placement), after raising (and checking) of the verbal form has taken place. If so, this "very late" fusion of the clitic must be quite costly for the grammar, given its cross-linguistic scarcity. Unfortunately, the two phenomena discussed in this note are beyond the scope of this work. We return briefly to clitic placement in gerunds and participles in note 36.

25. This closes the loop left open in notes 7 and 17. In the process of swallowing illustrated in (34)–(35), it is not the determiner clitic that fuses (leftward) with the verb in FP but, rather, *f* itself, heading the clitic cluster [ₒ*o-f*]. We assume that this indirect fusion of the determiner clitic buried within *f* does not fall under (65). See note 24 for an identical suggestion regarding enclisis to participles.

26. Although we have not studied this systematically—and we do not know of any study bearing on the topic—we have observed how Spanish-speaking children can place clitics enclitically onto infinitivals well before they have any noticeable functional syntax (at the beginning of the two-word stage) and before they place clitics proclitically. If these data turn out to be general, they would be very consistent with a direct placement of determiner clitics to the infinitival verb, with no mediation of functional structure or movement. A similar account might hold for the early-acquisition data of EP children reported by Duarte and Matos (2000), where enclisis is generalized to finite verbal forms. This may involve low leftward direct fusion to these forms in apparent violation of (65) if the "higher" functional categories responsible for verbal checking such as T are still not "active" at that early stage. Note that that EP children (contrary to Spanish children) have plenty of primary data in their linguistic environment (root clauses with enclisis) that might set them off in this "wrong" course, until the higher categories are activated. These are only speculations, however, and we cannot pursue these matters here.

27. Though infinitival *f* does not host displaced quantifier or focus phrases, it is compatible with negative and other aspectual adverbs. We leave open here whether the negative morpheme *não* is raised to FP from within TP, in an operation akin to Neg-raising. If *não* raises to FP, this would be a costly way of salvaging *f* in the ranking of (53), but it would still be permitted if *não* is the closest head to *f*; in particular, it would have to be higher than T within TP, or otherwise T with the verb would be attracted. Alternatively, *não* is base-generated within FP or independently displaced to FP as an affective element. We continue to assume that *f* cannot fuse rightward to the infinitival verb raised to T, which follows from the standard assumption that there is a spec containing a formative element (in this instance, PRO) between *f* and T in infinitival contexts (see the text after (33)). The same holds for rightward fusion of *f* to *não* in TP if this is base-generated within TP.

28. See Chomsky (2001) and references therein for extensive discussion of OS; see also Rivero (1986) for the idea that clitics may move as maximal projections to spec positions.

29. Again, we abstract away for expository purposes of verb raising to T or to *f*. If the verb adjoins to *f*, it will be under configuration (36), but this does not affect the proclitic outcome of the fusion operation. For clarification, we give the full structure of *f* in this case in (i), but we omit it in subsequent examples:

(i)   [_FP não [_f **a**-[_f [_T [_v convidar-*v*]-T]-*f*]] [_TP . . .]] > não+[_f**a**-[_f [_T [_v convidar-*v*]-T]-*f*]]

30. Observe also the ways in which derivation (70) comes out in Galician (compare with (66)):

(i) a. n'**a** convidar . . . /(Colloquial Galician)

   b. non-**a** convidar /(Formal Galician)

In (ia) negation reduces, its stress being realized on the clitic vowel. In (ib), *non* has incorporated *a*, as the normally velarized final [*n*] is in this context pronounced alveolarly, a hallmark of D incorporation in this language. In that case stress is being realized on the negative vowel. Either way, a phonological word results, providing a further PF argument for derivation (70).

31. Matters are more complicated for languages with systematic OS, such as Icelandic, but this is not the case for standard or conservative Romance. We address briefly the case of French in the appendix.

32. The derivations in the text that need adjustment are those of (18), (24), (33), (39), (45), and (46), as the reader can verify. Note that direct leftward fusion of the determiner clitic in [spec, *v*] (after OS) to the finite verb in T (i.e., without clitic placement) is also ruled out by condition (65).

33. Recall that leftward fusion of *f* to a finite verb does not fall under (65) (see note 25). Also see note 29.

34. See Kayne (1984: ch. 5) for prepositions inside the CP projection. One possibility is that such prepositions are "prepositional complementizers" (Kayne 1984). This is not necessary, though. For our purposes, all that is needed is that they are within the CP projection, either as head or spec.

35. Root *f* in "paratactic" contexts introducing *nominativus pendens* and allowing inflected infinitives is independent of all this, as observed in the text. These contexts include root-inflected infinitives (see (95a) in the text), complements to epistemic and declarative verbs (95b), and subject clauses (95c). Additional discussion of this matter is beyond the scope of this chapter.

36. A derivation similar to (89)–(90) may be justified for the clitic pattern in a combination of gerund plus participle such as (i):

(i) Incluso siendote   enviada por mí, la   carta   no   ha
     even   being-to-you-cl sent   by   me   the letter not has
     llegado. (*siendo enviadate)
     arrived

'Even having been sent to you by me, the letter has not arrived.'

Condition (65) prohibits "low" direct leftward fusion of *te* to the agreeing participle. OS then applies to the determiner clitic, placing it in the spec of the participle as in (ii):

(ii)   . . . siendo [$_{part}$ [$_{DP}$ **te** N] enviada *t*(DP)] > siendo+**te**

From this position, the determiner clitic leftward fuses with the gerund, yielding the enclitic pattern of (i). Note that this analysis, if correct, forces one to claim that participles in Spanish determine (strong) phases and can receive an EPP feature. A similar account might be invoked for the alternation in (iii), this time with two derivations available, one without and the other with OS (the outputs are trivially distinct):

(iii)   Para   estar**la**   enviando   repetidamente,   necesito
        for   to-be-her-cl   sending   repeatedly   (I-) need
        tiempo. (estar enviando**la**)
        time
        'In order to be sending it repeatedly, I need time.'

37. Another possibility for excluding (91) would be to claim that simple PF linear order of elements *within* fused complexes does not count for "distinctness" under (71). Then (91) (**la**+[$_v$ *invitar*-v]) is nondistinct from the fusion output of (88b) ([$_v$ *invitar*-v]+**la**) and the EPP feature on *v* that would result in (91) is not permitted by (71).

38. This contradicts Holmberg's generalization, which correlates object shift with verb movement (Holmberg 1986, 1999). See, however, Lasnik (1999) for an argument against the generalization. Chomsky (2001) also has a different approach to this matter.

39. Why French systematic OS is restricted to pronominal elements and does not extend to full DPs is a matter beyond the scope of this chapter.

40. These considerations do not extend to French finite clauses. In that case, as is standardly assumed (see Pollock 1989), the verb raises to T, and the low configuration for rightward fusion is destroyed. In turn, leftward fusion is now disallowed to the V-*v* complex in T by condition (65), forcing clitic placement in T.

REFERENCES

Ambar, M.-M. (1992) *Para uma sintaxe da inversão sujeito-verbo em português*. Colibri, Lisbon.

Anagnostopoulou, E. (1994) "Clitic Dependencies in Modern Greek." Ph.D. diss., University of Salzburg.

Anderson, S. (1992) *A-Morphous Morphology*. Cambridge University Press, Cambridge.

Anderson, S. (1993) "Wackernagel's Revenge: Clitics, Morphology, and the Syntax of Second Position." *Language* 69: 68–98.

Barbosa, P. (1996) "Clitic placement in European Portuguese and the position of Subjects," in A. L. Halpern and A. M. Zwicky (eds.) *Approaching Second: Second Position Clitics and Related Phenomena*. Center for the Study of Language and Information Publications, Stanford, Calif., 1–40.

Barbosa, P. (2000) "Clitics: A Window into the Null Subject Property." In J. Costa (ed.) *Portuguese Syntax: New Comparative Studies*. Oxford University Press, New York, 31–93.

Bobaljik, J. (1995) "Morphosyntax: The Syntax of Verbal Inflection." Ph.D. diss., MIT, Cambridge, Mass.

Bošković, Z. (2001) *On the Nature of the Syntax-Phonology Interface*. Elsevier, London.

Chomsky, N. (1994) *Bare Phrase Structure*. MIT Occasional Papers in Linguistics 5. MIT, Cambridge, Mass.

Chomsky, N. (1995) *The Minimalist Program*. MIT Press, Cambridge, Mass.

Chomsky, N. (2000) "Minimalist Inquiries: The Framework," in R. Martin, D. Michaels, and J. Uriagereka (eds.) *Step by Step: Essays in Minimalist Syntax in Honor of Howard Lasnik*. MIT Press, Cambridge, Mass.

Chomsky, N. (2001) "Derivation by Phase," in M. Kenstowicz (ed.) *Ken Hale: A Life in Language*. MIT Press, Cambridge, Mass.

Cinque, G. (1999) *Adverbs and Functional Heads*. Oxford University Press, New York.

Duarte, I., and G. Matos (2000) "Romance Clitics and the Minimalist Program," in J. Costa (ed.) *Portuguese Syntax: New Comparative Studies*. Oxford University Press, New York.

Galves, C. (2001) *Ensaios sobre as gramáticas do português*. Editorada Unicamp, Campinsa.

Guimarães, M. (1998) "Repensando a interface sintaxe-fonologia a partir do axioma de correspondência linear." Master's thesis, State University of Campinas.

Halpern, A. (1992) "Topics in the Placement and Morphology of Clitics." Ph.D. diss., Stanford University.

Holmberg, A. (1986) "Word Order and Syntactic Features in the Scandinavian Languages and English." Ph.D. diss., University of Stockolm.

Holmberg, A. (1999) "Remarks on Holmberg's Generalization." *Studia Linguistica* 53: 1–39.

Hooper, J. B., and S. A. Thompson (1973) "On the Applicability of Root Transformations." *Linguistic Inquiry* 4: 465–497.

Izvorski, R. (1995) "The Syntax of Clitics in the History of Bulgarian." Paper Presented at the Fourth Diachronic Germanic Syntax Conference, Université du Québec à Montréal.

Kayne, R. (1975) *French Syntax*. MIT Press, Cambridge, Mass.

Kayne, R. (1984) *Connectedness and Binary Branching*. Foris, Dordrecht.

Kayne, R. (1991) "Romance Clitics, Verb Movement, and PRO." *Linguistic Inquiry* 22: 647–686.

Kayne, R. (1994) *The Antisymmetry of Syntax*. MIT Press, Cambridge, Mass.

Lambova, M. (2001) "On A-bar Movements in Bulgarian and Their Interactions." *Linguistic Review* 18: 327–374.

Lasnik, H. (1999) *Minimalist Analyses*. Blackwell, Oxford.

Martins, A.-M. (1994a) "Clíticos na história do português." Ph.D. diss., University of Lisbon.

Martins, A.-M. (1994b) "Enclisis, VP-Deletion and the Nature of Sigma." *Probus* 6: 173–205.

Maurer, T.-H. (1968) *O infinito flexionado português (estudo histórico-descritivo)*. Companhia Editora Nacional, São Paulo.

May, R. (1985) *Logical Form*. MIT Press, Cambridge, Mass.

Nunes, J. (1998) "Bare X'-Theory and structures Formed by Movement." *Linguistic Inquiry* 29: 160–168.

Otero, C. (1996) "Head Movement, Cliticization, Precompilation and Word Insertion (Comments on Uriagereka's Paper)," in R. Freidin (ed.) *Current Issues in Comparative Grammar*. Kluwer, Dordrecht.

Pagotto, E. (1992) "A posição dos clíticos em português: um estudo diacrónico." MA diss., State University of Campinas.

Pesetsky, D. (2000) "Phrasal Movement and Its Kin." MIT Press, Cambridge, Mass.

Pires, A. (2001) "The Syntax of Gerunds and Infinitives: Subjects, Case and Control." Ph.D. diss., University of Maryland, College Park.

Pollock, J.-Y. (1989) "Verb Movement, Universal Grammar and the Structure of IP." *Linguistic Inquiry* 20: 365–424.

Postal, P. (1969) "On So-called 'Pronouns' in English," in D. A. Reibel and S. A. Schane (eds.) *Modern Studies in English: Readings in Transformational Grammar*. Prentice Hall, Englewood Cliffs, N.J., 201–224.

Raposo, E. (1973) "Sobre a forma *o* em português." *Boletim de Filologia* 22: 361–415.

Raposo, E. (1987) "Case Theory and Infl-to-Comp: The Inflected Infinitive in European Portuguese." *Linguistic Inquiry* 18: 85–109.

Raposo, E. (1994) "Affective Operators and Clausal Structure in European Portuguese and European Spanish." Paper presented at the 24th Linguistic Symposium on Romance Languages, University of California Los Angeles and University of Southern California.

Raposo, E. (1996) "Towards a Unification of Topic Constructions." Unpublished ms., University of California Santa Barbara.

Raposo, E. (1999) "Some Observations on the Pronominal System of Portuguese," in Z. Borras and J. Sola (eds.) *Catalan Working Papers in Linguistics* 6: 59–93.

Raposo, E. (2000) "Clitic Positions and Verb Movement," in J. Costa (ed.) *Portuguese Syntax: New Comparative Studies*. Oxford University Press, New York, 266–297.

Raposo, E. (2002) "Nominal Gaps with Prepositional Modifiers in Portuguese and Spanish: A Case for Quick Spell-Out," in M. J. Arche, A. Fébregas, and A. Trombetta (eds.) *Cuadernos de Lingüística* 9. Instituto Universitario Ortega y Gasset, Madrid, 127–144.

Raposo, E., and J. Uriagereka (1996) "Indefinite SE." *Natural Language and Linguistic Theory* 14: 749–810.

Rivero, M.-L. (1986) "Parameters in the Typology of Clitics in Romance and Old Spanish." *Language* 62: 774–807.

Rizzi, L. (1993) "Some Issues on Cliticization." Unpublished ms., University of Geneva.

Rizzi, L. (1997) "The Fine Structure of the Left Periphery," in L. Haegeman (ed.) *Elements of Grammar: Handbook of Generative Syntax*. Kluwer, Dordrecht, 281–337.

Sportiche, D. (1996) "Clitic Constructions," in J. Rooryck and L. Zaring (eds.) *Phrase Structure and the Lexicon*. Kluwer, Dordrecht, 213–276.

Terzi, A. (1999) "Clitic Combinations, Their Hosts and Their Ordering." *Natural Language and Linguistic Theory* 17: 85–121.

Torrego, E., and J. Uriagereka (1995) "Parataxis." Paper presented at the Second Georgetown Roundtable in Spanish Linguistics. Georgetown University.

Uriagereka, J. (1988) "On Government." Ph.D. diss., University of Connecticut.

Uriagereka, J. (1995a) "Aspects of the Syntax of Clitic Placement in Western Romance." *Linguistic Inquiry* 26: 79–123

Uriagereka, J. (1995b) "An F Position in Western Romance," in K. Kiss (ed.) *Discourse Configurational Languages*. Oxford University Press, New York.

Uriagereka, J. (1996a) "Determiner Clitic Placement," in R. Freidin (ed.) *Current Issues in Comparative Grammar*. Kluwer, Dordrecht.

Uriagereka, J. (1996b) "Formal and Substantive Elegance in the Minimalist Program," in C. Wilder, H.-M. Gärtner, and M. Bierwisch (eds.) *The Role of Economy Principles in Linguistic Theory*. Akademie-Verlag, Berlin.

Uriagereka, J. (1999) "Multiple Spell-Out," in S. D. Epstein and N. Hornstein (eds.) *Working Minimalism*. MIT Press, Cambridge, Mass., 251–282.

CHAPTER 16

COMPARATIVE ATHAPASKAN SYNTAX

Arguments and Projections

KEREN RICE AND
LESLIE SAXON

BETWEEN north and south in the vast territory in which Athapaskan languages are spoken, it is remarkable the extent to which patterns in the language recur and can be recognized as the same through an immense distance of space and time. In this chapter we offer an overview of syntactic patterns in the languages of the family, bringing together many earlier studies and using the frame of "arguments and projections" to give shape to our investigations.

In discussing syntactic patterns in this chapter, we limit ourselves for the most part to structures larger than the traditional word. This is not to deny that there may be significant syntax word-internally. Hale (2001), Rice (2000c), and Speas (1990), among others, in fact, take as their points of departure the central claim that the verb word is a syntactic construct of verb stem combining with a number of classes of clitics and the inflectional heads of functional projections.

The Athapaskan family is made up of approximately 40 languages, which, together with Eyak and Tlingit, form the larger Na-Dene stock (see Mithun 1999 and her references). Athapaskan languages are spoken in three noncontiguous areas of North America: in the American Southwest (the southern Athapaskan or Apachean branch), on the border of the Pacific Coast (Pacific Coast Athapaskan), and in the Canadian west and Alaska (the northern Athapaskan branch). Krauss and Golla (1981: 68) estimate the time since the breakup of the family at approximately 2,000 years. The Apachean branch shows great internal similarities in all respects; the other branches show some divergences within the group, while maintaining a basic coherence. In this chapter, we cite examples as illustrations from all branches and subbranches, including Navajo and Jicarilla Apache (Apachean), Hupa (Pacific Coast), Ahtna (Alaska), Koyukon (Alaska), Dena'ina (Alaska), Kaska (Yukon), Babine-Witsuwit'en (British Columbia), Tsuut'ina (or Sarcee) (often considered to represent a midstage between northern Athapaskan and Apachean), and the three languages forming the Mackenzie subgrouping of Canadian Athapaskan: Slave, Dogrib, and Dene Sųłiné (or Chipewyan). Most of these languages are well documented or are the subject of our fieldwork.

For reasons of space, we limit our investigation to basic clause structure as revealed by a study of pronouns and word order. We aim for a synthesis of the great body of research focusing on "the *yi-/bi-* alternation," an issue concerning the distribution of two third-person pronominal forms in Navajo and other languages of the Athapaskan family and the consequences for hierarchical relations.

Issues centering on other pronominal forms have also had a significant role in the development of the literature in Athapaskan linguistics: we broach the contrast between pronominals referring to speech-act participants and third persons in sections 1 and 3. Beside pronominals and clause structure, the next most investigated topics in Athapaskan syntax focus on questions and related operator constructions. The limits of the present work prevent us from doing more than referring in section 2.1.2 to some of the major work in this area of study.

1 CLAUSE STRUCTURE: SUBJECTS AND OBJECTS

A single topic has driven many aspects of the investigation of Athapaskan syntax: the morphological and syntactic expression of grammatical relations and argument structure. Patterns of variation in word order, inflectional marking, and information structure have highlighted how morphology, syntax, and semantic systems interlock.

In this section, we consider subject and object positions. Our view is that Athapaskan languages generally fit the established paradigm for clause structure, following the work of Fukui and Speas (1986), Kuroda (1988), Sportiche (1988), Pollock (1989), and subsequent investigations: clauses have two sets of subject and object positions defined, on the one hand, by argument structure and, on the other hand, by functional projections. Analysts of Athapaskan languages have disagreed about two things: (i) the role of nominal expressions (whether the arguments of predicates are limited to pronominals) and (ii) the nature of the functional projections (whether they are projections defining grammatical roles of subject and object or informational roles of topic and focus).

Speas (1995) has argued that the disagreements do not make a huge chasm, and we are in agreement. What we propose to do here is spell out in detail an analysis that highlights grammatical functions over information structure. This approach is quite satisfying to us, though it leaves some questions open, along with some holes. We hope to provide enough data and references in this chapter to leave lots of room for exploration by others.

We begin with subjects. The question of the position of subjects has commonly been broached in the general Athapaskanist literature in conjunction with issues of topicality and subject-object inversion (beginning with Hale 1973). (See Thompson 1996 for a recent overview of these matters from a historical-comparative perspective.) The question has also played a significant part in the literature on Apachean languages as Pronominal Argument or Discourse Configurational languages (see, e.g., Jelinek 1984; Willie 1989, 1991, 2000; Jelinek and Willie 1996; Willie and Jelinek 2000). We begin this section by arguing that in Athapaskan languages generally, more than one position is available for subjects, as in the following schematic structure, developing ideas from Rice and Saxon (1991, 1993, 1994), Saxon and Rice (1993), Saxon (1995, 2001), and Rice (2000a, b, c).[1]

(1)

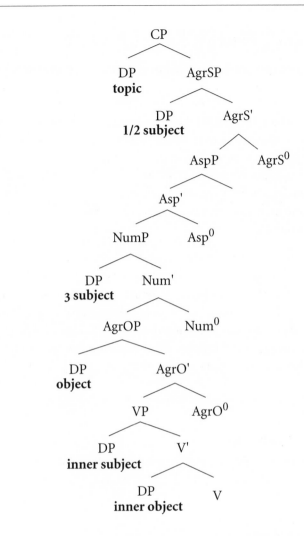

The structure in (1) shows three positions for subjects (specifier of AgrS, specifier of Num, and the VP-internal subject position), two object positions (one inside and one outside the VP),[2] and a position for quantificationally interpreted DPs (specifier of CP).

In the discussion here, we begin with arguments in favor of our proposal concerning subjects and objects (section 1) and then turn to a broad range of facts illuminating alternations between third-person object forms, which we argue crucially depend on the architecture we have proposed (sections 2 and 3).

We draw material principally from Navajo, Ahtna, Koyukon, Slave, and Dogrib, the languages that have been most studied in the areas of concern here. To our knowledge, other languages are similar, with the possible exception of the Pacific Coast languages Hupa and Kato, which appear to differ considerably. Hupa is discussed briefly in section 3.3.

1.1 Internal versus External Subject Positions

Subjects in most Athapaskan languages have a number of properties which are cross-linguistically somewhat unusual. In this section we recapitulate and augment evidence from the series of works previously referred to that argue that this patterning of subjects is a consequence of there being more than one subject position—one internal, and two external, to the verb phrase. The first two arguments, from the facts of idioms and noun incorporation, support the VP-internal subject hypothesis for Athapaskan languages. The third depends on evidence from word order. The last two arguments support the claim that there are separate positions for third-person and non-third-person subjects external to the VP. See Rice and Saxon (1994) for fuller discussion.

1.1.1 *Idioms*

Marantz (1984: 27) remarks that idioms in which the subject of a transitive verb contributes to the idiomatic meaning are cross-linguistically rare. This follows, Marantz assumes, from the fact that the domain of idioms is the VP.[3]

Athapaskan languages exhibit subject idioms, contrary to Marantz's prediction, as in the following examples:[4]

Ahtna

(2) C'eyuunı   sızkat.
      ghost   1sO-3S-pf-slap

      'I have a birthmark.' (lit. a ghost slapped me) (Kari 1990: 232)

Slave

(3) Mbeh   sedhéhxı̨.
      sleep   1sO-3S-pf-overcome

      'I am sleepy.' (lit. sleep killed me) (Rice 1989: 932)

Navajo

(4) Deeteel   yáábı'ıısha'.
      moose   3OO-3S-pf-toss in the air with pointed object

      'He died.' (lit. the moose tossed him in the air) (Young and Morgan 1987: 753)

(5) Dıchın   shá   yıdeezlá.
      hunger   1s-for   3O-3S-pf-carry along [pl O]

      'I got terribly hungry.' (lit. hunger started to carry them along for me) (Young and Morgan 1987: 758)

Under Marantz's assumption that only VP-internal arguments enter into idiom construction, one can conclude that these idioms have VP-internal subjects.

1.1.2 *Incorporation*

Many Athapaskan languages allow nouns to be incorporated into the verb. These nouns are commonly objects, but subjects, too, can be incorporated, as in the examples that follow. Ahtna, Koyukon, Slave, and Dogrib are among the languages with incorporation; incorporation of nouns is not productive in Navajo.[5]

Ahtna

(6) Uyıdlo'nesdyaa. (**dlo'**- 'laughter')
3-into-laughter-pf-go [s]
'He got the giggles.' (lit. laughter went into him) (Kari 1990: 423)

Koyukon

(7) Haa**hutl**deedaatl. (**hutl**- 'sled')
sled-pf-start off [pl]
'The sleds started off.' (Axelrod 1990: 188)

Slave

(8) K'ét**sı**etłah. (**tsı**- 'snow')
snow-pf-move on
'Snow drifted.' (Howard 1990: 519)

Dogrib

(9) Dah**dè**goeʔò. (**dè**- 'land')
land-A-imp-float up
'Land is boggy, swampy.' (Saxon and Siemens 1996: 9)

Like subject idioms, incorporated subjects are rare cross-linguistically. Assuming subjects to be VP-external, Baker (1988) predicts that subject incorporation does not occur, under the assumption that an incorporated noun must be lexically governed by the incorporating verb. If these subjects are actually internal to the VP, however, their potential to incorporate receives an account.

Although many Athapaskan languages allow incorporation of objects of transitive verbs and subjects of intransitive verbs, incorporation of subjects of transitives is unusual. Examples from Ahtna, Koyukon, and Dogrib follow:

Ahtna

(10) **hı**yızʔał. (**hı**- 'dog')
dog-3O-pf-bite [once]
'A dog bit him/her [once].' (Kari 1990: 79)

(11)   Uk'enaałyułghel. (naał- 'sleep')
        3O-sleep-3O-pf-move O
        'He took a nap.' (lit. sleep moved him past it) (Kari 1990: 218)

Koyukon
(12)   Tohebetaatltaanh. (to- 'water')
        water-3pO-pf-carry off [anim O]
        'They floated away.' (lit. water carried them off) (Axelrod 1990: 186)

Dogrib
(13)   Natłįyahte. (tłį-'dog')
        back-dog-3O-prog-carry [anim O]
        'Dogs are bringing him/her back.' (P. Rabesca, p.c. 2001)

1.1.3 *Word-order Variation*

Word-order variation provides a third type of evidence in support of subject
positions outside and inside the VP. We have discussed this type of argument in
Saxon and Rice (1993) and Rice (2000b). Consider the following examples from
Ahtna, Slave, and Navajo, each of which involves an intransitive verb, its subject,
and a locative adverbial expression. In the first set, the subject (in boldface) precedes the locative:

Ahtna
(14)   **Ts'en** uyıdah   nınıghel.
        bone   3-throat   3S-pf-stop moving
        'A bone got stuck in his throat.' (Kari 1990: 217)

(15)   **Tuu**   dayggu   tanel'aan.
        water   down   3S-imp-water line extends
        'The water level is down to a point.' (Kari 1990: 74)

(16)   **Debae** unenta   łooł'as.
        sheep   hill-among   3S-imp-[animals] move
        'The sheep are moving around on the hills.' (Kari 1990: 79)

Slave
(17)   **Tehmį** dechį chį   whe?ǫ.
        pack   tree   at base 3S-imp-be located [chunky O]
        'The pack is at the foot of the tree.' (Rice 1989: 281)

(18) **Sadzée** tu ké kenı̨dı̨.
sunshine water on 3S-imp-shine

'The sun is shining on the water.' (Rice 1989: 276)

(19) **Súhga** beta húle.
sugar 3-in 3S-not exist

'There is no sugar in it.' (Rice 1989: 270)

(20) **Et'ǫa** mek'eh dahthela.
branch 3-on above-3S-imp-be located [pl O]

'Branches are located on them [fish].' (Thom and Blondin-Townsend 1987: 15)

Navajo

(21) **Shı'éétsoh** bık'ıdah'asdáhí bıkaa'gı sıłtsooz.
1s-coat chair 3-on 3S-be located [cloth O]

'My coat is lying on the chair.' (Young and Morgan 1987: 687)

(22) **Tsídıı** sháátıs 'eet'a'.
bird 1s-over 3S-pf-fly

'The bird flew over me.' (Young and Morgan 1987: 149)

(23) Tł'éédą́ą́' **mą'ıı léı'** shıdááh gónaa ch'élwod.
last night wolf Indef 1s-in front of across 3S-pf-run out

'Last night a coyote crossed my path.' (Young and Morgan 1987: 278)

The subjects of these sentences are plausibly either internal or external to the VP, as word-order facts do not distinguish the two possibilities. In the following examples, in contrast, the subject follows the locative phrase and thus must be VP-internal on our assumptions:[6]

Ahtna

(24) Na'aaxe **hc'ae** looyaał.
outdoors dog 3S-imp-walk around [s]

'A dog is walking around outdoors.' (Kari 1990: 82)

(25) Ba'ane **tl'uuł** nı'unezc'et'.
outside rope 3S-imp-stretch

'A rope is stretched outside.' (Kari 1990: 125)

(26) Datsıít   **hwnax**   kuz'aan.
      by the water   house   3S-areal-imp-be located [chunky O]

'A house is nearby by the water.' (Kari 1990: 381)

Slave

(27) Tł'u   k'e   **yú**   ráyefa.
      rope   on   clothes   3S-imp-dry

'The clothes are drying on the line.' (Rice 1989: 275)

(28) Sılá   ké   **xay**   we?ǫ.
      1s-hand   on   scar   3S-be located [chunky O]

'There is a scar on my hand.' (Rice 1989: 276)

(29) Shí   ?óné   **?edee**   nı?á.
      mountain   beyond   caribou   3S-pf-[animals] move to a point

'Caribou gathered beyond the mountain.' (Rice 1989: 284)

(30) Yejaı   k'e   **gozo**   ?ajá.
      window   on   frost   3S-pf-become

'There is frost on the window.' (Rice 1989: 275)

Navajo

(31) Bıkáá'adánı   bıkáa'gı   **tó**   sıká̧.
      table   3-on   water   3S-be located [contained O]

'There is water on the table.' (Young and Morgan 1987: 686)

(32) 'Atıın   bą̧ąhgi   **tsın**   'íí'á.
      road   3-beside-Loc   tree   3S-imp-stand

'A tree stands beside the road.' (Young and Morgan 1987: 149)

(33) 'Ańt'ı'   bıyı'   **béégashıı**   naakaı.
      fence   3-inside   cattle   3S-imp-go around [pl]

'The cattle are inside the fence.' (Young and Morgan 1987: 259)

(In work on negation, Hargus 2002b argues for internal and external subject positions in Kwadacha (Ft Ware Sekani). See also section 1.3 on negation in Navajo and its significance for object positions.)

Taken together, the evidence in the preceding three subsections argues strongly for a subject position that is internal to the verb phrase. See section 1.2

for discussion of factors entering into the question of which subjects remain in VP.

1.1.4 *Morpheme Order for Subject Inflection*

Evidence also exists for two subject positions external to the VP. For example, it is very striking that subject inflection in Athapaskan languages appears in two different positions in the verbal complex. First- and second-person inflection is found directly before the verb stem, while third-person inflection occurs earlier in the word. This can be seen in the paradigm in (34), from Ahtna (Kari 1990: 682). See Willie and Saxon (1995), Jung (1999), and Rice (2000c) for exemplification from a range of other languages of the family:

Ahtna

(34) 'be alive' (imperfective)

kones	3
kosnes	1s
kunes	2s
kohnes	2p
'skones	human, 'someone'; 1p
hkones	3p

The morphologically unmarked form *kones* is interpreted as third person. The form *'skones* is polysemous—it is interpreted with either a third person unspecified human subject 'someone' or a first-person plural 'we', and it thus recalls French forms with the pronominal *on*. We regard it as essentially a third-person form, though this is a simplification.[7] In this paradigm, the second- and third-person plural prefixes differ only by their position relative to the morpheme *ko-*.

Rice and Saxon (1994) and Rice (2000c), starting from the observation that first-, second-, and third-person inflections occupy different morphological positions, argue that first and second person, on the one hand, and third person, on the other, represent different morphological *categories*. In particular, first and second person are identified as Agreement, essentially containing markings for person, while third person is identified as Number, with marking only for number and gender, but not for person. (For substantial justification for these observations cross-linguistically, see Benveniste 1946; for a recent treatment, see Ritter 1991, 1995. Rice and Saxon 1994 specifically address the issue of the designations "agreement" and "number" and provide evidence from the interrelations of inflection and DPs for support.) On the assumption that the position of these inflections relative to each other reflects distinct hierarchical positions in syntax, these facts, too, constitute evidence for two subject positions. (See later and the references cited for further discussion and argumentation.)

1.1.5 *Different Subjects: The Distribution of* y- *and* b- *as Oblique Objects*

Independent support for a third-person subject position as the specifier of NumP comes from anaphora. Saxon (1984, 1986) identifies a morpheme in Dogrib that she calls the disjoint anaphor—a morpheme that indicates that a third-person argument must be noncoreferential with another third-person argument in the clause, generally the subject. The examples in (35) through (38) show typical uses of the disjoint anaphor, which occurs throughout the family with this function.[8] We focus in this section on the disjoint anaphor as oblique object; similar facts hold of direct objects and possessors. The disjoint anaphor is **y**- and it is glossed *y-* (in the interlinear translations). It takes the form **ɪ**- or **zh**- in some contexts in some languages. See section 3 for further discussion.

Ahtna

(35)   Iʔeł   hghıya'.
       y-with   3S-pf-speak
       'She/He spoke with him/her (y).' (Kari 1990: 90)

Koyukon

(36)   John   yʉgh   neeneeyo.
              y-to   3S-pf-walk up to [s]
       'John walked up to him/her (y).' (Thompson 1989a: 40)

Dogrib

(37)   Yeka   k'eʔeeta.
       y-for   3S-imp-rummage around
       'She/He is rummaging around for it (y).' (Saxon and Siemens 1996: 109)

Navajo

(38)   Dıbé   łįį'   yıtah   yíghááh.
       sheep   horse   y-among   3S-pf-go [s]
       'The sheep went among the horses (y).' (Willie and Jelinek 2000: 262)

These examples show clauses with third-person subjects and noncoreferential oblique objects realized as **y**-, the disjoint anaphor. When the subject is non-third-person, **y**- is not used; instead, the form **b**- occurs. (In section 2 of this chapter we have to qualify this statement somewhat, though the generalization is an important one without exceptions in some branches of the family.) This pronominal form is realized as a labial **b, m, u, w,** or **v** in cognates throughout the family. (Both **b**- and **y**- are glossed as "3" earlier in this chapter.)

Koyukon

(39) **Beyeł**   heneehaayh.
      b-with   2sS-imp-talk

      'Speak to him.' (Jetté and Jones 2000: 704)

Tsuut'ina

(40) **Míyìsísdó.**
      b-1sS-wear

      'I'm wearing it.' (Cook 1984: 190)

Jicarilla Apache

(41) **Maa**   né'ą́.
      b-to   1sS-pf-give [chunky O]

      'I gave it to him.' (Sandoval and Jelinek 1989: 341)

We interpret these facts as showing that the disjoint anaphor **y-** occurs only in the scope of a specifier of NumP: this is the canonical position for third-person subjects, which license **y-** from this position. The marker **b-** occurs in any other context to mark a third-person oblique object. The facts in this section then provide independent support for the specifier of NumP as a grammatical position distinct from the specifier of AgrSP.[9]

The contrasting object forms, taken together with the facts of idioms and incorporation, thus provide evidence for three subject positions in the languages of the family, as in the structure shown in (1) at the beginning of this section.[10]

1.2 Conditions on External Subjects

The preceding section showed that Athapaskan languages license third-person subject in one of two positions: [Spec, VP] or [Spec, NumP]. In this section we argue that the languages differ in the interaction of the properties that determine the position of particular subjects in context. Whether the subject is realized internal to VP or externally depends to a large degree on properties of the subject: external subjects tend to be discourse topics, animate, or agentive, while internal subjects tend to be nontopical, inanimate, or nonagentive.

We appeal to three principles in explaining the moves that are possible. First, on the assumption that the predication relation entails a distinguished subject position, a subject moves to [Spec, NumP] to enter into this relationship with the predicate. Such subjects receive an interpretation as thematic or topical, what the sentence is about. Such interpretations are often associated with a definiteness effect (Diesing 1992, Runner 1993, Philippi 1997). Second, is Num itself. This functional category is restricted in Athapaskan languages to nominals high on an animacy scale: only humans or animates may be marked for number, and only these nominals may occupy [Spec, NumP]. As we will show, both topicality and animacy are relevant to the identification of nominals in [Spec, NumP]. Also relevant is, third, agency. If [Spec, AgrOP] and [Spec, NumP] are associated with accusative and nominative case, respectively, then agentive subjects may move to [Spec, NumP] to receive nominative case. (See Rice 2000a for some further discussion.)

In what follows we examine Ahtna, Slave and Dogrib, and Navajo, attempting to characterize subject movement from VP as closely as possible. We do this in semantic terms, relying on future work to pin down the syntactic sine qua non. See Rice (2000a, b), Rice and Saxon (1991, 1994, 2001), and Saxon and Rice (1993) for earlier treatments of the material in this section.

As a diagnostic for subject position, we depend on our assumption from section 1.1.5, that the realization of third-person oblique objects as **y-** is best explained in terms of a licensing subject in [Spec, NumP]. We use the object facts to diagnose the position of subjects. We would wish to supplement this test with data concerning the placement of adverbials, but there has been little study of this matter for Athapaskan languages. Potter (1997) on Western Apache and Hargus (2002b) on Kwadacha (Ft Ware Sekani) are pioneering works in this domain. We hope that our conclusions find support in future studies.[11]

1.2.1 *Ahtna*

In Ahtna, **y-** is used as an oblique object when the subject is human and agentive:

Ahtna

(42) **Ya**   atnaa.
      y-at   3S-imp-work
      'She/He is working on it.' (Kari 1990: 288)

Y- is also found with agentive, nonhuman animate subjects:

(43) Tıkaanı **yuka**   teznııc.
      wolf   y-for   3S-pf-reach
      'A wolf reached for [scared] him/her.' (Kari 1990: 307)

(44) **Ik'e**   dastbets.
      y-on   3S-pf-land
      'It [a bird] landed on top of it.' (Kari 1990: 106)

Human nonagentive subjects may cooccur in a sentence with **y**- as oblique object, too:

(45) Ic'aatse'   zdaa.
      y-opposite   3S-imp-sit [s]
      'She/He stays opposite from him/her.' (Kari 1990: 122)

Alternatively, such subjects may appear with **b**- as the oblique object form.[12]

(46) Uʔııdze'   zdaa.
      b-hidden by   3S-imp-sit [s]
      'He stays hidden by it.' (Kari 1990: 92)

(47) Udıdaa.
      b-touching-3S-imp-sit [s]
      'She/He is sitting, touching him/her (*b*).' (Kari 1990: 64)

Inanimate subjects, agentive (48a) or not (48b), always appear in a sentence with **b**- marking an oblique object:

(48) a. Nıget   **u**yughatkay.
          fear   b-into-3S-pf-leap
          'Fear leapt into him/her [she/he got nervous].' (Kari 1990: 237)

      b. Nıłdoxetah   del   uts'ınghes.
          sometimes   blood   b-from-3S-drip
          'Sometimes blood drips from it.' (Kari 1990: 216)

Our claim about the position of subjects in Ahtna is summarized in (49):

(49) **Subjects in Ahtna**
      Animate agentive subjects must occur in [Spec, NumP] while inanimate
      subjects must occur in the VP-internal subject position. Animate nonagen-
      tive subjects may occur in either position.

1.2.2 *Slave and Dogrib*

Conditions on subject raising in Slave and Dogrib differ slightly from Ahtna, with agency and animacy or humanness having more equal roles. In these languages, animate agentive subjects cooccur with **y**- as oblique object inflection:

Slave

(50)   Yets'ę́   rádı.
        y-to   3S-imp-help
        'She/He helps him/her.' (Rice 1989: 1008)

(51)   **Zh**ek'eenįhxá.
        y-on-3S-pf-chew
        'She/He/It chewed on it.' (Howard 1990: 231)

Dogrib

(52)   Tłį   yedzìįh?à.
        dog   yOO-3S-pf-bite up
        'The dogs bit him up / mauled him.' (Saxon and Siemens 1996: 124)

(53)   Kw'ıh   yek'alaedè.
        mosquito   yOO-3S-imp-[pl] bother
        'The mosquitoes are bothering her.' (Saxon and Siemens 1996: 128)

With animate nonagentive subjects, either **y-** (54) or **b-** (55) is possible to mark oblique objects, as in Ahtna:

Slave

(54)   **Y**eghǫ   ?eteredlį.
        y-for   3S-imp-have pity
        'She/He is sorry for him/her.' (Rice 1989: 270)

(55)   Mary   **b**ets'ę?óné   ?adéhshá.
                b-than   3S-imp-be bigger
        'Mary is bigger than him/her.' (Rice 1989: 1008)

With inanimate agentive subjects, **b-** occurs to mark oblique objects:[13]

Slave

(56)   Mehchįé   **m**etee   ?áhtła.
        truck   b-across   3S-pf-go [s]
        'A truck went over him/her/it.' (Rice 1989: 289)

(57)   Tthık'íí   **m**egohthe   déhk'é.
        gun   b-against   3S-pf-shoot
        'The gun shot him/her/it.' (Rice 1989: 290)

Dogrib

(58) Eneèko   nįhts'į   whek'òo   wexèedì.
      old man   wind   cold   bOO-3S-imp-touch

'The old man feels the cold wind.' (lit. the cold wind touches on the old man) (Saxon and Siemens 1996: 132)

B- is the only option for the oblique object when the subject is neither animate nor agentive:

Slave

(59) Beyúé   bek'e   naįtłole   Pajá.
      3-clothes b-on   3S-is loose 3S-pf-become

'His/Her clothes got loose on him/her.' (Rice 1989: 270)

(60) Tsę   bek'e   yįłǫ́.
      dirt   b-on   3S-pf-be lots

'There was lots of dirt on it.' (Rice 1989: 1008)

Dogrib

(61) SePeè   wek'enįįt'į   dìe.
      1s-jacket   b-on-3S-imp-be taut   very

'My jacket is too tight on her/him.' (Saxon and Siemens 1996: 110)

We therefore make the following claim about Slave and Dogrib subjects:

(62) **Subjects in Slave and Dogrib**
      Human agentive subjects must occur in [Spec, NumP] while inanimate, nonagentive subjects must occur in the VP-internal subject position. Other subjects may occur in either position.

(This statement anticipates some results concerning transitive subjects to be discussed in section 2.3.)

1.2.3 Navajo

For Navajo, unlike Ahtna, Slave, or Dogrib, the conditions on the distribution of **y-** and **b-** as oblique objects with intransitive verbs have been treated extensively in the literature: as in Ahtna and Slave, both **y-** and **b-** can occur. See Hale (1973), Perkins (1978), Speas (1990), Willie (1991), and others for important discussion. Agency and animacy both figure very importantly in determining the movement to [Spec, NumP].[14]

   First, abstracting away from (i) alterations of the basic SOV word order and

(ii) empty arguments, **y**- is found as oblique object inflection when the subject is agentive:

Navajo

(63) 'Ashkıı níbaal yíyah   nıızı́.
      boy   tent   y-under 3S-imp-stand

      'The boy is standing under the tent.' (Young and Morgan 1987: 257)

(64) Łı̨ı̨   naa'ahóóhaı yık'ı   ch'élwod.
      horse chicken   y-on   3S-pf-run [s]

      'The horse ran over the chicken.' (Young and Morgan 1987: 28 grammar)

Y- marks oblique objects also if an inanimate noun can be considered a controller of some sort.

(65) T'ııs tsé   yık'ııkę́ę́z.
      tree   rock   y-on-3S-pf-fall

      'The tree fell on the rock.' (Perkins 1978: 98)

(66) Níyol dóó tó   tsé   yıní'íígháázh.
      wind   and water rock   y-into-3S-pf-gnaw

      'The water and the wind gnawed [eroded] into the rock.' (Young and Morgan 1987: 237)

However, Young and Morgan (1987) show the verb in (66) with a **b**- also:

(67) **B**ıní'íígháázh.

      'It eroded into it.' (Young and Morgan 1987: 237)

Y- is found in clauses with animate nonagentive subjects:

(68) 'Ashkıı tsé   yık'ı dah neezdá.
      boy   rock   y-on   up   3S-pf-sit down [s]

      'The boy sat down on the rock.' (Young and Morgan 1987: 28 grammar)

(69) Mácí tsásk'eh yıkáá' / *bıkáá' ałhosh.
      cat   bed   y-top   b-top   3S-imp-sleep

      'The cat is sleeping on the bed.' (Perkins 1978: 119)

(70) Naa'ahóóhaı   'ayęęzhıı   yık'ı   naazdá.
     hen   egg   y-on   3S-imp-sit

     'The hens are sitting on the eggs.' (Young and Morgan 1987: 686)

In this context, replacing **y**- with **b**- results in ungrammaticality, as shown concretely in (69) (Perkins 1978: 119).

Strikingly, with inanimate nonagentive subjects, **b**- appears marking oblique objects, and **y**- is ungrammatical, opposite to what is true for sentences with animate subjects:

(71) Jooł   tsásk'eh   **bıkáá'** / *yıkáá'   yımas.
     ball   bed   b-top / y-top   3S-imp-roll

     'The ball is rolling on the bed.' (Perkins 1978: 120)

(72) Jooł   chıdí   **bıı'** / *yıı'   sıʔą́.
     ball   car   b-in / y-in   3S-imp-be located [chunky O]

     'The ball is in the car.' (Willie 1991: 97)

(73) Naaltsoos bık'ehgo na'abąąsí   shıbéeso bızıs   **bıyı'**
     driver's license   1s-billfold   b-in
     sıłtsooz.
     3S-imp-be located [cloth O]

     'My driver's license is in my billfold.' (Young and Morgan 1987: 687)

(74) **Bıníhííyį́.**
     b-indenting into-3S-imp-[water] lie

     'It [water] extends into it [to form a gulf or inlet].' (Young and Morgan 1987: 233)

We state the generalization concerning Navajo subjects as follows:

(75) **Subjects in Navajo**
     Animate subjects must occur in [Spec, NumP] while inanimate nonagentive subjects must occur in the VP-internal subject position. Inanimate agentive subjects occur in either position.

Willie (2000) makes the important point that animacy and agency are to be understood in context. She remarks on examples like those in (76), saying, "They contain agents, such as lightning or the rainbow, that are not strictly speaking animate but are endowed with volitionality as powerful sacred beings" (Willie 2000: 365 note 4).

(76) a. Nááts'íílıd   dzıł   **b**ınahaazlá.
         rainbow   mountain b-around-A-imp-surround

      'Rainbows surround the mountains.' (Young and Morgan 1987: 225,
      cited in Thompson 1996: 83)

      b. Nááts'íílıd   dzıł   yınahaazlá.
         rainbow   mountain y-around-A-imp-surround

      'Rainbows surround the mountains.' (Young and Morgan 1987: 225,
      cited in Thompson 1996: 83)

By our hypothesis 'rainbows' is VP-internal in (76a) but occupies [Spec, NumP]
in (76b). Perkins (1978: 101) comments on the flexibility of expression with such
examples. The ambiguous status of these examples with respect to animacy determines the grammatical variability we see with them.[15]

1.2.4 *Summary: Animacy Effects*

The previous discussion shows that subjects in Ahtna, Slave and Dogrib, and
Navajo pattern remarkably alike: as shown by the diagnostic of the choice between
y- and **b**- as third-person oblique object markers, in all of the languages animate,
agentive subjects raise to [Spec, NumP] while inanimate, nonagentive subjects do
not move, remaining in VP as indicated by pronominal marking. The languages
show some variation in the middle ranges, as shown in the following table:

(77) **Subject positions and semantic properties of subjects**

Properties of subjects	Agentive		Nonagentive	
	Language	Position	Language	Position
Animate	All languages	[Spec, NumP]	Navajo	[Spec, NumP]
			Ahtna	Variable
			Slave/Dogrib	Variable
Inanimate	Ahtna	[Spec, VP]	All languages	[Spec, VP]
	Navajo	Variable		
	Slave/Dogrib	Variable		

The languages show further variation, depending on information structure: we
show in section 3.2 that animate subjects in Ahtna and Koyukon may remain in
the VP under certain discourse conditions. Leaving these factors aside, the table
shows the primacy of animacy for subject raising in two of these languages: in
Navajo, animate subjects raise to [Spec, NumP], and in Ahtna, inanimate subjects
remain in VP. We return to these generalizations in section 4.

By our account, the effects attributed to an animacy hierarchy in many Athapaskan languages follow from conditions on subject raising. We develop this idea

in section 2.1 on Navajo, but here show examples from Koyukon as a preliminary. Compare the example in (78) with a human subject to the examples in (79) with *dineega* 'moose' as the subject:

Koyukon

(78)   John   yıneeł'aanh.
              y-3S-imp-look at

       'John is looking at him/her.' (Thompson 1989a: 40)

(79)   a. Dıneega   bıneeł'aanh.
          moose   b-3S-imp-look at

          'The moose is looking at him/her.' (Thompson 1989a: 42)

       b. ?Dıneega   yıneeł'aanh.
          moose   y-3S-imp-look at

          'The moose is looking at him/her.' (Thompson 1989a: 42)

The marginality of (79b) in comparison with (78) illustrates the animacy hierarchy effect. Thompson (1989a) analyzes such examples in the context of a three-level view of topicality: at a global, discourse level, the main participant(s) of a discourse will be the topic; at a local level, the topic is the most predictable and important participant within a span of 10 to 20 clauses; at a semantic or cultural level, humans are inherently more topical than nonhumans. The preference for (79a) over (79b) reflects topicality at the cultural level, where moose are inherently less topical than humans—the human participant is then more likely to be marked by **b-**, the sign of the topical object.

By our hypothesis, the subject *dıneega* 'moose' is an internal subject, ineligible as a licensor for **y-** object marking—which yields the marginal status of (79b). The animacy hierarchy effect follows from the fact that nonhuman subjects in Koyukon more commonly do not raise to the external subject position. We tie the effects to structural position rather than directly to topic status.

1.3 Direct Object Positions

In addition to claiming that there are multiple subject positions in Athapaskan clause structure, we claim that there are two positions for direct objects: as the complement to the verb and as the specifier of AgrOP. AgrOP is justified as a functional projection by the existence of full paradigms of object inflection in the languages of the family. Further, in many languages, the direct object noun phrase may occur either before or after an oblique argument or adjunct, which by assumption marks the left edge of VP. The facts then resemble what we saw in section 1.1.3 with subjects. In Navajo there is a further test for the position of the direct object: its position relative to NegP. On the assumption that the object may occur within the VP or as [Spec, AgrOP], these word order facts find a good account.

The following Navajo examples show word-order variation between a PP and the direct object.[16] In the first examples, the direct object (in boldface) appears adjacent to the verb:[17]

Navajo

(80)   Shɪmá   shádí   **'áwéé'**   yílák'eyííłtɪ́.
       1s-mother   1s-o sister   baby   3-at hand-3DO-3S-pf-give [anim O]

       'My mother handed the baby to my older sister.' (Young and Morgan 1987: 221)   .

(81)   Da'ɪɪdą́ągo   shɪdeezhí   **'abe'**   bílák'ééką́.
       1p-eat-conj 1s-yr sister   milk   3-at hand-1sS-give [contained O]

       'As we were eating I handed the milk to my little sister.' (Young and Morgan 1987: 221)

(82)   Naabeehó   bɪtahgɪ   **shɪghan**   'ashłaa.
       Navajo   3-among   1s-house   1sS-pf-make

       'I built my home among the Navajos.' (Young and Morgan 1987: 33)

(83)   Mą'ɪɪ   bɪnɪɪyé   hooghandɪ   **bee'eldǫǫh**   séłtą́.
       coyote   3-for   house-in   gun   1sgsS-imp-keep [sticklike O]

       'I keep a gun at home for coyotes.' (Young and Morgan 1987: 685)

In these examples, a postpositional phrase precedes the direct object. Assuming that the argumental PP marks the left edge of the VP, the direct object must be internal to the VP. In contrast, in the examples in (84)–(87), the direct object precedes the PP:

(84)   **'Aghaa'   hanoolchaadéę**   shɪmá sání
       wool   carded   1s-grandmother
       bílák'ééłjool.
       3-at hand-1sS-pf-give [mass O]

       'I handed my grandmother the carded wool.' (Young and Morgan 1987: 221)

(85) **Tl'óół** tsın bıgaan bınah dahsélé.
       rope   tree 3-arm 3-over 1sS-pf-hang

'I hung the rope over the tree limb.' (Young and Morgan 1987: 32)

(86) **Jooł** kın bıtıs 'ahííłhan.
       ball house 3-over 1sS-pf-throw

'I threw the ball over the house.' (Young and Morgan 1987: 32)

(87) **Bee'eldǫǫh bikǫ'** 'áłchíní bıts'ąą nanısh'ın.
       gunpowder   children 3-from 1sS-pf-hide

'I have the gunpowder hidden from the children.' (Young and Morgan 1987: 33)

In this case, the direct object is external to the VP. The same point is made for Slave in Rice (2000b: 121–122).

The same two patterns are also found in Koyukon. Examples (88)–(90) show the object adjacent to the verb:

Koyukon

(88) Hebets'e **kkenaa** est'aanh.
       3p-to   words   1sS-imp-own [chunky O]

'I direct [my] speech to them.' (Jetté and Jones 2000: 25)

(89) No'o **kkun'** deełtlaał.
       there wood   2sS-imp-split

'Split wood out there!' (Jetté and Jones 2000: 38)

(90) Betooledle **too** ts'edeenolghaas.
       3-bladder   water 1pS-refl-opt-melt

'Let's melt ourselves snow [water] in its bladder.' (Jetté and Jones 2000: 234)

The next ones show the direct object separated from the verb by a PP:[18]

(91) **Nelotsuł** yelo' ghʉ neenaanee'onh.
       ring   3-hand to   3S-pf-place [chunky O]

'He put a ring on her finger.' (Jetté and Jones 2000: 50)

(92) **Le'on** yʉgh needenaanee'onh.
       rock   3-to   3S-pf-place [chunky O]

'He attached a rock to it.' (Jetté and Jones 2000: 50)

(93) **Oyh**   tl'aah   aahaa   naalghʉh.
      snowshoe   sinew   with   3S-pf-web snowshoes

'She filled the snowshoes with sinew.' (Jetté and Jones 2000: 267)

Facts of negation in Navajo similarly show direct objects appearing in one of two relative positions, as shown next. In these examples, the negative particle and enclitic are shown in boldface. In (94) and (95), the negative particle **doo** precedes the direct object, and in (96) the order is opposite:

Navajo

(94) Jáan **doo** chıdí   yıyíı́łchǫ'-**da.**
            Neg   car   3O-3S-pf-wreck-neg

'John didn't wreck the car.' (Perkins 1978: 13)

(95) Díí   'ashkıı t'ah **doo** chı̨ı́h yę́ę̨ 'adılohıı   yıyııltsééh-**da.**
      this boy   yet   Neg   elephant   3O-3S-pf-see-neg

'This boy has never seen an elephant.' (Speas and Yazzie 1996: 76)

(96) Shızhé'é   béégashıı   **doo** nayıısnıı'-**da.**
      1s-father   cow   Neg   3O-3S-pf-buy-neg

'My father has not bought a cow.' (Hale and Platero 2000: 75)

If the unmarked situation is for **doo . . . -da** to embrace the VP, then the direct object may occur inside or outside the VP, as our tree in (1) shows.[19] See Perkins (1978: 13ff), Hale and Platero (2000), Potter (1997), and Hargus (2002b) for information about negation in Navajo, Western Apache, and Kwadacha (Ft Ware Sekani).

1.4 Cooccurrence of Third-person Objects and Object Inflection

Section 1.1.5 emphasized the similarities across the family in the analysis of oblique objects. In the general domain of objects, there is in addition a highly visible difference between Apachean and other languages. In the northern languages by and large, third-person object inflection is in complementary distribution with an overt noun phrase object. This is true of both direct and oblique objects. The Ahtna and Tsuut'ina examples shown next illustrate the typical northern pattern. Objects and object inflection are in boldface. All of these examples feature third-person subjects and **y**- object inflection; the facts with non-third-person subjects are parallel and are discussed next.

Ahtna

(97) a. **C'eghaeze'** naghı'aan.
    egg   3S-pf-lay

'It laid an egg.' (Kari 1990: 71)

  b. Naydghı'aan.
    3O-3S-pf-lay

'It laid it.'

Note how the object and object inflection are complementary in this pair.

Tsuut'ina examples are parallel:

Tsuut'ina

(98) a. **Dìní** tsììlìh.
    man   3S-imp-hire

'He'll hire the man.' (Cook 1984: 203)

  b. Tsìyìlìh.
    3O-3S-imp-hire

'He'll hire him.' (Cook 1984: 203)

Cook does not give the ungrammatical example comparable to (97c) but remarks on the complementarity of the object noun phrase and the inflectional form.

In the Apachean languages, in contrast, when an object noun phrase is present, it invariably cooccurs with inflection, as in (99) and many of the previous Navajo examples:

Navajo

(99) a. 'Ashkıı **'at'ééd** yınıł'į́.
    boy   girl   3O-3S-imp-see

'The boy sees the girl.' (Young and Morgan 1987: 65)

  b. *'Ashkıı **'at'ééd** nıł'į́.
    boy   girl   3S-imp-see

(The boy sees the girl.)

In the contrast between Apachean, on the one hand, and the typical northern languages, on the other, **y**- evidently marks agreement in Apachean with any class of third-person object, while in the rest of the family it marks agreement only with pronominal objects. The Apachean pattern then represents a generalization from the original.

Considering **b-**, the most basic cooccurrence facts are the same. In the Ahtna examples that follow, the objects of the postposition **naɬ'ıı** 'obscuring, hidden by, behind' are a referring expression in the first example and a pronominal in the second. Cooccurrence of **b-** with an overt noun phrase is disallowed. (In context, **b-** here takes the shape **u-** preceding a consonant.)

Ahtna

(100)   **Ts'abaelı   naɬ'ıı**   ngesdzen.
      spruce   behind   1sS-imp-stand

      'I am standing obscured by the spruce.' (Kari 1990: 92)

(101)   **Unaɬ'ıı**   hwghas'aan.
      3OO-behind   1sS-pf-handle a situation

      'I tricked him.' (lit. I handled a situation behind him) (Kari 1990: 92)

The Navajo example, on the other hand, shows the pattern ruled out in many of the northern languages, where a referring expression and agreement cooccur:

Navajo

(102)   Jooɬ   **chıdí   bıı'**   sı'á.
      ball   car   3OO-in   3S-be located [chunky O]

      'The ball is in the car.' (Willie 1991: 97)

Again, we propose that Navajo has extended the range of use of **b-** object inflection as agreement from pronominal third persons to all third persons.[20]

Saxon (1989) first suggested that the contrast we see here might be indicative of a major parametric difference between the Apachean branch and the rest of the family. We do not hold this view now. Evidence exists that a number of languages allow both patterns. Dena'ina, Babine-Witsuwit'en, and Slave have been discussed in the literature as having this character. While considerable work is required to investigate these cases in depth, such facts seem to cast doubt on the idea of a major parameter dividing northern languages and Navajo. See also note 21.

Dena'ina

(103)   John   **ch'anıksen**   ıɬjeh.
             baby   3S-pf-hit

       'John hit the baby.' (Thompson 1996: 91)

(104) Łik'a **John** yaghıdghach.
      dog   3O-3S-pf-bite

'The dog bit John.' (Thompson 1996: 91)

The Dena'ina sentence in (103) exemplifies the Ahtna pattern, in that when the object DP *ch'anıksen* 'baby' occurs, the verb is unmarked for object inflection. In (104), the object 'John' and object inflection cooccur. There is no indication in the literature as to whether the morphological contrast in Dena'ina correlates with a semantic distinction. For Babine-Witsuwit'en, Gunlogson (2001) suggests such a correlation: DPs cooccurring with inflection are characterized by definiteness. The following examples support this view:

Babine-Witsuwit'en

(105) **To**   hınılh'ën.
      water   3pS-imp-look at

'They're looking at water.' (Gunlogson 2001: 374)

(106) **Ts'enco** hıyınılh'ën.
      swan   3O-3pS-imp-look at

'They're looking at the swan.' (Gunlogson 2001: 374)

More work is required to fully understand the dynamics of such contrasts.[21] Considerations of space prevent us from exploring the ramifications of these observations for the parametric status of the languages of the family; we expect that this area will continue to be very fruitful in future research.

Subsequent sections of this chapter rely quite heavily on the conclusions of section 1 concerning the availability of a range of subject and object positions. Our arguments have mostly been empirical ones, to which we can perhaps add further arguments of a more theory-based sort. The theoretical model we are assuming posits universally available specifier positions for inflectionally related subject and object DPs (though AgrS and AgrO are not always the labels used for these functional projections). Our arguments thus not only provide support for our view of Athapaskan languages but also provide independent evidence for the theoretical model.

2 CLAUSE STRUCTURE AND ARGUMENT POSITIONS: THE *YI-/BI-* ALTERNATION

With this background in clause structure behind us, we now broach the most discussed topic in Athapaskan studies—that involving a word-order alternation and a morphological alternation in Navajo, which appear to correlate with each other. We use our discussion of this issue to further support the claims inherent in the tree structure given in section 1, first for Navajo and then for the languages of the family more generally.

Chad Thompson has long argued (1989a, 1989b, 1996) that the correlation alluded to in the preceding paragraph does not exist. We agree with him, and in fact the *lack* of a correlation is essential for the particulars of our analysis. While that analysis is quite different from what Thompson proposes, we aim to bring out parallels between our structural approach and his more functional one. We are indebted to his groundbreaking work in this area.

2.1 The *yi-/bi-* Alternation in Navajo and Related Phenomena

2.1.1 *Subject-object Inversion*

The most familiar data, discussed in many works including Hale (1973), Perkins (1978), Platero (1978), Sandoval and Jelinek (1989), Thompson (1989a, 1996), Speas (1990), Willie (1991, 2000), and Willie and Jelinek (2000), contrast clauses with SOV and OSV word order.[22] A concomitant contrast in morphology matches *yi-* object marking with the SOV structure and *bi-* with OSV. Ken Hale (1973) called the *bi-* construction "subject-object inversion." The inversion signals a difference in information structure, so that the OSV structure is often translated as a passive, as in (107b), though it is not a passive structure. Hale considers the most accurate term for it to be "inverse":

(107)   a. Łį́į́'   dzaanééz yıztał.
           horse   mule   y-kicked

           'The horse kicked the mule.' (Hale 1973: 300)

        b. Dzaanééz łį́į́'   bıztał.
           mule   horse   b-kicked

           'The mule was kicked by the horse.' (Hale 1973: 300)

Another classic pair illustrating subject-object inversion is shown in (108):

(108)   a. 'At'ééd   Jáan   yızts'ǫs.
           girl   John   y-kissed

           'The girl kissed John.' (Perkins 1978: 102)

       b. Jáan   'at'ééd   bızts'ǫs.
          John   girl   b-kissed

          'The girl kissed John.' (Perkins 1978: 102)

Inversion is limited so that if one of the nominals outranks the other on a scale
of animacy or potency, that nominal must be the first of the two in sequence,
regardless of grammatical relations. Grammatical relations are discerned from the
verbal morphology. We exemplify this restriction with the data in (109). The
inverse form (109b) is ruled out because of the ranking of *tó dılchxoshí* 'soda pop'
and *'ashkıı* 'boy':

(109)   a. 'Ashkıı   tó dılchxoshí   yoodlą́ą́.
           boy   soda pop   y-drank

           'The boy drank the soda pop.' (Hale 1973: 301)

       b. *Tó dılchxoshí   'ashkıı   boodlą́ą́.
          soda pop   boy   b-drank

          (The boy drank the soda pop.) (Hale 1973: 301)

The inversion process has been treated in different approaches as a type of topicalization (Speas 1990, Speas and Yazzie 1996, Willie and Jelinek 2000) and likened
to Italian Clitic Left Dislocation (Speas and Yazzie 1996). We feel that these approaches are on the right track but would like to be quite specific about the
position occupied by the inverted object. For the verbal morphology, we take both
yi- and *bi-* to be types of object inflection, following the discussion in section 1.

    As has been shown very clearly by Ellavina Perkins (1978), at most one DP
can be affected by subject-object inversion: at most, one instance of *bi-* can mark
an inversion. This is shown in (110):

(110)   a. Ashkıı   at'ééd   dzı'ızí   yıł   yoodzį́į́s.
           boy   girl   bike   y-with   y-pull

           'The boy is pulling the bike with the girl [on it].'

       b. Ashkıı   at'ééd   dzı'ızí   bıł   yoodzį́į́s.
          boy   girl   bike   b-with   y-pull

          'The girl is pulling the bike with the boy [on it].'

c. *Ashkıı   at'ééd   dzı'ızí   bıł   boodzı́ı́s.
   boy   girl   bike   b-with   b-pull

(The girl is pulling the bike with the boy [on it].) (Perkins 1978: 116)

Under a "topic" analysis, this fact follows when the limit on the number of topics that a clause can support is one. If we follow the lead of Speas and Yazzie (1996) and take "topicalization" in Navajo to be equivalent to Italian Clitic Left Dislocation, there is a problem in that the process in Italian is not limited to a single nominal in the way Navajo subject-object inversion is (Cinque 1990: 58).

In addition, evidence from questions in subject-object inversion suggests that the inverted element is not a topic in the usual sense of old information in the discourse. On this understanding of topic, a question phrase would be predicted never to be inverted, as a question phrase can be a discourse focus but not a topic. What we find is that inverted question phrases receive a discourse-linked interpretation in the sense of Pesetsky (1987). Mary Willie (1991) observes the following very significant contrast between questions with *yi-* as opposed to *bi-*:[23]

(111)   Háí-sh   Jáan   yızts'ǫs?
         who-Q   John   y-kissed

         'Who kissed John?' (Willie 1991: 204)

(112)   Háí-sh   Jáan   bızts'ǫs?
         who-Q   John   b-kissed

         'Which one (of you) was kissed by John?' (Willie 1991: 204)

In English 'which' is the mark of a discourse-linked question, one presupposing a set of individuals well defined in context who might satisfy the question, while ordinarily 'who' or 'what' is unlinked. The contrast between the two Navajo examples makes sense if *háí-sh* in the second example is discourse-linked.

Our view is that subject-object inversion involves discourse-linking of the inverted object, not only in the case of question phrases but also generally. This point of view accords with another fact about inversion: Willie (1991) makes the important discovery that there is a definiteness effect associated with the inverson construction. Let's consider first the direct construction with *yi-*.

(113)   a. 'Ashkıı   léı'   'at'ééd   yızts'ǫs.
            boy   Indef   girl   y-kissed

            'A boy kissed the girl.'

         b. 'Ashkıı   'at'ééd   léı'   yizts'ǫs.
            boy   girl   Indef   y-kissed

            'The boy kissed a girl.' (Willie 1991: 76)

Either subject or object can be indefinite; for this construction, no definiteness effect exists. (Bare nouns can be interpreted as indefinite, though the unmarked interpretation makes them definite; Fernald et al. 2000.) On the other hand, in inversion the inverted object must be definite, as with **'ashkıı** 'boy' in (114a), and not indefinite, as in the ungrammatical (114b):

(114)　a. 'Ashkıı　'at'ééd　léı'　**bı**zts'ǫs.
　　　　　boy　　　girl　　Indef　b-kissed

　　　　　'The boy was kissed by a girl.'

　　　b. *'Ashkıı　léı'　'at'ééd　**bı**zts'ǫs.
　　　　　boy　　Indef　girl　　b-kissed

　　　　　(A boy was kissed by the girl.) (Willie 1991: 77)

Fernald et al. (2000) show that N + *léı'*, like indefinites in many languages, must introduce a new character into the discourse. If 'a boy' in the (b) example is occupying a position which necessarily links to the previous discourse, the sentence cannot escape being ungrammatical. Thus our approach is able to account for the definiteness effect discovered by Willie.

　　We propose that the inverted object occupies the Specifier position of a functional category that we will call "Discourse Phrase" after a proposal by Rose-Marie Déchaine (2001). Déchaine, accounting for the prefixes marking first- and second-person agreement on the Algonquian verb which are unmarked for grammatical relation, posits a projection for discourse-linked arguments, in particular speech-act participants. For Navajo, we have just shown that the inverted object is necessarily discourse-linked, and therefore we broaden Déchaine's construct to accommodate also third-person forms under the rubric:

(115)

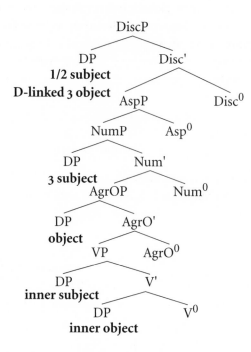

This proposal for Navajo is almost identical to our earlier proposal made in (1), based on a study of northern Athapaskan languages (Rice and Saxon 1994). The one difference lies in adopting the designation "DiscPhrase" rather than "AgrSP" and opening it up to discourse-linked third-person nominals in addition to speech-act participants. The specifiers of DiscP and AgrSP share the property of being L-marked positions, in the languages under discussion associated with overt agreement. From their status as A-positions, it is predicted that there will be at most one filler for the position, yielding the exclusivity effect noted by Perkins (1978). According to this approach, the characteristics of subject-object inversion are incompatible with first- or second-person subjects, as the inverted nominal and speech-act participant subjects are mutually exclusive, filling the same position.

The architecture in (115) yields the word-order facts of subject-object inversion, with the inverted object higher than (and to the left of) the subject in [Spec, NumP]. It should be compared with Willie and Jelinek's (2000) structures, which are in many ways very similar. (See also Speas 1990, 2000.) In (115) the canonical positions for third-person subject and object are the specifier positions of NumP and AgrOP, respectively. As argued previously, *yi-* as third-person object agreement is licensed in Navajo only when the subject is also third-person and c-commands the object. When the object occupies [Spec, DiscP], it is not in the c-command domain of the third-person subject. In this case *yi-* is not licensed as an object marker, and the default third-person object marker *bi-* must be used instead.

Our view has a lot in common with the work of Thompson (1989a, 1989b, 1996) and Aissen (2000), who regard the object linked to *bi-* as a proximate. A proximate can be defined as the discoursally most prominent third person. As our tree shows, [Spec, DiscP] is the hierarchically most prominent nominal position—here is where the two types of views come together.

2.1.2 *Focus Movement*

What has struck so many researchers has been the correlation of word order and morphology in Navajo subject-object inversion. In this section and the next, we conclude that, in fact, there is no such correlation. Object inflection with either *yi-* or *bi-* is independent of word order. We turn first to a little-discussed construction that we will call "focus movement" after Willie (1991: 207) and Willie and Jelinek (2000). It is characterized by *yi-* object inflection and OSV word order. In section 2.1.3, we examine the case where *bi-* object inflection is required regardless of word order.

Willie (1991: 199ff.) and Willie and Jelinek (2000) discuss some data from questions earlier treated by Schauber (1979). A pair of examples illustrating "focus movement" is shown next:

(116)   a. Ashkıı   ha'át'íísh   yıyıłtsą́?
            boy   what-Q   y-saw

         'What did the boy see?' (Schauber 1979: 118)

         b. Ha'át'íísh   ashkıı   yıyıłtsą́?
            what-Q   boy   y-saw

         'What did the boy see?' (Schauber 1979: 117)

As their term indicates, Willie and Jelinek propose that the word-order variation serves to put the question phrase in focus. From these examples, we can see that focus movement is not subject to the same types of restrictions as is subject-object inversion: the question phrase is not definite and in this construction does not receive a discourse-linked interpretation. Movement is not constrained by the "animacy hierarchy" illustrated in (109). And it isn't associated with any morphological change. The next examples further illustrate the phenomenon:

(117)   Ha'át'íísh   Jáan   neıdıyoołnıh?
         what-Q   John   y-will buy

         'What will John buy?' (Schauber 1979: 132)

(118) Háí-sh   Jáan   yızts'ǫs?
       who-Q   John   y-kissed

'Who kissed John?' or 'Who did John kiss?' (Willie and Jelinek 2000: 272)

The last example is interesting in that it shows that the possibility of ambiguity does not block focus movement. In this, focus movement again contrasts with subject-object inversion, about which it is often said that word order and morphology correlate in order to avoid ambiguity.

We would like to suggest that focus movement be analyzed as movement to [Spec, CP], like question movement in many other languages. This stance is in accord with recent treatments of questions in Athapaskan languages, including Rice (1989: ch. 38) on questions in Slave; Potter (1997), a full study of questions and related topics in Western Apache; Denham (1997) and Svendsen (2000), who provide analyses of questions in Babine-Witsuwit'en; and Perkins (2000), a study of Navajo questions. Anachronistically, this view is also compatible with Schauber's landmark (1979) study of questions in Navajo. Although we are not able to devote any further attention to questions in this chapter, we present data which, we argue, reflect the same structures but do not involve question phrases.

In the four examples (119)–(122), we find the word order OSV and a verb inflected with *yi-*, which we take as signs of focus movement in the absence of pertinent semantic evidence of focusing. The first two examples have a fronted nominal marked by the indefinite determiner *léı'*:

(119) Yıstłé   'ayóo   naats'ǫǫd   léı'   shádí   shá   nayısnıı'.
       sock   very   3s-stretch Indef   1s-ol sister 1s-for   y-bought

'My older sister bought me some very stretchy stockings.' (Young and Morgan 1987: 601)

(120) Dana L. Shipley   wolyéé   léı'   dıné   doo   yıł
                         named-Rel Indef   Navajo   Neg   y-with
       nda'asdįįd   da.
       3p-abide   Neg

'The Navajos couldn't stand a [person] named Dana L. Shipley.' (Young and Morgan 1987: 640)

Three of the four examples, including the two that follow, involve movement of an object which would be ineligible for subject-object inversion because of a conflict with the animacy hierarchy:

(121) Shıbee'ak'e'elchíhí   sıtsılí   t'óó   'átsé shá neıłtın.
       1s-pencil   1s-yr brother   merely   y-have on loan from-1s

'My younger brother has my pencil on loan from me.' (Young and Morgan 1987: 599)

(122)   Tsıghá bee yıılch'ílí   'áłchíní   yóó' 'adeıztą́ą́   lá.
        curling iron   children   y-3p-carry off   Evid

        'The children had carried off the curling iron.' (Young and Morgan 1987: 219)

Hale (1973) comments on the possibility for the type of structure we have been examining, without providing examples:

> Where the subject and object are clearly distinct in rank . . . the surface ordering of the subject and object is not absolutely fixed. Thus, I assume that, quite apart from the inversion rule, there is the possibility of reordering the subject and object, provided ambiguity does not result; where reordering of this secondary type has taken place, therefore, the higher ranking noun phrase may appear in a position other than the initial one in the surface structure. (Hale 1973: 309, fn 3)

As Hale states explicitly, the processes of focus movement and subject-object inversion are clearly distinct. In encompassing question movement, focus movement calls to mind A-bar operations, as does the lack of effect on inflection. Is focus movement unbounded? Schauber (1979) and Perkins (2000) show that for some speakers of Navajo, long-distance question movement is possible in certain grammatical contexts, as in the following examples:

(123)   Ha'at'íísh   Jáan   [_____   nahıdeeshnıh]   nízın?
        what   John   1s-fut-buy   wants

        'What does John want to buy?' (Schauber 1979: 131)

(124)   Háágóólá   Jáan   [doo   _____   jıdoogáał-da]
        where-to-Q   John   Neg   one-goes-Neg
        shó'ní ?
        1sOO-say of

        'Where is it that John expects me not to go?' (Schauber 1979: 181)

It is a question for empirical study as to whether focus movement more generally is possibly unbounded.

2.1.3   When bi- Is Required

Focus movement is a context in which the dislocation of a nominal does not affect object marking with *yi-*. Willie (1991) observes that contexts exist in which the *yi-/bi-* alternation is impossible and an object must be marked by *bi-*, regardless of word order. A minimal pair involving direct objects from Willie's work is given next, together with a near minimal pair with oblique objects from the Young and Morgan dictionary:

(125) a. lı'nı'   łį́į́'   **b**ıısxį́.
          lightning horse b-killed
          'Lightning killed the horse.' (Willie 1991: 90)

      b. Łį́į́   'ıı'nı'   **b**ıısxį́.
          horse lightning b-killed
          'Lightning killed the horse.' (Willie 1991: 90)

(126) a. 'Ak'ah   sıdogo shíla'   **b**ık'ésdááz.
          grease   hot   1s-hand   b-splash on
          'Hot grease splattered on my hand.' (Young and Morgan 1987: 200)

      b. ... shítáá'gı   tsídıı bıchaan   **b**ık'ésdááz.
          1s-forehead bird droppings b-splash on
          'Bird droppings splattered on my forehead.' (Young and Morgan 1987: 200)

Ellavina Perkins (1978) provides these examples:

(127) Jooł   tsın   **b**áhátıs   yılts'ıd.
        ball   log   b-over   3s-rolled
        'The ball rolled over the log.' (Perkins 1978: 55)

(128) Asaa'   tsé   **b**ıkáá'   sı'ą́.
        pot   rock   b-top   3s-be located [chunky O]
        'The pot is on the rock.' (Perkins 1978: 119)

She observes that "the appearance of the /yi/ or /bi/ form is conditioned by the animacy or inanimacy of the subject NP, such that the /yi/ form is used with animate subjects and the /bi/ form is used with inanimate subjects" (136). Further examples can readily be found in Young and Morgan (1987):

(129) Shıch'ah   tsın   bıgaan   **b**ınahıdé'ą́.
        1s-hat   tree   3-branch b-hang over
        'My hat is hanging over the tree limb.' (Young and Morgan 1987: 225)

(130) [Honıshgısh 'awéé' **bıná** sıtą́ągo]   'ájıłį́íh.
       poker   baby   b-beside 3s-be located [stick O]   UHS-let

       'One should leave the poker [sitting] beside the baby.' (Young and Morgan 1987: 223)

Our structural account of these facts is given in section 1.2. There we argued that this pattern of word order and morphology occurs when the inanimate subject remains in situ within the VP. Assuming this about the subjects, in the subject-first cases in (125a) and (126a), both the subject and the object are internal to the VP and thus *yi-* is not licensed. The fronted objects in (125b) and (126b) have one of two possible landing sites: [Spec, AgrOP], the usual position for moved objects in Navajo, or [Spec, DiscP], the landing site for subject-object inversion. In each of these configurations, object marking is *bi-*. There will be no option for the object to be marked by *yi-*, as its licensing condition is not met under the assumption that inanimate, nonagentive subjects do not move to [Spec, NumP].

Examples like (130), with its inanimate subject and animate oblique object, might tend to support the idea that *bi-* marks the proximate, or topical, object. Examples (127)–(129), with two inanimate participants in the situation, are neutral on the question. However, our next examples are striking in that they contain two instances of *bi-*, marking two different oblique objects:

(131) **Bıł**   **bıná'eeł.**
       b-with   b-float around

       'It [a boat] floats around it [e.g., an island] with him.' (Young and Morgan 1987: 227)

(132) ... shıcheıı 'ahbínídą́ą́'   tsınaabąąs   **bıł**   bíníbą́ą́z   lá.
       1s-gr.father this.morning   wagon   b-with   b-catch up to   emph

       ' ... this morning my grandfather caught up with them in the wagon.'
       (lit ... this morning the wagon rolled along catching up to them with my grandfather [driving]) (Young and Morgan 1987: 151)

What these sentences share is this: each contains a verb of motion whose inanimate subject is a conveyance (boat, wagon) for a rider who is represented in Navajo grammar as the object of the postposition *-ıł* 'with'.[24] The clause in each case also includes another oblique object which, like the object of *-ıł*, is marked by *bi-*. In (131) all of the elements of the situation are expressed by pronominals. In (132), the subject is *tsınaabąąs* 'wagon', and the rider is *shıcheıı* 'my grandfather'. The other oblique is a pronominal. In the following example, the motion of an object (the object of -*ił* 'with') is provided by the wind rather than a conveyance:

(133)   Bıdah   **bıł**   'anááyol.
         b-down from height   b-with   3S-pf-[wind] blow

       'It blew back down [from it].' (lit. [the wind] blew with it down from it) (Young and Morgan 1987: 487)

In our account, the facts of *bi-* follow from the assumption that the inanimate subject does not appear in [Spec, NumP] and therefore cannot license *yi-* for its object(s). An account like Perkins's (1978), Speas and Yazzie's (1996), or Willie and Jelinek's (2000) predicts that only one object may be marked by *bi-*, the single topic. Aissen (2000) predicts that a single proximate object, and nothing else, may be marked by *bi-*. In our account, *bi-* is the unmarked third-person object pronominal, occurring in the elsewhere condition, wherever *yi-* is not licensed. For other researchers, however, two environments have to be specified for *bi-*, an analytic move we would like to avoid.[25]

The tree (115) in section 2.1.1 gives the essence of our analysis of the *yi-/bi-* alternation in Navajo. We chose Navajo as our starting point because it has been more widely discussed in the literature and so is better known.[26] In the next several sections of the chapter, we would like to move beyond Navajo to other languages and other branches of the family. We first consider realizations of the *yi-/bi-* alternations in other languages, beginning with a look at how the *yi-/bi-* alternation is often regarded as being linked with information structure.

2.2 The *yi-/bi-* Alternation beyond Navajo

The following examples typify the shift in information structure that has been observed in Apachean languages. The English glosses show the topical objects in the (b) examples through a shift to forms of passives, though as we noted, the Apachean sentences are transitive and not passive:

Navajo
(134)   a. **yızts'ǫs** 'She/He kissed him/her.'

      b. **bızts'ǫs** 'She/He was kissed by him/her.' (Platero 1978: 119–120)

Jicarilla Apache
(135)   a. **yızkał** 'He kicked him.'

      b. **bızkał** 'He got kicked by him.' (Sandoval and Jelinek 1989: 349)

In this section we provide data comparing languages that pattern like Navajo and Jicarilla Apache in permitting the *yi-/bi-* alternation in the context of third-person subjects in the canonical [Spec, NumP] position. Our discussion here is strongly influenced by Thompson (1989a, 1996), who pioneered work in comparative Athapaskan syntax, and draws also on the important work by Leer (1990) on the system of anaphora in Proto-Athapaskan and beyond to Na-Dene. As Thompson (1989a, 1996) shows, Koyukon, a language of Alaska, appears very similar to the Apachean languages, in that topicality plays a critical role in the choice between the two forms:

Koyukon

(136)   a. John   yeneeł'aanh.
              y-3S-imp-look at

'John (topic) is looking at him/her (non-topic).' (Thompson 1996: 87)

     b. John   beneeł'aanh.
              b-3S-imp-look at

'John (non-topic) is looking at him/her (topic).' (Thompson 1996: 87)

We analyze the facts in Koyukon as we did for Navajo, taking the **b**- form to involve a canonical subject in [Spec, NumP] and a (null) object moved to [Spec, DiscP].[27]

As is observed by Willie (2000: 374ff.) and reinterpreted according to our claims, the option of a third-person object moving to [Spec, DiscP] is restricted to certain branches of the family, including Apachean and some Alaskan. The diagnostic is the existence of minimal pairs exhibiting the *yi-/bi-* alternation. Dena'ina, like Koyukon, has this character, as the following examples cited from Thompson (1996) show. Note how the Dena'ina sentences parallel Navajo (107)–(108):

Dena'ina

(137)   a. Łik'a John   yaghıdghach.
              dog   y-3S-pf-bite

'The dog bit John.' (Thompson 1996: 91)

     b. John   łık'a   baghıdghach.
              dog   b-3S-pf-bite

'The dog bit John.' (Thompson 1996: 92)

On the other hand, many languages, including Slave, Dogrib, and Tsuut'ina, do not permit such an alternation:

Slave

(138) a. John   ráyereyįht'u.
       　　　 y-3S-pf-hit

       'John hit him/her.'

       b. *John   rábereyįht'u.
       　　　　 b-3S-pf-hit

       (John hit him/her.)

Dogrib

(139) Ehtsèe   įle   yèhdı   /   *wèhdı.
       grandfather no   y-3S-pf-tell /   *b-3S-pf-tell

       'Grandfather told him/her no.' (Saxon and Siemens 1996: 133)

Tsuut'ina

(140) Yìʔàs.[28]

       y-3S-imp-kick

       'She/He'll kick him/her.' (Cook 1984: 200)

In those languages in which the alternation is ruled out, **y-** is the only possible realization, as seen here. In analyzing these languages, we assume that the highest A-projection is not to be reckoned as DiscP but, rather, as AgrSP. The effect is that only first- and second-person subjects occupy the specifier of this projection, leaving discourse-linked third-person objects without a distinctive landing site—and without a way to trigger agreement in the shape of **b-**.

2.3 The Role of Transitivity in *y-* Marking

Our discussion to this point depends on the assumption deriving ultimately from Saxon's (1984, 1986) work on Dogrib that the disjoint anaphor **y-** can be licensed only by a subject in [Spec, NumP]. For a range of languages and grammatical contexts, this view is too restrictive, a topic we explore in detail in section 3. Here we examine phenomena suggesting that transitivity plays a role in certain contexts. In Kaska, in fact, **y-** has been grammaticalized as third-person direct object marking, regardless of the nature or position of the subject.

Asymmetries between direct and oblique objects call to mind remarks by more than one linguist that Athapaskan languages seem to allow only a limited range of semantic roles for a direct object in relation to the verb (Petitot 1876: lxviii, §100; Speas 1996: 199). In a study of this issue in Navajo, Jelinek and Willie (1996) propose that direct objects in Navajo are assigned the "affected" θ-role, with the consequence that they are consistently interpreted as patients of active verbs. We agree that Athapaskan languages exhibit a robust tendency for transitive verbs to be interpreted as agentive. Canonical third-person subjects are typically agentive and occupy [Spec, NumP]. If these two properties don't go together, conflicts can arise. Particularly clear cases of conflicts involve idiomatic and incorporated subjects. (The examples in (141) and (142) are repeated from before.)

The Navajo subject idiom in (141) has its third-person direct object marked by **y**-:

Navajo

(141)   Dıchın   shá   yıdeezlá.
        hunger   1s-for   y-3S-pf-carry along

'I got terribly hungry.' (lit. hunger started to carry it along for me)
(Young and Morgan 1987: 758)

We take the position in section 1.2.3 that inanimate subjects in Navajo do not in general raise out of the VP and so remain in a syntactic configuration where they will not license the disjoint anaphor **y**-. As the inanimate subject in (141) clearly does license **y**- perhaps the exceptionality of this sentence can be explained in terms of the personification of *dıchın* 'hunger' and its assumption of the agent role due to the lexical semantics of the verb.

In the following Ahtna and Koyukon examples, involving incorporated subjects, the direct object is marked by **y**-, the prefix immediately following the incorporate:

Ahtna

(142)   Łıyız?ał. (**h**- 'dog')
        dog-y-pf-bite [once]

'A dog bit him/her [once].' (Kari 1990: 79)

Koyukon

(143)   Haatsehyedeełtaanh. (**tseh**- 'tears')
        away-tears-y-pf-carry [animate O]

'She/He went away crying.' (lit. tears carried him/her away) (Axelrod 1990: 185)

A conflict arises between the argument that an idiomatic or incorporated subject is VP-internal (section 1.1) and the assumption that **y**- is licensed only from outside VP. We resolve this conflict for Ahtna and Koyukon by showing in section 3.2 that the licensing of **y**- is not so limited: VP-internal licensors exist.[29]

Considering Slave and Dogrib, in most transitive cases **y**- is required for a direct object, even when the third person subject is inanimate, as in the following. In these cases, **b**- is ruled out, as it yields ungrammaticality:

Slave

(144)   Ɂıdı   łayatła.
      lightning   y-3S-pf-split

      'Lightning split it.' (Rice 1989: 1009)

Dogrib

(145)   Wek'èèt'ı̨   ełàyıhwhı   sǫ̀ǫ̀!
      laziness   y-3S-opt-kill   Prohib

      'May she/he not be lazy!' (lit. laziness had better not kill him/her!) (P. Rabesca, pers. comm., 2001)

By our account in section 1.2, we achieve this result by requiring agentive subjects of all types to move to [Spec, NumP], with a proviso in the next paragraph.[30] As transitive subjects are typically agentive while intransitive subjects are not, it follows that the objects of transitive verbs will show more marking with **y**- than will oblique objects in intransitive clauses.

An innovation in Slave and Dogrib grammar highlights the interplay between transitivity and agentivity: when the subject is one of a set of "afflictions," including a cold, cancer, snowblindness, or drowsiness, the object may be expressed by either **y**- (146a) or **b**- (146b) if the verb is transitive. (If it is not, the oblique object must be marked by **b**-.)

Dogrib

(146)   a. Dehko   ayı̨là.
         cold   y-3S-pf-do

         'She/He has a cold.' (lit. a cold did him/her)

      b. Dehko   awı̨là.
         cold   b-3S-pf-do

         'She/He has a cold.' (lit. a cold did him/her)

The pattern in (b) is innovative in Dogrib. It is also documented by Howard (1990) for Slave.[31] We would argue that the subject in the innovative pattern is not raised from VP, making object marking with **y**- impossible. The exceptional behavior of these subjects is evidently the beginning of a change in Dogrib and Slave away from patterning based strictly on transitivity.

Kaska shows a strikingly clear link between **y**- marking and transitivity. In

Kaska, **y**- marks third-person direct objects, while **b**- marks third-person oblique objects:

Kaska

(147) a. Yestsen.
      y-1sS-imp-smell
      'I smell it/him/her.' (Moore 2001)

    b. ... yedehsı̨.
           y-1sS-imp-tell
      'I said to him, ... ' (Moore 1999: 19)

    c. Nayedéhgu'.
      y-3S-pf-spill
      'She spilled it.' (Moore 1999: 11)

    d. I   dene   détsédle,   yedéhhı̄n   géhdı̄.
      that person that small y-3S-pf-kill 3pS-imp-say
      'That small person killed it, they say.' (Moore 1999: 29)

These examples show that **y**- is the general third-person direct object inflection, regardless of the person of the subject. (As Moore 2001 notes, certain verbs don't allow **y**- except with third-person subjects. 'Eat' is one such verb:

(148) Estsets/*Yestsets.
      1sS-imp-eat
      'I eat it.' (Moore 2001: 550)

These remnants represent the common Athapaskan pattern.) On the other hand, third-person oblique objects are marked by **b**-:

(149) a. Mets'úguseséyí.
      b-1sS-pf-cut open
      'I cut it open.' (Moore 1999: 13)

    b. Megấnahtãn.
      b-2pS-imp-watch
      'You all watch it.' (Moore 1999: 39)

    c. Mets'egúhtsehí.
      b-3S-pf-cut up
      'She cut it up.' (Moore 1999: 11)

    d. K'á'   kū   **meyāgelehı.**
       arrow also   b-to-3pS-pf-give [pl O]
       'They gave him arrows, too.' (Moore 1999: 25)

The rare exceptions show **y-** as oblique object when the subject is third person:

(150)   **Yeyēnezen.**
        y-3S-imp-love
        'She/He loves him/her.' (Moore 2001: 571)

    For this case-based reanalysis of **y-** and **b-** in Kaska to have taken place, **y-** must be understood to be the prototypical mark of a direct object. The prototypical direct object occurs in an agentive context. With this understanding, we regard the examples in this section as showing effects of grammaticalization based on this prototype.[32]

2.4 *B-* as Object Inflection

In the context of Kaska, we revisit our discussion of **b-** in section 1, where we argued that **b-** as object inflection occurs in those contexts in which **y-** is not licensed. Recognizing that **y-** is the marked option, we analyze **b-** as default third-person object agreement.

2.4.1 *Oblique Objects*

In much of the previous discussion, which is focused on sentences with third-person subjects, **b-** emerges as a contrastive form, used in preference to **y-** in special circumstances. In many contexts, the patterning of **b-** is not contrastive. This fact is very plain in the Kaska data in the previous section. In other languages, when the subject is first or second person, third-person oblique objects must be marked by **b-**. This pronominal form is realized as a labial **b, m, u, w,** or **v** in cognates throughout the family.

Ahtna

(151)   **Bako'ehı.**
        'I am afraid of him.' (Kari 1990: 279)

Slave

(152)   **Bets'ę́**   goyıde.
        b-to   1sS-pf-talk
        'I talked to him/her/it'

Navajo

(153)   Bık'ıısdzıl.

'I provide for them.' (Young and Morgan 1987: 210)

Based on the choice of oblique object marking in intransitive clauses with non-third-person subjects, Rice (2000b) argues that **b**- cannot always be understood as an indicator of topic in Slave. If **b**- were a topic marker, then the oblique objects with first-and second-person subjects would always be topics, an unlikely situation.[33]

Further, when the subject is first or second person, more than one **b**- can be present, as in the following examples:

Navajo

(154)   Bee   **b**ıł   hweeshne'.
         b-about b-with   1sS-pf-talk

'I told him about it.' (Young and Morgan 1987: 29)

Slave

(155)   Béyıge   **b**ets'ę́   goyıde.
         b-into   b-to   1sS-pf-talk

'I talked to him on it [telephone].' (Rice 1989: 277 (adapted))

In Navajo and Slave, there are no alternatives to these expressions with **y**- or zero in place of **b**-. Assuming that a single topic per clause is the unmarked situation, it isn't workable to regard **b**- as always an indicator of a topic.

This finding supports our claim that **b**- is the unmarked third-person affix. By our analysis, **y**- is limited and occurs only when licensed by a proper licensor: otherwise, the mark of the third person is **b**-.

2.4.2 *Direct Objects*

In fact, another option exists for the realization of third persons: no inflection at all. Third-person subjects are typically unmarked, as are third-person direct objects in clauses with non-third-person subjects. There is thus another alternation to be considered in this section, that between zero and **b**- as markers of direct objects.

Across the family, when the subject is first or second person, a pronominal direct object is typically phonologically null. The following verbs have identifiable subject inflection, but there is no mark of the pronominal direct object.[34]

Ahtna

(156)   Tnııłt'ot.

'I kissed her [once].' (Kari 1990: 351)

Koyukon

(157)   Nıtl'aanh.

'I am looking at him/her.' (Thompson 1989a: 45)

Dogrib

(158)   Wetakwì̧ı̧hk'ah.

b-in-head-2sS-move O roughly

'Dunk his head in it.' (lit. dunk him in it headwise) (P. Rabesca, pers. comm., 2001)

Slave

(159)   Ráreyıht'u.

'I hit him/her/it.' (Rice 1978)

Tsuut'ina

(160)   Nànìsgás.

'I'll brush him down.' (Cook 1980: 199)

Navajo

(161)   Nanı́łté.

'You are carrying it/him/her [anim O] around.' (Young and Morgan 1987: 65g)

Overt marking through the use of **b-** is also possible, as we see later. Thompson says that the direct object in the Koyukon (162) is understood "as being especially topical, perhaps contrastive" in comparison with (157) above lacking **b-** (Thompson 1989a: 45). The same is true of the Dogrib pair (158) and (163), where there is said to be emphasis on *him* in (163), with **b-** as direct object (realized as **w-** in Dogrib).

Koyukon

(162)   **B**ınıtl'aanh.

'I am looking at him/her.' (Thompson 1989a: 45)

Dogrib

(163)   Wetakwìw̧ı̧hk'ah.

b-in-head-b-2sS-move O roughly

'Dunk his head in it.' (lit. dunk him in it headwise) (P. Rabesca, pers. comm. 2001)

Slave

(164) Míhchú.

'I married her.' (Thom and Blondin-Townsend 1987: 21)

Tsuut'ina

(165) Mínìcùɬ

'You're blowing it.' (Cook 1980: 202)

Navajo

(166) Bɪníɬdaas.

'You're seating him.' (Young and Morgan 1987: 65g)

These examples can be contrasted with those in section 2.2, showing **y-** for object inflection when the subject is third person.

When can **b-** occur as direct object agreement with a first-or second-person subject? In Slave and Koyukon, **b-** can (but need not) occur if the object is third-person human or, at least in Slave, possesses human-like capabilities. (See Rice 1989: 627, 1007; Rice 2000a, 2000b, 2000c for discussion.) Evidence on Navajo from Young and Morgan (1987) shows that **b-** occurs marking direct object in the derived causative construction only, and only if the derived object is animate. This can be seen very clearly by comparing causatives of classificatory verbs. If the classificatory verb requires a human or animate argument, then with a first- or second-person subject **b-** can occur in the causative form (167)–(168). If it requires a nonanimate argument, then **b-** is not found (170)–(172). The verb is in boldface in the following examples:

Navajo

(167) Tsɪn bɪgaan bɪkáa'gɪ ɬééchąą yázhí dah
      tree 3-branch 3-on puppy above
      bɪséɬtį̜go . . .
      b-1sS-imp-keep [anim O] lying-conj

      'As I was holding the puppy lying on a tree branch . . . ' (Young & Morgan 1987: 245)

(168) 'Awéé' chɪdí bɪkáa'gɪ dah
      baby car 3-on top of above
      bɪséɬdáago 'anɪhɪ'doolkɪd.
      b-1sS-imp-keep [anim O] seated-conj 1p-pf-be photographed

      'Our picture was taken with me holding the baby in a sitting position on top of the car.' (Young and Morgan 1987: 245)

The verbs in these examples are inflected with **b-**. However, if the object is animate, **b-** marking is not always found:

(169) 'Azhą̄   doo   nıhılééchąą'í   da   ndı   t'áá
       even   Neg   1p-dog   neg   though   just
       sııltį́.
       1pS-imp-keep [anim O]

       'We keep him [here] even though he's not our dog.' (Young and Morgan 1987: 685)

With inanimate objects, the object is necessarily unmarked morphologically:

(170) Tó dılchxoshí   'aáłahjı'   **séł'ą̄,**   hoghandı.
       pop   always   1sS-imp-keep [chunky O]   house-in

       'I always keep pop [on hand] at home.' (Young and Morgan 1987: 685)

(171) Mą'ıı   bınııyé   hooghandı   bee'eldǫǫh   **séłtą̄.**
       coyote   3-for   house-in   gun   1sS-imp-keep [stick O]

       'I keep a gun at home for coyotes.' (Young and Morgan 1987: 685)

(172) 'Áłchíní   'ólta'déę̄'   nát'áazhgo   yıdooyı́ı̨ł   bınııyé
       child   school-from   3S-imp-return [du]-conj   3-fut-eat   3-for
       'atoo'   ła'   **séłką̄.**
       stew   some   1sS-imp-keep [contained O]

       'I keep some stew on hand for the two children to eat when they get home from school.' (Young and Morgan 1987: 685)

Rice (2000b) argues for Slave that the difference between **b-** and zero as direct object inflection has to do with the surface position of the object, with **b-** marking only those objects in [Spec, AgrOP]. Slave does not offer strong syntactic evidence in support of this proposal because, as noted, **b-** and an overt object noun phrase may not cooccur in this language. Word-order facts go against this analysis for Navajo (see (167), (170)).

What seems to be making the difference is a semantic distinction. In all of the languages we have examined, with the exception of Tsuut'ina (see (165)),[35] direct objects marked by **b-** invariably represent human or animate entities.[36] As we see in the previous section, **b-** also always marks oblique third person objects in the contexts where **y-** is ruled out. The Athapaskan facts then very closely parallel the situation in some dialects of Spanish and in Hindi (Aissen 2003) where the case marking of some direct objects—notably human direct objects—is identical to the ordinary marking of indirect objects. While we do not have a convincing structural account of the facts in Athapaskan languages, it is certainly significant that the patterning is not unique to this family.

3 THE LICENSING OF Y-

3.1 The Common Pattern: [Spec, NumP] as Licensor

Developing ideas from Saxon (1984, 1986), Rice and Saxon (1991, 1994), and Saxon and Rice (1993), we have assumed in this chapter that the distribution of the disjoint anaphor **y-** is limited by a structural licensing condition as shown in (173). This condition is common to all of the languages we know about, with the exceptions of Kaska, Hupa, and Kato:[37]

(173)   *y-* Licensing (Athapaskan)
        A DP α in [Spec, NumP] licenses **y-** inflection for a noncoreferential
        third-person clausemate DP β that it c-commands:

   a.   Apachean: β may be any DP.

   b.   Babine-Witsuwit'en: β must be definite.

   c.   Other languages: β must be pronominal.

We understand the conditions on β, the referent of **y-**, to reflect lexical properties of the affix in the languages in question. For Apachean, **y-** has the feature [third person]. For Babine-Witsuwit'en, it has the features [third person, definite] and for the other languages [third person, definite, pronominal]. Our discussion in section 1.4 supports this characterization.

Our focus here, however, is not on the subconditions that distinguish Apachean and Babine-Witsuwit'en from the rest of the family but, rather, on the licensor α. As (173) indicates, the classic situation is for a third-person canonical subject to license **y-** as an object or possessor. (In our view, this situation parallels the case of languages in which a reflexive anaphor must be licensed by a subject.) The remainder of this section is devoted to showing the range of possibilities that exist beyond this.

3.2 Object as Licensor

In Apachean, Slave, and Dogrib, the licensor of **y-** is strictly limited to subjects.
Y- agreement is never found in the absence of a third-person subject. The Slave
examples that follow are representative of these languages:

Slave

(174)   a.   Begháni?ǫ.
                b-to-1sS-pf-give [chunky O]
                'I gave it to him/her.'

         b.   *Begháyeni?ǫ
                b-to-y-1sS-pf-give [chunky O]
                (I gave it to him/her.)

In other branches of the family, objects may serve as licensors of **y-** under certain
conditions. (Compare the case of English, which permits an object to license a
reflexive, as in *I'm not going to introduce you to yourself!*) Continuing to regard
the licensing condition as governed by c-command, we offer a hierarchical account, while acknowledging that we are not able to resolve a number of questions.

We organize what follows in terms of the grammatical function of the referent
of **y-**.

3.2.1 Y- *as Object*

In ditransitive constructions in Koyukon, Ahtna, Dene Sųłiné (Chipewyan), and
Tsuut'ina with third-person direct and oblique objects and a non-third-person
subject, **y-** can appear marking the direct object. The licensor is the third-person
oblique object represented by **b-**.

Koyukon

(175)   **Bʉgh   yooghaskkaat.**
          b-from   y-1sS-pf-buy
          'I bought it from him/her.' (Thompson 1989a: 45)

(176)   **Betł'o   yens'oyh.**
          b-to   y-1sS-imp-give [chunky O]
          'I am giving it to him/her.' (Thompson 1989a: 45)

Ahtna

(177)   **Beydghełnen.**
          b-against-y-1sS-pf-strike
          'I struck it against it repeatedly.' (Kari 1990: 300)

Dene Sųłiné

(178) Bɛgháyénıłtı.

b-to-y-1sS-pf-give [anim O]

'I have given her to him.' (Li 1946: 419)

Tsuut'ina

(179) Mīts'ìʔ   yīdááʔóh.

b-to   y-1pS-send

'We will send him/her to him/her.' (Cook 1984: 205)

These data recall patterns in Kaska, where **y**- marks direct object and **b**- marks oblique objects. The structure being examined in this section is plausibly a stage in the grammaticalization which reaches its limit in Kaska, where properties of other event participants are immaterial to object forms. That is not the case here, however. Evidence from Koyukon, paralleled by the facts in the other languages, shows decisively that it is the third-person oblique object that is the licensor of **y**-, a point made clearly by Thompson (1989a):

Koyukon

(180) *yooghaskkaat

y-1sS-pf-buy

(I bought it.) (Thompson 1989a: 46)

The third-person direct object cannot be marked by **y**- in the absence of another third-person nominal in the clause, hence the ungrammaticality of this example. (Recall from section 2.3 how Kaska differs from all of the other languages of the family in permitting this pattern.) These facts show that the third-person property of the licensor is in the whole family ultimately more important to the patterning of **y**- than is grammatical function. This finding strongly supports the designation of **y**- as an obviative form, only occurring in contexts where there is more than one third-person nominal.

We propose that in Apachean and the languages like it, the licensor for **y**- must asymmetrically c-command **y**-. On the assumption that only the subject is in this hierarchical relation to other DPs in the clause, only the subject may license **y**-. In the other languages, the requirement is looser, and any c-commanding DP counts. In this case, an oblique object may license **y**- as a direct object. Both are within VP, so there is mutual c-command: this is all that is required.[38]

In Koyukon and Ahtna, however, there is an interesting trade-off between the featural content of the licensor and its grammatical function. A nonsubject noun phrase licenses **y**- (as in (175)–(179)) only if that licensing noun phrase is pronominal.[39] If the licensor is a subject, there is no such requirement. This is made clear by the ungrammaticality of (181) and the grammaticality of (182) (repeated):

Koyukon

(181)   *John   ghu   yooghaskkaat.
                 from   y-1sS-pf-buy

    (I bought it from John.) (Thompson 1989a: 46)

In (181) 'John', the oblique object, is a nonpronominal. This DP cannot license **y**-, and the example is ungrammatical.[40] When the licensor is a subject, no such restriction exists:

(182)   John   yeneeł'aanh.
                 y-3S-imp-look at

    'John is looking at him/her.' (Thompson 1996: 87)

(We will see further illustration of this contrast between subjects and nonsubjects in the following section.) Conceptually, we observe that the licensor of **y**- must have a certain level of prominence in the structure: it must be distinguished either hierarchically (as subject) or in terms of the discourse (as an entity identifiable by a pronominal). It is possible to give a structural account of this pairing, if the licensing positions are taken to be the VP-external subject and object positions: to explain the data in this section, one approach would be to say that the objects which license **y**- are those in [Spec, AgrOP], a position associated with overt agreement. Recall a similar proposal made for Slave in Rice (2001b), discussed before in connection with the choice of zero and **b**- for direct object inflection (section 2.4.2).

    However, the proposal has the same weakness as for Slave, and we cannot adopt it: because only pronominal objects trigger agreement in the languages under discussion, we do not have independent evidence apart from object agreement for the position of the object DP. In section 1.3, we used word order to establish the distinction between VP-internal and VP-external objects in Koyukon, so we feel that we have a firm footing for the broader structural proposal but less support in the treatment of pronominals. Therefore, we are at present without a structural account of these important findings and leave the problem for future research.

3.2.2 Y- *as Subject*

As shown by Thompson (1989a), **y**- has an additional role in Koyukon: it can be a subject marker. The following examples contrast sentences with zero-marked as opposed to **y**-marked subjects. In the examples, inflectional affixes referencing third persons are shown in bold type and indicated as well in the glosses. As far as interpretation goes, the two sentences in each pair differ in the reading of topicality. Thompson (1989a) identifies the construction in (a) as "direct" and the construction in (b) as "inverse." By a range of criteria discussed by Thompson, the subject of the (a) examples is the more topical nominal, while in the (b) examples the object is relatively topical:

Koyukon

(183)   a. **Y**ʉgh   neeneeyo.
      y-to   3S-pf-arrive walking [s]
      'She/He (zero) walked up to him/her (*y*-).' (Thompson 1989a: 40)

    b. **B**ʉgh   neeyeeneeyo.
      b-to   *y-pf-arrive walking [s]*
      'She/He (*y*-) walked up to him/her (*b*-).' (Thompson 1989a: 41)

(184)   a. **Y**ıneeł?aanh.
      y-3S-imp-look at
      'She/He (zero) is looking at him/her (*y*-).' (Thompson 1989a: 40)

    b. **B**ıyıneeł?aanh.
      b-y-imp-look at
      'She/He (*y*-) is looking at him/her (*b*-).' (Thompson 1989a: 40)

In the following examples taken from the *Koyukon Athabaskan Dictionary*, the glossing of the **y**-marked subject in (185b) as inanimate or nonhuman 'it' we take to be indicative of the reduced topicality of that subject in relation to the object:

(185)   a. **Y**edoltaał.
      y-3S-refl-imp-carry [anim O]
      'She/He (zero) is carrying it (*y*) for his/her own benefit.' (Jetté and Jones 2000: 93)

    b. **B**eyedoltaał.
      b-y-refl-imp-carry [anim O]
      'It (*y*) is carrying him/her (*b*) for its own benefit.' (Jetté and Jones 2000: 93)

As discussed in the preceding section, there are extra conditions on the licensing of **y**- if the licensor is not a canonical subject. Relevant here is the fact that **y**- cannot mark subject agreement if either the licensor or the licensee is an overt noun phrase rather than a pronoun. Thus, (186) is grammatical with zero subject marking but would be ungrammatical with a **y**-marked subject, in the absence of a pronominal object (Thompson 1989a: 39):[41]

(186) John ghu neeneeyo.
          to 3S-pf-walk

'She/He (zero) walked up to John.' (Thompson 1989a: 36)

Our analysis of **y**- as subject inflection depends on our earlier finding that subjects in Koyukon may remain internal to the VP. With the subject internal, an object may c-command it, giving the structural conditions required for the licensing of **y**-. The analysis of these examples is therefore the same as what we proposed in the preceding section for a **y**- object licensed by another object. The coincidence of a form and meaning contrast in these pairs we take as highly indicative of a structural contrast: we consider these examples strong evidence in support of our claim concerning subject and object positions.

According to our approach, the inverse constructions of Thompson's analysis involve internal subjects. In contrast, in the direct forms, the subject occupies the canonical subject position and, from this position, may license **y**- as an object but may not itself be marked by **y**-.

Ahtna allows **y**- as a subject in the same contexts as does Koyukon: Kari (1990: 57) notes that **y**- functions as "third person, non-topical subject." The **y**-subject occurs when a third-person pronominal direct or postpositional object is present in the same simple clause. The subject is understood as less topical than the object:

Ahtna

(187) **Bıınał'aen.**
        b-y-imp-look at

'It is looking at him.' (Kari 1990: 96)

In this example, **b**- is the direct object prefix, and it licenses **y**- as subject.[42] Pronominal postpositional objects may also license subject **y**-, again as in Koyukon.[43]

Ahtna

(188) **Bayuzdlaex.**
        b-past-y-pf-swim

'It [fish] swam past him.' (Kari 1990: 274)

(189) U'eł   yayaał.
        Cb-with y-prog-walk

'She/He is walking with him/her.' (Kari 1990: 419)

(190) **Ba**   tayghıghel.
       b-at   y-pf-fall in water
       'It fell in the water on him.' (Kari 1990: 217)

(191) **Uk'e'e**   yıghıłtsı'ı.
       b-less   y-imp-be small
       'She/He is smaller than him/her.' (Kari 1990: 419)

As Kari (1990: 419) remarks, **y**- occurs in an intransitive verb only in the presence of a pronominal object. If the object takes the form of a full DP, **y**- cannot occur:

(192) Dghelaay   taa   zdaa.
       mountain   among   3S-imp-stay
       'She/He stays in the mountains.' (Kari 1990: 326)

The restriction is the same as we saw in section 3.2.1 for third-person objects licensing a **y**- object. Only a pronominal object licenses **y**- marking of nominals inside the VP.[44]

(In an example like (189), an animate agentive subject is predicted to raise to [Spec, NumP], according to the generalization in (49). The discussion in the current section entails that subject raising depends on the topic status of subjects in a way not provided for previously.)

The crucial role of the pronominal form is evident from a further possibility in both Koyukon and Ahtna: a pronominal possessor may license **y**- as subject agreement. In the two Koyukon examples that follow, the possessor within a nonsubject argument of the verb licenses **y**- subject marking:

Koyukon
(193) **Bıtloogh**   yıtl'akk.
       b-hair   y-imp-comb
       'She/He (*y*) is combing his/her (*b*) hair.' (Thompson 1989a: 41)

(194) **Beyeh**   yeeldo.
       b-house   y-imp-stay
       'She/He (*y*) is staying at his/her (*b*) house.' (Jetté and Jones 2000: 93)

In the Ahtna examples that follow, the licensing DPs are the pronominal possessor of the object of **gha** 'to, at' in (195) and the pronominal possessor of the complement to **laen** 'be' in (196) (Kari 1990: 252):

Ahtna

(195) **Uzuuł**   gha   nıyıtkay.
       b-windpipe to   y-pf-leap

       'It leaped at his/her neck.' (Kari 1990: 419)

(196) **Bez'ae**   yılaen.
       b-uncle   y-imp-be

       'He is his/her uncle.' (Kari 1990: 419)

Such examples pose a problem in the theory of anaphors, which we have been implicitly assuming (see, for example, Chomsky 1986). We have argued that the pronominal **b-** licenses **y-** from a c-commanding position, taking **y-** to be a form that requires a c-commanding licensor. According to any interpretation of c-command, the c-command domain of a possessor will not extend beyond the DP properly containing the possessor. Yet we find here that a **y-** subject is licensed by a possessor structurally at a distance from it.

Interestingly, parallel facts have been observed in Mandarin (Tang 1989). (See also Maling 1984 on Icelandic.) In certain circumstances in Mandarin, the possessor within a subject can serve as the licensor for a reflexive elsewhere in the clause, as in (197) and (198):

Mandarin

(197) [Zhangsan   de   jiaoao] hai   le   **ziji**.
       (name)   DE   pride   hurt   pf   self

       'Zhangsan's pride hurt him [lit. himself].' (Tang 1989: 103)

(198) [[Zhangsan   de   tuisang]   de   yangzi]   shi   **ziji**   de
                     DE   depression DE   manner   make self   DE

       fumu   hen   danxin.
       parents   very   worried

       'Zhangsan's depression worried his [lit. self's] parents.' (Tang 1989: 106)

Tang (1989) proposes the term "subcommand" to encompass "c-command" and also the extension of c-command by which a relation is defined between a possessor, its containing DP, and other DPs in a structure.[45] The licensing condition for Ahtna and Koyukon can be stated in terms of subcommand, as in (199):

(199) **Licensing conditions on y- (Ahtna and Koyukon)**
       A third-person DP α licenses **y-** agreement for a clausemate DP β that it subcommands. If α is not in a subject position, α must be pronominal.

In this case, the possibility for a possessor licensing subject **y-** is provided for.

In Tsuut'ina, resembling Ahtna and Koyukon, **y-** can occur as subject agreement, as noted by Cook (1984: 201) and Thompson (1989a: 212–213):

Tsuut'ina

(200)   **Māyīt'ìh.**
      b-to-y-imp-like
      'It does like him/her.' (Cook 1984: 201)

In this example, the oblique pronominal object **b-** licenses **y-** as a subject prefix—by hypothesis, a subject in the internal subject position. This form can be used only in the case of a nonhuman subject. In this it recalls facts in the Alaskan languages already discussed, and it suggests that conditions similar to what we have previously seen govern licensors for **y-** as well as subject movement in Tsuut'ina.

We have found no evidence for **y-** functioning as a subject in languages such as Navajo and Slave or Dogrib. In other words, pairs such as the following are not found in these languages:

Slave

(201)   a. **Yets'ę́**   nínįya.
         y-to   3S-pf-walk [s]
         'She/He walked up to him/her.'

       b. *****Bets'ę́**   níyénįya.
           b-to   y-3S-pf-walk [s]
           (She/He/It walked up to him/her.)

(202)   a. **Ráyereyįta.**
         y-3S-pf-kicked
         'She/He kicked him/her.'

       b. *****Rábeyereyįta.**
           b-y-pf-kicked
           (She/He/It kicked him/her.)

If in these languages only external subjects can license **y-**, then this gap is expected. In contrast, for Koyukon and Ahtna, any c-commanding third-person noun phrase can license **y-**, and thus **y-** can occur as subject agreement when it is internal.

Jeff Leer (1990), working together with Eliza Jones, documents the full range of possibilities in Koyukon for subject and object inflection with ditransitive verbs. It is instructive to consider their paradigms. (In the translations, each argument is labeled as to its inflectional form in the Koyukon sentence. We also include Leer's indication of the relative positions of the three arguments of the verb on a hierarchy of salience.)[46]

Koyukon

(203)   a. **Yetl'o**   **yeghee'onh.** (S > DO, S <> PO)
        y-to   y-3S-pf-give [chunky O]

        'He (zero) gave it (*y-*) to her/it (*y-*).' (Leer 1990: 35)

    b. **Betl'o**   **yeyeghee'onh.** (S <> DO, S < PO)
        b-to   y-y-pf-give [chunky O]

        'He (*y*) gave it (*y-*) to her/it (*b-*).' (Leer 1990: 35)

These sentences involve the verb meaning 'give [chunky O]', whose object will be inanimate. That object will be no more salient than the subject or the object of the postposition. When the postpositional object is most salient, it is marked by **b-** with **y-** marking the other arguments. Other possibilities exist with the verb meaning 'give [animate O]':

(204)   a. **Yetl'o**   **yegheełtaanh.** (S <> DO, S <> PO)
        y-to   y-3S-pf-give [anim O]

        'He (zero) gave him (*y-*) to her/it (*y-*).' (Leer 1990: 35)

    b. **Yetl'o**   **beyegheełtaanh.** (S < DO, S <> PO)
        y-to   b-y-pf-give [anim O]

        'It (*y*) gave him (*b-*) to it (*y-*).' (Leer 1990: 35)

    c. **Betl'o**   **beyegheełtaanh.** (S < DO, S < PO)
        b-to   b-y-pf-give [anim O]

        'It (*y*) gave him (*b-*) to her (*b-*).' (Leer 1990: 35)

Leer describes the patterns in the (b) and (c) examples thus: "The cases where the subject (S) is . . . lower on the hierarchy than one of the non-subjects (DO or PO) are marked with *ye-* for the subject and *be-* for the non-subject(s)" (Leer 1990: 35). By our account these cases involve a VP-internal subject. Marking of this subject by **y-** can be licensed by either the pronominal direct or oblique object which c-commands it within VP. The objects can likewise appear as **y-**, being c-commanded by either of the other arguments of the verb.

    Notice from (204c) that Koyukon permits two instances of the **b-** pronominal in the environment of a VP-internal subject, as in Navajo and other languages.

Here, as for Navajo, this fact argues against a treatment of **b**- as a proximate form or as the marker of the sole topic of a sentence. Leer (1990) argues that the patterns seen are difficult to categorize as direct or inverse, because of the multiplicity of options available.

3.3 Hupa Reflexes of y- and b-

In all of the languages examined here except for Kaska, **y**-, whatever its grammatical function, occurs only in clauses that contain at least two third-person noun phrases. This fact is important in motivating our analysis of **y**- as essentially an anaphor in the Binding Theory understanding of this term. Hupa stands apart from this generalization, as the sentence in (205) shows:

(205)   yıWıłcis.

       y-1sO-imp-see

       'It sees me.' (Golla 1970: 99)

In this example, there are two participants in the event, but only one of them, the experiencer subject, is third person. This subject is marked by *y*-, and the first person singular direct object by *W*-.

    The conclusion that **y**- in Hupa is different is confirmed by the following examples, in which it functions as the subject of an intransitive verb.

(206)   Nayxe'ıne:W.

       y-imp-speak again [cust]

       'It always speaks again.' (Golla 1970: 99)

(207)   Yıwınchwıw.

       y-pf-cry

       'It cried.' (Thompson 1996: 93)

The *y*- form is restricted to marking subjects that are nonhuman or nontopical (Golla 1970, 1985; Thompson 1996). A form *ch'*- is the standard marker for third-person human subjects. In Hupa, then, the lexical specifications for **y**- contrast with those in the other languages. See Rice and Saxon (1993) for further discussion of this change from the Athapaskan prototype.

    Hupa also has a reflex of **b**-. Hupa *m*- indicates a nonhuman oblique object or possessor, contrasting with *y*- in case:

(208) **M**ıq'ıt ts'ısday.
      b-on 3HS-imp-sit

      'She/He is sitting/staying on it.' (Golla 1985: 65; Thompson 1996: 92)

(209) Dıgyaŋ **m**ıq'eh ch'ıteloːy'.
      here b-on 3HS-pf-lead

      'He led it along here.' (Golla 1970: 308)

(210) Xoŋ' **m**ınaːd na'xote'ıwıW hay k'yıteːt'aw.
      fire b-around 3HO-3pHS-imp-carry doctor

      'They carry the doctor around the fire.' (Golla 1970: 308)

It never appears as a direct object, nonhuman direct objects always being marked by zero in Hupa:

(211) Weːwahs.

      'I shaved it.' (Golla 1970: 105)

In Hupa, as in Kaska, the **y**-/**b**- contrast has been reinterpreted as a case contrast, limited in Hupa to nonhuman participants. In the two languages, **y**- marks direct verbal arguments: in Hupa, subjects; in Kaska, direct objects.

4 PARAMETERS IN THIRD-PERSON INFLECTION IN ATHAPASKAN LANGUAGES

We have tried to show in this chapter that Athapaskan languages are all made of the same fabric, despite the tailoring over time that has resulted in different-shaped garments.

Our major goal has been to make as strong a case as possible that the languages can be analyzed in terms of a common phrase structure and structural relations. As is clear at the end of this endeavor, third-person inflection has had an enormous role. This follows partly from a lack of other types of evidence—from word order, the placement of PPs and adverbials, the positioning of functional heads, or from more nuanced semantic interpretations—which we hope will emerge in future studies; partly it is because of the tremendous riches of previous works on **y**- and **b**-.

In this section we assemble our findings and identify parameters of difference among members of the family. We start with our frame—the functional categories that make up the extended projection of the Athapaskan VP.

4.1 Functional Categories

In section 1, recapitulating several of our earlier works, we argued for the functional projections AgrO, NumP, and AgrS, basing our arguments on the existence of paradigms of inflectional forms, on assumptions about the properties of idioms and incorporation, on word order, and on patterns of subject-object inflectional relationships. The essential motivation for these categories we take as the inflectional paradigms.

The languages differ only in specifics concerning the highest of these functional projections: under the term "AgrSP," it accommodates the discourse-linked first- and second-person subject forms; under the term "DiscP," it accommodates these and a discourse-linked third-person nonsubject. Following a suggestion in Willie (2000), we believe that the diagnostic for DiscP is a *yi-/bi-* alternation paralleling the Navajo contrast in (212), repeated from previously:

Navajo

(212) a. yɪzts'ǫs 'She/He kissed him/her.'

   b. bɪzts'ǫs 'She/He was kissed by him/her.' (Platero 1978: 119–120)

By this test, the languages we have examined are distinguished as follows:

(213) **AgrSP**   **DiscP**

   Mackenzie   Apachean
      Slave   Navajo
      Dogrib   Jicarilla Apache
      Dene Sųłiné   Alaskan
   Tsuut'ina   Ahtna
   Babine-Witsuwit'en   Koyukon
                        Dena'ina

(Our diagnostic is not applicable to Hupa [Pacific Coast] or Kaska [Yukon] because of their innovations in the lexical status of **y-** and **b-**.)

We do not understand exactly how a child is cued to the grammatical distinction. We assume that the semantic properties of the discourse-linked third person marked by **b-** in (212b) are critical to the setting of the parameter, as well as the potential for [O S **b**-V] word orders that exist in most of the languages

analyzed with DiscP. We note that Slave and Dogrib, with their recent innovations, allow the contrast represented in (214):

Dogrib
(214)   a. Rachel ayįlà. 'Rachel did it.'

      b. Dehko awįlà. 'A cold got him.'

Here the alternation in object form depends entirely on the contrast in the
subject DPs, a fact that we take to be essential to distinguishing (214) from (212).
It remains to be seen whether these languages will eventually be reanalyzed as
having DiscP rather than AgrSP—that is, permitting discourse-linked third-
person objects to occupy a distinguished phrase structure position shared with
first-and second-person subjects.

4.2 Subject Raising

We assume that all subjects are merged into the structure within the VP. Because
of the demands of first- and second-person agreement morphology in the head
of AgrSP (or DiscP), first- and second-person subjects must raise to the specifier
position of this category. Of more interest are third-person subjects, which show
cross-linguistic variability in their patterning across the family. In the following
table, repeated from section 1.2.4, we show how animacy and agency properties
of the subjects influence their potential for raising to [Spec, NumP].

(215) **Subject positions and semantic properties of subjects**

Properties of subjects	Agentive		Nonagentive	
	Language	Position	Language	Position
Animate	All languages	[Spec, NumP]	Navajo	[Spec, NumP]
			Ahtna	Variable
			Slave/Dogrib	Variable
Inanimate	Ahtna	[Spec, VP]	All languages	[Spec, VP]
	Navajo	Variable		
	Slave/Dogrib	Variable		

Naturally from (215) we ask: From what is subject raising predictable? The suggestion of an answer comes from the fact that in Navajo only animate (actually,
human) nouns can be specified for singular as opposed to plural number (Young
and Morgan 1987: 7–8 grammar; 492, 804), as in (216):

Navajo

(216) a. 'ashkıı 'boy'   'ashııké 'boys'

       b. hádı 'one's older sister'   hádí ké 'one's older sisters'

       c. shınálí 'my son's child'   shınálíké 'my son's children'

       d. shık'éí 'my relative'   shık'éíyóó 'my relatives'

Saxon (2001) assumes that features of Num⁰ attract only a subset of nouns, including those inflectable for number, and derives the restriction against inanimate subjects in [Spec, NumP] from this. There are a couple of difficulties with this approach. First, animate nouns rather than the narrower class of human nouns are the ones affected by subject raising, a matter without a direct explanation. Second, inanimate nouns that are understood to have a degree of agency may also be moved to [Spec, NumP].

The proposal for Navajo can be extended to the family more generally, but with the same problems. Next we show data from Koyukon (Jetté and Jones 2000: 323, 715)[47] and Slave (Rice 1989: 247f.) parallel to (216):

Koyukon

(217) a. be'o 'his wife'   be'o kkaa 'his wives'

       b. sode 'my older sister'   sode kkaa 'my older sister and her family'

       c. sode 'my older sister'   sode yoo 'my older sisters'

       d. denaa 'person'   denaa yoo 'people'

       e. eenaa' 'mother'   eenaa' kkaa yoo 'mom and the family'

Slave

(218) a. seya 'my son'   seyake 'my sons'

       b. t'eere 'girl'   t'eereke 'girls'

       c. dene 'person'   deneke 'people'

As in Navajo, DPs referring to humans may be inflected with the plural suffix, but not other DPs. We must ask, How do these facts contribute to restrictions on raising to [Spec, NumP]?

A further problem exists for languages like Ahtna and Koyukon in which even human agentive nominals may remain within VP if they are not topical. (See discussion in section 3.2.2.) For these languages, it is necessary to associate with Num⁰ a feature that will attract a subject to [Spec, NumP] only if it has certain properties defined over discourse structure. Given that [Spec, NumP] is the canonical (third person) subject position, and given that canonical subjects are also usually topics, this suggestion is not wildly unreasonable.

We proposed [Spec, AgrOP] as a position outside VP for moved objects (section 1.3); it remains for future research to explore the factors that determine object movement to this position.

4.3 Properties and Licensing of y-

As subjects in [Spec, NumP] license the disjoint anaphor **y-** for object marking in all languages apart from Hupa and Kaska, the incidence of **y-** depends on subject raising. In section 3.1, we gave the following summary of some of the properties of **y-** licensing:

(219) *y-* **Licensing (Athapaskan)**
       A DP α in [Spec, NumP] licenses **y-** inflection for a noncoreferential third-person clausemate DP β which it c-commands.

    a. Apachean: β may be any DP.

    b. Babine-Witsuwit'en: β must be definite.

    c. Other languages: β must be pronominal.

This characterization needs to be supplemented, following the additional findings of section 3. We turn first to the properties of the referent of **y-**.

In elaborating on (219), we consider first the ϕ-features of **y-** It is invariably a third-person inflectional form, but notable differences in what classes of DPs it shows agreement with exist across the family:

(220) ϕ-features of **y-** "third-person nonnominative inflection"
    a. Apachean, (Dena'ina): third person

    b. Babine-Witsuwit'en: third person, definite

    c. Mackenzie, Tsuut'ina, Kaska, Ahtna, Koyukon: third person, pronoun

The specifications in (220) show that except in Apachean and Dena'ina, **y-** marks agreement only with definite or pronominal DPs.

As far as case features go, there are three classes of languages:

(221) **Case features of *y-* "third-person nonnominative inflection"**

Accusative	*Objective*	*Nonnominative*
Kaska	Mackenzie	Tsuut'ina

Apachean   Babine-Witsuwit'en
                Alaskan
                Ahtna
                Koyukon
                Dena'ina
                Tanacross

In none of the languages does **y**- mark a canonical subject.[48] (We are not taking a position on the structural position of subject DPs in Hupa, and therefore we leave Hupa out of (221), referring the reader to section 3.3.) We take this to mean that **y**- has other than nominative case; it therefore cannot appear in [Spec, NumP] but must appear lower in the tree.[49] In Tsuut'ina and Ahtna, Koyukon, Dena'ina, and Tanacross, four languages of Alaska, **y**- is unrestricted in its non-nominative case. In Kaska, with rare exceptions detailed in section 2.3, **y**- is limited to accusative case. In the other languages, **y**- marks accusative or oblique object case.[50] As with the features outlined in (220), we consider those in (221) to be inherent features of **y**- in particular languages.

The languages differ in another respect: the nature of the licensor of **y**-. Saxon (1995) suggested that the obviative character of the reflex of **y**- in Dogrib, the "disjoint anaphor," is due to the complex internal structure of the pronominal, such that it carries an anaphoric feature specification for number, which must be bound by the clausal Num projection. The consequence of this is that Dogrib *y*-must be licensed by the DP in [Spec, NumP] and so is a dependent form understood in relation to the canonical subject. "Obviative" seems an appropriate term, given that both *y*- and its licensor must be third persons.

We propose to extend this analysis to Slave and the Apachean languages, which show the same pattern. In Hupa and Kaska, **y**- is not obviative: it is an independent form that appears whenever its own referential and case requirements can be satisfied, regardless of the presence of any other DPs in the clause. In the remaining languages, **y**- is obviative, but these languages differ from Dogrib in the licensor: as argued in section 3.2, a licensor within VP is possible, as long as it subcommands **y**- and is third person. We propose for these languages, too, that **y**- has a complex internal structure that includes an anaphoric element requiring a third-person antecedent. Our typology of obviation is shown in (222):

(222)   **Internal structure for *y*-: Properties of obviation**

Not obviative	**Obviative**	
No anaphoric element	*Anaphoric Num*	*Anaphoric 3*
Hupa	Slave, Dogrib	Dene Sųłiné
Kaska	Apachean	Tsuut'ina
		Babine-Witsuwit'en
		Alaskan

> Ahtna
> Koyukon
> Tanacross
> Dena'ina

In Dene Sųłiné, Tsuut'ina, Babine-Witsuwit'en, and the Alaskan languages Ahtna, Koyukon, Tanacross, and Dena'ina, the licensor for **y**- can be a canonical subject or a subcommanding object or possessor. We have not given an account here of the important fact introduced in section 3.2.1 that a nonsubject licensor for **y**- must be pronominal. This fact is very significant, but we are at a loss as to how to accommodate it in our analysis.

The features for **y**- that are laid out in (220)–(222) we understand to be inherent features of the form from which its behavior is determined. Variation across the three sets of properties yields quite an array of possibilities for **y**- in particular languages. Consider, for example, Dene Sųłine from the Mackenzie group, which includes also Slave and Dogrib. Dene Sųłine *y*- shares all its referential and case properties with its counterparts in Slave and Dogrib but permits a nonsubject licensor as shown in (222). In the set of four languages from Alaska, Dena'ina stands apart from Ahtna, Koyukon, and Tanacross only in that Dena'ina *y*- allows nonpronominal referents (220) while its counterparts do not. The variation that we can describe by disentangling ɸ-features from case and licensing features gives us confidence in the approach we have taken, as it is possible to imagine paths of diachronic change in **y**- that have resulted in the current picture.

NOTES

We acknowledge the great number of people who have contributed to this work by providing data, advice, suggestions, criticisms, and commentary, especially Judith Aissen, Sandra Chung, Henry Davis, Rose-Marie Déchaine, Ted Fernald, Victor Golla, Ken Hale, Sharon Hargus, Gary Holton, Nicole Horseherder, Eloise Jelinek, Alana Johns, S.-Y. Kuroda, Jeff Leer, Patrick Moore, Ellavina Perkins, Philip Rabesca, Betsy Ritter, Peggy Speas, Chad Thompson, Mary Willie, and Martina Wiltschko. We apologize to the people whose names we have missed. We have not been able to assimilate the findings of Hale (2003) and Jelinek and Carnie (2003) into the present chapter, but we hope that our work can be shown to support theirs.

In the 13 years and more that this chapter has steeped, we have received a tremendous amount of support and help, including the financial support of the University of Toronto, the University of Victoria, Memorial University of Newfoundland, the Dogrib Community Services Board (formerly the Dogrib Divisional Board of Education), the Social Sciences and Humanities Research Council of Canada (for grants to Leslie Saxon), the Killam Foundation (for a fellowship to Keren Rice), and the many universities and other organizations through which we have been invited to speak about this work.

    1. Our earliest work on this subject was done in 1991 in a paper prepared for the Athabaskan meeting held at the University of California, Santa Cruz. This present section depends heavily on that unpublished work. We are very grateful to participants at the conference for their contributions to our thinking, then and in the long interval since.

    2. We do not give a full analysis here of noun incorporation, which in Athapaskan languages may encompass the incorporation of subjects. (But see Rice 2000c: 68ff.) We discuss noun incorporation as an argument for our approach in section 1.1.2.

    3. This argument was originally given in Rice and Saxon (1994).

    4. We adopt the spellings of the original sources. As the sources make clear, these are usually orthographic and less commonly phonetic. C' represents an ejective consonant, and accents mark tone. Nasalization is frequently shown with the Polish hook. Verbs show primary marking for aspect and tense and reflect agreement with subjects and objects. Verbs of location or transfer and some others include lexical specification of attributes of the theme argument, indicated in square brackets after the verbal gloss, as in 'be located [pl O]'. Abbreviations are as listed here:

1	first person
2	second person
3	third person
A	areal prefix
anim	animate
conj	conjunction
cust	customary
d	dual
Dim	diminutive
DO	direct object
emph	emphatic
fut	future
H	human
imp	imperfective
Iter	iterative
Neg	negative
O	object
OO	oblique object
pst	past
pl	plural
pf	perfective
prog	progressive
Q	question marker
Refl	reflexive
s	singular
S	subject
U	unspecified participant

While we sometimes give detailed morphemic glossing of verbal forms as in the Ahtna verb *sızkat* 'he/she slapped me', it is not always possible to provide detailed segmentation for them on account of portmanteauism and prosodically marked elements. With this Ahtna verb, the verb stem 'slap' is *-kat, sı-* marks first-person singular direct object, and *z-* marks perfective viewpoint in an accomplishment. The third-person subject is morphologically unmarked.

5. This evidence was first discussed in Rice and Saxon (1994).

6. Guglielmo Cinque (pers. comm., 2002) notes that in most of the following examples the subjects are interpreted as indefinite in the construction. This observation merits further research. See Hargus (2002b) for relevant observations about Kwadacha (Ft Ware Sekani).

7. For discussion, see Thompson (1989a, 1990), Willie (1991, 2000), Saxon (1993), Willie and Saxon (1995), and Jung (1999).

8. In Hupa, the cognate form has been reanalyzed as subject inflection. See Rice and Saxon (1993) and the following section 3.3.

9. As Sharon Hargus (pers. comm., 2002) points out, the disjoint anaphor **y-** is not used in most languages of the family with clauses having a subject cognate with Ahtna *'s-* 'someone; we' seen in the paradigm for the verb 'to be alive' in section 1.1.4, despite our identifying it as a member of the grammatical category Num. This is a weakness of our account. An explanation for the difference between *'s-* (and its cognates) and other members of the category Num might come from discourse factors interacting with grammatical conditions. We leave this intriguing study to future research.

10. Hupa and Kato do not show evidence of this sort, so we limit our claims to the rest of the family until we find other ways of testing our hypothesis in Hupa and Kato, too.

11. We depend on the facts of oblique objects rather than direct objects in this section. See section 2.3 for discussion of some complications of transitive clauses.

12. In the sentence (46) the word *uʔudze'* 'hidden by it' is a postposition, despite appearances from its English gloss.

13. See section 4.3 for further discussion of inanimate subjects. We show there that for a certain class of subjects, either **y-** or **b-** occurs to mark a direct object, as in (146).

14. Our treatment here is shaped especially by the research of Ellavina Perkins (1978) and Mary Willie (1991).

15. Perkins (1978: 121ff.) makes some striking generalizations about the expression of locations that we have not been able to address in our model at all. In the contrast between **y-** and **b-** in that domain, telicity is involved, as Perkins makes clear. We refer the reader to Perkins's insightful discussion and analysis.

16. Speas (1990) accounts for parallel word-order facts without reference to a functional projection such as AgrOP, though she does assume such a projection. Her account depends on the analysis of ditransitives due to Larson (1988).

17. The Navajo verbs in (80), (81), and (84) incorporate *lák'e-*, meaning 'at the hand of' (Young and Morgan 1987: 221). *Bi-* and *yi-* prefixed to this form are possessors corresponding to the recipient.

18. In the following Koyukon example, we find adverbials on both sides of the direct object, which is boldface:

Koyukon

(i) Yoonaan **nendaale** tsook'aal   ghʉ   enodaange'onh.
     across   duck   grandmother   to   1sS-pf-transport by boat

   'I brought a duck to my grandmother across the river.' (Jetté and Jones 2000:
   56)

We assume that PPs and adverbials are possibly associated with different projections, so
that facts like these are not problematic for our view that there are two positions for
objects.

   19. Research into Navajo shows that the *doo* of negation may occur also preceding
the subject. A full treatment of NegP in Athapaskan languages goes beyond the scope of
our discussion.

   20. Works by Horseherder (1999) and Willie (2000) show that the facts of third-
person possessors are rather more complicated than third-person objects. See these
works for discussion and remarks on future directions for study.

   21. The facts are somewhat more complex; see Gunlogson (2001) and Hargus
(2002a) for very productive discussion. For similar facts in Slave, see Rice (2002, 2003).
Hargus (2002b) observes that Sekani allows such contrasts also. In Dogrib, too, it is
possible for **y-** and an object noun phrase to cooccur. We have not yet been able to
observe any uniform structural or semantic patterning to it.

   22. The discussion in section 2.1 derives in its detail from Saxon (2001).

   23. The example with *yi-* is ambiguous and may also mean 'who did John kiss?' We
discuss this fact in section 2.1.2.

   24. In doing research for this chapter, we have been limited to published data on
Navajo. Our crucial examples in this section are all of the same type and involve a verb
of motion with a conveyance as the inanimate subject and a human "rider." We predict
that a range of other examples yields the same potential for two *bi-* within a single
clause—for example, locative sentences such as 'the ball is beside the stick in the box'.
Essential for our proposal are sentences with inanimate subjects.

   25. How do we account for the facts originally motivating the ban against two instances of *bi-*, seen in (110)? By our account, in (110a) the subject 'the boy' is in [Spec,
NumP] and thus licenses *yi-* marking for the objects in its domain. In (110b), the object
'the boy' is in [Spec, DiscP], out of the domain of the subject 'the girl' in [Spec,
NumP] and ineligible for marking by *yi-*; the direct object is in the domain of [Spec,
NumP] and is marked by *yi-*. Finally, in (117c), ungrammaticality results because the
subject is in [Spec, NumP] and the direct object, which word order indicates is in its
domain, should be marked by *yi-* instead of by *bi-*, as we see.

   26. Thompson (1989a: 84) presents data from San Carlos Apache, which likewise
show that the *yi-/bi-* alternation and word-order facts are not correlated and, in fact,
cut across each other. His discussion highlights the role of topicality and animacy. Our
addition to his insights comes in attaching a structural account of the contrasts observed.

   27. Thompson (1996) finds that subject-object inversion in Koyukon is extremely
rare: he has come across just one nonidiomatic sentence with the word order O S b-V:

Koyukon

(i) Sołt'aanh   sis   dzaabedegheełghal.
     woman   bear   b-3S-pf-startle

'The woman was startled by the bear.' (Thompson 1996: 90)

The unusual word order and object inflection with **b-** is consistent with the analysis whereby 'woman' is moved to [Spec, DiscP] and 'bear' is moved to [Spec, NumP], and also with an analysis whereby 'bear' is an internal subject and doesn't license **y-** object inflection. Compare (79) in section 1.2.

28. Cook (1984: 196ff.) makes it clear that **b-** isn't a possible replacement for **y-** in this context in Tsuut'ina. But see later for a related construction.

29. If the subject is internal, it is expected that the object could instead be marked by **b-** In fact, **b-** is also possible in these contexts, as shown later.

Koyukon

(i) Hugho'ełts'eeyhbeetenaatltsonh. (**ełts'eeyh-** 'wind')
     wind-b-pf-tire out

'The wind tired him/her out.' (Axelrod 1990: 186)

As we show in section 4, alternations of **y-** and **b-** marking for objects and other arguments are the rule in Koyukon and Ahtna and are not governed by strictly grammatical constraints.

30. Interestingly, facts of noun incorporation bear on the claim that transitive subjects invariably raise out of the VP to [Spec, NumP] in Slave and Dogrib. Recall from section 1.1.2 that many Athapaskan languages allow incorporation of nouns and that subjects can be incorporated. In Koyukon, Ahtna, and Dogrib, we have seen examples of transitive subjects incorporated. We suggested on independent grounds that transitive subjects in Koyukon and Ahtna can remain in a VP-internal position—the only sort of position from which a subject can be incorporated following the assumptions about incorporation that we take from Baker (1988). If transitive subjects must raise in Slave and Dogrib, then the incorporation of transitive subjects in these languages is not expected unless statements about the ordering of grammatical operations can be specified.

31. The pattern in (b) is unknown in Rice (1989: 1216f.) and Howard and Leer (1980) but is now well attested in Howard (1990). We note that the discussion in Rice (1989) is based on a different dialect of Slave than that documented in Howard's work.

32. The Ahtna example here, repeated from (11), is interesting in light of our discussion in this section:

Ahtna

(i) Uk'enaałyułghel. (**naał-** 'sleep')
     3OO-past-sleep-3O-pf-move O

'He took a nap.' (lit. sleep moved him past it) (Kari 1990: 218)

Like (142) in the text, this example has an incorporated subject and a direct object marked by **y-**. It also has an oblique object which forms part of the idiom. This oblique object is marked by **b-** (here **u-**). The pattern recalls the facts of Kaska in terms of the distribution of cases and forms. See also discussion in section 3.2.1.

33. Cross-linguistically, Givón (1995) examines the likelihood that a particular grammatical and thematic relation will serve as a topic. He proposes that, in terms of gram-

matical relations, subjects are the most likely topics and indirect objects are the least likely. In terms of thematic relations, obliques, including locations, instruments, and others, are the least likely to be topics; agents are the most likely, followed by datives (or benefactives) and patients. Cross-linguistic facts thus make it unlikely that these oblique objects invariably are topics.

34. Hale et al. (2000: 111) note this particular complementarity: in the most widespread patterns in Athapaskan languages, when subject marking is overt, third-person object marking is null, and vice versa.

35. Babine-Witsuwit'en is also exceptional in this. Sharon Hargus (pers. comm., citing Hargus 2002a) notes that a few verbs in this language invariably require the presence of overt direct object inflection. The object referred to need not always be human or animate.

36. Our generalization here holds for direct objects in the context of non-third person subjects. Examples in the previous and following sections show that this is not true of **b-** generally.

37. See Rice (2003) on conditions on doubling of DP and inflection in Slave, showing a surface pattern similar to that in Babine-Witsuwit'en. Recall also from section 1.4 that Dena'ina and Dogrib show mixed patterns whose conditioning factors are not yet understood and consequently are not reflected in (173).

38. We intend the definition of c-command in which the first maximal projection dominating a node defines its c-command domain. Strictly speaking, postpositional objects do not c-command the other constituents of VP because of the intervening PP node. This well-known difficulty with adpositional objects in binding relations is not limited to Athapaskan languages; see the following English example:

(i)　I talked to John about himself.

It has been suggested in the face of data like these that binding relations be defined on thematic structure rather than phrase structure (Bach and Partee 1980; Wilkins 1988; Williams 1987, 1989; Reinhart and Reuland 1991). We note the problem but leave its solution open.

39. We do not have data which would tell us whether Dene Sułiné and Tsuut'ina show the same restriction.

40. We are not aware of parallel data in other languages, so we are not able to comment further on the geographical range of this pattern.

41. With an overt noun as subject, the relative topicality of the object is indicated through the use of **y-** for a relatively nontopical object or **b-** for a relatively topical object, as Thompson (1989a) shows. He also identifies the (a) pattern here as direct and (b) as inverse:

(i)　a. John yıneeɬʔaanh.
　　　'John (zero) is looking at him/her (*y*).' (Thompson 1989a: 40)

　　　b. John bıneeɬʔaanh.
　　　'John (zero) is looking at him/her (*b*).' (Thompson 1989a: 40)

With an overt noun as object, no pronominal agreement appears within the verb, and it is not possible to identify the topical nominal by inflection within the sentence.

42. We note that our analysis of this form is not in agreement with that of Kari (1990). See note 43 for further discussion.

43. Kari (1990: 419) uses the term "epenthetic object" in a description for what we are referring to as internal subject agreement. Under Kari's general editorship of the Koyukon dictionary (Jetté and Jones 2000), the use of **y-** as subject inflection in Koyukon is explicitly recognized, following Thompson (1989a).

44. There is some information available to us from Joan Tenenbaum's (1978) dissertation concerning the Alaska language Dena'ina. Here we see a Dena'ina example of the cross-linguistically most typical use of **y-** as nonsubject agreement in a clause with a third-person human subject.

Dena'ina

(i)   Yeł   nutasdyu.
      y-with   3S-pf-start back
      'She/He started coming back with him/her.' (Tenenbaum 1978: 83)

In (i) subject agreement is zero. In the following examples, subject agreement is **y-**. In both sentences **y-** as subject agreement is licensed by a pronominal direct or oblique object (marked by **b-**), just as in Koyukon and Ahtna:

(ii)   Tıqın   chıveydałyuq.
       wolf   b-y-pf-kill
       'The wolf (*y*) killed him/her (*b*).' (Tenenbaum 1978: 69)

(iii) Nunıgı   **veł**   yucheł.
       fog   b-with   y-imp-lift
       'The fog (*y*) was lifting with him/her (*b*).' (Tenenbaum 1978: 83)

The verb in (ii) shows agreement with a pronominal direct object (*v-*) and with the subject NP tıqın 'wolf' (*y-*). The facts are similar in (iii). (Note that in Dena'ina, unlike Koyukon and Ahtna, the prefixes *y-* and *v-* may mark agreement with either pronominal or full DPs, as in Apachean.) By hypothesis, *y-* occurs as subject agreement in Dena'ina only if the subject is occupying the internal subject position. The subjects in these examples are of just the sort that might be expected to remain within the VP. Fuller investigation of Dena'ina awaits future research.

45. Tang (1989: 101) defines subcommand as follows:

(i)   β SUBCOMMANDS α iff
      a. β c-commands α, or

      b. β is an NP contained in an NP that c-commands α or that subcommands a, and any argument containing β is in subject position.

By this definition (and assuming DP), possessors within DP and also a range of DPs within subject DPs subcommand other DPs in a structure. The data for Ahtna and Koyukon available to us is more limited than what Tang considers in Mandarin. To restrict the definition of 'subcommand' to possessors, what is required is changing clause (b) in the definition to (b'):

(ii)   b'. β is an NP daughter of an NP that c-commands α or that subcommands α.

46. Leer (1990) defines *salience* as "relative agency," a notion that is sometimes situationally determined. In (203a), the notation (S > DO, S <> PO) means that the

subject is more salient than the direct object, while the subject and postpositional object are equal in salience.

47. Jetté and Jones (2000) and Rice (1989) show that the suffixes in Koyukon and Slave can be used also with one or two classes of animals of great cultural importance, such as dogs and caribou.

48. Babine-Witsuwit'en and Tanacross are included in the table on the basis of information from Sharon Hargus (pers. comm., citing Hargus 2002a) and Gary Holton (pers. comm., 2002). Hargus reports that Babine-Witsuwit'en permits **y**- as subject inflection when its referent is inanimate and it occurs in a sentence with another third-person argument. An example is given in (i):

Babine-Witsuwit'en
(i)   Ləbot   **bı**   yəzdle.
       cups   b-in   y-imp-be located [pl O]

'The cups (*y*) are in it (*b*).'

We do not have detailed information on object marking in ditransitive clauses in this language. Holton (pers. comm., 2002) reports that Tanacross patterns like Koyukon and Ahtna on examples like (175)–(177) in respect of **y**- as an object form, and also permits **y**- as subject inflection in circumstances where the object is in focus, as in (ii):

Tanacross
(ii)   Doo   ch'e   **wu'eł**   yaahaał?
        who   b-with   y-imp-walk

'Who (*b*) is he (*y*) walking with?'

49. In fact, the same is true of **b**- with the added distinction that **b**- can never stand as a subject of any kind.

50. We do not discuss possessive uses of **y**-, which we have not examined in this chapter. Most of the languages in our sample allow possessive **y**-; it would be worthwhile to detail the facts fully. See Horseherder (1999) and Willie (2000) for discussion of possessives in Navajo.

REFERENCES

Aissen, Judith (2000) "Yi and Bi: Proximate and Obviative in Navajo," in Andrew Carnie, Eloise Jelinek, and MaryAnn Willie (eds.) *Papers in Honor of Ken Hale.* Working Papers in Endangered and Less Familiar Languages 1. MIT Working Papers in Linguistics, Cambridge, Mass., 129–150.

Aissen, Judith (2003) "Differential Object Marking: Iconicity vs. Economy." *Natural Language and Linguistic Theory* 21: 435–483.

Axelrod, Melissa (1990) "Incorporation in Koyukon Athapaskan." *International Journal of American Linguistics* 56: 179–195.

Bach, Emmon, and Barbara Partee (1980) "Anaphora and Semantic Structure," in

J. Kreiman and A. Ojeda (eds.) *Papers from the Parasession on Pronouns and Anaphora*. Chicago Linguistic Society, Chicago, 1–28.

Baker, Mark C. (1988) *Incorporation: A Theory of Grammatical Function Changing*. University of Chicago Press, Chicago.

Benveniste, Émile (1946) "Structure des relations de personne dans le verbe." *Bulletin de la societé de linguistique de Paris* 43: 1–12.

Chomsky, Noam (1986) *Barriers*. MIT Press, Cambridge, Mass.

Cinque, Guglielmo (1990) *Types of A-bar Dependencies*. MIT Press, Cambridge, Mass.

Cook, Eung-Do, (1984) *A Sarcee Grammar*. University of British Columbia Press, Vancouver.

Déchaine, Rose-Marie (2001) "Algonquian Agreement in Clausal Structure." Unpublished ms., University of British Columbia.

Denham, Kristin E. (1997) "A Minimalist Account of Optional wh-Movement." Ph.D. diss., University of Washington.

Diesing, Molly (1992) *Indefinites*. MIT Press, Cambridge, Mass.

Fernald, Theodore, Lorene Legah, Alyse Neundorf, Ellavina Tsosie Perkins, and Paul Platero (2000) "Definite and Indefinite Descriptions in Navajo," in Theodore B. Fernald and Kenneth L. Hale (eds.) *Diné bizaad naalkaah: Navajo language investigations*. MIT Working Papers on Endangered and Less Familiar Languages 3. MIT Working Papers in Linguistics, Cambridge, Mass. 31–53.

Fukui, Naoki, and Margaret Speas (1986) "Specifiers and Projections," in N. Fukui, T.R. Rapoport, and E. Sagey (eds.) *Papers in Theoretical Linguistics*. MIT Working Papers in Linguistics 8. MIT Working Papers in Linguistics, Cambridge, Mass., 128–172.

Givón, Talmy (1995) *Functionalism in Grammar*. John Benjamins, Amsterdam.

Golla, Victor (1970) "Hupa Grammar." Ph.D. diss., University of California, Berkeley.

Golla, Victor (1985) *A Short Practical Grammar of Hupa*. Hoopa Valley Tribe, Hoopa, Calif.

Gunlogson, Christine (2001) "Third Person Object Prefixes in Babine-Witsuwit'en." *International Journal of American Linguistics* 67: 365–395.

Hale, Kenneth (1973) "A Note on Subject-Object Inversion in Navajo," in B. Kachru et al. (eds.) *Papers in Honor of Henry and Renée Kahane*. University of Illinois Press, Chicago, 300–309.

Hale, Kenneth (2001) "Navajo Verb Stem Position and the Bipartite Structure of the Navajo Conjunct Sector." *Linguistic Inquiry* 32: 678–693.

Hale, Kenneth (2003) "On the Significance of Eloise Jelinek's Pronominal Argument Hypothesis," in Andrew Carnie, Heidi Harley, and MaryAnn Willie (eds.) *Formal Approaches to Function in Grammar: In Honor of Eloise Jelinek*. John Benjamins, Amsterdam, 11–43.

Hale, Kenneth, and Paul Platero (2000) "Negative Polarity Expressions in Navajo," in Theodore B. Fernald and Paul R. Platero (eds.) *The Athabaskan Languages: Perspectives on a Native American Language Family*. Oxford University Press, New York, 73–91.

Hale, Kenneth, Pamela Munro, and Paul Platero (2000) "The Navajo Inchoative Verb Form," in Theodore B. Fernald and Kenneth L. Hale (eds.) *Diné Bizaad Naalkaah: Navajo Language Investigations*. Working Papers on Endangered and Less Familiar Languages 3. MIT Working Papers in Linguistics, Cambridge, Mass. 97–116.

Hargus, Sharon (2002a) "Witsuwit'en Grammar: Phonology and Morphology." Unpublished ms., University of Washington.

Hargus, Sharon (2002b) "Negation in Kwadacha (Ft Ware Sekani)." Paper presented at the Athabascan Languages Conference, Fairbanks, Alaska.

Horseherder, Nicole (1999) "A Binding-Theoretic Analysis of Navajo Possessor *yi-*." Master's thesis, University of British Columbia.

Howard, Philip (1990) *A Dictionary of the Verbs of South Slavey*. Department of Culture and Communication, Yellowknife, Northwest Territories, Canada.

Howard, Philip, and Jeff Leer (1980) "Pronominal Inflection in Slavey." Unpublished ms. University of New Mexico.

Jelinek, Eloise (1984) "Empty Categories, Case, and Configurationality." *Natural Language and Linguistic Theory* 2: 39–76.

Jelinek, Eloise, and Andrew Carnie (2003) "Argument Hierarchies and the Mapping Principle," in Andrew Carnie, Heidi Harley, and MaryAnn Willie (eds.) *Formal Approaches to Function in Grammar: In Honor of Eloise Jelinek*. John Benjamins, Amsterdam, 265–296.

Jelinek, Eloise, and MaryAnn Willie (1996) " 'Psych' Verbs in Navajo," in Eloise Jelinek, Sally Midgette, Keren Rice, and Leslie Saxon (eds.) *Athabaskan Language Studies. Essays in Honor of Robert W. Young*. University of New Mexico Press, Albuquerque, 15–34.

Jetté, Jules, and Eliza Jones (2000) *Koyukon Athabaskan Dictionary*. Alaska Native Language Center, Fairbanks.

Jung, Dagmar (1999) "The Dynamics of Polysynthetic Morphology: Person and Number Marking in Athabaskan." Ph.D. diss., University of New Mexico.

Kari, James (1990) *Ahtna Athabaskan Dictionary*. Alaska Native Language Center, Fairbanks.

Krauss, Michael, and Victor Golla (1981) "Northern Athapaskan Languages," in June Helm (ed.) *Subarctic*. Smithsonian Institution, Washington, D.C., 67–85.

Kuroda, S.-Y. (1988) "Whether We Agree or Not: A Comparative Syntax of English and Japanese." *Lingvisticae Investigationes* 12: 1–47.

Larson, Richard (1988) "On the Double Object Construction." *Linguistic Inquiry* 19: 335–391.

Leer, Jeff (1990) "The Tlingit Anaphoric System and the Typology of Voice Systems." Paper presented at the Athapaskan Linguistics Conference, Vancouver, British Columbia.

Li, Fang-Kuei (1946) "Chipewyan," in Harry Hoijer (ed.) *Linguistic Structures of Native America*. Viking Fund Publications in Anthropology, New York, 398–423.

Maling, Joan (1984) "Non-Clause-bounded Reflexives in Modern Icelandic." *Linguistics and Philosophy* 7: 211–241.

Marantz, Alec (1984) *On the Nature of Grammatical Relations*. MIT Press, Cambridge, Mass.

Mithun, Marianne (1999) *The Languages of Native North America*. Cambridge University Press, Cambridge.

Moore, Patrick (ed.) (1999) *Dene gudeji: Kaska Narratives*. Kaska Tribal Council, Watson Lake, Yukon, Canada.

Moore, Patrick (2001) "Point of View in Kaska Historical Narratives." Ph.D. diss., Indiana University.

Perkins, Ellavina Tsosie. (1978) "The Role of Word Order and Scope in the Interpretation of Navajo Sentences." Ph.D. diss., University of Arizona.

Perkins, Ellavina Tsosie (2000) "Navajo H-Questions Revisited," in Theodore B. Fernald and Kenneth L. Hale (eds.) *Diné bizaad naalkaah: Navajo Language Investigations.* Working Papers on Endangered and Less Familiar Languages 3. MIT Working Papers in Linguistics, Cambridge, Mass., 117–128.

Pesetsky, David (1987) "Binding Problems with Experiencer Verbs." *Linguistic Inquiry* 17: 126–142.

Petitot, Émile, (1876) *Dictionnaire de la langue déné-dindjie.* Ernst Leroux, Paris.

Philippi, Julia (1997) "The Rise of the Article in Germanic Languages," in Ans van Kemenade and Nigel Vincent (eds.) *Parameters of Morphosyntactic Change.* Cambridge, University Press, Cambridge, 62–93.

Platero, Paul (1978) "Missing Noun Phrases in Navajo." Ph.D. diss., MIT, Cambridge, Mass.

Pollock, Jean-Yves (1989) "Verb Movement, Universal Grammar, and the Structure of IP." *Linguistic Inquiry* 20: 365–424.

Potter, Brian (1997) "Wh/Indefinites and the Structure of the Clause in Western Apache." Ph.D. diss., University of California, Los Angeles.

Reinhart, Tanya, and Eric Reuland (1993) "Reflexivity." *Linguistic Inquiry* 24: 657–720.

Rice, Keren (1978) *Hare Dictionary.* Northern Social Research Division, Department of Indian and Northern Affairs, Ottawa, Ontario, Canada.

Rice, Keren (1989) *A Grammar of Slave.* Mouton de Gruyter, Berlin.

Rice, Keren (2000a) "Monadic Verbs and Argument Structure in Ahtna, Navajo, and Slave," in Theodore Fernald and Paul Platero (eds.) *The Athabaskan Language: Perspectives on a Native American Language Family.* Oxford University Press, New York, 167–199.

Rice, Keren (2000b) "Another Look at the Athapaskan *y-/b-* Pronouns: Evidence from Slave for *b-* as a Case Marker," in Andrew Carnie, Eloise Jelinek, and MaryAnn Willie (eds.) *Papers in Honor of Ken Hale.* Working Papers in Endangered and Less Familiar Langauges 1. MIT Working Papers in Linguistics, Cambridge, Mass., 109–128.

Rice, Keren (2000c) *Morpheme Order and Semantic Scope: Word Formation in the Athapaskan Verb.* Cambridge University Press, Cambridge.

Rice, Keren (2003) "Doubling by Agreement in Slave (Northern Athapaskan)," in Andrew Carnie, Heidi Harley, and MaryAnn Willie (eds.) *Formal Approaches to Function in Grammar: In Honor of Eloise Jelinek.* John Benjamins, Amsterdam, 51–78.

Rice, Keren, and Leslie Saxon (1991) "A Structural Analysis of **y* in Athapaskan." Paper presented at the Athapaskan Conference, University of California at Santa Cruz.

Rice, Keren, and Leslie Saxon (1993) "Paradigmatic and Syntactic Mechanisms for Syntactic Change in Athapaskan," in David A. Peterson (ed.) *Proceedings of the Special Session on Syntactic Issues in Native American Languages, Nineteenth Annual Meeting of the Berkeley Linguistics Society.* Berkeley Linguistics Society, Berkeley, California, 148–159.

Rice, Keren, and Leslie Saxon (1994) "The Subject Position in Athapaskan Languages," in Heidi Harley and Colin Phillips (eds.) *The Morphology-Syntax Connection.* MIT Working Papers in Linguistics 22. MIT Working Papers in Linguistics, Cambridge, Mass., 173–195.

Rice, Keren, and Leslie Saxon (2001) "The *y-/b-* Pronouns in Athapaskan Languages: Perspectives on Content." Talk presented at the Workshop on American Indigenous Languages, University of California, Santa Barbara.

Ritter, Elizabeth (1991) "Two Functional Categories in Modern Hebrew Noun phrases," in Susan Rothstein (ed.) *Perspectives on Phrase Structure: Heads and Licensing.* Syntax and Semantics 25. Academic Press, New York, 37–60.

Ritter, Elizabeth (1995) "On the Syntactic Category of Pronouns and Agreement." *Natural Language and Linguistic Theory* 13: 405–443.

Runner, Jeff (1993) "Quantificational Objects and Agr-O," in V. Lindblad and M. Gamon (eds.), *Papers from the 5th Student Conference in Linguistics.* MIT Working Papers in Linguistics 20. MIT Working Papers in Linguistics, Cambridge, Mass.

Sandoval, Merton, and Eloise Jelinek (1989) "The Bi-construction and Pronominal Arguments in Apachean," in Eung-Do Cook and Keren Rice (eds.) *Athapaskan Linguistics: Current Perspectives on a Language Family.* Mouton de Gruyter, Berlin, 335–378.

Saxon, Leslie (1984) "Disjoint Anaphora and the Binding Theory," in M. Cobler, S. MacKaye, and M. Wescoat (eds.) *Proceedings of the West Coast Conference on Formal Linguistics* 3. Stanford Linguistics Association, Stanford, Calif., 242–251.

Saxon, Leslie (1986) "The Syntax of Pronouns in Dogrib (Athapaskan): Some Theoretical Consequences." Ph.D. diss., University of California, San Diego.

Saxon, Leslie (1989) "Lexical versus Syntactic Projection: The Configurationality of Slave," in Eung-Do Cook and Keren Rice (eds.) *Athapaskan Linguistics: Current Perspectives on a Language Family.* Mouton de Gruyter, Berlin, 379–406.

Saxon, Leslie (1993) "A Personal Use of the Athapaskan 'Impersonal' *ts'e-*. *International Journal of American Linguistics* 59: 342–354.

Saxon, Leslie (1995) "Complex Pronominals, Disjoint Anaphora, and Indexing." Talk presented at the Annual Meeting of the Linguistic Society of America, New Orleans.

Saxon, Leslie (2001) "On Two OSV Constructions in Navajo: Beyond Subject-Object Inversion," in Sunyoung Oh and Naomi Sawai (eds.) *Proceedings of WSCLA 6, The Workshop on Structure and Constituency in Languages of the Americas.* UBC Working Papers in Linguistics 7. UBC Working Papers in Linguistics, Vancouver, BC, Canada, 73–87.

Saxon, Leslie, and Keren Rice (1993) "On Subject-Verb Constituency: Evidence from Athapaskan Languages," in Jonathan Mead (ed.) *Proceedings of the Eleventh West Coast Conference on Formal Linguistics.* Center for the Study of Language and Information, Stanford, Calif., 434–450.

Saxon, Leslie, and Mary Siemens (1996) *Tłįchǫ yatiì enįhtł'è / A Dog-rib Dictionary.* Dogrib Divisional Board of Education, Rae-Edzo, Northwest Territories, Canada.

Schauber, Ellen (1979) *The Syntax and Semantics of Questions in Navajo.* Garland, New York.

Speas, Margaret (1990) *Phrase Structure in Natural Language.* Kluwer, Dordrecht.

Speas, Margaret (1995) "Clause Structure in Athapaskan Languages." Paper presented at the Workshop on the Morphology-Syntax Interface in Athapaskan Languages, University of New Mexico, Albuquerque.

Speas, Margaret (1996) "Null Objects in Functional Projections," in Johan Rooryck and Laurie Zaring (eds.) *Phrase Structure and the Lexicon.* Kluwer, Dordrecht, 187–211.

Speas, Margaret, and Evangeline Parsons Yazzie (1996) "Quantifiers and the Position of

Noun Phrases in Navajo," in Eloise Jelinek, Sally Midgette, Keren Rice, and Leslie Saxon (eds.) *Athabaskan Language Studies: Essays in Honor of Robert W. Young.* University of New Mexico Press, Albuquerque, 35–80.

Sportiche, Dominique (1988) "A Theory of Floating Quantifiers and Its Corollaries for Constituent Structure." *Linguistic Inquiry* 19: 425–449.

Svendsen, Melissa (2000) "The Typology of wh Questions: An Optimality Theoretic Approach." M.A. thesis, University of Victoria.

Tang, Chih-Chen Jane (1989) "Chinese Reflexives." *Natural Language and Linguistic Theory* 7: 93–121.

Tenenbaum, Joan (1978) "Morphology and Semantics of the Tanaina Verb." Ph.D. diss., Columbia University.

Thom, Margaret, and Ethel Blondin-Townsend (eds.) (1987) *Nahecho Keh / Our Elders.* Slavey Research Project, Government of the Northwest Territories, Canada.

Thompson, Chad (1989a) "Voice and Obviation in Athabaskan and Other Languages." Ph.D. diss., University of Oregon, Eugene.

Thompson, Chad (1989b) "Pronouns and Voice in Koyukon Athabaskan: A Text-Based Study." *International Journal of American Linguistics* 55(1): 1–24.

Thompson, Chad (1990) "The Diachrony of the Deictics in Athabaskan." Paper presented at the Athapaskan Conference, University of British Columbia, Vancouver.

Thompson, Chad (1996) "The History and Function of the *yi-/bi-* Alternation in Athabaskan," in Eloise Jelinek, Sally Midgette, Keren Rice, and Leslie Saxon (eds.) *Athabaskan Language Studies: Essays in Honor of Robert W. Young.* University of New Mexico Press, Albuquerque, 81–100.

Wilkins, Wendy (1988) "Thematic Structure and Reflexivization," in Wendy Wilkins (ed.) *Thematic Relations.* Syntax and Semantics 21. Academic Press, San Diego, 191–213.

Williams, Edwin (1987) "Implicit Arguments, the Binding Theory, and Control." *Natural Language and Linguistic Theory* 5: 151–180.

Williams, Edwin (1989) "The Anaphoric Nature of θ-roles. *Linguistic Inquiry* 20: 425–256.

Willie, MaryAnn (1989) "Why There Is Nothing Missing in Navajo Relative Clauses," in Eung-Do Cook and Keren Rice (eds.) *Athapaskan Linguistics: Current Perspectives on a Language Family.* Mouton de Gruyter, Berlin, 407–437.

Willie, MaryAnn (1991) "Pronouns and Obviation in Navajo." Ph.D. diss., University of Arizona.

Willie, MaryAnn (2000) "The Inverse Voice and Possessive *yi-/bi-* in Navajo." *International Journal of American Linguistics* 66: 360–382.

Willie, MaryAnn, and Eloise Jelinek (2000) "Navajo as a Discourse Configurational Language," in Theodore B. Fernald and Paul R. Platero (eds.) *The Athabaskan Languages: Perspectives on a Native American Language Family.* Oxford University Press, New York, 252–287.

Willie, MaryAnn, and Leslie Saxon (1995) "Third Person Forms in Athapaskan Languages: An Examination of the 'Fourth' Person." Paper presented at the Workshop on the Morphology-Syntax Interface in Athapaskan Languages, University of New Mexico, Albuquerque.

Young, Robert W., and William Morgan Sr. (1987) *The Navajo Language: A Grammar and Colloquial Dictionary.* 2nd ed. University of New Mexico Press, Albuquerque.

CHAPTER 17

....

NUMBER AGREEMENT VARIATION IN CATALAN DIALECTS

....

GEMMA RIGAU

THE aim of this chapter is to show that certain parametric properties and their interaction with UG principles allow us to differentiate between two main varieties of Catalan. I also show that the values of the parameter studied here are active in other Romance languages. That is to say, some dialects of Catalan are similar in this respect to certain dialects of Spanish and Portuguese, whereas others may be grouped with Occitan and French.

The theoretical aim of the chapter is to show that the functional category Tense is the locus of the parametric variation in number agreement in certain kinds of Catalan existential sentences. I concentrate on deontic existential sentences, because their complexity makes them a very interesting matter of study. However, the conclusions I draw here are equally valid in general terms for other existential constructions.

Section 1 is dedicated to some introductory remarks on Catalan syntax. In section 2 I introduce the relevant data for the analysis, concentrating on two Catalan dialects: Central Catalan (mainly the dialect spoken in the Girona area) and Ribagorçan Catalan, a dialect spoken in the northwest of Catalonia. In Ribagorçan Catalan no agreement is shown between the existential verb and its object; however, Central Catalan shows agreement between the verb and its object in existential constructions. I argue in section 3 that this agreement is in number, not in person. I then characterize the universal principles at the root of the presence or absence of verbal concord. These are principles taken from Chomsky (1999), and they are introduced in subsection 3.1. In 3.2 and 3.3, I determine the parameters of variation, placing them among the features of the functional category Tense (T). The Locative property of some of these features is the cause of this variation. The selection of one or the other value for number feature in T— that is, L-number or α-number—accounts for the bifurcation between Catalan dialectal grammars. Section 4 shows that the determination of the uninterpretable person and number features in T is not necessarily simultaneous: it is determined separately in some Romance existential constructions. Furthermore, empirical evidence is provided for Agree (and case determination) as an independent operation of the EPP-feature satisfaction. In section 5 I consider the concord phenomenon in other Catalan constructions. The clitic climbing phenomenon in some deontic existential constructions with an infinitive clause is briefly commented on in section 6. Comparison with other Romance languages is made in section 7. Finally, conclusions are summarized in section 8.

1 SOME INTRODUCTORY REMARKS

Catalan is a null subject language. This means that Catalan allows null subjects with definite pronominal interpretation. It also allows subjects to occur in postverbal position, leaving the preverbal subject position empty. The various options are shown in (1):[1]

(1) a. _____ parla.
         speaks
         'She/He speaks.'

     b. Ell parla.
         he speaks
         'He speaks.'

     c. Parla ell.
         speaks he
         'He speaks.'

The silent subject in (1a) is characterized as a phonologically empty nominative pronoun (*pro*), whereas the strong pronoun *ell* 'he' in (1b–c) is an overt nominative pronoun. Both pronouns agree with the verb in person and number.

Nevertheless, strong and null pronouns are not the only subject pronouns in Catalan. Like other Romance languages, Catalan allows constructions with an oblique clitic subject. They are existential constructions such as those in (2):

(2)   a. Hi ha una biblioteca nova.
          cl. has a library new

          'There is a new library.'

      b. Hi cal una biblioteca nova.
          cl. is-necessary a library new

          'A new library is needed (t)here.'

      c. Hi urgeix una biblioteca nova.
          cl. is-urgent a library new

          'A new library is urgently needed (t)here.'

Sentences in (2) have an existential verb—the presentational verb *haver*, and the deontic existential verbs *caldre* and *urgir*[2]—an object (*una biblioteca nova*) and an oblique clitic subject (*hi*). By the term "existential verb" I mean a verb with a static preposition incorporated in it (see section 2). I do not include the copulative verb *ser* 'be', which can appear in some presentational constructions instead of *haver* 'have':

(3)   a. No hi ha cap autobús.
          not cl. has any bus

          'There is no bus.'

      b. Els autobusos no hi són.
          the buses not cl. are

          'The buses are not here/there.'

In section 2 I argue that the locative clitic *hi* in (2) and (3a) acts as a clitic subject, whereas in (3b) it acts as a PP predicate with the copulative verb *ser* 'be'. Nevertheless, the oblique clitic *hi*, which is called an "adverbial pronoun" by traditional grammarians, shows other roles in Catalan. For example, in (4) the clitic *hi* acts as a verbal object. It can act either as a stative locative clitic, as in (4a), or as a directional locative clitic, as in (4b). It can also stand for a PP object, as in (4c), and in some dialects it stands for an inanimate dative, as in (4d). On these and other roles of this clitic in Catalan, see Fabra (1956), Bonet (1991), and Rigau (1982).

(4) a. Ell viu *a Banyoles*. / Ell hi viu.
         he lives in Banyoles / he cl. lives
         'He lives in Banyoles. / He lives there.'

     b. Ell va *a Banyoles*. / Ell *hi* va.
         he goes to Banyoles / he cl. goes
         'He is going to Banyoles.' / 'He is going there.'

     c. Ell pensa *en tu*. / Ell *hi* pensa.
         he thinks about you / he cl. thinks
         'He is thinking about you.'

     d. Ell dóna cops *al televisor*. / Ell *hi* dóna cops.
         he gives blows to the television-set / He cl. gives blows
         'He is hitting the television set. / He is hitting it.'

The clitic *hi* is the only oblique clitic that can appear in a presentational existential construction with *haver* 'have', such as in (2a). No other oblique clitic subject is available for this construction.[3] However, other impersonal existential constructions can show other oblique clitic subjects. This is the case of the deontic existential constructions in (2b–c). Their verbs express the existence of necessity, and—like their French and Sardinian equivalents, *falloir* and *kérrere*—they can coappear with an overt or covert animate dative clitic that indicates the person who is implicated or interested in the situation. In (5a) the clitic subject is a third-person singular dative pronoun, whereas in (5b) the dative clitic is first person plural. In (5c) the pronominal subject is covert and thus receives an arbitrary meaning (= 'to someone', 'to the people'):[4]

(5) a. Li cal una biblioteca nova.
         to-him/her is-necessary a library new
         'She/He needs a new library.'

     b. Ens urgeix una biblioteca nova.
         to-us is urgent a library new
         'We urgently need a new library.'

     c. Urgeix una biblioteca nova.
         is-urgent a library new
         'A new library is urgently needed.'

I regard the oblique clitic in existential constructions as the logical subject of the sentence.[5] Like other languages, such as Icelandic, Catalan shows "quirky subjects"—subjects that are considered internal arguments and marked with oblique (dative or locative) inherent case, plus an additional structural case feature (Chomsky 1998). For quirky subjects in Spanish and other Romance languages, see Masullo (1993), Fernández-Soriano (1999), and Longa et al. (1998).

The DP *una biblioteca nova* 'a new library' in (5) is an object, although in some dialects it can manifest agreement with the verb. (discussed later in this chapter). The fact that a nominative pronoun is not admitted in presentational and deontic existential sentences, as shown in (6), is a good proof that the element in the object position cannot be the subject of the construction and that the sentence is impersonal:

(6) a. *Hi ha/has tu
         cl. has/have$_{2d, sing.}$ you

     b. *Et calia/calíem nosaltres
         to-you was/were$_{1, pl.}$-necessary we

     c. *Vosaltres li cal/caleu
         you to-him/her is/are$_{2d, pl.}$-necessary

The object of a deontic existential verb can be an infinitive clause. In fact, this kind of verb follows the Latin pattern shown in (7), a sentence with a dative subject (*mihi*), an impersonal verb that means modality (*licet*), and an object (the infinitive clause *negligenti esse*).[6] Deontic existential constructions with infinitive clause in object position are introduced in section 6.

(7) In re publica mihi [negligenti esse] non licet. (Cic. *Att.* 1, 17, 16)
     in thing public to-me negligent to-be not is-permitted
     'In matters of state I may not be negligent.'

In Old Catalan there used to be many more such modal verbs that could appear in the impersonal form with a quirky subject. Most of them have now either disappeared or changed the syntactic behavior that they inherited from Latin (Par 1923: 147f). Thus, verbs like *convenir* 'to be advisable or necessary', *faltar* 'to be lacking or missing', or the complex verb *fer falta* 'to be necessary' have developed the capacity to check nominative case and have followed the strategy of converting the object into a derived subject. Therefore, sentences with these verbs are not always impersonal sentences, as shown in (8), where a nominative pronoun agrees with the verb:[7]

(8)   a. Jo no us convinc.
         I not to-you_pl. am-necessary
         'I am not useful to you.'

      b. Vosaltres no li feu falta.
         you_pl. not to-him/her make lack
         'She/He has no need for you.'

At present, the use of the deontic verb *caldre* 'to be necessary' is on the wane in several Catalan dialects. In some dialects, like the Catalan spoken in the Balearic Islands, it has been completely lost.[8]

The following section, concentrates on impersonal constructions with the verb *caldre* and on their agreement pattern in two Catalan dialects, specifically in Central Catalan and Ribagorçan Catalan.

2 VERB-OBJECT AGREEMENT PATTERNS

Catalan existential constructions follow two different strategies, as shown in (9) and (10):

(9)   a. Oblique D Vsing NPsing (Ribagorçan Catalan)

       b. Oblique D Vsing NPpl

(10)   a. Oblique D Vsing NPsing (Central Catalan)

       b. Oblique D Vpl NPpl

In Ribagorçan Catalan, no agreement is shown between the existential verb and its NP object.[9] However, Central Catalan shows agreement between the verb and its object in existential constructions. This agreement is in number, not in person. No nominative first-, second-, or third-person pronoun is allowed in (10), as shown in (6).

The divergence with respect to verbal agreement with the nominal object is visible in the examples in (11)–(12):[10]

(11)   a. Hi ha una cadira. (Ribagorçan Catalan)
           cl. has a chair
           'There is a chair.'

b. Hi ha tres cadires.
   cl. has three chairs
   'There are three chairs.'

c. Mos caleva una cadira.
   to-us was-necessary a chair
   'We needed a chair.'

d. Mos caleva tres cadires.
   to-us was-necessary three chairs
   'We needed three chairs.'

(12) a. Hi ha una cadira. (Central Catalan)
         cl. has a chair
         'There is a chair.'

      b. Hi han tres cadires.
         cl. have three chairs
         'There are three chairs.'

      c. Ens calia una cadira.
         to-us was-necessary a chair
         'We needed a chair.'

      d. Ens calien tres cadires.
         to-us were$_{3rd, pl.}$-necessary three chairs
         'We needed three chairs.'

In light of these data, two questions arise: Why is a quirky subject licensed in such sentences? Why do these dialects show such different behavior in existential sentences? The answers lie in the argument structure of the existential verbs and in the properties of the functional category T.

Existential sentences (11)–(12) show the same basic argument structure. Its verb is a light verb in the sense that it acts as the host of a real predicate: a covert static preposition. This preposition can be defined as a preposition of "central coincidence." According to Hale (1986) and Hale and Keyser (1993, 1997, 1998a), a preposition of central coincidence is a preposition that expresses the relation whereby some entity is associated or in contact with another entity. It defines a relation of spatial contiguity between one entity (i.e., a place) and another entity (i.e., a thing, a substance, a measure). The complement of the preposition incorporated into the light verb *haver* 'have' in (11a) and (12a) is the NP *una cadira* 'a chair'. The subject required by the preposition to complete the interrelation between the two entities is the clitic *hi,* a clitic expressing a locative circumstance, as shown in (13) (see also Freeze 1992, Kayne 1993).

(13)   [[v [*hi* [$_{P/V}$[*ha*] *una cadira*]]]]

The presentational existential verb *haver* 'have' is a pure light verb. It is in the sentence to allow the covert central coincidence preposition—namely, the real predicate—to be able to combine with temporal and aspectual morphemes. As represented in (13), the form *ha* is both a preposition and a verbal form (P/V). As a verb, it is able to move to T and to host temporal/aspectual morphemes. As a prepositional predicate it selects a complement and a locative clitic *hi* as its specifier, which can be defined as an impersonalizer (Rigau 1997, Longa et al. 1998).

The argument structure of deontic existential verbs in (11c–d) and (12c–d) is schematically represented in (14), and it is basically similar to (13). However, the host of the central coincidence preposition in (14) is not an empty light verb but a deontic verb. Because of their deontic property, those sentences express the existence of a need in some place or person for some entity (see Rigau 1999):

(14)   a.   [v [*mos* [$_{P/V}$[*caleva*] *una cadira*]]]

        b.   [v [*ens* [$_{P/V}$[*calia*] *una cadira*]]]

The lexical entry of the Catalan verb *caldre* in (14) contains an abstract preposition of central coincidence incorporated into a verb with a modal content. Etymologically, the Catalan verb *caldre* comes from the Latin verb *calere* 'to be hot, urgent', which comes from the Indo-European root **kel,* whose meaning was 'warm', but also 'cold'. In Latin this root acquired a modal content.[11]

As in (13), the inner predicate in (14) is not verbal, but prepositional, a predicate that has the property of being interrelational—that is, of requiring two arguments, one a complement, the other a subject (or specifier). However, as opposed to *haver* 'have', the modal verb acting as the host verb is not semantically empty.[12] The burden of its semantic properties are noted in the facts that the complement of P/V in (14) can be an NP, a DP, or an infinitive clause and that its specifier can be an inanimate or animate dative (or oblique) clitic: Central Catalan: *ens* 'to-us, *us*' to-you$_{pl.}$', *em* 'to-me', *hi* 'to-it, here', and so on; Ribagorçan Catalan: *mos* 'to-us', *vos* 'to-you$_{pl.}$', *mi* 'to-me', *hi* 'to-it, here', and so on.[13]

In other Romance languages, the abstract preposition in (14) can have phonological content. For instance, in Italian, the verb *bisognare* cooccurs with the verb *abbisognare* (= *a(d)-bisognare*). In contrast to the verb *bisognare*, the verb *abbisognare* appears with a dative argument, and the complement can be a NP, as shown in (15) from Benincà and Poletto (1994):

(15)   Mi abbisogna una certa somma.
       me$_{dat}$ is-necessary a certain amount
       'I need a certain amount of money.'

Consider now the case of the object of an existential verb. It can be partitive case, as shown by the fact that the object can be a bare NP, and it can be represented by the partitive clitic pronoun *en*:

(16)   a. Hi ha farina.
           cl. has flour
           'There is some flour.'

        b. N'hi ha.
           part. cl. has
           'There is some of it.'

        c. Ens caldrà farina.
           to-us will-be-necessary flour
           'We will need some flour.'

        d. Ens en caldrà.
           to-us part. will-be-necessary
           'We will need some of it.'

In Rigau (1997), it is argued that the incorporation of the stative preposition into the existential verbs allows them to assign partitive case. Hence, partitive case is considered an instance of the inherent case that the preposition is able to assign when incorporated into the host verb. Moreover, deontic existential verbs are able to coappear with a DP object in accusative case. This is visible in the grammatical Ribagorçan Catalan sentences in (17). Note that the animate direct object in (17b) is preceded by the preposition *a* 'to'. This preposition acts as an accusative marker in Spanish and in some Catalan dialects (see Torrego 1998).[14]

(17)   a. Hi cal istes cadires. (Ribagorçan Catalan)
           cl. is-necessary these chairs'
           'These chairs are needed here.'

        b. Mos cal a la teua veïna.
           to-us is-necessary to the your neighbor
           'We need your neighbor.'

c. No me les cal (, istes cadires).

not to-me them is-necessary these chairs

'(As for these chairs,) we don't need them.'

Sentences in (17) are ungrammatical in Central Catalan. As shown in (18), this dialect follows the strategy of showing number agreement between the verb and its object:[15]

(18)   a. Ens cal la teva veïna. (Central Catalan)

to-us is-necessary the your neighbor

'We need your neighbour.'

b. Hi calen aquestes cadires.

cl. are-necessary these chairs'

'These chairs are needed here.'

c. *No me les cal (, aquestes cadires).

not to-me them is-necessary these chairs

d. No em calen aquestes cadires.

not to-me are-necessary these chairs

'I don't need these chairs.'

Central Catalan grammatical sentences in (18) do not belong to Ribagorçan Catalan.

3 THE IMPERSONAL CHARACTER OF DEONTIC EXISTENTIAL SENTENCES AND THEIR AGREEMENT ABILITIES

To account for the facts depicted in (9) and (10), I now first characterize the universal principles that underlie the existence or nonexistence of agreement between the verb and its object. Second, I delimit the parameters of variation. The choice of one or the other value for these parameters accounts for the bifurcation between Catalan dialectal grammars.

3.1 Valuation of Uninterpretable Features

Following Chomsky (1999: 4), I assume that some categories have uninterpretable (or unvalued) features, which have to be assigned a value to be able to receive an interpretation at the interface of the computational system with other cognitive systems. When an uninterpretable feature is not valued, it is not erased, and the derivation crashes. A feature may receive a value and be erased as uninterpretable under Agree. According to Chomsky (1999: 4), the operation of Matching of two elements, a probe and a goal, induces Agree, which eliminates the uninterpretable features that activate those elements. However, both the element that acts as the probe and its goal must be active (i.e. visible) for Agree to apply. This means that the probe has to be nondefective. In Chomsky's words: the probe must have a complete set of φ-features.[16]

Moreover, according to Chomsky (1999: 3), structural case itself is not matched, but it is determined (and erased) under matching of φ-features. It is worth noting here that case determination (or case assignment) and EPP-feature deletion are independent phenomena.[17] Structural case correlates with agreement (Chomsky 1999: n. 18).

3.2 Oblique Clitic Subjects

The impersonalizer function of quirky clitic subjects in Catalan (and Romance) can be accounted for, assuming that oblique clitics have the L(ocative) property. As pointed out by Hale and Keyser (1998b: 11f.), many languages—such as Navajo—have "locative" or "areal" agreement, in addition to conventional person and number agreement. It seems convincing to analyze Romance quirky clitic subjects as overt or covert determiners with interpretable features with the property L, as in (19):[18]

(19)   Oblique clitic φ-features: L [person, number, ...]

L is a locative property of oblique (i.e., dative and locative) clitics. In other words, from a morphological point of view, a dative clitic can be first, second, or third person. However, because of its L property it will act as locative (i.e., impersonal) determiner. Similarly, a dative clitic can be morphologically singular or plural, but the property visible for the computational system is its L-number property. Hence, it acts as a determiner in the unmarked number.[19] This analysis of dative (and locative) clitics seems compatible with Kayne's dative clitics analysis. According to Kayne (1999), who follows a suggestion by A. Rouveret, the dative clitic has incorporated a covert dative preposition. For this reason, Romance dative clitic doubling necessarily involves preposition doubling, as shown in (20) for Catalan:

(20) a. Ens caldrà bona sort a tots.
          to-us will-be-necessary good luck to all
          'All of us will need good luck.'

      b. A la meva habitació hi cal una capa de pintura.
          in the my room cl. is-necessary a coat of paint
          'My room needs a coat of paint.'

The PP *a tots* 'to all' is doubling the animate dative clitic *ens*, whereas the PP *a la meva habitació* 'in my room' is doubling the inanimate dative clitic *hi*.

In parametric terms, I assume that the functional category T can manifest the L property in its person feature or in both person and number features.[20] In Romance existential sentences, T matches the oblique D in its L-person feature. This operation induces an agreement relationship between T and the oblique D, which it expresses morphologically as third person. According to Benveniste (1966), third person is the morphological expression of the default person feature in languages like Romance. Hence, L-person feature in T is valued under Agree, and T simultaneously determines the additional structural case in the quirky subject.

If in addition T has L-number, this feature matches L-number in oblique D. However, if number feature in T is not L-number feature (i.e., it is α-number[21]), it is unable to agree in number with oblique D and to receive a value. In this case, ϕ-features in T are not completely inactivated. Consequently, number feature is inactivated in T separately from person feature (see Chomsky 1998; Rigau 1991, 1997; Sigurdsson 1996, among others). In any case, oblique D erases the EPP feature in T under raising to the specifier position in T (i.e., spec-T).

The choice of L-number or α-number in existential constructions accounts for the bifurcation between Catalan dialectal grammars:

(21) a. Φ-features in T: [L-person, L-number] (Ribagorçan Catalan)

      b. Φ-features in T: [L-person, α number] (Central Catalan)

In Ribagorçan Catalan, L-person in T implies L-number—namely, when T is impersonal (i.e., L-person), its number property has the Locative property (L-number). However, in Central Catalan, number in T can be specified as singular or plural (i.e., α-number), even if T is impersonal.

3.3 Properties of v

Moreover, in Catalan as in other languages, T can select either a complete v (represented by v^*) or a weak verbal configuration v with or without ϕ-features but lacking the EPP feature (see Chomsky 1999).

Under the approach described in 3.2 and 3.3, T and v are the locus of parametric variation shown in (11)–(12) and (17)–(18).

Before proceeding to an analysis of the data, I must express my position relative to partitive NPs, such as the object NPs in (16). According to Chomsky (1998: n. 88), pure inherent case (i.e., partitive case) inactivates the ϕ-features set in a noun. My claim is that partitive case does not inactivate them, but that a noun with partitive case is unable to satisfy the EPP feature.[22]

4 ANALYSIS

This section analyzes the presence or absence of morphological concord between the existential deontic verb and its object in Catalan dialects. The sentences to analyze are those in (22):

(22)   a. Mos caleva cadires. (Ribagorçan Catalan)
      to-us was-necessary chairs
      'We needed some chairs.'

    b. Ens calien cadires. (Central Catalan)
      to-us were$_{3rd, pl}$-necessary chairs
      'We needed some chairs.'

    c. Mos caleva istes cadires. (Ribagorçan Catalan)
      to-us was-necessary these chairs
      'We needed these chairs.'

    d. Ens calien aquestes cadires. (Central Catalan)
      to-us were $_{3rd\ pl.}$-necessary these chairs
      'We needed these chairs.'

Sentences in (22a) and (22c) show that in Ribagorçan Catalan the deontic existential verb does not enter into agreement with its definite or indefinite object, whereas Central Catalan sentences in (22b) and (22d) show number agreement between the verb and its definite or indefinite object. In all these sentences, the oblique D satisfies the EPP feature in T (i.e., the need for a subject for the sentence) rising to the specifier position of T. The object cannot move to this position because oblique D is closer. See Chomsky (1998, 1999) on intervention effects.

Let us begin by analyzing the Ribagorçan Catalan sentence in (22a), in which the verb does not manifest morphological concord with the NP. This means that T matches its uninterpretable L-person and L-number features with the oblique D. Through this agreement operation, T is able to determine the structural case of the oblique D. Because the functional category v is not complete in these sentences, it has no uninterpretative features. In addition, other movement operations may take place: V moves to T, and probably the oblique clitic moves to a functional category for clitics (Kayne 1994: 42).[23] Consider the schematic representation in (23), where all uninterpretable features in T have to be erased for the convergence of the derivation:

(23) a. [. . . [T   [v [oblique D   P/V   N]]]]
           uninter. ɸ-features   inter. ɸ-features   inter. ɸ-features
                                    mos   *caleva*   *cadires*

      b. [. . . [$_T$ oblique D [$_T$ P/V T] . . . N]]
                      mos   *caleva*   *cadires*

Contrary to Ribagorçan, the Central Catalan equivalent sentence in (22b), repeated below shows morphological concord in number between the verb and its object, although the sentence is impersonal. There is no person agreement in these constructions, as shown in (6). What causes the divergence between Ribagorçan and Central Catalan is just one of the ɸ-features in T: number feature, which is not specified as a L(ocative) feature, but α-number. Consequently, T cannot match in number with the oblique D, and it has to find another element with an interpretable number feature in order to assign a value to its number feature. This element is the noun *cadires*, which is plural.[24]

(22) b. Ens calien cadires. (Central Catalan)
         to-us were$_{3rd}$, pl-necessary chairs
         'We needed some chairs.'

(24) a. [. . . [T   [v [oblique D   P/V   N   ]]]]
           uninter. L-person   inter. ɸ-features   inter ɸ-features
           uninter. α-number
                                    ens   *calien* *cadires*

b. [. . . [$_T$ oblique D   [$_T$ P/V T] . . .   N]]
      ens   *calien*   *cadires*

As in (23), in (24) T matches its L-person feature with oblique D. Because of this agreement operation, T determines the additional structural case in oblique D.

In (24) there is a matching split in Tense. L-person matches with oblique D, and number enters into agreement with N. All other operations are equal to (23). Therefore, features in T are the cause of the parametric variation shown in (22a–b).[25]

Nevertheless, another factor intervenes in the parametric variation shown in (22). It is another property of T: its ability to select a complete or incomplete verbal functional category (*v**/*v*). Consequently, T is the locus of parametric variation. It will be shown that in Central Catalan T selects *v* when T is impersonal. However, in Ribagorçan Catalan an impersonal T can select either an incomplete *v* or a complete *v** (see section 3.3).

Thus, in Ribagorçan Catalan sentences such as (22c), repeated here, where the verbal object is not partitive but a definite DP, T selects a complete *v**. A complete *v** is a head with its own uninterpretable EPP feature besides its φ-features, as shown in (25). The EPP feature in *v** is erased by the D object.[26] The φ-features in *v**—represented in italics in (25a)—receive their values from the φ-features in object D under Agree. Then the structural case feature in object D is determined by *v**, and it is accusative case. In contrast, T matches its φ-features with oblique D; consequently, the uninterpretable features in T are deleted, and the additional structural case feature in D is determined:

(22)   c. Mos caleva istes cadires. (Ribagorçan Catalan)
    to-us was-necessary these chairs

    'We needed these chairs.'

(25)   a. [. . .   [T   [*v* *   [oblique D   P/V
    D   ]]]]   *uninter.*   inter.
    inter.   uninter.   *φ-features*   φ-features
    φ-features   φ-features   *mos*
    caleva   istes cadires

   b. [. . . [$_T$ oblique D [$_T$ P/V T] . . .   D]]
       mos   *caleva*   *istes cadires*

Sentence (22d) is an example of the what happens in Central Catalan when the verbal object is D: the impersonal T selects an incomplete *v*. The uninterpretable feature L-person in T matches L-person interpretable feature in oblique D. Hence its unintepretable structural case feature is determined by T. However, α-number feature in T matches and agrees with number feature in D. Because of this, the structural case in D is determined (and erased) by T:[27]

(22)   d. Ens calien aquestes cadires. (Central Catalan)
             to-us were$_{3rd, pl}$-necessary these chairs
             'We needed these chairs.'

(26)   a. [. . . [T   [v [oblique D   P/V   D]]]]
                  uninter. L-person   inter. ϕ-features   inter. ϕ-features
                  uninter. α-number

                                               ens   calien   aquestes cadires

         b. [. . . [$_T$ oblique D [$_T$ P/V T] . . .   D]]
                  ens   calien   aquestes cadires

Briefly, consider the derivations in (27), which would crash in Ribagorçan Catalan:

(27)   a. [[T $_{[L-person, L-number]}$ v . . . D]]: It cannot converge because the unintepretable structural case feature in D is not determined, because there is no agreement between number feature in T and number feature in D.

         b. [[T $_{[L-person, L-number]}$ v^* . . . N]]: It cannot converge because the EPP feature in v^* is not erased (see n. 26).

The derivations in (28) show why an impersonal Central Catalan structure will crash if T selects v^*. The functional category v will always be incomplete in Central Catalan sentences with an impersonal T:

(28)   a. [[T $_{[L-person, \alpha-number]}$ v^* . . . N]]: It cannot converge because the EPP feature in v^* is not erased (see n. 26).

         b. [[T $_{[L-person, \alpha-number]}$ v^* . . . D]]: It cannot converge because D cannot match its ϕ-features both with v^* and (α-number) T.

The next sections show that the same pattern of parametric variation is followed by other existential sentences in Catalan, as well as other Romance languages.

5 SOME EXTENSIONS OF THE ANALYSIS

The behavior of *caldre* is not an isolated case but, rather, one instance of a phenomenon that is quite common in Catalan and other Romance languages. Compare the sentences in (29) and (30), sentences where dialectal divergence with respect to verbal agreement with the nominal object is also visible. Where Ribagorçan Catalan shows no agreement, Central Catalan has a strong tendency to show agreement between a verb and its object:

(29)　a.　Hi ha estudiants. (Ribagorçan Catalan)
　　　　　cl has students
　　　　　'There are some students.'

　　　b.　(Ens) ha fet uns dies molt assolellats.
　　　　　to-us has made some days very sunny
　　　　　'We've had some very sunny days.'

　　　c.　(En aquesta coral) hi canta nens.
　　　　　in this choir cl. sings boys
　　　　　'There are boys in this choir. / Some boys sing in this choir.'

　　　d.　Li ve ganes de dormir.
　　　　　to-him/her comes desires of to-sleep
　　　　　'She/He is getting sleepy.'

　　　e.　Sovint t'agafava atacs de tos.
　　　　　often to-you took$_{sing.}$ attacks of cough
　　　　　'You often used to have coughing fits.'

(30)　a.　Hi han estudiants. (Central Catalan)
　　　　　cl. have students
　　　　　'There are some students.'

　　　b.　(Ens) han fet uns dies molt assolellats.
　　　　　to-us have made some days very sunny
　　　　　'We've had some very sunny days.'

　　　c.　(En aquesta coral) hi canten nens.
　　　　　in this choir cl. sing boys
　　　　　'There are boys in this choir/Some boys sing in this choir.'

d. Li vénen ganes de dormir.
   to-him/her come desires of to-sleep
   'She/He is getting sleepy.'

e. Sovint t'agafaven atacs de tos.
   often to-you took$_{pl.}$ attacks of cough
   'You often used to have coughing fits.'

It was argued in Rigau (1997) that these sentences undergo the incorporation of an empty central coincidence preposition, which gives them a stative, or existential, meaning. All of them are impersonal, and the subject is an overt or covert clitic in the oblique case. In Ribagorçan no agreement is shown between the verb and the DP object. They are impersonal sentences. The construction in (29a) is a presentational existential sentence with the verb *haver* 'have'. In (29b) the verb *fer* 'to do, to make' has lost its agentive meaning and acts as a light verb that describes atmospheric conditions. In (29c) the abstract preposition of central coincidence is incorporated into the unergative verb *cantar* 'to sing'. Consequently, the verb loses its agentive meaning and becomes a stative verb that expresses the property of a place or an entity: in this case, the choir. It means that there are some boys who belong to the choir as singers.[28] The verb in (29d) is the unaccusative verb *venir* 'to come'. Because of the incorporation of the preposition of central coincidence, the sentence has a stative meaning: it expresses a property of the person to whom the pronoun refers—namely, that he is sleepy.[29] Sentence (29d) is a case of a transitive verb used as an existential predicate. An overt or covert dative clitic subject is obligatory when a transitive verb is used as a nonagentive verb. This implies that a static preposition has become incorporated into the verb.[30]

The sentences in (30) are as impersonal as those in (29). The only difference is that the DP object manifests number agreement with the verb. Like sentences with *caldre*, sentences in (29) and (30) show us the two different strategies that these two Catalan dialects follow to assign a value to the uninterpretable feature in T.

A few words must be said about the presentational existential verb *haver* 'to have'. In Ribagorçan and Central Catalan, when the object is an indefinite NP, the behavior of the verbs *haver* and *caldre* is parallel, as far as verbal concord is concerned (see (11) and (12)). But this is not the case when the object is a DP: Ribagorçan Catalan uses the copulative verb *ser* 'to be', whereas Central Catalan uses *haver* 'to have', as shown in (31) and (32).[31]

(31) a. Hi e Maria. (Ribagorçan Catalan)
         cl. is Mary
         'Mary is here/there.'

b. *Hi ha Maria.
cl. has Mary

(32) a. *Hi és la Maria.[32] (Central Catalan)
cl. is the Mary

b. Hi ha la Maria.
cl. has the Mary
'Mary is here/there.'

Note that Central Catalan uses the verb *haver* 'to have' when the DP is non-pronominal and in a postverbal position. Otherwise, the verb *ser* 'to be' is used. Therefore, in both dialects, the DP subject may appear in a preverbal position with the verb *ser*. In this construction, the clitic *hi* is not the only locative element that can appear in the sentence, as shown in (33), examples that belong to both Ribagorçan and Central Catalan:

(33) a. Les dones hi són.
the women cl. are
'The women are here/there.'

b. (La) Maria és a Lleida.
the Mary is in Lleida
'Mary is in Lleida.'

In (33a) the clitic *hi* is a true predicate, not a subject clitic, whereas in (33b) the predicate of the sentence is the locative preposition *a* 'in'. Therefore, *hi* in (33a) can stand for a PP, such as *a Lleida* 'in Lleida'. For motivation of this analysis, see Rigau (1997).[33]

Our analysis of existential sentences can be extended to constructions with the impersonalizer clitic *se*:

(34) a. Es pot tancar les finestres. (Ribagorçan Catalan)
cl. can/may$_{sing.}$ close the windows
'The windows can be closed.'

b. Es poden tancar les finestres. (Central Catalan)
cl. can$_{pl.}$ close the windows
'The windows can be closed.'

The clitic *se* has L-person and L-number features. In Ribagorçan, the node T assigns value to its L-person and L-number features through an agreement operation with the clitic. Hence, the finite verb does not agree with the DP object. Nevertheless, in Central Catalan, T is L-person but ga-number; consequently, T agrees with the DP object in number. Nevertheless, there is an important difference between the impersonal sentences in (34) and existential constructions. In (34) no central coincidence preposition has been incorporated into the verb. The clitic *se* originates in the specifier position of a complete v (or v^*) and occupies the position of an external argument.

When the clitic *se* coappears with an unergative verb, as in (35), T in Central Catalan has to check its α-number feature with an expletive *pro*. In Ribagorçan no expletive pronoun is necessary:

(35)   Es treballa massa.
        cl. works too-much
        'People work too much.'

6 Presence or Absence of Clitic Climbing

At first glance, the presence or absence of number agreement between the verb *caldre* and its object in Central Catalan and Ribagorçan seems to correlate with the absence or presence of the clitic-climbing property in *caldre* + infinitive clause constructions. Compare Central Catalan sentences in (36) with their Ribagorçan equivalents in (37):

(36)   a. No et caldria visitar-la. (Central Catalan)
            not to-you would-be-necesary to-visit her
            'You wouldn't need to visit her.'

       b. Ens calia fe'l. (= fer-lo)
            to-us was-necessary to-do it
            'We needed to do it.'

       c. No us cal anar-hi.
            not to-you$_{pl.}$ is-necessary to-go there
            'You don't need to go there.'

(37)   a. No te la caldria visitar. (Ribagorçan Catalan)
          not to-you her would-be-necesary to-visit
          'You wouldn't need to visit her.'

        b. Mos el caleva fer.
          to-us it was-necessary to-do
          'We needed to do it.'

        c. No vos hi cal anar.
          not to-you$_{pl.}$ cl. is-necessary to go
          'You don't need to go there.'

In Ribagorçan, clitics belonging to the embedded clause have to move to the main clause to reach a functional category that they may adjoin. This means that the embedded clause is defective in this dialect and that there is no C(omplementizer) node selected by V that determines a phase. However, in Central Catalan the object of the verb *caldre* is a nondefective embedded clause—namely, a CP. In this dialect, the infinitive clause has an active functional category for clitics:

(38)   a. [$_C$ [T [$_V$ cal [$_T$ T V clitic . . .] (Ribagorçan Catalan)

        b. [$_C$ [T [$_V$ cal [$_C$ [$_T$ T V clitic . . .] (Central Catalan)

The embedded node C in (38b) determines a phase. No clitic can move to the main clause, whereas in (38a) there is only one phase determined by C. In both structures in (38) the *v*P is a weak verbal configuration, so it does not determine a phase (see Chomsky 1999: 9).

In spite of the data in (36) and (37), it would be risky to claim that there is a correlation between the lack of morphological concord and the clitic climbing—for instance, that the L-number property in T is responsible for the defective character of the infinitive clause—and the fact that the embedded node T, which is defective, is linked to the matrix T. Other languages that follow the agreement pattern of Ribagorçan, such as French and Aragonese, do not show clitic climbing. The Aragonese verb *caler* does not have plural forms, yet the clitics selected by the embedded infinitive verb remain in the subordinate clause, as shown in the sentences in (39) from Nagore (1989: 207, 49).[34]

(39)   a. De diners no te'n caleba.
          of money$_{pl.}$ not to-you part. is-necessary
          'You didn't need money.'

b. No te cal sacar-lo.
   not to-you is-necessary to-take-out it
   'You don't need to take it out.'

c. (L'aragonés) cal fablar-lo y escribir-lo.
   the Aragonese is-necessary to-speak it and to-write it
   'As for Aragonese, it is necessary to speak and write it.'

On the other hand, the Ribagorçan reflexive clitic *si* 'herself/himself' remains in the embedded clause (see Rigau 1999):[35]

(40) a. *No li si cal rentar.
      not to-him/her himself/herself is-necessary to-wash

b. No (li) cal rentar-si.
   not to-him/her is-necessary to-wash himself/herself/oneself
   'She/He doesn't need to wash herself/himself.'
   'One doesn't need to wash oneself.'

Further data and studies are necessary to reach a firmly grounded conclusion about the possibility of correlation between the lack of agreement and clitic climbing.[36]

7 DEONTIC EXISTENTIAL SENTENCES IN OTHER ROMANCE LANGUAGES

The data analyzed in section 4 show us that Ribagorçan Catalan follows the strategy of other Romance languages and dialects like French, Occitan, and Benasquese—a dialect of transition between Ribagorçan and Aragonese. No morphological concord is manifested between the verb and its object, which shows accusative case, as illustrated by the accusative clitic in (41):

(41) a. Il   nous faut   ces   chaises. (French)
         expl to-us is-necessary these chairs
         'We need these chairs.'

b. Il   nous les   faut.
   expl to-us them$_{acc}$ is-necessary
   'We need them.'

c. Mos cau aguestes cagires. (Aranese Occitan)
 to-us is-necessary these chairs

 'We need these chairs.'

d. Mos les cau
 to-us them$_{acc}$ is-necessary

 'We need them.'

e. Mos cal istas sillas. (Benasquese)
 to-us is-necessary these chairs

 'We need these chairs.'

f. Mos les cal
 to-us them$_{acc}$ is-necessary

 'We need them.'

Because French is a non-null subject language, an expletive pronoun *il* has to appear in its impersonal sentences. This expletive element can be considered a parasitic element, in the sense that it has no role in the argument structure of the existential predicate.

The behavior of *kérrere* 'to be necessary' in Sardinian is partially similar to Ribagorçan. No morphological concord is manifested between the verb and its NP object, as shown in (42a), where *bi* is a locative clitic pronoun. However, when the object is a DP, it agrees in person and number with the verb, as shown in (42b). Both examples are from Jones (1993: 101f):

(42) a. Bi keret tres ovos.
 cl. is necessary three eggs

 'Three eggs are necessary.'

 b. Non bi keres tue inoke.
 not cl. are$_{2d\ sing.}$-necessary here

 'You are not needed here.'

Sentences in (42) show that in Sardinian the deontic verb *kérrere* has a double behavior. The sentence in (42a) is an existential construction with a quirky subject (the clitic *bi*), whereas (42b) is a personal sentence and the clitic *bi* is a clitic object. We assume that T has the Locative property only in (42a). Therefore, the Sardinian deontic verb *kérrere* acts similarly to the Catalan deontic verbs *convenir* 'to be advisable' and *fer falta* 'to be necesssary' mentioned in section 1. The DP object of these verbs acts as a derived subject but not its NP object, as shown in Ribagorçan Catalan examples in (43):

(43) a. Vosaltres no mos feu falta.
          you$_{pl.}$ not to-us make$_{2d, pl.}$ lack
          'We have no need for you.'

      b. Mos fa falta tres cadires.
          to-us makes lack three chairs'
          'We need three chairs.'

In contrast, deontic existential sentences in Central Catalan follow the strategy of Spanish, Galician, and Portuguese. The verb and the DP object show morphological concord, as in (44):

(44) a. Nos urgen estas sillas. (Spanish)
          to-us are-urgent these chairs
          'We urgently need these chairs.'

      b. Cómprenme estas cadeiras. (Galician)
          are-necessary to-me these chairs
          'I need these chairs.'

      c. Cumpren-nos os deveres que a Igreja impõe. (Portuguese)
          are-necessary to-us the obligations that the Church imposes
          'We are bound by the obligations that the Church imposes upon us.'

In light of what we see in (41) and (44), we can conclude that T in existential constructions in French, Occitan, and Benasquese is L-person and L-number, whereas in Spanish, Galician, and Portuguese, T is L-person but α-number.

8 CONCLUDING REMARKS

This chapter accounts for the dialectal variation in Catalan deontic existential constructions by showing that the deletion of φ-features in T is not necessarily simultaneous. The value of the person and number features in T is determined separately in existential constructions in Central Catalan and certain other Romance languages, whereas in Ribagorçan Catalan, like French or Occitan, φ-features in T are assigned values simultaneously. Furthermore, this chapter provides empirical evidence for Agree (and case determination) as an independent operation of the EPP-feature satisfaction. In Central Catalan, T and the object D agree even when D does not erase EPP feature in T.

NOTES

The issues discussed in this chapter were originally studied in Rigau (1997, 1999). Here they have been rethought and developed according to a minimalist account. For comments and suggestions, I am grateful to A. Belletti, N. Chomsky, G. Cinque, K. Hale, L. Rizzi, and my colleagues of the Grup de Gramàtica Teòrica at the Universitat Autònoma de Barcelona, especially to A. Gavarró, J. Mateu, C. Picallo, and X. Villalba. For providing me with data, I thank Z. Borràs, V. Longa, G. Lorenzo, F. Nagore, I. Pires Pereira, and very specially J. Suïls. Thanks to M. Kennedy for proofreading the manuscript. This research has been supported by Ministerio de Educación y Cultura (DGESIC: PR 1999–0211), Ministerio de Ciencia y Tecnología (BFF2003–08364-C02–01), and Generalitat de Catalunya (CIRIT: 1999BEAI400159; 2001SGR00150).

1. For other properties of Catalan as a null subject language, see Rizzi (1997), Solà-Pujols (1992), and references cited therein.

2. According to Lyons (1977: sec. 17.4), the term *deontic* refers to the logic of obligation and permission: "Deontic modality is concerned with the necessity or possibility of acts performed by morally responsible agents."

3. The same requirement applies for French presentational constructions with *avoir* 'have', where the pronoun *y* is needed (*Il y a une bibliothèque* 'There is a library'). However, French needs an additional expletive, namely, the nonreferential pronoun *il*, because it is a non-null subject language. See Rizzi (1997).

4. These constructions are called "relativized impersonal constructions" or "pseudo-impersonal constructions" by traditional Romance grammarians. See Benot (1910: 143f.) and Par (1923:147f.). See also Rigau (1999).

5. On the proximity between dative and locative, see Jespersen (1924: ch. 13).

6. Ernout and Thomas (1951: secs. 231, 272) claim that the infinitive clause that coappears with Latin verbs meaning possibility, necessity, or convenience is "more their object than their subject."

7. On the tendency of some Latin impersonal deontic verbs to become personal verbs accepting a neuter noun as a subject, and on the so-called partially impersonal Latin verbs, such as *decet* 'to be convenient', see also Ernout and Thomas (1951: sec. 231).

8. However, in those dialects where it enjoys good health, *caldre* is beginning to follow the strategy of marking the object with nominative case. Thus, some speakers use the verb *caldre* in agreement with a second-person singular pronoun, as in (ia), in spite of the fact that, in principle, other personal forms are not possible, as shown in (6). The same process is visible in Sardinian (see Jones 1993: 101f.). Nevertheless, Catalan speakers prefer other predicates when the personal pronoun is in the nominative case, as shown in (ib), where *fer falta* has the same meaning as *caldre*: 'to be necessary':

(i) a. ?Ens cals tu.
        to-us are$_{2nd, sing}$-necessary you
        'We need you.'

     b. Ens fas falta tu.
        to-us make$_{2nd, sing}$ lack you
        'We need you.'

9. The same behavior is visible with the existential verb *haver* and an indefinite NP object.

10. In Standard (or Prescriptive) Catalan, similarly to Ribagorçan Catalan, no agreement is shown between the presentational verb *haver* and its object. However, like Central Catalan, Standard Catalan shows number agreement between a deontic verb and its object. In fact, in this point Standard Catalan coincides with Balearic Catalan, as shown in (i):

(i) a. Hi ha estudiants. / *Hi han estudiants.
        cl. has students / cl. have students
        'There are some students.'

     b. Mos toquen tres exercicis. / *Mos toca tres exercicis.
        to-us is-obligated three exercises / to-us is-obligated three exercises
        'It is our turn to do three exercises.'

11. It probably became a noun or an ergative adjective. According to Cinque (1990: 7), most of the Italian modal adjectives belong to the ergative class. Actually, the behavior of *caldre* in some aspects is similar to the modal adjectival predicates like *ser probable* 'to be probable', *ser necessari* 'to be necessary' (see Rigau 1999). For the etymology of *caldre*, see Pokorny (1959).

12. The structure depicted in (14) agrees, broadly speaking, with that proposed by Hoekstra (1994) for some Hungarian and French modal verbs. According to Hoekstra, the structure underlying the Hungarian modal verb *kellet* 'to be necessary' and the French modal verb *falloir* 'to be necessary' is the following: MODAL [DP X YP], where X stands for a D/P. These deontic verbs select a dative argument.

13. In Catalan, when the verb *caldre* selects an inflective subjunctive clause, as in (i), it does not appear with a dative clitic. I argue that its argument structure is not so complex as in (14). In (i), the complement of the verb is a finite CP. No preposition is incorporated.

(i) a. Cal que estudiïs.
        is-necessary that (you) study
        'You really need to study.'

     b. *Em cal que estudiïs.
        to-me is-necessary that (you) study

14. Actually, the Latin impersonal verb *habet* could also select an accusative object, as argued by Ernout and Thomas (1956: sec. 230c): "Dès le début de l'époque impériale ... *habet* appairaît aussi au sens de 'il y a', avec un accusatif d'objet: par ex., Volpisc.,

Tac. 8. I (Script. H. Aug.): *habet in bibliotheca Vlpia librum elephantinum* 'il y a dans la bibliothèque Ulpia un livre d'ivoire'.

15. Number agreement is incompatible with the presence of the accusative preposition *a* 'to' or with an accusative clitic, as shown in the Spanish examples in (i) with the passive clitic pronoun *se*:

(i) a. Se buscan dos maestros. / *Se los buscan.
         cl. seek two teachers / cl. them seek

         'Two teachers are sought.'

     b. Se busca a dos maestros. / Se los busca.
         cl. seeks to two teachers / cl. them seek

         'Two teachers are sought.'

     c. *Se buscan a dos maestros.
         cl. seek to two teachers

In some Spanish dialects, the verbal object manifests number agreement with the verb when the passive clitic *se* absorbing the external argument is present, as in (ia). In other dialects, there is no agreement between the verb and its object in passive clitic *se* constructions, as shown in (ib), where the object is in accusative case. See Torrego (1998).

16. Φ-features are features of person, number, gender, and the like, which are interpretable in lexical categories but uninterpretable in functional categories.

17. EPP feature is the property that expresses the need of some functional category, such as Tense, to have a subject (or specifier). See Chomsky (1995).

18. Contrary to other Romance languages like Italian (*gli* 'to him/her'; *le* 'to them'), Catalan dative clitics do not manifest gender.

19. Nevertheless, usual morphological restrictions apply to constructions with the verb *caldre*—for example, the Person-Case constraint (Kayne 1975, Bonet 1991: 181f.), as shown in (i). The accusative clitic cooccurring with the dative clitic has to be third person:

(i) a. Me_{dat} la_{acc} cal (, a ta germana) (Ribagorçan Catalan)
         to-me her is-necessary (to your sister)

         'I need her.'

     b. *Me_{dat} te_{acc} cal / *Te_{acc} me_{dat} cal
         to-me you is-necessary / you to-me is-necessary

20. In Navajo examples in (i) the functional category manifesting L-property is *v*—for example, the Navajo Areal Agreement (example (14) in Hale and Keyser 1998b):

(i) a. Béégashii   yish'í.
         cow   3O.YPERF.1s.see.PERF

         'I see the cow.'

     b. Bikooh-góyaa   hweesh'í.
         arroyo-down along   AREALo.YPERF.1s.see.PERF

         'I see down along the arroyo.'

Hale and Keyser (1998b: 11f.) suggest that this type of agreement is involved in English constructions based on the *there*-insertion unaccusatives.

21. Where α-number has singular or plural value in Catalan.

22. EPP feature has to be satisfied by a DP. A bare NP or a PP is unable to do it. For the inability of a PP not related to an overt or covert clitic to satisfy EPP in French, see Kayne and Pollock (1999). Also, the possibility that nouns do not need case and that case is a necessity only for DPs has to be considered (N. Chomsky, pers. comm.).

23. Before moving to T, deontic verbs probably have to move to a Deontic Modal head, a functional category that expresses the deontic modality information of the sentence. Another possibility is to consider that the deontic verb is originated in the Deonty Modal head. See Cinque (1999).

24. Obviously T matches with singular number feature in N in the Central Catalan sentence: *Ens calia una cadira* (to-us was necessary a chair) 'We needed a chair'.

25. In Catalan, L-number cannot be implied by α-person feature.

26. Remember that we assume in section 3.3 that a partitive N is unable to satisfy the EPP feature.

27. The object D in (26a) can be a null D *pro*, as in (i):

(i)   (Aquestes cadires,) no ens calien *pro*.

       these chairs not to-us were-necessary *pro*

       '(As for these chairs) we didn't need them.'

28. See Mateu and Rigau (2002) for a detailed analysis of the argument structure of this existential construction.

29. If a referential DP appears in sentences (29c) and (30c), they lose their stative meaning, and the existential meaning is not possible:

(i)   Hi canten ells.

       cl. sing they

       'They are singing here/there.'

In (i), no static preposition is incorporated into the verb, and the person feature in T does not have the Locative property. Consequently, the verb agrees with the DP, even in Ribagorçan Catalan.

Like Ribagorçan, Sardinian does not manifest agreement in constructions such as (29c). Jones (1993: 195) also notes that the presence of a DP causes the ungrammaticality of the sentence:

(i)   a.   B'at ballatu tres pitzinnas.
             cl. has danced three girls

             'Three girls danced.'

       b.   *B'at ballatu cussos pitzinnas
             cl. has danced these girls

Regarding (29c) and (30c), see Torrego (1989), who argues that an initial locative phrase in Spanish and a locative clitic in Catalan allow a partitive NP with an unergative verb. See also Moro (1993), who considers the unaccusativity as an epiphenomenon.

30. I thank J. Mateu for calling my attention to this verb.

31. However, this is not a general fact in Northwestern Catalan dialects. Thus, in

the dialect spoken in Segrià, (32b) is grammatical and (32a) ungrammatical, unless the DP is right-dislocated.

32. In Central Catalan, personal proper nouns coappear with a definite determiner. Construction (32a) is ungrammatical as a declarative sentence. However, if *la Maria* is right-dislocated, the construction is grammatical: *Hi és, la Maria* 'As for Mary, she is here'.

33. The verb *haver* 'to have' shows sensitivity to tense and aspect in Ribagorçan. It cannot be used in imperfective past tense, and the verb *ser* 'to be' has to be used instead. This is true for indicative or subjunctive presentational constructions, as well as for the auxiliary selection in past perfect tense. On the sensitivity of auxiliary selection to tense in Romance, see Kayne (1993):

(i) a. Hi era moltes dones.
         cl. was many women
         'Many women were here/there.'

     b. Si hi fos molta gent, ballaríem.
         if cl. were$_{subjunctive}$ many people we would-dance
         'If there were many people, we would dance.'

     c. Ell era parlat. / Ell ha parlat.
         he was spoken / he has spoken
         'He had spoken. / He has spoken.'

34. Contrary to Ribagorçan Catalan, an accusative clitic cannot coappear with *caler* in Aragonese (F. Nagore, pers. comm.), as shown in (i). See Kayne (1989: 249) about the correlation between clitic climbing out of the infinitival complement of an impersonal verb and the possibility of accusative case on the postverbal DP:

(i) *Te las cal.
     to-you them is-necessary

35. It may be that the Ribagorçan reflexive clitic *si* is able to adjoin a defective (or partially active) functional category for clitics belonging to the embedded clause because of its zero-person and zero-number features. On the features of reflexive clitics, see Kayne (1993, 1998); see also Kayne (1975).

36. See Benincà and Poletto (1994) and Guéron (1999) for the Italian deontic verb *bisognare* 'to be necessary', which can select a finite or an infinitive clause.

REFERENCES

Benincà, P., and Poletto, C. (1994) "Bisogna and Its Companions: The Verbs of Necessity," in G. Cinque, et al. (eds.) *Paths towards Universal Grammar: Studies in Honor of Richard S. Kayne.* Georgetown University Press, Washington, D.C., 35–58.

Benot, E. (1910) *El arte de hablar: Gramática filosófica de la lengua castellana.* Anthropos, Barcelona, 1991.

Benveniste, É. (1966) "Structure des relations de personne dans le verbe," in É. Benveniste *Problèmes de linguistique générale*, Gallimard, Paris, 225–236.

Bonet, E. (1991) "Morphology after Syntax: Pronominal Clitics in Romance Languages." Ph.D. diss., MIT, Cambridge, Mass.

Chomsky, N. (1995) *The Minimalist Program*. MIT Press, Cambridge, Mass.

Chomsky, N. (1998) "Minimalist Inquiries: The Framework." MIT Occasional Papers in Linguistics. MIT Working Papers in Linguistics, 15. Cambridge, Mass.

Chomsky, N. (1999) "Derivation by Phase." MIT Occasional Papers in Linguistics. MIT Working Papers in Linguistics, 18. Cambridge, Mass.

Cinque, G. (1990) "Ergative Adjectives and the Lexicalist Hypothesis." *Natural Language and Linguistic Theory* 8(1): 1–40.

Cinque, G. (1999) *Adverbs and Functional Heads*. Oxford University Press, New York.

Ernout, A., and Thomas, F. (1951) *Syntaxe latine*. Klinscksieck, Paris.

Fabra, P. (1956) *Gramàtica catalana*. Teide, Barcelona.

Fernández-Soriano, O. (1999) "Two Types of Impersonal Sentences in Spanish: Locative and Dative Subjects." *Syntax* 2: 101–140.

Freeze, R. (1992) "Existentials and Other Locatives." *Language* 68: 553–595.

Guéron, J. (1999) "From Need to Necessity: A Syntactic Path to Modality." Unpublished ms., University of Paris III.

Hale, K. (1986) "Notes on World View and Semantic Categories: Some Walpiri Examples," in P. Muysken and H. van Riemsdijk (eds.) *Features and Projections*. Foris, Dordrecht, 233–254.

Hale, K., and S. J. Keyser (1993) "On the Argument Structure and the Lexical Expression of Syntactic Relations," in K. Hale and S. J. Keyser (eds.) *The View from Building 20*, MIT Press, Cambridge, Mass., 53–109.

Hale, K., and S. J. Keyser (1997) "On the Complex Nature of Simple Predicators," in A. Alsina et al. (eds.) *Complex Predicates*. CSLI Publications, Stanford, Calif. 29–65.

Hale, K., and S. J. Keyser (1998a) "The Basic Elements of Argument Structure." *MIT Working Papers in Linguistics* 32: 73–118.

Hale, K., and S. J. Keyser (1998b) "There-Insertion Unaccusatives and Other Complex Intransitives." Unpublished ms., MIT, Cambridge, Mass.

Hoekstra, T. (1994) "HAVE as BE Plus or Minus," in G. Cinque et al. (eds.) *Paths towards Universal Grammar: Studies in Honor of Richard S. Kayne*. Georgetown University Press, Washington, D.C., 199–216.

Jespersen, O. (1924) *The Philosophy of Grammar*. George Allen and Unwin, London.

Jones, M. A. (1993) *Sardinian Syntax*. Routledge, London.

Kayne, R. S. (1975) *French Syntax*. MIT Press, Cambridge Mass.

Kayne, R. S. (1989) "Null Subjects and Clitic Climbing," in O. Jaeggli and K. Safir (eds.) *The Null Subject Parameter*. Kluwer, Dordrecht, 239–262.

Kayne, R. S. (1993) "Toward a Modular Theory of Auxiliary Selection." *Studia Linguistica* 47: 3–31.

Kayne, R. S. (1994) *The Antisymmetry of Syntax*. MIT Press, Cambridge, Mass.

Kayne, R. S. (1998) "Person Morphemes and Reflexives." Unpublished ms., New York University.

Kayne, R. S. (1999) "A Note on Clitic Doubling in French." Unpublished ms., New York University.

Kayne, R. S., and Pollock, J.-Y. (1999) "New Thoughts on Stilistic Inversion." Unpublished ms. New York University and Centre National de la Recherche Scientifique, Lyon.

Longa, V. M., G. Lorenzo, and G. Rigau (1998) "Subject Clitics and Clitic Recycling: Locative Sentences in Some Iberian Romance Languages." *Journal of Linguistics* 34: 125–164.

Lyons, J. (1977) *Semantics*. Cambridge University Press, Cambridge.

Masullo, P. J. (1993) "Two Types of Quirky Subjects: Spanish versus Icelandic," in A. Schafer (ed.) *Conference Proceedings in Linguistics: NELS 23*, GLSA Publications, University of Massachusetts Amherst, 303–317.

Mateu, J., and Rigau G. (2002) "A Minimalist Account of Conflation Processes: Parametric Variation at the Lexico-Syntax Interface," in A. Alexiadov (ed.) *Theoretical Approaches to Universals*. John Benjamins, Amsterdam, 211–236.

Moro, A. (1993) *I predicati nominali e la struttura della frase*. Unipress, Padua.

Nagore, F. (1989) *Gramática de la lengua aragonesa*. Mira, Zaragoza.

Par, A. (1923) *Sintaxi catalana segons los escrits en prosa de Bernat Metge (1398)*. Max Niemeyer, Halle.

Pokorny, J. (1959) *Indogermanishes etymologisches Wörterbuch*. Francke, Bern.

Rigau, G. (1982) "Inanimate Indirect Object in Catalan." *Linguistic Inquiry* 13: 146–150.

Rigau, G. (1991) "On the Functional Properties of Agr." *Catalan Working Papers in Linguistics*. Universitat Autònoma de Barcelona, Bellaterra, 235–260.

Rigau, G. (1997) "Locative Sentences and Related Constructions in Catalan: *ésser/haver* Alternation," in M. Uribe-Etxebarria and A. Mendikoetxea (eds.) *Theoretical Issues at the Morphology-Syntax Interface*. Universidad del Pais Vasco, Bilbao, 395–421.

Rigau, G. (1999) "Relatived Impersonality: Deontic Sentences in Catalan," in E. Treviño and J. Lema (eds.) *Semantic Issues in Romance Syntax*. John Benjamins, Amsterdam, 193–230.

Rizzi, L. (1997) "A Parametric Approach to Comparative Syntax: Properties of the Pronominal System," in L. Haegeman, (ed.) *The New Comparative Syntax*. Longman, London, 268–285

Sigurdsson, H. (1996) "Icelandic Finite Verb Agreement." *Working Papers in Scandinavian Syntax* 57: 1–46.

Solà-Pujols, J. (1992) "Agreement and Subjects." Ph.D. diss., Universitat Autònoma de Barcelona.

Torrego, E. (1989) "Unergative-Unaccusative Alternations in Spanish." *MIT Working Papers in Linguistics* 10: 235–272.

Torrego, E. (1998) *The Dependencies of Objects*. MIT Press, Cambridge, Mass.

CHAPTER 18

CLASSIFIERS AND DP STRUCTURE IN SOUTHEAST ASIA

ANDREW SIMPSON

1 INTRODUCTION

SOUTHEAST Asia is a geographical area that is extremely rich from a linguistic point of view, being a Balkan-like region where a wide range of language families meet and interact with each other. This chapter's particular focus of interest is the internal structure of DPs and the specific problem of how to account for the considerable amount of cross-linguistic variation that appears to occur in the ordering of constituents in DPs. Some of the patterns found are schematized in (1)–(3) (RC = relative clause, CL = classifier):

(1) Thai, Khmer: N Adj RC Num CL Dem

(2) Burmese: Dem RC N Adj Num CL

(3) Hmong, Malay, Vietnamese: Num CL N Adj RC Dem

Of considerable interest here is the fact that the variation attested often does not seem to follow or correspond to the apparent headedness of the relevant languages. Thus, for example, Thai and Khmer are both canonical SVO head-initial languages, yet at first sight they seem to be head-final in their DPs with elements such as Num, CL, and Dem all following the head noun N (and in the postnominal placement of Num and CL, Thai and Khmer pattern with the canonical SOV language Burmese rather than the SVO languages listed in (3)). Other aspects of (1)–(3) can be similarly argued to be unexpected given the assumed general headedness of the languages in question. In this chapter, therefore, I set out to examine what factors might be responsible for the diversity attested, asking whether there are, indeed, any significant principles regulating the internal structure of DPs in Southeast Asian languages, or whether one has to concede that the patterns are really random and unconstrained.

2 THE STATUS OF CLASSIFIERS

Considering the syntax of DPs in Southeast Asian languages, a first important issue that needs to be examined and clarified is the syntactic status of the classifier elements that occur in DPs throughout the languages of the region. In the literature concerned with DP syntax in other classifier languages such as Japanese and Chinese, there are actually two quite different assumptions about classifiers and the relation they have to numerals. On the one hand, a number of works consider numbers and classifiers to instantiate distinct functional head positions, Num and CL (e.g., Pan 1990, Tang 1990). In other works, however, numbers and classifiers are treated as constituting a single functional head labeled simply CL, Num, or Q (e.g., Kawashima 1993, Muromatsu 1998). Somewhat surprisingly, there is often little explicit argumentation justifying one of the possible analyses over the other, and either one analysis or the other is frequently simply assumed without further discussion. Whether numbers and classifiers instantiate a single head or distinct heads is an important question with significant consequences, however, and it is therefore important to consider what arguments there are in favor of either of the two possible analyses.

Gil (1994) identifies the following observations as potential support for the view that numerals and classifiers comprise a single syntactic unit. First, as observed in Greenberg (1975), numbers and classifiers commonly occur together as a single *uninterrupted* sequence. Second, numbers and classifiers in many languages pattern phonologically as a single unit, suggesting that the classifier might perhaps be a suffix attached to the numeral. Third, in certain languages, the number+classifier sequence can appear separated and "floated" away from the rest of an NP, indicating (possibly) a particularly close linking of the number and classifier as a single unit. Such potential arguments in favor of a single-head analysis, however, are perhaps not particularly strong. The observation that numbers and classifiers are commonly adjacent and uninterrupted may just as easily be explained by the assumption that numbers and classifiers are perhaps in adjacent functional heads, Num⁰ selecting a complement CLP, and does not force one to assume that classifiers must necessarily be suffixes on numbers. The phonological dependence of classifiers on numbers (where attested) may possibly be attributed to classifiers coming to be enclitics as they grammaticalize, as indeed noted in Gil (1994), and again does not rule out the possibility that classifiers might encliticize from a discrete head position. Finally, the phenomena of numeral and classifier "floating" can, in fact, also be given plausible accounts under a two-head alternative and so do not obviously favor a single-head analysis.

The arguments supporting a two-head hypothesis are considerably stronger. First, there is the simple observation that two distinct morphemes occur in numeral–classifier sequences, which might naturally seem to suggest that two distinct head positions are projected. Classifiers in the many languages of Southeast Asia are also by and large phonologically quite unreduced and so appear to be fully independent functional words rather than inflectional affixes.

Second, classifiers are *functional* elements, argued by Muromatsu (1998), Cheng and Sybesma (1999), and others to have the primary semantic function of *individuating* NPs. Importantly, the two functions of individuation (provided by the classifier) and number specification (provided by numerals) are semantically distinct, and the use of a numeral with an NP does not, in fact, imply that the NP necessarily has to be conceived of as a set of discrete individuated entities. Instead, a numerated NP can be conceived of as a nonindividuated group whose total is simply specified numerically. This assumed distinction between the functions of numerals and classifiers has observable consequences in certain classifier languages, and one finds clear evidence of two types in favor of the separation of numerals and classifiers into two formally independent heads. In languages such as Vietnamese, Hmong, and Nung, one finds that a classifier can occur alone *without any numeral*, simply functioning to individuate an NP, as in (4):

(4) Tus   tsov   tshaib   tshaib   plab.
     CL   tiger hungry   hungry   stomach
     'The tiger is/was very hungry.' (Hmong; Jaisser 1987)

The converse situation, that numerals may sometimes occur without any accompanying classifier, typically is found when the numeral specification is rather vague and individuation is not necessarily implied. Thus, in Nung and Burmese, classifiers are optional with numbers that are multiples of ten; in Jingpo, classifiers are often omitted with numbers over ten; and "in Thai classifiers do not occur with large numbers like 1000 unless individuation is implied" (Aikhenvald 2000: 100). Hopper (1986) also points out that in Malay classifiers are omitted with numerals just when approximate and vague numeral reference is made and there is no specific individuation, as in (5):

(5) Adalah dua   tiga pondok kechil- kechil bersama-sama dekat
     be   2   3   hut   small   small   together   near
     rumah   Temenggong.
     house   Temenggong

     'There were two or three small huts close together near Temenggong's house.'

Finally, Bisang (1999) notes that in Vietnamese the classifier may similarly be omitted when a counted noun is not individualized, as in (6) and various other examples from Löbel (1996) (in (6) no classifier occurs individualizing *phong* 'room'):

(6) nha   ba   phong
     house   3   room

     'a three-room house'

Such patterns are good indications that classifiers and numerals perform distinct formal functions (numerical specification and individuation) and so should be assumed to occur in separate syntactic heads.

   A third argument in favor of the two-head hypothesis comes from the observation that in Nung, a northern Tai language, the number 'one' does not occur adjacent to the classifier at all but is actually separated from the classifier by the noun:

(7) An   ahn   tahng nuhng ma.
     take   CL   chair one   come

     'Bring a chair.' (Saul and Wilson 1980: 56)

A similar pattern is reported in Ejagham (Benue-Congo), and all numbers may be found nonadjacent to the classifier (NC = noun class marker):

(8) a-mege '   i-cokud   a-bae.
     NC-CL GEN   NC-orange seed   NC-two

     'two orange seeds' (Watters 1981: 310)

If numerical specification by any number is possible in a position distinct from the classifier position, this indicates again that the functions of counting and individuation can be assumed to relate to distinct functional head positions.

There are also languages that allow for a limited range of adjectives to be inserted between numerals and the classifier position, as in Chinese (9), this again indicating that the numeral and the classifier do not occur in a single functional head position:

(9) a. yi   xiao   ben   shu
        one   small CL   book

     'one small book'

     b. liu   da   jian   xingli
        6   big   CL   luggage

     'six big pieces of luggage' (T'ung and Pollard 1982)

Overall, then, the evidence suggests that numerals and classifiers do not occur together in a single-head position and that there are, instead, two distinct positions projected by numbers and classifiers, Num and CL, each associated with a distinct semantic function.

3 HEADEDNESS AND DIRECTIONALITY IN THE DP

The conclusion that Num⁰ and CL⁰ occur as the heads of distinct functional projections can now be shown to have important consequences for the analysis of DP-structure in many of the Southeast Asian classifier languages. Reconsider the ordering of elements in the Thai (and Khmer) DP (10) and compare this with Chinese (11):

(10) Thai: [$_{DP}$ N   Adj   Num   CL   Dem]

(11) Chinese: [$_{DP}$ Dem   Num   CL   Adj   N]

If one were to assume, contrary to the conclusions of section 2, that Num and CL combine to form a *single* functional head, then (10) and (11) would actually be mirror images of each other. The two orders could then possibly be accounted for by suggesting that (11) is a head-initial DP with Dem/D^0 and Num-CL^0 selecting complements to their right, and that the mirror-image pattern in (10) is simply a head-final DP ordered in the opposite way (though such a conclusion might be surprising, as Thai is elsewhere regularly head-initial). Significantly, once the single-head analysis of Num and CL is rejected (for the reasons given) in favor of the assumption that both Num and CL instantiate discrete functional heads, such an analysis of Chinese and Thai is no longer possible. Consider the Thai sequence in (10) once more. If the ordering in (10) is a result of simple base-generation of a head-final DP and if Num and CL are discrete heads, then it has to be assumed that CL^0 is located above Num^0. If this is so, then it becomes impossible to assume that the head-initial Chinese order in (11) is base-generated, because instead of (11) one would expect the sequence [Dem CL Num Adj N] with CL^0 selecting NumP to its right.

In fact, in all works distinguishing Num and CL as distinct heads, it is commonly assumed that Num/numerals and other quantifiers take scope over CL/classifiers, this reflecting the assumption that nouns may first be individuated by a classifier and then quantified over by a numeral or other quantifier (see Cheng and Sybesma 1999). If Num and CL project separate heads, such a scope relation therefore suggests that Num should be the higher of the two heads. Reconsidering the Thai order in (10) now, this results in the important conclusion that such a sequence cannot, in fact, be simply base-generated as it appears; in a head-final structure, one would (now) clearly expect the ordering to instead be [N CL Num Dem], with Num selecting CLP to its left.

If the surface linear sequence in Thai (10) is not simply base-generated, it has to be assumed that it results from certain movement. Because the ordering of the elements Num and CL with respect to N seems to be the problematic part of structure in need of explanation, consider now how the order [N Num CL] might be created. Essentially, there are three possibilities. If one assumes that the Thai DP is underlyingly head-final (despite this going against the headedness of Thai elsewhere), one would have to conclude that [N Num CL] sequences arise either via movement of the CL to a higher rightward head position above Num—namely, [N t$_i$ Num CL$_i$]—or that [N Num CL] results from lowering of the Num to a position below CL; namely, [N Num$_i$ CL t$_i$]. Neither of these possibilities seems plausible, however. The first would be expected to be blocked by the Head Movement Constraint (HMC) and the second barred by general restrictions on lowering. Consequently, it seems that one is forced to assume that Num and CL do not change positions, that the DP is therefore underlyingly head-initial, and that it is the N element that undergoes movement, raising leftward from a position base-generated as the rightward complement of CL. Because this raising might be expected to be blocked by the HMC if just the N^0 moved, and because adjectives and relative clauses also regularly intervene between the N in its DP-initial position and the Num CL sequence, it can be assumed that movement of the 'N' is actually movement of the entire NP rather than just the N^0, as represented in (12):

(12) $[_{DP} [_{NP}$ dek   naa-rak$]_i [_{NumP}$ soong $[_{CLP}$ khon $t_i]]]$
               child lovable   two   CL

    'two cute children'

Such a conclusion that NP-movement takes place within the DP will, in fact, also be forced by a consideration of the position of NP relative to demonstratives, if one assumes that there should be only a single direction of selection within a language, as in (13):

(13) $[_{DP} [_{NP}$ dek   naa-rak$]$ nii$]$
               child lovable   this

    'this cute child'

If one takes the general head-initial property of Thai to indicate that DPs should also be assumed to be head-initial, the sequence in (13) will also not allow for an analysis as being simply base-generated in its surface form. If the demonstrative is in a D^0 head position and Thai is head-initial, it has to be assumed that the NP has been moved leftward from an underlying complement position to the right of D^0—namely, $[_{DP} [_{NP}]_i$ Dem $t_i]$. If the demonstrative is alternatively suggested to be in a specifier position (perhaps SpecDP), because specifiers in Thai are projected to the left of phrasal heads, again it would have to be concluded that the NP has undergone leftward movement from a complement position to the right of D^0—namely, $[[_{NP}]_i [_{DP}$ Dem $[_D] t_i]]$.

The assumption that the demonstrative occurs in DP-final position due to leftward movement of its complement in Thai is one that, incidentally, also has to be made in other languages of Southeast Asia, such as Hmong, Vietnamese, and Indonesian. All of these languages are regular head-initial (and Spec-initial), and all have DP-final demonstratives. Considerations of headedness as noted with Thai therefore lead to the same assumption: that the complement of the D^0 is moved leftward, leaving demonstratives in surface-final position in the DP. What is significant to note about Hmong, Vietnamese, and Indonesian is that, unlike in Thai, Num, and CL, both precede the NP within DPs, and so these languages also appear to be regularly head-initial *inside* the DP, as illustrated in Indonesian (14):

(14)   tiga buah sepeda
      3   CL   bicycle

    'three bicycles'

As the sole exception to this headedness is the position of the demonstrative, the conclusion that its complement moves leftward leaving the demonstrative in DP-final position is rather straightforward to make, and any other attempted analysis faces serious difficulties in reconciling the different directions of headedness within the DP that would have to be assumed for D^0 versus Num^0, CL^0, and N^0. To the extent that such a conclusion is therefore well justified in Hmong, Vietnamese, and Indonesian, it adds extra plausibility to the similar assumptions made about Thai.

A further important comparative point concerns Nung, a northern Tai language. Significantly, Nung has exactly the same ordering of elements in the DP (and elsewhere in the language) as standard Thai does, with the exception of Num and CL, which *precede* the N (in the positions they are suggested to occur underlyingly in Thai):

(15)   Nung (northern Tai):   **Num**   CL   N   Adj
       Thai (southern Tai):   N   Adj   **Num**   **CL**

Supposing one were to attempt to argue that the ordering in standard Thai actually was base-generated as a head-final structure (despite all of the arguments against this given previously), it would then be very difficult to suggest that the same order could be base-generated in a related language except with the heads Num and CL located in quite a different position relative to the head-noun. To allow for both standard Thai and Nung, it seems that some kind of movement has to be assumed, and as all other arguments would seem to point toward an analysis of NP-movement in standard Thai, one can suggest that the [Num CL N] order in Nung simply encodes on the surface the underlying order in standard Thai.[1]

Finally, an NP-movement analysis of Thai receives further support from the fact that movement of this type is directly observable in certain other languages. For example, in Indonesian it is noted that the neutral order within the DP [Num CL NP Dem] may sometimes be converted into an order with the NP initial in the DP [NP Num CL Dem], as in:

(16)   Maka   adapun   mengerjakan   [lobang   sa   buah   itu]   sampai
       and   indeed   make   hole   one   CL   that   took
       lima   enam   hari.
       5   6   day

'Indeed it took 5 or 6 days just to dig that one hole.' (Hopper 1986: 317)

A similar alternation occurs in Vietnamese, as noted in Nguyen (1957). Vietnamese has the neutral order [Num CL NP] just as in Indonesian, but Nguyen points out that in poetry and literature and in "inventory forms," this may be converted into [NP Num CL], just as in Indonesian.[2]

The theoretical arguments and empirical support that can be brought together in favor of a head-initial analysis of DPs in Thai therefore turn out to be good. What needs to be done now is to see if there is any plausible motivation for the DP-internal movement of the NP. Before I do this, however, I briefly consider a potential alternative to the conclusion that (NP-)movement is involved and the possibility that Num and CL perhaps modify the NP in some other kind of non-head-complement way. Muromatsu (1998) suggests that rather than being functional categories selecting NP, numerals and classifiers may actually be small-clause *predicates*, predicating onto NP subjects within the DP. Considering Thai within such an approach, one would not be forced to assume movement of the NP to its surface position. Instead, it could be suggested that the NP is simply base-generated DP-initially as the subject of a rightward predicate consisting of Num + CL.

In support of the "predicate" theory is the observation that numerals and certain quantifiers seem to be able to occur as predicates in various languages such as English and (classical) Chinese, as noted in Higginbotham (1987) and Pulleyblank (1995):

(17)   a.   The apostles are twelve in number.
      b.   They are many (in number).

(18)   Mie-guo-zhe   wu-shi.
      destroy-country-NZL   50

      'His extinctions of countries were fifty.' (Meng 3B/9, in Pulleyblank 1995: 58)

In Thai, however, there is a good reason to believe that Num + CL does not, in fact, modify the NP in any kind of subject-predicate structure. Higginbotham (1987) points out that the possibility for numerals and quantifiers to occur as predicates is critically restricted and that only certain *weak* quantifiers are found in subject-predicate structures. Where predication is attempted with strong quantifiers as in (18), this is quite unacceptable:

(19)   *the men are all/each

Significantly in Thai, the Num position preceding CL also hosts various quantifiers (in alternation with numerals), and these include both weak and strong quantifiers:

(20) dek   soong khon / laai   khon / thuk   khon
      child   2   CL   several   CL   every   CL

      'two children/several children/all the children'

The possibility for strong quantifiers such as *thuk* 'all/every' to occur in Num preceding CL seems to clearly rule out the plausibility of any subject-predicate analysis of [NP Num CL] sequences. Such strong quantifiers are as impossible as predicates in Thai as they are in other languages:

(21) *Dek-law-nii   thuk-(khon).
      child-group-this   every-CL

      Intended: '*These children are all/every.'

Consequently, it seems that the NP-movement analysis of Thai DPs has to be maintained.

4 MOTIVATING THE MOVEMENT

The key to understanding what may cause the movement of the NP to DP-initial position can be suggested to lie in a frequently made observation about the use of [NP Num (CL)] sequences. In Greenberg (1975), Gil (1994), and various other works, it is pointed out that linear sequences of noun or NP before numeral (and classifier) are found to occur particularly often in written list or "inventory" forms, as well as when people are involved in situations such as ordering food in a restaurant or buying commodities in a store. Thus if both [Num CL NP] and [NP Num CL] forms are possible in a language, as in Indonesian, Vietnamese, Chinese, and various other languages, the latter [NP Num CL] ordering is frequently noted to be either a form preferred in lists or buying or food-ordering types of situations (as, for example, in Indonesian (22)), or, alternatively, it is only attested in such situations. This sequencing of noun or NP before a numeral is furthermore observed (J. Hurford, pers. comm., in Gil 1994) to occur as a conventional way of itemizing elements in written shopping lists in languages such as English which otherwise do not permit such orders, as shown in (23):

(22) Saya   mau   membeli   beras   dua   kilo.
      I   want   buy   rice   2   kilo

      'I want to buy two kilos of rice.'

(23)   Sugar, 3 pounds
       Bread, 2 loaves
       Wine, 4 bottles

Cross-linguistically, then, it can be noted that [NP Num CL] sequences are orders which are either found to be the only possible ordering of Num, CL, and NP in a language (as, e.g., in Thai, Khmer, and Burmese), or they occur frequently in certain situations as alternatives to a possibly more common [Num CL NP] order (as, e.g., in Indonesian, Vietnamese, Chinese, and also Japanese and Korean). [NP Num CL] orders are therefore considerably widespread and occur throughout the major classifier languages in Asia. This now raises the question of why such an ordering should be so widespread and why it should be favored in the situations noted. A possible answer here is that sequencing the noun or NP before the numeral and classifier may well be a natural and useful way of ordering this kind of information in certain types of *presentational* situations. What the placement of the NP in DP-initial position effectively does in [NP Num CL] forms is to ensure that in linear terms information about the identity of the NP is presented before information about its cardinality. Such an ordering is arguably practical and useful at certain times.

For example, in the case of a storekeeper receiving information about what goods a customer wishes to purchase, identifying the type of goods before the quantity (i.e., ordering noun or NP before Num CL) presents the information in a sequence that mirrors the actions of the storekeeper, who first needs to identify and locate the required goods and then select a certain quantity of them. The presentation of the information in this way may therefore be both naturally helpful and also efficient and logical. If this is indeed a plausible interpretation of why NP-initial orders are cross-linguistically particularly frequent in lists, ordering, and other presentational situations, the placement of the NP in DP-initial position can be likened to presentational focus or topicalization at the sentential level (as in fact hinted at in Greenberg 1975); in both CP and DP, nominal elements that are being newly presented may be fronted so that they linearly precede additional information being added on about them.

In this regard, note the following sequence from classical Chinese, which at one time had both [Num NP] and [NP Num CL] forms. In the initial presentation of the new referent, the fronted NP-initial order is used, while the [Num NP] order without NP-fronting occurs in the following sentence, as the referent has been established as old, identified information: (from Schafer 1948: 413):

(24)   You   da   jiang   er   ren.   Er   jiang...
       be   big   general   2   CL   2   general...

       'There were two great generals. The two generals . . .'

In some classifier languages such as Indonesian and classical Chinese, the DP-internal presentational focus is clearly optional, and the languages have both [Num CL NP] and [NP Num CL] orders. In other languages such as Thai, Khmer, and Burmese, there is no alternative to the [NP Num CL] order, and it can be suggested that the presentational focus movement has simply become obligatory, with all DPs having to be formed with the NP in prominent, DP-initial position.

If there is indeed a legitimate presentational focus–related motivation for the NP-movement, this now raises a further question. Supposing that the [NP Num CL] order results from NP-raising, it might be expected that this would have developed from earlier structures with no movement of the NP and that one would therefore find earlier forms with Num, CL, and NP simply remaining in their underlying base-generated positions—namely, [Num CL NP]. However, it does not seem possible to find such forms, and in Chinese, for example, [NP Num CL] sequences seem to have arisen spontaneously without any prior [Num CL NP] forms occurring. This therefore appears to challenge an NP-movement analysis and requires some further investigation.

A reasonable explanation of the lack of early [Num CL NP] forms can be offered here by considering a quite different theory of [NP Num CL] sequences, the "adverb" theory which suggests that postnominal Num-CL elements are actually not inside the DP at all but, rather, are adverbs base-generated in quite distinct adjunct-like positions. This approach to postnominal Num-CL sequences is developed in Fukushima (1991) and Ishii (2000) for modern Japanese, having originally been suggested in Greenberg (1975), and it is supported by a variety of evidence.

First, it is noted that in languages where Num and CL may occur following the NP, the Num and CL may also occur separated from the NP in other VP-/S-final adverbial type positions, as illustrated here in Thai (25) and classical Chinese (26):

(25) Mii **nisit**   maa   haa   khun **soong** **khon**.
      be   student   come   find   you   two   CL

      'Two students came to look for you.'

(26) Xi   sang   **di**   yu   Qin   **qi-bai-li**.
      west lose   land   to   Qin   700 li

      'On the west we lost 700 li's land to the Qin.' (Meng 1A/5, in Pulleyblank 1995: 58)

Second, it is well observed that classifiers develop from other independent nouns. Consequently, it can be suggested that in the earliest classifier-type constructions before the category of classifier may have formally been established as a DP-internal functional-category, "classifiers" would have actually been the heads of independent NPs occurring as adverbial-type elements modified by numerals. This is represented by the bracketing given to the early (oracle bone inscription) Chinese example (27) noted in Bisang (1999), where the classifier is simply a repetition of the first noun:

(27)   [$_{NP}$ ren]   [$_{NP}$ shi-you-wu ren]
            person   10-and-5   person
       '15 people'

Third, Fukushima (1991) points out that Num and CL in Japanese can actually be coordinated with adverbs, suggesting that Num and CL constitute separate adverbial elements base-generated outside the DPs they numerically modify:

(28)   Shoonin-ga   kinoo   [san-nin katsu tashika-ni]   sono
       witness-NOM   yesterday 3-CL   and   certainly   that
       jiko-o   mokugekishi-ta.
       accident-ACC witness-PAST

'Three witnesses certainly witnessed that accident yesterday.'

Fourth, there are instances of "floated" Num-CL pairs, which could not have been base-generated with the associated preceding NP and so which must be assumed to be base-generated independently. Although the Num-CL pair *ippatsu* 'one blast' can occur after the NP *pisutoru* 'pistol' in (29), it cannot be positioned before the NP, even though Japanese otherwise regularly allows the prenominal sequence [Num CL no NP]:

(29)   a. Taroo-ga   pisutoru-o   ippatsu   kinoo   utta.
           Taroo-NOM   pistol-ACC   one-CL(blast)   yesterday   shot
           'Yesterday Taroo shot off one blast of his pistol.' (Fukushima 1991: 73)

       b. *Taroo-ga   ippatsu-no-pisutoru   kinoo   utta.
           Taroo-NOM   one-CL-GEN-pistol-ACC   yesterday   shot

The adverb theory of postnominal Num-CL can now be suggested to provide a way of understanding how [NP Num CL] DP sequences might arise without there being any previous stage of [Num CL NP]. It can be suggested that under simple linear adjacency early sequences of argument NP and numerically quantified adverbial NP (the Num-CL pair) may have come to be significantly reinterpreted as parts of a single DP. When such a hypothetical reanalysis takes place in a language such as Thai, because of the ordering of Num before CL and the general headedness of the language, speakers who reanalyze [NP Num CL] as a

single DP will analyze the initial NP as undergoing movement to its surface position from a natural complement position following CL and interpret this movement as an instance of simple DP-internal presentational focus, effectively achieving the same linear ordering effect as the occurrence of an argument NP before
a numerically quantified adverbial NP in prereanalysis structures. The "occurrence" of NP-movement in the DP can consequently be suggested to arise not
from an earlier "unmoved" [Num CL NP] source but may actually be the direct
and instantaneous result of the reanalysis of a rather different two-NP structure.

If such a reanalysis approach can be maintained, it will clearly explain why
one does not find earlier sequences of [Num CL NP] in languages with [NP Num
CL] orders. Ironically, though, what one now needs to find is good evidence that
the suggested reanalysis has indeed taken place, as it could be argued as in Fukushima (1991) and Greenberg (1975) that, in fact, postnominal Num-CL sequences are still just adverbs and not part of the DP. In what remains of this
section, this chapter shows that there is indeed evidence of this kind, as well as
noting a certain interfering complication.

First, in Thai and Khmer there is clear evidence from the placement of demonstratives that Num and CL do occur inside the DP. As noted in an earlier
section, demonstratives in Thai (and Khmer) occur in final position in the DP,
following Num and CL:

(30) [_DP_ Dek   saam   khon   nan]   keng.
           child 3   CL   Dem   clever

      'Those three children are smart.'

Second, in Burmese, demonstratives are DP-initial and consequently cannot
be used to provide arguments for the occurrence of Num and CL inside DP.
However, the presence of case markers and postpositions following the Num and
CL in DP-final position again suggests that these elements are DP-internal rather
being base-generated as some kind of adverbial unit:

(31) Canaw [_DP_ saouq   hna   ouq]   **-ko**   weh   hta   teh.
      I   book   2   CL   ACC   buy   Asp   NON-FUTURE

      'I bought two books.'

(32) U-Win-Win [_PP_ [_DP_ meitswee   thoun   yauq]   **ne**]   Yangoun
      U-Win-Win   friend   3   CL   with   Rangoon

      thwaa   teh.
      go   NON-FUTURE

      'U-Win-Win went to Rangoon with three friends.'

Third, certain aspects of the interpretation of [NP Num CL] sequences suggest that Num and CL are DP-internal elements. Consider the clear contrast in interpretation between Thai (33), where Num and CL immediately follows the NP, and (34), where Num and CL occur sentence-finally in an adverbial type of position. Whereas (34) has a partitive type of interpretation, in (33) such an interpretation is significantly not available:

(33)   Dek   saam   khon   sia   chiwit   laew.
       child   3   CL   lose   life   ASP

      'The three children died already.'

(34)   Dek   sia   chiwit   laew   saam   khon.
       child   lose   life   ASP   3   CL

      'Three of the children died already.'

Partitive readings are generally assumed to be possible when numerical quantification is applied to a definite DP from a DP-external position, as in (35a) and are blocked when numerals occur under the scope of D^0 inside the DP as in (35b):

(35)   a.   [$_{QP}$ three of [$_{DP}$ the children]].

      b.   [$_{DP}$ the three children]

In Thai (34) the Num and CL are clearly in a DP-external position, and the result is a partitive reading. In (33), where the Num and CL occur adjacent to the NP, no partitive reading is possible. The natural conclusion to be made about [NP Num CL] sequences in examples such as (33) would therefore seem to be that Num and CL in such cases are indeed inside the DP, and this therefore blocks the possibility of a partitive interpretation. Furthermore, the only possible positioning of Num and CL relative to an overt demonstrative is before the demonstrative as in (30) and attempting to place Num and CL after a demonstrative as in (36) is simply ungrammatical, indicating that post-NP Num and CL in preverbal subject position must indeed be DP-internal:

(36)   *dek   nan   saam   khon   keng
       child   Dem   3   CL   clever

Turning to Burmese, there is similar interpretative evidence that the Num CL is inside the DP. In (37), with the sequence [Dem NP Num CL] there is only possible a nonpartitive interpretation. This once again clearly suggests that the Num and CL elements are DP-internal and under the scope of D^0:

(37) canaw eh-dii saouq hna ouq weh hta   teh.
      I   Dem   book   2   CL   buy Asp NON-FUTURE

'I bought those two books. / NOT:*I bought two of those books.'

Consequently, there is a range of evidence suggesting that if Num-CL sequences originated as adverbial elements, as seems likely, in Burmese and Thai, they have now allowed for reanalysis within the DP as suggested. Cross-linguistically, however, not all [NP Num CL] forms pattern in the same way, and there is a further complication. If one compares Burmese (37) with an apparently similar string of [Dem NP Num CL] in Japanese, one finds that the Japanese sequence actually has a different and opposite interpretation from the Burmese, as indicated:

(38) Jiro-wa   sono   hon-o   san satsu katta.
      Jiro-TOP   DEM   book-ACC   3   CL   bought

'Jiro bought three of those books. / NOT:*Jiro bought those three books.'
(Muromatsu 1998: 65)

Here Japanese and Burmese might seem to be significantly different, suggesting perhaps that postnominal Num CL sequences in Japanese are not inside the DP but adverbial, as argued in Fukushima (1991) and Ishii (2000). Interestingly, further patterns in Burmese show that Burmese may also still allow for such an adverbial possibility under certain explicit circumstances. Although it has been noted in (31) that case markers can occur after the Num CL sequence, it is actually also possible for a case marker to occur between the NP and Num CL, as in (39). Significantly, when this does occur (and case markers are used sparingly in Burmese), it allows for the same partitive-type interpretation that occurs in Japanese (38), suggesting that it is also still possible for Num CL in Burmese to occur and be interpreted outside of the DP:

(39) U-Win-Win eh-dii saouq **-ko** hna ouq weh teh.
      U-Win-Win Dem   book   **ACC**   2   CL   buy NON-FUTURE

'U-Win-Win bought two of those books.'

Consequently, while (30–34) allow for the conclusion that adverbial Num CL has indeed allowed for reanalysis in both Burmese and Thai, examples such as (34) and (39) suggest that it nevertheless may still be possible for Num CL to occur unreanalyzed and adverbially in DP-external positions in both languages (VP-finally in Thai and following case-marked DPs in Burmese), this having clear effects on the interpretations of such forms.

Before this section closes, one last pattern that can usefully be considered here is the historical development of modern-day [NP Num CL] forms in Khmer.

Briefly, old Khmer had two possible forms with numerals, either simply [NP Num] or alternatively [NP CL Num] with a classifier. In middle Khmer, as well as the latter [NP CL Num] forms, a second sequence [NP Num CL] is found, and it is this sequence that is now the sole modern form, as schematized in (40):

(40)   *Old Khmer*   *Middle Khmer*   *Modern Khmer*
    a. NP Num

    b. NP CL Num   NP CL Num

    c.   NP Num CL   NP Num CL

Such a sequence of development is both interesting and revealing and seems to suggest the following explanation. In old Khmer when "classifiers" first begin to occur, these elements were really just nouns and not grammaticalized as a distinct special category. NP CL Num forms were therefore simply sequences of two NPs, and Num was attached to the right of a second adverbial NP in the same rightward position that it otherwise attaches in in pattern (a). [NP CL Num] is therefore really [NP$_1$] [NP$_2$ Num], essentially in line with Greenberg (1975) and earlier proposals. Later on, in middle and modern Khmer, it can be suggested that there occurred natural grammaticalization of the classifier as a nominal functional category, and two-NP structures became reanalyzed as single DPs with Num and "CL" internal to the DP. Such a hypothetical grammaticalization process can now be suggested to be directly responsible for the otherwise puzzling and important change in CL Num word order which occurred, reversing the linear order of CL and Num and effectively replacing pattern (b) with pattern (c). What such a change seems to suggest is that when grammaticalization and reanalysis occurred, this significantly forced Num and CL as functional heads within the DP to be realigned in a *head-initial* order, following the general direction of headedness found elsewhere in Khmer. If correct as an explanation of the switch in CL Num word order, such a change is important in clearly showing the strong pressure that languages may be under to adopt consistent head-initial orders. One could imagine, for example, that it might be simpler for the original linear order [NP CL Num] to grammaticalize as a head-final structure without any reversal of the orders of Num and CL. That this did not happen, and CL seems to have grammaticalized in a specifically head-initial way, reinforces the view that grammaticalization and reanalysis do not occur in any random fashion and that there are clear principles of headedness governing the organization of DPs in the languages examined here.

Summarizing briefly the conclusions of sections 2–4 now, the general goal of the investigation here was to see whether there is any real regularity in DP structure in Southeast Asian languages and what factors might be responsible for surface variation. A significant cause of cross-linguistic word-order variation has now been identified as the obligatory application of DP-internal NP-movement in certain languages but not others. It has been suggested that such movement is essentially the result of the reanalysis of an earlier adverbial form, that similar adverbial forms may still exist in certain languages, and that the switch in CL Num word order in middle Khmer is understandable once one adopts such an account of the development of classifiers in DPs. In sections 5–7, the chapter now moves on to consider other aspects of the structure of DPs in Southeast Asian languages and suggests how, in certain cases, X^0-movement and grammaticalization may also be responsible for further surface variation attested.

5 BARE CLASSIFIERS AND DEFINITENESS

Although the use of classifiers with numerals is common and highly developed throughout the Southeast Asian area, one interesting classifier pattern is found in just a subset of the languages of the region: the occurrence of bare classifier-NP sequences without any accompanying numeral as in (48–50) from Vietnamese, Hmong, and Nung:

(41) Nguoi chong   rat   tot. (Vietnamese)
      CL   husband   very   good

      'The husband was very good.' (Daley 1998: 65)

(42) Tus tsov   tshaib   tshaib   plab. (Hmong)
      CL   tiger hungry   hungry   stomach

      'The tiger was very hungry.' (Jaisser 1987: 171)

(43) Leo   tu   me   da   tu   po   va ... (Nung)
      then CL   wife scold CL   husband   say

      'Then the wife scolded the husband and said ... ' (Saul and Wilson 1980: 160)

As such patterns do not occur in Thai, Khmer, Burmese, or Indonesian, this raises the question of whether classifiers should be assumed to have a different syntactic status in different languages and how the bare classifier phenomenon should be accounted for.

Considering the general patterns found in Vietnamese, Hmong, and Nung, an important observation is that bare classifier-NP sequences are commonly associated with referentiality and definiteness effects, so that when a DP has a definite interpretation, a bare classifier is generally found to occur with it, as in (41–43) (see Daley 1998, Löbel 1996, Bisang (1999), and Nguyen 1975). Cheng and Sybesma (1999) also note and investigate similar patterns in Cantonese and suggest that classifiers are used to express definiteness in Cantonese in a way similar to the use of definite determiners in other languages. As classifiers are assumed to occur in CL⁰, however, it is argued that bare-classifier nominal expressions with definite interpretations in Cantonese are simply Classifier Phrases (CLPs) and do not project any higher functional structure such as NumP or DP. Turning to examine the Southeast Asian languages now, this chapter will explore a slightly different approach and suggest that bare-classifier structures in these languages may be regular DPs resulting from raising of the classifier from CL⁰ up to D⁰.

A critical aspect of the general classifier patterning that needs to be accommodated in any analysis is the fact that although bare [CL NP] forms may naturally be interpreted as being definite, where a numeral occurs preceding the classifier, as in (44), such sequences have only indefinite interpretations:

(44) Toi   mua   tam   cai   ghe. (Vietnamese)
     I   buy   8   CL   chair

     'I bought eight chairs.'

Such a patterning is perhaps unexpected if classifiers are taken to regularly cause interpretations of definiteness when inserted into CL⁰. One might expect that either the definiteness of CL in (44) should become a property of the whole nominal expression leading to a definite interpretation or, if the numeral has quantificational scope over the definiteness of its CLP [CL NP] complement, one might alternatively expect a partitive interpretation 'three of the books', yet this is also not a possibility. Basically, there would seem to be a need to capture in some way the fact that classifiers in these languages may be definite or may express definiteness at some times but not at other times. A further observation relevant here is that when an otherwise indefinite sequence of [Num CL NP] is combined with a demonstrative, the result is that the whole expression is clearly definite:

(45) goh   saam   bo   sue (Cantonese)
     Dem   3   CL   book

     'those three books'

(46) slong   ahn   sleng   te (Nung)
     2   CL   province Dem

     'those two provinces' (Saul and Wilson 1980)

The definiteness effects induced by demonstratives in some position above Num and CL might seem to indicate that the locus of definiteness should indeed be taken to be a D^0 position above NumP, as often assumed, and that it is the occurrence of a particular morpheme in either the D^0 position or SpecDP which results in the interpretation of the DP as being definite. If this is indeed reasonable to assume, and if it is also reasonable to generalize further from structures with demonstratives to structures without demonstratives so that definiteness is assumed to be encoded in a constant position within nominals, it can now be suggested that bare classifier [CL NP] forms may perhaps be interpreted as being definite via the overt association of the classifier with the D^0 position through raising of the classifier up to D^0 in instances when a DP has a definite interpretation. It can be suggested that in the languages in question, either the D^0 or SpecDP must be overtly instantiated by a certain lexical element (a demonstrative or the classifier) for the definite interpretation to be triggered or signaled and that otherwise the DP will be interpreted as having a default indefinite value. [Num CL NP] forms such as (44) will consequently be automatically interpreted as indefinite, as the classifier remains in situ in CL and has clearly not been raised to D. Furthermore, when Num does occur, it will not be possible to raise CL (over Num) to D because of the Head Movement Constraint, explaining the nonoccurrence of forms such as [*CL_i Num t_i NP], and instead a demonstrative has to be inserted either into D^0 (or possibly SpecDP) to trigger a definite interpretation.[3]

The suggestion that CL may (sometimes) move to D and cause definite interpretations of the DP will certainly account for the basic patterns observed here and would also seem to be a reasonable way of explaining the ambivalent nature of CL, classifiers sometimes being associated with definite interpretations (when they raise to D^0) and sometimes not (when they remain in CL^0).[4] However, to be more convinced of the plausibility of a CL-to-D approach, one might hope to find additional empirical evidence of the higher D position. Such evidence interestingly exists in Vietnamese, and one finds examples where a second general classifier element occurs preceding the regular classifier, resulting in sequences with clear definite interpretations:

(47) Cai con dao [anh cho toi muon], no that sac.
      CL   CL   knife you give me borrow it real sharp

      'The knife you gave me is really sharp.' (Le 1968)

(48) cai chiec ban nay
      CL   CL   table Dem

      'this table' (Nguyen 1975)

What this shows is that there is indeed another X^0 head-position above CL^0, and, importantly, it is a head-position of just the type suggested, one that is both instantiated by a classifier and specifically associated with definite interpretations of the DP. Such patterns therefore seem to provide clear empirical support for the CL-to-D hypothesis and indicate that classifier elements may indeed sometimes occur in higher D^0-type heads in definite DPs. Historically, it can be suggested that the possibility of inserting a general classifier directly into the higher posited D^0 position has resulted from a sequence of movement and reanalysis. After a certain initial period of simple CL-to-D movement, with the classifier instantiating both heads CL and D, it can be suggested that frequent raising of the general classifier to D^0 may have allowed it to be reanalyzed as (potentially) just a D^0-element permitting simple insertion into D^0 and allowing CL^0 to be lexicalized and instantiated by a second classifier as in (47–49). In Simpson (1998), Simpson and Wu (2000), Wu (2004), and also Roberts and Roussou (2003), it is suggested that grammaticalization may indeed frequently consist in just this kind of movement and reanalysis sequence. In Wu (2000), one particularly relevant example of this is argued to be the reanalysis of the general classifier *ge* in Mandarin as an *indefinite* determiner in D^0 after similar raising from the CL^0 position. As shown in (49), the reanalysis of *ge* in D^0 now allows for the CL^0 position to be instantiated by a new classifier:[5]

(49) he   ge   san   ping   jiu
      drink GE   3   CL   wine
      'do a drinking of three bottles of wine'

Synchronically, it can be assumed that if the general classifier in Vietnamese occurs selected in the numeration, together with a second regular classifier, the general classifier will be inserted into D^0, and there will be no CL-to-D movement (47–48). Otherwise, however, if an additional general classifier is not selected, it can be argued that the classifier base-generated in CL^0 will instead have to undergo CL-to-D to give rise to the definite interpretation of a DP as suggested.[6] Consequently, then, CL-to-D, demonstrative insertion into D^0/SpecDP, and general classifier insertion into D^0 (where available) can all be suggested to achieve the same basic goal of overtly specifying the DP as being definite.

6 Num-Raising and Indefiniteness

Having argued that Vietnamese has come to have double classifier sequences as the result of head movement and reanalysis, I now consider another revealing case where head movement results in variation in DP surface structure: the patterning of number 'one' in Thai and Nung. In both these Tai languages, the regular position for numerals is preceding the classifier, as in (50). The number 'one,' however, is commonly placed *following* the classifier in Thai and can occur *only* in DP-*final* position in Nung (51a–b):

(50) a. dek   saam   khon (Thai)
         child   3   CL

      'three children'

      b. slam   ahn   vet (Nung)
         3   CL   spoon

      'three spoons' (Saul and Wilson 1980)

(51) a. dek   khon   nung (Thai)
         child   CL   one

      'one/a child'

      b. ahn   tahng   nuhng (Nung)
         CL   chair   one

      'one/a chair' (Saul and Wilson 1980)

Considering the placement of 'one' either before or after CL in Thai, it is unlikely that this results from a linear inversion rule, and simple inversion of the classifier with the number "one" clearly cannot account for the related postposing of 'one' in Nung. Importantly, what both Thai and Nung can be shown to share in their repositioning of the number 'one' is that 'one' is now commonly placed in the DP-final position where demonstratives otherwise occur, as in (52). The Thai example (53) shows that 'one' in this final position is indeed in complementary distribution with demonstratives, though it may nevertheless occur in the regular pre-CL Num⁰ position with a demonstrative following CL:

(52) a. dek   song   khon   nii (Thai)
         child   2   CL   Dem

      'these two children'

      b. slong   ohng   dehk   te (Nung)
         2   CL   child   Dem

      'those two children' (Saul and Wilson 1980)

(53) a. *dek   khon   nung   nii
          child CL   one   Dem

b. dek   nung   khon   nii
   child   one   CL   Dem

'this one child'

It can therefore be argued that the number 'one' in both Thai and Nung is coming to be an indefinite determiner that contrasts in its indefinite specification with the definiteness encoded by demonstratives.[7]

Before we see how 'one' comes to be in the Dem position, let us consider again briefly how the demonstrative and other DP-internal elements achieve their surface order in Thai and Nung. In sections 3 and 4, I argued at length for the occurrence of NP-movement over Num and CL in Thai—that is, [NP$_i$ Num CL t$_i$]. I have also suggested that when a demonstrative occurs in DP-final position in Vietnamese, Nung, Indonesian, Thai, and Khmer, the elements found to the left of the demonstrative are raised to this position as a single constituent from an underlying position to the right of the demonstrative, hence [[Num CL NP]$_i$ Dem t$_i$]. In Thai and Khmer, when a demonstrative occurs, there will effectively be two applications of leftward movement involved in the derivation, as illustrated in (54). First, the NP will raise over Num and CL to a position between these elements and Dem, and then the [NP Num CL] constituent will raise over Dem itself (as in Vietnamese, Nung, etc.), resulting in the surface linearization of examples, such as (52):[8]

(54)   Underlying structure: [Dem   Num   CL   NP]
        NP movement: [Dem   NP$_i$ Num   CL   t$_i$]
        movement over Dem: [[NP$_i$ Num   CL t$_i$]$_k$ Dem   t$_k$]

Concerning the occurrence of the number 'one' in the Dem position, it can be suggested that 'one' is first base-generated in Num^0 and then undergoes head-raising up to D^0. It is not possible to have any lexicalization of the Num position when 'one' is in the Dem position, suggesting that 'one' has indeed raised up from Num^0 (and semantically there is no reason that numbers should not co-occur with an indefinite determiner, as in Chinese (49)):

(55)   *dek   saam/nung   khon   nung
        child   3/one   CL   'one'

The derivation that results in 'one' occurring in D^0 in Thai can therefore be suggested to be as schematized in (56) with 'one' originating in Num^0. 'One' will first raise up to D^0, and then this will be followed by regular movement of the NP over Num and CL to its landing site below the Dem position. Finally, there will occur raising of the constituent to the right of Dem over Dem to its left, resulting in 'one' becoming final in the DP in a way entirely similar to the DP-final occurrence of demonstratives. Note that with the single exception of the suggestion that 'one' raises up to D^0, the analysis needs to make no new assumptions and simply makes use of mechanisms already argued for:

(56)   Underlying structure: ['one'   CL   NP]
       'One' raises from Num^0 to D^0:   [one$_i$ [t$_i$ CL   NP]]
       NP movement over Num CL: [one$_i$ [NP$_k$ t$_i$ CL   t$_k$]]
       Movement over the Dem position: [$\underline{NP_k\ t_i}$ CL t$_k$]$_m$ [one$_i$ t$_m$]
       (Containing 'one')

In addition to showing how the occurrence of head-movement results in further clear-surface variation in the DP, these patterns with 'one' in Thai and Nung also allow for three more general conclusions. First, the patterns can be argued to provide good support for the general underlying structures and movement suggested to occur in Thai, Khmer, and similar languages. If one assumes that simple classifier-number linear inversion is not possible as an analysis (and made more unlikely by the facts in Nung), and if it is assumed that 'one' raises up to D^0 from Num^0 (thus accounting for the fact that Num^0 may not be independently lexicalized when 'one' occurs in D^0), this indicates again strongly that Thai DPs with the surface order [N Num CL D] (D = Dem) cannot, in fact, be simple head-final structures. If such an ordering were to directly reflect the base-generated position of heads in the language, raising of 'one' from Num^0 to D^0 should be straightforwardly blocked by the intervening CL^0 head and the HMC. The fact that raising from Num^0 to D^0 does seem to occur can arguably be accounted for *only* if Num^0 occurs higher than CL^0, which itself then entails that the N(P) must be assumed to have undergone leftward raising from some other position lower than CL^0.

Second, the patterning here also provides further good support for the general assumption that Num^0 and CL^0 are independent functional heads. If the number 'one' is able to raise out of the regular position of numerals and up to a higher (D^0) position, this suggests that classifiers are not simply suffixes attached to numerals in a single head, as affixes and subparts of words are not normally stranded by operations of movement. Instead, it would seem to indicate that numerals and classifiers are independent words in discrete functional head positions.

Third, the fact that 'one' in Thai and Nung is becoming an indefinite determiner and is targeting the same position as definite D^0 elements (demonstratives) strongly supports the assumption that both definiteness and indefiniteness are encoded in the same D^0 position in DPs and, hence, that indefinite nominal expressions are indeed DPs in at least the Tai languages. In recent years there has been regular discussion about whether indefinite nominal expressions might possibly be constituents which are smaller than full DPs, being NPs or alternatively NumPs; however, often it is difficult to find clear empirical evidence in favor of either a DP or an NP or NumP analysis. Here in Thai and Nung, though, because of the interesting surface linearization of the DP, we find that the D^0 position is actually not adjacent to the NP or the NumP. Consequently it is possible to see the number 'one' developing as an indefinite determiner in a position that is quite distinct from the numeral position, and as this position otherwise hosts demonstratives, it is straightforward to make the important conclusion that indefinite nominal expressions can indeed be full DPs and of the same syntactic size as their definite counterparts. Furthermore, if the indefinite nature of *some* nominal expressions is expressed overtly in the D^0 position, it might be natural to assume that the D^0 position is indeed regularly the locus for the specification of indefiniteness and hence that there is a phonetically null counterpart to overt 'one' occurring with other numerals in indefinite DPs such as (50), for example.[9] The 'one' paradigm in Thai and Nung thus supports a variety of possible insights into the structure of DPs and provides important information about the derivation underlying DP surface order.

In the final section of the chapter now, I continue to examine how variation in surface structures may relate to the way that DP-internal heads are physically instantiated, this time looking further down in the DP below D^0 and Num^0.

7 N-TO-CL

A last set of clear classifier-related variation in the DP which remains in need of explanation is the occurrence of 'classifier-less' DPs—instances where no classifier occurs with a numerically quantified NP despite individuation being implied. This phenomenon essentially occurs in two basic forms. First, in a wide range of languages, certain *particular* nouns are commonly quantified without any apparent classifier. Frequently, the subset of nouns that pattern in this way is very similar and includes words for units of time such as 'year', 'day', and 'time'; sometimes the word for 'person', and certain other terms used with fairly high frequency, as illustrated in (57):

(57)   a. tu nam   b. ba lan (Vietnamese)
          4 year   3 time
          'four years'   'three times'

The second way that classifierless forms manifest themselves is not lexically restricted in this way, and in certain languages (e.g., colloquial Minangkabau and

Indonesian) the use of a classifier appears to be quite optional with a fully wide range of nouns, as, for example, in Nung (58):

(58)   slam   (tew)   kha-lo (Nung)
     3   (CL)   road
    'three roads' (Saul and Wilson 1980)

There might seem to be two possible analyses of the patterns here. Considering just the former lexically restricted type in (57), if the forms in (58) are taken to be genuinely classifierless and without any CL position, this might indicate a significant distinction among nouns in classifier languages and suggest that some nouns simply require no individuation. However, such an approach would not seem to be able to generalize further to cover the second type of classifierless forms in (58) as here the nouns certainly do have classifiers. The observation about this second type is just that the classifiers are used optionally, not that they are inherently individuated. A second approach to the former lexically restricted type might alternatively be to suggest that the elements 'year' and 'time' are actually base-generated in CL and that there is no N or NP in such constructions. However, this is somewhat unlikely as the nonoccurrence of an N-position and an NP-complement to CL would entail that there are classifiers which classify or individuate nothing. As classifiers are essentially by definition functions that apply to some second complement term, the presence of a classifier would therefore seem to require the presence of an N or NP. Furthermore, such an approach will again not generalize to cover the second type in (58), as the overt elements here are clearly nouns.

In addition to these two possible analyses of cases such as (57), there is a third potential analysis of these patterns suggested by the phenomena examined in sections 5 and 6. If the analysis of Thai and Nung 'one' moving from Num to D, and of Vietnamese CL moving from CL to D is correct, it could be that similar movement takes place in instances such as (57), with the elements 'year and time' being base-generated in the N position and then raising to the CL position, instantiating both in the same way that 'one' instantiates both Num and D in Thai and Nung, and that Vietnamese classifiers sometimes instantiate both CL and D. Considering the simple patterns in Vietnamese, Indonesian, and Chinese languages where CL and N are positions immediately adjacent to each other in the tree, there is no obvious way of finding empirical evidence in favor of one hypothesis rather than the other. However, Thai and Khmer, with their critically different surface linearization of DP structure, do provide a clear and useful means to check these hypotheses, as in these languages N and CL are not linearly adjacent in surface forms but commonly are separated by numerals in Num (i.e., in the order [N(P) Num CL]). As the Thai data in (59) show, in fact, elements such as 'year' and 'time' consistently appear to the right of Num in the CL position and not in the N-position, which occurs to the left of Num in surface word order:

(59) a. soong pii   b. saam khrang   c. sii khon
          2   year   3   time   4   person

          'two years'   'three years'   'four people'

This indicates that the first possible analysis that no CL position occurs in 'classifierless' forms cannot be correct: Thai and Khmer show that with elements such as 'year' and 'time' a CL position is indeed present and overtly occupied by these elements. As the second possibility that there is no N position in such structures is rather implausible for the reasons noted previously, and as 'year' and 'person' and the like also do appear very nominal and likely to be N-heads, it would seem that the most likely explanation of the forms in (57) and (58) is indeed the third possibility: that the patterns found in (57) and (58) are ultimately the simple result of movement from N to CL. Once again, then, as with the Num-to-D and CL-to-D raising considered in sections 5 and 6, it would seem that the surface variation attested (i.e., the difference between (57) and (58) and more regular forms such as, for example, (50)) is simply due to the application of overt head movement in certain instances and a single lexical element coming to instantiate two discrete syntactic head positions in the DP-tree.

The N-to-CL analysis of (57) is also given further plausibility and support by certain other patterns found. Such an analysis basically suggests that both N and CL positions are always projected in the DP structure and that various nouns raised from N to CL instantiate both N and CL positions in a single derivation. In some sense, this amounts to suggesting that some nouns might be able to function as their own classifiers and lexicalize the CL head, as well as the N head. Interestingly, in a range of languages such as Thai, Burmese, and Lahu, one finds exactly this possibility in a slightly different guise and the frequent occurrence of "self-classifiers" or "repeaters"—the simple repetition in CL of the element in N as in (60):

(60) a. hoong saam hoong (Thai)   b. cun   ta   cun (Burmese)
          room   3   room/CL   island   one   island/CL

          'three rooms'   'one island'

The idea of an element being used to classify or individuate itself is consequently both plausible and commonly attested. Assuming the "copy theory" of movement (Chomsky 1995), one might also suggest that in these repeater cases there may again quite possibly be movement between N and CL, with the difference between repeater and nonrepeater cases such as (57) being that in (60) the copy left in N by movement to CL is not deleted and is actually spelled out phonetically.

Finally, unlike the other two possible analyses of (57) I considered, the N-raising analysis of cases such as (57) will importantly also extend in a natural way to cover the second type of lexically unrestricted classifierless Ns (i.e., (58)), and it can be suggested that rather than assume that the CL position is not present in such cases, the N may instead be taken to raise up to CL to lexicalize this position. The optionality here would then relate to whether a classifier is selected from the lexicon for use or not, and if one is not selected, the N will simply be used to instantiate the CL position.[10] Furthermore, it can be suggested that if such N-to-CL movement does occur regularly and if the "movement and reanalysis" approach to grammaticalization is correct, one might expect that the frequent association of certain Ns with the CL position due to regular N-to-CL raising might ultimately allow for the reanalysis of such Ns as simple direct instantiations of CL, base-generated in CL *without* having first been raised there from N⁰ (just as Vietnamese *cai* (47–48) and Mandarin *ge* (49), both originally CLs, can now be base-generated in D). As noted earlier, it is well observed that in fact, classifiers do frequently develop from elements that were originally nouns. The assumption of N-to-CL movement, together with a movement and reanalysis view of grammaticalization, therefore provides a clear way of understanding how the creation of new classifiers from nouns may indeed occur. Continued use of N-to-CL results in the reanalysis of nouns in CL and allows for relexicalization of the lower N position with new nominal elements.

8 Concluding Remarks

This chapter has been concerned with attempting to understand how apparent variation in DP structure may be accounted for across a broad range of Southeast Asian languages. Sections 2–4 concluded that significant distortion of underlying DP structure is often caused by XP-movement inside the DP (i.e., NP-fronting). Sections 5–7 considered other aspects of DP-internal variation and argued that, in each case, the patterns result from simple X⁰-movement and the common raising of DP-internal heads to lexicalize and instantiate other higher head positions, a process which naturally leads to reanalysis and full grammaticalization of a head in a higher DP-internal position. In both parts of the chapter, then, variation has essentially been attributed to elements being in different stages of ongoing historical development and reanalysis, with both XP-movement and X⁰-movement becoming regularized, reanalyzed, and grammaticalized. Throughout the discussion, I attempted to show how important a role the classifier may often have in leading to possible explanations of the variation found. Finally, on a general level, the patterns investigated here not only suggest that the structure of DPs in Southeast Asian languages is far from random but also, in fact, arguably seem to indicate the opposite conclusion and suggest that DPs in the variety of languages examined here may actually share a single, basic, highly regular underlying structure.[11]

NOTES

1. Concerning the order N > Adj in Thai and Nung (and also Indonesian, Burmese, etc.), in many head-initial languages, either adjectives precede the N (e.g. English) or may follow the N, but it is or can be argued that the N raises over the adjectives that are present to some higher head position (e.g., French). One might therefore wonder if the N Adj orders of Thai, Nung, Indonesian, and the like are perhaps derived via movement of either N⁰ or NP over the adjective rather than being base-generated in this order. Though it is not possible to be fully sure here, there is certain evidence favoring the base-generation hypothesis over a movement analysis. In Thai, Nung, and Indonesian, it is not possible to stack adjectives behind the noun in the way that it is possible to stack prenominal adjectives in English (e.g., 'the big black dangerous dog'), and only a single adjective can occur in the post-N position (contra what is in fact reported about Thai in Sproat and Shih 1991). If two adjectival modifers are required, in Thai and Nung these critically have to be conjoined (e.g., 'dog big and black'), while in Indonesian a second adjective may be commonly added via a relative clause (e.g., 'dog big which is black'). This suggests that there is basically a single syntactic position available for adjectives following the N in these languages. It may therefore be appropriate to assume that the N(P) occurs in a base-generated predication structure with the following adjective/AdjP, essentially following Cinque's (1994) analysis of "predicative AdjPs" in Romance and Germanic languages. As further potential support for such an analysis, it can be noted that nonpredicative adjectives such as *adiid* 'former' have to precede the N in Thai.

2. See also Bhattacharya (1999) on Bangla for other clear evidence of optional NP-movement inside the DP.

3. Bare classifiers also occur with demonstratives in Hmong, Vietnamese, and Nung, such as:

> (i) tu   ma   nay   (Nung)
>   CL   N   Dem
>
>   'this dog'

As noted earlier, the DP-final position of demonstratives in Hmong, Vietnamese, and Nung is taken to result from leftward movement of the constituent following Dem. If it is assumed that the classifier in (i) is raised to D, there may be two possible analyses of structures such as (i). One possibility is to assume that demonstratives in Hmong, Vietnamese, and Nung are in SpecDP and that the D' constituent dominating CL (in D), Num, and NP raises leftward. Alternatively, one could assume the existence of a DP-shell structure, as suggested in Simpson and Wu (2002) to account for languages such as Spanish, which allow the clear cooccurrence of determiners and demonstratives. In such a DP-shell, both the determiner (or classifier) and the demonstrative may be generated in D^0 positions. Of course, it could also be the case that the classifier in forms such as (i) has not in fact raised to D^0 and simply remains in CL^0, and that the demonstrative alone identifies the DP as being definite.

4. How such an idea can be further technically implemented may be explained via a brief consideration of a rather different phenomenon found in Egyptian Arabic. As described in Wahba (1984), yes-no questions in Egyptian Arabic are signaled by the use of a *pronoun* in the +Q Comp position, which repeats or anticipates the φ-features of the following subject:

(i) Mona   ablit   il-talamiiz.
     Mona   met   the-students

     'Mona met the students.'

(ii) Il-talamiiz   ablu   Mona.
     the-students   met   Mona

     'The students met Mona.' (Wahba 1984)

(iii) Hiyya   Mona   ablit   il-talamiiz?
      she   Mona   met   the-students

      'Did Mona meet the students?'

(iv) Humma   il-talamiiz   ablu   Mona?
     they   the-students   met   Mona

     'Did the students meet Mona?' (Wahba 1984)

Such pronouns elsewhere do not encode interrogativity, and it is only when they are positioned in C^0/SpecCP that they cause sentences to be interpreted as questions. It can therefore be suggested (as in Wu 2004) that they are able to specify C^0 as being +Q due to a productive lexical process that allows for the optional addition of +Q interrogative features onto a pronoun when it is taken from the lexicon in Egyptian Arabic. When a pronoun is not to be used to type a clause as +interrogative, such +Q features will simply not be added. Considering the issue of how classifiers in Vietnamese, Hmong, and Nung may now sometimes encode definiteness via raising to the D^0 position and at other times remain in CL^0 without any definiteness specification, it can be suggested that a process of lexical feature-addition is available in these languages in a way that is very similar to the Egyptian Arabic case. It can be suggested that D^0-definiteness features may be optionally added to a classifier when it is taken from the lexicon in these languages, and that when such features are added on to a classifier, it will cause the classifier to raise up to D^0 to license or check these features against D^0. However, when such D-related features are not added onto a classifier, the classifier will simply remain in CL and not result in any definiteness interpretation in the structure. See Wu (2004) for further discussion of how the possibility that certain features may be optionally added to lexical hosts can be generally used to account for elements undergoing grammaticalization and change.

5. The fact that classifiers may potentially be reanalyzed as either definite or indefinite determiners would seem to indicate that such elements are not inherently definite or indefinite but come to be associated with either definiteness or indefiniteness because of their frequent use in certain constructions.

6. Another possibility is that individual speakers in Vietnamese consistently use different strategies, as the classifier-doubling strategy may be more common in older-generation speakers (Nguyen Binh, pers. comm.).

7. In this indefinite determiner position, 'one' can be used to refer to either specific or nonspecific indefinites.

8. If no NP over Num CL raising occurs, then the surface order is that of Vietnamese, Nung, and Indonesian, and if NP-movement but no movement over Dem occurs, the order is that found in Burmese.

With regard to the two applications of leftward XP-movement posited here, if these are both taken to be DP-internal topicalization-type movements, this may suggest that there are DP-internal topic-like positions, both below and above Dem/D⁰ in a way similar to Rizzi's (1997) suggestion that there are iterated topic positions both below and above the contrastive focus position within the clause.

9. It is possible that the number 'one' in English also raises to D^0. In contrast to other numerals, 'one' cannot cooccur with other instantiations of D^0 unless it is interpreted like the adjective 'unique' and is followed by a relative clause as in (iii):

(i)   The two/three/*one man left.

(ii)   These two/three books are mine/*/??This one book is mine.

(iii)   The unique/one person *(I like among them) is David.

10. In this sense, classifiers pattern a little like expletives. When an expletive such as 'there' is selected in a numeration, it will be inserted into SpecIP, but when no such expletive is selected, the subject of a clause has to raise to instantiate the SpecIP position.

11. See also Cinque (1996), who suggests the possibility of such a conclusion universally for DPs, and Tang (1999), who assumes such a conclusion in a rather different feature-based approach to DP-structure variation.

REFERENCES

Aikhenvald, Alexandra (2000) *Classifiers*. Oxford University Press, Oxford.

Bhattacharya, Tanmoy (1999) "The Structure of the Bangla DP." Ph.D. diss. University College London.

Bisang, Walter (1999) "Classifiers in East and Southeast Asian Languages: Counting and Beyond," in J. Gvozdanovic (ed.) *Numeral Types and Changes Worldwide*, Mouton de Gruyter, Berlin, 113–185.

Cheng, Lisa, and Rint Sybesma (1999) "Bare and Not-So-Bare Nouns and the Structure of NP." *Linguistics Inquiry* 30: 509–542.

Chomsky, Noam (1995) *The Minimalist Program*. MIT Press, Cambridge, Mass.

Cinque, Guglielmo (1994) "On the Evidence for Partial N-movement in the Romance DP," in G. Cinque, J. Koster, J.-Y. Pollock, L. Rizzi, and R. Zanuttini (eds.) *Paths towards Universal Grammar: Studies in Honor of Richard Kayne*. Georgetown University Press, Washington D.C., 85–110.

Cinque, Guglielmo (1996) "The 'Antisymmetric' Programme: Theoretical and Typological Implications." *Journal of Linguistics* 32: 447–464.

Daley, Karen (1998) *Vietnamese Classifiers in Narrative Texts*. Summer Institute of Linguistics, University of Texas at Arlington.

Fukushima, Kazuhiko (1991) "Generalized Floating Quantifiers." Ph.D. diss., University of Arizona.

Gil, David (1994) "Summary: Numeral Classifiers." *Linguist List* 5: 466

Greenberg, Joseph (1975) "Dynamic Aspects of Word Order in the Numeral Classifier," in C. Li (ed.) *Word Order and Word Order Change*. University of Texas Press, Austin, 27–46.

Higginbotham, James (1987) "Indefiniteness and Predication," in E. Reuland and A. ter Meulen (eds.) *The Representation of (In-)definiteness*. MIT Press, Cambridge, Mass., 43–70.

Hopper, Paul (1986) "Some Discourse Functions of Classifiers in Malay," in C. G. Craig (ed.) *Noun Classes and Categorization*. John Benjamins, Amsterdam, 309–325.

Ishii, Yasuo (2000) "Floating Quantifiers in Japanese: What Are They and What Do They Tell Us?" Talk presented at School of Oriental and African Studies, University of London.

Jaisser, Annie (1987) "Hmong Classifiers." *Linguistics of the Tibeto-Burman Area* 10: 169–176.

Kawashima, Ruriko (1993) "The Structure of NPs: Arguments for Quantifier Phrase and Number Phrase." *Cornell Working Papers in Linguistics* 11: 56–72.

Le Van Ly (1968) *So-thao ngu-phap Viet-Nam* [Sketch of Vietnamese grammar]. Trung-tam Hoc-lieu, Saigon.

Löbel, Elisabeth (1996) "Klassifikatoren: Eine Fallstudie am Beispiel des Vietnamesischen." Master's thesis, University of Cologne.

Muromatsu, Keiko (1998) "On the Syntax of Classifiers." Ph.D. diss., University of Maryland.

Nguyen Dinh Hoa (1957) "Classifiers in Vietnamese." *Word* 13: 124–152.

Nguyen Tai Can (1975) *Ngu-phap tieng Viet: tieng, tu ghep, doan-ngu*. [Vietnamese grammar: morphemes, compounds and phrases]. Dai-hoc and Trung-hoc Chuyen-nghiep, Hanoi.

Pan, Hai-Hua (1990) "Head Noun Movements in Chinese, the ECP and Minimality." Unpublished ms., University of Texas at Austin.

Pulleyblank, Edwin (1995) *Outline of Classical Chinese Grammar*. University of British Columbia Press, Vancouver.

Rizzi, L. (1997) "The Fine Structure of the Left Periphery," in L. Haegeman (ed.) *Elements of Grammar*. Kluwer, Dordrecht, 281–337.

Roberts, Ian, and Anna Roussou (2003) *Syntactic Change: A Minimalist Approach to Grammaticalization*. Cambridge University Press, Cambridge.

Saul, J. E., and N.F. Wilson (1980) *Nung Grammar*. Summer Institute of Linguistics, University of Texas at Arlington.

Schafer, Edward (1948) "Noun Classifiers in Classical Chinese." *Language* 24: 408–413.

Simpson, Andrew (1998) "On the Re-analysis of Nominalizers in Chinese, Korean and Japanese." Paper presented at the University of Southern California Symposium on East Asian languages, November.

Simpson, Andrew, and Zoe Wu (2000) "The Grammaticalization of Formal Nouns and Nominalizers in Chinese, Japanese and Korean, in T. E. McAuley (ed.) *Language Change in East Asia.* Curzon, London, 250–283.

Simpson, Andrew, and Zoe Wu (2002) "Agreement, Shells and Focus." *Language* 78 2: 287–313.

Sproat, Richard, and Chilin Shih (1991) "The Cross-linguistic Distribution of Adjective Ordering Restrictions, in C. Georopolous and R. Ishihara (eds.) *Interdisciplinary Approaches to Language.* Kluwer, Dordrecht, 565–593.

Tang, C.-C. Jane (1990) "Chinese Phrase Structure and the Extended X'-Theory." Ph.D. diss., Cornell University, Ithaca, N.Y.

Tang, Sze-Wing (1999) "Some Speculations about the Syntax of Noun Phrases." *UCI Working Papers in Linguistics* 5: 135–154.

T'ung, P. C., and D. E. Pollard (1982) *Colloquial Chinese.* Routledge, London.

Wahba, Wafaa (1984) "Wh-constructions in Egyptian Arabic." Ph.D. diss., University of Illinois at Urbana-Champaign.

Watters, J. (1981) "A Phonology and Morphology of Ejagham: With Notes on Dialect Variation." Ph.D. diss., University of California Los Angeles.

Wu, Zoe (2004) *Grammaticalization and Language Change in Chinese: A Formal View.* Routledge Curzon, London.

CHAPTER 19

THE CELTIC LANGUAGES

MAGGIE TALLERMAN

1 INTRODUCTION

THE Celtic languages are a subgroup of the Indo-European language family and are traditionally divided into two groups: Brythonic, containing Welsh (W), Breton, (B), and the extinct language Cornish; and Goidelic, containing Irish (I), Scottish Gaelic (SG), and the extinct language Manx. Scottish Gaelic and Irish are very similar syntactically, while Breton and Welsh display important differences. The terms P-Celtic and Q-Celtic are sometimes used to refer to Brythonic and Goidelic, respectively, because of the regular sound correspondences characterizing each group: the reflex of Indo-European *k^w is [p] in Brythonic but [k] in Goidelic, giving rise to such cognates as Welsh *pen* and Irish *ceann*, 'head'. The four living languages vary in status: although all are considered endangered, from the latter part of the twentieth century onward efforts have been made to secure their future. Welsh has around half a million speakers in Wales, Breton probably has somewhat fewer speakers, Scottish Gaelic has perhaps 80,000 native speakers, and Irish has less than half that number.

Interest in the Celtic languages among generative grammarians stems from the mid-1970s and initially was largely due to their relatively uncommon word order patterns. Finite clauses exhibit VSO(X) order, in common with perhaps 12% of the world's languages:

(1) Rhoddais   i   afal   i'r   bachgen   ddoe. (W)
     give:PAST:1SG I   apple   to-the   boy   yesterday

     'I gave an apple to the boy yesterday.'

(2) Thug   mé   ull   don   ghasúr   inné. (I)
     give:PAST I   apple   to:the   boy   yesterday

     'I gave an apple to the boy yesterday.' (McCloskey 1983: 10)

Unless a constituent is fronted (for example, for focalization), a finite verb must be clause-initial; unlike many VSO languages, then, Celtic has no SVO alternative order. Breton, however, displays a complication: apart from certain copula clauses which are V-initial, there is a general root clause verb-second requirement, resulting in patterns such as those in (3) and (4), where the finite verbs are in italic type:

(3) Gouzout   a   *ran*   [e   *lenn*   Anna   al
     know:NONFIN   PRT   do:PRES:1SG   PRT   read:PRES   A.   the
     levr]. (B)
     book

     'I know that Anna reads the book.' (Borsley, et al. 1996: 62)

(4) Al   levr   a   *lenn*   Anna. (B)
     the   book   PRT   read:PRES   A.

     'Anna reads the book.' (Borsley, et al. 1996: 62)

In (3), which represents an unmarked word order, the main clause has a nonfinite verb in initial position and a finite auxiliary (accompanied by a preverbal particle) in second position; in (4) the object is fronted, and the finite lexical verb is in second position. However, the embedded clause in (3) *is* VSO: for this reason, we can consider the constituent orders found in root clauses in Breton to be derived orders. I return to the issue of verb-second in Celtic in section 4.

In addition to clauses like (1) and (2), with a finite lexical verb in initial position, all the Celtic languages display a periphrastic pattern, with an initial finite auxiliary and a nonfinite lexical verb below the subject:

(5) Mae   ef   yn   adeiladu   tai   ym   Mangor. (W)
     is   he   PROG   build:NONFIN   houses   in   Bangor

     'He's building houses in Bangor.'

(6) Tá sé ag tógáil tithe i nDoire. (I)
     is he PROG build:NONFIN houses in Derry

'He's building houses in Derry.' (McCloskey 1983: 12)

The existence of what is often termed I-SVO order (where I indicates the inflected element) has been significant in generative analyses of Celtic clause structure, to which we now turn.

2 Word Order and Clause Structure: Finite Clauses

In some early generative transformational studies of Celtic, VSO order was taken to be basic; see Awbery (1976) and McCloskey (1979). However, around the same time, proposals emerged for an underlying SVO analysis: see Jones and Thomas (1977), Emonds (1979), Harlow (1981), and later, Sproat (1985). Following work on Germanic by den Besten (1983), Emonds proposed that the fronted verb in VSO languages raises to the complementizer position, C.

There is sound evidence for the SVO analysis, both from an empirical and theoretical standpoint, and it has become the accepted view of Celtic within transformational generative grammar. On the empirical side, first note that SV[NONFINITE]O order occurs in the I-SVO pattern in (5) and (6). It can then be argued that two alternatives derive from Celtic underlying SVO order: either a finite lexical verb raises to an initial position, giving VSO order as in (1) and (2), or else a finite auxiliary verb is fronted (or inserts) into I, and the nonfinite lexical verb remains in situ, giving surface I-SVO order. Furthermore, SVO order also occurs in nonfinite clauses (see section 3);[1] if there is no finite verb to raise, then the underlying word order surfaces. Second, VO forms a unit: all the Celtic languages have a surface nonfinite VP constituent, as Anderson and Chung (1977: 22), Stephens (1982: 132f.), and Timm (1989) demonstrate for Breton; McCloskey (1983) for Irish; and Sproat (1985) for Welsh. For instance, the nonfinite VP can be fronted under focalization.[2]

(7) [vp Ag péinteáil cathaoir] a bhí an fear. (I)
          PROG paint:NONFIN chair COMP was the man

'The man was *painting a chair*.' (Ó Siadhail 1989: 236)

(8) [$_{VP}$ Dont   deus   Gwengamp] o   deus   graet. (B)
         come:NONFIN from   G.   3PL   have   do:PASTPART

'They have *come from Gwengamp*.' (Stephens 1982: 185)

Although the verb, its object, and other complements clearly form a constituent, the finite verb and the subject (which are, of course, adjacent in VSO order) crucially do not; see McCloskey (1996a: 249) for Irish.

   On the theoretical side, the underlying SVO analysis correctly predicts the existence of subject/object asymmetries, which, given standard assumptions, a "flat" structure would not; see, for instance, Hendrick (1990) and McCloskey (1990). Second, the surface word orders are straightforwardly derived by a familiar process of verb raising.

   An obvious question concerns the landing site of the raised verb. There are two main contenders. One possibility considers Celtic as parallel to verb-second languages, raising V through I to C; this proposal first appears in Emonds (1979). As McCloskey (1996b: 48) notes, this treats VSO languages as underdeveloped verb-second languages, lacking the concomitant movement of XP to Spec, CP. Under this account, the position of the subject can be assumed to be that of SVO languages, namely, Spec, IP (ignoring for the moment the possibility of an articulated I structure). Raising to C specifically in Irish is proposed by Stowell (1989), with the kind of structure shown in (9):

(9) [$_{CP}$ [$_{C}$ V+INFL] [IP NP [$_{I}$ *t*] [$_{VP}$ [$_{V}$ *t*] (XP)]]]

However, the I-to-C analysis is effectively demolished for Irish by McCloskey (1996b). The main argument concerns the position of clause-initial sentential adverbs. In English these occur left-adjoined to IP: crucially, they follow a complementizer, as in (10)—the italic adverbials in (11) are intended to modify the lower clause:

(10) It's probable that [*in general / most of the time* [he understands what is going on]]

(11) *It's appalling *in general / most of the time* that he doesn't understand what is going on.

McCloskey attributes this contrast to the Adjunction Prohibition (Chomsky 1986: 6), which prohibits adjunction to a selected CP (a CP argument of a higher predicate) but allows adjunction to IP. The Adjunction Prohibition is indeed operative in Irish, as (12) shows: the adverbial (in italic) is intended to be an adjunct within the selected *wh*-CP and cannot adjoin to the left of it:

(12) *Ní   bhfuair   siad   amach   ariamh   *an   bhliain   sin*   [$_{CP}$ cé
       NEG   found   they   out   ever   the   year   DEMON   who
       a   bhí   ag   goid   a gcuid   móna]. (I)
       COMP was   PROG   steal:NONFIN   their   turf

'They never found out who was stealing their turf that year.' (McCloskey
1996b: 65)

However, surprisingly, Irish sentential adverbs appear obligatorily to the *left* of
the complementizer introducing the clause that they modify (compare the English
translation):

(13) Deiridís   *an   chéad   Nollaig   eile*   go   dtiocfadh
       they.used.to.say the   first   Christmas other   COMP   come:CONDIT
       sé   aníos. (I)
       he   up

'They used to say that next Christmas he would come up.' (McCloskey
1996b: 59)

McCloskey concludes that since the adverbial is indeed adjoined to IP, the only
way to derive structures like (13) is for the complementizer (*go* in (13)) to *lower*
over the intervening adverbial to form a complex with the finite verb in I:

(14) Deiridís [$_{CP}$ <go> [$_{IP}$ *an chéad Nollaig eile* [$_{IP}$ go dtiocfadh sé aníos]]].

Given these arguments, the finite verb (underlined) doesn't undergo I-to-C movement—the verb does not surface in C.[3] There are further reasons for rejecting an
I-to-C analysis of Celtic. In the Germanic languages, verb-second is generally
restricted to root clauses, a distribution that since den Besten (1983) has been
attributed to the presence of an overt complementizer introducing embedded
clauses, which blocks verb movement into C by occupying the potential landing
site; see (15)b. But if the complementizer is absent, I-to-C raising occurs, as in
(15)c: the finite verb and an overt complementizer are in complementary distribution. The items occupying C are in italic:

(15) a. [$_{CP}$ [Dieses   Buch]$_i$ [$_C$ *kaufte*]   [$_{IP}$ Karl t_i t_v]] (German)
             this   book:ACC   bought   K.

           'Karl bought this book.'

      b. Ich   meinte,   [*daß*   Karl   dieses   Buch   gekauft
           I   thought   that   K.   this   book:ACC   bought:PASTPART
           hatte]
           had

           'I thought that Karl had bought this book.'

c. Ich meinte, [*hätte*   Karl   dieses Buch
   I   thought had:SUBJCTV K.   this   book:ACC
   gekauft,   so . . .]
   bought:PASTPART   then

   'I thought, had Karl bought this book, then . . . '

In Celtic, however, finite embedded clauses have VSO word order and a co-occurring overt complementizer (in italic):

(16) Sílim   [*go*   dtuigeann   Bríd   Gaeilge] (I)
      think:PRES:1SG COMP   understand:PRES Bridget Irish

      'I think that Bridget understands Irish.' (Stenson 1981: 52)

Thus if the finite verb targets C, the fact that they are not in complementary distribution is unexplained. Given such arguments, the I-to-C analysis of Celtic has generally fallen from favor.[4]

The second and more recent proposal for the landing site of the raised verb is I (or one of the heads replacing a unified I). Theoretical advances made possible by the VP Internal Subject Hypothesis (for instance, Koopman and Sportiche 1991) have affected quite radically the views taken of VSO clause structure. There are two alternatives regarding the subject: either it is generated in Spec, VP, and remains in its underlying position or, alternatively, there must be more functional structure above VP than simply I, so that the verb can raise to the highest functional head position, and the subject to the specifier of the functional head immediately below.

The literature contains analyses of each type. In earlier work, McCloskey (1991) argued that the subject in Irish remained within Spec, VP. His evidence is that all the material following I in a finite clause behaves like a single constituent. For instance, this string undergoes shared constituent coordination:

(17) Níor   thug, nó is beag má thug, [an pobal
      NEG:COMP gave or almost-didn't-give the community
      aon aird   ar an   bhean   bhocht]. (I)
      any attention on the woman   poor

      'The community paid no attention, or almost no attention, to the poor woman.' (McCloskey 1991: 265)

Note that the subject and the object are both within the shared constituent, the verb having raised out of it. In the Irish equivalent of VP-ellipsis, the verb, of course, raises out of VP, but the VP material remaining to undergo elision appears

to include the subject, which obligatorily elides together with other arguments
and adjuncts of the verb (the antecedent material is in italic):

(18) Ni   tháinig   *muid* *'na bhaile* anuraidh ach
      NEG: COMP come:PAST   we   home   last.year   but
      tiochfaidh [vp‗‗‗]   i mbliana. (I)
      come:FUT   this.year

      'We didn't come home last year, but we will this year.' (McCloskey 1997:
      211)

Again, this is predictable if the subject remains within VP.

However, these data merely indicate that the subject and the following clausal
material form a constituent; the surface position of the subject is not, though,
necessarily within VP. In fact, there is good evidence in Celtic that subjects have
indeed raised from the underlying VP-internal position. In more recent work,
McCloskey (1996a, 1997, 2001b) rejects his earlier stance and argues that Irish
subjects do not have a surface position within VP.

McCloskey (1996a; 2001b) demonstrates convincingly that Case-driven DP
movement must occur, just as it does in English. Consider first the perfective
passive construction:

(19) a. Tá *sé*   críochnaithe *t* againn. (I)
         is it:NOM   finished   by:1PL

         'It has been finished by us.'

      b. *Tá críochnaithe *sé*   againn.
         is   finished   it:NOM   by:1PL (McCloskey 1996a: 268)

Since Irish pronominals have morphological case, it is clear that the nominative
pronoun *sé* of the perfective passive in (19)a is genuinely a surface subject, not
an object. Note crucially that nominative case cannot be licensed *within* VP, as
(19)b shows. So the nominative DP must raise for Case-licensing, if all A-
movement is Case-driven.

Second, consider the two different unaccusative constructions in (20):

(20) a. Neartaigh   ar   a   ghlór. (I)
         strengthen:PAST on his voice

         'His voice strengthened.'

      b. Neartaigh   a   ghlór.
         strengthen:PAST his voice

         'His voice strengthened.' (McCloskey 1996a: 268)

In (20)a the internal argument of the verb remains within VP and is Case-licensed by the preposition *ar*. But (20)b has no Case-licensing preposition: the bare DP *a ghlór* must then leave VP to be Case-licensed in subject position. Although this raising-to-subject is not directly visible from the word order of the finite clauses in (20), it can be clearly seen in the periphrastic constructions in (21):

(21) a. Tá ag   neartú   *ar* *a*   *ghlór*
         is   PROG   strengthen:NONFIN   on   his   voice
         'His voice is strengthening.'

      b. Tá *a*   *ghlór*   ag   neartú.
         is   his   voice   PROG   strengthen:NONFIN
         'His voice is strengthening.' (McCloskey 2001b: 170)

In (21)a, the internal argument of the unaccusative verb remains within VP, where it is Case-licensed by the preposition, whereas in (21)b, *a ghlór* has raised to the canonical subject position in Irish, above the progressive aspect marker that marks the left edge of the maximum verbal projection. McCloskey concludes that subjects in Irish necessarily raise out of VP; see also Bobaljik and Carnie (1996).

As supporting evidence, note that the class of adverbials which are typically considered to be left-adjoined to VP (since they modify material within VP) must appear immediately *after* the subject; the adverbial is in italics in (22), and the subject is underlined:

(22) Ní   bhfuair   <u>aon</u>   <u>bhean</u>   *riamh*   *roimhe*   greim
      NEG   take:PAST   any   woman   ever   before: 3MSG   grip
      láimhe   air. (I)
      hand:GEN   on: 3MSG
      'No woman had ever before taken his hand.' (McCloskey 1996a: 269)

McCloskey (2001b) demonstrates that these adverbials are indeed outside VP, since under VP-ellipsis they are retained rather than being deleted. If this is the correct interpretation of the position of the adverbial, then the subject must have raised out of VP.

Similar considerations have led researchers to the same conclusion for Welsh. Subjects again immediately precede VP-adverbials:

(23) Mae   <u>hogia</u>   *bob amser*   yn   brolio. (W)
      be:PRES:3SG   lads   always   PROG   boast:NONFIN
      'Lads are always boasting.' (Tallerman 1998: 105)

In (23), the adverbial is higher than the aspectual head *yn* (progressive), which itself takes a VP complement; the subject has then evidently raised to a position well outside VP; see also Koopman and Sportiche (1991: 232–235). The Brythonic languages provide additional evidence for the surface position of subjects, since they have split negation markers *ni . . . ddim* (Welsh) and *ne . . . ket* (Breton) (the first elements of which are often absent). The cognate items *ni/ne* appear clause-initially and are arguably complementizers (see Stump (1989: 466f.) on Breton, and also section 4 below);[5] but the second element occurs medially, in a position assumed to be outside the VP over which it has scope. Interestingly, Welsh and Breton differ with respect to the positions of their subjects and this medial negative element:

(24) Dydy   Mair *ddim* wedi gweld   y   ffilm. (W)
       NEG:be:PRES:3SG   M.   NEG   PERF see:NONFIN the film
       'Mair hasn't seen the film.'

(25) Ne   gann   *ket* Mari he   dilhad   war ar   stank. (B)
       NEG   wash:PRES:3SG   NEG   M.   her clothes on   the pond
       'Mari does not wash her clothes in the pond.' (Stephens 1982: 171)

The subject precedes the negator in Welsh but follows it in Breton. However, the Breton facts don't necessarily entail that the subject remains *within* VP; the negator *ket* itself might instead be in a higher position outside the VP than it is in Welsh.

The "Split INFL Hypothesis" (Pollock 1989, Belletti 1990, Chomsky 1991) suggests a satisfactory account of this array of facts. The verb is lower than C, so the subject, immediately following, cannot be in Spec, IP, but neither does the subject remain within VP. If there is more than one functional projection between C and V, then the verb can raise to the higher functional head, and the subject can move to the specifier position immediately below. This is diagrammed in (26), where F indicates a functional projection of some type:

(26)

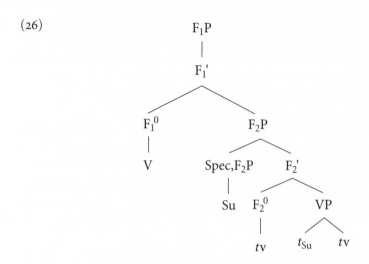

Analyses generally of this kind are proposed for Celtic languages by Rouveret (1991, 1994), Hendrick (1991), Duffield (1995), Bobaljik and Carnie (1996), McCloskey (1996a, 1997, 2001b), Tallerman (1998), and Willis (1998), among many others. However, there is no overall consensus on what should head each functional projection. For simple VSO structures such as (1) and (2), most analyses from the 1990s assume an articulated I consisting of T(ense) and Agr(eement) projections, possibly with the latter split further into AgrS (subject agreement) and AgrO projections, following Chomsky (1991). For instance, Rouveret, Hendrick, Tallerman, and Willis argue that for the Brythonic languages the highest functional head is AgrS; this has a TP complement hosting the raised subject in its specifier, roughly as schematized in (27):

(27) $[_{AgrSP} [_{AgrS} Verb] [_{TP} [_{DP} Subject] t_v [_{VP} t_{Su} [t_v' Object]]]]$

Such a proposal is also outlined for Irish by Bobaljik and Carnie (1996). Conversely, Duffield (1995) argues that TP is higher than AgrSP in Irish, as does McCloskey (1996a, 1997). In later versions of the Minimalist Program (see Chomsky 1995: ch. 4), there are no agreement projections, so alternative functional heads would be required in their place. Note, however, that from recent work it is clear that a satisfactory account of Celtic syntax requires a phrase structure sufficiently articulated to provide for a number of distinct core argument positions: see, for instance, McCloskey (2001b). In fact, current work on Celtic typically argues for the retention of the agreement projections (McCloskey (2001b); Roberts (2004); Carnie and Harley (2000)).

There are various additional considerations. Presumably, it is desirable to maintain a uniform clause structure across all clause types. But in addition to VSO clauses, all the Celtic languages have periphrastic I-SVO clauses of the type illustrated in (5) and (6), with aspectual heads between the subject and the VP. One possibility is that the finite auxiliary found in initial position starts off in a low position within the clause and raises through each of these aspectual positions: see, for instance, Hendrick (1991).[6] However, if the aspect markers are the heads of their projections, such a derivation will violate the Head Movement Constraint. Another possibility is that the auxiliary is inserted (rather than raised) into a position above the aspectual particles, in order to support the verbal morphology expressing Tense, agreement, and Mood; see, for instance, Cinque (1999: 66f.).

Second, as already noted, all the languages are subject-initial in nonfinite clauses. But in Scottish Gaelic and Irish, the word order is SOV, which suggests that the object has raised out of VP, at least in nonfinite clauses; see also Guilfoyle (1993) and Noonan (1995). OV order also occurs in certain finite clauses in both Irish and Scottish Gaelic. In the periphrastic construction (see (5) and (6)), a finite part of 'be' is in initial position, and there is an aspect marker immediately following the subject. Both VO (as in (6)) and OV orders occur, depending on the aspect. Example (28) illustrates OV in Scottish Gaelic, with the prospective aspect (the object is in italic):

(28) Tha   Calum   gus   *a'*   *chraobh* a ghearradh. (SG)
      be:PRES C.   PROSP the   tree   cut:NONFIN

     'Calum is about to cut the tree.' (Ramchand 1997: 72)

Ramchand (1997) provides extensive discussion of the syntax and semantics of aspect in Scottish Gaelic; see also Adger (1996). For Irish, Bobaljik and Carnie (1996) and McCloskey (2001b) propose an AgrO phrase between TP and VP, with raised objects moving to Spec, AgrOP, whereas Carnie and Harley (2000) propose that the AgrO projection is actually *within* a split VP.

3 WORD ORDER AND CLAUSE STRUCTURE IN NONFINITE CLAUSES

All the Celtic languages display nonfinite clauses, both with and without overt subjects. If we consider first clauses with overt subjects, the first major constituent is always the subject. However, overt subjects are licensed under different conditions on each side of the Celtic family. In Irish and Scottish Gaelic, nonfinite clauses with overt subjects occur freely in many different construction types, as illustrated in (29) and (30); the subjects of the nonfinite clauses are in italic:

(29) Ó   tharlaigh   [*iad*   ag   imeacht   an   lá
      since   happened   them:ACC   PROG   leave:NONFIN the   day
      sin . . .] (I)
      DEMON

      'Since they happened to be leaving that day. . . . ' (Chung and McCloskey
      1987: 177)

(30) Sheasadh   Iain   [ach   *Anna*   suidhe]. (SG)
      stand.up:CONDIT   I.   but   A.   sit.down:NONFIN

      'Iain would stand up provided that Anna sat down.' (MacAulay 1992:
      164)

As Chung and McCloskey (1987) outline, nonverbal "small clauses" with an overt
subject are also common:

(31) *Independent clauses in a narrative, following a finite clause:*
      Ghaibh   criú   naomhóige   isteach. *Iad*   righin
      come:PAST   crew   currach:GEN in   them:ACC   tough
      fadthruslógach. (I)
      with.long.loping.stride

      'The crew of a currach came in. They were tough and walked with a long
      loping stride.' (Chung and McCloskey 1987: 177)

(32) Chunnaic   Iain   Anna   [agus   *i*   aig   an   dorus]. (SG)
      see:PAST   I.   A.   and   her   at   the   door

      'Iain saw Anna at the door.' (MacAulay 1992: 169)

Chung and McCloskey (1987: 188) suggest that Irish (and by extension, Scottish
Gaelic) has a default accusative case-assignment rule that licenses the subjects of
nonfinite clauses and small clauses. Since third-person pronouns in Irish display
morphological case (nominative and accusative), it is clear that the subject pronouns are indeed accusative. Whatever mechanism licenses the (nominative) subjects of finite clauses is not operative in these examples.[7] Nor is there any other
Case-licenser, such as a preposition; nor are the accusative subjects restricted to
'exceptional Case-marking' environments. Although (29) is reminiscent of an
ECM embedded clause (cf. *We believed* [Kim *to be a liar*]) the remaining examples
could not plausibly be analyzed in this way, as there is no apparent Case-assigner
preceding the subjects.

Similar constructions in Welsh have different properties and distribution. For
instance, a finite clause can conjoin with a nonfinite clause, which is then un-

derstood to have the same tense as the first clause. But the nonfinite clause cannot have an overt subject; compare (32) with (33).[8]

(33)   Prynodd   Mair bapur   [a   mynd   (*hi)   allan]. (W)
       buy:PAST:3SG   M.   paper   and   go:NONFIN   she   out

       'Mair bought a paper and went out.'

All four Celtic languages, however, display a superficially homogeneous Case-licensing strategy which we could call the "prepositional subject" (P-subject) construction. Examples (34) through (37) illustrate it; the prepositional elements and subjects are in italics:

(34)   Disgwyliodd   Aled   [i   *Mair*   fynd   adre']. (W)
       expect-PAST:3SG A.   to   M.   go:NONFIN   home

       'Aled expected Mair to go home.'

(35)   Abalamour   *da Yann*   nompas   ankouaad . . . (B)
       because   to   Y.   NEG   forget:NONFIN

       'So that Yann doesn't forget. . . . ' (Tallerman 1997: 219)

(36)   Tar éis   *do lucht   na   Parlaiminte*   an   caisleán   a thógáil . . . (I)
       after   to   people   the   Parliament   the   castle   take:NONFIN

       'After the Parliamentarians took the castle. . . . ' (McCloskey 1997: 224)

(37)   Sheas   Iain   [an dèidh   *do Anna*   suidhe]. (SG)
       stand.up: PAST   I.   after   to   A.   sit:NONFIN

       'Iain stood up after Anna sat down.' (MacAulay 1992: 163)

An obvious first assumption is that the prepositional elements (which are, in fact, cognates in all four languages) are Case-licensers for the subjects of the nonfinite clauses. This seems straightforwardly true of Irish and Scottish Gaelic, but the situation in Welsh and Breton is more complex. I concentrate here on the contrast between Irish and Welsh; on Breton infinitival clauses, see Tallerman (1997).

One possibility is that the prepositional elements in (34) through (37) are complementizers, assigning Case down into the subject position below, as *for* does in English *For her to leave would be a pity*. But it is clear that Irish *do* is not a complementizer: all complementizers in Celtic occur in clause-initial position, but *do*-subjects have a certain positional freedom. As well as appearing in initial position, (38a), the *do*-subject can occur within VP, below both the raised object *é* and the nonfinite verb, (38b); see McCloskey (2001b):[9]

(38) a. le linn *dhom*   é   a fhágaint (I)
          when   to:1SG it   leave:NONFIN

      'when I leave it'

      b. le linn é   a fhágaint   *dhom*
          when   it   leave:NONFIN   to:1SG

      'when I leave it'

Since the P-subject sequence can appear in (at least) two different positions within the clause and can also be clefted (McCloskey 1984: 469), we have good evidence that it is a constituent. This suggests that *do* is a Case-marker, since it must accompany the subject.

Further evidence that Irish *do* (and Scottish Gaelic *do*) is simply a Case-assigning morpheme is that the *do* Case strategy alternates with other Case-licensing strategies, including the default accusative strategy outlined here, as shown in (39)b:

(39) a. le linn *dom*   bheith   go   mo   shearradh (I)
          while   to:1SG be:NONFIN   to   1SG   stretch

      'while I was stretching myself'

      b. le linn *mise*   a bheith   im'   bháb
          while   me:ACC be:NONFIN   in-my   baby

      'when I was a baby' (Ó Siadhail 1989: 282)

In contrast, the Welsh *i*-Subject sequence is not a constituent: although P+DP can normally pied-pipe, here it is impossible, suggesting also that *i* is not a Case marker:

(40) *I *bwy*   y   disgwyliodd   Aled _____   fynd
       to who   PRT   expected   A.   go:NONFIN
      adre'? (cf. (34)) (W)
      home

      'Who did Aled expect to go home?'

The question of whether *i* is a complementizer has received different answers; see particularly Rouveret (1994) and Tallerman (1998). Although Rouveret proposes that *i* is a complementizer, Tallerman argues that it does not display the typical behavior of complementizers in Welsh.[10] First, no element that is uncontroversially a complementizer inflects in Welsh. Second, complementizers in nonfinite clauses do not license overt subjects in Welsh. Third, complementizers in

Welsh are lexically selected by the matrix predicate and are subject to a certain amount of lexical, free, and dialectal variation. Consider the data in (41):

(41) a. Mae Aled yn   falch   [o   weld   Mair]. (W)
         is   A.   PRED pleased of   see:NONFIN M.
         'Aled is pleased to see Mair.'

      b. *Mae Aled yn   falch   [o   Gwyn/ ohono   fo
         is   A.   PRED pleased of   G.   of:3MSG him
         weld   Mair].
         see:NONFIN M.
         'Aled is pleased for Gwyn/for him to see Mair.'

      c. Mae Aled yn   falch   [i   Gwyn/ iddo   fo
         is   A.   PRED pleased to   G.   to:3MSG him
         weld   Mair].
         see:NONFIN M.
         'Aled is pleased for Gwyn/for him to see Mair.' (Tallerman 1998: 117)

The *o* element in (41)a is a complementizer; it occurs in a controlled infinitival clause with no overt subject (but presumably a PRO subject). This element cannot license an overt subject, nor can it inflect; see (41)b. In contrast, *i* in (41)c does license an overt subject and also inflects when the subject is pronominal. To illustrate the third property, note that the control adjective *balch* 'pleased, glad' selects complementizer *o*, but other adjectives exhibit different lexical selection properties. The control adjective *bodlon* 'willing, happy' generally selects a null complementizer but alternatively selects complementizer *i*. However, in constructions with 'inflectional' *i*, there is never any alternative: *i* is simply obligatory whenever it occurs and is subject to no variation whatever.

The relationship between Welsh *i* and abstract Case is an indirect one, according to Tallerman (1998). The proposal is that inflectional *i* is generated in T and raises to AgrS; evidence for the latter movement is that *i* inflects (e.g., *iddo* = *i* + 3MSG) as in (41)c. One benefit of this analysis is that the same Case-licensing mechanisms can be proposed for both finite and infinitival clauses in Welsh. In order to license the Case of subjects, AgrS must be lexically supported: either a finite verb raises to AgrS, or else inflectional *i* does so. Either element provides lexical support for AgrS. The subjects of both clause types are in the specifier of the projection immediately below AgrS, as shown in (42) and (43):

(42)

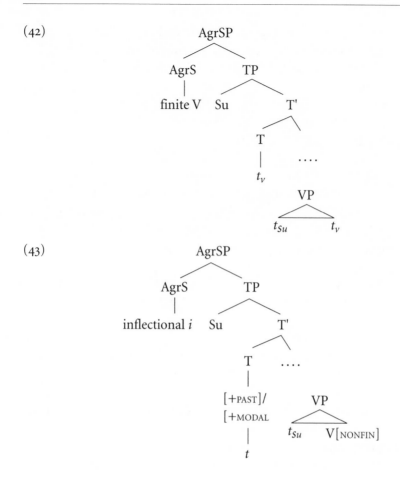

(43)

Support for the claim that the inflectional *i* cooccurring with overt subjects is generated in T° comes from the fact that it is associated with two different clause types. Both are infinitival and therefore formally nonfinite, but one displays the typical behavior of a finite clause, and the other that of a nonfinite clause. The former type occurs as the complement to epistemic and declarative predicates, such as verbs from the 'believe' and 'say' classes, as illustrated in (44). The *i*-clause is interpreted, obligatorily, as past tense and replaces a tensed complement clause (i.e., one with a finite lexical verb).[11] As Harlow (1992) notes, such clauses have the binding properties of ordinary finite clauses: their pronominal subject can be bound by an antecedent in the matrix clause, whereas an anaphor subject cannot (the English translations give the same effects):

(44) a. Dywedodd   Aled$_i$ [iddo   fo$_{i/j}$ fynd]. (W)
         say:PAST:3SG   A.   to:3MSG   him   go:NONFIN
         'Aled said that he'd gone.'

b. *Dywedodd Aled [iddo *ei hun* fynd].
  say:PAST:3SG A.   to:3MSG himself go:NONFIN

'*Aled said that himself had gone.' (Tallerman 1998: 90)

Furthermore, these *i*-clauses can conjoin with ordinary tensed clauses and they fail to display the negation properties of nonfinite clauses. It seems, then, that despite appearances, they are truly finite. Conversely, the type of *i*-clause in (41)c really is nonfinite: it is interpreted not as past tense but as modal or infinitival, it cannot conjoin with ordinary tensed clauses (see Sadler 1988: 40), it negates in the normal manner for nonfinite clauses, and it has the binding properties of nonfinite clauses. So a pronominal subject must be disjoint in reference to the matrix subject, and an anaphor subject can be bound within the matrix clause:

(45) a. Dymunai Aled$_i$ [iddo *fo$_j$/*fo$_i$* fynd] (W)
    wanted:3SG A.   to:3MSG him   go:NONFIN

   'Aled wanted him to go.'

  b. Dymunai Aled [iddo *ei hun* ddarllen   y   llyfr].
    wanted:3SG A.   to: 3MSG himself read: NONFIN the book

   'Aled wanted himself to read the book.' (Tallerman 1998: 92)

One additional complication in the treatment of infinitival clauses, particularly in Welsh and Breton, is that overt subjects occur in what appear to be identical environments to the empty category subjects of control and raising complement clauses, as noted by Borsley (1986). Compare the examples in (46): the embedded clause in (a) has an overt subject, (b) illustrates a control clause with a PRO subject, and (c) is a raising predicate with a trace in embedded subject position:[12]

(46) a. Mae   Aled yn   disgwyl   [*i* Elen ddarllen
    be:PRES:3SG A. PROG expect:NONFIN to E.   read:NONFIN
    y   llyfr]. (W)
    the book

   'Aled expects Elen to read the book.'

  b. Mae   Elen yn   ymdrechu   [*i*   *PRO*
    be: PRES:3SG E. PROG endeavor:NONFIN to
    ddarllen   y   llyfr].
    read:NONFIN the book

   'Elen is endeavoring to read the book.'

   c. Mae   [gwaed y   ceiliog]$_i$ yn   tueddi   [i   t$_i$
      be:PRES:3SG blood the cockerel PROG tend:NONFIN   to
      fod   yn y   cyw].
      be:NONFIN in the chick

   'The cockerel's blood tends to be in the chick.' (i.e., 'Like father like son.' (Tallerman 1998: 128)

In (46) each embedded clause is introduced by *i*. Borsley's Paradox is that if *i* assigns Case to the embedded subject in (46a), then it should also assign Case to the (traditionally Caseless) null subjects in (b) and (c). This is problematic because it predicts, among other things, that PRO and overt subjects should be freely interchangeable in such clauses and that raising to subject should be optional. Neither prediction is borne out. By arguing that the inflectional *i* in (46a) is not the same morpheme as complementizer *i* in (b) and (c), Tallerman (1998) provides one solution to Borsley's Paradox: complementizer *i* is never associated with abstract Case.

    In contrast, Irish *do* does not appear before the lower-clause subject position in control or raising structures,[13] predictably if it is indeed a Case-licensing morpheme as outlined previously. It inserts only if there is an overt subject requiring Case. Example (47) illustrates with a raising structure:

(47) Caithfidh sí$_j$ [gan   (*do) t$_j$ a bheith   breoite]. (I)
      must   she NEG:COMP to   be: NONFIN ill

   'She must not be ill.'

In fact, as McCloskey (1986a) shows, raising is optional in Irish, since the lower clause subject can always be Case-licensed by default accusative Case-assignment:

(48) Caithfidh [gan   í   a bheith   breoite]. (I)
      must   NEG:COMP her:ACC be: NONFIN ill

   'It must be that she is not ill.' (McCloskey 1986a: 200)

McCloskey (2001b) suggests that the two different positions of the Irish *do*-subject illustrated in (38) represent subject positions distinct from that of bare DPs in the language. The lower position seen in (38b) represents a position within VP—in fact, the thematic position of subjects. The higher position in (38a) represents the very highest position within the clause in which subjects can occur, and crucially, this is *above* the position occupied by ordinary accusative subjects in nonfinite clauses (see, for instance, (39b)). The evidence comes from negation: although accusative subjects appear below the negative marker *gan*, (49a), *do*-subjects appear above it, (49b). The subjects are in italic:

(49) a. B'fhearr liom   gan   *iad*   mé   a fheiceáil
          I-would-prefer NEG:COMP   them:ACC   me   see:NONFIN

      'I would prefer for them not to see me.'

      b. Conas   *d'aonaránach*   gan   a bheith   ag
          how   to solitary.person   NEG:COMP   be:NONFIN   PROG
          braistint   aonarach?
          feel:NONFIN   solitary

      'How could a solitary person not feel solitary?' (McCloskey (2001b: 184–185)

McCloskey (2001b) concludes, then, that the structure of nonfinite clauses in Irish is as in (50):

(50)

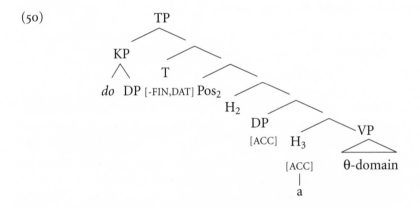

The higher position of *do*-subjects is the position in which they are Case-licensed; McCloskey argues persuasively that this position is not utilized for subjects in finite clauses. Position$_2$ is that of accusative subjects in nonfinite clauses, as well as nominative subjects in finite clauses.[14] Position$_3$ can be identified as the specifier of the AgrO projection and is occupied by the raised object in nonfinite clauses, giving SOV order. The lower position of *do*-subjects (cf. (38b)) is within the theta domain.

4 VERB-SECOND SYNTAX

All three Brythonic Celtic languages either have or had verb-second (V2) syntax at some point in their history: Breton retains V2 syntax, and both Middle Welsh and Middle Cornish exhibited it.[15] As noted in section 1, Breton generally requires some constituent to front in root clauses, giving rise to examples such as (51), from Schafer (1994), with a fronted subject, object, and VP, respectively:[16]

(51) a. [DP Ar   vugale]   o   deus   gwalc'het   ar   wetur
          the children 3PL   have   wash:PAST.PART   the   car
          dec'h. (B)
          yesterday

          'The children washed the car yesterday.'

     b. [DP Ar   wetur]   o   deus   ar   vugale   gwalc'het
          the car   3PL   have   the   children   wash:PAST.PART
          dec'h.
          yesterday

          'The children washed the car yesterday.'

     c. [VP Gwalc'hin   ar   wetur]   o   deus   graet.
          wash:NONFIN   the   car   3PL   have   do:PAST.PART

          'They really did wash the car.'

Any constituent may be fronted, including adverbials. In terms of discourse effects, fronted subjects are fairly unmarked, but the fronting of any constituent focalizes it to some extent. The finite verb, either an auxiliary or a lexical verb, comes in second position. The generally standard view of V2 syntax in Celtic sees it as parallel to the more familiar Germanic languages, in the sense that the fronted XP moves to Spec, CP; see Schafer (1994) and Borsley et al. (1996) on Breton, and see Willis (1998) on Middle Welsh. However, the position of the finite element in second position is far more controversial.

If Breton and Middle Welsh were analyzed as parallel to German, then the finite verb should be sited in C°. However, the following constructions indicate that in the Celtic languages, other elements can apparently occupy C° (see also (3)):

(52) [V Mynet]   a   oruc   serch   y   uorwyn   ym   pob
          go: NONFIN   PRT   do:PAST:3SG   love   the   maiden   in   every
          aleawt   itaw . . . (Middle W)
          limb   to: 3MSG

          'Love of the maiden entered into every limb of him . . . ' (Evans 1989: 167)

(53) [V Lennet]   en   deus   Tom   al   levr. (B)
          read: PAST.PART   3MSG   have   T.   the   book

          'Tom has read the book.' (Stephens 1982: 86)

(54)   [_A *Skuizh*]   int   da c'hortoz. (B)
      tired   are: 3PL   to wait: NONFIN

   'They are tired of waiting.'

In each example (52) through (54), the fronted element is a head, not an XP. Given standard assumptions concerning phrase structure (Chomsky 1986), heads must move to a head position and cannot occupy Spec, CP. Both fronted bare infinitives and past participles occur, as in (52) and (53). The fact that in each case their complements are left behind provides evidence that these, and the fronted adjective in (54), are all bare heads. A different possibility is that the fronted elements actually represent phrases from which constituents other than the head have been extracted, so that what remains looks like a bare head but in fact is not. This analysis, known as Partial XP Fronting or Remnant Topicalization, is discussed—and dismissed—by Borsley and Kathol (2000: 669f.) in relation to Breton. In contrast with remnant topicalization in German, the Breton example in (53), for instance, would not allow a full VP to be fronted as an alternative option—something we would expect to be possible under the remnant topicalization analysis. Furthermore, although neither German remnant topicalization nor ordinary topicalization in Breton is blocked by negation, the fronting of heads illustrated in (52) through (54) *is* blocked by negation. Borsley and Kathol (2000) thus conclude that the fronted elements are indeed heads and not phrases.

   Consider now (55):

(55)   [*Ne*]   lenn   ket   Anna   al   levr. (B)
      NEG   read: PRES:3SG   NEG   A.   the   book

   'Anna doesn't read the book.' (Borsley et al. 1996: 62)

The negative construction in (55) and its parallel in Middle Welsh have often been treated as an exception to V2, because no constituent has fronted; this is the position of Schafer (1994, 1995) and Willis (1998). However, Stump (1989: 466f.) argues that Breton negative *ne* should be seen as occupying C°, the initial position, and thus fulfilling the V2 requirement by ensuring that the verb is in second position.[17] If the negative particle is indeed in C°, then under standard assumptions, the finite verb must occupy a different (lower) position.[18]

   An obvious proposal is that the fronted heads in (52) through (54) also move to C°. Since the negative construction of (55) does not cooccur with a fronted head, we can take this as evidence that both fronted heads and *ne* are sited in C° and are thus in complementary distribution. The analyses of Borsley et al. (1996) and Schafer (1994) also assume that fronted heads move to C°, although for different reasons. Borsley et al. propose that Tense in Breton is licensed via the C-projection under one of four conditions: either C° is filled by a nonfinite verb or by the negator *ne*, or else the specifier position of CP is filled by a fronted XP, or alternatively the C° position heads a lexically selected CP (so accounting for the fact that embedded clauses are not V2, as (3) illustrates). Under these proposals, the finite element is consistently lower in the clause than C°. Schafer (1994), on the other hand, argues that V2 in Breton is a "fill C°" requirement: either a fronted head moves to C°, as in (52) through (54), with the finite verb remaining lower in the clause, or else in the XP-initial constructions (see (51)) the finite verb itself raises to C°. One problem with this analysis is that finite verbs are taken to occupy different positions in different clause types, yet there is no evidence that they do.[19] Borsley et al. take the finite element to be lower than C° in all clause types; we can assume it occupies the highest functional head position within the main clause. Whatever the correct analysis, it seems clear that Brythonic V2 is rather different in character to Germanic V2; see also Borsley and Kathol (2000) for a discussion of the similarities and differences.

Finally, both Breton (see Schafer 1994) and Middle Welsh allow "dummy" elements to fulfil the V2 requirement, as (56) illustrates:

(56) [*Sef*] y   clywei   arueu   am   ben
      SEF   PRT   perceive: IMPERF:3SG armour   on   head
      hwnnw. (Middle W)
      that.one

      'He could feel armour on that one's head.' (Watkins 1997: 587)

The item *sef* in (56) has no semantic or syntactic function apart from allowing the finite verb to be noninitial; presumably, we can say that *sef* occupies the initial position, C°, and thus satisfies V2 by relegating the finite element to second position.[20]

5 COPULAR CONSTRUCTIONS

The verb 'be' in each of the Celtic languages is astonishingly complex, both in morphology and syntactic behavior, and the syntax of the copula is one way in which the Brythonic and Goidelic languages differ significantly. Detailed analyses of the Irish copula are proposed by Doherty (1996, 1997), from whom the examples in this section are taken; on the related constructions in Scottish Gaelic, see Ramchand (1996) and Adger and Ramchand (2001). Traditional Irish grammar distinguishes between a copula (*is*), as in (57) and a substantive verb (*tá*) as in (58):

(57) Is   dochtúir é. (I)
      COP   doctor   him: ACC

      'He is a doctor.'

(58) Tá   sé   ar meisce. (I)
      is   he: NOM   drunk

      'He is drunk.'

The two constructions differ in various ways. First, the copular construction is subject-final, whereas the substantive construction has the usual finite V-Subject word order (the subjects are in italics in (57) and (58)). Second, the copula takes an accusative subject, whereas the substantive takes the usual nominative. Third, traditionally the copula is used when the predicate expresses a permanent property of its subject, whereas the substantive verb is used for temporary states, such as being drunk. As Doherty shows, this distinction can be profitably paralleled to the "individual-level" and "stage-level" distinction used by semanticists.[21]

Doherty (1997) proposes that the copular construction has the structure in (59):

(59)

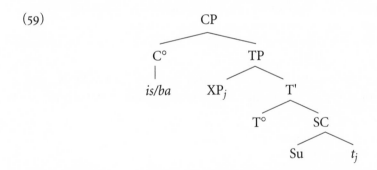

Here, there is an underlying small clause; its subject remains in situ (thus surfacing in final position), and its predicate raises to Spec, TP. However, in terms of binding facts, a reciprocal within the predicate can have the subject as its antecedent, but not vice versa, which is unexpected, given that in (59) the predicate is higher in the clause than the subject:

(60) a. Is   cosúil lena chéile   iad. (I)
         COP   like   with.each.other   them: ACC

         'They are like each other.'

      b. *Is   cosúil leofa   a chéile
         COP   like   with: 3PL   each.other

         '*Each other is like them.'

Doherty (1997) and Carnie (1997) account for such data by assuming that reconstruction occurs at LF (Huang 1993), so that the subject does indeed c-command the predicate at the appropriate level. That the subject is accusative is entirely consistent with the subjects of other small clauses (in fact, other nonfinite clauses). McCloskey's work argues that accusative is the default case for such subjects in Irish; see McCloskey (1986a), Chung and McCloskey (1987), and McCloskey (2001b).

As seen earlier, the proposal that finite verbs in general raise to C° lacks support. However, it might well be the case that the Celtic copula has a higher position than other finite verbs. In Irish, for instance, the copula combines with complementizers, giving rise to fusional forms such as *gur*:

(61) Dúirt siad   [*gur*   dhoctúir é]. (I)
      said   they   COMP:COP:PAST   doctor   him:ACC

      'They said he was a doctor.'

Rouveret (1996) proposes that the copula also raises to C° in Welsh, but only in constructions that have DP–copula–DP word order, as in (63). In Welsh, cleftlike fronting of a constituent is obligatory in copular clauses under certain conditions, optional in others, and impossible in yet others. With an indefinite predicate DP, as in (62), copula-initial word order—as in Irish—is possible. Unlike the Irish in (57), though, the subject is in the usual position, immediately after the finite verb. Rouveret argues that the copula in these V-initial cases raises only as far as AgrS. Note that this construction also contains an obligatory predicate marker, *yn*:

(62) Mae   Alys   yn   athrawes. (W)
      is   A.   PRED   teacher

      'Alys is a teacher.'

Alternatively, the indefinite predicate DP can be fronted; in this word order, the predicate marker disappears:[22]

(63) Athrawes   ydy   Alys. (W)
      teacher   is   A.

      'Alys is a teacher.'

However, the subject DP cannot be fronted in this case:[23]

(64) *Alys   ydy   athrawes. (W)
      A.   is   teacher

If the predicate DP is definite, the word order with an initial copula is ungrammatical, with or without predicative *yn*:

(65) *Mae Alys (yn) yr   athrawes. (W)
      is   A.   PRED the teacher
      'Alys is the teacher.'

Instead, DP-copula-DP order is obligatory, with either the predicate or the subject fronted; the unmarked word order is as in (66a), with the definite predicate DP fronted:

(66) a. Yr   athrawes ydy Alys. (W)
         the teacher   is   A.
         'Alys is the teacher.'

      b. Alys ydy'r   athrawes.
         A.   is-the teacher
         'Alys is the teacher./It's Alys who's the teacher.'

Rouveret (1996: 148ff.) proposes that constructions such as (63) and (66) involve movement of the initial XP to Spec, CP under focalization, with concomitant movement of the copula to C°; in effect, then, these are verb-second constructions. Support for the proposal that the copula is in C° comes first from the fact that it doesn't cooccur with other elements typically analyzed as complementizers in Welsh. Support for the claim that the fronted predicate DP raises to Spec, CP (rather than to a position within IP) comes once more from the binding facts. Rouveret points out that reconstruction affects only elements in an Ā-position, normally Spec, CP. As in Irish—see (60)—Welsh allows what at first glance appears to be a Binding Principle A violation, since the anaphor is higher than its antecedent:

(67) [Ei   elyn   pennaf ei   hun] ydy Siôn. (W)
       his enemy   chief   3MSG   self is   S.
      'Siôn is his own worst enemy.' (Rouveret 1996: 149)

But given reconstruction at LF, the binding facts are readily accounted for, since the antecedent then c-commands the anaphor.

Rouveret proposes that the stage-level/individual-level distinction is also important for Welsh and again has various syntactic effects. He suggests that bare nominals aren't inherently specified for the distinction, and so a DP in Spec, CP may receive either reading. However, the appearance of predicative *yn* forces a stage-level (temporary property) reading on a DP; in fact, only indefinite DPs can be stage-level predicates. So the indefinite predicates may occur in copula-initial clauses, as in (62), or else the predicate DP can raise to Spec, CP, as in (63). Since "definite nominals are canonically individual-level" (Rouveret (1996: 156)—that is, they encode permanent properties—it is not surprising that a definite predicate DP cannot occur in the *yn* construction, as we saw in (65).

The situation in Irish displays interesting parallels but uses the different 'be' verbs in conjunction with word-order differences to express the distinction. As noted in connection with (57) and (58), the copula *is* denotes permanent properties, whereas the verb *tá* is associated with temporary states.[24] Consider (68), from Stenson (1981: 94) and Doherty (1996: 39):

(68) a. Is   sagart é   mo dhearthái.   (I)
         COP priest   him:ACC my brother

      'He's a priest, my brother./My brother is a priest.'

      b. Tá mo dhearthái   ina   shagart.
         is my brother   in: 3MSG   priest

      'My brother is a priest.'

As the sources explain, these differ in that (68a) expresses a permanent state, classifying the brother as a member of the set of priests as a defining property, whereas (68b) expresses a more transient quality, indicating that being a priest is merely his profession.

6 AGREEMENT

All the Celtic languages display an absolute complementarity between overt lexical arguments and overt agreement morphology, sometimes known as the "anti-agreement effect." However, the details differ in important ways across the four languages. Compare the following data from Welsh in (69) and Irish in (70):

(69) a. Cafodd   y   merched   wahoddiad. (W)
         get:PAST:(3SG) the girls   invitation

      'The girls got an invitation.'

      b. *Cawson   y   merched   wahoddiad.
         get:PAST:3PL   the girls   invitation

      'The girls got an invitation.'

c. Cawson   (nhw)   wahoddiad.
   get:PAST:3PL   they   invitation

'They got an invitation.'

(70) a. Chuir   na   girseachaí   isteach   ar   an   phost. (I)
         put:PAST:∅   the   girls   in   on   the   job

      'The girls applied for the job.'

      b. *Chuireadar   na   girseachaí   isteach   ar   an   phost.
         put:PAST:3PL   the   girls   in   on   the   job

      'The girls applied for the job.'

      c. Chuireadar   (*siad)   isteach   ar   an   phost.
         put:PAST:3PL   they   in   on   the   job

      'They applied for the job.'

First, note that nonpronominal subjects do not cooccur with verbal agreement. In both Welsh and Irish, a plural lexical DP fails to trigger the third-person plural form of the finite verb; compare the (a) and (b) forms in (69) and (70). In Welsh, the form of the verb used in (69a) is identical to the third-person singular form of the verb—hence the gloss; it appears, then, that Welsh lacks number agreement with full DPs. The (c) forms illustrate a major difference between Welsh and the other Celtic languages. In Welsh, overt agreement morphology can cooccur with overt pronominal arguments, while in the remaining languages it generally cannot. So in Welsh, (69c), the third-person plural form of the verb can cooccur with an overt pronominal subject, whereas in Irish, it cannot; the subject in (70c) must be the null pronominal *pro*.[25] Breton and Scottish Gaelic pattern with Irish.

The second major difference within the Celtic languages concerns the availability of inflectional paradigms with rich-agreement morphology. Verbal paradigms in Irish comprise both "synthetic" and "analitic" forms: "The synthetic form . . . encodes information about tense and mood, as well as the person and number of its subject. The analytic form encodes only information about tense and mood, but not about the person-number characteristics of its subject" (McCloskey and Hale 1984: 489). The form in (70a), then, is an analytic form, containing no person/number marker. Verbal paradigms typically contain forms of both kinds, as illustrated in (71) (from McCloskey and Hale 1984: 489) where the forms in bold are synthetic and the remaining forms are analytic:

(71)   **Conditional paradigm of *cuir* 'put' in Ulster dialect:**

1SG	**chuirfinn** (*mé) 'I'	1PL	**chuirfimis** (*sinn) 'we'
2SG	**chuirfeá** (*tú) 'you':SG	2PL	chuirfeadh sibh 'you':PL
3MSG	chuirfeadh sé 'he'	3PL	chuirfeadh siad 'they'
3FSG	chuirfeadh sí 'she'		

Note that crucially, when fully inflected synthetic forms are available, these must be used, and they cannot cooccur with an overt pronominal subject; see (72)a. Where there is no synthetic form, then the analytic form must be used in conjunction with a pronominal subject.[26] In general, if a synthetic form is available, using the analytic form + pronoun is not an alternative: see (72b):[27]

(72) a. Chuirfinn   (*mé) isteach ar   an   phost sin. (I)
        put:COND:1SG   I   in   on   the job   DEMON

        'I would apply for that job.' (McCloskey and Hale 1984: 490)

     b. *Chuirfeadh mé   isteach ar   an   phost sin.
        put:COND:∅   I   in   on   the job   DEMON

        'I would apply for that job.' (McCloskey and Hale 1984: 491)

The conditions governing the appearance of overt agreement and overt arguments are parallelled throughout the syntax of Celtic. As already noted, prepositions (typically) have inflectional paradigms, but the inflected forms cannot cooccur with nonpronominal DPs. In Welsh, as with verbs, overt pronominals cooccur with inflected forms, as in (73a), whereas in Irish only null pronominals may do so, (74a). As there are no special analytic forms of prepositions, the canonical form cooccurs with lexical DPs:

(73) a. ganddi   hi   b. gan   y   ddynes   c. *ganddi'r   ddynes (W)
        with:3FSG her   with the   woman   with:3FSG-the woman

        'with her'   'with the woman'   'with the woman'

(74) a. léithi   (*í)   b. le   Máire   c. *léithi   Máire (I)
        with:3FSG her   with M.   with:3FSG M.

        'with her'   'with Máire'   'with Máire'

Further parallels occur in the agreement systems for both nouns and nonfinite verbs. These take a set of identical agreement proclitics, variant for person and number (and for third-person singular, gender) which occur under the same conditions as verbal and prepositional agreement inflections. They are obligatorily absent when the head has a lexical argument and obligatorily present otherwise, with overt pronominals cooccurring in Welsh and null pronominals in Irish. Thus *ei thŷ (hi)* (3FSG house her) 'her house' (W) versus *a teach (*í)* (3FSG house her) 'her house' (I).

Ideally, Celtic agreement facts require a unified treatment, since they are clearly a single phenomenon. McCloskey and Hale (1984) sketch two alternative accounts of Irish—the "agreement analysis" and the "incorporation analysis." The latter proposes that rich inflections arise when a pronominal argument is incorporated in the syntax into a lexical head, effectively *becoming* the agreement morphology; this accounts directly for the lack of cooccurrence between overt pronominals and overt agreement. But as they note, this analysis is unsuccessful in accounting for the patterns in Welsh, since pronouns do cooccur with rich agreement, and it also suffers from empirical problems in Irish, for instance, in the treatment of coordination. The agreement analysis suggests that the empty argument positions (subject, object of P, etc.) are occupied by *pro*, triggering agreement on the lexical heads, which are inserted into the derivation in their fully inflected forms. However, the differences between Welsh and the remaining languages in terms of appearance (or nonappearance) of overt pronominals aren't easily handled here either, as McCloskey and Hale note (1984: 526).

Rouveret (1991, 1994) presents a detailed treatment of agreement, based on Welsh. He takes the incorporation analysis as his starting point, but rather than an actual pronoun being incorporated, he proposes that, on the one hand, synthetic forms are derived by incorporating a NUMBER affix into the Agr category containing the PERSON affix. This ensures that full number agreement occurs. On the other hand, analytic forms (i.e., forms without full agreement) involve no incorporation into Agr; hence, they display no number agreement.[28] The analysis relies on the separation of the categories of Person and Number; in fact, Rouveret proposes that pronouns themselves are Number Phrases, not DPs, with the structure in (75):

(75)   [$_{NumP}$ Num° [$_{NP}$ pronoun]]

NumP is headed by the affix Num(ber) which has an NP complement containing the actual pronoun; this raises to Spec, NumP, leaving Num as an unsupported affix. Since affixes must be supported by adjoining to another head, Num raises to Agr. This accounts for rich agreement in the synthetic pattern. In the case of lexical DPs, the number affix never needs to raise to Agr (and hence cannot) because Num is not stranded but affixes to the head N, so there is no number agreement with lexical DPs. A remaining question is why the synthetic forms must be chosen when available and cannot be replaced by an analytic (or poor agreement) form + pronoun; see (72b). Rouveret considers various options: economy of derivation or the requirement for a more specific form to take precedence over a less specific form. McCloskey and Hale (1984) and McCloskey (1986b) also suggest a "blocking" effect of this type.

7 Ā-Dependencies, Agreement, and Successive Cyclic Movement

Section 6 discussed accounts of patterns of verbal agreement occurring in VSO sentences. However, much attention has also been paid to the rather different patterns in Ā-dependencies; see, for instance, Stump (1984, 1989), Borsley and Stephens (1989), Sadler (1988), Rouveret (1991, 1994), Tallerman (1996), and Willis (1998, 2000). As seen in section 4, both Breton and Middle Welsh are V2 languages: fronted XPs move to Spec, CP, normally considered to be an Ā-position. In affirmative constructions in Breton, the verb doesn't agree in number with a nonpronominal subject, whatever position the subject occupies:

(76) a. [Al levr]   a   lenne   / *lennent   ar
         the book PRT read:IMPERF:(3SG) / read:IMPERF:3PL   the
         baotred. (B)
         boys

         'The boys were reading the book.'

      b. [Ar baotred] a   lenne   / *lennent   al   levr
         the boys   PRT read:IMPERF:(3SG) / read:IMPERF:3PL   the book

         'The boys were reading the book.' (Stump 1989: 431–432)

Negative sentences differ: postverbal subjects trigger no verb agreement (so require the analytic verb form), whereas preverbal subjects trigger full number agreement:[29]

(77) a. Ne   lenne   / *lennent   ket   ar baotred
         NEG read:IMPERF:(3SG) / read:IMPERF:3PL   NEG   the boys
         al   levr. (B)
         the   book

         'The boys weren't reading the book.'

      b. [Ar baotred] ne   lennent   / *lenne   ket
         the boys   NEG read:IMPERF:3PL / read:IMPERF:(3SG) NEG
         al   levr.
         the   book

         'The boys weren't reading the book.' (Stump 1989: 431–432)

Stump's analysis uses the Empty Category Principle (ECP), which requires that the traces of moved constituents be properly governed. In brief, the contrast between (76b) and (77b) occurs because in (77b) Agr combines with the negative complementizer *ne*, allowing it to become a proper governor. The synthetic verb moves to C, which then governs the *wh*-trace in subject position. If the verb is in the analytic form, C[NEG] won't contain Agr and won't be "strong" enough to be a proper governor, but the presence of the overt complementizer also blocks antecedent-government by the fronted subject; an ECP violation results. On the other hand, the particle *a* in (76b) is not analyzed as a complementizer but merely a preverbal particle. (The distinction is not unreasonable: recall from section 4 that negative complementizers can appear in absolute initial position, as in (77a), whereas affirmative sentences require some element to front.) Even if a fully in-flected verb moved to C in (76b), Agr in C *without* Neg won't be "strong" enough to properly govern the subject trace, but given that C is empty in (76b), antece-dent-government of the trace by the fronted subject *ar baotred* satisfies the ECP instead. As for why overt subjects and full agreement can't cooccur—(76) and (77a)—Stump stipulates that Agr requires a null governee, so that only *wh*-trace or *pro* can appear with synthetic verbs.

In Middle Welsh, fronted subjects are associated with two distinct patterns, one with no verb agreement, (78), and one with full agreement, (79) (examples from Willis 1998: 91):

(78) [Mi] ae   heirch. (Middle W)
      I   PRT:3SG   seek:PRES:3SG

      '(It is) I (who) seek him.'

(79) A['r   guyrda]   a   doethant   y gyt.... (Middle W)
      and-the   noblemen   PRT   come:PAST:3PL   together

      'And the noblemen came together ...'

Willis suggests that the constructions differ in terms of the status of Spec, CP. In (78), the fronted subject occupies an Ā-position, moving directly there from Spec, TP (where it is Case-licensed) without passing through the intervening Spec, AgrSP. This accounts for the lack of agreement. In (79), however, Spec, CP is an A-position, and in order not to violate relativized minimality, the subject must pass through the intervening Spec, AgrSP, thereby triggering agreement. The syn-tactic differences correlate with a pragmatic distinction: movement to an Ā-position results in contrastive stress on the subject (giving a topic/focus interpre-tation in (78)), while movement to an A-position does not.

One of the difficulties in analyzing fronting constructions, relative clauses, and *wh*-questions—constructions with very similar syntax—in the Brythonic lan-guages is that the exact status of the preverbal particles such as *a* and *ne* etc. is extremely hard to diagnose. However, in Irish it seems clear that the cognate items are indeed complementizers, as argued cogently by McCloskey (2001a). In Irish, two different types of Ā-dependencies occur, one in which the extraction site contains a gap (a *wh*-trace, (80)) and one in which it contains a resumptive pronoun, (81). Each strategy is associated with a distinct complementizer (examples from McCloskey 2001a: 67):[30]

(80) an   ghirseach   a   ghoid   na   síogaí _____. (I)
      the girl   aL   stole   the   fairies

'the girl that the fairies stole away'

(81) an   ghirseach   ar   ghoid   na   síogaí   í. (I)
      the girl   aN   stole   the   fairies her

'the girl that the fairies stole away'

Notably, the complementizer *aL* must introduce every finite clause that has an application of *wh*-movement and so provides direct evidence of the successive cyclic nature of that process (see Chomsky 1977):

(82) a. an   rud   a   shíl   mé   a   dúirt   tú   a   dhéanfá
         the thing   aL   thought   I   aL   said   you   aL   do:COND:2SG
         _____ (I)

      'the thing that I thought you said you would do' (McCloskey 1990: 207)

      b. [$_{DP}$ DP [$_{CP}$ aL . . . [$_{CP}$ aL . . . [$_{CP}$ aL . . . *t* . . .]]]]

As McCloskey (1979, 1990, 2001a) shows, *aL* appears in the full range of constructions classically involving *wh*-movement: relative clauses, *wh*-questions, comparative and equative clauses, clefts, and others. It seems clear, then, that the pattern in (82b) reflects the operation of *wh*-movement constrained by subjacency: "We interpret the appearance of *aL* as a morphological signal that the gap has a local binder available in [Spec, CP]" (Chung and McCloskey 1987: 223). The following grammaticality contrast provides good evidence for this claim:

(83) *fear   nach   bhfuil   fhios   agam   [cén   cineál   mná
       man   NEG:COMP   is   knowledge   at:1SG   what   sort   woman
       a   phósfadh   _____] (I)
       aL   marry:COND

'*a man who I don't know what woman would marry' (McCloskey 1979: 32)

(84) ne   dánta   sin   nach   bhfuil   fhios   againn   [cén
      the   poems   DEMON   NEG:COMP   is   knowledge   at:1PL   what
      áit   ar   cumadh   iad] (I)
      place aN   compose:PASSIVE   them

'those poems that we do not know where they were composed' (McCloskey 1990: 209)

In (83) we find the gap pattern and the associated complementizer *aL*: as an extraction from an embedded question, this constitutes a subjacency violation. But (84) does not violate subjacency: the appearance of the resumptive pronoun *iad* (and the associated complementizer *aN*) indicate that no *wh*-movement has occurred.

8 CONCLUSION

Many more issues of theoretical and typological interest occur in the Celtic literature over the past quarter century than can be fitted into a short summary. Consonantal mutation, the structure of nominal phrases, and the syntax of A-movement (passive, raising) come to mind among much else. One conclusion is clear: despite the close genetic relationship between the four surviving Celtic languages, their syntax differs in nontrivial ways. Some traits are shared with other VSO languages (for instance, the antiagreement effect appears in Arabic), yet there is no general "VSO" syntax; the same point emerges clearly from the collection of papers in Carnie and Guilfoyle (2000). Still, much of the work in generative grammar over this same period has integrated the analysis of Celtic languages with that of more familiar SVO languages: the general conclusion is that the Celtic languages are not syntactically "exotic" but, rather, can be analyzed with existing syntactic apparatus.

NOTES

I am extremely grateful to the following for reading an earlier version of this chapter and for providing a wealth of perceptive and helpful suggestions: Bob Borsley, Guglielmo Cinque, Cathal Doherty, S. J. Hannahs, Jim McCloskey, Gary Miller, and David Willis. Remaining problems are due to my stubbornness. Welsh examples not cited with a source are provided by me.

1. In Scottish Gaelic and generally in Irish, the word order of nonfinite clauses is actually SOV. However, this is usually assumed to be derived from SVO via object rais-

ing; see, for instance, Bobaljik and Carnie (1996). Additionally, Southern Irish dialects (Connacht and Munster) can have SVO in nonfinite clauses.

2. The VP in the Welsh example in (5) can also be fronted, although idiosyncratically the progressive aspect marker *yn* deletes in this case. Other aspect markers, such as the perfect marker *wedi*, would be overtly present.

3. McCloskey does consider an alternative analysis involving CP-recursion; compare Rouveret (1996) and Tallerman (1996) on Welsh, which exhibits data parallel to that in Irish. However, McCloskey concludes that there are both empirical and theoretical problems with such an account of the Irish data and consequently rejects it. Another possible solution might involve a "split CP" along the lines of Rizzi (1997); see, for instance, McCloskey (2001a).

4. Carnie, et al. (2000) argue that Old Irish had both V-to-I movement and V-to-C movement, the latter motivated by a "filled C" requirement and responsible for the VSO word order.

5. The initial element of negation behaves just as in Irish (see (13)) in that an adverbial modifying the embedded clause precedes rather than follows the complementizer. See Willis (1998: 68ff.) on Middle Welsh and Tallerman (1996) on Modern Welsh.

6. Bob Borsley points out to me that the auxiliary verb 'be' occurring in periphrastic sentences appears to originate within a VP, since like other verbs it has nonfinite forms and also takes nonverbal complements. It may well be the case, then, that periphrastic sentences contain two VPs.

7. Various proposals are made concerning the Case-licensing of the subjects of Celtic finite clauses. Earlier analyses typically propose government by I^0 (or one of the functional heads replacing I) down into the specifier position below, which contains the subject; see, for instance, Chung and McCloskey (1987: 217) and Rouveret (1991: 375). Later analyses tend to assume that the subject raises covertly to Spec, AgrS, where it is Case-licensed under the Spec/head relation; see, for instance, Tallerman (1998).

8. In very formal varieties, Welsh does have a nonfinite "absolute" construction with overt subjects:

(i) *A'r*   *dydd* yn   gwawrio,   deffrodd   y   teithiwr. (W)
     and-the   day   PROG   dawn:NONFIN   wake-PAST:3SG   the   traveler

'And with the day dawning, the traveler awoke.' (Williams 1980: 114)

It is not clear how the subject in these constructions is Case-licensed; some solutions are suggested by Rouveret (1994: 312) and Tallerman (1998: 114ff.).

9. *Do* is inflected in (38); like most Celtic prepositions *do* has an inflectional paradigm. The Welsh prepositional element *i* in (34) also inflects. Overt inflections only cooccur with (null) pronominal subjects; see section 6.

10. The analysis in Tallerman (1998) proposes that, in fact, there are two distinct *i* elements: one is a true complementizer, occuring in control and raising infinitivals; the other ("inflectional" *i*) is a functional head within the I system. Clearly, it would be more satisfying if there were only one *i*; nonetheless, there is quite a body of evidence that there are actually two distinct morphemes, and the fact that they don't cooccur is predictable in view of the different clause types each occurs in.

11. Some speakers allow a past tense finite verb in these complement clauses, as in (i):

(i)   Mae   hi'n   gwbod   [gwelodd   o'r   broblem]. (W)
      is   she-PROG know:NONFIN see:PAST:3SG he-the   problem

'She knows that he saw the problem.'

12. Example (46c) contains the subject of a lower-clause idiom that is raised to matrix subject position, a traditional way of testing for raising predicates; the idiom is underlined.

13. Irish has a different version of Borsley's Paradox, since PRO subjects and overt subjects with default accusative case both occur in what looks like the same position in infinitival clauses, as (i) and (ii) show:

(i)   Níor   mhaith   liom   [é   a theacht   abhaile].
      NEG   good   with:1SG   him:ACC   come:NONFIN   home

'I wouldn't like him to come home.'

(ii) Níor   mhaith   liom   [PRO   a theacht   abhaile].
      NEG   good   with:1SG   come:NONFIN   home

'I wouldn't like to come home.' (McCloskey and Sells 1988: 151)

However, it is possible that PRO does not raise or does not raise to the same position as an overt subject.

14. The proposal that nominative subjects occupy the same position as the accusative subjects of nonfinite clauses cannot be tested by looking at the position of nominative subjects in relation to *gan*, since this negation marker occurs only in nonfinite clauses (including small clauses), where nominative subjects are not found. Although *gan* is generally considered a complementizer (see, for instance, Chung and McCloskey 1987), Duffield (1995: 151ff.) casts doubt on this assumption—and on the proposals discussed in the text for a distinct positioning of *do*-subjects versus accusative subjects—by showing that the subjects of nonfinite clauses may in fact *precede gan*. Compare (i) with (49a):

(i)   a. Ba mhaith liom   [gan   Máire   an   fear   sin   a phósadh].
         I-would-like   NEG   M.   the   man   DEMON   marry:NONFIN

'I would like for Mary not to marry that man.'

      b. Ba mhaith liom   [Máire   gan   an   fear   sin   a phósadh].
         I-would-like   M.   NEG   the   man   DEMON   marry:NONFIN

'I would like for Mary not to marry that man.' (Duffield 1995: 154)

15. There's also some evidence that Old Irish was V2 at an archaic stage: see Doherty (2000).

16. The verb *kaoud* 'have' in Breton is morphologically different from other verbs in the language. The base (*deus* in (51)) is preceded by an element agreeing with the subject (here *o*). Elsewhere in the grammar of Breton, these items function as proclitics, but in the verb *kaoud* they are typically reduced or elided or amalgamated with the base: *o deus*, for example, is generally pronounced [døs]. Borsley and Stephens (1989: 416) conclude that "we are dealing not with a combination of clitic and verb but with a verb

that varies in its form." Thus, the examples in (51) are not considered to deviate from the generalization that the verb is in second position.

17. However, negative sentences can also have a fronted constituent, as in (77b), perhaps suggesting that *ne* does not itself satisfy V2 by occupying first position.

18. An alternative would be that the finite verb adjoined to the negative particle, or vice versa.

19. The problem of finite verbs occupying different positions in different clause types is obviated in Schafer (1997), an account that does not involve movement of the fronted head but, rather, a deletion operation at PF. See Borsley and Kathol (2000) for some criticism of this analysis.

20. The assumption here is that the affirmative preverbal particles (glossed PRT) in the Welsh and Breton examples are not complementizers, whereas the negative particle is. (See Stump 1989 for some justification of this position.) The particles are proclitic on the following verb and do not count separately in the calculation of verb-second placement.

21. The traditional distinction in the use of copula versus substantive 'be' is not strictly maintained in modern spoken Irish, according to Ó Dochartaigh (1992: 41); see also the comments surrounding the discussion of (68).

22. The fact that there are different forms of the copula in (62) and (63) is one of the intriguing puzzles of the construction; see Rouveret (1996), Hendrick (1996), and Zaring (1996) for proposals.

23. The correct construction requires another special form of the copula, *sy(dd)*, and the predicate marker *yn*:

(i)   Alys   sy'n   athrawes. (W)
      A.   COP-PRED   teacher

      'It's Alys who's a teacher.'

24. However, Doherty (1996: 37) points out that whereas nominal predicates, as in (68), are productive with the copula, adjectival predicates are not. This has the consequence that many adjectives expressing a permanent state must cooccur with the substantive verb *tá* instead.

25. None of the languages are *pro*-drop or null argument languages in the classical sense: in Irish, overt pronominals don't cooccur with a richly inflected verb, while in Colloquial Welsh, overt pronominals are normally present, since the verbal morphology is so degraded. A very minor pattern found in some dialects of both Breton and Irish allows overt agreement to cooccur with overt arguments, as is standard in Welsh; see Borsley and Stephens (1989) and McCloskey and Hale (1984). Breton formerly patterned more like Welsh.

26. Scottish Gaelic formerly patterned with Irish but has now lost the majority of synthetic verbal inflections, leaving just the analytic forms, which, of course, require a cooccurring pronoun—for example, *buailidh mi/tu/e/iad* 'I/you/he/they will strike' (Gillies 1993).

27. McCloskey and Hale (1984) report that occasional doublets are available in some dialects, but these represent the exception.

28. Rouveret suggests that analytic forms do display agreement, but this is agreement specified for person only and not number. An "overt" and "null" Agr contrast is

also proposed by Hendrick (1988) and criticized by Stump (1989); McCloskey (1986b) also suggests that analytic verbs have Agr but lack a value for it.

29. Modern Literary Welsh patterns like Breton in requiring full agreement with a preverbal subject in negative relative clauses and other "fronting" constructions. However, Colloquial Welsh requires no agreement.

30. The notation in the glosses *aL* and *aN* indicates the different mutation-triggering properties of the two complementizers (which are otherwise often homophonous): L = lenition; N = nasalization.

REFERENCES

Adger, David (1996) "Aspect, Agreement and Measure Phrases in Scottish Gaelic," in Robert D. Borsley and Ian Roberts (eds.) *The Syntax of the Celtic Languages: A Comparative Perspective*. Cambridge University Press, Cambridge, 200–222.

Adger, David, and Gillian Ramchand (2001) "Predication and Equation." Unpublished ms., University of York and University of Oxford.

Anderson, Stephen, and Sandra Chung (1977) "On Grammatical Relations and Clause Structure in Verb-Initial Languages," in Peter Cole and Jerry Sadock (eds.) *Grammatical Relations*. Syntax and Semantics 8. Academic Press, New York, 1–25.

Awbery, Gwenllian (1976) *The Syntax of Welsh*. Cambridge University Press, Cambridge.

Belletti, Adriana (1990) *Generalized Verb Movement: Aspects of Verb Syntax*. Rosenberg and Sellier, Turin.

Bobaljik, Jonathan, and Andrew Carnie (1996) "A Minimalist Approach to Some Problems of Irish Word Order," in Robert D. Borsley and Ian Roberts (eds.) *The Syntax of the Celtic Languages: A Comparative Perspective*. Cambridge University Press, Cambridge, 223–240.

Borsley, Robert D. (1986) "Prepositional Complementizers in Welsh." *Journal of Linguistics* 22: 67–84.

Borsley, Robert D., and Andreas Kathol (2000) "Breton as a V2 Language." *Linguistics* 38: 665–710.

Borsley, Robert D. and Janig Stephens (1989) "Agreement and the Position of Subjects in Breton." *Natural Language and Linguistic Theory* 7: 407–427.

Borsley, Robert D., Maria-Luisa Rivero, and Janig Stephens (1996) "Long Head Movement in Breton," in Robert D. Borsley and Ian Roberts (eds.) *The Syntax of the Celtic Languages: A Comparative Perspective*. Cambridge University Press, Cambridge, 53–74.

Carnie, Andrew (1997) "Two Types of Non-verbal Predication in Modern Irish." *Canadian Journal of Linguistics* 42(1–2): 57–73.

Carnie, Andrew, and Eithne Guilfoyle (eds.) (2000) *The Syntax of Verb Initial Languages*. Oxford University Press, New York.

Carnie, Andrew, and Heidi Harley (2000) "Clausal Architecture: The Licensing of Major Constituents in a Verb Initial Language." Unpublished ms., University of Arizona and University of Pennsylvania.

Carnie, Andrew, Heidi Harley, and Elizabeth Pyatt (2000) "VSO Order as Raising out of IP? Some Evidence from Old Irish," in Andrew Carnie and Eithne Guilfoyle (eds.) *The Syntax of Verb Initial Languages.* Oxford University Press, New York, 39–59.

Chomsky, Noam (1977) "On *wh*-Movement," in Adrian Akmajian, Peter Culicover, and Thomas Wasow (eds.) *Formal Syntax.* Academic Press, New York, 71–132.

Chomsky, Noam (1986) *Barriers.* Linguistic Inquiry Monograph 13. MIT Press, Cambridge, Mass.

Chomsky, Noam (1991) "Some Notes on Economy of Derivation and Representation," in Robert Freidin (ed.) *Principles and Parameters in Comparative Grammar.* MIT Press, Cambridge, Mass., 417–454.

Chomsky, Noam (1995) *The Minimalist Program.* MIT Press, Cambridge, Mass.

Chung, Sandra, and James McCloskey (1987) "Government, Barriers and Small Clauses in Modern Irish." *Linguistic Inquiry* 18: 173–237.

Cinque, Guglielmo (1999) *Adverbs and Functional Heads: A Cross-linguistic Perspective.* Oxford University Press, New York.

den Besten, Hans (1983) "On the Interaction of Root Transformations and Lexical Deletive Rules," in Werner Abraham (ed.) *On the Formal Syntax of the Westgermania.* John Benjamins, Amsterdam, 47–138.

Doherty, Cathal (1996) "Clausal Structure and the Modern Irish Copula." *Natural Language and Linguistic Theory* 14: 1–46.

Doherty, Cathal (1997) "Predicate Initial Constructions in Irish," in Brian Agbayani and Sze-Wing Tang (eds.) *WCCFL 15: The Proceedings of the Fifteenth West Coast Conference on Formal Linguistics.* Center for the Study of Language and Information, Stanford, Calif., 81–95.

Doherty, Cathal (2000) "Residual Verb Second in Early Irish: On the Nature of Bergin's Law." *Diachronica* 17: 5–38.

Duffield, Nigel (1995) *Particles and Projections in Irish Syntax.* Kluwer, Dordrecht.

Emonds, Joseph (1979) "Word Order in Generative Grammar," in G. Bedell, E. Kobayashi, and M. Muraki (eds.) *Explorations in Linguistics.* Kenkyusha Press, Tokyo, 58–88.

Evans, D. Simon (1989) *A Grammar of Middle Welsh.* Dublin Institute of Advanced Studies, Dublin.

Gillies, William (1993) "Scottish Gaelic," in Martin J. Ball (ed.) *The Celtic Languages.* Routledge, London, 145–227.

Guilfoyle, Eithne (1993) "Nonfinite Clauses in Modern Irish and Old English," in Katharine Beals, Gina Cooke, David Kathman, Sotaro Kita, Karl-Erik McCullough, and David Testen (eds.) *Proceedings of the Twenty-Ninth Regional Meeting of the Chicago Linguistic Society.* Chicago Linguistic Society, Chicago, vol. 1, 199–214.

Harlow, Stephen (1981) "Government and Relativization in Celtic," in Frank Heny (ed.) *Binding and Filtering.* Croom Helm, London, 213–254.

Harlow, Stephen (1992) "Finiteness and Welsh Sentence Structure, in Hans-Georg Obenauer and Anne Zribi-Hertz (eds.) *Structure de la phrase et théorie du liage.* Presses Universitaires de Vincennes, Paris, 93–119.

Hendrick, Randall (1988) *Anaphora in Celtic and Universal Grammar.* Kluwer, Dordrecht.

Hendrick, Randall (1990) "Breton Pronominals, Binding and Barriers," in Randall Hendrick (ed.) *The Syntax of the Modern Celtic Languages*. Syntax and Semantics 23. Academic Press, San Diego, 121–165.

Hendrick, Randall (1991) "The Morphosyntax of Aspect." *Lingua* 85: 171–210.

Hendrick, Randall (1996) "Some Syntactic Effects of Suppletion in the Celtic Copulas," in Robert D. Borsley and Ian Roberts (eds.) *The Syntax of the Celtic Languages: A Comparative Perspective*. Cambridge University Press, Cambridge, 75–96.

Huang, James C.-T. (1993) "Reconstruction and the Structure of VP: Some Theoretical Consequences." *Linguistic Inquiry* 24: 103–138.

Jones, Bob Morris, and Alan Thomas (1977) *The Welsh Language: Studies in Its Syntax and Semantics*. University of Wales Press, Cardiff.

Koopman, Hilda, and Dominique Sportiche (1991) "The Position of Subjects." *Lingua* 85: 211–258.

MacAulay, Donald (1992) "The Scottish Gaelic Language," in Donald MacAulay (ed.) *The Celtic Languages*. Cambridge University Press, Cambridge, 137–248.

McCloskey, James (1979) *Transformational Syntax and Model Theoretic Semantics: A Case Study in Modern Irish*. D. Reidel, Dordrecht.

McCloskey, James (1983) "A VP in a VSO language," in Gerald Gazdar, Ewan Klein, and Geoffrey K. Pullum (eds.) *Order, Concord and Constituency*. Foris, Dordrecht, 9–55.

McCloskey, James (1984) "Raising, Subcategorization and Selection in Modern Irish." *Natural Language and Linguistic Theory* 1: 441–485.

McCloskey, James (1986a) "Case, Movement and Raising in Modern Irish," in J. Goldberg, S. MacKaye, and M. Wescoat (eds.) *WCCFL 4: Proceedings of the Fourth West Coast Conference on Formal Linguistics*. Stanford Linguistics Association, Stanford, Calif., 190–205.

McCloskey, James (1986b) "Inflection and Conjunction in Modern Irish." *Natural Language and Linguistic Theory* 4: 245–281.

McCloskey, James (1990) "Resumptive Pronouns, Ā-binding and Levels of Representation in Irish," in Randall Hendrick (ed.) *The Syntax of the Modern Celtic Languages*. Academic Press, San Diego, 199–248.

McCloskey, James (1991) "Clause Structure, Ellipsis and Proper Government in Irish." *Lingua* 85: 259–302.

McCloskey, James (1996a) "Subjects and Subject Positions in Irish," in Robert D. Borsley and Ian Roberts (eds.) *The Syntax of the Celtic Language: A Comparative Perspective*. Cambridge University Press, Cambridge, 241–283.

McCloskey, James (1996b) "On the Scope of Verb Movement in Irish." *Natural Language and Linguistic Theory* 14: 46–104.

McCloskey, James (1997) "Subjecthood and Subject Positions, in Liliane Haegeman (ed.) *Elements of Grammar: Handbook of Generative Syntax*. Kluwer, Dordrecht, 197–235.

McCloskey, James (2001a) "The Morphosyntax of *wh*-Extraction in Irish." *Journal of Linguistics* 37: 67–100.

McCloskey, James (2001b) "The Distribution of Subject Properties in Irish," in William Davies and Stanley Dubinsky (eds.) *Objects and Other Subjects: Grammatical Functions, Functional Categories and Configurationality*. Studies in Natural Language and Linguistic Theory 52. Kluwer, Dordrecht, 157–192.

McCloskey, James, and Kenneth Hale (1984) "On the Syntax of Person-Number Inflection in Modern Irish." *Natural Language and Linguistic Theory* 1: 487–534.

McCloskey, James, and Peter Sells (1988) "Control and A-Chains in Modern Irish." *Natural Language and Linguistic Theory* 6: 143–189.

Noonan, Máire (1995) "VP Internal and VP External AgrOP: Evidence from Irish," in Raul Aranovich, William Byrne, Susanne Preuss, and Martha Senturia (eds.) *WCCFL 13: The Proceedings of the Thirteenth West Coast Conference on Formal Linguistics*. Center for the Study of Language and Information, Stanford, Calif., 318–333.

Ó Dochartaigh, Cathair (1992) "The Irish Language," in Donald MacAulay (ed.) *The Celtic Languages*. Cambridge University Press, Cambridge, 11–99.

Ó Siadhail, Mícháel (1989) *Modern Irish: Grammatical Structure and Dialectal Variation*. Cambridge University Press, Cambridge.

Pollock, Jean-Yves (1989) "Verb Movement, Universal Grammar and the Structure of IP." *Linguistic Inquiry* 20: 365–424.

Ramchand, Gillian (1996) "Two Types of Predication in Scottish Gaelic: The Syntax-Semantics Interface." *Natural Language Semantics* 4: 165–191.

Ramchand, Gillian (1997) *Aspect and Predication: The Semantics of Argument Structure*. Clarendon Press, Oxford.

Rizzi, Luigi (1997) The Fine Structure of the Left Periphery," in Liliane Haegeman (ed.) *Elements of Grammar: Handbook of Generative Syntax*. Kluwer, Dordrecht, 281–337.

Roberts, Ian (2004) *Principles and Parameters in a VSO Language: A Case Study in Welsh*. Oxford University Press, New York.

Rouveret, Alain (1991) "Functional Categories and Agreement." *Linguistic Review* 8: 353–387.

Rouveret, Alain (1994) *Syntaxe du gallois: principes généraux et typologie*. CNRS Éditions, Paris.

Rouveret, Alain (1996) "*Bod* in the Present Tense and in Other Tenses," in Robert D. Borsley and Ian Roberts (eds.) *The Syntax of the Celtic Language: A Comparative Perspective*. Cambridge University Press, Cambridge, 125–170.

Sadler, Louisa (1988) *Welsh Syntax: A Government-Binding Approach*. Croom Helm, London.

Schafer, Robin (1994) "Nonfinite Predicate Initial Constructions in Breton." Ph.D. diss., University of California, Santa Cruz.

Schafer, Robin (1995) "Negation and Verb-Second in Breton." *Natural Language and Linguistic Theory* 13: 135–172.

Schafer, Robin (1997) "Long Head Movement and Information Packaging in Breton." *Canadian Journal of Linguistics* 42(1–2): 169–203.

Sproat, Richard (1985) "Welsh Syntax and VSO Structure." *Natural Language and Linguistic Theory* 3: 173–216.

Stenson, Nancy (1981) *Studies in Irish Syntax*. Gunter Narr, Tübingen.

Stephens, Janig (1982) "Word Order in Breton." Ph.D. diss., School of Oriental and African Studies, University of London.

Stowell, Tim (1989) "Raising in Irish and the Projection Principle." *Natural Language and Linguistic Theory* 7: 317–359.

Stump, Gregory (1984) "Agreement vs. incorporation in Breton." *Natural Language and Linguistic Theory* 2: 289–348.

Stump, Gregory (1989) "Further Remarks on Breton Agreement." *Natural Language and Linguistic Theory* 7: 429–471.

Tallerman, Maggie (1996) "Fronting Constructions in Welsh," in Robert D. Borsley and

Ian Roberts (eds.) *The Syntax of the Celtic Language: A Comparative Perspective.* Cambridge University Press, Cambridge, 97–124.

Tallerman, Maggie (1997) "Infinitival Clauses in Breton." *Canadian Journal of Linguistics* 42(1–2): 205–233.

Tallerman, Maggie (1998) "The Uniform Case-Licensing of Subjects in Welsh." *Linguistic Review* 15: 69–133.

Timm, Leonora (1989) "Word order in 20th century Breton." *Natural Language and Linguistic Theory* 7: 361–378.

Watkins, T. Arwyn (1997) "The *sef*... Realization of the Welsh Identificatory Copula Sentence," in Anders Ahlqvist and Věra Čapková (eds.) *Dán do oide: Essays in Memory of Conn R. Ó Cléirigh.* Institiúid Teangeolaíochta Éireann, Dublin, 579–591.

Williams, Stephen J. (1980) *A Welsh Grammar.* University of Wales Press, Cardiff.

Willis, David W. E. (1998) *Syntactic Change in Welsh: A Study of the Loss of Verb-Second.* Clarendon Press, Oxford.

Willis, David W. E. (2000) "On the Distribution of Resumptive Pronouns and *wh*-Trace in Welsh." *Journal of Linguistics* 36: 531–573.

Zaring, Laurie (1996) " 'Two Be or Not Two Be': Identity, Predication and the Welsh Copula." *Linguistics and Philosophy* 19: 103–142.

CHAPTER 20

PREVERBAL ELEMENTS IN KOREAN AND JAPANESE

JOHN WHITMAN

1 PREVERBAL AND POSTVERBAL NEGATION IN OV LANGUAGES

Dahl (1979) (see also Dryer 1988, 1992) observes that SOV languages evince two typical negation patterns: one where the marker of negation immediately precedes the verb and one where it follows. Inflected negative markers appear in the latter pattern; preverbal negators are uninflected particles. These two patterns are shown in (1–2) with examples from Korean and Japanese:

(1) Preverbal negation

    a. Mica ka   hakkyo ey *an*   ka-ss-ta. (Korean)
       Mica NOM school to NEG go-PAST-INDIC

       'Mica didn't go to school.'

    b. Tuki   *na*   mi-tamaɸ-i   so!
       moon NEG see-HONORIFIC-CONTINUATIVE PRT
       (Japanese; *Taketori Monogatari* 859)

       'Please don't look at the moon!'

(2) Postverbal negation
    a. Mica ka   hakkyo ey   ka-ci   *anh*-ass-ta. (Korean)
       Mica NOM   school to   go-SUSP   NEG-PAST-INDIC

    'Mica didn't go to school.'

    b. Yooko ga   gakkoo ni   ik-*ana*-katta   koto (Japanese)
       Yôko   NOM   school to   go-NEG-PAST   that

    'that Yôko didn't go to school'

The preverbal negation pattern in (1b) is limited to negative imperatives in Old and Early Middle Japanese (eighth–twelfth centuries). Dryer (1988, 1992) shows that the SONegV pattern in (1) and the SOVNeg pattern in (2) are overwhelmingly the most common patterns in verb-final languages. Of the 117 verb-final languages in Dryer's (1988) sample, 39 (15 families) show SONegV, while 64 (19 families) show SOVNeg. In contrast, 8 languages (5 families) have NegSOV, while 6 (3 families) have SNegOV (1988: 96).

There is an obvious parallel between the uninflected negative particle in the SONegV pattern and nonhead negators such as French *pas*. At the same time, there is a parallel between the postverbal negators in the SOVNeg pattern, which may be inflected, and head-type negators such as French *ne*. For a concrete comparison, consider Pollock's (1989: 414) analysis of French negation. The nonhead negator *pas* occupies the specifier position of a projection above VP, while *ne* originates as the head of this projection. *Pas* has the properties of a maximal projection: it does not block movement of the verb. *Ne* is analyzed by Pollock as a clitic, which moves with the verb to Tense:

(3) $[_{TP}$ Paul $[_{T'}$ ne mange $[_{NegP}$ pas t_{ne} $[_{VP}$ $t_v]]]]$
     "Paul doesn't eat."

Like *ne*, the postverbal negators *anh-* (2a) and *-ana-* (2b) are heads. Korean *anh-* is inflected for tense and selects a verbal complement in suspective *-ci*. It may optionally assign overt case to this complement (Song 1971):

(4) Mica ka   hakkyo ey   ka-ci   lul   anh-ass-ta.
     Mica NOM   school to   go-SUSP   ACC   NEG-PAST-INDIC

    'Mica didn't go to school.'

Japanese *-ana-* also inflects for tense and shares the adjectival inflectional pattern of the independent negative adjective *na-(i)* 'not exist.'

In a standard left-branching analysis of Korean or Japanese clause structure, these parallels are difficult to capture. Postverbal negators in the SOVNeg pattern may be straightforwardly analyzed as heads (see Park 1990, Ahn 1991, and Choi 1991 for head analyses of postverbal negation in Korean). But preverbal negators in the SONegV pattern may not be analyzed as specifiers.[1] In a base-generated analysis of verb-final word order in an SONegV sentence like (1a), for example, the negative particle *an* must be analyzed as sister to the verb, in the position of a complement, not a head.[2]

(5)   (= 1a)

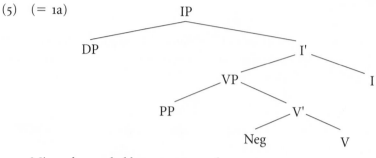

Mica	ka	hakkyo ey	*an*	ka-ss-ta.
Mica	NOM	school to	NEG	go-PAST-INDIC

'Mica didn't go to school.'

The analysis in (5) fails to explain how it is possible for the negative particle to be realized as a complement of V, a position normally reserved for arguments. But more directly to the current point, it fails to capture the parallelism between preverbal negators in the SONegV pattern and uninflected negative particles like *pas* in VO languages.

This parallelism can be captured under the account of Object–Verb–Infl order in Kayne (1994: sec. 5.5), according to which head final order is derived by movement of VP to the left.[3] Under this approach, uninflected negative particles in the SONegV pattern of (1a) are generated in the specifier of a projection which selects VP as its complement, parallel to *pas* in the specifier of NegP in (3):

(6)   (= 1a)

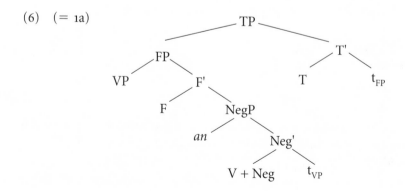

[Mica ka   hakkyo ey t$_v$]   ka-ss-ta.
Mica   NOM   school   to   NEG go-PAST-INDIC

The verb first raises to the head of NegP. The remnant VP then moves past the negative particle *an* into the specifier of a higher projection,[4] FP in (6); FP then moves to the specifier of TP.[5]

In the Korean SOVNeg pattern in (2a), the negative head *anh-* is generated in NegP; the complement of NegP, containing the lexical verb suffixed with *-ci*, moves beyond Neg.[6] Finally, the entire NegP moves to the specifier of TP:

(7) (= 2a)

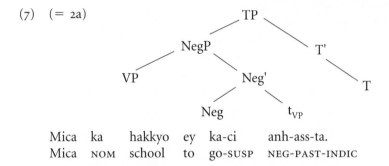

Mica ka   hakkyo ey ka-ci   anh-ass-ta.
Mica NOM   school to go-SUSP   NEG-PAST-INDIC

The Japanese SOVNeg pattern in (2b) represents a variation on this basic derivation, where the head of Neg is the bound suffix *-ana-*. In Japanese the lexical verb raises and adjoins to Neg; the rest of the derivation is as in (7):

(8) (= 2b) [$_{TP}$ [$_{VP}$ Yooko ga   gakkoo ni t$_v$] [$_{NegP}$ ik-ana-t$_{VP}$]-katta]
            Yôko   NOM   school   to   go-NEG-   -PAST

koto
that

'that Yôko didn't go to school'

A final pattern of variation is presented by the Korean negative potential particle *mos* 'cannot'. *Mos* appears in a preverbal pattern parallel to (6), as well as in a postverbal pattern:

(9) a. Mica ka   hakkyo ey *mos*   ka-ss-ta. (Korean)
        Mica NOM   school to cannot   go-PAST-INDIC
        'Mica couldn't go to school.'

     b. Mica ka   hakkyo ey ka-ci   *mos*   hay-ss-ta. (Korean)
        Mica NOM   school to go-SUSP   cannot   do-PAST-INDIC
        'Mica couldn't go to school.'

The preverbal pattern in (9a) can be derived in the same way as (6): the lexical verb raises to the head of the projection hosting *mos*, and the remainder of the VP moves over *mos* in Spec, NegP. Cinque (1999) suggests a derivation for the postverbal pattern in (9b) where *mos* occupies the head of a modal projection; *mos* blocks raising of the lexical verb to T, which must therefore be supported by insertion of dummy *ha-* 'do.'

The occurrence of *mos* in the preverbal pattern (9a) and the parallelism with negative *an* and *anh-* suggests a slightly different approach. Suppose that *mos*, like *an*, is uniformly a specifier.[7] The heads of the projections hosting *mos* and *an* optionally select a lexical verb suffixed with supective *-ci*. The form V-*ci* is ineligible for head raising, perhaps because of its nominal character (cf. Song 1971). Thus the only licit derivation when V-*ci* is selected is to move the entire projection containing V-*ci* to the left of *mos* or *an*. In the case of *anh-* (7) a lexical head of NegP is available to support Tense, but *mos* occurs with no lexical head of its projection; thus dummy *ha-* 'do' is inserted, as Cinque proposes.

The cooccurrence possibilities of *an* and *mos* confirm that these items occupy distinct projections and indicate that *an* is in a higher projection than *mos*.[8] Of the four combinations in (10), only the pattern in (d) is acceptable (albeit awkward) to most speakers:

(10) a. *Mica ka   hakkyo ey *mos an*   ka-ss-ta.
         Mica   NOM   school to   cannot NEG   go-PAST-INDIC

      b. *Mica ka   hakkyo ey *an mos*   ka-ss-ta.
         Mica   NOM   school to   NEG cannot   go-PAST-INDIC

      c. *Mica ka   hakkyo ey *an ka-ci*   *mos hay-ss-ta.*
         Mica   NOM   school to   NEG-go-SUSP   cannot do-PAST-INDIC

      d. ?Mica ka   hakkyo ey *mos ka-ci*   *anh-a-ss-ta.*
         Mica   NOM   school to   cannot go-SUSP NEG-PAST-INDIC

         'It is not the case that Mica couldn't go to school.'

Example (10d) is derivable on the assumption that the projection including *mos* is selected by negative *anh-*. Within that projection, preverbal *mos* is derived as in (9a); the projection containing *mos* is then fronted to the left of *anh-*, as in (7). Examples (10a) and (10c) can be ruled out on the assumption that the underlying order of *an* and *mos* is fixed: the projection containing *mos* does not select the NegP projection containing *an*.

Particularly interesting is the unacceptability of (10b). We might expect this pattern to be derivable from the same basic order of negative elements as (10d)— that is, *an* . . . *mos*, by successive cyclic verb raising to T, followed by fronting of the remnant projection of Spec, TP. This is shown in (11):

(11) (= 10b) *[$_{TP}$ [$_{FP}$ [$_{VP}$ Mica   ka   hakkyo   ey t$_V$] [$_{NegP}$ an t$_v$
                    Mica   NOM   school   to   NEG-
            [$_{ModP}$ mos t$_v$ t$_{VP}$]]]   ka-ss-ta]
             cannot   go-PAST-INDIC

In (11), the verb -ka- 'go' raises first to the head of ModP, then through the head of NegP to adjoin to T. Meanwhile, the remnant VP moves past *mos* and *an* to the specifier of FP, as in (6). Finally FP moves to Spec, TP. Such a derivation would depend crucially on the ability of the verb to move though NegP, ModP, and other intermediate projections to adjoin to T, a potential derivation for S-O-V-Tense order mentioned by Kayne (1994: sec. 5.5, note 14).

Evidence in this section shows that verb movement to the left does occur in Korean and Japanese, specifically in the derivation of the SONegV pattern. But the unacceptability of (10b) indicates that the verb and Tense suffixes are not composed by head movement and adjunction of the former to the latter. Instead, composition of the verb and Tense affixes is the result of what Kayne calls "pure agglutination": fronting of the projection containing the verb to the specifier of T, followed by a postsyntactic operation that converts the verb and tense suffixes into a single phonological word.[9] This conclusion, combined with the assumption that *an* occupies a position structurally higher than *mos*, accounts for the cooc-currence patterns of these two negators in (11).

Summing up the discussion so far: under the antisymmetric account, the SONegV pattern corresponds to the configuration with negator in Spec, like French *pas*. The SOVNeg pattern corresponds to the configuration with a negator in head position. This configuration may either block raising of the lexical verb if the negator is a free morpheme, as in the Korean pattern (7), or host the raised verb if the negator is a bound morpheme, as in the Japanese negation pattern (8).

The basic analysis of where negation may be realized either as a specifier or head predicts in principle that there may be two negative morphemes, one in each position. Although neither Japanese nor Korean evinces such a pattern, it occurs in Burmese, a Sino-Tibetan OV language. As predicted by the antisymmetric analysis, the preverbal negative particle in Burmese is in immediate preverbal position. The postverbal negative suffix immediately follows the verb and precedes discourse modal suffixes:

(12) a. K'inbya   ma   thwà   bù   là?   (Burmese)
          you   NEG   go   NEG   Q
          'Are you not going?'

    b. Diné   ma   thwà   néh.
        today   NEG   go   NEG.IMPERATIVE
        'Don't go today.'

The Burmese pattern is naturally analyzed with the negative particle *ma* in the specifier of NegP and the negative suffix (matrix nonimperative *bu*, negative imperative *néh*) in the head of NegP. Derivation of (12a–b) proceeds as in (8): the verb raises and adjoins to the negative heads *bù* or *néh*.

Thus far, I have shown that an antisymmetric analysis of SOV negation can account for the following facts:

- OV languages attest both preverbal and postverbal negation.
- Preverbal negators are typically immediately preverbal.
- Preverbal negators are always uninflected.
- Postverbal negators may be inflected.
- OV languages may have "bipartite" negation; when they do, the preverbal negator is immediately preverbal and uninflected.

I have also shown that the preverbal SONegV pattern is not straightforwardly accounted for under base-generated left-branching (symmetric) analysis. Next, I adduce further evidence from Korean and Japanese for the antisymmetric analysis of OV negation.

2 Preverbal Negation in Korean Periphrastic Causatives

Bratt (1993), citing Lee (1988) and Sells and Cho (2000), observes that Korean periphrastic causatives are ambiguous when the preverbal negative particle *an* precedes the embedded verb and the causee argument is marked with accusative case:[10]

(13) Emeni   kkeyse ttal   ul   an   mek-key   ha-si-ess-ta.
     mother   NOM   daughter ACC   NEG   eat-COMP do-HON-PAST-INDIC
     (Bratt 1993: 245)

     'The mother made the daughter not eat.' / 'The mother didn't make the daughter eat.'

This ambiguity disappears when the causee is marked nominative:

(14) Emeni   kkeyse ttal   i   an   mek-key   ha-si-ess-ta.
     mother   NOM   daughter NOM   NEG   eat-COMP do-HON-PAST-INDIC
     (Bratt 1993: 245)

     'The mother made the daughter not eat.'

The ambiguity in (13) can be explained by two distinct derivations. In the derivation in (15), the complement of the matrix causative verb *ha-* (labeled CP in (15)) contains the negative specifier *an*, which therefore takes embedded scope. Word order internal to the complement is derived as in (6), by raising the embedded verb to Neg and raising the remnant VP past *an*. The entire complement clause then raises past the matrix causative verb *ha-*:

(15)   Emeni   kkeyse [_{CP} [_{VP} ttal   ul t_v] an   mek-key t_{VP} t_{CP}] ha-t_{CP}.

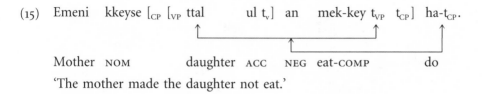

Mother NOM   daughter ACC   NEG eat-COMP   do
'The mother made the daughter not eat.'

In the derivation in (16), the negative specifier *an* is in the matrix clause and therefore takes scope over the matrix causative verb. This derivation proceeds as in (15), except that preceding raising of the complement CP, the embedded verb (suffixed with *-key*) raises and adjoins to causative *ha-*:

(16)   Emeni   kkeyse [_{CP} [_{VP} ttal   ul t_v] t_v t_{VP}] an   mek-key + ha-t_{CP}.

Mother NOM   daughter ACC   NEG eat-COMP + do
'The mother didn't make the daughter eat.'

The analysis in (15–16) is based on the assumption that head raising and adjunction of the embedded verb to matrix causative *ha-* is optional, thus predicting that the derivation in (16) could proceed without raising of embedded 'eat' and producing the reverse order of the embedded verb and negative *an*. This is indeed the case *in* (17); as predicted, (17) is unambiguously interpreted with matrix scope for negation:

(17)   Emeni   kkeyse   ttal   ul   mek-key   an   ha-si-ess-ta.
       mother NOM   daughter ACC   eat-COMP NEG   do-HON-PAST-INDIC
'The mother didn't make the daughter eat.'

The unavailability of matrix scope for negation in (14), where the embedded subject (causee) is marked with nominative case, can be accounted for by applying the generalization expressed by Baker's (1988) Government Transparency Corollary (GTC). The GTC permits a raised head to inherit the case assigning properties of the X⁰ category it raises and adjoins to. In (16), the embedded verb raises through Infl in the embedded clause to adjoin to matrix *ha-* 'do'. Under the GTC, embedded Infl (more precisely, the trace t_{v+Infl}) thus inherits the ability to assign accusative case. However, when embedded Infl assigns nominative case, as in (14), the embedded verb has not raised. In such cases the only available derivation is the non-head-raising one in (15), associated with embedded scope of negation.[11]

More generally, the analysis in (15–16) predicts that if verb raising is blocked, embedded scope of negation must result. Verb raising in the periphrastic causative construction is blocked by insertion of an association with focus particle between *ha-* and its complement, as noted by J.-S. Lee (1992):

(18) Emeni   kkeyse   ttal   ul   an   mek-key   to
      mother   NOM   daughter   ACC   NEG   eat-COMP   also
      ha-si-ess-ta.
      do-HON-PAST-INDIC

      'The mother also made the daughter not eat.'

(19) Emeni   kkeyse   ttal   ul   an   mek-key   kkaci
      mother   NOM   daughter   ACC   NEG   eat-COMP   even
      ha-si-ess-ta.
      do-HON-PAST-INDIC

      'The mother even made the daughter not eat.'

As predicted, (18) and (19) have unambiguous embedded scope for negation.

Bratt (1993), working with a Head-driven Phase Structure Grammar framework, accounts for the contrast in (13–14) by claiming that the periphrastic causatives with an accusative-marked causee are monoclausal, while the same causatives with a nominative-marked causee are biclausal. In the monoclausal case (13), the embedded verb and causative *ha-* form a compound verb; negative *an* may attach either to the entire compound, resulting in matrix scope, or to the first verb in the compound, resulting in embedded scope. In the biclausal case (14), negative *an* preceding the embedded verb must be in the embedded clause.

Examples like (18) and (19) show that even with an accusative-marked causee, the embedded verb and the matrix causative verb cannot always be analyzed as a compound verb. However, the problem posed by the periphrastic causative facts for a movement-based analysis based on a left-branching tree such as (5) is even more severe:

(20) (= 17)

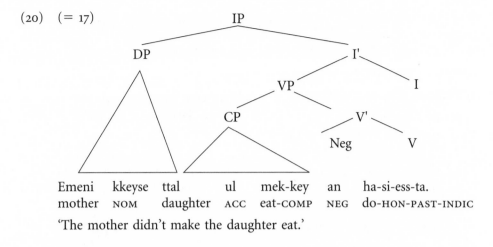

Emeni	kkeyse	ttal	ul	mek-key	an	ha-si-ess-ta.
mother	NOM	daughter	ACC	eat-COMP	NEG	do-HON-PAST-INDIC

'The mother didn't make the daughter eat.'

Example (20) shows negative *an* in the sister-of-V position of (5). This representation accounts for the matrix interpretation of *an* in (17). But it is unclear how
to derive (13), where *an* precedes the embedded verb, on the matrix interpretation
of *an*. A derivation where the embedded verb *mek-* 'eat' in (20) incorporates into
causative *ha-* would run counter to the generalization that incorporation occurs
from complement, not from specifier position. Alternatively, *an* might be analyzed
as a (V^0) internal prefix rather than a complement of V. Incorporation of the
embedded verb would then take the form of infixation from complement position,
as in (21):

(21)

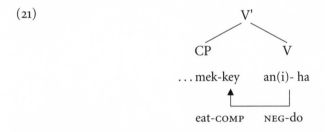

However, such an account would have to explain why the raised verb is infixed
after *an*, in a language that otherwise lacks infixation.

In general, the ability of negative *an* to take matrix scope in a context like
(13), where it is preceded by the entire complement clause except for the complement verb, strongly suggests that Korean has both a mechanism of complement
raising past a negative specifier and a mechanism of verb-to-verb raising.

3 NEGATIVE IMPERATIVES IN EARLIER JAPANESE

In Old and Early Middle Japanese, the uninflected negative imperative particle *na* appears in two positions: the immediate preverbal position in (1b) and the clause-final position as in the second line of (22):

(22) Me₂gusi mo na   mi₁ so₂ / ko₂to₂ mo to₂gam-u   na.
      worry   too NEG see PRT   deed   too blame-CONCLUSIVE   NEG
      (*Man'yôshû* 1759)

'Don't pity me. / Don't blame me.'

Only the latter, clause-final pattern survives in modern Tokyo Japanese.[12] Clearly, it is desirable to relate these two occurrences of the uninflected particle *na*, both of which have the same negative imperative function. The key to relating them has to do with the shape of the lexical verb. In the preverbal pattern of (1b), the verb appears in a compound form, either the continuative stem pattern in (1b) or, for the two irregular verbs *ku* 'come' and *su* 'do' (23), the irrealis stem. The irrealis stem is normally a bound form, while the continuative is the normal stem for forming verb–verb compounds. A further characteristic of the preverbal pattern is that the lexical verb typically (although not always: see (24)) appears immediately before the etymologically obscure clause-final particle *so₂* or *so₂ne*:

(23) Iza   ko₁domo tapa   waza   na   se   so₂.
      hey   children foolish trick NEG   do.IRREALIS   PRT
      (*Man'yôshû* 4487, 8th century)

'Hey kids, don't try any foolish tricks.'

(24) Titi   papa   mo   upe pa   na   sakar-i.
      father mother   too me   TOPIC NEG   depart-CONTINUATIVE
      (*Man'yôshû* 904, 8th century)

'Father, mother, don't leave me.'

In contrast, in the postverbal pattern, the lexical verb always occurs in a finite (nonpast) form—either the conclusive form, as in (22), or the adnominal (subordinate) form in the case of the verb 'be' and its derivatives. These two are the normal forms for clausal subordination: the conclusive for subordination under the complementizer *to₂* 'that' and certain modals and the adnominal for participial subordinate forms.

The appearance of compound forms in the preverbal negative imperative pattern and subordinate forms in the postverbal pattern suggests that both verb raising and adjunction take place in the former pattern and that clausal complementation without verb raising takes place in the latter. This is exactly the difference proposed for preverbal and postverbal negation in Korean in section 1. The occurrence of the particle so_2 immediately after the verb in the preverbal pattern further supports the hypothesis that uninflected *na* occupies a specifier position in this pattern. The derivation of (1b) thus proceeds as in (25), parallel to (6):

(25) (= 1b)   [[$_{VP}$ Tuki t$_V$] [$_{NegP}$ *na*   mi-tamaɸ-i + so   t$_{VP}$]

           moon   NEG   see-HON-CONT   PRT
        'Please don't look at the moon!'

In the preverbal pattern, in contrast, the lexical verb remains in its expected shape inside a complement clause. It is difficult to determine in this pattern whether *na* occupies a head or specifier position, but, in either case, the surface word order and the inflectional form of the verb are accounted for by raising the projection containing the verb past *na*, parallel to (7):

(26) (= 22)   [[$_{VP}$ ko$_2$to$_2$ mo   to$_2$gam-u] [$_{NegP}$ *na* t$_{VP}$]

           deed   too   blame   NEG
        'Don't blame me.'

This section has shown that the inflectional forms of the verbs in the two negative imperative patterns of earlier Japanese support the two derivations for preverbal and postverbal negation proposed in section 1.

4 LANGUAGES WITH SNEGOV

As noted in section 1, Dryer lists six languages with SNegOV order: Yaqui (Aztec-Tanoan), Bambara, Mandinka, Vai (Mande, Niger-Kordofanian), Berta, and Songhai (Nilo-Saharan) (1988: 123). Of these six, the two Nilo-Saharan languages are actually SVO (Triulzi et al. 1976, Prost 1956).

However, the three Mande languages listed by Dryer do indeed attest the order SNegOV, as shown in the Bambara example in (27):

(27)   À   té   jége sàn. (Bambara; Anschütz 1989: 48)
       3S   NEG.IMPERF fish buy

       'She/He isn't buying fish.'

Thus in these languages, negation might superficially appear to occupy the predicted position for a specifier (or adjunct) negator on a symmetric left-branching
picture of verb-final syntax, as in (28):

(28) (= 27)

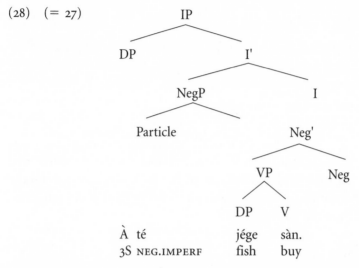

À té   jége sàn.
3S NEG.IMPERF   fish buy

In section 1. I argued that the SONegV pattern was the counterpart in VO languages to patterns involving a specifier or adjunct negator, such as French *pas*, in
VO languages. But the preponderance of SONegV languages over SNegOV is,
after all, only statistical. If it could be shown that (28) is the correct representation
for the SNegOV pattern, we would be forced to recognize it as the true counterpart of *pas*-type negation in OV languages.

    In fact, (28) is not an adequate representation for the Mande SNegOV lan-
guages listed by Dryer. As Koopman (1992) shows in her study of Bambara, the
basic word order is Subject–Infl–Object–Verb–noncasemarked Complement.
Koopman shows that OV (and NP-P, NP-N, NP-Infl) order in Bambara is derived
by movement of an NP complement to the left of its governing head for case
purposes. Thus the surface order in (27) is derived by movement of the subject
and object NPs, as shown in (29):

(29) [$_{IP}$ À [$_{I'}$ bé [$_{VP}$ t$_A$ jége sàn t$_{jege}$]]]]
          3S   IMPERF fish buy

      (Anschütz 1989: 48; structure from Koopman 1992: 558)

      'She/He is buying a fish."

Most crucially for our purposes, Koopman analyzes negators as Infl elements.
Each of the tense, aspect, and mood indicators that appears in the position of Infl

in (29) has a negative counterpart that appears in exactly the same position (and with which it is therefore in complementary distribution). Thus the negative counterpart of (29) is (30), with negative imperfective *té* in Infl:

(30) (= 27) $[_{IP}$ À $[_{I'}$ té $[_{VP}$ t$_A$ jége   sàn t$_{jege}$]]]]
                        3S   NEG.IMPERF   fish   buy

'She/He is buying a fish.'

The clause structure in (29–30) provides an immediate explanation for why the surface order of negation in Bambara is SNegOV rather than SONegV. We derived SONegV order by raising the verb to the head of the projection containing negation and moving the remnant VP to the left past negation. But in Bambara, neither the verb nor the verb phrase moves to the left of negation. More generally, we associated SONegV order with movement of VP to the left of Infl; clearly, Bambara does not move VP to the left of Infl. This contrast suggests the following typological generalizations:

(31)   SONegV is restricted to OV–Infl languages.

(32)   SONegOV is restricted to Infl–OV languages.

Note that (32) is not predicted by the nonderived left-branching structure in (28) at all. This structure predicts that a specifier or adjunct negator should be able to appear to the left of the object in an OV language with clause-final Infl.

Mandinka and Vai show the same complementarity between affirmative and negative tense, aspect, and mood markers as Bambara. All occur before the VP, as in Bambara. The Mandinka examples here are from Wilson (2000/2001):

(33)   a. Siisewo   ye   kiloo   laa.
           chicken   INFL   egg   lay

       'The chicken laid an egg.'

       b. Siisewo   man   kiloo   laa.
           chicken   INFL.NEG   egg   lay

       'The chicken didn't lay an egg.'

(34)   a. Asi   taa   suu.
           he INFL   go   home

       'He is to go home.'

b. Akana   taa   suu.
   he INFL.NEG   go   home

'He isn't to go home.'

Dryer's remaining example of an SNegOV language is the Uto-Tanoan (Tara-Cáhitic) language Yaqui. Yaqui also attests surface SNegOV order:

(35)   'Emé'e   káa   hunúen   'án-nee. (Dedrick and Casad 1999: 56)
       you-PL   NEG   thus   do-fut

'You must not do *that*.' (Do it rather in some other way.)

On the basis of data like (35), Lindenfeld (1973) posits a rule that inserts the negator *kaa* directly after the subject. Once again, Yaqui might appear to attest the left-branching symmetric structure in (28) that was ultimately rejected for Mande; in the Yaqui case, *kaa* would occupy the specifier of a left-branching Neg P.

However, Dedrick and Casad (1999) show that *káa* and its imperative counterpart *kát* do not occupy a position directly to the right of the subject. They show that Yaqui is a language with second-position clitics. Clitics include subject pronouns, emphatic and dubitative particles, and negative *kaa*. Clitics are preceded by a topicalized phrase, although as in other clitic-second languages, there is some leakage to this phenomenon: in certain sentence patterns, clitics may appear in initial position; in others, some other item (such as certain adverbs) may precede the clitic string in addition to the topic. Thus in contrast to (35), which topicalizes 'you' and focuses 'thus', (36) focuses 'you':

(36)   Káa   'emé'e   hunúen'   án-nee. (Dedrick and Casad 1999: 56)
       NEG   you-PL   thus   do-FUT

'*You* must not do that.' (Others may.)

Example (37) shows negative imperative *kát* preceded by an adjunct clause and followed by the clitic form of the second-person pronoun. Note that negation precedes pronominal clitics:

(37)   Née   muku-k-o   kát=e'em   hi'osia-ta   née   sewá-tua.
       I   die-PERF-when   NEG=you:PL   paper-ACC   me   flower-cause
       (Dedrick and Casad 1999: 59)

'When I die, don't put paper flowers on me.'

These facts show that negation in Yaqui is not the specifier of a left-branching projection between the subject and the VP but, rather, a second-position clitic. Its surface position appears to be the head of the projection that hosts topics.

Summarizing the results of this section: even among the small number of languages in Dryer's sample that superficially attest the order Subject–Negation–Object–Verb, none appears actually to attest a structure corresponding to (28), where the preverbal negative particle occupies the a specifier (or adjunct) position above VP. This result is totally unexpected on a conventional, left-branching picture of the syntax of head-final languages. As we have seen, however, it is readily explained by an account that derives head final order by raising the verb to the left and moving the remnant VP past it.

5 Preverbal Auxiliaries in OV Languages

Dryer (1992) observes that tense and aspect markers display the same dual positioning as negative markers in OV languages. When the tense or aspect marker is a particle (specifically, when it lacks inflection), the marker tends to precede the verb, although some cases of SOVTense/Aspect also occur. Dryer shows 18 instances of SOTense/AspectVerb and 6 instances of SOVTense/Aspect in his genetically and areally balanced sample (1991: 99). More important, the generalization is almost categorical in the case of inflected Tense or Aspect Dryer auxiliaries; these tend overwhelmingly to follow the verb in OV languages. Dryer lists 36 examples of SOVAux and 3 examples of SOAuxV (1992: 100). Although Dryer does not specify which languages in his sample are SOAuxV, all three are in Africa. As six Mande languages (Susu, Vai, Mandinka, Gambian Mandinka, Bambara, Mende) are in Dryer's sample, it seems likely that these are the source of the SOAuxV pattern. Although the pattern in question in Mande languages is in fact SAuxOV, Dryer does not distinguish preverbal and immediate preverbal position in his discussion. Needless to say, Koopman's (1992) analysis of Bambara accounts for SAuxOV order in these cases.

Further research is required to fully explore the range of tense, aspect, and mood markers that occur as preverbal particles in OV languages. In the remainder of this chapter, I explore three such particles in Japanesese and Korean.

5.1 Preverbal *e* 'can' and *ari* 'be . . . ing' in Earlier Japanese

Premodern Japanese had two preverbal modal/aspectual markers, *e* 'can', expressing (nondeontic, nonepistemic) possibility (i.e. ability), and *ari*, expressing ongoing action. I label the former "potential" and the latter "progressive" here. Both *e* and *ari* are identical to the continuative forms of the corresponding verbs, *u* 'be able to' and *ari* 'exist', respectively.

(38) Sa-wo-pune   no₂ *e*   yuk-i₁te pat-e-mu.
      PREF-small-boat GEN POT go-ing   stop-IRR-CONJECTURE
      (*Man'yôshû* 2091, 8th century)

      'The small boat will likely be able to go and dock.'

(39) Sima no₂ sakizaki *ari*   tat-er-u   panatatibana
      island GEN capes   PROG stand-IMPERF-ADNOM flower
      (*Man'yôshû* 3239, 8th century)

      'the flowers that are standing on the capes of the islands'

Already predominantly in Old Japanese and exclusively in later stages of the language, *e* occurs in negative potential sentences:

(40) Sato toɸo-ki   ɸa e   tugeyar-a-z-u. (*Makura no sôshi*, 995)
      home far-ADNOM TOP POT word-send-IRR-NEG-CONCLUSIVE

      'We were unable to send word to those whose homes were far off.'

Two properties of preverbal *e* and *ari* are relevant to our concerns. First, both of these items correspond to "low" mood and aspect markers, $Mod_{possibility}$ and $Asp_{generic/progressive}$ in the scheme of Cinque (1999); that is, they are positioned under Tense. Second, the interpretation of examples like (40) shows that preverbal *e* always takes scope under negation.

Both of these properties are accounted for if it is assumed that *e* and *ari* are specifiers. The verb moves to the head of the projections containing *e* and *ari*; the remnant VP then moves to the left of these specifiers. In a negative sentence such as (40), the verb moves past the modal projection containing *e* to adjoin to the head of NegP, *z-*. The complement of NegP then moves past V+Neg, parallel to (8). This is shown in (41), omitting material in the remnant VP complement of Mod:

(41) (= 40) [$_{TP}$ [$_{ModP}$ [$_{VP}$ e t$_V$ t$_{VP}$] [$_{NegP}$ tugeyar-a-z t$_{MODP}$]   -u]
                       POT   word-send-IRR-NEG   -CONCLUSIVE

The low scope of *e* is consistent with this derivation, where it originates in a projection c-commanded by negation.

5.2 Preverbal *cal* 'well' in Korean

Earlier, I sketched a derivation of preverbal modal/aspect markers in premodern Japanese, accounting for their type ("low") and scope (lower than negation). Korean lacks preverbal aspect or modal markers, but it has a preverbal adverb corresponding to another "low" functional head in Cinque's (1999) system: *cal* 'well'.[13]

As observed by many authors, *cal* is restricted to the immediate preverbal position. The following examples are from J.-H. Lee (1993: 434):

(42) a. Chelswu nun sayngsenhoy lul   *cal* mek-nun-ta.
        Chelswu TOP raw fish   ACC   well   eat-PRES-INDIC

      'Chelswu often eats raw fish.'

     b. *Chelswu nun *cal*   sayngsenhoy lul   mek-nun-ta.
        Chelswu   TOP well   raw fish   ACC   eat-PRES-INDIC

      'Chelswu often eats raw fish.'

The distribution of *cal* can be accounted for in the same fashion as the premodern Japanese mood and aspect markers discussed in the previous section. The verb moves to the head of the projection hosting *cal* in its specifier; the remnant then moves to the left of *cal*.

Korean, however, contains another possibility not present in modern Japanese: the preverbal negation pattern of (6). We see in (43) that *cal* must precede preverbal *an* or *mos*:

(43) a. Mica ka   hakkyo ey   *cal* *mos/an*   ka-ss-ta.
        Mica NOM   school to   well   cannot/NEG   go-PAST-INDIC

      'Mica didn't/couldn't often go to school.'

     b. *Mica ka   hakkyo ey   *mos/an*   *cal*   ka-ss-ta.
        Mica   NOM   school to   cannot/NEG   well   go-PAST-INDIC

The ordering in (43) is predicted by the derivation of preverbal negation in (6) and the account of potential *e* and negation in premodern Japanese sketched in the previous section. The projection containing *cal* is generated as a complement of Neg. The verb moves through the head of the projection containing *cal* to the head of NegP. The remnant VP moves to the left of *cal*; finally, the larger remnant containing VP and *cal* moves to the left of negation.

While the facts concerning preverbal mood and aspect markers discussed in the previous section are mildly problematic for a base-generated left-branching representation of Japanese phrase structure (as with preverbal negation; they require generating the mood or aspect marker in the VP complement position), the relative positioning of *cal* and *mos/an* is more problematic. Consider an analysis where *cal* and *an/mos* are generated as iterated sisters of the verbal projection:

(44)

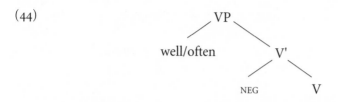

The structure in (44), if it makes any prediction about the relative scope of 'well/often' and negation, predicts that the former should take scope over the latter. As we have seen, this is exactly the wrong prediction. The appropriate descriptive generalization would appear to be (45):

(45)   Functional items immediately preceding or following the verb in Verb–Infl languages take scope from right (higher) to left (lower).

While a base-generated left-branching analysis of Verb-Infl languages can handle the generalization in (45) for items that follow the verb, it appears to be unable to handle the generalization for items that precede the verb.

6 CONCLUSION

One of the major accomplishments of Dryer (1992) is to show that noninflected negative and tense/aspect/modal particles are as likely—in fact, more likely—to precede the verb as follow it in V-final languages. As Dryer argues, these facts militate against a uniform treatment of these items as "verb-patterners," that is, as heads. The alternative is to treat such preverbal functional elements as specifiers. As we have seen, however, this move alone is insufficient: on a base-generated left-branching analysis of verb-final syntax, both their position (immediately before the verb) and their scope (always low) are unexpected. I have argued that these typological generalizations support a view where V–Infl order is derived and that the relevant derivations involve both verb and remnant movement.

NOTES

1. In an ingenious analysis, Lee (1992) analyzes preverbal *an* in Korean as a right-branching specifier. The surface order in (1a) is then derived by movement of the lexical verb rightward over *an*. The chief difficulty with Lee's analysis is the lack of independent evidence for specifiers on the right, in Korean or other languages. But in important ways his analysis anticipates the antisymmetric analysis of Korean negation.

2. Sells (1998) explicitly analyzes preverbal *an* as a complement.

3. The implications of Kayne's proposal for Dahl and Dryer's typological generalizations are pointed out by Whitman (1995, 2001), who implements an analysis of Korean negation based on the specific proposal in Kayne (1994: sec. 5.5, note 14. See Hagstrom (2000) as well for a different leftward phrasal movement analysis of Korean negation and Cinque (1999) for a leftward VP movement analysis of the postverbal negative modal *mos*. A modification of Cinque's analysis of *mos* is presented later.

4. I assume that movement past *an* in the specifier of NegP is possible for the same reason that phrasal movement past "adverbial" specifiers is generally possible: the fronted VP and the negative element differ with respect to some crucial feature, thus avoiding a Relativized Minimality violation. See Cinque (1999) for relevant discussion.

5. As Kayne (1994: 141, note 14) notes, head-final languages such as Korean and Japanese must contain some projection with a nonfinal head to host, elements such as subjects and topics, if these are to c-command the rest of the clause. Whitman (1998, 2001), adopting a suggestion of Kayne's, argues that the nominative markers *i/ka* (Korean) and *ga* (Japanese) head the projections hosting subjects in their surface position. On this view the surface representation of (6) is as follows:

(i) (= 6) $[_{kaP}$ Mica   *ka* $[_{TP}$ $[_{FP}$ $[_{VP}$ t_{Mica} hakkyo   ey $t_v]$ $[_{NegP}$ an
Mica   NOM   school   to   NEG
$[_{Neg'}$ ka-$t_{VP}]]]$-ss-ta]]
go-   -PAST-INDIC
'Mica didn't go to school.'

The phrasal projection kaP in (i) may be identified as an Agreement projection, or perhaps the Finiteness Phrase of Rizzi (1997).

6. In (7) I have shown Spec, Neg as the landing site of the complement of Neg^0 and labeled this projection VP for simplicity. But the fact that the complement of Neg^0 takes the supective suffix -*ci* and may be case marked, as we saw in (4), suggest that VP-*ci* has nominal properties, as first pointed out by Song (1971). One possibility is that VP-*ci* moves on to the specifier of projection where accusative (and in certain instances, nominative) case is assigned.

7. J.-H. Lee (1992) also analyzes *mos*, together with preverbal *an*, as specifiers.

8. This indicates that *mos* is located in a projection corresponding to Cinque's Mod$_{possibility}$, under Tense and negation, rather than a higher modal projection.

9. Sakai (1998) argues that verbal affixes in Japanese are composed postsyntactically

with the verb by the operation of Morphological Merger (Halle and Marantz 1993). While Sakai's conclusion seems correct for the particular case of tense suffixes discussed in this section, we have seen that a stronger conclusion—that Korean and Japanese lack verb movement altogether—is not supported.

10. Not all speakers accept this ambiguity. Some speakers report only an embedded scope interpretation for (13). Such speakers presumably disallow raising of the embedded verb suffixed with -*key*.

11. The Government Transparency Corollary (or its successor) cannot account for all instances of accusative case assignment to the embedded causee in periphrastic causatives. As we see in (18–19), accusative case may be assigned to the causee even when raising of the embedded verb is blocked. Lee (1992) argues that accusative case can be assigned to the causee under a mechanism of Exceptional Case Marking (ECM). Lee's mechanism cannot explain the matrix scope interpretation of negation in (10), but it is possible that ECM is responsible for accusative case assignment to the causee in other contexts, when verb raising does not occur and only an embedded interpretation is available for negation.

12. Maeda's (1977: 39–40) description of the Osaka negative imperative V-CONTINUATIVE *na* (e.g., *iki na* 'Don't go') suggests that it is the successor to the earlier preverbal negative imperative pattern.

13. *Cal* corresponds to 'well' with statives, accomplishment, and achievement verbs and 'often' with activity verbs. Both correspond to relatively low functional heads in Cinque's (1999) system: voice in the case of 'well', frequentative in the case of 'often'. As my examples in this section involve an activity interpretation, I label the projection hosting *cal* FreqP.

REFERENCES

Ahn, Hee-Don (1991) "Light Verbs, VP-Movement, Negation, and Clausal Architecture in Korean and English." Ph.D. diss., University of Wisconsin, Madison.

Anschütz, Susanne (1989) *Aktantenfunktionen und Thema-Rhema im Bambara*. Julius Groos, Heidelberg.

Baker, Mark (1988) *Incorporation: A Theory of Grammatical Function Changing*. University of Chicago Press, Chicago.

Bratt, Elizabeth Owen (1993) "Clause Structure and Case Marking in Korean Causatives," in S. Kuno, I.-K. Lee, Y.-S. Kang, Y. Kim, J. Maling, and J. Whitman (eds.) *Harvard Studies in Korean Linguistics V*. Hanshin, Seoul, 241–252.

Choi, K. (1991) "A Theory of Syntactic X^0 Subcategorization." Ph.D. diss., University of Washington, Seattle.

Cinque, Guglielmo (1999) *Adverbs and Functional Heads: A Cross-Linguistic Perspective*. Oxford University Press, New York.

Dahl, Östen (1979) "Typology of Sentence Negation." *Linguistics* 17: 79–106.

Dedrick, John, and Eugene Casad (1999) *Sonora Yaqui Language Structures*. University of Arizona Press, Tucson.

Dryer, Matthew (1988) "Universals of Negative Position," in M. Hammond, E. Moravcsik, and J. Wirth (eds.) *Studies in Syntactic Typology*. John Benjamins, Amsterdam, 93–124.

Dryer, Matthew (1992) "The Greenbergian Word Order Correlations." *Language* 68(1): 81–138.

Hagstrom, Paul (2000) "Phrasal Movement in Korean," in S. Robinson, L. Veselinova, and L. Antieau (eds.) MIT Working Papers. *Proceedings of SCIL 9*. Department of Linguistics, MIT, Cambridge, Mass.

Halle, Morris, and Alec Marantz (1993) "Distributed Morphology and the Pieces of Inflection," in Ken Hale and Samuel J. Keyser (eds.) *The View from Building 20: Essays in Linguistics in Honor of Sylvain Bromberger*. MIT Press, Cambridge, Mass., 111–176.

Kayne, Richard (1994) *The Antisymmetry of Syntax*. MIT Press, Cambridge, Mass.

Koopman, Hilda (1992) "On the Absence of Case Chains in Bambara." *Natural Language and Linguistic Theory* 10(2): 555–594.

Lee, Jae-Hong (1992) "Postverbal Adverbs and Verb Movement in Korean," in P. Clancy, (ed) *Proceedings of the Second Southern California Conference on Japanese and Korean Linguistics*. Center for the Study of Language and Information, Stanford, Calif., 428–446.

Lee, Jeong-Shik (1992) "Case Alternation in Korean: Case Minimality." Ph.D. diss., University of Connecticut.

Lee, Young-Suk (1988) "The Korean Causative: A TAG Analysis." Paper given at the 63rd Annual Meeting of the Linguistic Society of America, New Orleans.

Maeda, Isamu (1977) *Ôsaka ben*. Asahi sensho 80. Asahi shinbunsha, Tokyo.

Park, Kabyong (1990) "Negation, Verb Movement, and Light Verbs in Korean," in E.-J. Baek (ed.) *Papers from the Seventh International Conference on Korean Linguistics*. University of Toronto Press, Toronto, 387–398.

Pollock, Jean-Yves (1989) "Verb Movement, Universal Grammar and the Structure of IP." *Linguistic Inquiry* 20(3): 365–424.

Prost, R. P. A. (1965) *La langue sonay et ses dialectes*. Mémoires de l'Institut Français d'Afrique Noire, 47. Ifan, Dakar.

Rizzi, Luigi (1997) "The Fine Structure of the Left Periphery," in Liliane Haegemann, (ed.) *Elements of Grammar*. Kluwer, Dordrecht, 281–338.

Sakai, Hiromu (1998) "Feature Checking and Morphological Merger," in David Silva (ed.) *Japanese/Korean Linguistics 8*. Center for the Study of Language and Information, Stanford, Calif., 189–208.

Sells, Peter (1998) "Structural Relationships within Complex Predicates," in B.-S. Park and James Yoon (eds.) *The 11th International Conference on Korean Linguistics*. Hanguk, Seoul, 115–147.

Sells, Peter, and Young-me Yu Cho (2000) "On the Distribution of X^0 Elements in Korean," Chungmin, Lee, and John Whitman (eds.) (2000) *Korean Syntax and Semantics: Papers from the LSA Institute Workshop, UC Santa Cruz, 1991*. Tahehaksa, Seoul.

Song, Seoul Choong (1971) "A Note on Negation in Korean." *Linguistics* 76: 59–76.

Triulzi, A. A., A. A. Fafallah, and M. L. Bender (1976) "Berta," in M. Lionel Bender (ed.) *The Non-Semitic Languages of Ethiopia*. Michigan State University African Studies Center, East Lansing, 513–532.

Whitman, John (1995) "Apparent Discontinuities in the Acquisition of Verbal Morphology in Korean." Paper presented at the Daewoo Symposium on Child Acquisition of Korean, Seoul National University.

Whitman, John (1998) "Gojun to ku kôzô [Word order and phrase structure]," in Kô-ichi Takezawa and John Whitman, (eds.) *Nichieigo hikaku sensho*. Vol. 9: *Kaku to gojun to tôgo közô* [Case, word order, and syntactic structure]. Kenkyûsha, Tokyo,

Whitman, John (2001) "Kayne 1994: p. 143, fn. 3," in G. Alexandrova and O. Artunova (eds.) *The Minimalist Parameter*. John Benjamins, Amsterdam, 77–100.

Wilson, W. A. A. (2000/2001) "Creissel's Mandinka Grammar." *Journal of West African Languages* 28(2): 109–124.

CHAPTER 21

CONTINENTAL WEST-GERMANIC LANGUAGES

JAN-WOUTER ZWART

1 INTRODUCTION

THE Continental West-Germanic languages form a subgroup of the Germanic branch of the Indo-European language family, spoken in the area of Northwest Europe defined by the river basins of the Scheldt, the (lower) Meuse, the Rhine, the Ems, the Elbe, the Weser, the Oder, and the upper Danube. Outside of this area, Continental West-Germanic dialects are spoken in pockets in Northern Italy, in South Africa, and in German and Jewish settlements and immigrant communities around the world (mainly in Siberia and the Americas).

The group is best known for its national languages High German (of Germany and Austria, referred to here as "German") and Dutch (of the Netherlands and Belgium). Other official languages included are Frisian (of the Netherlands), Luxembourgeois (of Luxemburg), Alemannian or Swiss German (of Switzerland), and Afrikaans (of South Africa).[1]

Ignoring official language status, we can say that the Continental West-Germanic languages constitute two dialect groups, the Frisian group and the Dutch-German group, and two offspring languages, Yiddish and Afrikaans, with slightly more deviating syntax due to the effects of contact with non-Indo-European languages.

Within the Frisian group, three dialect groups exist, North-, East-, and West-Frisian, of which only the latter, referred to here as Frisian, is widely spoken (in the province of Friesland in the Netherlands).[2]

Within the Dutch-German dialect group, a division is made in High, Central, and Low dialects, roughly corresponding to the fall of the rivers flowing to the north or west through the area where these dialects are spoken.[3] The High West-Germanic dialect group includes Bavarian, Alemannic (Swiss German), Swabian, and Rhine Franconian. The Central West-Germanic dialect group includes Central Franconian, Palatinatian (Pfälzisch), Hessian, Thuringian, and Upper Saxon. The Low West-Germanic dialect group includes Lower Franconian, Lower Saxon, East- and Westphalian, Brandenburgish, and Mecklenburgish.

The official language of Germany and Austria, called High German, is based on High and Central West-Germanic dialects. The Dutch spoken in the Netherlands is a mixture of Lower Franconian and Lower Saxon dialects; the Dutch spoken in Belgium, also called Flemish, is Lower Franconian.[4] Low German is the collective term for the Low West-Germanic dialects spoken in Germany (i.e., not Lower Franconian). Luxembourgeois is a Central Franconian (Central West-Germanic) dialect. Swiss German and Alsatian are alternative names for the (High West-Germanic) Alemannian dialect group.

In the remainder of this chapter, the syntax of the Continental West-Germanic dialects is illustrated mainly by the example of Dutch, with variation indicated as much as space limitations allow.

2 GENERAL SYNTACTIC TYPOLOGY

The Continental West-Germanic dialects display largely identical syntax, characterized (1) by an asymmetry between main and embedded clauses with respect to the position of the finite verb (second in main clauses, final in embedded clauses), (2), by clause-final position of (clusters of) nonfinite verbs (*verb raising*) (3) by nonadjacency of the verb and its internal argument (*scrambling*), (4) by subject-verb inversion in fronting constructions (*verb second*), and (5) by clause-final position (i.e., to the right of the verb in final position) of complement clauses (*extraposition*). These phenomena, illustrated in the following in Dutch, are in evidence in all Frisian and Dutch/German dialects, as well as in Afrikaans, but not in Yiddish, where the verb invariably precedes the object.[5]

(1) *Main clauses (SVO)* (Dutch)

a. Jan   kust   Marie. (*Jan Marie kust)
   John   kiss-3SG Mary

   'John kisses Mary.'

Embedded clauses (SOV)

b. . . . dat Jan   Marie kust (* . . . dat Jan kust Marie)
        that John   Mary   kiss-3SG

   ' . . . that John kisses Mary.'

(2) *Verb clustering (SOVVV)*

. . . dat Jan   Marie zou   willen   kussen.
      that John   Mary   will-PAST.SG want-INF   kiss-INF

   ' . . . that John would like to kiss Mary.'

(3) *Scrambling (SOxV)*

. . . dat Jan   Marie nooit kust.
      that John   Mary   never kiss-3SG

(4) *Verb second (xVSO)*

Waarom   kust   Jan   Marie? (*Waarom Jan kust Marie?)
why   kiss-3SG John   Mary

   'Why does John kiss Mary?'

(5) *Extraposition (SxVO)*

. . . dat Jan   niet   wist   [dat hij   Marie kuste].
      that John   not   know-PAST.SG that he-NOM   Mary   kiss-PAST.SG

   ' . . . that John did not know that he kissed Mary.'

   (* . . . dat Jan niet [dat hij Marie kuste] wist)

The clause-final position of the verb in (1b), (2), (3), and (5) can be shown to be its basic position, the fronted position in (1a) and (4) appearing only in the circumscribed context of a finite main clause. Nonfinite elements of a verb cluster (6a), as well as verbal particles (6b), are not fronted along with the finite verb, betraying the finite verb's origin at the end of the clause (Koster 1975):

(6) a. Jan   zou   Marie willen   kussen. (Dutch)
        John   will-PAST.SG Mary   want-INF   kiss-INF

        'John would like to kiss Mary.'

        (*Jan zou willen kussen Marie.)

     b. Jan   belt   Marie op.
        John   ring-3SG   Mary   up

        ('op+bellen' = lit. up-ring, 'call by telephone')

'John calls Mary by telephone.'
(*Jan opbelt Marie)

The clause-final position of the verb suggests that the Continental West-Germanic languages are typologically SOV languages, but this is not necessarily correct. Two considerations suggest that the Continental West-Germanic languages are more properly described as fundamentally head-initial (Zwart 1994): first, the nonadjacency of the object and the verb in embedded clauses, illustrated in (3), suggests that the object is in a derived position (VandenWyngaerd 1989), perhaps displaced from the position occupied by the embedded clause in (5); second, heads in Continental West-Germanic typically precede rather than follow their complement, as illustrated in the Dutch examples in (7), which are representative of the entire language group:

(7)   *head-complement order (heads in italics, complements between brackets)*
    a. Complementizer + embedded clause: ... *dat* [Jan Marie kust].
                                              that John kisses Mary.

    b. Preposition + complement   *op* [de tafel]
                                              on the table

    c. Determiner + noun phrase   *de* [kern van de zaak]
                                              the heart of the matter

    d. Noun + complement   de *kern* [van de zaak]
                                              the heart of the matter

    e. Adjective + complement   (Jan is) *dol* [op Marie].
                                              John is crazy about Mary.

It appears, then, that the Continental West-Germanic languages are head-initial languages, featuring various displacement processes (including object movement and verb movement) yielding SOV (cf. (1b),(3)), (derived) SVO (cf. (1a)), and VSO orders (cf. (4)).[6]

3 WORD CLASSES

The lexical word classes noun (N), verb (V), and adjective (A) are all productive within the grammar of Continental West-Germanic. Their form and distribution characteristics are as follows.

Nouns may be marked for number (singular vs. plural; e.g., Dutch *boek-boeken*, German *Buch-Bücher* 'book(s)'); gender (common vs. neuter, as in Dutch; or masculine, feminine, neuter, as in German); dependent marking on the determiner or the attributive adjective (e.g., Dutch *de man/de vrouw/het kind*; German *der Mann/die Frau/das Kind* 'the man/the woman/the child'); and (limited) Case (see section 4). *Nouns* appear in combination with determiners, numerals, and attributive adjectives (Dutch *de twee rode boeken* 'the two red books'); *noun phrases* may appear as subjects (see section 4) and in the complement of prepositions (as in (7b)).

Verbs may be marked for person and number (1 through 3 singular and plural, with generally some syncretism—as in Dutch *ik loop, jij/hij loop-t, wij/jullie/zij lop-en*,[7] German *ich lauf-e, du läuf-st, er läuf-t, wir lauf-en, ihr läuf-t, sie lauf-en* 'I/you/he/we/you-PL/they walk')—and (limited) tense (only present (actually, nonpast) and past tense, as in Dutch *ik loop-ik liep*; German *ich laufe-ich lief* 'I walk-PRES/PAST', with all other tenses expressed analytically, as in Dutch *ik heb gelopen*; German *ich bin gelaufen* [I walk-PERF] 'I have walked'). Nonfinite verb forms include the infinitive, often accompanied by a grammaticalized locative preposition (Dutch *(te) lop-en*; German *(zu) lauf-en* '(to) walk'), the perfective participle (Dutch *ge-lop-en*; German *ge-lauf-en*), and the present participle (Dutch *lop-end*; German *lauf-end* 'walking').[8] The distributional characteristic of verbs in the Continental West-Germanic languages is that they participate in the subject-verb inversion illustrated in (1a) versus (4).

Adjectives show gender and number agreement with nouns, as previously illustrated, and may be marked for the comparative or superlative (Dutch *groot/grot-er/groot-st* 'big/big-COMP/ big-SUP'). Positionally, they enter into a predicative or attributive alternation (Dutch *het boek is groot* 'the book is big' vs. *het grote boek* 'the big book'), where it is remarkable that only the predicatively used adjective may be followed by a complement PP (as in (7e)).

Adpositions (P) are not productive. They show no form alterations and generally appear before their complement noun phrase (as in (7b)), although most dialects feature a limited number of postpositions and circumpositions (Dutch *in de sloot* 'in (locational) the ditch' vs. *de sloot in* 'into (directional) the ditch', Dutch *tegen de muur op* [against the wall up] 'up against (directional) the wall'). In some dialects, prepositions may command different case forms on their complements (e.g., German *ins* (< *in das) Zimmer* [in the-ACC room] 'into (directional) the room' vs. *im* (< *im dem) Zimmer* [in the-DAT room] 'in (locational) the room'). Adpositions may also appear as secondary predicates (generally called "particles") in constructions like (8), from Dutch (also (6b)) (cf. Den Dikken 1995):

(8) Hij   trapte   [de deur in].
     he   kick-PAST.SG   the door in

     'He kicked the door in.'

Adverbs (Adv) are generally not morphologically marked. They may show up in various positions between the verb-second and verb-final positions, but not to the right of the verb-final position (cf. (1b))(except with a marked backgrounding intonation); they can, however, be fronted (cf. section 7). The class of adverbs includes negation markers (Dutch *niet*; German *nicht* 'not'), as well as a range of modal particles (Dutch *maar*; German *mal* 'just').

The functional elements include complementizers (C), determiners (D), and degree words (Deg).

The *complementizers* are clause initial but can be preceded by a single fronted phrase in embedded interrogatives:

(9) Ik   vroeg   me   af... (Dutch)
    I-NOM   ask-PAST.SG   me-ACC.WEAK   off

    a. [of iemand   mij   gezien   had].
       if   someone me-ACC see-PART.PERF have-PAST.SG
    'I wondered if anyone saw me.'

    b. [wie of mij   gezien   had].
       who if me-ACC see-PART.PERF have-PAST.SG
    'I wondered who saw me.'

Complementizers in many dialects display the typologically rare phenomenon of subject agreement (Zwart 1993, Hoekstra and Smits 1997) (e.g., West-Flemish *da-n-ze komen* [that-3PL+they-NOM.WEAK come-PL] 'that they come'; Frisian *dat-s-to komst* [that-2SG+you-NOM.WEAK come-2SG] 'that you come'). The complementizers in Continental West-Germanic come in various types, including: (1) demonstrative (Dutch *dat*; German *daß* 'that'), (2) interrogative (Dutch *of*; German *ob* 'if, whether'), (3) conditional (Dutch *als, zo* 'if, when'), and (4) prepositional (Dutch *om*; German *um* 'about, for'; Flemish *van* 'of'—all used only in nonfinite clauses). They can be combined with prepositions to yield a variety of clausal connectives (e.g., Dutch *door dat* [by that] 'because'; German *ohne daß* [without that] 'without') and, especially in nonstandard varieties, with each other as well (e.g., Dutch *als of* 'as if').[9]

Determiners display gender and number agreement with the head noun (see previously), as well as case morphology, if present (see section 4). There are definite and indefinite determiners, the latter identical to the numeral 'one' (Dutch *een*; German *ein*). Determiners precede the remainder of the noun phrase, with the possible exception of degree elements (e.g., Dutch *heel de wereld* [whole the world] 'the entire world'; Yiddish *zeyer an interesant bukh* [very an interesting book] 'a very interesting book').

Degree words include extent markers (like Dutch *zo*; German *so* 'so') and excess markers (like Dutch *te*; German *zu* 'too'), which precede the adjectives they belong to (Dutch *zo/te groot* 'so/too big') (cf. Corver 1991).

4 Grammatical Functions

Subjects in Continental West-Germanic show person and number agreement with the finite verb (e.g., Dutch *ik loop, jij/hij loop-t, wij/jullie/zij lop-en*; German *ich lauf-e, du läuf-st, er läuf-t, wir lauf-en, ihr läuf-t, sie lauf-en*, 'I/you/he/we/you-PL/ they walk'). Where case is in evidence, the subject invariably takes the unmarked nominative case.

Positionally, the subject precedes the object and the verb (cf. (1)) but may be preceded, especially in main clauses, by fronted topics or focused elements (in which case the subject is also preceded by the finite verb, cf. (4))(see section 7).

The subject may correspond to the external argument of the verb it agrees with (10a) but also to its internal argument (passive, (10b))—though not the recipient in a ditransitive construction (10c)[10]—or to an argument of the verb of an embedded clause (raising, (10d, e)).

(10) a. Jan   geeft   de kinderen   het boek. (Dutch)
         John   give-3SG   the children   the book

    'John gives the children the books.'

   b. Het   boek   wordt   de kinderen   gegeven.
      the   book   become-3SG   the children   give-PART.PERF

    'The book is being given to the children.'

   c. *De kinderen   worden   het boek   gegeven.
      the children   become-PL   the book   give-PART.PERF

    'The children are being given the book.'

   d. Jan   schijnt   [de kinderen   het boek   te geven].
      John   seem-SG   the children   the book   to give-INF

    'John seems to be giving the book to the children.'

   e. Het boek   schijnt   [de kinderen   gegeven   te worden].
      the book   seem-SG   the children   give-PART.PERF   to become-INF

    'The book appears to be given to the children.'

Nonargument subjects ("expletives") are of two types, corresponding to the locative (Dutch *het*; German *es*) and nonlocative (Dutch *er*; German *da*) inanimate pronouns (see section 6)(cf. Bennis 1986). In what appears to be their core use, the nonlocative expletive anticipates a clause (11a), while the locative expletive anticipates a nonspecific ("indefinite") noun phrase (the "associate", (11b)):[11]

(11) a. Het/*er is   duidelijk [dat hij   een genie is]. (Dutch)
          it/there be-3SG   clear   that he-NOM   a genius   be-3SG

          'It is clear that he is a genius.'

      b. Er/*het is   een genie in de zaal.[12]
          there/it be-SG   a genius   in the room

          'There is a genius in the room.'

The nonlocative expletive is also used as the subject in weather constructions (Dutch *het regent*; German *es regnet* 'it is raining').

Subject drop is generally limited to nonlocative expletives in subject-verb inversion constructions (12)—but not in weather constructions—and to expletives more generally in embedded clauses (13):

(12) Is   (het) duidelijk [wat   jullie   moeten   doen]? (Dutch)
      be-3SG   it   clear   what   you-PL   must-PL   do-INF

      'Is it clear what you have to do?'

(13) ... daß (da/*es) viele Leute   anwesend   waren. (German)
      that   there/it   many people   present   be-PAST.PL

      '... that there were many people present.'

Frisian, in addition, allows subject drop of the second-person singular pronoun:

(14) Moatst   Pyt   helpe. (Frisian)
      must-SG   Pete   help-INF

      'You must help Pete.'

Objects appear in the area between the verb-second position (cf. (1a)) and the verb-final position (cf. (1b)) (the *Mittelfeld*). Their exact position with respect to adverbs, modal particles, and negation markers depends on a number of factors, including specificity or definiteness, discourse linking, and intonation (see, e.g., Lenerz 1977). In general, specific or definite, discourse-linked objects tend to precede other Mittelfeld material, and nonspecific or indefinite, non-discourse-linked objects tend to follow other Mittelfeld material.

Indirect objects may be expressed as noun phrases or as PPs. Indirect object noun phrases tend to precede direct object noun phrases (cf. (10a)), but indirect object PPs enjoy greater positional freedom.[13]

Where case is in evidence—in particular, in the pronominal system—direct objects are marked in comparison with subjects (e.g., Dutch *hij* [he-NOM] vs. *hem* [he-OBJ]). A case distinction between direct and indirect object pronouns exists in High West-Germanic but is obliterated in Dutch and in most Low West-Germanic dialects (e.g., German *er* [he-NOM], *ihn* [he-ACC], *ihm* [he-DAT]; Lower Saxon *he* [he-NOM] vs. *em* [he-OBJ]; Yiddish *er* [he-NOM] vs. *im* [he-OBJ]; Frisian *hy* [he-NOM] vs. *him* [he-OBJ]; Afrikaans *hy* [he-NOM] vs. *hom* [he-OBJ]).[14] Outside the pronominal system, the direct and indirect object are not morphologically marked in Frisian, Dutch, and Afrikaans, and the case system is much reduced in Yiddish and all German dialects except Standard High German.[15]

There is abundant syntactic evidence for a structural asymmetry between subjects and objects in Continental West-Germanic: subjects may bind reflexive objects, but objects may not bind reflexive subjects (15); similarly with licensing of negative polarity items (16):[16]

(15) a. . . . dat Jan   z'n   eigen haat. (Colloquial Dutch)
              that John POSS.MASC own   hate-SG

      '. . . that John hates himself.'

      b. *. . . dat   z'n   eigen hem   haat.
                 that POSS.MASC own   he-OBJ hate-SG

(16) a. . . . dat niemand ook maar iets wist. (Dutch)
              that nobody   anything-NPI   know-PAST.SG

      '. . . that nobody knew a single thing.'

      b. *. . . dat ook maar iemand niets   wist.
                 that anybody-NPI   nothing know-PAST.SG

However, there is no "superiority" effect to prohibit the fronting of an interrogative object across an interrogative subject (17), and subjects and objects can be relativized equally well (18):

(17) a. Wie heeft   wat   gedaan? (Dutch)
           who have-3SG what do-PART.PERF

      'Who did what?'

      b. Wat   heeft   wie gedaan?
           what have-3SG who do-PART.PERF

      'Who did what?'

(18) a. de man   die   het boek   geschreven   heeft
         the man   DEM-CG   the book   write-PART.PERF have-3SG

         'the man who wrote the book'

      b. het boek   dat   de man   geschreven   heeft
         the book   DEM-NTR   the man   write-PART.PERF have-3SG

         'the book that the man wrote'

An asymmetry comparable to the one between subjects and objects exists between indirect objects and direct objects, indirect objects binding anaphoric direct objects (19), and licensing negative polar direct objects (20):

(19) a. ...dat   ik   Piet   z'n   eigen   toonde. (Coll. Dutch)
                  that I   Pete   POSS.MASC own   show-PAST.SG

         '...that I showed Pete himself.'

      b. *...dat   ik   z'n   eigen   Piet   toonde
                   that I   POSS.MASC own   Pete   show-PAST.SG

(20) a. *...dat   Jan   niemand   ook maar iets   gaf. (Dutch)
                   that John   nobody   anything-NPI   give-PAST.SG

         '...that John didn't give anyone anything.'

      b. *...dat   Jan   ook maar iemand   niets   gaf.
                   that John   anyone-NPI   nothing   give-PAST.SG

These facts are taken to indicate that the displacement operation taking the objects to positions nonadjacent to the verb (in clause final position) is of the A-movement type (Vanden Wyngaerd 1989).

5 TYPES OF COMPLEMENTATION

5.1 Full and Reduced Complement Clauses

Propositional internal arguments of a verb can be expressed in full (i.e., CP-type) and reduced (i.e., IP-type) clauses: full complement clauses are finite (containing a tense-marked verb) or nonfinite; reduced complement clauses are always nonfinite.

Full complement clauses are realized in "extraposition"—that is, to the right of the verb-final position (cf. (5)). The arguments of reduced complement clauses are realized as subjects ("raising," with verbs of appearance like Dutch *schijnen* "seem") or objects ("raising to object" or "Exceptional Case-Marking" (ECM)), with perception verbs (Dutch *zien* 'see') and causative verbs (Dutch *laten* 'let') of the embedding ("matrix") clause. In particular, the raising to object cases yield various patterns of clausal intertwining, illustrated schematically in (21):[17]

(21)   a. [$_\text{CLAUSE-1}$ ADVERB–EXT.ARG–VERB [$_\text{CLAUSE-2}$ EXT.ARG–VERB–INT.ARG]]

      b. EXT.ARG$_1$–EXT.ARG$_2$–INT.ARG$_2$–ADVERB$_1$–VERB$_1$–VERB$_2$

      c. EXT.ARG$_1$–VERB$_1$–EXT.ARG$_2$–INT.ARG$_2$–ADVERB$_1$–VERB$_2$

Example (21a) is an approximation of the deep structure of a Continental West-Germanic perception verb construction involving a reduced complement clause; (21b) is a schematic representation of the realization of such a construction, with the matrix clause shown in embedded clause word order (i.e., with the verb in final position); (21c) represents the same construction with the matrix clause showing main clause word order (i.e., with the verb in second position). The position of the matrix clause adverb (ADVERB$_1$), to the right of the arguments of the embedded clause, shows that the clausal intertwining is still intact, even though superficially undone by the displacement of the matrix clause verb. These constructions are illustrated in (22), from Dutch:

(22) a. [. . . dat   Jan   gisteren   zag   [*Piet   kussen*
                 that   John   yesterday   see-PAST.SG   Pete   kiss-INF
        Marie]. (= (21a))
        Mary

     b. . . . dat   Jan   *Piet   Marie*   gisteren   zag
              that   John   Pete   Mary   yesterday   see-PAST.SG
        kussen. (= (21b))
        kiss-INF

        '..that John saw Pete kiss Mary yesterday.'

     c. Jan   zag   *Piet   Marie*   gisteren   *kussen*. (= (21c))
        John   see-PAST.SG   Pete   Mary   yesterday   kiss-INF

The patterns illustrated in (22) can be described as resulting from the same displacements needed to describe the word order of the simple clause illustrated in (1)–(5), namely, leftward movement of noun phrases and (in (22c)) of the finite verb.

Multiple embedding of reduced clauses yields essentially the same surface syntax, with the arguments lining up as objects in the Mittelfeld, and the verbs forming what looks like a cluster in the verb-final position (except the finite verb if the highest embedding clause has main clause word order):

(23) a. [. . . dat   Jan   nooit   zou   [moeten   [laten   [*Piet*
                that   John   never   shall-PAST.SG   must-INF   let-INF   Pete
           kussen   Marie]]]].
           kiss-INF   Mary

      b. . . . dat   Jan   *Piet   Marie*   nooit   zou   moeten
               that   John   Pete   Mary   never   shall-PAST.SG   must-INF
           laten   *kussen.*
           let-INF   kiss-INF

           ' . . . that John should never let Pete kiss Mary.'

      c. Jan   zou   *Piet   Marie*   nooit   moeten   laten
           John   shall-PAST.SG   Pete   Mary   never   must-INF   let-INF
           kussen.
           kiss-INF

           'John should never let Pete kiss Mary.'

Example (23) also illustrates the use of modal verbs taking bare infinitive complements, an extremely common pattern, where the modal verb can be deontic or epistemic (Dutch *zullen* 'shall', *moeten* 'must', *mogen* 'may', *kunnen* 'can', *willen* 'will, want'), aspectual (Dutch *gaan* 'go', *komen* 'come', *blijven* 'stay'), or postural (*staan* 'stand', *zitten* 'sit', *liggen* 'lie down').[18]

The clausal intertwining and verb clustering are also in evidence in perfective constructions involving an auxiliary (either *have* or *be*) and a perfective participle, albeit that the participle in some dialects occupies a different position from the infinitive (see (24)):

(24) . . . dat   Jan   *het boek*   niet   *gelezen*   heeft.
            that   John   the book   not   read-PART.PERF   have-SG

      ' . . . that John hasn't read the book.'

5.2 Verb Clusters

The Continental West-Germanic dialects display a bewildering variety of word orders in the verb clusters, although the order of the verbs is never random, and some orders are never found (cf. Zwart 1996).[19] Also, a distinction must be made between infinitival and participial constructions. The facts are summarized in table 21.1.

A further complication arises when recuded infinitive clauses are embedded in an auxiliary-participle construction (cf. English *have* [AUXILIARY] *wanted* [PARTICIPLE] *to see* [INFINITIVE]). These constructions allow additional verb orders not reflected in table 21.1 (e.g., *1-3-2* in Standard High German and *2-3-1* in West-Flemish), though not in all dialects (not in Frisian, e.g., or in Low Germanic dialects showing the effects of Frisian substratum influence, such as the Low Saxon dialect spoken in the Dutch province of Groningen). In all but the fully "descending" (i.e., *3-2-1*) orders, the participle is replaced by an infinitive (*Infinitivus pro participio* [IPP], or "Ersatzinfinitiv"):[20]

(25) a. ... dat Jan het boek had *kunnen* lezen. (Dutch)
        that John the book have-PAST.SG can-INF read-INF

       '... that John had been able to read the book.'

    b. ... daß Johann das Buch hätte lesen
        that John the-NOM/ACC have-CONJ.3SG read-INF
       können (German).
       can-INF

       '... that John should have been able to read the book.'

The replacement of the participle by the infinitive does not take place when the reduced nonfinite clause appears in extraposition, in which case the embedded

Table 21.1. Order of the verbs in "verb clusters"

Language	Auxiliary-participle	Single infinitive	Multiple infinitive
Frisian	*2-1*	*2-1*	*3-2-1*
Standard Dutch	2-1/1-2	1-2	*1-2-3*
Standard German	*2-1*	*2-1*	*3-2-1*
Low Germanic (West-Flemish)	2-1	1-2	1-2-3
Central Germanic (Luxembourgeois)	2-1	1-2	1-2-3
High Germanic (Bavarian, Swabian)	2-1	1-2/2-1	3-2-1/1-3-2
Afrikaans	*2-1*	*1-2*	*1-2-3*
Yiddish	d.n.a.	d.n.a.	*2-3*

Numbers refer to the status of the verbs in terms of embedding, with the more embedded verb receiving a higher number (e.g., *must do* = 1-2, *gelezen heeft* [read-PART.PERF have-3SG] = 2-1). Obligatory word orders are in italics. d.n.a. = does not apply.

verb and its arguments appear to the right of the embedding verb (i.e., in extra-position, cf. (5)):

(26) ...dat   Jan   heeft   beloofd/*beloven   (om)   het boek
         that John have-3SG   promise-PART.PERF/INF   for   the book
      te zullen   lezen.
      to shall-INF   read-INF

      '...that John has promised to read the book.'

In similar contexts, when the embedded clause has an infinitive with *te/zu* 'to' but no complementizer, the arguments of the embedded clause are again displaced into the matrix clause and the infinitive (with *te/zu*) is included in the verb "cluster," but (with a few exceptions like Dutch *proberen* 'try') the participle is not replaced by the infinitive:[21]

(27) ...dat   Jan   het boek   heeft   beloofd/*beloven
         that John the book   have-3SG   promise-PART.PERF/INF
      te zullen   lezen.
      to shall-INF   read-INF

      '...that John has promised to read the book.'

5.3 "Verb Projection Raising"

The syntax of infinitival complementation is further complicated by the phenomenon, present in many dialects, that a string of two (or more) verbs in ascending order (1-2-3, 1-3-2, etc.) may be broken up by adverbs, negation markers, stranded prepositions, or arguments and predicates originating in the more embedded clause:[22]

(28) a. We   zullen   *der*   een keer   moeten   *voor*
         we-NOM   shall-PL   there   one time   must-INF   for
         zorgen. (East-Flemish)
         care-INF

         'We will have to take care of it some time.'

      b. ...daß   er   es   hätte   *genau*   durchsehen
            that he-NOM   it   have-CONJ.3SG   exact   through-see-INF
         müssen. (German)
         must-INF

         '...that he should have looked it through carefully.'

5.4 Small Clauses

Propositional complements involving nonverbal predicates ("small clauses"), typically locative or resultative phrases, are productively formed in Continental West-Germanic. The predicate, which can be a noun phrase, an adjective phrase, or a prepositional phrase (including the class of verbal particles or "intransitive prepositions"), appears to the immediate left of the verb-final position—that is, following all other Mittelfeld material:[23]

(29) a. ... dat   Jan   de kast   leeg   vond. (Dutch)
　　　　　　that   John   the closet empty   find-PAST.SG

　　　'... that John found the closet empty.'

　　　b. ... dat   Jan   (toen)   de sloot   (weer)   in sprong.
　　　　　　that John   then   the ditch again   in jump-PAST.SG

　　　'... that John then jumped into the ditch again.'

As can be seen in (29b), both the subject of the small clause predicate and the noun phrase contained in the small clause predicate are separated from the head of the small clause predicate (*in* 'into').[24]

In constructions with transparent reduced infinitival clauses, a predicate originating with the most deeply embedded verb appears to the immediate left of the verb cluster or, in dialects allowing the cluster to be broken up, somewhere inside the verb cluster:

(30) Maar ik   zou$_1$ hem   ook   eerst laten$_3$ *vuil*
　　　but   I-NOM will-PAST.SG   he-OBJ also first let-INF   dirty
　　　worden$_4$ ebben$_2$. (East Flemish)
　　　become-INF   have-INF

　　　'But I would have let it get dirty first, too.'

6 PRONOUNS

The Continental West-Germanic pronouns can be organized by using the feature oppositions in figure 21.1. In Dutch, for example, the pronouns are (1) [+ ANIMATE] *iedereen/elk/allen*, [−ANIMATE] *alles*, [LOCATIVE] *overal*; (2) *wie, wat, waar*; (3) *iemand, iets, ergens*; (4) *deze, dit, hier*; (5) *die, dat, daar*; (6) [−ANIMATE] *ət* (spelled *het*), [LOCATIVE] *ər* (spelled *er*); and (7) the set of personal pronouns,

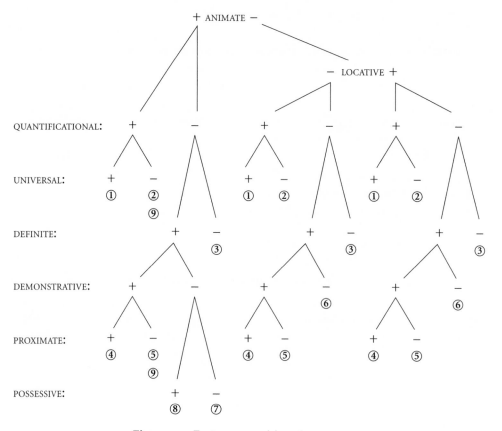

Figure 21.1 Feature oppositions in pronouns

see later; (8) the set of possessive pronouns, see later, including (9) the archaic [+ANIMATE] interrogative *wiens* and distal demonstrative *diens*.

The *personal pronouns* (7) show person (1, 2, 3), number (SG, PL), and, in third-person singular, gender (MASCULINE, FEMININE) distinctions (in addition to case, for which see section 4).[25] These pronouns generally have strong and weak variants (see table 21.2).

The *possessive pronouns* are Dutch *mijn, jouw, zijn, haar, ons, jullie, hun* [my, your, his, her, our, your-PL, their], with weak variants in the singular *mən, jə, zən, dər* [my-WEAK, your-WEAK, his-WEAK, her-WEAK]; Frisian *myn, dyn, syn, har, ús, jimme, har/harren*; and Bavarian *mai, dai, zai, iarɐ, insɐ, eŋgɐ, eɐnɐ*. On their use, see section 8.

The placement of weak pronouns is somewhat different from that of strong pronouns and full noun phrases. Weak pronouns may not be coordinated, modified, isolated, backgrounded (via "right dislocation"; see section 7), or fronted (via "topicalization"; see section 7).[26] Weak direct object pronouns precede indirect objects (unlike with full noun phrases, cf. (10a)), and a weak pronoun cor-

Table 21.2 Strong versus weak pronouns

Language	Variant	Case	1SG	2SG	3SG.M	3SG.F	1PL	2PL	3PL
Dutch	Strong	NOM	ik	jij	hij	zij	wij	jullie	zij
		OBJ	mij	jou	hem	haar	ons	jullie	hun
	Weak	NOM	ək	jə	-/ie	zə	wə	-	zə
		OBJ	mə	jə	əm	dər	-	-	zə
Frisian	Strong	NOM	ik	do	hy	sy	wy	jimme	sy
		OBJ	my	dy	him	har	ús	jimme	harren
	Weak	NOM	ək	-to	ər	sə	wə	jim	sə
		OBJ	mi	di	əm	ər	-	jim	har
Bavarian	Strong	NOM	i:	du:	eɐ	zi:	miɐ	e:z	ze:
		ACC	mi:	di:	eɐm	zi:	unz	diɐ	ze:
		DAT	miɐ	diɐ	eɐm	iɐ	unz	eŋg	eɐnɐ
	Weak	NOM	-e	-d	-ɐ	-s	-mɐ	-z	-z
		ACC	-me	-de	-n	-s	-	-	-z
		DAT	-me	-dɐ	-	-	-	-	-

responding to the internal argument of the infinitive in an ECM-construction may precede the infinitive's external argument:

(31) a. ...dat ik   Piet de afwas zag   doen. (Dutch)
        that I-NOM Pete the dishes see-PAST.SG do-INF
    '...that I saw Pete do the dishes.'

   b. ...dat ik   ət   Piet zag   doen.
        that I-NOM it-WEAK Pete see-PAST.SG do-INF
    '...that I saw Pete do it.'

More generally, weak object pronouns enjoy greater positional freedom than strong object pronouns or full noun phrases, in some dialects even preceding the (nonclitic) subject:

(32) a. ...daß sich etwas   ändert. (German)
        that REFL something change-3SG
    '...that something changes.'

   b. Ziede   ze   gije? (South-East Flemish)
      see-2SG.INV they-OBJ.WEAK you
    'Do you see them?'

Weak subject pronouns in many dialects coalesce with the complementizer (e.g., Frisian *dat-st-ə* (*<dat-st-do*) *komst* [that-2SG+you-SG.WEAK come-2SG] 'that you come'; Bavarian *dam-ma* (< *das+ma*) *farn* [that+we-NOM.WEAK go-PL] 'that we go'). Sometimes the weak subject pronoun may be doubled by a strong pronoun (e.g., West-Flemish *da-n-k ik komen* [that-1SG+I-NOM.WEAK I-NOM come-1SG] 'that I come'; Bavarian *dam-ma miɐ farn* [that+we-NOM.WEAK we-NOM go-1PL] 'that we go').

Remarkably, (some or all) nonlocative inanimate pronouns in the complement of prepositions are replaced by their locative counterparts, appearing to the left of the preposition:[27]

(33) a. 1 *met   alles   >   overal   mee. (Dutch)
             with   everything   everywhere with 'with everything'

      b. 2 *met   wat   >   waar   mee
             with   what   where   with 'with what'

      c. 3 *met   iets   >   ergens   mee
             with   something   somewhere   with 'with something'

      d. 4 *met   daat   >   daar   mee
             with   that   there   with 'with that'

      e. 5 *met   dit   >   hier   mee
             with   this   here   with 'with this'

      f. 6 *met   ət   >   ər   mee
             with   it   there-WEAK with 'with it'

Dialects differ in the range of this phenomenon (e.g., German lacks the replacement with pronouns of types 1 and 3), and for some dialects a preference for the nonlocative, noninverted variant is reported (Swiss German, West-Flemish). In Dutch and (colloquial) German, the locative pronoun can be separated from the adposition (preposition stranding), but in other dialects the locative and the adposition are said to be inseparable (e.g., Luxembourgeois; Bertrang 1921: 310).

The nonlocative *demonstratives* are also used as deictic determiners (as in Dutch *deze/die man* 'this/that man', etc.), which cannot be combined with nondeictic determiners or possessive pronouns. In Afrikaans, the demonstrative determiners are necessarily combined with a proximate (*hier* 'here') or distal (*daar* 'there') locative marker (e.g., *hierdie man* 'this man', *daardie man* 'that man'), as the demonstrative determiner itself lacks the proximate/distal distinction.[28]

Standard High German, Central and High West-Germanic dialects, and Yiddish have a special third-person reflexive pronoun (German *sich*, Yiddish *zikh*). In other persons, as more generally in Frisian, Afrikaans, and the Low West-

Germanic dialects, the (objective case) weak pronoun also functions as a reflexive pronoun, but an exception is often made for the third person, which may use a special reflexive pronoun under High German influence (e.g., Modern Dutch *zich*).[29] A reflexive (or reflexively used) pronoun combined with an emphasis marker yields a locally bound anaphor (e.g., Dutch *zich-zelf*, Frisian *əm-sels*); a weak pronoun combined with the same emphasis marker yields what has been analyzed as a logophor (e.g., Dutch *əm-zelf*).[30]

Reciprocity may be expressed by using the reflexive pronoun (34a), a special reciprocal pronoun (34b), or a combination of the two types (34c):

(34)   a. Die Freunde   begegnen   sich. (German)
           the-NOM friend-PL meet-PL   REFL
           'The friends met each other.'

       b. De vrienden   ontmoetten   elkaar. (Dutch)
           the friend-PL meet-PAST.PL   each-other
           'The friends met each other.'

       c. Ze   schlowe *zech* noch *èèn den aner* dowt.
           they-NOM   beat-PL REFL yet one the other   dead
           (Arlon, Luxembourgeois)
           'They will beat each other to death.'

The reflexive pronoun is furthermore used in middle constructions (35a) but not in Low West-Germanic dialects, where the special reflexive pronoun is either absent or a late borrowing from Central or High West-Germanic (35b):

(35)   a. Dieses Buch   liest   sich   gut. (German)
           this-NOM book   read-3SG   REFL   good
           'This book reads well.'

       b. Dit boek   leest   (*zich) lekker. (Dutch)
           this book   read-3SG   REFL   good
           'This book reads well.'

Obviation is not marked in the pronoun system.[31] Pronouns interpreted coreferentially or as "bound variables" are not marked by special morphology in the Continental West-Germanic languages.

7 ALTERNATIONS, DISPLACEMENTS, AND SPECIAL WORD ORDER TYPES

7.1 Alternations

Alternations commonly found in the Continental West-Germanic dialects include the passive, the middle, the causative, the applicative, the dative alternation, the locative alternation, and an object placement alternation relating to definiteness or specificity.

The *passive* is generally formed by a combination of an auxiliary verb meaning 'become' (Dutch *worden*, German *werden*; Luxembourgeois uses *gin* 'give') and a perfective participle (36a).[32] Transitive and intransitive unergative verbs can be passivized (the latter yielding "impersonal passives" with an expletive subject, (36b)).[33] Ditransitives yield asymmetric passives, with only the direct object passivizing (cf. 10b, c).

(36) a. De hond   wordt   geslagen. (Dutch)
         the dog   become-3SG   beat-PART.PERF

         'The dog is being beaten.'

      b. Er   wordt   gedanst.
         there   become-3SG   dance-PART.PERF

         'People are dancing.'

Psych verbs (ascribing a mental state to one of their arguments) come in two classes: one allowing passivization (37), and the other disallowing it (38):

(37) a. Het nieuws   verontrust   Jan. (Dutch)
         the news   disturb-SG   John

         'The news disturbs John.'

      b. Jan   wordt   door het nieuws   verontrust.
         John   become-3SG   by the news   disturb-PART.PERF

         'John is disturbed by the news.'

(38) a. Het nieuws   bevalt   Jan.
         the news   please-3SG   John

         'The news pleases John.'

      b. *Jan   wordt   door het nieuws   bevallen.
         John   become-3SG   by the news   please-PART.PERF

The *middle* construction shows two varieties in Continental West-Germanic. In one type, the construction is reflexive (cf. (35a)), and the subject can only be an internal argument, not an adjunct. In the other type, no reflexive is used (cf. (35b)), and the subject can be both an internal argument or an adjunct (usually instrumental or locative; cf. (39a)). The first type is found in Standard High German, and the second in Standard Dutch.[34] Middle constructions also have an expletive locative or instrumental variant (also showing the ±reflexive split) (39b) and a periphrastic causative variant (always reflexive and always with the internal argument as subject)(39c):

(39) a. Deze stad   woont   prettig. (Dutch)
          this town   live-3SG pleasant

          'It is pleasant living in this town.'

      b. Het   woont   prettig   in deze stad.
          it   live-3SG pleasant in this town

          'It is pleasant living in this town.'

      c. Zo'n woord   laat   zich   gemakkelijk vertalen.
          such+a word   let-SG REFL   easily   translate-INF

          'Such a word allows for easy translation.'

The middle is never marked morphologically.

The *causative* is always formed periphrastically, using a causative verb (Dutch *laten*; German *lassen* 'let') and a reduced infinitival complement. In embedded contexts, the causative shows similar transparency effects as the ECM construction (cf. (21)):

(40) a. Jan   liet   Piet   Marie kussen. (Dutch)
          John   let-PAST.SG Pete   Mary   kiss-INF

          'John let Pete kiss Mary.'

      b. ...dat   Jan   *Piet*   *Marie*   liet *kussen*.
             that   John   Pete   Mary   let-PAST.SG kiss-INF

          '... that John let Pete kiss Mary.'

The causative construction does not allow for passivization.[35]

The *applicative* alternation is formed with the verbal prefix *be*:

(41) a. De printer   spat   inkt   op het papier. (Dutch)
          the printer spit-3SG   ink   on the paper

      b. De printer   be-spat   het papier met inkt.
          the printer APPL-spit-3SG   the paper   with ink

          'The printer spits ink on the paper.'

The *dative* alternation is commonly found, as in Dutch (42) next to (10a):

(42) Jan   geeft   het boek   aan de kinderen.
      John   give-3SG the book   to the children

      'John gives the book to the children.'

The presence of a *locative* alternation (involving displacement of a locative to subject position) is not easy to establish because of possible confusion with to-picalization (see later in this section) and, in embedded clauses, with "scrambling" (relatively free word order in the Mittelfeld). The word order type in (43) may be an example (cf. Zwart 1992):

(43) ... dat   in de kast   een lijk   zit. (Dutch)
            that   in the closet a body   sit-SG

      '... that a body is in the closet.'

In the Mittelfeld, a *specificity* alternation is found, with specific objects preceding discourse particles and nonspecific objects following them:

(44) a. Pak   het boek   maar. (Dutch)
         take-IMP   the book   just

         'Why don't you take the book?'

      b. Pak   maar   een boek.
         take-IMP   just   a book

         'Why don't you take a book?'

Indefinite objects preceding discourse particles take on a specific or generic reading:[36]

(45) Je   moet   een boek   maar   niet   opeten.
      you   must-SG   a book   just   not   eat-INF

      'You don't want to eat a book.'

The same tendency exists with other adverbial material in the Mittelfeld (sentence adverbs, VP-adverbs), but here the interpretive effects can be undone by marked intonation patterns (cf. Zwart 1997: 92f).

7.2 Displacements

This section covers the positioning of question words and phrases, as well as the distribution of focused, topicalized, and backgrounded material.[37]

Question words and phrases are fronted in all Continental West-Germanic dialects. In main clauses, the fronting is accompanied by inversion of the subject and the finite verb ("verb second," cf. (4)). In embedded clauses, the verb stays in the verb-final position, but the question word or phrase is still fronted and may be followed by one or more complementizers in a number of dialects (including Frisian and colloquial Dutch):[38]

(46) (Ik vraag me af) waarom of dat Jan Marie kust. (Dutch)
      (I wonder)   why   if that John Mary   kiss-3SG

      'I wonder why John is kissing Mary.'

The parallelism between the position of the finite verb in main clause interrogatives and the position of the complementizer in embedded interrogatives suggests that the inverted verb is in the head position of CP and the question phrase is in the specifier position of CP (essentially den Besten 1977).

With multiple question words or phrases, only one is fronted, and the others stay in the position expressing their grammatical function (in situ, cf. (17)). The question phrase in situ receives the high pitch intonation associated with focus. Without the high pitch intonation, the in situ question word *wat* (Dutch) / *was* (German) receives the interpretation of an indefinite inanimate pronoun ('something'):

(47) Ik   weet   wat. (Dutch)
      I-NOM know-SG   what

      'I know something'; 'I have an idea.'

The fronting of question words allows for considerable pied-piping:[39]

(48) a. [Waar   over]   heb   je   gesproken? (Dutch)
          where about   have-2SG.INV you   speak-PART.PERF

          'Who did you talk about?'

      b. [De ouders van welke student]   heb   je
          the parents of which student   have-2SG.INV you
          beledigd?
          insult-PART.PERF

          'The parents of which student did you insult?'

On the other hand, fronting of just the question words leads to "preposition stranding" (49a) and subextraction (49b):

(49) a. *Waar* heb   je   *over*   gesproken? (Dutch)
         where have-2SG.INV you   about   speak-PART.PERF

      'What did you talk about?'

      b. *Welke student* heb   je   *de ouders van*
         which   student   have-2SG.INV you   the parents of
         beledigd?
         insult-PART.PERF

      'Which student did you insult the parents of?'

The same pattern is displayed in questions addressing kinds (as in *what kind of books*):

(50) a. *Wat   voor   boeken*   heb   je   gelezen? (Dutch)
         what   for   book-PL   have-2SG.INV you   read-PART.PERF

      b. *Wat*   heb   je   *voor   boeken*   gelezen?
         what   have-2SG.INV you   for   book-PL   read-PART.PERF

      'What kind of books did you read?'

Long-distance movement of question words and phrases (i.e., subextraction from a nonreduced embedded clause) takes place and is sensitive to the usual opacity factors. Thus, there is no long-distance extraction out of subject clauses and adjunct clauses or out of embedded interrogatives or embedded clauses with main clause word order.[40] The following special features may be noted.

Long-distance movement of subject question words generally shows no "*that-trace effect*" (omission of the complementizer in the context of an extracted subject):[41]

(51) Wie   denk   je   dat   het boek   geschreven
      who   think-2SG.INV you   that   the book   write-PART.PERF
      heeft? (Dutch)
      have-SG

      'Who do you think wrote the book?'

In Frisian and German, long-distance interrogatives may involve doubling of the question word (52a) or displacement of the question word to the edge (Spec,CP) of the embedded clause and insertion of an invariant operator in the Spec,CP of the main clause (52b):

(52) a. Wen   denkst   du   wen   sie
          who-ACC   think-2SG   you (SG)   who-ACC   she-NOM
          liebt? (German)
          love-3SG

      b. Was   denkst   du   wen   sie   liebt? (German)
          what   think-2SG   you (SG)   who-ACC   she-NOM   love-3SG

          'Who do you think she loves?'

Topicalization generally shows the same syntax as question phrase movement—
namely, fronting of the topic, possibly over longer distance, accompanied by inversion of the main clause subject and finite verb.[42] "Topics" are understood here
as discourse-familiar elements, prototypically demonstrative pronouns, or noun
phrases headed by a deictic determiner. There is a strong preference for these
elements to be fronted:

(53) a. ??Ik   weet   dat   niet. (Dutch)
          I   know-SG   DEM.DIST.NTR   not

      b. Dat   weet   ik   niet.
          DEM.DIST.NTR   know-SG   I   not

          'I don't know that.'

A fronted element (with or without deictic determiner) can also be resumed by
a distal demonstrative pronoun, which appears between the fronted element and
the (inverted) finite verb:[43]

(54) Jan / Die jongen   (die)   ken   ik   niet. (Dutch)
      John / DEM.DIST.CG boy   DEM.DIST.CG   know-1SG   I   not

      'I don't know John/that guy.'

Note that the resumptive d-word turns locative when extracted from out of a
prepositional phrase:[44]

(55) Bananen (daar)   ben   ik   niet   dol   *op*. (Dutch)
      bananas there   be-1SG   I-NOM   not   wild   on

      'I'm not crazy about bananas.'

The fronted element and the resumptive d-word fail constituency tests (e.g., they
cannot appear together in any other position), suggesting that only the d-word

has been fronted and that the phrase in front is a 'base-generated' sentence satellite.

The tendency to front topics (deictic elements) is absent from embedded clauses:[45]

(56) * . . . dat   die jongen   (die)   jij   wel
          that   DEM.DIST.CG boy   DEM.DIST.CG   you   DISC-PRT
       kende. (Dutch)
       know-PAST.SG

       ' . . . that you knew that guy.'

Focus is expressed by high pitch intonation on the pitch-bearing syllable of the focused element. In the default case, focus is on the most deeply embedded complement or predicate (cf. Cinque 1993).[46] Marked ("narrow") focus can be on any constituent and may or may not be accompanied by additional displacements of the focused constituent ("focus scrambling").

Backgrounding is marked by both position (to the right of the verb-final position) and intonation (level and low pitched).[47] Backgrounded arguments are doubled by a weak pronoun in the position associated with the argument's grammatical function (subject or object position) ("right dislocation"). Backgrounded clausal arguments are doubled by the inanimate nondemonstrative pronoun (Dutch *ət*; German *es* 'it'). Adverbs can only appear in postverbal position when backgrounded. Weak elements (such as weak pronouns and discourse particles) cannot appear in postverbal position at all, not even as backgrounded material.

Clauses and PPs also appear in postverbal position without backgrounding (i.e., without the level low pitch intonation) ("extraposition").[48] PPs interpreted as secondary predicates ("small clause predicates") must appear in the preverbal position designated for embedded predicates. Embedded (nonreduced) complement clauses must appear in extraposition; adjunct clauses enjoy more freedom.

Extraposed clauses and backgrounded clauses differ in a number of respects, most significantly in that backgrounded clauses are opaque, and extraposed clauses are not (pitch accent indicated by small capitals; low-level pitch by smaller print):[49]

(57) a. *Wie   heb   je   het   beTREURD   dat   je
          who   have-2SG.INV   you   it   regret-PART.PERF that   you
       gekust   hebt? (Dutch, backgrounding)
       kiss-PART.PERF   have-2SG

       'Whom did you regret it that you kissed?'

b. Wie   heb   je   (%het) betreurd   dat je
   who   have-2SG.INV   you   it   regret-PART.PERF that you
   geKUST   hebt? (Dutch, extraposition)
   kiss-PART.PERF have-2SG

   'Whom did you regret it that you kissed?'

Extraposed PPs are always opaque (i.e., no preposition stranding in postverbal position, cf. (49a)):

(58) *Waar   heb   je   gesproken   over? (Dutch)
      where   have-2SG.INV   you   speak-PART.PERF   about

      'What did you talk about?'

Other elements appearing in extraposition include relative clauses (59a), specifications (59b), and the second member of coordinations (59c):

(59) a. . . . dat ik   iemand   ken   die   kan
              that I-NOM   someone   know-1SG   REL.CG   can
         voetballen. (Dutch)
         play.soccer-INF

         '. . . that I know someone who can play soccer.'

      b. . . . dat ik   iemand   ken,   een   voetballer.
              that I-NOM   someone   know-1SG   a   soccer.player

         '. . . that I know someone, a soccer player.'

      c. . . . dat ik   een   tennisser   ken   en   een
              that I-NOM   a   tennis.player   know-1SG   and   a
         voetballer.
         soccer.player

         '. . . that I know a tennis player and a soccer player.'

Extraposed elements are interpreted as associated with material which may be deeply embedded within preverbal constituents:

(60) . . . dat   ze   de hoogte   van de letters   op de kaft   van rapporten
              that they   the height   of the letters   on the cover   of reports
         voorschrijven   van de regering. (Dutch)
         prescribe-PL   of the government

         '. . . that they prescribe the height of the letters on the cover of government reports.'

7.3 Special Word-Order Types

Subject-verb inversion is also featured in various construction types not involving preposing, such as yes-no questions (61a), narrative inversion (61b), conditionals (61c), and imperatives (61d):[50]

(61) a. Heb   je   iemand   gezien?
         have-2SG.INV you   someone   see-PAST.PERF
         'Did you see anyone?'

      b. (Sam en Moos lopen op straat.)   Zegt   Sam
         (Sam and Moos are walking in the street)   say-3SG   Sam
         opeens...
         suddenly

      c. Heb   je   geluk   dan   speel   je   quitte.
         have-2SG.INV you   luck   then   play2SG.INV   you   even
         'When you are lucky you will break even.'

      d. Kom   jij   eens   hier!
         come-2SG.INV you-STRONG   DISC.PRT here
         'You come here!'

Imperatives (61d) are alternatively formed with infinitives (e.g., Dutch *hierkomen, jij!* [here-come you] 'come here, you!').

Relative clauses are "externally headed," with the relative clause following the head noun (when not appearing in extraposition). The distal demonstrative pronoun, and sometimes the interrogative pronoun, functions as relative pronoun.[51] In many dialects, it may be followed by a (full or reduced) complementizer (e.g., Frisian *dy 't* (<*dat*), Limburgian *die-wad of*).

Many dialects use an invariant relative pronoun (Yiddish *vos*, Alemannic *wo*, Afrikaans *wat*, etc.), often in combination with a resumptive pronoun:[52]

(62)   äine, won   em   alls   toktere   nüüt   gnützt
       one   REL   he-DAT   all   doctor-PL   not   profit-PART.PERF
       hät. (Zurich Swiss German)
       have-3SG

       'someone who all the doctors could not help'

When the relativized phrase is a possessive, or is part of a PP, more elaborate circumscriptions are used:

(63) a. de puur   won   em   s häime   verbrunen   isch
          the farmer REL   he-DAT.WEAK   the farm burn-PART.PERF be-3SG
          (Zurich Swiss German)

          'the farmer whose farm burned down'

      b. de suu   wo   d mueter   irer läbtig gspaart
          the son REL   the mother her life   save-PART.PREF
          hät   für   en
          have-3SG   for   he-ACC.WEAK

          'the son for whom his mother has been saving all her life'

In *free relatives* (relative clauses lacking a head noun), the relative pronoun is of
the interrogative type:

(64) a. de man   die/*wie   ik   zie. (Dutch)
          the man DEM.DIST.CG / INT.CG   I-NOM see-1SG

          'the man I see'

      b. Ik   weet   wie/*die   ik   zie.
          I-NOM   know-1SG   INT.CG / DEM.DIST.CG   I-NOM see-1SG

          'I know whom I see.'

In these cases, the relative pronoun shows a matching effect that is absent from
ordinary relative clauses, where the case morphology of the head noun and the
relative pronoun need not match (65a). In free relatives, the case morphology of
the relative pronoun needs to satisfy the case requirements set on the free relative
itself (functioning as subject or object of the matrix clause), as well as the case
requirements associated with the gap inside the relative clause (65b, c):

(65) a. Ich   kenne   *den* Mann   *der*   dort
          I-NOM   know-1SG   the-*ACC* man DEM.DIST.MASC.*NOM*   there
          wohnt. (German)
          live-3SG

          'I know the man who lives there.'

      b. *Ich   kenne   *wer/wen*   dort   wohnt.
          I-NOM   know-1SG   INT.MASC.*NOM/ACC*   there live-3SG

          'I know who lives there.'

      c. Ich   liebe   *wen*   ich   küsse.
          I-NOM   love-1SG   INT.MASC.*ACC* I-NOM   kiss-1SG

          'I love whom I kiss.'

8 NOUN PHRASE STRUCTURE

The order of elements in the noun phrase in Continental West-Germanic dialects is DETERMINER–NUMERAL–ADJECTIVE–NOUN–PP/CP. The PP and CP may have adjunct or argument status and may also appear in extraposition (see section 7).

Possession is expressed in four different ways: (i) by a possessive pronoun (e.g., Dutch *mijn boek*; German *mein Buch* 'my book') or (much more limited) a genitive case-marked noun phrase (e.g., Dutch *Jans boek*; German *Johanns Buch* 'John's book'); (ii) by a weak possessive pronoun preceded by the (unmarked or objective case-marked) possessor (e.g., Dutch *Jan z'n boek* [John his book], German *Johann sein Buch*, 'John's book'),[53] (iii) by a PP headed by a preposition expressing the relation of possession (e.g., Dutch *het boek van Jan* [the book of John] 'John's book'); and (iv) by a genitive case–marked noun phrase following the head noun (e.g., German *das Buch des Schülers* [the book the-GEN pupil-GEN] 'the pupil's book').[54]

The languages also feature a pseudopossessive construction, illustrated in (66), where the head noun functions as a predicate of the noun phrase contained in the "possessive" PP:

(66)   een   schat   van   een   kind (Dutch)
       a   treasure   of   a   child

    'a lovely child'

Other pseudopossessive constructions involve classifiers (67a) and measure phrases (67b):[55]

(67)   a. twee   *(stuks)   vee (Dutch)
        two   pieces   cattle

      'two head of cattle'

    b. een   aantal   deelnemers[56]
       a   number   participant-PL

      'a number of participants'

Noun phrases may also (seem to) be headed by a (nominalized) adjective or numeral, or possessive pronoun, as in Dutch *een oude* [a old-NOM] 'an old one'; *de vijf* [the five] 'the group of five'; German *der Alte* [the-MASC old-NOM] 'the old man'; Swiss German *der Alt* [the-MASC old] 'the old man'; and Bavarian *da reiche* [the-MASC rich-NOM] 'the rich one'.[57] Similar are the various types of possessives with understood head noun (e.g., Dutch *de jouwe* [the you.POSS-NOM] 'yours'; German *der meine* [the-MASC I.POSS-NOM] 'mine'; Luxembourgeois *men-*

ges [I.POSS-GEN] 'of mine'; Swiss German *syni* [he.POSS-NOM] 'his'; Bavarian *(an Sepp) da sei* [the Sepp the-MASC he.POSS] '(Sepp) his'; Afrikaans *hulle s'n* [they he.POSS] 'theirs', *daardie tafel s'n* [that table his] 'the one of that table').

The Continental West-Germanic dialects feature productive processes of *nominalization* and *adjectivalization* best described as involving a verb phrase (or some other subpart of a clause including the verb phrase) embedded within a noun phrase or adjective phrase. The prototypical nominalization is illustrated in (68a), with just a neuter determiner (or inanimate distal demonstrative) and a verb nominalized by infinitive morphology, but both the nominal and the verbal part can be expanded significantly (68b), as long as they do not mix (as in (68c), where the verbal part is in italics):[58]

(68) a. het   lezen (Dutch)
          the-NTR   read-INF

          'the [activity of] reading'

      b. dat   vervelende   alsmaar   in bed
          DEM.DIST.-AN   irritating-NTR.DEF   all-the-time   in bed
          stripboeken   lezen
          comic-books   read-INF

          'that irritating habit of reading comic books in bed all the time'

      c. *dat   *alsmaar*   vervelende   *in bed*   *stripboeken*
           DEM.DIST.-AN   all-the-time   irritating   in bed   comic-books
           lezen
           read-INF

Adjectivalization yields two types of construction, depending on whether the adjective functions as a predicate of the internal argument or of the subject of the adjectivalized verb. If the adjective predicates a property of the verb's internal argument, the adjectivalization process involves perfect participle formation, as in (69a). If the adjective predicates a property of the verb's subject, the process involves gerundive formation, and the result looks like an internally headed relative construction (69b):

(69)   de man   leest   het boek (Dutch) →
          the man   reads   the book

      a. het   (door de man)   gelezen   boek
          the   by the man   read-PART.PERF   book

      b. de   het boek   lezende   man
          the   the book   read-GER   man

          'the man who is reading the book'

The adjectivalization in (69b) may reach similar complexity as the nominalization in (68b):

(70) een   vervelende alsmaar   in bed stripboeken   lezende
      a   irritating   all-the-time in bed comic-books   read-GER
      man (Dutch)
      man

      'an irritating man who reads comic books in bed all the time'

The sensitivity of the adjectivalization process to the argument status of the head noun can be used as a test to gauge the unaccusativity or unergativity status of intransitive verbs. Thus, only unaccusative verbs (where the single argument is an internal argument, such as Dutch *sterven* 'die') allow perfective adjectivalization (as in *de gestorven man* [the die-PART.PERF man] 'the man who died'), and unergative verbs (where the single argument is an external argument, such as Dutch *dansen* 'dance') do not (**de gedanste man* [the dance-PART.PERF man], intended meaning 'the man who danced').[59]

9 NEGATION

Sentential negation is expressed by a negative adverb appearing in the Mittelfeld (Dutch *niet*; German *nicht* 'not') (71a). In older stages of the Continental West-Germanic languages, negation was expressed by a negative particle *en/ne* immediately preceding the verb, which still survives in Flemish dialects (71b). "Negative concord" (noncanceling multiple negation) is very common in the Continental West-Germanic dialects (though disallowed in the standard varieties)(71c):

(71) a. Ik   heb   het boek niet gelezen. (Dutch)
         I-NOM have-1SG   the book not   read-PART.PERF

         'I have not read the book.'

      b. . . . da   Valère ier   niemand en   kent. (West-Flemish)
               that Valery here no one   NEG know-3SG

         '. . . that Valery doesn't know anyone here.'

c. Mia   hod   neamad koa   stikl   broud   ned
   we-NOM   have-1PL   no one   no   piece   bread   not
   kschengt. (Bavarian)
   give-PART.PERF

   'We didn't give anyone a piece of bread.'

Nonspecific arguments in negative clauses are marked by a negative determiner
(Dutch *geen*; German *kein* 'no'), which may or may not cooccur with the negative
adverb (depending on the status of negative concord in the dialect):

(72) a. Ik   heb   geen   boek   gelezen. (Dutch)
         I-NOM   have-1SG   no   book   read-PART.PERF

         'I haven't read a book.'

      b. Koa   mensch   is   ned   kema. (Bavarian)
         no   man   be-3SG   not   come-PART.PERF

         'No one came.'

Nonspecific expressions more generally are negated by prefixation of *n-* (as in
Dutch *iets* vs. *niets* 'something/nothing'; *iemand* vs. *niemand* 'someone/no one';
ergens vs. *nergens* 'somewhere/nowhere'; *ooit* vs. *nooit* 'ever/never'). When more
than one of these negative nonspecific expressions occurs, the negative prefix
surfaces on the highest (leftmost) expression only, and the generic negative adverb
(Dutch *niet*) is left out, except in varieties featuring negative concord:

(73) a. Niemand   heeft   (*n)iemand   (*n)iets   (*niet)
         no one   have-3SG   (no) one   (no)thing   (not)
         gegeven. (Dutch)
         give-PART.PERF

         'No one has given anyone anything.'

      b. ...da   Valère   niemand   niets   nie   getoogd   en
            that Valery   no one   nothing   not   show-PART.PERF   NEG
         eet. (West-Flemish)
         have-3SG

         '...that Valery didn't show anything to anyone.'

Afrikaans has a double negation type (deviating from the Continental West-
Germanic negative concord pattern) where the invariant negative element *nie* is
repeated in sentence final position:[60]

(74) a. Hy   kom   nie   terug   nie. (Afrikaans)
         he   come   not   back   not

      'He's not coming back.'

      b. Ons   het   niks   te doen   nie.
         we   have   nothing   to do   not

      'We have nothing to do.'

      c. Jan   het   nie   gesê   dat   hy sal   kom   nie.
         John   have   not   say-PART.PERF   that   he will   come   not

      'John didn't say that he will come.'

This type of double negation is probably of non-Indo-European origin (Bouman 1926: 60, den Besten 1986).

10 COORDINATION AND ELLIPSIS

Coordination follows the pattern *[(&) α [& β]]*:

(75) a. Jan   en/of   Piet (Dutch)
         John   and/or   Pete

      b. EN/OF   Jan   EN/OF   Piet
         and/or   John   and/or   Pete

      'both John and Pete/either John or Pete'

The second member of the coordination may appear in extraposition, together with the conjunction (cf. (59c)), suggesting its constituent status.

The first constituent of the second of two conjoined clauses (whether subject or preposed topic) may be left out under identity with a parallel constituent in the first clause:[61]

(76) a. *Jan*   pakte   een pen   en   begon
         John   take-PAST.SG   a pen   and   start-PAST.SG
         te schrijven. (Dutch)
         to write-INF

      'John took a pen and started to write.'

b. Toen pakte   *Jan*   een pen en   begon
   John take-PAST.SG John   a pen   and   start-PAST.SG
   te schrijven.
   to write-INF

   'Then John took a pen and started to write.'

Gapping (verb deletion in coordinate structures) operates from left to right in main clauses but bidirectionally in embedded clauses (with the embedded clause word order illustrated in (1b)):[62]

(77) a. Jan   kuste   Marie   en   Piet   Truus. (Dutch)
         John kiss-PAST.SG Mary   and   Pete   Truus

         'John kissed Mary and Pete Truus.'

      b. ... dat   Jan   Marie kuste   en   Piet   Truus

      c. ... dat   Jan   Marie   en   Piet   Truus kuste
             that John Mary   kiss-PAST.SG and   Pete Truus kiss-PAST.SG

         ' ... that John kissed Mary and Pete Truus.'

The Continental West-Germanic languages lack VP-deletion of the English type (as in *John kissed Mary before Bill did/tried to*) and use a paraphrastic verb phrase instead:[63]

(78) Jan   kuste   Marie   voor   dat   Wim   dat
      John kiss-PAST.SG Mary   before that Bill that
      deed/probeerde. (Dutch)
      do/try-PAST.SG

      'John kissed Mary before Bill did/tried to.'

ABBREVIATIONS USED

ACC = accusative	EXT.ARG = external argument	NEG = negation
AN = animate	GEN = genitive	NOM = nominative
APPL = applicative	GER = gerund	NPI = negative polarity item
CG = common gender	IMP = imperative	NTR = neuter
CONJ = conjunctive	INF = infinitive	OBJ = objective
DAT = dative		

DEF = definite	INT = interrogative	PART = participle
DEM = demonstrative	INT.ARG = internal ar-	PERF = perfect
DISC-PRT = discourse	gument	PL = plural
particle	INV = inversion	POSS = possessive
DIST = distal	IPP = Infinitivus Pro	REFL = reflexive
ECM = exceptional Case-	Participio	REL = relative
marking	MASC = masculine	SG = singular

NOTES

Thanks to John Durbin for reading the manuscript and suggesting additions.

1. Frisian is traditionally included in the Insular West-Germanic language group, together with English. The syntax of Old English is not much different from the syntax of the Continental West-Germanic languages, but the development of English has since taken it in a radically different direction, whereas Frisian has preserved the syntactic features characteristic of West-Germanic. For this reason, Frisian is included in the Continental West-Germanic group here.

2. In Dutch dialectology, West-Frisian is also the name of a Dutch dialect spoken in the north of the Dutch province North Holland, which shows effects of Frisian substratum influence (Hoekstra 1993).

3. *Central* West-Germanic refers to a region of the West-Germanic speech area, whereas *Middle* West-Germanic refers to a time period between Old and (Early) New West-Germanic.

4. Strictly speaking, Flemish dialects (West-Flemish, East-Flemish) are spoken only in the West of Belgium. Other Dutch dialects spoken in Belgium include Brabantish and Limburgian, which are also spoken across the border in the south of the Netherlands.

5. Thus, Yiddish has *SVO* order in (1), *SVVO* in (2), and *SVOx* in (3). Inversion (4) and extraposition (5) are as in all Continental West-Germanic dialects, albeit that inference from Slavic or Hebrew (or both) may give rise to "verb-third" constructions (Weissberg 1988: 155), also found in the Low German spoken in the Altai region in Siberia (Jedig 1969: 168).

6. Yiddish may be analyzed as differing from the other Continental West-Germanic languages in that it generalizes the main clause finite verb movement to all verbs in all types of clauses:

(i) . . . az   ikh   *vil*   *leyenen*   nokh   dray   bikher. (Yiddish)
        that   I   want-SG   read-INF   still   three   book-PL

'. . . that I want to read three more books.'

7. A note on Dutch orthography: a double vowel in a closed syllable and a single vowel in an open syllable both indicate the same (tensed) vowel; a double consonant following a single vowel indicates that the vowel is lax.

8. Frisian has two infinitives, ending in -*e* (following modal and causative verbs)

and -*en* (following perception verbs, aspectualizers, and the infinitival marker *te*), respectively.

9. Other clausal connectives (historically) include one of the four types described in
the text (e.g., German *weil* (<*die wile daz*) 'because' (Paul 1920: IV, 264)).

10. A recipient subject construction generally involves the active form of a verb of
receiving (Dutch *krijgen*; German *bekommen* 'get') with the source argument expressed
in a PP:

(i) De kinderen   krijgen   het boek   van Jan. (Dutch)
    the child-PL   get-PL   the book   from John

    'The children get the book from John.'

11. This distinction between locative and nonlocative expletives is in evidence in
German dialects and in colloquial German (nonlocative expletive *es*, locative expletive
da), but the Standard High German language employs the nonlocative expletive *es*
where other Continental West-Germanic dialects would use the locative expletive, apparently with concomitant relaxation of the requirement of nonspecificity on the associate.
In Afrikaans, where the weak forms *er* and *het* are absent, the locative expletive is *daar*,
and the nonlocative expletive is *dit*.

12. Locative expletive constructions may be intransitive, as in (11b), or transitive, as
in (i):

(i) Er   heeft   iemand   een huis   gekocht. (Dutch)
    there   have-3SG   someone   a house   buy-PART.PERF

    'Someone bought a house.'

13. In Afrikaans, animate (direct and indirect) objects may be preceded by an object marker (a grammaticalized preposition) *vir* (< Dutch *voor* 'for'):

(i) Ek   sien   vir   hom. (Afrikaans)
    I-NOM   see   FOR   he-OBJ

    'I see him.'

The presence of the object marker is apparently also related to focus (i.e., *vir* is obligatory when the object appears to the right of sentence adverbs and negation and is
"strongly preferred" with fronted pronouns; cf. Robbers 1997: 18).

14. Elsewhere, the distinction between accusative and dative is intact, but the accu-
sative is not distinguished from the nominative (e.g., Luxembourgeois *hien* [he–NOM/
ACC] vs. *him* [he-DAT]) and mixed systems are also attested (e.g., Westphalian *se* [she-
NOM] and [they-NOM/ACC] vs. *iär* [she-OBJ] and [they-DAT], also Yiddish *zi* [she-NOM/
ACC] vs. *ir* [she-DAT]).

15. Where present, case is marked on the determiner or the adjective (or both) and
on the head noun in a few cases. German distinguishes four morphological cases (NOM
der, ACC *den*, DAT *dem*, GEN *des* 'the'), but the dialects and Yiddish express possession
without making use of a genitive case (see section 8) and maintain no more than a two-
way case opposition (NOM vs. OBJ or NOM/ACC vs. DAT) elsewhere.

16. The colloquial Dutch reflexive *z'n eigen* (lit. 'his own') is used here because, in
principle, it could be used both as a subject and as an object.

17. The pattern in (21) and the discussion of it in the text do not apply to Yiddish,

where the verb does not appear in the verb-final position and the ECM-complement clause follows the matrix verb (Santorini 1993: 234).

18. In Swiss German, the modal verbs may be repeated or doubled (or both):

(i) Gönd   go(ge) en guete Platz go(ge) sueche. (Zurich Swiss German)
     go-IMP go(go) a good place   go(go) find-INF

'Go find a good place.'

19. The term "verb cluster" is used in a descriptive and somewhat inaccurate sense here. It is clear from various phenomena—for example, the displacement of the finite verb out of the cluster to the verb-second position and the interlacing of verbs with other material in dialects like West-Flemish—that the verbs do not form a cluster in any technical sense of the word (i.e., a string of elements behaving as a group).

20. The "IPP effect" is optional in certain dialects (e.g. Luxembourgeois; Bertrang 1921: 348) and in Afrikaans (Robbers 1997: 186f.); it is absent from Yiddish. Lange (1981: 64) correlates the presence of the IPP effect with the presence of a perfective prefix (*ge-*) in the participle (which is absent from Luxembourgeois and optionally present in Afrikaans). (Yiddish has the perfective prefix but lacks the verb clustering to begin with.)

21. Thus, infinitival complementation in Continental West-Germanic shows three types: (i) transparency of the embedded clause and IPP-effect (traditionally called "verb raising"), (ii) no transparency of the embedded clause and no IPP-effect ("extraposition"), and (iii) the mix of transparency without IPP-effect ("third construction"). The last may be described as the result of a combination of object shift and extraposition ("remnant extraposition").

22. The technical term for the phenomenon is "verb projection raising," assuming that the word order is the result of rightward movement of part of a verb phrase. This type of analysis assumes a head-final structure for Continental West-Germanic, with the verb clusters resulting from rightward movement and adjunction to the embedding verb of either a verb ("verb raising") or the projection of a verb ("verb projection raising"). As discussed in Zwart (1996), the phenomena, including their dialectal variations, are more economically described starting from a head-initial structure, with object shift of arguments of the more deeply embedded verb moving across both the embedded and the embedding verb (yielding the effects of verb raising) or to a position between the two verbs (yielding the effects of verb projection raising).

23. With one exception: the embedded predicate and the verb may be separated by stranded prepositions in dialects that allow them. This suggests that the surface position of predicates is derived rather than basic.

24. It can be shown by standard tests (see section 8) that the verb *springen* as used in (29b) is unaccusative, suggesting that the subject *Jan* originates within the complement domain of the verb—that is, as part of the small clause *[Jan [de sloot in]]* (Hoekstra and Mulder 1990).

25. The neuter pronoun *ət* forms a separate category (cf. (6) in Figure 21.1), essentially a weak variant of the inanimate distal demonstrative pronoun *dat*.

26. Weak subject pronouns are not in general banned from the first sentence position, but some appear only in enclisis, like Dutch third-person singular -*ie* and the Bavarian weak pronouns (cf. Table 21.2).

27. Pronouns introducing free relative clauses in the complement of a preposition (as in *based on what you are saying*) are not replaced by their locative counterparts:

(i) gebaseerd {op wat / *waar op} jij zegt (Dutch)
    based   on what where on you say

28. Such demonstrative-locative combinations are also possible in other Continental West-Germanic dialects, but in the order DEMONSTRATIVE–NOUN–LOCATIVE, such as Dutch *dit boek hier* 'this book here', *dat boek daar* 'that book there'. On the locative-demonstrative alternation, see Kayne (2000).

29. Some Lower Franconian dialects (e.g., Brabantish, Amsterdams) employ, by way of locally bound reflexive, a possessive structure *z'n eigə*, lit. 'his own', where the possessive element (*z'n*) varies according to the person, number, and gender of the antecedent (cf. (15)).

30. The elements identified here as logophors (e.g., Dutch *əmzelf*) cannot be locally bound and are not in complementary distribution with nonreflexive pronouns (cf. Reinhart and Reuland 1993).

31. The one exception appears to be the type exemplified by the Dutch possessive distal demonstrative *diens*, which is necessarily obviative with respect to local and non-local subjects (cf. Postma 1984).

32. The past tense of the passive is expressed by putting the auxiliary in the past tense (i), but Yiddish and the Central and High West-Germanic dialects lacking a simple past use the perfective construction in (iii). The perfect of a passive employs the auxiliary 'to be' (Dutch *zijn*; German *sein*) with the perfective participle (ii)—in German combining with a participle of the passive auxiliary 'to become' (iii)—which can be put in the past tense to express the past perfect (iv). The future passive forms employ the future auxiliary (Dutch *zullen*; German *werden*) in combination with the passive auxiliary and the perfective participle (v):

(i)   De hond werd   geslagen. (Dutch)
      the dog become-PAST.SG beat-PART.PERF

      'The dog was beaten.'

(ii) De hond is   geslagen. (Dutch)
      the dog be-3SG   beat-PART.PERF

      'The dog has been beaten.'

(iii) Der Hund   ist   geschlagen   worden. (German)
      the dog   is-3SG   beat-PART.PERF   become-PART.PERF

      'The dog has been beaten.'

(iv) De hond was   geslagen. (Dutch)
      the dog be-PAST.SG   beat-PART.PERF

      'The dog had been beaten.'

(v)   De hond zal   geslagen   worden. (Dutch)
      the dog will-SG   beat-PART.PERF become-INF

      'The dog will be beaten.'

33. As shown by the translation, the unexpressed agent in impersonal passives is interpreted as animate.

34. A mixture of the two types is found in the Limburgian dialects in the Nether-

lands—these are Low/Central Rhine Franconian varieties with considerable Standard Dutch influence (cf. Cornips 1996).

35. Neither does the ECM construction (cf. Bennis and Hoekstra 1989).

36. Likewise, definite objects following discourse particles are interpreted as discourse-new.

37. See section 5 for displacement to subject or object position ("A-movement"). A-movement in Continental West-Germanic is subject to the standard locality restrictions; that is, it takes place out of reduced (nonfinite) complement clauses only.

38. When more complementizers are present, the sequence of complementizer types is invariably CONDITIONAL (Dutch *als/as*)–INTERROGATIVE (Dutch *of*)–DEMONSTRATIVE (Dutch *dat*); cf. De Rooij (1965). This may be taken to suggest that CP consists of a number of functional projections, headed by various grammatical features corresponding to these complementizer types (cf. Müller and Sternefeld 1993 for German; Hoekstra and Zwart 1994 for Dutch).

39. Note the conversion of the inanimate interrogative *wat* into its locative counterpart *waar* (cf. section 6).

40. This is accepting the argumentation in Reis (1996) that German clauses of the type in (i) involve parenthesis rather than long-distance extraction.

(i)	Wer	glaubst	du	hat	recht?
	who-NOM	believe-SG	you-NOM	has-SG	right

'Who do you think is right?'

Yiddish, which lacks the main clause-embedded clause asymmetry in example (1), does allow extraction out of embedded clauses with main clause word order and, more strikingly, also out of embedded clauses with subject-verb inversion, as in (ii):

(ii)	Vos	hot	er	nit	gevolt	az	in shul	zoln
	what	have-SG	he-NOM	not	want-PART.PERF	that	in school	shall-PL
	di	kinder	leyenen?					
	the-PL	child-PL	read-INF					

'What did he not want the children to read at school?'

41. With intransitive verbs in Dutch, the combination of a complementizer and a subject gap feels awkward, which is mitigated by including the locative expletive *ər*:

(i)	Wie	denk	je	dat	??(ər)	komt?
	who	think-2SG.INV	you	that	there	come-3SG

'Who do you think is coming?'

42. However, in some dialects (e.g., in the Southwest of Belgium) some cases of topicalization do not require subject-verb inversion, whereas the inversion is obligatory with question word fronting (see Zwart 1997: 255 and references cited there).

43. The resumptive pronoun agrees in gender with the fronted phrase, except where the fronted phrase corresponds to the subject of a copula construction (or the external argument of a small clause), in which case the default neuter gender form is obligatory. This neuter demonstrative also appears in deictic copula constructions:

(i)   Dat   zijn   kooplieden. (Dutch)
      DEM.DIST.NTR be-PL   merchant-PL

      'Those are merchants.'

In comparison with the "resumptive d-word" strategy illustrated here, the "left disloca-tion" strategy (where the fronted element is resumed by a personal pronoun in the po-sition corresponding to its grammatical function) appears to be rather awkward and not in common use.

44. Note that extraction out of a PP in Dutch requires locative morphology on the extracted element (cf. (i)). This suggests that even when the "optional" resumptive d-word is not spelled out, it is nevertheless present in zero form:

(i)   *Ik   ben   *bananen*   niet   dol   *op.*
      I-NOM   be-SG   bananas   not   wild   about

45. This can be understood if the "sentence satellite" analysis of topicalization is correct (Zwart 1997: 250).

46. The most deeply embedded complement or predicate need not be, and very often is not, the rightmost element, because of the obligatory placement of objects and embedded predicates to the left of the verbfinal position. This suggests that the algo-rithm by which (unmarked) focus is assigned applies to the "deep structure," not to the "surface structure."

47. These remarks on backgrounding and extraposition do not immediately apply to Yiddish, where reference to the verb-final position is difficult because of the general-ized verb movement characteristic of Yiddish syntax.

48. Standard High German disfavors PP extraposition, but the phenomenon does not seem absent from the spoken language and is common in all West-Germanic dia-lects.

49. See also Bennis (1986). Bennis ties the opacity effect to the presence of the dou-bling pronoun, but pronoun doubling is not (in all cases) restricted to backgrounding, whereas the opacity effect is.

50. Yiddish uses a clause-initial question particle *tsi* in (main and embedded clause) yes-no questions.

51. Some dialects, including Limburgian and Bavarian, use a special relative pro-noun composed of the distal demonstrative pronoun and an invariant interrogative ele-ment (Limburgian *die-wad*, Bavarian *der-wo*).

52. In Alemannic, the resumptive pronoun is used only when the relativized phrase is dative or genitive. In Yiddish, it can also be used when the relativized phrase is a subject or direct object (Birnbaum 1979: 306).

53. The weak possessive pronoun has the properties of a "phrasal clitic," like En-glish *'s*, in that it attaches to phrases (as in Dutch *[de vader van Jan] z'n boek* [the father of John] his book, 'John's father's book').

54. The fourth type of possessive construction is archaic in Dutch and German.

55. In Dutch and German, the measure phrase fails to agree with the numeral in a number of cases (e.g., *twee kilo(*s) bananen* [two kilo(-PL) bananas], German *drei Stück Kuchen* [three piece cake] 'three pieces of cake'); this is also the case with independent measure phrases (e.g., *twee kilo(*s)* [two kilo(-PL)], *vijf jaar/#jaren* [five year-SG/PL] 'a five-year period' (with plural marking, the meaning is rather 'five one-year periods').

The form used here is unmarked for number rather than marked for singular (Mattens 1970).

56. Verbal agreement with these noun phrases containing a measure phrase is *ad sensum*; that is, when a distributive reading is intended, the verbal takes on plural agreement:

(i) Een aantal   deelnemers   zijn   gevallen.
     a   number   participant-PL be-PL   fall-PART.PERF

     'A number of participants fell.'

57. In Frisian, *ien* 'one' may be added with indefinite determiners, which also trigger a "strong" adjectival ending in *-en* instead of *-e* (e.g., *in goeden (ien)* [a good-STRONG one] 'a good one', *it âlde* [the-NTR old-WEAK] 'that which is old').

58. The arguments of the verb can appear in an extraposed possessive PP as well (with the internal argument preceding the external argument):

(i) dat   (vervelende alsmaar in bed) lezen   van stripboeken van jou
     that irritating all-the-time in bed read-INF of comic-books   of you

     'that irritating habit of yours of reading comic books in bed all the time'

59. Gerundive adjectivalization is possible with both types of verbs (e.g., *de stervende/dansende man* 'the dying/dancing man'). An unergative verb like Dutch *dansen* 'dance' behaves like an unaccusative verb when it is combined with a directional secondary (small clause) predicate (e.g., *de kamer in* [the room into] 'into the room'): *de *(de kamer in) gedanste man* [the the room into dance-PART.PERF man] 'the man who danced into the room' (cf. Hoekstra and Mulder 1990).

60. The second *nie* is dropped when it is adjacent to the first *nie*:

(i) Ek ken   hom   nie (*nie).
     I   know   him   not not

     'I don't know him.'

61. See Zwart (1997: 263f.) for discussion of the differences between the type of construction illustrated in (76a), which probably involves coordination of the subject's sister category, and that in (76b), which forces a bound variable reading on the empty subject of the second conjunct. Note that the empty subject in (76b) must be taken to precede the verb, since the verb doesn't show the special second-person singular inversion morphology in Dutch (cf. (48)).

62. The complementizer *dat* 'that' can be inserted in the second conjunct of (77c), but not in (77b), suggesting that (77b) and (77c) illustrate different phenomena (cf. Neijt 1979).

63. Consequently, Continental West-Germanic also lacks the phenomenon of Antecedent Contained Deletion (as in *John kissed everyone Bill did*).

REFERENCES

Bennis, Hans (1986) *Gaps and Dummies.* Foris, Dordrecht.

Bennis, Hans, and Teun Hoekstra (1989) "Why Kaatje Was Not Heard Sing a Song," in D. Jaspers et al. (eds.) *Sentential Complementation and the Lexicon.* Foris, Dordrecht, 21–40.

Bertrang, Alfred (1921) *Grammatik der Areler Mundart.* Académie Royale de Belgique, Brussels.

Birnbaum, Solomon A. (1979) *Yiddish: A Survey and a Grammar.* University of Toronto Press, Toronto.

Bouman, A. C. (1926) *Onderzoekingen over Afrikaanse syntaxis.* Nasionale Pers, Cape Town.

Cinque, Guglielmo (1993) "A Null Theory of Phrase and Compound Stress." *Linguistic Inquiry* 24: 239–297.

Cornips, Leonie (1996) "The Spread of the Reflexive Adjunct Middle in the Limburg Dialects: 1885–1994." *Linguistics in the Netherlands 1996*: 49–60.

Corver, Norbert (1991) "Evidence for DegP." *Proceedings of NELS* 21: 33–47.

den Besten, Hans (1977) "On the Interaction of Root Transformations and Lexical Deletive Rules. Unpublished ms., MIT and University of Amsterdam.

den Besten, Hans (1986) "Double Negation and the Genesis of Afrikaans," in P. Muysken and N. Smith (eds.) *Substrata versus Universals in Creole Genesis.* John Benjamins, Amsterdam, 185–230.

Den Dikken, Marcel (1995) *Particles.* Oxford University Press, New York.

de Rooij, Jaap (1965) "*Als–of–dat.*" Ph.D. diss., University of Nijmegen.

Hoekstra, Eric (1993) "Over de implicaties van enkele morfo-syntactische eigenaardigheden in West-Friese dialecten." *Taal en Tongval* 45: 135–154.

Hoekstra, Eric, and Caroline Smits (eds.) (1997) *Vervoegde voegwoorden.* Meertens Instituut, Amsterdam.

Hoekstra, Eric, and Jan-Wouter Zwart (1994) "De structuur van de CP: functionele projecties voor topics en vraagwoorden in het Nederlands." *Spektator* 23: 191–212.

Hoekstra, Teun, and René Mulder (1990) "Unergatives as Copular Verbs: Locational and Existential Predication." *Linguistic Review* 7: 1–79.

Jedig, H. H. (1969) *Očerki po sintaksisu nižnenemeckogo govora Altayskogo kraya.* Zapadno--sibirskoe knižnoe izdatel'stvo, Omsk.

Kayne, Richard S. (2004) "Here and There" in E. Laporte, C. Leclère, M. Piot & M. Silberztein (eds.), *Syntaxe, Lexique et Lexique-Grammaire. Volume dédié à Maurice Gross. Lingvisticae Investigationes Supplementa 24,* Amsterdam/Philadelphia: John Benjamins Publishing Co.

Koster, Jan (1975) "Dutch as an SOV Language." *Linguistic Analysis* 1: 111–136.

Lange, Klaus-Peter (1981) "Warum Ersatzinfinitiv?" *Groninger Arbeiten zur germanistischen Linguistik* 19: 62–81.

Lenerz, Jürgen (1977) *Zur Abfolge nominaler Satzglieder im Deutschen.* Gunter Narr, Tübingen.

Mattens, Willy H. M. (1970) "De indifferentialis: een onderzoek naar het anumerieke gebruik van het substantief in het Algemeen Bruikbaar Nederlands." Ph.D.diss., University of Nijmegen.

Müller, Gereon, and Wolfgang Sternefeld (1993). "Improper Movement and Unambiguous Binding." *Linguistic Inquiry* 24: 461–507.

Neijt, Anneke (1979) *Gapping: A Contribution to Sentence Grammar.*" Foris, Dordrecht.

Paul, Hermann (1920) *Deutsche Grammatik.* Max Niemeyer, Halle.

Postma, Gertjan (1984) "The Dutch Pronoun Diens; Its Distribution and Reference Properties." in H. Bennis and W. U. S. van Lessen Kloeke (eds.) *Linguistics in the Netherlands 1984.* Foris, Dordrecht, 147–158.

Reinhart, Tanya, and Eric Reuland (1993). "Reflexivity." *Linguistic Inquiry* 24: 657–720.

Reis, Marga (1996) "Extractions from Verb-Second Clauses in German?, in U. Lutz and J. Pafel (eds.) *On Extraction and Extraposition in German.* John Benjamins, Amsterdam, 45–88.

Robbers, Karin (1997) "Non-finite Verbal Complements in Afrikaans." Ph.D. diss., University of Amsterdam.

Santorini, Beatrice (1993) "Jiddisch als gemischte OV/VO-Sprache," in W. Abraham and J. Bayer (eds.) *Dialektsyntax.* Westdeutscher Verlag, Opladen, 230–245.

Vanden Wyngaerd, Guido (1989) "Object Shift as an A-movement Rule." *MIT Working Papers in Linguistics* 11: 256–271.

Weissberg, Josef (1988) *Jiddisch: Eine Einführung.* Peter Lang, Bern.

Zwart, C. Jan-Wouter (1992) "Dutch expletives and Small Clause predicate raising." *Proceedings of NELS* 22: 477–491.

Zwart, C. Jan-Wouter (1993) "Verb Movement and Complementizer Agreement." *MIT Working Papers in Linguistics* 18: 297–340.

Zwart, C. Jan-Wouter (1994) "Dutch Is Head-Initial." *Linguistic Review* 11: 377–406.

Zwart, C. Jan-Wouter (1996) "Verb Clusters in Continental Westgermanic Dialects," in J. Black and V. Motapanyane (eds.) *Microparametric Syntax and Dialect Variation.* John Benjamins, Amsterdam, 229–258.

Zwart, C. Jan-Wouter (1997) *Morphosyntax of Verb Movement: A Minimalist Approach to the Syntax of Dutch.* Kluwer, Dordrecht.

LANGUAGE INDEX

Name Index

SUBJECT INDEX